TRANSFORM AND ROLL OUT

The Unofficial and Unauthorised
Guide to the *Transformers* Franchise
1984-1992

TRANSFORM AND ROLL OUT

The Unofficial and Unauthorised
Guide to the *Transformers* Franchise
1984-1992

Ryan Frost

Published in 2018 by Telos Publishing
139 Whitstable Road, Canterbury, Kent CT2 8EQ, United Kingdom.

www.telos.co.uk

ISBN: 978-1-84583-974-1

Telos Publishing Ltd values feedback. Please e-mail any comments you might
have about this book to: feedback@telos.co.uk

British Library Cataloguing in Publication Data.
A catalogue record for this book is available from the British Library.

ACKNOWLEDGEMENTS

In writing this book, I've had assistance from a number of people and organisations who have provided facts, information and general help. I'm extremely grateful to everyone who has helped make this book a reality, especially:

Simon Coward at Kaleidoscope.org.uk, Richard Gentle at the Audit Bureau of Circulations, Gill Hanhart and all the staff at the Westminster Reference Library, James Kearney at the Associated Press Archive, Stuart Webb (for general advice and fact-checking) and Ian White at the TV-am Archive and Museum.

Thanks also to Stephen James Walker and everybody at Telos Publishing, for their guidance and wisdom, and for taking a punt on a first-time author.

For my friends and family, and everyone else who's offered patience and encouragement along the way, especially Mum, Dad, Charmayne, Ricki and Jason. Cheers!

CONTENTS

Foreword

For more than thirty years, my association with the *Transformers* franchise has been a source of great pride, and eternal 'bragging rights'. I have had the honour and privilege of being the Animated Voice of Grimlock, Dinobot Leader, throughout the G1 episodes and in additional return appearances over the years, including as the current voice of Grimlock in *Transformers: Power of the Primes*. Over the decades, I have watched, as fandom has fuelled, sustained … and allowed for the twists, turns, variations and realignments of the Cybertronian lore. The franchise has never ceased to build on its legacy and standing as a cornerstone of iconic pop culture. My Special Guest appearances at *Transformers* conventions and comic conventions around the world (planet Earth LOL), have introduced me to new *global* generations of fandom as they – along with the veteran fans – reach ages where they first discover *Transformers*, and immediately claim it as 'their own'.

Archiving this ever-expanding universe of near virtual reality over its long history is an epic feat, to which the author of this work will undoubtedly attest. This is an informative and enjoyable read that appears meticulous in its attention to detail, as it chronicles and organises the 'historical documents' of the phenomenon that is … *Transformers*. For the fan who wants to invest more deeply in how it all came to be and how it all continues 'being' … enjoy.

Gregg Berger
@greggberger on Twitter
facebook.com/greggberger
imdb.com search Gregg Berger

Introduction

The Transformers first appeared in 1984 as a range of toys. Since then, the franchise has grown to become a global phenomenon. Although forever linked with its '80s roots, it has continued and developed throughout the rest of the 20th Century and into the present, maintaining relevance by continually adapting and evolving, all the while entertaining children and adults alike. Arguably its popularity has never been higher than it is today, thanks to the recent record-breaking series of live-action blockbuster movies.

However, it's not just the modern-day, updated Transformers who are getting all the limelight. Interest in the classic original Transformers has also grown, thanks in part to new fans discovering the franchise via the movies, but also as part of the general '80s-nostalgia boom of the early 21st Century.

Because of this renewed interest in the original incarnation of the Transformers (known officially as the 'Generation One' era), fans now have many ways they can relive those old memories – every episode of the classic cartoon has been released on DVD, many of the original toys have been rereleased, and the old Marvel comics have been collected and reprinted in trade paperback format.

This book will serve as an in-depth look at all aspects of the Transformers franchise prior to its (temporary, as it turned out) cancellation in the early '90s, including the toys, the comics and the cartoon, with plot synopses, reviews and the most detailed notes ever written on the stories' continuity. As well as all this, US and UK popular culture of the '80s will be explained to modern and overseas readers who might not otherwise understand references to Ted Koppel or Gary Davies. Furthermore, this book contains various essays on aspects of the fiction and its production; biographical data for all key personnel; and much more besides. In short, this book contains everything you'd ever need to know about the original incarnation of the Transformers.

So here it is, whether you're a long-time fan with your battered old comics and VHS tapes, or a new reader coming to the franchise for the first time thanks to the pristine DVDs and trade paperback reprints, there should be something here for everyone. Let's travel in time back to 1984 …

Notes

… actually, let's not travel back to 1984. Not yet, anyway. Before we do, I'd best explain how this book is going to work.

The text is divided into sections dedicated to each of the three main iterations of the '80s Transformers phenomenon – the toys, the cartoons and the comics. The toy section will be self-explanatory – for each year of releases, there will be an overview and essay, followed by a run-down of every Transformer released in that period. The comic and cartoon segments require a bit more in the way of explanation:

The Comics:

As this book is focused on the combined US and UK Transformers comic universe, stories will generally (though not always) be tackled in the order of their presentation in the UK comics – the UK being the only place where all of these adventures were published. US-originated stories are identified with their US issue number (for example [16] 'Plight of the Bumblebee'); UK-only stories are identified by the inclusion of a decimal point denoting how they fit within the overall story. For example, the UK story 'Salvage' was printed between the American stories [39] 'The Desert Island of Space' and [40] 'Pretender to the Throne', so it's been given the number [39.1], denoting that it slots in between those US issues.

Information about each adventure will be split into various sections as follows:

Dates and **Credits:** The cover dates of the US and UK issues in which the story appeared, followed by a list of production credits. To avoid unnecessary repetition, cover credits are provided only for a story's debut appearance (some of the British stories got a second printing in the comic).

Plot: A plot summary of the story in question.

Notes: General discussion about each story; how it fits in with established continuity, explanations of pop-culture references etc.

Sometimes the American entries will have additional sections: **UK Notes,** with details of how the stories fit into the combined UK/US continuity, and **UK Changes,** which identifies any edits made to the stories as they were reprinted in the UK.

Roll Call: A list of all the Transformers (and other significant recurring humans and aliens) who appear in the story.

Review: A short critical summary of the adventure, followed by a mark out of five.

On occasion I'll also be making points about the comics that merit a heading of their own, so the above categories will be occasionally joined by others as applicable. The story entries will generally be interspersed with **Data Files** of production staff.

The Cartoons:
Aimed at a slightly younger audience, *The Transformers* cartoon show eschewed the comics' penchant for long story arcs in favour of telling exciting, mostly stand-alone stories. Because of this, the cartoons will be tackled in a slightly different way. The **Plot**, **Credits**, **Roll Call**, **Data Files** and **Review** sections will all still be present, but due to the show's more simplistic nature, there is no real need for every episode to have an extensive notes section.

To make up for this omission, every third episode (or more frequently where necessary) will feature a section entitled **Spotlight**, where I will discuss a specific aspect of the franchise not covered elsewhere – all sorts of topics are discussed, including toy release dates, end credit mix-ups and histories of the various animation studios.

Additionally there will be two (slightly frivolous) categories unique to the analysis of the cartoons. **Megatron's Rants** and **Witty Put-Downs** will contain amusing or bizarre quotes from the show, and will act as a means to convey the general sense of fun inherent in even the worst episodes.

Putting the show into some sort of a viewing order has long been a problem for fans (and indeed the compilers of the official DVD releases). Watching the episodes in strict production or broadcast order doesn't make for the most satisfactory of experiences, and with that in mind, the episodes have been sorted into what could be considered a 'best viewing order', based primarily on the production order but with a few episodes shifted around for continuity as necessary.

Throughout this book, a numerical code is used to identify each episode: season number, then a hyphen, followed by the episode number within that season. So for example {2-44} 'Cosmic Rust' is the forty-fourth episode of Season Two. To ensure that comic stories aren't confused with cartoon episodes, square brackets [] indicate a comic and braces {} indicate a cartoon.

PART ONE: THE TOYS

Origins

The very first 'transformer' was Magma, lead character in the 1966-67 Japanese television show *Ambassador Magma*. The idea of robots changing their appearance was admittedly nothing new by this point – the 1927 film *Metropolis* had depicted a robot taking the form of a human – but this was the first time that one had been seen to transform from a humanoid mode into a vehicle (in this case a rocket ship).

The idea caught on in Japan, culminating in the development of the very first transforming robot toy, Brave Raideen, the title character of a 1975 anime series. Made by the Popy toy company, the heavy, die-cast action figure could convert into a bird creature (albeit with the help of some detachable parts).

By the early '80s, Japanese televisions and toy aisles were filled with transformable robots, with lines such as Beast King GoLion (1981), Machine Robo (1982) and most notably the smash hit franchise Macross (1982). Some of these would later find their way to foreign shores via licencing agreements with American toy companies like Tonka and Mattel, who rebranded them with new, Westernised names such as Voltron and GoBots.

The Japanese toy manufacturer Takara decided to get in on the act, and as part of their Diaclone range of toys, introduced robot action figures that, with a few twists and turns, could convert into cars, planes … even insects and dinosaurs.

But this wasn't Takara's only foray into transforming figures. Since 1974 they had been producing a line of action figures called Microman. In 1983 a spin-off line, MicroChange, was introduced, and featured life-size facsimiles of everyday items (cassettes, microscopes, guns etc) that could be converted into robots.

Both the Diaclone and MicroChange ranges were on display at the 1983 Tokyo Toy Show, where representatives of Rhode Island, US-based toy company Hasbro were in attendance. Hasbro were impressed enough to acquire the licences to both lines; rather than market them individually, however, they decided to sell the two ranges under a single banner, The Transformers.

The 1984 Toy Range

Launched in 1984, the first wave of Transformers figures included some of the line's most iconic and enduring characters. All the figures were repurposed from Takara's Diaclone and MicroChange lines, although many sported newly-designed colour schemes created especially for the Western market.

Betraying their origins, the Diaclone-based figures generally featured openable cabs, doors or cockpits that were intended for use with their original mini driver/pilot figures (which Hasbro had decided to dispense with). Other toys (such as Huffer and Brawn) featured a stylised 'M' logo moulded into the plastic, a holdover from their earlier MicroChange incarnations.

The bulk of the figures were packaged in rectangular window boxes, which were either red or purple depending on whether the figure was a Heroic Autobot or an Evil Decepticon. The front of every package featured an attractive painting of the character in an action pose; the rear of the box featured more artwork, plus a cut-out-and-keep profile of the toy's character and abilities ('Tech Specs'), which was fully-readable only when viewed through a piece of red-tinted transparent plastic also included in the box.

As well as the red decoder piece and the figure itself, each Transformers box included a set of instructions, a small fold-out catalogue depicting other available figures, a sticker sheet and a host of various weapons and accessories.

The weapons generally included a working projectile launcher and a set of 'missiles'. The power and range of the firing mechanisms were deliberately weakened by Hasbro under new safety guidelines introduced following an incident in 1979 where a four-year-old boy died of asphyxiation after accidentally firing such a projectile (from a Mattel Battlestar Galactica Colonial Viper toy) into his throat.

Smaller Transformers (such as Mini-Cars and the Decepticon Cassettes) were sold on simpler cardboard-backed blister packs, came with fewer accessories (if any) and had the instructions printed on the back of the packaging.

As this was just the beginning of the Transformers toy range (and without access to modern-day tools such as 3D modelling programs), the toy designs were understandably quite primitive – the robot modes were often poorly-articulated and oddly-proportioned. However, it can be argued that this actually worked to the benefit of the early figures – their statuesque quality and weird body-shapes actually gave them an eerie alien quality (which became lost when the comics and cartoons depicted them as much more anthropomorphic). Other unique features of these early figures included some die-cast metal parts, chromed (vacuum metallised) plastic, and rubber tyres – all of which served to give the earlier toys a heft and lustre that later waves of figures were unable fully to replicate.

In order to get the most out of the toy moulds, Hasbro decided at the outset to sell multiple versions of a single toy in different colour schemes, ensuring that kids had to buy the same figure multiple times (albeit in alternative liveries and marketed as different characters) in order to get the complete set. This practise of releasing 'repaints' continues in Transformers toys even today.

One final point to note: with a few exceptions, most of the 1984 Transformers were based on recognisable, real-world vehicles. Although this benefited the toys greatly, neither Hasbro nor Takara actually paid any monies to the relevant manufacturers. The iconic Autobot Bumblebee, for example, clearly transforms into a Volkswagen Beetle, and yet no legal permission was ever sought from Volkswagen themselves. This has resulted in some problems in recent years – between 1989 and 2014 (when Volkswagen finally granted a licence), no new Bumblebee toy could be based on a VW Beetle without fear of litigation.

Autobot Commander:

- **Optimus Prime**. Transforms into red/blue truck cab (specifically, a Freightliner FL86). Not that much larger than the regular Autobot Cars, he was made more impressive by his array of accessories, most noticeably his Combat Deck battle platform (which becomes the truck trailer in vehicle mode), and Roller, a non-transforming toy car designed for use with the trailer's launching gimmick. The figure was known as 'No. 17 Battle Convoy' when originally released in Japan as part of the Diaclone line.

Autobot Mini Cars:

Small, cheap toys, specifically aimed at the pocket-money market. When originally conceived as MicroChange figures, the Mini Cars were intended to represent life-size, tiny robots that transformed into toy cars. As such, their vehicle modes are deliberately mis-proportioned ('super-deformed') – they were designed to resemble cutesy toy versions of cars, rather than actual vehicles.

- **Brawn**. Originally the MicroChange '05 Jeep'. The Transformers release is green and orange; the original version was a tan brown colour.
- **Bumblebee**. Originally the MicroChange '03 Volkswagen Beetle'. Although best known as a yellow toy, it was also available in red. The original Japanese figure was additionally available in blue.
- **Cliffjumper**. Originally the MicroChange '01 Porsche Turbo 924'. As with Bumblebee, he was sold in both red and yellow variants, although in Cliffjumper's case he's best remembered in his red incarnation. Again, when first released in Japan he was also available in blue. Although they transform into two completely different cars, Bumblebee and Cliffjumper had similar robot modes and identical transformations.
- **Gears**. Originally the MicroChange '04 4WD', a red/blue four-wheel drive truck. The Japanese MicroChange version featured a slightly darker shade of blue.
- **Huffer**. Based on the MicroChange '07 Truck', he's an orange and blue truck cab in vehicle mode, and is identical to his Japanese equivalent.
- **Windcharger**. A red/grey Pontiac Firebird, the toy is identical to its Japanese forebear, the MicroChange '06 Transam'.
- **'Bumblejumper' aka 'Bumper'**. Originally the MicroChange '02 [Mazda] Familia 1500 XG'. Never officially released, examples of this yellow toy are known to have been sold by Hasbro in Cliffjumper packaging; the name is an unofficial one coined by fans. Again, the toy shares design cues with both Bumblebee and Cliffjumper, and the original Japanese release was available in yellow, red and blue versions.

Autobot Cars:

Forming the bulk of the Autobot troops, the medium-sized cars were, like Optimus Prime, originally part of Diaclone's Car Robot line.

- **Bluestreak**. Originally the 'No. 7 Fairlady Z' toy, his alternate mode was that of a Datsun 280ZX. Despite his name, this figure was actually silver, although box art and early toy catalogues depict him as blue (as per an earlier Japanese release). Because of this, it is generally assumed that the switch to a silver livery was a last-minute decision. His Diaclone counterpart was also commercially available in black/sliver; an *extremely* limited-edition gold chrome version was also made.
- **Hound**. In Japan he was originally known as 'No. 12 J59 Jeep' where, as per his Hasbro release, he was green.
- **Ironhide**. His Diaclone release ('No. 2 Onebox Cherry Vanette') was black, however Hasbro decided to release the figure in red. The toy has no head. It was designed so that a mini-pilot figure would sit in place of a head, but because the pilot figures were not included with Hasbro's Transformers, an alternative solution

was found – a sticker depicting a face was applied to the robot's upper body.

- **Jazz**. Originally the 'No. 14 Porsche 935 Turbo', this white toy was released by Hasbro unchanged. Like other Autobots whose alternate modes were sponsored race cars, the sponsor logos were deliberately misspelt – Jazz's Porsche mode is sponsored by 'Martinii' [sic].
- **Mirage**. In Japan, this blue-and-white race car was known as 'No.16 F-1 Ligier JS11'. Hasbro retained the original colour scheme (although a red version was also sold in Japan as part of a gift set). As with Jazz, some of the sponsor logos are misspelt – the French cigarette company Gitanes becomes 'Citanes' on the toy.
- **Prowl**. Known as 'No. 13 Police Car Fairlady Z' in Japan; the Hasbro version featured only minor changes from his original black and white deco. But for the light-bar atop his police car mode, this a straight repaint of the Bluestreak figure.
- **Ratchet**. The Western equivalent of Diaclone's 'No. 4 Onebox Ambulance Type', he was a white van and shared Ironhide's body type (with the addition of a light-bar on the vehicle roof). The Japanese version (and indeed some of Hasbro's initial runs) featured the logo of the International Red Cross Movement on the roof and sides, but this was soon removed, presumably to avoid potential litigation.
- **Sideswipe**. A red version of the Diaclone 'No. 15 New Countach LP500S', his car mode was that of a Lamborghini. In Japan he was additionally available in yellow, and also (as part of a larger gift set) black.
- **Sunstreaker**. Originally the 'No. 1 Countach LP500S', this yellow Lamborghini has a similar vehicle mode to Sideswipe but a completely different transformation and robot mode. As the earliest-numbered of Diaclone's Car Robot toys, this figure is often credited as being the very first Transformers toy. The Japanese edition was coloured red.
- **Trailbreaker**. A black version of the Car Robot 'No. 5 4WD Hi-Luxe', in other words a Toyota camper van. The original Japanese toy was also available in blue or yellow.
- **Wheeljack**. Aka 'No. 18 Lancia Stratos Turbo', he transforms into a white sports car (with the sponsor – Italian airline Alitalia – misspelt as 'Alitalla').

Decepticon Leader:

- **Megatron**. Transforms into a black and silver handgun, and originally retailed in Japan as the MicroChange 'MC-13 Walther P-38 U.N.C.L.E.' – so named because he was packaged with a sight, stock and silencer that replicated the look of a weapon seen on the television show *The Man from U.N.C.L.E.* (1964). These accessories could themselves combine into a large weapon for Megatron to wield. Although the function was disabled in Hasbro's Megatron, the Japanese version could fire spring-loaded projectiles in gun mode.

Decepticon Planes:
The three original Decepticon planes share the same mould – the only physical difference between them is their colour scheme. The original Diaclone releases had hard plastic nosecones in jet mode; for safety reasons, these were replaced with softer plastic for their Hasbro release.

- **Skywarp**. Like the other Decepticon Planes, he was based on the 'F-15 Robo' body type. His black colour scheme, however, was created specifically for the Transformers line.
- **Starscream**. Again, he was an F-15 jet in vehicle mode. His grey and red colours were retained from his Diaclone release, 'Acrobat Type'.
- **Thundercracker**. When originally released in Japan, this blue Transformer was known as 'Super-High-Speed Fighter Type'.

<u>Decepticon Cassettes:</u>

- **Soundwave**. Originally the MicroChange 'MC-10 Cassette Man', Soundwave transforms from a blue robot into an audiocassette player/recorder. His cassette tray could hold any one of his cassette minions, such as …
- **Buzzsaw**. Transforms from a gold cassette into a robotic bird. The toy had previously seen release in Japan as 'MC-03 Condor', which was available in red and blue versions. As with all the cassette Transformers, Buzzsaw was made to resemble a 1:1 scale microcassette (the kind used in answering machines and Dictaphones) rather than a standard full-size music cassette. Buzzsaw was packaged with Soundwave figures and not available individually.
- **Frenzy**. Originally sold as the MicroChange 'MC-01 Micross', this blue microcassette transformed into a humanoid robot and was largely unchanged from his Japanese release.
- **Laserbeak**. A red repaint of Buzzsaw. Laserbeak and Frenzy were sold together in a two-pack.
- **Ravage**. Originally the 'MC-02 Jaguar'. As the name suggests, he transformed from a black cassette into a robotic cat. A blue version was also sold in Japan.
- **Rumble**. A red repaint of Frenzy. Rumble and Ravage were sold only as a two-pack.

The 1985 Toy Range

In 1985, the number of different Transformers toys more than doubled, as many new figures saw release during the course of the year. As we shall see in the notes to the cartoon episode {1-09} 'Fire on the Mountain', the Jetfire, Shockwave and Skids figures were actually released in late 1984, but as they appear in Hasbro's 1985 toy catalogues they are generally considered to be part of the 1985 range.

1985 saw the introduction of many new and popular features that would become mainstays of the franchise for years to come. For the first time we had robots that transformed into animals (the Dinobots and Insecticons), robots that could be connected together to make a larger, combined robot (the Constructicons), transforming vehicles with pull-back-and-go engines (Mini-Spies, Powerdashers and Jumpstarters), plus the ingenious Triple-Changers, robots who could convert into two different vehicle modes.

The majority of these 'new' figures were again repurposed from Takara's MicroChange and Diaclone lines, but with so many additional characters being introduced, Hasbro were in danger of exhausting Takara's entire back catalogue of transforming robot toys. With this in mind, they decided to branch out and cut deals with other Eastern manufacturers such as Bandai, Toybox and ToyCo, to contribute towards the 1985 Transformers range in addition to their original partners Takara.

It was during 1985 that Hasbro came up with another innovation: 'rub-signs'. These were heat-sensitive black-and-silver stickers that, when gently rubbed, would display either an Autobot or a Decepticon logo. As well as being a successful gimmick, they were hard to counterfeit. The Transformers franchise was by now a roaring success, and many other toy companies began producing their own transforming robot figures; the rub-signs became a way for the public to tell which robot toys were imitations and which were genuine Transformers.

Also introduced in 1985 was the concept of mail-away figures – the backs of all Transformers packages featured cut-out-and-collect 'Robot Points' that could now be redeemed against mail-order toys, some of which were unavailable in the shops.

Although the American market could cope with this glut of new releases, countries with smaller populations declined to stock the entire range. Consequently, popular 1985 Transformers such as Blaster and Swoop went unreleased in a number of European markets, including the United Kingdom.

In Japan however, the Transformers concept was embraced with open arms. Delighted with Hasbro's success, Takara dropped their old Diaclone and MicroChange lines in favour of Transformers. They even began developing toys specifically for the franchise; with this new stream of purpose-made figures from Takara, Hasbro's brief flirtation with other Japanese manufacturers was more or less ended almost as soon as it had begun.

With the exception of the 'Bumblejumper' figure, the entire 1984 range continued to be available for purchase for the time being; this list concerns itself solely with new figures making their debuts in 1985.

Autobot Mini Vehicles:
In 1984 this sub-line was known as the 'Autobot Mini Cars', but with the introduction of other types of vehicles into the range, the description had to be altered.

- **Beachcomber**. A grey and blue dune buggy. Not previously released in Japan, this and the other 1985 Mini Vehicles were specifically created by Takara for the Transformers line.
- **Cosmos**. A green flying saucer.
- **Powerglide**. A red aeroplane (an A-10 Thunderbolt II).
- **Seaspray**. A blue/white/yellow hovercraft.
- **Warpath**. A red tank.

The Mini Vehicles each came packed with a **Mini Spy**, an extremely small and simple car Transformer with pull-back-and-go motorised action. There were four body-types: 4WD, Buggy, FX-1 and Porsche. Each body type was available in three different colours – white, yellow and blue – and depending on the rub-sign could be either an Autobot or a Decepticon, resulting in a total of 24 possible variations. They were originally released in Japan by Takara as Mecha Warriors, where they were also available in red.

Autobot Cars:
Again, these figures all originated from Diaclone's Car Robot line.

- **Grapple**. Originally the 'No. 20 Crane' toy, Grapple was a yellow truck crane.
- **Hoist**. A green and orange tow truck. His original Japanese release ('No. 8 4WD Wrecker Type') was available in either blue (standard release) or red (gift set edition). This was a variant of the Trailbreaker toy, with a different rear section and head.
- **Inferno**. Like his Diaclone counterpart, 'No. 10 Fire Engine', Inferno was red. His design was near-identical to that of Grapple, but featured an extending ladder in lieu of Grapple's hook arm.
- **Red Alert**. A predominantly white version of 1984's Sideswipe figure, his vehicle mode was supposed to represent a fire-chief's car, complete with light-bar on the roof. This version was originally sold in Japan as a police car, 'No. 19 New Countach Police Car'.
- **Skids**. A blue car, also available in both black and red versions in Japan, where it was sold as 'No. 9 Honda City Turbo'.
- **Smokescreen**. A red and blue car, originally the 'No. 11 Fairlady Z Racing Type'. He was a slightly modified version of the Datsun design shared by Prowl and Bluestreak.
- **Tracks**. Prior to his Transformers incarnation, this toy was known as 'No. 21 Corvette Stingray'. Although the original Diaclone version was red, the Transformers version was blue. As well as his car and robot modes, Tracks featured some fold-out wings and gun accessories that, when deployed, gave him a third 'flying car' mode. As the latest-numbered (and therefore last released) of the Diaclone Car Robot toys, it has been claimed that Tracks was developed with the Transformers phenomenon in mind, hence his very American vehicular mode.

Autobot Jumpstarters:
Chunky alien vehicles with a pull-back-and-go engine, designed to transform the toy into robot mode automatically, after a brief forward surge.

- **Topspin**. A blue and grey futuristic jet, he was originally the 'Baku-Ten Attack Robo Jet Type'. His original Diaclone version was available in either grey and blue (a reversal of the Hasbro colour scheme) or red and blue.
- **Twin Twist**. A grey and blue 'drill-tank', previously the 'Baku-Ten Attack Robo Drill Type'. Again, the Japanese version was available in two colour schemes, blue/red and blue/grey.

Autobot Deluxe Vehicles:
Unlike the majority of Transformers, the Deluxe Vehicles were not created by Takara. Instead, they were originally part of the Special Armoured Battalion Dorvack line created by Takatoku Toys. When Takatoku went bust in 1984, the rights to their designs were snapped up by Bandai, a major Japanese toy manufacturer little-known in the West at the time.

Hasbro were able to negotiate only a temporary licence to distribute these toys for Western markets. In the intervening years Bandai have become a large multinational and a direct rival of Hasbro. As such, the likelihood of such a deal being cut again (and therefore the chance of seeing these classic figures reissued) is incredibly slim.

- **Roadbuster**. An orange and green off-road vehicle of made-up type, Roadbuster was originally released in Japan as the red/orange 'Mugan Calibur'.
- **Whirl**. Originally known as 'Ovelon Gazette' when released as part of the Dorvack line. Although both versions of the toy are blue, the Transformers version is a lighter shade.

(Autobot) Dinobots:
Originally released as the Diaclone Dinosaur Robo team in a similar grey colour scheme to their Transformers counterparts, but with some of the secondary colours changed around (blues and blacks swapped for reds).

- **Grimlock**. Known simply as 'Tyrannosaurus' when originally released.
- **Slag**. 'Triceratops'.
- **Sludge**. 'Brontosaurus'.
- **Snarl**. 'Stegosaurus'.
- **Swoop**. 'Pteranodon'.

(Autobot) Omnibots:
These were smaller car Transformers that boasted a third mode – a super-weaponised car mode that entailed the use of flip-out armaments and wings. All three Omnibots were identical to their Diaclone equivalents, collectively known in Japan as the Double Changers.

The Omnibots were available only via mail order (in exchange for $5 and four Robot Points).

- **Camshaft**. As with all the Omnibots, his original Japanese 'name' was just a description of his car model, in this case a grey 'Savannah RX-7'.
- **Downshift**. A white 'Celica XX'.
- **Overdrive**. A red 'Ferrari BB'.

Autobot Powerdashers:
Crude, simplistic transforming robots with pull-back motorised action in vehicle mode. Like the Omnibots, they were available only via mail order, in this case for the sum of $3 and two Robot Points. The Diaclone versions were known simply as 'Dashers'.

The Transformers versions were never officially named, so for the purposes of this list, the original Diaclone names have been used.

- **Sky Dasher** (aka 'Powerdasher Jet', 'Jet Type' or 'Cromar'), a red/black futuristic aircraft. The original Diaclone version had a blue colour scheme.
- **Drill Dasher** (aka 'Powerdasher Drill Tank', 'Drill Type', 'Drill Tank Type' or 'Zetar'), a black/yellow drill tank.
- **F-1 Dasher** (aka 'Powerdasher Car', 'F1 Type', 'Race Car Type' or 'Aragon'), a red/black futuristic car. The Japanese version was red and blue.

Other Miscellaneous Autobots:

- **Blaster**. A red/grey/yellow cassette player, the Autobot equivalent of the

Decepticon Soundwave. The original MicroChange version, the blue/grey 'MC-21 Radicasse Robo' actually contained a working radio.

- **Jetfire**. A transforming jet figure originally developed by Takatoku for their Super Dimensional Fortress Macross line, Jetfire is a (slightly modified) version of the 1/55-scale 'VF-1S Valkyrie' toy. While the Hasbro version is white and red, the original Macross edition was light grey. As with the Deluxe Autobots, the design is now owned by Bandai.
- **Omega Supreme**. Made up of 26 individual parts, Omega Supreme consisted of a rocket, a launch pad, a battery-powered tank and a circular track around which the tank was able to navigate. The entire set could be disassembled and then re-combined into Omega Supreme, a grey, yellow and red robot with motorised walking action. The figure was licenced from the Japanese manufacturer Toybox, who originally released it in a red / grey scheme as 'Super Change Robo Mechabot-1'.
- **Perceptor**. Transforms into a red/blue microscope (which actually works, with a magnification of 12x). Originally the MicroChange 'MC-20 Micro Scope', he was first released in a black livery. The toy has a bonus third mode, an alien tank-like vehicle.

(Decepticon) Insecticons:
Originally released by Takara as part of the Diaclone line, where they were collectively known as the Insecter Robo.

- **Bombshell**. A purple and black rhinoceros beetle, his Japanese equivalent was red/black and named 'Kabutron' (also sometimes anglicised as 'Kabtoron').
- **Kickback**. This predominantly black figure transforms into a robotic grasshopper. His Japanese forerunner was called 'Battas' and was coloured red and black.
- **Shrapnel**. A black and purple stag beetle, he was based on the Diaclone 'Kuwagattler' (aka 'Kuwagatorer') which was red and black.

(Decepticon) Deluxe Insecticons:
Another group of non-Takara figures, the Deluxe Insecticons were Takatoku designs, originally created for the Armoured Insect Squadron Beetras line.

- **Barrage**. A green and yellow rhinoceros beetle. His original Beetras release was named 'Beet-Gadol' and was grey and black.
- **Chop Shop**. A brown stag beetle. In Japan he was coloured black and grey and was named 'Beet-Gugal'.
- **Ransack**. A black and yellow locust, Ransack was originally due for release in Japan as 'Beet-Vadam' (in a green and grey livery) – however Takatoku went out of business just prior to the planned release date, so the Beetras version was never made commercially available.
- **Venom**. Transforming into a green and orange cicada, he was originally the black/brown coloured 'Beet-Zeguna' when released by Takatoku in Japan.

(Decepticon) Constructicons:

The six Constructicons were originally manufactured by Takara under the Diaclone banner, where they were marketed as the Construction Robo Build Combination Set – six robots who could convert into construction vehicles, and also combine (with the aid of numerous connector pieces and accessories) into a single giant robot, **Devastator**.

- **Bonecrusher.** Like all the Constructicons, Bonecrusher is coloured a vibrant lime green and purple. He transforms into Devastator's left arm. His Diaclone counterpart was yellow, and named 'No. 1 Bulldozer'.
- **Hook.** In Japan he was called 'No. 4 Truck Crane' and available in two colour schemes, orange or blue. He becomes the upper body of Devastator.
- **Long Haul.** The lower body of Devastator, in Japan he was orange and went by the name 'No. 5 Dump Truck'.
- **Mixmaster.** Devastator's left leg, he was originally the 'No. 6 Concrete Mixer' and available in either orange or blue.
- **Scavenger.** The original Diaclone release was yellow/black and named 'No. 2 Power Shovel'. He becomes the right arm of Devastator.
- **Scrapper.** The right leg module of Devastator, his original Japanese release ('No. 3 Shovel-Dozer') was yellow.

The Constructicons were available to buy either singly or as a complete set of six.

Decepticon Triple Changers:

- **Astrotrain.** A white and purple robot who can transform into either a steam locomotive or a space shuttle. This figure was originally intended to be released as part of the Diaclone range, but put on hold when Takara dropped their other robot lines to concentrate on Transformers. Some early examples of Japanese Astrotrain figures have a unique black/white colour scheme – these versions are generally assumed to be unreleased Diaclone figures sold to the public in Transformers packaging.
- **Blitzwing.** A purple and beige robot who can convert into a tank or a jet. Originally released in white and green as 'No. 1 Jet Fighter Type' as part of Takara's Diaclone Triplechanger sub-line.

Decepticon Planes:

As with the 1985 Autobot Mini Vehicles, these figures were created especially for the Transformers line by Takara. Although heavily based on the 1984 Decepticon Plane figures (which were themselves old Diaclone designs), these new toys featured newly-designed wings and weapons.

- **Dirge.** A blue/orange F-15 with customised canard-type wings.
- **Ramjet.** A white/red F-15 with customised delta-type wings.
- **Thrust.** A red/black F-15 with customised wings housing VTOL engines.

Other Miscellaneous Decepticons:

- **Shockwave**. Transforms from a purple and silver robot into a futuristic laser gun. He is the only Transformers design to originate from the South Korean ToyCo company, who originally marketed him as the 'Gun-Borg Astro-Magnum' (in a grey colour scheme)

The 1986 Toy Range

1986 was a transitional period for the Transformers toy line. As in previous years, many of the new figures came from Takara's old Diaclone range; there was a single figure (Sky Lynx) that was a non-Takara toy licensed from a third party manufacturer, and some figures still had die-cast metal parts and rubber tyres. By the time 1986 was over, all these practices would cease – future Transformers would be bespoke toys, designed specifically for the range; Takara would be Hasbro's sole Eastern partner; and in a push to make the toys cheaper (and sturdier), Transformers would from now on be predominantly plastic.

The 1986 roster of characters was dominated by two contrasting sets of figures: the 'Scramble City' combiners and the new movie line.

The Scramble City combiners began life as a range called 'Free Combination' (or 'Jizai Gattai', in the original Japanese). This was an old Diaclone concept, put on hold when Takara ditched that brand in order to concentrate on Transformers. These were combiners, similar to the 1985 Constructicon figures but with an added twist. Each combiner team consisted of five robots: a larger Transformer who would form the torso, and four smaller limb-bots. Each limb robot was interchangeable, allowing children to create their own unique super-robots using different combinations of figures. In the US, there was no specific marketing term used to describe these 'Free Combination' toys; in Europe they were marketed as 'Special Teams' and in Japan they were part of the 'Scramble City' line. This latter term has since been adopted as the *de facto* name for this type of combiner team.

In addition to these came the largest individual Transformers yet, the two city playsets Metroplex and Trypticon. Both of these were scaled to work with the new Scramble City combiners, and each had a combining gimmick of its own.

Meanwhile, 1986 saw the release of the animated theatrical feature film, *The Transformers: The Movie*. To coincide with the movie, Hasbro released a wave of toys based on the new characters introduced therein. As the movie was set in the near-future (the year 2005), the movie figures had completely fictional vehicular forms. Whereas the majority of Transformers toys up to this point had been based on real-world vehicles and machines, the movie line featured abstract, alien cars and jets. To accommodate these new figures, many of the older 1984 and 1985 toys were discontinued – this point was emphasised in the animated movie, which saw the deaths of long-standing characters such as Optimus Prime and Starscream.

The year's special offers and pack-ins included a series of posters (included with the larger figures), part of a promotion entitled 'Decipher the Decepticon'. Smaller figures came with free sew-on patches advertising yet another competition, 'Prizes in Disguise'. Many of the figures, including Hot Rod and the Predacons, were initially manufactured with die-cast content. By year's end, many of these toys had been reissued in all-plastic variants.

Autobot Mini Vehicles:
The five Mini-Vehicles released in 1985 remained available to buy in 1986, as did 1984's Bumblebee figure. All other 1984 Mini-Vehicles were discontinued. Their ranks were bolstered by:

- **Hubcap**. As with the majority of the new Mini-Vehicles, Hubcap was a re-coloured and modified version of one of the now-discontinued 1984 toys. Hubcap was basically a yellow Cliffjumper (a Porsche), but with a different head and no spoiler.
- **Outback**. Essentially a tan and brown re-release of Brawn (a Jeep), with a new face, arms and chest.
- **Pipes**. A blue truck cab, Pipes is an extensively modified version of the old Huffer toy.
- **Swerve**. A red and white four-wheel-drive truck, this toy is a re-coloured Gears, but with a new head and chest.
- **Tailgate**. As with his predecessor, Windcharger, the toy is a Pontiac sports car. Now coloured white, he sports a new head and chest design.
- **Wheelie**. The solitary original figure in this year's line-up of Mini-Vehicles, Wheelie is a new character introduced for *The Transformers: The Movie*, and converts into a space-age orange car.

Autobot Cassettes
A series of Autobot cassettes was released to provide the 1985 Blaster toy (still available as part of the 1986 range) with some additional play value.

- **Eject**. Transforms from a blue and grey microcassette into a robot.
- **Ramhorn**. A brown microcassette that transforms into a rhinoceros. Ramhorn and Eject were available only as a twin-pack.
- **Rewind**. Identical to Eject, but with a black and grey livery.
- **Steeljaw**. This microcassette transforms into a yellow lion. Again, Rewind and Steeljaw were available only as a two-pack.

Autobot Cars:
All previous Autobot Cars were now discontinued, with the exception of Mirage, Ratchet, Sunstreaker and Wheeljack, which were available via mail-order in exchange for cash and Robot Points.

- **Blurr**. As with all of the new Autobot 'Cars', Blurr was a new character created especially for the movie, and as such transformed into a futuristic blue vehicle.
- **Hot Rod**. A red futuristic sports car.
- **Kup**. A futuristic turquoise pickup truck.

Autobot Triple Changers:

- **Broadside**. A grey and red robot with two vehicle modes: a futuristic jet and an aircraft carrier.

- **Sandstorm**. Transforms into either a helicopter or a dune buggy. He is orange and black in colour.
- **Springer**. This grey and green Transformer is another to have featured prominently in the theatrical movie. His vehicle modes are both futuristic: a helicopter and a car.

Autobot Heroes:
Deluxe figures, slightly bigger than the standard Autobot Cars.

- **Rodimus Prime**. A red and yellow futuristic van, which splits into two components, a robot and a battle platform. In *The Transformers: The Movie*, Rodimus Prime is an upgraded version of the Hot Rod character, who leads the future Autobots after Optimus Prime's death.
- **Wreck-Gar**. A brown and orange motorcycle, and another new character created for the movie.

(Autobot) Aerialbots:
One of the 'Scramble City' combiner teams, the five figures combine to form the giant Autobot **Superion**.

- **Air Raid**. Transforms from robot mode into a black F-15 Eagle jet. Can also transform into a combiner limb (either an arm or leg) compatible with any of the other Scramble City teams. He is usually depicted as Superion's left leg.
- **Fireflight**. A red and white F-4 Phantom jet, he is also a combiner limb, and usually forms the right arm of Superion.
- **Silverbolt**. The Aerialbot leader, Silverbolt is a white Concorde SST and forms the head and torso of Superion. He also has a fourth mode, a launching ramp for his fellow Aerialbots.
- **Skydive**. An F-16 Falcon, Skydive is grey and black, and in limb mode is most often seen as Superion's right leg.
- **Slingshot**. Transforms into a Harrier jumpjet. Can also become a limb, where he's nominally the left arm of Superion.

Autobot) Protectobots:
The second Autobot Scramble City combiner team, the theme here is rescue vehicles. The five figures can merge to form **Defensor**.

- **Blades**. Transforms from robot to rescue helicopter and back. This red and white Autobot is also a combiner limb, and is usually the right arm of Defensor.
- **First Aid**. A white ambulance. Can also become a limb, and is most commonly seen as Defensor's left arm.
- **Groove**. A white police motorcycle, Groove is predominantly depicted as Defensor's right leg.
- **Hot Spot**. A light blue fire truck, Hot Spot is the team leader and therefore becomes Defensor's head and torso. As with the other team leaders, Hot Spot boasts a fourth 'base' mode, and becomes a repair bay. He can also become a (very

rudimentary) car carrier.
- **Streetwise**. Transforms into both an off-white police car and a combiner limb, where he's most often depicted as Defensor's left leg.

Other Miscellaneous Autobots:

- **Metroplex**. A giant white Transformer, Metroplex can become either a rolling battle station or an Autobot City, where he's scaled for compatibility with smaller figures such as the Mini Vehicles and combiner limbs. He has ports in his shoulders and knees that can accommodate four combiner limbs; when attached, these give him a 'super' robot mode. Also included in the box are three small figures: **Scamper**, who transforms from a robot into a black race car; **Slammer**, a grey tank that can be reconfigured into a tower and weapon for Metroplex's city mode; and **Six-Gun**, a robot that's the combined mode of Metroplex's various guns and weaponry.
- **Sky Lynx**. A rarity in 1986 – a Transformer not designed by or in conjunction with Takara. The Sky Lynx figure was designed by Tomy and licenced from Toy Box – a partnership that had also begat the Omega Supreme figure a year earlier. Unlike Omega Supreme, the original iteration of Sky Lynx had never seen release in Japan, as Toy Box had cancelled their range of transforming figures due to poor sales. Sky Lynx is a white space shuttle that transforms into a 'dino bird', while the shuttle's undercarriage/payload can detach and transform into a lynx. Both elements can then recombine into a griffin-like four-legged bird.
- **Ultra Magnus**. One of the last Diaclone toys to be co-opted as a Transformer, this was a red, white and blue re-release of Takara's old 'Powered Convoy' figure (originally released in blue, red and grey). Ultra Magnus is a car carrier, the front cab being a repaint of the Optimus Prime robot. The cab can then combine with the carrier trailer to form a larger robot.

Although by now unavailable in stores, Optimus Prime could still be obtained (as a 'Movie Edition') via the mail-order Robot Points scheme.

Decepticon Planes:
Starscream, Dirge, Ramjet and Thrust were all still available in 1986. Thundercracker could also be obtained, but only via mail order from Hasbro.

- **Cyclonus**. A purple futuristic jet.
- **Scourge**. A blue and white futuristic vehicle, reminiscent of a hovercraft.

Decepticon Cassettes:

- **Ratbat**. Transforms from a magenta-coloured microcassette into a robotic bat creature. Unavailable to buy individually, he was sold only as part of a two-pack with a re-released Frenzy.

Decepticon Triple Changers:
The 1985 Triple Changers Astrotrain and Blitzwing remained available into 1986. Their numbers were bolstered by …

- **Octane**. An off-white/purple robot with two vehicle modes, a tanker truck and a jumbo jet.

(Decepticon) Combaticons:
A Scramble City combiner team with a military theme, the five robots combined to form **Bruticus**.

- **Blast Off**. This combiner limb can become a brown/purple robot and a space shuttle. He's regularly depicted as the right arm of Bruticus.
- **Brawl**. A green tank Transformer, Brawl is nominally the left leg of Bruticus.
- **Onslaught**. The Combaticon leader, Onslaught is a purple and green missile transport, and forms Bruticus's torso. He also has a 'battle station' mode.
- **Swindle**. A tan-coloured 4x4 off-road vehicle, and also a Scramble City combiner limb, in which mode he's usually the right leg of Bruticus.
- **Vortex**. This grey helicopter is also a combiner limb, and is often depicted as Bruticus's left arm.

(Decepticon) Stunticons:
The fourth and final Scramble City team of 1986, the Stunticons were all road vehicles. They combined to form **Menasor** and, as with the Aerialbots and Protectobots, were also available as a gift set.

- **Breakdown**. A cream-coloured Lamborghini and limb-bot; predominantly used as Menasor's right leg.
- **Dead End**. Transforms from red robot to Porsche to combiner limb. Usually the left arm of Menasor.
- **Drag Strip**. A yellow F-1 racer, Drag Strip is also a Scramble City-type limb, and is nominally the right arm of Menasor.
- **Motormaster**. A black and grey truck, Motormaster is the Stunticon leader and as such forms the torso of their combined form, Menasor. He also has a 'ramp' mode, and his accessories include an unnamed black scout car, which becomes a chest plate for Menasor.
- **Wildrider**. A grey Ferrari and combiner limb, Wildrider is usually Menasor's left leg.

Decepticon Battlechargers:
Car Transformers with pull-back-and-go motors and automatic transformation, similar in concept to the 1985 Jumpstarter figures.

- **Runabout**. A black Lotus.
- **Runamuck**. A white Pontiac.

(Decepticon) Predacons:
Another combiner team – this time, all the robots transform into animals. Unlike the Scramble City combiners, the individual members are not interchangeable

with other groups, and can combine only with each other. Furthermore, each robot transforms into a specific body part (arm, leg or torso), whereas in the Scramble City teams any of the smaller robots could form either an arm or a leg. The combined mode is named **Predaking**.

- **Divebomb**. A black and orange eagle. Can also become an arm for Predaking (usually the left).
- **Headstrong**. A red and yellow rhinoceros, and can also form either of Predaking's legs (though usually the left).
- **Rampage**. An orange tiger and the other arm for Predaking.
- **Razorclaw**. A yellow and black lion, Razorclaw is also the torso of Predaking.
- **Tantrum**. Predaking's other leg, Tantrum becomes an orange bull.

Other Miscellaneous Decepticons:

- **Gnaw**. Another movie character, Gnaw represents one of the Sharkticon warriors who attack the Autobots on the planet Quintessa. He transforms into a purple amphibious monster.
- **Trypticon**. A grey Transformer with three modes: a battle station, a city, and a robotic dinosaur. In creature mode, Trypticon has a battery-powered motor that allows him to walk. In his city configuration he can combine with the ramp and battle station modes of Motormaster and Onslaught respectively to become a 'super Trypticon'. Accessories include **Brunt**, a tank that splits up into various towers and parts for Trypticon's city mode; and **Full-Tilt**, a small robot who becomes either a futuristic car or Trypticon's chest plate in dinosaur mode.
- **Galvatron**. A grey and purple Decepticon, and one of the most prominent characters in *The Transformers: The Movie*. He can transform from a robot into either a futuristic tank or a laser pistol, with battery-powered lights and sounds.
- **Reflector**. A re-release of an old Takara MicroChange toy ('MC-05 Microx'), this is a black and grey camera that splits into three separate robots, **Spectro**, **Spyglass** and **Viewfinder**. As we shall see in the notes to the cartoon episode {1-15} 'A Plague of Insecticons', Reflector was originally due for a 1984 release (hence his appearance in early cartoon episodes and comics), but then cancelled until 1986. He was available only via the mail-away Robot Points scheme.

As with Optimus Prime, Megatron was also available as a 'Movie Edition', albeit through the Robot Points programme only.

The 1987 Toy Range

So far as the Transformers toy range was concerned, 1987 was the 'year of the gimmick'. It was no longer enough that a Transformer could switch between two modes – there had to be another selling point added to the mix. Of all the figures launched in 1987, just two – the Decepticon Cassettes Slugfest and Overkill – were designed simply to convert between their two modes.

Some of these new gimmicks had been seen before – the Throttlebots featured pull-back-and-and-go motors that harked back to the 1985 Powerdashers and Mini Spies; and the Technobots and Terrorcons were new Scramble City-type combiner teams.

The Headmaster and Targetmaster teams formed the core of the 1987 range, and featured some interesting new concepts. The Headmasters were robots with removable heads; while the body could convert into a vehicle (or robotic animal) as per usual, the head could transform into a small humanoid, which could then ride or pilot the larger figure. The Targetmasters were a similar concept; the toys' weapons could transform into small mini-figures.

Another departure from the norm was marked by the figures' vehicle modes, which continued the aesthetic introduced in *The Transformers: The Movie*, in that they were predominantly alien or futuristic. Although the Throttlebots, Duocons and Punch/Counterpunch all had present-day vehicle modes, the vast majority of the toys were unabashedly space-age.

On a related note, another notable aspect of the figures this year was that they featured more lurid colour schemes than ever before, almost as if the figures' designers had highlighter pens in mind when deciding upon the toys' final look. In the early days of the Transformers, when they were designed to resemble realistic vehicles, the colour schemes had been chosen to suit. No longer constrained by the need for verisimilitude, these alien cars and futuristic jets were now bedecked in dazzling pinks, yellows and oranges.

For the first time, all the figures introduced this year were designed by Takara specifically for the Transformers range.

(Autobot) Throttlebots:
Small, simple transforming cars with pull-back-and-go motors. They effectively replaced the old Mini-Vehicle range. Although each was a unique and individual figure, they shared the same basic transformation scheme.

- **Chase**. A red Ferrari.
- **Freeway**. A blue Corvette.
- **Goldbug**. A gold VW Beetle.
- **Rollbar**. A green Jeep.
- **Searchlight**. A white Ford RS2000.
- **Wideload**. An orange and blue dump truck.

(Autobot) Technobots:
A new Scramble City combiner team, the five figures could clip together to form **Computron**. The figures were available singly or as a gift set. The theme for the group is futuristic vehicles.

- **Afterburner**. A futuristic orange motorcycle. He could also form a combiner limb, usually Computron's right arm.
- **Lightspeed**. A red futuristic car. Also transforms into Computron's right leg, or indeed the limb of any Scramble City combiner.
- **Nosecone**. A brown drill tank. As a combiner limb, he's normally depicted as the left leg of Computron.
- **Scattershot**. A red spaceship, and the torso of Computron. He also has a third

mode, that of a rocket launcher emplacement.

- **Strafe**. A white futuristic jet. Can become a Scramble City-compatible arm or leg, usually the left arm of Computron.

Autobot Clones:
A novel concept, the clones were Autobot figures with identical robot modes (from the front, at least), but had different transformations and different vehicle modes. To differentiate between the two figures when in robot mode, each featured a rub-sign that, when activated, revealed an icon depicting the figure's vehicle mode.

- **Cloudraker**. Transforms from a red and grey robot to a futuristic jet. Available only as part of a two-pack with –
- **Fastlane**. A red/grey robot that converts to a futuristic car.

(Autobot) Monsterbots:
The Monsterbots transformed from robots into monster creatures. Their special gimmick was that they could generate harmless sparks via a friction mechanism (similar to those in cigarette lighters).

- **Doublecross**. A grey two-headed dragon.
- **Grotusque**: A pink, winged monster, with a head reminiscent of a sabre-toothed tiger.
- **Repugnus**: A yellow/orange insect monster.

Autobot Targetmasters:
Each figure came complete with a gun that could transform into a small humanoid figure. (The name of the smaller figure is listed in brackets after that of the main toy.) The previously-released Hot Rod, Kup and Blurr were also reissued as part of the Targetmaster range.

- **Blurr** (with **Haywire**). For this re-release of the 1986 figure, the toy was slightly retooled to accommodate the new Targetmaster weapon.
- **Crosshairs** (with **Pinpointer**). A red/blue futuristic truck.
- **Hot Rod** (with **Firebolt**). As with Blurr, Hot Rod was slightly modified from his 1986 release.
- **Kup** (with **Recoil**). Again, this re-release was re-tooled, given fists with larger holes to accommodate the thicker handle of the Targetmaster weapon, and a new weapon mounting-point in vehicle mode.
- **Pointblank** (with **Peacemaker**). A red futuristic car.
- **Sureshot** (with **Spoilsport**). A yellow/orange futuristic dune buggy.

Autobot Headmasters:
Each figure's head was detachable; the head could transform into a mini-figure, which could pilot the main toy when in vehicle mode.

- **Brainstorm** (with **Arcana**). A turquoise-coloured futuristic jet.
- **Chromedome** (with **Stylor**). A brown and cream futuristic car.

- **Hardhead** (with **Duros**). A green alien tank.
- **Highbrow** (with **Gort**.) A futuristic blue helicopter.

Other Miscellaneous Autobots:

- **Punch**. Marketed as a 'Double Spy', Punch was a triple-changer – as well as his normal robot mode and his (blue) car mode, he could also transform into a second, Decepticon robot mode, thereby allowing him to spy on his enemies. The Decepticon robot mode was named **Counterpunch**.
- **Fortress Maximus**. By far the biggest Transformer figure of the original run (22 inches, or 56 centimetres tall), and indeed the tallest Transformer figure ever until it was finally bested by 2013's Titan-Class Metroplex. Fortress Maximus could convert from a robot into either a city or a battle station. As a Headmaster, his head could detach and become a smaller robot, **Cerebros**. Also, the head of Cerebros could itself detach and form an even smaller figure, **Spike**. Cerebros could also transform into an attachment for the Fortress Maximus city mode. Also included were **Gasket** (an armoured car) and **Grommet** (a tank-like vehicle), which could combine to form the robot **Cog**.

Also remaining in the Autobot range were the following 1986 toys: the cassettes (Eject, Ramhorn, Rewind and Steeljaw), the Aerialbots, the Protectobots, plus Metroplex, Rodimus Prime, Sky Lynx, Ultra Magnus and Wreck-Gar.

Mail-away Autobots included Cliffjumper, Cosmos, Mirage, Optimus Prime, Ratchet, Sunstreaker, Warpath and Wheeljack, all available via the Robot Points scheme.

Decepticon Cassettes:

- **Overkill**. Transforms from a microcassette into a blue/white tyrannosaurus.
- **Slugfest**. A green cassette that transforms into a stegosaurus. Slugfest and Overkill were available only as a two-pack.

(Decepticon) Terrorcons:
A five-robot Scramble City combiner team. The theme of the group was 'monsters'. Unlike their Autobot equivalent (the Technobots), they were available only individually; there was no gift set option in the Western world. When combined they formed the giant Decepticon **Abominus**.

- **Blot**. Transforms from a robot into a blue and purple monster, vaguely mole-like in appearance. Also a combiner limb, usually Abominus's right arm.
- **Cutthroat**. His alternative mode is that of a bird-monster. As a combiner limb, he can form the arm or leg of any Scramble City-type robot, but is predominantly the right leg of Abominus.
- **Hun-Gurrr**. Converts between grey robot and two-headed dragon modes. Also forms the torso of Abominus.
- **Rippersnapper**. This white robot can transform into a shark monster or a combiner limb. He's best known as the left arm of Abominus.

- **Sinnertwin**. A yellow two-headed monster and combiner limb, usually the left leg of Abominus.

NB: Although his box and instructions call him 'Hun-Gurrr', the spelling of the Terrorcon leader's name has been variable to say the least. 'Hun-Grr' and 'Hun-Grrr' have also been used in officially-sanctioned media, including comics, cartoon scripts and Hasbro toy catalogues.

(Decepticon) Duocons:
Another new concept – each Duocon figure comprised of two separate vehicle components that clipped together to form a robot.

- **Battletrap**: A blue van and grey helicopter that combine to form a single robot.
- **Flywheels**: A green tank and a red jet merge to form a robot.

Decepticon Clones:
As with the Autobot Clones above, these were two Transformers packaged together, with identical robot modes but completely different transformations. The Decepticon two-pack included:

- **Pounce**. Transforms into a green and purple puma.
- **Wingspan**. A green and purple hawk.

Decepticon Targetmasters:
As per the Autobot Targetmasters, these toys included weapons that could themselves transform into mini figures.

- **Cyclonus** (with **Nightstick**). A toy carried over from the previous year's range, now packaged with a bonus Targetmaster and modified to hold or mount the new weapon.
- **Misfire** (with **Aimless**). A pink alien jet.
- **Scourge** (with **Fracas**). Another 1986 figure, re-released and modified.
- **Slugslinger** (with **Caliburst**). A grey and blue twin-nosed jet.
- **Triggerhappy** (with **Blowpipe**). A blue futuristic jet.

NB: Scourge's Targetmaster partner Fracas is the only Transformer from the original run whose name varies considerably in pronunciation throughout the English-speaking world. In American English, it's pronounced fray-cass, whereas in British English it's frac-car (closer to the original French).

Decepticon Headmasters:
As with the Autobot Headmasters, these figures had detachable heads that could themselves turn into humanoids.

- **Mindwipe** (with **Vorath**). A magenta and brown bat.
- **Skullcruncher** (with **Grax**). A green and pink alligator.
- **Weirdwolf** (with **Monzo**). A yellow wolf.

(Decepticon) Headmaster Horrorcons:
A twist on the Headmaster concept: the core robots were triple changers, with a jet and animal mode. The small mini-figures could act as pilots in jet mode, or could transform into the heads of either the robot or animal.

- **Apeface** (with **Spasma**). A grey/black robot with alternative ape and futuristic jet modes.
- **Snapdragon** (with **Krunk**). A grey/black robot that can transform into either an alien jet or a tyrannosaurus-like dinosaur.

Other Miscellaneous Decepticons:

- **Sixshot**. A green and white Decepticon who could transform from a robot into a star fighter, or a futuristic armoured car, or an alien tank, or a laser pistol, or a winged wolf. He was marketed as a 'Six Changer', reflecting his impressive and unprecedented rage of modes.
- **Scorponok**. A giant purple and green robot that could transform into either a city mode or a scorpion. As a Headmaster, his head could transform into a smaller figure called **Zarak**. Also packaged with another robot, **Fasttrack**, which transformed into a six-wheeled armoured car.

Other Decepticons that remained available from previous years were the Predacon, Combaticon and Stunticon combiner teams, plus the Ratbat/Frenzy cassette two-pack, Galvatron, Gnaw and Trypticon.

Robot Points could be redeemed against Megatron, Reflector and Thundercracker, who all remained available, albeit as mail-away exclusives.

Decoys:
The smaller Transformers of the 1987 range (the Throttlebots and combiner limbs) were sometimes available with free 'Decoy' figures also included in the pack. Decoys were small, unpainted, unarticulated figures, made of a rubbery plastic. The Autobot Decoys were available only in red, while the Decepticons were purple (although some red Decepticon Decoys were on sale for a short time). Each decoy was individually numbered.

The Decoys were originally designed for the Japanese market, where they were marketed under the 'Hero Collection' banner. Because of this, Megatron's Decoy has a sword (which matches his Japanese appearance) and there is no Gears figure (as Gears was never released in Japan under the Transformers brand). A Laserbeak Decoy was sold in Japan, but was never officially released as part of the American line-up (although rumours abound that some Laserbeaks did, in fact, see a US release).

Autobot Decoys: 1) Grimlock; 2) Snarl; 3) Swoop; 4) Sludge; 5) Slag; 6) Ratchet; 7) Ironhide; 8) Smokescreen; 9) Grapple; 10) Trailbreaker; 11) Sunstreaker; 12) Skids; 13) Jazz; 14) Inferno; 15) Tracks; 16) Red Alert; 17) Hound; 18) Sideswipe; 19) Prowl; 20) Mirage; 21) Hoist; 22) Wheeljack; 23) Bluestreak; 24) Brawn; 25) Windcharger; 26) Bumblebee; 27) Huffer; 28) Cliffjumper; 29) Blaster; 30) Perceptor; 31) Optimus Prime.

Decepticon Decoys: 32) Megatron; 33) Skywarp; 34) Thundercracker; 35) Starscream;

36) Soundwave; 37) Blitzwing; 38) Astrotrain; 39) Kickback; 40) Shrapnel; 41) Bombshell; 42) Hook; 43) Scavenger; 44) Bonecrusher; 45) Long Haul; 46) Mixmaster; 47) Scrapper; 48) Devastator; 49) Ravage; 50) Frenzy; 51) Shockwave; 52) Reflector.

The 1988 Toy Range

The 1988 range of Transformers could essentially be considered '1987, part 2': many of the gimmicks introduced the previous year (figures that could generate harmless sparks, Headmasters, Targetmasters, six-changers, etc) continued to form the bulk of the line. There was another Scramble City combiner team (the Seacons), and yet more cassettes.

There was still room for innovation, however: following on from the success of the Headmasters and Targetmasters, a new gimmick was introduced: Powermasters. These Transformers were 'locked' into their vehicle modes, but included small mini-figures that could convert into plug-in 'engines' for the vehicles. When in place, these would unlock the simple latch mechanism and allow the larger figure to be transformed.

While the Powermaster idea would prove to be short-lived, one other innovation in 1988 would last a bit longer: the Pretenders. These were hollow, non-transforming action figures that could split open, revealing a smaller Transformer figure stored inside. Although the outer shells often boasted extremely impressive designs, the inner Transformers were by necessity simple affairs.

Away from the gimmicks, there were other noteworthy aspects of the 1988 range. After the brief flirtation with futuristic vehicles, the majority of new toys introduced this year had more Earthly, contemporary-looking vehicle modes (the main exception being the Pretenders, whose simplistic nature meant that many of them could convert only into crude, abstract 'alien' vehicles). Also, the launch of a new Optimus Prime toy (as a Powermaster) would pave the way for further classic characters to be similarly re-imagined in the remaining years of the toy line. (Although Goldbug, Rodimus Prime and Galvatron were all reincarnations of other characters, Powermaster Optimus Prime was the first to reuse an old name.)

Furthermore, with the exception of the Powermasters (most of which were quite involved), the Transformers of 1988 were generally less complex than in previous years. The new Headmaster and Targetmaster figures (as well as the solitary six-changer) were noticeably smaller and simpler than their 1987 counterparts. Although this made the toys cheaper to produce and more accessible to smaller children, the move set a precedent: without exception, the remaining years of the line would see Transformer designs and engineering that were noticeably simpler than in years past.

(Autobot) Sparkabots:
These were small, cheap, pocket-money figures. When rolled across a flat surface, sparks were generated from the rear of the figures' vehicle modes.

- **Fizzle**. A blue race car.
- **Guzzle**. A grey tank.
- **Sizzle**. A black/red sports car.

Autobot Cassettes:
In a novel twist on the formula, this year's cassette packs included two figures that could combine into a larger robot.

- **Grand Slam**. A red microcassette that transforms into an alien tank.
- **Raindance**. Transforms from a blue microcassette into an alien jet.

The two cassettes combined to form the larger robot, **Slamdance**. For the third consecutive year, the Rewind/Steeljaw and Ramhorn/Eject cassette two-packs from 1986 continued to be available.

(Autobot) Triggerbots:
Another group of low-cost figures, these were notable for incorporating hidden, spring-loaded weapons that would pop out at the touch of a button.

- **Backstreet**. An orange race car.
- **Dogfight**. A blue jet.
- **Override**. A red and blue motorcycle.

(Autobot) Headmasters:
Similar to the 1987 Headmaster figures, but simpler and smaller. Again the toys featured detachable robot heads that could themselves transform into mini-figures.

- **Hosehead** (with **Lug**). A red fire engine.
- **Nightbeat** (with **Muzzle**). A blue and yellow car.
- **Siren** (with **Quig**). A grey fire-chief's car.

Brainstorm, Chromedome, Hardhead and Highbrow remained available from the previous year.

(Autobot) Targetmasters:
Again, these were less complex figures than the 1987 Targetmasters. However, this was partially mitigated by the addition of a second Targetmaster weapon – each toy now came with two mini-figures, each of which could either transform into a weapon, or combine to form a larger 'super weapon'. These figures were sometimes referred to as 'Double Targetmasters' to reflect this fact.

- **Landfill** (with **Flintlock** and **Silencer**). A tan dump truck.
- **Quickmix** (with **Boomer** and **Ricochet**). A red cement mixer.
- **Scoop** (with **Holepunch** and **Tracer**). An orange tractor shovel.

The new-mould Targetmasters from the previous year's assortment (Crosshairs, Pointblank and Sureshot) remained available.

(Autobot) Powermasters:
As described above, these toys included mini-figures that could transform into the main robot's engine.

- **Getaway** (with **Rev**). A white car.
- **Joyride** (with **Hotwire**). A teal dune buggy.
- **Slapdash** (with **Lube**). A yellow and blue race car.

(Autobot) Pretenders:

Each robot came complete with a larger 'shell' figure that could split open and store the Transformer within. Details of the outer shell are given in brackets after the main description.

- **Catilla**. A grey sabre-toothed tiger (yellow sabre-toothed tiger).
- **Chainclaw**. A yellow bear (brown bear).
- **Cloudburst**. A red alien jet (human in red armour).
- **Groundbreaker**. A grey alien car (human in orange armour).
- **Gunrunner**. An orange alien jet (red alien car).
- **Landmine**. A futuristic, grey, wheeled tank-like vehicle (human in yellow armour).
- **Sky High**. A red and grey alien helicopter (human in red armour).
- **Splashdown**. A grey and red futuristic hovercraft (human in teal armour).
- **Waverider**. A black alien submersible (human in grey armour).

Catilla and Chainclaw, with their animal transformations and shells, were known as 'Pretender Beasts'. Gunrunner was a 'Pretender Vehicle', whose robot mode could either store within the car shell, or sit in its openable cockpit like a driver.

Other Miscellaneous Autobots:

- **Optimus Prime** (with **Hi-Q**). The new version of Optimus Prime was, like his original version, a red truck cab with a grey trailer. Like the original, the cab transformed into the core robot, while the trailer could become a battle station. As a Powermaster, a small mini-figure/engine (named Hi-Q) was also included. Cab and trailer could combine to form a larger robot.
- **Quickswitch**. As with the larger Sixshot figure the previous year, Quickswitch was a six-changer. He could transform from a grey, red and teal robot into an alien jet, a drill tank, a futuristic hovercraft, a laser pistol and a flying puma.

Also still in the shops from the 1987 Autobot range: Fortress Maximus, the Technobots, Monsterbots and Autobot Clones. Also available via the mail-order Robot Points scheme: Cosmos, Hubcap (erroneously billed as Cliffjumper on the order form), Mirage, Ratchet, Sunstreaker, Warpath and Wheeljack.

(Decepticon) Firecons:

The Decepticon equivalent of the Sparkabots; each figure transformed into a robotic monster that, when rolled along the ground, emitted harmless sparks from the creature's mouth.

- **Cindersaur**. A purple dinosaur-like creature.
- **Flamefeather**. A blue bird-monster.
- **Sparkstalker**. A pink insect-monster.

Decepticon Cassettes:
As per this year's Autobot cassettes, the tapes in this Decepticon two-pack could combine to form a single robot, **Squawkbox**. The 1986 Overkill and Slugfest two pack was also still available.

- **Beastbox**. A purple microcassette that transforms into an ape.
- **Squawktalk**. A green cassette/bird.

(Decepticon) Triggercons:
The Triggercons shared the same gimmick as the Triggerbots: spring-loaded weapons.

- **Crankcase**. A grey 4x4.
- **Ruckus**. A purple/tan dune buggy.
- **Windsweeper**. A brown jet.

(Decepticon) Seacons:
A group of Decepticons who could transform into sea-monsters. Uniquely for a Scramble City combiner team, there were six members to collect – the leader/torso plus five limb-bots. As well as their standard robot, creature and limb modes, the smaller limb-robots also had the ability to transform into a weapon – so when the combined mode, **Piranacon**, was formed (from the torso plus any combination of the other five), the spare sixth member would become the giant robot's weapon. A Seacon gift set was available, but it did not include Nautilator.

- **Nautilator**. A green and grey robot/combiner limb/gun/lobster creature. Although he can form the limb of any Scramble City combiner team, he's most commonly found as the right arm of Piranacon.
- **Overbite**. A purple and green robot/limb /gun/shark creature. As the 'odd-man-out' of the team, colour-wise (he's the only purple Seacon), he's usually depicted as Piranacon's gun.
- **Seawing**. A green and grey robot/combiner limb/gun/manta creature. Typically the left arm of Piranacon.
- **Skalor**. A blue and pink robot/limb/gun/coelacanth creature. Nominally Piranacon's right leg.
- **Snaptrap**. Transforms from a robot into a green and pink turtle-monster. As the Seacon leader, he forms the torso of Piranacon.
- **Tentakil**. A blue and pink robot/limb/gun/squid monster, usually the left leg of Piranacon.

(Decepticon) Headmasters:
As was the case with the year's new Autobot Headmasters, these were smaller and simpler than the Headmaster figures introduced in 1987.

- **Fangry** (with **Brisko**). A black and purple winged wolf-monster.
- **Horri-Bull** (with **Kreb**). A blue and grey bull-monster.
- **Squeezeplay** (with **Lokos**). A purple/blue crab-monster.

All the previous year's Decepticon Headmasters (including Scorponok) remained available in 1988.

(Decepticon) Targetmasters:
Again, these were 'Double Targetmasters', smaller than the previous year's range but including two transforming guns.

- **Needlenose** (with **Sunbeam** and **Zigzag**). A grey jet.
- **Quake** (with **Heater** and **Tiptop**). A red tank.
- **Spinister** (with **Hairsplitter** and **Singe**). A blue helicopter.

The new-mould Decepticon Targetmasters from the previous year (Misfire, Slugslinger and Triggerhappy) remained available.

(Decepticon) Powermasters:

- **Darkwing** (with **Throttle**). A dark grey jet.
- **Dreadwind** (with **Hi-Test**). A light grey jet.

The two Decepticon Powermasters can combine to form **Dreadwing** – not a robot, but a combined super-jet mode.

(Decepticon) Pretenders:
Again, the descriptions of the outer shells are listed in brackets after the main figure.

- **Bomb Burst**. A blue futuristic jet (grey bipedal bat-monster).
- **Bugly**. A purple futuristic jet (black bipedal insect-monster).
- **Carnivac**. A purple wolf (grey wolf).
- **Finback**. A lilac futuristic submarine (burgundy bipedal fish-monster).
- **Iguanus**. A purple alien motorcycle (purple bipedal iguana-monster).
- **Roadgrabber**. An indigo alien jet (purple/pink futuristic car).
- **Skullgrin**. A grey alien tank (grey bipedal, skeletal bull-monster).
- **Snarler**. A brown boar (green boar).
- **Submarauder**. A purple futuristic submarine (blue bipedal fish-monster).

With their animal shells, Carnivac and Snarler were classed as 'Pretender Beasts'. As was the case with Gunrunner (his Autobot counterpart), Roadgrabber was a 'Pretender Vehicle', who could either be stored within his space-age car shell, or ride on it as a pilot.

Other Miscellaneous Decepticons:

- **Doubledealer**. (Technically a mercenary who could work for either faction, but sold in Decepticon packaging.) A green/grey missile launcher truck with two Powermaster engine mini-figures. **Knok** is the Autobot engine, and unlocks Doubledealer's (Autobot) robot mode, whereas **Skar** is a Decepticon engine (which itself transforms into a bat creature rather than a standard humanoid), and unlocks Doubledealer's Decepticon mode – a robotic falcon.

Other Decepticons still available this year included the Terrorcons, Sixshot and the Decepticon Clones. Megatron, Reflector and Thundercracker were still available via the Robot Points scheme.

The 1989 Toy Range

1989 saw the Transformers line narrow its focus down to two main gimmicks – Micromasters and Pretenders. The initial batch of Pretenders launched in 1988 had obviously been popular, so much so that it was decided to build the franchise around them. But while 1988's Pretenders had been a novel idea – non-transforming, hollow figures that could open up to reveal a Transformer hidden inside them – in 1989 the concept was taken to a whole new level.

There were Classic Pretenders, Mega Pretenders, Ultra Pretenders and combining Pretender Monsters. Some robots came with multiple shells, nested within each other like Russian dolls. Others had shells that could transform into a vehicle mode. One group even had shells made of a soft, rubbery plastic. What had begun as a unique but simple idea had now been taken to extremes – and with the concept now fully-mined, these would be the last Pretender figures produced by the range.

The other subset of Transformers this year, the Micromasters, were developed as a means to mimic the runaway success of a rival toy line, Micro Machines. Produced by Galoob, Micro Machines were extremely small, scaled-down vehicles that at the time were outselling more established toy car brands such as Matchbox and Hot Wheels. Their combination of small size and good detail was a major selling-point. Hasbro decided to take the winning formula of Micro Machines and adapt it for use within the Transformers franchise.

The result was the Micromasters – tiny figures (roughly two inches in height) that could transform into vehicles. Unlike the Pretenders, which for the most part were futuristic vehicles, animals and monsters, the Micromasters transformed into recognisable, real-world cars, planes and other vehicles. Micromasters were usually sold as 'patrols' (packs of multiple figures), but larger playsets were also introduced, for maximum playability. All these bases and playsets were part of a modular system (they could be connected together via a series of interlocking ramps), so that children could create a giant 'Micromaster City'.

Aside from this new direction for the toys themselves, another big change was to the packaging, with the franchise getting a bold new logo. In contrast to the rigid, square lettering of the original, this new one was positively dynamic, all curves and angles. Though an excellent design, it was in play for only two years before the line was cancelled, and therefore never got the chance to establish itself in the minds of the public.

Despite such radical changes (both intrinsic and cosmetic), Transformers sales had begun to dwindle quite considerably. The end was in sight …

Autobot Pretenders:
The 'standard' Pretenders from 1989 differed from the previous year's range, in that they were slightly smaller. However, thanks to the judicious use of clip-on accessories for the inner robot, their vehicle modes were more cohesive-looking than before.

- **Doubleheader**. A grey/red alien twin-nosed aircraft (two-headed human in blue armour).
- **Longtooth**. A grey/red futuristic truck (grey walrus-monster).
- **Pincher**. A grey/blue scorpion (human in yellow armour).

Autobot Classic Pretenders:
After the success of the Powermaster Optimus Prime toy the previous year, more 'classic' characters got updated figures, this time as part of the Pretender range. The Classic Pretenders were also available to buy without their outer shells – these shell-less versions were billed as 'Legends' and sold exclusively by the Kmart department store chain.

- **Bumblebee**. A yellow VW Beetle (human in yellow armour).
- **Grimlock**. A grey tyrannosaurus (human in grey armour).
- **Jazz**. A white Porsche (human in blue armour).

Autobot Mega Pretenders:
While Pretender shells were usually non-transformable, the Mega Pretenders had shells that had vehicle modes of their own. The shell and the inner robot could combine into a larger vehicle.

- **Crossblades**. A beige/orange futuristic dragster (human in beige armour that transforms into a helicopter). The inner robot can attach to the shell as an extended nose for its helicopter mode.
- **Vroom**. A red futuristic car (human in white armour that transforms into a motorcycle). When in vehicle form, the inner robot can attach to the shell's motorbike mode as a sidecar.

Autobot Ultra Pretender:
Ultra Pretenders featured a transformable inner robot, plus a humanoid shell that could also transform into a vehicle (which the inner robot could either be stored inside of, or ride in like a pilot). There was also a second (non-transforming) vehicular shell inside which both the robot and the first shell could be stored. Again, the outer vehicle could be piloted by the inner robot.

- **Skyhammer**. A gold/red/grey alien car (smaller transformable shell: human in red armour/alien jet; outer shell: red/grey alien jet).

Autobot Micromaster Patrols:
Packs of four extremely tiny figures.

Battle Patrol:

- **Big Shot**. A brown/cream wheeled tank.
- **Flak**. A green missile tank.
- **Sidetrack**. A cream/brown anti-aircraft tank.
- **Sunrunner**. A cream/green bomber plane.

Off Road Patrol:

- **Highjump**. A grey SUV.
- **Mudslinger**. A blue monster truck.
- **Powertrain**. An orange truck cab.
- **Tote**. A red van.

Race Car Patrol:

- **Free Wheeler**. A yellow Lamborghini.
- **Roadhandler**. A red Pontiac.
- **Swindler**. A grey DeLorean.
- **Tailspin**. A blue Porsche.

Rescue Patrol:

- **Fixit**. A white ambulance.
- **Red Hot**. A red fire engine.
- **Seawatch**. A blue hydrofoil.
- **Stakeout**. A black police car.

Autobot Micromaster Stations:
Single Micromaster figures with a small transforming 'Station' accessory.

- **Hot House**. A white bomber plane (sharing a mould with Tailwind, a 1989 Decepticon Micromaster from the Air Strike Patrol pack). Comes packed with a red 'Fire Station', which transforms into a tank-like battle platform.
- **Ironworks**. A yellow truck cab (a repaint of Powertrain, a 1989 Autobot Micromaster from the Off Road Patrol). Complete with 'Construction Station', a small grey/yellow building site playset that can convert into a communications bay.

Autobot Micromaster Transports:
These packs consisted of a single Micromaster figure with a larger 'Transport' accessory, designed to be used with the Micromaster in vehicle form. These Transports could also convert into a battle mode.

- **Erector**. A yellow truck cab. The transport accessory was 'Crane', a yellow-and-grey crane trailer, which could attach to the Micromaster when in vehicle mode. The trailer could also transform into a gun emplacement.
- **Overload**. A blue truck cab. Packaged with 'Car Carrier Trailer', a red/grey trailer that attached to the Micromaster cab. The trailer could transform into a futuristic aircraft for the Micromaster robot to pilot.

Autobot Micromaster Bases:
The Micromaster Bases were large vehicles (large enough for the smaller Micromasters to 'pilot') that could convert into a base. Each came packed with an exclusive

Micromaster figure.

- **Groundshaker**. A green jet (sharing a mould with Whisper, a 1989 Decepticon Micromaster from the Air Strike Patrol set). Packaged with 'ATV', a large blue six-wheeled all-terrain vehicle that converts into a battle station.
- **Countdown**. A red moon buggy. The centrepiece of the 1989 Transformers range, this impressive set also included a large 'Rocket Base', a mobile rocket launchpad (complete with rocket) that transforms into a giant base playset.

Other Autobots available in the shops this year included the the previous year's six humanoid Pretenders (Cloudburst, Groundbreaker, Landmine, Sky High, Splashdown and Waverider), plus Powermaster Optimus Prime, and the cassette two-packs Grand Slam/Raindance, Ramhorn/Eject and Rewind/Steeljaw. (These last two cassette packs had been on sale continuously since 1986, and as such boasted the longest period of availability of all the toys in the original line.)

Decepticon Pretenders:
As per this year's standard Autobot Pretenders, these were smaller figures than the previous year's assortment, but the inner robots were better-designed.

- **Bludgeon**. A green tank (orange-armoured skeletal samurai warrior).
- **Octopunch**. An orange robotic crab (green/maroon humanoid octopus creature).
- **Stranglehold**. An orange rhinoceros (a cream/purple human).

Decepticon Classic Pretender:

- **Starscream**. A grey jet (human in turquoise armour).

Decepticon Mega Pretender:

- **Thunderwing**. Grey futuristic jet (alien in grey armour that transforms into a spaceship). When in jet mode, the inner robot can attach to the nose of the shell's spaceship form to create a larger spacecraft.

Decepticon Ultra Pretender:

- **Roadblock**. A gold/grey futuristic tank (smaller transformable shell: purple insect monster/alien jet; outer shell: turquoise futuristic snowplough).

Decepticon Pretender Monsters:
This was a team of six Decepticon Pretender figures. Smaller than regular Pretenders, their shells were uniquely made from a soft, rubbery plastic. The six inner robots could combine to form **Monstructor**.

- **Birdbrain**. A purple/black warthog monster, and Monstructor's lower body (black bird-monster).
- **Bristleback**. A green/gold monster, and a Monstructor arm (beige turtle monster).

- **Icepick**. A claret/green monster, also a leg for Monstructor (orange ice monster).
- **Scowl**. A yellow/lilac dog-headed monster, and a Monstructor leg (blue rock monster).
- **Slog**. A black/gold monster, also Monstructor's upper body (red monster).
- **Wildfly**. A yellow/claret bird monster, and a Monstructor arm (purple winged monster).

Decepticon Micromaster Patrols:
Packs of four small toys.

Air Strike Patrol:

- **Nightflight**. A grey jet.
- **Storm Cloud**. A lilac jet.
- **Tailwind**. A grey bomber plane.
- **Whisper**. A black stealth fighter.

Sports Car Patrol:

- **Blackjack**. A black Ford Probe.
- **Detour**. A yellow Corvette Indy.
- **Hyperdrive**. A blue Mitsubishi X2S.
- **Road Hugger**. A purple Ferrari.

Decepticon Micromaster Stations:

- **Airwave**. A red jet (sharing a mould with Nightflight from the Air Strike Patrol). Comes complete with 'Airport', a small airport playset that transforms into a missile battery.
- **Greasepit**. A grey monster truck (a repaint of Mudslinger from the Off Road Patrol). Packaged with 'Gas Station', which transforms from a garage into a battle station.

Decepticon Micromaster Transports:

- **Flattop**. A burgundy jet. Comes with an 'Aircraft Carrier' accessory for use in vehicle mode, which can convert into an interstellar jet for Flattop to pilot.
- **Roughstuff**. A green truck cab with a 'Military Transport' trailer. The trailer can transform into a jet for the smaller Micromaster figure to ride in.

Decepticon Micromaster Bases:

- **Skyhopper**. A grey jet (a repaint of Storm Cloud from the Air Strike Patrol). Packaged with 'Helicopter', a large khaki helicopter that converts into a battle station.
- **Skystalker**. An orange Porsche. The larger of the two Decepticon base playsets, it included 'Interstellar Shuttle', a spaceship that converts into a battle station.

Other Decepticons still in the shops included the previous year's six 'large' Pretenders (Bomb-Burst, Bugly, Finback, Iguanus, Skullgrin and Submarauder), plus the cassette two-packs Overkill/Slugfest and Beastbox/Squawktalk.

The 1990 Toy Range

1990 was the final year of the original Transformers line (at least, in its North American incarnation). For various reasons, the brand had suffered a slow decline from its peak around 1986, and Hasbro were finally pulling the plug. They didn't go down without a fight, however: as well as a whole slew of new Micromasters figures, Hasbro introduced a unique new type of Transformers toy, known as Action Masters. These were Transformers that didn't transform.

Fans have for years debated the relative merits of the Action Masters. According to their detractors, these figures violated one of the main principles of the franchise. Although they came packaged with transformable accessories, this wasn't enough for some. Given that the Action Masters formed a major proportion of figures in the final year of the toy line, they have often been cited (perhaps unfairly) as one of the reasons for its cancellation.

On the other hand, unencumbered by the need to transform, the Action Masters were brilliantly accurate representations of some of the franchise's best-loved characters. Optimus Prime, Bumblebee, Megatron, Jazz and many other classic characters were rendered as Action Masters, most looking as if they had just stepped out of the cartoon.

Meanwhile, the Micromasters sub-line (originally introduced in 1989) made up the remainder of the Transformers released this year. A new gimmick was the notion of Micromaster Combiners. These were vehicles made up of two Micromasters. For example, the Autobot Micromaster named Phaser transforms into the front half of a space shuttle, while his partner Blast Master converts into the rear half. Not only could the two connect to form a completed space shuttle, but they could be mixed and matched with other Micromaster Combiners to form all sorts of combinations of bizarre hybrid vehicles.

Yet again, this appears to have been a ploy to ape a rival toy manufacturer – the year before, Matchbox had introduced a line of toy vehicles called Connectables, which could also be split into various parts and recombined in different configurations.

In previous years, Transformer names, tech-specs and biographies were the purview of Marvel's Bob Budiansky, the chief writer of the American Transformers comic. With his departure from the comic in 1989, such work was now done in-house by Hasbro themselves. This may account for the fact that three Transformers in the 1990 range – the Micromasters Sky High, Tracer and Barrage – were given names that were already taken by other characters.

(Autobot) Action Masters:
The basic Action Master sets were sold on carded blister packs and included a single figure (roughly 10cm tall) packaged with a handgun and a small transformable accessory (which could convert into an extension for the small handgun, to create a 'super weapon'). In the Action Master listings, an asterisk (*) indicates a re-imagined

'classic' character, and a dagger (†) indicates an entirely new character.

- **Blaster***. A grey/red action figure, with **Flight Pack**, a blue jetpack/gun extension.
- **Bumblebee***. A yellow/black action figure, with **Heli-Pack**, a blue helicopter backpack/gun extension.
- **Grimlock***. A grey/black action figure, with **Anti-Tank Cannon**, a red weapon emplacement/gun extension.
- **Inferno***. A red/black action figure, with **Hydro-Pack**, an orange backpack/gun extension.
- **Jackpot†**. A black/yellow action figure, with **Sights**, a black bird of prey /gun extension.
- **Jazz***. A white/blue action figure, with **Turbo Board**, a grey skateboard/gun extension.
- **Kick-Off†**. A black/white action figure, with **Turbo-Pack**, a black backpack/gun extension.
- **Mainframe†**. A red/blue action figure, with **Push-Button**, a blue robot/gun extension.
- **Rad†**. A red/grey action figure, with **Lionizer**, a red lion/gun extension.
- **Rollout†**. An orange/white action figure, with **Glitch**, a grey robot/gun extension.
- **Skyfall†**. A crimson/white action figure, with **Top-Heavy**, an orange rhino/gun extension.
- **Snarl***. A grey/red action figure, with **Tyrannitron**, a black dinosaur/gun extension.

The release of Bumblebee as an Action Master meant that the character had a toy available in every year (1984-1990) of the American Transformers toy line: the original Mini-Vehicle version was in the shops from 1984-1986; the Throttlebot Goldbug was in the shops from 1987-88; in 1989 the Pretender Classics version was released; and now in 1990 we had the Action Master version. Goldbug was also in the shops in 1991, as part of the European 'Classics' range.

(Autobot) Action Master Action Blasters:
Action Master figures packaged with small pilotable (and transformable) vehicles.

- **Over-Run†**. A red action figure, with **Attack Copter**, a green helicopter/gun emplacement.
- **Prowl***. A white action figure, with **Turbo Racer**, a white motorcycle/gun emplacement.

(Autobot) Action Master Vehicles:
Action Master figures packaged with medium-sized transformable vehicles.

- **Sprocket†**. A black/white action figure with **Attack Cruiser**, a green car/jet.
- **Wheeljack***. A white action figure with **Turbo Racer**, a red car/jet.

(Autobot) Action Master Armored Convoy:
An Action Master figure packaged with a large transformable vehicle.

- **Optimus Prime***. A red/blue action figure with **Armored Convoy**, an articulated truck. The truck cab transforms into a jet, while the trailer becomes a battle station.

(Autobot) Micromasters:
Standard four-packs of small Micromaster figures, similar to those released the previous year.

Air Patrol:

- **Blaze Master**. A mustard-coloured helicopter.
- **Eagle Eye**. A sky blue jet.
- **Sky High**. A white Concorde.
- **Tread Bolt**. A blue stealth bomber.

NB: Sky High shouldn't be confused with the 1988 Autobot Pretender of the same name.

Construction Patrol:

- **Crumble**. A grey crane.
- **Groundpounder**. An orange tractor shovel.
- **Neutro**. A yellow bulldozer.
- **Takedown**. A red cement mixer.

Hot Rod Patrol:

- **Big Daddy**. A black 1950s Chevrolet.
- **Greaser**. An orange 1930s coupé.
- **Hubs**. A lime green 1940s coupé.
- **Trip-Up**. A white 1960s Mustang.

Monster Truck Patrol:

- **Big Hauler**. A green monster truck.
- **Heavy Tread**. An orange dragster-type monster truck.
- **Hydraulic**. A blue monster truck.
- **Slow Poke**. A yellow tow truck.

(Autobot) Micromaster Combiners:
Packs of three Micromaster Comber vehicles, each of which could split into two halves – these halves could then transform into robots. The various halves could be mixed and matched to create hybrid vehicles.

Astro Squad:

- **Barrage**. A grey robot /front half of moon buggy.
- **Heave**. Grey robot/rear half of moon buggy.

- **Moonrock**. A red robot/front half of rocket transport.
- **Missile Master**. A red robot/rear half of rocket transport.
- **Phaser**. A white robot/front half of space shuttle.
- **Blast Master**. A white robot/rear half of space shuttle.

NB: Barrage shouldn't be confused with the 1985 Deluxe Insecticon of the same name.

Metro Squad:

- **Oiler**. A blue robot/front half of tanker truck.
- **Slide**. A white robot/rear half of tanker truck.
- **Power Run**. A yellow and white robot/front half of hovercraft.
- **Strikedown**. A blue and white robot/rear half of hovercraft.
- **Wheel Blaze**. A yellow robot/front half of fire engine.
- **Roadburner**. A yellow robot/rear half of fire engine.

Autobot Micromaster Combiner Transports:

Transformable trailer vehicles that came packed with a Micromaster Combiner pair. The trailers had connector ports at the front and back, allowing the Micromasters to plug into them. The trailers could convert into battle platforms (which were compatible with the connectable ramp system used by the Micromaster Stations and Bases the previous year). The trailers could also split into two transformable vehicles, which could be piloted by the Micromaster figures included in the pack.

- **Missile Launcher**. A black/yellow trailer that could either transform into a battle station, or split into two mobile artillery vehicles. Packaged with:

  - **Retro**. A red robot/front half of truck crane.
  - **Surge**. A red robot/rear half of truck crane.

Retro and Surge were repaints of Stonecruncher and Excavator respectively, from the Decepticon Constructor Squad set.

- **Tanker Truck**. A blue/white tanker trailer that could either transform into a battle station, or split into two mobile cannon vehicles. Packaged with:

  - **Pipeline**. An orange robot/front half of excavation vehicle.
  - **Gusher**. An orange robot/rear half of excavation vehicle.

Pipeline and Gusher were repaints of Grit and Knockout respectively, from the Decepticon Constructor Squad set.

Autobot Micromaster Combiner Battlefield Headquarters:

- **Battlefield Headquarters**. A large blue and white truck. The front half transforms into a jet, while the rear section becomes a shuttle. Jet and shuttle can recombine to form a larger spacecraft. Packaged with:

   o   **Full-Barrel**. A blue and grey robot/front half of truck.
   o   **Overflow**. A blue and grey robot/rear half of truck.

The Autobot Micromasters Countdown, Erector, Hot House, Ironworks and Overload (plus their respective bases/transports) remained available in the shops, having been carried over from the 1989 range.

(Decepticon) Action Masters:
As per their Autobot equivalents, each came packaged with a small transformable accessory.

- **Banzai-Tron**†. A grey/green action figure with **Razor-Sharp**, a black crab/gun extension.
- **Devastator***. A green/purple action figure with **Scorpulator**, a black scorpion/gun extension.
- **Krok**†. A grey/blue action figure with **Gatoraider**, a grey alligator/gun extension.
- **Shockwave***. A purple/grey action figure with **Fistfight**, a black robot/gun extension.
- **Soundwave***. A blue/silver action figure with **Wingthing**, a black bat/gun extension.
- **Treadshot**†. A black/grey action figure with **Catgut**, a black puma/gun extension.

(Decepticon) Action Master Action Blasters:
Just like their Autobot counterparts, these were Action Master figures packaged with small transformable vehicles.

- **Axer**†. A grey/blue action figure with **Off-Road Cycle**, a red motorbike/gun emplacement.
- **Starscream***. A grey/blue action figure with **Turbo Jet**, a black jet/'battle chariot'.

Decepticon Action Master Attack Vehicles:
Action Master figures with larger transformable vehicles.

- **Gutcruncher**†. A green/mustard action figure with **Stratotronic Jet**, a blue and orange jet that transforms/separates into a tank, a flying scout drone and a battle station.
- **Megatron***. A grey action figure with **Neutro-Fusion Tank**, a black/purple tank that transforms/separates into a jet and a battle station.

Decepticon Micromasters:
Military Patrol:

- **Bombshock**. A green robot/tank.
- **Dropshot**. A blue robot/armoured personnel carrier.
- **Growl**. A brown robot/armoured car.
- **Tracer**. A black robot/helicopter. (NB: Tracer shouldn't be confused with the 1988 Autobot Targetmaster weapon of the same name.)

Race Track Patrol:

- **Barricade**. A blue robot/F1 race car.
- **Ground Hog**. A purple robot/dragster.
- **Motorhead**. A yellow robot/stock car.
- **Roller Force**. A pink robot/off-road buggy.

Decepticon Micromaster Combiners:

Battle Squad:

- **Direct-Hit**. A sky blue robot/front half of cannon transport.
- **Power Punch**. A sky blue robot/rear half of cannon transport.
- **Fireshot**. A black robot/front half of stealth plane.
- **Vanquish**. A black robot/rear half of stealth plane.
- **Meltdown**. A purple robot/front half of half-track truck.
- **Half-Track**. A purple robot/rear half of half-track truck.

Constructor Squad:

- **Grit**. A violet robot/front half of excavation vehicle.
- **Knockout**. A violet robot/rear half of excavation vehicle.
- **Sledge**. An orange robot/front half of dump truck.
- **Hammer**. An orange robot/front half of dump truck.
- **Stonecruncher**. A yellow robot/front half of truck crane.
- **Excavator**. A yellow robot/rear half of truck crane.

Decepticon Micromaster Combiner Transport.

- **Cannon Transport**. A magenta/purple weapons trailer that could either transform into a battle station, or split into two mobile gun emplacements. Packaged with:

  - o **Terror-Tread**. A turquoise robot/front half of dump truck.
  - o **Cement-Head**. A turquoise robot/rear half of dump truck.

Terror-Tread and Cement-Head were repaints of Sledge and Hammer respectively, from the Decepticon Constructor Squad set.

Decepticon Micromaster Combiner Base:

- **Anti-Aircraft Base**. A mustard-coloured tank that transforms into a battle station. Packaged with:

  - o **Blackout**. A blue robot/front half of bomber plane.
  - o **Spaceshot**. A blue robot/rear half of bomber plane.

The Decepticon Micromasters Airwave, Flattop, Greasepit, Roughstuff and Skystalker (plus their respective bases/transports) remained available in the shops, having been originally introduced as part of the 1989 range.

European Transformers, 1990-1993

While the original Transformers toy line drew to a close in the USA in 1990, it continued unabated in Europe, where sales were still in sufficient numbers to make continued production worthwhile. These later European figures were a mixture of re-releases of older characters (dubbed 'Classics' or 'Classic Heroes'), releases of figures originally intended for the Japanese market, plus a tranche of toys exclusive to Europe. It's possible that at least some of these were initially earmarked for release in North America, but remained unreleased when the line was cancelled there.

In 1993, the successor franchise Transformers: Generation 2 was launched, which is outside of this book's purview. However, a number of the early Generation 2 figures saw release in Europe in old-style packaging. As they straddle the line between the original Transformers range and Transformers: Generation 2, they are included here for the sake of completeness.

Classics

Re-releases of old figures in new packaging. These are reissues of the *original* versions of each character, so for example the Classic Optimus Prime is a new release of the 1984 figure (rather than the Powermaster or Action Master Optimus Primes that came later).

Autobots:

- **Optimus Prime** (1991).
- Aerialbots (1990): **Air Raid, Fireflight, Silverbolt, Slingshot** and **Skydive**.
- Dinobots (1991): **Grimlock, Sludge** and **Snarl**.
- Heroes (1990): **Inferno, Ironhide, Jazz, Prowl, Sunstreaker** and **Wheeljack**.
- Heroes (1991): **Sideswipe** and **Tracks**.
- Protectobots (1991): **Blades, First Aid, Groove, Hot Spot** and **Streetwise**.
- Throttlebots (1991): **Chase, Freeway. Goldbug, Rollbar, Searchlight** and **Wideload**.
- Triple Changers (1991): **Sandstorm** and **Springer**.

Decepticons:

- Combaticons (1991): **Blast Off, Brawl, Onslaught, Swindle** and **Vortex**.
- Stunticons (1990): **Breakdown, Dead End, Drag Strip, Motormaster** and **Wildrider**.
- Triple Changers (1991): **Astrotrain** and **Octane**.

In 1992, the Constructicons (**Bonecrusher, Hook, Long Haul, Mixmaster, Scavenger** and **Scrapper**) were reissued, but modified from their original 1985 releases. Now coloured yellow and purple, each was packaged in universal 'Constructicon' packaging, with no reference whatsoever to each character's individual name. These new versions lacked the accessories necessary to form their combined mode, Devastator.

Japanese Transformers

In 1987, the Transformers franchises in the East and West began to diverge quite considerably. There were Japanese-exclusive cartoon episodes, and a great many Japanese-exclusive toys. Some of these figures later saw official release in the West as part of the tail end of the Transformers toy line in Europe.

* **Galaxy Shuttle** (Autobot, 1990). Originally part of the Japanese sub-line Transformers: Victory, Galaxy Shuttle was a white robot that transformed into a space shuttle. The European release was exclusive to Italy.
* **Overlord** (Decepticon, 1991). Like Doubledealer before him, Overlord was a double Powermaster (or Godmaster, as they were known in Japan), with two Powermaster engines (billed as 'Energon Figures' for the European release). Overlord is a blue/black/grey robot that can transform into a city mode, or split into two parts that can transform into a jet and a tank respectively. The mini Energon Figures were given no individual names (but in Japan were known as Mega and Giga).

Motorvators (Autobots, 1991)
The Motorvators were recoloured versions of Japanese 'Brainmaster' figures. Each one came complete with a mini-figure that slotted into the chest cavity of the larger robot. When the door to the chest cavity was closed, a mechanism inside the toy would slide the mini-figure up into the robot head, and reveal the robot's face. The small mini-figures were given no individual names for their European release, and were billed merely as 'Energon Figures'.

* **Flame**. A yellow robot/Lamborghini. A repaint of the Japanese figure 'Laster'. In Japan his Energon Figure was known as the 'Brain of Skill'.
* **Gripper**. A black robot/dune buggy. A repaint of the Japanese Brainmaster 'Blacker'. In Japan his unnamed Energon Figure was billed as 'Brain of Strength'.
* **Lightspeed**. A red robot/Ferrari. A repaint of the Japanese toy 'Braver'. His Energon Figure was called 'Brain of Intelligence' when released in Japan. Not to be confused with the Technobot of the same name.

The Japanese versions of these toys could combine to form a larger robot, Road Caesar. However, the European versions lacked the additional combiner parts required to form the gestalt robot.

(Autobot) Rescue Force (1992):
These were a series of individually-carded figures, originally released in Japan as a subline called 'Breastforce' (where they came packaged with mini-figures that converted into chestplates for the larger robot). The European releases were modified (different colours, weapons etc), did not include the mini-figures, and used identical artwork and packaging for all four toys, meaning that none of them was individually named.

- A yellow robot/drill tank. Originally released in Japan as '**Drillhorn**'.
- A blue robot/dune buggy. Originally released in Japan as '**Jallguar**'.
- A blue robot/tank. Originally released in Japan as '**Killbison**'.
- A white robot/jet. Originally released in Japan as '**Leozack**'.

The original Japanese releases could combine to form a super-robot, Liokaiser; however, the European release was missing two members (Guyhawk and Hellbat), meaning that a complete European Liokaiser could never be formed.

European Exclusives

Action Masters:
As with the American Action Masters, these were non-transforming figures that came packaged with convertible accessories. Unlike the standard Action Masters (whose accessories transformed into weapon extensions), these European exclusives boasted accessories that transformed into backpacks. As before, an asterisk (*) indicates a re-imagined 'classic' character, and a dagger (†) an entirely new character.

- **Bombshell** (1991, Decepticon)*. A purple/grey action figure with **Needler**, a green crab that converts into a helmet/backpack assembly.
- **Charger** (1991, Decepticon)†. A green/grey action figure with **Fire Beast**, a black rhino that converts into a helmet/backpack assembly.
- **Powerflash** (1991, Autobot)†. A yellow/grey action figure with **Road Rocket**, a black tank that converts into a helmet/backpack assembly.
- **Sideswipe** (1991, Autobot)*. A red/grey action figure with **Vanguard**, a blue tank that converts into a helmet/backpack assembly.
- **Take-Off** (1991, Decepticon)†. A grey/blue action figure with **Screech**, a blue bird that converts into a helmet/backpack assembly.
- **Tracks** (1991, Autobot)*. A blue/black action figure, with **Basher**, a green tank that converts into a helmet/backpack assembly.

Exo-Suit Action Masters:
These were vehicles that could transform into battle armour that could be worn by the accompanying Action Master figure.

- **Circuit** (1991, Autobot)†. A yellow/blue action figure with **Supersonic Racing Car**, a red race car/battle armour. Circuit himself was a repaint of the 1990 wide-release Action Master Axer.

- **Thundercracker** (1991, Decepticon)*. A purple/crimson/green action figure with **Solo Mission Jet Plane**, a purple stealth fighter/battle armour. Thundercracker was a repaint of the 1990 Action Master Starscream.

Exo-Suit Action Masters – with Motorised Action:
Similar to the standard Exo-Suit Action Masters, but their vehicles/armour featured a battery-powered, motorised gimmick.

- **Rumbler** (1991, Autobot)†. A grey/blue action figure with **4WD All-Terrain Vehicle**, an orange motorised buggy/battle armour. Rumbler was a repaint of the 1990 Action Master Sprocket.
- **Slicer** (1991, Decepticon)†. A blue/grey action figure with **4WD Assault Vehicle**, a pink motorised buggy/battle armour. Slicer was a repaint of the 1990 Action Master Wheeljack.

Action Master Elites:
Unlike regular Action Masters, the Elites are actually transformable (although the transformations were simplistic and the vehicle modes rudimentary). Each one featured an action gimmick, for extra play value.

- **Double Punch** (1991, Decepticon). A black/magenta robot that converts into a scorpion. Gimmick: claws/arms go up and down at the touch of a button. The design of this toy is an homage to the Japanese-exclusive figure BlackZarak (1988), which itself was based on the 1987 Scorponok toy.
- **Omega Spreem** [sic] (1991, Autobot). A yellow/magenta robot that converts into a tank. Gimmick: turret/torso spins at the touch of a button. Although the colours are radically different, the design of this toy is based on that of Omega Supreme.
- **Turbo Master** (1991, Decepticon). A purple/pink robot that transforms into a helicopter. Gimmick: propellers/wrists spin at the touch of a button. The head and chest of the figure (plus the cannons on his back) are designed to resemble the Scramble City combiner, Bruticus.
- **Windmill** (1991, Autobot). A blue robot that transforms into a helicopter. Gimmick: the propeller turns at the touch of a button. Unlike the other Action Master Elites, Windmill is not an homage to any pre-existing Transformer.

(Autobot) Turbomasters:
Transformers with large hand-held missile launcher weapons that integrated into the toy's vehicle mode. Not technically European exclusives, as they were released simultaneously in Japan.

Smaller Turbomasters:

- **Boss** (1992). A sky blue robot/sports car.
- **Flash** (1992). A red robot/sports car.
- **Hurricane** (1992). A white robot/sports car.
- **Scorch** (1992). A yellow robot/pickup truck.

Larger Turbomasters:

- **Rotorstorm** (1992). A blue robot/helicopter. This toy would eventually see a North American release (albeit modified, re-coloured and re-named) in 1997.
- **Thunder Clash** (1992). The largest toy of the 1992 range, Thunder Clash is a red/white/turquoise truck. The cab transforms into a robot, while the trailer becomes a base. As with Rotorstorm, this toy was modified and released in North America in 1997 (and renamed as Optimus Prime, no less).

(Decepticon) Predators:
As with the Turbomasters, these were Transformers with missile launcher weapons. Additionally, the four smaller Predator figures also incorporated the 'Megavisor' gimmick. This consisted of a flip-down panel, almost like a photographic slide. When the smaller Predators were attached to either of the two larger Predators, kids could look through an eyepiece and view an image, meant to represent the jets' 'target lock' display.

Smaller Predators:

- **Falcon** (1992). A blue-grey robot/stealth fighter.
- **Skydive** (1992). A purple robot/jet. Not to be confused with the Aerialbot of the same name.
- **Snare** (1992). A red robot/jet.
- **Talon** (1992). A green robot/jet.

Larger Predators:

- **Skyquake** (1992). A turquoise/copper robot/bomber plane. The largest Decepticon toy of the year, Skyquake was later released in the USA in 1997 (albeit modified, re-coloured, and re-named as Starscream).
- **Stalker** (1992). A turquoise/red tank. Later released in modified form in the USA as Soundwave (in 1997).

The 1993 Transition Year

In 1993 the Transformers line was relaunched in America under the new brand name Transformers: Generation 2. Generation 2 wouldn't be unveiled in Europe until later in the year, so for the time being the Generation 2 figures were released in old-style packaging.

These, then, were the final figures to see release as part of the original Transformers toy line. By 1994, all these figures would be reissued in Europe, this time in proper Generation 2 packaging.

(Autobot) Aquaspeeders:
Transformers with a colour-changing gimmick – certain parts of the toy were designed to change colour with a change in temperature. These figures included water-squirting

weapons. Assuming one used warm water, 'shooting' the figures with these weapons would cause them to change colour. When released in the USA as part of Generation 2, these figures had different names and colour schemes.

- **Aquafend**. A pink robot/dune buggy. USA release: 'Jetstorm'.
- **Deluge**. A green and blue robot/race car. USA release: 'Drench'.
- **Jetstorm**. A red robot/car. USA release: 'Gobots'.
- **Speedstream**. A blue/white robot/F1 race car. USA release: 'Deluge'.

(Autobot) Axelerators:
Also released outside Europe as part of the Generation 2 line, Axelerators were car Transformers whose detachable engines doubled as the robots' weapons. Unlike their American release, the European Axelerators used pink-tinted plastic for the windshields rather than the usual grey.

- **Hotrider**. A turquoise robot/pickup truck (released in the USA as 'Turbofire').
- **Rapido**. A red robot/race car.
- **Skram**. A blue robot/sports car.
- **Zap**. An orange robot/sports car (released in the USA with the unfortunate name 'Windbreaker').

(Autobot) Lightformers:
Transformers with a weapon that doubles as an eyepiece accessory. Looking through the eyepiece and activating a geared mechanism will give the illusion of laser beams firing.

- **Deftwing**. A blue and grey robot/jet.
- **Ironfist**. A beige robot/military truck.

(Autobot) Obliterator:
The Obliterators were large vehicle Transformers, whose front halves converted into a robot, while the back half could become a missile platform. They were exclusive to Europe.

- **Pyro**. A red fire engine/robot and missile platform. Renamed 'Spark' when re-released in 1994 as part of the Generation 2 range.

(Decepticon) Skyscorchers:
The Decepticon equivalents of the Autobot Axelerators, these were jet Transformers whose radar assemblies could detach and be used as handguns when in robot mode.

- **Hawk**. A green robot/jet (released in the USA as 'Eagle Eye').
- **Snipe**. A blue robot/jet (released in the USA as 'Afterburner').
- **Terradive**. A black robot/jet.
- **Tornado**. A grey robot/jet (released in the USA as 'Windrazor')

(Decepticon) Stormtroopers:

As with their Autobot equivalents, the Aquaspeeders, these figures featured water-squirting weapons and colour-changing plastic parts.

- **Aquablast**. A dark green robot/sports car.
- **Drench**. A red robot/sports car.
- **Hydradread**. A blue robot/sports car.
- **Rage**. A black robot/sports car.

(Decepticon) Trakkons:

The Decepticon equivalents of the Autobot Lightformers, with an identical gimmick.

- **Calcar**. A pink robot/car.
- **Fearswoop**. A yellow robot/jet.

(Decepticon) Obliterator:
Featured the same gimmick as his Autobot counterpart Pyro listed above.

- **Clench**. A blue tow truck/robot and missile platform. Renamed 'Colossus' for its 1994 Generation 2 re-release.

PART TWO: THE COMICS

Creation And Launch

The Transformers comic was launched in the USA by Marvel Comics in May 1984. It was originally intended to be a four-issue limited series, but good early sales figures resulted in its quick promotion to the status of an ongoing title.

Marvel Comics was founded in 1939 as Timely Publications, famous for its strong roster of superhero titles, including *Captain America* and *Namor the Submariner*. Interest in superheroes waned in the post-war years; the company changed its name to Atlas Comics and concentrated on other genres. However, after rival company DC Comics successfully revived the superhero format in the late '50s, Atlas jumped on the bandwagon: they changed their name to Marvel Comics (in 1961) and began producing classic titles such as *The Fantastic Four* and *The Amazing Spider-Man*.

Although best-known for producing comics based on their own original creations, Marvel were no stranger to toy tie-ins – titles such as *Rom: SpaceKnight*, *Micronauts* and *G.I. Joe* had all previously made the crossover from toy shelves to comic books with some success. *G.I. Joe*, especially, was seen as the ideal model for a successful tie-in – that comic's main writer Larry Hama worked with toy manufacturers Hasbro to develop names and character profiles for the various action figures, which would then be worked into the comic and also turned into an animated series by Marvel Productions. *G.I. Joe* was a great success, and both Marvel and Hasbro were eager to make lightning strike twice.

Having bought the licence to market the newly-dubbed Transformers figures outside of Japan, Hasbro appointed Marvel staff editor Denny O'Neil to be 'the next Larry Hama', and set about developing personalities and backstories for these 'Robots in Disguise'.

However, toy tie-in comics didn't have the same respect in the industry as Marvel's superhero titles; as a well-regarded and proficient editor, O'Neil can be somewhat forgiven for thinking that, as an assignment, *The Transformers* was perhaps a little beneath him. For whatever reason, the treatment he came up with was deemed sub-par by Marvel's editor-in-chief Jim Shooter, who also briefly had a go at developing the franchise himself. At least two of O'Neil's ideas survived the re-writes – the Autobot computer was nicknamed 'Aunty', and the Autobot leader was dubbed 'Optimus Prime'.

In the end, it was another Marvel staffer, Bob Budiansky, who stepped in and saved the day. Like Larry Hama on *G.I. Joe*, he named most of the characters and developed their personalities, powers and abilities. He was given the editorship of the fledgling comic, and experienced Marvel writers such as Bill Mantlo, Ralph Macchio and Jim Salicrup were drafted in to write the initial issues based on his notes.

[1] THE TRANSFORMERS
US#1, 'September 1984' (published May 1984), 25 pages.

British reprint: UK#1, 3 October 1984 (Part One), 11 pages; UK#2, 17 October 1984 (Part Two), 12 pages.

The two pages excised from the UK reprint instead formed the basis of a pull-out poster in UK#2. See the **UK Changes** section below for further details.

NB: The cover dates used on the American issues were usually well in advance of the actual publication dates. The intention was to lengthen the shelf-life of the comics, by creating the illusion of them being still 'new' even after they had been sitting on the newsstands for a few months.

The date listed on most of the UK issues is the 'off' date, i.e. the date the comic was withdrawn from sale to make way for the following issue. On the covers of the earliest UK issues, two dates were provided: the on-sale and the off-sale dates. To ensure consistency throughout, I have used the latter.

To start with, the US comic ran bi-monthly and the UK comic fortnightly.

Credits:
Bill Mantlo (plot); Ralph Macchio (script); Frank Springer (pencils); Kim DeMulder (inks); Nel Yomtov (colours); Michael Higgins, Rick Parker (letters); Bob Budiansky (editor); Jim Shooter (editor-in-chief); Bill Sienkiewicz (cover). **UK:** Jerry Paris (cover, UK#1); John Ridgway (cover, UK#2).

Plot:
The Transformers are a race of robots from the metallic alien world Cybertron. Civil war erupts between two factions – the Heroic Autobots, led by the noble warrior Optimus Prime, and the Evil Decepticons, commanded by the ruthless tyrant Megatron. The war is so cataclysmic that the planet is flung from its regular orbit, into the path of an asteroid belt.

Optimus Prime and a group of Autobots take off in a spaceship, the *Ark*, the weaponry of which is sufficiently powerful to blast a path through the asteroids and ensure Cybertron's safe passage. However, once the mission is successfully completed, the Decepticons mount an attack and board the vessel.

The *Ark* crash-lands on prehistoric Earth, lying dormant until 1984, when a volcanic eruption re-awakens both factions. The ship's computer reformats the now-stranded Transformers so that they are able to disguise themselves as cars, jets, communications devices and other machinery, to blend in with their new surroundings.

A group of Autobots set out to explore their new home, but are attacked by the Decepticons at a drive-in movie screening. After a pitched battle, the Autobots manage to lure the Decepticons away from the terrified and defenceless moviegoers.

One such moviegoer is student Buster Witwicky, who is intrigued by the heavily-damaged Autobot car named Bumblebee. Buster drives Bumblebee home to his father's workshop, where both father and son are amazed when the car begins to talk …

Notes:
The opening scenes on Cybertron (described here as a Saturn-sized machine world) give us a beginner's guide to its Autobot/Decepticon War, offering very few specifics and leaving a lot tantalisingly vague – although some of the gaps in this potted history will be elaborated upon in future issues. There's no exact timeframe given, although we are told that Cybertron circled the star Alpha Centauri 'ages ago'; that the Decepticons have been gathering their strength for 'eons'; that they spent 'weeks' amassing their forces; and that after Optimus Prime came onto the scene, the war raged for 'over one thousand years'. Clearly, the opening five pages of the comic depict an *incredibly* long

passage of time.

(Alpha Centauri – located 4.24 light years from our own Sun – is actually a binary system comprising two stars, Alpha Centauri A and Alpha Centauri B. It's never made clear which of the two stars was orbited by Cybertron. Only a single star is depicted in the comic.)

We are told that Optimus Prime hails from the city-state of Iacon (a fact that future writers will latch onto and elaborate upon), and that his Cybertronian vehicle mode is that of a blocky, wheeled tank (although the later story [48] 'The Flames of Boltax' will have an alternative take on Prime's pre-Earth vehicle mode). Megatron's home base on Cybertron is known simply as 'Castle Decepticon'.

According to this issue, the *Ark* spends 'over four million years' dormant and entombed in Mount St Hilary, Oregon before it is awakened by a volcanic eruption in 1984. However, we later learn that's not the whole truth, and that the ship wasn't completely inactive during that time – soon after the crash, the *Ark*'s computer reawakened the Dinobots to investigate the arrival of Shockwave (as detailed in [4] 'The Last Stand').

Buster Witwicky is a high-school student, old enough to drive, so he's a minimum 16-and-a-half years old by this point, assuming he's fully compliant with Oregon state driving laws (however, see the notes to '[22.1] The Gift'). His (as-yet-unnamed) father runs the S Witwicky Auto Repair shop. Buster has a friend nicknamed 'O' and a girlfriend, Jessie (whose name is sometimes also spelt 'Jesse').

There's no concrete indication as to exactly when in 1984 these events take place, but it's presumably a Friday night during school term time (as we see Buster coming home from school and going to the movie later that evening), and both Buster and the drive-in attendant are wearing short sleeves at night. (The hitchhiker seems dressed for colder weather, but he's walking a mountain path, where the temperature is presumably lower.)

Megatron at one point describes Earth as a 'brave new world', a turn of phrase coined by William Shakespeare in his play *The Tempest*, later used by Aldous Huxley as the title of his seminal 1932 novel. The name of the volcano, Mount St Hilary, is a play on Mount St Helens, a real-life volcano in Washington State (near the border with Oregon), which famously erupted in 1980.

The frame showing the *Ark* crashing to earth four million years ago (seen again in [5] 'The New Order') appears to depict a palm tree (or something very similar) in the foreground; this is historically inaccurate – palm trees and their like are not native to Oregon.

UK Changes:
NB: Page numbers refer to the comic strip itself, *excluding* adverts, covers etc.
Page 2, panel 2: 'eons' is changed to 'æons'.
Page 3, panel 1: 'defenseless' is altered to 'defenceless' and 'armored' to 'armoured'. Nelson Yomtov's credit is changed from 'coloring' to 'colours'.
Page 4, panel 1: 'valor' becomes 'valour'.
Page 4, panel 6: 'vigor' is amended to 'vigour'.
Page 5, panel 6: 'labored' is changed to laboured'.
Page 6, panel 4: 'demoralize' becomes 'demoralise'.
Page 8, panel 2: 'fueled' is altered to read 'fuelled'.
Page 9, panel 6: 'lay' is changed to 'lie'.

Page 10, panel 8: 'indiginous' [sic] is corrected as 'indigenous'.
Page 13, panel 1: 'maneuverable' is re-written as 'manoeuverable' [sic] (the proper UK spelling is 'manoeuvrable').
Page 20, panel 3: 'reconnoiter' is changed to 'reconnoitre'.
Page 20, panel 6: 'Dad'll cream me!' becomes 'Dad'll kill me!'

Pages 14 and 15 (the Autobot roll-call double spread) were excised from the main narrative of the UK comic, and placed in the centre of UK#2 as a pull-out poster (with a big Transformers logo covering the first two panels and the hand-lettering replaced by a Letraset font). The resulting gap in the story was covered by the caption 'Their exit does not go unnoticed ... the Autobots, too, have risen.'

Roll Call:
(Characters making their debuts are listed in **bold**.)

Autobots: **Optimus Prime, Jazz, Prowl, Bluestreak, Ironhide, Ratchet, Sideswipe, Sunstreaker, Hound, Wheeljack, Mirage, Trailbreaker, Bumblebee, Cliffjumper, Brawn, Huffer, Gears** and **Windcharger.**

Decepticons: **Megatron, Starscream, Skywarp, Thundercracker, Soundwave, Rumble, Frenzy, Laserbeak, Buzzsaw** and **Ravage.**

Other: **Buster, Sparkplug, Jessie** and **'O'.** Plus various unnamed Transformers in the Cybertron sequences.

Optimus Prime makes mention of a mysterious 'Aunty', who is ordered to transmit data to the *Ark*'s big screens. The meaning is unclear here but the reference will be explained (to UK readers, at least) in [4.3] 'Raiders of the Last *Ark*'.

The famous 'roll-call' sequence in this story, where the Autobots and Decepticons introduce themselves, would on the face of it seem to be a complete checklist of all the Transformers currently active on Earth at this point. However, this soon proves not to be the case – over the course of this and the next three stories we see a number of background characters whose silhouettes seem not to match those of any of the main characters, and in later issues we see additional characters pop up from time to time, presumably having also been on the *Ark* when it crashed. Notable examples include Red Alert in [4.2] 'The Enemy Within', Reflector in [4] 'The Last Stand' and Inferno in [8.1] 'Decepticon Dam-Busters'.

Data File: Bill Mantlo (writer)
Mantlo was well-prepared to write for *The Transformers*, having previously written for the toy tie-in comics *Micronauts* and *ROM: SpaceKnight*. He co-created the character Rocket Raccoon, and also the superhero duo Cloak and Dagger. Other titles he worked on included *The Spectacular Spider-Man*, *The Incredible Hulk* and *Iron Man*. Sadly, Mantlo (who was also a trained lawyer) suffered severe brain damage in a hit-and-run accident in 1992, and has been institutionalised ever since.

Review:
Introducing over thirty new characters and their backstory in just sixteen pages would

be a hard task for any writer. Scribes Mantlo and Macchio make a decent fist of it, but from the evidence on the page, it seems the challenge was just too great.

Such is the level of exposition needed to make this work that one of the most notable facets of this issue is the sheer amount of text crammed inside huge bloated captions and speech-bubbles; it's little wonder that two letterers were hired to share the burden. At times it feels more like an illustrated text story than a comic; this verbosity is never more apparent than in the faintly-ridiculous roll-call sequences, as the characters take turns to introduce themselves using the clunkiest dialogue imaginable.

Another mark against this comic is the rather haphazard artwork. We can forgive penciller Frank Springer for not having yet gotten the look of the robots quite right, but there are huge inconsistencies here – some of the characters (notably Gears) vary considerably in design from scene to scene. This can bewilder even hardcore fans, so imagine what it must have been like for new readers.

When looked at dispassionately, then, there are some obvious flaws here. It's overly wordy, and very rough around the edges. But given that this is the iconic launch issue of a book that captured the imagination of kids around the globe, it's difficult to review this comic without being swayed by the glow of nostalgia.

Although it was inevitable that the series would take time to settle down and find its feet, in telling the galaxy-spanning history of a group of alien robots who have warred for eons, there's no doubt that this issue is epic in scope and ambition. It's a solid (if imperfect) platform for the franchise to build upon and flourish. Given this story's assured place in the history of the Transformers universe, this low score is given grudgingly and through gritted teeth. 2/5

Wherefore *Ark* Thou?

Pinpointing the exact location of the fictional Mount St Hilary is, at first glance, quite easy. We know from [7] 'Warrior School' that the mountain is probably located near Mount Hood National Forest in northern Oregon, and [5] 'The New Order' tells us that the Greater Portland Medical Center is 'nearby'. There are quite a few extinct volcanoes on the outskirts of Portland (part of what's known as the Boring Lava Field), and it's tempting to think that Mount St Hilary is one of these.

However, some confusion arises from the inconsistent way that Mount St Hilary is drawn. Some stories (e.g. [12.2] 'Crisis of Command') depict it as arid and surrounded by desert, whereas others (e.g. the hitchhiker scene in [1] 'The Transformers') show it as tree-lined and verdant. The mountains around Portland generally fall into the latter category.

If we prefer the barren 'Crisis of Command' depiction, then the most likely location is on the dryer, eastern side of the Cascade range, around 70 miles (110 km) east of the centre of Portland.

Neither of these two possible locations (the Boring Lava Field or the eastern side of the Cascades) contradicts the assertion in [6] 'The Worse of Two Evils' that the Blackrock offshore oil platform is 146 miles (253km) from the *Ark*'s position.

(The 'volcano in the desert' depiction of Mount St Hilary is more-or-less confined to the UK-originated stories; the UK illustrators were basing their designs on *The Transformers* cartoon show, which during its first season was mostly set in desert regions.)

[2] POWER PLAY!
US#2, 'November 1984' (published July 1984), 23 pages.

British reprint: UK#3, 31 October 1984 (Part One), 14 pages; UK#4, 14 November 1984 (Part Two), 9 pages.

Credits:
Bill Mantlo (plot); Jim Salicrup (script); Frank Springer (pencils); Kim DeMulder (inks); Nel Yomtov (colours); Janice Chiang (letters); Bob Budiansky (editor); Jim Shooter (editor-in-chief); Michael Golden (cover). **UK:** Jerry Paris (cover, UK#3); Michael Golden (cover, UK#4 – a reuse of the US cover).

Plot:
That same night, the Decepticons attack a nuclear power plant, strip it of all vital components and then make their escape.

Meanwhile, Sparkplug Witwicky is able to patch up Bumblebee, who assumes robot mode and explains that the Autobots are low on fuel. Sparkplug offers to aid the Autobots in setting up a process whereby standard gasoline can be made compatible with the Transformers' systems. Bumblebee signals the Autobots to rendezvous at Sparkplug's garage.

The Decepticons, meanwhile, have constructed a new base of operations from the components taken from the power plant. Thanks to intelligence gathered by the Decepticon spy Ravage, they learn of the Autobots' alliance with Sparkplug. They, too, journey toward the garage.

A fierce battle between the Autobots and Decepticons ensues, with both factions desperate to secure Sparkplug's services. In the end, the Decepticons are defeated and forced into retreat – but not before Sparkplug is kidnapped and carried away by the Decepticon Starscream.

Buster urges the Autobots to pursue and rescue his father, but it is no use – the Autobots, out of fuel, weakly collapse to the ground …

Notes:
This issue's story follows on directly from the events of [1] 'The Transformers', with Sparkplug (named here for the first time) working overnight to fix Bumblebee. The rest of the action takes place during the course of the following day; the conversation between Buster, Jessie and 'O' seems to confirm this (it's presumably a Saturday – they apparently don't have school), with the trio discussing the events at the drive-in the previous night. However, we later see that the Decepticons have already managed to half-complete an impressive-looking new HQ using the power-plant technology – so either the Decepticons are impossibly quick at building sinister lairs, or more time has passed than is evident from the dialogue.

'O' refers to the cancellation of the US reality show *That's Incredible!* (in which John Moschitta, later to voice Blurr in *The Transformers* animated series, came to national prominence). This last aired in April 1984, confirming that these events take place after that date. He also listens to an artist known as the Dazzler on his boom-box; this is a reference to a fictional female pop star with super powers, who had her own Marvel comic in the early 1980s. (At the time of this story's publication, Marvel were soliciting a new graphic novel, *Dazzler: The Movie*, which was advertised within the pages of US#2.)

Bumblebee states that the events on Cybertron we saw in the first issue occurred four million years previously; this is also confirmed later by Megatron.

UK Changes:
Page 1, panel 1: Nel Yomtov's credit changes from 'colors' to 'colours'.
Page 15, panel 5: 'honored' becomes 'honoured'.
Page 19, panel 1: 'logic-center' is amended to 'logic-centre'.
Page 23, panel 6: 'refueling' changed to 'refuelling'.

Roll Call:
Autobots: Optimus Prime, Jazz, Prowl, Ironhide, Ratchet, Sideswipe, Sunstreaker, Hound, Wheeljack, Mirage, Bumblebee, Cliffjumper (flashback only), Brawn and Windcharger.

Decepticons: Megatron, Starscream, Skywarp, Thundercracker, Soundwave, Rumble, Frenzy, Laserbeak, Buzzsaw and Ravage.

Other: Buster, Sparkplug, Jessie and 'O'.

Data File: Jim Salicrup (writer)
Although Salicrup is a proficient writer and artist, he's best known for his editorial stints at Marvel (and later also Topps Comics and Papercutz). Comics edited by Salicrup include *The Fantastic Four*, *Spider-Man* and *The X-Files*.

Review:
With all the set-up out of the way, this is theoretically where the good stuff ought to kick in. However, after the intergalactic first issue, here we're reduced to watching Optimus Prime and Megatron squabble over a gruff car mechanic. For a comic about powerful robots stranded on Earth, this is surprisingly small-scale stuff.

The main thing to notice about 'Power Play' is just how clinical it all feels. It might well have been an intentional ploy by the writers to make this cold and soulless – it's a story about machines, after all – but it's hard to engage with characters that think and talk in bold proclamations rather than proper dialogue. (Example: 'While the battle rages on – the time has come for Megatron to take matters into his own hand!') There are some token attempts at leavening the atmosphere, but the 'comedy' humans who foolishly gawk at the Transformers are more annoying than humorous.

What's frustrating is that it *nearly* gets things right. The artwork, though still patchy, is much closer now to the familiar 'look' of the Transformers. There's a valiant attempt at fleshing out some of the characters – Starscream is devious but clever, Mirage's loyalties are questionable, and so on. The final battle in the junkyard is an improvement on issue 1's drive-in skirmish, and the whole thing feels a little more polished than last time out.

Frustratingly stilted and lacking in sparkle, 'Power Play' should at least get points for effort. It's another tentative step on the uphill road to greatness, as the writers and artists slowly begin to build confidence and settle into some sort of stride. 2/5

The Back-Up Strips, Part 1: *Machine Man*
The UK iteration of the *The Transformers* comic was a very different beast from its

American cousin. Throughout most of its run, a good chunk of the British comic was filled out by a secondary strip on top of the continuing adventures of the Transformers themselves. For many British fans, these back-up strips formed a vital part of the UK reading experience.

The first was *Machine Man*, which first ran between issues 1 and 42 in the UK. Machine Man was a creation of the legendary Jack Kirby, and debuted in *2001: A Space Odyssey* #8 (dated July 1977). As well as guesting in a couple of other titles, the character has had his very own comic, which has run sporadically since 1978 in various guises. X-51, aka Machine Man, is a human-built android, fending for himself in a cynical, crime-filled world. Disguising himself as a human, he is an office worker by day and a superhero by night. A relatively minor Marvel character, then; but as a powerful robot, he was seen as the ideal accompaniment to the adventures of the Transformers.

In this and the other UK back-up strip entries throughout this book, there will be no in-depth analysis or synopses – even a less-celebrated Marvel character such as Machine Man boasts a number of dedicated fan sites and web pages that go into much more detail than is possible here.

- 'Byte of the Binary Bug!' (UK#1-3), originally printed in *Machine Man* Vol. 1 #11 (October 1979). Machine-Man battles the Binary Bug, and is rewarded with a job at an insurance firm. Because the first couple of *The Transformers* stories were a few pages longer than the norm, this story had to be split into three instalments, rather than the usual two.
- 'Where Walk the Gods!' (UK#4-5), from *Machine Man* Vol. 1 #12 (December 1979). Super-evolved, golden beings judge Machine Man's worthiness (cf [4.3] 'Raiders of the Last *Ark*').
- 'Xanadu!' (UK#6-7), from *Machine Man* Vol. 1 #13 (February 1980). A dying criminal attempts to transplant his consciousness into Machine Man's body (cf '[23.5] Resurrection').
- 'The Man Who Could Walk Through Walls' (UK#8-9), from *Machine Man* Vol. 1 #14 (April 1980). A shady senator sets out to discredit Machine Man, who is framed for a series of crimes.
- 'Kill Me or Cure Me' (UK#10-11), from *Machine Man* Vol. 1 #15 (June 1980). Machine Man enlists the help of the Fantastic Four to defeat a scientist who has mutated into a green blob-monster. Humorously, a reference to the Fantastic Four being a famous foursome like the rock band Kiss has been changed to an ABBA reference for the UK reprint.
- 'Baron Brimstone and his Sinister Satan Squad!' (UK#12-14), from *Machine Man* Vol. 1 #16 (August 1980). A villain with magical abilities steals a powerful energy gizmo. The introduction of another strip, *The Chromobots*, meant that fewer pages could be allocated to *Machine Man*; these stories were now split into smaller chunks and spread over three issues.
- 'Arms and the Robot!' (UK#15-17), from *Machine Man* Vol. 1 #17 (October 1980). Machine Man's arm has been stolen by the evil villainess Madam Menace.
- 'Alone Against Alpha Flight!' (UK#18-20), from *Machine Man* Vol. 1 #18 (December 1980). Machine Man is hunted by the Canadian superhero team, Alpha Flight.
- 'Jolted by Jack O'Lantern!' (UK#21, 23-25), from *Machine Man* Vol. 1 #19 (February

1981). During Halloween, Machine Man defends an embassy building from a bizarre new villain.

From issue 27, *The Transformers* UK began printing some more recently-published Machine Man stories – in which the eponymous hero had been put into storage, only to wake up again nearly forty years in the future. These stories saw a second UK printing toward the end of the comic's run.

- 'He Lives Again!' (UK#27-30, re-printed UK#309-312), from *Machine Man* Vol. 2 #1 (October 1984). Machine Man is brought out of storage in the year 2020, only to discover that Madam Menace is now head of a powerful, sinister corporation.
- 'If This Be Sanctuary?!' (UK#31-34, re-printed UK#318-321), from *Machine Man* Vol. 2 #2 (November 1984). Madam Menace hires Arno Stark, the Iron Man of 2020, to hunt down Machine Man.
- 'Rime of the Ancient Wrecker!' (UK#35-38, re-printed UK#322-325), from *Machine Man* Vol. 2 #3 (December 1984). Machine Man discovers that the mysterious Ancient Wrecker is a familiar face from his own past, while the Iron Man of 2020 prepares to attack.
- 'Victory' (UK#39-42, re-printed UK#326-329), from *Machine Man* Vol. 2 #4 (January 1985). Machine Man makes a final stand against Sunset Bain.

[3] PRISONER OF WAR!
US#3, 'January 1985' (published October 1984), 23 pages.

British reprint: UK#5, 30 November 1984 (Part One), 12 pages; UK#6, 14 December 1984 (Part Two), 11 pages.

Credits:
Jim Salicrup (script); Frank Springer (pencils); Kim DeMulder, Mike Esposito (inks); Nel Yomtov (colours); Janice Chiang and others (letters); Bob Budiansky (editor); Jim Shooter (editor-in-chief); Mike Zeck (cover). **UK:** John Ridgway (cover, UK#5); Mike Zeck (cover, UK#6 – reuse of US cover).

Plot:
Sparkplug is taken back to the Decepticon fortress and forced at gunpoint to concoct a fuel solution for the Decepticons.

Meanwhile, the appearance of the Transformers has sparked a media frenzy, with even newspaper photographer Peter Parker (aka Spider-Man) arriving on the scene to get a closer look.

Thinking him to be an enemy, Spider-Man ambushes the Autobot Gears, but quickly comes to realise that not every Transformer is evil. He agrees to help the Autobots get past the human military blockade of the Decepticon fortress and, with Gears in tow, infiltrates the enemy stronghold.

Having gotten past Ravage and Soundwave, Spider-Man and Gears rescue Sparkplug. However, they are no match for Megatron, who sends the trio plummeting down through a hole in the floor of the mountaintop lair.

Spider-Man saves both himself and Sparkplug with his webs, but Gears crashes down to the valley floor below – seemingly to his death.

They regroup back at the *Ark*, where Sparkplug is finally reunited with his son, and Spider-Man bids the Autobots farewell. Gears is repaired, the groggy Autobot revealing to a disbelieving Buster that Sparkplug has betrayed them all and provided the Decepticons with the fuel formula ...

Notes:
Again, these events all seem to be occurring within a short space of time. The world's media would presumably react instantaneously to the news of the giant robots, and it's difficult to believe that Peter Parker would delay too long chasing down this story. Nor, for that matter, is it likely that the fuel-depleted Autobots would waste much time before setting out to rescue Sparkplug.

Megatron states here that he's been in power for 'countless millennia' (presumably this doesn't include his four million years buried in Mount St Hilary), which confirms assertions in [1] 'The Transformers' that the war on Cybertron raged for millions of years prior to the *Ark* mission.

Sparkplug's name is revealed here to be William Witwicky (although presumably no-one ever calls him anything other than Sparkplug – hence the 'S Witwicky' sign on the front of his garage). He's a retired US army sergeant who was a POW in the Korean War (1950-53), which means he's probably in his late fifties when we see him here.

Other contemporary pop-culture references abound: 'O' makes mention of film director George Lucas (the famous *Star Wars* creator who came to prominence in 1973 following the release of his movie *American Graffiti*); the Cold War (c.1945-1991) is said to be in full swing; the US 'Star Wars' military defence program (a major news story in 1983) is namechecked; and Spider-Man not only quotes US comedienne Joan Rivers' 'Can we talk?' catchphrase, but also refers to Megatron as 'Bazooka Joe', the cartoon mascot of the Bazooka bubblegum brand.

Spider-Man is seen to sing the first few lines of 'Heigh-Ho' (although in the comic it's misspelt as 'Hi-Ho') from the 1937 Walt Disney animated film *Snow White and the Seven Dwarves*. He refers to Rumble and Frenzy as 'Tweedledum and Tweedledee', characters best known from Lewis Carroll's 1871 book *Through the Looking-Glass, and What Alice Found There*. Finally, he quotes the 'Thought I saw a pussycat' catchphrase made famous by the classic Warner Brothers cartoon character Tweety (created 1942).

Spider-Man sees Gears transform and wonders if 'Detroit's training trucks to be quick-change artists'. Detroit is popularly known as the Motor City because of its close association with the automobile trade, and is the home of many US vehicle manufacturers such as General Motors, Ford and Chrysler.

From Spider-Man's point of view, these events are explicitly said to take place prior to *The Amazing Spider-Man* #258 (notable for being the issue where the web-slinger discovers that his black costume is actually a living being), which had a cover date of November 1984 (concurrent with *The Transformers* #2 in the US) but was set in 'the middle of summer'. Joe Robertson is referred to as the *Daily Bugle*'s 'new' editor-in-chief – he was promoted to the job in *The Amazing Spider-Man* #251 (April 1984).

Also from the wider Marvel Universe, we see Nick Fury and Timothy 'Dum Dum' Dugan of the SHIELD organisation discussing a 'big green fire-snorting lizard' – a reference to the 1977-79 comic *Godzilla, King of the Monsters*. Depicted in the background of one panel is the sentient truck 'US 1', the star of Marvel's *US 1* comic, which ran for 12 issues from May 1983. Reed Richards, of *The Fantastic Four* fame, is mentioned in passing.

Ratchet has something important to tell Prime, but is cut off before he can finish; we will find out what's so important in [4] 'The Last Stand'.

Sparkplug, as well as being an experienced mechanic, also appears to have some professional knowledge of chemistry, being able to convert petroleum into Transformer fuel, and to identify exactly which computers and refining equipment he would need to undertake the work. The Decepticons steal fuel-conversion gear from the University of Oregon (whose real-life campus is located in the town of Eugene, around 100 miles south of Portland).

UK Changes:
Page 1, panel 3: 'colorist' is changed to 'colours'.
Page 3, panel 2: a reference is changed from *The Transformers* #2 to *The Transformers* #4.
Page 5, panel 2: 'see last issue' becomes 'see issue 3'.
Page 6, panel 2: 'refueled' is anglicised as 'refuelled' and 'neighborhood' to 'neighbourhood'.
Page 11, panel 4: 'rumors' has become 'rumours'.
Page 11, panel 6: the asterisk and reference to *Spider-Man* #258 have been omitted entirely.
Page 14, panel 2: 'facade' becomes 'façade' (yes, the UK comic made the effort to add the cedilla!)
Page 17, panel 5: 'traveling' is amended to read 'travelling'.
Page 23, panel 4: 'valor' is changed to 'valour'.

Roll Call:
Autobots: Optimus Prime, Prowl, Ironhide, Ratchet, Sideswipe, Sunstreaker, Hound, Trailbreaker, Bumblebee, Cliffjumper, Brawn, Huffer, Gears and Windcharger.

Decepticons: Megatron, Starscream, Skywarp, Thundercracker, Soundwave, Rumble, Frenzy, Laserbeak, Buzzsaw and Ravage. **Shockwave** is seen as a background character in the Decepticon base, but this is a blatant error (the character isn't properly introduced until next issue), and as such can be ignored as a *bona fide* appearance.

Other: Buster, Sparkplug, Jessie and 'O'.

Review:
Included as part of a publicity drive to drum up extra readers, Spider-Man's appearance completely overshadows the Transformers' adventures here, making for a rather unbalanced read. The Transformers themselves are shunted to the sidelines, and the threat of the Decepticons is trivialised as Spider-Man, aided by his sidekick Gears, makes short work of Soundwave, Rumble, Frenzy and Ravage. Moreover, the appearance of the agile Spider-Man only serves to highlight how flat and 'non-kinetic' the artwork has been thus far in the series' run.

We're only just getting to know these characters; relegating them to the status of supporting cast does the book no favours at all – which is rather a shame, as the early scenes of the Decepticons scheming and torturing Sparkplug are actually rather good.
1/5

Why Were There So Few Crossovers?

It was extremely rare for Marvel superheroes to be restricted to just one regular comic; they would regularly cross over into each other's titles without anyone batting an eyelid. Often, crossover stories would begin in one particular comic series, and then you'd have to switch to another, completely different series in order to see the conclusion. Even Superman and Batman would drop by every now and then for a Marvel/DC team-up.

So when Spider-Man appears here, it's not at all surprising to anyone with even the slightest knowledge of the Marvel Universe. Spider-Man showed up in other comics all the time, to the extent that readers were almost blasé about such cross-title appearances. Indeed, the UK comic made no special effort to advertise his arrival. Given all this, it's perhaps surprising that in the entire original run of *The Transformers* comics, Spider-Man was the only pre-existing Marvel-owned character to join the Autobots in their battle with the Decepticons. So, why was this the case?

Well, the main problem was that the Transformers brand was owned by toy manufacturers Hasbro, and they were extremely protective of their property. Hasbro wanted *The Transformers* to be a showcase for their own toys, and frowned upon rival franchises muscling in. Look at the list of back-up strips used to fill out the UK comic: aside from a few inclusions of standard Marvel fare such as *Iron Man*, *Hercules* and *Rocket Racoon*, the rest were all based on Hasbro-originated toy franchises such as *G.I. Joe*, *Visionaries*, *Inhumanoids* and *Robotix*.

Indeed, Spider-Man himself nearly didn't make it into the pages of *The Transformers*: Hasbro were reluctant to see the character showcased in the comic, as their arch-rivals Mattel had the rights to make Spider-Man action figures as part of their Secret Wars range. In the end, a compromise was reached, whereby Spider-Man could be featured, but only in his old-style black costume – but ironically Hasbro's intervention proved to be in vain: the American *The Transformers* issue starring Spider-Man still featured a full-page advertisement for Mattel's Secret Wars toys.

So although the earliest *The Transformers* stories made mention of Marvel characters such as Nick Fury, Dazzler and the Avengers (to name but a few), these meta-references eventually stopped and the comic began to forge ahead in its own isolated continuity. These days, the '80s *The Transformers* comics are deemed to have taken place in a parallel dimension from the mainstream superhero comics, an offshoot world officially designated by Marvel as 'Earth-91274' or 'Earth-120185'.

The last word on the subject was had by Don Daley, one of the editors of the US *The Transformers* comic. In the letters page in #64 he wrote: '*Transformers* and Marvel Universes are separate from each other. What about issue #3? Can we just forget that one? Please.'

The Back-Up Strips, Part 2: *Matt and the Cat*

The second back-up strip to be featured in the pages of the UK comic, *Matt and the Cat* (UK#5-UK#73) was the first to be written and drawn especially for *The Transformers*. (Most of the other back-up strips were just reprints of American material.)

Matt and the Cat was based on a short cartoon strip of the same name that featured in local newspaper *The Bradford Telegraph & Argus*. The strip focused on Matt, a naive young boy, and Humph, his sardonic, wisecracking pet cat.

Writer and artist Mychailo 'Mike' Kazybrid was asked to bring the strip over to the UK *The Transformers* comic, but in doing so took the story away from its more domestic roots and planted the two characters into the middle of a sci-fi epic. As these strips have never been reprinted elsewhere (and there don't appear to be any online guides), a full synopsis can be justified on this occasion ...

Plot:

Matt is watching television one evening when he is told to put his cat Humph out for the night. As Matt lives on the top floor of a five-storey block of flats, this involves flinging Humph out of a window and into a metal dustbin on the ground below. A passing alien robot mistakes the bin for a probe, and takes it away for inspection (UK#5). Matt goes outside to investigate, and demands that Humph be let go (UK#6). Humph initially manages to escape, and helplessly watches on as Matt is taken aboard the robots' spacecraft (UK#7), but the cat cannot evade capture for long, and is himself eventually beamed up (UK#8).

While wandering the corridors of the ship, Humph is accosted by a small robot (UK#9), while Matt ends up in the company of some sinister aliens (UK#10), who reveal that the ship is en route to Darkon. Matt and Humph are finally reunited, but are sent to the vessel's slave quarters (UK#11). While Matt ponders their fate, Humph is more interested in taking out a comic subscription (UK#12). Meanwhile the ship's captain, the Slavemaster, gloats that the pair will fetch a good price on Darkon – assuming they survive the trip, that is (UK #13).

Slave-bot Olia-Cym is sent to bring food to the Earthling captives, but upon entering the cell, he is ambushed by Matt and Humph (UK#14). However, Olia-Cym soon manages to convince the pair of his good intentions (UK#15). The ship prepares to land, as Matt and Humph consider the prospect of being sold as slaves on Darkon (UK#16).

Olia-Cym agrees to help the reluctant travellers, and provides them with spacesuits so they might make their escape (UK#17). At the same time, the slave vessel comes under fire from a squadron of Myzoni star fighters (UK#18). In the confusion, Olia-Cym activates a trap door, and the trio plummet toward the surface of Darkon (UK#19).

Matt and Humph land on Darkon, but Olia-Cym is nowhere to be seen (UK#20). While exploring the planet, Humph is briefly captured by the Myzoni (UK#21), but soon rescued by Olia-Cym and his fellow slave-bots (UK#22). Meanwhile, Matt is accosted by the evil Darkonians (UK#23). The slave-bots convince Humph to lead an uprising against their Darkonian masters (UK#24) – his first target is the Myzoni patrol car (UK#26) in which Matt is being held hostage (UK#26). Humph zaps the Myzoni with his new ray-gun and is finally reunited with Matt (UK#27).

Now out of immediate danger, Matt and Humph reflect on their current situation, stranded light-years away from Earth (UK#28). Humph wanders off, falls into a hole (UK#29) and ends up in the underground lair of a were-mouse (UK#31). Fleeing from the creature, Humph falls into another hole, leading to yet another underground level (UK#32).

There he finds a spooky-looking castle (UK#33), home to the Slavemaster of Darkon, the evil alien who originally kidnapped Matt and Humph from Earth (UK#34). He chains up the feline, and gloats that the approaching Matt and Olia-Cym will be next (UK#36). While the Slavemaster is distracted, Humph manages to slip free of his bonds (UK#37) and meets the friendly robot Digbeth (UK#39). Matt is captured by the slave master's robotic bats (UK#40) and brought to the castle (UK#41).

The Slavemaster reveals his plan – the 'ultimate experiment'. By harnessing the cosmic energy of the planet itself, he will easily triumph against the Myzoni and the rebelling slave-bots. Humph is recaptured and thrown into a cell alongside Matt and Digbeth (UK#42). However, when their cell door is opened to provide them with food, Matt and the cat make their escape (UK#43) and venture through the castle's corridors (UK#44).

Once again they confront the Slavemaster, and only narrowly avoid being hit by his energy blasts (UK#45). They are saved by the intervention of Olia-Cym and Digbeth, who usher the Earthlings to safety (UK#46). The four friends flee the castle aboard a Darkonian skim-craft, but are pursued by the Slavemaster's killer robot, Doomsmere (UK#47).

Doomsmere destroys the skim-craft, but the four friends are able to jump clear of the explosion (UK#48). With our heroes now forced to flee on foot (UK#49), Doomsmere prepares to attack (UK#50). While Humph and Doomsmere tussle (UK#51), the Slavemaster has meanwhile created a robotic replica of Humph, named 'Scratchit', with which he hopes to fool Matt (UK#52).

Humph escapes from Doomsmere, only to fall foul of a strange alien plant, which traps the feline in its creepers and petals. Humph can only look on in horror as Matt is duped by his evil duplicate (UK#53). Thankfully, however, Olia-Cym and Digbeth are able to free Humph from the plant's clutches (UK#54), and the cat confronts his doppelganger (UK#55). Unable to discern between the real and fake Humphs, Matt suggests the two rivals fight it out between themselves (UK#56). The fight is ended by Digbeth, who crashes out of the sky, landing on Scratchit (UK#58). The four friends aren't safe from harm yet, though – with his new powers, the Slavemaster is able to conjure up a violent cosmic storm, from which our heroes are only narrowly able to escape (UK#59).

Finally safe from the Slavemaster, the gang arrive at the coast of the Great Sea. However, a robot Amphibicon lurks in the waters (UK#61). The robot, named Solarfin, captures Humph (UK#64) and transports him to the Amphibicons' undersea city (UK#65). It transpires that Humph's bravery has become legendary, and that the Amphibicons want him to help defend them from the Piratrons (UK#66). Right on cue, the Piratrons attack (UK#67), and their leader Octus Alpha threatens to kill Humph unless the Amphibicons install him as their new overlord (UK#68).

Meanwhile, Matt, Digbeth and Olia-Cym approach the Amphibicon dwellings (UK#69), and are met by one of the Piratrons, who takes the trio to Lagoon City (UK#70), where they are reunited with Humph (UK#71). Once there, Octus Alpha uses his 'time disc' to dematerialise the four friends (UK#72). Matt, Olia-Cym and Digbeth end up back at Matt's house, but to his delight the comic-mad Humph instead finds himself in the Avengers Mansion … (UK#73)

[4] THE LAST STAND
US#4, 'March 1985' (published December 1984), 22 pages.

British reprint: UK#7, 28 December 1984 (Part One), 12 pages; UK#8, 11 January 1985 (Part Two), 10 pages.

Credits:
Jim Salicrup (script); Frank Springer (pencils); Ian Akin, Brian Garvey (inks); Nel

Yomtov (colours); John Workman (letters); Bob Budiansky (editor); Jim Shooter (editor-in-chief); Mark Texeira (cover). **UK:** Mark Texeira (cover, UK#7 – reuse of US cover); Barry Kitson (cover, UK#8).

Plot:

The Autobots engage in heated arguments over what to do with Sparkplug, whom they now feel has betrayed them by furnishing the Decepticons with fuel. The stress is too much for the mechanic, who suffers a heart attack. He is whisked off to the nearest hospital in the Autobot Ratchet's ambulance mode.

(N.B. As discussed under the entry for [4.1] 'Man of Iron', I'm assuming that the events of the next three stories take place around this point in the narrative.)

While unconscious, Sparkplug has flashbacks to his time in the Korean War, where he was captured and forced to repair enemy vehicles. Meanwhile, the Autobots learn that there are other Transformers on Earth – a recording made by the *Ark* millions of years ago shows the Dinobots doing battle with the Decepticon Shockwave, with the final outcome unknown. Optimus Prime sends a probe to investigate the site of the battle, but the probe unwittingly ends up awakening the long-dormant Decepticon.

Megatron's refuelled Decepticons attack the *Ark*, where the depleted Autobots – still themselves starved of energy – prove to be seriously outgunned and on the verge of final defeat. However, just as Sparkplug sabotaged the Korean vehicles that he had ostensibly repaired while a POW in the 1950s, it transpires that he has also sabotaged the Decepticons' fuel formula – by introducing a corrosive agent that now totally debilitates Megatron and his forces.

With the redeemed Sparkplug revealed to be recovering in hospital, and the Decepticons defeated, the Autobots finally appear to have victory in their grasp …

… that is, until Shockwave appears, blasts Optimus Prime's forces to the ground and proclaims 'The Autobots are no more!'

Notes:

Again, we pick up exactly where the previous issue left off, with the revelation that Sparkplug has provided the Decepticons with a fuel formula.

In terms of popular culture, 'O' is seen watching the renowned ABC weeknight news/current affairs programme *Nightline* (1980-present), whose then-presenter Ted Koppel is named in dialogue. There's also a mention of *People*, a popular celebrity gossip magazine published since 1974.

In the Korea sequences, set in 1952, we hear tell of the 4067th MASH (Mobile Army Surgical Hospital) unit, a sly reference to the 4077th unit, which featured in the popular US sitcom *M*A*S*H* (1972-83). This tallies with what we learnt about Sparkplug's war exploits in [3] 'Prisoner of War'. These events are said to take place 'thirty years ago', which must be rounding down (it's actually 32, assuming the present-day events are all still taking place in 1984).

One of the captions reads 'Meanwhile, all's quiet on the Decepticon front', a reference to Erich Maria Remarque's 1929 novel *All Quiet on the Western Front*.

The Dinobot sequences are set 'shortly after we crashed on this planet four million years ago', and take place in a bizarre secluded tropical jungle in Antarctica known as the Savage Land, where dinosaurs are still the dominant life form. The Savage Land is a staple of the Marvel Comics universe, first introduced in *X-Men* #10 (March 1965). Basically it's a science experiment-cum-game reserve set up by aliens in order to study evolution. This issue's editorial notes explain that the Savage Land is home to Ka-Zar – a Tarzan-like character who's popped up in various Marvel titles since the mid-1960s, including his own comic, *Ka-Zar the Savage* (1981-84), which ended its 34-issue run just as *The Transformers* was beginning. This entire sequence was portended in [3] 'Prisoner of War', when Ratchet tried in vain to tell Optimus Prime about the Dinobot footage.

This will be restated below in the Roll Call section, but it also bears noting here: there are a number of Decepticons seen in this issue that bear no resemblance to the standard set of ten that were introduced in the first issue. Again, this seems to confirm that there are more Transformers on Earth than we see named in [1] 'The Transformers'.

Focusing on continuity with previous issues, the US military are still camped outside the Decepticon base (as established in [3] 'Prisoner of War'). The Decepticons Frenzy, Rumble, Skywarp and Soundwave are shown nursing injuries we saw sustained in the last story – Skywarp at the hands of Sunstreaker; the remainder at those of Spider-Man and Gears …

UK Notes:
… at least, from the perspective of US readers. As surmised below, we have to slot the UK 'flashback stories' during these events, so on that basis these injuries must instead be the result of the battle in [4.3] 'Raiders of the Last *Ark*'. This is the first – but by no means the last – divergence between the US-only plot and the combined UK/US narrative.

UK Changes:
Page 1, main panel: 'colors' is changed to 'colours'.
Page 8, panel 1: 'refueled' becomes 'refuelled'.
Page 9, panel 3: 'refueling' is amended to read 'refuelling'.
Page 10, panels 3 and 4: with this page printed in black and white in the UK, the two maps displayed on the Autobot screen are no longer visible.
Page 15, panel 1: the reference to issue #2 is changed to issue #4.

Roll Call:
Autobots: Optimus Prime, Jazz, Prowl, Bluestreak, Ironhide, Ratchet, Sideswipe, Sunstreaker, Wheeljack, Mirage, Trailbreaker, Bumblebee, Brawn, Huffer, Gears, Windcharger, **Grimlock**, **Snarl**, **Slag**, **Sludge** and **Swoop**. These last five listed, known collectively as the Dinobots, appear only in flashback.

Decepticons: Megatron, Starscream, Skywarp, Thundercracker, Soundwave, Rumble, Frenzy, Laserbeak, Buzzsaw, Ravage and **Shockwave**. Although this is Shockwave's first proper appearance, he actually appeared, in error, as a background character in [3] 'Prisoner of War'.

Additional, unnamed Decepticons are also seen in some sequences. These closely resemble the characters Spectro, Spyglass and Viewfinder (collectively known as **Reflector**), who appeared often in the cartoon episodes of *The Transformers* and who were also represented in the toy line. They are never seen again (except in flashback), so are presumably killed here by the effects of the corrosive fuel.

Other: Buster, Sparkplug, Jessie and 'O'. The Rolands, neighbours of the Witwickys who we first saw in [2] 'Power Play', are seen again here.

Data File: Frank Springer (artist)
Springer began his comic career in the '50s, and his art has appeared in titles as diverse as *Batman*, *Playboy*, *Captain Britain*, the New York *Daily News*, *Star Wars*, *National Lampoon*, *Tales of the Zombie* and *Nick Fury, Agent of SHIELD*.

Review:
And here's where it all comes together. The decision to continue the comic beyond the initial four-issue limited run seems to have galvanised all involved. Gone are the uncertainties and mis-steps, replaced with a newfound confidence and swagger.

Mirage's mini character arc concludes, as the previously-reluctant Autobot is galvanised into action. Shockwave and the Dinobots are brought into play, a set-up for future adventures. The disgraced Sparkplug is not only redeemed, but gets a wonderful flashback sequence set during the Korean War.

It's still not a perfect issue by any means – the first half is a pretty disjointed affair, with a number of scenes that seem like pure filler: Megatron facing off against the human troops; some 'comedy' business involving Mr 'O'; and Jessie making a trip to a ballet class.

But when the final battle begins in earnest, the action and adventure are unceasing until the game-changing final panel where Shockwave wipes out the Autobots with a single shot.

It might be a bit uneven in places, but the various twists and turns ensure that it remains incredibly enjoyable throughout. 4/5

A Four-Issue Limited Series
[4] 'The Last Stand' marked the end of the original four-issue limited series. Although not the best-regarded of story arcs, it nevertheless set up many themes and ideas that would continue through the comic's run.

Noticeable already is the prevalence of regular human characters, who are given pivotal parts to play in the action. Although the titular Transformers are clearly the main attraction, their human acquaintances Buster, Jesse and Sparkplug form the emotional core of the story, and indeed prove vital to the plot.

Although the robots themselves will develop a bit more personality over the coming years (especially in the UK stories), here they are definitely cold and alien; even the supposed 'good guys', the Autobots. Jazz's predilection for Earth culture and Grimlock's primitive diction are still around the corner, so for now all the personality on display comes from the human cast. Even when the robots themselves became better-established, the comic's writers (especially Bob Budiansky) would continue to make judicious use of supporting human characters.

Behind the scenes, it was becoming clear that the sheer number of different characters was quite confusing to outside authors, and that only one man had the depth of knowledge required to write them successfully. Concurrent with the announcement that the comic's four-issue run was being extended, editor Bob Budiansky was appointed chief writer. Because of Marvel rules about editors not being allowed to commission scripts from themselves, Budiansky stepped down as editor, being replaced in this role by Jim Owsley. It was all change going into 1985 …

MARVEL UK: A BACKGROUND

While Marvel Comics continued to publish the *The Transformers* comic in the USA, a sister title was also launched by Marvel UK in Britain featuring new and exclusive UK-only stories nestled between reprints of the American material.

Marvel UK was the British subsidiary of the American Marvel Comics, repackaging US material for the local market as well as producing some of its own original titles. At this stage, Marvel UK weren't exactly new to the world of licensed tie-ins, having already tasted success with titles based on *Doctor Who* and *Star Wars*.

The UK *The Transformers* comic was published to take advantage of the already-produced US strips, but also to provide stories of its own, especially given that the US book was not at first guaranteed to continue past issue four. Although the American *The Transformers* comic was eventually green-lit for an extended run, there was still a requirement for UK-produced stories: given that the UK comic had a much quicker release rate, more material was needed than Marvel US could provide.

Editorship of the British title was given to Sheila Cranna, with guidance from the experienced Alan MacKenzie, who was credited as 'editorial advisor' for the first few issues. As well as running reprints of the American strips, Cranna commissioned a variety of other features to fill out the comic, making it a surprisingly diverse read.

Indeed, the first thing most readers notice about the early UK issues of the *The Transformers* is how eclectic it all was. The actual *The Transformers* strip took up only about a third of the comic's 32 pages, while the rest of the page-count was filled with news articles about robots, competitions, puzzles, posters and a back-up strip (years-old reprints of *Machine Man*). Rather than being a dedicated Transformers comic, it read more like a general publication about robots, which just happened to have *The Transformers* as the lead strip.

This sort of format was quite normal in the UK industry, where many comics consisted of multiple strips rather than being dominated by a single story. Some of the best-loved British comics (such as *The Beano*, *2000AD* and *Eagle*) were anthologies in this vein, as were the British versions of *M.A.S.K.* and *Masters of the Universe*, both of which (much like *The Transformers*) were based on popular boys' toys and cartoon series.

So, although by this time the US comic was gradually steering toward what would become its regular format (Budiansky taking over as writer, the introduction of a letters page), by early 1985 the UK version was still very different from the streamlined behemoth that would come to be a major player in British newsagents over the next few years.

[4.1] MAN OF IRON
- UK#9, 25 January 1985 (Chapter One), 11 pages
- UK#10, 8 February 1985 (Chapter Two), 11 pages
- UK#11, 22 February 1985 (Chapter Three), 11 pages
- UK#12, 8 March 1985 (Chapter Four), 11 pages

American reprint: US#33, 'October 1987' (published June 1987 – Chapters One and Two), 22 pages; US#34, 'November 1987' (published July 1987 – Chapters Three and Four), 22 pages.

The US printing – more than two years after the initial UK run – was a last-minute filler to cover a production delay. The choice of this story for reprinting was probably due to a combination of reasons: as a UK four-parter it would fit neatly within two US issues; it was continuity-light, containing no references to any other stories; and finally, as a highly regarded story, it made for an excellent showcase of what the UK series could do.

The original UK printing lacked any captions identifying the various segments of this story. The description of each instalment as a 'Chapter' (rather than the usual 'Part') originated in a later single-issue compilation (the UK 85/86 Winter Special – aka Collected Comics #3). Each chapter was also given an individual title: 'First Encounter', 'Kidnapped!', 'You've Got Friends?' and 'Battlefield Castle Stansham'. The US printing had no individual title for the first instalment, but confusingly called the remaining segments 'Chapter Two', 'Part 3' and 'The Conclusion'.

Credits:
Steve Parkhouse (script); John Ridgway (art, chapters 1-2); Mike Collins (art, chapters 3-4); Josie Firmin (colours, chapters 1-2); Gina Hart (colours, chapters 3-4); Richard Starkings (letters); Sheila Cranna (editor); John Ridgway (cover, UK#9 and 10); Mike Collins (cover, UK#11 and 12). **US:** Nel Yomtov (re-colouring); Don Daley (editor); Tom DeFalco (editor-in-chief); Charles Vess (cover, US#33); Tom Morgan (cover, US#44).

The UK covers were just blow-ups of selected interior art.

Plot:
The Decepticons attack a castle in England, where a mysterious alien ship is found buried nearby. After the attack, the military are called in and the curator, Roy Harker, is contacted. Roy's son, Sammy, encounters the Autobots while playing in the woods, and links them to the legendary Man of Iron, a robot who was apparently known to the local Saxons in the 11th Century.

The Autobots contact Sammy, who fills them in on the Man of Iron legend, and they deduce that the mythical robot was in fact an ancient Transformer sent to Earth from Cybertron in an attempt to ascertain the fates of the *Ark* crew.

In a second attack on the castle, the Decepticons have the Man of Iron killed, but the Autobots manage to drive them away. The Man of Iron's ship still remains buried beneath the castle, but the Autobots destroy it to prevent it from falling into Decepticon hands.

Notes:
This is one of the 'flashback stories' that, as discussed below, are assumed to have taken place at some point during the events of [4] 'The Last Stand'.

The Autobots that remained on Cybertron sent a rescue ship to Earth 'millions of years' ago, in an attempt to make contact with Optimus Prime and his forces. The ship (about the size of 'an ocean-going liner') was manned by a robot known as Navigator (who would lay dormant in the craft) and a scout, the eponymous Man of Iron, who would regularly emerge and survey the local area. All the while, the ship would emit a homing signal that could be detected by the Earth-bound Transformers.

As the aeons passed, the ship became buried and a castle was built on the site. We see a flashback to the year 1017, when the Man of Iron emerged from the ship amidst an attack by the Saxons, who were led by a man named Godwin the Strongarm. By this time, the local area was known as Stenshame. A local landmark – Eldric's Cross – is mentioned, the surrounding forest is called Stanewood, and there is also a nearby abbey, manned by the priest Aethelric.

It should be noted that this sequence is not particularly accurate from an historical standpoint – castles were not introduced to England until the the 1050s. Some old Roman forts still existed at this time, but Saxon fortifications were generally limited to burhs and hill forts, rather than *bona fide* castles. If we assume that this entire sequence is just Sammy picturing the events in his head (and therefore that the castle's appearance in these sequences is just part of his misplaced imagination), we can ignore the anachronism and assume that the actual battle took place around a much less impressive Saxon burh. The present-day Stansham Castle was most likely built by the Normans years after the Saxons' encounter with the Man of Iron. The Normans were, after all, known to build castles on the sites of Saxon burhs (such as the real-world Tamworth Castle). Another possibility is that the manuscript that Roy reads from (dated 1070 and written 53 years after the event), is simply confused.

The present-day events are said to take place in late summer/early autumn (1984) in the (fictional) village of Stansham; the Harkers live at 10 Millbank Road. Internal evidence suggests that Stansham is somewhere in the southwest of England: Jazz passes a road sign showing that a town ending in the letters '-ston' is 14 miles away; given that the story is set in Southern England (in what was once Saxon territory), this could only really refer to the towns of Helston or Launceston, both located in the county of Cornwall. Furthermore, the motorway battle is said to take place on the M4, the major road link between London and the southwest of the country. Finally, the army jeep that we see has a licence plate SAB 710B, which tells us the vehicle was registered in the south-western town of Worcester.

The Autobots travel to England in an impressive shuttlecraft (presumably a short-range escape shuttle that was carried to Earth aboard the *Ark*). The Transformers' names appear to be just nicknames or code-names – Jazz indicates that his real name would be unpronounceable to human tongues. Sammy has a copy of a *Spider-Man* comic in his room.

In the first instance of the UK letters page being used to explain a plot point, the Openers section in UK#13 clarifies that Sammy's weird dream (at the start of chapter 2) was in fact partially caused by Mirage's powers of illusion, so that the Autobot could steal the Man of Iron drawing undetected. In other words, 'Sammy was half-dreaming and half under the influence of Mirage.'

This story takes place over at least three days; there is also a coda set one year later.

Both the plot and title of this story are heavily reminiscent of the 1968 Ted Hughes novel *The Iron Man* (renamed *The Iron Giant* in the US), in which a young boy befriends a mysterious giant robot.

US Changes:
In a reversal of the usual format, here follows a list of changes made to a British story for its American reprint:

Page 2, panel 6: 'realised' is changed to 'realized'.
Page 3: two of the panels (the first and third) are re-sized.
Page 3, panel 2: again, 'realised' is replaced with 'realized'.

Page 9, panel 3: 'Stenshame' is changed to 'Stansham' and 'neighbouring' to 'neighboring'.

Page 11: the 'To Be Continued' caption has been omitted.

Page 23: the caption boxes have been moved around, and the credits made bigger to accommodate the American editors.

Page 23, panel 1: 'awoken' is amended to 'awoke'

Page 25, panel 1: 'unpronounceable' is re-rendered as 'unpronouncable' [sic]

Page 25, panel 2: 'Trailbreaker' is changed to 'Tailbreaker' [sic]

Page 33: the 'To Be Continued' caption is again removed.

Page 34, panel 1: the credits panel is excised, and the tree behind it increased in size.

Page 34, panel 2: 'emphasise' is changed to 'emphasize'.

Page 35, panel 6: the colloquial 'alright' is changed to the formal 'all right'.

Page 37, panel 3: 'Oh, Lord' is replaced by 'Oh, criminy'

Page 38, panel 1: 'Good God!' is changed to 'Good gravy!'

Page 44, panel 2: 'vapourised' becomes 'vaporized'.

Careful study of the lettering on page 18 seems to indicate that this issue was censored even prior to its original UK printing. In each instance of the exclamation 'What the heck?' the last two letters seem to have been rewritten in another hand. This leads one to believe that the original script read 'What the hell?' (a phrase considered somewhat offensive at the time), and was amended before going to press.

The chequered reprint history of this story has resulted in the identities of some characters being changed between versions. Starscream, Skywarp and Thundercracker are identical but for their colour schemes, so when this (largely black-and-white) story was recoloured in subsequent editions, the various colourists have had their own ideas as to which Decepticon was which. There is one notable scene in which an unidentified jet Decepticon is rammed by Jazz. On the cover to UK#12, this Decepticon is coloured as Skywarp; in the UK Winter Special/Collected Comics reprint, it is coloured as Thundercracker; and finally, in the US reprint, it is bedecked in Starscream's colours.

Roll Call:
Autobots: Optimus Prime, Jazz, Bluestreak, Mirage and Trailbreaker.

Decepticons: Starscream, Skywarp, Thundercracker, Laserbeak and Buzzsaw.

Data File: Steve Parkhouse (writer)
Parkhouse is best known for having written comic strips for *Doctor Who Magazine* (including stories such as 'Stars Fell on Stockbridge' and 'Voyager'), but also contributed to *2000 AD*, *Nick Fury, Agent of SHIELD* and *Night Raven*. He is married to fellow *The Transformers* contributor Annie Halfacree.

Review:
It's a testament to the flexibility of the format that we can get two such different takes on the franchise in back-to-back stories. Whereas [4] 'The Last Stand' was full of excitement and adventure, this by contrast is an exercise in atmosphere, suspense and wonder.

What differentiates this story from most other *The Transformers* tales is its depiction of the alien robots as truly otherworldly – they creep about at night, show very little emotion and can kill or maim each other with just a single shot. Forget the almost unimaginable lengths of time discussed in [1] 'The Transformers' – placing a single Autobot in the 11th Century gives the Cybertronian war more historical weight than any mention of a 'four million year conflict'.

Beautifully illustrated, and written with a real fairytale quality, this is pure *The Transformers* magic. 5/5

The Early UK Stories: Continuity Nightmares?

Only five stories in, and we're already having to tackle one of the most hotly-debated topics in the comic's history. The US issues from [1] 'The Transformers' to [4] 'The Last Stand' tell a single seamless story of robotic adventures. Each ends on a cliffhanger that is immediately picked up in the very next issue.

However, to mess things up for continuity-obsessed fans, three UK-only tales – [4.1] 'Man of Iron', [4.2] 'The Enemy Within' and [4.3] 'Raiders of the Last *Ark*' – were published, and although they're *supposed* to be set roughly around this same time period, it's an absolute nightmare to fit them into the US continuity, given that there appears to be no gap in the narrative where they can have taken place.

Everyone seems to have their own ideas about fitting these UK 'flashback stories' into the wider continuity, and indeed the UK comic itself had a few stabs at making it work in an occasional series of plot summaries.

So how *can* we fit them in? Well, they're obviously set during the very earliest days of the Transformers' Earth exile: they depict the Decepticons as being based in their mountaintop Fortress Sinister, which was all but abandoned after [4] 'The Last Stand'; and Sunstreaker, effectively killed off in [5] 'The New Order', is alive and well. The key piece of evidence comes from [4.2] 'The Enemy Within', where Megatron makes mention of his recent encounter with Spider-Man – so these stories must be set at some point *after* Spider-Man rescues Sparkplug from the Decepticons in [3] 'Prisoner of War'.

Furthermore, the Autobot Gears features in these 'flashback stories'. Gears, if you remember, was badly injured during the Spider-Man adventure, and his revival is part of the cliffhanger that spans [3] 'Prisoner of War' and [4] 'The Last Stand' – so these events must take place at some point during that latter story, after Gears has fully recovered.

The presence of Ratchet in these 'flashback stories' also gives us some clues. Near the beginning of [4] 'The Last Stand', Ratchet dashes to the local hospital and drops off the ailing Sparkplug (pages 5-7 of that issue) and is not seen again until page 17, where he's still at the hospital. From then on, Ratchet remains away from the other Autobots.

Therefore, we can assume that the chain of events goes something like this: Ratchet drops Sparkplug off at the hospital and returns to the *Ark*. Then, while Sparkplug remains on the critical list (perhaps for a week or two), the 'flashback stories' take place. Afterwards, Ratchet goes back to the hospital to check on Sparkplug's condition, and is therefore safe from Shockwave's attack. In this scenario, the 'flashback stories' take place at some point between pages 7 and 17 of [4] 'The Last Stand' – most likely after the sixth panel on page 7, straight after Buster heads toward the hospital telephones and just before the 'Meanwhile, all's quiet on the Decepticon front ...' caption.

However, this solution isn't perfect. Throughout much of the first few issues, the Autobots and Decepticons are suffering from fuel starvation, a plot strand that drives most of the early narrative. After the climax of [2] 'Power Play', the Autobots are always depicted as being near-crippled by their lack of energy – and yet this doesn't seem to be much of a problem in the 'flashback stories'.

The best possible rationalisation is to assume that the Man of Iron's buried spacecraft contains enough fuel reserves to power the Autobots for an extra week or so. The Autobots take this fuel – off-panel – before destroying the ship. This provides the Autobots with sufficient energy resources to tide them over through the events of [4.2] 'The Enemy Within' and [4.3] 'Raiders of the Last *Ark*'.

One final point to note: [4.1] 'Man of Iron' contains no references to any other stories and features only a minimal Transformer cast. As such, it could theoretically fit pretty well anywhere. 'Robot War!' a story-so-far feature in UK#22, suggested that [4.1] 'Man of Iron' takes place soon after Sparkplug's abduction, between [2] 'Power Play' and [3] 'Prisoner of War'. However, it seems extremely unlikely that Optimus Prime would drop everything and travel to England while Sparkplug remained in Decepticon captivity.

The Back-Up Strips, Part 3: *The Chromobots*

When the UK *The Transformers* comic went up in price from issue #11 (rising 2p to 27p), editor Sheila Cranna was determined to give readers more value for their money. At the time, half of all the comic's pages were printed in black-and-white. Putting a new two-page strip, *The Chromobots*, into a regular slot on pages 4 and 5 pushed the main *The Transformers* strip further toward the interior of the comic, where it would have a higher number of colour pages.

As with *Matt and the Cat*, this strip was the brainchild of writer/artist Mike Kazybrid, and especially commissioned and exclusive to *The Transformers* UK. Never reprinted and rarely discussed online, presented here is the full synopsis for *The Chromobots* ...

Plot:

Dudley is a comic-obsessed bookworm, whose reading is interrupted by a small alien cyborg crahsing in through his bedroom window (UK#12). The new arrival is a Chromobot by the name of Mikros, who reveals that the crash was caused by jet pack failure (UK#13).

Putting Mikros in a shopping bag, Dudley goes for a walk in the park, thereby giving the lost alien the opportunity to scan for the signals of his fellow Chromobots. Dudley narrowly avoids being tricked by a second Chromobot, named Transmute, who uses his shape-shifting powers to disguise himself as an old man (UK#14). However, it was all a test of Dudley's loyalty: Transmute is actually a good guy. He and Mikros are on an urgent mission, one in which both Earth and the Chromobot Empire are at stake (UK#15).

Transmute tells Dudley of an evil Chromobot named Predator, who has escaped from prison and plans to create a super-weapon by combining alien technology with human nuclear weapons (UK#16). Predator kidnaps Tessa Stone, head of Stone Industries, a nuclear arms developer. However, Tessa's cries for help are heard by Transmute, who leaps into battle with the evil Chromobot (UK#17). Despite their best efforts, both Transmute and Mikros are unable to beat Predator in hand-to-hand combat (UK#18).

While Predator teleports away to continue his dastardly plan, Dudley is introduced to a third good Chromobot, named Shield (UK#19). They regroup back at Dudley's house to come up with a plan. Opting to return to their spaceship, the Chromobots are nearly spotted by Dudley's father, but Transmute manages to disguise himself as a 'Humph the Cat' soft toy and avoids discovery (UK#20).

From the safety of the Chromobot spaceship, Shield contacts his home planet. It transpires that Predator's teleporting ability can be traced: it seems the villain has activated a time slip, travelling forward in time to the year 2535 (UK#21). Dudley and the Chromobots follow Predator's trail, and are themselves warped into the 26th Century (UK#22).

Future-Earth is a nuclear wasteland, populated by aggressive mutants (UK#23), who are minions of Predator. A fight breaks out between the mutants and the Chromobots (UK#24), but is interrupted by the arrival of Predator himself, who reveals that, in this future, his plan was successful and both Earth and the Chromobot world have been devastated (UK#25).

However, Dudley steals the Time Modulator from a distracted Predator, and escapes back to the present with his Chromobot friends. They opt to destroy the modulator, which not only prevents Predator's apocalyptic future from ever occurring, but also erases the villain from existence. With the Earth now safe, the Chromobots tend to the recovering Tessa Stone. (UK#26).

[4.2] THE ENEMY WITHIN!
- UK#13, 22 March 1985 (Part 1), 11 pages
- UK#14, 5 April 1985 (Part 2: 'The Best Laid Plans …'), 11 pages
- UK#15, 19 April 1985 (Part 3: 'Crime … and Punishment!'), 11 pages
- UK#16, 3 May 1985 (Part 4: 'Trial … and Error!'), 6 pages
- UK#17, 17 May 1985 (Part 5: 'Endings … and Beginnings!'), 5 pages

The entire story was reprinted in full colour in 1991, near the end of the original UK run. Parts 2 and 3 were split in half and each spread across two issues; the individual segments were now listed as 'Chapters', having been renamed as such for a prior colour reprinting in the 1986 Summer Special, aka Collected Comics #4. In that Special, the first part was retrospectively given the title 'Solo Strategy!'

- UK#308, 9 February 1991 (Chapter 1), 11 pages
- UK#309, 2 March 1991 (Chapter 2: 'The Best Laid Plans …'), 5 pages
- UK#313, 27 April 1991 (Chapter 3), 6 pages
- UK#314, 11 May 1991 (Chapter 4: 'Crime … and Punishment!'), 5 pages
- UK#315, 25 May 1991 (Chapter 5), 6 pages
- UK#316, 8 June 1991 (Chapter 6: 'Trial … and Error!'), 6 pages
- UK#317, 22 June 1991 (Chapter 7: 'Endings … and Beginnings!'), 5 pages

As can be seen above, the reprint series took a break during issues 310-312; a shake-up in the comic's format meant that a back-up strip – *Machine Man* – had to be concluded before the reprints could resume again in issue 313.

Credits:
Simon Furman (script); John Ridgway (art, part 1); Mike Collins (art, parts 2-5); Gina Hart (colours); Richard Starkings (letters); Sheila Cranna (editor); John Ridgway (cover, UK#13); Mike Collins (cover, UK#14-17).

For stories such as this, which had a second printing within the UK comic, the format of the credit lists will be such that the part numbers refer to the original printing only.

As with [4.1] 'Man of Iron', there was no specially-commissioned cover art for these issues; instead the covers consisted of interior art panels expanded to fit the page.

Plot:

Both factions of the Transformers face a threat from an enemy within their own ranks – the Autobot Brawn has gone berserk after being zapped by a faulty piece of equipment, and Starscream deserts the Decepticons after a heated argument with Megatron.

Both rebels run amok – Brawn causes chaos in a small town, while Starscream attacks an airbase. The Autobots and Decepticons come together to discuss what to do about the two problem robots, and agree on a trial-by-combat – Brawn and Starscream will do battle to the death; the winner will have their honour restored and be allowed to return to their comrades.

The battle begins, with a repentant Brawn now having fully recovered from his breakdown. After a long, brutal struggle, Starscream apparently kills Brawn and is welcomed back into the Decepticon ranks.

However, Brawn's death was faked by the Autobots (as part of a plan to counteract suspected Decepticon treachery), and he too is redeemed.

Notes:

Starscream attacks a top-secret airbase in Oregon, which is a new installation (it's yet to see action) codenamed Oregon Four-Alpha. In reality, there are two US Air Force bases in Oregon – Portland Air National Guard Base and Kingsley Field – both of which are locally well-known and therefore unlikely to be the location of the classified base depicted here.

The town Brawn attacks – St Petersburg – is also fictional. There are towns with that name in other US states (Florida and Pennsylvania), but none in Oregon. A fictional television station, OBTV, reports on these events.

The Decepticons have the ability to review footage of old Cybertronian gladiatorial competitions; we see a fight between the two robots Tornado and Earthquake, which results in their mutual annihilation. Presumably this recording is taken directly from Megatron's own memory banks – it seems unlikely that the Decepticon troops took computers or archives with them when they boarded the *Ark*.

As noted already, Megatron makes a direct reference to his meeting with Spider-Man in [3] 'Prisoner of War'. Furthermore, the news anchor reports that the Transformers have been 'terrorising parts of Oregon recently'.

The uppermost panel on page 8 of Chapter 2 is a visual reference to the famous Roy Lichtenstein painting *Whaam!* (1963). Some of the individual chapter titles are literary references – *Crime and Punishment* is the title of an 1688 novel by Fyodor Dostoyevsky, and 'The Best Laid Plans' is a quotation from the 1785 Robert Burns poem 'To A Mouse'.

The whole story appears to take place during the course of a single day, and leads directly into the following adventure, with Megatron preparing for an all-out assault on the Autobots.

Roll Call:

Autobots: Optimus Prime, Jazz, Prowl, Bluestreak, Ratchet, Sideswipe, Sunstreaker,

Hound, Mirage, Bumblebee, Brawn, Huffer, Gears, Windcharger and **Red Alert**.

Decepticons: Megatron, Starscream, Skywarp, Thundercracker, Soundwave, Rumble, Frenzy, Laserbeak, Buzzsaw and Ravage.

As with the one-shot appearances of the Reflector robots in [4] 'The Last Stand', we can assume that this rare appearance by Red Alert is another indication of additional Transformers (mostly background characters) being active on Earth but not specifically named in the roll-call sequences of [1] 'The Transformers'.

Other Transformers featured here include Tornado and Earthquake, non-toy characters created specifically for a cameo appearance in this story. Tornado would also play a part in the Annual story [A2.4] 'State Games'.

Data File: John Ridgway (artist)
Ridgeway's long career spans multiple titles, including *Doctor Who Magazine*, *Spider-Man and Zoids*, *Commando*, *Babylon 5* and, for *2000 AD*, *Judge Dredd* and *Strontium Dog*.

Data File: Sheila Cranna (editor)
After leaving *The Transformers*, Cranna's other editorial work included stints on *Doctor Who Magazine* and the *Indiana Jones* comic.

Review:
A relatively straightforward tale brought to vivid life by the excellent artwork – as with [4.1] 'Man of Iron', visually this story puts its American counterparts to shame.

On the surface, this is a tale that plays safe: the by-the-numbers plot (good guy goes rogue) is probably the first example in *The Transformers* comics of a well-worn cliché being utilised. That the adventure climaxes in a traditional duel-to-the-death only adds to the familiarity of the scenario.

However, these classic tropes aren't the only focus here; they're a 'way in' to the story, a framing device to allow us to look into the minds of some of these characters. The depictions of Starscream and Ravage here are never bettered in the original comic's run, which is no mean feat.

Debutant writer Simon Furman also manages to spice up proceedings via the use of some interesting storytelling flourishes, notably some 'split-screen' pages at the climax of Part 2. Even from the outset, he's obviously having fun playing with the format, seeing what he can get away with. 3/5

Openers
Openers was the name of the introductory double-page spread found on pages 2 and 3 of the UK comic under the editorship of Sheila Cranna (UK#1-21). It would generally include an editorial, readers' letters, fact files and other information. Notable editions include …

- UK#1: First edition. Featured readers' letters (by kids who had visited Marvel UK's offices on a school trip and seen a pre-sale copy of the issue).
- UK#3: There are letters bemoaning the lack of a Megatron toy in the UK ('He may be appearing on the shelves next year'), and the switch from full-colour to a mix of colour and black and white ('The all-colour *Transformers* was a first-issue bonus; to

keep it up would mean we'd have to put up the cover price.') There's also the first of a regular series of fact-files, of which the Autobot Hound is this week's subject.

- UK#4: A Gears fact file, and a reader's letter advocating getting rid of the back-up strip, *Machine Man*.
- UK#5: Megatron fact-file. There's a notable reader's letter here requesting a Transformers annual and cartoon show. In reply, an annual is promised for 'next year' and it's reported that Marvel are 'already working on a series'. (The cartoon show would debut in the UK in 1985.) The 'Penpals' column begins, wherein kids could request postal correspondence with like-minded fans.
- UK#6: Optimus Prime fact-file. First appearance of the Stock Exchange feature, in which readers are invited to trade toys and comics with each other.
- UK#7: There's a Bumblebee fact file, and a short piece by Hasbro representative Anthony Temple, who reveals that a Megatron toy will be 'in your toy shops from Easter'. Temple also reveals that the three top-selling toys in the range are Jazz, Optimus Prime and Starscream.
- UK#8: Ravage fact file.
- UK#9: Sideswipe fact file. Openers extends into an unprecedented third page this issue, to accommodate two lists of competition winners and a complete checklist of the currently-available toys.
- UK#10: Starscream fact file. Hasbro's Anthony Temple writes in again, informing readers of some new toys in the pipeline: Beachcomber, Seaspray, Powerglide, Warpath, Cosmos and the Insecticons.
- UK#11: Sunstreaker fact file. There's an apology from the editor, for putting the price up by two pence. Also included is a reader's letter asking about the cliffhanger ending to issue 8 ([4] 'The Last Stand'); editor Sheila Cranna insists that these dangling plot points 'will be answered in future issues of *The Transformers*.'
- UK#12: Skywarp fact file.
- UK#13: Windcharger fact file. Hasbro's Anthony Temple tells us about the Jumpstarters (Topspin and Twin Twist).
- UK#14: Humph (a character from back-up strip *Matt and the Cat*) fact file. In the letters section, we have the first instance of a reader complaining that the comic's regular Robot Round-Up feature is a waste of 'two precious pages.' Another reader asks when he'll see Ironhide, Wheeljack and Trailbreaker in toyshops. ('This year,' comes the reply, 'along with Prowl and other favourites.')
- UK#15: Laserbeak fact file. Openers gets a slight re-design.
- UK#16: Prowl fact file. First appearance of the Your Choice feature, in which readers nominate their favourite *The Transformers* issues, stories, covers etc.
- UK#17: Soundwave fact file.
- UK#18: Jazz fact file. Hasbro's Anthony Temple reveals that the Dinobots are now in the shops.
- UK#19: The final edition of the fact file series, this time focusing on Rumble.
- UK#21: The final Openers, with editor Sheila Cranna saying her goodbyes: 'So much is happening here at Marvel, it's time to move on to new projects.'

Robot Round-Up

In the early days of the UK comic (UK#1-14, 16, 18 and 20), this was a regular two-page feature, covering the subject of real-life robots. It included articles about crazy inventors who'd built robots in their garage, cutting-edge science from Japan, and hippy American academics making bold predictions of future technological progress. Writer Johnny Black is a sci-fi enthusiast and still works today as a music journalist – so from time to time the column would focus on robots within popular culture as well. The edition in UK#9 took the form of a special report from Disney's EPCOT Center in Florida.

The section was occasionally complemented by a third page, not written by Black; in UK#2 this comprised a feature about fictional robots that had appeared in the UK television show *Doctor Who*, and in UK#5 it covered Sieve-Head, a robot from the kids' magazine show *Saturday Superstore*. UK#10 featured an additional two-page feature, written by Alan McKenzie, about *Forbidden Planet*'s Robby the Robot.

In one notable edition, UK#14, Robot-Round Up was used as the location of the comic's April Fool joke, telling of a robot named Jasper, built by one 'O Pilfarlo'.

[4.3] RAIDERS OF THE LAST *ARK*

- UK#18, 31 May 1985 (Part One), 6 pages
- UK#19, 14 June 1985 (Part Two), 5 pages
- UK#20, 28 June 1985 (Part Three), 6 pages
- UK#21, 12 July 1985 (Part Four), 5 pages

Credits:
Simon Furman (script); Mike Collins (pencils); Jeff Anderson (inks); Gina Hart (colours); Richard Starkings (letters, parts 1, 3-4); John Aldrich (letters, part 2); Sheila Cranna (editor); Mike Collins and Jeff Anderson (covers, UK#18-21).

For the final time, the cover images were blow-ups of the interior strip art.

Plot:
The Decepticons attack the *Ark*, and the Autobots are in very real danger of being defeated. As a last resort, Optimus Prime decides to activate the ship's computer (nicknamed 'Auntie') and with it the *Ark*'s automated defence systems.

Unfortunately, having taken some damage, Auntie has been driven completely mad, trapping Autobots and Decepticons alike in a magnetic field, threatening death and destruction on both factions.

The Autobot Windcharger and the Decepticon Ravage are unaffected, as they themselves also have the ability to control electromagnetic forces. Reluctantly teaming up, the mismatched duo make their way to the computer's core, past many devious traps – including a web of laser beams, a deadly electrical hazard and a powerful Guardian sentry robot.

Ravage is eventually able to deactivate Auntie, thereby freeing the rest of the stricken Transformers. The Decepticons break off their attack after Windcharger uses his magnetic powers to repel Megatron, sending him flying out of the top of the volcano.

Notes:
The title is an obvious homage to that of the film *Raiders of the Lost Ark* (Steven Spielberg, 1981). Ravage's and Windcharger's journey through the *Ark*'s various hazards is very reminiscent of the quests through perilous booby-trapped tunnels

undertaken by that film's hero, Indiana Jones.

This story is continuity-heavy: in a flashback to the Decepticons' attack on the *Ark* (originally depicted in [1] 'The Transformers'), it's implied that it was Auntie who advised Optimus Prime to crash the ship on Earth. This is problematic in hindsight – later stories depict the crash as Prime's decision alone. (The apparent contradiction can be easily reconciled: Prime had the help of Auntie in planning the crash prior to take-off, as a contingency plan in the event of an attack, and when the Decepticons were on the verge of victory, Prime ordered the ship's destruction on Auntie's recommendation.)

The attack by the Decepticons we see here is a direct reprisal for their being conned by the Autobots at the end of the previous story, [4.2] 'The Enemy Within'. Megatron displays here a seldom-seen ability – he is able to tap into black holes remotely and interdimensionally summon antimatter for use as a weapon.

We get our first little bit of foreshadowing as well: after the Decepticons flee the battle, the Autobots find the words 'We'll be back' graffitied onto a wall; this references the Decepticons' attack in [4] 'The Last Stand', to which this story is a prequel. The style of writing is visually similar to the 'Are all dead' slogan etched onto the *Ark*'s wall on the front cover of the next issue, [5] 'The New Order'.

It's unclear whether the damage to Auntie is due to the *Ark*'s planetfall four million years ago, or to Megatron's shot just before she is reactivated here. Given that the *Ark*'s computer was shown to be working in previous stories (notably in [1] 'The Transformers' – where she was referred to as 'Aunty'), it would seem that Optimus Prime is only awakening the computer's higher brain functions here, and that Auntie has always been active, albeit in a more basic mode (to which she presumably returns after her defeat). The ship is here described as the 'last of the great *Ark*s', the first suggestion that there is more than one vessel of its type.

For the first time in the UK-originated stories, mention is made of the Autobots' ongoing fuel crisis ('We're lower on fuel than ever'). Optimus Prime confirms that Windcharger, Jazz, Prowl, Hound and Brawn all suffer major damage during the battle; this is a nice touch on the part of the UK writing team, as these Autobots are indeed missing in the latter stages of [4] 'The Last Stand'. Presumably there are Decepticon injuries too – Frenzy, Rumble, Skywarp and Soundwave are also on the casualty list in that story.

Roll Call:
Autobots: Optimus Prime, Jazz, Prowl, Sideswipe, Sunstreaker, Hound, Mirage, Trailbreaker, Bumblebee, Huffer, Gears and Windcharger.

Decepticons: Megatron, Starscream, Skywarp, Thundercracker, Soundwave, Rumble, Frenzy, Laserbeak, Buzzsaw and Ravage.

Thundercracker's appearance in this story is unconfirmed; much of this story is drawn in black-and-white, and in monochrome it's near-impossible to tell him from Skywarp. In the sections that *do* have colour, he's never clearly shown; taking into account the fact that all the other original Decepticons are present and correct here, he deserves the benefit of the doubt.

In the flashback section near the beginning of Part Three, the silhouette of **Thrust,** one of the Decepticon jet Transformers, can be seen in the background – his distinctive

VTOL wing engines are plainly visible. As with the appearance of Red Alert in [4.2] 'The Enemy Within', this is another example of the UK art team placing new characters in the early UK stories despite them not yet being a part of the regular character roster. We have to ignore this as an error because, at this point in the continuity, Thrust is still on Cybertron.

Data File: Mike Collins (artist/writer)
As well as working on a slew of English strips (including *Spider-Man*, *Doctor Who* and *Judge Dredd*), Collins successfully made the crossover to American comics, working for both DC (*Batman*, *Superman*, *Wonder Woman*) and Marvel USA (*Uncanny X-Men*). Other work includes cover art for licensed *Star Trek* novels, and illustrations for Ladybird's range of *The Transformers* books. More recently, he has worked as a storyboard artist for television, for shows such as *Doctor Who*, and its spin-off *Class*.

Review:
The first real misstep from *The Transformers* UK, 'Raiders of the Last *Ark*' is more a succession of set-pieces than a story in its own right. Although it's quite diverting and adds some neat concepts to the Transformers universe (Auntie and the Guardian robot), it's not really substantial enough and comes across as being very much a filler. 2/5

The Back-Up Strips, Part 4: *From the Fact Files*
These were short (four to six page) dramatisations of actual historical events, printed in a few of the early UK *The Transformers* comics. They were Belgian-produced, French-language strips, with new English captions and dialogue. For the most part they had been previously published as part of the *Histoire Vrai* ('True Stories') segment in *Tintin* magazine.

- UK#15: 'Trapped Beneath the Waves!' – The rescue of the USS *Squalus*, an American submarine that sank in 1939. Previously published as 'SOS le *Squalus* a coulé!'
- UK#17: 'The Truth about Alcatraz!' – A potted history of the notorious island. Previously published as 'La Dramatique Histoire d'Alcatraz'.
- UK#19: 'The Battle of Hastings – The True Story' – A retelling of the Norman invasion. Previously published as 'La Bataille de Hastings'.
- UK#21: 'The Saga of Erik the Red' – Erik leads the Vikings to Greenland. Previously published as 'Eric le Rouge, la Viking'.

The Back-Up Strips, Part 5: *Robo-Capers*
Written and illustrated by Lew Stringer, *Robo-Capers* began in UK#15 as a short, three-panel humour strip, and was eventually promoted to a half-page slot in UK#75 after the cancellation of *Matt and the Cat*.

The majority of the *Robo-Capers* strips told of the alien King No-Nose (aka King Kruel in earlier appearances), and an unnamed inventor who would build various robots to aid the King's planned invasion of Earth – robots that would invariably backfire with hilarious results.

Another strand would see new inventions trialled on Earth – a robot lawnmower, a robot pen, a robot receptionist etc, each of which would have an unforeseen flaw in their programming.

Notable editions included:

- UK#15: The first *Robo-Capers* focuses on Thugatron, the Ultimate Robot.
- UK#37: In which we meet Drinko the vending machine robot (pre-dating Dispensor from the 2007 live-action *Transformers* movie by over 20 years).
- UK#51: This issue's edition of Robo-Capers was beset by a printing error, making it near-unreadable. It was reprinted without any problems in UK#57.
- UK#74: A one-off full-page special, as Grimlock takes over as the comic's resident letter-answerer; from UK#75 *Robo-Capers* takes over *Matt and the Cat*'s regular slot, doubling in size to a half-page strip.
- UK#88, 97 and 114: 'Transformers Who Never Made the Grade' – a three-part series showcasing such characters as a transforming lamp-post who hates dogs.
- UK#107-113: 'Forgotten Robots of History' – a seven-part series showcasing an alternative history of robots, from the Stone Age to the present-day.
- UK#127-152: For its final stretch, *Robo-Capers* presents a continuing story, as King No-Nose and the inventor have adventures on the Moon, before finally getting to Earth and meeting British Prime Minister Margaret Thatcher. They then arrive on Robotworld, and attempt to mould its meek and mild robot inhabitants into an invasion force. Finally realising that all their schemes are inevitably doomed to failure, the King and the inventor attempt to reach Earth again – not as invaders but as holidaymakers.
- UK#183: 'Wind of Change' – a one-off *Robo-Capers* special. Written by Simon Furman and drawn by Lew Stringer, it shows Grimlock leaving his role as resident letter-answerer, and his replacement by Dreadwind.
- UK#200: A special Robo-Capers/Combat Colin crossover: King No-Nose and the Robot Inventor wave 'goodbye for good!'

Half-Measures

From UK#16 to UK#21, *The Transformers* strip was reduced from its usual 11 pages, down to a measly five or six. A new back-up strip, *Planet Terry*, was introduced to make up the page count. So why the sudden change in format? Why produce a 32-page *The Transformers* comic and include only, at most, six pages of actual *The Transformers* action?

The change was a last-minute decision. UK#15 promised that the next issue would include 'the final exciting instalment of "The Enemy Within"', indicating that the last 11 pages of that story were originally set to be printed in their entirety in UK#16, before the decision was made to split them over two issues. Similarly, the following story ([4.3] 'Raiders of the Last Ark') also appears to have been chopped up into four segments, having initially been a two-parter.

With no official explanation for the reduced page-count, all we can do is speculate. One theory is that the UK comic wanted to delay the next batch of US reprints for as long as possible, in order to create a bigger stockpile of material. However, the more likely scenario is that another UK story fell though at the last minute, and the existing ones had to be extended in order to fill the gap. The original intention was for Steve Parkhouse and Simon Furman to alternate as writers; it's therefore possible that Parkhouse's sudden departure after just one story, [4.1] 'Man of Iron', was the cause of the muddle.

Whatever the case, these six issues are a true anomaly in *The Transformers'* publishing history, packed with filler material and little in the way of Transformers action. A revamp of the title in UK#22 couldn't come fast enough ...

[5] THE NEW ORDER
US#5, 'June 1985' (published February 1985), 22 pages.

British reprint: UK#22, 26 July 1985 (Part One), 9 pages; UK#23, 9 August 1985 (Part Two), 13 pages.

From #5 onwards, the US comic became a monthly rather than bi-monthly title.

Credits:
Bob Budiansky (script); Alan Kupperberg (art); Nel Yomtov (colours); Rick Parker (letters); Jim Owsley (editor); Jim Shooter (editor-in-chief); Mark Bright (cover). **UK:** Mark Bright (cover, UK#22 – reuse of US cover); Robin Smith (cover, UK#23).

Plot:
Shockwave has seized the *Ark*, taken over leadership of the Decepticons and set about repairing his fallen comrades. Megatron, still too weak to move, secretly plots to usurp Shockwave and retake command.

Shockwave monitors human television broadcasts, and sees a news report detailing a new, state-of-the-art oil platform owned by millionaire industrialist G B Blackrock; he sets off to attack it.

Meanwhile, Sparkplug is recovering well in hospital. Ratchet, unable to get a radio response from the other Autobots, takes Buster and heads off to the *Ark*, where they are shocked to discover that the Decepticons have taken over. Buster slips inside the ship unnoticed.

He is astonished by what he sees – the defeated, inactive Autobots are strung up from the ceiling, and Optimus Prime reduced to the status of a disembodied head ...

Notes:
The television broadcasts watched by Shockwave are a mix of real-life and invented shows. The main programme featured on the very first page is classic '50s sitcom *The Honeymooners*, which is often repeated on US television to this day and is cited as the inspiration for the cartoon show *The Flintstones*. The programme's lead characters Ralph Kramden, Alice Kramden and Ed Norton are depicted here. The other real-world show on display is the US game show *Let's Make a Deal* (1963-present), where oddly-costumed audience members are chosen by host Monty Hall to compete for prizes, culminating in the Big Deal round, where players pick a prize hidden behind one of three doors.

Aside from the news programme about the oil rig, the other two shows we see are entirely made-up – an American football game involving the fictional tailback Otis Parsley, and a daytime US soap featuring a character called Brad – a pastiche of popular shows such as *The Young and the Restless* (1973-present) or *Days of Our Lives* (1965-present).

As Megatron discusses recent events with Shockwave, we see flashbacks to all the previous US-originated stories thus far – the *Ark*'s landfall ([1] 'The Transformers)', the construction of the Decepticon fortress ([2] 'Power Play'), Sparkplug's capture by the Decepticons ([3] 'Prisoner of War'), and finally Shockwave's arrival ([4] 'The Last Stand').

Megatron mentions the 'divine weld', the first hint that the Transformers' origin involves a godlike creator. In a story full of firsts, we also see the introduction of the Creation Matrix as a concept – we're told it can 'construct new Transformer life' and that it is 'encoded' into a new Autobot leader 'every ten millennia'. It's quite clear from the dialogue here that the Matrix is just a computer program, rather than the physical object we're shown later in the comic's run.

A helpful sign outside the hospital tells us that it's the (fictional) Greater Portland Medical Center, the first reference in the comics to the city of Portland, which is said to be 'nearby' the *Ark*.

With Shockwave now in command, this story marks the first time we see a change in Decepticon leadership – it certainly won't be the last.

UK Notes:
As *The Honeymooners* was too obscure a reference to be recognised by UK readers (it remained unseen in the UK until a run on the BBC2 channel between 1989 and 1991), in the original British printing all references to the show were removed and replaced with photographic images from the sci-fi miniseries *V* (1983), depicting the character Mike Donovan in a struggle with one of the alien Visitors.

UK Changes:
Page 1: as mentioned, the *Honeymooners* splash page has been replaced with an image from *V*.
Page 2: again, *The Honeymooners* is replaced by *V*.
Page 3, panel 4: 'gas' is changed to 'petrol'.
Page 7: 'colors' has been amended to read 'colour'.
Page 7: the caption is changed from 'As seen last issue – Jim' to 'As seen in issue 8'.
Page 13, panel 2: 'carburator' becomes 'carburettor'.
Page 15: the caption 'As seen in *Transformers* #3 – Ows.' Is changed to 'As seen in *Transformers* #6'

Roll Call:
Autobots: Optimus Prime, Jazz, Prowl, Bluestreak, Ironhide, Ratchet, Sideswipe, Sunstreaker, Hound, Wheeljack, Mirage, Trailbreaker, Bumblebee, Cliffjumper, Brawn, Huffer, Gears and Windcharger. All of these appear as lifeless bodies only, except Ratchet (fully functional) and Optimus Prime (decapitated but conscious).

Notably, Sunstreaker's body is zapped by Shockwave as a show of force; this results in the character becoming essentially irreparable and thus written out of the story at this point.

Decepticons: Megatron, Starscream, Skywarp, Thundercracker, Soundwave, Rumble, Frenzy, Ravage and Shockwave. Of these, Ravage, Thundercracker and Starscream appear only in unconscious form in a life-support machine. Megatron is also in life support, but able to talk.

Shockwave confirms here that there are only 11 active Decepticons currently on Earth. Thus we can now be sure that any other generic background Decepticons who made it to Earth (such as the Reflector-style robots seen in [4] 'The Last Stand') have now been fully wiped out by Sparkplug's corrosive fuel formula.

Other: Buster, Sparkplug, **G B Blackrock** and **Josie Beller**. Blackrock and Beller, seen here for the first time, appear only on the television news reports watched by Shockwave.

Data File: Mark Bright (artist)
Responsible for the most iconic *The Transformers* cover ever (US#5), Bright later returned to the franchise, providing art for *Spotlight: Nightbeat*, a 2006 *The Transformers* comic from IDW Publishing. His other work includes stints on *Batman*, *Green Lantern*, *Captain America* and *Iron Man*.

Review:
Brilliantly grim and atmospheric, the sight of the Autobots strung up in the *Ark* is an era-defining image. The introductions of Blackrock, Beller and the Creation Matrix mark the beginning of many new and exciting story arcs; and with the death of Sunstreaker, Buster's discovery of Prime's head and some amazing cover art, this story is nothing if not iconic.

That said, nothing much happens here – this basically consists of Shockwave, Prime and Megatron explaining the story to each other, while Buster discovers things that we the readers already know. The 'comedy' scene in which the ambulance drivers search in vain for the source of Ratchet's voice is not only awful, but also out of place in an otherwise sombre tale.

A classic story – if not necessarily a great one – 'The New Order' scores highly for its incredible imagery and doom-laden tone, which are (almost) excellent enough to make up for its other deficiencies. 4/5

The Back-Up Strips, Part 6: *Planet Terry*
Planet Terry told the adventures of the eponymous young space-boy on an intergalactic quest to find his parents. Aimed squarely at younger readers, it was released in America as part of Marvel's Star Comics imprint. Each original *Planet Terry* comic was split into three or four mini-adventures, which made it ideal for serialisation in short chunks.

- 'The Search' (UK#16), from *Planet Terry* #1 (April 1985). Terry searches for his parents, but instead finds a new robot friend.
- 'A Clue' (UK#17), from *Planet Terry* #1 (April 1985). Terry and Robota meet an old man who knows of Terry's parents.
- 'Some Answers' (UK#18), from *Planet Terry* #1 (April 1985). In flashback, we see Terry's birth and accidental abandonment.
- 'Malt Shop Menace' (UK#19), from *Planet Terry* #1 (April 1985). Terry and Robota encounter the gruff alien Omnus at a milkshake bar.
- 'The Saga of Princess Ugly' (UK#20), from *Planet Terry* #2 (May 1985). Terry's spaceship crashes on an alien planet. The natives offer to repair the ship if Terry and his friends rescue the captive Princess Ugly.

- 'Too Close (Enough) For Comfort' (UK#21) from *Planet Terry* #2 (May 1985). Terry and his pals make a perilous quest to the Domed City.
- 'The Doom of the Domed City' (UK#22-23) from *Planet Terry* #2 (May 1985). Terry rescues Princess Ugly.
- 'The Secret of the *Space Warp*' (UK#24-25) from *Planet Terry* #3 (June 1985). Terry finds his parents' spacecraft, which gives him a clue to their whereabouts.

In order to bring the story to a satisfactory conclusion, the original *Planet Terry* #3 (containing the stories 'The Secret of the *Space Warp*', 'Deadly Games' and 'Found') was heavily edited; it was this condensed omnibus version that was serialised across UK#24-25. The UK edit comprised pages 1-3 and 18-22 of the original issue, with some dialogue edits (and a slight rearrangement of the panel order) to smooth over the gap.

Although the American comic was cancelled after 12 issues, with Terry's quest unresolved, the UK reprint had a happy ending in which Terry is reunited with his family. This was the cliffhanger ending to the original *Planet Terry* #3. Sadly for American readers, the first story of #4 ('The Monster of the Cave'), revealed that these were not, in fact, his parents – just inanimate statues.

[6] THE WORSE OF TWO EVILS!
US#6, 'July 1985' (published March 1985), 22 pages.

British reprint: UK#24, 23 August 1985 (Part One), 11 pages; UK#25, 6 September 1985 (Part Two), 11 pages.

Credits:
Bob Budiansky (script); Alan Kupperberg (art); Nel Yomtov (colours); Rick Parker (letters); Jim Owsley (editor); Jim Shooter (editor-in-chief); Alan Kupperberg (cover). **UK:** John Higgins (cover, UK#24); Alan Kupperberg (cover, UK#25 – reuse of US cover).

Plot:
Shockwave's attack on the oil platform is completely successful; during the battle, the rig's designer – the prodigious Josie Beller – is electrocuted.

Shockwave returns to the *Ark*, only to be met by an enraged Megatron, still injured but desperate to regain his status as leader of the Decepticons. The pair do battle in a nearby town, causing widespread damage and panic, but the already-weakened Megatron is no match for the fully-fit Shockwave.

Meanwhile, Buster agrees to help Optimus Prime, but doesn't reckon on having his brain zapped by the bodiless Autobot leader – an action that Prime mysteriously refers to as a 'mind link'.

As Shockwave sets about preparing the oil rig for use as a new base of operations, the rest of the Decepticons pledge their loyalty to him.

Notes:
G B Blackrock's offshore oil platform is '146 miles' from the *Ark*. In reality, there are no oil rigs off the Oregon coast.

The events of the previous issue must have had a duration of only minutes – a caption informs us that the live news report we saw Shockwave watching at the beginning of [5] 'The New Order' was 'less than an hour ago'.

At the base of Mount St Hilary lies the (fictional) town of Vallemont. Oddly, despite it being so close to the *Ark*, this is the town's one and only appearance in the comics.

Ratchet is able to recognise Shockwave on sight, suggesting that the Decepticon was well-known to the Autobots back on Cybertron four million years ago.

Although unexplained here, this issue marks the point where the Creation Matrix is passed from Optimus Prime to Buster, an action that will fuel many future plotlines.

The title is a play on the old idiom, 'the lesser of two evils'.

UK Changes:
Page 2, panel 2: the caption is changed from 'Last issue – Ows.' to 'Issue #22'.
Page 3: the credit for 'coloring' is changed to 'colours'.
Page 6, panel 1: 'armor' is amended to 'armour'.
Page 10, panel 4: editor Jim Owsley's tag is removed from the 'last issue' caption.
Page 12, panel 2: another re-written caption – 'Details of his arrival on Earth were revealed last issue – Owsley' becomes 'Details of his arrival on Earth will be revealed soon!'
Page 16, panel 3: correcting a mistake in the original version, Megatron's speech about not being at full strength is now spoken by Shockwave in the UK reprint.

Roll Call:
Autobots: Optimus Prime (still a disembodied head) and Ratchet.

Decepticons: Megatron, Starscream, Skywarp, Thundercracker, Soundwave, Rumble, Frenzy, Laserbeak, Buzzsaw, Ravage and Shockwave.

Other: Buster, G B Blackrock and Josie Beller.

Data File: Alan Kupperberg (artist)
Kupperberg's many art credits include *Iron Man*, *Justice League of America* and *The Amazing Spider-Man*.

Review:
The focus of this story is firmly on action and adventure, with two major battles (the attack on the oil rig and the Megatron/Shockwave battle) taking up the majority of the page count – although the continuing plotlines are kept ticking along nicely.

The end result is professional and functional – it does its job well but lacks the flair or spark to be considered amongst the best the series has to offer. 3/5

[7] WARRIOR SCHOOL!
US#7, 'August 1985' (published March 1985), 23 pages.

British reprint: UK#26, 14 September 1985, 23 pages.

Uniquely, the UK comic reprinted the entirety of this story in a single issue (usually the US strips were split across two UK issues).

Credits:
Bob Budiansky (script); William Johnson (pencils); Kyle Baker (inks); Nel Yomtov (colours); Rick Parker (letters); Jim Owsley (editor); Jim Shooter (editor-in-chief); Mark Bright and Brad Joyce (cover). **UK:** Mark Bright and Brad Joyce (cover – reuse of US cover).

What Do the Credits Actually Mean?
For those not well-versed in the making of comics, some explanation might be required for the various credits used in this book, and the various crafts that go into making a completed comic book.

- **Script:** Comics are often written in a similar manner to film and television screenplays, complete with dialogue and descriptions of the action. Sometimes the scriptwriter will just be credited as a 'Writer' (especially in the American comics), but for the sake of consistency the term 'Script' will be used throughout.
- **Pencils:** Once the script was completed, it would then go to a penciller, who, as the title suggests, would draw the comic with a pencil (although nowadays many comics are produced digitally). The penciller would generally be responsible for the composition of images, framing, layouts and vantage points (or 'camera angles').
- **Inks:** Due to the printing process, the penciller's subtle lines and shading did not translate well onto the finished page. Therefore an inker would trace over the pencil in solid blacks. The inker's role was an important one, being responsible for shading, detail, shadow and the overall mood of the art.
- **Art:** Sometimes (especially in the UK comics), a single artist would be responsible for both pencils *and* inks. In these cases, the persons involved are credited as providing simply the 'Art'.
- **Colours:** The colourist was responsible for adding colour to the inked art, in the form of special dyes. This would then be translated into a CMYK (cyan, magenta, yellow, key) colour model for printing. This was the standard for the American and later British Transformers comics, however the earlier UK issues used actual painted art, allowing for additional subtleties of shade.
- **Letters:** The letterer would be responsible for any text seen on the page, including speech bubbles, story titles, sound effects etc.
- **Editor:** The main 'overseer' of the comic, who would check it at every stage of the creative process, from script to finished page. It was their job to iron out mistakes, check continuity and above all ensure the quality of the final comic.
- **Editor-in-Chief:** One of the most senior positions within the comics industry, the editor-in-chief at Marvel was an executive-level role, with responsibility for the overall creative direction of all titles published by that company.
- **Cover:** This credit indicates the artist(s) responsible for the comic's cover.

The UK and US strips differed in how they were put together. The UK comics used the more traditional method – the writer would produce the script, which would then be brought to life by the artists to produce the final piece. Marvel US had a different way of working: the writer would produce a story treatment or synopsis only (rather than a full script), which the artists would interpret as they saw fit. The finished art would then go back to the writer, and it was at that point that the full script (captions, dialogue etc) would be added to the already-completed art.

Plot:
Ever since his mindlink with Prime, Buster has been getting painful headaches – the alien power of these headaches is so strong that they cause nearby objects to levitate.

The Decepticons attack yet another facility owned by G B Blackrock – this time they add an aerospace plant to their portfolio of captured assets. Blackrock, infuriated that the Decepticons seem to be targeting him, vows revenge. He visits the critically-ill Josie Beller in her hospital bed. She has been ordering electronic equipment for her mysterious new project …

Ratchet, the only Autobot still active, ventures into the *Ark* and comes face to face with Megatron. Ratchet proposes a deal – the lives of his fellow Autobots in exchange for the destruction of Shockwave. Megatron readily accepts, leaving Ratchet to figure out how he can possibly hope to defeat the all-powerful Shockwave …

Notes:
It's finally confirmed here that Buster lives in a 'suburb of Portland', which retroactively confirms that the city scenes in stories such as [2] 'Power Play' and [4] 'The Last Stand' must have taken place in the city (Oregon's largest). Another Portland suburb is home to Blackrock Aerospace Plant Number One, and G B Blackrock's office building is located downtown. Blackrock owns a hospital, Blackrock Chronic Care Institute, 'nearby'. At the beginning of the issue, Buster and Ratchet are wandering through Mount Hood National Forest, to the east of the city.

Reference is made to Lee Iacocca, the renowned US businessman and former president of Ford and Chrysler who designed the Mustang and Escort cars. In the same scene, a can of soda from a vending machine costs 'O' fifty cents (which in 1985 equated to 40 GB pence).

Jessie considers Buster to be (maybe) the smartest kid in school. (Jessie could well be exaggerating, but it's true to say that Buster does seem quite intelligent.) Buster states that his father has been a mechanic for over 30 years, which ties in with what we see of Sparkplug's military back-story in [4] 'The Last Stand'.

As a result of Josie Beller's electrocution in [6] 'The Worse of Two Evils', she now has extensive nervous tissue damage and suffers from bodily paralysis, except for her head and some limited movement in her right arm.

More of Cybertron's background is revealed here: we see the events of [1] 'The Transformers' recapped again, but this time from the Decepticons' point of view. Shockwave's briefing is held in a dome-like building that may or may not be situated in the environs of the Castle Decepticon we saw in the first issue.

It's confirmed that there are no trees on Cybertron, and that Ratchet enjoyed partying back on his home planet. Despite being a medical officer in the Autobot army, he's not trained for combat; instead of built-in armaments he can call upon the use of only a medical laser scalpel and what appears to be a jet of cryogenic fluid built into his wrists.

At one point Ratchet makes the exclamation 'By the Primordial Program!' a reference to the semi-mythical Creation Matrix. Furthermore, we see a Cybertronian custom performed. This is the Rite of Oneness, a highly ceremonial oath shared by two Transformers that must be upheld on pain of death (although the dishonourable Decepticons have been known to renege on such bargains).

Ratchet's outburst 'I'm a doctor … not a warrior!' mirrors the various catchphrases (such as 'I'm a doctor, not an escalator!' and 'I'm a doctor, not a bricklayer!') of the Dr McCoy character from the television show *Star Trek* (1966-69).

Finally, there are a number of flashbacks and other references to previous issues: Prime's mindlink with Buster, the attack on the oil rig, Shockwave carrying the beaten Megatron back to the *Ark* (all from [6] 'The Worse of Two Evils'), Buster's discovery of the Autobot corpses ([5] 'The New Order'), Sparkplug's heart attack, Shockwave's defeat by the Dinobots in the Savage Land (both from [4] 'The Last Stand') and the *Ark*'s planetfall ([1] 'The Transformers').

Oddly, in the frame showing the *Ark* crashing to Earth, there is a pteranodon-like creature depicted in the air nearby; this must be a mistake as, with the exception of the Savage Land's inhabitants, no pterosaurs existed on Earth four million years ago.

UK Changes:

Page 1, panel 1: 'rigors' is changed to 'rigours' and 'color' to 'colour'.

Page 3, panel 7: 'pasttime' [sic] is corrected to 'pastime'.

Page 6, panel 1: the caption is changed from 'last issue – Ows' to 'issue #24'.

Page 7, panel 4: '… did it last issue – Owz' becomes '… did it in issue #24'.

Page 8, panel 5: 'labor' is amended to 'labour'.

Page 12, panel 2: 'last issue – Owz' again becomes 'issue #24'.

Page 13, panel 6: 'harbor' is changed to 'harbour'.

Page 14, panel 2: Editor Jim Owsley's tag is removed from the caption box.

Page 15, panel 2: 'valor' is changed to 'valour' (two instances).

Page 16, panel 1: '*Transformers* #4 – Owz' becomes '*Transformers* #7'.

Page 20, panel 3: again, Jim Owsley's tag is erased from the caption.

Page 20, panel 5: 'defend Shockwave' is corrected to 'defeat Shockwave'.

Page 22, panel 2: Owsley's tag is again excised.

Page 22, panel 4: correcting a mistake in the original printing, Ratchet's speech bubble ('This much I knew …') is now reassigned to Megatron.

Page 23, panel 2: 'honor' is changed to 'honour'.

Roll Call:

Autobots: Ratchet, Optimus Prime (as a decapitated head), Jazz, Prowl, Ironhide, Sideswipe and Cliffjumper (as lifeless corpses), Grimlock, Slag and Sludge (in flashback).

It's difficult to tell exactly whether one of the corpses is Prowl or Bluestreak (the pair look very similar), but given that it lacks Bluestreak's shoulder-mounted missile launchers, it's most likely to be Prowl.

Decepticons: Megatron, Soundwave, Rumble (flashback only), Laserbeak and Shockwave.

Other: Buster, Jessie, 'O', G B Blackrock and Josie Beller.

This is the fifth and final appearance of 'O', the previous ones having come only in the first four US issues.

Data File: Jim Owsley (editor)
Credited as the first black editor in American comics, Owsley (who has since legally changed his name to Christopher J Priest) also edited *Captain America, Iron Man* and Marvel's range of *Spider-Man* comics (and indeed helped launch *Web of Spider-Man*). He also wrote for *Green Lantern, Wonder Woman* and *Batman*. Outside of comics, he is an ordained Baptist minister.

Review:
Excluding the first six pages, in which Ratchet and Buster lark about in a forest, explaining the plot to some bewildered campers, this is brilliant stuff. The overarching story finally feels like it's moving somewhere, not only in terms of the plotting but also in terms of character – Ratchet's confrontation with Prime and then Megatron, and Buster's scene in the garage, are all tremendous. There's also some nice action as Soundwave and Laserbeak take over the factory.

But those awful first six pages – nearly a quarter of the story's overall page count – sadly mar what's otherwise a great piece. 4/5

[8] REPEAT PERFORMANCE!
US#8, 'September 1985' (published May 1985), 22 pages.

British reprint: UK#27, 21 September 1985 (Part One), 11 pages; UK#28, 28 September 1985 (Part Two), 10½ pages.

For the UK printing, the final half-page of this adventure was omitted entirely (see the **UK Notes** section below).

From issue 27, the UK comic changed from a fortnightly to a weekly publication schedule.

Credits:
Bob Budiansky (script); William Johnson (pencils); Kyle Baker (inks); Nel Yomtov (colours); Rick Parker (letters); Jim Owsley (editor); Jim Shooter (editor-in-chief); Mark Bright and Kyle Baker (cover). **UK:** Robin Smith (cover, UK#27); Mark Bright and Kyle Baker (cover, UK#28 – reuse of US cover).

Plot:
Ratchet travels to the Savage Land, hoping to find the Dinobots – the only Transformers thus far to have beaten Shockwave. The mission is a success; Ratchet discovers that the Dinobots' random brute force was able to match Shockwave's logical battle strategies.

Meanwhile, the Decepticons are setting their plans in motion at the aerospace factory, where they intend to use the power of the Creation Matrix in Prime's brain to instil life into newly-constructed Decepticon troops. A bed-ridden Josie Beller watches the Decepticons' activities on the television news, and swears to exact revenge for the attack that paralysed her.

Ratchet contacts Megatron by view-screen, and shows the Decepticon visual proof of Shockwave's defeat. It's actually a trick – the footage is four million years old and shows only the original battle between Shockwave and the Dinobots.

Megatron prepares to kill Ratchet but is surprised when the Dinobots show up and join in the battle. The force of Ratchet's attacks destabilises a mountaintop ledge, and

Megatron is sent plummeting to the valley floor below.

Notes:
Ratchet traverses the rough terrain of the Savage Land thanks to the MARB – Mobile Autobot Repair Bay – a floating medical platform equipped to revive the Dinobots.

A caption informs us that these events are set prior to *The Avengers* #257 (July 1985), in which the Savage Land is destroyed by the characters Terminus and Jorro.

We see more of Josie Beller here – she is shown to be developing some kind of metal exoskeleton that coats her skin, allowing her to move previously-paralysed limbs and fire what look like electrical rays from her hands. She's now well on the route to becoming Circuit Breaker, and will be fully unveiled as such in the next US issue ([9] 'Dis-Integrated Circuits').

Shockwave reveals that he is constructed from 'nuclear-hardened steel', and mentions that he plans to create six new Decepticons. (These six, the Constructicons, will debut in [10] 'The Next Best Thing to Being There'.)

As is usual, there are many references to previous issues for the benefit of new readers fresh to the series. Ratchet recalls the events of [7] 'Warrior School', specifically his discovery of the Autobot corpses in the *Ark* and his deal with Megatron. We hear of Josie Beller's electrocution in the oil rig attack of [6] 'The Worse of Two Evils'. Also, most notably, we see an extended sequence showing full details of the Shockwave/Dinobot battle, originally described in [4] 'The Last Stand'.

UK Notes:
Ratchet travels to the Savage Land in a shuttlecraft – it looks very different from the one the Autobots used in [4.1] 'Man of Iron', but then again, it might well be the same one, either rebuilt or with some transforming abilities of its own.

The short epilogue showing Beller getting ready to 'check out' of the hospital was omitted from the UK printing; when she next appears in the UK comics ([8.1] 'Decepticon Dam-Busters'), she's still bed-ridden.

UK Changes:
Page 1, panel 1: 'colors' is changed to 'colour', and the reference to *The Avengers* #257 is excised.

Page 3, panel 4: 'valor' becomes 'valour'.

Page 10, panel 5: the caption 'see *Transformers* #4 – Owz' is replaced by 'see *Transformers* #8'.

Page 12, panel 5: 'armor' is amended to 'armour'.

Page 14, panel 3: the caption is changed from '*Transformers* #6 – Owz' to '*Transformers* #24'.

Page 14, panel 5: the description of Beller's right arm, 'She cannot lift or move it on her own' is corrected to 'Moving it causes her great pain' ([7] 'Warrior School' confirmed that she did in fact have some 'limited' movement in the arm).

Page 20, panel 6: 'honor' is changed to 'honour'.

Page 22: as previously mentioned, the final four panels are omitted from the UK version.

Roll Call:
Autobots: Optimus Prime (as a decapitated head), Jazz, Sunstreaker (as corpses),

Wheeljack, Bumblebee, Gears (as corpses; flashback-only), Ratchet, Grimlock, Snarl, Slag, Sludge and Swoop.

Decepticons: Megatron, Soundwave, Laserbeak and Shockwave.

Other: G B Blackrock and Josie Beller.

Review:
The decision in recent issues to focus on just a few select robots (Ratchet, Megatron, Shockwave) continues to pay dividends – all three are now familiar, developed characters, and serve as excellent protagonists/antagonists.

On top of that, the plot continues to twist and turn; again there are some excellent action sequences, and as an added bonus we have the full introduction of the Dinobots.

Top-notch stuff indeed. 5/5

US Straplines, Part 1
It's not just the cover art that sells a comic – an exciting or shocking slogan splashed across the front cover can also lure in customers. Here is a list of all such slogans that appeared on the American *The Transformers* comic, from US#2 to US#30. (Issues #1, 6, 14, 22-23 and 27 had no such straplines.)

- US#2: Optimus Prime vs. Megatron!
- US#3: Guest-starring Spider-Man
- US#4: The Autobots' last stand!
- US#5: Are all dead.
- US#7: 'Flee while you can, Buster! Megatron is the mightiest of Decepticons! I may not survive!'
- US#8: And now ... the Dinobots!
- US#9: The lady's name is – Circuit-Breaker! She's out to destroy all robots ... that is, if Starscream doesn't get her first!
- US#10: Dawn of the Devastator!
- US#11: Jetfire soars supreme!
- US#12: Optimus Prime: Autobot killer!
- US#13: The menace of Megatron!
- US#15: The man behind the machines!
- US#16: Bumblebee's last stand!
- US#17: Into the smelting pool!
- US#18: Blaster and Straxus battle ... between two worlds!
- US#19: You asked for him – you got him! Omega Supreme!
- US#20: 'This town ain't big enough for the both of us, Autobot – draw!'
- US#21: Aerialbots over America
- US#24: Game over, Optimus Prime!!
- US#25: Megatron's last stand!
- US#26: Introducing: The Mechanic! 'No job too big ... or too small ...'
- US#28: The Mechanic strikes again... and the Autobots strike out!
- US#29: Scrapped – by the Scraplets! And introducing the Triple Changers!
- US#30: Introducing ... the Throttlebots!

[8.1] DECEPTICON DAM-BUSTERS!

- UK#29, 5 October 1985 (Part One), 11 pages
- UK#30, 12 October 1985 (Conclusion!), 11 pages

Credits:

Simon Furman (script); John Stokes (art); Steve Whitaker (colours); Richard Starkings (letters); Ian Rimmer (editor); John Ridgway (cover, UK#29); Mike Collins (cover, UK#30).

Plot:

Traversing a small town on their way back to the *Ark*, Ratchet and the Dinobots inadvertently frighten one of the natives. The Dinobots ask why humans are scared of them. By way of explanation, Ratchet recounts one of the Transformers' previous adventures …

Ratchet tells of the Decepticon attack on Sherman Dam. Although defeated, Megatron destroys the dam, and the ensuing wave of water threatens to engulf a nearby town.

The Autobots use various methods to save the townspeople: they blast trenches and channels in the ground to divert the water; they cause a rock-fall to halt the water's progress; and finally they evacuate the townspeople to higher ground.

The town is saved, but rather than hail the Autobots as heroes, the humans blame them for all their woes – unable to tell the difference between the two factions. It seems that the Autobots will be forever blamed for the Decepticons' evils.

Ratchet and the Dinobots eventually return to the *Ark*, only to find their path blocked by a Guardian robot …

Notes:

The story recounted by Ratchet presumably takes place around the time of the so-called 'flashback stories' ([4.1] 'Man of Iron' to [4.3] 'Raiders of the Last *Ark*') – the Decepticons we see here are still based at their mountaintop HQ, which served them prior to Shockwave's arrival in [4] 'The Last Stand'.

The Sherman Dam story is adapted from a sequence in the cartoon episode {1-02} 'More Than Meets the Eye, Part Two'. Given the divergence in styles between the two media, this means that a few elements unique to the cartoon show make a rare appearance in the comics:

- Both Prime and Megatron are able to transform their hands into melee weapons (an axe and a flail respectively) – in the cartoon, the Transformers could often sprout weapons and other useful devices from their hands, but this ability is rarely demonstrated in the comics.
- Prime has some rather out-of-character dialogue ('Stick it in neutral, Megatron!' and 'You're old …yesterday's model – fit only for scrap!') – fine for the all-action hero of the cartoon show, but not really befitting the more introverted Prime depicted in the comic series.
- Rumble causes the wave of water by transforming his arms into pile drivers. This was a trademark ability often demonstrated in the cartoon show; in the comics, however, Rumble creates earthquakes by emitting 'low frequency ground waves' (see [2] 'Power Play' or [3] 'Prisoner of War').

There is actually a real-world Sherman Dam, located near Loup City in Nebraska. However, this exists purely for flood control and irrigation purposes, and is not a power station. The dam shown in the comic and cartoon is clearly based on Hoover Dam, near Boulder, Colorado. (At one point, the comic actually refers to the dam as 'Boulder Dam', but this is corrected in later reprints.) [The 2004 video game *Grand Theft Auto: San Andreas* also depicts Hoover Dam and renames it as Sherman Dam – presumably one of the game's designers was a Transformers fan].

At one point, Prime utters the exclamation, 'By the Celestial Spires!' – the first of what will become many exclamations referencing the spires of the Celestial Temple of Iacon on Cybertron, a setting previously seen in the annual story [A1.3] 'And There Shall Come … A Leader'.

As ever, there are links to other stories: camcorder footage of the Megatron/Ratchet/Dinobot battle from [8] 'Repeat Performance' is shown on a news broadcast; Josie Beller and G B Blackrock are shown plotting attacks that we'll eventually witness in [9] 'Dis-Integrated Circuits'; and in the final panel we see a Guardian, one of the robot defence drones that protect the Ark, as previously seen in [4.3] 'Raiders of the Last *Ark*'.

The title is a reference to the seminal British war movie *The Dam Busters* (Michael Anderson, 1955).

Interface

A series of fact-files of various Transformers, similar in style to the ones previously featured in the Openers section (UK#4-19) but with more detail. The strand was eventually cancelled to make way for the more exhaustive 'Transformers A to Z' series of character profiles.

- UK#25: Warpath and Ramjet
- UK#28: Snarl
- UK#31: Bombshell
- UK#32: Inferno
- UK#39: Scavenger
- UK#42: Blitzwing and Tracks
- UK#45: Cosmos and Beachcomber
- UK#52: Smokescreen and Mixmaster
- UK#55: Kickback and Slag
- UK#61: Devastator
- UK#65: Blaster and Sovndwave [sic]
- UK#67: Perceptor
- UK#68: Longhaul [sic]
- UK#69: Swoop
- UK#70: Omega Supreme
- UK#71: Thrust
- UK#73: Ravage

Roll Call:

Autobots: Optimus Prime, Jazz, Prowl, Bluestreak, Ironhide, Ratchet, Sideswipe, Hound, Wheeljack, Mirage, Trailbreaker, Bumblebee, Brawn, Grimlock, Snarl, Slag,

Sludge, Swoop and **Inferno**. (Apart from Ratchet and the Dinobots, all these characters appear in flashback only.)

Yet again in a UK story, we have a 1985 Autobot – on this occasion, Inferno – depicted as part of the original *Ark* crew (similar to Red Alert's appearance in [4.2] 'The Enemy Within'). Although this is his debut so far as the comics are concerned, Inferno had previously appeared in [A1.2] 'Missing in Action', a text-only story from the UK 1986 Annual.

Decepticons: Megatron, Starscream, Skywarp, Thundercracker, Soundwave, Rumble and Frenzy (flashback only).

Although they aren't drawn clearly enough to make out properly, it's assumed that the Reflector robots are amongst those helping to load up the Energon cubes in Part One.

Other: G B Blackrock and Josie Beller.

Data File: Steve Whitaker (colourist)
Whitaker is best known for being the colourist on the seminal graphic novel *V for Vendetta*. His other credits include *Action Force* and *Spider-Man and Zoids* (both for Marvel UK), and later *Death's Head II*, *Turok: Dinosaur Hunter*, *Tank Girl: Apocalypse* and *What If …?*

Review:
A lazy rehash of one of the cartoon episodes. The nice artwork is probably this tale's only redeeming feature. Worse still, by crafting a story around the concept that humans have trouble telling Autobots from Decepticons, it's also stealing the thunder from (and lessening the impact of) the upcoming Circuit Breaker storyline, which will explore similar themes. 1/5

The 'NEXT' Box, Part 1
One of the many changes instigated by new UK editor Ian Rimmer in UK#22 was the introduction of the iconic 'NEXT' box – a yellow box at the bottom of the final page, containing a dramatic slogan or phrase hinting at the events of the following issue. Here is a list of all such slogans plus (for completeness) the longer taglines from earlier issues that predated the introduction of the 'NEXT' box.

- UK#1: Giant-size problems for Earth when the Transformers come out fighting!
- UK#2: Big problems for Bumblebee – and Buster has plenty of his own!
- UK#3: 'The humans shall not be taken!' So swears Optimus. But … there's plenty scrapping in the scrap yard next issue!
- UK#4: Poor Buster's dad's in BIG trouble with the Decepticons, but an unexpected ally appears on the scene!
- UK#5: Spidey reckons he has the problem all tied up – but things aren't that easy!
- UK#6: Has Sparks [sic] Witwicky given Megatron the advantage he needs in his deadly war? Find out in the next instalment of *The Transformers*!
- UK#7: With their fuel supply desperately low, the Autobots face an overwhelming attack!

- UK#8: Jazz gives one particular boy the blues – when he appears in a quiet British woodland …
- UK#9: Sammy's dream is larger than life – and very strange things happen!
- UK#10: Man of Iron Part 3
- UK#11: The final exciting instalment of the Transformers story, Man of Iron
- UK#12: Both Optimus Prime and Megatron find they have trouble within their ranks!
- UK#13: The best laid plans …
- UK#14: Crime … and punishment!
- UK#15: Trial … and error!
- UK#16: Endings … and beginnings.
- UK#17: Raiders of the last *Ark*!
- UK#18: Auntie: judge, jury … and executioner?
- UK#19: Unholy alliances!
- UK#20: The final battle!
- UK#21: What happened to Shockwave? Have the Autobots survived? Where is Ratchet?
- UK#22: [First appearance of the NEXT box] The last Autobot!
- UK#23: Oil rig assault!
- UK#24: Megatron v Shockwave!
- UK#25: Warrior school!
- UK#26: In search of – Dinobots!
- UK#27: Cliffhanger!
- UK#28: Decepticon dam-busters!
- UK#29: Wave of destruction!
- UK#30: The wrath of Guardian!
- UK#31: Death in the flames!
- UK#32: Dis-integrated circuits!
- UK#33: Circuit training!
- UK#34: Introducing: the Constructicons!
- UK#35: Constructicons – combine!
- UK#36: Brainstorm!
- UK#37: Jetfire's in the sky!
- UK#38: Prime time!
- UK#39: The logical conclusion!
- UK#40: Christmas Break*er*!
- UK#41: Crisis of command!
- UK#42: Bumblebee alone!
- UK#43: Primed for action!
- UK#44: The Icarus theory!
- UK#45: Dreams die hard!
- UK#46: Dinobot-hunt!
- UK#47: Swamp-thing!
- UK#48: Robot rustlers!
- UK#49: The final rage!
- UK#50: Shooting star!
- UK#51: Megatron = megabucks!
- UK#52: Rock and roll-out!
- UK#53: Cover me!
- UK#54: I, Robot-Master!
- UK#55: I, master-robot!

- UK#56: Plight of the Bumblebee!
- UK#57: Fighting back!
- UK#58: Robot-Buster!
- UK#59: Baptism of fire!
- UK#60: Devastation derby!
- UK#61: Devastated!
- UK#62: Second generation!
- UK#63: Electric dreams!
- UK#64: Return bout!
- UK#65: The smelting pool!
- UK#66: Into the smelting pool!

[8.2] THE WRATH OF GRIMLOCK!

- UK#31, 19 October 1985 (The Wrath of Guardian!), 11 pages
- UK#32, 26 October 1985 (The Wrath of Grimlock!), 11 pages

NB: This story has no overall title; instead, each instalment is individually named. In such cases, this book will represent the story using as a single 'unofficial' title for ease of reference.

In this instance, the first reprint of these issues (in Collected Comics #6, aka *The Transformers* Summer Special 1987) has 'The Wrath of Grimlock!' splashed across the front cover, so that is the name this book will use to refer to this particular adventure.

Credits:
Simon Furman (script); Barry Kitson (art, part 1); Barry Kitson and Mark Farmer (art, part 2); Gina Hart (colours, part 1), Steve Whitaker (colours, part 2); Annie Halfacree (letters, part 1); Mike Scott (letters, part 2); Ian Rimmer (editor); Will Simpson (cover, UK#31 and 32).

Plot:
The Guardian robot has been reprogrammed by Shockwave to attack the Autobots, but is eventually driven off after being damaged by Ratchet. Ratchet sets about repairing the remainder of the Autobots, while the Dinobots chase after Guardian.

The Autobots discover that Shockwave has hidden a bomb inside the Guardian robot, and, using a remote control device, they use Optimus Prime's headless body to prevent the Dinobots from unwittingly detonating it.

Unable to defuse the bomb in time, the Dinobot Swoop transforms into his pterosaur mode and lifts Guardian safely out of range of the *Ark*. However, Swoop is caught in the blast, presumed destroyed.

The remainder of the Dinobots leave the *Ark*, believing their destiny lies elsewhere.

Notes:
This story sees the return of the Guardian-type drone robot, which previously appeared in [4.3] 'Raiders of the Last *Ark*'. It's impossible to say whether or not this particular Guardian is the same as the one seen previously, or indeed how many Guardians are stationed on the *Ark*.

We learn here that the Guardian is an Omega-class battle droid, is vulnerable to magnetism (as seen in [4.3] 'Raiders of the Last *Ark*' – referred to here as 'that Auntie business') and can also be harmed via a cerebral access port on the robot's neck. It boasts two-foot-thick armour-plating, neural hydraulic musculature, and 'enough stored energy to power a space transit'.

We also get some additional information regarding the Creation Matrix: it's confirmed here that the 'mindlink' with Buster in [6] 'The Worse of Two Evils' was Optimus Prime's method of transmitting the bulk of the Creation Matrix into the human's brain. However, a residual vestige of the program remains in Prime's head, which Shockwave is using to create his six new Decepticons.

Buster's Matrix-induced powers now extend to him being able to repair damaged machinery (in this case, an audio cassette player), using only his thoughts. The song Buster listens to is 'Glory Days' by Bruce Springsteen, a track from the record-breaking album *Born in the USA*, released in June 1984. Buster has a *Spider-Man* poster on his bedroom wall.

Ratchet confirms that the damage to Sunstreaker is so severe that he 'might never be operational again.' This is due to the hapless Autobot being zapped by Shockwave in [5] 'The New Order'.

Following on from the references to the Celestial Spires of Iacon in the previous story ([8.1] 'Decepticon Dam-Busters'), the Autobot Prowl mentions the alien landmark on two occasions here, speaking of 'Iacon's Great Dome' and later 'the Great Dome'.

We learn that, without a brain module, any Transformer body can be operated remotely (which indicates that Guardian can't be completely unintelligent, or else the Autobots could presumably control him, too).

Demonstrating for the first time that Shockwave's logic isn't always infallible, the Decepticon commander calculates here that the Autobots will be destroyed with '100%' certainty.

Josie Beller is also seen briefly in this story, using her exoskeleton suit to zap a computer terminal. This replicates a similar scene from [8] 'Repeat Performance', which was excised from the UK printing of that story.

It's presumed that Ratchet is able to fix all the Earthbound Autobots, with the exception of Sunstreaker, Optimus Prime (whose head is still held by the Decepticons), and maybe also Red Alert and Inferno, who won't appear again in the comic for a number of years.

The title is possibly a reference to the movie *Star Trek II: The Wrath of Khan* (Nicholas Meyer, 1982).

Roll Call:
Autobots: Optimus Prime (seen separately as both a lifeless decapitated body and as a bodiless head), Jazz, Prowl, Ratchet, Wheeljack, Windcharger, Grimlock, Snarl, Slag, Sludge and Swoop.

Decepticons: Soundwave (flashback only) and Shockwave.

Other: Buster and Josie Beller.

Data File: Ian Rimmer (editor/writer)
Rimmer scripted strips in *Action Force*, *2000 AD* and *Eagle*, and also penned the revived *Roy of the Rovers* strips in the BBC's *Match of the Day* magazine. As an editor, he worked on *Captain Britain*.

Review:

A highly satisfying tale, which not only tells a decent story in its own right, but weaves some of the ongoing US plot threads into the mix as well.

Another plus point is the characterisation – this is a landmark story in the depiction of the Dinobots, and Grimlock is especially well-served here.

All in all, this is a great entry in the UK canon, and one that more than makes up for the disappointments of [8.1] 'Decepticon Dam-Busters'. 4/5

UK Straplines, Part 1

Just like the equivalent lists for the American comic, here's a run-down of all the cover straplines for *The Transformers* UK, taking in issues #1 through #66.

- UK#1: Robot invaders! They're evil machines from another world! They want our planet! How can the Autobots save us? The fight begins inside.
- UK#2: The robots have landed – the metal invasion has begun.
- UK#3: Bumblebee, friend or foe? The sting in the tale!
- UK#4: Optimus Prime vs. Megatron! [As per the cover of US#2.]
- UK#5: Into the evil Decepticons' stronghold!
- UK#6: Guest-starring Spider-Man. [As per US#3.]
- UK#7: The Autobots' last stand! [As per US#4.]
- UK#8: Looks like it's the end for the heroic forces ...
- UK#9: A fantastic new Transformers adventure!
- UK#10: A night-time visitor for Sammy!
- UK#11: Action and adventure inside!
- UK#12: Showdown!
- UK#13: Has Brawn changed sides?
- UK#14: Shock developments!
- UK#15: A head-on clash for the warring Transformers inside!
- UK#16: The enemy within!
- UK#17: It's a gloomy outlook for the Autobots in The Enemy Within!
- UK#18: The *Ark* is invaded!
- UK#19: Introducing Auntie – a force to be reckoned with!
- UK#20: Electric issue!
- UK#21: The might of Megatron!
- UK#22: Are all dead. [As per US#5.]
- UK#23: Discover Prime's fate – inside!
- UK#24: Shockwave's act of war ... Offshore strike.
- UK#25: 'CF-One to base, CF-One to base ... You ain't gonna believe this ...'
- UK#26: Ratchet registers for warrior school!
- UK#27: Now weekly!
- UK#28: Introducing – the Dinobots!
- UK#29: Decepticon dam-busters!
- UK#30: The Decepticon dam-busters unleash a tidal wave of terror!
- UK#31: The Dinobots – no more mister nice guys!
- UK#32: In the flames of battle ... the wrath of Grimlock!
- UK#33: Autobots – Decepticons – Humans! Stand by for Circuit Breaker.
- UK#34: Starscream vs. Circuit Breaker – battle of the Autobot haters!
- UK#35: Creating the Constructicons!
- UK#36: Dawn of the Devastator!

PART TWO: THE COMICS

- UK#37: In search of Buster ... and the Creation Matrix!
- UK#38: Introducing Jetfire! Fast – furious – and fatal?
- UK#39: Optimus Prime: Autobot killer!
- UK#40: Head on clash ... the logical conclusion!
- UK#41: Merry Christmas everyone!
- UK#42: Ravage's resolution: anarchy in the *Ark*!
- UK#43: '... Ooops!'
- UK#44: Jet trap!
- UK#45: Giant free poster inside!
- UK#46: In one savage Swoop ...
- UK#47: The Dinobot hunt is on!
- UK#48: To slay the swamp thing!
- UK#49: Robot rustlers!
- UK#50: War zone!
- UK#51: The return of Megatron!
- UK#52: The menace of Megatron!
- UK#53: Free *Transformers* stickers from Panini inside!
- UK#54: Stage fight!
- UK#55: The man behind the machines. [As per US#15.]
- UK#56: none
- UK#57: 'Bring me the head of Bumblebee!'
- UK#58: Bumblebee's last stand! [As per US#16.]
- UK#59-60: none
- UK#61: 'Who is he?' 'Buster Witwicky.' 'What is he?' 'Dead!'
- UK#62: Devastated!
- UK#63: The incredible new teams!
- UK#64: All in the mind ...!
- UK#65: 'Seconds out – round two!'
- UK#66: Meanwhile, on Cybertron ...

[9] DIS-INTEGRATED CIRCUITS!
US#9, 'October 1985' (published June 1985), 22 pages.

British reprint: UK#33, 2 November 1985 (Part One), 11 pages; UK#34, 9 November 1985 (Part Two), 11 pages.

Credits:
Bob Budiansky (script); Mike Manley (pencils); M. Hands (inks); Nel Yomtov (colours); Rick Parker (letters); Jim Owsley (editor); Jim Shooter (editor-in-chief); Mike Manley (cover). **UK:** John Higgins (cover, UK#33); Mike Manley (cover, UK#34 – reuse of US cover).

M Hands was an in-house pseudonym used by Marvel from the 1970s to the mid-1990s, and indicates that three or more different Marvel staffers contributed to the inks on this issue (which presumably was in danger of missing its deadline). The name is derived from the adage 'Many hands make light work'. Other comics bearing the 'M Hands' name include *The Avengers* #325, *G.I. Joe* #143 and *The Spectacular Spider-Man* #110.

Plot:

Still upset about the loss of his oil platform and aerospace plant, G B Blackrock has developed a new weapon that he believes can defeat the Transformers. However, after a meeting with the Autobot Jazz, in which Jazz offers him protection from the Decepticons in return for fuel, Blackrock comes to realise that not all the Transformers are evil.

Starscream and Frenzy arrive on the scene, with the aim of destroying Blackrock's weapon; Jazz and Wheeljack attempt to stop them. However, all four robots are stopped in their tracks when Josie Beller makes an entrance.

Beller, her crippled body now augmented by an electronic suit, takes down the Transformers with ease, unable to distinguish Autobot from Decepticon. Now calling herself Circuit Breaker, she is prevented from destroying the robots only by an impassioned plea from Blackrock.

Circuit Breaker departs, vowing that she will show no mercy the next time she encounters a Transformer.

Notes:

Again, some time seems to have passed in between stories – Blackrock has had the chance to build a new weapon (the Anti-Robot Photonic Multi-Cannon), and Ratchet has fixed the majority of the Autobots. It's revealed here that the Autobots have been living on fuel left in the *Ark* from when it was occupied by the Decepticons ([5] 'The New Order' *et seq*). Heard playing on the radio is the Madonna song 'Material Girl' from the album *Like a Virgin*, which was released in November 1984.

We discover here that G B Blackrock also owns his own speedway and is a keen race driver. He seems to have had prior dealings with US Army General Capshaw, who believes the Transformers to have been built on Earth, possibly by Communists. Capshaw reads the *Daily Bugle* newspaper, as featured heavily in the *Spider-Man* comics.

Buster's new abilities have developed to the extent that he is now able to fix cars using only his mind; again this is due to the effects of the Creation Matrix. The sign on the garage has changed since we last saw it – it now reads 'Witwicky Auto Repair' (instead of 'S Witwicky Auto Repairs').

Ratchet is briefly shown piloting the MARB mobile repair bay previously seen in [8] 'Repeat Performance'. Megatron's disappearance in the same issue is referenced, as is Beller's electrocution from [6] 'The Worse of Two Evils'.

This is actually Circuit Breaker's second appearance in the Marvel Universe – she was previously seen in a cameo role in #3 of *Secret Wars II* (September 1985). One of the terms of Marvel's Transformers licence was that the rights to any new character debuting in the *The Transformers* comic, even if not based on a toy, would be owned by Hasbro. To get round this, they had her feature in the *Secret Wars* franchise first, thereby ensuring she remained a Marvel property and not a Hasbro one.

UK Changes:

Page 1, panel 1: 'colors' is changed to 'colours'.

Page 3, panel 3: 'as seen in *Transformers* #6 – Owz' is amended to 'as seen in *Transformers* #24'.

Pages 4, 5, 9, 16 and 21: a printing error in the UK comic has resulted in these pages being mis-coloured; reds have become greens and vice versa, and blues have become pinks.

Page 5, panels 5 and 6: correcting a mistake in the US printing, in which some of Prowl's lines have been misattributed to Ratchet, the speech bubble that begins '– but it's premature to even consider …' has now been given to Prowl, and Ratchet's line 'As long as I'm in command, I will not sanction Autobots stealing fuel from humans!' has been changed to 'And no matter who's in command, we cannot sanction Autobots stealing fuel from humans!'

Page 6, panel 6: 'labor' has been altered to 'labour', and the caption 'see last issue – Owz' has been amended to 'issue 28'.

Page 9, panel 2: oddly, the caption 'suffered in *Transformers* #4 – Owz' has been changed to 'suffered in *Transformers*', with no issue number given.

Roll Call:
Autobots: Optimus Prime (again, as a decapitated body and as a bodiless head), Jazz, Prowl, Bluestreak, Ironhide, Ratchet, Sideswipe, Hound, Wheeljack, Mirage, Bumblebee, Cliffjumper, Brawn, Huffer, Gears and Windcharger.

Trailbreaker is conspicuous by his absence – presumably it's taking longer to repair him than the other Autobots.

Decepticons: Starscream, Frenzy, Buzzsaw and Shockwave.

Other: Buster, G B Blackrock and Josie Beller/Circuit Breaker.

Data File: Mike Manley (artist)
The Transformers was one of Manley's first credited jobs in the comics industry; he later worked on titles such as *Captain America*, *Superman*, *Wolverine*, and on the celebratory five-hundredth issue of *Batman*. He has also worked in the field of television animation, and was a storyboard and background artist on shows such as *Batman Beyond* and *Clerks: The Animated Series*.

Review:
The problem with this story is that too much emphasis is placed on the human characters. This wouldn't be an issue if they were nuanced and well-written, but Circuit Breaker is such a bland, one-note villain that it's a mistake to have her carry the story. What makes it worse is that the really interesting characters of the last few issues – Ratchet and Shockwave – are sidelined and reduced to supporting roles. 2/5

[10] THE NEXT BEST THING TO BEING THERE!
US#10, 'November 1985' (published July 1985), 22 pages.

British reprint: UK#35, 16 November 1985 (Part One), 11 pages; UK#36, 23 November 1985 (Part Two), 11 pages.

Credits:
Bob Budiansky (script); Ricardo Villamonte (pencils); Brad Joyce (inks); Nel Yomtov (colours); Janice Chiang (letters); Michael Carlin (editor); Jim Shooter (editor-in-chief); Kyle Baker (cover). **UK:** John Ridgway (cover, UK#35); Kyle Baker (cover, UK#36 –

reuse of US cover).

Plot:

Having harnessed the power of the Creation Matrix within Prime's head, Shockwave creates the Constructicons, six new Decepticon warriors whose alternate modes are those of construction vehicles. Their first mission: to hijack and augment a radio telescope, which Soundwave can then use to contact Cybertron.

The Autobots track the Decepticons to the radio telescope, as does Bomber Bill, a human trucker whose vehicle was taken by the Constructicons, who have been using stolen machinery to upgrade the radio dish.

The Autobots are met by the Constructicons, who demonstrate an amazing ability: the six individual Transformers are able to merge and combine into a giant gestalt robot, Devastator. The Autobots are no match for the behemoth, and are seemingly unable to prevent Soundwave from sending his message to Cybertron.

However, Bomber Bill drives his truck into the dish, which cuts off Soundwave's transmission. Content that most of their message got through, the Decepticons retreat.

Meanwhile, the Autobots have tapped into the telephones at the aerospace plant where the Decepticons are based. They overhear Shockwave threatening to kill Optimus Prime ...

Notes:

This story is best known for the introduction of the Constructicons, an event foreshadowed in [8] 'Repeat Performance'. Other than various one-off cameos in the UK comics and annuals, this marks the first time since the debuts of Shockwave and the Dinobots in [4] 'The Last Stand' that new, regular Transformers have been introduced into the series.

The radio telescope we see here is situated within a short distance of Interstate 15 in south-eastern Idaho. Interstate 15 is a real-life road, stretching north-south from Montana to California, and it does indeed pass through Idaho. However in the real world there are no radio telescopes in the state. Idaho lies immediately to the east of Oregon, so isn't too far away from the Transformers' usual stomping grounds.

Bomber Bill claims to have driven for eight days straight without rest. He's said to have travelled 12,000 miles in that time, which averages out to 62.5 mph, assuming he has indeed driven continuously for an eight-day period. (Presumably this is an exaggeration, and he's trying to impress the waitress.)

G B Blackrock makes another appearance in this story – he makes mention of the fuel deal he has in place with the Autobots, negotiated in the previous issue.

The Autobots are unsure if Sunstreaker will ever again be operational – this after he was blasted by Shockwave in [5] 'The New Order'. (A similar claim was made in the UK story [8.2] 'The Wrath of Grimlock'.)

The title of this story is taken from a slogan for a series of US television commercials by Bell System, famous in the '70s and '80s, advertising the benefits of long-distance telephone calls.

UK Changes:

Page 1, panel 1: 'penciler' is changed to 'pencils', 'colorist' to 'colours', and the reference to issue '#7' to '#26'.

Page 6, panel 5: 'center' becomes 'centre'.

Page 7, panel 1: 'endeavor' is edited to 'endeavour'.
Page 8, panel 4: 'armored' is changed to 'armoured'.
Page 9, panel 3: the reference to issue #6 is changed to issue #24.
Page 10, panels 4 and 5: the imposition of the 'NEXT' box over the bottom of the page results in one of Buster's thought-bubbles, plus a caption, being completely obscured.
Page 12, panel 1: the 'But outside …' caption has been excised.

To improve the cliffhanger, so that Part One ends on Buster using his new powers, rather than Bomber Bill flirting with a waitress, the page order has been juggled around – the UK comic presents the pages in the order 8, 11, 9, 10 (i.e. the original page 11 is now slotted in between pages 8 and 9).

Roll Call:
Autobots: Optimus Prime (as decapitated head and headless body), Jazz, Prowl, Bluestreak, Ironhide, Ratchet, Sunstreaker (as a corpse), Hound, Bumblebee, Brawn and Huffer.

Decepticons: Soundwave, Laserbeak, Shockwave, **Scrapper**, **Scavenger**, **Mixmaster**, **Bonecrusher**, **Long Haul**, **Hook** and **Devastator**.

Other: Buster, Sparkplug and G B Blackrock.

A half-built **Jetfire** is also seen here, but at this point he's still lifeless.

Data File: Ricardo Villamonte (artist)
Villamonte's other comic credits include issues of *Uncanny X-Men*, *Thor*, *Conan the Barbarian* and DC Comics' adaptation of *Beowulf*.

Review:
Despite the introduction of the Constructicons, this feels very much like a small-scale, understated affair. The continuing storylines such as Buster's new powers and Prime's continued captivity are left to drag on while the focus here is firmly on side issues such as the human trucker, Bomber Bill.

On the plus side, the story of the Autobot Huffer and his desire to get home makes for a good emotional centre to this story. The introduction of the Constructicons is well-handled, and Soundwave's message to Cybertron tantalisingly hints that the Transformer home world might yet play a part in future proceedings.

All in all, not the worst story to this point, but certainly the most underwhelming.
2/5

What's the Origin of the Constructicons?
For UK readers, the Constructicons' origin story is simple. Shockwave has captured the head of Optimus Prime, repository of the life-giving Creation Matrix. Shockwave's plan is to use the Matrix to bestow consciousness unto six new troops, the Constructicons.

However, unbeknownst to Shockwave, the Creation Matrix no longer resides in Prime's head – it's been transferred to the human, Buster Witwicky. Fortunately for Shockwave, some small remaining vestige of the Matrix remains with Optimus Prime, and it's this energy – the dregs, if you will – that is used to give birth to the

Constructicons.

This version of events is confirmed elsewhere: the Constructicons' creation 'used up all but the last vestiges of the Matrix', muses Prime in [8.2] 'The Wrath of Grimlock'; 'The creation of these six used up all the Matrix's power left in Prime's mind', says the Decepticon Mainframe Computer in [A2.1] 'In the Beginning'.

This all seems fairly clear-cut from the UK point of view; but what if we take only the US stories into account?

Well, for American readers there were no references whatsoever to 'last vestiges' or 'residual Matrix energy' – odd, when you consider that the UK-only stories mentioned this plot point on a number of occasions.

So what explanation did the US comics present? Well, from the dialogue, it seems clear that the Matrix is used to create the Constructicons *before* it's transferred to Buster. There's no need for Shockwave to scrape the bottom of the barrel (so to speak) – he has the full, entire program to work with. It's only *after* the Constructicons' brains are created that Prime passes the Matrix to Buster.

Let's look at the evidence. Prime gives the Matrix to Buster in [6] 'The Worse of Two Evils', by which time Prime's head is already rigged up to some brain-tapping machinery (which we see for the first time in [5] 'The New Order').

In [8] 'Repeat Performance', Shockwave says he wants to 'continue the manufacture of a new generation of Decepticons', indicating that the process has already begun in earnest. In the same issue, he states that 'already, I have tapped his programming'. When the manufacture of the Constructicons finally takes place in [10] 'The Next Best Thing to Being There', Shockwave boasts that each of the new Decepticons' brain modules 'already pulsates with the life infused [past tense] within them by your legendary Creation Matrix'.

So, to summarise: the US and UK timelines of the Matrix appear to differ, as follows:

US reading of events:

- Shockwave beheads Prime.
- Shockwave taps the Matrix, infusing the Constructicon brain modules with life.
- Prime gives the Matrix to Buster.
- Shockwave constructs bodies for – and activates – the Constructicons.

UK reading of events:

- Shockwave beheads Prime.
- Prime gives the Matrix to Buster, but a little of its power remains.
- Shockwave uses up this power and creates the Constructicons.

[11] BRAINSTORM!
US#11, 'December 1985' (published August 1985), 22 pages.

British reprint: UK#37, 30 November 1985 (Part One), 11 pages; UK#38, 7 December 1985 (Part Two), 11 pages.

Credits:
Bob Budiansky (script); Herb Trimpe (pencils); Tom Palmer (inks); Nel Yomtov (colours); Diana Albers (letters); Michael Carlin (editor); Jim Shooter (editor-in-chief); Herb Trimpe (cover). **UK:** John Ridgway (cover, UK#37); Herb Trimpe (cover, UK#38 – reuse of US cover).

Plot:
With Optimus Prime unable to give life to Shockwave's latest creation Jetfire, the Decepticons realise that Prime must have transferred the Creation Matrix to another recipient. Going back though old footage of the *Ark*, Shockwave discovers that the Matrix was indeed passed onto Buster. He programs the otherwise mindless Jetfire to capture the boy.

Thanks to their phone-tap, the Autobots learn of Shockwave's interest in Buster, and send Bumblebee and Bluestreak to rescue him. Battle commences between the two Autobots and the mindless Decepticon jet.

Upon realising that Jetfire is little more than a drone, the Autobots tell Buster that he is therefore vulnerable to the powers of the Matrix. With just a thought, Buster dismantles his attacker.

Although Buster and the Matrix are now safe and secure, the same cannot be said for Optimus Prime – the time has come for Shockwave to kill the Autobot leader …

Notes:
Buster is revealed here to be a straight-A student, which confirms Jessie's assertion in [7] 'Warrior School' that he was perhaps the smartest kid in school. His bedroom contains a book on calculus, as well as the tomes *Advanced Physics* and *The Key to the Computer*. His calculator is apparently made by a company called Austar – although in real life Austar is an Australian television and telecoms provider – nothing to do with calculators. However, the batteries to his personal cassette player are made by the real-world company Energizer.

We see many references to recent events in Buster's life: his argument with Jessie in [7] 'Warrior School' (incorrectly attributed to issue 8 in the editor's note); his being given the Creation Matrix in [6] 'The Worse of Two Evils'; and his car repairs in [9] 'Dis-Integrated Circuits' onwards. We also see recorded footage of him sneaking past Rumble into the *Ark*, as happened in [5] 'The New Order'. Bumblebee shows concern for Sparkplug's internal organs: a reference to the heart attack he suffered in [4] 'The Last Stand'. The sign on his garage has changed yet again from when we last saw it in [9] 'Dis-Integrated Circuits': it now reads 'S Witwicky Auto Repair and Tow Service'.

Both Sparkplug and Mozzarella Mike, a pizza delivery guy, have telephone numbers that begin with 555. 555 is a prefix commonly used for fictional telephone numbers in films, television and other media. The explanation is that, under the old exchange-name system, no US place names began with a combination of the letters J, K and L – all assigned to the digit '5' on a telephone. So the prefix 555 went largely unused, and Hollywood was encouraged to use the code to ensure that their made-up numbers wouldn't have a real-life match.

There are many references to the previous issue's story: Prime's initial refusal to breathe life into Jetfire is mentioned, as is the Autobots' wiretap operation; and the aerospace technicians Ferdy and Gabe are seen again here.

Laserbeak now appears to communicate only in squawks and caws; originally he and Buzzsaw could talk properly, as seen in the first couple of issues.

Some of the aircraft in the aerospace plant closely resemble the vehicle modes of the Decepticons Thrust, Ramjet and Dirge – so it's possible that when these three characters arrive from Cybertron in [21] 'Aerialbots over America', they base their Earth modes on the jets seen here.

UK Changes:
Page 1, panel 1: 'penciler' is changed to 'pencils' and 'colorist' to 'colours'.
Page 2, panel 2: the reference to issue #6 is changed to issue #24.
Page 6, panel 1: the reference to issue #5 is amended to issue #23 (although the misspelling of Optimus as 'Opitmus' remains unchanged).
Page 10, panel 2: 'in *Transformers* #8' has been altered to read 'in *Transformers* #26'.
Page 14, panel 3: the minor typo 'tridimen ional' has been corrected to 'tridimensional'.

The Transformers Calendars
In the years 1985 and 1989, the UK *The Transformers* comic printed a series of pull-out posters that doubled as monthly calendars. The 1985 set consisted of painted artwork of key Transformers characters; the 1989 posters featured classic cover art from previous issues. A complete list of the calendars can be found below:

January 1985 (Optimus Prime) – UK#8
February 1985 (Megatron) – UK#10
March 1985 (Jazz) – UK#12
April 1985 (Starscream) – UK#14
May 1985 (Sideswipe) – UK#16
June 1985 (Laserbeak) – UK#18
July 1985 (Sunstreaker) – UK#21
August 1985 (Skywarp) – UK#23
September 1985 (Ratchet) – UK#25
October 1985 (Shockwave) – UK#29 (art based on the cover of US#5)
November 1985 (Prowl) – UK#33
December 1985 (Soundwave) – UK#38

January 1989 (reprints the cover of UK#177) – UK#200
February 1989 (reprints the cover of UK#134) – UK#204
March 1989 (reprints the cover of UK#138) – UK#208
April 1989 (reprints the cover of UK#152) – UK#212
June 1989 (reprints the cover of UK#133) – UK#216
May 1989 (reprints the cover of UK#136) – UK#220
July 1989 (reprints the cover of UK#129) – UK#224
August 1989 (reprints the cover of UK#142) – UK#229
September 1989 (reprints the cover of UK#130) – UK#234
October 1989 (reprints the cover of UK#153) – UK#237
November 1989 (reprints the cover of UK#135) – UK#243
December 1989 (reprints the cover of UK#145) – UK#247

In quite a major error, the June 1989 calendar was printed in May and vice versa. The November 1989 calendar was printed a week late, as it had to make way for a sponsored competition page that appeared in UK#242.

Roll Call:
Autobots: Optimus Prime (head only), Jazz, Prowl, Bluestreak, Ironhide, Ratchet, Sideswipe, Hound, Bumblebee, Brawn, Huffer and Gears.

Decepticons: Rumble, Laserbeak and Shockwave.

Other: Buster, Sparkplug and Jessie.

Jetfire makes another appearance, but at this stage he's still only a mindless drone, so it's debatable whether or not this counts as a 'proper' sighting of the character.

Data File: Tom Palmer (artist)
Renowned inker Palmer has been in the comics business since the '60s, his work featuring in *Doctor Strange*, *Uncanny X-Men* and *The Avengers*, to name just a few. More recently, he was the inker on *Kick Ass*, which was adapted into a hit movie (Matthew Vaughn, 2010).

Review:
And the interminable Prime/Matrix story arc trudges onward, just as it has for the last eight months. The scenes in which Shockwave gloats or rants at Optimus Prime's severed head have by now become terribly boring.

There is some resolution here – Buster's story is wrapped up, as he finally comes clean to his father about his new powers. It's nice to focus on some genuinely interesting human characters for a change, given that previous issues have given us creations such as Bomber Bill and Circuit Breaker.

There's some good stuff here, sadly overshadowed by the now tiresome 'Prime's head' storyline. 2/5.

[12] PRIME TIME!
US#12, 'January 1986' (published September 1985), 22 pages.

British reprint: UK#39, 14 December 1985 (Part One), 11 pages; UK#40, 21 December 1985 (Part Two), 11 pages.

Credits:
Bob Budiansky (script); Herb Trimpe (pencils); Al Gordon (inks); Nel Yomtov (colours); Janice Chiang (letters); Michael Carlin (editor); Jim Shooter (editor-in-chief); Herb Trimpe (cover). **UK:** Herb Trimpe (cover, UK#39 – reuse of US cover); Jeff Anderson (cover, UK#40).

Uncovered
Working out who produced the cover art for the early issues of *The Transformers* is quite tricky. In the US, no credits were ever provided in the comic itself. It wasn't until UK#53 that British cover artists began getting formal credit for their work; the same issue also provided credits for previous covers going back to UK#40. For the early issues, then, I have had to rely on the various credit lists published, after the fact, in

online guides, comics websites, reprint compilations etc, corroborating these and correcting errors where necessary.

It is believed that the colours on the US covers were the uncredited work of George Roussos, who was Marvel's resident cover colourist for the duration of the comic's life.

Plot:

Buster flies back to the aerospace plant in Jetfire. His plan is to trick the Decepticons by letting them think that he's been captured by Jetfire, when in reality the mindless Transformer has now been reprogrammed to follow his orders. However, the plan hits a snag when they are confronted mid-flight by the Air Force; Jetfire's quick manoeuvring to avoid the attacking aircraft causes Buster to lose consciousness, and the human is captured upon arrival at the Decepticon HQ.

Shockwave discovers the wiretap, and so sets a trap – he allows the Autobots to get hold of a fake Prime head, which, when attached, gives the Decepticons control of the Autobot leader's body. The Autobots are mercilessly gunned down by the ersatz Prime, who has also been joined by a crew of Decepticon troops.

Back at the aerospace plant, Buster finally awakens, and uses his Matrix powers to take control of Jetfire. After first attacking Shockwave, he orders Jetfire to deliver the real Prime head to the Autobots. His proper head and body reunited, Optimus Prime turns on the Decepticons. Shockwave is thrown into a swamp, his reign of terror over for the time being.

The human workers regain control of the aerospace plant and free Buster, who gladly relinquishes the Creation Matrix to the newly-restored Optimus Prime.

Notes:

The events of this issue pick up only moments after those of [11] 'Brainstorm' – Buster is *en route* to the Decepticon HQ, and the Autobot convoy is still on the move.

Here we finally tie up all the ongoing plot threads begun back in [5] 'The New Order' – Shockwave is banished to the bottom of a swamp, Optimus Prime gets his head back, and Buster finally returns the Creation Matrix to its rightful owner.

There are overt references to the events of two previous stories – Buster's mindlink with Prime in [6] 'The Worse of Two Evils', and the first encounter with Jetfire in [11] 'Brainstorm'.

This is the first appearance of Trailbreaker alive and well since Shockwave's arrival in [4] 'The Last Stand', reinforcing the idea that his repairs took a bit longer than those of his fellow Autobots.

Shockwave's master plan is fully revealed here. Using the facilities of the aerospace plant and his human slaves, he planned to build 'thousands' of new Decepticons, which were to have been given life by the Creation Matrix. By the time of his defeat, he has already overseen the construction of a 'hundred new jet warriors', who, thanks to Buster's intervention, are prevented from being infused with consciousness.

UK Changes:

Page 1, panel 1: the 'penciler' and 'colorist' credits are changed to 'pencils' and 'colours' respectively.

Page 2, panel 5: 'see issue #6' is changed to 'issue #24'.

Page 18, panel 4: 'vaporize' becomes 'vapourize' [sic]. The UK spelling is actually 'vaporise'.

Roll Call:
Autobots: Optimus Prime, Jazz, Prowl, Ironhide, Sideswipe, Hound, Trailbreaker, Bumblebee (flashback only), Cliffjumper, Brawn, Huffer, Gears, Windcharger, and Jetfire (still a mindless drone).

Decepticons: Soundwave, Rumble, Frenzy, Laserbeak, Buzzsaw, Ravage and Shockwave.

Other: Buster and Sparkplug (flashback only).

Data File: George Roussos (cover colourist)
With a career dating back to the 1930s, Roussos worked on many prestigious comics in both the Golden and Silver Ages, including the second ever issue of *Batman* (1940) and the fourth issue of *The Avengers* (which saw the return of Captain America). His other credits include *Flash Gordon*, *The Phantom*, *The Lone Ranger* and *Fantastic Four*. In the early '80s he became Marvel's in-house cover colourist, and it was in this role that he contributed to *The Transformers*.

Review:
All the ongoing plotlines and story arcs of the past year finally come to a head in this, an absorbing and action-packed entry in *The Transformers* canon.

Although a satisfying conclusion, it's not quite worthy of an 11-month build-up. Rumble's turn as comic relief isn't funny in the slightest, and it's a bit of an anti-climax to see Shockwave defeated by a mere swamp.

All in all, though, this is fitting finale to the comics' opening stretch. With more and more characters introduced during the next few issues, the feel of the comic will change dramatically as the cast of characters expands and evolves.

In a way, it's sad to wave goodbye to this simpler phase in the comic's history – a phase that saw it rise from awkward beginnings and grow into a confidently-written, enjoyable series. However, it's nice to know that, in this last issue of the original storyline, we're bowing out on a high note. 4/5

[12.1] CHRISTMAS BREAKER!
UK#41, 28 December 1985, 11 pages

Credits:
James Hill (script); Will Simpson (art); Gina Hart (colours); Richard Starkings (letters); Ian Rimmer (editor); Mike Collins and Mark Farmer (cover).

Plot:
It's Christmas Eve, and Buster is trying to teach the Autobots about the magic of Christmas – going so far as to help them erect a Christmas tree in the *Ark*, and suggesting that Optimus Prime wear a Santa outfit.

Meanwhile, Circuit Breaker is having a hard time of it. Still haunted by her near-death experience at the hand of Shockwave, her mood isn't helped by being labelled a 'freak' by passers-by after she saves a young girl from drowning.

When Jazz and Buster cross her path, Circuit Breaker attacks the Autobot. However, Buster pleads with her not to continue the assault, appealing to her Christmas spirit just as the clock strikes midnight. Grudgingly acceding to Buster's request, she ceases her attack and flies off into the night.

Jazz is left to reflect that perhaps Christmas *is* magical, after all.

Notes:
The local newspaper seen here is issue #2394 of the (fictional) *Portland Chronicle*. It's presumably a weekly paper that began around February 1940, assuming a constant release rate.

The majority of the story is set in St Petersburg, here described as a suburb of Portland. The town was previously seen in [4.2] 'The Enemy Within'.

A close-up of Buster's wristwatch shows the manufacturer as the real-world Swiss company Buler.

There are many flashbacks to previous issues:

- Soundwave's and Laserbeak's attack on the aerospace plant (from [7] 'Warrior School').
- Shockwave's attack on the oil rig (from [6] 'The Worse of Two Evils').
- Beller lying in hospital (multiple stories, beginning with [7] 'Warrior School').
- Circuit Breaker revealing herself to G B Blackrock, and her later tussle with Jazz and Wheeljack (from [9] 'Dis-Integrated Circuits').

Roll Call:
Autobots: Optimus Prime, Jazz, Prowl, Bluestreak, Wheeljack (flashback only), Brawn and Huffer.

Decepticons: Starscream, Soundwave, Frenzy, Laserbeak and Shockwave. The Decepticons appear only in flashback; Shockwave appears both in a flashback and as a ghostly hallucination.

Other: Buster, G B Blackrock (flashback only) and Circuit Breaker.

Data File: Mark Farmer (artist)
Eagle and Inkpot Award winner Farmer is another British artist who made the move to America. His other UK credits include *2000 AD*, *Doctor Who Magazine* and *Action Force*. He also contributed to the Ladybird *The Transformers* book range. In the US, he worked on *The Avengers*, *The Incredible Hulk*, *Batman* and *Superman: True Brit* (which was co-written by Monty Python member John Cleese).

Review:
It might be a lightweight Christmas story padded out with flashbacks, but 'Christmas Breaker', surprisingly, still has something to offer.

Here we get under the skin of Circuit Breaker and, unlike in her appearances in the US comics, she's written with a touch of depth. Her confident, bullish facade is peeled back to reveal a pitiful, anguished woman, clearly suffering from post-traumatic stress. Her US appearances normally paint her as a one-note obstacle in the Autobots' path, but here she's almost a fully-fledged *person*.

The plot is straightforward and the art is decent enough ... but it's the intriguing psychological profile of Circuit Breaker here that elevates this story above the status of festive fluff. 3/5

Eighteen Months in Portland – a Timeline

With 1985 now almost over, this is as good a time as any to take stock and look back at the events depicted in the comics up to this point. Cannily, the American writers deliberately steered clear from pinning down these stories to any definitive dates. (Donny Finkleberg's cheque – seen in [23] 'Decepticon Graffiti' – is the first time the US comic presents us with any sort of specific dating.) This intentional vagueness meant that, from the point of view of American readers, there were no continuity or time problems in these opening issues. Unfortunately for UK readers, a date *did* appear in [12.2] 'Christmas Breaker' and, rather than clarify matters, actually created a number of problems. UK readers had now been effectively told that the comic was moving in real time: that 18 months of comics equated to 18 months in the fictional universe of *The Transformers*. The opening tranche of issues was almost certainly intended to depict events happing in quick succession, not over a timespan of a year and a half.

Taking the UK-supplied dates as definitive, here then is one possible chronology of events. It's not ideal, and relies on gaps of many months between certain adventures, but when trying to spread these stories over a year and a half, such gaps are inevitable.

Late August/Early September 1984: [1] 'The Transformers' to [4] 'The Last Stand'
It's definitively '1984'. The events of these stories (including the UK 'flashback stories', which also take place around this time) occur in very quick succession, with the cliffhanger ending of each story segueing into the opening scenes of the next. We have three clues about the dating of these stories. First, Spider-Man's appearance in [3] 'Prisoner of War' takes place before the events of *The Amazing Spider-Man* #258, which is set during the 'summer'. Secondly, [4.1] 'Man of Iron' takes place in late summer/early autumn. Lastly, we see Buster come home from school in [1] 'The Transformers', which means that the US summer break, which ends in late August at the absolute earliest, is already over. The only way all three things can be true is if we set these stories over a couple of weeks beginning in late August.

Sparkplug's Stay in Hospital
In the mid-'80s, the average stay in hospital for a heart attack victim was around a week and a half, so it's generally assumed that the stories in which Sparkplug is laid up ([4] 'The Last Stand' to [10] 'The Next Best Thing to Being There') take place over a very short space of time. However, all the evidence suggests that Sparkplug had a substantial period of recuperation. While he was hospital, we saw:

- Josie Beller design and build her Circuit Breaker costume from scratch, while lying crippled in a hospital bed;
- the Decepticons take over two industrial installations and build six new warriors;
- G B Blackrock design and build an anti-robot cannon from scratch; and
- Ratchet repair an army of fallen Autobots.

Intuitively, such events must have taken place over a time period of a few months, or a few weeks at the absolute least, implying that there was more to Sparkplug's illness than just a heart attack. Furthermore, the Madonna track 'Material Girl' from the album *Like a Virgin*, released in November 1984, is heard in [9] 'Dis-Integrated Circuits', meaning that, at the absolute least, Sparkplug spends a couple of months, September to November, in hospital.

Notably, all future references to Sparkplug's illness (e.g. in [31] 'Buster Witwicky and the Car Wash of Doom') will continue to insist that his heart attack was only 'mild', despite evidence to the contrary.

About a Week Later, Mid-September 1984: [5] 'The New Order' and [6] 'The Worse of Two Evils'

These two stories occur on the same day, 'less than an hour' apart. In the time since [4] 'The Last Stand', Shockwave has had time to establish a Decepticon base in the *Ark*, revive his comrades, attach Optimus Prime's head to a Matrix-extracting device and string up the remaining Autobot corpses. Meanwhile Ratchet, oblivious to the Autobots' plight, appears to be having a whale of a time acting as a real ambulance, and only realises there's a problem when his radio signal meets with no response.

One Day Later, Mid-September 1984: [7] 'Warrior School' and [8] 'Repeat Performance'

As an inexperienced warrior, Ratchet initially decides against making an attempt to rescue the rest of the Autobots ('I bury my responsibilities'); it's an off-the-cuff remark by Buster that eventually galvanises him into action. While tracking down the Dinobots in Antarctica, Ratchet reflects on all that's happened to him recently, including his discovery of Prime's head and the pact with Megatron. These events are said to have happened in 'the last 24 hours', the implication being that this is still the same day as [6] 'The Worse of Two Evils'.

Since the last issue, Josie Beller has regained consciousness (and is busy working on her new costume), having suffered a paralysing electric shock during that story's oil rig attack. Also in the wake of the oil rig hijack, G B Blackrock has been fortifying his aerospace plant; and installing a hi-tech security system and an impressive array of weaponry throughout a large industrial facility cannot have been a quick and easy task. However, the '24 hours' line is in the comic, so we have to take it at face value.

Now well into the autumn, the weather is visibly worsening, though there are a few holidaymakers still about (the campers in [7] 'Warrior School' and the skiers in [8] 'Repeat Performance'), and Megatron falls into a temporary snowdrift that has melted away by the time of [13] 'Shooting Star'.

That Same Day, Mid-September 1984: [8.1] 'Decepticon Dam-Busters' (framing sequence) and [8.2] 'The Wrath of Grimlock'

The victory of Ratchet and the Dinobots over Megatron takes place on a mountainside not far from the *Ark*; their walk back to Mount St Hilary probably lasts a day at most.

Two Months Later, Mid-November 1984: [9] 'Dis-Integrated Circuits'

Josie Beller has now completed her Circuit Breaker costume, G B Blackrock has designed and constructed his Anti-Robot cannon, and Ratchet has had time enough to rebuild the majority of the Autobot troops. As previously mentioned, Jazz is seen listening to the Madonna track 'Material Girl' from the *Like a Virgin* album, released on 12 November 1984.

Despite Sparkplug's long-term hospitalisation, Buster still appears to be accepting repair jobs at the garage, even if he's not yet able to fix any of the cars. (One vehicle has been in the repair shop for 'three weeks'.) (Although we never see them, it's likely that

Sparkplug employs at least one other staff member to work at the garage, even if only to man the shop while he's away. It's possible that this other mechanic is currently on vacation, leaving Buster to fend for himself for a while.)

That Same Week, Mid-November 1984: [10] 'The Next Best Thing to Being There'
Jazz is still undergoing repairs from the injuries he received in the previous issue. G B Blackrock is taken on a tour around the *Ark* – the fuel deal he struck with the Autobots in [9] 'Dis-Integrated Circuits' is still very new.

Sparkplug comes home from hospital in this story; he dismisses his heart attack as 'only a little one'. He's aware that Mr Fishbein's car has been in for repair. (In the previous issue it was said to have been dropped off at the lot three weeks prior.) Presumably Buster has been keeping his father updated on matters pertaining to the garage.

Shortly Afterwards, late November 1984: [11] Brainstorm and [12] Prime Time
These two stories appear to take place on the same day; little time can have passed since [10] 'The Next Best Thing to Being There', as Sparkplug is still convinced that Buster is able to repair cars. It's revealed that Buster and Jessie have not spoken since their argument in [7] 'Warrior School', a couple of months before.

Which brings us back to …

Thirteen Months Later, Christmas 1985: [12.1] 'Christmas Break*er*'
This story is definitively dated to Christmas Eve night 1985. The author's intent was for this story to be set only a short time after the aerospace workers were freed in [12] 'Prime Time' (as their story is headline news in the local paper). However, we know this cannot be accurate because, as discussed above, the events of [12] 'Prime Time' must surely have occurred in 1984. One possible explanation is that the aerospace workers had been under a gagging order that prevented them from talking to the press and has only recently been rescinded (perhaps due to a legal challenge).

[12.2] CRISIS OF COMMAND!
- UK#42, 4 January 1986 (Part One), 11 pages
- UK#43, 11 January 1986 (Part Two), 11 pages
- UK#44, 18 January 1986 (Part Three), 11 pages

Credits:
Mike Collins (script, parts 1 and 3); James Hill (script, part 2); Geoff Senior (art, parts 1-2); John Stokes (art, part 3); Steve Whitaker (colours, part 1); John Burns and Stuart Place (colours, part 2); Gina Hart and Stuart Place (colours, part 3); Mike Scott (letters); Ian Rimmer (editor); Will Simpson (cover, UK#42); John Ridgway (cover, UK#43); Jeff Anderson (cover, UK#44).

NB: Gina Hart was credited as the (sole) colourist on parts 2 and 3; a correction/apology was later printed on the Transformation page of UK#52.

Plot:
Optimus Prime is troubled. He is hesitant, indecisive and self-pitying, and his time spent in Decepticon captivity weighs heavily upon him. Even his own troops are

questioning Prime's decisions – Prowl insists that the Creation Matrix be used to make an army of Ultimate Autobot warriors, despite Prime's weak arguments to the contrary.

Ravage allows himself to be captured by the Autobots. His plan is to escape, and then lure any pursuers into a Decepticon trap. Sure enough, Bumblebee chases Ravage down, only to be met by a horde of Decepticons, who easily take him prisoner.

In the end, it's Optimus Prime himself who rescues Bumblebee. His crisis of confidence over, Prime single-handedly storms the Decepticon base, taking down a number of Decepticons in the process.

The reinvigorated Autobot leader returns to the *Ark*, and immediately vetoes Prowl's 'Ultimate Autobot' idea, explaining that the Autobots should always put compassion and morality first. Being a warrior is just a means to that end; warfare in itself should never be the sole purpose of any Autobot.

Notes:

Optimus Prime's malaise here was foreshadowed in [12.1] 'Christmas Break*er*', in which it was stated that something 'troubles' him.

The Decepticons, meanwhile, have regrouped back to their power-plant base; officially named here as 'Fortress Sinister', it was built in [2] 'Power Play', and last seen in [4.2] 'The Enemy Within'. Soundwave is their stand-in commander during the absence of both Megatron and Shockwave.

Jazz's argument against the Ultimate Autobot proposal is that they 'barely have enough fuel' for themselves, indicating that the energy deal with G B Blackrock ([9] 'Dis-Integrated Circuits') is suffering a few teething problems.

This story is heavily influenced by the *Transformers* cartoon show (a deliberate ploy by the production team), and as such there are some curious scenes that appear out of whack with normal comic continuity. As per the television episodes, Mount St Hilary is depicted as being in the middle of the desert (the comics usually show it as being located in more verdant environs). Also, Rumble has his pile drivers (which, as discussed in the notes to [8.1] 'Decepticon Dam-Busters', is a concept usually restricted to the cartoons). On a similar theme, Mirage and Hound team up to capture Ravage, in a scene lifted wholesale from the television episode {1-03} 'More Than Meets the Eye, Part Three'.

As is the norm, there are a few flashbacks here: we see Shockwave's deadly arrival at the *Ark* (from [4] 'The Last Stand'), Optimus Prime's capture and decapitation ([5] 'The New Order' *et seq*), and the Decepticon-controlled Prime's attack on the Autobots ([12] 'Prime Time').

There are a couple of references back to the Annual story, [A1.3] 'And There Shall Come … A Leader': Emirate Xaaron is name-checked, and there's another reference to the 'Spires of Iacon'.

Roll Call:

Autobots: Optimus Prime, Jazz, Prowl, Bluestreak, Ironhide, Ratchet, Sideswipe, Hound, Wheeljack, Mirage, Bumblebee, Huffer and Gears.

On the final page of this story, Sunstreaker appears as a background character, despite him having been killed off in [4] 'The Last Stand'. Furthermore, Tracks and (a miscoloured) Beachcomber appear in the opening *Ark* scenes, although in story terms neither Autobot should be active on Earth at this point. These three cameos must surely rate as art errors rather than bona fide appearances.

Decepticons: Starscream, Skywarp, Thundercracker, Soundwave, Rumble, Frenzy, Laserbeak, Buzzsaw, Ravage and Shockwave (flashback only).

Additionally, there are mentions of Megatron, Jetfire and the Constructicons.

Data File: James Hill (writer)
Hill's other writing credits include strips for *Action Force, Spider-Man and Zoids, Thundercats* and the *Red Dwarf Smegazine*. He was later the editor of the UK *Masters of the Universe* comic.

Review:
No-holds-barred action and adventure? Check! Juicy sub-plot about a hero who embarks on an emotional journey of self-discovery and redemption? Check! Clichéd in the extreme, but realised with much aplomb. 3/5

Transformation
'Transformation' was the title of the editorial introduction that comprised page 2 of the British *The Transformers* comic from UK#22 until the end of its run. It replaced the previous 'Openers' page – see [4.2] 'The Enemy Within'. More often than not, it would include a run-down of the comic's contents, hype-up future stories and events, and offer news and information. Editions of special note are listed below:

- UK#22: The very first Transformation.
- UK#26: The editorial is giddy with excitement about some amazing news: from next issue, *The Transformers* will become a full-colour weekly!
- UK#27: Transformation celebrates the comic's first birthday.
- UK#37: Soundwave takes over the Transformation page, explaining that the humans are all off doing their Christmas shopping. The Decepticon boasts of demonstrating 'how a Transformation page should be put together'. Ironically, his text is yellow on a white background, making it barely readable …
- UK#39: For the first time, we get a lowdown of upcoming stories to look forward to, including a mention of [17] 'The Smelting Pool', which wouldn't even be published in America for another two months.
- UK#40: This week Transformation addresses readers' most frequently-asked questions, covering the availability of US-only toys such as Shockwave, and what to do if you break your Transformers toys.
- UK#41: For the very first time, other Marvel comics are plugged on the Transformation page; readers are encouraged to try out *Secret Wars II* and *Spider-Man and Zoids*.
- UK#45: The first hint that the comic is a runaway success: 'We're pleased to say that *Transformers* [sic] is one of the most popular comics on the market!'
- UK#50: A celebratory tone this week as the comic reaches its fiftieth issue. There are references also to the Special Teams, whose upcoming introduction will usher in a 'new era' and 'shape the future of *The Transformers*'.
- UK#57: Another run-down of forthcoming stories, this time covering up to issue #65.

- UK#69: News of the latest Transformers toys to be launched, including first mentions in the comic for Hubcap, Swerve, Outback, Wheelie and Tailgate.
- UK#71: News of future issues – UK#74 will feature a 'bright new look'; humour strip *Matt and the Cat* is being dropped; and there are teasers for upcoming stories [20.1] 'In the National Interest' and [20.2] 'Target: 2006'.
- UK#72: More toy news this week, as the Cyclonus and Scourge figures get a mention. It's all rather redundant, though, as the pair had been featured in toy ads running in the comic since issue #67 …
- UK#74: Transformation gets a new look. Confidence in the comic is sky-high, the editorial promising great things as far ahead as issue #100 …
- UK#78: News that *The Transformers* UK is now on sale in Australia. Plus, the Transformers movie is set for release in 'late November/early December' 1986.
- UK#84: A plug for two forthcoming Transformers publications from Marvel: *Transformers Universe*, plus the movie adaptation.
- UK#85: Part one of a complete list of currently-available Transformers figures.
- UK#86: The second and final part of the toy checklist.
- UK#87: News that the movie's release has been delayed until 12 December 1986.
- UK#88: Teasers for upcoming stories and issues, up to issue #100.
- UK#89: Confirmation that the *Transformers Universe* series will not see stand-alone release, and will instead be serialised within the comic itself.
- UK#99: UK readers are introduced to *Action Force*.
- UK#102: A plug for the latest title from Marvel UK, *Thundercats*.
- UK#107: Clarifying a plot point, the editor confirms that Megatron's madness this issue can be attributed partly to his failed mind-swap with Straxus.
- UK#111: A call for *The Transformers* readers to check out the *Action Force* comic – the first indication that sales figures for the junior title were not so good.
- UK#120: Details of upcoming stories (up to issue #130), including the first mention of Headmasters and Targetmasters.
- UK#122: Attempts to convince *The Transformers* readers to pick up its flagging sister title *Action Force* get increasingly desperate.
- UK#131: Teasers for upcoming stories, through to issue #136
- UK#137: Yet another plug for the doomed *Action Force*.
- UK#140: A teaser for the upcoming epic, [36.2] 'The Legacy of Unicron'.
- UK#153: A recap of the story so far, for the benefit of new *Action Force* readers coming fresh to the comic after the recent *The Transformers/Action Force* merger.
- UK#156: News of the latest titles to be added to Marvel UK's roster: *The Real Ghostbusters*, *Visionaries* and *Action Force Monthly*.
- UK#158: First UK mention of the upcoming Transformers Pretenders figures.
- UK#168: Announcing yet another Marvel UK title, *Adventures of the Galaxy Rangers*. It would last nine issues before merging with *Thundercats* due to poor sales.
- UK#173: Notification that Marvel UK have moved from 'the wilds of Bayswater' to Arundel House near London's Temple underground station.
- UK#178: A tribute to long-standing designer John Tomlinson, who recently left the comic after 99 issues, and news that the comic is in line for a design overhaul from issue #183.
- UK#183: A daring new look for the Transformation page.
- UK#211: Notice that the comic's format will be changing from issue 213.

- UK#213: A brand new look, and an apology for the price increase.
- UK#215: The change to a partly black-and-white format is announced rather nonchalantly: 'No, that isn't a mistake with the colour – that's the way it's supposed to be!'
- UK#240: 'Yes it's true – Simon Furman is now writing for the Americans! Here's to continuity at last!'
- UK#250: 'There is some important news on the future of Transformers but we're keeping stumm on that for now. Stay tuned for further developments!'
- UK#276: Notice that the original pages of [20.2] 'Target: 2006' have gotten lost in the post, meaning that they can't be reprinted.
- UK#304: Announcement that the *G.I. Joe* back-up strip is to be cancelled, and replaced with 'a full chronological back-up from our earliest issues (#1-100) which many of you will never have seen before'. However ...
- UK#305: 'We've got fifteen people and an Apple-Mackintosh working flat-out, 24 hours a day, in our film vaults at the moment, to bring you the new(?) pre-Furmanian back-up strip (as mentioned last week). The bad news is we've also got gremlins down there ... film-eating gremlins!' Ultimately, just three further stories would get the reprint treatment.
- UK#308: The news that the comic will be going fortnightly from issue #309.

[12.3] THE ICARUS THEORY
- UK#45, 25 January 1986 (Part One), 11 pages
- UK#46, 1 February 1986 (Part Two), 11 pages

Credits:
Simon Furman (script); Barry Kitson (art); Gina Hart (colours, part 1); Stuart Place (colours, part 2); Richard Starkings (letters); Ian Rimmer (editor); Kev Hopgood (cover, UK#45); Jeff Anderson (cover, UK#46).

Plot:
A disgraced employee of Roxxon Oil, Professor Morris, has developed a control helmet with which he is able to remotely command robots. Having discovered Swoop's body at the bottom of a lake, he uses the Dinobot to attack the Autobots – he believes the Transformers to be the creations of Roxxon's biggest corporate rival, G B Blackrock.

A confused Swoop is able to regain a semblance of control over his body, and breaks off the attack. He flies back to Roxxon HQ, where he confronts a repentant Morris. The Autobots also arrive on the scene, but Swoop – although now free of Morris's control – attacks them again before being restrained.

It transpires that the Dinobots' four-million-year period of dormancy in a tar pit has affected their brain circuitry, regressing them to a state of mindless savagery. The Autobots realise they must track down the remaining four Dinobots before they, too, begin to wreak havoc ...

Notes
The title is a reference to the mythological story of Icarus, who took to the skies with wings made from wax. Icarus flew too close to the sun, his wings melted, and he fell into the sea and drowned. In this story it is Morris who takes on the role of Icarus, arrogant and proud. The dizzying experience of flight blinds him to reality, and like

Icarus he over-reaches himself, leading to his eventual downfall. There are also parallels between Icarus and Swoop – instead of heat from the Sun, it is the explosion of the Guardian drone that sends the Dinobot falling towards a watery end.

As with [12.1] 'Christmas Breaker', we are given specific dates here. The old copy of the *Daily Bugle* used to illustrate the menace of the Transformers is dated September 1985 and reads 'Giant Robots on Rampage! Invasion from Space'.

The actual story takes place over a period of eight days, 19-26 January 1986 (Sunday to Sunday). Morris's disastrous meeting with his Roxxon colleagues takes place on the 19 January, after which he takes out his ire on the stuffed dummy. Swoop is fished out of the water on 20 January, and the attack on the Autobots (and much of the ensuing action) occurs on 25 January. Finally, there is a brief coda set the following day.

There are references to a number of previous stories: Morris's presentation shows stills of Megatron being attacked by the army near Fortress Sinister from [4] 'The Last Stand', and Shockwave outside the Blackrock aerospace plant from [8] 'Repeat Performance'.

Bumblebee is still undergoing repairs after his capture by the Decepticons in [12.2] 'Crisis of Command', and Optimus Prime is still repentant for his bout of indecision in the same story.

There's a flashback to [8.2] 'The Wrath of Grimlock', where we see Swoop carrying the booby-trapped Guardian robot. Although Swoop gets clear of the drone prior to its explosion, he is still caught up in the blast, and crash lands in the (fictional) Lake Dena, a nearby Oregon reservoir.

This is Optimus Prime's first encounter with Swoop on Earth (the Autobot leader was in Decepticon captivity during all the Dinobots' previous appearances). However we learn here that, back on Cybertron, Prime was commander of the Elite Flying Corps, of which Swoop (then known as Divebomb) was a member.

Swoop is confirmed to be smaller than the Decepticon Planes (i.e. Starscream and his ilk), but larger than cassette Transformers such as Laserbeak. This is real-world accurate - consider the size of Swoop's alternate mode, a pterosaur (wingspan around 7.5 metres) relative to Starscream's alternative mode, an F-15 Eagle (wingspan 13.05 metres), and Laserbeak's alternative mode, a condor (wingspan around 3 metres).

It's stated that the Dinobots are suffering from a burn-out of the 'cybo-dendrons', caused by their internment in the tar pit for four million years (as described in [8] 'Repeat Performance').

Professor Morris's first initial is given as 'P', but his full name is as yet unrevealed. Roxxon Oil are a staple of the Marvel Universe – a shady and nefarious energy company, first seen in *Captain America* #180 (December 1974). The name is a riff on that of the real-world oil company Exxon.

Read All About It

The *Daily Bugle* newspaper is a staple of the Marvel Universe. First seen in *The Fantastic Four* #2 (January 1962), it is best known as the employer of Spider-Man's alter ego Peter Parker, who famously worked there as a photographer.

It's no surprise to see the *Bugle* featuring in a UK Transformers story. Although Marvel US had begun to sever ties between *The Transformers* and its regular superhero titles (see the essay 'Why Were There So Few Crossovers?' under [3] 'Prisoner of War'), this was far from the case in the UK, where the team-up title *Secret Wars II* was being heavily advertised in the pages of *The Transformers* and Marvel icon *Iron Man* was starring in the back-up strip.

To ensure that the *Bugle's* appearance here looked authentic, the art department used an old American comic as a template. *The Amazing Spider-Man Annual* #15 (December 1981) famously featured a full-size *Daily Bugle* front page (headline: 'Spider-Man: Threat or Menace?'), and it's this front page we see here, albeit edited to suit the needs of the Transformers story. Despite the new headline, the copy of the *Bugle* used here is mostly identical to its appearance in the *Spider-Man* issue. The weather report ('High in the 70s') is present and correct, and the issue date ('Saturday Sept 12') is also retained. The only other alteration is the year. In the original version the year was given as 1981, but here it's been amended to 1985 – which results in a slight error, as 12 September was a Thursday in 1985, not a Saturday.

Roll Call:
Autobots: Optimus Prime, Jazz, Prowl, Bluestreak, Ironhide, Ratchet, Sideswipe, Hound, Wheeljack, Trailbreaker, Bumblebee, Cliffjumper, Brawn, Huffer, Grimlock, Snarl, Slag, Sludge and Swoop.

With the obvious exception of Swoop, the rest of the Dinobots appear only in a single illustrative flashback-style panel, and take no part in the main action. The presence of Cliffjumper and Bluestreak in this story is debatable; the inconsistent way the Autobots are drawn and coloured makes identification a little awkward here.

Decepticons: Megatron and Shockwave, who appear only in photographic slides as part of Professor Morris's presentation.

Other: G B Blackrock (again, appearing only in a photographic slide) and **Professor Morris**.

Data File: Barry Kitson (artist)
Kitson worked on *Captain Britain* and *Spider-Man Weekly* for Marvel UK and *2000 AD* for Fleetway before hitting the big time in America. Working for DC Comics and Marvel US, his credits include *The Adventures of Superman, JLA: Year One, Superman, The Amazing Spider-Man* and *Fantastic Four*.

Data File: Kev Hopgood (artist)
Hopgood's credits include *Action Force, Doctor Who Magazine* and *Judge Dredd*. He got his big break working on the *Iron Man* comic for Marvel US, where he co-created the character War Machine, as played by Don Cheadle in films such as *Iron Man 2* (John Favreau, 2010) and *Avengers: Age of Ultron* (Joss Whedon, 2015).

Review:
A taut little psychological drama. Professor Morris is a brilliant addition to the human cast of characters, and there's a definite sense here that the UK stories are broadening in scope, beginning to push at storytelling boundaries that the safer US series seems reluctant to do.

That said, there are a couple of complaints: the artwork is not up to the usual standard we've come to expect in the UK strips (the Autobot troops fare especially badly here), and the Icarus references are perhaps a bit overbearing – the metaphors are somewhat forced and obvious, when a touch of subtlety might have made the point better.

All in all, this is a fine little two-parter, setting the scene nicely for the Dinobot saga that follows. 4/5

[12.4] DINOBOT HUNT!

- UK#47, 8 February 1986 (Part One), 11 pages
- UK#48, 15 February 1986 (Part Two), 11 pages
- UK#49, 22 February 1986 (Part Three), 11 pages
- UK#50, 1 March 1986 (Conclusion!), 11 pages

Credits:

Simon Furman (script); Will Simpson (art, parts 1 and 3); Barry Kitson (pencils, part 2; art, part 4); Marc Griffiths (inks, part 2); Stuart Place (colours, parts 1, 3 and 4); Jeff Anderson and Stuart Place (colours, part 2), Annie Halfacree (letters, parts 1, 2 and 4); Mike Scott (letters, part 3); Ian Rimmer (editor); David Lloyd (cover, UK#47); Jeff Anderson (cover, UK#48); Geoff Senior (cover, UK#49); John Higgins (cover, UK#50).

NB: Tim Perkins, an inker by trade, is additionally credited for 'Art Assist' on part 4. Stuart Place's contribution to part 2 went uncredited; a correction was published in UK#52.

Plot:

Having determined that the remaining four Dinobots must all be suffering from the same mental affliction that plagues Swoop, the Autobots divide into teams and search across America for their damaged colleagues. Matters are complicated by the fact that the Decepticons are out to hinder their progress.

Snarl is located near a secret US missile installation in the middle of the desert. The base commander elects to auto-destruct the facility rather than let it fall into enemy hands. The resulting explosion knocks out Snarl and allows the Autobots to retrieve him.

Meanwhile, another Autobot team tracks Sludge to a Californian swampland; however it is the Decepticons who find him first. A third team locates Slag in Idaho, and are able to pacify him despite the best efforts of the Decepticon Laserbeak.

The final Dinobot, Grimlock, is discovered in the snows of Canada. The Autobots' efforts to subdue him are hindered by the appearance of Sludge, who thanks to a Decepticon control device attacks both Grimlock and his fellow Autobots. Bumblebee is able to nullify the Decepticons' hold over Sludge, while Optimus Prime deals with Grimlock. The Dinobot hunt completed, the weary and damaged Autobots return to their base.

Although the Dinobots have been retaken by the Autobots, it is the Decepticons who are the true victors – during the course of the quest they have caused havoc, dealt injuries to multiple Autobots, and used the whole thing as a distraction to steal fuel from a nearby oil rig.

Notes:

Of all the four locations visited in this story, only one – Black Rock Desert in Nevada – exists in the real world. Although the other places are all fictional, from internal evidence it's possible to guess their rough whereabouts.

Sludge's woodland-and-river refuge, the fictitious Little Wood in Northern California, is drawn to resemble Six Rivers National Forest, a region nicknamed the 'Everglades of the West'. Slag's location, Old River Valley in Idaho, is probably supposed to represent the Owyhee Desert in the far south-western corner of the state. Finally, the Autobots locate Grimlock in Doonstown, Canada, which boasts an oil rig nearby. Considering that all the other Dinobots are found within a 350 mile (560 km) radius of the *Ark*, it's likely that Doonstown is in Southern British Columbia.

Of course, this isn't the first time the Transformers' adventures have led them to cross the Oregon-Idaho state border; the events of [10] 'The Next Best Thing to Being There' were also set in the Gem State.

In the Nevada/Snarl segment, we see an advanced secret military base, commanded by General Carl Thompson (he wears three stars, so he's actually a Lieutenant General). His forces seem much better-equipped than the previous army troops we saw in stories such as [3] 'Prisoner of War' – they are armed with laser-saws and disintegrator bombs, and are able to positively identify Snarl's back-plates as solar collectors. Given G B Blackrock's known links to the military (as seen in [9] 'Dis-Integrated Circuits'), it's tempting to theorise that the advanced tech seen here has been funded by the millionaire industrialist. The troops speak of a 'force 11 storm' – a 64-73mph (103-117km/h) violent storm, according to the Beaufort scale.

There are a couple of notable introductions in this story. In the California segment we get our first glimpse of Sludge's pal, LCTV reporter Joy Meadows. (The real LCTV, by the way, is a local public-access station operating out of New York, and is presumably unrelated to the fictional television station mentioned here.) Also seen for the first time is a fully-conscious Jetfire. He's still sporting his Decepticon insignia here, at least until it's skewered by Slag's horns. (There was apparently no time to perform the 'Rite of the Autobrand', a ritual we'll eventually witness in [14] 'Rock and Roll-Out'.) It's presumed that Optimus Prime used the Creation Matrix to instil him with life sometime after the events of [12] 'Prime Time'.

In order to find the Dinobots as quickly as possible, the Autobots are split into four teams: team A (California/Sludge) consists of Windcharger, Gears and Cliffjumper; the B team (Nevada/Snarl) is Mirage, Brawn and Trailbreaker; team C (Canada/Grimlock) is made up of Sideswipe, Bluestreak and Huffer; and finally, team D (Idaho/Snarl) comprises Jetfire, Jazz and Ironhide.

As always, there are copious references to previous stories. Swoop's mental breakdown in [12.3] 'The Icarus Theory' is referenced, as is Iacon's Great Dome, last seen in [A1.3] 'And There Shall Come … A Leader'. The MARB hover-platform (last spotted in [9] 'Dis-Integrated Circuits') is seen again here. The Autobot shuttles are of the same design as those seen in [8] 'Repeat Performance', and two of their number are seen to be destroyed here.

On the cover of UK#48, Sludge is described as a 'Swamp Thing', a reference to the 1982 Wes Craven movie of the same name, which itself was based on a DC Comics title.

Roll Call:
Autobots: Optimus Prime, Jazz, Prowl, Bluestreak, Ironhide, Ratchet, Sideswipe, Wheeljack, Mirage, Trailbreaker, Bumblebee, Cliffjumper, Brawn, Huffer, Gears , Windcharger, Grimlock, Snarl, Slag, Sludge, Swoop (flashback only) and Jetfire.

Of all the currently-active Autobots, the only one not to appear in this story is Hound. (It's possible he was injured during the events of [12.3] 'The Icarus Theory'.)

Decepticons: Skywarp, Soundwave, Laserbeak and Scavenger.

A feature in issue #48, the 'Decepticon Who's Who' confirms that Shockwave is currently 'missing, but presumed still functional', and that Megatron is 'missing, presumed destroyed'. Scavenger's appearance here is the first by a Constructicon since their debut story, [10] 'The Next Best Thing to Being There'.

Other: **Joy Meadows**

Data File: Jeff Anderson (artist)
A well-known name in the '80s UK comics scene, Anderson contributed to *Captain Britain, Spider-Man and Zoids, Death's Head* and *Knights of Pendragon*. He also worked on *Judge Dredd, Judge Anderson* and *Halo Jones* strips for *2000 AD*. After becoming inspired by his work on *The Graphic Bible* (basically, the Bible in graphic novel format), he later became an ordained curate.

Data File: David Lloyd (artist)
Lloyd is best known as the artist on the much-loved graphic novel *V for Vendetta*. His other credits include *Wasteland* and *Hellblazer*, plus comics based on the *Aliens* and *James Bond* franchises.

Review:
A bit of a mixed bag, this one – the first and last instalments are excellent, but the middle two sections are disappointing to say the least.

The Sludge segment is notable only for its introduction of the recurring character Joy Meadows, although here she's unmemorable and nondescript, and a far cry from the well-written and fully-fledged General Thompson – the star of the show in the Snarl section.

Part three fares even worse, some excellent action sequences being the saving grace of an issue wherein a couple of cowboys implausibly attempt to 'rustle' a robotic dinosaur. Despite these faults, each mini-adventure lasts only a single issue, so even the poorer ones admittedly don't outstay their welcome.

Boasting a grand scale, two truly brilliant issues plus a variety of locations and situations, 'Dinobot Hunt' is guaranteed 'epic' status – it's just a shame that parts two and three are unable to match the standards set by the instalments that bookend them. 3/5

The Back-Up Strips, Part 7: *Iron Man*

A character that needs no introduction, Iron Man is one of Marvel Comics' most enduringly popular creations.

The first two stories chosen to be reprinted here were from the anthology title *Marvel Fanfare*, a comic intended to be more highbrow and classier than Marvel's usual fare. This ethos is certainly evident in these two *Iron Man* tales, which boast some absolutely stunning artwork.

- 'Night of the Octopus' (UK#43-46), from *Marvel Fanfare* #22 (September 1985). Doctor Octopus attempts a prison break using his new indestructible robot arms.
- 'From the Ashes' (UK#47-50), from *Marvel Fanfare* #23 (November 1985). Iron Man tracks down the recently-escaped Doctor Octopus.

The next *Iron Man* adventure to be reprinted featured a future incarnation of the character: the Iron Man of 2020 (actually 2015, but the date was changed to tie in with the character's appearance in the old *Machine Man* back-up strips, which were set in 2020).

- 'Man of the Year' (UK#119-125) from *The Amazing Spider-Man Annual* #20 (November 1986). To prevent a terrorist attack, the Iron Man of 2020 travels back in time to the present day.

After this, the remaining two stories once again featured the present-day Iron Man:

- 'Deep Trouble!' (UK#126-129) from *Iron Man* #218 (May 1987). Iron Man travels to England to investigate a canister of death gas that sunk on board the *Titanic*.
- 'Stratosfire!' (UK#146-152) from the *Iron Man Annual* #9 (1987). The evil Roxxon Oil Company create their own 'super hero'.

[13] SHOOTING STAR!
US#13, 'February 1986' (published October 1985), 23 pages.

British reprint: UK#51, 8 March 1986 (Part One), 12 pages; UK#52, 15 March 1986 (Part Two), 11 pages.

Credits:
Bob Budiansky (script); Don Perlin (pencils); Al Gordon (inks); Nel Yomtov (colours); Janice Chiang (letters); Michael Carlin (editor); Jim Shooter (editor-in-chief); Don Perlin and Al Gordon (cover). **UK:** Geoff Senior (cover, UK#51); Don Perlin and Al Gordon (cover, UK#52 – reuse of US cover).

Plot:
Small-time hoodlum Joey Slick discovers Megatron, but the Decepticon leader isn't his usual self: damaged by his battle with Ratchet and the Dinobots, he no longer has a will of his own.

Joey goes on a crime spree with Megatron as his 'super gun'. With even the army unable to prevent him from robbing banks and hijacking shipments of gold, it seems no-one can stop this one-man crime wave.

Eventually it is Joey himself who sees reason, and he confronts his old nemesis, mob boss Jake Lomax, in a bid to end the cycle of violence. During the struggle, Megatron is thrown to the floor, the jolt restoring his mental capacity.

Impressed by Joey's audacity, Megatron spares the human's life and walks off into the night. Now shorn of his 'super gun', the repentant gangster is finally arrested by the authorities.

Notes:
We see a lot more of the Portland area in this issue. Lomax lives in an exclusive, private estate, while Slick lives in the south-west of the city.

The bank raided by Joey is the First National Bank. Although a popular and generic name, there actually was a real-life First National Bank of Oregon located in Portland in the '80s (at 1300 SW Fifth Avenue). Since 1996 it has been part of the Wells Fargo bank chain.

Outside the city – but presumably still in the general vicinity – we see the Port Street overpass. (Although Port Street is fictional, the Portland area does indeed have more than its fair share of overpasses, as the city is criss-crossed by major highways such as the I-5 and the I-84.) Other landmarks include the Cascade Motor Court motel and a '6-12' convenience store (obviously based on the real-world 7-Eleven chain).

Megatron is located in a shallow stream near what appears to be a sewage outlet, the implication being that, after landing in the snow in [8] 'Repeat Performance', which we see here in flashback, he was somehow swept away into a river. This all seems a bit improbable – the chances of a gun on a mountainside glacier reaching shallow water fifty miles downstream are surely next to nil. (Even if Megatron made it as far as a river, he would surely sink to the bottom.) It's likely that some sort of natural defence mechanism kicked in, and Megatron involuntarily 'guided' himself towards a populated area.

Joey's landlady, Mrs Peréz, offers to make him some menudo soup, a traditional Mexican broth made from beef stomach. Joey compares his notoriety with that of legendary gangster Alphonse 'Al' Capone (1888-1947). The nearest NFL franchise, the Seattle Seahawks, are given a namecheck. They were a pretty decent team in the early-mid '80s; their head coach Chuck Knox was awarded Coach of the Year in 1984, as they twice reached the play-offs.

This story appears to take place over the course of a number of months (time enough for Joey to build up a cult celebrity status). Using the previously-established timeline (see [12.1] 'Christmas Breaker'), we can say that the opening scenes take place around Winter 1984 (the fictional *Globe Journal* newspaper has the headline 'Robots Leave Plane Plant', a reference to the events of [12] 'Prime Time'), and the final scene, in which Megatron finally regains his faculties, probably happens a few weeks prior to his return to the Decepticon ranks in [15] 'I, Robot Master' in the spring of 1986. (From here on in, I'll be assuming that, unless stated otherwise, the events of the comics are roughly contemporaneous with the UK cover dates of their relevant issues.)

UK Changes:
Page 1, panel 1: 'colorist' is changed to 'colours'.
Page 5, panel 4: a reference to issue #8 is changed to issue #28.
Page 18, panel 2: 'neighborhood' is amended to 'neighbourhood'.

Roll Call:
Autobots: Ratchet (flashback only)

This is the first ever story from which Optimus Prime is absent entirely.

Decepticons: Megatron, plus, in flashback, Starscream, Soundwave, Frenzy and Ravage.

Data File: Don Perlin (artist)
A cartoonist since the '40s, Perlin joined Marvel Comics in 1974 and enjoyed lengthy stints on titles such as *Ghost Rider* and *The Defenders*. While working as an artist on *Werewolf by Night*, he co-created the character Moon Knight.

Review:
It's an obvious thing to say, but to hang the entire plot on such terribly clichéd human characters dooms this story from the start. Putting Megatron in the midst of all this ought theoretically to help a bit, but instead he is dragged down to their level – the Decepticon's refusal to kill Joey at the end might well be rationalised as a result of his mental problems, but it serves only to cheapen the character.

The issue describes itself as 'weird' and 'offbeat'. It's certainly an atypical story, but contrary to the build-up, it's all played straight, with the exception of some obligatory 'comedy' henchmen. The writers seem to think that putting Megatron in amongst some stereotypical mobsters is a funny story in and of itself – which quite plainly is not the case.

That said, this issue still has some merit. It rattles along nicely, there's lots going on, and the action keeps up at a nice pace. Even though it's a pretty horrid comic, there's enough here to keep one interested (which is more than can be said for the better, but blander, [10] 'The Next Best Thing to Being There'). And of course any issue that reintroduces Megatron into the mythos – however cackhandedly – can't be *entirely* devoid of merit. 1/5

The Back-Up Strips, Part 8: *Robotix*
An adaptation of a kids' cartoon show that, like *The Transformers* itself, was based upon a line of boys' toys sold by Hasbro (or rather, their subsidiary Milton Bradley). The US comic lasted just a single issue.

• 'A World in Chaos' (UK#51-54), from *Robotix* #1 (February 1986). Survivors of a crashed spaceship encounter two warring factions of alien robots.

[14] ROCK AND ROLL-OUT!
US#14, 'March 1986' (published November 1985), 22 pages.

British reprint: UK#53, 22 March 1986 (Part One), 11 pages; UK#54, 29 March 1986 (Part Two), 11 pages.

Credits:
Bob Budiansky (script); Don Perlin (pencils); Al Gordon (inks); Nel Yomtov (colours); Janice Chiang (letters); Michael Carlin (editor); Jim Shooter (editor-in-chief); Bob Budiansky and Mike Esposito (cover). **UK:** Robin Smith (cover, UK#53); Bob Budiansky and Mike Esposito (cover, UK#54 – reuse of US cover).

Plot:
The US military send a fleet of ships in an attempt to retake G B Blackrock's oil rig, which is still occupied by the Decepticons. Ultimately, the Decepticons depart of their own volition, but not before reminding the humans how hopelessly outgunned they are. The altercation is witnessed first-hand by Walter Barnett, a US government

intelligence agent assigned to a group named Triple-I (Intelligence and Information Institute) and charged with keeping a lid on the Transformer situation.

Meanwhile, Shockwave has returned to claim leadership of the Decepticon ranks, and his first plan is to harness sonic energy from a rock concert. The Autobots get wind of this scheme, and send a group of new Autobots – Hoist, Tracks, Smokescreen and Skids – to investigate. A further new Autobot, the architect Grapple, stays behind in the *Ark* to work on a special project.

Eventually, the new Autobots sabotage the Decepticons' efforts to hijack the concert, and a brief firefight ensues. Thankfully, however, mass panic is averted – the 80,000-strong crowd of rock fans believe the whole battle was nothing more than an extravagant lightshow.

Notes:
This story sees the first appearances of the Autobots Skids, Tracks, Grapple, Hoist and Smokescreen. It's explained that their minds had been copied onto crystals for reanimation in case the Autobots ever required additional reinforcements. The implication in the word 'copied' is that these are mental clones of five Autobots who stayed behind on Cybertron. Their minds were presumably duplicated onto the hard-drive-like crystals so that they could be given life, in the event that anything went wrong on the original *Ark* mission.

It's revealed that the Autobots have an extremely long injury list. In addition to Sunstreaker, we have confirmation that Hound, Gears, Cliffjumper, Jazz, Bluestreak, Sideswipe and Huffer are currently inoperative, a result of the battle at the conclusion of [12] 'Prime Time'.

This issue marks the final appearance of G B Blackrock's offshore oil platform. First seen in a television report in [5] 'The New Order', it was conquered by the Decepticons in [6] 'The Worse of Two Evils'. Here we learn that the rig is located two miles from the Oregon coast, and is 87.3 miles from the rock concert in Portland (which doesn't quite gel with the claim in previous issues it was 146 miles from the *Ark*).

The aircraft carrier we see here has a number visible on its runway, either 59 or 65, depending on which way up you look at it. This means that the ship could be the USS *Forrestal*, (registry number CV-59) built in 1955 and decommissioned in 1993. However, it's preferable from a pop-culture standpoint to believe that this is actually the USS *Enterprise* (CVN-65), the world's first nuclear vessel. The ship was featured in numerous popular media in the mid-'80s, including cinematic appearances in *Star Trek IV: The Voyage Home* (Leonard Nimoy, 1986) and *Top Gun* (Tony Scott, 1986).

The Transformers' fuel crisis is now well and truly over – the Decepticons can now convert any fuel into Energon cubes (thanks to Shockwave's power siphon), while the Autobots now have built into their bodies devices that convert gasoline into Transformer fuel. Thanks to their deal with G B Blackrock, they can obtain fuel free of charge from Blackrock-affiliated forecourts via the use of a Blackrock Gold Priority Card. Other changes to the Autobots include panels that hide their faction logos, and lifelike animated mannequins to act as fake drivers. The concept of Energon cubes originates from a *Transformers* cartoon episode, {1-01} 'More Than Meets the Eye, Part One'.

The (fictional) Municipal Stadium we see here is said to be in northwest Oregon, and has a capacity of 80,000. This would appear to be based on Portland's real-life Civic Stadium (currently known as the Jeld Wen Field because of sponsorship agreements), at which Elvis Presley famously played in 1957. A sign in the stadium parking lot states that next week's live concert is by the Bangles, a pop-rock band famous in the '80s for hits including 'Eternal Flame', 'Manic Monday' and 'Walk Like an Egyptian'. However, the main rock group featured in this issue is the fictitious Brick Springstern and the Tenth Avenue Band, clearly based upon the real-world Bruce Springsteen and the E-Street Band. We first hear the group's music playing on a Portland radio station broadcasting at 1270 kHz. (In real life, there is no Portland station on that particular AM frequency.) On one occasion the singer is referred to as 'Brick Spring*horn*', but this error was corrected in later reprints.

The singer is drawn to resemble Springsteen, down to the trademark sweatband, and the group features an African-American saxophonist based on E-Street Band member Clarence Clemons. Furthermore, many of the songs are based on real Springsteen hits, as follows:

'Dancing in the Night' (lyrics: 'Can't start a fire without a light … even if we're just dancing in the night) is based on 'Dancing in the Dark' (released in May 1984, from the album *Born in the USA*, a US #2 and UK #4 single). Actual lyrics: 'Can't start a fire without a spark … even if we're just dancing in the dark.'

'Born to Ride' ('Cause chumps like us/baby we were born to ride') is based on 'Born to Run' (released August 1975, from the album *Born to Run*, a US #23 and UK #16 single). Actual lyrics: 'Cause tramps like us/baby we were born to run.'

We also see him sing 'Born in America' (based on 'Born in the USA', released October 1984, from the album of the same name, a US #9 and UK #5 single) and 'Margarita' (based on 'Rosalita (Come out Tonight)', a track from the 1973 album *The Wild, The Innocent & The E Street Shuffle*).

Here Jetfire is officially welcomed into the Autobot ranks, thanks to the 'Rite of the Autobrand'. Grapple plays no part in the battle at the stadium; instead Optimus Prime has him working on a special project (namely the construction of Omega Supreme, as will be revealed in [19] 'Command Performances').

Businesses located in Portland include Gloria & Roz's Diner, Fred & Manny's Garage (where full tanks for five Autobots cost $82.40/£56.00) and Burger Shed (home of the $1.99 Humongous Burger – £1.35 GBP at 1986 rates).

Finally, this issue sees the introduction of the III organisation, which is based out of the Capitol Building in Washington DC. We meet two of its members, Walter Barnett and his superior Forrest Forsythe.

UK Notes:
For the first time, the events of the UK comic can be used to explain plot holes and inconsistencies that arise in the American adventures. For example, the concept of Autobot mind-cloning raises an obvious question: if Transformer brains can be so easily duplicated, then why isn't this technique used more often? Well, it's entirely possible that these crystals are extremely rare – as we shall see in [A1.4] 'Hunted', the Decepticons are desperate to get their hands on this kind of technology. It's also possible that the procedure is too risky to perform *en masse* – note here that Wheeljack has concerns about the cloned Autobots' minds being intact.

Another point to note is that the new Autobots seem terribly naive here, taking a while to come to terms with human culture and custom. Considering that the other Autobots gleaned this knowledge from listening in to to human broadcasts and transmissions via Auntie ([1] 'The Transformers'), it would appear that this method of learning is no longer available – perhaps a legacy of the computer problems experienced in [4.3] 'Raiders of the Last *Ark*'.

At this point, the US writers were busy sidelining many of the original Autobots so that new characters could be introduced in their stead. It's suggested that the massive battle at the end of [12] 'Prime Time' resulted in heavy casualties, hence the Autobot corpses seen in this story. However, the UK comics ignored these injuries and continued to include the likes of Jazz and Bluestreak in subsequent adventures such as [12.1] 'Christmas Break*er*' and [12.2] 'Crisis of Command'. It wasn't until [12.4] 'Dinobot Hunt' that some of these original Autobots were finally rendered inactive in the UK continuity.

In other words, there are two different explanations for the Autobot corpses here: for US readers they are a result of the battle with the fake Prime in [12] 'Prime Time', but for UK readers these Autobots succumbed later, during the [12.4] 'Dinobot Hunt'.

It's stated here that Hound is one of the deactivated Autobots, despite him not taking part in [12.4] 'Dinobot Hunt'. The cause of his injury is therefore a mystery to UK readers; but as he hasn't been seen since the battle with Swoop in [12.3] 'The Icarus Theory', that would appear to be the most likely cause of his current malaise.

In the UK, these issues also included a feature called 'The Autobot Who's Who'. It confirms that the Autobot wounded (including the Dinobots and Windcharger) are currently 'injured; undergoing treatment'. Sunstreaker's injuries, sustained in [5] 'The New Order', are confirmed as being more severe, with his status listed as 'injured; little possibility of revival'.

The Decepticons claim to have been stationed aboard the oil platform for 'weeks'. (It can be assumed that the bulk of the Decepticon forces are still based in Fortress Sinister at this point – as seen in [12.2] 'Crisis of Command' – and that Starscream's troops are only temporarily stationed on the rig, perhaps on sentry duty.)

Shockwave's time spent trapped in the swamp, as established in [12] 'Prime Time', is not referenced here at all, although his escape will later be shown in a flashback sequence in [16.1] 'Robot Buster'. In neither issue is it confirmed for exactly how long he's absent. (Note though that from the US point of view he's never actually been away. The only issue he's skipped is [13] 'Shooting Star', which aside from flashbacks featured no Transformers other than Megatron anyway. It is only in UK comics such as [12.2] 'Crisis of Command' and [12.4] 'Dinobot Hunt' that he is confirmed lost for any period of time.)

Starscream here states that Shockwave had 'abandoned' the Decepticons. That could be a reference to Shockwave's time in the swamp; it might also refer to him having left the Decepticons briefly while constructing the power siphon; or it could refer to Starscream and company having been left alone on the oil rig.

Although they make their American debut here, Energon cubes were previously mentioned in the UK story [8.1] 'Decepticon Dam-Busters' (which seems to indicate that the Decepticons must have already possessed at least a rudimentary version of the power siphon before this point). Similarly, the Rite of the Autobrand was previously mentioned in [12.4] 'Dinobot Hunt'.

This is the second reference to Bruce Springsteen in the comics; Buster was seen listening to his song 'Glory Days' in [8.2] 'The Wrath of Grimlock'.

UK Changes:
Page 1, panel 1: 'honored' and 'colorist' are replaced by 'honoured' and 'colour'

respectively.
Page 2, panel 1: 'honored' is again changed to 'honoured'.
Page 6, panel 3: the reference to issue #6 is changed to issue #24.
Page 20, panel 2: 'harbor' is altered to read 'harbour'.

Roll Call:
Autobots: Optimus Prime, Jazz (as a corpse), Prowl, Bluestreak (corpse), Ratchet, Sideswipe (corpse), Hound (corpse), Wheeljack, Mirage, Bumblebee, Cliffjumper (corpse), Huffer (corpse), Gears (corpse), Jetfire, **Grapple**, **Hoist**, **Smokescreen**, **Skids** and **Tracks**.

Although making their comic debuts, Grapple, Hoist and Tracks had all previously appeared in the UK Annual story [A1.2] 'Missing in Action'.
    On the final page of the comic, the Autobot road convoy led by Optimus Prime appears to include Jazz (in the first panel; look for his distinctive spoiler), Windcharger (in the second panel, note the car with the horizontal slats over the rear windscreen) and Sideswipe (third panel, far right). This is surely an error, given that all three characters are definitively stated to be inactive here.

Decepticons: Starscream, Skywarp, Thundercracker and Shockwave.

Other: G B Blackrock, **Walter Barnett** and **Forrest Forsythe**.

Data File: Michael Carlin (editor)
Carlin is an Eisner Award-winning editor who has helmed a staggering array of titles, including stints on *Batman*, *Captain America*, *Fantastic Four*, *Superman* and *Thor*. He later took on an executive role at DC Comics.

Review:
Arguably, this story is more offbeat than the deliberately-weird [13] 'Shooting Star' that preceded it. There's lots of comedy as the new Autobots have difficulty adjusting to their new surroundings; we also have the appearance of the outrageously-named Brick Springhorn; and then there is the Decepticons' frankly bizarre plan to power themselves using sonic energy stolen from a rock concert. Add in Shockwave's return, the introduction of Triple-I, Jetfire's Auto-branding and the revelation that almost half the Autobots are effectively dead, and you have a comic that is frankly all over the place, both plot-wise and tonally.
    In theory then, this issue ought to be a disaster ... and yet somehow, almost despite itself, it succeeds. The various disparate parts combine to form an oddly-satisfying whole. It's a lurid, stupid pick 'n' mix of a story, presented with much verve and wit.
4/5

[15] I, ROBOT-MASTER!
US#15, 'April 1986' (published December 1985), 22 pages.

British reprint: UK#55, 5 April 1986 (Part One), 11 pages; UK#56, 12 April 1986 (Part Two), 11 pages.

Credits:
Bob Budiansky (script); Don Perlin (pencils); Keith Williams (inks); Nel Yomtov (colours); Janice Chiang (letters); Michael Carlin (editor); Jim Shooter (editor-in-chief); Herb Trimpe (cover). **UK:** Herb Trimpe (cover, UK#55 – reuse of US cover); Robin Smith (cover, UK#56).

Plot:
Desperate for fuel, Megatron attacks a mine in Wyoming. The coal is insufficient to quench his thirst for energy, and the lack of power renders him motionless and inert.

Meanwhile, Triple-I are desperate to curtail the widespread national panic caused by the Transformers' presence. They concoct an elaborate cover story, suggesting that the robots have been created by a mad terrorist, Robot-Master. Comic-book writer Donny Finkleberg, who originated the Robot-Master concept, is asked to play the part of the villain.

The Autobots arrive at the mine in order to secure Megatron, but they are fired upon by the US military, who are unable to tell the difference between the two Transformer factions. When the Decepticons arrive to rescue their stricken leader, Optimus Prime's forces are in no fit state to oppose them.

Megatron, now restored to full health, grudgingly spares Finkleberg's life in the hope that the Robot-Master persona can continue to bad-mouth the Autobots and ensure the humans continue to mistake friend from foe.

Notes:
The mine we see in this and subsequent stories is the (fictional) Culverton Mine in Eastern Wyoming's Powder River Basin. In the real world, this area is indeed coal-rich – 20% of the USA's entire electricity supply comes from power stations running on coal from the Powder River Basin.

This issue sees the introduction of Donny Finkleberg, aka Robot-Master. His name and appearance are based upon those of real-life comic writer Danny Fingeroth. Here Finkleberg is seen working for Marvel Comics, who are said to be based out of 387 Park Avenue South in New York. (In the real world, Marvel were indeed based in offices at that address, having taking out a ten-year lease on floors 10 and 11 in 1981). Although his face is never seen, the extremely tall editor who bundles Finkleberg out of the office is presumably based upon the similarly tall real-life Marvel editor-in-chief Jim Shooter.

One of Finkleberg's proposed projects is a *Potato Salad Man* graphic novel entitled 'This Man, This Mayonnaise'. The title obviously spoofs that of 'This Man … This Monster', an iconic story originally published in *Fantastic Four* #51 (June 1966). The main character in that issue was the Thing, a regular member of the Fantastic Four, whose textured orange-brown skin looks not unlike a mustard-based potato salad. This isn't the first time (nor the last) that Marvel Comics would homage that particular title: for example *Ms. Marvel* #1 (Jan 1977) was entitled 'This Woman, This Warrior', and more recently *The Amazing Spider-Man* #611 (Jan 2010) boasted the moniker 'This Man, This [Expletive Deleted]'.

The Triple-I meeting takes place in a futuristic building in the foothills of the Cascades (the same mountain range that's home to the *Ark*). Forsythe, Barnett and Blackrock are all present – we later see that Barnett has a wife, and a son named Stevie.

While some television viewers suspect that Robot-Master might be a communist (the Cold War was still rumbling on in 1986), others believe him to be working for the

PLO. The Palestinian Liberation Organisation was, at the time, involved in hostilities with US-supported Israel. Incidents such as the 1982 Lebanon War and 1985's Operation Wooden Leg helped ensure that the PLO was barely out of the news during the mid-'80s.

The broadcasting company we see here is called ZBS News (presumably based on the real-world CBS News). Blackrock makes a disparaging remark about the President's attempts at 'balancing the budget', a reference to the government's programme of economic reforms colloquially known as 'Reaganomics'.

As ever, there are references to previous issues – we're shown images of the Megatron/Shockwave battle ([6] 'The Worse of Two Evils'), Soundwave taking over the aerospace plant ([7] 'Warrior School'), and Hoist at the rock concert ([14] 'Rock and Roll-Out'). Blackrock states that the Autobots helped him to retake the oil rig – an inaccurate description of events; the Decepticons left willingly.

Bizarrely, Soundwave's rather low-tech method of gaining intel on the Megatron situation involves him loitering in tapedeck mode in an electrical store.

Appropriately for an issue published in December (in the US), it's seen to be snowing (in the panel showing G B Blackrock's skyscraper).

The story's title is based on that of *I, Robot*, a 1950 book by Isaac Asimov, which itself was based on an identically-titled story by Eando Binder that first appeared in the January 1939 issue of *Amazing Stories* magazine.

UK Changes:
Page 1, panel 1: 'colorist' is changed to 'colours'.
Page 8, panel 6: Wheeljack's colour is altered from green to blue (although neither scheme is correct; he should be predominantly white).
Page 10, panel 3, 'neighborhood' becomes 'neighbourhood'.

Roll Call:
Autobots: Optimus Prime, Wheeljack, Bumblebee, Hoist, Skids and Tracks.

Decepticons: Megatron, Starscream (flashback only), Soundwave, Laserbeak, Buzzsaw, Ravage and Shockwave (flashback only).

The above list is based on the assumption that the Decepticon jet shown on Triple-I's big screen in footage from [14] 'Rock and Roll-Out' is Starscream, although to be fair it could just as easily be Skywarp or Thundercracker.

Other: G B Blackrock, Walter Barnett, Forrest Forsythe and **Donny Finkleberg**.

Review:
For the third issue in a row, we're presented with a comedy story. It worked well in the previous issue (where the humour developed naturally from the new Autobots and their reactions to their alien surroundings), but here we're straight back into 'Joey Slick' territory: Donny Finkleberg is so annoying and unfunny in his debut appearance that the whole issue is marred by his irksome schtick.

There's little to enjoy in the remainder of the comic, either. As was the case with Circuit Breaker in previous issues, Triple-I and the US Military are so stupid here that it's unbelievable. They fire upon and damage the Autobots while the Decepticons emerge unscathed.

We've seen before that well-written human supporting characters can add a lot to a Transformers story; making some badly-written ones the main focus is a recipe for disaster. 1/5

1985 in Comics: The First Full Year

Although some concessions were made to ensure all the individual issues were enjoyable out of context, for long spells in 1985 the emphasis was firmly on the year's ongoing story arc rather than standalone adventures. The American comics told of Shockwave's attempts to build a Decepticon army, the origins of Circuit Breaker, the resurrection of the Autobots, Buster's struggles with the Matrix and the quest to restore Optimus Prime's head. By year's end all these threads would be brought to a conclusion, and entirely new plot strands (involving Triple-I and Robot-Master) be set up for further development in 1986.

This being the comic's first full year of publication, however, not everything went without a hitch. It's arguable that the first US story arc, culminating with [12] 'Prime Time', was dragged out a bit too much. And as the climax of a year's worth of stories, the final Prime versus Shockwave battle came across as a little underwhelming.

However, the positives far outweighed the negatives: interesting human characters such as Buster and G B Blackrock continued to flourish, and the Transformers themselves began to develop individual personalities. The star of the show was clearly Shockwave, the cold logician who so callously defeated Sunstreaker and Megatron – not out of spite or ambition but simply because it was the optimal course of action.

With the UK comic printing stories at double the rate of the American one (roughly 44 pages per month as opposed to 22), this was the year when the former began producing its own original set of adventures. The first three, from [4.1] 'Man of Iron' through to [4.3] 'Raiders of the Last *Ark*', were in stark contrast to those *The Transformers* US was producing at the time, both stylistically and in terms of continuity. These were self-contained, atmospheric adventures with sumptuous painted art that seemed a world away from their transatlantic counterparts.

When the chance for further original stories came later in the year, the UK creative team were more experienced and better-prepared; while the first few months of 1985 had seen them struggling to integrate their additions into the mix, by year's end their stories were confidently expanding in scope, while simultaneously remaining true to the source material from across the pond.

Behind the scenes, the American comic was getting into its stride. Bob Budiansky (scripts), Nel Yomtov (colours) and Jim Owsley (editor) formed a core team, maintaining consistency of vision despite a revolving door of artists. (Covers excepted, no artist worked on more than two of the first twelve issues of *The Transformers*.) Owsley departed part-way through the year to take over Marvel's two Spider-Man comics (and indeed launch a third, *Web of Spider-Man*), and was replaced by Michael Carlin, in a seamless handover that had little impact on the style or quality of the series.

The UK comic, on the other hand, altered drastically over the course of the year. Here a change in editorship was readily apparent. Sheila Cranna left to take up the reins at *Doctor Who Magazine* and was replaced by Ian Rimmer, who immediately set to work re-imagining the comic. The many back-up features (such as *Planet Terry*, *The Chromobots* and *Robot-Round-Up*) were quickly ditched, the contents whittled down to just two main strips, *The Transformers* and *Machine Man*. By year's end the comic had been completely revamped: it was sleeker, more streamlined and aimed at a slightly older audience. Cranna, meanwhile, continued her association with the brand by editing the very first Transformers annual, a project so successful that she was asked back to helm the subsequent edition the following year.

Soon after Rimmer took over, there was another change to contend with: a sharp rise in readership meant that the comic could be relaunched as a full-colour weekly, albeit with a reduced page count.

With the departure of Steve Parkhouse after just a single story, [4.1] 'Man of Iron', rookie Simon Furman took over as *The Transformers* UK's main writer, and it was soon apparent that he was a perfect fit for the role. Writing good action stories to tight deadlines is never the easiest of tasks, but also to weave them seamlessly into Bob Budiansky's American storylines was another feat entirely. Furman would go on to be the main writer throughout the rest of the UK run, and to great success.

Beginning the year as a feature-packed fortnightly anthology, printed partly in black-and-white, *The Transformers* UK ended it with a sharp new look and a talented young production team. By the end of an eventful 1985, both the British and the American iterations of the comic were well set for further successes …

[16] PLIGHT OF THE BUMBLEBEE!
US#16, 'May 1986' (published January 1986), 22 pages.

British reprint: UK#57, 19 April 1986 (Part One), 11 pages; UK#57, 26 April 1986 (Part Two), 11 pages.

Credits:
Len Kaminski (script); Graham Nolan (pencils); Tom Morgan (inks); Nel Yomtov (colours); Bill Oakley (letters); Michael Carlin (editor); Jim Shooter (editor-in-chief); Herb Trimpe (cover). **UK:** John Stokes (cover, UK#56); Herb Trimpe (cover, UK#57 – reuse of US cover).

'Special thanks to Eliot Brown, for splash page design and art.' (Brown contributed a schematic drawing of Bumblebee for the comic's first page.)

Plot:
The Decepticons pinpoint Bumblebee as the weak link in the Autobot army. Their plan: capture the diminutive Autobot, take control of his body and then program him to attack his fellow Autobots.

Bumblebee manages to escape the initial attack by hiding in a used car lot, but he doesn't reckon on being 'stolen' by a pair of car thieves. The Decepticons track him down again, and move in for the kill.

Thankfully, the sight of a yellow VW being chased through the city by the Decepticons makes headline news on television. The Autobots see the footage and rush to the scene, where the Decepticons are eventually driven off.

Notes:
Dialogue in the original printing of this issue set these events in Wisconsin, a state in north central United States that (even at its most westerly point) is over a thousand miles away from the *Ark*'s location near Portland. More recent reprints have amended

the text to read 'Oregon' instead.

The Autobots are suffering from injuries received in battle 'yesterday'. Although a caption seems to indicate that this is the same battle seen in [15] 'I, Robot-Master', the fact that both Wheeljack and Prowl are recovering from recent damage appears to contradict this (as neither was involved in battle at any time during the events of that issue).

Here we get a few welcome facts and statistical data about Bumblebee: his height is stated as 5' (1.52m) in car mode and 15' (4.57m) in robot mode. He weighs in at 2,200lbs (997kg), which is at the very least 20% heavier than a real-world Beetle (depending on what model of the car he's supposed to represent). Here he's seen to travel at least 200mph (322km/h), which doesn't seem all that impressive (given that real-world – albeit custom – Beetles can reach these sorts of speeds). Presumably his speed here is being curtailed by his injuries.

The Decepticons use a bizarre tracking system of 'bearings' and 'vectors'. In the real world, the numbers in navigational bearings are limited to 360 (as bearings are given in degrees and there are 360 degrees in a circle). However, the Decepticons (and later, the human pilots) exceed this limit (e.g. 'bearing 770', 'bearing 575').

A poster on a wall is shown advertising a Jimmy Buffett concert. The renowned singer/restaurateur is famous for such songs as 'Margaritaville' (1977) and 'Cheeseburger in Paradise' (1978).

The story's title is derived from 'Flight of the Bumblebee' (Russian: *Polyot Shmelya*), an interlude from the opera *The Tale of Tsar Saltan, of his Son the Renowned and Mighty Bogatyr Prince Gvidon Saltanovich and of the Beautiful Princess-Swan*, written by Nikolai Rimsky-Korsakov in 1899-1900.

UK Notes:

The Decepticons are based in what is described as a 'makeshift fortress'. From the US point of view, there's no reason to believe that this is anything other than Fortress Sinister. Although unseen in the US comics since [4] 'The Last Stand', it had also been the Decepticons' base of operations in UK-only stories such as [12.2] 'Crisis of Command'. Presumably the Decepticons returned there after being ejected from the aerospace plant in [12] 'Prime Time'. From the UK perspective, however, this cannot be Fortress Sinister. When next we see the latter, in [16.1] 'Robot Buster', it's completely deserted, and appears to have been vacant for quite some time. In that story Shockwave even demonstrates an irrational hatred for the place. So it's difficult to imagine that the makeshift base we see here – which Shockwave appears to have no problem with – can be the same place.

UK readers of this comic might be feeling a sense of *déjà vu*: this plot is extremely reminiscent of some previous UK-only stories. Shockwave's 'electro-calcinator module' appears identical in function to the mind-controlling cerebro-shells previously seen in [A1.1] 'Plague of the Insecticons'; the idea of an Autobot being commandeered by car thieves originated in [A1.2] 'Missing in Action'; and Bumblebee deserting his fellow Autobots has strong parallels with events in [12.2] 'Crisis of Command'.

UK Changes:

Page 1, panel 1: 'colors' is changed to 'colours'.
Page 7, panel 6: 'totaled' is altered to 'totalled'.
Page 11, panel 3: 'maneuvers' is amended to read 'maneoeuvres' [sic]. (The correct UK

spelling is 'manoeuvres'.)

Roll Call:
Autobots: Optimus Prime, Prowl, Ratchet, Wheeljack, Bumblebee and Jetfire.

Decepticons: Starscream, Skywarp, Thundercracker, Laserbeak, Buzzsaw and Shockwave.

It's possible that one of either Skywarp or Thundercracker is actually absent from this story. We never see more than two of the Decepticon jets at any one time, and due to some poor colouring in this issue, it's hard to tell who is who.

Data File: Len Kaminski (writer)
Following his work on *The Transformers*, Kaminski wrote for a number of prestigious titles, including *Web of Spider-Man*, *The Avengers* and *Iron Man*, on the latter of which he had a long run. He also edited *Captain America*, *Fantastic Four* and *Thor*.

Data File: Graham Nolan (artist)
Best known for his work with DC Comics, Nolan provided art for a great many *Batman*-related titles over the years, and co-created the villain Bane. His other credits include *The Phantom*, *X-Men Forever* and *Green Lantern*.

Review:
After the rather wacky adventures of recent months, this is a refreshing change of pace – we're finally getting back to the straight-out action stories of the earlier issues.

That said, this story is perhaps a little *too* straightforward. It plays safe – it's solid and entertaining but lacks the spark usually evident in other issues. Read straight after [15] 'I, Robot-Master' this feels like a breath of fresh air, but in the grand scheme of things it is as generic as the comic ever gets. 2/5

The Back-Up Strips, Part 9: *Rocket Raccoon*
Deliciously bizarre tales of an anthropomorphic alien raccoon. The character finally reached a wider audience as a major character in the movie *Guardians of the Galaxy* (James Gunn, 2014).

- 'Rocket Raccoon' (aka 'Animal Crackers') (UK#55-57), from *Rocket Raccoon* #1 (May 1985). Ranger Rocket investigates the assassination of Lord Dyvyne's chief toysmith.
- 'The Masque of the Red Breath' (UK#58-61), from *Rocket Raccoon* #2 (June 1985). Against the backdrop of the Great Masquerade, Rocket searches for his kidnapped girlfriend, the otter Lylla.
- 'The Book of Revelations' (UK#62-65), from *Rocket Raccoon* #3 (July 1985). Fed up with the constant attacks, Rocket teams up with former enemy Blackjack O'Hare and goes on the offensive.
- 'The Age of Enlightenment' (UK#66-69), from *Rocket Raccoon* #4 (August 1985). Uncle Pyko has a plan to cure the Loonies of their insanity.

[16.1] ROBOT BUSTER!
- UK#59, 3 May 1986 (Part 1), 11 pages
- UK#60, 10 May 1986 (Part 2), 11 pages

Credits:
Simon Furman (script); Barry Kitson (plot idea; art, part 1; pencils, part 2); Tim Perkins (inks, part 2); Josie Firmin (colours, part 1); TM Cooks (colours, part 2); Annie Halfacree (letters); Ian Rimmer (editor); Geoff Senior (cover, UK#59); Barry Kitson (cover, UK#60).

Rather than use traditional painted colours, for Part 2 Marvel experimented with the American-style colour separation technique, with unsatisfactory results. The colouring credit went to T M Cooks, an in-house pseudonym (the T M standing for Too Many). (The only other recorded usage of this moniker came just a few months later, for the cover art of Marvel UK's *Spider Man and Zoids* #47.)

Plot:
Ratchet and Wheeljack build a robotic 'battle-suit' for Buster, so that he can defend himself if attacked by Decepticons. Optimus Prime orders the suit destroyed, arguing that Buster's safety would be better served by keeping a low profile.

In a bid to prove Prime wrong, Buster sneaks into the repair bay and steals the battle-suit. He travels to Fortress Sinister, hoping to salvage some Decepticon equipment. However, the Decepticons have the same idea, with Shockwave and Frenzy also present at the now-derelict HQ.

Thanks to the battle-suit, Buster is able to survive an encounter with the relatively small and weak Frenzy, but is completely outmatched by Shockwave. After a game of cat-and-mouse around the nearby mountains, Shockwave finally corners the human, and moves in for the kill.

However, the Autobots arrive just in time. Outgunned, Shockwave lets Buster go – but he now knows that the Autobots have a special affinity for the human, which may just prove to be their downfall ...

Notes:
This story shows us some never-before-seen areas of the *Ark*: the battle-suit is constructed in Repair Bay Two, and we also discover that Buster has a bedroom on board, complete with bed and dresser. Wheeljack is currently working on the ship's 'stellar drive boosters', the first hint that the *Ark* will once again leave the Earth.

Prime makes a reference to the 'Argon Nebulae'. The most abundant elements found in standard stellar nebulae are hydrogen and helium, so perhaps the Autobots have knowledge of some incredibly bizarre nebulae in which argon is instead the primary constituent. Another possibility is that Prime is referring to nebulae located in the ancient constellation of Argo (aka Argo Navis), which represented the vessel crewed by Jason and the Argonauts. Nebulae within this constellation include the Carina, Keyhole and Homunculus nebulae.

(While on the subject of the *Argo*, compare the name of Jason's mythical vessel with that of the Autobots' own ship. In the Jason stories the *Argo* contains a selection of mighty warriors on a great quest. Clearly this is a much better thematic match for the Autobot *Ark* than its biblical namesake.)

Prime refers to Ratchet as a 'seasoned and trusted warrior' – compare this with Ratchet's lack of fighting skills in [7] 'Warrior School'. One possible explanation for the discrepancy is that Ratchet lied about his military qualifications in order to secure a spot on the *Ark*.

The idea of humans piloting giant robots (or mecha, to use the proper terminology) was quite popular in the 1980s - indeed many of the earlier Transformers toys contain cockpits as a holdover from their origins as part of the Japanese Diaclone toy line (1980). Other contemporary media showcasing mecha included *Macross/Robotech* (1982), *Zoids* (1982) and most famously *Aliens* (James Cameron, 1986).

Buster mocks the Autobot leader's orders by sarcastically commenting, 'Prime hath spoken'. This is another biblical reference – Psalms 62:11 'God hath spoken' and Isaiah 1:2 'The Lord hath spoken' being two examples.

Shockwave recalls his previous defeats. He remembers being buried under tons of rock following his skirmish with the Dinobots (originally depicted in [4] 'The Last Stand'). He also recalls 'days or months' of interment in a swamp (into which he sank during the events of [12] 'Prime Time'), during which he nearly succumbed to insanity.

Oddly, Shockwave is neither mentioned by name, nor clearly seen, until the final panel of part one. This was presumably intended to keep the villain's identity a mystery for as long as possible, but it's very obvious that Shockwave is the 'surprise' antagonist long before the cliffhanger reveal.

The title is a reference to that of the movie *Ghostbusters* (Ivan Reitman, 1984), and the front cover artwork to issue 59 pays homage to that film's famous logo.

Base Jumping

The Decepticons seem to have so many bases that it's not easy to keep track of them all. Here's a handy guide to locating the Decepticon forces:

Fortress Sinister:
Built in [2] 'Power Play', this is the Decepticons' first HQ on Earth. It's also seen in [3] 'Prisoner of War', [4] 'The Last Stand' and the 'flashback stories' [4.3] 'The Enemy Within' and [8.1] 'Decepticon Dam-Busters'.

The *Ark*:
After the arrival of Shockwave, the Decepticons deactivate the Autobots and decamp to the *Ark*, in [5] 'The New Order'. Even though they take over the oil platform and the aerospace plant (see below), they maintain a presence in the Autobot vessel until [8] 'Repeat Performance', when the Decepticons leave of their own volition. Megatron stays behind to hold the fort, but when he is defeated by Ratchet and the Dinobots, the *Ark* is reclaimed by the Autobots.

Blackrock offshore oil platform:
First sighted in [5] 'The New Order', it's annexed by Shockwave in [6] 'The Worse of Two Evils'. It's not seen again until [14] 'Rock and Roll-Out', when the Decepticons abandon the rig.

Blackrock Aerospace Plant Number One:
This complex is commandeered by the Decepticons in [7] 'Warrior School', and appears to be their main base of operations until Shockwave's defeat in [12] 'Prime Time'.

Fortress Sinister (again):
With the *Ark* and the aerospace plant both lost, Soundwave sets up camp in Fortress Sinister, as seen in [12.2] 'Crisis of Command'. Presumably this is also base camp throughout [12.4] 'Dinobot Hunt'.

'Makeshift Fortress':
Shockwave is seen ransacking Fortress Sinister in [16.1] 'Robot Buster', ostensibly because he sees it as symbolising Megatron's rule over the Decepticons. In that story the HQ is described as 'untouched' and completely vacant but for Shockwave and Frenzy. Due to this hatred of Fortress Sinister, Shockwave sets up the temporary HQ we see in [16] 'Plight of the Bumblebee'.

Roll Call :
Autobots: Optimus Prime, Prowl, Ratchet, Wheeljack, Trailbreaker, Bumblebee and Tracks.

Although it can be assumed that one of the block-coloured Autobots seen near the end of part two is Prowl, it could just as easily be Smokescreen, who has a similar body-type.

Decepticons: Frenzy and Shockwave.

Other: Buster.

Data File: Tim Perkins (artist)
Perkins' credits include issues of *2000 AD*, *Doctor Who Magazine*, *Biker Mice from Mars* and *Action Force*.

Review:
Human-centric stories have thus far been amongst the comic's weakest instalments, but fortunately – despite the predictable plotting – this one isn't a complete disaster. It is helped by the fact that the likeable Buster is placed centre-stage. He has been absent from the series since [12.1] 'Christmas Breaker', and it's nice to see him return to the action, although the story itself isn't particularly involving. 2/5

[16.2] DEVASTATION DERBY!
* UK#61, 17 May 1986 (Part 1), 11 pages
* UK#62, 24 May 1986 (Part 2), 11 pages

Credits:
Simon Furman (script); Will Simpson (art); John Burns (colours); Mike Scott (letters); Ian Rimmer (editor); Will Simpson (cover, UK#61); Robin Smith (cover, UK#62).

Plot:
Following his recent encounter with Buster, Shockwave has determined that the Autobots' devotion to their young friend could prove to be their Achilles' heel. He sends Soundwave and the Constructicons on a mission to kidnap the boy.

Meanwhile, Buster has recently been having some strange nightmares, populated by special combining Transformers of a new and sophisticated design. In order to take his mind off recent events, he seeks fun and relaxation at a local demolition derby. The Autobots also go, hoping to keep an eye on the troubled human. However, the Decepticons turn up, and all-out carnage ensues. When the Constructicons unite to form Devastator, this reminds Buster of the combining Transformers in his recent nightmares; the mental strain is too much for the youngster, who falls unconscious.

On the point of capturing the human, Soundwave scans Buster's mind – only to see for himself Buster's dreams of a new breed of Transformer. Realising that the visions could be used to create new Decepticons, he calls off the attack and lets Buster leave unharmed.

Notes:
Peaking in popularity in the 1970s, the demolition derby (or 'banger racing', as it's known in the UK) is a sport where drivers deliberately crash into their opponents' vehicles, the winner being the one who has the last car remaining functional. Contestants regularly give themselves over-the-top nicknames (much like those of professional wrestlers) – 'Mike Mayhem' is mentioned on a poster seen here. Events occur primarily during the summer months, usually as part of a county or state fair, so Sparkplug's assertion that the derby comes round 'once a month' is a bit odd. One can only presume that in the spring/summer of 1986 these fairs were spaced out quite regularly. Those local to Portland would have included the Washington County Fair in Hillsboro, the Clackamas County Fair in Canby and the Multnomah County Fair in Portland itself.

This story features the second example of native Cybertronian writing seen in the comic. The first was in [7] 'Warrior School' – there it was inscribed on the ceremonial urn used in the Rite of Oneness. Here the lettering is written on Smokescreen's handheld communicator. It appears stylistically different from the glyphs that have been seen previously (and will be seen again in [23] 'Decepticon Graffiti'), indicating that there is more than one language on the planet.

(As an aside, it seems odd that the Transformers would have a written language, given that, as robots, they can presumably store and transmit information electronically. Even if a written language *were* required, the likelihood is that it would be in a very concise, functional format, like a modern-day Quick Response (QR) code or even microdots.)

The Autobots' dummy drivers, introduced in [14] 'Rock and Roll-Out', are referred to here as Facsimile Constructs. This is the comics' very first use of that phrase, which will later be applied to any lifelike copy or decoy, even including faux-Transformers (see also [20.2] 'Target: 2006' and [23.1] 'Prey').

The ever-changing sign on Sparkplug's garage has reverted back to 'Witwicky Auto Repair' in this story, as per [9] 'Dis-Integrated Circuits'; different wordings have been seen in the interim, most recently in [11] 'Brainstorm'.

There are many references to the previous story, [16.1] 'Robot Buster'. Soundwave mentions the Constructicons' poor showing in [10] 'The Next Best Thing to Being There', and Buster's nightmares are explained as an after-effect of his time spent as holder of the Creation Matrix, as seen in the sequence of stories from [6] 'The Worse of Two Evils' to [12] 'Prime Time'.

Roll Call:
Autobots: Optimus Prime, Ironhide, Ratchet, Wheeljack, Brawn, Smokescreen and Tracks.

An image of the yet-to-be-created **Superion** is also seen here.

Decepticons: Soundwave, Shockwave, Scrapper, Scavenger, Mixmaster, Bonecrusher, Long Haul, Hook and Devastator.

Although Scavenger appeared in [12.4] 'Dinobot Hunt', this is the first sighting of the remainder of the Constructicons since their debut in [10] 'The Next Best Thing to Being There'.

Other: Buster, Sparkplug and Jessie.

This is the first appearance of Sparkplug and Jessie in a UK-only story.

Data File: Will Simpson (artist)
Simpson's many and varied credits include art on *Judge Dredd*, *Hellblazer*, *Batman* and *The Punisher 2099*. He has since become a storyboard artist, working on films such as *Reign of Fire* (Rob Bowman, 2002) and *Unknown* (Jaume Collet-Serra, 2011) and the television series *Game of Thrones* (from 2011).

Review:
As a precursor to [16.3] 'Second Generation', this is more of an extended prologue than a story in its own right. On those terms, however, it works pretty well.

The action scenes at the demolition derby are excellent, and the artwork is fantastic throughout. Soundwave fares especially well here, featuring prominently and having most of the best lines. His 'empty speech bubble moment' (the character is so choked with outrage that he's left speechless) is an especially great touch. 3/5

Competition Time!
One of the selling-points of the UK *The Transformers* comic was the regular competitions it used to run. Prizes ranged from the very unimpressive to the very desirable ...

- UK#1: win an Autobot Jazz figure.
- UK#2: win a Transformer toy (the Thundercracker pictured is the Japanese Diaclone version with alternative decals).
- UK#2: win *Space Olympics*, a Corgi book.
- UK#3: win an Autobot mini-vehicle (illustrated by a photo of a yellow Cliffjumper variant).
- UK#4: win a copy of the soundtrack album to *The A-Team*.
- UK#4: win the Mandala board game.
- UK#5: win the Four-In-Line board game (an electronic version of Connect Four).
- UK#6: win a Bontempi synthesizer.
- UK#9: win the book *Get Into Space!*
- UK#11: win an Insecticon figure.
- UK#12: win a Crayola stencil set.

- UK#13: win the book *Draw and Colour Moving Books: Robots.*
- UK#14: win a Transformers Stunt Flyer.
- UK#15: win the book *50 Facts about Robots.*
- UK#15: win a Kodak 4000 automatic disc camera.
- UK#16: win a computer peripheral, the Valiant Turtle.
- UK#17: win a Model 8 construction kit.
- UK#19: win a watercolour paint set.
- UK#20: win a Bontempi synthesizer.
- UK#21: win a magnetic Ludo set.
- UK#22: win a Ladybird Transformers book and cassette set.
- UK#23: win a Bontempi Memo Bunny music game.
- UK#24: win Transformers transfer sets (similar to those given away free with UK#1 and 2).
- UK#25: win an aircraft model kit.
- UK#26: win a Kodak camera (in conjunction with Cadbury's Wildlife Bars).
- UK#31, 35: win some original Marvel art (in conjunction with Save the Children).
- UK#33: win a Transformers Stunt Flyer (as per UK#14).
- UK#34: win a weekend in Blackpool (in conjunction with Ty-Phoo tea).
- UK#37: win a Ladybird Transformers book and cassette set.
- UK#38: win the novelisation of *Santa Claus: The Movie.*
- UK#41: win a bundle of various Transformers goodies (books, toys etc).
- UK#60-62: win animal-themed gifts (in conjunction with Cadbury's Wildlife Bars).
- UK#68: win some Transformers Adventure Game Books.
- UK#77: win the book *How to Draw Comics the Marvel Way.*
- UK#90: win a *The Transformers: The Movie* poster.
- UK#91: win a Sony Walkman (in conjunction with Ready Brek cereal).
- UK#92: win *The Transformers: The Movie* soundtrack album.
- UK#93: win some *Transformers* VHS tapes.
- UK#98: win a *The Transformers: The Movie* book and audiocassette pack.
- UK#100: win some Transformers toys.
- UK#103: win some *Transformers* VHS tapes.
- UK#104: win some Battle Beasts figures.
- UK#105-107: win a set of felt-tip pens (in conjunction with Ricicles cereal).
- UK#114: win a wildlife gift set (in conjunction with Cadbury's Wildlife Bars).
- UK#125: win an art kit (in conjunction with Ricicles cereal).
- UK#126: win a duffle bag, joke book and ruler (in conjunction with Curly Wurly chocolate bars).
- UK#130-131: win a Headmasters videocassette.
- UK#133: win *The Transformers: The Movie* on videocassette.
- UK#133: win a portable hi-fi system (in conjunction with Rice Krispies cereal).
- UK#134: win a set of Marvel annuals.
- UK#135: win a set of Transformers books, from Corgi.
- UK#138: another chance to win a set of the Corgi books.
- UK#139: win a Dragon Lock puzzle game.
- UK#141: win a Ladybird Transformers book and cassette set.
- UK#145: win a *Transformers* videocassette.
- UK#148: win a set of adventure game books, from publishers Puffin.
- UK#152: win a set of Seacon figures.
- UK#155: win stickers and a poster (in conjunction with Ricicles cereal).

- UK#158: win *Visionaries* videocassettes.
- UK#160: win a compact camera (in conjunction with Ready Brek cereal).
- UK#162: win some Pretenders figures.
- UK#170: win *Action Force* videocassettes.
- UK#178: win a *Transformers* videocassette.
- UK#182: win a bicycle (in conjunction with Kellogg's Frosties cereal).
- UK#184: win an Optimus Prime toy.
- UK#185: win a Trypticon toy.
- UK#189: win a clock radio (in conjunction with Ready Brek cereal).
- UK#198: win a set of Marvel annuals.
- UK#200: win a set of Micromasters.
- UK#225: another chance to win a set of Micromasters.
- UK#232-235: win Micromaster Bases and Transports.
- UK#242: win an activity pack – pencils, toys etc (in conjunction with Fiendish Feet yoghurts).
- UK#250: win a Micromaster rocket base.
- UK#260-261: win a set of Transformers Classic Heroes figures.
- UK#264: win Micromaster bases.
- UK#265: win a microscope (in conjunction with Weetos breakfast cereal).
- UK#277-279: win Micromaster Combiner bases.
- UK#283: win a Peugeot mountain bike (in conjunction with Monster Munch corn snacks).
- UK#287: win a plush animal toy (in conjunction with the charitable event, World Animal Day).
- UK#288: win some *Incredible Hulk* videocassettes.
- UK#289: win a *Transformers* videocassette.
- UK#294: win some Halloween-themed goodies (in conjunction with Fiendish Feet yoghurts).
- UK#296: win a 'Wildlife Explorer's Kit' (in conjunction with NatWest Bank and the WWF).
- UK#296: win videocassettes of the *RoboCop* animated series.
- UK#311: win a set of Transformers Triple Changers and Classic Heroes figures.
- UK#316: win some *Beetlejuice* action figures.
- UK#319: win tickets to Thorpe Park (a theme park).
- UK#321: win a Go Green! board game (in association with NatWest Bank and the WWF).
- UK#321: win a radio (in conjunction with Robinsons fruit drinks).
- UK#325: win Happy Cube puzzle games (in conjunction with Weetos breakfast cereal).
- UK#327: win a Halloween Pack (pens, face-paints etc – in conjunction with Fiendish Feet yoghurts).
- UK#328: win a Transformers Overlord figure, with videos for the runners-up.

[16.3] SECOND GENERATION!
- UK#63, 31 May 1986 (Part 1), 11 pages
- UK#64, 7 June 1986 (Part Two), 11 pages
- UK#65, 14 June 1986 (Part 3), 11 pages

Credits:

Simon Furman (script); John Stokes (art, part 1); Barry Kitson (pencils, part 2); Tim Perkins (inks, part 2); Jeff Anderson (art, part 3); Josie Firmin (colours, part 1); Steve Whitaker and Stuart Place (colours, part 2); Tony Jozwiak (colours, part 3); Mike Scott (letters, parts 1-2); Annie Halfacree (letters, part 3); Ian Rimmer (editor); Alan Stevens (cover design, UK#63); Geoff Senior (cover, UK#64); Robin Smith (cover, UK#65).

NB: There was no new cover art for issue 63, instead pictures from the toys' box art were pasted onto a blue and white background – hence the unusual 'cover design' credit.

At this point in the UK comic's history, Stuart Place appears to have been the 'go-to guy' for helping out in the colouring department, presumably when the original colourist was in danger of missing their deadline. Place was also given co-colouring credits on issues #43, #44 and #46.

In part 2, the change in colourists is particularly noticeable. Whitaker paints Megatron's chest gold, Buster's T-shirt is white and the clouds billowing from the power station chimneys are grey. When Place takes over for the last three pages, the smoke clouds are now a pale brown, Buster's T-shirt has changed to green and Megatron is now sporting his familiar grey chest.

Plot:
In order to get to the bottom of Buster's nightmarish visions, Optimus Prime once more links his brain with the young human's mind.

The two experience a dream – or possibly a vision of the future – and witness a battle between the Autobot and Decepticon Special Teams, groups of robots with the ability to combine into larger, gestalt Transformers. However, utilising the equipment previously employed to extract the Creation Matrix from Prime's brain, Shockwave also monitors the dream and puts his own plan in motion to build these powerful new Transformers.

At the Wyoming coal mine, Megatron and Shockwave finally come face to face, but are convinced by Soundwave to put their animosity aside and share leadership duties.

Notes:
This story was written at the behest of Hasbro, who wanted some product placement for their new combining Special Teams figures. They are seen here only in an extended dream sequence, so as not to contradict their 'proper' introduction, in the US-originated [21] 'Aerialbots over America', which was not due to be printed in the UK comic for another five months.

The dream sequence shows the Autobots helping to evacuate a stricken power station, only to run into the Decepticons, who are attacking the plant as a diversion to cover a simultaneous attack on the *Ark*. The dream is described as a 'vision of the future', but it never actually comes to pass in later comics. (After the Special Teams are built, the Decepticons never attack the *Ark* while Optimus Prime is alive.) However, future-history is possibly scrambled somewhat by Galvatron's time-travelling in [20.2] 'Target: 2006' *et al*, so it's possible that all this might have actually happened were it not for Galvatron's tinkering with history.

This story was heavily trailed in UK#54 (the second part of [14] 'Rock and Roll-Out'), which included a free pull-out mini-comic, 'The Special Teams Have Arrived', which expanded on the events of the dream sequence. There we discover that the station's name is the (fictional) Pullen Power Plant, and that its evacuation comes as a result of some landslides in the vicinity. This information is brought to us by *NTV News*

– actually a real-life programme broadcast on Nebraska television, an affiliate of the US broadcasting giant ABC. Nebraska borders Wyoming, where the Decepticons are based, and so would make an ideal local target for the Decepticons.

Given Shockwave's aversion to Fortress Sinister, as seen in [16.1] 'Robot Buster', the Decepticon HQ seen here is probably the 'Makeshift Fortress' that first appeared in [16] 'Plight of the Bumblebee'.

This story sees the return of the Dinobots, who were left comatose following their mental breakdown in [12.4] 'Dinobot Hunt'. A caption advises readers to check out the latest *The Transformers* Annual for more details of their recent malaise – a reference to the story [A2.5] 'Victory'.

Megatron becomes joint leader of the Decepticons here, marking the first time he's really been in a command position since [4] 'The Last Stand'.

As is to be expected by now, there are copious mentions of prior events. There are references to Soundwave scanning Buster's mind (and Ratchet 'kidnapping' the boy) in [16.1] 'Robot Buster'. Donny Finkleberg is still in Decepticon custody as per [15] 'I, Robot-Master'. Reference is made to the previous Megatron/Shockwave battle in [6] 'The Worse of Two Evils'. There are also flashbacks to Buster's story so far: his encounter with Bumblebee in [1] 'The Transformers', his first mindlink with Prime in [6] 'The Worse of Two Evils', and his relinquishing of the Creation Matrix in [12] 'Prime Time'.

As well as the usual recaps of previous stories, there are also many portents of future events. In order to perfect the creation of the Special Teams, Optimus Prime will need to find 'some way of observing' the combination process – this is a reference to [19] 'Command Performances', in which Bumblebee records details of the Constructicons' transformation sequence.

Also, Megatron's and Shockwave's temporary reconciliation here acts as a rationale for their more cordial (but still strained) relationship we shall see in [18] 'The Bridge to Nowhere'. The final panels show Soundwave's electromagnetic message, sent in [10] 'The Next Best Thing to Being There', arriving at its Cybertronian destination, leading into [17] 'The Smelting Pool'.

Stop the World, I Want to Get off

In [10] 'The Next Best Thing to Being There', the Transformers' home planet Cybertron was described as being 'hundreds of light-years away', albeit couched in terms of 'inter-dimensional space'. Here Cybertron is referred to as being 'in a galaxy far, far beyond our own'. Can this be right?

Well, it depends on the speed at which Cybertron is travelling away from our galaxy (remember, it was knocked out of its orbit around Alpha Centauri, a star system relatively close to our own). For comparison, Earth is shooting through space at around 575,000mph (taking into consideration its orbit around the Sun, the Sun's path through the Milky Way and the Milky Way's speed through the cosmos relative to other galaxies). This equates to a speed of around 0.00086 light years per year. So assuming that Cybertron has been hurtling through space at the same speed as Earth, then in four million years it would travel 3425 light years, which considering the Milky Way is 120,000 light years across, is not exactly an intergalactic distance. Even if Cybertron's journey began four million years *before* the *Ark* mission (i.e. a total journey time of eight million years), and it was flying through space at a hundred times the speed of Earth, that's still only a distance equivalent to 57% of the Milky Way's circumference.

Presumably, then, the planet must have navigated through a wormhole or suchlike in order to get so distant; perhaps the creation of the Space Bridge – see [18] 'The Bridge to Nowhere' – could also have had some kind of space-warping effect.

US *The Transformers* writer Bob Budiansky would eventually provide a much more reasonable location for Cybertron – in [29] 'Crater Critters' the planet is said to be only 'several dozen' light years away from Earth.

Roll Call:
Autobots: Optimus Prime, Jazz (in a dream), Ratchet, Hound, Wheeljack, Bumblebee (flashback only), Grimlock, Slag, Sludge and Swoop. Plus (in a vision) the Aerialbots: **Silverbolt**, **Air Raid**, **Fireflight**, **Skydive**, **Slingshot** (and their combined form, **Superion**); and the Protectobots: **Hot Spot**, **Streetwise**, **Blades**, **Groove**, **First Aid** (and their combined form, **Defensor**).

Hot Spot is incorrectly named 'Hotspot' (a single word) both here and in the 'Special Teams Have Arrived' mini-comic.

Superion had previously been depicted in [16.2] 'Devastation Derby', in one of Buster's drawings.

Although seen in Buster's dream, Jazz is presumably still dead due to the injuries received in [12.4] 'Dinobot Hunt'; his corpse was last sighted in [14] 'Rock and Roll-Out'. In a similar vein, this is the first appearance of Hound since he was presumably damaged in [12.3] 'The Icarus Theory'; again, his inactive body was sighted in [14] 'Rock and Roll-Out'.

Decepticons: Megatron, Soundwave, Ravage, Shockwave and Mixmaster. Plus (in a vision) the Combaticons: **Onslaught**, **Brawl**, **Blast Off**, **Swindle**, **Vortex** (and their combined form, **Bruticus**). The Stunticons: **Motormaster**, **Drag Strip**, **Dead End**, **Wildrider**, **Breakdown** (and their combined form, **Menasor**).

Buzzsaw is mentioned in passing, but not seen.

Other: Buster, Sparkplug, Jessie and Donny Finkleberg.

Data File: Josie Firmin (colourist)
Josie Firmin is the daughter of Peter Firmin, co-creator of many classic British television series for children, including *The Clangers* and *Bagpuss*. Her other comics work includes *Care Bears*.

Review:
Although it's just a glorified toy advertisement, introducing no fewer than 24 new Transformers, the shameless marketing is thankfully limited to the terrible middle issue. Either side of that, there's a surprising amount of fun to be had here.

The first part contains a wonderfully scary dream sequence, unnerving and surreal, while part three takes us back to the main plot – the Dinobots return, there's a power-struggle for the Decepticon leadership, and Soundwave is once again on top form.

However, the narrative structure is terribly disjointed (part three, oddly, is pretty much unrelated to the rest of the story) and, coupled with the awful second issue, that makes this story difficult to recommend. 2/5

[17] RETURN TO CYBERTRON PART 1: THE SMELTING POOL!
US#17, 'June 1986' (published February 1986), 22 pages.

British reprint: UK#66, 21 June 1986 (Part One), 11 pages; UK#67, 28 June 1986 (Part Two), 11 pages.

Credits:
Bob Budiansky (script); Don Perlin (pencils); Keith Williams (inks); Nel Yomtov (colours); Janice Chiang (letters); Michael Carlin (editor); Jim Shooter (editor-in-chief); Herb Trimpe (cover). **UK:** Herb Trimpe (cover, UK#66 – reuse of US cover); John Higgins (cover, UK#67).

Plot:
Cybertron, the present day. Since the disappearance of the *Ark* and the Autobot leader Optimus Prime, the tide of war has turned in the Decepticons' favour. Small, rag-tag groups of Autobots commit raids from secret underground lairs, while the Decepticon Lord Straxus commands from his impressive citadel, Darkmount.

The diminutive Autobot Scrounge receives a tip that something big is happening at Decepticon HQ. He infiltrates the base and records a mysterious encoded transmission that the Decepticons are in the process of decrypting. However, before he can deliver the information to his Autobot contact Blaster, he is captured by the Decepticons and flung into the Smelting Pool – a pit of molten metal.

Blaster is concerned when Scrounge fails to make the scheduled rendezvous, and defies the orders of his commander, Perceptor, in order to track down the missing informant.

Blaster allows himself to be captured and is himself hurled into the Smelting Pool. There he meets a dying Scrounge, whose last act is to give Blaster a copy of his recording. Blaster is rescued from the pool by his fellow Autobots, who return to their base and decode the transmission.

It is a message from the Decepticons on Earth – Optimus Prime is alive!

Notes:
This is the first story to be set entirely on Cybertron, and we find out an awful lot about the planet, its geography and its culture.

The province of Polyhex is commanded by its Lord High Governor, Straxus, from his seat of power at Darkmount. There appears to be an acute energy crisis; Straxus' Decepticons routinely round up Autobots and neutralist Cybertronians, smelting them down into raw materials to be used in the construction of new Decepticon troops (and also, presumably, the space bridge, which we see here in an incomplete state, although its name and function are not yet revealed).

This is the first we hear of neutral Cybertronians, who have no alignment to either the Autobot or the Decepticon cause. They are still referred to as 'Transformers', however, so it's likely they have the same shape-changing abilities as their warrior compatriots.

One group of neutralists, known as the 'Empties', are beggars who conglomerate in a Skid Row-esque area known as Dead End; they spend their days pleading for fuel and circuit-boards from passers-by. Another neutral is mentioned in dialogue but not seen – Spanner, a renowned interdimensional engineer.

A small band of Autobots is based in an underground lair named Autobase. They are led by Perceptor, and their complex includes a Hall of Fame, which contains statues of presumed-dead Autobot heroes such as Optimus Prime, Bumblebee and Wheeljack.

This is arguably the first Transformers comic strip to have been influenced by the upcoming theatrical release *The Transformers: The Movie*, which would come out in August 1986 but was in production throughout 1985. (The US comic's creative staff would have had insider knowledge of this. The movie was mentioned in the letters page in US#17.) Cybertron is for the first time depicted with two moons, as featured prominently in the movie, and Beachcomber's Cybertronian vehicle mode strongly resembles that of the Movie Autobot Kup. (It could perhaps be claimed that the two moons were first glimpsed in Huffer's hologram in [10] 'The Next Best Thing to Being There', but the artwork there is not at all clear.)

It's probable that, despite having not been shown (clearly) before, the moons have always orbited Cybertron. It's just about feasible that they could instead be relatively recent artificial constructs, but given the current Cybertronian fuel crisis, this seems very unlikely. Another outside possibility is that they are objects that have been naturally caught up in Cybertron's gravitational pull, but it would be a huge coincidence for the planet to have attracted two stray moons that just happen to look like mini-versions of itself.

Blaster's skin here is described as being of steel, confirming Shockwave's assertion in [8] 'Repeat Performance' that Transformers (or at least some of them) are constructed from a nuclear-hardened version of the compound. Presumably, the elements in alien Cybertronian steel are quite different from those used in the creation of the Earthly version (iron, carbon, manganese etc). 'Smelting' is a real-world metallurgical term, and refers to the process of reducing ores to their base metal constituents.

This is the first time we hear mention of Cybertronian time units. One vorn is approximately equal to 83 Earth years; the *Ark*'s disappearance occurred 'almost 50,000 vorns ago' (nearly 4,150,000 years). A breem is equivalent to around 8.3 Earth-minutes. It's probable that, just like human cultures, the Transformers base these units of time on celestial motion. (Scrounge at one point refers to 'millennia', i.e. thousands of Cybertronian years.) A vorn, therefore, could well be the length of time it took for Cybertron to orbit Alpha Centauri.

Aside from the new regulars that debut here, we meet some one-off Transformers. Telus and Rotorbolt are neutrals, killed and taken to the Smelting Pool via a Decepticon Harvester Unit. Wheezel is one of the unfortunate inhabitants of Dead End, and provides information in exchange for fuel. Ferak is a Decepticon who pilots (or possibly transforms into) a 'hunter-seeker skyship'.

Finally (and most memorably) we have the Autobot Scrounge, who transforms into a yellow disc. He has a special arm with extendable fingers equipped with monitoring devices. He intercepts Soundwave's message – sent in [10] 'The Next Best Thing to Being There' – of which we finally see the contents. The message is a brief description of Earth and the Transformers' adventures there, plus details of how the planet's resources could be used to refuel Cybertron. The two Earthbound factions are described as having been 'led' (past tense) by Megatron and Optimus Prime. (At the time of Soundwave's transmission, Megatron was presumed dead and Optimus Prime in captivity.)

UK Notes:
When it's stated that the materials gleaned from the Smelting Pool will be used to create new Decepticon troops, this is probably a reference to mindless drones (such as the harvester vehicles); it's unlikely that Straxus has access to the Matrix Flame (which gives consciousness to new Transformers – see '[20.2] Target: 2006'.)

UK Changes:
Page 1, panel 1: 'penciler' and 'colorist' are changed to 'pencils' and 'colour' respectively.
Page 4, panel 8: 'maneuver' is edited to read 'manoeuvre'.
Page 8, panel 1: 'favour' is amended to 'favour'.
Page 22, panel 3: the reference to issue 10 is changed to issue 36.
Page 22, panel 5: 'endeavor' is altered to 'endeavour'.

Roll Call:
Autobots: Optimus Prime (depicted in Soundwave's message), **Blaster**, **Powerglide**, **Cosmos**, **Seaspray**, **Warpath**, **Beachcomber** and **Perceptor**.

Although he makes his comics debut here, Cosmos had previously appeared in the Annual story [A1.2] 'Missing in Action'. Statues of Optimus Prime, Bumblebee and Wheeljack are also seen here.

Decepticons: Megatron, Starscream, Soundwave, Laserbeak, Ravage (all of whom appear only in Soundwave's communiqué), **Shrapnel**, **Bombshell**, **Kickback**, **Ramjet**, **Thrust**, **Dirge** and **Straxus**.

Shrapnel, Bombshell and Kickback (or possibly clones thereof) had featured in the Annual story [A1.1] 'Plague of the Insecticons'. Thrust and Dirge had likewise been seen in [A1.4] 'Hunted'.
   In Soundwave's message, the Decepticons are block-coloured, so the condor Decepticon could just as easily be Buzzsaw. Equally, the jet Transformer could well be Skywarp or Thundercracker. However, I've assumed they are Laserbeak and Starscream, the most 'famous' of their respective body-types.

Data File: Janice Chiang (letterer)
A prolific letterer, at one stage Chiang was performing this task on up to ten comics per month. Her CV reads like a *Who's Who* of comics, with credits on *Batman*, *The Adventures of Superman*, *The Amazing Spider-Man* and *The Incredible Hulk*.

Review:
An extraordinarily grim tale, 'The Smelting Pool' depicts Cybertron as a bleak, hopeless society, replete with beggars, overlords, torture and despair. The two (anti-)heroes of the piece are Blaster, despondent and angry, and the tragic Scrounge, a classic boy-who-cried-wolf character, who has his arm ripped off before being smelted to death in a pit of lava.
   It's an interesting departure for the US comic, especially considering that three of its past four issues have been very light-hearted in tone. However, it works very well here – Cybertron's terrible fate seems all the more grim for coming after a run of 'funny'

Earth-based stories. We can almost forgive the excesses of Joey Slick and Donny Finkleberg – if nothing else, they work now in hindsight as a stark contrast to the darker tone used here, making it seem even grimmer by comparison.

Where this story really excels is in its world-building. Writer Bob Budiansky pulls out all the stops here, creating cities, provinces, slums, characters and even alien time-units, in order to presnt an overall picture of Cybertron that is at once both awe-inspiring and grotesque. One of the very best *The Transformers* instalments. 5/5

US Advertisements, Part 1: Food and Drink
If you re-read the old *The Transformers* comics, you'll find a lot more than just action and adventure – it gives one a warm glow of nostalgia to pore through advertisements for '80s products such as the Nintendo Cereal System, *George Brett's Secrets of Baseball* and the *ALF* fan club. Below is a list of all the food and drink products advertised within the pages of the American comic. (NB: The regular pages of miscellaneous classified ads aren't included in these lists. Cross-promotions of the 'Eat Cheerios and win a chance to see *The Muppets Take Manhattan*' type are listed under the company that *placed* the ad (in this case, Cheerios).

Bonkers! (fruit candy) – US#3, 5, 7-8, 10, 18-23, 28-29; MOV#1
Bubble Yum (bubblegum) – US#47
Campbell's (tinned soup) – US#51-53
Candilicious (fruit candy) – US#43-45
Cap'n Crunch (breakfast cereal) – US#12, 24-25, 27-28; MOV#2-3; GIJ#1-2, 4
Capri Sun (fruit drink) – US#75-77, 80
Cheerios (breakfast cereal) – US#1
Chips Ahoy! (cookies) – US#28, 32-33, 35, 37, 43, 45-46, 58-66; HDM#2
Cocoa Puffs (breakfast cereal) – US#75
David (seed snacks) – US#20
Dorman's (processed cheese slices) – US#7, 12
Fruity Pebbles/Cocoa Pebbles (breakfast cereals) – US#58
Gum Dingers (gum-filled lollipops) – US#21-27; MOV#1-3; GIJ#1-4
Honey Nut Cheerios (breakfast cereal) – US#71, 76
Honeycomb (breakfast cereal) – US#10
Jolly Rancher (fruit candies) – US#21, 26, 42; GIJ#3
Lucky Charms (breakfast cereal) – US#58-66, 76, 79
M&M's (chocolate candies) – US#15-38, 45-46; MOV#1-3; GIJ#1-4; HDM#1-4
Mars confectionary (Skittles, Starburst) – US#22
Morning Funnies (breakfast cereal) – US#53
Nabisco confectionary (Charleston Chew, Sugar Daddy, Sugar Babies) – US#12, 19
Nestlé Quik (chocolate milk mix) – US#7-9, 12-14, 58-61
Newtons (fruit chewy cookies) – US#1-4, 8-9, 11-12
Nintendo Cereal System (breakfast cereal) – US#56
Oreo (cookies) – US#5-7, 10-11, 30; HDM#1
Payday (candy bars) – US#7
Quaker Instant Oatmeal – US#62-66
Rain-Blo and Super Bubble (bubblegum) – US#29-31; HDM#1
Reese's Pieces (peanut butter candy) – US#5-6, 8, 10
Starburst (fruit chews) – US#12

Tang (breakfast beverage crystals) – US#30, 36; HDM#1, 4
Teenage Mutant Ninja Turtles Cereal – US#78
Tootsie Rolls (chewy chocolate candy) – US#6, 9
Trix (breakfast cereal) – US#59-66, 77
Twizzlers (fruit candy sticks) – US#7, 9
Yummy Mummy (breakfast cereal) – US#48

[18] THE BRIDGE TO NOWHERE!

US#18, 'July 1986' (published March 1986), 22 pages.

British reprint: UK#68, 5 July 1986 (Part One), 11 pages; UK#69, 12 July 1986 (Part Two), 11 pages.

Credits:

Bob Budiansky (script); Don Perlin (pencils); Keith Williams and Vince Colletta (inks); Nel Yomtov (colours); Janice Chiang (letters); Michael Carlin (editor); Jim Shooter (editor-in-chief); Herb Trimpe (cover). **UK:** Phil Gascoine (cover, UK#68); Herb Trimpe (cover, UK#69 – reuse of US cover with some modifications to the background).

Vince Colletta was well known in the comics industry as an extremely fast inker, and would often be called upon to help meet deadlines if a particular comic was in danger of running late. It would appear that this issue is another such instance.

Plot:

Lord Straxus sends a message to the Decepticons on Earth – tapping the knowledge of the captive scientist Spanner, he has built a space bridge, a portal allowing instantaneous transport between Cybertron and Earth.

Perceptor's Autobot resistance cell learns of Straxus' plan, and mounts a two-pronged assault on the Decepticon forces – while the bulk of the Autobots enter into a diversionary attack on Darkmount, Blaster attempts to destroy the bridge.

Blaster is stopped in his tracks when the bridge itself transforms into Spanner – not only was the luckless scientist forced into designing the bridge, but he was forced into literally *becoming* the bridge as well. Blaster is reluctant to destroy Spanner, and his hesitancy allows the Decepticons time to realise that the bridge is under attack.

The space bridge becomes the scene of a massive Autobot/Decepticon battle. The Autobots appear defeated, but a last effort by Blaster results in the death of Straxus and some major damage to the bridge. Perceptor, Blaster and five other Autobots escape to Earth just as the space bridge dematerialises for good.

Notes:

The Earth terminus of the space bridge materialises across the Columbia River, a designated National Scenic Area on the border of Oregon and Washington. More specifically, this would seem to be set in and around the forests due north of Mount Hood, about 40 miles east of Portland.

The Decepticons' mine camp in Wyoming has undergone a bit of a facelift since last we saw it in [15] 'I, Robot-Master'. Its landscape and rock walls are now strewn with Decepticon machinery and fortifications. One such device is Soundwave's Interspace Transmitter/Receiver, which can broadcast Robot-Master's propaganda to the entirety of the North American continent.

Soundwave can also contact Straxus on Cybertron via a console set into the cliff-face; it seems he's perfected the transdimensional radio wave technology that was used to transmit his initial message in [10] 'The Next Best Thing to Being There' (presumably this time without needing to hijack a human radar dish).

Shockwave offers to construct a device to convert the mine's coal deposits into Energon cubes; it's likely he has in mind a machine similar to the power siphon destroyed by the Autobots in [14] 'Rock and Roll-Out'.

In the original American version of this story, Megatron states that he sent Laserbeak and Buzzsaw on a scouting mission. This was an attempt to correct retrospectively an error in previous issues; when the Decepticons were divided into two separate groups – Shockwave's faction and the Megatron/Soundwave group – Laserbeak and Buzzsaw were allied with Soundwave in [15] 'I, Robot-Master', but were seen with Shockwave in [16] 'Plight of the Bumblebee'.

On Cybertron, we discover that the Autobase seen in [17] 'The Smelting Pool' is, like Darkmount, located in the province of Polyhex. One-shot Transformers seen here include the ill-fated Decepticon Crosscut, and the Autobot tunnellers Corkscrew and Borebit. One of the Decepticon casualties in the climactic battle is a hunter-seeker sky ship similar to those seen at the beginning of the previous story.

Both Straxus and his Darkmount citadel are destroyed here.

UK Changes:
For the first time, some of the dialogue was heavily rewritten for the UK printing. In the UK-only stories, specifically in [16.3] 'Second Generation', Megatron and Shockwave had grudgingly put aside their differences and agreed to a joint leadership of the Decepticons, but from the US perspective the two tyrants were still at odds. Here's a comparison of the altered text (page 9, panels 5-6, and page 10, panels 1-2):

US Version:
SHOCKWAVE: How like you, Megatron, to be foolishly expending your energy on emotional outbursts … and, even worse, on a lowly human!

MEGATRON: Shockwave! I sent Laserbeak and Buzzsaw to find Starscream, Thundercracker and Skywarp – not you!

SHOCKWAVE: Then you should congratulate yourself for outperforming even your own paltry expectations … and for bringing me back to reclaim my rightful – and logical – position as leader of the Decepticons!

UK Version (changes in **bold**):
SHOCKWAVE: How like you, Megatron, to be foolishly expending your energy on emotional outbursts … and, even worse, on a lowly human!

MEGATRON: Shockwave! **Though we both command the Decepticons, I suggest you use a different tone to address me!**

SHOCKWAVE: **Perhaps the alliance was a mistake. A mistake that I must rectify! Stand aside and I shall** reclaim my rightful – and logical – position as leader of the

Decepticons!

The remainder of the changes are only minor, as follows:
Page 2, panel 1: 'penciler' and 'colorist' become 'penciller' and 'colourist'.
Page 8, panel 4: the American slang term 'shilling' is replaced by the UK slang word 'grafting'. Either term works as a description of Robot Master's work under Decepticon duress.
Page 8, panel 4: the reference to issue #15 is changed to issue #56.
Page 10, panel 5: the reference to issue #10 is changed to issue #36.
Page 16, panel 2: 'favor' is amended to read 'favour'.
Page 20, panel 1: the reference to 'last issue' is altered to 'issue 67'.

Roll Call:
Autobots: Blaster, Powerglide, Cosmos, Seaspray, Warpath, Beachcomber and Perceptor.

There's also an appearance by Scrounge, in a flashback to [17] 'The Smelting Pool'.

Decepticons: Megatron, Starscream, Skywarp, Thundercracker, Soundwave, Laserbeak, Buzzsaw, Ravage, Shockwave, Shrapnel, Bombshell, Kickback, Ramjet, Thrust, Dirge and Straxus.

Although it's likely that all three of the 'coneheads' (Ramjet, Thrust and Dirge) appear in this story, only two are ever shown at once; frustratingly, the block-colouring once again hinders attempts at positive identification.

Other: Donny Finkleberg.

Data File: Vince Colletta (artist)
Best known for his work in the so-called Silver Age of Comics, Colletta frequently inked the pencils of the legendary Jack Kirby. His impressive CV includes inks on early issues of *Daredevil* and *Fantastic Four* (for which he inked the wedding of Reed Richards and Susan Storm), as well as a run on *Thor*.

Review:
In the previous issue, we had a brilliant subplot in which an unsung Transformer endured a brave but tragic fate. Although the Spanner revelation here is well-handled (and the design of his 'robot mode' is excellent), this storyline is just too similar to the recent Scrounge plot to make as much of an impact.

Straxus, too, is a problem: here he comes across as needlessly stupid, knowingly sending Decepticons to their doom in the middle of an energy crisis, refusing to listen to good advice from Shrapnel, and clumsily demolishing the space bridge power lines. It just weakens the character and takes some of the sheen off a previously impressive creation.

On the plus side, some of the art and imagery here are brilliant. As well as the aforementioned Spanner scene, we have the memorable sight of a robot materialising and exploding in the middle of a national park, and the lurid pink interdimensional void to feast our eyes on.

There are other good moments: the final battle scenes are a feast of death and destruction, and the bickering between Megatron and Shockwave continues to amuse.

This is a decent issue, but not really in the same league as 'The Smelting Pool'. 3/5

[19] COMMAND PERFORMANCES!

US#19, 'August 1986' (published April 1986), 22 pages.

British reprint: UK#70, 19 July 1986 (Part One), 11 pages; UK#71, 26 July 1986 (Part Two), 11 pages.

Credits:
Bob Budiansky (script); Don Perlin (pencils); Ian Akin, Brian Garvey (inks); Nel Yomtov (colours); Janice Chiang (letters); Michael Carlin (editor); Jim Shooter (editor-in-chief); Herb Trimpe (cover). **UK:** John Stokes (cover, UK#70); Herb Trimpe (cover, UK#71 – reuse of US cover).

Plot:
Grapple unveils his new creation – Omega Supreme, a giant Transformer whose function is to guard the *Ark* against intruders. Leaving their base in Omega Supreme's capable hands, the remainder of the Autobots travel to the Decepticons' base in Wyoming. Their mission: to record the Constructicons' transformation sequence – this information will then assist them in building combining Transformers of their own.

The Decepticons' mine base is besieged by Autobots; Megatron figures that the *Ark* has been left unguarded and so leads a platoon of Decepticons to Mount St Hilary. They are met by Omega Supreme, who destroys most of the Decepticon attackers.

At the Wyoming mine, the Autobots' attack finally goads the Constructicons into uniting. Bumblebee records the combination process, and the Autobots beat a hasty retreat, their objective completed. Realising he has been duped, Shockwave cedes the Decepticon leadership to Megatron.

Meanwhile, Donny Finkleberg has used the battle to his advantage, and managed to escape the Decepticons while they were distracted. Ravage, however, picks up his scent and goes after him. While hunting the missing human, Ravage finds and attacks the Autobot Skids, who is presumed dead by the other Autobots.

Notes:
Yet another Transformer character is introduced to the comics, as Omega Supreme appears for the first time. He's the end result of the project that Grapple was set to work on in [14] 'Rock and Roll-Out' His skin is 'tougher than a block of triple-strength durabyllium steel'; his wing shields are impervious to Megatron's blasts and are made from a hyper-dense crystalline alloy. (Most metal alloys are crystalline or at least polycrystalline in structure, so it's only the hyper-dense part that's particularly noteworthy.)

Another notable aspect of this story is the destruction by Omega Supreme of six of the original Decepticons: Rumble, Frenzy, Buzzsaw, Starscream, Skywarp and Thundercracker. However, as is the norm (see the section **Dead or Alive** below), three of these characters – Starscream, Thundercracker and Frenzy – will return to action in the UK much sooner than in the US. It's stated here that the Decepticon wrecks have been placed in storage within the *Ark*.

It's confirmed here that the Decepticons' converted mine base is 'steel-rimmed', and that the Decepticons speak to each other in English. (Donny Finkleberg overhears them scheming.) The language was probably programmed into the Transformers when they were re-built by the *Ark* in [1] 'The Transformers'. We know that the *Ark* has the ability to monitor human broadcasts, so presumably all their knowledge of English language and idioms comes from television and radio transmissions – this would also explain the use of human slang terms by Autobots such as Jazz.)

There are, once again, references to other stories. Megatron goes to greet the newly-arrived Transformers from Cybertron, only to discover that – as seen in [18] 'The Bridge to Nowhere' – it is Blaster's Autobot group, aka the Cybertron Seven, who have travelled across. Skids' admiration of the way humans interact with their own machinery, plus his envious glance at a car getting a hose-down, foreshadow his own forthcoming antics in [20] 'Showdown'. Optimus Prime is wounded by a giant axe weapon that forms part of the Decepticon defences; this injury will become a plot point in future issues.

UK Notes:
Optimus Prime's plan to record Devastator's transformation (via an 'electro signal interceptor') was prefigured in [16.3] 'Second Generation'.

UK Changes:
For the second story running, dialogue was altered for the British printing so as better to fit into the UK continuity. From the US point of view, the story marks the first appearance of the Dinobots since they were awakened in [8] 'Repeat Performance'. It's explained that Prime has kept them hidden away in the *Ark* due to their overly-conspicuous alt-modes. The Dinobots resent this, and decide here to secede from the Autobot ranks. They aren't seen again in the US stories until their return in [27] 'King of the Hill'.

From the UK perspective, of course, the Dinobots had featured extensively in stories such as [8.2] 'The Wrath of Grimlock' and [12.4] 'Dinobot Hunt'. As well as this exchange being reworded to reflect the Dinobots' UK adventures, it was also toned down so that the Dinobots don't yet leave the Autobot ranks, allowing for their upcoming appearance in [20.1] 'In the National Interest'.

Another point to note is that in the US comics, Grimlock has a simple, childish speech pattern, clearly modelled on his popular representation in the cartoons. The UK comic, however, has thus far had Grimlock speak normally; consequently the edits to this story also serve to provide Grimlock with some rather better diction:

Page 3, panels 2-4:

US Version:
GRIMLOCK: Bah! You are a coward, Optimus Prime! You do not fight!

PRIME: Fighting is not this mission's purpose, Grimlock. You and your Dinobots must understand that.

GRIMLOCK: Dinobots understand we are warriors – but because you say we would stand out among humans we never go to war! Now you tell us go to war, but do not fight! Commander who attacks to run away cannot command Dinobots!

UK Version (changes in **bold**):
GRIMLOCK: **Enough talk. When do we get to hit something?**

PRIME: Fighting is not this mission's purpose, Grimlock. You and your Dinobots must understand that.

GRIMLOCK: **Oh, we understand, alright. Once again, you've clearly demonstrated how unfit you are to lead the Dinobots. We'll have no part in this fool's errand. Back to the *Ark*, Dinobots. We've got some talking to do …**

Another, minor dialogue alteration occurs later in the story (page 4, panel 3). Shockwave has managed to track down and retrieve the Constructicons, who haven't appeared in the US comics since their debut in [10] 'The Next Best Thing to Being There'. No other explanation is given for their absence. However, from the UK perspective, the Constructicons have been present in stories such as [12.4] 'Dinobot Hunt' and [16.2] 'Devastation Derby', so the exchange had to be re-worded slightly:

US Version – SHOCKWAVE: Even you, Megatron, must admit my finding and bringing back the Constructicons was eminently logical!

UK Version – SHOCKWAVE: Even you, Megatron, must admit **the work done by the** Constructicons was eminently logical!

One final continuity edit was made to another piece of Shockwave dialogue. His US reference to Megatron as 'our commander' was changed in the UK printing to 'co-commander' (page 10, panel 8).

Other minor changes are as follows:

Page 1, panel 1: 'penciler' and 'colorist' are changed to 'pencils' and 'colour' respectively. The reference to Grapple's project 'beginning in *Transformers* #14' is amended to read '*Transformers* #15'. This is a mistake; the relevant UK issue was in fact #53.
Page 4, panel 5: 'humors' is altered to read 'humours'.
Page 11, panel 6: 'center' becomes 'centre'.

Dead or Alive?
The subject of Autobot casualties is addressed in this story. Ratchet has 'over a dozen' injured Autobots, and the Dinobots make up 'a third' of the remaining Autobot forces. Inspired by this information, this is as good a time as any to take stock of the current Autobot injury list. Don't forget that the causes of these injuries differed by continuity – for US readers there had been a mass cull of Autobots in [12] 'Prime Time'; in the UK stories most Autobots survived this massacre only to die in [12.4] 'Dinobot Hunt':

Still Alive (16):
Optimus Prime, Ratchet, Wheeljack, Bumblebee, Grimlock, Snarl, Slag, Sludge,

Swoop, Jetfire, Grapple, Hoist, Smokescreen, Skids, Tracks, Omega Supreme

All of these characters appear in this story. The five Dinobots do indeed comprise roughly one-third of the total active Autobot troops at this point.

Confirmed Long-Term Inactive (9):
Bluestreak, Sideswipe, Cliffjumper, Huffer, Gears

These Autobots' corpses were seen in [14] 'Rock and Roll-Out'; they were also confirmed as injured in 'The Autobot Who's Who' printed in UK #53 and #54.

Windcharger: Confirmed as injured in the 'Who's Who', he was presumably killed in [12.4] 'Dinobot Hunt'.

Sunstreaker: Destroyed by Shockwave in [5] 'The New Order'. Confirmed as 'beyond repair' in [8.2] 'The Wrath of Grimlock' and [10] 'The Next Best Thing to Being There'.

Red Alert, Inferno: Both were part of the original *Ark* crew – Red Alert was seen just once in [4.2] 'The Enemy Within', likewise Inferno in [8.1] 'Decepticon Dam-Busters'. It was confirmed in Soundwaves (UK#62) that Red Alert was a casualty of Shockwave's attack on the *Ark* in [4] 'The Last Stand' and had been out of commission ever since – Grapple's situation was presumably the same.

Ambiguous (7):
Jazz: Initially presumed to be one of the casualties of [12] 'Prime Time'/[12.4] 'Dinobot Hunt' (delete according to your preference), he's later seen in UK stories such as [20.2] 'Target: 2006' and [23.5] 'Resurrection'.

Prowl: There's no sign of him in this issue, so it's assumed that he's incapacitated for reasons unknown. He survived the mass deaths of [12] 'Prime Time'/[12.4] 'Dinobot Hunt', featuring in later stories such as [14] 'Rock and Roll-Out' and [16] 'Plight of the Bumblebee'. From the UK perspective, he's definitely still active, appearing in stories such as [23.1] 'Prey', but in the US-only narrative he seems to be a longer-term casualty, and is confirmed disabled in [28] 'Mechanical Difficulties'.

Ironhide: From the US perspective, Ironhide is certainly a long-term casualty. He was last seen being attacked by the fake Prime in [12] 'Prime Time'. However in the UK-only narrative he's still around at this point, appearing in stories such as [16.2] 'Devastation Derby' and [20.2] 'Target: 2006'.

Hound: Another US victim of the [12] 'Prime Time' massacre who survived in the UK comics. Although his body appeared in the 'corpse scene' of [14] 'Rock and Roll-Out', the 'Autobot Who's Who' later confirmed that he had been reactivated, and he featured in [16.3] 'Second Generation'.

Mirage: He's generally assumed to have died in [12.4] 'Dinobot Hunt' (or [12] 'Prime Time', if you follow only the US comics); however, he was listed as active in the 'Who's Who' and made a fleeting appearance during Jetfire's Autobrand ceremony in [14]

'Rock and Roll Out' before being killed off in [20.2] 'Target: 2006'.

Trailbreaker: Like Hound, he continued to play a part in UK-only stories such as [16.1] 'Robot Buster' and [20.2] 'Target: 2006', despite his US demise in [12] Prime Time.

Brawn: Another Autobot written out of the US comics in [12] 'Prime Time', he continued to be involved in UK stories such as [16.2] 'Devastation Derby' and [20.2] 'Target: 2006'.

Roll Call:
Autobots: Optimus Prime, Ratchet, Wheeljack, Bumblebee, Grimlock, Snarl, Slag, Sludge, Swoop, Jetfire, Grapple, Hoist, Smokescreen, Skids, Tracks, Blaster, Powerglide, Cosmos, Seaspray, Warpath, Beachcomber, Perceptor and **Omega Supreme**.

Decepticons: Megatron, Starscream, Skywarp, Thundercracker, Soundwave, Rumble, Frenzy, Laserbeak, Buzzsaw, Ravage, Shockwave, Scrapper, Scavenger, Mixmaster, Bonecrusher, Long Haul, Hook and Devastator

Other: Donny Finkleberg.

Review:
A hugely enjoyable action story, featuring two excellently-staged battle sequences – the Autobot attack on the mine and Omega Supreme's battle against the Decepticons. But that's not all: we still have time to further the overarching plot, as both Donny and Skids go AWOL, Megatron regains the Decepticon leadership, and we get another step closer to the introduction of the Special Teams.

The only real drawback is the introduction of (yet) another annoying human character in the form of road-rage antagonist Jake Dalrymple. However, this is only a minor niggle in an otherwise highly satisfactory instalment. 4/5

[20] SHOWDOWN!
US#20, 'September 1986' (published May 1986), 22 pages.

British reprint: UK#72, 2 August 1986 (Part One), 11 pages; UK#73, 9 August 1986 (Part Two), 11 pages.

Credits:
Bob Budiansky (script); Herb Trimpe (pencils); Ian Akin, Brian Garvey (inks); Nel Yomtov (colours); Janice Chiang (letters); Michael Carlin (editor); Jim Shooter (editor-in-chief); Herb Trimpe (cover). **UK:** Geoff Senior (cover, UK#72); Herb Trimpe (cover, UK#73 – reuse of US cover).

Plot:
Stuck in van mode, the damaged Autobot Skids is found and repaired by Charlene, a grocery store worker from a small Wyoming town. Tired of war, Skids begins to embrace the simple life of just being Charlene's car – until he is forced to reveal his true identity when he saves Charlene from Jake Dalrymple, a man with a vendetta against Skids after his sports car suffered some minor damage in a traffic accident involving the

Autobot.

Skids and Charlene become firm friends, but their idyllic life together is shattered when they are tracked down by Donny Finkleberg, who wants to defect to the Autobots. Finkleberg is being hunted by Ravage, who quickly arrives on the scene. The two Transformers face off in an abandoned mining town.

Ravage appears to have the upper hand, but Skids manages to hurl the Decepticon to his doom, down an abandoned mineshaft. Skids, realising that his first responsibility is to his Autobot comrades, bids Charlene goodbye and heads back to the *Ark* with Finkleberg.

Notes:

This story follows directly on from the events of [19] 'Command Performances': road-rage motorist Jake Dalrymple is still bitter about his altercation with Skids, who begins the adventure injured following his defeat at the hands of Ravage. Donny Finkleberg is still on the run, and has Ravage hot on his trail.

This is the final appearance of the Robot-Master costume, which Finkleberg destroys here in a campfire. It was originally introduced in [15] 'I, Robot-Master'. Skids' story here – found by a curious human who takes him to a local repair shop – mirrors that of Bumblebee in [1] 'The Transformers'.

Following the demise of six Decepticons in the previous story, another is dispatched here, as Ravage is sent tumbling down a mineshaft – leaving Megatron, Soundwave and Laserbeak as the only Decepticons remaining of the original batch of ten introduced in issue #1.

This story has a Wild West theme to it, culminating in a dream sequence in which Skids and Megatron engage in a quick-draw gun duel.

Charlene's employer is Wild Bill's Market, named after notorious gunman Wild Bill Hickok (1837-76), who for a time lived in Cheyenne, Wyoming – the state in which this story is set. Charlene is a fan of the classic Western movie *High Noon* (Fred Zinnemann, 1952). She shows Skids the climactic gunfight at the end, in which Marshal Kane (Gary Cooper) faces off against the Miller Gang – Frank Miller (Ian MacDonald), Ben Miller (Sheb Wooley), Jack Colby (Lee van Cleef) and Jim Pierce (Robert J Wilke).

The final scenes of the story are set in a ghost town (a mining settlement completely abandoned because the mine dried up), of which there are a great many real-world examples in Wyoming.

One of the signs in the ghost town reads:

------N WATSON
------Y GOODS SINCE 1810

This is a possible reference to Ellen Watson (1861-89; aka 'Cattle Kate'), a nefarious cow-rustler and outlaw based in Wyoming in the late 19th Century. (It'd be fun if the second obscured word was in fact 'Dairy', considering her predilection for cows.)

UK Changes:

This and the subsequent US issue, [21] 'Aerialbots Over America', were written with the intent that they should be read consecutively – at the end of this story, Skids resolves to return to the Autobots, and in the very next issue he has just arrived back at the *Ark*. In Britain however, there was a lengthy 16-week gap between the two stories' publication, as Marvel UK took the opportunity to run a couple of their own original *The Transformers* tales in the gap between American reprints. As such, a small change was made to the dialogue here, explaining to UK readers why it would take so long for Skids to return home: the original line 'I'm going back with Donny – back to my people, the Autobots' is replaced in the British comic by 'When my wounds heal, I'm going back to the Autobots' (see page 22, panel 3).

Other, minor changes are as follows:
Page 1, panel 1: 'penciler' and 'colorist' become 'pencils' and 'colour'.
Page 6, panel 2: both instances of the word 'totaled' are changed to 'totalled'; the reference to 'last issue' is altered to '*Transformers* #70'.
Page 15, panel 4: correcting a mistake in the original printing, the plural 'Decepticons' is changed to a singular 'Decepticon'.

Roll Call:
Autobots: Skids.

Decepticons: Megatron and Ravage.

Megatron doesn't actually appear 'properly' in this story; he's seen in Skids' dream sequence, and also as a hologram. There are other Transformers depicted in the hologram (including possibly Jetfire, Sideswipe and Starscream), but they are indistinctly drawn, making positive identification difficult.

Other: Donny Finkleberg.

Data File: Nel Yomtov (colourist)
Yomtov was the only member of the creative team to have worked on every single issue of the American *The Transformers* comic. His other credits include *The Amazing Spider-Man* and *Uncanny X-Men*. He was also an editor, helming runs of *Fantastic Four*, *Iron Man* and *Hawkeye*. A massive baseball fan, he has written a number of books on the subject, and also worked as a consultant for the MLB.

Review:
As obligatory cowboy stories go, this one's not so bad – the relationship between Skids and Charlene is actually rather cute, and many of the Wild West references are quite subtle. However, the cover artwork is a bit of cheat, promising a Megatron/Skids duel that disappointingly turns out to be just a dream.

A pleasant, slower-paced interlude in amongst the action-packed instalments that surround it; thankfully not every issue of the comic is this languid, but as a one-shot it works quite well. 3/5

[20.1] IN THE NATIONAL INTEREST
- UK#74, 16 August 1986 (Part 1), 11 pages
- UK#75, 23 August 1986 (Part 2), 11 pages
- UK#76, 30 August 1986 (Part 3), 11 pages
- UK#77, 6 September 1986 (Part 4), 11 pages

This story was also reprinted later in the comic's run, as follows (NB: the original parts 1 and 2 were each divided into two and spread across a couple of issues):

- UK#302, 29 December 1990 (Part 1), 6 pages
- UK#303, 5 January 1991 (Part 2), 5 pages
- UK#304, 12 January 1991 (Part 3), 6 pages
- UK#305, 19 January 1991 (Part 4), 5 pages
- UK#306, 26 January 1991 (Part 5), 11 pages
- UK#307, 2 February 1991 (Part 6), 11 pages

Credits:
Simon Furman (script); Will Simpson (art, parts 1 and 4; pencils, parts 2-3); Dave Hine (inks, part 2); Tim Perkins (inks, part 3); Andrew Leary (art assist, part 3); John Burns (colours, parts 1-2); Gina Hart (colours, part 3); Tony Jozwiak (colours, part 4); Annie Halfacree (letters); Ian Rimmer (editor); Alister Pearson (cover, UK#74); John Stokes (cover, UK#75); Dave Hine (cover, UK#76); Phil Gascoine (cover, UK#77).

Plot:
TV news reporter Joy Meadows has information that Robot-Master is not the leader of the Transformers and is, in fact, a government plant. Realising that the story threatens to undermine his plans, Megatron decides to kill Meadows.

Meanwhile, Triple-I aren't too happy about the latest revelations, either. They, too, decide that the reporter must be silenced before her special report can be aired. As well as a team of highly-trained masked gunmen, Triple-I have another weapon in their arsenal – Centurion, a powerful robot under the mental control of the reluctant Professor Morris.

It is the Dinobots who find Meadows first, Sludge having taken a shine to the woman when last they met. The Dinobots agree to be interviewed for television, but first Meadows must summon her camera crew. Swoop finds the camera crew, but is met by both Megatron and Centurion, and a three-way fight ensues. Remembering his previous encounter with Swoop, Morris determines to defy his Triple-I masters and help the Dinobots.

The Decepticons find Meadows and the Dinobots, and engage in yet more hostilities. The Dinobots appear on the brink of defeat, until Centurion appears again and turns the tide of the battle. The deadlock is broken by Soundwave, who threatens to kill the reporter unless they agree not to televise the report. The Dinobots grudgingly agree – Meadows is safe for now, but unable to reveal the truth about Robot-Master for fear of her life.

Notes:
This story is a sequel to two previous adventures: [12.3] 'The Icarus Theory', in which we are first introduced to Professor Morris and his robot-control machinery; and [12.4] 'Dinobot Hunt', specifically its second part, in which Sludge encounters Joy Meadows and her crew for the first time.

Morris is on trial for the murder of the security guard that we saw in his previous appearance; he's still repentant, but Triple-I have tampered with the evidence to ensure his acquittal. (In the event, he is kidnapped from the trial before a sentence can be reached.) The courtroom scenes are said to take place in the (fictional) Central Criminal

Court in Portland. (In real life, such a trial would have been held in the city's US District Court.)

The Professor's full name is here given as Peter Anthony Morris, and his equipment has been repaired and relocated since the events of [12.3] 'The Icarus Theory'. Triple-I, represented by returning characters Forrest Forsythe and Walter Barnett, have locked him in a near-impenetrable room in a subterranean laboratory beneath the streets of Portland. From there, Morris controls Centurion, a Transformer-sized military robot, with power and strength enough to match that of most Decepticons.

Joy Meadows, plus Tony and Rick, her LCTV cameramen, are planning to run a story discrediting Robot-Master. Meadows' informant is G B Blackrock, who previously expressed his displeasure with Triple-I's methods in [15] 'I, Robot-Master'. Meadows remembers the Decepticons' attacks on two of Blackrock's industrial installations, in [6] 'The Worse of Two Evils' and [7] 'Warrior School'.

Although Robot-Master/Donny Finkleberg has escaped from the Decepticons, as seen in [19] 'Command Performances', neither Triple-I nor Meadows are aware of this fact as yet. Meadows is met by the Dinobots at a (fictional) location called Talon's Point (presumably somewhere between Portland city and Mount St Hilary, on the banks of the Columbia River).

The Dinobots begin this story still angry with Prime after the argument they had in [19] 'Command Performances', especially irked by the Autobot leader's assertions that the Dinobots' lack of vehicular modes makes them conspicuous. (The line about the Dinobots' egregious alt-modes was actually excised from the UK printing of that story, but it is a valid point all the same, and no doubt one that's been debated by the characters many times off-panel.)

Roll Call:
Autobots: Grimlock, Snarl, Slag, Sludge and Swoop.

Decepticons: Megatron, Soundwave, Laserbeak, Scrapper, Scavenger, Mixmaster, Bonecrusher, Long Haul and Hook.

Other: G B Blackrock (voice only), Professor Morris, Joy Meadows, Walter Barnett, Forrest Forsythe, Donny Finkleberg and **Centurion**.
Finkleberg's appearance is only via archive television footage of Robot-Master seen on the fictional news programme *Between the Lines*.

Data File: Dave Hine (artist)
Hine boasts credits for both Marvel and DC. His work can be seen in such titles as *Batman*, *Spawn*, *Civil War: X-Men*, *2000 AD* and *Doctor Who Magazine*.

Data File: Gina Hart (colourist)
Hart's work includes stints on *Doctor Who Magazine*, *2000 AD*, *Sonic the Comic* and the *Rupert Bear* strips.

Data File: Alister Pearson (artist)
Pearson is best known as an artist for *Doctor Who*-related merchandise, including over a hundred covers for Target Books' range of novelisations of television episodes, plus covers for script books, original fiction and non-fiction books, and *Doctor Who*

videocassette and audiobook releases. He has also provided a number of covers for Titan's range of *Star Trek* novels.

Review:
In one respect, this story is ahead of its time – the late 20th Century mistrust of governments and corporations (which notably manifested itself in the sci-fi conspiracy show *The X-Files* in the 1990s) is presaged here in a story that begins with a shady group of politicians plotting the death of a journalist and forcibly extracting a prisoner from a public trial.

After such a promising beginning, however, the story goes quickly downhill, choosing unwisely to focus on the Dinobots' various battles rather than the more interesting goings-on at Triple-I. The action sequences are generally well done, and the addition of Centurion adds some novelty to proceedings, but given such a promising start, the resolution is a bit of a let-down.

What's worse is that the Dinobots – who were so well-developed in [8.2] 'The Wrath of Grimlock' – are written like they're a bunch of five-year old kids, totally ruining their previous depiction as gruff, badass warriors. When they begin spouting phrases such as 'twerp', 'sad case' and 'ooh 'eck' (no, really), it makes even their American 'Me Grimlock' personalities seem sophisticated by comparison. The fact that Sludge has implausibly fallen head-over-heels in love with the rather characterless Joy Meadows is just further evidence of how far the Dinobots have fallen. Granted, this newfound immaturity might be a symptom of their recent mental problems dating back to [12.4] 'Dinobot Hunt', but even so, it's galling to read such brilliant characters being totally undermined like this. 2/5

The Back-Up Strips, Part 10: *Hercules, Prince of Power*
The Avengers' very own demi-god stars in his own title (albeit set in the far future and in an alternate reality).

- 'What Fools These Immortals Be!' (UK#70-73), from *Hercules, Prince of Power* #1 (September 1982). The arrogant Hercules is exiled from Olympus by his father Zeus.
- 'For the Love of Gods' (UK#74-77), from *Hercules, Prince of Power* #2 (October 1982). After losing a bet, Hercules needs to earn some money – so he decides to rescue a sexy heiress from a group of pirates and pocket the reward …
- 'Whom the God Would Destroy!' (UK#78-81), from *Hercules, Prince of Power* #3 (November 1982). Hercules investigates a case of disappearing planets.
- 'Not Just Another Galactus Story!' (UK#82-85), from *Hercules, Prince of Power* #4 (December 1982). Hercules comes face to face with the world-devourer, Galactus.

[20.2] TARGET: 2006
- UK#78, 13 September 1986 (Prologue), 11 pages
- UK#79, 20 September 1986 (Part 1), 11 pages
- UK#80, 27 September 1986 (Part 2), 11 pages
- UK#81, 4 October 1986 (Part 3), 11 pages
- UK#82, 11 October 1986 (Part 4: Wreck and Rule!), 11 pages
- UK#83, 18 October 1986 (Part 5: The Devil You Know …), 11 pages
- UK#84, 25 October 1986 (Part 6: Trios), 11 pages

- UK#85, 1 November 1986 (Part 7), 11 pages
- UK#86, 8 November 1986 (Part 8), 11 pages
- UK#87, 15 November 1986 (Part 9), 11 pages
- UK#88, 22 November 1986 (Epilogue: Aftermath), 12 pages

Credits:
Simon Furman (script); Jeff Anderson (art, prologue and parts 1, 3, 9); Ron Smith (art, part 4); Geoff Senior (art, parts 5-6, 8); Will Simpson (pencils, parts 2, 7 and epilogue); Tim Perkins (inks, parts 2, 7 and epilogue); Tony Jozwiak (colours, prologue and parts 1-3, 7, 9); John Burns (colours, part 4); Gina Hart (colours, parts 5-6, 8 and epilogue); Richard Starkings (letters, prologue, parts 4-7 and epilogue); Annie Halfacree (letters, parts 1-3, 8-9); Ian Rimmer (editor); Alister Pearson (cover, UK#78); John Higgins (cover, UK#79); John Stokes (cover, UK#80); Will Simpson (cover, UK#81); Phil Gascoine (covers, UK#82, 84 and 87); Robin Smith (covers, UK#83 and 85-86); Geoff Senior (cover, UK#88).

Plot:
Three Decepticons from twenty years in the future – Galvatron, Scourge and Cyclonus – travel through time and arrive on Earth in 1986. However, due to the mechanics of time-travel, three beings of similar mass must be displaced into a limbo dimension.

The Autobots are thrown into chaos when Prime, Ratchet and Prowl duly disappear, leaving them leaderless and panicked. Meanwhile, Galvatron takes command of the 1986 Decepticons by burying Megatron under a rockfall. The Autobots attack the Decepticons, but the super-powerful Galvatron defeats them easily.

Meanwhile, on Cybertron, Emirate Xaaron is planning Operation: Volcano – an elaborate plan to lure many powerful Decepticons into a trap, where they can be defeated once and for all. His plans are thrown into disarray when news reaches him that something has happened to the Matrix – and by extension to Optimus Prime. Jeopardising the Volcano mission, Xaaron sends his most powerful warrior, Ultra Magnus, to investigate what's happened to Prime on Earth.

Realising that they are hopelessly outclassed by the three new super-Decepticons, the Autobots retrieve Megatron from the rubble and join forces with the usurped tyrant in an attack against Galvatron and his minions. This, too, proves unsuccessful.

Galvatron reveals that he is a future incarnation of Megatron, having been rebuilt in the year 2006 by a sentient planet, Unicron. However, this came at the expense of Galvatron essentially becoming Unicron's slave; his plan here is to build a weapon powerful enough to destroy Unicron in the future.

Another trio of future-Transformers arrive in 1986, and this time the newcomers are Autobots – Hot Rod, Kup and Blurr. They hatch an elaborate scheme to trick Galvatron into returning to 2006, and while Ultra Magnus distracts the Decepticon, the future-Autobots set their plot in motion.

Galvatron is fooled into believing that he has killed Starscream twenty years too soon – in which case, he muses, he has altered history and created an alternate timeline, wherein his actions will have no effect on history as he knows it. Believing that he is unable to influence his future, he and his two henchmen return to their own time.

Galvatron's return means that Prime and the other displaced Autobots rematerialise, and they bid Ultra Magnus farewell as he returns to Cybertron, where Operation: Volcano hits a snag – rather than wander into a trap, the Cybertronian

Decepticons instead head to Earth, at Megatron's behest.

Notes:
This is the first UK comic story to have been significantly influenced by the events of *The Transformers: The Movie*. However, writer Simon Furman had available only an early draft of the film script, which dated its events to 2006. The movie would eventually be re-dated to 2005 for its theatrical release, but in this and all subsequent future-set stories, the UK comic would continue with the idea that – as far as they were concerned – its events happened in 2006.

The story opens where the previous comic left off; Prowl recounts how the Autobots arrived at the scene of the Dinobot battle in the aftermath of [20.1] 'In the National Interest'. This flashback marks the point at which the Dinobots temporarily secede from the ranks of the Autobots. (From the US point of view, this had already happened in [19] 'Command Performances'.)

A huge chunk of the action here takes place back on Cybertron; this story serves as another instalment of the Cybertron saga begun in [1] 'The Transformers' and continued in stories such as, most recently, [18] 'The Bridge to Nowhere'. Emirate Xaaron, here making his comics debut (although he had previously appeared in the annual story [A1.3] 'And There Shall Come a Leader'), is revealed as the leader of the Autobot resistance network that included Blaster and the rest of the Cybertron Seven.

Since we last saw it four million years ago, the Autobot city-state of Iacon has become a smouldering ruin, and beneath its surface there now exists a secret Autobase, where Xaaron commands a crack group of Autobot freedom fighters, the Wreckers. (Given that the Autobase previously seen in [17] 'The Smelting Pool' was said to be located near Polyhex, this is presumably a completely different complex to the one that Blaster called home.) Later in the story, the name of the Wreckers' base is given as 'Debris', but whether this is another term for the Iacon Autobase, or the name of yet another secret hideout, is not confirmed.

Other Cybertronian locations include Iacon's Imperial Amphitheatre, which was presumably home to the ancient Cybertronian gladiatorial battles such as those seen in [4.2] 'The Enemy Within' and [A2.4] 'State Games'. We also get a glimpse of Maccadam's Old Oil House, a robotic equivalent of a Wild West saloon, where Transformers can sip black-market fuel to the backdrop of bar-brawls and a robot piano. A 'cycle' is a Cybertronian time unit, said to be roughly equivalent to two Earth days.

The Wreckers hone their skills by fighting against Facsimile Constructs: detailed replicas of real Decepticon troops (presumably a similar technology to the faux humans seen in [16.2] 'Devastation Derby'). They are preparing for Operation: Volcano, wherein the Wreckers hope to lure key Decepticon troops into an ambush, planned to occur on the anniversary of Iacon's fall.

The destruction of Iacon is recounted in a text feature in UK#83, 'Cybertron: The Middle Years'. There it's revealed that a Decepticon warlord, Trannis, filled the power vacuum left by Megatron when he departed the planet four million years previously. Over the millennia, Trannis took over the entire planet, decimating the Autobot forces and murdering their high council – with the exception of Xaaron, who survived and set up the Autobot resistance cells. Trannis himself is said to have been replaced by Straxus, whom we saw in [17] 'The Smelting Pool', upon his assassination at the hands of the Wreckers.

Another tidbit of information gleaned from outside the comic strip – specifically, in a profile printed in UK#81 – is that Ultra Magnus is a recently-created Transformer, born from the Matrix Flame (of which, more later). Magnus is so new, in fact, that the senior Wrecker, Impactor, doubts his readiness for the mission ahead.

Galvatron and the other time-travellers are from the year 2006, and much is revealed of future events here. As will be discussed in the notes to [27.1] 'Wanted: Galvatron – Dead or Alive', Galvatron and company are from what this book will henceforth call Timeline A, and their meddling in the past here changes the course of history, creating Timeline B.

So far as Galvatron's original Timeline A is concerned, we learn that Earth has a weather control system in place by the year 1992. Unicron, a powerful sentient planet, has reformatted a dying Megatron into Galvatron – a new, more powerful Decepticon. Cyclonus and Scourge have been through the same process; Cyclonus's previous incarnation was named Life Spark. Unicron's upgrades have made Galvatron resistant to Soundwave's mind-scans, although Laserbeak seems instinctively aware of the future Decepticon's true identity.

Polyhex still exists in 2006, and Galvatron has only a vague memory of Lord Straxus ('Oh yes, I remember him ...'), indicating that, in Timeline A, the whole Megatron/Straxus/Clone storyline – see [23.3] 'Under Fire, [57.1] 'Two Megatrons' et al – never occurs. Galvatron and company have travelled back in time from around the mid-point of *The Transformers: The Movie* – see the entry for [MOV2] 'Judgment Day' for further details – but suffice it to say that the journey occurs after Starscream's death in the film but prior to Galvatron stealing the Matrix. (From Hot Rod's point of view, the 2006 incarnation of Ultra Magnus is the current Matrix-bearer.)

Notably, Cyclonus is very surprised that Ultra Magnus is active on Earth in 1986. This makes sense: were it not for the time-travellers displacing Optimus Prime, Magnus would not have been sent to Earth. However, given the continued existence of the Insecticons, Ramjet, Thrust and Dirge in 2006 (as seen in the movie), it would appear that Operation: Volcano was *inevitably* doomed to failure, regardless of Magnus's presence on Cybertron. (Presumably Megatron always planned to recall his troops from Cybertron and unwittingly save them from the Wreckers, whether Galvatron had shown up or not.)

There's some confusion as to when exactly in 1986 these events occur. A visible readout on the time machine displays '11/10/86'. However, the very next comic adventure, [21] 'Aerialbots over America', will be set on 4 July. In addition, the opening caption to Part 1 makes reference to the 'late summer air'. All things considered, it's better to assume that '11/10/86' is not supposed to represent a date, and that these events take place in late June/early July. (Astronomically, the Northern Hemisphere summer begins in early May; the solstice is the *mid-point* of summer, not the beginning as is sometimes claimed. Given this rather pedantic definition, early July can just about be described as 'late summer'.)

Galvatron's arrival in 1986 creates a weather disturbance (the only time this happens); he lands in a cereal farm somewhere in Oregon. Other locations seen here include the Portland Iron and Steel Foundry and an unnamed spot in Northern Oregon, presumably somewhere in Mount Hood National Park, where Galvatron builds his solar weapon – thanks to Unicron's influence, this is also the site where the Autobots eventually build their city (which has been completed by the time of the movie – see also [A3.4] '*Ark* Duty'). The solar weapon is used to destroy the spacecraft that ferried the Decepticons from Cybertron to the *Ark* in [1] 'The Transformers'.

Other events recalled from previous issues include Omega Supreme's victory over the Decepticons in [19] 'Command Performances', and Optimus Prime's flashback that relates Sparkplug's capture by Starscream in [2] 'Power Play'. However, the flashback shows those events as occurring against a backdrop of rocky terrain; in reality the kidnapping took place at the site of Sparkplug's garage in Portland.

It's confirmed that the Decepticons injured by Omega Supreme have been taken in for repair by the Autobots, lying dormant in pod-like stasis/healing units. Starscream, Thundercracker and Frenzy are revived here, although Starscream ends the story having been returned to stasis. Rumble and Buzzsaw are both confirmed as 'too far gone', along with Skywarp, whose corpse is blown to smithereens by Galvatron.

Ultra Magnus travels to Earth via a prototype Space Bridge, which as depicted here seems more akin to a teleport beam than a bridge per se. It causes great pain to those who use it, but in future it will become the Autobots' main way of getting to and from Cybertron (see also [40.5] 'Wrecking Havoc' and the notes to [A1.4] 'Hunted').

Galvatron's torture device, although not named as such here, bears some resemblance to the Variable Voltage Harness seen in [41] 'Totaled'. With Optimus Prime, Prowl and Ratchet all missing, and Jazz captured, command of the Autobots falls to Jetfire. (This is in keeping with the 'Autobot Who's Who' of UK#53, which placed Jetfire as being amongst the 'High Command'. But from an in-fiction point of view it's odd that such a relatively young Transformer would be given the leadership over one of the more senior Autobots such as Ironhide, Hound or Trailbreaker.)

Some of the Cybertronian natives, such as Whirl, Sandstorm and Broadside, are shown transforming into human vehicles. It's to be assumed that, thanks to Soundwave's transmission from Earth – seen by both factions in [17] 'The Smelting Pool' – the Transformers now have knowledge of terrestrial alt-modes and have started using them in preparation for possible future missions to Earth.

One final note: when Optimus Prime returns to Earth in the epilogue, the final frame shows him sporting an injury to the side of his torso. This leads into the following story, [21] 'Aerialbots over America', which contains a scene where Prime is receiving treatment for this injury. From the UK point of view, we'll see how Prime incurs this wound in [23.4] 'Distant Thunder'. (He's struck down by the illusory alien Zenag.) However, for US readers, it is explained as having been received during the battle in [19] 'Command Performances'.

You Got the Torch! What's the Matrix Flame?
The Matrix Flame makes its one and only appearance here. It's a burning torch, located on Cybertron and tended by a monk-like Transformer dressed in a ceremonial fabric tunic. It's inextricably linked to the Creation Matrix – it ceases to burn when Optimus Prime is banished to the limbo dimension. The fact that this news is reported to Emirate Xaaron – and that the Flame's extinction is investigated only by the Autobots – would seem to imply that it's under the control and protection of the Autobots alone.

Given that Cybertron is perhaps hundreds of light-years away from Earth (see the notes section of [16.3] 'Second Generation'), it would appear that the Creation Matrix and the Matrix Flame can remain linked no matter how far they are apart spatially. It's only when the Creation Matrix enters another dimension entirely that the Flame dwindles.

The Matrix Flame can be used to 'tap' the life-giving properties of the Creation

Matrix in order to create new Autobot troops. So why doesn't Xaaron just use the Flame and create armies of new troops, as he did with Ultra Magnus? Well, given the lack of energy and resources currently faced by Cybertron's inhabitants, creating a whole new Transformer might well be an extremely costly process. Furthermore, it's possible that the Flame needs to 'recharge' for extended periods of time in between births.

You Got The Notion! What's Galvatron's Plan?

Galvatron's plan is, on the surface, quite simple. However, the more one thinks about it, the less sense it starts to make. Is there any logic behind the scheme? Could he possibly have succeeded? Or is he just a raving lunatic?

Let's recap. In the year 2006, Galvatron lives under the thrall of Unicron, a powerful sentient planet that's threatening to eat Cybertron. The new Decepticon leader wants none of this, and so travels back in time to 1986 for two reasons. First, being in the past appears to provide Galvatron with some immunity – although Unicron still has *some* mental influence here, he's unable to remote-torture Galvatron like he does in 2006. Secondly, Galvatron now has the opportunity to build a weapon that he hopes can destroy Unicron in the future ... and this is where things start to get a bit confusing.

Galvatron's idea is to build a solar-powered weapon beneath the site of the future Autobot City and then return to the year 2006, whereupon he will activate the weapon, destroying both Unicron *and* the Autobot HQ. The thing is, his plan relies on him successfully altering history – in the original timeline, there is no cannon beneath Autobot City, and Galvatron has gone back in time in an attempt to alter that fact. So the question is: if Galvatron's main reason for being in the past is to rewrite the course of history, why does he flee at the first sign that his actions are, in fact, changing things?

Surely he must know that his very presence is having a profound effect on causality? He's giving the Autobots and Decepticons foreknowledge of the future, he's influencing the actions of his past self (Megatron), and his actions have caused Ultra Magnus to arrive from Cybertron, amongst other things. If Galvatron has any claim to be a sane, intelligent individual, he *must* realise that he's having massive ramifications on future events. Starscream's apparent destruction must surely just be confirmation of what he already suspects – that he is irrevocably changing the future as he knows it. However, instead of it being just another in a long line of running changes, Galvatron sees this as a deal-breaker, and promptly hot-foots it back to 2006. Eh?

Well, let's for one moment give Galvatron the benefit of the doubt here, and attempt to rationalise his sudden volte-face. One explanation could be that Galvatron has factored some minor alterations into his plan already. As will be discussed in the notes to [27.1] ' Wanted: Galvatron – Dead or Alive', the universe does appear to be somewhat self-correcting, with some 'fixed events' that always happen, no matter how much time is altered. This accounts for the failure of Operation: Volcano in both timelines (as discussed above), the creation of Galvatron in a parallel dimension ([67] 'Rhythms of Darkness'), and also the creation of Goldbug in two realities (although the circumstances differ between the two accounts – see [GIJ4] 'All Fall Down' (GIJ) and [27.4] 'Hunters'). It seems that some things are always destined to happen, no matter how much one messes about with time travel. So Galvatron figures that the universal history takes a roughly fixed path, and that a few ripples here and there won't affect much in the grand scheme of things. It's only when a cataclysmic change occurs, with the apparent death of the pivotal character Starscream, that Galvatron realises that too much has altered for his plan to work properly.

(As we shall see, if Galvatron believes the above then he's completely wrong. No matter how much he alters the past, he'll always end up in his 'own' timeline. Any changes he makes will have no impact whatsoever upon the future to which he returns.)

So, what other apparent flaws in his plan can we attempt to rationalise?

1) Why does Galvatron travel to 1986, of all times? Why not go further back to a pre-Transformer Earth, where he'll meet virtually no resistance? This could be for the simple reason that he needs the Constructicons to build the anti-Unicron gun. Look at the current state of the Earthbound Transformers in mid-1986 – troop numbers are at their all-time lowest. A great many of the original Autobots and Decepticons who survived the *Ark* crash are either dead, incapacitated or deserted. (For the full list, see [19] 'Command Performances'.) The Special Teams are yet to be built and reinforcements from Cybertron not yet arrived. The Autobot and Decepticon forces are never weaker than here. It's arguably the ideal time to recruit the Constructicons and at the same time minimise resistance.

2) How can he expect Autobot City to be built on top of a ginormous planet-destroying gun? Well, it's possible that the initial plan was to construct the weapon in secret, and then fill in the surrounding crater (seen on the opening page of Part 2) so that nobody knows it's even there. Use some kind of future tech to make it undetectable to Autobot sensors, and – hey presto – there's your secret concealed weapon. Trouble is, he doesn't factor in the possibility that the Autobots just happen to be spying on him.

However, even after he realises he's been rumbled, he doesn't seem to care – most likely because he thinks he can just wipe out all the Autobots who have knowledge of his plan.

3) How can he expect Unicron to be destroyed by a solar-powered gun? Everybody knows that Unicron can be destroyed only by the Matrix! That may be true with the benefit of hindsight, but remember at this point Galvatron doesn't know that the Matrix is Unicron's one and only Achilles' heel. Unicron himself knows about the threat and seems quite unfazed by it all: 'He [Galvatron] sought to destroy me ... he has since been made to understand that Unicron cannot be destroyed ... Galvatron had ... underestimated me!'

So, in conclusion: Galvatron completely misunderstands the mechanics of time travel. His actions will have no consequences on his own future (Timeline A). All he's doing is creating a parallel reality (Timeline B). Besides which, the gun probably wouldn't have harmed Unicron anyway. But because he's ignorant of these facts, his plan is actually feasible so far as he knows.

Roll Call:
Autobots: Optimus Prime, Jazz, Prowl, Ironhide, Ratchet, Hound, Wheeljack, Mirage, Trailbreaker, Bumblebee, Brawn, Gears, Grimlock (flashback only), Snarl (flashback only), Slag (flashback only), Sludge (flashback only), Swoop (flashback only), Jetfire, Grapple, Hoist, Smokescreen, Tracks, **Emirate Xaaron, Impactor, Ultra Magnus, Roadbuster, Whirl, Topspin, Twin Twist, Rack and Ruin, Springer, Sandstorm, Broadside, Hot Rod, Kup** and **Blurr.**

Sideswipe appears in a single frame, in the epilogue. He's supposed to be dead at this point – see [19] 'Command Performances' – so, much like Shockwave's cameo in [3] 'Prisoner of War', it's probably an art error rather than a *bona fide* appearance.

This story sees the comic debut of some previously Annual-only characters: Emirate Xaaron was in [A1.3] 'And There Shall Come a Leader', and both Topspin and Twin Twist featured in [A1.4] 'Hunted'.

This story sees the deaths of Mirage and Trailbreaker, who make their last appearances here for some time (although Trailbreaker will have a one-off cameo in [22.1] 'The Gift'). Trailbreaker is mortally wounded during the fight at the steelworks, while Mirage is strafed to death by Cyclonus and Scourge.

Impactor also dies here, but considering his importance (and the fact that he crops up later as a zombie), he merits a spot on the list of recurring Autobots ... unlike the one-off Skater, who has a brief cameo here.

Decepticons: Megatron, Starscream, Skywarp (as a corpse), Thundercracker, Soundwave, Frenzy, Laserbeak, Shockwave, Scrapper, Scavenger, Mixmaster, Bonecrusher, Long Haul, Hook, Shrapnel , Bombshell, Kickback, Ramjet, Thrust, Dirge, **Galvatron, Cyclonus, Scourge, Astrotrain, Blitzwing** and **Octane.**

Named, one-off Decepticons featured here include Fang and Macabre.

Other: Buster (flashback only), Sparkplug (flashback only), Joy Meadows (flashback only), Centurion (flashback only) and **Unicron.**

Data File: Simon Furman (writer/editor)
Furman started out on the comic *Scream* before decamping to Marvel UK to write their scripts for *The Transformers*. His knowledge and enthusiasm for the brand meant that he soon became writer-editor on the comic, while also finding time to work on other British titles such as *Doctor Who Magazine*, *Thundercats*, *Action Force*, *Dragon's Claws* and *Death's Head* (the latter two of which he co-created). Furman was then hired by Marvel US to write for their version of *The Transformers*, from which he broke into more mainstream titles such as *Sensational She-Hulk*, *Alpha Flight* and *What If ...?* Despite attempts to forge a career outside of *The Transformers*, he has become synonymous with the brand, writing comics based on *Transformers: Generation 2*, *Beast Wars: Transformers* and also the official *Transformers: Revenge of the Fallen* movie adaptation. He has also written *Transformers: The Ultimate Guide* and *Transformers: The Movie Guide* for Dorling Kindersley books. In other media, he has penned a *Doctor Who* audio play, 'The Axis of Insanity', for Big Finish Productions, and a television script, 'Nemesis, Part 2', the final episode of the animated series *Beast Wars: Transformers*.

Data File: Ron Smith (artist)
Former World War II Spitfire pilot Smith began his comics career in the '40s and worked on much-loved titles such as *Hotspur*, *Bunty*, *Eagle* and *The Dandy*. He's best known for his run on the *Judge Dredd* strips in *2000 AD*, contributing to classic stories such as 'The Day the Law Died and 'The Judge Child'.

Review:
This is a tricky one to review, considering it's the most influential and talked-about

Transformers comic story ever. What more praise can possibly be heaped on a story that for thirty years has been rightly heralded by fans around the world as one of the all-time greats?

It's easy to forget that this is, at its heart, a kids' comic. The layers of plot and wealth of storytelling techniques on display here are very much reminiscent of a book for older readers. The mind-boggling time travel ideas work well, and overall this is of a quality well above what one would expect for a toy tie-in.

Writer Simon Furman can't be praised highly enough here. Although there's a single over-arching story, each instalment is satisfying in its own right. The experience is akin to watching a serialised US television show such as *Breaking Bad* or *Fringe*. Each issue works as an individual piece of work, but the overall effect is of a story greater than the sum of its parts.

And every issue brings a different ingredient to the table. Part 3 is told completely in flashback and with a running commentary by the Autobot Ironhide. The twist ending to that issue goes unresolved for two weeks, because in the meantime we have Part 4, an interlude set completely apart from the main action. Integral background information is provided by character bios and a prose story about Cybertron's history. Every single cliffhanger is a game-changer. It really is a stunning piece of work.

It's not just the script that's noteworthy – some of the images here are mind-blowing. Special praise must go to the rendering of the action sequences, which come across as vicious and bloodthirsty without the presence of actual blood. The Ultra Magnus/Galvatron battle in Part 8 is absolutely electrifying. It's a real creative tour de force from all concerned.

There are some areas of imperfection; the ending could be a little tighter, for one. And for kids reading the comic in 1986, this story contained numerous spoilers for the yet-to-be released theatrical movie (Megatron turns into Galvatron and kills Starscream!). But such niggles are minor – this is indisputably one of the best and most influential *The Transformers* comic stories of all-time; a relative masterpiece. 5/5

[21] AERIALBOTS OVER AMERICA!
US#21, 'October 1986' (published June 1986), 23 pages.

British reprint: UK#89, 29 November 1986 (Part One), 11 pages; UK#90, 6 December 1986 (Part Two), 12 pages.

Credits:
Bob Budiansky (script); Don Perlin (pencils); Ian Akin, Brian Garvey (inks); Nel Yomtov (colours); Janice Chiang (letters); Michael Carlin (editor); Jim Shooter (editor-in-chief); Herb Trimpe (cover). **UK:** Robin Smith (cover, UK#89); Herb Trimpe and Robin Bouttell (cover, UK#73 – re-coloured adaptation of US cover).

Plot:
Using one of his mind-controlling cerebro-shells, Bombshell commands Hoover Dam engineer Ricky Vasquez. The Decepticons' plan: use Vasquez to infiltrate the dam and take command of the main computer there, then send a giant turbine/drill through the space bridge to destroy the dam and tap the power of the resulting deluge.

The Autobots see the commotion on a TV news report and send the new Aerialbots to save the day; however there has been insufficient time to complete the programming of their brains – when combined in Superion mode, the giant Autobot is paralysed with confusion.

In the end it is Vasquez himself who saves the day, using Megatron's gun mode to blast at the space bridge. The appearance of his young daughter Maria has helped him fight the Decepticons' hold over him.

Meanwhile, in an aircraft hangar, Circuit Breaker is putting finishing touches to her new display – the heads of Blaster and his six Cybertronian friends have been mounted on the wall …

Notes:

For American readers, this story sees the introduction of the Aerialbots, who have just been created by the Autobots using combination technology stolen from the Decepticons in [19] 'Command Performances'. Also joining the fray are the Insecticons and the new Decepticon Planes, who arrive from Cybertron having previously been featured in Cybertron-based stories such as [17] 'The Smelting Pool'.

This is our first sighting of the newly-repaired space bridge since it was sabotaged by Blaster in [18] 'The Bridge to Nowhere'. Here it's seen to materialise near Hoover Dam, which means that its terminus isn't tied to a single location (as, when last seen, it materialised over the Columbia River, about 750 miles (1,200km) from Hoover Dam).

Skids rejoins the Autobots here after his apparent death in [19] 'Command Performances' and his solo adventure [20] 'Showdown', where he hooked up with the defector Donny Finkleberg. Donny reveals the existence of Blaster's 'Cybertron Seven', making the Earthbound Autobots aware of their presence on Earth for the first time.

Sent to find the new Autobots, Jetfire tells Finkleberg of 'basketrek', a game he used to play on Cybertron, perhaps indicating that (at least some of) his memories and personality existed prior to his creation on Earth (perhaps stored in a crystal like those seen in [14] 'Rock and Roll-Out'). Another possibility is that he's drawing upon Torrent Memory, a cloud-like pool of knowledge shared between Autobots according to a later sequel comic series, *Transformers: Regeneration One* (see Appendix 3 for more on this). According to the letters page in UK#102, Jetfire was merely lying to Finkleberg in an attempt to unsettle the human.

The Cybertron Seven have in fact been shipped to southern New Jersey, home of RAAT (Rapid Anti-robot Assault Team), who, as we'll see, are the military wing of Triple-I. (Given that most of the Transformers' adventures have taken place in western USA, it seems counter-intuitive to base RAAT on the opposite side of the continent, 2,500 miles from the *Ark*.) The RAAT troops are commanded by Circuit Breaker, here making her first US appearance since [9] 'Dis-Integrated Circuits'.

This is the first US-originated story to give a definitive date to the events therein: it's 4 July (1986).

This story's title is possibly a play on that of *Wings Over America*, the US #1 triple live album by Paul McCartney's band Wings, released in 1976.

UK Notes:

Although they are 'properly' introduced here, British readers had seen the Aerialbots before, as part of Buster's Matrix-induced vision in [16.3] 'Second Generation' and in [A2.3] 'The Return of the Transformers', an out-of-continuity annual story. Similarly, British readers last saw Circuit Breaker in the UK-only story [12.1] 'Christmas Break*er*'.

The UK comic provided an explanation for the sudden appearance of the

Insecticons and the 'conehead' jets – they were recalled to Earth by Megatron at the end of [20.2] 'Target: 2006'.

Hoover Dam becomes the second such structure to be targeted by the Decepticons, following the battle of Sherman Dam in [8.1] 'Decepticon Dam-Busters'.

If, as discussed above, Jetfire had a previous life prior to his construction on Earth, this would also go some way to explaining why he's so high up in the Autobot hierarchy – see also [20.2] 'Target: 2006'.

As previously discussed in [20.2] 'Target: 2006', Optimus Prime is suffering from a wound received in [19] 'Command Performances'/[23.3] 'Distant Thunder' (delete according to taste). This is the first time in the comics that we see Bombshell use one of his mind-altering cerebro-shells, although they had previously seen action in the annual story [A1.1] 'Plague of the Insecticons'. It's confirmed here that Silverbolt has a fear of heights, previously alluded to in another annual story, [A2.3] 'The Return of the Transformers'.

UK Changes:
Page 1, panel 1: 'colorist' is changed to 'colourist'.
Page 3, panel 5: the '*Transformers* #18' caption is amended to read 'after last issue.'
Page 6, panel 2: another caption change – 'suffered in *Transformers* #19' becomes 'see Transformation for details.'
Page 7, panel 2: 'center' is altered to 'centre'.
Page 7, panel 3: 'rumor' becomes 'rumour'.
Page 7, panel 5: the reference to issue #19 is changed to issue #71.
Page 11, panel 4: the caption has been moved to the top of the panel to avoid it being obscured by the 'Next' box.

Roll Call:
Autobots: Optimus Prime, Ratchet, Wheeljack, Bumblebee, Jetfire, Skids, Silverbolt, Air Raid, Fireflight, Skydive, Slingshot, Superion, and as corpses: Blaster, Powerglide, Cosmos, Seaspray, Warpath, Beachcomber and Perceptor.

Decepticons: Megatron, Shrapnel, Bombshell, Kickback, Ramjet, Thrust and Dirge.

Other: Circuit Breaker and Donny Finkleberg.

Review:
Messy and uninspired. There are a number of bizarre plot-holes, and the story is hardly original, yet again involving the Decepticons attacking a dam/power station. Added to that is a groan-inducing cliffhanger, in which we discover that Circuit Breaker still can't recognise good from evil. This is a story that's very difficult to like.

That said, the main point of this adventure is to act as a showcase for the new Aerialbots, and in this respect it works well – the main set piece is a rather exciting air battle between the new Autobots and the Decepticon 'conehead' planes, set against the iconic backdrop of Hoover Dam. 2/5

[22] HEAVY TRAFFIC!
US#22, 'November 1986' (published July 1986), 23 pages.

British reprint: UK#91, 13 December 1986 (Part One), 12 pages; UK#92, 20 December 1986 (Part Two), 11 pages.

Credits:
Bob Budiansky (script); Don Perlin (pencils); Ian Akin, Brian Garvey (inks); Nel Yomtov (colours); Hans IV (letters); Don Daley (editor); Jim Shooter (editor-in-chief); Herb Trimpe (cover). **UK:** Phil Gascoine (cover, UK#91); Lee Sullivan (cover, UK#92).

The name 'Hans IV' is a variant of the 'M Hands' pseudonym previously used on [9] 'Dis-Integrated Circuits', indicating that multiple staffers worked on the lettering in this issue.

Plot:
Following their not-entirely-successful mission to Hoover Dam, the Aerialbots are finally provided with proper personalities thanks to the Matrix. However, unbeknown to the Autobots, Prime has been secretly injected with one of Bombshell's brain-tapping cerebro-shells, which means that the Decepticons are able to siphon off some of the Matrix energy for themselves. They use this power to give life to the Stunticons.

Following the trail of Blaster's 'Cybertron Seven', Skids and Donny Finkleberg head across America in a bid to locate the recent Autobot arrivals. However, they are soon halted in their tracks by the new Stunticons.

A fight ensues; the Aerialbots get involved and the two combining teams do battle on the freeway as Menasor and Superion. The altercation is finally ended by Circuit Breaker, who is able to deactivate the gestalt Autobot, giving the Decepticons a chance to escape.

Skids and Finkleberg, meanwhile, continue their quest for Blaster and company. While stopped at a motel for the night, Finkleberg calls up Triple-I and asks them what sort of reward he would get in exchange for Skids' location …

Notes:
This is the first of two consecutive US issues featuring a road trip across the USA, as Skids and Finkleberg head out from the *Ark* in Oregon toward the Cybertron Seven, who are being held in southern New Jersey. Skids' rescue of a driver threatened by a fallen power cable is later featured on local Colorado news, which means that their route wasn't necessarily the most direct one they could have taken.

That said, it is possible to work out the rough location of the Superion/Menasor freeway battle. Assuming that RAAT's helicopters have taken off from New Jersey at the same moment that the Aerialbots leave the *Ark*, and also that the Aerialbots are flying at ten times the speed of the RAAT helicopters, then the battle possibly takes place on the Pennsylvanian stretch of the I-76. (The 'nearby cliff' where the Aerialbots initially spot Skids is probably part of the Appalachian mountain range.)

One of the most interesting points of note here is the fact that the Aerialbots' brains have been wiped by the Autobots following their previous adventure, [21] 'Aerialbots over America', which seems morally dubious, even taking into account that their programming was said to be incomplete in that story. However, it is of course possible that their original personalities weren't completely erased, just temporarily excised and then loaded back into their bodies following a successful reboot.

The Creation Matrix is still being referred to here as a 'program'; its reconceptualisation as a quasi-mystical talisman is still to come. Optimus Prime proves to be immune from the brain-controlling effects of Bombshell's cerebro-shells; the reason for this is not revealed – the presence of the Matrix might have had some effect, although in [21] 'Aerialbots over America' it was implied that a strong enough will was sufficient to fight the effects.

Last issue's cliffhanger excepted, this is our first full sighting of the Cybertron Seven since [19] 'Command Performances'; an extensive flashback here explains how they came to be prisoners of RAAT. Bombshell begins this issue inside the *Ark*, having surreptitiously hitched a ride on Silverbolt in [21] 'Aerialbots over America'. Optimus Prime's now-famous armpit wound ([19] 'Command Performances'/[23.3] 'Distant Thunder') is again mentioned.

Skids refers to having conducted close observation of humans ([20] 'Showdown'); Finkleberg still has an uncashed cheque for $25,000 which was given to him (off-panel) as payment for playing the super-villain in [15] 'I, Robot-Master'.

And finally, we have the best exchange of dialogue yet seen in the comics – Barnett: 'D-did that thing just shatter an overpass into dust?' Finkleberg: 'No, I … I think it was an entrance ramp …'

UK Notes:

This new information about Prime's immunity to cerebro-shells retroactively reduces the impact of [A1.1] 'Plague of the Insecticons', in which he narrowly avoids being injected with one.

UK Changes:

Page 1, panel 1: 'penciler' and 'colorist' are changed to 'penciller' and 'colourist' respectively.

Page 2, panel 1: 'the humor' becomes 'any humour'.

Page 3, panel 7: the reference to issue #5 is changed to issue #24.

Page 4, panel 3: another altered caption – from 'suffered in *Transformers* #19' to '*Transformers* #100 for details'.

Page 5, panel 6: the previous issue reference is changed from #18 to #69.

Page 6, panel 5: the reference to issue #15 becomes issue #52.

Page 12, panel 1: Motormaster's line 'I see him, Drag Strip!' is amended to read 'Indeed, Drag Strip!'

Page 12, panel 2: to ensure a strong mid-story cliffhanger, this panel has been moved to last on the page in the UK printing.

Marvel Team-Up

As part of Marvel Comics' 25th Anniversary celebrations (the first comics under the Marvel banner, *Journey into Mystery* #69 and *Patsy Walker* #95, were dated June 1961), the covers of this and most other concurrent Marvel titles were decorated with a special border featuring a number of famous superheroes. They were as follows (clockwise from top right): Thor, the Human Torch, Mr Fantastic, the Invisible Woman, She-Hulk, the Thing, Luke Cage, Hawkeye, Vision, the Scarlet Witch, Daredevil, the Beast, Angel, Cyclops, Marvel Girl, Iceman, Nightcrawler, Phoenix, Storm, Colossus, Wolverine, Rogue, Kitty Pryde, Puck, Henry Pym, Wasp, Captain America, Namor the Sub-Mariner, Dr. Strange, Captain Marvel, Iron Man, Hulk and Spider-Man.

Roll Call:
Autobots: Optimus Prime, Ratchet, Wheeljack, Skids, Silverbolt, Air Raid, Fireflight, Skydive, Slingshot, Superion, Blaster, Powerglide, Cosmos, Seaspray, Warpath, Beachcomber and Perceptor.

These last seven listed, the so-called Cybertron Seven, are seen alive only on a video screen; otherwise they are headless corpses.

Decepticons: Megatron, Soundwave, Motormaster, Drag Strip, Dead End, Wildrider, Breakdown, Menasor and Bombshell.

This is the 'proper' debut of the Stunticons, following their appearance in Buster's dream ([16.3] 'Second Generation').

Other: Circuit Breaker, Walter Barnett and Donny Finkleberg.

Data File: Ian Akin and Brian Garvey (artists)
The inking team of Akin and Garvey gained credits on many issues of *The Transformers*. They worked together for a ten-year period, from 1982 to 1992, on comics such as *Iron Man*, *Vision and the Scarlet Witch*, *Jessica Rabbit* and *ROM: SpaceKnight*. Since they went their separate ways, Garvey has worked with DreamWorks Animation on films such as *The Prince of Egypt* (Brenda Chapman, Steve Hickner and Simon Wells, 1998) and *The Road to El Dorado* (Eric Bergeron and Don Paul, 2000).

Review:
This story has a smart sense of humour – the Barnett/Finkleberg joke transcribed above is brilliant, and Skids' constant use of Donny's wallet as leverage is equally amusing. The cross-country nature of the adventure gives it a more epic scope than most Earthbound tales, and the final cliffhanger is great.

However, the presence of the infuriatingly stupid Circuit Breaker – who attacks the Autobots in the face of all evidence – ruins an otherwise decent issue. 2/5

[22.1] THE GIFT
UK#93, 27 December 1986, 11 pages

Credits:
James Hill (script); Martin Griffiths (pencils); Tim Perkins (inks); Steve White (colours); Robin Riggs (letters); Ian Rimmer (editor); Robin Smith (cover).

Plot:
December 1986: Jetfire visits Buster at his house. The Autobot is troubled. In a recent battle with the Decepticons at a NASA facility, his rashness resulted in an injury to Trailbreaker and allowed Soundwave to escape. However, in another skirmish, this time at a Blackrock chemical plant, his performance was exemplary; he saw off most of the Decepticons before preventing an explosion of toxic chemicals. He concludes that his unique standing as the first Autobot born on Earth has clouded his judgment, and that he performs well only when humans are being directly threatened. Buster, however, asserts that Jetfire's

unique point of view is actually a virtue, and something to be proud of.

Notes:
Published in the UK's 1986 Christmas issue, this special festive story is set in late December 1986 (Buster has an end-of-term history exam 'tomorrow'), and therefore some months in advance of the other ongoing storylines. (The next story printed, [23] 'Decepticon Graffiti', takes place during the summer of 1986.) Optimus Prime is mentioned in the present tense (the Autobot leader is presumed dead between [23.1] 'Prey' and [23.5] 'Resurrection'), so these events are best placed immediately afterwards. Jazz refers to the Decepticons having a singular Special Team at this point, so the action must be set prior to the Combaticons' debut in [24] 'Afterdeath'.

The ever-changing sign on Sparkplug's garage today reads 'S Witwicky Auto Repair Tow Service', which is almost (give or take an ampersand) how it looked in [11] 'Brainstorm'. Buster is reading up on the American War of Independence, specifically the decisive Siege of Yorktown (1871).

Jetfire claims ignorance of the Primal Program (i.e. the Creation Matrix) and the Celestial Spires (of Iacon). (He's presumably exaggerating for effect – we already know he has some knowledge of Cybertron; see the notes under [21] 'Aerialbots over America' for more on this.)

The Decepticons raid a NASA monitoring facility (apparently quite close to Mount St Hilary) in order to use the radio telescope there to make contact with Cybertron. (The Decepticons had the ability to contact Cybertron via a console set into the wall of their coal mine base in [18] 'The Bridge to Nowhere'. Presumably this new console has hit a few teething problems, hence the Decepticons having to make do with a human transmitter. The fact that this NASA base in Oregon wasn't a target in [10] 'The Next Best Thing to Being There' would seem to indicate that it's a newly-built facility. When next the Decepticons contact Cybertron in [25] 'Gone but Not Forgotten', they will again do so from the comfort of their own base.)

We're provided with new information about the fuel deal the Autobots have in place with G B Blackrock (negotiated in [9] 'Dis-integrated Circuits'). As well as providing them with regular gasoline for free (as seen in [14] 'Rock and Roll-Out'), Blackrock produces huge vats of Transformer fuel for the Autobots.

There are references to Jetfire's creation in [11] 'Brainstorm', and also [20.2] 'Target: 2006' ('all this business with Galvatron'), and the appearance of Menasor in [22] 'Heavy Traffic'.

Perhaps as a result of it not being the work of regular UK writer Simon Furman, this story features an appearance by Trailbreaker, despite him having succumbed to fatal injuries in [20.2] 'Target: 2006'. His appearance in the flashback sequences can be best attributed to Jetfire having a slightly unreliable memory of events.

Jetfire's top speed is cited as Mach 4.2, a detail from the US *Transformers Universe* comic series, which at this point had yet to be fully published in the UK.

How old is Buster?
In the Transformation page in UK#23, we're explicitly told that Buster was 17 years old during the events of [5] 'The New Order', set in 1984. This makes sense, considering that we know he's in high school, and that he was legally driving a car in [1] 'The Transformers'. However, in [50] 'Dark Star', set early in 1989, it's unambiguously stated that Buster is *still* 17, which can't be right. That would make him 13 when we first saw

him, which patently wasn't the case. There are three ways we could explain away this discrepancy. First, we could ignore the age given in [50] 'Dark Star' and just assume that he's now 21. Secondly, we could invoke a time travel explanation – perhaps everyone on Earth was de-aged by five years as an effect of the time rift that caused so much havoc in [48.2] 'Time Wars'. Thirdly, we could ignore the inconsistency entirely and just go with the flow. With a few notable exceptions, such as Judge Dredd, comic and cartoon characters don't really tend to age. Bart Simpson is always ten years old; Bruce Wayne ought to be a pensioner by now. This should be borne in mind when considering the fictional history of Buster Witwicky, who appears to spend at least six years stuck in his mid-teens.

Roll Call:
Autobots: Jetfire, plus, in flashback, Optimus Prime, Jazz, Prowl, Wheeljack and Trailbreaker.

Decepticons: (all in flashback) Soundwave, Bombshell, Kickback, Thrust and Dirge.

Other: Buster and, in flashback, G B Blackrock.

Data File: Steve White (artist/colourist)
Writer, artist and editor White cut his teeth at Marvel UK, working on titles such as *The Real Ghostbusters*, *Captain Britain* and *Thundercats*, and editing *Death's Head*, *Action Force* and *The Knights of Pendragon*. He is best known for his stint at *2000 AD*, where he wrote many *Rogue Trooper* scripts. He later became a senior editor at Titan Magazines, overseeing *Adventure Time*, *Simpsons Comics*, *Wallace and Gromit* and their range of Transfomers titles

Data File: Robin Riggs (letterer)
Riggs got into comics after winning a competition in the *Marvel Try-Out Book*. After breaking through at Marvel UK, he later moved into artwork, gaining credits on titles including *Batgirl*, *The Avengers*, *Superman*, *X-Men* and *2000 AD*.

Review:
As a story set a couple of months in advance of the other ongoing storylines and yet containing flashbacks, this has a hint of *A Christmas Carol* about it. The scenes with Jetfire peeking through Buster's window are quite fun, and pre-date similar sequences in the first Transformers live-action movie by about 20 years.

Fluffy and inconsequential it might be, but it's also light-hearted and full of festive cheer. 3/5

[23] DECEPTICON GRAFITTI!
US#23, 'December 1986' (published August 1986), 22 pages.

British reprint: UK#94, 3 January 1987 (Part One), 11 pages; UK#95, 10 January 1987 (Part Two), 11 pages.

Credits:
Bob Budiansky (script); Don Perlin (pencils); Ian Akin, Brian Garvey (inks); Nel Yomtov (colours); Janice Chiang (letters); Don Daley (editor); Jim Shooter (editor-in-chief); Herb Trimpe (cover). **UK:** Lee Sullivan (cover, UK#94); Herb Trimpe (cover, UK#95 – re-use of US cover).

Plot:
Megatron summons from Cybertron two Decepticons, Runabout and Runamuck, and orders them to deliver a message to Optimus Prime, inviting the Autobot leader to a duel to the death.

The Decepticon duo – collectively known as the Battlechargers – defy Megatron and decide on an alternative course of action: they follow an unsuspecting family on a road trip across the USA, and graffiti over all the national monuments they come across.

Meanwhile, guilt weighs heavily on the shoulders of Donny Finkleberg, the writer having accepted a cheque from RAAT after helping them capture Skids. Circuit Breaker's methods – which involve gruesome scientific experiments on the captured Autobots' bodies – are a little too heavy-handed for Donny's liking. Circuit Breaker attempts to halt the Battlechargers' progress in Philadelphia, but is unsuccessful. As a last resort she makes a deal with her captive Autobots – in exchange for their freedom, she makes a robotic battle suit out of their bodies. After a shootout at Liberty Island, Circuit Breaker emerges victorious.

Donny, still plagued by a guilty conscience, donates his money to help pay for restoration work on the defaced Statue of Liberty.

Notes:
This story takes place over at least a week, during the summer holidays ('We've been taking this cross-country trip before the kids have to go back to school'), with a coda set on 4 October 1986 (going by the date on Donny's cheque). Locations vandalised by the Battlechargers include: a football stadium in Wyoming (possibly the War Memorial Stadium in Laramie, home of the Wyoming Cowboys), the Mount Rushmore National Memorial (the famous sculpture near Keystone, South Dakota, completed in October 1941), the Gateway Arch (in St Louis, Missouri; completed in 1965, it's the tallest man-made monument in the Western Hemisphere), the Washington Monument (the 169 metre-tall obelisk in Washington DC, completed in 1884), Independence Hall (in Philadelphia, Pennsylvania, where the Declaration of Independence and the US Constitution were drafted and signed) and finally the Statue of Liberty (aka *Liberty Enlightening the World*, the iconic French-built statue in New York City, designated in 1886).

It's stated that the Statue of Liberty has been 'recently renovated'. This is a reference to works begun in 1984, including replacement of the torch, and some realignment of the head, which had been installed 61 centimetres off-centre. The renovation was completed in 1986 and the statue re-opened in July that year.

Once again we see inside the RAAT headquarters in New Jersey. Notably, the sign on the hangar door reads 'Rapid Anti-robot Attack Team'. (In all other explanations of the acronym, the second A is said to stand for 'Assault'.) With the addition of Skids, the number of Autobots held captive there stands at thirteen: Skids and the five Aerialbots (captured off-panel following the events of [22] 'Heavy Traffic'), plus Blaster, Cosmos, Warpath, Beachcomber, Powerglide, Seaspray and Perceptor (whose abductions were revealed in [21] 'Aerialbots over America'). Circuit Breaker confirms that she has been diagnosed as a 'quadriplegic' (or tetraplegic, to use the correct medical terminology). After she frees the Autobots, her employment at RAAT is terminated.

Here it's established that Transformer brains are tiny, marble-sized spheres, a plot-point that will form the basis of [37] 'Toy Soldiers'. Although Megatron's offer of a duel to the death with Optimus Prime is never delivered, the idea of a final battle between the two leaders foreshadows their unconventional showdown in [24] 'Afterdeath'.

Circuit Breaker recalls the moment when she was injured by Shockwave's attack on the oil rig, as previously seen in [6] 'The Worse of Two Evils'. The Battlechargers' sloppy calligraphy recalls previous Transformer attempts at writing in English, in [4.3] 'Raiders of the Last Ark' and on the cover of [5] 'The New Order'. Circuit Breaker's jury-rigged Autobot is conceptually similar to a robot seen previously in the *Transformers* cartoon series, the titular {2-01} 'Autobot Spike'.

The title is a possible reference to that of *American Graffiti* (George Lucas, 1973); and like that film, this issue features a secondary character named Judy.

UK Notes:
Megatron's increasing propensity to lash out at his own troops (in this story, he nonchalantly smacks Soundwave over the head with a car exhaust) will be picked up on by the UK comics. In [23.1] 'Prey', he will nearly kill Motormaster in a fit of pique, and will also make an attempt on Optimus Prime's life, which seems to be an evolution of the 'duel to the death' plan he concocts here.

UK Changes:
Page 1, panel 1: 'penciler' and 'colorist' credits are changed to 'penciller' and 'colourist'.
Page 2, panel 4: 'last issue' becomes 'issue #92'.
Page 21, panel 1: 'humor' is amended to 'humour'.

Roll Call:
Autobots: Optimus Prime (as an image on a viewscreen), Skids, Silverbolt, Air Raid, Fireflight, Skydive, Slingshot, Blaster, Powerglide, Cosmos, Seaspray, Warpath, Beachcomber and Perceptor. Optimus Prime aside, the other Autobots in this story appear only as corpses.

Decepticons: Megatron, Soundwave, Laserbeak, **Runabout** and **Runamuck**.

Other: Circuit Breaker, Walter Barnett and Donny Finkleberg (final appearance).

Review:
Despite this being a story that ties up three ongoing storylines (the captured Autobots, Circuit Breaker, Finkleberg) and introduces two new characters to the mix, it's a pleasant surprise to find that what could have been a cluttered and busy instalment is actually rather straightforward and fun.

The Battlechargers make an instant impression, thanks to some well-written interplay and great dialogue from writer Bob Budiansky. Visually it's quite appealing too, with the defaced Statue of Liberty going down as one of the most iconic images of the entire run. 4/5

The Back-Up Strips, Part 11: *Spitfire and the Troubleshooters*
Part of Marvel's 'New Universe' subline, this comic told of MIT Professor Jenny Swensen (aka 'Spitfire') and her robotic exo-suit, MAX.

- 'Beginnings' (UK#86-90), from *Spitfire and the Troubleshooters* #1 (October 1986). Jenny Swensen investigates the mysterious death of her father.
- 'Behemoth' (UK#91-94), from *Spitfire and the Troubleshooters* #2 (November 1986). Spitfire comes face to face with a Death Tank.
- 'Counter Attack' (UK#95-98), from *Spitfire and the Troubleshooters* #3 (December 1986). Jenny takes the fight to her father's killer, Fritz Krotze.

[23.1] PREY!
- UK#96, 17 January 1987 (Part 1), 11 pages
- UK#97, 24 January 1987 (Part 2), 11 pages

Credits:
Simon Furman (script); Will Simpson (pencils, part 1); Tim Perkins (inks, part 1); Jeff Anderson (art, part 2); Steve White (colours); Annie Halfacree (letters); Ian Rimmer (editor); Jeff Anderson (cover, UK#96); Geoff Senior (cover, UK#97).

Plot:
Optimus Prime's scheme: concerned that his troops performed poorly when he wasn't there to lead them (see [20.2] 'Target: 2006'), he plans to fake his own death and then see for himself how well or badly the Autobots fare on their own.

Shockwave's scheme: realising that the increasingly irrational Megatron is no longer fit to lead the Decepticons, he concocts a complex ruse to depose him with the help of the Predacons, a team of elite hunters from Cybertron.

Megatron leads the Predacons in an attack on Optimus Prime, unaware that his minions are part of Shockwave's secret plot against him. Meanwhile Optimus Prime struggles to put his own plan in motion, desperately avoiding the Predacons' attacks while readying his fake 'corpse'. The Predacon leader, Razorclaw, leaps in for a final attack …

The Autobots eventually arrive on the scene – Megatron and the Predacons are nowhere to be found, and what appear to be Optimus Prime's remains are strewn across the landscape …

Notes:
The story opens with Optimus Prime using the *Ark*'s monitor screens to review recent events; specifically Megatron's attack on Hoover Dam from [21] 'Aerialbots over America', and Scourge's attack on the foundry from [20.2] 'Target: 2006'. The recent arrival of the Battlechargers in [23] 'Decepticon Graffiti' is also mentioned.

This is the first appearance of Shockwave since his brief cameo in [20.2] 'Target: 2006'. Here he's shown skulking and plotting in a cave, away from the main Decepticon group – the implication being that he's been in a sulk ever since he lost the Decepticon leadership in [19] 'Command Performances', and only now that Megatron begins acting irrationally does he seize his chance once more.

Here Megatron loses his temper with Motormaster, attacking him with a boulder and using him as target practice for the Predacons. This is more evidence of the

Decepticon leader's increasingly erratic behaviour, following [23] 'Decepticon Graffiti', where he took a swipe at Soundwave.

There is another indication of Optimus Prime feeling pain when his combat deck/trailer is shot; only the second time this particular weakness has been referenced within a story. (For the first, see [A1.1] 'Plague of the Insecticons'.)

Shockwave mentions having fought Prime in a 'murky little dimension', a teaser for the upcoming [23.3] 'Distant Thunder', where we will finally discover what Prime and company got up to when they dematerialised in [20.2] 'Target: 2006'.

The presence of Silverbolt amongst the Autobot troops confirms that the Aerialbots have already returned to the *Ark* after their release from captivity in [23] 'Decepticon Graffiti'. The fate of the remaining eight RAAT detainees will be explored in [23.4] 'Fallen Angel'.

The basic plot of this story (a noble leader fakes a disappearance in order to assess his subjects) is derived from William Shakespeare's play *Measure for Measure* (c1603).

Split Decision

The eleven-part epic [20.2] 'Target: 2006' set the standard for stories in the UK comic, which for the next hundred issues or so would consist mostly of long runs of home-originated stories (roughly eight-to-ten issues in a row) interrupted by reprints of the American material. One of the drawbacks of these longer sagas was that they were generally off-putting to new readers – picking up in issue for the first time, even the most dauntless reader might baulk at reading a strip advertised as a 'part nine', for example. To avoid this problem, most subsequent UK story arcs would be split into smaller chunks of one or two issues with their own individual titles, to disguise the fact that they were just single chapters in a long-running storyline. Ostensibly a two-parter, this story, [23.1] 'Prey', is just the first chapter of a nine-issue arc that will continue through to [23.5] 'Resurrection'.

Roll Call:

Autobots: Optimus Prime, Jazz (flashback only), Prowl, Ironhide (flashback only), Ratchet, Wheeljack, Bumblebee, Brawn, Jetfire, Hoist, Smokescreen, Tracks and Silverbolt.

Decepticons: Megatron, Soundwave, Shockwave, Motormaster, Drag Strip, Dead End, Wildrider, Breakdown, Ramjet (flashback only), Thrust (flashback only), Dirge (flashback only), Galvatron (flashback only), Scourge (flashback only), Runabout (flashback only), Runamuck (flashback only), **Razorclaw**, **Rampage**, **Tantrum**, **Headstrong**, **Divebomb** and **Predaking**.

In both of Smokescreen's appearances here, he's drawn off-model. First, during the flashback on page 3, panel 1, he's drawn to look like Bluestreak, despite Bluestreak not having been present at the battle in the steelworks. Then, on page 7, panel 6, he's missing his trademark shoulder cannons; and again, this cannot be the similar-looking Bluestreak, given that he has been inactive in the UK strips since the injury he sustained in [12.4] 'Dinobot Hunt'.

Data File: Annie Halfacree (letterer)

Now known as Annie Parkhouse following her marriage to fellow *The Transformers* contributor Steve, the Eagle Award-winning Halfacree is best known these days as the resident letterer on the *Judge Dredd* strips. Other credits include *Tank Girl*, *Lion*, *Hellblazer*, *Hellboy* and *Star Wars*.

Review:
Another colourful and eventful entry in the UK canon, and an intriguing first chapter in the 'leaders go to Cybertron' arc. The plotting and scheming of Optimus Prime and Shockwave elevate this story above the usual action fare. The only major negative is the ending, where it's all too obvious that the corpse isn't Prime's real body. 3/5

[23.2] UNDER FIRE!
- UK#98, 31 January 1987 (… The Harder They Die!), 11 pages
- UK#99, 7 February 1987 (Under Fire!), 11 pages.

NB: As with [8.2] 'The Wrath of Grimlock', here are two issues essentially forming a two-part story, despite each having its own individual title. As such, they will be analysed together, using the 'Under Fire' moniker as an umbrella title.

Credits:
Simon Furman (script); Geoff Senior (art, part 1); Jeff Anderson (art, part 2); Steve White (colours); Annie Halfacree (letters); Ian Rimmer (editor); Phil Gascoine (cover, UK#98); Lee Sullivan (cover, UK#99).

Plot:
Optimus Prime is not dead. The Predacons broke off their attack as part of Shockwave's power-play against Megatron, who was able to destroy only the fake Prime. Megatron and Prime were transported to Cybertron after the Decepticon leader activated the space bridge.

Megatron teams up with the commander of Cybertron's Decepticon forces – Lord Straxus. Having narrowly survived death in [18] 'The Bridge to Nowhere', Straxus now exists as a head inside a life-support machine. Megatron feeds false information to the Cybertron-based Autobots, telling them that Optimus Prime is not himself but rather a disguised Decepticon spy.

The Wreckers capture Prime, having fallen for Megatron's misinformation. He is saved by a diminutive Autobot named Outback, the only one that believes him to be the genuine Optimus Prime. Ultra Magnus gives chase, backed up by a gang of Guardian drones. Although Prime and Outback are eventually able to evade their pursuers, Outback is gravely wounded when the Guardians attack.

Ultra Magnus hides out of view and looks on as a defiant Prime vows to save his new friend …

Notes:
Despite this being a Cybertron-set story, we learn very little more about the planet. Straxus presides over the Decepticons from a fortress in the province of Polyhex. (The previous Decepticon fortress, Darkmount, was destroyed in [18] 'The Bridge to Nowhere' – it's unclear if this is a rebuilt Darkmount or a different building entirely.)

Straxus survived the explosion of his body – again, in [18] 'The Bridge to Nowhere' – and now exists as a head in a life-support system. He's planning some kind of strike against Megatron, the nature of which will become clear in [23.5] 'Resurrection'.

It's confirmed that the Autobot city-state of Iacon has been destroyed, as revealed in [20.2] 'Target: 2006', and that a breem is a Cybertonian unit of time, as previously used in [17] 'The Smelting Pool'.

Ultra Magnus's bizarre behaviour here, when he almost executes Prime without first verifying the facts, is explained as a being a result of the guilt he still feels following the death of Impactor in [20.2] 'Target: 2006'. He commands a group of Guardian drones, similar (but not identical) to the model previously seen in [4.3] 'Raiders of the Last Ark' and [8.2] 'The Wrath of Grimlock'. These Cybertronian Guardians are equipped with powerful blaster weapons built into their arms, but seem less durable than those seen in previous stories.

It's confirmed that Optimus Prime's 'corpse' was in fact a Facsimile Construct, a type of fake Transformer last seen in [20.2] 'Target: 2006'. The handcuff-like 'energy restraints' used on Optimus Prime are reminiscent of similar devices seen in {3-00} *The Transformers: The Movie*, which was released theatrically in the UK around a month prior to this story's publication.

Roll Call:
Autobots: Optimus Prime, Ratchet (flashback only), Wheeljack (flashback only), Bumblebee (flashback only), Gears (flashback only), Hoist (flashback only), Blaster (flashback only), Ultra Magnus, Roadbuster, Twin Twist, Rack and Ruin, Springer, Sandstorm and **Outback**.

Decepticons: Megatron, Straxus, Octane, Razorclaw (flashback only), Rampage (flashback only), Tantrum (flashback only), Headstrong (flashback only), Divebomb (flashback only) and **Ratbat**.

Data File: Geoff Senior (artist)
A Transformers fan-favourite, Senior co-created *Death's Head* and *Dragon's Claws* (with Simon Furman). His other comic work includes *2000 AD* and *Action Force*. He later moved out of the comics industry and now works in advertising, although he has made brief returns to the Transformers franchise, including on the UK *Transformers* title for Titan Publishing and *Transformers: Regeneration One* for IDW.

Data File: Phil Gascoine (artist)
Gascoine's long and distinguished career took in titles such as *Battle Action*, *Commando*, *Knights of Pendragon*, *The Unknown Soldier* and *Look-In* (for which he contributed art based on the *Knight Rider* and *Robin of Sherwood* television series).

Review:
This looks really lovely, but plot-wise nothing much happens. Megatron and Straxus rant at each other, the Wreckers act irrationally, and Prime and Outback spend the story getting in and out of scrapes. As a set-up to [23.3] 'Distant Thunder' and [23.5] 'Resurrection', this is a more of a chess play than an actual story – the pieces are being moved into position for the battles yet to come. Functional, but nothing more. 2/5

The Back-Up Strips, Part 12: *Action Force/G.I. Joe*
Action Force (the UK equivalent of the American *G.I. Joe* franchise) would prove to be

the longest-running back-up strip in the UK comic by quite some distance. For further details regarding *Action Force*, see the notes to [27.3] 'Hunters', [36.3] 'Enemy Action' and especially the essay 'Fighting for Freedom' that prefaces the entry for [29.1] 'Ancient Relics'.

- 'Improvisation on a Theme' (UK#99-102), from *G.I. Joe: A Real American Hero* #44 (February 1986). A group of new Action Force recruits are attacked by Cobra during a training mission.
- 'Dummy Run!' (UK#122), from *Action Force* #18 (4 July 1987). Action Force battle Cobra near Stonehenge.
- 'Slaughter' (UK#153-156), from *G.I. Joe: A Real American Hero* #48 (June 1986). The master of disguise, Zartan, infiltrates Action Force HQ.
- 'Serpentor' (UK#157-160), from *G.I. Joe: A Real American Hero* #49 (July 1986). Cobra set about creating an ultimate warrior.
- 'Road Safety – From the Air!' and 'Battle Island' (UK#161). Two mini-strips. The first is a public service ad, produced in conjunction with the UK's Department of Transport. The second is a story of which the final few panels were written and drawn by a competition winner.
- 'The Battle of Springfield' (UK#162-165), from *G.I. Joe: A Real American Hero* #50 (August 1986). Action Force lay siege to Cobra's base in Springfield.
- 'Thunder Machine' (UK#166-169), from *G.I. Joe: A Real American Hero* #51 (September 1986). A swamp battle between the Thunder Machine and HAVOC vehicles.
- 'Snap Decisions' (UK#170-173), from *G.I. Joe: A Real American Hero* #52 (October 1986). Cobra Commander orders the assassination of Serpentor.
- 'Pit-Fall' (UK#174-177), from *G.I. Joe: A Real American Hero* #53 (November 1986). Cobra invade and destroy Action Force's base of operations.
- 'Launch Base' (UK#178-181), from *G.I. Joe: A Real American Hero* #54 (December 1986). Cobra sell a hi-tech base to a Latin American dictator.
- 'Unmaskings' (UK#191-194), from *G.I. Joe: A Real American Hero* #55 (January 1987). Destro and Cobra Commander escape from the ruins of the Pit.
- 'Jungle Moves' (UK#195-198), from *G.I. Joe: A Real American Hero* #56 (February 1987). Action Force launch an attack on a Cobra Terror-Drome.
- 'Hush Job' (UK#199, 201-203), from *G.I. Joe: Yearbook* #3 (March 1987). Scarlett embarks on a daring rescue mission to save Snake-Eyes.
- 'Strange Bedfellows' (UK#204-207), from *G.I. Joe: A Real American Hero* #57 (March 1987). Flint and Lady Jaye foil a plot to impersonate Destro.
- 'Desperate Moves' (UK#208-212), from *G.I. Joe: A Real American Hero* #58 (April 1987). Cobra Commander gains a new battle suit, while GI Joe attack a Terror-Drome in the Middle East.
- 'Divergent Paths' (UK#220-224), from *G.I. Joe: A Real American Hero* #59 (May 1987). Cobra Commander teams up with an eccentric accountant in order to locate Action Force.
- 'Cross Purposes' (UK#225-229), from *G.I. Joe: A Real American Hero* #60 (June 1987). A group of new Action Force recruits are thrown in at the deep end, when they come under attack from the Dreadnoks.
- 'Airshow' (UK#230-231, 233-235), from *G.I. Joe: Special Missions* #12 (August 1988).

When a new Action Force jet is stolen from an air show, Maverick chases after it –
in a biplane.

- 'Beginnings ... and Endings' (UK#236-240), from *G.I. Joe: A Real American Hero* #61
(July 1987). A quartet of Action Force members go undercover to rescue a
kidnapped journalist.
- 'Evasion' (UK#241-245), from *G.I. Joe: Special Missions* #6 (August 1987). Trapped in
Eastern Europe and hunted by a Communist army, Action Force must escape out
of the country.
- 'Divided We Fall!' (UK#245), a four-page mini-comic included with UK#245 (and
also *The Incredible Hulk Presents* #8, as well as being given away free in toy shops); it
was designed to provide an in-fiction explanation for the rebranding of *Action
Force* to *G.I. Joe: The Action Force*.
- 'Law of the Jungle!' (UK#246-247), from *Action Force* #40-41 (5-12 December 1987).
Snake-Eyes and Storm Shadow attempt to retrieve a record tape from a crashed
spy satellite.

From UK#248, the strip was renamed as *G.I. Joe: The Action Force*, as part of a
rebranding of the franchise that took place in 1989.

- 'The Lower Depths' (UK#248-249, 251-253), from *G.I. Joe: Special Missions* #21 (May
1989). GI Joe and Cobra do battle in the New York sewers.
- 'Transit' (UK#254-257), from *G.I. Joe: A Real American Hero* #62 (August 1987).
While Billy trains with Jinx, Outback returns to a frosty reception. Meanwhile, the
captured Joes are sent to a prison work camp.
- 'Going Under' (UK#258-261), from *G.I. Joe: A Real American Hero* #63 (September
1987). Snake Eyes and Scarlett fake their own deaths. Meanwhile, Billy meets the
GI Joe team.
- 'Manoeuvreing [sic] for Position' (UK#262-265), from *G.I. Joe: A Real American Hero*
#64 (October 1987; originally published as 'Maneuvering for Position'). Having
killed Cobra Commander, Fred VII assumes the identity of the villainous leader.
- 'Shuttle Complex' (UK#266-269), from *G.I. Joe: A Real American Hero* #65
(November 1987). The discovery of Cobra's spy satellite network leads to a space
battle against GI Joe.
- 'The Tenth Letter' (UK#270-273), from *G.I. Joe: A Real American Hero* #66
(December 1987). Storm Shadow, Snake-Eyes and Scarlett stage a prison escape.
- 'Cold Snap' (UK#274-277), from *G.I. Joe: A Real American Hero* #67 (January 1988).
Cobra hatch a plot to start civil wars all over the world.
- 'Cut and Freeze Dried' (UK#278-281), from *G.I. Joe: A Real American Hero* #68
(February 1988). The Joes arrive in Frusenland in an attempt to foil Cobra's
scheme.
- 'Into the Breach' (UK#282-285), from *G.I. Joe: A Real American Hero* #69 (March
1988). Both GI Joe and Cobra have forces in the volatile country of Sierra Gordo, a
country gripped by civil war.
- 'Fair Trade' (UK#286-289), from *G.I. Joe: A Real American Hero* #70 (April 1988). A
hijacked plane containing both GI Joe and Cobra troops crash-lands in the jungle.
- 'Bailout' (UK#290-293), from *G.I. Joe: A Real American Hero* #71 (May 1988).
Trapped behind enemy lines, the Joes struggle to escape from Sierra Gordo.

- 'Stiletto' (UK#294-297), from *G.I. Joe: A Real American Hero* #72 (June 1988). Dr Mindbender's latest creation, an enhanced type of human known as a Star Viper, infiltrates G.I. Joe headquarters.
- 'Divided We Fall' (UK#298-301), from *G.I. Joe: A Real American Hero* #73 (July 1988). Civil war breaks out on Cobra Island.
- 'Alliance of Convenience' (UK#302-305), from *G.I. Joe: A Real American Hero* #74 (August 1988). As the battle continues on Cobra Island, the Joes are forced to ally themselves with Dr Mindbender.

[23.3] DISTANT THUNDER!
UK#100, 14 February 1987, 19 pages

Credits:
Simon Furman (script); Will Simpson (pencils); Tim Perkins (inks); Steve White (colours); Annie Halfacree (letters); Ian Rimmer (editor); Alan Davis and Thomas Davis (cover).

NB: Renowned comic writer and artist Alan Davis was the sole contributor to the cover art, but requested that his young son Thomas (a big Transformers fan) be given a co-credit.

Plot:
Optimus Prime and Outback hide underground as the Wreckers close in for the kill. To lift the spirits of his badly-wounded companion, Prime tells a story of when he and a number of other Transformers were transported to another dimension …

The dimension is home to two races of techno-organic beings: the heroic Cloran; and a group of simian invaders, led by a tyrant named Zenag. The stranded Autobots (Prime, Prowl and Ratchet) vow to help the Cloran fight the invaders, but the Decepticons (Shockwave, Frenzy and Thundercracker) would rather cut a deal with Zenag in return for a route home.

Goaded by Zenag into fighting the Decepticons, Prime realises that things are all-too-familiar – the history of the Cloran mirrors that of the Autobots themselves, and Zenag is just as calculating as Shockwave. Prime realises that the entire scenario is a deception, designed to get the stranded Transformers fighting amongst themselves. Realising they have been duped, the Autobots and Decepticons cease fighting, and the real culprits soon show themselves – alien parasites who feed on negative emotions.

Back in the present, the Wreckers finally discover Prime's and Outback's hiding-place, but Ultra Magnus – who overhears Prime making a speech about non-violent solutions – realises that this is in fact the real Optimus Prime, who is welcomed back into the Autobot ranks.

Notes:
Optimus Prime finally reveals what happened to him and the five other Transformers who were shunted into another dimension to make way for the arrivals of Galvatron, Hot Rod and company in [20.2] 'Target: 2006'.

This story also addresses the subject of the wound on Optimus Prime's torso. From the American point of view, the damage is done in [19] 'Command Performance', and is seen again in stories such as [21] 'Aerialbots over America' and [22] 'Heavy Traffic'.

According to the UK stories, the damage in [19] 'Command Performances' is only minor, and the wound seen in later stories is caused by the illusory Zenag during the battle we see in this issue.

Optimus Prime's hiding-place is in an underground tunnel located beneath the Dead End region (the home of the destitute Empties seen in [17] 'The Smelting Pool'). Aside from the main flashback, Prime also remembers the events of [23.2] 'Under Fire', specifically his trip though the space bridge, his capture by the Autobots and Megatron's alliance with Straxus.

This is our first sighting of the void-like dimension that will in later issues be referred to as 'limbo'. It's populated by green blob-like aliens who feed on negative emotions by creating nightmarish visions that, if not interrupted, can manifest as physical reality.

This was a special nineteen-page strip contained within a celebratory bumper issue #100 of the UK comic.

Roll Call:
Autobots: Optimus Prime, Prowl (flashback only), Ratchet (flashback only), Emirate Xaaron, Ultra Magnus, Roadbuster (flashback only), Whirl, Twin Twist (flashback only), Springer, Sandstorm, Broadside and Outback.

Decepticons: Megatron, Thundercracker, Frenzy and Straxus – all flashback-only.

Data File: Alan Davis (artist)
Davis is a huge name in the world of comics, having either written for or drawn many notable titles, including *Batman*, *Detective Comics*, *Avengers*, *Captain America*, *Fantastic Four*, *Uncanny X-Men*, *Captain Britain*, *Thor*, and *2000 AD*.

Review:
Considering this is a milestone issue, 'Distant Thunder' is disarmingly low-key. Despite not being a particularly momentous or game-changing story, it's still a fitting celebration of all that's good about the UK comic.

On the negative side, some of the plotting is quite familiar – the idea of aliens who feed on negative emotions is not a new one in science fiction (the 1968 *Star Trek* episode 'Day of the Dove' being a notable prior example), and the notion that dreams might be dangerous has already been explored in the pages of *The Transformers*, in [A2.5] 'Victory' and [16.2] 'Second Generation'.

But all that is window-dressing in a story that is resolutely about Optimus Prime and what he stands for. Here is a flawed but noble character, laid bare. His nobility, his courage and his intelligence are all put to the test and, through it all, he remains true to his beliefs, even willing to die for them. Despite the clichéd sci-fi tropes that act as backdrop, this is essentially a character piece, and an excellent one at that. 4/5

UK Straplines, Part 2
Another collection of straplines from the cover of *The Transformers* UK, this time from issues #67 to #132.

- UK#67: 'Eat molten metal, Decepticons!'
- UK#68: Bridging the gap between … the war of the worlds!

- UK#69: Duel!
- UK#70: 'Autobots – attack!'
- UK#71: Omega … Supreme!
- UK#72: Robot mastered …?
- UK#73: 'This town ain't big enough for the both of us, Autobot – draw!' (as per US#20)
- UK#74: The Dinobots … cut loose!
- UK#75: Double jeopardy!
- UK#76: Swoop – up, up … and blown away?!
- UK#77: This one … has it all!
- UK#78: Going … going … gone! The shocking fate of Optimus Prime!
- UK#79: Galvatron … Ultra Magnus … the new leaders are here!
- UK#80: Arrival!
- UK#81: To be continued …?
- UK#82: Meet the Wreckers … and get wrecked!
- UK#83: Scourge is scrapped … and not by an Autobot!
- UK#84: At last! The awesome origin of … Galvatron!
- UK#85: Galvatron's Autobot zombie!
- UK#86: It's crunch time!
- UK#87: 'Lights!' 'Camera!' 'Action!'
- UK#88: Volcano erupts without Magnus! Maybe it doesn't matter!
- UK#89: Slave of the Insecticons!
- UK#90: 'Autobots!' 'Wrong, Decepticon, we're Aerialbots'
- UK#91: Stunticons make Menasor … make trouble!
- UK#92: Robot roadworks!
- UK#93: Christmas greetings from Galvatron … 'I'll be back!'
- UK#94: Battle Chargers [sic] … the fastest Transformers on Earth!
- UK#95: 'What are we doing here, Runamuck?' 'Taking liberties, Runabout?'
- UK#96: Prime's the prey … and he hasn't got a prayer!
- UK#97: Terror of the Predacons!
- UK#98: 'Home, sweet home …!'
- UK#99: 'Any last requests, prisoner …?'
- UK#100: none
- UK#101: 'I'm back … and I'm mad!'
- UK#102: 'His name's Galvatron …' 'He's real powerful … and completely insane!' 'Now all we gotta do is … stop 'im!'
- UK#103: Prime and Magnus … side by side on Cybertron!
- UK#104: No mercy for Megatron!
- UK#105: Deadlock!
- UK#106: … And one shall die!
- UK#107: Rampage!
- UK#108: 'Strike two, Megatron …' 'You're out!'
- UK#109: All in a day's work for … The Mechanic!
- UK#110: Under attack … from the *Ark*!
- UK#111: The Autobots want a new leader! 'Vote for me!'
- UK#112: Dinosaur war!
- UK#113: Rodimus Prime speaks out … 'Bring me the head of Galvatron!'
- UK#114: Introducing: the all-new Rodimus Prime! 'What's yours called?'
- UK#115: none
- UK#116: Galvatron victorious!

- UK#117: The good … the mad … and the ugly!
- UK#118: 'Eat particle cannon, Prime!'
- UK#119: 'Galvatron!' 'Come on Down!'
- UK#120: 'I've won!' Who can stop Galvatron?
- UK#121: 'Surrender, Autobots!!' The Mechanic … is back!
- UK#122: Goldbug – on the dis-assembly line!
- UK#123: Trouble – times three!
- UK#124: Scrapped by the Scraplets! 'Yum! Yum!'
- UK#125: And now … *Action Force*
- UK#126: At Ratbat's command!
- UK#127: 'Foood!' Throttlebots – on the menu!
- UK#128: 'Fetch!'
- UK#129: none
- UK#130: 'Hi there!' 'We're' 'The' 'Headmasters!'
- UK#131: Scorponok's sting!
- UK#132: 'Sorry, kid – you're on your own!'

[23.4] FALLEN ANGEL
- UK#101, 21 February 1987 (Part One), 11 pages
- UK#102, 28 February 1987 (Part Two), 11 pages

Also reprinted in the 1991 *Transformers Annual*

Credits:
Simon Furman (script); Geoff Senior (art, part 1); Jeff Anderson (art, part 2); Steve White (colours); Annie Halfacree (letters); Ian Rimmer (editor); Lee Sullivan (cover, UK#101); Geoff Senior (cover, UK#102).

Plot:
No longer imprisoned by RAAT, Skids leads Blaster and the rest of the Cybertron Seven back towards the *Ark*. However, at that moment Galvatron arrives from the future, displacing Skids into the limbo dimension.

Blaster and his friends prove no match for the deranged Decepticon, who is on the verge of destroying them when the Dinobots arrive on the scene. The Dinobots are out for revenge following the destruction of Centurion, whom Galvatron beheaded soon after his arrival on Earth.

Despite initially faring well, the Dinobots soon lose the upper hand – and they, too, are nearly destroyed. They are saved when Professor Morris, the brains behind the remote-controlled Centurion robot, takes mental control of Swoop's body and attacks again.

Eventually the Decepticons show up, and also attack Galvatron – their leader Shockwave fears being usurped by the unhinged time-traveller. Unwilling to fight back against his fellow Decepticons, Galvatron retreats.

Notes:
In this story the scene switches back to Earth, as we discover the fate of those Autobots who were captured by RAAT in [21] 'Aerialbots over America' and [22] 'Heavy Traffic', and then later released in [23] 'Decepticon Graffiti'. There is no mention of the

Aerialbots – the presence of Silverbolt in [23.1] 'Prey' indicates that they flew on ahead while the rest of the Autobots travelled on foot.

This is the first appearance of Galvatron since [20.2] 'Target: 2006'. It's revealed that, after he left the present-day in that story, he returned to his own time period. Immediately after the events of *The Transformers: The Movie*, in which he is defeated by being hurled into space, he reactivates his time-jump mechanism and travels to 1987. His planetfall, plus a couple of sonic attacks courtesy of Blaster, has made the future Decepticon mentally unstable.

Also returning in this story are the Dinobots and Centurion, who have been in a self-imposed exile following the events of [20.1] 'In the National Interest'. With them comes Centurion's controller, Professor Morris, making his final appearance in the comic, although Centurion will be rebuilt in [29.1] 'Ancient Relics'.

As in [20.2] 'Target: 2006', Galvatron's arrival in the present means that a Transformer of similar mass is displaced into the limbo dimension (see also [23.3] 'Distant Thunder'). Skids is the unfortunate victim on this occasion, and will be confined to that void for a *very* long time (returning only when Galvatron is killed – see [53.1] 'Survivors').

This story apparently takes place in the Powder River Basin area of Wyoming – explosions from the battle with Galvatron are visible from the Decepticons' coalmine base. Shockwave sees the explosions and fears that they're being caused by Megatron, whom Shockwave double-crossed in [23.1] 'Prey'. It's confirmed that Shockwave is now the leader of the Decepticon army on Earth (a position he previously held between [5] 'The New Order' and [19] 'Command Performances').

Although he had previously appeared in Marvel's comic adaptation of *The Transformers: The Movie*, released as a mini-series in the US and as a Winter Special in the UK, this story sees the first appearance of Rodimus Prime in the comics proper.

Roll Call:
Autobots: Grimlock, Snarl, Slag, Sludge, Swoop, Skids, Blaster, Powerglide, Cosmos, Seaspray, Warpath, Beachcomber, Perceptor and **Rodimus Prime** (flashback only).

Decepticons: Soundwave, Shockwave, Shrapnel, Thrust, Dirge, Galvatron, Razorclaw and Rampage.

The appearance of Thrust here is by no means confirmed – he is seen only in the background, block-coloured and missing his distinctive wings. This could possibly be an appearance by Ramjet instead. However, since this mystery Decepticon is coloured quite darkly, it's more likely to be the deep red Thrust than the white Ramjet.

Other: Circuit Breaker (flashback only), Professor Morris, Walter Barnett (flashback only), Centurion and Unicron (flashback only).

Review:
Essentially, this is just a 22-page fight scene, reintroducing a few characters that haven't been seen for a while. The star of the show is Galvatron himself, who is unstoppable, insane, and a great deal of fun. Story-wise there's not much to chew on here, but this is entertainment on a purely visceral level, with no pretentions of being anything more. A guilty pleasure. 4/5

The Back-Up Strips, Part 13: *The Inhumanoids*

The Inhumanoids was another Hasbro/Sunbow toy line/cartoon tie-in comic, under Marvel's Star Comics imprint. An adaptation of the cartoon mini-series, it was cancelled after four issues, ending on a cliffhanger. As the UK printing was so close to the original American publication, the cancellation came as a surprise to the UK production team, who subsequently included in the comic's letters page many complaints from readers, begging for the cliffhanger to be resolved. Never again would a back-up strip be taken from so recent a publication.

- 'The Coming of the Inhumanoids!, Part 1' (UK#103-106), from *The Inhumanoids* #1 (January 1987). The Earth Corps investigate the appearance of giant monsters on Earth.
- 'The Coming of the Inhumanoids!, Part II (or, "I Left My Monsters in San Francisco")' (UK#107-110), from *The Inhumanoids* #2 (March 1987). The Earth Corps learn about the Inhumanoids' origins.
- 'The Coming of the Inhumanoids: The Battle Down Below!' (UK#111-114), from *The Inhumanoids* #3 (May 1987). The Earth Corps venture underground into the Inhumanoids' domain.
- 'Metlar Unleashed' (UK#115-118), from *The Inhumanoids* #4 (July 1987). The third and final Inhumanoid, Metlar, escapes from his centuries-long imprisonment.

[23.5] RESURRECTION!
- UK#103, 7 March 1987 (Part 1), 11 pages
- UK#104, 14 March 1987 (Part 2), 11 pages

This story was also reprinted later in the comic's run, as follows (NB: each original instalment was divided in half and spread across a couple of issues):

- UK#229, 5 August 1989 (Part 1), 5 pages
- UK#230, 12 August 1989 (Part 2), 6 pages
- UK#231, 19 August 1989 (Part 3), 6 pages
- UK#232, 26 August 1989 (Part 4), 5 pages

Credits:
Simon Furman (script); Will Simpson (art, part 1); Jeff Anderson (art, part 2); Steve White (colours); Annie Halfacree (letters); Ian Rimmer (editor); Martin Griffiths and Robin Bouttell (cover, UK#103); Geoff Senior (cover, UK#104).

Plot:
On Cybertron, the Decepticons are in disarray. The local Autobots, united under the twin leadership of Optimus Prime and Ultra Magnus, have made numerous successful raids against them. Furthermore, the increasingly dangerous and unstable Megatron threatens the Decepticons from within.

The decapitated Straxus has a plan to get rid of Megatron, using a mind-transfer device to exchange bodies with him. However, the transfer goes wrong – there are now two personalities in Megatron's body, vying for control.

Prime and Magnus attack the Decepticon stronghold in Polyhex, but Ratbat kills three birds with one stone by summoning the space bridge, sending the two Autobots and the confused Megatron back to Earth.

Notes:
This story features the first mention of Energon cubes (a powerful energy source) since [18] 'The Bridge to Nowhere'. In the Cybertron sequences, Straxus measures time in days, indicating that as well as the alien-sounding measurements such as breems and vorns, Cybertron's (former) period of rotation is also used to measure time on the planet.

Prime's address to the Autobots takes place in the Wreckers' Autobase located beneath Iacon, last seen in [20.2] 'Target: 2006' (and possibly also in [23.2] 'Under Fire', though it's unclear). It's confirmed that Straxus came to power following the assassination of Megatron's successor (the warlord Trannis, as described in [20.2] 'Target: 2006').

Optimus Prime's funeral on Earth sees his remains buried – apparently it's 'what he would have wanted', although the usual practice is to send Autobot cadavers into space via a small rocket. (Note that other 'dead' Autobots such as Sunstreaker and Bluestreak never got such a funeral, and are later seen lying in stasis modules aboard the *Ark* – it would appear that such ceremonies are held only in those rare cases where there is zero chance of repair.)

In attendance at the funeral are the 'Cybertron Seven' (Blaster, Perceptor, Beachcomber, Cosmos, Seaspray, Warpath and Powerglide), who have finally made it back to the *Ark*. They arrived on Earth in [18] 'The Bridge to Nowhere' and were immediately captured by RAAT. Having been released in [23] 'Decepticon Graffiti', they recall how they got lost on their voyage to the *Ark*, were attacked by Galvatron, but saved by the Dinobots, who gave them directions back to the Autobot base (as seen in [23.4] 'Fallen Angel').

Here Megatron attempts to use his seldom-seen ability to tap into the power of a black hole (last seen in [4.3] 'Raiders of the Last *Ark*'). Straxus's attempted body swap is unsuccessful, resulting in both personalities being trapped inside Megatron's body (according to Soundwave's mind scan). Although the Megatron personality would seem to be the dominant one, it has left the Decepticon leader suffering from amnesia, and he has no memory of Shockwave's attempted coup (in [23.1] 'Prey').

There are flashbacks to [23.2] 'Under Fire' (Prime and Megatron falling onto the space bridge; Prime's capture by the Wreckers) and [23.3] 'Distant Thunder' (Emirate Xaaron arriving on the scene as Prime cradles Outback's prone body). There is also a reference to Galvatron's original arrival on 20th Century Earth (as seen in [20.2] 'Target: 2006').

Counter-Plot
In the recent run of UK-only stories, from [23.1] 'Prey' through to [23.5] 'Resurrection', we've seen a number of memorable events, such as: Optimus Prime's 'death' and subsequent funeral, Megatron's descent into insanity, Shockwave's attempt to usurp Megatron, and the introduction of the Predacons.

In the next three US-originated stories, from [24] 'Afterdeath' to [26] 'Funeral for a Friend', we'll see some even more iconic storylines, such as ... Optimus Prime's death and subsequent funeral, Megatron's descent into insanity, Shockwave's attempt to usurp Megatron, and the introduction of the Predacons. So, what's the reason for the repetition of these storylines? And did it spoil the reading experience for British fans who saw all these similarly-themed stories printed in the UK comic?

We already know that the UK production team had early access to upcoming American storylines – for example, the events of [17] 'The Smelting Pool' were teased in the Transformation page in UK#39 in December 1985, two full months before that story saw its print debut in the US. So UK writer Simon Furman must have known how future American strips were going to play out, and yet still decided to duplicate many of their story beats. This was especially harsh on American writer Bob Budiansky, whose original stories looked derivative and recycled when published in the UK *after* the Furman versions.

What's interesting is how much effort it took to reconcile multiple versions of the same events. A lot of text in [25] 'Gone But Not Forgotten' had to be rewritten for its UK printing, and the UK stories had Megatron suffer amnesia, so he could be surprised when Shockwave made a play against him for a second time. The Predacons, meanwhile, were called to Earth in [23.1] 'Prey', only for them to be sent back to Cybertron at the end of [23.5] 'Resurrection', so it wouldn't contradict the events of [25] 'Gone but Not Forgotten' when they were recalled to Earth once more. So clearly the duplication of plots was not only intentional, but was deemed such a good idea that Furman didn't mind bending over backwards to shoehorn everything (rather clumsily) into a single canon for UK readers.

But why do it in the first place? Well, for one thing, there's an argument to be made that it was intended to enhance the impact of the upcoming US storylines. We already knew from [20.2] 'Target: 2006' that the Autobots were a shambles when robbed of Optimus Prime's leadership. These UK stories had Prime fake his own death (in [23.1] 'Prey'), to test whether or not the Autobots were ready should he ever go missing again. Yet again, the Autobots were found wanting, with [23.5] 'Resurrection' showing them as unsure of what to do, and arguing amongst themselves. So when Prime is killed again – for real, this time – in [24] 'Afterdeath', it gives his death much greater impact, as it's just been hammered home to us how badly the Autobots fare when devoid of their leader.

Another point to note is that Optimus Prime was, at this point, the cornerstone of the Transformers franchise. Although he had been killed off in *The Transformers: The Movie*, that film was set in the 21st Century, and so for UK readers at least (the stories in their version of the comic having been tied in to the events of the movie), it was taken for granted that the Autobot leader was safe for at least the next twenty years. Having Prime 'die' in [23.1] 'Prey' only to return unscathed (as he did previously in [20.2] 'Target: 2006') just lent more credence to the feeling that he was nearly immortal, and could escape from pretty much anything. Again, this made his real death in [24] 'Afterdeath' all the more affecting, simply because, prior to this point, readers had been hoodwinked into believing that Prime was more or less indestructible.

As regards Megatron, his descent into madness came pretty much out of the blue for American readers. Other than his impatience with Soundwave in [23] 'Decepticon Graffiti', there were no other signs of his paranoia until he finally snapped in [25] 'Gone but Not Forgotten'. When the UK stories are added to the American canon, then, we get a much slower, more gradual slide into insanity, as Megatron gets more and more paranoid until [23.5] 'Resurrection', where he's the victim of a failed attempt to swap his mind with that of Straxus. It is in that moment that Megatron finally loses his last vestige of sanity; and this gives us a proper technological explanation for his behaviour in [25] 'Gone but Not Forgotten'.

It can be argued, then, that despite the repetition of ideas, having these UK stories pre-empt the American ones actually worked to the comic's benefit overall, heightening the emotion of Prime's later death, and giving us a greater understanding of Megatron's growing insanity.

Roll Call:
Autobots: Optimus Prime, Jazz, Prowl, Ironhide, Ratchet, Hound, Wheeljack, Bumblebee, Brawn, Jetfire, Smokescreen, Silverbolt, Blaster, Powerglide, Cosmos, Seaspray, Warpath, Beachcomber, Perceptor, Omega Supreme, Emirate Xaaron, Ultra Magnus, Roadbuster, Topspin, Twin Twist, Springer, Sandstorm, Broadside, Outback (flashback only), **Pipes** and **Tailgate**.

With the exception of the absent Gears, Fireflight, Skydive, Air Raid and Slingshot, the Autobots in attendance at Optimus Prime's funeral represent the entirety of the Earth-based Autobot army. This is Omega Supreme's first appearance since his debut in [19] 'Command Performances'.

Two of the new mini-Autobots make blink-and-you'll-miss-them cameos as background characters in this story – Pipes on the second page of Part 1 (on the far left, block-coloured and partially obscured by scenery), and Tailgate on the seventh page (in the first panel, amongst the Autobots in the crowd scene at Prime's speech).

Decepticons: Megatron, Soundwave, Frenzy, Shockwave, Straxus, Galvatron (flashback only), Astrotrain, Blitzwing, Octane, Razorclaw, Tantrum, Headstrong and Ratbat.

Data File: Robin Bouttell (colourist)
Bouttell coloured many covers for the UK *The Transformers* comic. He later became an artist and sculptor, concentrating on lifelike representations of animals.

Review:
The final chapter in the latest run of UK-originated stories, this story works well as a closure to recent arcs and as a set-up to the stories that follow. It's a great last hurrah for Prime and Megatron, who would soon be killed off in the American strips. Optimus Prime gets to be truly heroic, a fearless, inspirational freedom fighter, while Megatron finally snaps after undergoing a failed mind-swap. Witty, clever and action-packed. 5/5

[24] AFTERDEATH!
US#24, 'January 1987' (published September 1986), 23 pages.

British reprint: UK#105, 21 March 1987 (Part One), 11 pages; UK#106, 28 March 1987 (Part Two), 12 pages.

Credits:
Bob Budiansky (script); Don Perlin (pencils); Ian Akin, Brian Garvey (inks); Nel Yomtov (colours); Janice Chiang (letters); Don Daley (editor); Jim Shooter (editor-in-chief); Herb Trimpe (cover). **UK:** Lee Sullivan (cover, UK#105); Herb Trimpe and Robin Bouttell (cover, UK#106 – re-coloured adaptation of US cover).

Plot:

The Decepticons attack a branch of high-tech firm Energy Futures Industries, who have developed a new power generator, the Hydrothermocline, which draws energy from thermal layers in the ocean. Inevitably, the Autobots arrive on the scene in an attempt to stop the Decepticons.

To prevent an all-out battle and risk the destruction of the Hydrothermocline, computer expert Ethan Zachary proposes an alternative solution – the Autobots and Decepticons will battle it out safely within a virtual-reality computer game, with the Decepticons getting to keep the Hydrothermocline if they win. Megatron requests raising the stakes so that either his or Prime's life will be forfeit, depending on who loses the game.

Upon entering the game, Optimus Prime insists that the Autobots stay true to their principles, despite the unreality of their situation. This stipulation works to the Autobots' advantage – after they save the lives of some of the native in-game characters, those characters then return the favour and help them against the Decepticons.

Prime is initially victorious, but Megatron uses a 'cheat code' that puts him back in the game. The Autobot leader defeats Megatron again, this time for good, but in doing so, inadvertently kills some of the game's other virtual characters.

Zachary prepares the kill-switch to destroy Megatron, but is overruled by Prime, who insists that, by killing some of the in-game characters, it was in fact *he* who 'cheated'. Optimus Prime is destroyed and the Hydrothermocline is given to the Decepticons.

The final scene shows Zachary filing away a floppy disc marked with the name 'Optimus Prime' …

Notes:

The video game craze was just taking off in the mid-1980s (thanks to the launch of affordable home computers and consoles such as the Nintendo Entertainment System and the Commodore 64), and movies featuring them as a major plot point had become a popular Hollywood sub-genre, examples including *WarGames* (Jon Badham, 1983), *Tron* (Steven Lisberger, 1982) and *The Last Starfighter* (Nick Castle, 1984).

The (fictional) video game played by Ethan Zachary in this story is named *Multi-World* (created by 'Flippy-Floppy Industries'), and has a number of zones or levels including Metropipe, Cloud-Steppes, Vineland and Slimepit. Zachary's lab contains a giant viewscreen, the Spectramax 2000, which he uses to play the game. Characters in the game include Formulak the Compuzoid, and the Hordes of Hazzak. These characters (and indeed Optimus Prime) can be saved to a floppy disk for potential reuse.

By 1987 commercial floppy disks had capacities up to 2.88MB (not even large enough to hold a three-minute pop song at low 128kbps quality), which would imply that Optimus Prime has a very small brain. However, it's possible that Zachary has access to higher-capacity disks than were commercially available.

Almost overshadowed by Optimus Prime's death, this story sees the US debut of two more combining teams, the Protectobots and the Combaticons. They had previously appeared in the UK-only story [16.3] 'Second Generation', but only as part of Buster's Matrix-induced visions. No explanation is given for their sudden appearance – at the time of publication, it was presumed that they were created on Earth (like the

Aerialbots and Stunticons as seen in [22] 'Heavy Traffic), but a flashback in [47] 'Club Con' will depict Defensor as having been active on Cybertron 'hundreds of years ago' (a flashback that is probably unreliable, given that it also shows Sunstreaker on Cybertron).

It's in this story that the cerebro-shell implanted into Prime's brain in [22] 'Heavy Traffic' is finally removed. It seems to have had a limited range, as in [23.3] 'Fallen Angel', Shockwave seemed oblivious to the whereabouts of Megatron (which he would have known had he been able to tap into Prime's cerebro-shell while the Autobot leader was on Cybertron).

The Hydrothermocline is based on a real-world OTEC (Ocean Thermal Energy Conversion) system, which uses the heat differential between surface water and deep water in the oceans to produce electricity. Such systems are usually expensive and inefficient however, so it would appear that Zachary's Hydrothermocline is a particularly advanced form that has solved such issues. (See also [A2.3] 'The Return of the Transformers' for another example of Decepticons targeting advanced sea-based energy generators.)

UK Changes:
Page 1, panel 1: 'colorist' is changed to 'colourist'.
Page 5, panel 3: the reference to issue 22 is changed to issue 91.
Page 11, panel 6: to ensure that the UK mid-story cliffhanger doesn't come in the middle of a conversation, Hot Spot's speech bubble ('No, Optimus Prime') is omitted.
Page 12, panel 1: similarly, Optimus Prime's initial response to Hot Spot ('No?') is also excised.

Why Does Optimus Prime Die?
From a behind-the-scenes point of view, the reasoning for Optimus Prime's demise is clear: by 1987 the figure was no longer on sale, and Hasbro insisted that the comic focus on those characters who still had toys on the shelves. The cartoon had killed the Autobot leader in dramatic fashion (in {3-00} *The Transformers: The Movie*), and now the comic had to follow suit.

But while Optimus Prime's demise in 'Afterdeath' is suitably dramatic, it makes little sense from a narrative point of view. Optimus Prime wins the computer game, despite Megatron having cheated, but nevertheless concedes victory because, in beating Megatron, he unwittingly caused the deaths of the in-game inhabitants of Metropipe. In other words, Optimus Prime asks to be destroyed because he killed some unreal characters.

In previous issues, it's been demonstrated that Optimus Prime has an almost religious adherence to his moral principles. In [19] 'Command Performances', he is inconsolable when he thinks Skids has been killed: 'One life lost is one life too many,' he says. 'I have failed in my role as Autobot commander.'

Prime's way of thinking is expanded upon in the UK-only stories. In [4.1] 'Man of Iron', he orders the destruction of an Autobot spacecraft (and its sentient Navigator), rather than let it fall into the hands of the Decepticons for possible use against humans. In [12.2] 'Crisis of Command' he rejects the idea of building new Autobots for fear of the effect they would have on the Earth and its people. More recently, [23.3] 'Distant Thunder' had him willing to make the ultimate sacrifice: 'If, as a result of my death, just one … life is saved … the real victory will be mine!'

However, while it's within reason to expect Prime to lay down his life for other beings, it strains credulity that he would sacrifice himself for some non-sentient characters in a computer game, especially when his death results in the Decepticons getting their hands on the state-of-the-art Hydrothermocline.

So perhaps there's an external reason for Prime's bizarre behaviour here. Since the comics began, Optimus Prime has had to endure a number of attacks that could have caused damage to his mind. He was decapitated by Shockwave, who subjected his head to a number of invasive procedures ([5] 'The New Order' *et seq*); he connected his brain to that of the human Buster Witwicky in order to experience a shared dream ([16.2] 'Second Generation'); he was forcibly transported to a limbo dimension where his brain was attacked by emotion-sapping parasites ([20.2] 'Target: 2006' and [23.3] 'Distant Thunder'); his mind was invaded by a cerebro-shell ([22] 'Heavy Traffic'); and, finally, his brain was affected by the PARD device ([A2.2] 'To a Power Unknown'). Any one of these traumas might have caused Prime to exhibit some illogical behaviour; having undergone *all five* is bound to have had a cumulative effect on his psyche. While, on its own terms, the ending to 'Afterdeath' is quite absurd (and the story certainly seems to be written on the basis that Prime is *compos mentis*), we can just about make it work if we assume that he is suffering from mental trauma as a result of the events of previous stories.

Roll Call:
Autobots: Optimus Prime, Wheeljack, Hot Spot, Streetwise, Blades, Groove, First Aid and Defensor.

Decepticons: Megatron, Onslaught, Brawl, Blast Off, Swindle, Vortex and Bruticus.

Other: **Ethan Zachary.**

Data File: Don Daley (editor)
Daley served as editor on many Marvel titles, including runs of *Captain America*, *Fantastic Four*, *G.I. Joe: A Real American Hero* and *The Punisher*.

Review:
Up until its twenthieth page, 'Afterdeath' is a really good story. Having the Autobots and Decepticons battle each other inside a computer game is a brilliant idea, and the depiction of the CGI Multi-World is suitably weird. Megatron, with his use of the cheat code, has never been more devious; and the script is aided by regular penciller Don Perlin, who gives Megatron some priceless facial expressions (his smug grin at the top of page 20 being a highlight). However, everything is overshadowed by that horrendous ending, in which Optimus Prime sacrifices himself because he killed some computer game characters. The shock of seeing Prime die (and it's a gorgeously-drawn death, with pieces flying everywhere) cannot compensate for the utter stupidity of the ending. 1/5

[25] GONE BUT NOT FORGOTTEN!
US#25, 'February 1987' (published October 1986), 22 pages.

British reprint: UK#107, 4 April 1987 (Part One), 11 pages; UK#108, 11 April 1987

(Part Two), 11 pages.

Credits:
Bob Budiansky (script); Don Perlin (pencils); Ian Akin, Brian Garvey (inks); Nel Yomtov (colours); Janice Chiang (letters); Don Daley (editor); Jim Shooter (editor-in-chief); Herb Trimpe (cover). **UK:** Dave Hine and Robin Bouttell (cover, UK#107); Herb Trimpe and Robin Bouttell (cover, UK#108 – re-coloured adaptation of US cover).

Plot:
With the Hydrothermocline now under their control, the Decepticons prepare to swap their old coal-mine base for a new island headquarters off the coast of Florida. The increasingly-unhinged Megatron still suspects that Optimus Prime might be alive, and attacks his fellow Decepticon Brawl in a mad rage. Megatron also destroys a passing truck, just because it bears a resemblance to the former Autobot leader's vehicle mode.

Shockwave, having grown increasingly weary of Megatron's mood swings, decides to act – he recalls the Predacons from Cybertron via the space bridge and has them attack the erratic Decepticon leader. Megatron manages to win the battle.

Manic, paranoid and dangerously unstable, Megatron begins indiscriminately firing his fusion cannon, destroying himself and the space bridge.

Notes:
The story begins with the US military, under the aegis of Triple-I, making an attempt at attacking the Decepticon base. As per previous efforts (see, for example, [4] 'The Last Stand' and [14] 'Rock and Roll-Out'), the humans prove no match for the Decepticons.

It's in this story that the Decepticons finally give up their coal-mine base in Wyoming (occupied since [15] 'I, Robot Master') and set up a new base on an uninhabited island in the Florida Keys. The location of this new island base is shown on Shockwave's map – however, because the map is drawn quite vaguely (perhaps deliberately so), it's impossible to pin it down to an actual real-world location.

Writer Bob Budiansky must certainly have consulted some maps prior to scripting this story; it's stated that the Decepticons take two days to drive from Wyoming to Florida, which seems reasonable; and that they travel via US Route 1, which runs north-south along the east coast of the USA, from Maine to Florida.

For the Predacons' mission on Earth, Shockwave has recorded some instructions (and indeed, elements of his own brain) onto a format known as Laser Disk (not to be confused with LaserDisc, a real-world optical storage solution introduced in 1978).

The clam bar destroyed during the fight between Megatron and the Predacons is called Conch Republic. This has been a nickname for the Florida Keys since 1982, when a dispute over a roadblock prompted the Florida city of Key West to stage a tongue-in-cheek 'secession' from the United States.

In dialogue, Shockwave refers to the nefarious terrorist organisation Cobra, with whom the Decepticons forged an uneasy alliance in [GIJ2] 'Power Struggle'. (The *G.I. Joe and the Transformers* comic series is set around the same time as the events of this story.)

There are many references back to the previous story, [24] 'Afterdeath' – Shockwave mentions the theft of the Hydrothermocline, and great play is made of Optimus Prime's recent demise. With Megatron dying in an explosion here, it means that, within the space of two issues, both original Transformer faction leaders have been written out of the comic.

UK Notes:
For its UK printing, this story had to be heavily edited to reflect the fact that the Predacons had already made one previous attempt at Megatron's life, in [23.1] 'Prey'. Furthermore, the *G.I. Joe and the Transformers* comic would not be printed in the UK for a number of years, so all references to that title were excised. As such, there were many more changes made to the text than was usually the case …

UK Changes:
Page 1, panel 1: 'penciler' and 'colorist' were anglicised to 'penciller' and 'colourist' respectively.
Page 2, panel 7: Shockwave's dialogue changes, as follows:

US version:
SHOCKWAVE: '… and radio Cobra. Tell them we're moving our base of operations closer to their Caribbean island. We must maintain this pretence of cooperation with these fleshlings … at least for now.'

UK version:
SHOCKWAVE: '… **but let us not trouble Megatron with the news that communications with Cybertron are now so simple. He, er … seems to be less interested in day to day Decepticon affairs since the death of Prime.**'

In the same panel, the editorial note has also been altered. Original US printing: 'For more on the Cobra/Decepticon alliance, see the *G.I. Joe/Transformers* limited series, on sale now.' UK version: 'This most shocking event – the demise of the Autobot leader, Optimus Prime – was shown in full in last week's *The Transformers!*'
Page 4, panel 7: 'last issue' is changed to 'issues 105/106'.
Page 8, panel 4: correcting a mistake in the US printing, the Decepticon Dead End is coloured red and given his proper name. (In the US version, he was coloured yellow and misidentified as Drag Strip.)
Page 9, panels 5-6: more dialogue is altered, as follows:

US version:
SHOCKWAVE: 'You'll find coordinates to which you'll send the space bridge. There is also an additional assignment. As leader of the Predacons you'll appreciate this, Razorclaw. It involves your team's speciality – hunting.'

RAZORCLAW: 'Who's our prey?'
SHOCKWAVE: 'The most dangerous prey of all – Megatron. Needless to say, a successful hunt will earn you a most generous reward.'

UK version:
SHOCKWAVE: 'You'll find coordinates to which you'll send the space bridge. **I will be there to meet you and your Predacons. Your team's special hunting talents are needed again – and once more it is Megatron who is your prey!**'

RAZORCLAW: '**But he knows us!**'
SHOCKWAVE: '**No – he's so deranged he's forgotten your first attack.** Needless to say, a successful hunt still earns you a most generous reward.'

Page 11, panel 4: to make for a more satisfying mid-story cliffhanger, Dead End's line, 'But … but commander … he's already dead' is now reattributed to Megatron and changed to 'And death will come to Optimus Prime'.
Page 12, panel 1: the 'Meanwhile …' caption is deleted.
Page 12, panel 2: another altered conversation –

US Version:
HEADSTRONG: 'Yeah, but why'd we have to modify our body forms, Razorclaw? I liked the way I was just fine.'
RAZORCLAW: 'Because Shockwave says we'll be better suited to fight in an Earthen environment this way, Headstrong – and I can't wait!'

UK version:

HEADSTRONG: 'Yeah, but why'd we have to **stay in these modified body forms?** I liked the way I was just fine.'

RAZORCLAW: '**Same reason we changed before – we're better suited to fight on Earth** this way, Headstrong – and I can't wait!'

Page 12, panel 5: A caption is reworded. Original US version: 'And as they touch down on this new world they convert to their new forms.' UK version: 'Returning for a second hunt, they transform to their relatively new modes.'
Page 13, panel 1: Razorclaw's line is changed. US version: 'Yes, Shockwave. Since Megatron has never dealt with us, he won't recognise us …' UK version: 'Yes, Shockwave. Since Megatron doesn't remember us, he won't know what's hit him …'

Roll Call:
Autobots: Optimus Prime, Hot Spot, Streetwise, Blades and First Aid (all flashback only).

Decepticons: Megatron, Soundwave, Laserbeak, Shockwave, Onslaught, Brawl, Blast Off, Swindle, Vortex, Motormaster, Drag Strip, Dead End, Wildrider, Breakdown, Razorclaw, Rampage, Tantrum, Headstrong, Divebomb and Predaking.

Breakdown's appearance in this story is debatable – it's likely, however, that he's one of the car-shaped silhouettes seen in the convoy on the first panel of page 10. This story marks the first US appearance of the Predacons.

Other: Walter Barnett, and Ethan Zachary (flashback only).

Review:
After the rather disappointing exit of Optimus Prime in the previous story, Megatron's demise is far better handled. His descent into madness is simultaneously funny and

horrific, and the contrast between the maniacal Megatron and his usurper – the cold, logical Shockwave – is nicely played.

The Florida Keys make for an interesting new backdrop for the action, and the Predacons come off quite well here, ripping Megatron into shreds before ultimately succumbing to his attacks. 4/5

[26] FUNERAL FOR A FRIEND!
US#26, 'March 1987' (published November 1986), 22 pages.

British reprint: UK#109, 18 April 1987 (Part One), 11 pages; UK#110, 25 April 1987 (Part Two), 11 pages.

Credits:
Bob Budiansky (script); Don Perlin (pencils); Brett Breeding (inks); Nel Yomtov (colours); Janice Chiang (letters); Don Daley (editor); Jim Shooter (editor-in-chief); Herb Trimpe (cover). **UK:** Herb Trimpe (cover, UK#109 – reuse of US cover); Jeff Anderson (cover, UK#110).

Plot:
The Autobots leave to conduct the funeral ceremony for Optimus Prime. To safeguard the *Ark* in their absence, they have set up a powerful arsenal of weapons to deter any would-be attackers.

Ratchet, meanwhile, still feels bad about being unable to repair Prime. Rather than attend the funeral, he decides instead to travel to a local junkyard, to find parts he can use to repair some of the other fallen Autobots.

The junkyard is the scene for a police sting operation, where they are in the process of arresting the Mechanic, a master criminal and car thief. Spotting Ratchet in vehicle mode, the Mechanic and his sidekick Juan use the Autobot as a getaway vehicle, and then use the Autobot to sneak into the *Ark* and activate the defence grid. As the rest of the Autobots return from the funeral, the activated weapon system attacks them indiscriminately.

With weapons and technology from the *Ark* at his disposal, the Mechanic hunts Ratchet through the ship's corridors. However, the Autobot is able to repair Prowl, who in police car mode is able to take advantage of the Mechanic's phobia of the law.

The Mechanic flees in terror, while Ratchet disables the *Ark*'s defences, allowing his fellow Autobots to return home.

Notes:
This story sees the introduction of the Mechanic, a notorious car thief operating out of Forbes's Garage in southeast Portland. Route 26, which passes through Portland, is referenced, perhaps an in-joke related to the fact that this story appeared in issue #26 of the US comic.

There is a 'Vote Now' flyer visible on a wall during the car chase sequence; probably a reference to the 1986 US Senate election that took place in November 1986, just as this issue was going on sale – Oregon's seat was won by the (later disgraced) Republican candidate, Bob Packwood.

This story implies that the Autobots present are the only ones still active, and that the remainder are either dead or severely injured within Ratchet's storage chambers. In the US continuity, the bulk of these are casualties of the battle in [12] 'Prime Time', plus Bumblebee, killed in [GIJ1] 'Blood on the Tracks', and Optimus Prime, destroyed in [24] 'Afterdeath'. However, that still doesn't explain the injuries to Prowl, who was alive and well in [16] 'Plight of the Bumblebee', or Mirage, who was in [14] 'Rock and Roll-Out'.

Ratchet is said to have been working on repairing Optimus Prime for 238 hours, indicating that roughly ten days have passed since the events of [24] 'Afterdeath'.

The title is probably a reference to an Elton John instrumental piece of the same name, released as a single in 1973.

UK Notes:

The UK situation with regard to Autobot injuries was even more complex than the American one by this point, as the UK comic had continued to use many of the original Transformer characters despite them having been killed off in the US one. We know that Bumblebee is definitely still alive in the UK continuity at this point (his UK death will occur in [27.1] 'Wanted: Galvatron – Dead or Alive'), so on that basis we can be sure that there are more Autobots currently active than the few seen in this story. In the UK, Prowl was last seen alive and well as recently as in [23.5] 'Resurrection', so as in the American continuity, there seems to be no good reason for his injuries here.

At this point in the UK narrative, Skids had been displaced into limbo (in [23.4] 'Fallen Angel'), so his appearance here was edited out.

When Prime was last believed to be dead (in [23.5] 'Resurrection') it was decided that he should be buried on Earth. Here, however, we see him get a more conventional Cybertronian send-off, as his corpse is blasted into space.

UK Changes:

Page 1, panel 1: 'penciler' and 'colorist' are changed to 'penciller' and 'colourist' respectively. The reference to issue #24 is amended to #106.

Page 2, panel 4: Skids is erased and replaced with black background.

Page 2, panel 6: 'center' becomes 'centre'.

Page 5, panel 7: the reference to Ironhide being injured is changed to Bluestreak (as Ironhide was still alive according to recent UK stories such as [23.5] 'Resurrection').

Page 10, panel 3: 'fueled' is changed to 'fuelled'.

Pages 10 and 11 are switched in the UK printing, to make for a better cliffhanger.

Page 19, panel 1: 'center' is again amended to 'centre'.

Roll Call:

Autobots: Optimus Prime (as a corpse), Prowl, Ratchet, Wheeljack, Jetfire, Grapple, Hoist, Smokescreen, Skids (excised from UK printing), Tracks, Silverbolt, Air Raid, Fireflight, Skydive, Slingshot, Hot Spot, Streetwise, Blades, Groove, First Aid, Blaster, Powerglide, Cosmos, Seaspray, Warpath, Beachcomber, Perceptor and Omega Supreme.

Other: **The Mechanic** and **Juan.**

For the first time ever, no Decepticons appear in this story, not even in flashback.

Review:
The funeral scenes are great, and it's nice to have a story that focuses on Ratchet, one of the major players in the title's early days.

Unfortunately, however, the Mechanic sub-plot is terrible, and he becomes another in a long list of human characters (Joey Slick, Circuit Breaker, Bomber Bill etc) who don't really work. That such a terrible villain causes so much damage to the Autobot ranks strains credulity. 1/5

US Advertisements, Part 2: Film, Television and Video Games (A-G)
As before, a list of all advertisements for films, television shows or video games that appeared in the American *The Transformers* comic, listed alphabetically from A to G:

1943: The Battle of Midway (video game) – US#49-51
3-2-1 Contact (educational television show) – US#39
Abadox (video game) – US#67
Acclaim Double Player (wireless video game controller) – US#62-66, 73
Acclaim Remote Controller (wireless video game controller) – US#57
Acclaim's range of video game releases – US#71
Activision's range of video game releases – US#67
Activision Decathlon, The (video game) – US#3
Adventures of the Galaxy Rangers, The (home video release of cartoon show) – US#29
Arachnophobia (1990 movie) – US#69
Back to the Future Part II & III (video game) – US#72
Battletoads (video game) – US#79-80
Beetlejuice (video game) – US#79-80
Bionic Commando (video game) – US#62-68
Bonk's Adventure (video game) – US#69, 71
Bubble Bobble (video game) – US#54-56
Captain Planet and the Planeteers (cartoon show) – US#71
Castlevania III: Dracula's Curse (video game) – US#76
CBS's schedule of Saturday morning cartoons – US#11
Challenge of the Gobots (cartoon show) – US#13
Code Name: Viper (video game) – US#67-68, 70
Destiny of an Emperor (video game) – US#75-76
Dick Tracy (1990 movie) – US#67-68
Double Dragon (video game) – US#43
Double Dragon II: The Revenge (video game) – US#67
Double Dragon III: The Sacred Stones (video game) – US#77-78
Epyx 500XJ (video game controller) – US#50
FCI (video game publisher) – US#48-49, 51
Freedom Stick (video game controller) – US#45-47, 49
Gargoyle's Quest (video game) – US#72, 74, 76
George Brett's Secrets of Baseball (videocassette) – US#34; HDM#3
G.I. Joe: A Real American Hero (video game) – US#78
Gun Smoke (video game) – US#43-44, 47

[27] KING OF THE HILL!
US#27, 'April 1987' (published December 1986), 22 pages.

British reprint: UK#111, 2 May 1987 (Part One), 11 pages; UK#112, 9 May 1987 (Part Two), 11 pages.

Credits:
Bob Budiansky (script); Don Perlin (pencils); Ian Akin, Brian Garvey (inks); Nel Yomtov (colours); Janice Chiang (letters); Don Daley (editor); Jim Shooter (editor-in-chief); Herb Trimpe (cover). **UK:** Lee Sullivan (cover, UK#111); Herb Trimpe and Tim Perkins (cover, UK#112 – re-coloured adaptation of US cover).

Plot:
With Optimus Prime gone, the Autobots agonise over who is the best choice to be their new leader. The Dinobots arrive at the *Ark*, and Grimlock puts forward a claim, but he is rebuffed – although he is a fearsome warrior, it's agreed that he lacks the necessary compassion and wisdom for the role.

The Decepticons, meanwhile, are also having leadership problems. Their fuel auditor Ratbat can no longer support inefficient Decepticon operations on Earth. However, as a sop to Shockwave, Ratbat agrees to send the giant Decepticon dinosaur Trypticon to attack the *Ark*.

The Autobots are unable to withstand Trypticon's attack, and are on the verge of defeat. At that moment Grimlock steps into the battle and, with the rest of the Dinobots, is able to drive Trypticon back across the space bridge to Cybertron.

Impressed with the qualities shown by Grimlock in defeating the Decepticon gargantuan, the Autobots accept Grimlock as their new commander.

Notes:
This is quite a landmark issue for the comic: the Autobots and Decepticons get new leaders; the Decepticons are now based in their new headquarters; the Dinobots reappear after a lengthy absence; and the giant Decepticon Trypticon makes his debut (in what would actually prove to be his only appearance in the American material).

For US readers, this is the Dinobots' first appearance since their secession in [19] 'Command Performances'. No details are given as to what they've been doing in the interim, but as this story begins they are camped out near the *Ark*, having been spying on the Autobots. (Hence they are aware of Prime's recent death.)

Grimlock meets Rachel Becker, part of a team of palaeontologists on a fossil-hunting expedition. (Oregon is actually a good hunting-ground for fossils, although contrary to her claims, Rachel would be lucky to find a trilobite fossil anywhere near the *Ark*'s location.)

It's revealed here that the new Decepticon island base is actually a giant undersea tower, with the tropical island as its 'top floor' on the surface. Like the previous base in Wyoming, it contains equipment capable of contacting Cybertron.

Shockwave is being assessed by a Cybertron-based Decepticon called Ratbat who, in his role as a 'fuel auditor', has the ultimate say in whether or not any Decepticon plan gets the go-ahead. As a glorified accountant, he is unwilling to authorise any scheme without first performing a cost/benefit analysis, much to Shockwave's chagrin.

The giant Decepticon Trypticon makes a brief trip to Earth via the space bridge (which was obviously not damaged beyond repair when Megatron shot at it in [25] 'Gone but Not Forgotten'). He brings with him a loyal assistant called Wipe-Out (who was invented especially for this story and not available as a toy).

The Dinobots are not above stealing fuel tankers to feed on; Swoop steals one from a truck '158 miles to the southeast' (presumably a diner somewhere on Route 20). This isn't the first time that the comic has shown Transformers stealing vehicles from truck stops (see also [10] 'The Next Best Thing to Being There').

The 'Pacific Northwest University' mentioned in this story is entirely fictional (or was until a real-world institution of that name was founded in 2008). Its palaeontology professor is named for the real-word professor and prominent civil engineer Robert Paaswell, a former tutor of writer Bob Budiansky.

UK Notes:
In the UK stories, the Dinobots actually left the rest of the Autobots in the aftermath of [20.1] 'In the National Interest', but had been seen wandering around Wyoming in [23.4] 'Fallen Angel'.

Likewise, although this was Ratbat's first appearance in the US stories, he was part of Straxus's inner circle on Cybertron, and thus made his UK debut in [23.2] 'Under Fire'.

The UK cover to issue 111, showing Grimlock requesting that the Autobots 'Vote for me!', is a reference to the then-imminent UK local elections, which were swiftly followed by the General Election of June 1987, which was won by Margaret Thatcher's Conservative Party.

UK Changes:
Page 1, panel 1: 'penciler' and 'colorist' become 'penciller' and 'colourist' respectively.
Page 4, panel 1: 'monstrosity' is changed to 'dinosaur'.
Page 4, panel 2 *et seq*: in the US printing, Snarl's dinosaur head is coloured blue throughout, but the English printing corrects this mistake and presents it as gold.
Page 4, panel 4: in the original version, Sludge was given a blue dinosaur head here, but in the UK printing, his head is white.
Page 4, panel 5: the reference to issue #19 is changed to issue #78.
Page 7, panel 5: 'equaled' is amended to read 'equalled'.
Page 12, panel 6: correcting a typo in the original US version, 'Tyrpticon' is changed to 'Trypticon'.
Page 13, panel 8: 'armor' becomes 'armour'.

Roll Call:
Autobots: Optimus Prime (hologram only), Ratchet, Wheeljack, Grimlock, Snarl, Slag, Sludge, Swoop, Jetfire, Silverbolt, Hot Spot, Streetwise, Blaster, Powerglide, Cosmos, Seaspray, Warpath, Beachcomber, Perceptor and Omega Supreme.

Decepticons: Soundwave, Shockwave, Drag Strip, Ratbat and **Trypticon**.

Review:
Once you get past the fact that the Autobots are really, really stupid for electing Grimlock as their new leader, there's some good stuff here. After the silliness of the Mechanic, the human characters in this issue are far more realistic and restrained, thankfully. The Trypticon battle is a well-rendered action sequence, and Ratbat steals the show in his two small scenes. 3/5

[27.1] WANTED: GALVATRON – DEAD OR ALIVE!

NB: Within the strip itself, the title of this story is parsed as 'Wanted Galvatron Dead or Alive' (note the lack of punctuation). The full title is taken from the contents pages of the issues in question.

- UK#113, 16 May 1987 (Part One), 11 pages
- UK#114, 23 May 1987 (Part Two), 11 pages

This story was also reprinted later in the comic's run, as follows. (NB: each original instalment was divided into halves and spread across a couple of issues):

- UK#221, 10 June 1989 (Part 1), 6 pages
- UK#222, 17 June 1989 (Part 2), 5 pages
- UK#223, 24 June 1989 (Part 3), 6 pages
- UK#224: 1 July 1989 (Part 4), 5 pages

Credits:
Simon Furman (script); Geoff Senior (art, part 1); Will Simpson (pencils, part 2); Tim Perkins (inks, part 2); Steve White (colours); Annie Halfacree (letters, part 1); Richard Starkings (letters, part 2); Geoff Senior (cover, UK#113); Jeff Anderson (cover, UK#114).

This is the first UK strip not to carry an editor's credit. The previous editor, Ian Rimmer, had by now left the comic, and the editorship was now shared between lead writer Simon Furman, and regular letterer Richard Starkings. However, because of Marvel rules about writers not being allowed to edit their own material, Starkings was the sole editor for 'official' purposes. Starkings essentially became Furman's script editor (some of Furman's original scripts still exist today, complete with Richard Starkings' hand-written annotations), while Furman undertook the day-to-day running of the title.

Plot:
The year is 2007. In the aftermath of Unicron's attack on Cybertron (see [MOV3] 'The Final Battle'), the Autobot/Decepticon battle has begun anew. With their leader Galvatron missing, Shockwave now commands the Decepticon forces.

The new Autobot leader Rodimus Prime is determined to find out what happened to Galvatron, and to that end has put a 10,000-shanix bounty on his head. The offer is taken up by the alien robot Death's Head, a self-styled 'freelance peacekeeping agent' (in reality a bounty hunter), who determines that Galvatron has fled back in time to the year 1987 (as seen in [23.4] 'Fallen Angel').

Death's Head's arrival in 1987 is witnessed by Bumblebee, who decides to return to the *Ark* and inform the Autobots what's happened. 'Can't allow that,' says Death's Head, who destroys the diminutive Autobot with a single shot.

Notes:
This story is a sequel to *The Transformers: The Movie*, and is the first of many UK stories set in the early 21st Century (exactly twenty years in the future); the story begins with an alien bartender recounting recent events. Just as the 'Leaders go to Cybertron' arc was split into smaller chunks ([23.1 'Prey' *et seq*), this story is itself the first chapter in a larger tale, the 'Volcano' arc.

The bar scene is set on the planet Elpasos, presumably a reference to the Spaghetti Western *For a Few Dollars More* (Sergio Leone, 1965), set in El Paso, Texas and featuring a couple of bounty hunters as its lead characters. A possible influence on this story's title is the song 'Wanted Dead or Alive' by Bon Jovi, released as a single in March 1987.

Death's Head is a robotic bounty hunter, although he hates being referred to as such. His right hand is removable, and can be replaced with a number of interchangeable weapons, such as an axe and a spiked club. He drinks three quarts of oil (roughly three litres) in a single sitting, and is around the same size as a Transformer. He keeps a verbal record of all his missions, dictating to his spaceship's on-board computer. The Galvatron job is designated 'mission 531'. He is able to best both Scourge and Cyclonus in combat, and his gun makes light work of Bumblebee.

As is now customary, one Transformer is transported to the limbo dimension upon Death's Head's arrival in 1987; in this instance the Protectobot First Aid is the unlucky victim (see also [20.2] 'Target: 2006' and [23.4] 'Fallen Angel').

In a flashback, it's confirmed that the 'Matrix of Leadership' seen in the animated movie is one and the same thing as the comic's 'Creation Matrix'. This is the first time in the comics that the Creation Matrix is depicted as a physical object, rather than just a powerful computer program.

This is the first appearance of the Junkion Wreck-Gar, whose speech patterns are based upon 20th Century TV broadcasts. Often the references are generic (e.g. 'Full report and pictures in our ten o'clock bulletin'), but sometimes his speeches are based on actual specific broadcasts:

- 'Eyes down ... for Bob's Full House!' *Bob's Full House* was a bingo-themed game show broadcast in the UK between 1984 and 1990, hosted by legendary British comedian Bob Monkhouse.
- 'What's yours called?' A slogan from a long-running series of 1980s TV advertisements for the Renault 5 automobile, narrated by British comedian Griff Rhys Jones.

How Does Time Travel Work?
'When travelling through time, the possibility exists of arriving, not in the dimension you left, but in a *parallel dimension*. It is one identical to your own, until history alters dramatically at a given point.'
- editorial caption, 'Target: 2006', Part 9

'He was on a *parallel dimension* Earth, where nothing he accomplished would have any bearing on the future.'
- Unicron, 'Target: 2006', Epilogue

If the thorny subject of time travel in *The Transformers* can be summed up in just a couple of sentences, than those above do it as concisely and accurately as can be. Galvatron might have arrived at this conclusion only after becoming the victim of an Autobot trick, but it's nevertheless accurate – this, in *The Transformers*, is exactly how time travel works. It's the only possible way to reconcile two facts we are given during the course of the comics' run:

1) Time *can* be changed

2) Time *can't* be changed

If that sounds confusing, perhaps some further explanation is required ...

It's an incontrovertible fact that history can be altered by the actions of time travellers from the future. In Galvatron's version of the future, Unicron attacks Cybertron in the year 2006 but is defeated ([MOV3] 'The Final Battle'); however, in a parallel dimension, Unicron is successful ([67] 'Rhythms of Darkness'). In yet *another* version of events, Unicron attacks Cybertron in the year 1991 but is again defeated ([75] 'On the Edge of Extinction').

Indeed, in [27.1] 'Wanted: Galvatron – Dead or Alive', we get more evidence of this. Bumblebee is alive and well in 2007 despite his death in 1987 (and although Bumblebee would eventually be resurrected a couple of years later, writer Simon Furman wasn't to know this at the time). Furthermore, the Ultra Magnus of 2007 has no idea where Galvatron is, despite having encountered the Decepticon in 1987 – it's quite clear both here and in [27.2] 'Burning Sky' that the 2007 version of Magnus has different memories from his 1987 counterpart. Another example: the story [A3.4] '*Ark* Duty', set in 2003, shows that the Autobots' spacecraft, the *Ark*, as still buried within Mount St Hilary on Earth, despite it having left Earth in 1988 in [35] 'Child's Play' (comic).

But although time travelling and history bending are enough to create parallel dimensions, in another respect history *cannot* be changed. Take a look at the chain of events from Galvatron's point of view. After he messes up history in [20.2] 'Target: 2006', he goes back to his own time, and arrives in *exactly the same dimension that he left*, taking part in the second half of the movie with the future precisely as he remembered it. He might have messed up the past, but it's quite clear that the future he returns to has been completely unaffected by his meddling.

So the rules seem to be as follows:

1) If you travel back in time, you can play around with history and create alternative timelines. However ...

2) ... when you return to your point of origin, you arrive in exactly the same universe you left.

All this was pretty much confirmed in the letters page of UK #97: 'As soon as Galvatron started mucking about in the time-stream, he created an entirely new history. The Galvatron that was once Megatron had no memory of battling himself, because in his past it simply didn't happen. If the "now" Megatron becomes Galvatron in the future, then he *will* have those memories. This is what is known as the theory of parallel dimensions. The same planet, same characters, different events.'

This is reiterated in the letters page of UK#156, when a reader suggests that Megatron's death in the present would cause his future self, Galvatron, to be erased from existence. The reply: 'No-one's quite sure whether taking out Megatron would get rid of Galvatron' – implying that the present-day Megatron is not necessarily the same entity as the Galvatron from the future timeline.

The letters page of US#65 tackles the problem of Unicron's two invasions, one in 1991 and the other in 2005: 'The movie is only one possible version of Unicron's attack on Cybertron ... The comic is *not* leading up to the movie, 2005 in the comic will be completely different.'

This actually makes perfect sense. Imagine being the inventor of a time machine: time travel is great but there are a whole host of possible side effects – you could prevent yourself from having ever been born (the old 'Grandfather Paradox'). So it's no surprise that the original inventor of Galvatron's time machine put in a failsafe device. This lets you create as many parallel dimensions as you like, but for safety reasons makes the current timeline immutable. Look how many times Galvatron, Death's Head, Hot Rod and company go back to the past and have a big impact on events there, and yet still the post-movie 21st Century remains intact.

As we now know that there are multiple timelines, we can use this to explain away a few plot holes and inconsistencies. For example, Buster's dream in [16.3] 'Second Generation' is described as a vision of the future, but it never actually comes to pass. As previously discussed, the attack on the power plant in that story might be from an alternative timeline in which Galvatron never altered history. We can also now explain Bumblebee's two deaths, here in [27.1] 'Wanted: Galvatron – Dead or Alive', but also in [GIJ1] 'Blood on the Tracks'. Some of the stories in the UK Annuals are completely incompatible with the comic's continuity unless we start talking about parallel dimensions.

Assuming that there are only two parallel universes shown thus far (let's call them Timeline A and Timeline B), let's look at them and see how they differ:

Timeline A:
This is the original timeline, before Galvatron started meddling with history. All stories set prior to [20.2] 'Target: 2006' are part of Timeline A. Without Galvatron's involvement in past affairs, Bumblebee is not killed by Death's Head, but instead destroyed by GI Joe. Adventures such as [A2.3] 'The Return of the Transformers' also take place. In the 21st Century, the planet-devourer Unicron attacks Cybertron and creates Galvatron. We then get the cycle of future-set UK stories such as [27.1] 'Wanted: Galvatron Dead or Alive' *et seq*.

Timeline B:
This is the new reality, created by Galvatron's meddling. It is identical to Timeline A until it branches off with Galvatron's arrival in [20.2] 'Target: 2006'. After that, events unfold differently – in this timeline, Bumblebee is killed by Death's Head and Unicron attacks Cybertron in 1991 ([75] 'On the Edge of Extinction').

As was touched upon in the notes to [20.2] 'Target: 2006', although these altered timelines can differ quite a bit, it seems that some events are always destined to happen – 'fixed points', if you will.

These include:

- Operation: Volcano is unsuccessful in both timelines (as previously discussed in the entry for [20.2] 'Target: 2006')
- Bumblebee is destroyed (in Timeline A by GI Joe, in Timeline B by Death's Head) and becomes Goldbug. In both timelines he eventually reverts to being Bumblebee.
- Targetmasters are created in Timeline B ([HDM1] 'Ring of Hate' *et seq*), but the Timeline A post-movie Rodimus was also once a Targetmaster (as he remembers

his Targetmaster partner Firebolt in [31.3] 'Headhunt').

The 'future stories happen in a parallel reality' concept was first postulated in the letters page of UK#212, after a reader asked how the Wreckers could die in [48.2] 'Time Wars' and yet still be alive in the future-set [A4.5] 'Peace'. The response: 'It could be that the timeline was upset by Galvatron's dabblings. Therefore, they may well have survived – in another timeline. Sounds simple, really. I think.'

If this sounds confusing, don't worry – with the exception of those comics set in the 21st Century (in the aftermath of the movie), most stories going forward will be assumed to take place in the revised Timeline B, and those that aren't will be clearly explained as such in the relevant story notes.

It must also be remembered that this alternate realities theory only ever affects the UK stories – for US readers, the Transformers comics are nice and linear: Unicron attacks only once, Bumblebee dies only once, and so on. It's only when we factor in the British stories, with their tales of time travel, parallel universes and future histories, that we need to invoke this rule.

Roll Call:
Autobots: Jazz, Bumblebee, Cliffjumper, First Aid (flashback only), Ultra Magnus, Hot Rod (flashback only), Kup, Blurr, Rodimus Prime and **Wreck-Gar**.

The one-off Autobot Nautilus also makes an appearance.

Decepticons: Shockwave (flashback only), Galvatron (in flashback, also as an image on a poster and on a computer monitor), Cyclonus and Scourge.

Other: Unicron (flashback only) and **Death's Head**.

All the characters listed above are their 2007 versions, with the exception of First Aid, the 1987 version of whom is seen, and Bumblebee, whose 1987 and 2007 versions both appear.

Review:
An important story, this one, it marking the introduction of a major new character in Death's Head and also being the first of many UK stories set in a parallel-universe 21st Century. The high concept could well have died on its feet had the execution not been right. Thankfully, then, this is a mini-masterpiece.

It was a bit of a risk to concentrate so much on this new character, and throw readers in at the deep end. (Outside of flashbacks, no Transformers appear in this story until just under half way through.) Thankfully, though, Death's Head is so well-written and drawn that he's an absolute joy to read and behold. 5/5

[27.2] BURNING SKY!
- UK#115, 30 May 1987 (Part One), 11 pages
- UK#116, 6 June 1987 (Part Two), 11 pages

Credits:
Simon Furman (script); Dan Reed (art, part 1); Geoff Senior (art, part 2); Steve White

(colours); Richard Starkings (letters); Lee Sullivan (cover, UK#115); Jeff Anderson (cover, UK#116).

Plot:
Having arrived on Earth (in [23.5] 'Resurrection'), Ultra Magnus is enjoying some well-deserved peace and quiet. His rest is interrupted by a blast emanating from the nearby Mount Verona; Magnus comes to the rescue of geologist Cindy Newell, whose van had overturned as a result of the shockwave.

Galvatron is also in the vicinity, having built a massive power siphon around the mouth of the volcano – he seeks to tap the energies of the Earth's core. He and Ultra Magnus do battle.

In 2007, Rodimus Prime and a group of Autobots decide to journey into the past, in an attempt to stop Galvatron and Death's Head.

Back in 1987, the victorious Galvatron drags Ultra Magnus up the side of Mount Verona; Galvatron gloats that tapping the volcano's power will turn him into a god …

Notes:
This is a showcase for Ultra Magnus and Galvatron, who last appeared in [23.5] 'Resurrection' and [23.4] 'Fallen Angel' respectively. The two characters had previously met in [20.2] 'Target: 2006' where, as here, a vicious battle ensued. It's stated that Ultra Magnus has been on Earth for a 'few months', providing confirmation that these stories are generally happening in real time relative to the comic's publication schedule – this was printed nearly three months after Magnus's previous appearance.

Geologist Cindy Newell debuts here; she will go on to play a major role throughout this 'Volcano' story arc and also in a later adventure, [31.5] 'Ladies' Night'.

Mount Verona is a fictional volcano located in the Cascade Range in Oregon (like Mount St Hilary, where the *Ark* is located). It's presumably named for the city of Verona in Italy. Galvatron's power siphon device would seem to work on the same principle as the ones developed by Shockwave (see, for example, [14] 'Rock and Roll-Out'), but on a much larger scale. (As evidenced by this power siphon, and also his time travel machinery, it would seem that Cybertronian technology in 2007 is far in advance of present-day levels.)

In a flashback, Ultra Magnus remembers kneeling over Impactor's dead body (in a scene presumably set in the immediate aftermath of [20.2] 'Target: 2006').

How Did the Movie Affect the Comics?
The Transformers: The Movie, the 1986 animated feature film, had a profound impact on the UK *The Transformers* comic – despite its failure at the box office.

The British iteration of the comic had long produced its own homegrown strips, which would be set in the 'gaps' between American stories. By 1987, however, it had become clear that there were certain problems with this way of working.

When writer Bob Budiansky plotted the American comics, he did so with little to no knowledge of what was occurring in the UK title – the onus was squarely on British writer Simon Furman to weave his own stories in between Budiansky's tales, and make them fit. This was fine in the early days of the title – the American comic tended to ignore the Dinobots, for example, which allowed the UK title to feature them quite prominently without fear of creating too many continuity problems. Now though, making the two comics mesh seamlessly was becoming harder and harder. Some characters that had been killed off in the US comics were still alive and well in the UK stories. Moreover, the US writing team had occasionally produced stories that – unknown to them – covered similar ground to strips that had already seen print in the UK (notably [16] 'Plight of the Bumblebee' and [25] 'Gone but Not Forgotten'). Many US stories were now being heavily edited for their British printing, in order to better fit into the overall continuity (notable examples incluing [18] 'The Bridge to Nowhere' and, again, [25] 'Gone but Not Forgotten'). The whole thing was getting more than a little messy.

The Transformers: The Movie, set in the early 21st Century, proved to be a godsend for Simon Furman. While the American comic stayed firmly rooted in the present day (more or less), the UK stories could be set in the future, in the aftermath of the movie, without fear of being contradicted. Not only did this give Furman a freer rein in writing new adventures, but it also pleased Hasbro, who were understandably delighted that the new movie figures such as Rodimus Prime and Cyclonus, who barely featured in the American strips, were being showcased in the UK comics.

Roll Call:
Autobots: Impactor (flashback only), Ultra Magnus, Kup, Blurr, Rodimus Prime and Wreck-Gar.

Kup, Blurr, Rodimus Prime and Wreck-Gar are those characters' 2007 incarnations. Ultra Magnus appears in both his 1987 and 2007 iterations.

Decepticons: Galvatron (2007 version).

Other: **Cindy Newell.**

Data File: Richard Starkings (letterer/writer/editor)
Not many contributors to The Transformers can claim to have helped redefine an entire industry, but Starkings, via his font company Comicraft, paved the way for the use of electronic fonts in comics in lieu of traditional hand-drawn calligraphy. His name has appeared in the credits of hundreds of titles, including 2000 AD, Batman: Hush, The League of Extraordinary Gentlemen, Captain America, Doctor Who Magazine, Spawn and Superman – he having either hand-lettered those titles or provided fonts. As an editor, he has helmed titles such as Death's Head, Action Force and Captain Britain.

Review:
On the plus side, this is a visual feast – part two sees the always-reliable Geoff Senior in fine form, while part one marks the debut of Dan Reed, whose organic, expressionistic art is a major departure from any style seen previously in the comic. However, the artwork cannot disguise a seriously padded story, which could have been told just as easily in half the page count. The Ultra Magnus v Galvatron fight isn't a patch on their previous battle in [20.2] 'Target: 2006'. 2/5

[27.3] HUNTERS
- UK#117, 13 June 1987 (Part One), 11 pages
- UK#118, 20 June 1987 (Part Two), 11 pages

Credits:
Simon Furman (script); Will Simpson (pencils, part 1); Jeff Anderson (pencils, part 2) Tim Perkins (inks, part 1); Stephen Baskerville (inks, part 2); Steve White (colours); Richard Starkings (letters, part 1); Mike Scott (letters, part 2); Geoff Senior and John Burns (cover, UK#117); Lee Sullivan (cover, UK#118).

Jeff Anderson is oddly credited for 'Art' on part two, despite Stephen Baskerville also getting a credit for inks on that issue. It's likely that Anderson was the penciller only, and the 'Art' credit was a mistake. In another mix-up, Steve White was uncredited for his work on part two.

Plot:
With Cindy as their guide, Rodimus Prime, Kup and Blurr arrive at Mount Verona. Realising that Ultra Magnus is in trouble, Rodimus attacks Galvatron. Matters are complicated when Death's Head shows up. He's insistent that he be allowed to execute Galvatron, so that he can claim the reward money. He makes it plain that if any Autobots get in his way, they too will be killed.

Galvatron and Rodimus fight – however, Ultra Magnus shoots at the power siphon, creating a distraction that allows the Autobots (and indeed Death's Head) to retreat and regroup.

Meanwhile, Wreck-Gar happens upon the body of the recently-destroyed Bumblebee, and sets to work rebuilding the Autobot. Some time later, his work is complete – Bumblebee has a new body and a new name: Goldbug.

Notes:
While searching for Galvatron, Death's Head is initially under the impression that the Decepticons are still based in Wyoming (whereas in fact they recently decamped to Florida in [25] 'Gone but Not Forgotten'). It's revealed that the Decepticons are monitoring Galvatron's actions while he's active in 1987.

There are references here to previous stories, including flashbacks to the events of the movie, and to those of [27.1] 'Wanted: Galvatron – Dead or Alive'. Events of the previous story, [27.2] 'Burning Sky', are recapped, and the explosion therein is confirmed to have been a small controlled eruption of Mount Verona. Ultra Magnus remembers meeting Kup and Blurr before, in [20.2] 'Target: 2006'.

More Wreck-Gar-isms abound:

- 'What "B" …? That's Blockbusters!' Catchphrases of Bob Holness, host of the TV game show *Blockbusters* (the original run of which lasted from 1983 to 1993).
- 'Your starter for ten …' A quote from yet another British game show, this time *University Challenge*. (First broadcast in 1962, its original cancellation in December 1987 occurred just a few months after this story was published.)
- 'Jim'll Fix It!' A reference to *Jim'll Fix It* (1975-1994), a light entertainment show in which viewers would get their wishes granted.

<u>No Joe!</u>
In America, the destruction of Bumblebee and his subsequent reconstruction as Goldbug occurred in a four-issue spin-off comic, *G.I. Joe and the Transformers*. By 1987,

Marvel's *G.I. Joe* comic was finally seeing print in the UK, under the title *Action Force*; however, there was a significant lag between the two titles – in June 1987, for example, the *Action Force* comic was in the process of reprinting the American *G.I. Joe* story, 'Beached Whale', which was by then *three years* old.

Printing the *G.I. Joe and the Transformers* series in the UK was always going to be problematic, given that it referenced *G.I. Joe* characters and situations that, due to the lag, had yet to be introduced to British readers. To avoid confusing UK *Action Force* fans, the decision was taken to skip the crossover series entirely (for now, at least). However, this meant that writer Simon Furman had to come up with an alternative method of writing out Bumblebee and introducing Goldbug, and used the 'Volcano' story arc as a means to do so.

As mentioned in the notes to [27.1] 'Wanted: Galvatron – Dead or Alive', this poses a problem – if we are to consider the entirety of the UK and US comics as a single canon, we are left with the fact that Bumblebee is killed and reborn into Goldbug on two separate occasions. However, thanks to Galvatron's time travelling antics, we have the ability to rationalise this seeming incompatibility; we can assume that the events of *G.I. Joe and the Transformers* occur in a parallel dimension, the one that existed prior to Galvatron tampering with history. Indeed, there is some evidence for this in the comics themselves: in [40] 'Pretender to the Throne', Goldbug claims to have attended Optimus Prime's funeral, which flatly contradicts the events of the *G.I. Joe* story, making it all the more likely that it never actually 'happened' in the main timeline.

Roll Call:
Autobots: Bumblebee (as a corpse), Ultra Magnus, Kup, Blurr, Rodimus Prime, Wreck-Gar and **Goldbug**.

Decepticons: Soundwave, Laserbeak, and Galvatron.

Other: Unicron (flashback only), Death's Head and Cindy Newell.

Bumblebee, Ultra Magnus, Goldbug, Soundwave, Laserbeak and Cindy are from 1987, all other characters are 2007 versions. The 2007 iteration of Ultra Magnus appears in a flashback.

Review:
A step in the right direction, this latest chapter in the 'Volcano' saga has a bit more impetus than the rather lacking [27.2] 'Burning Sky'. Whereas that previous story featured the rather wet Ultra Magnus as its main character, here we're reintroduced to Rodimus Prime, Wreck-Gar and Death's Head, who are much more engaging. That said, the plot is once again rather flimsy – characters show up, have a fight, and then retreat again; other than the creation of Goldbug, nothing of note really happens here.
3/5

[27.4] FIRE ON HIGH!
- UK#119, 27 June 1987 (Part 1), 11 pages
- UK#120, 4 July 1987 (Part 2), 11 pages

Credits:
Simon Furman (script); Dan Reed (art, part 1); Geoff Senior (art, part 2); Steve White (colours); Mike Scott (letters, part 1); Richard Starkings (letters, part 2); Will Simpson, Dave Harwood and John Burns (cover, UK#119); Jeff Anderson (cover, UK#120).

Plot:
Geology expert Cindy Newell tells the Autobots how Galvatron's volcano plan could potentially kill millions, by causing a chain reaction of volcanoes and earthquakes along America's Pacific coast, possibly destroying San Francisco in the process. The Autobots devise a dangerous plan – while Ultra Magnus distracts Galvatron, Wreck-Gar will steal the insane Decepticon's handheld time travel device, and rig it to return everyone to their proper place in history.

Although Ultra Magnus is easily defeated – hurled into the mouth of the volcano and presumably killed – Galvatron is met by Rodimus Prime and Death's Head, both of whom take their turn at attacking the tyrant, to no avail.

However, Wreck-Gar has had the time he needs to rig the time travel device, although he's unsure it will work exactly as planned. Sure enough, the device is activated and all the time travellers are returned to 2007 – all, that is, except Galvatron, whose sole remaining challenger is the small Autobot Goldbug …

Notes:
It's revealed here that the augmented eruption of Mount Verona has the potential to cause havoc along the west coast of America. This is a reference to the so-called Ring of Fire, a horseshoe-shaped area of geologic instability that includes the Cascade Range of mountains (home to Mount Verona) and the San Andreas Fault; a boundary between tectonic plates and the cause of earthquakes such as the one that ravaged San Francisco in 1906.

There are references to the events of [27.2] 'Burning Sky' (including a mention of the volcano's initial explosion), and [27.3] 'Hunters' (specifically Ultra Magnus sabotaging the power siphon).

Controversially, the cliffhanger ending to this story (and indeed the entire 'Volcano' story arc) was not resolved within the comic itself. As part of a marketing strategy, the concluding part, [A3.3] 'Vicious Circle', was exclusive to the 1988 *The Transformers Annual*.

As is now customary, Wreck-Gar's speech is full of cultural references:

- 'If you want to do it, B&Q it!' A misquote of a series of advertisements for B&Q, Britain's leading DIY chain store. (The actual slogan was 'You can do it if you B&Q it'.)
- 'It's Childsplay!' Probably a reference to the title of a series hosted by UK comedy double act Morecambe and Wise, which consisted of short plays scripted by children (1976). Alternatively, it could be a reference to the quiz show *Child's Play*, hosted by Michael Aspel from 1984 to 1988.
- 'Jus' like that!' Catchphrase of much-loved British comedian Tommy Cooper.
- 'Nudge, nudge … wink, wink – know what I mean?' A misquote from 'Candid Photography', a sketch from the *Monty Python's Flying Circus* episode 'How to Recognise Different Types of Trees from Quite a Long Way Away' (1969). The sketch was written and co-performed by Eric Idle, who provided the voice of

Wreck-Gar in *The Transformers: The Movie*.

- 'Come on down!' The catchphrase of Leslie Crowther, host of the British version of the game show *The Price is Right* (when it originally ran from 1984 to 1988).
- 'Vorsprung durch Technik' Or 'Advancement through Technology', the advertising slogan of vehicle manufacturer Audi.
- 'Boldly going where no man has gone before' From the opening narration of the TV series *Star Trek* (1966-69).

Death's Head – A History

The Death's Head character was originally intended to appear only in the 'Volcano' arc in *The Transformers* UK (from [27.1] 'Wanted: Galvatron – Dead or Alive' to [27.4] 'Fire on High'). However, it soon became evident that this marvellous creation – a cold-blooded killer robot with a deadpan delivery – was good enough to warrant his own comic. Plans were quickly set in motion for his return.

One stumbling-block was Hasbro, who as part of their deal with Marvel claimed the rights to all characters created for *The Transformers*. This legal point would later be extremely beneficial to fans, as toys based on comic characters such as Straxus and Impactor saw retail release because of this very clause. However, Marvel UK were understandably reluctant to cede ownership of Death's Head to the American toy manufacturer. To that end, they used a tried-and-trusted method previously employed by Marvel US, who were able to retain the rights to Circuit Breaker by ensuring she made her debut outside of the Transformers franchise (in an issue of *Secret Wars II*). So Death's Head was swiftly written into a short strip, 'High Noon Tex', which was eventually published from May 1988 across a number of different Marvel UK titles (including in *The Transformers* UK#167).

Death's Head made two more appearances in *The Transformers* (in [31.2] 'Headhunt' and [36.2] 'The Legacy of Unicron') before flying the coop. He next appeared in 'Crossroads of Time', a strip in issue #135 (April 1988) of *Doctor Who Magazine* (then helmed by former *Transformers* editor Sheila Cranna), and also in issues of another Marvel UK title, *Dragon's Claws* (1988).

December 1988 saw the launch of Marvel UK's *Death's Head* title. The freelance peacekeeping agent had finally got a comic all to himself, but it was shortlived: it ran for just ten issues before cancellation. The early 1990s, though, saw the character crossing over to the mainstream of Marvel US, with guest appearances in titles such as *Fantastic Four* (issue #338) and *The Sensational She-Hulk* (issue #24, written by Simon Furman).

1992 saw the launch of *Death's Head II*, a Marvel UK comic that saw a rather different version of the character than fans had been used to. The original Death's Head was killed off, his mind absorbed into a gestalt cyborg that, although having a different appearance and personally, carried on the Death's Head name. This ran for twenty issues.

Things then went quiet on the Death's Head front until 2005, when the character won a reader's poll, as a result of which he was showcased in the Marvel US title *Amazing Fantasy*. These stories featured a third version of the character (Death's Head 3.0), this time as an alien cyborg based on Earth a thousand years in the future.

2014 proved to be a momentous year for the bounty hunter. First, a one-shot comic entitled *Revolutionary War: Death's Head II* saw print. Published by Marvel US, it featured various incarnations of the character meeting each other. Then, in the summer,

Death's Head finally got his own action figure. Produced by Hasbro, it was part of the *Marvel Infinite Series* toy line.

Roll Call:
Autobots: Ultra Magnus, Kup, Blurr, Rodimus Prime, Wreck-Gar and Goldbug.

Decepticons: Galvatron.

Other: Death's Head and Cindy Newell.

Ultra Magnus, Goldbug and Cindy are their present-day selves; the remaining characters are their 2007 versions.

Data File: Dan Reed (artist)
An ex-pat American who lived in France, Reed had a distinctive style that graced titles such as *The Incredible Hulk* and *Alpha Flight*, as well as both the UK and American Transformers comics.

Review:
After four issues of running on the spot, the 'Volcano' arc finally wakes from its dormancy – Cindy's dire warnings of the threat Galvatron poses, coupled with the fact that the Autobots finally have a proper plan in place (as opposed to their random attacks on Galvatron earlier in the saga), give this story a gravitas and impetus that the last two stories sorely lacked.

Although the decision to conclude the arc in a later annual was a cynical one, on its own merits this is the most successful chapter of the Volcano story since the opening instalment. 3/5.

[28] MECHANICAL DIFFICULTIES!
US#28, 'May 1987' (published January 1987), 22 pages.

British reprint: UK#121, 11 July 1987 (Part One), 11 pages; UK#122, 18 July 1987 (Part Two), 11 pages.

Credits:
Bob Budiansky (script); Don Perlin (pencils); Ian Akin, Brian Garvey (inks); Nel Yomtov (colours); Janice Chiang (letters); Don Daley (editor); Jim Shooter (editor-in-chief); Ian Akin (cover). **UK:** Jeff Anderson (cover, UK#121 & 122).

From this point forward, the UK comic edited the credits on all the American stories it reprinted – no longer would the editor or editor-in-chief be credited in the UK reprints of US-originated stories.

Plot:
One of Grimlock's first commands as Autobot leader is to order the death of the Mechanic, the human criminal who caused so much trouble recently. Blaster and Goldbug are sent on the mission, and it's made clear that failure is not an option.

The first attempt by Blaster and Goldbug is foiled by the police, who blunder onto the scene and allow the Mechanic to escape. The criminal retreats to his new base, an abandoned factory on the outskirts of Portland, where he plans to sell new, weaponised super cars to local mob bosses.

After clear-the-air talks, the police join forces with Blaster and Goldbug, and ensure the destruction of the super-cars and the arrests of the mobsters. Realising that the Mechanic has escaped, Blaster and Goldbug elect to desert rather than face Grimlock's wrath.

Notes:

This story sees the second and final appearance of the Mechanic and his sidekick Juan, who first appeared in [26] 'Funeral for a Friend'. There are a number of references back to that earlier story, including a flashback to the Mechanic's attack on Ratchet. The Mechanic still has possession of the Autobot tools he stole in that story; he is now using them to commit crimes on a larger scale than ever before. His real name is revealed as Nestor Forbes.

The opening scene of this adventure takes place in Portland International Airport (code: PDX), a real-world location. There's a full moon, so it's possible that these events occur on 11 July 1987, coinciding with the cover date of the UK printing.

The Pacific Northwest has a large criminal underworld, with at least eight mobsters willing to pay $50,000 for their cars to be souped-up by the Mechanic. (As in [13] 'Shooting Star', the City of Portland would appear to be a hotbed of crime. See also [A1.2] 'Missing in Action'.)

The computer stolen by the Mechanic is a '256 thousand kilobyte' (i.e. 256 megabyte) Formax model, said to be the most powerful of its kind. Assuming this is a reference to its RAM, that would make it the equivalent of a home desktop computer from roughly around the turn of the 21st Century – extremely powerful from a 1987 point of view.

In a slight geographical error, the *Ark* is said to be 'east' of the Mechanic's factory in Portland; the *Ark* is in fact located in the Cascade Range to the *west* of the city; the City of Portland lies in the Willamette Valley with the Cascades to the west and the Northern Oregon Coast Range of mountains to the east.

UK Changes:

Page 1, panel 1: the hand-lettered credits are excised completely, replaced with a set of printed credits at the bottom of the page.

Page 5, panel 2: correcting a mistake in the US printing (in which Goldbug responds to a non-existent question), Grimlock is given a new line, 'What do you think?'

Page 5, panel 6: the reference to issue #26 is changed to '109/110'.

Roll Call:

Autobots: Ratchet (flashback only), Wheeljack, Grimlock, Blaster and Goldbug.

From the American point of view, this is the first *The Transformers* issue to feature Goldbug (who had been introduced to US readers in a *G.I. Joe* crossover comic).

Other: the Mechanic and Juan (both making their final appearances).

Review:

A sequel to the terrible [26] 'Funeral for a Friend' was never going to be a classic, but on the plus side this is a stronger story than its predecessor in a number of ways – the Grimlock/Blaster/Goldbug conflict adds some personal drama to the story, the Mechanic comes across as more of a threat, and there are some nice bits of humour.

The problem, however, it that this is a story that doesn't really know if it's supposed to be a serious one or a 'funny' one. On the one hand, Grimlock demands the death of a human, Blaster and Goldbug desert the Autobot ranks, and a convoy of SWAT vans swoop in and arrest some of the country's deadliest criminals. On the other hand, we have Grimlock in full-on buffoon-mode, and a notorious scene in which one of the cops decides to perform a song-and-dance routine in the middle of a gangland meeting.

This is a story unsure of tone, in which the comedy serves only to undermine any sense of threat it tries to invoke. 2/5

<u>Next Issue, Part 1</u>

To whet readers' appetites, the American *The Transformers* comic would often hint at the events of the following issue (sometimes a little over-enthusiastically, it has to be said). These missives were sometimes located on the final page of the strip, and sometimes at the bottom of the letters page. Here is a list of all such 'next issue' teasers, issues #1 through #30 (except #6 and #16, neither of which had one):

US#1: Hey, buddy, can ya spare some fuel?

US#2: And along came a … Spider-Man!

US#3: Continued next issue!

US#4: *Not* the end …

US#5: Megatron vs. Shockwave – to the death!

US#7: In search of – Dinobots!

US#8: Hide your personal computer! Trade in your VCR! No machine is safe from: Circuit Breaker!

US#9: Constructicons – phone home!

US#10: Heads up, Autobots, Jetfire is in the air!

US#11: Prime time!

US#12: The malevolent Megatron returns – in the weirdest *Transformers* story yet!

US#13: What happens when the biggest rock star in the world meets the biggest robots in the world? Find out in – Rock and Roll Out!

US#14: Can it be – a human who can control the Transformers? Meet … I, Robot-Master!

US#15: Plight of the Bumblebee

US#17: The cosmic conclusion of Return to Cybertron – The Bridge to Nowhere! (75¢ toll, exact change not necessary.)

US#18: Optimus Prime versus the Decepticons! Megatron versus the Autobots! And the coming of … Omega Supreme!

US#19: *The Transformers* meets the Wild West in – Showdown!

US#20: The Aerialbots! Estimated time of arrival, 30 days.

US#21: The Stunticons arrive! The Aerialbots return! Circuit Breaker strikes! (All this – and Donny Finkleberg, too!)

US#22: Skids' fate revealed! Plus: introducing the riotous Runamuck and Runabout in Decepticon Graffiti!

US#23: The Protectobots! The Combaticons! And … Optimus Prime vs. Megatron in a battle to the death!! (No kidding!)

US#24: Is Optimus Prime truly dead? The answer to that question just might prove fatal to Megatron in: Gone but Not Forgotten!

US#25: Introducing the Mechanic – his tune-ups can be fatal!

US#26: Introducing the biggest, baddest Decepticon yet – Trypticon! And the return of the Dinobots!

US#27: The Mechanic returns!

US#28: The Triple Changers arrive – but they're infected with a deadly disease – the Scraplets!

US#29: Introducing the Throttlebots in – 'The Cure!'

US#30: What's wrong with G B Blackrock? What's in the cargo? Find out this and more in – Buster Witwicky and the Car Wash of Doom!

[29] CRATER CRITTERS
US#29, 'June 1987' (published February 1987), 22 pages.

British reprint: UK#123, 25 July 1987 (Part One), 11 pages; UK#124, 1 August 1987 (Part Two), 11 pages.

Credits:
Bob Budiansky (script); Don Perlin (breakdowns); Ian Akin, Brian Garvey (finishes); Nel Yomtov (colours); Janice Chiang (letters); Don Daley (editor); Jim Shooter (editor-in-chief); Bob Budiansky, Ian Akin and Brian Garvey (cover). **UK:** Lee Sullivan (cover, UK#123); Will Simpson and John Burns (cover, UK#124).

Note that Don Perlin was credited for 'breakdowns' only (i.e. just basic art and layouts), rather than full pencils; likewise regulars Akin and Garvey were credited for finishes (i.e. more than their usual inking duties, turning Perlin's breakdowns into final art). The UK reprint eschewed this terminology and credited Perlin for pencils and Akin and Garvey for inks.

Plot:
After receiving a tip from G B Blackrock, Blaster and Goldbug investigate a meteorite crash in northern Arizona, which turns out to be a downed Decepticon cargo ship, sent from Cybertron. The two Autobots team up with Charlie Fong, one of the researchers investigating the resultant crater.

Back on Cybertron, Ratbat becomes aware that the ship has crashed on Earth, so sends the Triple Changers to investigate what became of it. While Goldbug protects Charlie, Blaster takes on the Decepticons alone.

It transpires that the cargo ship crashed because it's been infected by Scraplets – a swarm of tiny robots who have the ability to replicate, and who feed on metal. Blaster and the Decepticon Triple Changers are all infected, so Goldbug leaves the area with Charlie in an attempt to find a cure.

Goldbug doesn't get far, however – he, too has been infected …

Notes:
This story sees the first US appearance of the Decepticon Triple Changers (Astrotrain,

Blitzwing and Octane), although they had previously featured in a couple of the British stories set on Cybertron (including [20.2] 'Target: 2006' and, more recently, [23.5] 'Resurrection'). This is the first US appearance by G B Blackrock since [15] 'I, Robot-Master'; his last UK-only appearance was in the Christmas story, [22.1] 'The Gift'.

This story lays a lot of groundwork for an upcoming adventure, [31] 'Buster Witwicky and the Car Wash of Doom', in which the crashed ship's mysterious cargo will finally come into play. The Triple Changers mention that they plan to enlist the services of a wealthy human involved in the automobile trade, a reference to their mindcontrol of G B Blackrock in that story. Finally, Blackrock mentions that some oil tankers have gone missing in the Caribbean, a reference to the Decepticon attacks seen in that issue.

It's stated here that Cybertron is 'several dozen' light-years from Earth, a far cry from the 'hundreds' of light years distance mentioned in [10] 'The Next Best Thing to Being There' (see also the notes to [16.3] 'Second Generation'). It is said that the Scraplets ravaged the planet 'thousands of vorns ago' (i.e. after the *Ark* crashed on Earth) but that a 'rare chemical' proved to be a cure. (For more on this remedy, see the notes to [30] 'The Cure'.)

There are references to the desertion of Blaster and Goldbug (in [28] 'Mechanical Difficulties'), and an extended flashback showing Scrounge's death in [17] 'The Smelting Pool'.

The majority of this story is set in northern Arizona (probably the Mojave Desert).

UK Changes:
Page 1, panel 1: credits replaced.
Page 5, panel 6: the reference to issue #17 is changed to issue #67.
Page 18, panel 3: correcting a typo in the original printing, 'they'l' is amended to 'they'll'.

Roll Call:
Autobots: Grimlock (flashback only), Blaster and Goldbug.

Blaster's friend Scrounge also appears, in flashback.
Decepticons: Astrotrain, Blitzwing, Octane and Ratbat.

Other: G B Blackrock.

Review:
The stars of this story are the titular Scraplets, a brilliant concept, realised with aplomb. The mismatched duo of Blaster and Goldbug have a rather strained relationship, which adds an additional layer of tension to their scenes together. There's also a lovely cameo from Ratbat, who once again is on fine form. 4/5

FIGHTING FOR FREEDOM: An Introduction to GI Joe and Action Force

Launched in 1964, GI Joe was a range of military toys developed by the Hassenfeld Brothers, a company now better known as Hasbro. They were essentially dolls aimed at boys (a macho equivalent of Barbie and the like), but for marketing purposes the phrase 'action figure' was coined. Around twelve inches in height, GI Joe was available in several varieties covering all the armed forces, and featured interchangeable uniforms, weapons and vehicles. He had a distinctive scar on his right cheek. Later versions featured flocked hair and movable eyes (operated via a lever on the back of the head). In the UK, the licence to produce the figure was granted to Palitoy, who rebranded him as Action Man.

By the early 1980s, flagging sales on both sides of the Atlantic meant that a rethink was in order. Both Hasbro and Palitoy decided to scale down their figures to three and three-quarter inches tall, matching Kenner's highly successful range of *Star Wars* action figures.

For American audiences, this resulted in GI Joe: A Real American Hero (1982), a popular and varied toy line that included not only military and martial arts heroes and villains, but also a large variety of vehicles for use in conjunction with the toys. The relaunched GI Joe was given a Marvel comic, and a cartoon show by Sunbow Productions. These were highly successful in their home country, running even longer than the later Transformers equivalents did.

In the UK, meanwhile, Palitoy were independently developing their own scaled-down Action Man spin-off, known as Action Force (1982). Once again, comics were used to market the figures – an *Action Force* strip ran in the children's adventure title *Battle Picture Weekly*. Such was the popularity of the *Action Force* strip that the comic was renamed *Battle Action Force*.

In May 1985, Palitoy ceased trading, the rights to Action Force passing to Hasbro UK. Rather than continue the range of original figures, Hasbro instead decided to import GI Joe toys from America and package them as part of the Action Force line. Over time, Action Force transmuted from a British-developed toy range with its own unique identity into, essentially, GI Joe under a different name. It came as no surprise, then, that Hasbro quickly decided to move the comic rights to Marvel UK, where *The Transformers* had become a huge success for them. Launched in March 1987, Marvel's *Action Force* comic featured a mix of British-originated stories and reprints of American *G.I. Joe* material (albeit heavily edited to suit the *Action Force* continuity). Similarly, the Sunbow cartoon was re-dubbed as *Action Force* for UK consumption.

By the middle of 1987, sales of the *Action Force* comic were beginning to flag, the imported GI Joe toys and fiction failing to attract as big an audience as had been hoped. Marvel tried their best to stoke up interest, running a couple of *Action Force* back-up strips in *The Transformers* and funding a heavy advertising push.

As part of Marvel UK's plan to promote the *Action Force* comic in the UK, the decision was taken to create a crossover story, which would begin in *The Transformers* and be concluded in *Action Force*, with the hope that fans of the former title would begin buying the latter as well. The strategy proved unsuccessful; *Action Force* comic eventually folded after fifty issues.

[29.1] ANCIENT RELICS!
- UK#125, 8 August 1987 (Part 1), 11 pages
- *Action Force* #24, 15 August 1987 (Part Two), 5 pages
- *Action Force* #25, 22 August 1987 (Part Three), 5 pages
- *Action Force* #26, 29 August 1987 (Part Four), 5 pages
- *Action Force* #27, 5 September 1987 (Part Five), 5 pages

Credits:
Simon Furman (script); Geoff Senior (pencils); Dave Harwood (inks); Steve White (colours); Annie Halfacree (letters); Jeff Anderson (cover, UK#125, plus Action Force #24-27).

Plot:
Still searching for the deserters Blaster and Goldbug, Grimlock follows a Transformer life signal to London. Also present are the Protectobot Blades, and the rebuilt mechanoid, Centurion. Centurion's very existence is resented by some of the Autobots, who feel that he is an ancient relic, and that the resources spent on his repair might have been better used on healing some of the fallen Autobots.

The life force signal belongs to Megatron, who has been deposited in the sewers beneath the city. After he kills the colleagues of archaeologist Susan Hoffman, the counter-terrorist organisation Action Force are sent in to investigate.

Both Action Force and the Autobots attack Megatron, to no avail. Action Force plan to target the Decepticon with a bomb, which will also ignite some nearby gas containers and surely destroy him. However, Grimlock is engaged in combat with Megatron and is in danger of being caught up in the explosion.

It is Centurion who orders Grimlock clear of the target area, sacrificing his own life to ensure that Megatron is caught up in the blast.

Notes:
This story marks the first Transformers/Action Force crossover in the UK; it wouldn't be the last time the two franchises would cross paths in Britain – after the cancellation of the UK *Action Force* comic, the series would linger on as a regular back-up strip in *The Transformers* from issue #153; and the *G.I. Joe and the Transformers* story would (belatedly) see print much later in the comic's run (in issues #265 to #281).

This story sees two old characters return from the dead. The first is Megatron, who makes a comeback after his apparent demise in [25] 'Gone but Not Forgotten'. He would continue to show up in the UK stories. From the American point of view, however, he would remain dead – for now. This would create a major continuity headache when Megatron eventually returned in the US series (see [57.1] 'Two Megatrons').

The other returnee is Centurion, who was last seen being beheaded by Galvatron in [23.4] 'Fallen Angel'. Curiously, there's no mention of his human controller Professor Morris. It's possible that Morris is still holed up in his bunker beneath Portland and controlling the mechanoid remotely, but given that his room contained only enough water for a year (and that exiting the room would mean certain death at the hands of Triple-I), it's possible that the Professor is dead.

(Writer Simon Furman has since gone public regarding the confusion surrounding Morris, postulating that the Professor might have been rescued by the Dinobots. However, this is never confirmed in the comic itself. Another possibility is that Morris's physical body is dead, but his consciousness remains intact within the body of the Centurion robot. In any case, [23.4] 'Fallen Angel' remained Morris's final appearance, despite Centurion's continued existence. The letters page in UK#135 confirmed that Morris was definitely still in control of the robot.)

Grimlock and Centurion travel to London aboard a shuttle, perhaps similar to those previously seen in the comic (most recently in [12.4] 'Dinobot Hunt'). This is the third story to be set in the UK (after [4.1] 'Man of Iron' and [A2.2] 'To a Power Unknown'), and it sees the debut of a new recurring human character, Susan Hoffman (whose name is a play on that of Susanna Hoffs, singer and guitarist with pop/rock band the Bangles).

Mention is made of the Mechanic, and of the desertion of Blaster and Goldbug (as seen in [28] 'Mechanical Difficulties'). Centurion remembers his previous battle with Megatron in [20.1] 'In the National Interest'. It's confirmed that the Autobots were aware of Megatron's supposed destruction in [25] 'Gone but Not Forgotten'.

Roll Call:
Autobots: Wheeljack, Grimlock and Blades.

Decepticons: **Clone Megatron**. (A continuity mix-up later in the comic's run will lead to the retroactive reveal that this is a clone, and not the real Megatron as originally intended. Until that retcon occurs in [57.1] 'Two Megatrons', the clone is written and presented as if it were the genuine article.)

Other: Centurion, **Susan Hoffman**. (Also Action Force: Flint, Scarlett, Bazooka, Airtight, Barbecue, Wild Bill, Heavy Metal, Dusty and Crankcase, plus the Dragonfly, Mauler and Sky Striker vehicles.)

Review:
On paper this should have been a momentous adventure, featuring an exciting crossover and the return of Megatron. However, it isn't quite as epic as it wants to be, and ends up feeling a little lightweight and inessential. That said, this is still a fun little interlude and a good showcase for the Action Force characters – pacy, well-drawn and suitably action-packed. 3/5

[30] THE CURE!
US#30, 'July 1987' (published March 1987), 22 pages.

British reprint: UK#126, 15 August 1987 (Part One), 11 pages; UK#127, 22 August 1987 (Part Two), 11 pages.

Credits:
Bob Budiansky (script); Don Perlin (breakdowns); Ian Akin, Brian Garvey (finishes); Nel Yomtov (colours); Janice Chiang (letters); Don Daley (editor); Jim Shooter (editor-in-chief); Herb Trimpe (cover). **UK:** Lee Sullivan (cover, UK#126); Robin Smith (cover, UK#127).

As with [29] 'Crater Critters', the UK reprint credited Perlin for pencils and Akin and Garvey for inks.

Plot:
On Cybertron, Ratbat captures a group of Autobots known as Throttlebots, and gives them an ultimatum – either they travel to Earth and eradicate the Scraplet menace (and, by extension, all Transformers infected by them) or Ratbat will destroy all life on the planet. Naturally, the Throttlebots go for the first option, and head to Earth.

Meanwhile, Bumblebee and Charlie Fong happen upon a garage. Parched by the arid conditions, Charlie gulps down a glass of water. Some of it spills onto Goldbug and destroys the Scraplets; it would appear that water is the cure for the Scraplet menace.

Charlie and Goldbug convince the Throttlebots not to destroy Blaster, and instead use the water to cure him (and also the afflicted Decepticons). The tiny Scraplet robots combine into a giant creature, which is no match for the Autobots and Decepticons present, who join forces to defeat it.

The Triple Changers make off with their mysterious cargo, but not before tagging G B Blackrock with a hypnotic device.

Notes:
This story is notable for marking the debut of the Throttlebots – Wideload, Rollbar, Chase, Freeway and Searchlight. (In the Transformers toy range, Goldbug was a Throttlebot too, but while he joins forces with them in this and a few subsequent issues, so far as the comic is concerned he never *officially* joins the team.)

This story is a direct sequel to [29] 'Crater Critters', and as such contains numerous references to that story. (In the USA, the two stories were published back-to-back.) There's also a mention of the Smelting Pool from [17] 'The Smelting Pool', and we get another view of G B Blackrock's distinctively-shaped office building, previously depicted in stories such as [7] 'Warrior School'.

As in [29] 'Crater Critters', there is some foreshadowing of the next story, [31] 'Buster Witwicky and the Car Wash of Doom', with the Decepticons retrieving their mysterious cargo and G B Blackrock falling under the influence of the Decepticon hypno-chip.

Water Works
It transpires that the cure for the deadly Scraplet infestation is something as mundane as water, a compound that is naturally abundant throughout the universe. Despite coming from an apparently waterless planet, The Transformers are definitely aware of the existence of water: Bumblebee's very first line back in [1] 'The Transformers' was: 'So much of [the Earth] is water, and Bumblebee's little levers love a good swim.'

In the letters page of UK#162, Grimlock elucidated further: 'There are seas on Cybertron, but not water based ones. The Great Rust Sea, for instance, stretches from the borders of Tyrest to Polyhex. The Seacons [a group of Decepticons that transform into sea monsters] were created primarily for off-world combat, on planets where there are water based oceans.'

So while the Transformers are aware of water, what they *don't* know is that it acts as a remedy for their plague. In [29] 'Crater Critters', it's revealed that the planet Cybertron was stricken by a Scraplet outbreak 'thousands of vorns ago' (one vorn being roughly equal to 83 Earth years). Despite the fact that water was presumably used to cure the plague, the exact nature of the cure was later forgotten.

This is problematic – Transformers have a lifespan of millions of years, so even if the Scraplet outbreak on Cybertron occurred, say, fifty thousand vorns ago (i.e. 4,150,000 years), that's still well within the living memory of most of the population. It's possible that records were lost (the planet is war-torn, after all), or never made public, but when the likes of Megatron are able to access data files concerning relative minutiae (the old gladiatorial footage seen in [4.2] 'The Enemy Within'), it's doubly odd that such an important event – the entire planet saved from certain death at the hands of the Scraplets – has been lost to the mists of time.

Some possibilities present themselves. First, it could be that the original plague didn't spread very far before it was cured, and that only a few Transformers were aware of the incident. As news of the infestation leaked, the story became exaggerated, Chinese Whispers-style, so that in the minds of modern Transformers, it's become a mythical apocalyptic event. Alternatively, the Scraplets could have mutated since their first encounter with the Transformers (it's confirmed that they have the ability to evolve), and although they are currently vulnerable to water, their Achilles' heel could have changed since the last time they attacked, hence the uncertainty surrounding the exact nature of the cure.

UK Changes:
Page 1, panel 1: the credits are painted out, the result being that Rollbar's feet are now visible.
Page 3, panel 3: 'As seen last issue' becomes 'in issue 123'.
Page 5, panel 1: 'See last issue for more details' is changed to 'see issue 124 for details'.
Page 7, panel 2: 'travelers' is amended to 'travellers'.
Page 13, panel 1: righting a mistake in the original printing, Goldbug's and Wideload's oddly-conjoined speech bubbles are separated.
Page 13, panel 6: 'see last issue' is changed to 'see issue 123'.

Roll Call:
Autobots: Blaster, Goldbug, **Chase**, **Searchlight**, **Freeway**, **Rollbar** and **Wideload**.

Decepticons: Astrotrain, Blitzwing, Octane and Ratbat.

Other: G B Blackrock.

Review:
The second part of the Scraplet story is every bit as good as the first. Again the concepts and visuals are first rate – the combined form of the Scraplets is well realised, and the Triple Changers' reactions when Blaster tells Goldbug to release the acid are priceless.

Although the usual action scenes are present and correct, what really makes this work is Goldbug's moral dilemma, as he is pressed to decide whether to kill Blaster or to cure him. It's not often that *The Transformers* poses such weighty questions; to see it done so well here is extremely satisfying. 4/5

[31] BUSTER WITWICKY AND THE CAR WASH OF DOOM
US#31, 'August 1987' (published April 1987), 23 pages.

British reprint: UK#128, 29 August 1987 (Part One), 11 pages; UK#129, 5 September 1987 (Part Two), 12 pages.

Credits:
Bob Budiansky (script); Don Perlin (breakdowns); Jim Fern (finishes); Nel Yomtov (colours); Rick Parker (letters); Don Daley (editor); Jim Shooter (editor-in-chief); Bob Budiansky (cover). **UK:** Dave Hine and John Burns (cover, UK#128); Robin Smith

(cover, UK#129).

The British version credited Perlin for pencils and Fern for inks.

Plot:
A Decepticon attack on an oil tanker proves embarrassing for Shockwave when it's discovered that the tanker is empty. Ratbat decides to take matters into his own hands, and prepares a more convoluted plan.

Ratbat has set up 'Wash and Roll', a series of car washes with hypnotic flashing lights that make mental slaves of all humans that use them. Once hypnotised, the victims will then siphon the fuel from their own vehicles and into Decepticon-controlled fuel storage facilities.

Buster Witwicky investigates when his girlfriend Jessie becomes affected by one such car wash, and he follows her to the Decepticon facility. There, he learns that the Decepticon-controlled G B Blackrock has been running the operation at Ratbat's behest.

Ratbat attempts to kill Buster within one of the car washes, but the young human is saved when Jessie rams Ratbat with her car. Buster then causes a neon sign to explode; the resulting flash snaps the mesmerised humans out of their stupor, thwarting the Decepticons' plans.

Notes:
This story follows on from the last two, [29] 'Crater Critters' and [30] 'The Cure'. We finally see what the Decepticons wanted with Blackrock, and now we see what their mysterious cargo was: the prototype car wash.

We are also reintroduced to the Witwicky family. Buster had not appeared in an American story since [12] 'Prime Time'; Sparkplug and Jessie hadn't featured since [11] 'Brainstorm'. Here a hypnotised Sparkplug says that his forename is 'Irving', contradicting [3] 'Prisoner of War', in which his name was given as William. (The simplest explanation is that his name is Irving William Witwicky and that – like actors Orson Welles and Sean Connery – he prefers to go by his middle name. Under hypnosis, however, his real name is revealed.)

The Decepticon island base is here confirmed to be 'mobile', apparently able to move around the ocean floor. Its exact nature will be revealed in [39] 'The Desert Island of Space'. Ratbat is now overseeing Decepticon operations on Earth, having been based on Cybertron when last we saw him in [30] 'The Cure'. Their preferred method of hypnotising humans is via a 'stroboscopic opticon', in other words a series of quickly-flashing lights.

The newspaper that reports on the fuel shortage is the (fictional) *Portland Express* (presumably a rival to the *Portland Chronicle* seen in [12.1] 'Christmas Breaker').

This story has much in common with the *Transformers* cartoon episode {2-36} 'Auto-Bop'. In both adventures, the Decepticons use flashing lights and music to hypnotise humans into assisting them. Here, though, the story is based around a car wash rather than a discotheque.

The title is play on that of *Indiana Jones and the Temple of Doom* (Steven Spielberg, 1984), and indeed the title caption uses the same font used on that film's poster.

UK Notes:
In the British comics, the Witwickys had continued to make sporadic appearances since

they were last seen in the US, in stories such as [16.2] 'Devastation Derby' and more recently [22.1] 'The Gift'.

The UK comic had already sought inspiration from the *Indiana Jones* franchise – [4.3] 'Raiders of the Last *Ark*' had a title based on that of the first film in the series.

UK Changes:
Page 1, panel 1: credits replaced.
Page 6, panel 3: '*Transformers* #'s 1-12' is changed to 'numerous past issues'.
Page 6, panel 5: the reference to issue #4 is amended to issue #7.
Page 9, panel 2: 'colored' is anglicised as 'coloured'.
Page 15, panel 3: 'as seen last issue' becomes 'in issue 127'.
Page 18, panel 3: 'tire' is changed to 'tyre'
Page 20, panel 3: again, 'tire' is changed to 'tyre'.

Roll Call:
Autobots: Bluestreak (flashback only) and Bumblebee (flashback only).

Bluestreak and Bumblebee appear in flashback (in a scene from [11] 'Brainstorm'), however Bluestreak is missing his shoulder rockets and is coloured like Prowl.

Decepticons: Laserbeak, Shockwave, Vortex, Shrapnel, Bombshell, Kickback, Ramjet, Thrust, Astrotrain (flashback only), Blitzwing (flashback only), Octane (flashback only) and Ratbat.

Other: Buster, Sparkplug, Jessie and G B Blackrock.

Review:
Previous attempts at comedy stories have been hit and miss, and this is no exception. While some of it is genuinely funny (Ratbat is, as always, hilarious), the wacky central concept of hypnotic disco car washes, on top of the already light-hearted tone, adds up to an instalment that, to put it mildly, is a bit over the top. While it can be quite fun if one is in the right frame of mind, overall this adventure is just a tad too silly for its own good. 2/5

US Advertisements, Part 3: Film, Television and Video Games (H-Z)
As before, a list of all advertisements for films, television shows or video games that appeared in the American *The Transformers* comic, listed alphabetically from H-Z:

Hanna-Barbera cartoons – US#13
Heavenly Kid, The (1985 movie) – US#9
House II: The Second Story (1987 movie) – US#30-31; HDM#1
Hydlide (video game) – US#55
Infocomics (interactive adventure software) – US#42
John Elway's Quarterback (video game) – US#51-52, 55
Konami (hand-held LCD games) – US#67
Konami (video game publisher) – US#36-38, 40-43, 45-46, 52, 69-70; HDM#4
Laser Invasion (video game) – US#80
LaserScope (light gun video game accessory) – US#74

Last Starfighter, The (1984 movie) – US#1
Mario Bros. (video game) – US#2
Marvel Action Universe (television show) – US#48
Marvel mail-away videocassette offer – US#51-53
MegaMan 3 (video game) – US#75, 77
Metal Gear (video game) – US#44, 54, 57
Mission: Impossible (video game) – US#71
Montezuma's Revenge (video game) – US#3
Narc (video game) – US#70
NBC's schedule of Saturday morning cartoons – US#11, 23, 59-61; MOV#1
Nemesis (video game) – US#68
Nickelodeon (clothes and accessories based on shows from the television channel) – US#47
Nickelodeon (fan club) – US#69
Nintendo *Game & Watch* (portable handheld video games) – US#47-50, 52
Operation C (video game) – US#78
Operation: Wolf (video game) – US#54-57
Pac-Man (video game) – US#51
Punisher, The (video game) – US#74-75
Questprobe (a series of video games featuring Marvel characters) – US#15-16
Quickshot (video game controllers) – US#48-53
Rambo (video game) – US#43
Sega Master System – US#38
Ski or Die (video game) – US#75
Silver Surfer (video game) – US#75-77
Splatterhouse (video game) – US#72
Star Wars: The Arcade Game – US#1-2
Street Fighter 2010: The Final Fight (video game) – US#73-74
Super Off-Road (video game) – US#67-68
Taito (video game publisher) – US#48-50, 52
Teenage Mutant Ninja Turtles (video game) – US#55
Tengen (video game publisher) – US#54-55, 57
Thrashin' (videocassette release of the 1986 movie) – US#29
Thundercats videocassettes – US#19
Total Recall (video game) – US#71
Transformers videocassettes – US#9
Transformers and *G.I. Joe* videocassettes – US#13
Ultragames (video game publisher) – UK#45, 47-50
Uncanny X-Men, The (video game) – US#68-69
WCW World Championship Wrestling (video game) – US#62-66
Wizards & Warriors (video game) – US#42
Wrath of the Black Manta (video game) – US#67-72, 74
WWF Wrestlemania (video game) – US#50

[31.1] WORLDS APART!
* UK#130, 12 September 1987 (Part 1), 11 pages
* UK#131, 19 September 1987 (Part 2), 11 pages

This story was also reprinted later in the comic's run, as follows. (NB: each original instalment was divided into halves and spread across a couple of issues):

- UK#255, 3 February 1990 (Part 1), 5 pages
- UK#256, 10 February 1990 (Part 2), 6 pages
- UK#257, 17 February 1990 (Part 3), 5 pages
- UK#258, 24 February 1990 (Part 4), 6 pages

Credits:
Simon Furman (script); Will Simpson (pencils); Tim Perkins (inks); Steve White (colours, part 1); Nick Abadzis (colours, part 2); Annie Halfacree (letters); Geoff Senior and John Burns (cover, UK#130); Lee Sullivan (cover, UK#131).

Plot:
On the planet Nebulos, the Decepticons have captured three Autobots, ostensibly to study and perfect the new Targetmaster process, in which native Nebulans are 'binary-bonded' to Transformer companions and engineered to convert into their hand-held weapons.

The Autobot Headmasters, whose own Nebulan companions convert into their robot heads, go on a mission to rescue their friends from the Decepticons' grasp. However, the whole set-up is a trap: it's not the Targetmaster process the Decepticons are having trouble with, it's the Headmaster process. Scorponok duly captures the Autobot Headmaster Highbrow for further study.

Highbrow is an interesting case. He and his Nebulan companion, Gort, are a mismatched duo, almost unworkably so. However, they actually work well as a pair as, despite all their differences, they have the same ultimate goals – liberty and peace. This combined strength of will means that Highbrow is able to escape Scorponok's clutches.

Notes:
This story acts as a quick introduction to (most of) the new Headmaster and Targetmaster characters, as well as the basic concept behind them. UK issue #130, which included part one of this story, saw the launch of a new back-up strip for the title, namely reprints of the American *The Transformers: Headmasters* four-issue limited series, which would delve deeper into the origins of these exciting new Transformers.

This story is set at some point during that *Headmasters* comic series; the events occur after the Headmasters and Targetmasters have been created, but prior to both factions leaving Nebulos and heading for Earth – i.e. between pages 20 and 21 of [HDM4] 'Brothers in Armor'.

Scorponok is having trouble perfecting the Headmaster process. (This is undoubtedly a reference to his own bonding with the Nebulan Lord Zarak, which is a troubled partnership, to say the least. [HDM4] 'Brothers in Armor' showed us that the bonding process was affecting Zarak's sanity, while in [HDM3] 'Love and Steel' Scorponok hesitated in the midst of battle due to Zarak's effect on him. This, then, would seem to be a last-ditch attempt by Scorponok to iron out these problems.)

The Decepticons are holed up in a 'notorious' complex on Nebulos dubbed the 'Fortress of Despair'. (This is the fortress's one and only appearance; it never featured in the *Headmasters* comic series. It's unclear if this is a new facility, purpose-built by the Decepticons after their arrival on Nebulos, or a pre-existing Nebulan building that's been annexed. What's certain is that it demonstrates the Decepticons' predisposition towards overly dramatic appellations for their headquarters (consider also Fortress Sinister, built in [2] 'Power Play', and Darkmount, seen in [17] 'The Smelting Pool').)

Roll Call:
Autobots: **Highbrow, Chromedome, Hardhead, Brainstorm, Crosshairs, Pointblank** and **Sureshot**.

Decepticons: Cyclonus, Scourge, **Scorponok, Skullcruncher, Mindwipe, Weirdwolf, Apeface, Snapdragon, Slugslinger, Triggerhappy** and **Misfire**.

Nebulans: **Galen** (flashback only), **Gort, Stylor, Duros, Arcana, Pinpointer, Peacemaker, Spoilsport, Zarak, Krunk, Fracas, Caliburst, Blowpipe** and **Aimless**.

Of these Nebulans, only Galen (in flashback), plus Gort, Stylor, Pinpointer, Peacemaker and Spoilsport are shown in their humanoid modes. All other Nebulan appearances in this story are as either the heads or the weapons of their Transformer partners.

Although the majority of these characters are making their debuts in the comic proper, all had previously appeared in the *Headmasters* spin-off comic.

Data File: Nick Abadzis (artist/letterer)
Abadzis's credits include *The Real Ghostbusters*, *Thundercats* and *Action Force*. He is also a writer, and has penned strips in *2000 AD*, *Doctor Who Magazine* and *Torchwood Comic*.

Review:
A slight and forgettable story that introduces the Headmasters and Targetmasters but does little else. An efficient piece of writing, it succeeds in getting the job done, but it's fairly mundane stuff. 2/5

The 'NEXT' Box, Part 2
More teases and tag-lines from the iconic 'NEXT' box that appeared in the UK *The Transformers* comic – issues UK#67-132.

- UK#67: The bridge to nowhere!
- UK#68: Dead duel!
- UK#69: Omega Supreme!
- UK#70: Omega ... Supreme!
- UK#71: Showdown!
- UK#72: Skids – all washed up?!
- UK#73: In the national interest!
- UK#74: Gauntlet!
- UK#75: Holocaust
- UK#76: The Dinobots' last stand?
- UK#77: Target 2006!
- UK#78: Apocalypse then ... now!
- UK#79: Construction time again!
- UK#80: Defeat!
- UK#81: 'Wreck and rule!'

- UK#82: The devil you know …
- UK#83: Trios!
- UK#84: Prisoners of war!
- UK#85: You haveta ask?!
- UK#86: Back to the future!
- UK#87: Aftermath!
- UK#88: Aerialbots over America!
- UK#89: Dogfight!
- UK#90: Heavy traffic!
- UK#91: Clash of the Special Teams!
- UK#92: The gift!
- UK#93: Decepticon graffiti!
- UK#94: 'Give me liberty…!'
- UK#95: Prey!
- UK#96: Running scared!
- UK#97: … The harder they die!
- UK#98: Under fire!
- UK#99: Distant thunder!
- UK#100: Fallen angel!
- UK#101: A kind of madness!
- UK#102: Resurrection!
- UK#103: Whose death is it anyway?
- UK#104: Afterdeath!
- UK#105: And the loser is …!
- UK#106: Megatron's last stand!
- UK#107: The hunter hunted!
- UK#108: The Mechanic!
- UK#109: Dark *Ark*!
- UK#110: King of the hill!
- UK#111: Dinosaur-war!
- UK#112: Wanted: Galvatron!
- UK#113: First blood!
- UK#114: Burning sky!
- UK#115: Fire storm!
- UK#116: Hunters!
- UK#117: … Trouble, yes?
- UK#118: Fire on high!
- UK#119: Out of time!
- UK#120: To be concluded! See this year's *Transformers* Annual for the shocking climax!
- UK#121: Dis-assembly!
- UK#122: Crater critters!
- UK#123: Scrapped!
- UK#124: And now … *Action Force*!
- UK#125: To be continued … in the pages of *Action Force* 24
- UK#126: Scraplets – combine!
- UK#127: Car wash of doom!
- UK#128: All washed up!
- UK#129: [Main strip] Worlds End! [Headmasters back-up] Headmasters!
- UK#130: [Main strip] Scorponok's sting! [Headmasters back-up] Exodus!

- UK#131: [Main strip] Kup's story! [Headmasters back-up] War or peace!
- UK#132: [Main strip] Head hunt! [Headmasters back-up] … Heads you lose!

[31.2] KUP'S STORY!
UK#132, 26 September 1987, 11 pages

Credits:
Simon Furman (script); Dan Reed (art); Steve White (colours); Annie Halfacree (letters); Dan Reed and John Burns (cover).

Plot:
Several hundred years ago. The old Autobot warrior Kup is in self-imposed exile, drifting through space aboard a 'crate' of a spaceship. Although he was once one of Cybertron's greatest heroes, his strength and bright attitude have waned due to old age.

Kup's craft happens upon a space battle and, against his better judgment, the Autobot intervenes and saves a ship in distress. Its passenger is Hot Rod, a young Autobot on a mission to save his friend Blurr from captivity on the planet Tyroxia.

Hot Rod commandeers Kup's vessel and takes it to Tyroxia. Once there, however, he is overwhelmed by the Tyroxian forces and is on the verge of defeat until saved by Kup. It transpires that some of Hot Rod's youthful exuberance and enthusiasm have rubbed off on the old-timer, enabling him to rescue Hot Rod and Blurr from the Tyroxians' clutches.

Notes:
This is a story written with a specific purpose in mind. UK readers were already familiar with the future versions of Hot Rod, Kup and Blurr, so the introduction of their present-day counterparts (as Targetmasters) might have confused some readers. This then, was an attempt to establish the Autobot trio as having been friends for hundreds of years.

Hot Rod and Blurr were captured while on a scouting mission for 'our leader, Fortress Maximus, looking for habitable worlds', a reference to the events of [HDM1] 'Ring of Hate', in which a group of Autobots led by Fortress Maximus depart Cybertron for Nebulos.

At the beginning of this story, Kup is suffering from 'combat fatigue'. He is one of the oldest and most experienced Autobots, and his skills have begun to diminish with age. Rather than put comrades at risk in a battle situation, war veterans such as this are provided with ships and allowed to live out their final days travelling the cosmos. The affliction would appear to have a substantial psychological element to it, with Kup's problems stemming more from a lack of self-belief than anything physical.

The Tyroxians are powerful, fanged aliens, whose cyborg-like, techno-organic appearance extends to their ships and planet. Their language, as written, consists of simple geometric shapes such as circles, triangles and rectangles.

Roll Call:
Autobots: Hot Rod, Kup and Blurr.

Data File: John Burns (artist)
Burns is an artist with other fifty years' industry experience. From the year 2000, he was

lead artist on the *Nikolai Dante* strips in *2000 AD*. Other comics boasting his artwork include *TV Century 21*, *Look-In*, *Eagle* and *Epic*. He also drew daily cartoon strips for British newspapers *The Sun* and the *Daily Mirror*.

Review:

This story borrows heavily from [12.2] 'Crisis of Command': an Autobot suffering from self-doubt regains his confidence after single-handedly saving a junior warrior from certain death, against overwhelming odds. This is a rehash, then, but a forgivable one: it's an important story for the development of Hot Rod and especially of Kup, who in the space of eleven pages is turned from a bit-part player into one of the most memorable characters yet seen in the comic.

As in [4.2] 'The Enemy Within' and [23.3] 'Distant Thunder', writer Simon Furman again proves that he's not afraid to use clichéd plots, so long as they can adequately service the real purpose of the story: a character study. 4/5

The Back-Up Strips, Part 14: *Spider-Man*

- 'Children in Danger!' (UK#132), a special, one-off, four-page strip, part funded by the British Home Office. It was basically a PSA (public service ad) in which Spider-Man saves a child who gets into a car with a stranger – readers are encouraged not to do the same. The strip ran in a number of UK Marvel titles, including *Action Force* #31.

[31.3] HEADHUNT
- UK#133, 3 October 1987 (Part 1), 11 pages
- UK#134, 10 October 1987 (Part 2), 11 pages

This story was also reprinted later in the comic's run, as follows. (NB: each original instalment was divided into halves and spread across a couple of issues):

- UK#225, 8 July 1989 (Part 1), 6 pages
- UK#226, 15 July 1989 (Part 2), 5 pages
- UK#227, 22 July 1989 (Part 3), 5 pages
- UK#228, 29 July 1989 (Part 4), 6 pages

Credits:
Simon Furman (script); Dan Reed (art, part 1); Geoff Senior (art, part 2); Steve White (colours); Richard Starkings (letters); Dave Gibbons (cover, UK#133); Lee Sullivan (cover, UK#134).

Plot:
Cybertron, the year 2007. The Autobot/Decepticon war continues to drag on, neither side able to gain the upper hand. Decepticon leader Shockwave hires the bounty-hunter Death's Head to kill Rodimus Prime, and manipulates Cyclonus and Scourge into also going after Prime, hoping that they, too, will be killed in the crossfire.

The four robots battle in the sewer-like utility ducts beneath Cybertron; Scourge and Cyclonus flee the scene when they realise that Death's Head is after *them* too. Death's Head then chases a wounded Rodimus Prime through the underground tunnels, but fails to realise he's being tricked – Prime lures the mercenary through the underground entrance of the Autobase and into the sights of the waiting Autobots.

Rodimus Prime gives Death's Head a counter-offer – he pays the bounty-hunter ten thousand shanix to bring him the heads of Cyclonus and Scourge …

Notes:
This is the first story to be set in the post-movie future since [27.2] 'Burning Sky', and acts as a prequel to, and set-up for, the forthcoming epic [36.2] 'The Legacy of Unicron'.

The Decepticon envoy Blot meets Death's Head on the planet Scarvix (although it's unclear whether this is Death's Head's base of operations or simply a neutral venue). The mercenary claims that his axe holds 'sentimental value' to him, but given the character's deadpan delivery, this could be just a joke. His energy weapon is identified as a 'titanium shott blaster'. There is a reference to Death's Head's previous altercation with Cyclonus and Scourge in [27.1] 'Wanted: Galvatron – Dead or Alive'; indeed Scourge still bears a scar on his chest from the wound he incurred in that skirmish.

Like the Autobases previously seen in [17] 'The Smelting Pool' and [20.2] 'Target: 2006', this one incorporates a secret underground entrance. The surface-level approach is surrounded by a series of trenches guarded by an array of (automated?) weapon emplacements. Rodimus Prime himself conducts periodic inspections of these trenches. At the beginning of this story, Prime is seen within a gold-coloured tower on Cybertron – it's unclear whether this building is separate from the Autobase seen later, or part of the same complex.

Rodimus Prime recalls that his Nebulan Targetmaster partner, Firebolt, died on Earth at some point prior to the events of the movie.

Roll Call:
Autobots: Hot Rod (flashback only) and Rodimus Prime.

Decepticons: Shockwave, Galvatron (sort of, see below), Cyclonus, Scourge and **Blot**.

Nebulans: **Firebolt** (flashback only).

Other: Death's Head.

This story marks the debut appearances of Blot and Firebolt in the main *The Transformers* strip; they had already featured in the *Headmasters* mini-series.

All these characters are their 21st Century future versions. Galvatron appears only as part of an artistic flourish – when Shockwave talks about the missing Decepticon in part one, an image of Galvatron's devilish eyes appears in the background.

Data File: Dave Gibbons (artist)
The Jack Kirby Award-winning Gibbons provided art for the very first issue of *2000 AD*, and is the co-creator of that title's *Rogue Trooper* strip. He also provided art for *Doctor Who Weekly*, again from the very first issue. His other credits include *Green Lantern*, *Superman*, *Batman* and *Captain America*. He is best known, however, as the artist and letterer on the seminal comic classic *Watchmen*. His lettering on that series has been cited as one of the key influences in the development of the ubiquitous computer typeface Comic Sans.

Review:
The best Transformers stories are those that manage to combine action and excitement with a good storyline and characterisation, and 'Headhunt' falls firmly into this category.

Not only is this a good study of Rodimus Prime (weary of war, haunted by Firebolt's death and longing for better days), but the plot is also of great interest, as first the Decepticons, then the Autobots, seek the services of the bounty-hunter Death's Head, while the Machiavellian Shockwave plots the deaths of Scourge and Cyclonus.

But where this story really excels is in its action sequences, as the four robots hunt each other within a claustrophobic rat's maze of tunnels and sewers. Gripping stuff. 5/5

UK Advertisements, Part 1: Food and Drink

Like the American comic, the British one included some deliciously retro advertisements within its pages, for products and companies such as Battle Beasts, Woolworth's and a Ladybird book based upon the 1986 FIFA World Cup. Here then is a list of all advertisements for food and drink that appeared in *The Transformers* UK:

Cadbury's (chocolate bars) – UK#161
Cherry Coca-Cola – UK#118, 120, 123, 127, 131
Chomp (chocolate bar) – UK#269
Crosse & Blackwell (pasta shapes) – UK#231
Curly Wurly (chocolate bar) – UK#134, 214, 236, 239, 243
Fiendish Feet (yoghurts) – UK#246, 248, 318, 321, 325
Findus Crispy Pancakes – UK#259
Heinz Bean Street Kids (tinned baked beans) – UK#138
Heinz Haunted House (pasta shapes) – UK#79-80
Heinz Invaders (pasta shapes) – UK#95-96
Golden Wonder (crisps and snacks) – UK#87-88
Jawbreakers (gobstopper sweets) – UK#17, 28, 155, 157
Kraft Titans (meatballs in tomato sauce) – UK#173, 176
Kia-Ora (fruit drink) – UK#137, 140, 143
Knorr Mysteries of the Deep (soup) – UK#245, 248, 253
Marmite (yeast-extract food paste) – UK#102
Matlow's Refreshers (chewy sweets) – UK#314
McCain *Teenage Mutant Ninja Turtles* pizza slices – UK#299
Milky Way (chocolate bar) – UK#280, 283, 291, 295, 314, 317, 326, 328
Nerds (fruit-flavoured sweets) – UK#219, 237, 240
Nesquik (milkshake mix) – UK#69, 72, 74
Nestlé Animal Bars (chocolate bar) – UK#157
Pez (fruit-flavoured sweets) – UK#173, 175, 178, 180
Quosh (orange-flavoured soft drink) – UK#166, 168, 170
Ready Brek (breakfast cereal) – UK#155
Real Ghostbusters potato snacks – UK#154
Rice Krispies (breakfast cereal) – UK#226, 228, 245, 250
Ricicles (breakfast cereal) – UK#105-107, 125, 162, 164
Shredded Wheat (breakfast cereal) – UK#301
Smarties (chocolate sweets) – UK#283
Sugar Puffs (breakfast cereal) – UK#158-159

Sun-Pat (peanut butter) – UK#242, 246
Teenage Mutant Hero Turtles frozen pizzas (from Tesco) – UK#289-290
Thundercats potato snacks – UK#103
Weetabix (breakfast cereal) – UK#2, 85, 88, 92, 98, 102, 106, 110, 113, 118, 122, 126, 134, 143, 147, 149, 154, 159, 162, 171-172, 184, 193, 196, 201, 205, 207, 209, 217, 223, 227, 240
Weeto's (breakfast cereal) – UK#120, 128, 133, 164, 166, 183, 185, 194, 196

[31.4] GRUDGE MATCH!
- UK#135, 17 October 1987 (Part 1), 11 pages
- UK#136, 24 October 1987 (Part 2), 11 pages

Credits:
Simon Furman (script); Jeff Anderson (pencils); Stephen Baskerville (inks); Steve White (colours); Annie Halfacree (letters); Jeff Anderson, Stephen Baskerville, Robin Bouttell (cover, UK#135); Robin Smith (cover, UK#136).

Plot:
Bored out of their minds, the Predacons decide to have a little fun by causing havoc in a circus. Swoop, viewing the attack on television, recognises the Predacon Divebomb as an old nemesis from his Cybertron days.

It transpires that Swoop himself was once known as Divebomb. After he was defeated in battle many years ago, the victor 'stole' the Divebomb name and has been using it ever since. The pair also clashed a second time on Cybertron; an event that Swoop is clearly embarrassed about and has kept secret for millions of years.

Seeking revenge, Swoop attacks Divebomb, but when the rest of the Predacons show up, Swoop is outnumbered and facing death. Swoop's Dinobot comrades arrive on the scene, however, and the two teams do battle.

Divebomb, on the verge of defeat, reveals Swoop's embarrassing secret – when last they clashed on Cybertron, Swoop's life was saved by Optimus Prime (the commanding officer that Swoop hated with a passion).

Grimlock, however, was already aware of this information, and tells Divebomb that it doesn't matter – whatever happened in the past, the Dinobots always stick together. The defeated Predacons are allowed to flee, with both Swoop and Divebomb hoping for a rematch in the future.

Notes:
This story is a tie-in to an adventure from the 1988 *The Transformers Annual*, [A3.1] 'What's in a Name', which is set during these events and features a flashback to the previous Swoop/Divebomb battle.

The origins of this adventure can be traced to a short sequence in [12.3] 'The Icarus Theory', where it was revealed that Swoop was previously known as Divebomb, and that he was a member of the Elite Flying Corps, serving under Optimus Prime, whom Swoop hated and rebelled against. (There's evidence to suggest that Divebomb was an early name for Swoop behind the scenes, too – an internal production document written for the cartoon series has the Dinobot's name typed as 'Divebomb', which is then crossed-out and replaced with a handwritten 'Swoop'. It's likely that Bob Budiansky, who named the majority of the 1980s Transformers characters, decided against using the Divebomb name for Swoop, but kept it in mind when christening the

Predacons. These internal documents, with their last-minute alterations, might well have been the inspiration for the whole Swoop/Divebomb name plot in the first place.)

It's revealed that, as the current Autobot leader, Grimlock has access to all of Optimus Prime's old mission files, including some off-the-record reports that were never officially logged.

The action takes place in and around the (fictional) town of Calusa, Florida (presumably the closest mainland settlement to the Decepticons' island base). (In the real world, Calusa is the name of a Native American tribe that lived in the Florida region until the 18th Century.)

Roll Call:
Autobots: Grimlock, Snarl, Slag, Sludge and Swoop.

Decepticons: Razorclaw, Rampage, Tantrum, Headstrong, Divebomb and Predaking (flashback only).

Review:
This is a strange story; one that invites the reader to care about the petty, childish Swoop, whose 'big secret' is nothing more than the fact that he was once bested in battle and needed Optimus Prime to save him. With the personal stakes so small, it's difficult to muster much enthusiasm for what is otherwise just 22 pages of action and fight scenes (albeit quite fun fight scenes). The ending, too, in which Grimlock and Swoop allow the Predacons to withdraw, is an anticlimax that recalls a similar grudging truce at the end of [20.1] 'In the National Interest'. 2/5

[31.5] LADIES' NIGHT
- UK#137, 31 October 1987 (Part 1.), 11 pages
- UK#138, 7 November 1987 (Part 2.), 11 pages

Credits:
Simon Furman (script); Dan Reed (art, part 1); Geoff Senior (art, part 2); Euan Peters (colours, part 1); Nick Abadzis (colours, part 2); Annie Halfacree (letters); Lee Sullivan (cover, UK#137); Barry Kitson, Robin Bouttell (cover, UK#138).

Plot:
Investigating the recent eruption of the 'dormant' Mount Verona in Oregon, the adventurer Susan Hoffman discovers the inert bodies of Ultra Magnus and Galvatron, perfectly preserved within the now-solidified lava. Her discovery is featured on a Joy Meadows-hosted television programme, *Ladies' Night*, which is viewed by a number of interested parties.

Goldbug and the Throttlebots arrive on the scene, hoping to rescue Ultra Magnus. Cindy Newell is also present, having also seen the TV footage. The Combaticons show up too, with orders to blow up the volcano and ensure the destruction of both Magnus and the insane Galvatron. The Throttlebots initially decide to allow the Decepticons to proceed – although it will mean the death of Ultra Magnus, at least Galvatron will also be destroyed.

Appalled at the Autobots' decision, Susan, Joy and Cindy join forces in a bid to sabotage the Decepticons' plan, setting traps and attacking them with tanks. The

Autobots change their minds and try to stop the Decepticons, but only to save the lives of the humans.

Although the Decepticons are driven away, it appears that the various battles have destabilised some of the volcanic rock; Galvatron's hand begins moving …

Notes:
This story sees the return of Blaster, Goldbug and the Throttlebots, who are still on the run from Grimlock (and who were last seen in [30] 'The Cure'). It would appear that, in an attempt to evade Grimlock's clutches, the band of deserters are zigzagging their way across America. ([30] 'The Cure' was set in Arizona, here they are in Oregon, and in their next appearance – [32] 'Used Autobots' – they will have relocated to California.) When we first see them in this adventure, they are 'some two hundred miles east' of Mount Verona (probably in or near Pendleton, Oregon).

The Throttlebots are watching a movie from Walt Disney's *Herbie* franchise, a series of films depicting a sentient VW Beetle – the same model as the Throttlebot Goldbug, who comments that Herbie is 'my kinda hero'. It's unclear exactly which film they are watching, but it could be any one of *The Love Bug* (Robert Stevenson, 1968), *Herbie Rides Again* (Robert Stevenson, 1974), *Herbie Goes to Monte Carlo* (Vincent McEveety, 1977) or *Herbie Goes Bananas* (Vincent McEveety, 1980).

Ultra Magnus and Galvatron are trapped inside Mount Verona following its eruption in [A3.3] 'Vicious Circle'. The eruption is said to have taken place 'four months ago'. (Assuming this story is set around the time it was published, i.e. late October/early November 1987, this would place the eruption in late June/early July, which ties in with the publication date of [27.4] 'Fire on High' – the last comic story to feature the volcano.) It's confirmed here that Mount Verona was a dormant volcano prior to Galvatron's tampering.

This adventure is notable for seeing some of the comic's favourite human characters team up in an attempt to thwart the Decepticons. Joy Meadows was introduced in [12.4] 'Dinobot Hunt', and returned in [20.1] 'In the National Interest'. She also appeared in Sludge's dream in [A2.5] 'Victory'. Cindy Newell had a central role in the aforementioned 'volcano' storyline, having appeared in [27.2] 'Burning Sky', [27.3] 'Hunters' and [27.4] 'Fire on High'. Susan Hoffman (whose characterisation as a female Indiana Jones type pre-dated the creation of Lara Croft by nine years) had previously appeared in the *The Transformers/Action Force* crossover story [29.1] 'Ancient Relics'. Of these, only Hoffman would make a further appearance, in [52.2] 'Race with the Devil'. Writer Simon Furman saved a few lines of exposition by not explaining these characters' backgrounds within the story itself. Instead, it was left to the Transformation editorial in issue #137 to explain to new readers that the three women had all made previous appearances in the comic.

Hoffman discovers the bodies of Ultra Magnus and Galvatron 'one week' prior to the live transmission of *Ladies' Night* ('the programme for today's working woman'). The show is broadcast during the early hours, probably around four or five in the morning, Pacific Time – Cindy and the Throttlebots watch the programme in Oregon at night; whereas for Soundwave, watching the show in Florida, it's daylight – Eastern Time being three hours in advance of Oregon.

This is the first appearance of the Decepticon Brawl since he incurred what looked like serious damage in [25] 'Gone but Not Forgotten', when his head was crushed by Megatron. This story was written to segue seamlessly into the next American story, [32]

'Used Autobots', which opens with the Combaticons again attacking Blaster and the Throttlebots. (Onslaught states here that 'you [Autobots] become our priority targets!')

Roll Call:
Autobots: Blaster, Ultra Magnus, Goldbug, Chase, Searchlight, Freeway, Rollbar and Wideload.

Decepticons: Soundwave, Shockwave, Onslaught, Brawl, Blast Off, Swindle, Vortex and Galvatron.

Other: Joy Meadows, Cindy Newell and Susan Hoffman.

Ultra Magnus and Galvatron appear only as petrified corpses, as nightmarish visions in Cindy's dream, and in a brief flashback.

Data File: Euan Peters (colourist/editor)
Peters coloured many comics for Marvel UK, including *Action Force*, *Death's Head* and *The Knights of Pendragon*.

Review:
A little gem. This tale has all the action and excitement one would expect in a Transformers adventure, but there's a lot more to this than just thrills and spills. It's a witty script (Meadows' line about how she learned to operate a tank is knowingly ludicrous), and the Combaticons (who are always a fun team) are ideal villains for this type of yarn. Despite it being a bit of a romp, this story also has a serious side, as Goldbug contemplates sacrificing Magnus so that Galvatron might be destroyed – echoing the dilemma he had in [30] 'The Cure', where he contemplated letting Blaster die for the greater good. 4/5

[32] USED AUTOBOTS
US#32, 'September 1987' (published May 1987), 22 pages.

British reprint: UK#139, 14 November 1987 (Part One), 11 pages; UK#140, 21 November 1987 (Part Two), 11 pages.

Credits:
Bob Budiansky (script); Don Perlin (pencil breakdowns); Ian Akin, Brian Garvey (finishes); Nel Yomtov (colours); Pat Brousseau (letters); Don Daley (editor); Jim Shooter (editor-in-chief); Frank Springer (cover). **UK:** Robin Smith (cover, UK#139); Lee Sullivan (cover, UK#140).

In the UK printing, the pencil breakdowns and finishes roles were re-described as 'pencils' and 'inks' respectively, and Diana Albers was incorrectly credited as letterer.

Plot:
Blaster and the Throttlebots are attacked by the Combaticon Vortex, but are able to drive him off. Stopping at a garage to recuperate, they once again come under fire – this time from RAAT, who have placed traps within all Blackrock-owned gas stations.

The Autobots flee again, and this time find respite within a used car lot. However, the lot's owner discovers that the Autobots are wanted by RAAT, and so betrays them to the authorities in exchange for a reward.

The Throttlebots, incapacitated because the car salesman filled their tanks with soda, can only look on as RAAT, the Combaticons and the Protectobots all converge on the car lot, and a mass battle ensues. Amidst the chaos, the Throttlebots are captured by RAAT.

Although the Combaticons are driven off, Blaster still isn't safe – the Protectobots are there not to rescue him but to *arrest* him for his act of desertion …

Notes:

The Autobots are now no longer reliant on G B Blackrock for fuel (effectively ending the partnership that began all the way back in [9] 'Dis-Integrated Circuits'). This is down to their new geothermal generator (a device similar in function to the Decepticons' power siphon technology), that can convert heat energy beneath Mount St Hilary into Energon.

On the subject of Blackrock, at least one of his gas stations is under military control and hides a RAAT vehicle that lies in wait for any unsuspecting Autobots. (As a friend of the Autobots, Blackrock presumably has no knowledge that these stings are happening – RAAT are acting behind his back.) Rollbar suggests that RAAT have traps at every Blackrock-owned filling station, but this seems very unlikely, as Blackrock must have thousands of stations across the USA. This is the first appearance of RAAT and their commander, Walter Barnett, since [23] 'Decepticon Graffiti'.

It's stated here that the Autobots have 'finished repairing the *Ark*' – the Autobots' ship had been buried beneath Mount St Hilary since [1] 'The Transformers'. There are references to [30] 'The Cure': the Throttlebots theorise that the Combaticons have been pursuing them since those events, and Blackrock's intervention in that story is also mentioned. Blaster's and Goldbug's failed mission and subsequent desertion in [28] 'Mechanical Difficulties' is also alluded to.

Goldbug's plan, that the Throttlebots hide in plain sight amongst other cars, recalls [16] 'Plight of the Bumblebee', in which, as Bumblebee, he tried the very same trick, with similarly dire consequences. Lee Iacocca is mentioned again (c.f. [7] 'Warrior School').

UK Notes:

The Autobots' new method of extracting power from a volcano is a smaller-scale version of Galvatron's plan to tap the energies of Mount Verona in [27.2] 'Burning Sky' *et seq*. The idea that the Autobots had been working on making the *Ark* space-ready came out of the blue for American readers, but in the UK this plan had been previously referred to in [16.1] 'Robot Buster'.

Changes were made to some of the text in the UK reprint, establishing that the Combaticons were chasing the Throttlebots because of their previous confrontation in [31.5] 'Ladies' Night'.

UK Changes:

Page 1, panel 1: credits replaced.

Page 3, panel 5: 'tie-up' is changed to 'jam'.

Page 4, panel 1: 'Decepticons' and 'the crater in Arizona' are altered to read

'Combaticons' and 'Mount Verona' respectively, plus the references to issues #30 and #9 are changed to #138 and #34.

Page 7, panel 5: 'see *Transformers* #28' becomes 'see *Transformers* #121'.

Page 8, panel 1: the reference to issue #30 is changed to #126.

Page 8, panel 3: 'sunup' is replaced by 'dawn'.

Page 12, panel 1: the reference to Lee Iacocca is excised.

Page 14, panel 1 'refueled' is changed to 'refuelled'.

Page 22, panels 1 and 2: to make sure the strip filled the page, these panels were extended upwards and extra background added.

The Transformers US: The Ident Box

An 'ident box' is a part of a comic's cover where one can find the issue number, date and pricing information. On Marvel comics, it was also customary for the box to accommodate a piece of art – usually one of the title's main characters.

The artwork used in the ident boxes on the American *The Transformers* comics was as follows:

US#1: Optimus Prime
US#2: Megatron
US#3: Gears
US#4: Megatron
US#5-14, 27-29, 50-75: Optimus Prime (a different image from that of US#1)
US#15-26: as above, but with the addition of the Marvel 25th Anniversary logo
US#30-32, 34-37: Grimlock
US#33: Grimlock (with a Union Jack in the background)
US#38-49: Fortress Maximus (from the cover art of *Headmasters* #1)
US#76: Optimus Prime's corpse (taken from the interior artwork)
US#77-79: Action Master Grimlock (based on interior art from US#76)
US#80: the Decepticon insignia

The Transformers: The Movie #1-3: Optimus Prime with Marvel 25th Anniversary logo (as per US#15-26)

G.I. Joe and the Transformers #1-4: the heads of Snake-Eyes and Bumblebee (and issues #1-3 also incorporated the Marvel 25th Anniversary logo)

Headmasters #1: Optimus Prime (as per US#5-29)
Headmasters #2: Zarak and Galen (based on interior art from *Headmasters* #1)
Headmasters #3-4: Fortress Maximus (from the cover art of *Headmasters* #1)

The Transformers Universe series used a smaller ident-box with no additional artwork other than Marvel's 25th Anniversary logo.

Looking at the ident boxes, we can also see how the pricing of the comic fluctuated over the years:

US#1-12: 75¢ (UK 50p, CAN $1)
US#13: 75¢ (UK 50p, CAN 95¢)

US#14-27: 75¢ (UK 40p, CAN 95¢)
US#28-39: $1 (UK 40p, CAN $1.25)
US#40-49, 51-56: $1 (UK 50p, CAN $1.25)
US#50: $1.50 (UK 50p, CAN $2.00) – special issue with higher page-count
US#57-74, 76-80: $1 (UK 60p, CAN $1.25)
US#75: $1.50 (UK60p, CAN $2.00) – special issue with higher page-count

The Transformers: The Movie #1: 75¢ (UK 40p, CAN 95¢)
The Transformers: The Movie #2-3: 75¢ (UK 40p, CAN $1.25)

All *The Transformers Universe* issues were priced at $1.25 (UK 40p, CAN $1.50)
All *G.I. Joe and the Transformers* issues were priced at 75¢ (UK 40p, CAN 95¢)
All *Headmasters* issues were priced at $1 (UK 40p, CAN $1.25)

In other cover-rated trivia, there were two Transformers logos used on the comic. The original version was used for US#1-50. All issues from US#51 onwards featured the new logo introduced in 1988.

Roll Call:
Autobots: Wheeljack, Grimlock, Slag, Hot Spot, Streetwise, Blades, Groove, First Aid, Blaster, Goldbug, Chase, Searchlight, Freeway, Rollbar and Wideload.

Decepticons: Onslaught, Brawl, Blast Off, Swindle and Vortex.

Other: Walter Barnett.

Review:
The action sequences here are some of the best seen in the comic for a while, and there are some interesting twists to savour – Grimlock's plan to launch the *Ark*, the trap at the gas station, and of course the cliffhanger ending.

Unfortunately, any plus points are more than cancelled out by the 'comedy' scenes at the used car lot; its owner Big Steve can be safely filed alongside Joey Slick and Bomber Bill in the list of light-relief human characters that never quite worked. Furthermore, RAAT's continued insistence that all robots are evil, in the face of so much contrary evidence now, is grating. 1/5

[33] and [34] MAN OF IRON (re-print)
After 32 issues in three years, the makers of the American *The Transformers* comic finally missed a deadline. At the end of [32] 'Used Autobots', a caption promised readers that the following issue would see a Defensor v Bruticus battle; however, due to unavoidable production delays, publication of the next story, 'Child's Play' was deferred for two months, a reprint of a UK story [4.1] 'Man of Iron' appearing in its stead.

Unscheduled reprints were by now a rarity within Marvel Comics, thanks mostly to practices put in place by Jim Shooter, the company's Editor-in-Chief from 1978 to 1987, but they had been a regular occurrence in the 1970s, plaguing even some of Marvel's best-known titles, such as *The Fantastic Four* (#180 and #189), *Thor* (#254), *Iron Man* (#76) and *The Avengers* (#150).

[35] CHILD'S PLAY (comic)

NB: Not to be confused with {2-28} 'Child's Play' (cartoon episode).

US#35, 'December 1987' (published August 1987), 23 pages.

British reprint: UK#141, 28 November 1987 (Part 1), 12 pages; UK#142, 5 December 1987 (Part 2), 11 pages.

Credits:
Bob Budiansky (script); Don Perlin (pencils); Ian Akin, Brian Garvey (inks); Nel Yomtov (colours); Jack Morelli (letters); Don Daley (editor); Tom DeFalco (editor-in-chief); Frank Springer (cover). **UK:** Stephen Baskerville and Lee Sullivan (cover, UK#141); Dan Reed and Robin Bouttell (cover, UK#142).

Plot:
As the Protectobots journey back to the *Ark* with their prisoner, the deserter Blaster, they are ambushed by the Combaticons at a railway yard. Blaster is in tape deck mode and has been fitted with a 'mode lock', a device that prevents him from transforming. The Protectobots stash Blaster in a nearby pipe while they do battle with the Decepticon combiner team.

Also at the rail yard are a group of four children – Sammy, Allan, Jed, and Robin – playing at 'Space Wars', only to find themselves in the midst of a real space war. Blaster persuades the kids to remove the mode lock, which enables him to assume robot mode and keep them out of danger.

The Protectobots and Combaticons, meanwhile, have assumed their combined modes – Defensor and Bruticus respectively. Although Defensor's protective shield gives him the initial edge, Bruticus's continued attacks soon deplete the giant Autobot's defences. However, Blaster turns the tide by hitting Bruticus with an electricity pylon, and the Combaticons are defeated.

The fact that Blaster saved the day, coupled with his determination that the children not be harmed, convinces the Protectobots to let him go rather than turn him over to Grimlock. Blaster gives the kids a ride into orbit around the Earth, thanks to the mode-locked Combaticon Blast-Off, who is now stuck in space shuttle mode. Their pleasure-cruise is short-lived, however, as the Autobots' newly-repaired spacecraft, the *Ark*, shows up and starts shooting at them …

Notes:
After the brief interregnum that was [4.1] 'Man of Iron', the American stories resume exactly where they left off – this is a direct continuation of [32] 'Used Autobots', with Blaster in the Protectobots' custody and Grimlock still readying the *Ark* for take-off.

The Protectobots' course back to the *Ark* takes them through a railyard in Northern California. The freight train featured on the issue's cover art bears the name of Union Pacific, the largest freight railway company in the USA; it's therefore possible that these events are set in the city of Roseville, CA, the site of a major Union Pacific rail hub. Oddly, the trains we see in this story are old-style steam locomotives with wooden box cars. (Perhaps they are part of a museum or restoration facility.)

The Autobots' spaceship, the *Ark*, finally leaves Earth, four million years after crashing there in [1] 'The Transformers'. Grimlock has installed within the craft a new torture device, the Variable Voltage Harness, which he hopes to use on the 'traitor' Blaster. There's a direct reference to the events of [28] 'Mechanical Difficulties', the story in which Blaster and Goldbug defied Grimlock and seceded from the Autobots' ranks.

This adventure sees the debut of the so-called 'Spacehikers', Jed, Allan, Sammy and Robin, four children who will continue to make appearances in the comic until [45] 'Monstercon from Mars'.

There's a reference to Christopher Columbus, the Italian explorer who famously voyaged to the Americas in 1492.

UK Changes:

Page 1, panel 1: the original credits are replaced, the artwork is extended upwards (so that there is more sky on the page) and the title caption is aligned to the top centre of the page (whereas in the original printing it's aligned to the top left).

Page 4, panel 5: a 'last issue' caption is added.

Page 8, panel 6: 'armor-piercing' becomes 'armour piercing'.

Page 19, panel 3: 'favor' is amended to 'favour'.

Page 20, panel 3: 'defenseless' becomes 'defenceless'.

Page 21, panel 3: the reference to issue #28 is altered to issue #122.

Page 22, panel 4: the 'to be continued!!' caption is excised.

Roll Call:

Autobots: Wheeljack, Grimlock, Hot Spot, Streetwise, Blades, Groove, First Aid, Defensor, Blaster, Powerglide, Cosmos and Beachcomber.

Decepticons: Onslaught, Brawl, Blast Off, Swindle, Vortex and Bruticus.

Other: The **'Spacehikers'** (**Allan, Jed, Sammy** and **Robin**).

Review:

The main problem with this story is that it's pitched at a much lower age level than usual. While admittedly *The Transformers* was a comic for children, the tone here is far lighter and 'kid-friendly' than in any previous adventure.

The battle between the giant combiners Bruticus and Defensor is merely a secondary concern; the main focus here is on the quartet of children who become embroiled in the action. Unfortunately these youngsters are bratty, argumentative and downright annoying, which makes for a rather unpleasant reading experience. 1/5

US Straplines, Part 2

A list of all the slogans that graced the cover of the American *The Transformers* comic between issues #31 and #60. (NB: issues #35-36, 38 and 41 carried no such straplines.)

US#31: It's wet! It's wild! It's – the car wash of doom!

US#32: Used Autobots.

US#33: You won't believe it! Your eyes will bug out!! An explosive saga from the House of Ideas!!!

US#34: Man of Iron!!! More amazing Marvel majesty!!!

US#37: Suburban shootout! Mayhem at the mall!

US#39: Fort Max gets the shaft!

US#40: Introducing the Pretenders … At last – the return of Optimus Prime!

US#42: Optimus Prime – Powermaster!!

US#43: A saga from the future, starring – Rodimus Prime vs. Galvatron – deadly duel in the promised land!

US#44: Cosmic Carnival!

US#45: The return of Circuit Breaker!

US#46: The Sparkabots battle the Roadjammers

US#47: Assault of the savage Seacons!

US#48: The Return of Megatron – the end of Optimus Prime?!?

US#49: Decepticon fights Decepticon! … while Starscream conquers all!

US#50: Starscream triumphant!

US#51: Slaughter on the slopes!

US#52: Menace of the Mecannibals!

US#53: 'Next!'

US#54: King 'con!

US#55: It's man vs. machine – in a duel to the death! Plus: introducing – the Decepticon Micromasters!

US#56: Attack of the Air Strike Patrol!

US#57: The Autobots' worst nightmare comes true – Megatron returns!

US#58: Megatron alive! Ratchet a prisoner! Optimus out of control!

US#59: Not a hoax – not a dream – this issue, an Autobot dies!

US#60: They're back! Jazz! Grimlock! Bumblebee! The Classic Pretenders! The Autobots have three great heroes … 'But not for long!'

[36] SPACEHIKERS!

US#36, 'January 1988' (published September 1987), 22 pages.

British reprint: UK#143, 12 December 1987 (Part 1), 11 pages; UK#144, 19 December 1987 (Part 2), 11 pages.

Credits:

Bob Budiansky (script); José Delbo (pencils); Ian Akin, Brian Garvey (inks); Nel Yomtov (colours); Diana Albers (letters); Don Daley (editor); Tom DeFalco (editor-in-chief); Frank Springer, Ian Akin and Brian Garvey (cover). **UK:** Martin Griffiths and John Burns (cover, UK#143); Barry Kitson and Robin Bouttell (cover, UK#144).

Plot:

Growing increasingly troubled by Grimlock's leadership of the Autobots, Wheeljack contacts his friend Sky Lynx, asking him if he can help out. In the meantime, the *Ark* is easily able to capture the mode-locked Blast-Off and its passengers, the four young Spacehikers.

As part of a plot to capture Blaster, Grimlock sets up a fake execution for the humans, hoping that the deserter will come to their aid. In the event it is Sky Lynx who rescues the humans. The Dinobots pursue him into an asteroid field.

Meanwhile, Blaster sneaks aboard the *Ark* and quickly gains the support of the rest of the Autobots. However, he's forced to surrender to Grimlock when the humans' lives are again threatened.

Notes:
This story sees the debut of the Autobot Sky Lynx, who has the capability to travel through 'warp space', probably a variation of the interdimensional technology that allows the Space Bridge to function.

Cybertron is once more implied to be 'a few hundred light years' away, as it was in [10] 'The Next Best Thing to Being There', when in [29] 'Crater Critters' it was only 'several dozen' light years from Earth. Tying up with the timescales described in [HDM1] 'Ring of Hate', Sky Lynx makes reference to 'nearly 50,000 vorns of war'. One of the Decepticons Sky Lynx fought on Cybertron was the Earth-built Stunticon Breakdown, indicating that the Decepticons have, on occasion, sent troops across the Space Bridge. (It's likely that, as a member of a combiner team, Breakdown's mission to Cybertron was to allow the Cybertron-based Decepticons to study him and develop new combiner teams of their own, such as the Predacons, Terrorcons and Seacons. Prior to this, combining Transformers existed only on Earth.)

This adventure is a direct sequel to the previous one, [35] 'Child's Play' (comic), and resolves that story's cliffhanger ending. There's yet another cliffhanger ending to this story, but it won't be resolved until [41] 'Totaled', the comic instead choosing to focus on other storylines in the interim.

There's a sequence in which Blaster hijacks a television satellite to propel him through space. We then cut to the Alzamora family of Parsippany, New Jersey, who are seen watching an episode of *Sledge Hammer!* when the transmission is cut off. *Sledge Hammer!* was a police sitcom that ran for two seasons between 1986 and 1988; the eponymous Inspector Sledge Hammer is here shown uttering his catchphrase, 'Trust me. I know what I'm doing.' Marvel published a two-issue tie-in to the show, in February and March 1988. (Writer Bob Budiansky lived in New Jersey and would often choose the state as a location in his comics – it's also home to the RAAT base last seen in [23] 'Decepticon Graffiti'. The town of Parsippany would later be namechecked in another Budiansky piece, 'Sing a Song of Sin', from *Sleepwalker* #9 (February 1992).)

This story features a number of Autobots not seen in the comic for a long while; Gears and Sideswipe make their first American appearances since [12] 'Prime Time' (although their corpses were seen in [14] 'Rock and Roll Out'), Prowl and Skids appear for the first time since [26] 'Funeral for a Friend', and there are US debuts for Twin Twist and Sandstorm (whose sudden appearance amongst the Autobot ranks is unexplained).

It's established here that, according to Autobot law, all sentient beings have the right to a trial when accused of a crime. Sky Lynx mentions that there are nine planets in the solar system (as this story was penned before Pluto's 2006 reclassification as a 'dwarf planet'). Blaster makes an offhand reference to swimming in the 'smelting pools of Polyhex', a reference to [17] 'The Smelting Pool'.

UK Notes:
In the British narrative, Gears and Sideswipe had appeared a bit more recently. Sideswipe made a one-panel cameo in [20.2] 'Target: 2006' – though if we assume that to be an art error, his last *bona fide* appearance was in [12.4] 'Dinobot Hunt' – and Gears was briefly in [23.2] 'Under Fire'.

It's well-established that Cybertron-based Autobots can teleport to Earth (as per [20.2] 'Target: 2006' and [40.1] 'City of Fear'), so we can assume that Twin Twist and Sandstorm arrived on Earth using that method. Although this was their US debut, both had made a number of appearances in the UK comic, most recently in [23.5] 'Resurrection'.

As discussed in the notes to [14] 'Rock and Roll Out', it was implied that Skids was a clone of an Autobot who had been left behind on Cybertron, and who had allowed his mind to be copied onto a data crystal. In the UK stories, this clone-Skids was banished to a limbo dimension in [23.4] 'Fallen Angel', so the Skids who appears in this story must therefore be the original, who has presumably just arrived from Cybertron alongside Twin Twist and Sandstorm. (Skids' disappearance didn't happen in the American comics, so for US readers there was no reason to suspect that the Skids seen here is anything other than the same clone-Skids introduced in [14] 'Rock and Roll-Out'.)

UK Changes:
Page 1, panel 1: Credits replaced. The frame was extended downwards to fill out the page, so some extra space background was painted in.
Page 9, panel 4: 'maneuver' is re-spelt 'manoeuvre'.
Page 11, panels 4, 6 and 7: the bottom of the image was cropped to make way for the 'Next' box. As a result, the lines 'Wheeljack-!' and 'Er, yes, Slag' were excised, and another, 'But you forgot Daisy!', was moved upwards.

Roll Call:
Autobots: Prowl, Ratchet, Sideswipe, Wheeljack, Gears, Grimlock, Snarl, Slag, Sludge, Swoop, Jetfire, Grapple, Hoist, Smokescreen, Skids, Tracks, Silverbolt, Fireflight, Skydive, Hot Spot, Blades, First Aid, Blaster, Powerglide, Cosmos, Seaspray, Warpath, Beachcomber, Perceptor, Omega Supreme, Twin Twist and **Sky Lynx**.

Decepticons: Blast Off, Breakdown (flashback only), Bombshell (flashback only) and Razorclaw (flashback only).

Other: The 'Spacehikers' (Allan, Jed, Sammy and Robin).

Review:
The kids are still irksome in their second appearance, but otherwise this is a pretty good story. The Blaster/Grimlock schism that's rumbled on since [28] 'Mechanical Difficulties' comes to a head, and it's nice to see a few classic original Autobots make cameo appearances. Sky Lynx is a decent addition to the cast of characters, and the unique setting – the entire story takes place in space – gives the adventure a distinctive look. It's a bit rough around the edges, but all in all this is a decent instalment. 3/5

[36.1] STARGAZING
UK#145, 26 December 1987, 11 pages

Credits:
Simon Furman (plot); Ian Rimmer (script); Jeff Anderson (pencils); Stephen Baskerville (inks); Euan Peters (colours); Annie Halfacree (letters); Barry Kitson, Robin Bouttell (cover).

Plot:
Christmas Eve. Having been in stasis for over a year, Starscream escapes the 'deep sleep capsule' in which he was imprisoned. In a melancholy mental state, he dreams of one day returning to Cybertron. His reverie is broken by a passing human, who attempts to cheer up the Decepticon by appealing to his Christmas spirit.

Starscream remains unimpressed, but is urged by the human to turn over a new leaf and save a bus stuck in a snowdrift. The Autobot Streetwise appears on the scene, and is suitably nonplussed when Starscream goes against type and frees the bus.

When the human questions him about his newfound altruism, however, Starscream reveals that he's still as evil as ever – he freed the bus only so as to humiliate Streetwise.

Notes:
This story continues the tradition of one-off Christmas stories, as per [12.1] 'Christmas Breaker' and [22.1] 'The Gift'. Like those two previous examples, this was scripted by an outside writer (ex-Transformers editor Ian Rimmer), although regular writer Simon Furman does get a 'plot' credit.

Furman was probably responsible for the choice of Streetwise as this issue's sole Autobot representative (barring flashbacks); he's one of the very few Autobots not seen on board the *Ark* after it takes off (in either [36] 'Spacehikers' or its sequel [41] 'Totaled'), and therefore is one of the few still left on Earth by this point.

Starscream has no idea what Christmas is, but is able to access an 'internal data file' and look up the information from there. It's possible that this file was programmed into all the Transformers who crash-landed on Earth in the *Ark* (after Aunty scanned human broadcasts in [1] 'The Transformers'), or perhaps he's accessing 'torrent memory' (see the notes section under [21] 'Aerialbots over America' for more on this).

Starscream was originally put into stasis after his defeat in [19] 'Command Performances', but briefly revived in [20.2] 'Target: 2006' before being interred again, by Hot Rod, Kup and Blurr, in that same story.

<u>Rise and Shine</u>
One of the most intriguing questions raised by this story concerns the nature of Starscream's slumber. Why does he suddenly wake up, and why now? And why was his stasis pod just lying, exposed, in the middle of a field?

The simplest explanation is the one that makes the least sense – that Hot Rod, Kup and Blurr decided to place Starscream in the sleep chamber and just leave him in a field for anyone to find. This seems very odd – when one of the deadliest Decepticons is at your mercy, why dump him in field, when the possibility exists that he will one day awaken and attack again?

It's possible that the three Autobots were still under the mental influence of Unicron, who, it was established, had some form of control over them in [20.2] 'Target: 2006'. However, this raises even more questions – if the Autobots were being directed to keep Starscream in play, then why put him in a stasis pod at all, when they could just as easily have let him run free?

However, there's an alternative scenario: that Starscream was put back in stasis aboard the *Ark*, but for whatever reason was left behind. (The ship took off in a hurry, after all.) Alternatively, the pod might have been aboard the *Ark* when it took off, but then mistakenly identified as junk and jettisoned. This would also explain why it was just lying out in the open; and the impact with the Earth might have been the trigger that woke the Decepticon.

Roll Call:
Autobots: Streetwise, Hot Rod (flashback only) and Blurr (flashback only).

Decepticons: Starscream.

Review:
It's tricky to review Christmas stories – they're deliberately written as inconsequential fluff pieces, to be all-but-forgotten by the time January rolls around, and as such it's hard to criticise them for being slight and vacuous, when that seems to have been the intention all along. However, this is a particularly poor instalment, even when its seasonal nature is taken into consideration. The art is fine, but that's about all. 1/5

[36.2] THE LEGACY OF UNICRON!
- UK#146, 2 January 1988 (Part 1), 11 pages
- UK#147, 9 January 1988 (Part 2), 11 pages
- UK#148, 16 January 1988 (Part 3), 11 pages
- UK#149, 23 January 1988 (Part 4), 11 pages
- UK#150, 30 January 1988 (Part 5), 11 pages
- UK#151, 6 February 1988 (Part 6), 11 pages

To conceal the identity of the story's main villain, the title wasn't revealed until the final page of part 1. To avoid spoiling the cliffhanger, the contents page for issue 146 gave the title simply as 'The Legacy of', with the final word concealed by a number of question marks.

This story was also reprinted later in the comic's run, as follows. (NB: each original instalment was divided into halves and spread across a couple of issues).

- UK#290, 6 October 1990 (Part 1), 5 pages
- UK#291, 13 October 1990 (Part 2), 6 pages
- UK#292, 20 October 1990 (Part 3), 5 pages
- UK#293, 27 October 1990 (Part 4), 6 pages
- UK#294, 3 November 1990 (Part 5), 6 pages
- UK#295, 10 November 1990 (Part 6), 5 pages
- UK#296, 17 November 1990 (Part 7), 6 pages
- UK#297, 24 November 1990 (Part 8), 5 pages
- UK#298, 1 December 1990 (Part 9), 5 pages
- UK#299, 8 December 1990 (Part 10), 6 pages
- UK#300, 15 December 1990 (Part 11), 6 pages
- UK#301, 22 December 1990 (Part 12), 5 pages

Credits:
Simon Furman (script); Geoff Senior (art, parts 1-2; inking assist, part 6); Dan Reed (art, parts 3-4); Jeff Anderson (pencils, part 5); Stephen Baskerville (inks, part 5); Bryan Hitch (art, part 6); Steve White (colours); Annie Halfacree (letters, parts 1-5); Richard Starkings (letters, part 6); Lee Sullivan (cover, UK#146); Jeff Anderson, Stephen Baskerville and

John Burns (cover, UK#147); Dan Reed and John Burns (cover, UK#148); Barry Kitson and Robin Bouttell (cover, UK#149); Jerry Paris and John Burns (cover, UK#150); Lee Sullivan (cover, UK#151).

Issue 149's cover artists were initially uncredited – a correction and apology was later published in issue 156.

Plot:
The year is 2008. Death's Head hunts down Scourge and Cyclonus on the planet of Junk, but all are powerless to withstand the will of Unicron, who takes mental control of them. Although his body was destroyed, Unicron's head survived, and the planet-devourer now commands the native Junkions, forcing them to build a new body for him.

Unicron plans to attack Cybertron once his new body is fully completed, but in the meantime sends his new puppets to pave the way for his arrival. Death's Head assassinates the Decepticon leader Shockwave, and Scourge and Cyclonus are installed as the faction's joint commanders. At Unicron's behest, they launch an all-out attack on the Autobots, the intention being that the two sides will annihilate each other.

The Autobots get wind of what's happening on the Junkion planet, and so Rodimus Prime travels there. Death's Head explains that Unicron's mental control over his subjects is a two-way street – already Death's Head has been able to connect mentally with Unicron and learn the origins of the Transformers.

Rodimus tries the same trick and ventures into Unicron's mind, but elsewhere Wreck-Gar has set a countdown to an explosion at the base of Unicron's head. Rodimus Prime leaves Unicron's mind just as the bomb goes off, destroying the tyrant. Thanks to the mind-link, Unicron's consciousness survives, albeit now trapped and subsumed within the Autobot Matrix.

Death's Head, Scourge and Cyclonus escape the explosion by diving through a time-portal that Unicron had built in an attempt to summon Galvatron from the past. In their absence, Soundwave assumes command of the Decepticons and orders them into retreat.

Notes:
This adventure opens on New Year's Day 2008; which, as with most of the UK's future-set stories, was exactly twenty years after the comic's original publication date. It is a sequel to [31.3] 'Headhunt', our previous foray into the future. As per the end of that story, Death's Head is hunting Scourge and Cyclonus, having been paid ten thousand shanix by Rodimus Prime to assassinate the two Decepticons.

Chronologically, this is Unicron's first appearance in *The Transformers* continuity since his apparent destruction at the end of *The Transformers: The Movie* – although, as his head was seen to survive at the end of the latter, the door was always left open for a return. (The cartoon series also saw the decapitated Unicron continuing to blight the Transformers, in episodes such as {3-16} 'Ghost in the Machine'.) As per [20.2] 'Target: 2006', Unicron demonstrates the ability to take mental control of other robots. (This is an invention of the comics – Unicron never actually demonstrates this ability in the movie itself, instead using the threat of torture as his means of bending Galvatron to his will.)

The Junkions' homeworld is referred to as 'Junk' throughout, rather than 'Junkion'.

(In *The Transformers: The Movie*, both Unicron and Perceptor separately refer to the world as the 'planet of junk'; it would seem that comic writer Simon Furman misinterpreted these lines and assumed that Unicron and Perceptor were naming the planet, rather than simply describing it.) The Junkion leader Wreck-Gar finally returns home in this story, having departed to aid the Autobot cause in 2005 (in *The Transformers: The Movie*).

One subplot in this story, Unicron's time portal, was born out of necessity – the *Headmasters* comic series had established that Cyclonus and Scourge were active in the present day, despite not having been created until 2005. As this story ends, Scourge and Cyclonus are thrown back through time, explaining their appearance as Targetmasters in the spin-off comic. The time portal is also a means to explain Death's Head's departure from the comic; his next appearance would be in the pages of Marvel UK's *Doctor Who Magazine*. (See the notes section under the entry for [27.4] 'Fire on High' for more details on what Death's Head did next.)

This story confirms that Transformers (and other similarly advanced races) can detach their consciousnesses from their bodies and journey to the 'astral plane', a dream-like dimension where other such intelligences can meet, interact, and indeed do battle. The concept was first explored in [16.3] 'Second Generation', in which Optimus Prime and Buster shared a dream via the Creation Matrix. In both instances, the experience is depicted as trippy and nightmarish. (This combination of two concepts – a virtual reality 'matrix' and a metaphysical meeting of minds – is very reminiscent of ideas explored in the *Doctor Who* television series, especially in the 1976 serial 'The Deadly Assassin'. Given the large number of other *Doctor Who* references within the UK *The Transformers* comic, it's very possible this was an intentional homage. All this, of course, was many years before the Wachowski siblings' *Matrix* film franchise (1999-2003), which covered similar territory.)

The Decepticon stronghold depicted here is the same as that seen in [31.3] 'Headhunt'. A caption at the beginning of part 3 states that 'there's a kind of hush all over the world', a reference to the song 'There's a Kind of Hush', popularised by Herman's Hermits in 1967 and the Carpenters in 1976.

The Junkions' speech patterns are again littered with cultural references. On the cover of UK#146, Unicron's Junkion agent says 'G'day,' an Australian greeting popularised in the UK by the imported antipodean soap opera *Neighbours* (1985-present). Tellingly, however, this particular Junkion makes no such cultural references within the strip itself; a signifier that his mind is under Unicron's control. Other pop-culture references include:

- 'And tonight on Question Time ...' *Question Time* (1979-present) is a British political debate show, then hosted by Robin Day.
- 'Quite remarkable!' The catchphrase of legendary British sportscaster David Coleman, OBE.
- 'Your mission, Wreck-Gar, should you choose to accept it ...' A reference to the US television show *Mission: Impossible* (1966-73).
- 'Analysis, Mister Spock.' A catchphrase of Captain James T Kirk in the American sci-fi classic *Star Trek* (1966-69).
- 'Countdown to today's prize.' A possible reference to the game show *Countdown* (1982-present); however the show offered no daily prize until 1998, after which point winners were rewarded with special teapots.

- 'Goodnight from me ... and goodnight from him!' A catchphrase of the celebrated British comedy act the Two Ronnies.
- 'Th- th- that's all folks!' Porky Pig's regular sign-off, signalling the end of a *Looney Tunes* cartoon (1930-69).

Gods of Metal: The Origin of the Transformers

When one considers that the Transformers franchise is essentially an American-Japanese co-production, it's perhaps surprising that the definitive fictional origin story for the characters and concepts was invented in England.

Although the cartoon series had postulated an alternative history of the Transformers, in {3-04} 'Five Faces of Darkness, Part 4', that version of events was a little underwhelming, suggesting that they had been created by the evil Quintessons. As such, it's no surprise that the comic's rather more epic origin story has been officially endorsed by Hasbro and used as the starting point for later iterations of the franchise, such as *Transformers: Cybertron* (2005-06).

This origin story wasn't exclusive to the UK strips, however. When British writer Simon Furman took over the American comic, he made sure to retell the story there too. Overall, there were three tellings of the genesis story in the comics – first in [36.2] 'The Legacy of Unicron' in the UK, and later in the American adventures [61] 'The Primal Scream' and [74] 'The Void'.

According to Unicron in 'Legacy', he was alive 'when the universe was in its infancy', a 'primal force of evil' who led an army against Primus, 'lord of the Light Gods'. The original versions of Primus and Unicron are depicted as golden, glowing humanoids, doing battle in space. Unicron, much like his later robotic aspect, is depicted as suitably satanic, with horns, wings and a beard. Primus, on the other hand, bears an uncanny resemblance to Rodimus Prime. Unfortunately, neither Unicron's army nor Primus's fellow Light Gods are ever shown.

The battle between the two deities was so intense that it shook the universe: 'worlds were destroyed, suns imploded.' To ensure that no more innocents were harmed in the crossfire, Primus fled to the astral plane and Unicron followed; the struggle continued anew, as a literal battle of wills. Close to defeat, Primus fled back into the real world, followed by Unicron. However, it was all a trap – Primus had set it up so that their consciousnesses did not return to their physical bodies, but instead rematerialised inside 'tiny, barren lumps of space rock'.

Both beings had the strength of will to reshape these small worlds in their own image. Unicron eventually reconfigured himself as a giant robot. Primus, however, shaped himself into a planet – Cybertron. He populated himself with the Transformers and 'instilled his essence' into a 'genetic matrix', aka the Creation Matrix, which had but two functions – to create new Transformer life and also, when the time came, to destroy Unicron. In other words, the Transformers were created with a specific purpose, a manifest destiny – to rise up one day and destroy the world-devourer, Unicron.

The first retelling of this story, in [61] 'The Primal Scream', differs only in some small details. Here, Primus and Unicron are said to have been the last of their kind, and Unicron's army are specifically named as the Gods of Darkness. Primus knew he had to defeat Unicron before he could 'take his place within the Omniversal Matrix'. (This concept is never expanded upon, but in context it would appear to be either some sort of final resting place or perhaps some higher state of being.) Here the battling Primus and Unicron are coloured not gold, but rather red/yellow and orange/grey respectively.

The third version, in [74] 'The Void' (US), goes even further. Apparently there was another universe that existed before this one, but it was completely devoured by Unicron, who remained as the sole surviving entity existing within an otherswise infinite void. However, some small elements of the old universe endured, and 'reacted with each other' to create an explosion that restarted the universe anew, 'countless trillions of your years' ago. (In the real world, our present universe is only 13.8 billion years old, implying that there have been many other universes in existence prior to 'our' one.) The universe has a 'sentient core', which created Primus as a guardian against the 'threat posed by Unicron'. In this telling of the story, there is no mention of any other gods of Light or Darkness as described in the other two versions.

While the general gist of the story remains the same, there are some key differences, which can probably be put down to unreliable narrators – the first time we hear the origin story, it's from the lips of the evil Unicron; the second time, it's told by the 'Keeper' (who was probably not even present for the events in question); and on the third occasion, the storyteller is Primus himself. The decision as to which version to take as 'gospel' is left to the individual reader.

Magic 'Trix

According to [5] 'The New Order', the Creation Matrix is simply a very powerful computer program. It's able to 'construct new Transformer life' and is 'encoded' into a new Autobot leader 'every ten millennia'.

Fast forward four years, and the concept has evolved. Now the Matrix is a glowing energy crystal, protected by a metal casing that only a Prime can open. It's the 'instilled essence' of the Transformers' creator Primus, and the one weapon capable of defeating the planet-devourer, Unicron.

From a behind-the-scenes point of view, the sudden change was completely understandable. When American writer Bob Budiansky was writing [5] 'The New Order' and other early stories, the Matrix was just a computer program; its life-giving powers were simply a means by which he could introduce new characters into the series, such as the Constructicons ([10] 'The Next Best Thing to Being There') and the Stunticons ([22] 'Heavy Traffic').

However, all that changed when *The Transformers: The Movie* was released. The cartoon version of the Matrix – a powerful talisman with mystical powers – was such a strong image that UK writer Simon Furman based his interpretation of the Matrix on what he'd seen in the film, even though it didn't exactly align with what had been previously established in the comics.

So that's why there are two different representations of the Matrix within the comics. But are the two mutually exclusive? Or is there a way to marry the two concepts into a unified theory of the Matrix?

Thankfully, the letters page of US#66 clarified (retconned) matters: 'The Matrix is a tangible object, housed (normally) in the chest compartment of an Autobot leader. Point one: this is not common knowledge among the rank and file of Autobot and Decepticon. It had long been assumed that because the Matrix power was focused through the mind of the Autobot leader, the energy lay there. What Shockwave got [in [10] 'The Next Best Thing to Being There'] was the stored Matrix force in Prime's mind. Without the Matrix itself, in time this store would have run dry ...

'Point two: Prime (because of the suddenness of his death) didn't have a chance to pass the Matrix on. And because the true nature and location of the Matrix was such a closely guarded secret, the Autobots didn't know it was there to remove. They simply assumed it had died with Prime's mind.'

This is confirmed by dialogue within the stories themselves. Prime 'kept the Matrix's true location from my fellow Autobots' ([54.3] 'Deathbringer') and 'the Autobots… had no idea the Matrix was a tangible object' ([62] 'Bird of Prey'). However, this explanation brings its own problems: it turns out that sending dead Autobots into space is actually an ancient Cybertronian tradition (as per [26] 'Funeral for a Friend'), which makes one wonder how the Matrix has never before been lost under similar circumstances.

Indeed, it seems very odd that the Matrix should be entrusted to an Autobot leader at all. In any war, the prime target (excuse the pun) is always the leader of the opposition. Placing such a valuable artefact inside the body and mind of the Autobot warrior at the top of the Decepticons' hit-list is just asking for it to be lost or captured.

The only way this makes any sense is if the Matrix is fitted with some sort of guidance system, allowing it to teleport home if lost or stolen. The Matrix Flame (seen in [20.2] 'Target: 2006') might be part of that locator system (as it stays alight when the Matrix is within its range and blinks out when the Matrix is lost). However, the Matrix is sentient and can be corrupted (see [65] 'Dark Creation'). Perhaps after millions of years of conflict, the Matrix no longer 'wants' to return home when required.

So far as the majority of Transformers are concerned, the Matrix is just another means of creating new Transformer life, no different from the Matrix Flame on Cybertron (which might, after all, be one of many such flames). It's only when faced with their impending doom at the hands of Unicron, that the Matrix makes itself known, so to speak, and finally fulfils its destiny.

Roll Call:
Autobots: Optimus Prime (flashback only), Grimlock, Snarl, Slag, Sludge, Swoop, Inferno, Grapple, Smokescreen, Hot Spot, Perceptor, Ultra Magnus, Springer, Sandstorm, Kup, Blurr, Rodimus Prime, Wreck-Gar and Scattershot.

Inferno (or rather his 2008 version) dies here. It's the character's first appearance since [8.1] 'Decepticon Dam-Busters'. Scattershot makes his first appearance in the regular strip, having previously featured only in the *Headmasters* mini-series. Optimus Prime's mysterious predecessor also appears, in flashback (see the notes under [65] 'Dark Creation' for more on this robot's identity).

Decepticons: Shockwave, Hook, Blast Off, Motormaster (only as part of Menasor), Drag Strip (only as part of Menasor), Dead End, Wildrider (only as part of Menasor), Breakdown, Menasor, Galvatron (flashback only), Cyclonus, Scourge, Blitzwing, Octane, Scorponok and Hun-Gurrr.

A statue of Megatron is briefly seen in the background of the Decepticon stronghold. The future Shockwave is killed here. As with Scattershot, this is Hun-Gurrr's first appearance outside of the *Headmasters* limited comic. In the huge battle sequence in part 3, the Decepticon blasted by Blades is possibly a miscoloured Sinnertwin (as the head is the right design but the colours are wrong). Of all the characters who appear in this story, Scorponok is the only one who is the 'present day' version of the character – all the rest are their 2008 incarnations.

Other: Unicron, Death's Head and **Primus** (flashback only).

Data File: Bryan Hitch (artist)
Now a massive name in the comics industry, via titles such as *Stormwatch, The Authority, The Ultimates, Fantastic Four, Kick Ass 2* and *The Amazing Spider-Man*, Hitch began his career as a teenager at Marvel UK. Outside of comics, he was a concept artist for the relaunched *Doctor Who* television series between 2005 and 2013 and also contributed designs to the movie *Star Trek* (J J Abrams, 2009).

Review:
After [20.2] 'Target: 2006', this is the second-best story that the classic *The Transformers* comics ever presented. Indeed, in certain aspects it is superior – the pace is quicker, the plot is more streamlined, and the character work is better.

If this is a last hurrah for Death's Head, it's a brilliant one. Yet again he's the star of the show, and it's no surprise that he went on to feature in a comic of his very own. Highlights include Part two, with its amazing action sequences, stunningly rendered by Geoff Senior, and of course the brutal death of Shockwave.

The fourth chapter concentrates on Inferno's and Smokescreen's escape from Junkion, and Inferno's noble sacrifice. What could easily have been just a 'filler' issue is made so much more by the brilliant characterisation of the two leads.

Part five – the comic's one hundred and fiftieth issue – includes the stunning origin story, Furman's imagination matched only by some lovely surreal imagery. The finale, too, is notable for its visuals, with newcomer Bryan Hitch wowing on his debut.

If there's any criticism to be made, it's that the opening instalment is mostly superfluous (almost like a James Bond pre-credit sequence), and that the ending seems a little rushed.

But such quibbles are minor – this is one of the true *The Transformers* greats. 5/5

[36.3] ENEMY ACTION!
* UK#152, 13 February 1988 (Part One), 11 pages
* UK#153, 20 February 1988 (Part Two), 11 pages

Credits:
Simon Furman (script); Jeff Anderson (pencils); Stephen Baskerville (inks); Steve White (colours); Gary 'Glib' Gilbert (letters); Lee Sullivan (covers, UK#152 and 153).

Plot:
The present day. Galvatron has broken free from the bowels of Mount Verona, and makes his way to the Decepticon undersea base. He is followed by the Autobot Sparkabots and the Decepticon Firecons – groups of Transformers sent to Earth from Cybertron to keep tabs on the future tyrant.

Shockwave, fearful that Galvatron seeks to overthrow him and take command of the Decepticons, sends the Seacons to intercept. Galvatron is easily able to fend them off, and then embarrasses Shockwave by declaring that he came in peace – there was no need for the Seacon attack.

Galvatron's intention all along was to undermine Shockwave's position, rather than face him in combat. Having successfully sown seeds of doubt in the minds of Shockwave's troops, Galvatron departs.

Notes:
This story sees the debut of no fewer than thirteen new characters, reflecting the new 1988 range of Transformers toys that were just creeping into the shops at the beginning of the year: the six Seacons (and their combined mode, Piranacon), plus the Firecons and Sparkabots.

This is the first appearance of Galvatron alive and well since he was caught up in the eruption of Mount Verona in [A3.3] 'Vicious Circle'; the explosion that awoke him occurred in [31.5] 'Ladies' Night'. His time spent trapped in the volcano seems to have done him some good – no longer merely a ranting maniac, here he comes across as calm and calculating – an intellectual match for Shockwave as well as a physical one.

Transformer communications technology has come a long way in three years – in [10] 'The Next Best Thing to Being There', the Decepticons needed access to a space telescope in order to contact Cybertron, but now such communications are commonplace, via the use of two-way hand-held videophones. Though based on Cybertron, Springer has been keeping a watchful eye on events taking place on Earth and knows all about Ultra Magnus and Galvatron being interred within Mount Verona (as per [31.5] 'Ladies' Night').

Galvatron escapes the volcano (in Oregon) at 15:23 (Eastern Time?), and when he arrives in Florida it is still daylight – therefore it would seem that Galvatron is able to travel the 2,500 miles between the two locations in a couple of hours.

Shockwave refers to the time when Galvatron wrested control of the Decepticons from Megatron in [20.2] 'Target: 2006', also to his decisive intervention in the battle with Galvatron in [23.4] 'Fallen Angel', and to his attempts to destroy Galvatron in [31.5] 'Ladies' Night'.

The story ends with Shockwave determined to seek out Megatron, a plot line that will be picked up again in [39.1] 'Salvage'.

Great News, Pals!
In the UK publishing industry, sometimes a failing comic would not be cancelled entirely but instead subsumed into another title. For example, one of the best-known British comics, *2000 AD*, has itself absorbed two failed titles, *Tornado* and *Starlord*, during the course of its run. With the type of spin that would make even a politician blush, soon-to-be-cancelled titles would traditionally break the news of their impending absorption by treating it as something to be celebrated: 'Great news, pals: two great papers, *Lion* and *Eagle*, are teaming up to bring you all these top stories in one action-packed weekly.'

A major benefit of this sort of merger was that the 'parent' title would improve in quality, being able to take all the best elements and strips from the cancelled comic. Sometimes the cancelled title would have had access to better printing technology, personnel etc, which would also enhance the successor. Of course, the main driver in this process was sales – when the cancelled comic was absorbed into a more successful one, most of its readers would also make the move, thereby improving the circulation of the new hybrid.

In 1988, Hasbro were in something of a quandary. They were desperate to sell Action Force figures in the UK, but although they had paid for a strong media presence

– with TV advertisements, videocassette releases and a computer game tie-in – Marvel UK's *Action Force* comic was a slow seller. *The Transformers*, which was in rude health at the time, was often used to plug the *Action Force* franchise, either by advertisements, editorial mentions, back-up strips or indeed the big franchise crossover event [29.1] 'Ancient Relics'. None of this was enough, however, and the *Action Force* comic folded in February 1988 after fifty issues.

Because of their shared heritage as Hasbro-owned properties, it was deemed that *The Transformers* would be the perfect title in which to continue the adventures of *Action Force*. It was seen as a no-brainer – Marvel UK were still paying Hasbro for the comic book rights to the property, and Hasbro wanted a way to push their current range of Action Force toys in the shops.

So, from issue 153, the UK *The Transformers* comic was relaunched as *The Transformers and Action Force* (although, as evidenced by the indicia on page two of every issue, for official purposes the title was still simply *The Transformers*). Despite the fanfare (and some cover art featuring *Action Force* characters Hawk and Snake-Eyes alongside the Sparkabots), the change was essentially minimal – *Action Force* took over from *Iron Man* as the new back-up strip, and *Codename: Combat Colin* (which had begun in *Action Force*) replaced *Robo-Capers* as the resident humour strip.

Roll Call:
Autobots: Springer, **Sizzle**, **Fizzle** and **Guzzle**.

Decepticons: Megatron (only as an image on a viewscreen), Shockwave, Drag Strip, Ramjet, Thrust, Galvatron, Razorclaw, Rampage, **Snaptrap**, **Seawing**, **Skalor**, **Overbite**, **Nautilator**, **Tentakil**, **Piranacon**, **Sparkstalker**, **Flamefeather** and **Cindersaur**.

Perhaps due to the UK production team having early access to the new figures, a number of the details are slightly askew: the Seacons and Sparkabots have incorrect colour schemes, Snaptrap is referred to as 'Snap Trap', Piranacon is called 'Pirranacon' and Overbite is named 'Jawbreaker'. The Sparkabot team are referred to as 'Sparkler Mini-Bots' throughout.

Data File: Gary 'Glib' Gilbert (letterer/designer)
As well as being a letterer for the UK *The Transformers* comic, Gilbert was also for a time its designer. His other work at Marvel UK came on titles such as *Thundercats*, *Doctor Who Classic Comics* and *The Real Ghostbusters*. He later went on to become an art editor at Eaglemoss Publications, contributing to partworks such as *The Classic Marvel Figurine Collection* and *The DC Comics Superhero Collection*.

Review:
A game of two halves. The main plot, in which Galvatron just waltzes up to Decepticon HQ and gets the better of Shockwave, is brilliant, aided by some good 'underwater' art by Jeff Anderson. The B-story, however, in which the Sparkabots and Firecons do battle on a beach, is pretty banal stuff. 3/5

The Back-Up Strips, Part 15: *Combat Colin*
A humour strip developed by Lew Stringer for the *Action Force* comic, *Combat Colin* replaced Stringer's other strip, *Robo-Capers*, when *Action Force* comic merged with *The*

Transformers. Originally billed as *Codename: Combat Colin*, it was retitled *Combat Colin co-starring Semi-Automatic Steve* from UK#171. Notable stories included:

- UK#153: The first instalment. Combat Colin and Semi-Automatic Steve introduce themselves.
- UK#154-158: The daring duo have trouble defeating a giant robot.
- UK#160-163: 'Combat Colin Versus the Gwanzulums' – Colin faces off against the shape-shifting alien Gwanzulums. (The Gwanzulums were a bit of a running joke across Marvel UK's output, also appearing in titles such as *Doctor Who Magazine* (issues #141-142) and *The Real Ghostbusters* (issue #9).)
- UK#164-168: 'Combat Colin Meets the Loch Ness Monster'.
- UK#170-174: Colin and Steve come up against the evil Mr Magno, and his Mega Magnet.
- UK#175-180: Colin meets the legendary Bigfoot.
- UK#182: To bridge the one-issue gap between the end of *Action Force* and the beginning of *Visionaries*, six pages of *Combat Colin*, in which he battles against the evil Aunt Arctic of the Anatarctic, were printed in lieu of a 'proper' back-up strip. (The strips originated in *Action Force* issues 34-40.)
- UK#187-192: Semi-Automatic Steve is kidnapped by Aunt Arctic; Colin teams up with Steve's landlady Mrs Frumpy to rescue him.
- UK#200: A special *Combat Colin/Robo-Capers* crossover.
- UK#201-206: Combat Colin is kidnapped by Professor Madprof and replaced by an evil duplicate.
- UK#208-211: Colin is terrorised by his ex-girlfriend, Gladys Blemish.
- UK#220: Explaining a major production error within the comic (the calendar for May was printed in June and vice versa), it's revealed that the mistake was caused by Professor Madprof's time machine.
- UK#224: Combat Colin goes full page (albeit in black and white).
- UK#228-230: The Brain uses bad television to soften humans' minds, as a prelude to an invasion of Earth.
- UK#235-236: Colin attends a magic show, but 'the Amazing Dave' turns out to be arch-villain the Mountain Man.
- UK#238-241: Combat Colin goes up against a radioactive mutant known only as the Gunge.
- UK#243: The Giggly Sisters – Colin's and Steve's girlfriends – take over the page this week, defeating a monster by inviting him round for tea and fairy cakes. There's also a problems column, and some knitting hints.
- UK#244-248: 'Prisoners of the Place of No Return'. In a spoof of cult television show *The Prisoner*, Colin and Steve awake to find themselves trapped in a mysterious village.
- UK#250: 'Christmas with Combat Colin'. Colin hosts a Christmas party, and invites a number of Marvel superheroes.
- UK#253-256: 'Combat Colin in Space!' Colin and the Brain travel to Mars, and meet the all-powerful Pyramid-Head.
- UK#257-259: 'Combat Colin meets Combat Kate!' Combat Colin returns to Earth, only to find that he has been supplanted by a new hero, Combat Kate.
- UK#264-266: 'Combat Colin and Semi-Automatic Steve vs. The Deadly Duo'

Professor Madprof and Mr Magno sabotage construction of the Solent Tunnel.

- UK#267: As Colin is 'off sick with the gout', this week's strip becomes *Combat Kate co-starring Headline Howard!*.
- UK#270-271: Combat Colin goes up against Marvel super-villain Doctor Doom.
- UK#272-274: 'The Day the Giggling Stopped'. Wallytown becomes embroiled in a series of strange incidents: Julie Giggly turns evil, and Steve is transformed into a carrot.
- UK#275-277: 'Return to Mars'. Colin and pals journey to Mars in a bid to defeat the evil Megabrain.
- UK#278-281: 'Combat Colin's Prehistoric Adventure'. Colin and chums are sucked through a time warp and into the age of the dinosaurs.
- UK#287-289: 'The Secret of the Combat Trousers!' Villainous spy Jane Bondski goes undercover as one of the Giggly Sisters to steal the secrets of the Combat Trousers. Plus: the origin of Combat Colin.
- UK#290-292: 'Combat Colin versus the Mechanical Might of Robocol 2'. Professor Madprof creates another robot version of Combat Colin.
- UK#294-299: 'Invasion of Megabrain!' Now with a new body, Megabrain attempts to invade Earth once again.
- UK#301-303: Weirdo warlock Doctor Peculiar has accidentally conjured forth demons to attack Earth.
- UK#306-308: 'Combat Colin and Semi-Automatic Steve Meet the Mutant Master'. The evil Mutant Master and his band of mutants attack the Ministry of Daft Ideas.
- UK#309-311 'Combat Colin and the Bobble Hat of Doom!' Colin turns 'yampy' when the villainous Bad Hatter supplies Colin with a new hat.
- UK#312-315: 'One of our Gigglies is Missing'. When Julie Giggly mysteriously disappears, Colin suspects that Mutant Master may be responsible.
- UK#316-318: 'The New Combat Colin'. After exposure to cosmic rays and gamma radiation, Colin is transformed into a musclebound superhero.
- UK#320-323: 'The Defeat of Combat Colin'. Combat Colin is tricked into retiring, leaving the Earth defenceless as Mutant Master attacks yet again.
- UK#324-326: 'Secret of the Mutant Master!'. Combat Colin finally unmasks the evil Mutant Master, only to find that the villain is a duplicate of Colin himself. Or is he?
- UK#327-332: 'The Last "Ooer"!' Megabrain has journeyed to the future, and presents Colin with a future newspaper that proves that Colin will shortly die in battle.

[37] TOY SOLDIERS!

US#37, 'February 1988' (published October 1987), 22 pages.

British reprint: UK#154, 27 February 1988 (Part 1), 11 pages; UK#155, 5 March 1988 (Part 2), 11 pages.

Credits:

Bob Budiansky (script); José Delbo (pencils); Ian Akin, Brian Garvey (inks); Nel Yomtov (colours); Bill Oakley (letters); Don Daley (editor); Tom DeFalco (editor-in-chief); José Delbo, Ian Akin and Brian Garvey (cover). **UK:** Bryan Hitch (covers, UK#154 and 155).

Plot:

Having captured the Throttlebots, Triple-I declare that the six Autobots will be destroyed unless all Transformer attacks cease. With most of the Earth-based Autobots having left the planet in the *Ark*, there is nothing to stop the Decepticons from causing havoc. Triple-I, still unaware that there are two Transformer factions, execute the Throttlebots in a car-crusher.

Except that the Throttlebots are not dead – Triple-I employee Walter Barnett has come to the realisation that not all the robots are evil, and managed to retrieve the sextet's brain modules before their bodies were crushed. With the brains now connected to radio-controlled toy cars, the Throttlebots' next problem is that the toys' batteries are starting to run low.

Barnett teams up with Buster Witwicky, and the pair elect to take the Throttlebots to the *Ark*, not realising that it has left the planet. Stopping off at a mall for batteries, the humans and Throttlebots only narrowly avoid destruction at the hands of the Predacons, who are tracking the Autobots' scent.

Buster and the Throttlebots eventually reach Mount St Hilary, to find the *Ark* gone and the area deserted. Goldbug sends a radio message requesting reinforcements, but before any help can arrive, Ratbat shows up and attacks …

Notes:

This story follows up on events in [32] 'Used Autobots', which saw the Throttlebots captured by RAAT, the military wing of Triple-I. That organisation's Oregon base is seen again here, having previously featured in [15] 'I, Robot Master'. Triple-I operatives Walter Barnett and Forrest Forsythe make a return appearance, as do Barnett's son and wife (last seen in [15] 'I, Robot Master; the latter finally gets a first name: Charlene).

With the main Autobot forces in space, the Decepticons are free to attack without interference. They steal liquid oxygen from a chemical storage depot in Huntsville, Alabama. (In the real world, Huntsville is home to a thriving aerospace, military and technology economy. The home of NASA's Marshall Space Flight Center, it's at the forefront of rocket propulsion research and therefore the obvious place from which to steal liquid oxygen.)

The second Decepticon target is Atlanta, Georgia, where the Constructicons seize steel girders from a building site. (It's less obvious why the Decepticons go all the way to Georgia for their steel supplies; there is a steel mill in Jacksonville, Florida, that would have been ideally suited for their needs, and also is closer to the Decepticon base in the Florida Keys.)

The newspaper read by Forrest Forsyth is *The Record* (a generic name, but also possibly another of Bob Budiansky's New Jersey references – there's a paper by that name published in Bergen County). There are references to Buster foiling Ratbat's plans in [31] 'Buster Witwicky and the Car Wash of Doom', and also to Sparkplug's repair of Bumblebee in [2] 'Power Play'. Sparkplug's garage, first seen in [1] 'The Transformers', is finally destroyed here by the Predacons. Transformers' brains are the size of peas, as previously established in [23] 'Decepticon Graffiti'. There's a first mention of Buster's brother Spike, who is 'at college back east'.

Buster attempts to buy batteries from a store called 'Radio Shed', a reference to the real-world RadioShack chain. (See the piece on Alternative Transformers, in the notes to {2-24} 'A Decepticon Raider in King Arthur's Court', for more on RadioShack.)

At one point Ratbat suggests that 'the report of the death of these Autobots is greatly exaggerated', a reference to the the phrase coined by oft-misquoted author Mark Twain (pen-name of Samuel Clemens, 1835-1910), 'The report of my death was an exaggeration.'

The radio message sent by Goldbug here is the same one intercepted by the Nebulos-based Autobots in [HDM4] 'Brothers in Armor'.

UK Changes:
Page 1, panel 1: the credits are replaced, and the sky is extended upwards so that the image fills the entire page.
Page 3, panel 2: the very American 'boondoggle' is changed to the very English 'bodge up'.
Page 4, panel 5: the reference to issue #32 is altered to issue #140.
Page 10, panel 8: 'fibers' becomes 'fibres'.
Page 11, panel 5: the reference to issue #2 is changed to issue #3, and Don Daley's sign-off is excised.
Page 18, panel 2: '*Transformers* #31, remember?' becomes simply '*Transformers* #129'.
Page 20, panel 1: the editorial caption is painted out.
Page 22, panel 8: '*Headmasters* 4' becomes '*Transformers* #145'.
Page 22, panel 10: the editorial caption is again excised.

Roll Call:
Autobots: Goldbug, Chase, Searchlight, Freeway, Rollbar and Wideload.

Decepticons: Scrapper, Scavenger, Bonecrusher, Long Haul, Hook, Blitzwing, Razorclaw, Rampage, Tantrum, Headstrong, Divebomb and Ratbat.

Other than a single-panel cameo for Hook in [36.2] 'The Legacy of Unicron', this is the first appearance of the Constructicons since [20.2] 'Target: 2006' (or [19] 'Command Performances' in the US).

Other: Buster, Sparkplug, Walter Barnett and Forrest Forsythe.

Review:
With the comic beginning to branch out in terms of storytelling, it's a pleasant surprise to get back to something a bit more retro. With all the feel of an adventure from two years prior, we have Triple-I's Walter Barnett teaming up with Buster Witwicky, and Decepticons plundering the Earth for fuel. The central conceit of the Throttlebots' brains being implanted into toy cars is a really interesting one, and the whole story is simply a blast from start to finish. Even better, RAAT annoyance-in-chief Forrest Forsythe comes to the realisation that there are two Transformer factions, finally putting an end to all those tired 'US Government vs the Autobots' stories.

For this to work, however, the Decepticons have to be incredibly inept. The Predacons, once billed as Cybertron's elite team of hunters, here fail to retrieve six toy cars from a shopping mall, and Ratbat suffers the ignominy of getting clobbered by a roller-shutter. It's a bit of a cheat, and cheapens the characters quite a bit, but it's all in good fun. 4/5

[38] TRIAL BY FIRE!
US#38, 'March 1988' (published November 1987), 22 pages.

British reprint: UK#156, 12 March 1988 (Part 1), 11 pages; UK#157, 19 March 1988 (Part 2), 11 pages.

Credits:
Bob Budiansky (script); José Delbo (pencils); Dave Hunt (inks); Nel Yomtov (colours); Bill Oakley (letters); Don Daley (editor); Tom DeFalco (editor-in-chief); Frank Springer and Dave Hunt (cover). **UK:** Dougie Braithwaite (cover, UK#156); Lee Sullivan (cover, UK#157).

Plot:
Tracking Goldbug's distress signal, Fortress Maximus and his Autobot Headmasters arrive on Earth and investigate Mount St Hilary. Also present at the volcano is one Spike Witwicky, searching for his missing brother Buster. Despite Spike's pleas for help, the Headmasters have better things to do than search for a missing boy.

After the Autobots depart the volcano, the Decepticon Headmasters arrive on the scene, having tracked the Autobots to that location. They threaten Spike's life, but the young man is able to activate a radio signal and draw the attention of Fortress Maximus's group. The ensuing battle destabilises the volcano, which is now on the verge of erupting.

Spike is cornered by Scorponok but saved by Fortress Maximus's Nebulan partner Galen, who is himself killed by a rock fall, after admitting that it was a mistake not to heed Spike's earlier plea for help.

Spike uses Galen's control helmet to take mental command of Fortress Maximus; the Decepticons are forced into retreat, and the Autobots also flee the scene as the volcano erupts behind them.

Notes:
This story sees a number of characters from the *Headmasters* comic make their debuts within the main series, as the Autobots and Decepticons that had been based on the planet Nebulos make their first visit to Earth.

The Fortress Maximus seen here is slightly different from how he appeared in *Headmasters* – he's now much bigger, and his head transforms into the (apparently mindless) Cerebros. Galen, Fort Max's Nebulan companion, now forms the head of Cerebros, rather than the head of Fortress Maximus himself.

The Headmaster process now appears to be complete, resulting in a true merging of personalities. Zarak is now completely evil, displaying no sympathetic traits whatsoever, indicating that his own mind has been completely subsumed – indeed, at one point Mindwipe absentmindedly refers to Scorponok as 'Lord Zarak', heavily implying that the two are now, for all intents and purposes, indistinguishable as separate entities.

The Headmasters' arrival on Earth is as a result of them hearing Goldbug's distress signal sent in [37] 'Toy Soldiers' and received in [HDM4] 'Brothers in Armor'. Thanks to Goldbug's memory bank, we discover what happened in the aftermath of [37] 'Toy Soldiers': Goldbug was left for dead by Ratbat, and Buster was kidnapped by the Decepticon. Also following on from the events of the previous issue, we discover that

Sparkplug's garage has been completely demolished by the Predacon attack. Sparkplug's eldest son Spike, mentioned but not seen in [37] 'Toy Soldiers', makes his debut here, and takes Galen's place as Fortress Maximus's companion upon the Nebulan's death.

When the Autobot Headmasters are scanning Earth from orbit, they view images of New York's iconic Times Square intersection, and also the Eiffel Tower (completed 1889) in Paris, France.

Oh, Brother

When Hasbro released the Fortress Maximus toy in 1987, they made the canny decision to link the toy to the popular *Transformers* cartoon show, and the giant figure's Headmaster companion was named Spike, presumably intended to represent Spike Witwicky, the Autobots' human friend in that show. While undoubtedly a brilliant marketing ploy, this proved problematic for the production team of *The Transformers* comic. In that continuity, the Autobot's human friend was *Buster* Witwicky, rather than Spike.

The name Spike Witwicky had been originally coined by Marvel's then-editor-in-chief Jim Shooter, who had helped to develop the Transformers backstory before handing the project over to Bob Budiansky. (Indeed, Shooter had used the surname 'Witwicky' before, in issue #31 of Marvel's *Dazzler* comic, dated March 1984.) Allegedly, in a curious turn of events, Marvel had been persuaded to rename the character Buster at the behest of Sunbow, the producers of the then forthcoming cartoon show, who had felt the name Spike sounded too aggressive. So in *The Transformers* comic, it had been Buster Witwicky, rather than Spike, who had become the Autobots' closest human ally. Oddly, however, Sunbow had then reversed their earlier decision, and decided to use the name Spike in the cartoon show, which began transmitting later in 1984.

Of course, this put the comic in a bit of a bind – their human character was called Buster, but now they had to include a Headmaster character called Spike. Their solution was a simple one: Spike Witwicky was introduced as Buster's older brother, who had just returned from college.

Pothole or Plot Hole?

In a very convenient turn of events, it transpires that the cave in the side of Mount St Hilary that formerly housed the *Ark* is one that Spike used to frequent when he was a Boy Scout. This raises the question, if Mount St Hilary was on a popular hiking route (a supposition fuelled by the appearance of a backpacker in [1] 'The Transformers'), why is it that nobody ever noticed the *Ark* before?

According to the comics, the *Ark* was completely entombed within the volcano, and not visible from the outside – there was access via a cave system in [5] 'The New Order', but the main exits from the ship were via the mouth of the volcano, or by means of a newly-built road made by the Autobots after they awakened in 1984 (as seen in [2] 'Power Play' and [3] 'Prisoner of War') – a road that wouldn't have been present when Spike was hiking there as a young child. After that, it would seem that the Autobots set to work extending their HQ, spreading throughout the mountain. It's not until [9] 'Dis-Integrated Circuits' that this expansion is so great that the Autobots' base is visible from the outside of the volcano.

It's also possible, of course, that the *Ark* – at least initially – had some form of cloaking technology that prevented it from being detected. It's likely that, if such technology existed, it was damaged when the volcano erupted in 1984.

UK Notes:
Although this was the Headmasters' first appearance in the American *The Transformers* comic, they had already featured in the UK-only story [31.1] 'Worlds Apart'.

UK Changes:
Page 1, panel 1: credits replaced; artwork extended upwards to take up a full page.
Page 8, panel 3: references to *The Transformers* #37 and *Headmasters* #4 are changed to *The Transformers* #155 and #145 respectively.
Page 18, panel 2: 'armored' becomes 'armoured'.

Roll Call:
Autobots: Goldbug (as a brain in a toy car), Fortress Maximus, **Cerebros**, Highbrow, Chromedome, Hardhead, Brainstorm, Pointblank, Sureshot and **Grotusque** (flashback only).

Grotusque had previously appeared in the *Headmasters* comic series.

Decepticons: Ratbat (flashback only, also in a photograph), Scorponok, Skullcruncher, Mindwipe, Weirdwolf, Apeface and Snapdragon.

Nebulans: Galen, Gort, Stylor, Duros, Arcana, Zarak, Grax*, Vorath, Monzo*, Spasma* and Krunk.

* Seen only in combined Headmaster mode, not as an individual. Llyra, Galen's love interest in the *Headmasters* series, is seen in flashback.

Other: Buster, Sparkplug and **Spike**.

Although making his first appearance in the main comic, the future version of Spike had previously been depicted in the comic adaptation of *The Transformers: The Movie*.

Review:
As an 'important' story – featuring the introduction of the Headmaster characters in the main comic, the death of Galen and the first appearance of Spike – this is a little underwhelming, despite its pivotal role in the ongoing storylines. Basically, it boils down to Spike skulking around in a cave until the Transformers converge on the volcano and do battle. The first half, especially, is as boring and talky as the comic ever gets.

Thankfully, then, the final battle is superb. The inside of a volcano makes for a great backdrop to a battle, with collapsing caves and rivers of molten lava adding spice to the sequence. Galen's death, too, lends weight to the proceedings. (Until this point, only the minor character Reflector had truly been killed off, never to return.) 3/5

[39] THE DESERT ISLAND OF SPACE!
US#39, 'April 1988' (published December 1987), 22 pages.

British reprint: UK#158, 26 March 1988 (Part 1), 11 pages; UK#159, 2 April 1988 (Part 2), 11 pages.

Credits:
Bob Budiansky (script); José Delbo (pencils); Dave Hunt (inks); Nel Yomtov (colours); Bill Oakley (letters); Don Daley (editor); Tom DeFalco (editor-in-chief); José Delbo and Dave Hunt (cover). **UK:** Dan Reed (cover, UK#158); Will Simpson and David Elliot (cover, UK#159).

Plot:
The Decepticons have captured Buster and taken him to their island base in the Florida Keys – knowing full well that the presence of a hostage will dissuade Earth's authorities from launching an attack on the island.

In the meantime, Spike has undergone the binary-bonding process and is now officially the Headmaster partner of Fortress Maximus. After learning of Buster's whereabouts, he leads the Autobot Targetmasters in a rescue attempt. However, everyone is surprised when the island suddenly jets out of the ocean and into the sky – the Decepticon base is, in fact, a spacecraft.

The Targetmasters are beaten back by the island's defences, but Fortress Maximus, undeterred, follows the craft into space. Wounded when the Decepticons shoot at him, Fortress Maximus is nevertheless able to get the better of Shockwave, and sends the Decepticon plummeting to the Earth below, where he is seen to burn up in the atmosphere.

Spike and Fortress Maximus are rescued by the Targetmasters, but Buster remains in Decepticon captivity.

Notes:
This story is notable for the 'death' of Shockwave, who burns up in Earth's atmosphere. (It eventually transpires that he survives; but he does not reappear until [65] 'Dark Creation'.) Although Pointblank and Sureshot appeared as background characters in the previous story, the remainder of Autobot Targetmasters (and their Nebulan companions) make their main strip debuts here (though all had previously featured in the *Headmasters* mini-series).

This is also the final appearance of Walter Barnett, Forrest Forsythe, and the organisations RAAT and Triple-I. (They were initially set up to be misguided human adversaries, oblivious to the fact that the Autobots weren't as evil as the Decepticons. As soon as Triple-I became aware that the Autobots were good guys, they could no longer fulfil their original plot function and so were quickly dropped from the comic.)

This is the last time that the Throttlebots are depicted as being stuck as toy cars – presumably, at some point between this and their next appearance, in [50] 'Dark Star', they are retrieved by the Autobots and provided with replacement bodies.

Fortress Maximus's group of Autobots have access to an 'All-Terrain Turbo-Transport', a small vehicle capable of accommodating a number of Transformers and making short-range trips into Earth orbit. It fulfils much the same function as the *Ark*'s shuttlecraft as seen in [8] 'Repeat Performance'.

There are references to the events of [37] 'Toy Soldiers' (the Decepticon raids, Barnett's theft of the Autobot brain modules, Buster's capture and the destruction of Sparkplug's garage), and also to those of [38] 'Trial by Fire' (Galen's death, and Spike's involvement with the Autobots).

Kup mentions having battled the Decepticons on the planet Deneb IV, a possible reference to the pilot episode of *Star Trek: The Next Generation*, 'Encounter at Farpoint' (broadcast in September 1987), in which a planet of the same name featured prominently. (Deneb is a real star, located in the constellation of Cygnus.)

One of the Decepticons seen here as a background character has the same body-type as Rumble and Frenzy and yet cannot be either, as both went off-line in [19] 'Command Performances'. Although this is probably just an art error, it could also be the case that this is an entirely new character, having just arrived from Cybertron. (In the mid-1980s, the electronic toy manufacturer Nasta acquired a licence to make Transformers tie-in merchandise, including an AM radio and an electronic voice changer. Both products were modelled after a made-up Decepticon character named simply 'Enemy', who bore a striking resemblance to Rumble and Frenzy. It's possible that the mystery Decepticon seen here is, in fact, this Enemy character. Enemy was finally released as a bona fide Transformers figure in 2012 – a predominantly red repaint of the 1980s Rumble/Frenzy mould.)

UK Notes:
Shockwave was a major player in the UK comic, and consequently the British production team were loath to see the character killed off. Dialogue was rewritten (see the UK Changes section below) so that he simply fell to Earth in this story, rather than burned up – which allowed him to feature in the very next UK adventure, [39.1] 'Salvage'.

Although in the US continuity both Rumble and Frenzy had been written out of the series in [19] 'Command Performances', the later story [20.2] 'Target: 2006' showed Frenzy being revived and rejoining the Decepticon forces. From the UK point of view, then, the mystery cassette Transformer isn't a mystery at all: he's Frenzy (not Rumble or Enemy).

Although this story marked the first US appearances of Hot Rod, Kup, Blurr, Crosshairs and the Nebulan Targetmaster weapons in the regular strip, most were already familiar to UK readers thanks to stories such as [31.1] 'Worlds Apart' and [20.2] 'Target: 2006'.

UK Changes:
Page 1, panel 1: credits replaced; art extended downwards (additional ocean painted in) to make the panel fit the page.
Page 2, panel 3: the reference to issue #37 is changed to issue #155. Editor Don Perlin's tag is removed from the caption.
Page 3, panel 6: 'insure' is corrected to 'ensure'.
Page 4, panel 2: 'defense' becomes 'defence'; the reference to issue #37 is again changed to issue #155, and again Perlin's sign-off is excised.
Page 4, panel 7: 'seven Autobots' is corrected to 'six Autobots'.
Page 5, panel 2: 'six toy cars' is amended to 'five toy cars'.
Page 5, panel 3: 'six' is once again changed to 'five'; 'the seventh one' is altered to 'the sixth one'.
Page 5, panel 4: the reference to issue #37 again becomes issue #155, and for the third time editor Don Perlin's name is erased.
Page 8, panel 3: 'Galen's Autobot body' is changed to 'Fort's Autobot body'; Perlin's tag

is again excised.

Page 9, panel 6: 'Sparks' is corrected to read 'Firebolt'.

Page 19, panel 5: 'maneuverability' is changed to 'manoeuvrability'.

Page 21, panel 3: 'that I burn up' is amended to 'that I fall to Earth'.

Page 21, panel 7: 'falling to your doom' becomes 'falling to Earth' and 'save you' is changed to 'get you'.

Page 22, panel 8: 'the end' – caption removed.

Roll Call:

Autobots: Hot Rod, Kup, Blurr, Rollbar, Fortress Maximus, Cerebros, Chromedome (flashback only), Crosshairs, Pointblank and Sureshot.

A number of the Throttlebots are seen in this story, but it's unclear which ones (as their brains are trapped in near-identical toy cars). Consequently, there could also be appearances here for Chase, Freeway, Wideload and/or Searchlight. (Rollbar is the only one who can be positively identified, as he has a speaking part.)

Decepticons: Soundwave, Frenzy (or possibly 'Enemy' – see above), Shockwave, Scavenger, Hook, Onslaught, Blast Off, Vortex, Wildrider, Breakdown, Shrapnel, Kickback, Razorclaw, Tantrum (flashback only), Headstrong (flashback only) and Ratbat.

Nebulans: Stylor (in flashback, and only as Chromedome's head), Firebolt, **Haywire**, **Recoil**, Pinpointer, Peacemaker and Spoilsport.

Haywire and Recoil had previously appeared in the *Headmasters* mini-series, but make their debuts in the main strip here.

Other: Buster, Sparkplug, Walter Barnett, Forrest Forsythe and Spike.

Data File: José Delbo (artist)

The Argentinian Delbo is best known for his five-year stint on DC's *Wonder Woman* (the popularity of which was boosted by the launch around the same time of a popular television show based on the character). Other books to showcase his talents included *Green Lantern*, *Superman* and *Detective Comics*. He seemed to specialise in licensed tie-in comics: as well as *The Transformers*, he also contributed to *Thundercats*, *The Twilight Zone*, *Yellow Submarine* and *Rainbow Brite and the Star Stealer*.

Review:

A solid slice of action, helped immeasurably by yet another excellent central concept – that of a desert island that can convert into a spaceship. The island's transformation and take-off stands out as one of the most striking images in this phase of the comic's life. 3/5

The Back-Up Strips, Part 16: *Visionaries*

Like *Transformers*, *G.I. Joe* and *The Inhumanoids*, *Visionaries* was a Hasbro toy line that was translated into a comic and a cartoon. The figures were futuristic knights in armour, with the same size and articulation as contemporary *G.I Joe* toys. As a gimmick, each toy included at least two working holograms. The comic and cartoon explained that the characters were forced to turn to magic after all technology stopped working on their planet.

- 'The End – The Beginning' (excerpt) (UK#158), from *Visionaries* #1 (November 1987). A brief teaser from the strip, part of an ad campaign for the *Visionaries* comic, action figures and videocassettes.

Following this teaser, Marvel UK launched its own *Visionaries* comic. It soon folded due to lack of sales, so the remaining American *Visionaries* stories were run as a back-up strip in *The Transformers* UK:

- 'Quest of the Four Talismans' (UK#183-186), from *Visionaries* #5 (July 1988). The Spectral Knights and Darkling Lords embark on a multi-issue quest for some mystical talismans (c.f. [62]-[66], the 'Matrix Quest' arc).
- 'Wings: Quest of the Four Talismans – Part Two' (UK#187-190), from *Visionaries* #6 (September 1988). The second Talisman is guarded by a tribe of flying people.

This was the final story of the American *Visionaries* comic; planned as a four-part story, the 'Four Talismans' arc was never completed. Later, the UK *The Transformers* comic reprinted the *Visionaries*' origin story:

- 'The End – The Beginning' (UK#213-219) from *Visionaries* #1 (November 1987). A new Age of Magic begins on the planet Prysmos, where two factions of knights compete for new powers. *Visionaries* #1 was a giant-sized issue with a higher than usual page-count, hence the story being spread across seven issues rather than the usual four.

[39.1] SALVAGE!
- UK#160, 9 April 1988 (Part 1), 11 pages
- UK#161, 16 April 1988 (Part 2), 11 pages

Credits:
Simon Furman (script); Lee Sullivan (art); Euan Peters (colours); Tom Frame (letters, part 1) Gary 'Glib' Gilbert (letters, part 2); Bryan Hitch (covers, UK#160 and 161).

Plot:
As part of a new environmental project, businessman Richard Branson retrieves the bodies of Megatron and Centurion from the bottom of the Thames. However, the bodies are subsequently stolen by the Decepticons, as part of Shockwave's plot to defeat Galvatron.

Shockwave plans to turn Megatron into his puppet by using a 'psycho probe' to implant commands directly into his brain. However, the probe causes Megatron to retreat into a dream-like state, in which he sees representations of Optimus Prime and Lord Straxus.

Meanwhile, the Sparkabots have unearthed Ultra Magnus, who was buried within Mount Verona when that volcano erupted. After months of confinement, Ultra Magnus has developed a phobia of Galvatron, the Decepticon who defeated him time and again.

In his dream, Megatron finally composes himself and destroys Straxus – a catharsis that allows him to awaken from his coma. Ultra Magnus is also able to overcome his psychosis, and defeats Galvatron when the two meet outside the Decepticons' Fortress Sinister.

Notes:

This story features a cameo from businessman Richard Branson, founder of the various Virgin companies, who at the time had been appointed to the role of 'litter tsar' by the then-current UK Prime Minister, Margaret Thatcher, as part of the Keep Britain Tidy campaign. His appearance in *The Transformers* was authorised by Branson himself.

The previous UK-only story, [36.3] 'Enemy Action', set up many plot threads that are revisited here. Galvatron is once again keeping a keen eye on Shockwave's plans, which, as previously hinted, now involve the revival of Megatron. The Sparkabots are still active, and they free Ultra Magnus from the volcano in which he's been trapped since [A3.3] 'Vicious Circle'.

Megatron and Centurion make their first appearances since they fell into the River Thames at the end of [29.1] 'Ancient Relics'. While Megatron is successfully revived, Centurion is not, and therefore this marks the final appearance of the human-controlled mechanoid that debuted in [20.1] 'In the National Interest'. Following the botched attempt at a mind-swap in [23.5] 'Resurrection', Megatron still has an element of Straxus's mind within him. Megatron's symbolic defeat of Straxus within in the dream sequence would appear to indicate that Megatron's mind is now completely his own.

(It will eventually transpire that this is not, in fact, the real Megatron, merely a clone built by Straxus as a contingency plan in case the mind-swap went wrong. This plot-twist – revealed in [57.1] 'Two Megatrons' – had not yet been conceived, however, so the clone-Megatron seen here is written as if he were the real deal. Also in [57.1] 'Two Megatrons', it will be revealed that Straxus's mind is not destroyed here, instead remaining dormant within the clone-Megatron's subconscious.)

Since crashing to Earth at the end of [39] 'The Desert Island of Space', Shockwave has been holed up in the old Fortress Sinister base. (His previous dislike for the base, revealed in [16.1] 'Robot Buster', has obviously been overcome out of necessity.) Fortress Sinister was first built in [2] 'Power Play', named in [12.2] 'Crisis of Command' and last seen in [16.1] 'Robot Buster'.

The Decepticon Dirge continues to be active in the UK stories; from the US point of view, he was killed in [GIJ3] 'Ashes, Ashes' (an adventure not published in Britain until 1990).

Roll Call:

Autobots: Optimus Prime (only as part of Megatron's dream), Ultra Magnus, Sizzle, Fizzle and Guzzle.

Decepticons: Shockwave, Ramjet, Thrust, Dirge, (a mental avatar of) Straxus, Galvatron, Blitzwing, Clone Megatron, Snaptrap and Overbite.

Other: Centurion and **Richard Branson.**

As per [36.3] 'Enemy Action', Overbite is referred to as 'Jawbreaker', Snaptrap as 'Snap Trap' and the Sparkabots as 'Sparklers'.

Data File: Lee Sullivan (artist)

Lee Sullivan is best known for his *Doctor Who* art, including comic strips in *Doctor Who Magazine* (including 'Nemesis of the Daleks' and 'The Mark of Mandragora') and *Radio Times*; cover art for the novel 'Love and War'; and background illustrations for the webcasts 'Shada' and 'Death Comes to Time'. A frame of his comics work, depicting the character Abslom Daak, even appeared in a *Doctor Who* television episode, 'Time Heist' (2014). Outside of *Doctor Who*, his other comic work includes *Judge Dredd* and *William Shatner's TekWorld*.

Review:

A necessary evil, this story sees the reintroduction of Megatron and Ultra Magnus and confirmation that Shockwave is still alive – this is all about making sure that the pieces are in place for future adventures. Despite the rather mechanical nature of the plotting, however, it works reasonably well, with some good material for Ultra Magnus and Megatron and some excellent artwork. 3/5

[40] PRETENDER TO THE THRONE!

US#40, 'May 1988' (published January 1988), 22 pages.

British reprint: UK#162, 23 April 1988 (Part 1), 12 pages; UK#163, 30 April 1988 (Part 2), 10 pages.

Credits:

Bob Budiansky (script); José Delbo (pencils); Dave Hunt (inks); Nel Yomtov (colours); Bill Oakley (letters); Don Daley (editor); Tom DeFalco (editor-in-chief); José Delbo and Dave Hunt (cover). **UK:** Jeff Anderson and David Elliott (cover, UK#162); Lee Sullivan (cover, UK#163).

Plot:

Optimus Prime lives – but only as a computer program. It transpires that programmer Ethan Zachary made a back-up of Prime's mind prior to his destruction. Unfortunately, however, Prime's mind is a little scrambled – he believes himself to be a fictional character from a computer game. Zachary makes an attempt to contact the Autobots for help, and succeeds in enlisting the aid of Goldbug.

Meanwhile, Scorponok's forces take over a genetics lab and use it to create six very special Decepticons: Pretenders – robots that have the ability to encase themselves within 'synthoplasmic outer shells' resembling giant monsters. Their scheming is overheard by Optimus Prime, who has hacked into the Decepticons' computer systems.

The Autobots decide to fight fire with fire, and create some Pretenders of their own. The two factions do battle but, guided by Optimus Prime, the Autobot Pretenders are able to triumph.

Notes:

This story is notable for two main reasons: first, barring flashbacks and dream sequences, it marks Optimus Prime's first appearance (albeit in a non-corporeal state) since his destruction in [24] 'Afterdeath'; and secondly, it sees the introduction of the Pretenders.

Since the events of [24] 'Afterdeath', Ethan Zachary now owns a videogame publishing company, Alternate Reality, Inc. In an attempt to help the confused Optimus Prime remember that he is a great warrior, Zachary has been placing Prime in specially-programmed computer games, designed to trigger old memories.

It's heavily implied that the Pretenders are Scorponok's invention; their shells are created from 'synthesised protoplasm' in a 'biochemical reaction'. While the Decepticon shells resemble animal-like monsters, the Autobot Pretenders have shells that resemble giant humans.

Zachary reads a newspaper entitled *The Sentinel* (indicating that his company could be based in the state of Pennsylvania, which boasts two different periodicals bearing that name). Goldbug is given a new body here, replacing the one destroyed by Triple-I in [37] 'Toy Soldiers'. He claims that he was present for Optimus Prime's funeral (in [26] 'Funeral for a Friend'), and that Prime's body was launched into the sun. (This further supports the theory that *G.I. Joe and the Transformers* takes place in a parallel universe – see [27.1] 'Wanted: Galvatron – Dead or Alive'. According to those comics, Bumblebee was in a state of disrepair while the funeral was taking place. Later stories will establish that Prime's body was simply launched into space, rather than specifically aimed at the sun.)

During his telephone conversation with Zachary, Sparkplug recalls his heart-attack (from [4] 'The Last Stand'), the destruction of his garage, Buster's kidnapping (both from [37] 'Toy Soldiers') and Spike becoming a Headmaster (from [39] 'The Desert Island of Space'). There's also a mention of his first encounter with Bumblebee (from [1] 'The Transformers').

UK Changes:
Page 1: credits replaced, artwork extended.

Page 3, panel 3: the reference to issue #24 is changed to issue #106. Editor Don Perlin's signature in the caption is removed.

Page 5, panel 4: the reference to issue #4 is changed to issue #7. Perlin's tag is excised.

Page 5, panel 5: 'totaled' becomes 'totalled'. The reference to issue #37 is altered to issue #155. Perlin's name is omitted.

Page 5, panel 6: '*Transformers* #37' becomes '*Transformers* #155'. Again, Don Perlin's name is removed.

Page 5, panel 7: the reference to issue #39 is changed to issue #158. Perlin's tag is omitted.

Page 6, panel 5: 'Damaged last issue' is amended to 'Damaged in issue 159'. Perlin's name is excised from the caption again.

Page 6, panel 7: the reference to issue #37 is changed to issue #154. Perlin's sign-off is erased.

Page 12, panel 6: to make for a better cliffhanger, the ellipsis is changed to a full stop.

Page 13, panel 1: '… and' is omitted entirely.

Page 16, panel 1: 'traveled' becomes 'travelled'

Page 21, panel 2: Optimus Prime's miscoloured head is corrected.

Roll Call:
Autobots: Optimus Prime (as a computer program; also in flashback), Grapple (flashback only), Air Raid (flashback only), Hot Spot (flashback only), Goldbug, Fortress Maximus, Cerebros, Highbrow, Brainstorm, **Landmine**, **Cloudburst**, **Waverider**, **Groundbreaker**, **Sky High** and **Splashdown**.

Cerebros's appearance is only as the head of Fortress Maximus, rather than an individual sighting. Fortress Maximus's appearance is only as a body on an operating table, still recovering from the injuries sustained in [39] 'The Desert Island of Space'.

Decepticons: Ratbat (flashback only), Scorponok, Mindwipe, **Bomb Burst**, **Skullgrin**, **Submarauder**, **Iguanus**, **Bugly** and **Finback**.

Nebulans: Gort, Arcana, Zarak and Vorath.

Gort and Arcana appear only as the heads of Highbrow and Brainstorm respectively.

Other: Buster (flashback only), Sparkplug, Ethan Zachary and Spike.

Data File: Bill Oakley (letterer)
A regular contibutor to *The Transformers*, Oakley is perhaps best known for his lettering on *The League of Extraordinary Gentlemen*. His other credits include *The Avengers*, *X-Men* and *Batman: Gotham Knights*.

Review:
The meat of this story is in the Optimus Prime plot, as his friends try unsuccessfully to get him to remember his true identity. Though Prime retains his resourcefulness, strength of will, compassion and tactical nous, it's interesting to see these balanced with his new child-like innocence, making for an interesting fresh take on the character. There's also a great cameo from Sparkplug, understandably bitter after his recent bad experiences.

However, it's the Pretenders who let the side down: while they made for popular toys, unfortunately they didn't translate well into the comics – though, to be fair to author Bob Budiansky, it would be difficult for any writer to rationalise why the Decepticons would want to disguise themselves as organic monsters. 2/5

US Advertisements, Part 4: Books and Comics (A-H)
A list of all advertisements for books and comics (plus comic retailers) that appeared in the American comic, listed alphabetically from A-H:

A.I. Gang, The (a series of game books by Signet Books) – US#20
Academic Industries (comic book adaptations of classic novels) – US#13, 17-18, 25; MOV#3; GIJ#2
Alpha Flight – US#49
Alternate Realities (comic wholesaler) – US#21, 26
Amazing Spider-Man, The – US#17, 32; HDM#2
American Comics (retailer) – US#18, 21, 26, 29, 33, 35, 37, 39, 41, 44, 50, 53, 57, 69, 72-73; GIJ#1, 3
Asgardian Wars, The (graphic novel) – US#50
Atlantis Attacks (Marvel cross-title story arc) – US#54
Avengers, The – US#41
Bantam Books' *Choose Your Own Adventure* book series – US#5
Bullwinkle and Rocky (comic series) – HDM#3
Captain America – US#16, 30

Comet Man – US#28
Comic Book Price Guide, The – US#20
Complete Guide to Nintendo Video Games (book) – US#75
Count Duckula – US#49
Crestohl/Ross (retailer) – US#55
Dakota North – US#17
Damage Control – US#51
Daredevil – US#41
Dazzler: The Movie (graphic novel) – US#2
Deadly Foes of Spider-Man, The (comic series) – US#78
Direct Comics and Games (retailer) – US#34, 36; HDM#3-4
Disney's DuckTales Magazine – US#58-61
Dragonlance (series of fantasy novels) – US#30; HDM#1
Dragon's Den/Big Apple Comics (retailer) – US#45
East Coast Comics (retailer) – US#13, 19, 25, 28, 31, 35, 39, 43, 45, 50, 56, 70, 80; MOV#3; GIJ#2
Elfquest – US#7
Endless Quest (a *Dungeons & Dragons* book series) – US#2
Epic Comics (a Marvel imprint for predominantly creator-owned properties) – US#15
Escape from Tenopia (a series of game books by Bantam Books) – US#20, 24; MOV#2; GIJ#1
Evolutionary War, The (Marvel cross-title event) – US#42
Fallen Angels – US#26; GIJ#3
Fall of the Mutants, The (a 1987 storyline running across several Marvel titles) – US#35
Firestar – US#15
Fred Hembeck Destroys the Marvel Universe – US#6
Forgotten Realms (novel series) – US#41-42
G.I. Joe Yearbook #2 – US#15
Graphiti (retailer) – US#72
Groo the Wanderer – US#28
Hayden Books (range of video game guides) – US#72
Heroes for Hope starring The X-Men – US#11
How to Become a Comic Book Artist – US#15, 18

[40.1] CITY OF FEAR!
- UK#164, 7 May 1988 (Part 1), 11 pages
- UK#165, 14 May 1988 (Part 2), 11 pages

Credits:
Simon Furman (script); Dan Reed (art); Euan Peters (colours); Annie Halfacree (letters); Dan Reed (covers, UK#164 and UK#165).

Plot:
Ultra Magnus and the Sparkabots return to the city-state of Kalis on Cybertron, home to the Autobase. Upon arrival, they discover that the Autobase has been deserted, and find signs that a battle took place within the complex. Exploring the city beyond, the newly-arrived Autobots find it strangely quiet, its few remaining inhabitants clearly spooked.

Crossing the border into the neighbouring settlement, Tyrest, the four Autobots capture a Decepticon, Flywheels, and bring him back with them to Kalis. Flywheels explains what's been going on: Transformer corpses are rising from the dead and attacking the living.

Flywheels forms a temporary alliance with Magnus and the Sparkabots and suggests that the animated cadavers are being controlled via a remote signal. Ultra Magnus sets up a jamming frequency, thereby rendering the corpses inactive once more. Magnus has traced the source of the zombie-signal – it emanated from below the surface of Cybertron …

Notes:
In this story we finally see the mechanism whereby the Autobots are able to transport themselves from Cybertron to Earth, as previously used by Ultra Magnus in [20.2] 'Target: 2006'. A 'prototype' version of the space bridge, it resembles a glowing yellow portal that allows one simply to step through to travel great distances. As in [20.2] 'Target: 2006', the main drawback to this mode of transport is that it causes extreme pain to anyone using it.

Emirate Xaaron and the Wreckers are now headquartered in an Autobase in the city-state of Kalis, having relocated from Iacon due to a 'security breach'. The Iacon Autobase was last seen in [23.5] 'Resurrection'. Kalis is described as a city-state (as per Iacon, Vos and Tarn – see [A2.4] 'State Games'), and it borders a region known as Tyrest (which could also be a city-state, but is not confirmed as such). (Although it here makes its debut appearance in the comics, Tyrest was first mentioned in the letters page in UK#162 – see [30] 'The Cure'.)

It's reasserted that Transformer bodies can be remotely controlled when not connected to a living brain, as previously evidenced in [8.2] 'The Wrath of Grimlock' and [HDM2] 'Broken Glass'.

The Empties – the caste of tramp-like Transformers first seen in [17] 'The Smelting Pool' – are again featured here. A complex known as the Baird Beaming Transmitter is able to send a jamming transmission that nullifies the effects of the 'zombie-signal'. (Possibly it is named after John Logie Baird (1988-1946), the inventor of the television. Compare with Maccadam's Oil House, the bar seen in [20.2] 'Target: 2006' – another Cybertronian location with a very Scottish-sounding name.)

Barring a (very) brief cameo in the *Headmasters* comic, this story marks the first appearance of the Decepticon Duocons, Flywheels and Battletrap. While the toy versions of these characters each consisted of two vehicles that connected together to form a single robot, here the pair are presented more like standard triple-changers. It's unclear why the Duocons ended up on Cybertron, given that they were previously established as being part of Scorponok's group; presumably they returned to the planet via the space bridge, having initially arrived on Earth with the rest of Scorponok's forces in [38] 'Trial by Fire'.

Roll Call:
Autobots: Ultra Magnus, Sizzle, Fizzle and Guzzle.

Decepticons: **Flywheels** and **Battletrap**.

There are many other nameless Transformers seen here (although one would be retrospectively dubbed 'Chuffer' in the letters page of UK#175). An Autobot called J'Muk is mentioned but not seen.

Review:
A great little zombie story, helped immensely by the art of Dan Reed, who is at his best when called upon to draw monsters and alien landscapes (see also [31.2] 'Kup's Story'). Although it's just the first chapter in a larger 'Magnus on Cybertron' story arc, it's also satisfying enough as a story in its own right, a neat trick to pull off. 4/5

[40.2] LEGION OF THE LOST!
- UK#166, 21 May 1988 (Part 1), 11 pages
- UK#167, 28 May 1988 (Part 2), 11 pages

Credits:
Simon Furman (script); Jeff Anderson (pencils); David Elliott (inks); Euan Peters (colours); Tom Frame (letters, part 1); Annie Halfacree (letters, part 2); Lee Sullivan (cover, UK#166); Jerry Paris (cover, UK#167).

Plot:
Investigating a massive explosion, the Wreckers – an Autobot commando unit – trace the source to a subterranean reactor built millions of years ago by Megatron as part of a plan to turn Cybertron into a giant spacecraft; this reactor was to have been the planet's engine.

The Wreckers' subterranean probes unwittingly activate an alarm system: a signal is sent out, awakening dead Transformers who then, zombie-like, seek out and attack the Autobots. Before they can jam the signal, the Wreckers are taken prisoner by the zombies – one of which is the reanimated corpse of the former Wrecker leader, Impactor.

Taken down into the underground complex, the Wreckers come face to face with Flame, a renegade Autobot scientist who plans to make Megatron's dream of a planetary engine come true – and who has created an undead army to help achieve his ambitions.

Though the Autobots seem powerless stop Flame, Springer is able to escape from his cell and head toward the surface ...

Notes:
The bulk of this story is set three weeks prior to the events of [40.1] 'City of Fear', and serves to explain why Ultra Magnus and the Sparkabots found the Autobase and its environs deserted. As well as Flame's zombie army killing the inhabitants (or at least forcing them to flee the city), a nuclear explosion added to the death toll. (The blast yield is said to have been 1.5 megatons – one hundred times that of the atomic bomb that devastated Hiroshima in 1945.)

We hear further details of Cybertron's past: the Decepticons were originally considered to be 'harmless cranks' when first founded (see [A2.4] 'State Games' for more on their rise to prominence), but Megatron soon moulded them into an army. However, it wasn't until Megatron announced his plan to convert Cybertron into a cosmic dreadnought that war was declared. Only 'a hundred or so' years after the declaration of war, 'Megatron disappeared' to Earth.

(It seems reasonable to assume that the Decepticons were involved in a number of skirmishes and battles with the Autobots for many years prior to the official declaration of all-out war. In [3] 'Prisoner of War' Megatron speaks of having been in power for 'countless millennia'; and in [A1.3] 'And There Shall Come ... A Leader' the fighting is established to have been already in full-swing when Optimus was anointed Autobot leader, an event stated in [1] 'The Transformers' to have taken place 'over a thousand years' prior to the *Ark* mission.)

Xaaron claims that Megatron 'rose to power within [the Decepticons'] ranks', which contradicts [A2.4] 'State Games', in which he was said to have been the Decepticons' founder member and leader from the very beginning. It could be that early Autobot intelligence regarding the fledgling Decepticon faction was a little hazy, due mostly to the fact that the Decepticons were initially dismissed as harmless.

As well as being chairman of the Autobot Council of Elders, Xaaron also held a position at the Academy of Science and Technology in Iacon. (It's possible that all the Elders held dual roles in society. Whereas Xaaron was a scholar, another member, Traachon, was a military leader, and held the rank of General (as per [A2.4] 'State Games'). Xaaron considered Megatron's planet-engine scheme to be flawed and dangerous, and had Flame cast out of the Academy when he insisted on continuing Megatron's line of research.

The Wreckers were first introduced in [20.2] 'Target: 2006'; the death of their leader Impactor during that story becomes a major plot point here. There's also a reference to the Wreckers having once mistaken Optimus Prime for a Decepticon spy (in [23.2] 'Under Fire').

World in Motion

One of the silliest ideas in the first issue of *The Transformers* is that the Autobot/Decepticon War resulted in Cybertron being 'shaken loose' from its natural orbit and sent plummeting through the universe. In a lovely piece of continuity, the annual story [A2.4] 'State Games' sees Megatron planning to do just that – he wants to turn Cybertron into a 'mobile battle-station' with which he can conquer the galaxy (harking back to his line about a 'cosmic dreadnought' in [1] 'The Transformers'). Presumably it's his ill-fated attempts to turn Cybertron into a giant spaceship that force the planet off-course.

The idea of a mobile battle-planet is nothing new in fiction – even in *The Transformers* itself we have Unicron, who works along the same sort of lines. There were the Death Stars in *Star Wars* (George Lucas, 1977) and its sequels, and in the television show *Doctor Who* (see [A2.2] 'To a Power Unknown'), the alien Daleks tried to turn Earth into a giant spaceship in a serial entitled 'The Dalek Invasion of Earth', broadcast in 1964.

So it's a nice idea ... but unfortunately it's also complete nonsense.

Let's look at just how much energy it would require to move Cybertron. We know its size (it's as big as Saturn, as established in [1] 'The Transformers'), so we can make an assumption as to its mass. Given that it is made of metal and that the Transformers are made of steel (as confirmed in [17] 'The Smelting Pool'), let's assume that Cybertron has a density similar to that of iron – 7.874 grams per cubic centimetre. This gives a total mass of 6.51×10^{27} kg – about 1090 times the mass of Earth.

Now, at what speed would the planet be travelling? Well, in order to get around the galaxy in short order it would need to travel at speeds many times greater than that of light. But let's be ultra-conservative here and say that it is moving at 'just' the speed of light, i.e. 299,792,458 metres per second. Given that energy = 0.5 x mass x velocity x velocity, we can calculate that it would require 2.93×10^{44} Joules to make Cybertron travel at the speed of light. That's equivalent to the energy output of a *supernova*. And even then, it would take the planet over four years to reach the nearest star system.

Despite its absurdity, and the fact that even Emirate Xaaron thought it unworkable, in this story we learn that the mad scientist Flame intends to bring Megatron's old plan to fruition, via the use of nuclear fusion.

We know that stars are powered by nuclear fusion, and also that the energy equivalent of a supernova would be required to move Cybertron at the speed of light. So could a suitably-advanced fusion reactor produce such energy, if it worked on the same principle as a star? Unfortunately for Flame, that's not the case; the reactions in a star depend upon its extreme mass and temperature – conditions unlikely to be replicated in laboratory conditions.

Considering that Cybertron is gripped in an almost permanent energy crisis, all things considered it seems extremely unlikely that any Transformer would be able to harness energy equivalent to that found in a stellar explosion – and even then, we're assuming that the tremendous forces this unleashed wouldn't rip the planet to shreds. And of course, a similarly gargantuan amount of energy would be required to stop the planet or make it change direction.

Roll Call:
Autobots: Optimus Prime (flashback only), Emirate Xaaron, Impactor (as a reanimated corpse), Ultra Magnus, Roadbuster (flashback only), Topspin, Twin Twist, Rack and Ruin, Springer, Sandstorm, Broadside, Sizzle, Fizzle and Guzzle.

The renegade Autobot **Flame** is the main villain of the story.

Decepticons: Megatron (flashback only) and Flywheels.

Data File: Jerry Paris (artist)
As well as providing the cover art for the very first issue of the UK *The Transformers* comic, Paris also contributed to *Doctor Who Magazine*, *Action Force* and *Penthouse Comix*.

Review:
As the middle chapter of the 'Flame' story arc, the lacks the mysteriousness and creepiness of the opening instalment, and the gripping excitement of the conclusion. Instead, it's all about exposition, as we find out exactly what's been going on, who the villain is, and what he's scheming.

Although it's mostly talk and flashbacks, there's an attempt to make this a bit more worthy – although it has to be said that Springer's throughline (an Autobot leader crippled by self-doubt who comes good in the end) is noteworthy only for its unoriginality (see also [12.2] 'Crisis of Command', [39.1] 'Salvage' et al.) On the plus side, the reappearance of Impactor as a zombie is smartly done, and makes for the best cliffhanger since [36.2] 'The Legacy of Unicron'.

Although it's the weakest instalment of the 'Flame' saga, 'Legion of the Lost' is still good fun, and paves the way for the epic conclusion to follow. 3/5

[40.3] MELTDOWN!

- UK#168, 4 June 1988 (Part 1), 11 pages
- UK#169, 11 June 1988 (Part 2), 11 pages

Credits:

Simon Furman (script); Robin Smith (art); Euan Peters (colours); Gary 'Glib' Gilbert (letters, part 1); Gordon 'GLOP' Robson (letters, part 2); Jerry Paris (cover, UK#168); Jeff Anderson (cover, UK#169).

Plot:

Springer escapes from Flame's underground lair and joins forces with Ultra Magnus, the Sparkabots and Flywheels, the latter of whom flies away to summon additional help. The remainder of the Wreckers fight their way through the zombies and gain access to a weapons locker. The two groups meet up in the tunnels, but their progress is halted by a blast door.

Meanwhile, Emirate Xaaron confronts Flame and inspects the renegade scientist's handiwork. As Xaaron predicted, the nuclear reactor is unstable, and begins a countdown to a complete meltdown. Flywheels returns with Trypticon in tow, and the giant Decepticon bashes through the blast door as Autobots and Decepticons alike join forces in a bid to save Cybertron from destruction.

Unfortunately, the only way to prevent the reactor from going critical is to activate the controls manually from within a radioactive chamber – whoever deactivates the reactor and saves the planet will sacrifice themselves in the process. Xaaron volunteers, but is stopped in his tracks by Impactor's reanimated corpse. The Autobot zombie's strength of will is such that he remembers his past life as a member of the Wreckers. Impactor kills Flame, and then braves the deadly radiation in order to shut down the reactor and save the planet.

Safe at last, Xaaron mourns for Impactor, the Autobot who died twice so that others might live.

Notes:

This is a story of 'lasts': it's the final ever appearance of Trypticon, whose only other sighting was in the US-only [27] 'King of the Hill'. It's also farewell to Impactor, whose second death scene is just as affecting as the first in [20.2] 'Target: 2006'. It's also the last instalment of the 'Flame' trilogy, which began in [40.1] 'City of Fear.

It's revealed that Emirate Xaaron has not transformed in 'hundreds of years'; attempting to transform after such a long time can be fatal. His alternative form is/was a 'vehicular combat mode'. Xaaron confirms the Autobot Council of Elders is now 'long gone', a reference to 'Cybertron: The Middle Years', a feature in UK#83 that provided background information to [20.2] 'Target: 2006'; this revealed that with the exception of Xaaron, who was able to survive, the Council members were massacred by a Decepticon warlord named Trannis.

The entirety of this story takes place over an extremely short period of time: 4.86 breems (roughly equivalent to 40 minutes and 35 seconds), according to Flame's countdown timer that ticks down over the course of the action.

The Story So Far ...

When American *The Transformers* issues were split into multiple parts for their UK printing, the first page of the second part was usually shrunk down in size and surrounded by an additional border, with the Transformers logo and a précis of the previous issue's plot at the top and a piece of specially-commissioned artwork down the left-hand side. Details of the various different versions of this border are as follows:

From UK#2: Optimus Prime in robot mode, by Barry Kitson.
From UK#52: Optimus Prime transforming, by Geoff Senior.
From UK#140: Galvatron, by Will Simpson.
From UK#214: Megatron, by Lee Sullivan.
Headmasters back-up strip (from UK#132): Gort transforming, by Robin Smith.
UK#265-281 (*G.I Joe* crossover): Optimus Prime, Shockwave, Hawk and Snake Eyes, by Lee Sullivan.

The borders were eventually phased out; UK#310 was the first 'part 2' of a US strip not to have a recap border.

Roll Call:
Autobots: Emirate Xaaron, Impactor, Ultra Magnus, Topspin, Twin Twist, Rack and Ruin, Springer, Sandstorm, Broadside, Sizzle, Fizzle, Guzzle and Flame.

Decepticons: Trypticon and Flywheels.

Data File: Gordon 'GLOP' Robson (letterer)
Robson lettered *Action Force Monthly*, *Doctor Who Magazine* and *The Real Ghostbusters* for Marvel UK, but is best known for his work on *2000 AD*, on such strips as *Judge Dredd*, *Strontium Dog* and *Nemesis the Warlock*.

Review:
An excellent end to the 'Flame' trilogy. All the staples of a classic *The Transformers* story are present: a strong villain, some excellent action sequences, a superb mid-story cliffhanger, tension, twists and a brilliant conclusion. It's this conclusion that's especially worthy of praise. In a comic about giant robots, one of the biggest difficulties is in provoking an emotional response in the reader, in getting people to empathise with these aliens. The task is even more onerous when you consider that, with 250-plus characters on the go, many of them never get a chance to shine.

It's a wonder, then, that the death of Impactor (who prior to this trilogy had appeared in just a single story) is so well done, so beautifully executed, that it ranks as one of the strongest pieces of 'emotional' writing the comic will ever see. 5/5

[40.4] DEADLY GAMES!
- UK#170, 18 June 1988 (Part 1), 11 pages
- UK#171, 25 June 1988 (Part 2), 11 pages

Credits:
Simon Furman (script); Dan Reed (art); Euan Peters (colours); Gary 'Glib' Gilbert (letters); Jeff Anderson (cover, UK#170); Jerry Paris (cover, UK#171).

Plot:
While the Wreckers prepare to travel to Earth for an assault on Galvatron, Ultra Magnus and the Sparkabots investigate the disappearance of an Autobot named Chameleon. Their search brings them to an old amphitheatre in Tyrest, where an alien businessman named Zabra has been capturing Autobots and forcing them to fight to the death in the arena.

Ultra Magnus is taken prisoner and forced to fight against the reigning champion, and Chameleon's killer, an alien named Hooligan. Ultra Magnus wins but – true to his ideals – refuses to kill his opponent. Magnus then turns his attentions to Zabra, and forcefully 'convinces' him to disband his operations on Cybertron.

Notes:
Ultra Magnus and the Sparkabots are still on Cybertron, following the events of the last story, [40.3] 'Meltdown'. We also see the Wreckers preparing for a journey to Earth; this will be shown in [40.5] 'Wrecking Havoc'. This is our final glimpse of the present-day Ultra Magnus in the *The Transformers* comic; all subsequent appearances will be by his 21st Century, post-movie incarnation.

The Jekka Amphitheatre dates from the pre-war era on Cybertron, when Transformers did battle in the state games (see also [4.2] 'The Enemy Within and [A2.4] 'State Games', amongst others). It's located in a region known as Tyrest (previously seen in [40.1] 'City of Fear'), which is here described as a 'quadrant of Cybertron' (implying that the region comprises one fourth of the entire surface area of the planet).

The cover of issue #171 states that Hooligan hails 'from the planet of Mil-Wal'; a reference to the association football club Millwall FC, based in London, England, whose fanbase had a reputation for hooliganism – a notion contested by the club's supporters, who sent a letter of protest to Marvel UK after this issue's publication.

Ultra Magnus makes a reference to the 'golden spires of Iacon', an architectural feature first seen in [A1.3] 'And There Shall Come … A Leader'. The Firecons refer to their previous battle with the Sparkabots, in [36.3] 'Enemy Action'.

Issue 170 saw the comic rise in price by 3p to 35p; to soften the blow, an additional one-page Transformers strip was printed. Listed simply as 'A Bonus Story' in the contents page, it was in fact a glorified advertisement run in other Marvel comics to showcase *The Transformers* (similar to the 1-page *Dragon's Claws* strip/ad that ran in issue 171).

Roll Call:
Autobots: Emirate Xaaron, Ultra Magnus, Springer, Sandstorm (flashback only), Broadside (flashback only), Sizzle, Fizzle and Guzzle.

Decepticons: Sparkstalker, Flamefeather and Cindersaur.

Review:
The 'fight to the death in a gladiatorial arena' story is such a well-worn trope that it's a wonder the comic hasn't featured it previously. There's little here that hasn't been done before in dozens of other shows and films, but the ending – in which Ultra Magnus refuses to kill his opponent – is especially reminiscent of the *Star Trek* episode 'Arena' (1967).

But while the script is uninspired, at least the art is good. Dan Reed is in his element here, his organic style perfectly suited to the array of monsters and aliens in the arena and in the audience. Sadly, though, that's not enough to make up for this story's other shortcomings. 1/5

UK Straplines, Part 3
A third collection of straplines from the cover of *The Transformers* UK, covering issues #133 to #198.

- UK#133: 'Warned you, yes?'
- UK#134: 'You're next!'
- UK#135: Swoop vs. Divebomb! 'This sky ain't big enough for the both of us!'
- UK#136: 'Game over!'
- UK#137: The silent scream!
- UK#138: 'Back off, Autobots! This is a job only we can handle!'
- UK#139: 'Aaaaaa!'
- UK#140: 'What am I bid?' 'Whaddaya mean – no takers?'
- UK#141: 'Knock, knock!'
- UK#142: The 8.24 from Portland ... has been cancelled!
- UK#143: 'Relax! There's no way they can catch us now!'
- UK#144: 'Huh! If you want something done properly ... you just gotta do it yourself!'
- UK#145: It's Christmas! 'So what?'
- UK#146: 'G'day!' Junk culture!
- UK#147: none
- UK#148: 'Ah, this is the life!'
- UK#149: Smokescreen ... through the windscreen! 'I knew I should'a worn a seatbelt!'
- UK#150: The origin of the Transformers
- UK#151: Side by side ... against Unicron!
- UK#152: Sea scrape!
- UK#153: none
- UK#154: Throttlebots ... the final transformation!
- UK#155: Predacons on the rampage – inside!
- UK#156: Headmasters ... on Earth!
- UK#157: none
- UK#158: 'Don't shoot!' The hostage!
- UK#159: Dead in space?
- UK#160: Molten madness!
- UK#161: 'No! It can't be you ... you're dead!'
- UK#162: Introducing the Pretenders – inside!
- UK#163: Pretenders – the ultimate warriors!
- UK#164: 'Face it, Sparklers, no-one's home!'
- UK#165: Night of the living dead!
- UK#166: The end?
- UK#167: 'Ach! D-does this mean we're not friends anymore?'
- UK#168: Under pressure!
- UK#169: 'Let's party, Trypticon!'
- UK#170: 'Game on!'
- UK#171: Tonight only! From the planet Mil-Wal ... Hooligan vs. Ultra Magnus
- UK#172: 'And this ...' '... is just the start!'
- UK#173: 'One side, Wreckers ... Galvatron's coming through!'

- UK#174: 'Wotta revoltin' development this is!'
- UK#175: 'Behind me? Haw – me not fall for that old trick!'
- UK#176: 'Who wants the world?'
- UK#177: Optimus Prime is back … '… and I'm here to stay!'
- UK#178: 'Roll up! Roll up! For the greatest show …' '… in outer space!'
- UK#179: 'Your mouthwash ain't making it, lizard breath!'
- UK#180: 'Are you sitting comfortably … then I'll begin …'
- UK#181: 'Once upon a time …'
- UK#182: 'Ours!'
- UK#183: Arcee … deceased?
- UK#184: 'What is going on around here!'
- UK#185: No way out!
- UK#186: The awakening!
- UK#187: Matrix master!
- UK#188: 'Keep your eyes peeled, it could be anywhere!'
- UK#189: 'No problem!'
- UK#190: Coming soon – *Monster from Mars* starring Skullgrin
- UK#191: Skullgrin vs. Skullgrin!
- UK#192: 'Sizzle, Fizzle, Backstreet … kill them!'
- UK#193: White line nightmare!
- UK#194: The Seacons are back! 'Wait – can't we chew on this first?'
- UK#195: Tape scrape!
- UK#196: 'They just don't understand, Dogfight … it's a jungle out here!'
- UK#197: Blast from the past!
- UK#198: '"You're new on Earth", they said!' '"You don't know what Christmas is all about", they said!' '"We'll explain all about peace and the spirit of goodwill", they said!'

[40.5] WRECKING HAVOC!
- UK#172, 2 July 1988 (Part One), 11 pages
- UK#173, 9 July 1988 (Part Two), 11 pages

Credits:
Simon Furman (script); Bryan Hitch (art); Euan Peters (colours); Steve Parkhouse (letters, part 1); Annie Halfacree (letters, part 2); Jerry Paris (cover, UK#172); Jeff Anderson (cover, UK#173).

Plot:
Having arrived on Earth as part of Scorponok's forces, Cyclonus and Scourge seek out Shockwave and make him an offer – in exchange for their loyalty (and safe harbour), the future Decepticons request permission to go after Galvatron. Their ultimate aim is to wrest control of Galvatron's time-jump trigger device and return to their own time period, the year 2008. However, unbeknown to them, the trigger device has been destroyed.

Cyclonus and Scourge meet with Galvatron in the middle of a small American town, but before they can engage in combat, the Wreckers arrive from Cybertron. A battle ensues in the middle of town, the Wreckers desperately trying to avoid human casualties.

Realising that Galvatron no longer has the time-jump device, Springer lures

Cyclonus and Scourge out of the town by pretending to have stolen it. Realising they have been duped, Cyclonus and Scourge retreat. Galvatron, too, manages to sneak away.

Notes:

The story opens with an air battle between Scourge, Cyclonus, and some Grumman F-14 Tomcats. This takes place above the Cascade Range in Oregon, home of Mount St Hilary ([1] 'The Transformers' *et seq*) and Mount Verona ([27.2] 'Burning Sky'). Used by the USA between 1974 and 2006, the Tomcats were, at the time, the US Navy's primary air-superiority fighter. Oddly, this story shows them with Air Force markings (the F-14 was never used by the US Air Force, only the Navy). It's possible they are a special detachment, launched from Oregon Four-Alpha (the secret Air Force base seen in [4.2] 'The Enemy Within').

The battle between the Wreckers, Galvatron, Cyclonus and Scourge takes place in an unnamed 'small mid-western town', making this story the first to be set in America's midwest since [16] 'Plight of the Bumblebee', which (in its original printing) was set in Wisconsin.

Galvatron's time-jump trigger device was destroyed by Wreck-Gar in [27.4] 'Fire on High'. The Wreckers were seen preparing for the trip to Earth in [40.4] 'Deadly Games', in which Ultra Magnus's absence was also explained.

This is the first appearance of Scourge and Cyclonus as Targetmasters in the main comic, although they were seen as such in the *Headmasters* limited series. They recall how they were sent back in time to the present day (in [36.2] 'The Legacy of Unicron') and subsequently became Targetmasters (in [HDM4] 'Brothers in Armor').

Roll Call:

Autobots: Emirate Xaaron, Topspin, Twin Twist, Rack and Ruin, Springer, Sandstorm and Broadside.

Decepticons: Shockwave, Galvatron, Cyclonus and Scourge.

Nebulans: Nightstick and Fracas.

Review:

After the plot-heavy stories of recent months, this all-out action/adventure comes as a breath of fresh air. The opening air battle, despite not being particularly vital to the story, is especially well-written and drawn.

The new, post-volcano Galvatron continues to impress – his powers of manipulation are matched only by his prowess on the battlefield. Despite this being an action story, Galvatron has a meaty part and gets all the best lines.

There's little depth or subtext here, just fights and explosions – but when it's as well-realised as this, who cares? 4/5

The UK Letters Page

The UK letters page went through a number of different iterations, all hosted in-character by a particular Transformer. Where the letters pages add to or provide background information for particular stories, those editions are mentioned within the notes sections of the stories themselves. Other editions of special note are described below:

Soundwaves (host: the Decepticon, Soundwave)

Soundwave's responses to readers' letters were generally knowledgeable, and often tongue-in-cheek. One of his foibles was to spit ('puttup!') after mentioning any Autobots by name.

- UK#22: The first edition. A reader bemoans the recent shortening of the *The Transformers* strips (which occurred between issues UK#16-21), and calls for the axing of regular features such as Robot Round-Up and *From the Fact Files*. He'll get his wish …
- UK#28: Here we get the first reader to provide feedback on the *Transformers* cartoon show. Although in future Soundwave will become less enamoured with it (as more and more confused readers write in to ask why it contradicts the comic stories), for now he describes the show as a 'big hit'.
- UK#29: Just one issue later, Soundwave contends that the comics relate the 'accurate' story of the Transformers, and that the cartoons are less reliable; they 'use the basic facts, and then build up stories around them.'
- UK#39: Soundwave reveals why there are no female Transformers ('they'd just get in the way'), and confirms that the current *Machine Man* story, set in the year 2020, occurs in the 'original' timeline, not an alternative future or parallel dimension.
- UK#41: Because Soundwave got drunk on 'high grade lubricating oil' at the office party, he's too hung over to host the letters page, which for one week becomes 'Rat-Chat', presided over by the Autobot Ratchet.
- UK#44: A classic exchange. Reader: 'Dear Soundwave … There is a *Beano* fan club, so please could you start one as well.' Soundwave: 'I refuse point blank to start up a *Beano* fan club!'
- UK#48: Soundwave is getting increasingly snappy when it comes to the *Transformers* cartoon show. It 'manages to get almost everything wrong', apparently.
- UK#51: Soundwave promises readers that all *The Transformers* stories will eventually see print again. He would be proven correct, although in the case of [4.3] 'Raiders of the Last *Ark*' it would take 26 years …
- UK#52: Soundwave takes the week off; he's 'taking the Constructicons out into the desert for some combat training', a reference to the forthcoming story [16.2] 'Devastation Derby'.
- UK#61: A reader asks about the inconsistency of the comic's art. (Readers at this point were generally ignorant that half of the *The Transformers* stories were imported US reprints that used the mechanical colour separation method.) Soundwave replies that the team are 'experimenting with different colouring methods'.
- UK#63: Soundwave answers questions about the story [4.1] 'Man of Iron', which has just been reprinted. It's confirmed that Thundercracker is the Decepticon who kills the Man of Iron (due to the way in which the reprint was coloured, the Decepticon's identity is unclear in the story itself), and that the navigator Autobot in the rescue ship is named simply 'Navigator'.
- UK#64: The first clear hint about the upcoming movie and the comic tie-in, [20.2] 'Target: 2006'. When asked about Ultra Magnus and Galvatron, Soundwave replies, 'Perhaps we shall encounter these two in *future* stories. As they say, who knows what *tomorrow* may bring!'
- UK#66: Another classic one-liner. A reader asks about Bumblebee's eight senses: 'What am I missing by only having a mere five senses?' Soundwave: 'The answer to your question.'

- UK#69: For the first time in the UK, mention is made of the *Transformers Universe* comic series. They 'might even decide to serialise it in this comic'.
- UK#73: The final edition.

Grim Grams (host: the Autobot, Grimlock)

Probably fandom's best-loved letter answerer, Grimlock was generally amiable and sharp-witted. His nickname for the human team at Marvel UK was 'dumb stubbies', and he would threaten to torture them if they made any mistakes.

- UK#75: The first edition.
- UK#83: Apparently, the first part of *Transformers Universe* will be 'on sale in late November'.
- UK#89: Some hints about future adventures. On Optimus Prime: 'I wonder what would happen if he ever disappeared permanently?'; and later: 'Optimus Prime on Cybertron? Nah, couldn't possibly happen ... could it?' – references to an upcoming storyline beginning in [23.1] 'Prey'.
- UK#91: For one issue only, Grimlock presents 'Film 2006', a review of {3-00} *The Transformers: The Movie* in his usual witty style.
- UK#96: The first reference to Season Three of the *Transformers* cartoon show: 'The fate of all the movie characters will be explored in a new TV series (now in production).'
- UK#128: Readers aren't happy that they'll have to fork out for *The Transformers Annual* to read the resolution to the cliffhanger ending of [27.4] 'Fire on High'. Grimlock: '[Concluding the story in the Annual] was bound to provoke comment – not all of it favourable'.
- UK#182: The final edition.

Dread Tidings (host: the Decepticon, Dreadwind)

The most controversial letter-answerer, Dreadwind was prone to mood swings – sometimes jokey, sometimes irascible and downright rude. His reign wasn't helped when Simon Furman – chief writer of the UK strips and a font of information – left to write for the American comic. After that, Dreadwind became increasingly clueless and seemed visibly irritated when readers wrote in to correct mistakes in his previous answers. (For more on Dread Tidings, see the notes under [53.4] 'The Hunting Party'.)

- UK#184: The first Dread Tidings.
- UK#190: Dreadwind is in a particularly bad mood, refusing to answer questions directly and rudely dismissing correspondents who want to organise a readers' poll.
- UK#198: The page features an order coupon for the *Transformers Universe* book.
- UK#249: Dreadwind is asked about Stormcloud's mysterious 'purpose', hinted at in [55] 'The Interplanetary Wrestling Championship'. Later stories would make it clear that Stormcloud and the rest of the Air Strike Patrol were working as double agents for Megatron, but Dreadwind seems oddly ignorant of this plotline.
- UK#272: More evidence of Dreadwind's lack of knowledge: 'What's all this about Jumpstarters then? Never heard of 'em!'
- UK#280: Dreadwind is asked about the five-part story that opened Season Three of the *Transformers* cartoon series: 'I haven't heard of this 'Five Faces of Darkness' – anybody out there got any comments?'
- UK#281: More ignorance of Transformers lore: 'Who exactly are these Pretender Monsters? ... Somebody out there care to tell me?'

- UK#282. If any single issue sums up Dreadwind's tenure as letter-answerer, it's this one: asked if Powermaster Optimus Prime was featured in any of the *Transformers* home video releases, he incorrectly replies, 'Yes, but don't ask which one.' He's obviously getting fed up with knowledgeable readers correcting him; when asked if the Classic Heroes range of Transformers figures would see release as a giftset of all six toys, he responds: 'Not that I know of, but I dare say someone in the Outer Hebrides will write in saying they've seen one!'
- UK#299: the final edition.

Darn 'n' Blast (host: the Autobot, Blaster)
More genial, friendly and upbeat than Dreadwind, but prone to giving silly, jokey answers to questions. Blaster's tenure is often seen as the 'dumbing-down' of the letters page, with more space given to frivolity and readers' drawings.

- UK#300: First Darn 'n' Blast. 'I am an Action Master, summoned from yet another alternative future.'
- UK#305: 'What are the chances of a new *Transformers* film?' 'We are talking to David Lynch at this moment.'
- UK#306: Confirmation that the comic will soon be using a lot more Kympress paper, a cheaper stock that apparently 'absorbs more ink' and 'improves reproduction'.
- UK#313: A reader writes in, confused about the multiple Megatrons, Galvatrons and timelines presented in the UK comic. Blaster's white lie: 'I know that Simon [Furman] is working hard to tie up the loose ends in future issues'.
- UK#332: the final edition.

[41] TOTALED!
US#41, 'June 1988' (published February 1988), 22 pages.

British reprint: UK#174, 16 July 1988 (Part 1), 11 pages; UK#175, 23 July 1988 (Part 2), 11 pages.

For the UK printing, the title was changed to 'Totalled!'

Credits:
Bob Budiansky (script); José Delbo (pencils); Danny Bulanadi (inks); Nel Yomtov (colours); Bill Oakley (letters); Don Daley (editor); Tom DeFalco (editor-in-chief); José Delbo and Dave Hunt (cover). **UK:** Jeff Anderson (cover, UK#174); Lee Sullivan (cover, UK#175).

Plot:
Two groups of Autobots meet for the first time – Grimlock's crew aboard the *Ark*, and Fortress Maximus's team aboard the *Steelhaven*. Fortress Maximus asks Grimlock for help rebuilding Optimus Prime, using the personality disc recently obtained from Ethan Zachary.

Grimlock, his leadership threatened, reacts angrily and claims trial by combat to determine who should be the Autobot leader. With Fortress Maximus still recovering from his recent altercation with Shockwave, Blaster volunteers to fight in his stead.

The Autobots look on as Grimlock and Blaster do battle, and are caught unawares as Ratbat and his Decepticon army choose that moment to launch an attack. As the battle rages, the Constructicons free those Decepticons who had previously been captured and placed in storage aboard the *Ark*.

Keen to ensure Optimus Prime's survival, Fortress Maximus orders Goldbug and three other Autobots to flee the battle and travel to Nebulos. Grimlock and Blaster put aside their differences and launch an assault on the Decepticon ship, forcing them into retreat.

Notes:

This issue sees the culmination of a number of plotlines, and so features many references to past stories. This is the conclusion of the 'Blaster and Goldbug as traitors' story arc, which began when they defied Grimlock's orders in [28] 'Mechanical Difficulties'. Blaster begins this story in captivity, having finally been captured by Grimlock at the end of [36] 'Spacehikers'. This is also the final story of Grimlock's reign as leader, before he is supplanted by the soon-to-be-resurrected Optimus Prime. Grimlock was promoted to the rank of Autobot leader back in [27] 'King of the Hill'.

Fortress Maximus's ship finally gets a name here – the *Steelhaven*. The ship no longer has the means to rebuild Optimus Prime, its resources having been spent rebuilding Goldbug and creating the Pretenders (in [40] 'Pretender to the Throne'; Goldbug's body was destroyed in [37] 'Toy Soldiers'). Fortress Maximus has still to recover fully from the injuries he sustained in [39] 'The Desert Island of Space'; he sends Goldbug and three other Autobots – Joyride, Getaway and Slapdash – to Nebulos in the hope of rebuilding Optimus Prime, who was destroyed in [24] 'Afterdeath'. Optimus Prime's personality disc is also aboard the *Steelhaven*, Goldbug having retrieved it from Ethan Zachary in [40] 'Pretender to the Throne'.

The Decepticons free a number of prisoners from the *Ark*, these being Buzzsaw, Thundercracker, Rumble, Skywarp, Frenzy and Starscream, all of whom had been defeated by Omega Supreme in [19] 'Command Performances'. Buster Witwicky is still a captive of the Decepticons, having been kidnapped in [37] 'Toy Soldiers'.

Many of the original Autobots make a return appearance here, having been previously killed off. Most notably there is Sunstreaker, who has not been seen in the comic since [5] 'The New Order'. This is probably due to the introduction of a new medic, the Protectobot First Aid, to lighten Ratchet's burden, and also to the Autobots' new energy self-sufficiency (see [32] 'Used Autobots').

(Grimlock may have been a terrible leader – and left the Earth unprotected – but his overall contribution to the Autobot cause was generally quite positive. Under his watch, the *Ark* was repaired, new power reserves were found, and many previously-deactivated Autobots were returned to service.)

UK Notes:

Grimlock and Blaster engage in trial by combat – 'an ancient Autobot tradition' – previously invoked in the UK story [4.2] 'The Enemy Within', wherein Brawn battled Starscream.

In the UK stories, most of those Decepticons captured in [19] 'Command Performances' had already returned to action. Frenzy, Thundercracker and Starscream were reactivated in [20.2] 'Target: 2006' (although Starscream was placed back into stasis, only to reawaken again in [36.1] 'Stargazing'). Furthermore, Skywarp had been blown to smithereens by Galvatron (also in [20.2] 'Target: 2006'). So while in the original American version of this story, at least six Decepticon prisoners of war were retaken, in the UK reprint this number was reduced to just two named characters – Rumble and Buzzsaw.

Another problem encountered by the UK production team was the appearances of Skids and Broadside, neither of whom should have been present on the *Ark* – in the UK continuity, Skids had been trapped in a limbo dimension since [23.4] 'Fallen Angel', and Broadside was part of the Cybertron-based commando unit, the Wreckers. To fix this continuity issue, in the UK reprint both characters were heavily modified so as to make them appear less recognisable and more like generic background characters. (That said, it's relatively simple to reconcile the appearance of both characters. The Skids seen here is the original incarnation; the version trapped in limbo is a clone (as explained in the notes to [36] 'Spacehikers'), and for Broadside these events are occurring prior to his recently-printed adventures set on Cybertron (see the notes to [44.2] 'Firebug').)

UK Changes:

Page 1, panel 1: credits replaced, artwork extended upwards, title changed from 'Totaled!' to 'Totalled!'

Page 2, panel 4: 'see last issue – Doctor Don' becomes 'see issues 162/163'.

Page 2, panel 5: 'see last issue – Database Don' is changed to 'see issue 163'.

Page 4 panel 4: 'honored' is amended to read 'honoured'; and 'Grotusque' is changed to 'Grotesque'. (The correct spelling of the Autobot's name is Grotusque, a play on the fact that the character has tusks when in animal mode, but as that figure was never released in the UK, the British editors were unfamiliar with the character and so assumed incorrectly that the oddly-spelt name was a typo.)

Page 7, panel 2: the reference to issue #39 is changed to issue #159. Editor Don Perlin's sign-off is excised from the caption.

Page 7, panel 5: 'see *Transformers* #36 – Detained Don' is changed to 'see *Transformers* 144'.

Page 7, panel 6: a reference to issue #28 is changed to issue #121. Perlin's tag is removed.

Page 9, panel 3: 'see *Transformers* #39 – Dueling Don' becomes 'see *Transformers* #159'.

Page 10, panel 2: Skids' appearance is edited.

Page 11, panel 6: to make for a better cliffhanger, Omega Supreme's line is changed from 'Let the combat …' to 'Let the combat begin!'

Page 12, panel 1: the leading ellipsis is deleted from Omega Supreme's speech bubble.

Page 13, panel 6: Broadside's appearance is altered.

Page 16, panel 1: 'outmaneuvered' is amended to 'outmanoeuvred'.

Page 18, panel 1: the stencilled names on the stasis pods are changed – where the names of Buzzsaw, Thundercracker, Rumble, Skywarp, Frenzy and Starscream were visible, now only Rumble and Buzzsaw are seen. Long Haul's line is changed from 'We have a lot more of these damaged Deceps to load!' to 'We have a lot more work to do!' The reference to issue #19 is changed to issue #71, and Don Perlin's tag is removed.

Roll Call:

Autobots: Optimus Prime (corpse only), Jazz, Prowl, Bluestreak, Ironhide, Ratchet, Sideswipe, Sunstreaker, Hound, Wheeljack, Mirage, Trailbreaker, Cliffjumper, Brawn, Huffer, Gears, Windcharger, Grimlock, Snarl, Slag, Sludge, Swoop, Jetfire, Grapple, Hoist, Smokescreen, Skids, Tracks, Silverbolt, Air Raid, Fireflight, Skydive, Slingshot, First Aid (flashback only), Blaster, Powerglide, Cosmos, Seaspray, Beachcomber,

Perceptor, Omega Supreme, Sandstorm (flashback only), Broadside, Hot Rod, Kup, Blurr, Outback, Goldbug, Fortress Maximus, Cerebros, Highbrow, Chromedome, Hardhead, Brainstorm, Crosshairs, Pointblank, Sureshot, Scattershot, Lightspeed, Nosecone, Afterburner, Grotusque, Doublecross, Repugnus, Sky Lynx (flashback only), Landmine, Cloudburst, Waverider, Sky High, **Joyride**, **Slapdash** and **Getaway**.

Decepticons: Soundwave, Laserbeak, Scrapper, Scavenger, Mixmaster, Bonecrusher, Long Haul, Hook, Onslaught, Brawl, Swindle, Vortex, Motormaster, Drag Strip, Dead End, Wildrider, Breakdown, Shrapnel, Bombshell, Kickback, Ramjet, Thrust, Astrotrain, Blitzwing, Octane, Razorclaw, Rampage, Tantrum, Headstrong, Divebomb and Ratbat.

Other: Buster and Spike.

Nebulans: Gort, Stylor, Duros and Arcana (none of whom is shown individually, only as the head of their Autobot partner).

Stasis pods containing the bodies of Buzzsaw, Frenzy, Rumble, Starscream, Skywarp and Thundercracker are also seen. This is Outback's first appearance in the American strips, although he had already featured in some UK-only stories.

It's entirely likely that more Transformers appear than are listed above, but given that many are block-coloured and seen only in the background, further positive identification is difficult.

Review:
Like [40.5] 'Wrecking Havoc', the UK story that preceded it, this is basically an extended action sequence, stretched out to 22 pages; and, as before, that's no bad thing.

It's quite refreshing to see numerous dangling plot threads finally pay off, with the promise of another – the return of Optimus Prime – just around the corner. The battle scenes are positively cathartic, symbolising the end of one era and the dawn of another. The Autobot forces are united, Grimlock is no longer leader, Goldbug and Blaster are redeemed, Starscream and his cronies are rescued – there are a number of major turning-points in the American comic, and this is one of them.

Thankfully, this isn't all just action and plotting – there's some welcome humour here too; Grimlock and Blaster get some of the funniest lines seen in the comic for many months. 5/5

[42] PEOPLE POWER!
US#42, 'July 1988' (published March 1988), 22 pages.

British reprint: UK#176, 30 July 1988 (Part 1), 11 pages; UK#177, 6 August 1988 (Part 2), 11 pages.

Credits:
Bob Budiansky (script); José Delbo (breakdowns); Dave Hunt, Don Hudson (finishes); Nel Yomtov (colours); Bill Oakley (letters); Don Daley (editor); Tom DeFalco (editor-in-chief); José Delbo and Dave Hunt (cover). **UK:** Kev Hopgood (cover, UK#176); Jeff Anderson (cover, UK#177).

In the UK printing, José Delbo was credited for 'pencils' and Dave Hunt for 'inks'. Don Hudson went uncredited in the UK.

Plot:
Goldbug, Joyride, Getaway and Slapdash arrive on Nebulos in the hope that the planet's scientists can rebuild Optimus Prime. However, their plan hits a snag. After the Headmasters and Targetmasters left the planet, the native Nebulans came up with a plan to prevent their world from ever again being blighted by Transformers – the planet's atmosphere has been infused with a special radiation that is harmless to Nebulans but renders all fuel on the planet deadly to Transformers.

To get around this, two Decepticons, Darkwing and Dreadwind, have become Powermasters – they are binary-bonded to a pair of Nebulan criminals who become the Transformers' engines, enabling them to function despite the poisoned energy supply.

Joyride, Getaway and Slapdash also undergo the Powermaster process (Goldbug is more resistant to the radiation than the others), and the newly-rebuilt Optimus Prime is engineered to be a Powermaster also.

The reinvigorated Autobots are able to defeat the marauding Decepticons, and they too leave the planet.

Notes:
This story is set on Nebulos, the main location in the *Transformers: Headmasters* comic series. The planet's capital city Koraja is seen again (although it looks very different, having been rebuilt since the battle in [HDM4] 'Brothers in Armor'), and two of the series' supporting characters, Sorgen and Soriza, appear in cameo roles (having originally featured in [HDM1] 'Ring of Hate' and [HDM3] 'Love and Steel' respectively).

Nebulos is located 'several dozen' light years from Earth. There are many real-world solar systems that distance from Earth. If we assume that Nebulos's sun is similar in type to our own, potential locations could include 59 Virginis, 51 Pegasi, and GI 777 A.

After a number of teases, dream sequences and flashbacks, Optimus Prime finally returns as a physical being, following his destruction in [24] 'Afterdeath' (though his disembodied consciousness has been seen in [40] 'Pretender to the Throne'). His return was presaged in [41] 'Totaled', in which Fortress Maximus sent a quartet of Autobots to Nebulos with the specific mission of rebuilding the Autobot leader.

The death of the Nebulan leader Galen in [38] 'Trial by Fire' is mentioned.

Charged with Battery
The description of the Powermaster process in this story is a bit strange. Hi-Q states that the 'atmosphere was filled with an invisible radiation' that 'tainted all fuel on Nebulos so that it would be poisonous to any living robot'. The Decepticons Darkwing and Dreadwing ingested this fuel and were nearly killed as a result. The Powermaster process saved them. Not only were they completely healed, but they now draw 'all their energy needs' from their new Nebulan companions, Throttle and Hi-Test, who transform into the Decepticons' engine blocks. This explanation is problematic. Although the converted Nebulans consume 'at least ten times as much food as they had before', an intake of around 25,000 kilocalories per day would equate to just 105.6 megajoules, about as much energy as you'd find in two-and-a-half kilograms of

gasoline. Obviously, this would be nowhere near enough to power a Transformer. So how can we rationalise this?

The most likely explanation is that the Nebulans act as power collectors, sucking energy from nearby surroundings – heat, light, movement, radiation and so on – similar in theory to the power siphon devices used by Shockwave in [14] 'Rock and Roll-Out' and by the Autobots in [32] 'Used Autobots'. The Nebulans must also act as a filtration system, preventing harmful radiation from being absorbed.

Radiation is the key here. When the Autobots start getting low on fuel, Joyride begins literally to fall apart. This isn't a standard symptom of fuel deprivation in Transformers – in [15] 'I, Robot Master', we find that they freeze like statues when starved. It's likely, then, that the radiation in Nebulos's atmosphere does more than just taint the planet's fuel supplies – it also acts as a corrosive agent that affects 'living' robots.

UK Changes:
Page 1, panel 1: credits replaced, artwork extended upwards.
Page 6, panel 3: 'see *Headmasters* 1-4 – D-Day Don' is changed to 'see issues 130-145'.
Page 6, panel 4: 'see *Transformers* #38 – Dearly Departed Don' is changed to 'see issue 157'.
Page 13, panel 4: 'armor' becomes 'armour'.

Roll Call:
Autobots: Optimus Prime, Goldbug, Hardhead (flashback only), Joyride, Slapdash and Getaway.

Decepticons: Skullcruncher (flashback only), Fasttrack (flashback only), **Darkwing** and **Dreadwind**.

Nebulans: **Hi-Q**, **Hotwire**, **Lube**, **Rev**, **Throttle** and **Hi-Test**.

Dreadwing (the combined jet form of Darkwing and Dreadwind) is also seen (however it's not a separate character as such). A number of Autobots and Decepticons appear in Hi-Q's flashback, but unfortunately only Skullcruncher, Fasttrack and Hardhead are drawn distinctly enough to make out.

Data File: Dave Hunt (artist)
An inker by trade, Hunt has credits on many Marvel and DC titles, including *The Amazing Spider-Man*, *Batman*, *Superman* and *Uncanny X-Men*.

Review:
The *Headmasters* comic series was a brilliant success; in this (sort-of) sequel, the Transformers return to Nebulos and face the consequences of their previous actions. While the Autobots flounder, we also get another look at the Nebulans themselves, who have rebuilt their planet only to see it threatened again. It's a great hook for a story.

The problem, however, is that this single issue also has to introduce the Powermasters and the new Optimus Prime, and features a sub-plot about a disgraced scientist who turns to crime. There's so much going on that all of these plot strands end up feeling rushed and/or underdeveloped. A rough-and-ready instalment that would have worked so much better if spread over more issues. 3/5

[43] THE BIG BROADCAST OF 2006 (comic)
This is a comic adaptation of an episode {3-19} of the *Transformers* cartoon series.

US#43, 'August 1988' (published April 1988), 22 pages.

British reprint: UK#180, 27 August 1988 (Part 1), 12 pages; UK#181, 3 September 1988 (Part 2), 12 pages.

The UK reprint bookended the story with two additional pages. See the **UK Notes** section below for more on this.

Credits:
Ralph Macchio (script), adapted from a television script by Michael Reaves (uncredited); Alan Kupperberg (pencils); Dave Elliott (inks); Nel Yomtov (colours); Kurt Hathaway (letters); Don Daley (editor); Tom DeFalco (editor-in-chief); Herb Trimpe (cover). **UK:** Simon Furman (script [framing sequence]); Lee Sullivan (art [framing sequence]); Gary 'Glib' Gilbert (letters [framing sequence]); Steve White (colours [framing sequence]); Lee Sullivan (covers, UK#180 and UK#181).

Although there were two new pages of content in the UK reprint (one at the beginning and one at the end of this story), the UK creative team were credited only for their work on Part 1.
   This is the only story from the main American *The Transformers* comic to be published out of sequence in the UK, where it went out *after* [44] 'The Cosmic Carnival' (UK#178-179).

Plot:
For story details, see the entry for the animated episode from which this issue was adapted, {3-19} 'The Big Broadcast of 2006' (cartoon episode).

Notes:
After the production problems that resulted in [4.1] 'Man of Iron' being reprinted in the US comic, the editorial team took it upon themselves to commission a number of 'contingency' stories – adaptations of episodes of the *Transformers* cartoon show – that could be drawn upon in the event of any further problems. 'The Big Broadcast of 2006' was the only one to see print, but at least one other is known to have been held in reserve: a comic version of {3-22} 'The Dweller in the Depths', pencilled by Ian Akin and inked by Dave Hunt.
   As with the original cartoon version of this story, there are a great many pop-culture references in the script. Most of those are verbal but a few are visual: ships seen in orbit around Junkion include the *USS Enterprise* from the television series *Star Trek* (1966-69) and *Thunderbird 3* from the television series *Thunderbirds* (1965-66). Other visual jokes include *Crambo*, a movie watched by the Junkions, clearly based on the *Rambo* series of films that began in 1982; and *Space Age Jack*, a parody of *G.I. Joe*, although the homage is clearer in the original cartoon episode. The entertainment is being broadcast by UBS, a play on the name of real-world broadcaster CBS. The

network's jingle is a rendition of Strauss's *Also Sprach Zarathustra*, the opening fanfare of which was memorably used in the 1968 Stanley Kubrick film *2001: A Space Odyssey*.

The dialogue includes references to many American cultural icons, as follows. (Those marked with an asterisk were also present in the television script.)

- *Casablanca* (Michael Curtiz, 1942) 'Here's looking at you, kid.' *
- *Meet the Press* (television news/interview show, 1947-present) 'For a transcript send one dollar to Merkle Press.' *
- *Saturday Night Live* (television variety show, 1975-present) 'Live from New York! It's –' *
- *ALF* (television sitcom, 1986-90). 'No problem!'
- *Jeopardy!* (television gameshow, 1964-present). 'I'll take American History for five hundred, please.'
- *Sledge Hammer!* (television sitcom, 1986-88). 'Trust me … I know what I'm doing' (see also [36] 'Spacehikers').
- *Taxi* (television sitcom, 1978-83). 'Tenk you veddy much.' *
- *Mission: Impossible* (action/adventure series, 1966-73). 'Your mission, should you decide to accept it …' *
- *Get Smart* (secret agent sitcom, 1965-70). 'Right chief', 'Sorry about that, chief' *
- *Superman* (comic book, launched 1939). 'Don't call me chief!', 'Jeepers, Mr Kent!' *
- *The Price is Right* (game show, 1972-present). 'Name that price.'
- *The Avengers* (British fantasy/espionage show, 1961-69). 'Mrs Peel, we're needed!' *
- *Star Trek* (science fiction show, 1966-69). 'Our five-year mission …' *
- *Chico and the Man* (sitcom, 1974-78). 'Lookin' Gooood!' *
- *Mary Hartman, Mary Hartman* (soap opera parody, 1976-77). 'Waxy yellow build-up.' *
- *Star Wars* (George Lucas, 1977). 'Star wars … nothing but star wars!' (a reference to a Bill Murray *Star Wars* skit on the 28 January 1978 episode of *Saturday Night Live*) (This song was included in the cartoon version, but changed to 'Laser wars … nothing but laser wars.')
- *Leave It to Beaver* (sitcom, 1957-63). 'Ward, I think we've been a little rough on the Beaver.' *
- *Sudden Impact* (Clint Eastwood, 1983). 'Go ahead … make my day!' *
- The Three Stooges (comedy act, 1925-75). 'I was a victim of soicumstances!' A catchphrase of Curly Howard, as heard in numerous short films such as *Disorder in the Court* (Preston Black, 1936). *

Other, non-specific references include:

- 'This concludes our broadcast day.' A traditional sign-off (spoken by an announcer and usually followed by the American national anthem) when television stations ceased broadcasting overnight. *
- 'It is better to light a candle than to curse the darkness.' An ancient Chinese proverb, best known as the motto for the Amnesty International organisation.

Betraying this story's origins as a cartoon episode, it's stated that the Quintessons are 'a highly-evolved race who once ruled Cybertron itself'. That said, as this line is never actually contradicted in the rest of the comics, it's possible to take it at face value. If it *is* true, it's likely that the Quintessons invaded Cybertron at some point in the distant past, but were later driven out.

Some real world star systems are mentioned: Beta Hydra [sic], which could be a reference to either Beta Hydrae or, more likely; Beta Hydri; Delta Pavonis; and Cygnus 7, properly known as Iota[1] Cygni. This story is set in 2006, after *The Transformers: The Movie*, the events of which are mentioned by Rodimus Prime. ('I've defeated you before, Galvatron, when we fought in the machine world, Unicron!')

The story's title is derived from the *Big Broadcast* film series, such as *The Big Broadcast of 1936* (Norman Taurog, 1935). Blaster's jamming signal is likened to the music of Mantovani (1905-80), a light orchestra conductor whose records sold millions in the '50s and '60s.

UK Notes:
The British comic had already presented its own version of events post-2006, for instance in [27.1] 'Wanted: Galvatron – Dead or Alive' and [36.2] 'The Legacy of Unicron', so this story represented something of a continuity headache. However, for purely financial reasons, the UK title couldn't really afford to skip any of the American material.

A novel solution was found: the material would be presented to UK audiences as a lie told by Wreck-Gar to a would-be interrogator. A new one-page prologue was produced, setting up the story as an invention of Wreck-Gar's, and a one-page epilogue was appended, confirming that these events never actually happened. In a nice piece of continuity, these scenes were designed to segue into the upcoming epic, [44.1] 'Space Pirates'.

To avoid letters from confused readers, the Transformation (editorial) page made it abundantly clear what was going on: 'Please, please don't leap for pen and paper after reading this and last issue's Big Broadcast of 2006 story. We know there are many seeming mistakes in its depiction of the Transformers' future. For the real story behind the Big Broadcast, we suggest you check out [the newly-written epilogue on] page 14.'

The exact contents of the canister sought by the Quintessons were never made clear in the American comic. In the cartoons, it contained data pertaining to their shady business deals, as revealed in {3-20} 'The Quintesson Journal'. According to the UK comic, the capsule contained details of the Quintessons' colonisation plans, as seen in [44.1] 'Space Pirates'.

Further cultural references unique to the UK sequences include: 'I'll squeal, Mister Regan,' alluding to British cop show *The Sweeney* (1975-78); 'Are you sitting comfortably? Then I'll begin', a famous introductory line from children's television programme *Watch with Mother* (1950-74); and 'Goodnight children everywhere,' from the UK radio show *Children's Hour* (1922-64).

The whole sequence, consisting of a preposterous tale related by a heroic yet unreliable narrator, was heavily influenced by 'The Girl Who Was Death', a 1968 episode of *The Prisoner*, which also included the 'Goodnight children everywhere' line. The shadow of a penny-farthing bicycle, an iconic image in *The Prisoner*, is cast over Wreck-Gar's face in the final panel.

As per the precedent set in [36.2] 'The Legacy of Unicron', all references to the planet Junkion are changed to 'Junk'.

UK Changes (excluding the new material added to the beginning and end of the story, as described above):

Page 1: artwork extended upwards, credits replaced.

Page 1, panel 2: 'Junkion' changed to 'Junk'.

Page 1, panel 4: 'Wreckgar' is corrected to 'Wreck-Gar'.

Page 5, panel 1: 'Wreckgar' is again edited to read 'Wreck-Gar'.

Page 6, panel 1: 'Junkion' is again renamed as 'Junk'.

Page 6, panel 7: 'reconaissance' is corrected to 'reconnaissance'; 'Junkion' is amended to 'Junk'.

Page 7, panel 4: 'Junkion' is again substituted with 'Junk'.

Page 11, panel 8: 'Junkion' is changed to Junk'.

Page 12, panel 3: 'Junkion's surface' becomes 'Junk's surface'.

Page 12, panel 4: 'Junk-Gar' is changed to 'Wreck-Gar'.

Page 13, panel 7: 'Junkion' becomes 'Junk'.

Page 14, panel 1: In one of the stranger edits, 'Junkions' omni-directional relay' is changed to 'Junkion's omni-directional relay' (note the placement of the apostrophe).

Page 14, panel 4: 'neighboring' is amended to 'neighbouring'.

Page 15, panel 1: 'Junkion!' is changed to 'Junk'.

Page 15, panel 2: 'And on Junkion, all the junk has been neatly stacked' becomes 'And on Junk, all the debris has been neatly stacked'.

Page 15, panel 6: 'Junkion' is again changed to 'Junk'.

Page 16, panel 1: 'Junkion' becomes 'Junk'.

Page 16, panel 3: 'Junkion' is amended to 'Junk'.

Page 17, panel 3: 'Wreckgar' is changed to 'Wreck-Gar'.

Page 17, panel 4: 'Meet your end, Galvatron' is changed to 'Meet your end, Cyclonus'.

Page 19, panel 7: 'Sweeps' becomes 'Scourge'.

Page 20, panel 3: 'Junkion' is changed to 'Junk'.

Page 22, panel 1: Again, 'Junkion' is switched to 'Junk'.

Page 22, panel 3: 'Wreckgar' is changed to 'Wreck-Gar'.

Page 22, panel 6: For the final time, 'Junkion' is changed to 'Junk'.

Page 22, panel 9: The 'next issue' caption is changed to a speech, designed to lead into the newly-created epilogue: 'Does that answer your question, torturer?'

Roll Call:

Autobots: Silverbolt, Air Raid, Fireflight, Skydive, Slingshot, Superion, Blaster, Omega Supreme, Ultra Magnus, Kup, Rodimus Prime, Wreck-Gar and Sky Lynx.

Decepticons: Soundwave, Blast Off, Galvatron, Cyclonus, Scourge and Astrotrain.

Plus various unnamed Junkions, Quintessons and Sharkticons.

Although they had been in the comic adaptation of *The Transformers: The Movie*, this was the first time that the Quintessons and Sharkticons had appeared in the comic proper. This was also the first American sighting of Ultra Magnus, Rodimus Prime, Wreck-Gar, Galvatron, Cyclonus and Scourge outside of the movie adaptation.

Data File: Dave Elliott (artist)

Elliott was another artist to have worked on both the UK and US *The Transformers* comics. His other credits include *Doctor Who Magazine*, *2000 AD* and *Viz*. He later co-founded Radical Comics, and was the editor of their *Hercules* title that was later adapted into a blockbuster movie (Brett Ratner, 2014).

Review:
'The Big Broadcast of 2006' wasn't exactly a shining example of the *Transformers* cartoon show, but like all episodes of that series, the exceptional performances of the voice cast helped inject a bit of urgency, sharpness and indeed comedy timing into proceedings. The comic adaptation lacks any sort of sparkle whatsoever; the colourful cartoon episode is turned into a drab sludge. 1/5

[44] THE COSMIC CARNIVAL
US#44, 'September 1988' (published May 1988), 22 pages.

British reprint: UK#178, 13 August 1988 (Part 1), 11 pages; UK#179, 20 August 1988 (Part 2), 11 pages.

As stated above, the UK comic amended the running order of the American stories; this story was printed prior to [43] 'The Big Broadcast of 2006'.

Credits:
Bob Budiansky (script); Frank Springer (pencils); Danny Bulandi (inks); Nel Yomtov (colours); Bill Oakley (letters); Don Daley (editor); Tom DeFalco (editor-in-chief); Frank Springer and Dave Hunt (cover). **UK:** Stephen Baskerville (cover, UK#178); Jerry Paris (cover, UK#179).

Plot:
Goldbug and the Powermasters are aboard the *Steelhaven, en route* back to the Moon to pick up the Autobots stranded there. They intercept a transmission from the Cosmic Carnival, 'the greatest show in the galaxy', an interplanetary circus. Optimus Prime's interest is piqued when he notices that the Autobot Sky Lynx is listed as one of the performers, so the *Steelhaven* makes a detour to investigate.

It transpires that, when ferrying the human Spacehiker children to safety, Sky Lynx was cajoled into visiting the carnival with them. Unable to pay their entrance fee, Sky Lynx and the children signed a contract, agreeing to work as performers at the show until such time as their debt was paid. However, the Autobot and the children have been working at the circus for a while now, and are still nowhere near earning their freedom.

Optimus Prime and Goldbug team up with Berko, another human working at the carnival, and conspire to rescue Sky Lynx and the children during a performance. The carnival's cruel boss, Mr Big Top, is trapped in a cage by Berko and becomes an exhibit in his own circus.

Notes:
This story picks up on a number of ongoing plot threads from previous issues. Goldbug and the new Powermasters are still aboard the *Steelhaven*, having previously left the planet Nebulos in [42] 'People Power'. They are heading back to the Moon to pick up the Autobots who were stranded there in [41] 'Totaled'. The fates of Sky Lynx and the

Spacehikers are finally addressed, their last appearance having come in [36] 'Spacehikers'; once Blaster surrendered to Grimlock at the end of that story, Sky Lynx and the children were allowed to go free. Goldbug refers to some 'war-weary Autobots who left Cybertron to go to your peaceful world [Nebulos]', a description of Fortress Maximus's voyage in [HDM1] 'Ring of Hate'.

The fate of the Spacehikers recalls an episode of *The Twilight Zone*, 'People Are Alike All Over' (1960), in which a human space traveller (played by Roddy McDowall) is placed in a zoo on the planet Mars, his cage decorated to look like the interior of an Earth house. The final twist, in which Mr Big Top is incarcerated within his own zoo, recalls the conclusion of the film *Freaks* (Tod Browning, 1932), in which a would-be murderess is reduced to the status of a sideshow exhibit.

UK Changes:
Page 1, panel 1: credits replaced, artwork extended upwards.
Page 3, panel 2: Don Perlin's tag is omitted.
Page 4, panel 1: the reference to issue 41 is changed to 175. Perlin's sign-off is again deleted.
Page 12, panel 1: 'favor' becomes 'favour'.
Page 12, panel 2: the reference to issue #36 is changed to issue #144. Don Perlin's tag is removed.

Roll Call:
Autobots: Optimus Prime, Goldbug, Sky Lynx, Joyride, Slapdash and Getaway.

Other: The Spacehikers (Allan, Jed, Sammy and Robin) and **Berko**.

Nebulans: Hi-Q, Hotwire, Lube and Rev. The Nebulan Hi-Test is also featured (in a flashback scene), but this would seem to be an art error.

A number of Decepticons (including possibly Starscream, Skywarp and Thundercracker) appear in flashback, though none is clearly recognisable.

Review:
This is fun and frothy, the production team getting the most out of the 'alien circus' setting – the visuals are a delight, and some of the one-liners are brilliant: 'No, son! That stuff'll rot your fangs!' However, the story is pretty inconsequential in the grand scheme of things; if it weren't for the return of Sky Lynx and the Spacehikers, it's one that could easily be skipped.

A detour, then, but a charming one nonetheless. 3/5

US Advertisements, Part 5: Books and Comics (I-Z)
A list of all advertisements for books and comics, plus comic retailers, that appeared in the American *The Transformers* comic, listed alphabetically from I-Z:

Inferno (a cross-title Marvel epic) – US#47
J&S Comics (retailer) – US#5, 9, 13, 17, 22, 28, 30, 35, 42, 51; HDM#1
Lazer Tag Official Game Handbook – US#29
Marvel Comics (various titles) – US#18, 56

Marvel Comics subscription offer – US#1-6, 8-13, 15-49, 51-56, 58-80; MOV#1-3; GIJ#1-3; HDM#1-4
Mile High Comics (retailer) – US#1, 4, 8-10, 12, 14-15, 17, 21-22, 26, 28, 32-33, 44, 53, 57, 78; GIJ#3; HDM#2
'Nam, The – US#27
NBA Hoops Collect-A-Books – US#76
New England Comics (retailer) – US#27, 31, 33, 38, 40, 42, 45, 52; GIJ#4; HDM#3
New Universe, The (collective term for several Marvel titles, launched 1986) – US#16, 19-21, 25-26, 38
Nth Man: The Ultimate Ninja – US#55
Official Marvel Comics Try-Out Book, The – US#36-38; HDM#4
Peter Porker, the Spectacular Spider-Ham – US#10
Pro Set NFL Collect-A-Books – US#73-74
Punisher War Journal, The – US#52
Quasar – US#57
Science Fiction Book Club, The (mail order retail scheme) – US#71, 78-79
Secret Wars II – US#6-9, 11, 13
Sleeze Brothers, The – US#58
Star Brand, The – HDM#4
Star Comics (Marvel's junior imprint) – US#4-6, 8, 13-14, 16, 18, 20
Star Wars: Droids – US#17
Sword of Solomon Kane, The – US#8
Swords of the Swashbucklers (graphic novel) – US#4
Time Machine (book series) – US#31
War, The – US#52
West Coast Avengers – US#50
West Coast Avengers/Vision and the Scarlet Witch crossover – US#9
Westfield Comics (retailer) – US#16, 23, 31, 45, 55; MOV#1
Wheels and Wings (partwork/periodical) – US#64-66
X-Factor – US#12

[44.1] SPACE PIRATES!
- UK#182, 10 September 1988 (Part 1), 11 pages
- UK#183, 17 September 1988 (Part 2), 11 pages
- UK#184, 24 September 1988 (Part 3), 11 pages
- UK#185, 1 October 1988 (Part 4), 11 pages
- UK#186, 8 October 1988 (Part 5), 11 pages
- UK#187, 15 October 1988 (Part 6), 11 pages

Credits:
Simon Furman (script); Dan Reed (art, parts 1-2); Dougie Braithwaite (pencils, parts 3-4); Dave Harwood (inks, parts 3-4); Lee Sullivan (art, parts 5-6); Euan Peters (colours, parts 1-5); Steve White (colours, part 6); Gary 'Glib' Gilbert (letters, parts 1, 3-6); Annie Halfacree (letters, part 2); Lee Sullivan (cover, UK#182); Andrew Wildman (covers, UK#183, 185-187); Jerry Paris (cover, UK#184).

Glib was erroneously credited as the letterer for all six parts; a correction and apology was printed in the letters page of UK#197.

314

Plot:

2008. The planet Quintesson is dying. When the native Quintessons' plan to colonise other worlds falls through, after a vital data canister is lost to them, they initiate plan B – a convoluted plan to claim the planet Cybertron as their own.

The first phase takes the form of an attack on Autobot City on Earth. Upon realising that the city has been besieged, the Autobots leave a skeleton crew on Cybertron while the bulk of their forces travel to Earth in a bid to save the city. Rodimus Prime arrives on the scene but is tricked into parting with the Matrix, which is quickly seized by the Quintesson General Ghyrik. Now shorn of the Matrix, Rodimus Prime reverts to his smaller, weaker, Hot Rod form.

The second phase sees the Quintessons lead the Decepticons into a trap on Cybertron. With the Autobot and Decepticon forces now otherwise occupied, the path is clear for the Quintessons to invade.

However, their assault on Earth hits a snag: Hot Rod awakens Metroplex – a giant Autobot who has lain dormant for years, hidden beneath Autobot City. Metroplex single-handedly defeats the Quintessons on Earth, and Hot Rod outwits Ghyrik to recover the Matrix.

The Quintesson forces are defeated on Cybertron also: the Autobots and Decepticons there temporarily join forces to drive the invaders away.

There's yet more bad news for the Quintessons – the data canister containing their colonisation plans is recovered by Wreck-Gar, who beams its contents to every planet in the galaxy – hundreds of alien races learn that they were also potential invasion targets, making the Quintessons very unpopular indeed.

Defeated, dishonoured and now homeless, the Quintessons evacuate their planet as it explodes. The cause of the planet's destruction: a mysterious rift in the fabric of time and space …

Notes:

Although this isn't the first UK story to be set after *The Transformers: The Movie* (others include [31.3] 'Headhunt' and [36.2] 'The Legacy of Unicron'), it is the one that arguably owes the greatest debt to that film. This is the first UK comic appearance of movie characters such as Arcee, Wheelie, Eject and Steeljaw; many of the film's locations, including Quintesson, Autobot City and Lookout Mountain, are revisited, and there are even some parallels in dialogue ('blitzing Autobot City') and action (planets destroyed; the Matrix stolen by a villain).

This story's main focus is the Quintessons and the destruction of their planet. Quintesson is experiencing an 'orbital decay', which will see it either torn apart by gravitational forces or consumed by its sun. The decay is being caused (or at least accelerated by) a rift in space and time (of which more will be revealed in [44.3] 'Dry Run' and [48.2] 'Time Wars'). The Quintessons' initial survival plan involved secret visits to alien words, gathering intelligence before picking the best candidate and invading it. These intelligence reports were sent to a communications uplink satellite, which would then correlate all the scouts' findings into a physical data canister, which would be launched through space back to the Quintesson home world. However, a cosmic storm diverted the canister to the planet of Junk, where it was retrieved by Wreck-Gar (as per [43] 'The Big Broadcast of 2006').

The Quintessons' back-up plan involved an invasion of Cybertron, something they were initially loath to do for fear of the Autobot Matrix – however the loss of the canister has now forced their hand. Many of the different Quintesson species are seen – Sharkticons, Allicons, plus the Executioner and Judge castes. Named Quintesson characters include Kledji (a large Judge, and the brains of the operation), Sevax (a smaller Judge, who commands the hunt for the canister), Ghyrik (the Executioner who leads the attack on Earth) and Jolup (another Executioner).

At the beginning of this story, Autobot City is fully intact (although a different colour than in its movie appearance), indicating that it has been fully repaired following the various attacks it suffered. The city has the ability to transform into a more armoured, weaponed-up fortress, thanks to the presence of Metroplex, a massive, city-sized Autobot buried beneath it. Metroplex has lain dormant 'for five years now', which ties in to the City's initial foundation in 2003 (as per [A3.4] 'Ark Duty').

The Autobot and Decepticon headquarters on Cybertron are both the same as seen in previous future-set stories (such as [36.2] 'The Legacy of Unicron'). One of the ill-fated Autobots who dies in Autobot City during the Quintesson attack is named Hopper. The scenes of the deactivated Autobots strung up around the city echo similar images in [5] 'The New Order'.

A sequence in Part 6 in which Ultra Magnus and Soundwave discuss their temporary alliance pays homage to one in the 1988 graphic novel *Batman: The Killing Joke* (which was edited by Denny O'Neil, the man who coined the name 'Optimus Prime'), even down to the composition and framing of the individual panels.

Wreck-Gar plays a major part in the action here, and as with all his appearances, his speech is littered with pop-culture references:

- 'Great balls of fire!' – a reference to the 1957 hit single of the same name, recorded by Jerry Lee Lewis.
- 'L.A. Law this ain't!' – *L.A. Law* was an American-produced television drama series (1986-94).
- 'Are you suffering from a tense, nervous headache? … Nothing acts faster than Anadin!' – from a series of UK television commercials for Anadin painkiller tablets.
- 'Bite it, crunch it, chew it!' – slogan for a series of UK television commercials for Rowntree's Lion Bars (a type of chocolate bar).
- 'Tonight, on *The Clothes Show* …' – a reference to a television fashion programme broadcast in Britain from 1986.
- 'Awayday Special to the coast …' – the Awayday Special was a discounted day-return train ticket launched by British Rail in the 1970s.
- 'Must deliver a government health warning to Prime … Quintessons can seriously damage your health!' – a play on the mandatory health warnings appended to cigarette and tobacco advertisements (which were still legal in '80s Britain).
- '… they've re-scheduled the order of play' – a reference to the annual Wimbledon tennis tournament, which often fell foul of the notoriously unreliable British weather.
- 'Batten down the hatches, Jim lad' – a homage to Robert Louis Stevenson's classic novel *Treasure Island* (1881-82).
- 'Top of the pops on the Quintessons' hit-list …' *Top of the Pops* was a weekly pop music programme, broadcast in the UK from 1964 to 2006.
- '… it's still not safe to go back in the water' – a misquote of the tagline from the movie *Jaws* (Steven Spielberg, 1975).

- 'For up to 20% fewer fillings, use Gibbs SR!' – Gibbs SR was a UK toothpaste brand.
- 'Made the great escape from the Quintessons' prison ...' – *The Great Escape* (John Sturges, 1963) is a classic war film.
- '... the sweet you can eat between meals!' – advertising slogan for the Milky Way chocolate bar (not to be confused with the American confection of the same name).
- 'Frying tonight!' – a quote from the comedy film *Carry On Screaming!* (Gerald Thomas, 1966).
- 'Shot my bolt, Bernie' – Bernie was the armourer on UK crossbow-based game show *The Golden Shot* (1967-75).
- 'It'll take more than Five Alive to pep me up' – Five Alive is a fruit-flavoured soft drink.
- 'I was so impressed I bought the company!' – catchphrase of Victor Kiam, who in the '80s owned Remington, a company famous for their grooming products.
- 'The needs of the many must take precedence over the needs of the one, captain' – a reference to the film *Star Trek II: The Wrath of Khan* (Nicholas Meyer, 1982).
- 'Autobots must be warned of Quintessons' university challenge!' – *University Challenge* is a British game show (launched 1962).
- 'It'll be winner takes all' – another game show reference; *Winner Takes All* was originally broadcast 1975-88.
- 'It's time for a closedown!' – a reference to when British television stations used to cease transmitting overnight.
- 'When Bob says opportunity knocks!' – *Bob Says Opportunity Knocks* (1987-89) was a UK talent show hosted by Bob Monkhouse.
- 'We follow the Green Cross Code' – the Green Cross Code was a series of road safety instructions issued to children in the UK.
- '*Run Silent, Run Deep*' – the name of a classic submarine movie (Robert Wise, 1958).
- 'You know it makes sense' – a slogan for a series of road safety advertisements, later co-opted as a catchphrase in the sitcom *Only Fools and Horses* (1981-2003).
- 'Why slo-mo ... when you can Flymo!' – advertising slogan for the Flymo range of lawnmowers.
- 'Need extra-strength Daz' – Daz is a laundry detergent sold in Britain.
- 'Reaches the parts of engines other powders can't stir' – a (badly mangled) version of the advertising slogan for Heineken beer, which allegedly 'refreshes the parts other beers cannot reach.'
- 'Points mean prizes!' – a catchphrase of British entertainer Bruce Forsyth, when he was the host of game show *Play Your Cards Right* (1980-2003).
- 'Oh, she flies through the air with the greatest of ease!' – lyrics from the song *The Daring Young Man on the Flying Trapeze* (published 1867), famously sung in the film *It Happened One Night* (Frank Capra, 1934).
- 'I'm afraid I'm going to have to offer that to the other side!' – a line often spoken by game show hosts when offering a question to another team after it's answered incorrectly by the original recipient. Shows of this format include the aforementioned *University Challenge*.
- 'Today, the *Wish You Were Here* team visits a small asteroid in the Delta Six quadrant' – *Wish You Were Here ...?* was a British television series about holidays and travel, running between 1974 and 2003.

- 'We are not alone' – tagline of the movie *Close Encounters of the Third Kind* (Steven Spielberg, 1977).
- 'Your verdict, Brian?' 'Over the moon, Jimmy' – a reference to *The Big Match*, a UK television programme about association football (1968-92), hosted by (amongst others), Brian Moore and Jimmy Hill.
- 'The Junkion World Service is ready to transmit' – an allusion to the BBC World Service. Launched in 1932 and transmitted from London, it's the world's largest radio broadcast service.
- '*That's Life!*' – the name of a British television magazine programme that ran between 1973 and 1994.

Transforming *The Transformers*

In late 1988 it became clear that the UK *The Transformers* comic was haemorrhaging readers; the sales figure was down almost 40% from its 1986 peak. So it was decided to make an attempt to stem the flow.

Around the time of 'Space Pirates', a number of changes were made, constituting a mini-relaunch of sorts, in an attempt to renew interest in the title. The most notable innovation was a cosmetic one: from UK#183, the Transformation editorial page was completely revamped – the previous colourful design being replaced by a stark white look. While distinctive, this was far less welcoming and attractive.

Another change was to alter the regular letter-answerer character. After more than a hundred issues, from UK#184 the popular Autobot Grimlock was replaced by the relatively obscure Decepticon Powermaster Dreadwind, whose responses were brusquer, and on occasion even slightly condescending.

The back-up strip was changed also. Hasbro were desperately trying to plug their new range of action figures, the Visionaries. As with Action Force before it, Visionaries struggled to catch on in Britain, and its own comic title was cancelled after six issues. This didn't deter Hasbro or Marvel UK, who ensured that the Visionaries were featured within *The Transformers* comic, and even given a regular billing on the front cover.

As a further incentive to readers, a number of prizes and free gifts were given away. UK#184 offered the large Powermaster Optimus Prime toy as a competition prize, and UK#185 went even further, offering up the even larger Trypticon figure, which did not get an official British release (at least, not until a 2016 reissue came along). UK#186 and 187 contained freebies (Action Force sticker books and stickers), and UK#188 promised a free can of Tango (a fruit-flavoured soft drink) for every reader. UK#189 ran a competition in conjunction with Ready Brek cereal. This meant that there was either a free gift or a prize given away for six consecutive issues.

Frailty, Thy Name Is ...

This is the first *The Transformers* comic other than the movie adaptation to feature the female Autobot, Arcee.

Transformers was an oddity amongst boys' toy lines, in that there were no female characters available to buy. Masters of the Universe had Teela, GI Joe had Scarlett and the Baroness, and *Star Wars* had Princess Leia. The introduction of the Arcee character, then, was a chance to right that particular wrong, to present a strong female character in a franchise dominated by males, and to act as an audience relation figure, someone to inspire the children reading the comic, for them to look up to.

And then we got 'Space Pirates'.

Arcee's role in her comic debut is troubling, to say the least. She's partly to blame for the Quintesson attack on Autobot City, deserting her scouting post simply because she's bored. She's then used as a pawn by the Quintessons, and unwittingly forms part of their ruse to steal the Matrix from Rodimus Prime. She's a weak, flawed character, as demonstrated by the opening splash page of UK#186, in which Hot Rod is almost dragging her down the corridor and away from danger. Her first priority is clearly her unrequited love for Rodimus Prime. Sample quote: 'When he was Hot Rod, he and I were very good friends. I miss him so ...'

So, rather than being the equal of her peers, she's defined solely by her inadequacies as a warrior, and by her relationship to Rodimus Prime – a woeful introduction for what should have been a breakthrough character. On the final page of UK#183 she's even treated as a sex object, artist Dan Reed's drawing of her posterior having to be seen to be believed.

So is there any way we can justify this depiction? Well, Arcee wouldn't be the first Autobot to flagrantly defy orders and leave her post – Hot Rod did the same in [A3.4] 'Ark Duty'. Besides, the Quintessons pretty much annihilated the Autobot forces on Earth – it would have made little difference to the end result, anyway, had Arcee remained standing guard. Furthermore, she isn't the first Autobot to be used as bait in a Decepticon trap – see, for example, [31.1] 'Worlds Apart'. Neither is she the first Autobot to be besotted by a love-interest – Skids in [20] 'Showdown' and Sludge in [20.1] 'In the National Interest' being two memorable precedents.

But, while it could be argued that she's getting the same rough ride as some of her male counterparts, it still leaves a bitter taste in the mouth. In the age of Ripley from the *Alien* franchise, Cheetara from *Thundercats*, Sarah Connor from the *Terminator* films and of course *She-Ra: Princess of Power*, there's simply no excuse for having the one and only female Transformer be presented to impressionable kids as a sexy, pink cry-baby.

Roll Call:
Autobots: Wheeljack, Trailbreaker, Grimlock, Smokescreen, Air Raid, Skydive, Slingshot, Blades, Blaster, Cosmos, Beachcomber, Perceptor, Ultra Magnus, Springer, Hot Rod, Kup, Blurr, Rodimus Prime, Wreck-Gar, Chase, Wideload, Scattershot, Nosecone, Strafe, **Arcee, Wheelie, Eject, Rewind, Ramhorn, Steeljaw** and **Metroplex**.

Additionally, shown strung up at the end of part three there's an Autobot who's difficult to identify. He's coloured like Brawn (orange and green), yet doesn't look anything like him.

Decepticons: Soundwave, Ravage, Scrapper, Mixmaster, Onslaught, Blast Off, Vortex, Motormaster, Wildrider, Ramjet, Thrust, Dirge, Astrotrain, Blitzwing, Razorclaw, Rampage and Hun-Gurrr.

Other: Unicron (flashback only).

Data File: Dougie Braithwaite (artist)
Braithwaite worked his way up the ranks, beginning at Marvel UK before moving onto *2000 AD* and then to Marvel and DC Comics in America. His CV is an illustrious one, and contains titles such as *Doctor Who Magazine, Captain America, Judge Dredd, Green Lantern, The Incredible Hulk, Justice* and *Thor*.

Review:
A real curate's egg, 'Space Pirates' gets as much wrong as it gets right. In places it's brilliant – the Wreck-Gar/Wheelie sub-plot is hilarious, and the Quintessons' convoluted plan is an excellent example of how to construct a plot. There's a lot of emotion too, as Hot Rod, Arcee and even Soundwave all go through the wringer. Intended as an epic to rival [20.2] 'Target: 2006' and [36.2] 'The Legacy of Unicron', it's nothing if not big – the fate of whole worlds is in the balance.

However, there are severe flaws in the execution. As already discussed, the depiction of Arcee is ill-judged. The battles for Autobot City and Cybertron are fought by just fifty Transformers in total, a far cry from the hundreds involved in [41] 'Totaled' and [36.2] 'The Legacy of Unicron'. The main problem, though, is the villains – the Quintessons are one-dimensional, moustache-twirling tyrants, undone by their own stupidity. It's hard to work up any enthusiasm for this story, when the main threat is a race of beings so utterly inept that they can be outmanoeuvred by comedy characters such as Wheelie and Wreck-Gar. 2/5

[44.2] FIREBUG!
UK#188, 22 October 1988, 11 pages

Also reprinted in the 1991 *Transformers Annual*

Credits:
Simon Furman (plot); Dan Abnett (script); Jeff Anderson (art); Euan Peters (colours); Tom Frame (letters); Jeff Anderson (cover).

Plot:
Three Autobots from Cybertron – Sandstorm, Broadside and Inferno – arrive on Earth with the intention of setting up a base. Their project is interrupted when they become aware of a fire in a nearby town.

The three Autobots attempt to put out the flames, but this is no ordinary fire – it's being caused by an alien Firebug. After some initial trouble, the three Autobots capture the creature and transport it to a safe location: the hot planet Mercury, where the Firebug can live in freedom without risking any more lives.

Notes:
The cause of all the trouble in this story is a Firebug, a former native of the planet Furnacia, which has since burnt itself out. The species is now virtually extinct, after an incident on the ice planet Thessin.

The town seen here is unnamed, but it could well be Vallemont, which according to [6] 'The Worse of Two Evils' is located extremely near Mount St Hilary. This is Inferno's first appearance in a present-day story since [8.1] 'Decepticon Dam-Busters' (although his future self was sighted in [36.2] 'The Legacy of Unicron', and he also appeared in the annual story [A1.2] 'Missing in Action'). It's likely that he was amongst those Autobots damaged by Shockwave at the end of [4] 'The Last Stand', and that he was only recently repaired by Ratchet and First Aid (like many other long-term injured Autobots who returned to the ranks in [41] 'Totaled').

Sandstorm implies that his Earth alternative modes are new ('These Earthen forms Xaaron prepared for us are really neat'), even though he assumed helicopter mode in [20.2] 'Target: 2006'. (It's possible that Sandstorm had reverted to his original Cybertronian form following the events of [20.2] 'Target: 2006', and that he had only recently been refitted to assume Earth modes again.)

The Firebug's arrival on Earth goes unnoticed by either NASA or Wright-Patterson Air Force Base (home of the Air Force Research Laboratory) near Dayton, Ohio. The Autobot spacecraft lands in a grassy area and turns invisible via the use of a 'scan cloak'; Sandstorm then jokes about remembering where they parked. This scene echoes a near-identical moment in the film *Star Trek IV: The Voyage Home* (Leonard Nimoy, 1986).

Wrecked Continuity
The adventures of the Wreckers, the Cybertron-based Autobot strike force, are difficult to place into chronological order. [36] 'Spacehikers' and [41] 'Totaled' depicted some of their number as being part of the *Ark* crew, but according to [40.2] 'Legion of the Lost', they were on Cybertron at this time, fighting zombies. So how can we reconcile these two accounts?

Here's one reading of events, which relies on the assumption that some stories occur in a different order from that in which they were published:

- The Wreckers arrive on Earth, via their usual teleport technology. While there, they temporarily team up with Grimlock's forces on the *Ark*.
- [36] 'Spacehikers': Some of the Wreckers, including Twin Twist and Sandstorm, are aboard the *Ark* as Grimlock hunts down Blaster.
- The events of [37] 'Toy Soldiers', [38] 'Trial by Fire', [39] 'The Desert Island of Space', [39.1] 'Salvage' and [40] 'Pretender of the Throne' occur, in that order. Then:
- [41] 'Totaled': The Wreckers travel with the rest of the *Ark* crew to the moon. Sandstorm is seen amongst the Autobot ranks (and also Broadside, but his appearance was edited out of the UK printing of that story).
- During their time aboard the *Ark*, the Wreckers meet and befriend the Autobot Inferno, who had been one of the original crew of the *Ark* four million years ago, and he joins their ranks.
- [44.2] 'Firebug': After the *Ark* crew are rescued from the moon, at some point after [44] 'The Cosmic Carnival' but before [47] 'Club Con', Sandstorm, Broadside and their new friend Inferno set up a base on Earth. After this adventure, Inferno stays behind at this new base while Sandstorm and Broadside (and Twin Twist) briefly return to Cybertron.
- This allows all the Wreckers to be back on Cybertron for the events of [40.1] 'City of Fear', [40.2] 'Legion of the Lost', [40.3] 'Meltdown', [40.4] 'Deadly Games' and [40.5] 'Wrecking Havoc'. After all this, Sandstorm and Broadside rejoin Inferno in time for [48.1] 'Cold Comfort and Joy'.

Roll Call:
Autobots: Inferno, Sandstorm and Broadside. Emirate Xaaron is also mentioned.

Review:
A decent one-shot adventure with a sweet ending, but it's the very definition of a filler

story. 2/5

The 'NEXT' Box, Part 3
More slogans from the 'NEXT' box that appeared in the UK *The Transformers* comic – issues UK#133-198.

- UK#133: [Main strip] ... ? [Headmasters back-up] Broken glass!
- UK#134: [Main strip] Grudge match! [Headmasters back-up] Calling ... Cybertron!
- UK#135: [Main strip] True confessions! [Headmasters back-up] Nebulans ... transform!
- UK#136: [Main strip] Ladies' night! [Headmasters back-up] What price victory?!
- UK#137: [Main strip] Sisters in arms! [Headmasters back-up] Love and steel!
- UK#138: [Main strip] Used Autobots! [Headmasters back-up] The bubble bursts!
- UK#139: [Main strip] Auction stations! [Headmasters back-up] The Decepticon Headmasters!
- UK#140: [Main strip] Child's play! [Headmasters back-up] Goin' up!
- UK#141: [Main strip] Off the rails! [Headmasters back-up] Brothers in armour!
- UK#142: [Main strip] Space hikers! [Headmasters back-up] No mercy!
- UK#143: [Main strip] Judge, jury ... and executioner? [Headmasters back-up] Targetmasters!
- UK#144: [Main strip] Stargazing! [Headmasters back-up] Earthbound!
- UK#145: Junk culture!
- UK#146: Shock tactics!
- UK#147: Total war!
- UK#148: The hard fall!
- UK#149: Mind games!
- UK#150: In fact – to be concluded!
- UK#151: Enemy action!
- UK#152: Firebathing!
- UK#153: Toy soldiers!
- UK#154: Throttlebot hunt!
- UK#155: Headmasters – on Earth!
- UK#156: Battle beneath the Earth!
- UK#157: Hostage!
- UK#158: Dead in space?
- UK#159: Salvage!
- UK#160: The greatest fear of all!
- UK#161: Pretender to the throne!
- UK#162: Pretenders – on the rampage!
- UK#163: City of fear!
- UK#164: Legion of the lost!
- UK#165: Legion of the lost! (repeated caption, possibly due to a technical error)
- UK#166: Friend or fiend!
- UK#167: Meltdown!
- UK#168: Mayhem!
- UK#169: Deadly games!
- UK#170: Game on!
- UK#171: Wrecking havoc!
- UK#172: Smalltown nightmare!
- UK#173: Totalled!

- UK#174: Moon madness!
- UK#175: People power!
- UK#176: Master-blaster!
- UK#177: The Cosmic Carnival!
- UK#178: Ring for action!
- UK#179: The big broadcast!
- UK#180: The whole truth!
- UK#181: Space pirates!
- UK#182: Plan of attack!
- UK#183: Pursuit!
- UK#184: The tender trap!
- UK#185: The awakening!
- UK#186: The end of the world!
- UK#187: Firebug!
- UK#188: Dry run!
- UK#189: Monstercon from Mars!
- UK#190: Contract breaker!
- UK#191: Cash and carnage!
- UK#192: Hell on wheels!
- UK#193: Club Con!
- UK#194: Tape scrape!
- UK#195: The flames of Boltax!
- UK#196: Up goes Underbase!
- UK#197: Cold comfort and joy!
- UK#198: Time wars!

[44.3] DRY RUN!
UK#189, 29 October 1988, 11 pages

Credits:
Simon Furman (plot); Dan Abnett (script); Jeff Anderson (pencils); Cam Smith (inks); Euan Peters (colours); Tom Frame (letters); Jeff Anderson (cover).

Plot:
The present day. With the hypnotised Megatron now completely under his control, Shockwave plans an attempt on Galvatron's life – however, he still isn't sure if his puppet is up to the job.

Cyclonus accidentally lets slip that, twenty years in the future, he and Cyclonus will kill Shockwave. Calculating that their deaths in the here and now might prevent his own demise in the future, Shockwave sees this as an ideal opportunity to test Megatron in proper battle conditions.

Megatron brutally attacks the two Targetmasters, who are hesitant to fight back – if Megatron is killed twenty years too early, it might have serious repercussions for their own futures. Scourge manages to escape, but both Cyclonus and Nightstick are brutally murdered.

Shockwave is satisfied that Megatron is finally ready to take on Galvatron. Meanwhile, Cyclonus's death – twenty years before he is created – causes a rift to open in the fabric of time and space …

Notes:

This story sees many ongoing plot threads come to a head. Shockwave and Galvatron became enemies in [36.3] 'Enemy Action', which is also where Shockwave began formulating his plan to use Megatron to assassinate the future Decepticon. Megatron was recovered and hypnotised in [39.1] 'Salvage'; Scourge and Cyclonus joined forces with the present-day Shockwave in [40.5] 'Wrecking Havoc'. There's a reference to Shockwave's future death in [36.2] 'The Legacy of Unicron', and an oblique reference to Death's Head's participation in that killing ('We, er, had help last time.')

The rift caused by Cyclonus's demise is the same one that resulted in the destruction of the Quintesson planet in [44.1] 'Space Pirates'. Megatron's training involves him battling against a Facsimile Construct built to resemble Galvatron (similar to those used to train the Wreckers in [20.2] 'Target: 2006'). The Megatron seen in this story is in fact the clone Megatron introduced in [29.1] 'Ancient Relics', but nobody knows this yet (not even the writers).

Galvatron's showdown with the clone Megatron would eventually happen within the pages of the 1989 *The Transformers Annual*, in the story [A4.2] 'Altered Image'.

Time Slip?

The mechanics of time travel (at least, the way in which it's presented within *The Transformers*) have already been covered in the notes to [27.1] 'Wanted: Galvatron – Dead or Alive', but this story poses a couple of questions that put those theories to the test.

'To preserve my life … I must end yours!'

Shockwave appears to be under the impression that he can prevent his death in the future by killing Scourge and Cyclonus in the present. That's clearly not the case, as from their perspective, Cyclonus and Scourge have already done the deed. Shockwave would be killing them after they have already performed the act.

Another point to note is that Cyclonus and Scourge are from an alternate future that, thanks to all the time travelling and rewriting of history that's been going on, will not now come to pass from the perspective of those living in the present day. However, Shockwave is unaware of any of this (perhaps due to his absence during the events of [20.2] 'Target: 2006').

'If I kill him now, I may cease to exist!'

Scourge thinks that, by killing Megatron in the present, it will radically change the chain of events that led to his own creation in 2006. What he doesn't know is that those events have *already* been drastically altered, but thanks to the fail-safes built in to the time travel device, Scourge himself is immune to such changes, and his own future remains intact. He's also ignorant of the fact that this isn't the real Megatron. However, as he himself admits, 'I can't know for sure'. Rather than place his life in the hands of his own tenuous grasp of temporal mechanics, he decides to play safe and flee the scene.

Roll Call:

Decepticons: Shockwave, Galvatron (or rather, a replica thereof), Cyclonus, Scourge and Clone Megatron.

Nebulans: Nightstick and Fracas.

Data File: Tom Frame (letterer)
Frame was best known for his work on *2000 AD*, on which he worked from 1977 until his death in 2006. He contributed to strips such as *Judge Dredd* (including classic stories 'The Day the Law Died' and 'The Judge Child'), *Judge Anderson*, *Strontium Dog*, *Rogue Trooper* and *A.B.C. Warriors*.

Review:
A tightly-plotted, pivotal story that manages to fit an awful lot into just eleven pages. As well as setting up two upcoming adventures, [A4.2] 'Altered Image' and [48.2] 'Time Wars', it also memorably sees the deaths of Cyclonus and Nightstick.

Nightstick's death is all the more impactful because it's underplayed – there's no screaming or blood, just a faintly-ridiculous 'krikt' sound effect as he's crushed to death. It's just a single panel, but this is one of those stories where every panel is important. 5/5

[45] MONSTERCON FROM MARS!
US#45, 'October 1988' (published June 1988), 22 pages.

British reprint: UK#190, 5 November 1988 (Part 1), 11 pages; UK#191, 12 November 1988 (Part 2), 11 pages.

Credits:
Bob Budiansky (script); José Delbo (breakdowns); Dave Hunt (finishes); Nel Yomtov (colours); Bill Oakley (letters); Don Daley (editor); Tom DeFalco (editor-in-chief); Bob Budiansky and Dave Hunt (cover). **UK:** Stephen Baskerville (cover, UK#190); Art Wetherell and Stephen Baskerville (cover, UK#191).

Plot:
Sent to Earth to secure a supply of fuel for Scorponok's group of Decepticons, the Pretender Skullgrin, disguised in his monster shell, initially causes fear and panic. He is approached by film director and studio owner Rollie Friendly to appear in a new movie. As he is to be paid in fuel, Skullgrin figures that starring in motion pictures will be an ideal way of completing his mission.

Circuit Breaker, meanwhile, has been watching Skullgrin's rise to fame with interest. Suspicious of the beast, she wonders why he's so insistent on being paid in fuel, and also muses that he is the same size as a Transformer.

Circuit Breaker follows the film crew to a shoot taking place at the Grand Canyon. There, Skullgrin lowers his guard and exits his shell, revealing himself to be a Decepticon. Her suspicions confirmed, Circuit Breaker swoops in for the kill.

Rollie Friendly is still filming the action, and offers to make Circuit Breaker a celebrity, just as he's done with Skullgrin. Circuit Breaker, unwilling to be used in such a fashion, breaks off her attack and flies away.

Notes:
Skullgrin is sent to Earth by Scorponok on a mission to establish a secret fuel depot. This is our first sighting of Scorponok's group of Decepticons (as opposed to Ratbat's

faction) since [40] 'Pretender to the Throne'. In exchange for fuel, Skullgrin signs a contract with Friendly Films International, who appear to specialise in B-movies such as *Monster from Mars* and *Creepozoids of the Crab Nebula*. (There is a real-world film named *Creepozoids* (David DeCoteau, 1987), which is *exactly* the sort this story seems to be parodying.)

Skullgrin first comes to public attention when he is mistaken for Bigfoot, a mythical creature said to inhabit the forests of North America, and photographs are printed in *The Inquirer*, a (fictional) tabloid newspaper. After signing for Friendly Films, Skullgrin makes the cover of *People* (cf [4] 'The Last Stand'), *Time* (a weekly news magazine, first published 1923) and *Newsweek* (another news magazine, launched 1933). Skullgrin's fuel of choice is Blackrock gasoline (a brand owned by entrepreneur G B Blackrock, introduced in [5] 'The New Order').

There are a number of references to the film *King Kong* (Merian C Cooper and Ernest B Schoedsack, 1933), which also revolves around an ambitious film director determined to film a monster that becomes infatuated with an actress. Another plot point in *King Kong*, where the giant ape confuses cameras for weapons, is neatly subverted here: 'Put the camera down, Ralph, he thinks it's a weapon!' 'Fleshlings insult me! I know that is camera, not weapon!' This story also shares some plot ideas with the *Transformers* cartoon episode {2-39} 'Hoist Goes Hollywood'.

This story sees the final appearance of the Spacehiker children who made their debut in [35] 'Child's Play' (comic), as they are finally returned to Earth by Sky Lynx. Their full names are revealed here: Allan Silver, Samuel Wainwright, Jed Lindley and Robin Lindley. Sky Lynx mentions the Scraplets, a plague deadly to Transformer life as first seen in [29] 'Crater Critters'. Circuit Breaker is the main villain of this story; it's her first appearance (barring flashbacks) since [23] 'Decepticon Graffiti'. Once again, she recalls the attack by Shockwave that paralysed her, as seen in [6] 'The Worse of Two Evils'.

There's a reference to Frank Purdue (1920-2005), the famous American businessman and poultry-farming magnate. *Beauty and the Beast* (originally *La Belle et la Bête*), the 1756 fairytale by Jeanne-Marie Leprince du Beaumont, is also mentioned, as is the movie *Star Wars* (George Lucas, 1977). Locations seen in this issue include California (home state of the Spacehikers), the Great Smoky Mountains National Park (specifically its North Carolina section) and the Grand Canyon in Arizona (a state previously visited by Transformers in [30] 'The Cure').

One of the reporters at the Skullgrin press conference (page 12, panel 5) appears to be holding an issue of *The Transformers* comic.

UK Changes:
Page 1, panel 1: credits replaced, artwork extended downwards.
Page 3, panel 4: 'favorite' becomes 'favourite'.
Page 4, panel 3: 'see last issue to find out where they've been – Don' is changed to 'see *Transformers* issues #178/179'.
Page 5, panel 9: a new caption is added to Circuit Breaker's flashback: 'issues 33/34'
Page 6, panel 3: 'favor' becomes 'favour'.
Page 9, panel 3: 'nix the close-ups!' is changed to 'forget close-ups!'
Page 9, panel 7: 'plus points' is amended to 'plus bonuses'.
Page 12, panel 1: 'favor' is again changed to 'favour'.

Roll Call:
Autobots: Sky Lynx

Decepticons: Shockwave (flashback only), Scorponok (flashback only) and Skullgrin.

Other: Circuit Breaker and the Spacehikers (Allan, Jed, Sammy and Robin).

Nebulans: Zarak (flashback only, and shown only as Scorponok's head rather than as an individual character).

Review:
In a way, this is quite clever: 'Monstercon from Mars' satirises the Hollywood B-movie industry. It does this by aping exactly what it lampoons – replete with a knowingly absurd premise, awful dialogue and some truly atrocious characterisation. There's a fine balance to be struck between being terrible and being deliberately cheesy in order to make a point, and it works on that basis.

The problem is that it's so cynical. The directors and stars of these B-movies are portrayed as unlikeable and unprofessional, making even Skullgrin seem sympathetic by comparison. The comedy here is constantly underpinned by a layer of bitterness that seems almost savage in its dismissal of the low-budget horror genre.

A story that's admirable on a technical level, but difficult to read on any other. 1/5

TransMissions
TransMissions was the letters page that featured semi-regularly throughout the run of the American *The Transformers* comic. Not every issue had particularly notable letters; only editions of particular interest are listed below.

- US#4: The first instance of a letters page in the comic. Editor Bob Budiansky reveals that the comic will run for more than its initial four-issue run. (His claim that the series is now spectacularly popular is confirmed by readers' letters full of praise for the title.) He reveals an all-new art line-up for issue #5, featuring Vince Giarrano (*Batgirl*, *Manhunter*) and Brad Joyce. (For whatever reason, this would fail to materialise: Giarrano would never work on *The Transformers*, and Joyce would ink only US#10.)
- US#17: First mention of the forthcoming *Transformers Universe* comic series, and also of the animated movie.
- US#18: A reader asks why there are no female Transformers; editor Michael Carlin explains that one will appear in the upcoming theatrical movie, and reveals there are plans to adapt the movie into comic-book form. Elsewhere, a running joke is born: a reader explains that he was introduced to *The Transformers* comic by his cousin Shingo; Carlin asks why Shingo himself doesn't write in …
- US#19: The letters page hints at the upcoming *The Transformers/G.I. Joe* crossover comic. Also: 'We're still waiting to hear from you, Shingo.'
- US#26: First reader feedback on the movie; a sequel is suggested as a possibility.
- US#27: Reader feedback on Optimus Prime's death. 'Sorry we upset you so much.'
- US#31: There's a brilliant letter here, from a reader whose friend was diagnosed with thrombotic thrombocytopenic purpura (a blood-clotting disease). Inspired by the adventures of the Transformers, the kid pulled through.

- US#34: There are letters praising the *Headmasters* mini-series. Don Daley replies: 'If there's a big enough demand for it, a *Headmasters* unlimited series wouldn't be out of the question.'
- US#38: A correspondent claiming to be the legendary Shingo writes in. It's a great letter, calling for better characterisation in the writing: 'Action alone will not immortalize a comic, but create an unforgettable dramatic scene and people will remember it forever.'
- US#41: The editor responds to questions about gender in Transformers: 'Most people … assume two things: first, that Transformers are either male or female, and second, that unless a character is explicitly female, the Transformer is male.' There are also two competitions – the first to find the word 'Shingo' hidden somewhere within the comic (page 10, panel 1, just beneath the uppermost crater), the second to name all the Autobots who appear on page 10, panel 2.
- US#42: It's revealed that another *Transformers Universe* comic series will begin in the summer. (This will never happen, although excerpts from the abandoned series will eventually see print within the comic proper.)
- US#43: Solution to the 'Bot Roster' competition from issue 41.
- US#44–46: A list of winners of the competitions set in issue 41.
- US#57: 'We hope to bring the UK and US continuities closer together'. (Some wishful thinking from the letters page; continuity with the UK comic post-US#57 would become more muddled than ever.)
- US#68: For the first time, a piece of reader-submitted artwork is printed on the letters page.
- US#70: A letter from one Rob Tokar, of New York City: 'I think *Transformers* stinks! Geoff Senior's artwork is the pits, and Simon Furman couldn't write a check!' The letter was actually in jest: Tokar had just been installed as the new editor of *The Transformers* comic.
- US#73: The letters page becomes a showcase for reader-submitted art.
- US#80: As it's the final issue, there are farewell letters by writer Simon Furman and colourist Nel Yomtov.

[46] CA$H AND CAR-NAGE!
US#46, 'November 1988' (published July 1988), 22 pages.

British reprint: UK#192, 19 November 1988 (Part 1), 11 pages; UK#193, 26 November 1988 (Part 2), 11 pages.

Credits:
Bob Budiansky (script); José Delbo (pencils); Danny Bulanadi (inks); Nel Yomtov (colours); Bill Oakley (letters); Don Daley (editor); Tom DeFalco (editor-in-chief); Frank Springer (cover). **UK:** Stephen Baskerville (cover, UK#192); Andrew Wildman (cover, UK#193).

Plot:
The mysterious Z Foundation hires four bounty-hunters and equips them with jamming devices that can render Transformers immobile. The Foundation sends this new team – the Roadjammers – to New York State in a bid to capture three Autobots.

The Roadjammers perform their task perfectly, successfully disabling and securing the Autobots – Backstreet, Sizzle and Fizzle. However, the Autobots realise that only the Decepticons could have known their location, and this must mean that the Z Foundation are in league with the Decepticons.

Sure enough, the Z Foundation is run by Zarak, as part of a grander scheme to get humans to attack the Autobots. Realising they have been duped, the Roadjammers reactivate their captured Autobots, and manage to escape with their lives.

Notes:
This is the second successive story to focus on Scorponok's Decepticon faction. We meet three new Decepticon Headmasters here – Fangry, Squeezeplay and Horri-Bull. (The implication is that these were among Scorponok's troops all along – ever since [HDM1] 'Ring of Hate' – but like the Pretenders before them, it's assumed they were just lurking in the background prior to their full reveal.)

This story also marks the first appearance of the Triggerbots – Backstreet, Override and Dogfight – and the first American appearance of the Sparkabots – Sizzle, Fizzle and Guzzle – and the Firecons – Sparkstalker, Flamefeather and Cindersaur. Some of these new characters are drawn to resemble closely their action figures (more so than is usual), indicating that penciller José Delbo didn't have access to any of the standard character reference material, instead having to base his drawings on the actual toys.

Locations seen here include the states of Pennsylvania and Arizona, and also New York City. The three Autobots are captured near the Shawangunk Ridge in New York State. (An editorial caption informs us that Shawangunk should be pronounced 'Shon-gum', but that's only partly true. 'Shon-gum' is a vernacular contraction that became popular in the 18th Century; the original Lenape pronunciation is closer to 'Shah-wang-gunk'. Both pronunciations are valid.)

Cybertron is again said to be 'several dozen' light-years from Earth, as per [29] 'Crater Critters'. (Other stories, including [36] 'Spacehikers', suggest that the distance is significantly greater.) This is the final appearance of the space bridge, which was introduced in [18] 'The Bridge to Nowhere'.

The 'jammer' devices are similar in function to the Transfixatron weapon from the cartoon episode {2-07} 'The Autobot Run'.

UK Notes:
British audiences had already seen the Sparkabots in a number of stories, including [36.3] 'Enemy Action' and [40.4] 'Deadly Games', meaning that some of the dialogue had to be altered to reflect that they had visited Earth before.

UK Changes:
Page 1, panel 1: credits replaced; artwork extended upwards.
Page 7, panel 2: Don Perlin's tag is excised from the caption.
Page 10, panel 6: 'center' is changed to 'centre'.
Page 10, panel 8: numerous changes, as follows:

- Backstreet's line: 'I don't know, but there's no going back – the bridge is already disappearing behind us' is now reattributed to Fizzle, and reads: 'Earth, Backstreet, a small carbon-based planet!'
- Fizzle's line: 'This matches the description of the planet where many other Autobots have gone – Earth' is altered to 'We came here once before to battle

Galvatron.*'

- Sizzle's speech bubble is changed to an editorial caption: '*in issues 152/153'.

Page 10, panel 9: 'Maybe we'll find one of 'em' becomes 'Maybe we'll find other Autobots'.

Roll Call:
Autobots: Sizzle, Fizzle, Guzzle, **Backstreet, Dogfight** and **Override**.

Decepticons: Scorponok, Sparkstalker, Flamefeather, Cindersaur, **Fangry, Horri-Bull** and **Squeezeplay**.

Nebulans: Zarak, **Brisko, Kreb** and **Lokos**.

Data File: Danny Bulanadi (artist)
Inker Danny Bulanadi is unique amongst the contributors to *The Transformers* comic, in that he also worked (as a storyboard artist) on the animated cartoon show. His other comic credits include *Captain America, Fantastic Four* and *The Punisher*. In the field of animation, he also provided storyboards for *Johnny Quest* and *Extreme Ghostbusters*.

Review:
This is less a fully-fledged story and more a means to an end. Its foremost aim is to introduce twelve new Transformers to American audiences, as well as a new human team, the Roadjammers. These bounty-hunters are obviously being set up as recurring villains – but oddly all the build-up will ultimately go to waste, because they will never be seen again.

The introductions are generally well handled, and the mystery of the Z-Foundation is a nice twist, but there's nothing here to get super-excited about. 2/5

[47] CLUB CON! (THE UNDERBASE SAGA! Part One)
US#47, 'December 1988' (published August 1988), 20 pages.

British reprint: UK#194, 3 December 1988 (Part 1), 10 pages; UK#195, 10 December 1988 (Part 2), 10 pages.

Credits:
Bob Budiansky (script); José Delbo (pencils); Dave Hunt (inks); Nel Yomtov (colours); Bill Oakley (letters); Don Daley (editor); Tom DeFalco (editor-in-chief); Bob Budiansky and Kevin Nowlan (cover). **UK:** Bob Budiansky and Kevin Nowlan (cover, UK#194 – re-coloured and mirrored version of US cover); Stephen Baskerville (cover, UK#195).

Plot:
A few hundred years ago, the Autobots on Cybertron detected something headed toward Earth. Realising that this was the likely location of the *Ark* and its crew, the Autobots sent two cassette Transformers – Raindance and Grandslam – to the planet in an attempt to warn Optimus Prime of the mysterious arrival.

In the present day, the Decepticons have relocated their island base to the Caribbean Sea, where they search the oceans for the two cassettes. As a cover for their hunt, they have marketed the island as a tourist resort – Club Con. Jessie and Blaster go undercover on the island in an attempt to find the kidnapped Buster and also work out what the Decepticons are planning.

Blaster and Jessie learn of the cassettes, and manage to steal them. However, Blaster is forced to hand them over when the Decepticons begin threatening the holidaymakers. Jessie and Blaster are forced to leave the island empty-handed ... but at least now they are aware that the Decepticons are hatching a dastardly scheme ...

Notes:

According to Buster, who has overheard some Decepticon conversations, the Autobots on Cybertron were aware of the *Ark*'s location on Earth 'a few hundred years ago'. This information was not made publically available, and shared only with a select few. (The Autobots in [17] 'The Smelting Pool' were certainly unaware that anyone had survived the *Ark* mission.) Three possibilities present themselves. First, Earth's location could have been relayed to Cybertron by Shockwave, who wasn't part of the *Ark* crew. (He remained behind on a Decepticon ship in orbit around Earth for a period – see [4] 'The Last Stand'.) Secondly, the *Ark* itself could have sent an automated distress call prior to crash-landing on Earth (in [1] 'The Transformers'). Thirdly, it's possible that the *Ark* was detected by the Man of Iron, who relayed this information back to Cybertron (see [4.1] 'Man of Iron' – a UK-original story that was also printed in the American *The Transformers* comic).

(Buster's flashback shows Sunstreaker and Defensor on Cybertron at this time, which is clearly incorrect – Sunstreaker was part of the *Ark* crew on Earth, and Defensor had yet to be created. It's obvious these 'flashbacks' are no more than Buster's own interpretation of what he's overheard.)

The Autobot tapes were lost at sea after being retrieved by an 18th Century pirate ship that sank in the Caribbean Sea. (The Caribbean was a popular destination for such buccaneers; their number included the famous pirate Blackbeard [c1680-1718].)

This is Starscream's first appearance in the American stories since his defeat at the hand of Omega Supreme in [19] 'Command Performances'; his body was recovered in [41] 'Totaled' and has since been fully repaired. This story also sees the American debut of the Seacons, and the first appearance of Jessie since [31] 'Buster Witwicky and the Car Wash of Doom'. The Decepticon Runamuck makes only his second appearance in the comic, following his debut in [23] 'Decepticon Graffiti'; oddly, he appears as a background character within both the Decepticon *and* the Autobot ranks. (As the Runamuck aboard the *Ark* appears to be a part of Blaster's exercise routine, it's likely this is simply a facsimile construct, as per the fake Galvatron in [44.3] 'Dry Run', rather than the genuine article.)

Following his recent adventures aboard the *Steelhaven* (see [44] 'The Cosmic Carnival'), Optimus Prime is reunited with the Autobot forces and has been installed as leader, ahead of Grimlock, Blaster and Fortress Maximus. The *Ark* is in orbit around the Earth, having been repaired since taking heavy damage in [41] 'Totaled'.

Although Ratbat is the leader of the Decepticon island faction, he still answers to 'Decepticon Imperial Headquarters' back on Cybertron. There's a reference to the destruction of Sparkplug's garage in [37] 'Toy Soldiers' – although the comic misattributes it to issue [38] 'Trial by Fire', in which we see the aftermath of the devastation.

Starscream's line 'I'm Starscream. Fly me!' is a reference to a 1971 advertising campaign by National Airlines. Fronted by one of their flight attendants, the original slogan was 'I'm Cheryl. Fly Me.'

UK Notes:
Although this was Starscream's first US appearance since [19] 'Command Performances', he had already returned twice in the British comics, most recently in [36.1] 'Stargazing'. Similarly, UK readers were already aware of the Seacons; they had been previously seen in stories such as [36.3] 'Enemy Action'.

Rabat's mention of the Decepticon Imperial Headquarters would seem to be a reference to Helex, the Decepticon capital (according to [52.1] 'The Fall and Rise of the Decepticon Empire').

Given that the 'Underbase Saga', comprised of this and the next three US issues, up to [50] 'Dark Star', would be interrupted in the UK by the stories [48.1] 'Cold Comfort and Joy' and [48.2] 'Time Wars', the subtitle was edited out of the UK printing.

UK Changes:
Page 1, panel 1: credits replaced, artwork extended upwards, captions 'Beginning a 4-part epic!' and 'The Underbase Saga! Part One' painted out.
Page 5, panel 1: the reference to issue #38 is changed to issue #154. Editor Don Perlin's sign-off is deleted.
Page 6, panel 2: a mention of issue #1 is amended to issue #2. Again, Perlin's tag is excised.
Page 7, panel 3: Starscream's line: 'Having been so recently repaired – for which you have my eternal gratitude and everlasting loyalty, of course ...' is changed to 'After my long spell in an Autobot life support pod ...'
Page 9, panel 1: 'snorkeled' becomes 'snorkelled'.
Page 11, panel 1: the 'soon ...' caption is deleted entirely.

Short Stories
Prior to this adventure, every US issue of *The Transformers* contained at least 22 pages of strip. As with the British version, however, sales were falling (see the notes to [44.1] 'Space Pirates'), and so the comic's production costs needed to be cut. The novel solution? Reduce the page count of the strip.

[47] 'Club Con' was only twenty pages long. Aside from the usual advertisements and Bullpen Bulletins page, the rest of the comic was filled up with content from the ill-fated *Transformers Universe, Volume 2*. *Transformers Universe* was a limited four-issue comic series originally published in 1986, consisting of profiles and information about the various Transformers characters. A follow-up series covering the newer characters was mooted, and indeed partly finished, in 1988. However, because of waning interest in the franchise, the second *Transformers Universe* series was never published.

From this point onwards, the US strip would vary in length from issue to issue, sometimes – as with [56] 'Back from the Dead' – being reduced to a mere 16 pages. Unpublished *Transformers Universe* entries would then be added to the issue as necessary, to bring it up to the correct length.

Roll Call:
Autobots: Optimus Prime, Jazz, Bluestreak (largely off-panel, though his arm and gun are seen), Sunstreaker, Mirage, Grimlock, Grapple, First Aid, Defensor, Blaster, Beachcomber, Perceptor, Outback, Fortress Maximus, Cerebros, **Raindance** and

Grandslam.

Cerebros' appearance is only as the head of Fortress Maximus, rather than an individual sighting. Sunstreaker, Defensor, Beachcomber and Perceptor appear only as part of Buster's (factually dubious) flashback.

Decepticons: Starscream, Skywarp, Swindle, Vortex, Drag Strip, Wildrider, Breakdown, Ramjet, Thrust, Runamuck, Ratbat, Snaptrap, Seawing, Skalor, Overbite, Nautilator and Tentakil.

Other: Buster, Sparkplug, Jessie and Spike (only as the head of Fortress Maximus).

Review:
After years of big UK stories billed as 'epics' or 'sagas', the American comic now presents one of its own. It certainly feels grandiose, with its tale of Autobot Cassettes stuck in a treasure chest for hundreds of years, and a desperate search to get the vital information recorded thereon.

After the recent misadventures of Arcee in the British comic, it's refreshing to see a well-written female character take centre stage here – Jessie is smart and proactive, defying Blaster's orders to investigate the Decepticon scheme, and sneaking though the Decepticon base in an attempt to retrieve Buster and the cassettes.

Some of it doesn't quite work (the Decepticons' holiday-resort scheme is on a par with their earlier car wash plan on the ridiculousness scale – see [31] 'Buster Witwicky and the Car Wash of Doom'), but it's an enjoyable story overall, and a promising start to the arc. 4/5

[48] THE FLAMES OF BOLTAX! (THE UNDERBASE SAGA! Part Two)
US#48, 'January 1989' (published September 1988), 18 pages.

British reprint: UK#196, 17 December 1988 (Part 1), 9 pages; UK#197, 24 December 1988 (Part 2), 10 pages.

The story's page count was padded out for its UK reprint by inserting the US cover art (albeit modified and recoloured) into the story between the original pages 15 and 16.

Credits:
Bob Budiansky (script); José Delbo (pencils); Danny Bulanadi (inks); Nel Yomtov (colours); Bill Oakley (letters); Don Daley (editor); Tom DeFalco (editor-in-chief); José Delbo and Dave Hunt (cover). **UK:** Art Wetherell and Stephen Baskerville (cover, UK#196); Anthony Williams and Stephen Baskerville (cover, UK#197).

Plot:
Having recovered the Autobot tapes, the Decepticons replay their contents using the Realvision system – a virtual reality environment in which viewers can experience computer-generated environments as if they were really there.

Starscream, Ratbat and Buster, who has temporarily escaped his cell, find themselves in a recording of ancient Cybertron, millions of years ago, when the Autobot/Decepticon war was in its infancy. A group of Autobots led by a young

Optimus Prime travel to meet the reclusive Boltax, a neutral Transformer who is reckoned to own a huge database of knowledge, one that could turn the tide of the war.

After overcoming a series of traps guarding Boltax's tower, Optimus Prime finally comes face to face with the mechanoid. Boltax's database – known as the Underbase – proves too large for any single Transformer to comprehend, but Megatron and a group of Decepticons arrive on the scene in a bid to seize it for themselves. The Decepticons shoot Optimus Prime, but the Autobot is able to recover and launch the database into space.

With the projection completed, Ratbat muses that the Underbase's trajectory means it is headed for Earth, and will arrive within the week ...

Notes:
This story casts more light on the early days of the Autobot/Decepticon war. At that time, there were designated neutral zones, into which neither faction was allowed to encroach (indicating that, despite the onset of war, there were still some laws and treaties that were respected by both parties – the grab for the Underbase here might have been the final nail in the coffin for any such rules).

High Circuitmaster Boltax was part of a 'circuit sect' – a cult group of which some Transformers (even Autobots) were highly suspicious. He was the keeper of the Underbase, 'a collection of knowledge that underlies all databases, much greater and broader in scope than anything in the universe'. (It's never made clear whether Boltax himself compiled the Underbase or whether he was just its caretaker.)

Boltax has converted himself into a gigantic, sentient mountain, the Temple of Knowledge, in which the Underbase is contained. He can communicate with other beings via a series of avatars, the Disciples of Boltax. The titular Flames of Boltax are the result of the Underbase's excess energies burning off. Closing the outer vents results in these flames being unable to escape; this build-up of energies is what sends the Underbase flying into space.

At this time, Optimus Prime was a mere lieutenant in the Autobot army – specifically, part of the Fourth Computerised Division. His actions here, preventing the Underbase from falling into Decepticon hands, made his reputation, and he would advance through the ranks as a result. His pre-Earth alternate mode is a futuristic-looking truck, very different from the tank-like form that he assumed in [1] 'The Transformers' (so either Optimus Prime was a triple-changer, or he was assigned different alternate modes as his role in the Autobot army changed over time).

The timing of the story is too neat to be mere coincidence; the Autobot tapes have been on Earth for hundreds of years, yet they are recovered only a few days before the Underbase is due to arrive. It's therefore likely that they were fitted with some form of homing beacon, which was set to activate when the Underbase approached the planet, hence the Decepticons becoming aware of their existence.

The Decepticons are no longer allowing tourists to visit their island (as in [47] 'Club Con') – now the cassettes have been recovered, there's no longer any need to keep up the subterfuge. Buster has been in Decepticon captivity since the events of [37] 'Toy Soldiers'.

This story marks the first appearance (albeit as part of the Realvision projection) of the Decepticon Triggercons – Cankcase, Ruckus and Windsweeper.

UK notes:

According to the later UK story [A6.1] 'The Magnificent Six', the Underbase was linked to Primus himself, indicating that it's an ancient and intrinsic part of the Transformers' very fibre, rather than a creation of Boltax.

In the chronology of early Cybertron, the events of this story occur after the rise of the Decepticons in [A2.4] 'State Games', but before Optimus Prime's rise to the rank of commander of the Elite Flying Corps as per [A3.1] 'What's in a Name?'. Given that Prime seems to have had two different alternative modes while on Cybertron, it's not unreasonable to assume that, as leader of the Elite Flying Corps, he was at one point given a further mode, capable of flight.

UK Changes:
Page numbers below refer to the original US printing, not the extended UK version.
Page 1, panel 1: credits replaced, artwork extended upwards, 'Underbase Saga' caption deleted.

Page 3, panel 3: editor Don Perlin's tag is removed from the caption.

Page 8, panel 7: the caption is changed from 'He disappeared in an explosion in *Transformers* #25 – Disaster-Prone Don' to 'Megatron is believed – mistakenly – to be dead.'

Between pages 15 and 16: a revised version of the US cover is inserted into the strip here, recoloured to blend in better with the surrounding pages. A speech bubble: 'At last! With Optimus Prime dead nothing can stop me!' is added.

Page 18, panel 6: the 'To be continued' caption is painted out.

Roll Call:
Autobots: Optimus Prime, Backstreet, Dogfight, Override, Raindance and Grandslam.

Decepticons: Megatron, Starscream, Soundwave, Onslaught, Drag Strip, Blitzwing, Ratbat, **Crankcase**, **Ruckus** and **Windsweeper**.

Other: Buster.

Optimus Prime, Backstreet, Dogfight, Override, Megatron, Crankcase, Ruckus and Windsweeper appear only as part of the Realvision projection.

Data File: Anthony Williams (artist)
Williams began his career at Marvel UK, where his work included *Doctor Who Magazine*, *The Real Ghostbusters* and *Action Force*. He also boasted a long association with *2000 AD*, having contributed to *Judge Dredd*, *Robo-Hunter* and *Sinister Dexter* strips. He later worked in the American comics industry, on titles such as *The Amazing Spider-Man*, *Captain America*, *Fantastic Four*, *Superman* and *X-Men*.

Review:
The 'Underbase Saga' continues with another good instalment. It's always nice to see stories set in Cybertron's past, and this one deftly adds to the series' mythology. The Underbase is being set up as an all-powerful source of knowledge, and is an intriguing concept worthy of a four part story.

Some of the story doesn't really work – the various traps faced by the Autobots scream of filler (and are similar to the traps encountered by Windcharger and Ravage back in [4.3] 'Raiders of the Last *Ark*') – but on the whole it is solid. Plus, it's always great to see a Megatron/Prime showdown, even an illusory one. 3/5

Next Issue, Part 2

Next issue teasers, as printed in issues #31-60 of the US *The Transformers* comic:

US#31: How much is a four million-plus years old Transformer with several trillion miles on him worth? Find out in … Used Autobots!

US#32: Blaster's fate revealed! And – the battle you've been craving – Bruticus vs. Defensor!!

US#33: Mighty Marvel moves on with the cataclysmic conclusion of Man of Iron!

US#34: Back to America! Child's Play.

US#35: Hitch a ride through the solar system with the Spacehikers! Plus Sky-Lynx!

US#36: A child's playthings are all that stand between the Decepticons and world conquest in 'Toy Soldiers!'

US#37: Headmasters on Earth!

US#38: Shockwave battles Fortress Maximus in a conflict to end all conflicts!!!

US#39: Is it really Optimus Prime, or just an incredible simulation? Also, the Pretenders!

US#40: The battle you demanded! Grimlock vs. Blaster! (And about 100 more Transformers dukin' it out, too!)

US#41: Optimus Prime returns! (No kidding!) Plus – the newest, strongest Transformers yet – the Powermasters!

US#42: The Sharkticons battle the Junkions at the behest of the Quintessons! Appearances by Ultra Magnus, Galvatron and Rodimus Prime! A veritable *Transformers* extravaganza!

US#43: We flash back to the present! Do not miss 'The Cosmic Carnival!'

US#44: Flash! Decepticon Skullgrin becomes Hollywood's latest movie star! 'Monstercon from Mars' premieres at a newsstand near you in 30 days!

US#45: The bounty-hunting Roadjammers stalk the Autobots for – 'Ca$h and Carnage!'

US#46: Vacation at Club Con – the tropical paradise that offers sun, sand, surf … and the savage Seacons!

US#47: Optimus Prime vs Megatron! The secrets of the Autobot tapes revealed! And more robots than you can shake a microchip at!

US#48: In the frozen Arctic, Decepticon battles Decepticon in an all-out 'Cold War'!

US#49: Does Buster live? Does the Earth die? Find out in the giant-sized cataclysmic conclusion of the Underbase Saga – 'Dark Star!'

US#50: Fortress Maximus vs the Decepticon Pretender Beasts!

US#51: They're mean, they're nasty and they're hungry – the Mecannibals!

US#52: The main course!

US#53: The newest – and smallest – Transformers yet: the Micromasters!

US#54: Mecha-wrestlemania!

US#55: Guess who's back from the dead?!

US#56: Megatron! 'Nuff said!

US#57: Ratchet might be able to save his patients – but can he save himself?!?

US#58: Ratchet vs. Megatron! Grimlock's Pretenders vs. the Sports Car Patrol! Optimus Prime and Scorponok vs. Starscream! Don't miss this big battle issue as metal meets metal when titans clang!

US#59: You should be worried, Optimus Prime! Judging by what happened to the Decepticon base, it looks like Ratchet is one of Yesterday's Heroes! On sale in 30 days!

US#60: The honest-to-gosh origin of the Transformers!

[48.1] COLD COMFORT AND JOY!

UK#198, 31 December 1988, 11 pages

Credits:

Simon Furman (plot); Ian Rimmer (script); Andrew Wildman (pencils); Stephen Baskerville (inks); Euan Peters (colours); Gary 'Glib' Gilbert (letters); Andrew Wildman (cover).

Plot:

Christmas Day, 1988. Optimus Prime travels to Earth for the first time since being rebuilt as a Powermaster. His demeanour is as cold as the weather – dying and being brought back to life appears to have changed him mentally. He no longer feels any affinity for the Earth, or for its people.

Meanwhile, the rest of the Powermasters watch a news broadcast revealing that a nearby town has been decimated by giant robots. Naturally assuming that some Decepticons were responsible, they dash to the scene. However, it transpires that the culprits were in fact Autobots – Inferno, Sandstorm and Broadside – who accidentally flattened the town due to their own clumsiness.

Optimus Prime thinks back to how the Transformers brought their battle to Earth in the first place – it was he who pressed the button and caused their ship to crash into the planet, thereby placing Earth in danger. His resolve restored, Prime orders the Autobots to help repair the damaged town.

Notes:

Much of this story is set in and around the (fictional) town of Border Flats. This is presumably located somewhere in Oregon, as the Advance Surveillance Unit were said to have been based in the area in their last appearance (in [44.2] 'Firebug'). The television news crew filming in the area are from the (again, fictional) station SFTV (perhaps named after writer Simon Furman). The Powermasters are seen watching a broadcast of '*Miami Metal Clamp* … or something like that', a reference to the cop show *Miami Vice* (1984-89).

Optimus Prime refers to his destruction (in [24] 'Afterdeath') and subsequent resurrection (in [42] 'People Power'). It's stated that the binary-bonding process involves a 'mixing of minds', implying for the first time that Powermasters (and possibly also Targetmasters) are mentally linked to their Nebulan companions, in a similar vein to the Headmaster process (although what this means for Transformers whose Nebulan partners are later killed is not addressed).

There are flashbacks and references to the Transformers' arrival on Earth (from [1] 'The Transformers'), and the kidnapping of Sparkplug Witwicky (in [2] 'Power Play'), which are said to have occurred 'four years ago'. The Autobot shuttle seen here is of a new design (and presumably part of the rebuilt *Ark's* complement of ancillary craft); this type of ship will continue to be used throughout the next twenty years (as seen in the future-set [44.1] 'Space Pirates').

One of the inhabitants of Border Flats is wearing a smiley badge on his hat. At the time of publication, the symbol had become synonymous with the contemporary acid house scene.

Roll Call:
Autobots: Optimus Prime, Prowl (flashback only), Inferno, Sandstorm, Broadside, Joyride, Slapdash and Getaway.

Decepticons: Megatron, Starscream, Soundwave, Frenzy, Laserbeak and Ravage (all flashback only).

Other: Sparkplug (flashback only).

Nebulans: Hi-Q, Hotwire, Lube and Rev.

Review:
The now-traditional UK Christmas issue comes round again, and while it's not the greatest of efforts, it does a decent job, as far as festive fluff stories go.
    The twist ending, in which it turns out that the devastation was caused by Autobots, is a neat idea, and Optimus Prime gets some good character work. 3/5

[48.2] TIME WARS
- UK#199, 7 January 1989 (Part 1), 11 pages
- UK#200, 14 January 1989 (Part 2), 11 pages
- UK#201, 21 January 1989 (Part 3), 11 pages
- UK#202, 28 January 1989 (Part 4), 11 pages
- UK#203, 4 February 1989 (Part 5), 11 pages
- UK#204, 11 February 1989 (Part 6), 11 pages
- UK#205, 18 February 1989 (Part 7), 11 pages

Credits:
Simon Furman (script); Andrew Wildman (pencils, part 1); Stephen Baskerville (inks, part 1); Robin Smith (art, parts 2-3); Dan Reed (art, parts 4-5); Lee Sullivan (art, parts 6-7); Euan Peters (colours); Gary 'Glib' Gilbert (letters, parts 1, 5 & 7); Annie Halfacree (letters, parts 2-3); Gordon 'GLOP' Robson (letters, part 4-5); Peter Knight (letters, part 6); Art Wetherell and Dave Harwood (cover, UK#199); Lee Sullivan (cover, UK#200); Dougie Braithwaite and Dave Harwood (cover, UK#201); Andrew Wildman (covers, UK#202-203 & 205); Jeff Anderson and Dave Harwood (cover, UK#204).

The lettering in part 5 was a collaboration between 'Glib' and 'GLOP'. Incidentally, although Gary Gilbert's 'Glib' nickname is a simple corruption/shortening of his surname, his colleague Gordon Robson assumed it to be an acronym, for Greatest Letterer In Britain. In a piece of jokey one-upmanship, Robson asked to be credited as 'GLOP': Greatest Letterer On (the) Planet.
    Andrew Wildman's credit as cover artist was missing from issue 203; an apology and correction was printed the following week.

Plot:

A rift in time and space, exacerbated by Cyclonus's death years before he was even created, threatens to destroy Earth and Cybertron, both in 1989 and in 2009. A group of Autobots from the future travel back to 1989 in a last-ditch attempt to close the rift, and a group of future Decepticons follow them.

Meanwhile, Galvatron has formed an alliance with his own previous incarnation, Megatron. A group of Autobots and Decepticons from Cybertron arrive on Earth and launch an assault on the two tyrants, but they are easily defeated, suffering a great many casualties.

Autobots and Decepticons from both time zones realise that the only way to close the rift is to ensure that Galvatron and Scourge (and Cyclonus's remains) are thrown into it. Optimus Prime battles Galvatron hand to hand as Earth verges on destruction, and Galvatron is sucked into the rift. To save the universe, Scourge willingly sacrifices himself and jumps into the anomaly. The world's ultimate saviour is Shockwave, who throws Cyclonus's body into the rift before sealing it with a blast from his space gun mode.

Past and future are saved, but the victory comes at a great cost – many present-day Transformers have been killed in the battle.

Notes:

The present-day sequences of this story appear to be set in and around Wyoming; Ravage wakes from his underground dormancy (which began after he fell down a Wyoming mine in [20] 'Showdown') and finds Galvatron's base soon afterwards. (Rather than being an entirely new underground base, this could well be another appearance of Shockwave's makeshift fortress last seen in [16] 'Plight of the Bumblebee'.)

All seven parts of this story open with an image of the rift as it gradually increases in size and threatens to engulf Earth. The rift appears to have been caused not just by Cyclonus's untimely death, but also by Scourge and Cyclonus time-travelling to the present day (at the end of [36.2] 'The Legacy of Unicron') without using the standard mass-displacement procedure. It was established in [20.2] 'Target: 2006' that beings of equivalent mass have to be shunted off to a limbo dimension to make way for any incoming time travellers.

To make way for the Transformers of the future, a total of twelve robots from the present day are transported to limbo – Optimus Prime, Snarl, Blaster, Hardhead, Highbrow, Brainstorm, Horri-Bull, Fangry, Skullcruncher, Weirdwolf, Misfire and Triggerhappy. The 2009 Cybertronians who take their places are Rodimus Prime, Arcee, Kup, Blurr, Ultra Magnus, Red Alert, Soundwave, Hun-Gurrr, Blot, Sinnertwin, Cutthroat and Rippersnapper.

Optimus Prime, having visited the limbo dimension before (as seen in [23.3] 'Distant Thunder'), is now immune to the effects of the mind parasites who live there. Thanks to their connection via the Matrix, Optimus Prime is able to communicate with Rodimus and view events on Earth through his eyes. Skids is still alive within the limbo dimension, having been there since he made way for Galvatron in [23.4] 'Fallen Angel'.

Optimus Prime surmises that he is effectively a past incarnation of Rodimus Prime, and therefore returning to Earth and existing side by side with Rodimus will make the rift grow wider. (Although Optimus and Rodimus are two separate beings, they have both 'become one with' the Matrix, and as such can be considered as two aspects of the same entity, on a metaphysical level at least. Although Optimus Prime is not currently in possession of the complete Matrix, it was established in previous stories that a small vestige remains within him, even when the majority has been removed – see the notes to [10] 'The Next Best Thing to Being There'.)

Ultra Magnus states that the planet Quintesson was 'swallowed whole' by the rift – contradicting the events of [44.1] 'Space Pirates', in which it was destroyed by 'orbital decay'. The future Autobots' time travel mechanism isn't as flexible as that used by Galvatron – they have to wait until 'dimensional vectors come into alignment' before they can attempt to travel through time; such periods of alignment appear to occur only once every month.

This is the first time we get a good look at future-Earth (away from the environs of Autobot City, seen in [44.1] 'Space Pirates' and [A3.4] 'Ark Duty') – the architecture is a mix of traditional brick buildings and space-age towers. The future-set events are said to take place on New Year's Day 2009, and there we have our first sighting of the future version of Spike and his son Daniel, both of whom were present during the events of *The Transformers: The Movie*. The future Decepticons have constructed a device called an energy leach, which threatens the Earth's very existence. It consists of a giant 'laser bore', a massive drill-like contraption. (The implication is that the Decepticons' plan is to extract energy from the Earth's core – a scheme similar to that of Galvatron in [27.4] 'Fire on High'.)

In this story we see the Autobot Advance Surveillance Unit (introduced in [44.2] 'Firebug') join forces with the Wreckers and also a new team, the Decepticon Mayhem Attack Squad. This latter force consists of Carnivac, Catilla, Venom, Chop Shop, Flywheels and Battletrap.

Scourge refers to his previous meeting with Springer ('I suppose you've seen this trick before, haven't you?'), which occurred in [40.5] 'Wrecking Havoc'. The Transformation editorial page in UK#203 erroneously claims that this story is set after [50] 'Dark Star'; that's clearly impossible, as some of the characters in this story, such as Goldbug and the Dinobots, are killed during the events of [50] 'Dark Star'.

At the beginning of this adventure, Highbrow is still in possession of Scorponok's head, which he stole in [A4.4] 'All in the Minds'. Apeface's crash in that story is also referred to. An issue of the Marvel UK comic *Dragon's Claws* is seen in the 2009 sequences (wishful thinking on the part of the creative team – *Dragon's Claws* would be cancelled in April 1989 after just ten issues).

Shockwave was driven mad after learning that he was destined to die. (His future self was killed in [36.2] 'The Legacy of Unicron', and he learnt of it in [44.3] 'Dry Run'.) However, he recovers his senses in time to save the day, after Ravage convinces him that he has the power to change the future and avoid his fate.

Remembering the First Time

This book has demonstrated on a number of occasions how the 'future' stories and the 'present' stories are taking place in parallel dimensions – see the notes to [27.1] 'Wanted: Galvatron – Dead or Alive'. In the future-set stories, or Timeline A, the *Ark* will remain stuck in Mount St Hilary (as per [A3.4] 'Ark Duty') and Unicron will attack Cybertron in the year 2006 (in *The Transformers: The Movie*). However, by travelling into the past (in [20.2] 'Target: 2006'), Galvatron creates a different chain of events: Timeline B.

What's odd in this story is that Galvatron (from Timeline A) begins to remember events from the point of view of Megatron (from Timeline B). Not only does this contradict the established 'rules' of time travel (it's confirmed in the letters page of UK#97 that Galvatron and Megatron don't share the same memories, now that their respective timelines have diverged), but we will later discover that this isn't even the real Megatron, but a clone created by Straxus (see [57.1] 'Two Megatrons'). So why is Galvatron reliving memories of a clone from a parallel universe?

There are a number of possible answers. The simplest one is that Galvatron is just mad – he does, after all, have a history of mental instability (as seen in stories such as [23.4] 'Fallen Angel'). Another possibility is that Galvatron is being affected by the rift – his time-travelling is the ultimate cause of the anomaly, and it could be that these alternative memories are somehow 'bleeding through' from the rift.

The latter would seem to be the best explanation. Galvatron begins the story quite sane, and it's only as a result of the phantom memories that he begins his decent into madness. When Megatron queries how Galvatron can have these recollections, Galvatron seems as bemused as anybody: 'Uh? What? I don't understand ...'

One popular fantheory is that Galvatron is not in fact Megatron, but is instead the future version of Straxus's Megatron clone. However, this doesn't quite work – it is only in the divergent Timeline B that Megatron is cloned by Straxus; Galvatron is from Timeline A, and so does not experience those events.

Let's look at the chronology: Galvatron travels into the past and starts messing around with the timelines ([20.2] 'Target: 2006'). As a direct result of his incursion, Optimus Prime is transported to limbo. Upon his escape, Optimus Prime discovers that the Autobots have fared badly in his absence. Prime decides to fake his own death to see if the Autobots can survive without him, and it's in setting up that plan that he and Megatron are transported to Cybertron, where Megatron is cloned ([23.1] 'Prey' *et seq.*) In other words, by interfering with the past, Galvatron sets up a chain of events that results in the clone being created. If Galvatron had stayed in his own time, Prime would never have attempted to fake his death, he and Megatron would never have gone to Cybertron, and the clone wouldn't exist. Therefore Galvatron cannot be a future incarnation of the clone, as the clone was never created in the original timeline.

Grimlock's New Brain
As part of the two-hundredth issue celebrations, *The Transformers* readers were treated to a free gift: a booklet entitled *Transformers: The Facts*. This gave a brief overview of the Transformers' origins, as previously presented in [36.2] 'The Legacy of Unicron', and featured profiles of some of the comic's production staff. There was also a 'Transformers Book of Records' section, identifying the strongest, biggest, fastest and deadliest Transformers – Grimlock, Metroplex, Blurr and Galvatron respectively.

One of the more interesting segments was a page entitled 'The Transformers Q & A!' This provided definitive answers to readers' most frequently asked questions. One of the subjects tackled was the thorny issue of Grimlock's intelligence.

In the earlier days of *The Transformers* comic, Grimlock and the Dinobots were used only sparingly in the American strips, which allowed for them to be prominent characters in the UK stories. While the *Transformers* television series depicted the Dinobots as comic relief simpletons, the writers of the UK comic strips made them a bit more astute. Grimlock became the 'face' of the UK letters page, and was soon having to explain why he was clever in the comics but dumb in the cartoons. From Grim Grams, UK #75: 'The cartoon series gets everything wrong. This is most clearly shown in their depiction of the Dinobots ... "Me Grimlock! Me not speak too good!'

Do me a favour ..."'

Just five issues later (UK#80), he was at it again. Reader: 'In the cartoon series they say you are stupid.' Grimlock: 'The cartoon series has got it wrong – it's as simple as that!'

In UK#91, 'Grimlock' reviewed the newly-released animated feature film, *The Transformers: The Movie*: 'They ... depict the Dinobots as slow-witted and semi-literate! It's just too much! I'm off to bust some heads over this!' This then was the position of the UK editorial team: Grimlock and the Dinobots were of decent intelligence, and their 'dim' portrayal in the cartoon was wrong.

However, problems arose when the Dinobots started getting a bigger slice of the action in the American strips. The US writers had no idea that the British comics were depicting Grimlock as smart, and so when he became Autobot leader in [27] 'King of the Hill', the American stories portrayed him as childish and brutish, more in line with his cartoon persona. Again, this caused confusion in the UK letters pages, as seen in this response from 'Grimlock' in the letters page in UK#152: 'I sorta go from bein' sorta thick ... and then getting mind-expandingly clever ... and finally end up as my street-wise, 'con-crushing, wisecracking self. If you think you're confused, spare a thought for poor old confused me!'

Thankfully, then, *Transformers: The Facts* gives readers a definitive answer: 'Grimlock possesses a brilliant mind, but considers intellectuals as weak (he despises weakness). He often chooses to act and talk dumb.' If that seems like a massive fudge on the part of the UK writing staff, that's because it is – however it's probably the best they could have come up with, given the circumstances.

After UK writer Simon Furman began working on the American strips, this 'Grimlock acts dumber than he really is' explanation was reiterated in the US comic. From the letters page of US#63: 'Grimlock is intelligent, he just chooses not to show it ... Friend and foe alike tend to underestimate Grimlock because of this, giving him a considerable edge.'

Roll Call:
Autobots: Optimus Prime, Ironhide, Wheeljack, Grimlock, Snarl, Slag, Sludge, Swoop, Red Alert (future version), Inferno, Hoist, Skids, Blaster (seen in both future and present-day incarnations), Ultra Magnus (future version), Roadbuster, Topspin, Twin Twist, Rack and Ruin, Springer, Sandstorm, Broadside, Kup (future version), Blurr (future version), Rodimus Prime (future version), Goldbug, Fortress Maximus, Cerebros, Highbrow, Hardhead, Brainstorm, Scattershot, Arcee (future version), and **Catilla**.

Cerebros appears only as the head of Fortress Maximus, rather than as a discrete individual. Catilla is presented here as a Decepticon (but he will later switch his allegiance, and his toy is labelled as an Autobot, so he's listed with the other Autobots for the sake of consistency).

Decepticons: Soundwave (future version), Ravage, Shockwave, Galvatron (future version), Cyclonus (future version – seen only in flashback and as a corpse), Scourge (future version), Clone Megatron, Scorponok, Skullcruncher, Mindwipe, Weirdwolf, Snapdragon, Slugslinger, Triggerhappy, Misfire, Hun-Gurrr (future version), Cutthroat (future version), Blot (future version), Sinnertwin (future version), Rippersnapper (future version), Flywheels, Battletrap, Fangry, Horri-Bull, **Carnivac**, **Venom** and **Chop Shop**.

Additionally, Bruticus (the combined form of Onslaught, Brawl, Swindle, Blast Off and Vortex) and Divebomb appear on the cover of UK#205, in an image meant to represent Galvatron's warped memories.

Other: Spike (seen in both present-day and future incarnations) and **Daniel** (future version).

The present-day Spike appears only as part of Fortress Maximus, rather than as an individual character.

Nebulans: Gort, Duros, Arcana, Zarak, Grax, Vorath, Monzo, Krunk and Fracas.

With the exception of Fracas, the remainder of the Nebulans appear only in their 'head' modes.

Death count (confirmed):

- Chop Shop: shot full in the chest. Makes no further appearances.
- Flywheels: killed by Galvatron, his right arm torn off. Makes no further appearances.
- Galvatron: sucked into the temporal rift. Makes no further appearances (in that incarnation, at least).
- Rack and Ruin: shot by Galvatron; the blast is so intense that one of his heads flies off. Makes no further appearances.
- Roadbuster: dies using an experimental 'pathblaster' weapon, which feeds back and explodes. Makes no further appearances.
- Sandstorm: blown to bits by Galvatron. Makes no further appearances.
- Scourge: willingly flies into the temporal rift. Makes no further appearances.
- Topspin: shot in the head by Megatron. Makes no further appearances.
- Twin Twist: head torn off by Galvatron. Makes no further appearances.
- Venom: shot full in the chest by Galvatron. Manages to get back to his feet, only for Galvatron to tear away a huge chunk of his body. Makes no further appearances.

Death count (ambiguous):

- Battletrap: Galvatron tears a hole in his chest and flings him against a wall. Flywheels seems to think his friend has been killed and swears revenge. Later repaired; shows up in [74] 'The Void'.
- Ultra Magnus (future version): set upon by three Decepticons, out for blood. Other Autobots are later seen carrying his body away. It's unclear whether he's been killed or just gravely injured. Makes no further appearances. (The letters page in UK#216 states that he was 'badly damaged', but whether that damage was fatal or not is never clarified.)

Data File: Robin Smith (artist)
Smith is best known for his work on *2000 AD*, his art having graced strips such as *Judge Dredd*, *Judge Anderson* and *Bogie Man*. As well as the original UK *The Transformers* comic, he also worked on the UK version of *Transformers: Generation 2*, and on the 2007 UK *Transformers* comic from Titan Magazines.

Review:
The last hurrah for the UK comics – one final epic before the decline in sales resulted in a massive change in format. As the final 'traditional' UK story, it's a great way to bow out: the Galvatron story arc begun in [20.2] 'Target: 2006' is properly tied up, there are a number of well-drawn (and brutal) action sequences, and the stakes are higher than ever – the fate of two worlds and two time zones hangs in the balance.

While it's undoubtedly an 'epic', there are a few elements that don't quite work: the Autobot-on-Autobot battle in part 3 is pure padding, the future Decepticons are superfluous to the plot (they don't actually do anything after they arrive in the present), and the whole 'Galvatron remembers a parallel timeline' subplot is messy and ill-defined.

It takes a while to get going, but despite a few niggles, 'Time Wars' is a memorably exciting way for the 'big' UK colour stories to bow out. 4/5

[49] COLD WAR! (THE UNDERBASE SAGA! Part Three)
US#49, 'February 1989' (published October 1988), 18 pages.

British reprint: UK#206, 25 February 1989 (Part 1), 10 pages; UK#207, 4 March 1989 (Part 2), 10 pages.

The story's page-count was padded out for its UK reprint by the addition of the first two pages of the next story, [50] 'Dark Star'. Surprisingly, the reshuffle actually works rather well, the two new pages making for a decent coda.

Credits:
Bob Budiansky (script); José Delbo (pencils); Danny Bulanadi (inks); Nel Yomtov (colours); Bill Oakley (letters); Don Daley (editor); Tom DeFalco (editor-in-chief); José Delbo and Danny Bulanadi (cover). **UK:** Andrew Wildman (cover, UK#206); Lee Sullivan (cover, UK#207).

Plot:
Ratbat's Decepticon faction are holed out in the Arctic, waiting for the Underbase to arrive. The duplicitous Starscream has his own plans for the database, and so sets in motion a convoluted plan to obtain it first. He invites Scorponok's group of Decepticons to the Arctic, and when the captive Buster lets slip about the Underbase, Scorponok and Ratbat turn on one another. As the two Decepticon factions battle each other, Starscream escapes during the confusion, stranding Buster on an iceberg with a device capable of summoning the Autobots.

Buster has a dilemma – does he summon the Autobots, in which case they would probably be demolished by the combined armies of Scorponok and Ratbat, or does he stay silent and remain on the iceberg, where he will die if not rescued?

Starscream manages to steal Scorponok's ship while the Decepticons are fighting each other, and launches into space to intercept the Underbase. Buster, meanwhile, makes the decision to summon the Autobots …

Notes:
This is a very action-heavy story, with very little to note other than the giant Decepticon-on-Decepticon battle. It marks the first meeting of Scorponok's and Ratbat's Decepticon factions; thanks to Starscream's machinations, it doesn't go well.

Both Blaster and Starscream recall the events of [47] 'Club Con', and Buster's knowledge of the Underbase comes from his spying on the Decepticon simulation in [48] 'The Flames of Boltax'. Buster has been in Decepticon captivity since he was snatched by Ratbat at the end of [37] 'Toy Soldiers'.

This story features the first appearance of Buzzsaw since way back in [19] 'Command Performances'.

UK Changes:
Page 1, panel 1: artwork extended downwards, credits replaced.
Page 5, panel 1: '*Transformers* #47 – Don' becomes '*Transformers* #194 & 195'.

Roll Call:
Autobots: Optimus Prime, Blaster and Fortress Maximus.

Decepticons: Starscream, Skywarp, Thundercracker, Soundwave, Laserbeak, Buzzsaw, Breakdown, Blitzwing, Octane, Razorclaw, Rampage, Tantrum, Headstrong, Divebomb, Ratbat, Scorponok, Skullcruncher, Mindwipe, Weirdwolf, Apeface, Snapdragon, Triggerhappy, Hun-Gurrr, Cutthroat, Blot, Sinnertwin, Rippersnapper, Snaptrap, Seawing, Skalor, Overbite, Nautilator, Tentakil, Piranacon, Bomb Burst, Skullgrin, Submarauder, Iguanus, Bugly, Finback, Horri-Bull and Squeezeplay.

Other: Buster and Spike.

Nebulans: Zarak, Grax, Vorath, Monzo, Spasma, Krunk, Kreb and Lokos.

Kreb and Lokos appear only as the heads of Horri-Bull and Squeezeplay, rather than as individual characters.

A great many Decepticons appear in crowd scenes in this story. Because they are inked/coloured indistinctly, it's entirely possible that they include more than those listed above.

Review:
Starscream is at his manipulative and calculating best here, making a grab for the Underbase while skilfully playing two sets of Decepticons against each other. But while his power play is nicely written, the whole thing is let down by the visuals. The art is grubby-looking and indistinct, which isn't a huge problem in a plot-driven story, but here, in what is essentially a giant battle sequence, it becomes a major failing. 2/5

[50] DARK STAR (THE UNDERBASE SAGA! Part Four: The Electriying Conclusion)

US#50, 'March 1989' (published November 1988), 38 pages. As the fiftieth issue of the American *The Transformers* comic, this was a special 'giant sized' issue with a larger-than-usual page-count.

British reprint: UK#208, 11 March 1989 (Part 1), 12 pages; UK#209, 18 March 1989 (Part 2), 12 pages; UK#210, 25 March 1989 (Part 3), 12 pages.

The British reprint of this story was only 36 pages long, as the two-page 'prologue' sequence had been appended to the previous one, [49] 'Cold War'.

Credits:
Bob Budiansky (script); José Delbo (pencils); Dave Hunt (inks); Nel Yomtov (colours); Rick Parker (letters); Don Daley (editor); Tom DeFalco (editor-in-chief); José Delbo and Danny Bulanadi (cover). **UK:** Andrew Wildman (covers, UK#208 and 210); Geoff Senior (cover, UK#209).

Andrew Wildman was uncredited for his cover on issue #208.

It was at this point that Euan Peters took over as editor of the UK comic, having previously worked under Simon Furman as assistant editor; his first editor's credit was given on the Transformation page of issue #208.

Plot:
The Autobots arrive in the Arctic to rescue Buster and are set upon by the Decepticons. After a brief battle, they all realise they've been duped by Starscream, who is about to seize the power of the Underbase.

The Autobots and Decepticons arrive on the scene just as Starscream begins absorbing the Underbase's awesome energies. Although the contact is interrupted by a well-placed cannon blast from Optimus Prime, he is too late – Starscream's power is still magnified.

The newly-enhanced Decepticon goes on the rampage, attacking New York, Tokyo and Buenos Aires. Most of the Transformers who stand against him are annihilated, although those with an organic component (Pretenders, Headmasters etc) have an immunity.

Optimus Prime, meanwhile, has plans of his own. He launches a special rocket that deflects the Underbase into a collision course for Earth. Starscream intercepts the ancient database and absorbs it completely, growing into a powerful, mutated behemoth.

However, it was all a ruse on the part of Optimus Prime – realising that the Underbase is too powerful for any single being to control, he has deliberately engineered events to ensure that Starscream absorbs it all and is overwhelmed by its power, destroying him.

Notes:
In the final instalment of the 'Underbase Saga', which began in [47] 'Club Con', we are

given a detailed description of the Underbase itself. It's a database encoded in patterns of light. Its 'gathered energies' have 'swelled beyond measure', and it exists in a state 'somewhere between energy and mass'. It's depicted as a glowing yellow cuboid crisscrossed by beams of light. It is so powerful that it can burn planets and turn suns nova.

(For the Transformers, knowledge equates to power on a quite literal level, so the combined knowledge of the Cybertronians, and possibly also Primus and his Light Gods, is a powerful force indeed.)

It's confirmed here that Buster is 17 years old (but see the notes to [22.1] 'The Gift' for more on this). There are mentions of the Decepticon-on-Decepticon battle in [49] 'Cold War', and the Underbase being launched into space millions of years ago, as seen in [48] 'The Flames of Boltax'.

The battle against Starscream takes place across three cities; in New York, there is a confrontation on the Brooklyn Bridge (which was opened in 1883 and spans the East River). The action then switches to Tokyo, Japan, where the natives initially assume that the Dinobots are props in a monster (*kaiju*) movie – a popular genre in Japan, the most famous example being *Godzilla/Gojira* (Ishirō Honda, 1954). The sequence would appear to take place on the western outskirts of the city – there is a forest nearby (possibly the environs of Mount Takao). The attack on Buenos Aires is centred on the famous thoroughfare Avenida 9 de Julio (which translates as Ninth of July Avenue, after Argentina's independence day), the widest avenue in the world. The monument that Starscream throws at Fortress Maximus is the Obelisco de Buenos Aires (constructed 1936).

This story sees the first appearance of the five original Throttlebots since [39] 'The Desert Island of Space', where their brains were stuck inside toy cars. Their sudden reappearance is never explained, though it would seem that the Autobots have somehow retrieved and rebuilt them in the interim.

The 'alien' creature burned to death in the prologue looks suspiciously like a tapir.

UK Changes:
When the opening two pages were printed in the UK as a coda to [49] 'Cold War', the original page 1 was heavily edited: the art was extended to fill the page, the credits were removed, the 'Underbase Saga' caption was painted out, some of the other captions were moved around, the reference to issue #48 was changed to issue #197, and editor Don Daley's sign-off was excised.

Page 3, panel 1: the 'Chapter One' caption is removed. Credits are added to the bottom of the page.

Page 4, panel 5: Don Perlin's tag is removed from the caption.

Page 9, panel 1: the 'Chapter Two' caption is omitted.

Page 15, panel 1: the uppermost caption is painted out.

Page 16, panel 1: the 'Chapter Three' caption is removed.

Page 21, panel 4: 'armored' becomes 'armoured'.

Page 23, panel 7: the reference to issue #42 is amended to #177. Perlin's signature is erased.

Page 28, panel 1: Don Perlin's name is again deleted, this time from the 'translated from Spanish' caption.

Page 30, panel 2: the reference to issue #19 is changed to issue #71. Perlin's tag is erased.

Page 31, panel 1: the 'Chapter Four' caption is painted out.

PART TWO: THE COMICS

Page 38, panel 5: the 'The End' caption is omitted.

Roll Call:
Autobots: Optimus Prime, Jazz, Prowl, Bluestreak, Ratchet, Sideswipe, Hound, Mirage, Brawn, Gears, Grimlock, Snarl, Slag, Sludge, Swoop, Jetfire, Hoist, Tracks, Silverbolt, Air Raid, Fireflight, Skydive, Slingshot, Blaster, Powerglide, Cosmos, Warpath, Beachcomber, Perceptor, Omega Supreme, Goldbug, Chase, Searchlight, Freeway, Rollbar, Wideload, Fortress Maximus, Cerebros, Scattershot, Lightspeed, Nosecone, Afterburner and Strafe.

Decepticons: Starscream, Skywarp, Thundercracker, Soundwave, Laserbeak, Buzzsaw, Astrotrain, Blitzwing, Octane, Razorclaw, Rampage, Tantrum, Headstrong, Divebomb, Ratbat, Scorponok, Skullcruncher, Mindwipe, Weirdwolf, Apeface, Snapdragon, Slugslinger, Hun-Gurrr, Cutthroat, Blot, Rippersnapper, Snaptrap, Seawing, Skalor, Overbite, Nautilator, Tentakil, Bomb Burst, Skullgrin, Iguanus, Bugly, Finback and Horri-Bull.

Other: Buster and Spike.

Nebulans: Zarak, Grax, Vorath, Monzo, Spasma, Krunk and Hi-Q.

Of the Nebulans, only Hi-Q is shown in his humanoid mode (all the others are seen as heads only).

Death count:

- Aerialbots – Air Raid, Fireflight, Slingshot, Skydive and Silverbolt. Zapped by Starscream over New York. Later rebuilt ([75] 'On the Edge of Extinction' et al).
- Blaster. Shot in the chest by Starscream. Later rebuilt ([75] 'On the Edge of Extinction').
- Bluestreak. Killed by Starscream in New York. Last appearance.
- Brawn. Destroyed by Starscream on the Brooklyn Bridge. Last appearance (except as a corpse).
- Buzzsaw. Killed by Starscream in Buenos Aires. No further appearances.
- Decepticon Triple-Changers – Astrotrain, Blitzwing and Octane). Shot down by Starscream over Buenos Aires. Later resurrected ([62.9] 'The Bad Guys' Ball').
- Dinobots – Grimlock, Snarl, Slag, Sludge and Swoop. Killed by Starscream in Tokyo, except Grimlock, who is killed by the Decepticon Pretenders. Grimlock is rebuilt as a Pretender in [58] 'All the Familiar Faces'; the remainder of the Dinobots are resurrected in [72] 'All This and Civil War 2'.
- Gears. Zapped by Starscream in New York. Last appearance (except as a corpse).
- Goldbug. Blown to pieces by Starscream. Later rebuilt as Pretender Bumblebee in [58] 'All the Familiar Faces'.
- Hoist. Killed by Starscream during the battle in New York. Final appearance.
- Hound. Killed by Starscream on the Brooklyn Bridge. Last appearance (except as a corpse or in flashbacks).
- Jazz. Terminated by Starscream. Later rebuilt as a Pretender in [58] 'All the

Familiar Faces'.

- Jetfire. Destroyed by Starscream in New York. Final appearance.
- Laserbeak. Downed by Starscream over Buenos Aires. Final appearance.
- Mirage. Killed by Starscream on the Brooklyn Bridge. Last appearance.
- Omega Supreme. Destroyed by Starscream in Buenos Aires. Never seen (alive) again.
- Perceptor. Crushed by Tentakil. Confirmed killed in [60] 'Yesterday's Heroes'.
- Predacons – Rampage, Razorclaw, Tantrum, Headstrong and Divebomb. Blasted by Starscream in Tokyo. Later rebuilt ([62.1] 'Snow Fun').
- Prowl. Killed (off-panel) by Starscream during the New York sequence. Though not seen here, his death is later shown in the aptly-titled [62.2] 'Flashback'.
- Ratbat. Killed by Scorponok. Final appearance.
- Seacons – Snaptrap, Tentakil, Nautilator, Skalor, Overbite and Seawing. Killed by Starscream in the East River. Last appearance (barring flashbacks).
- Skywarp. Shot down by Starscream over Tokyo. Final appearance.
- Soundwave. Blasted by Starscream in Buenos Aires. Later repaired ([58.3] 'Fallen Star').
- Starscream. Destroyed after absorbing the Underbase. Later rebuilt as a Pretender ([58] 'All the Familiar Faces').
- Technobots – Scattershot, Strafe, Afterburner, Nosecone and Lightspeed. Zapped by Starscream in Buenos Aires. Last appearance.
- Terrorcons – Hun-Gurrr, Blot, Cutthroat, Rippersnapper and Sinnertwin. Massacred by Starscream in Buenos Aires. Never seen again.
- Throttlebots – Searchlight, Freeway, Rollbar, Chase and Wideload. Destroyed by Starscream in Tokyo. Last appearance.
- Thundercracker. Shot out of the air above Tokyo. Last appearance.
- Tracks. Bathed in acid by Blot. Later repaired ([62.20] 'Makin' Tracks').

It's implied that many other Transformers are killed during these events, whether in the Arctic battle at the beginning of the story, or in the destruction of the Decepticon island spaceship, or at the hands of Starscream. Later adventures will work on the assumption that most Earth-based Transformers were destroyed, the exceptions being Ratchet, the Pretenders, the Headmasters, the Targetmasters and the Powermasters. The Protectobots and the Combaticons, however, will show up in an Annual story set after these events ([A4.3] 'Prime Bomb'), and Seaspray will appear in the very next issue ([51] 'The Man in the Machine').

A number of characters who are permanently killed here later show up in the alternate future timeline (Skywarp in *The Transformers: The Movie*, Hoist in [A3.4] '*Ark Duty*' etc), implying that the events of this story do not occur in that reality.

Data File: Rick Parker (letterer)
Regular *The Transformers* letterer Rick Parker is also a noted writer, cartoonist and artist. He has won a *Comic Buyer's Guide* award for his lettering, which has been seen in hundreds of different titles, including *The Avengers*, *Captain America* and *Uncanny X-Men*. His cartoons have appeared in publications such as *Life*, *Time* and the *New York Times*, and he has created works of fine art displayed in many prestigious American galleries.

Review:
The artwork here is often poor, the plotting is mechanical, and the whole thing has a cold, emotionless feel to it. This is simply a 38-page massacre, written with as little feeling as possible.

The cull was nothing if not practical: with over 250 characters running around, killing off most of the older ones, whose toys were no longer available to buy, would help shift the focus onto the newer ones, which were still in the shops.

That said, there is a certain morbid fascination to be had in seeing this many recurring characters being wiped out in one fell swoop. The story certainly makes an attempt at being epic, spanning four continents and two space battles.

Do this story's importance and grand scale make up for its other deficiencies? Not quite, but if you're going to have an adventure in which over fifty characters get unceremoniously bumped off, this is probably the best way to go about it. 3/5

US Advertisements, Part 6: Toys and Games
A list of all advertisements for toys and games that appeared in the US *The Transformers* comic:

Advanced Dungeons & Dragons (role-playing game) – US#32-33, 36-37, 39, 45, 48, 54-57, 67-70; HDM#2, 4
Adventures of Indiana Jones, The (role-playing game) – US#4
Airwolf remote-controlled helicopter – US#47, 49, 51, 58-66
Buck Rogers: Battle for the 25th Century (board game) – US#45-46, 51
Buck Rogers: XXVc (role-playing game) – US#76
Captain Power and the Soldiers of the Future (interactive videocassette game) – US#37-40
Dungeon! (board game) – US#72-75
Dungeons & Dragons (role-playing game) – US#22-24, 27, 31, 34, 48, 77-80; MOV#1-2; GIJ#1, 4; HDM#3
Gammarauders (role-playing game) – US#34; HDM#3
GI Joe figures – US#41, 44, 46, 49
Helen of Toy (mail order war games) – US#1
Hunt for Red October, The (board game) – US#43
Lazer Tag – US#23-25; MOV#1-3; GIJ#1-2
Lego – US#77
Magestones (board game) – US#71, 79
Marvel Secret Wars (action figures by Mattel) – US#3
Marvel Super Heroes (role-playing game) – US#27, 38, 80; GIJ#4
MASK action figures – US#11-12, 15, 19
Model Expo (mail order war games) – US#11
Monogram (plastic model kits) – US#3, US#4
Morphodroids (remote-controlled transforming cars) – US#11
MPC (model car kits) – US#27-30, 35-38; GIJ#1; HDM#1, 4
Onslaught: D-Day to the Rhine (board game) – US#32, HDM#2
Risk (board game) – US#4
Robotech role-playing game – US#30-32; HDM#1-2
Spacetubes (glow-in-the dark, glittery wand-shaped trinkets) – US#14
Spinjas (spinning top battle game) – US#54
Star Games (role-playing games retailer) – US#40

Tak-a-Toy (toy/game manufacturer) – US#53
Tomy Aurora motorised toy race track – US#30; HDM#1
Top Gun remote-controlled airplane – US#48, 50
Top Secret/S.I. (role-playing game) – US#35-36, 40, 44; HDM#4
TSR board games (Buck Rogers/Dragonlance) – US#47, 49

[51] THE MAN IN THE MACHINE!
US#51, 'April 1989' (published December 1988), 22 pages.

British reprint: UK#211, 1 April 1989 (Part 1), 11 pages; UK#212, 8 April 1989 (Part 2), 11 pages.

Credits:
Bob Budiansky (script); José Delbo (pencils); Dave Hunt (inks); Nel Yomtov (colours); Bill Oakley (letters); Don Daley (editor); Tom DeFalco (editor-in-chief); José Delbo and Danny Bulanadi (cover). **UK:** Andrew Wildman (cover, UK#211); John Stokes (cover, UK#212).

Plot:
Despite the Autobot forces having been decimated, Spike Witwicky wants out. Leaving the headless body of Fortress Maximus aboard the *Ark*, he returns home to his family. In an attempt to resume a 'normal' life, he later goes on a skiing trip with his college friend Cliff, but is haunted by bad dreams. The pair are attacked by Carnivac and Snarler, the Decepticon Pretender Beasts, who have orders to destroy Fortress Maximus – and therefore also Spike.

Spike realises that his nightmares represent his current bad feelings toward being binary-bonded to Fortress Maximus. Realising that he has to embrace that aspect of himself, he sends a mental command to his giant Autobot partner, and together again the pair are able to defeat the Decepticon attackers.

Notes:
Spike returns home, to a building he describes as 'my dad's house in Portland'. (When we first saw the building, in [40] 'Pretender to the Throne', it was described as a run-down boarding house. Presumably Sparkplug later purchased the building, using the insurance money from his destroyed garage perhaps, and renovated it.)

There are references to some famous glasses-wearers: Franklin D Roosevelt (1882-1945), the thirty-second President of the United States of America; Albert Einstein (1879-1955), the Nobel Prize-winning theoretical physicist; and Elton John (1947-), the perennially popular British singer/songwriter.

Optimus Prime is still counting the cost of the massacre in [50] 'Dark Star', and so is reluctant to let Spike leave the Autobot ranks. There is a flashback to Spike undergoing the binary-bonding surgery (which occurred at some point between [38] 'Trial by Fire' and [39] 'The Desert Island of Space'). Buster's recent capture by the Decepticons ([37] 'Toy Soldiers' to [49] 'Cold War') also gets a mention. Although Spike's helmet magnifies his telepathic connection to Fortress Maximus, he is able to achieve a modicum of control without it.

This story sees the first appearance of the Decepticon Pretender Beasts in the US comic. The ski resort visited by Spike and Cliff is said to be in the Sierra Nevada

Mountains in California.

UK Notes:
Spike goes to meet his college friend Cliff in San Francisco, the third time the Californian city had been referenced, after mentions in the UK-only stories [27.4] 'Fire on High' and [A2.6] 'The Mission'.

Although this story marked the US debut of Carnivac, he had previously appeared in the UK-only story [48.2] 'Time Wars'. Later, in [53.1] 'Survivors', it will be revealed that Catilla was also involved in the Decepticon attack on Spike in this story, but merely 'monitored' in the background, hence his non-appearance in the action. Snarler, Catilla and Carnivac were given their pretender shells as a 'reward' from Scorponok for taking part in the mission.

UK Changes:
Page 1, panel 1: artwork extended downwards; credits replaced.
Page 4, panel 1: the reference to issue #39 is changed to issue #157. 'See last issue – Don' becomes 'see issues 208 + 210'.
Page 13, panel 4: 'criticize' is changed to 'criticise'.
Page 18, panel 4: 'realize' is altered to 'realise'.
Page 22, panel 8, the 'the end' caption is painted out.

Roll Call:
Autobots: Optimus Prime, Blaster (as a corpse), Seaspray, Fortress Maximus and Cerebros.

Decepticons: Carnivac and **Snarler**.

Other: Buster, Sparkplug and Spike.

Review:
After the excesses of the last few stories, this is a refreshing change of pace. Primarily a character piece, it works well as an exploration of the Spike/Fortress Maximus dynamic; and the settings, a ski resort and nightmare world, are memorably different. The threat is provided in the form of the Pretender Beasts, who shine in what would prove to be their only American appearance.

This story works best when read straight after [50] 'Dark Star', to which it acts as a counterpoint. When taken out of context, it's far less impressive, the stakes being not high enough to get overly excited about. As with [20] 'Showdown', it does 'quiet interlude' well enough, but not enough as to be wholly satisfying. 3/5

[52] GUESS WHO THE MECANNIBALS ARE HAVING FOR DINNER?
US#52, 'May 1989' (published January 1989), 21 pages.

British reprint: UK#213, 15 April 1989 (Part 1), 5 pages; UK#214, 22 April 1989 (Part 2), 6 pages; UK#215, 29 April 1989 (Part 3), 5 pages; UK#216, 6 May 1989 (Part 4), 5 pages.

Credits:
Bob Budiansky (script); José Delbo (pencils); Dave Hunt (inks); Nel Yomtov (colours);

Manny Manos (letters); Don Daley (editor); Tom DeFalco (editor-in-chief); José Delbo and Danny Bulanadi (cover). **UK:** John Stokes (covers, UK#213 and 214); Jeff Anderson (cover, UK#215); Art Wetherell (cover, UK#216).

'Manny Manos' is another variation on Marvel's in-house 'Many Hands' pseudonym, as previously used on [9] 'Dis-Integrated Circuits' (*'manos'* being the Spanish word for 'hands').

Plot:
Repairing the masses of inactive Autobots will require vast quantities of microchips, so Optimus Prime sends the Pretenders Cloudburst and Landmine to a sleazy spaceport, Grand Central Space Station, to procure some. As robots are unwelcome on the station, the two Autobots go aboard disguised in their human shells.

The Autobots strike a deal with the Nebulans Throttle and Hi-Test, unware that they are Decepticon Powermaster engines. Fortunately, however, the Nebulans are equally ignorant of the fact that Cloudburst and Landmine are Autobots.

Throttle and Hi-Test are working as middle men for the Mecannibals, sphere-shaped and heavily-fanged mechanoids who like to eat robots. Next on their menu is Sky Lynx, but Cloudburst and Landmine manage to free their Autobot colleague and secure the microchips they need.

Unfortunately, Throttle and Hi-Test realise that the two humans are in fact disguised Autobots. Informed of this development, the Mecannibals have Cloudburst and Landmine captured. The Mecannibals prepare to feed …

Notes:
The opening scene is set in a cantina, with a gruff bartender refusing to serve a robot. This mirrors a famous scene in *Star Wars* (George Lucas, 1977), in which a cantina barman refuses to serve the droids R2D2 and C-3PO. The robot in this story looks remarkably like C-3PO, and the line 'We don't serve your kind here' is an exact quote from *Star Wars*.

Other *Star Wars* homages abound – Master Mouth, the lead Mecannibal, is a black marketeer reminiscent of movie villain Jabba the Hutt, and Landmine frees Sky Lynx using a weapon called a 'laser saber'.

The title is an allusion to *Guess Who's Coming to Dinner* (Stanley Kramer, 1967), which tackled the issue of interracial marriage; given that context, the spaceport's general attitude toward robotic life-forms would seem to be a thinly-veiled anti-racism message on the part of writer Bob Budiansky.

The barman in the cantina is named J'oh, presumably a reference to Joe the Bartender, a character from *The Jackie Gleason Show* (1952-57). This wasn't the first Jackie Gleason allusion in *The Transformers*; his sitcom *The Honeymooners* was memorably referenced in [5] 'The Last Stand'.

Grand Central Space Station would appear to be named after Grand Central Station (or Grand Central Terminal, to give it its proper name), a major transport hub in New York City. It is home to a number of undesirables, including gamblers, con-artists and prostitutes – or Antaresian pleasure slaves, as the script calls them. Antares is a real-life star, in the constellation of Scorpio.

After the Mecannibals eat the Chromite, Master Mouth exclaims that his meal was 'finger lickin' good', a reference to an advertising slogan for Kentucky Fried Chicken.

This is the first appearance of the Decepticon Powermasters since [42] 'People Power'; it's revealed that they've been working for the Mecannibals since their exile from Nebulos. Sky Lynx is seen again for the first time since his brief appearance in [45] 'Monstercon from Mars'; he is still travelling with Berko, who was last sighted in [44] 'The Cosmic Carnival'.

Triple Changes

This story's UK printing coincided with major format change for the UK *The Transformers* comic. New editor Euan Peters had boarded a sinking ship, as the title was haemorrhaging readers at an alarming rate – there was a real danger that sales would fall to a point where basic production costs couldn't be met.

The solution adopted by the publishers was two-fold. First, from UK#213, they raised the cover price by 3p to 38p. Then, from UK#215, the title went back to being partly black-and-white, as it had been between issue #2 and issue #26. Rather than have individual stories presented in a mix of colour and black-and-white, Peters took the bold step of splitting the comic into three strips – the first a full-colour American reprint, the second a UK-originated story in black-and-white, and finally a back-up strip in full colour.

Also debuting in UK#213 was a new design for the comic; the Transformation page was re-vamped yet again (far more successfully than the previous redesign in UK#183), as were the letters and 'Next Time' pages.

All in all, it was a dashing new look. However, as we shall see, the changes were not enough to stem the decline in sales. Ironically, if the negative feedback printed in the letters page is anything to go by, it would seem that the introduction of the black-and-white pages actually exacerbated the problem and ultimately hastened the title's demise.

UK Changes:

Page 1, panel 1: artwork extended upwards, credits replaced.
Page 4, panel 6: the reference to issue #50 is changed to #208-210. Editor Don Perlin's sign-off is excised.
Page 9, panel 3: 'Darkwind' is corrected to 'Dreadwing'.
Page 9, panel 4: the caption is deleted.
Page 9, panel 5: 'Darkwind' is again changed to 'Dreadwing'.
Page 21, panel 3: the 'To be continued' caption is painted out.

Roll Call:

Autobots: Optimus Prime (flashback only), Gears (corpse), Grimlock (corpse), Blaster (corpse), Goldbug (corpse), Sky Lynx, Landmine, Cloudburst, Groundbreaker (flashback only) and Sky High (flashback only).

Decepticons: Darkwing and Dreadwind.

Darkwing and Dreadwind appear only in their combined 'Dreadwing' mode.

Other: Berko and the **Mecannibals**.

Nebulans: Throttle and Hi-Test.

Review:

The Autobot Pretenders get some much-needed focus in this story, as they are thrown in at the deep end, on an undercover mission for Optimus Prime. They make for intriguing and unusual heroes, and their abilities are showcased well, especially in the scene where they rescue Sky Lynx.

Writer Bob Budiansky excels in world-building (prominent examples include [17] 'The Smelting Pool' and [HDM2] 'Broken Glass'), and the seedy space station setting allows him to go to town on the little details, like an alien bartender whose specialities include 'zygotic fermented slime slurpees with a twist of fungus'.

The plot is workmanlike rather than original, but the good work on the Pretenders and the well-realised setting more than make up for any shortcomings. 4/5

[52.1] THE FALL AND RISE OF THE DECEPTICON EMPIRE.

- UK#213, 15 April 1989 (Part 1), 6 pages
- UK#214, 22 April 1989 (Part 2), 5 pages

Credits:

Simon Furman (script); Lee Sullivan (art); Stuart Place (colours); Gary 'Glib' Gilbert (letters). For cover credits, see the entry for [52] 'Guess Who the Mecannibals are Having for Dinner' above.

Due to a production error, the credits for part two were missing, accidentally replaced by the credits for [52] 'Guess Who the Mecannibals are Having for Dinner'. A correction and apology was printed in UK#221

Plot:

Megatron and Ravage have returned to Cybertron, and are aghast at what they find there – Autobots walk the streets openly, and there is little sign of any Decepticon presence. Investigating, they travel to the Decepticon capital Helex, where they discover that, since the death of Straxus, the Decepticons have been ruled by a corrupt, decadent triumvirate.

Megatron confronts the three new rulers – Legonis, Octus and Seizer – and argues the point that the Decepticons on Cybertron have lost their way. Megatron is thrown into a gladiatorial arena and forced to battle another Decepticon, Quake. However, rather than finishing off his opponent, he makes another plea to the Decepticon audience.

Megatron's words strike a chord with those present, and the triumvirate are blasted to smithereens. now in control of the Decepticon forces on Cybertron, Megatron dreams of conquest once again.

Notes:

Picking up on the Cybertron-as-Rome parallel (see the notes to [A2.4] 'State Games'), this story sees the Decepticons ruled by a triumvirate (repeatedly misspelled 'triumverate' throughout) consisting of Legonis, Octus and Seizer. The names seem to be derived from famous Roman monikers. Seizer is an obvious play on Caesar and Octus on Octavius. It has been theorised that they are supposed to represent Julius Caesar and Gaius Octavius, better known as the Emperor Augustus, who were both members of ruling triumvirates. However, neither of those could be characterised as 'bloated and complacent'. There were many noted people named Caesar and Octavius in Ancient Roman history, so it's unclear if these Decepticons are supposed to be based on any specific historical characters, or just named so as to give a general sense of Ancient Rome. 'Caesar' was a title given to many Roman Emperors, and 'Octavius' was both a family name and a popular given name, usually bestowed upon the eighth-born child of the family.

Tracing the roots of Legonis's name is a little trickier. Some commentators have assumed that it's a reference to Marcus Aemilius Lepidus, also a member of a Roman triumvirate, but the name sounds more like Gaius Cassius Longinus, who plotted the assassination of Julius Caesar, or simply *legionis*, a Latin word for a legion or army.

To complete the link, the title of this story is derived from the book *The History of the Decline and Fall of the Roman Empire* (Edward Gibbon, 1776-89).

Megatron (or rather, his Straxus-created clone) and Ravage are seen here for the first time since [48.2] 'Time Wars'; they travelled to Cybertron in a 'craft'. (It will be revealed in [53.1] 'Survivors' that it's the ship that was previously owned by the Decepticon Mayhem Attack Squad.) Megatron refers to his previous visit to Cybertron, as seen in [23.2] 'Under Fire'.

The Decepticon capital is called Helex. This is its first mention in the comics; previous Decepticon commanders on Cybertron such as Straxus and Ratbat were based out of Polyhex. Helex is likely to be the 'Decepticon Imperial Headquarters' mentioned by Ratbat in [47] 'Club Con', and possibly also the location of Castle Decepticon, seen in [1] 'The Transformers'.

This is the first appearance of the Decepticon Triggercons in the present day. (They had previously figured in the extended flashback sequences in [48] 'The Flames of Boltax'.)

Octus is designed to resemble a Dalek, an alien monster from the British television series *Doctor Who* (1963-); this story's artist, Lee Sullivan, also drew Daleks for Marvel UK's *Doctor Who Magazine*, contributing to strip stories such as 'Nemesis of the Daleks'.

Outside of annual stories, this was to be the final UK-originated Transformers story to have its print debut in full colour. Originally intended as a one-shot, 11-page story, it was split into two following the introduction of the new three-story format adopted by *The Transformers* comic in UK#213.

Roll Call:
Decepticons: Ravage, Clone Megatron, Crankcase, Ruckus, Windsweeper and **Quake**.

Data File: Stuart Place (colourist)
Place did the rounds on Marvel UK's '80s output, with credits on *Captain Britain*, *Death's Head*, *Action Force* and *The Real Ghostbusters*.

Review:
Megatron is fantastic here, waltzing into the Decepticon base and turning the faction upside-down, all within the space of 11 pages. Fun, sharp and to the point. 4/5

UK Advertisements, Part 2: Transformers Toys
Unlike its American counterpart, the UK *The Transformers* comic would regularly carry advertisements for Transformers action figures:

Selected 1984 figures (Sideswipe, Bumblebee, Rumble etc) – UK#1.

Selected 1984 Autobot figures (Jazz, Mirage, Hound etc) – UK#3-14, 16.

Insecticons – UK#17, 19.

Selected 1985 Autobot figures (Red Alert, Tracks, Grapple etc) – UK#18, 46, 49, 52-53.

Selected 1985 Decepticon figures (Thrust, Ramjet, Ravage etc) – UK#20-22, 27-29, 47, 50, 55. (The first three appearances of this ad featured an error: the names of some of the toys were mixed up.)

Dinobots – UK#30-32, 45, 48, 51, 54.

Optimus Prime and Megatron – UK#33-44.

The Incredible New Teams (Stunticons, Aerialbots etc) – UK#59-63, 65, 97, 99, 101, 103, 105, 107, 109, 111, 114-116, 119-120.

Selected 1986 figures (Hot Rod, Cyclonus etc) – UK#67-73, 87, 93.

Triple Changers – UK#74-76, 86, 88.

The New Leaders (Ultra Magnus and Galvatron) – UK#77-85, 92, 96, 138.

Autobot Heroes (Rodimus Prime and Wreck-Gar) – UK#112-113, 118, 124.

Headmasters – UK#128, 132, 134, 144, 146, 148, 153, 157, 160, 162, 164, 187.

Targetmasters – UK#130-131, 133, 136, 140 (double-sized 'poster' version), 142, 150, 152, 155, 185, 193, 201, 204, 208, 211.

Pretenders – UK#167, 169, 173, 179, 191, 199, 202, 206, 209, 214, 216, 218, 227.

Powermasters – UK#172, 175, 177, 182, 188, 200, 203, 207, 210.

Micromasters – UK#219-220, 222, 226, 229, 232-233, 235, 237, 243, 248, 250, 252-255.

Pretender Classics – UK#223, 225, 230, 234, 239, 242, 249, 251, 256.

Classic Heroes – UK#258, 262, 266, 282, 285, 288, 294, 296, 302, 311-312, 315-316, 322-323, 329, 331-332. (From issue 311, the advertisement was amended slightly: Tracks and Sideswipe replaced Sunstreaker and Ironhide.)

Micromaster Combiners – UK#270, 274, 276-277, 279, 281, 284, 291, 293, 299.

[52.2] RACE WITH THE DEVIL
- UK#215, 29 April 1989 (Part 1), 6 pages
- UK#216, 6 May 1989 (Part 2), 5 pages
- UK#217, 13 May 1989 (Part 3), 6 pages
- UK#218, 20 May 1989 (Part 4), 5 pages

Credits:
Simon Furman (script); Andrew Wildman (art); Gary 'Glib' Gilbert (letters); Jez Hall (cover, UK#217); Lee Sullivan (cover, UK#218). For cover credits to issues 215 and 216, see the entry for [52] 'Guess Who the Mecannibals are Having for Dinner' above.

Jez Hall was credited only as 'J Hall'; his forename was revealed in the following issue.

Plot:
The Triggerbots are sent to Earth to find out what Darkwing and Dreadwind are up to. It seems the Decepticon Powermasters are engaged in a mysterious mission, and the Autobots are investigating who sent them and what they're after.

After a chase through space, both parties end up in Peru, where archaeologist and adventurer Susan Hoffman is also present, searching for a native shrine worshipped by the local Juluth tribe. The Decepticons soon find what they were looking for – the body of Starscream – but are shocked to discover that his corpse has been reanimated by the

Underbase energies he absorbed before he died.

This zombie Starscream is just as dangerous as ever, and attempts to kill both the Autobots and Decepticons present. Backstreet attempts to reason with the creature, with some success. However, as soon as the zombie lets its guard down, the Nebulans Throttle and Hi-Test absorb the remaining Underbase energy. Starscream's power source depleted, the Decepticons swoop in and make off with his now inert remains.

The Autobots, meanwhile, rescue Hoffman's team of explorers after they were captured by tribespeople.

Notes:
This was the first completely black-and-white UK strip, and the first to have any uncoloured pages since the UK printing of [7] 'Warrior School', when the comic was still a fortnightly publication. As with [52.1] 'The Fall and Rise of the Decepticon Empire', this story was hastily chopped into smaller chunks to fit the new three-story format introduced in UK#213. (It was originally to have consisted of two 11-page segments.)

The majority of this story is set in Peru, in the environs of (the fictional) Mount Ancayo. The name recalls that of Ankayuq K'uchu, a real-world mountain in Southern Peru, part of the Andes range. However, the names of the tribe and of their devil god – Juluth and Myaz respectively – are completely made up. Apparently the Juluth are a 'tribe unchanged since the time of the Incas' (i.e. since the 16th Century), although their clothing appears very dissimilar to real-world Incan dress.

Adventurer Susan Hoffman makes her final appearance here, having previously featured in [29.1] 'Ancient Relics' and [31.5] 'Ladies' Night'. As a bit of an in-joke, three of her assistants are drawn to resemble Egon Spengler, Peter Venkman and Ray Stantz, characters from *The Real Ghostbusters* (the comic version of which was one of Marvel UK's most popular titles at that point).

This is the first appearance of the Triggerbots in the present-day since [46] 'Ca$h and Car-nage', which ended with Backstreet on Earth while Dogfight and Override were prisoners of the Decepticons. Given that the Decepticons were shown to be in complete disarray in [52.1] 'The Fall and Rise of the Decepticon Empire', it's no wonder they were able to escape. The Triggerbots had also appeared in the flashback sequences in [48] 'The Flames of Boltax'.

Starscream was destroyed in [50] 'Dark Star'. This isn't the first time that Transformer zombies had appeared in the UK comic (see also [40.1] 'City of Fear').

Imperfect Timing
This story throws up two problems regarding the chronology of the events depicted therein. The first is an internal dating issue, the second concerns how this story relates to the others around it.

The internal problem is this: the opening to Part 1 states that it is 24 April 1989, but later in Part 3 it is 1 May 1989, and there is no obvious point in the action for the seven-day gap to occur. While not a perfect solution, the best place for the gap would probably be immediately after the initial chase through space (after the first panel on Part 2). We can postulate that it took a week for the Decepticons to track Starscream's corpse to Peru. Alternatively, it could be the case that Starscream's remains were spread over a wide area, and the Decepticons spent a week collecting various parts elsewhere before returning for his 'skeleton'.

With the internal chronology sorted, the other issue remains. It eventually transpires that the Powermasters' paymaster is none other than Megatron (the real one, not the clone), who doesn't become active for a good while yet. Also, it takes Darkwing and Dreadwind until [57] 'The Resurrection Gambit' to return Starscream's body to Megatron. This would seem to indicate that this story is set quite a bit later than many of the others that surround it. The order of events, therefore, must go something like this …

- The real Megatron awakens on Cybertron and resumes control from the clone ([57.1] 'Two Megatrons').
- Megatron then sets in motion his plan to reactivate Starscream, and in April 1989 sends Darkwing and Dreadwind to collect his corpse ([52.2] 'Race with the Devil').
- Megatron reveals that he has returned ([56] 'Back from the Dead').
- Darkwing and Dreadwind meet with Megatron, having completed their mission to recover Starscream's body ([57] 'The Resurrection Gambit').

All of which means that this story is actually set roughly contemporaneously with [56] 'Back from the Dead', which wouldn't be published in the UK for another five months. This was the first continuity headache that the new three-story format would throw up – it wouldn't be the last …

Roll Call:
Autobots: Backstreet, Dogfight and Override.

Decepticons: Starscream (as an animated corpse), Darkwing and Dreadwind.

Other: Susan Hoffman.

Nebulans: Throttle and Hi-Test.

Darkwing and Dreadwind appear both individually and as part of the 'Dreadwing' combined super jet.

Data File: Jez Hall (artist)
After the briefest of stints at Marvel UK, Hall provided the art for the *Count Duckula* strips in the *News of the World* newspaper. He later broke into the field of animation, as a storyboard artist, concept artist, director and animator. His credits include *Gargoyles*, *Hurricanes*, *Noddy*, *Dexter's Laboratory*, *Thunderbirds* and *Red Dwarf*, plus the 2017 reconstruction of the abandoned *Doctor Who* serial, 'Shada'.

Review:
A rather back-loaded story. The final part is great, with Backstreet managing to talk Starscream round, only to be gazumped by Throttle and Hi-Test. The problem is that the rest is utterly vacuous – the pursuit through space, the reappearance of Susan Hoffman, and the added threat of a native tribe … all these elements are used to bulk out the story, marking time until the conclusion. An oddly-structured adventure, which ultimately works best if you just ignore all but its final five pages. 2/5

[53] RECIPE FOR DISASTER!

US#53, 'June 1989' (published February 1989), 22 pages.

British reprint: UK#217, 13 May 1989 (Part 1), 5 pages; UK#218, 20 May 1989 (Part 2), 6 pages; UK#219, 27 May 1989 (Part 3), 6 pages; UK#220, 3 June 1989 (Part 4), 5 pages.

Credits:
Bob Budiansky (script); José Delbo (pencils); Dave Hunt (inks); Nel Yomtov (colours); Jade Moede (letters); Don Daley (editor); Tom DeFalco (editor-in-chief); Jim Lee (cover). **UK:** John Stokes (cover, UK#219); Jeff Anderson (cover, UK#220). For cover credits to issues 217 and 218, see the entry for [52.2] 'Race with the Devil' above.

Plot:
Captured by the Mecannibals and on the verge of being eaten, Landmine and Cloudburst manage to talk their way out of trouble – in exchange for procuring some delicious lead sulfide crystals, the Mecannibals agree to free them. While Berko remains a captive as collateral, Landmine and Cloudburst head to the planet Femax to collect the lead sulfide.

Femax is a planet ruled by giant, Transformer-sized warrior women, and so the two Autobots in their human Pretender shells are able to blend in – however, on Femax men are forbidden to enter the paradise-like Golden Realm, and Landmine and Cloudburst are arrested for trespassing.

The Femaxian commander, or First One, falls for Cloudburst, and asks the Autobot to be her mate. Cloudburst is forced to reveal that he is, in fact, a robot ... and is summarily executed, his head chopped off.

However, Landmine is able to placate the Femaxians, who, after a heated argument, agree to repair Cloudburst and give the Autobots the crystals they require. Back on the Mecannibal ship, the Autobots are allowed to go free, and point the hungry mechanoids in the direction of Decepticons Dreadwind and Darkwing, who are forced to flee through space with the Mecannibals in hot pursuit.

Notes:
The main talking point of this story is the US comic's position on Transformer gender and sex, revealed here for the first time – both within the strip itself and in the letters page. When the First One attempts to seduce Cloudburst, he reveals that sex is a concept alien to him: 'You don't understand. Where I come from, there are no men, no women.' Cloudburst feels no attraction to the Femaxian woman whatsoever – when asked if he finds the First One desirable, his response is simply: 'You're asking the wrong person.' The letters page clarifies the point: 'Transformers have no gender! Since the Transformers do not reproduce sexually, they have no need to be male or female. Most have characteristics that are commonly associated with males, so they are referred to as "he's". On a rare occasion, one might come across as female and is referred to as a "she". Arcee fits into this latter category, but referring to themselves as "he's" and "she's" is a convention the Transformers probably picked up from hanging around Earthlings too long'.

This story is a direct sequel to [52] 'Guess Who the Mecannibals are Having for Dinner', and picks up from the cliffhanger ending to that adventure, with the Autobots on the verge of being eaten.

Lead (II) sulfide crystals – the Mecannibals' garnish of choice, apparently – are also known as galena, and occur naturally on Earth.

UK Changes:
Page 1, panel 1: artwork extended upwards, credits replaced.
Page 2, panel 4: 'see last issue – Don' becomes 'issue 215'.
Page 6, panel 3: 'savory' and 'flavorful' are amended to read 'savoury' and 'flavourful'.
Page 12, panel 1: the word 'meanwhile' is painted out.
Page 13, panel 5: 'apologize' is twice changed to 'apologise'.
Page 16, panel 3: 'armor' is altered to 'armour'.
Page 20, panel 4: 'honored' is changed to 'honoured'.

Roll Call:
Autobots: Sky Lynx, Landmine and Cloudburst.

Decepticons: Darkwing and Dreadwind.

Other: Berko and the Mecannibals.

Nebulans: Throttle and Hi-Test.

Review:
A group of Transformers arrive on a planet where women are the powerful dominant gender and men are 'weak of body and mind'. It's a standard sci-fi trope, and is usually a springboard for the author to delve into weighty themes such as gender equality and sexism, shedding light on our own society.

How refreshing, then, that writer Bob Budiansky plays against type, aiming at gentle comedy rather than weighty, issue-based drama. The scene in which the Femaxian First One tries to get Cloudburst into bed, not realising that he's an alien robot with no interest in sex, is pure farce.

However, despite the light-hearted nature of the story, it doesn't really come off. At times it's just too absurd for its own good – notably in the sequence where, just as they're about to feed on Landmine and Cloudburst, the Mecannibals let the Autobots go because they're all out of condiments. Also, the sequence where Cloudburst has to prove his worthiness by undergoing a number of physical tests is pure padding.

An amiable tale that's difficult to actively hate, but far too flimsy to work properly. 2/5

[53.1] SURVIVORS!
- UK#219, 27 May 1989 (Part 1), 6 pages
- UK#220, 3 June 1989 (Part 2), 5 pages
- UK#221, 10 June 1989 (Part 3), 5 pages
- UK#222, 17 June 1989 (Part 4), 6 pages

Credits:
Simon Furman (script); Dan Reed (art, parts 1-2); John Stokes (art, parts 3-4); Gary 'Glib' Gilbert (letters); Jeff Anderson (cover, UK#221); Simon Coleby (cover, UK#222). For cover credits to issues #219 and #220, see the entry for [53] 'Recipe for Disaster' above.

Plot:
Two groups of Autobots and Decepticons, isolated and forgotten after the Time Wars, discuss joining forces to form a new group of their own. While the Autobots (what remains of the Wrecker commando unit) are eager for the alliance, the Decepticons (previously members of the Mayhem Attack Squad) aren't so sure. When the group hears of trouble at a nearby nuclear power plant, the Autobots head off to avert the disaster while the Decepticons remain behind, still arguing amongst themselves as to the benefits of the proposed coalition.

The cause of the problems at the power plant is the Autobot Skids, who was returned to Earth when Galvatron died, having been trapped in limbo for two years. The mind-parasites that infected Skids during his stay in limbo have the ability to turn dreams into reality – unfortunately, horrific creatures from Skids' nightmares have become manifest and have pursued him to the power plant.

The ex-Wreckers arrive on the scene, but are reticent to fight, for fear that any stray shots might cause the nuclear reactor to go into meltdown. Ultimately, however, the day is saved by Carnivac and Catilla, who arrive just in time to defeat the nightmare creatures.

Although the Decepticon Snarler wants no part of the alliance (and swears to kill the defectors when he next sees them), Carnivac and Catilla join the small band of Autobots, and the new group – the Survivors – is complete.

Notes:
This story sees the formation of the Survivors, an alliance of Autobots and Decepticons who survived being attacked by Megatron and Galvatron in [48.2] 'Time Wars'. The group consists of the Autobots Inferno, Springer, Broadside and Skids, plus the Decepticon Pretender Beasts Catilla and Carnivac (although Catilla converts to the Autobot faction by the end of the story). They are stranded on Earth since their ship was stolen by Megatron and Ravage in [52.1] 'The Fall and Rise of the Decepticon Empire'.

Skids has returned to our dimension, having been displaced to limbo when Galvatron travelled back in time to the present day, as part of the mass-substituton effect. With Galvatron now dead ([48.2] 'Time Wars'), Skids is returned to Earth. (Skids was displaced way back in [23.4] 'Fallen Angel', though he has been glimpsed a few times in the interim, in stories such as [36] 'Spacehikers' and [48.2] 'Time Wars'.) The mental parasites who inhabit limbo, and their ability to turn dreams into reality, were first seen in [23.3] 'Distant Thunder'.

Catilla becomes an Autobot in this story, and wears the Autbot insignia from here on (although there's no Rite of the Autobrand – see [14] 'Rock and Roll-Out' – so his affiliation is only 'honorary'). The Pretender Beasts were given their shells by Scorponok in exchange for their recent attack on Spike Witwicky, as seen in [51] 'The Man in the Machine'.

The Hudden Nuclear Power Plant, said to be located in California, is fictional (although, coincidentally, a real-world Californian nuclear plant, Rancho Seco, was closed in June 1989 – at the same time this story was being published in the UK).

This was the final UK story written with the old 11-page format in mind. (It was originally written as a two-parter, but split into four parts due to the format change of UK#213.) From now on, all UK stories would be written specifically for the new, shorter slot.

Repeat to Fade

When readers wrote in to the UK letters page clamouring for the return of fan favourite character Death's Head, UK#221 was probably not what they had in mind. Instead of a new story featuring the popular bounty-hunter, the UK *The Transformers* comic re-ran his debut outing, [27.1] 'Wanted: Galvatron – Dead or Alive'. This was the first time the UK comic had re-run strips that had already seen print within its pages, and was another sign of the book's declining sales. At the turn of the year, readers were being treated to 11 pages of new, full-colour Transformers action every week; now around half of the 11 pages were reprints of old material, and the rest were in black and white.

Although the American stories would resume in UK#232, with the publication of [54] 'King Con', this wouldn't be the last time that old strips would be reprinted as cheap filler material. While the policy undoubtedly helped the comic stave off cancellation and continue on past its three hundredth issue, it was an unpopular move with some long-time readers who were already familiar with these stories.

The full list of reprints is as follows:

- [29.1] 'Wanted: Galvatron – Dead or Alive' (originally published in UK#113-114, reprinted in UK#221-224).
- [31.3] 'Headhunt' (originally published in UK#133-134, reprinted in UK#225-228).
- [23.5] 'Resurrection' (originally published in UK#103-104, reprinted in UK#229-232).
- [31.1] 'Worlds Apart' (originally published in UK#130-131, reprinted in UK#255-258).
- [36.2] 'The Legacy of Unicron' (originally published in UK#146-151, reprinted in UK#290-301).
- [20.1] 'In the National Interest' (originally published in UK#74-77, reprinted in UK#302-307).
- [4.2] 'The Enemy Within' (originally published in UK#13-17, reprinted in UK#308-309, 313-317).
- [53.5] 'The Big Shutdown' (originally published in UK#230-231, reprinted in UK#330-331).
- [59.2] 'The Greatest Gift of All' (originally published in UK#250, reprinted in UK#332).

Roll Call:
Autobots: Skids, Springer, Broadside and Catilla.

Decepticons: Carnivac and Snarler.

Data File: John Stokes (artist)
Another British artist to successfully make the move to American titles, Stokes began his career working on comics such as *Buster* (notably their *Fishboy* strips), *Lion*, *Doctor Who Magazine* and *2000 AD*. Other works include *Batman*, *Alpha Flight*, *Justice League of America* and *Wonder Woman*.

Review:
Despite being quite a small-scale affair, this is a story that has the perfect blend of adventure and characterisation. The action scenes are well done, and the unusual

villains – a group of creatures from Skids' nightmares – are memorably chilling.
But the real key to this story is in the various dilemmas faced by the characters – Skids considers suicide, hoping that his death will also destroy the creatures his mind has unwittingly created; Carnivac deliberates whether or not to join with the Autobots, at the cost of becoming a traitor; and Springer has to defeat the monsters, even though he knows that doing so could risk Skids' life, or even cause a nuclear explosion.
The first true classic of the black-and-white era. 5/5

[53.2] ASPECTS OF EVIL!
- UK#223, 24 June 1989 (1), 5 pages
- UK#224, 1 July 1989 (2), 5 pages
- UK#225, 8 July 1989 (3), 5 pages
- UK#226, 15 July 1989 (4), 5 pages
- UK#227, 22 July 1989 (5), 5 pages

Credits:
Simon Furman (script); Jeff Anderson (art, part 1); Art Wetherell (pencils, part 2), Simon Coleby (inks, part 2; pencils, part 5); Andrew Wildman (art, part 3); Lee Sullivan (art, part 4); Cam Smith (inks, part 5); Helen Stones (letters, part 1); Gary 'Glib' Gilbert (letters, parts 2-3 and 5); Nick Abadzis (letters, part 4); Jeff Anderson (covers, UK#223 and 225-226); Geoff Senior (covers, UK#224 and 227).

Plot:
The year 2356: Rodimus Prime lies on a hospital bed, deathly ill. Speaking to a young student, he muses on the nature of evil, and gives five examples of the most evil creatures he has ever met.

Prime's first example is Scorponok, with his famous cunning; he recounts a confrontation from the year 1991 when, during the Decepticon Civil War, Scorponok came under attack from Megatron's Air Strike Patrol. Scorponok manoeuvres a situation whereby he is captured by Hot Rod – and therefore Hot Rod is duty-bound to protect the Decepticon from attack. While Hot Rod is busy battling the Air Strike Patrol, Scorponok makes his escape.

The next flashback involves Galvatron. After triumphing in the Time Wars, Rodimus Prime returns to 2009, only to find that reality has been drastically changed – Galvatron is still alive, and Cybertron is under Decepticon control. Galvatron goads Rodimus Prime into attacking him – Prime's uncontrolled rage 'taints' the Matrix within him, causing pain to the other Autobots present. Rodimus realises that he must break off the attack in order to save his friends.

The cold, logical Shockwave is the next subject. Rodimus Prime recalls an incident in 2004, when Shockwave attacked the opening ceremony of Autobot City on Earth. Shockwave had planned and predicted everything to the letter, thought of every contingency. The operation was going perfectly, the Autobots and humans present seemingly doomed. However, Shockwave didn't reckon on the rash young Autobot Hot Rod, whose illogical actions could never have been foreseen. Hot Rod confronted Shockwave directly, forcing the Decepticon into retreat.

Megatron is the focus of the fourth flashback: Hot Rod remembers events from 1990, when Megatron suspected that one of his troops was really an Autobot agent. Bludgeon seemed the most likely culprit, but he swore his innocence and demanded the right to trial by combat. During the resulting battle, one of the Decepticons, Warmonger, hesitated when he had a kill-shot. Megatron immediately realises that Warmonger is the traitor, and kills him. Megatron reveals that he was unaware whether Bludgeon was the traitor or not – he was merely using him to flush out the *real* traitor.

The final example is evil incarnate – the chaos-bringer Unicron. Rodimus Prime recalls how, in the year 2010, Unicron made a third attempt to destroy Cybertron, but was defeated when Rodimus Prime unleashed the power of the Matrix. However, Unicron somehow survived within Prime, having been absorbed by the Matrix.

Back in 2356, the student storms out – Rodimus's stories have corrupted him, and now he seeks Unicron for himself. Rodimus Prime screams in horror as he realises that Unicron still exists within him and his evil powers will soon 'hold sway once more'.

Notes:
This tale takes the form of five stories-within-a-story; each part focuses on a different villain, in the form of a flashback told by a wizened Rodimus Prime to a young student. The framing sequences are set in the year 2356, so chronologically speaking this is the penultimate *The Transformers* adventure (with only [A4.5] 'Peace', set in 2510, occurring later).

The Scorponok flashback is set in 1991, 'near to the end of the Decepticon Civil War'. This doesn't neatly fit into continuity, and indeed contradicts events of later adventures that are set in 1991. While a Decepticon Civil War does indeed occur, it involves Shockwave versus Scorponok (as seen in adventures such as [72] 'All This and Civil War 2') or Megatron versus Shockwave (as per [61.1] 'Starting Over'), rather than Megatron versus Scorponok as seen here. If it actually happened (and we have to consider that a confused, tormented Rodimus Prime could be an unreliable narrator), this story must have taken place in Timeline A – the parallel reality in which Galvatron never altered history (see [27.1] 'Wanted: Galvatron – Dead or Alive' for more on this).

The Shockwave sequence, on the other hand, is set in 2004 and ties in neatly with events we've already seen. It shows Shockwave launching an attack on the newly-completed Autobot City, which was still in the planning stages in 2003 (according to [A3.4] 'Ark Duty').

The Megatron segment is again problematic. Ostensibly set in 1990, it features Megatron alive and well – but according to the US stories, Megatron will be largely inactive during that year, between the explosion in [59] 'Skin Deep' and his resurrection in [77] 'Exodus'. Again, this is a story better placed in Timeline A.

Hot Rod's Nebulan companion Firebolt is present in the 1991 sequence, indicating that his death (reported in [31.3] 'Headhunt') happened at some point after that date.

Time After Time
The two segments not covered above, featuring Galvatron and Unicron respectively, deserve an essay all of their own, seeing as they are set in a strange, post-Time Wars future, in which Galvatron still exists.

How was the post-Time Wars future created?
After the events of [48.2] 'Time Wars', Rodimus Prime and his fellow Autobots from the future (Timeline A) attempt to return to their own time. However, rather than returning to Timeline A, they instead find themselves in this new, altered future.

In [48.2] 'Time Wars', a rift in the space-time continuum threatened to destroy both

Earth and Cybertron, but the Transformers were able to seal it and allow time to correct itself. The rift was inadvertently created by Galvatron, whose meddling in history (from [20.2] 'Target: 2006' onwards) created the splinter reality Timeline B. When time corrected itself, it readjusted so that the root cause of the rift – Galvatron's time travelling – now never happened. So when Rodimus and company return to the future, they find a new reality in which Galvatron never left, and in which he has managed to conquer Cybertron.

All future stories set after [48.2] 'Time Wars' – 'Aspects of Evil' (parts 2 and 5, plus the framing sequence), [59.3] 'Shadow of Evil' and [A4.5] 'Peace' – take place in this 'readjusted' post-Time Wars future.

The Galvatron of this future shall henceforth be referred to as 'Galvatron III', to avoid confusion with the original Galvatron of timeline A (who perished in [48.2] 'Time Wars') and Galvatron II (who will be introduced in [67] 'Rhythms of Darkness').

The Future Matrix

In the future timelines, Rodimus Prime used the Matrix to destroy Unicron; although the chaos-bringer was physically dead, his evil was absorbed by the Matrix (as per [36.2] 'The Legacy of Unicron'). The will of Unicron remained dormant within the Matrix until 2009 (in the revised post-Time Wars future), when Rodimus Prime was goaded into attacking Galvatron – this rage fuelled the darkness that was growing within the Autobots' sacred talisman.

Events came to a head a year later, in [59.3] 'Shadow of Evil', by which time Unicron had amassed enough power to attempt to take over the Matrix completely, and with it the body of Rodimus Prime. He was stopped, albeit temporarily.

Later in 2010 (as per the Unicron segment of 'Aspects of Evil'), Unicron awakens again, but this time he is able to manifest himself physically. Once more, Rodimus Prime uses the Matrix to destroy Unicron's body, but again, the toll is great. (The last panel of this sequence sees Rodimus ordering his troops to fall back: 'Stay away from me, it's not safe' – implying that Unicron's essence survived again within the Matrix.)

When next we see Rodimus (the 'Aspects of Evil' framing sequence), he is desperately ill (probably a result of Unicron's growing influence within him): 'I'm weakening – letting his evil powers hold sway once more!' Presumably Rodimus is able to win the battle of wills against Unicron (just as he nearly did in [59.3] 'Shadow of Evil'): when he later appears in [A4.5] 'Peace', he is back on his feet and looking healthy.

Aspects of Earthforce?

The final UK-only stories (beginning with [60.1] 'Perchance to Dream'), collectively dubbed 'The Earthforce Saga', are set around 1990 and showcase a team of Earth-based Autobots who defend the planet from the combined forces of Shockwave and Megatron. While the continuity is a bit iffy (see the essay under [61.1] 'Starting Over' for more on this), the general point is that a version of Megatron is shown to be active in 1990. So while the Scorponok and Megatron segments don't mesh well with the American comics, is there a case to be made for them being a part of the Earthforce storyline?

At first glance, the answer is a resounding yes. When last we see the Earthforce Megatron (in [63.3] 'Assassins'), he is working in cahoots with Stranglehold, Bludgeon and Octopunch, just as he is here. In that story he had been usurped as Decepticon leader by Soundwave and Starscream, and a plan to retake command was thwarted by the Autobots. It's possible, then, that following the events of 'Assassins', Megatron, Bludgeon and company decamped to Cybertron and took part in the events of this 'Aspects of Evil' segment.

This leaves two groups of Decepticons on Earth, post-Earthforce – Scorponok's group of Headmasters, Targetmasters and Pretenders (mentioned in [62.5] 'The Living Nightlights') and the older, classic Decepticons. It's entirely possible that, early in 1991, Shockwave re-took command of the classic group, and led them in a brief war against Scorponok's group for ultimate supremacy of the Earth-based Decepticons.

Unfortunately, however, there is a major snag in this argument – the Rodimus Prime of 'Aspects' is from Timeline A, and therefore should have no memory of the Earthforce era, which occurred in Timeline B. Unless the events of Earthforce happened in both timelines (which in itself would cause all kinds of continuity headaches), we have to accept that all of the 'Aspects of Evil' segments are set in Timeline A and its post-Time Wars offshoot.

Roll Call:
Other than Rodimus Prime and his unnamed student, all other characters appear in flashback only. A year in brackets after a character's name indicates the setting of the flashback in which they feature.

Autobots: Optimus Prime (2004), Ultra Magnus (2004), Hot Rod (1991, 2004), Kup (2004, 2009, 2010), Blurr (2004, plus 2009 as a decapitated head), Rodimus Prime, Arcee (2004, 2009, 2010), **Landfill** (1991), **Quickmix** (1991), **Flak** (2009) and **Sunrunner** (2009).

Decepticons: Megatron (1990), Shockwave (2004), Thrust (2004), Galvatron III (2009, 2010), Astrotrain (2004), Blitzwing (2004), Scorponok (1991), Crankcase (2009), Ruckus (2009), Windsweeper (2009), **Stormcloud** (1991), **Whisper** (1991), **Tailwind** (1991), **Nightflight** (1991), **Stranglehold** (1990), **Bludgeon** (1990) and **Octopunch** (1990).

Other: Unicron (2010).

Nebulans: Firebolt (1991).

It's unclear whether or not Landfill's and Quickmix's Targetmaster companions – Flintlock, Silencer, Boomer and Ricochet – make appearances here; the Autobots' weapons are drawn indistinctly.

Many Decepticon jets appear in the 2004 sequence, but only Thrust, Astrotrain and Blitzwing are shown closely enough as to be distinguishable.

Data File: Cam Smith (artist)
Eisner Award-winning inker Cam Smith is another who went onto bigger and better things after his work on *The Transformers*. After leaving Marvel UK (where his inks featured in titles such as *Doctor Who Magazine*), he went on to have a good career in America, on titles such as *Superman*, *Supergirl*, *The Incredible Hulk*, *Fantastic Four* and *X-Men*.

Review:

The Megatron sequence is a brilliant vignette, and the best use of the five-page format thus far. Unfortunately, however, the rest of the flashbacks are generally poor. Shockwave fares especially badly, launching an attack on Autobot City before deciding to retreat at the first sign of trouble. Scorponok's sequence, rather than being a demonstration of pure evil, is merely small-time villainy by his standards. The Galvatron segment suffers from some less-than-stellar art, and readers are left scratching their heads at the new altered future, which comes out of nowhere, with little explanation. The Unicron sequence isn't bad, but suffers from having to wrap up the plot too quickly, making for a rather unsatisfactory ending.

The basic premise is sound, and there are many memorable moments, but – Megatron sequence notwithstanding – it's frustrating that such an interesting concept is squandered on such unworthy material. 2/5.

[53.3] [DOUBLE] DEAL OF THE CENTURY!
UK#228, 29 July 1989, 5 pages

Credits:

Simon Furman (script); Andrew Wildman (art); Stuart Bartlett (letters); Jeff Anderson (cover).

Plot:

The Pretender Chainclaw has been entrusted with some Autobot battle plans, but before he can deliver them to Optimus Prime, he is kidnapped by a mysterious Decepticon named Dealer. Optimus Prime receives a message from Dealer, asking for five thousand Energon units for the safe return of the plans and Chainclaw. Prime reluctantly accepts, and sends an Autobot named Double to make the exchange.

Meanwhile, Dealer meets with Scorponok and offers him the plans, in exchange for five thousand Energon units. Scorponok agrees to the transaction and gains access to the plans. Later, Double returns to Optimus Prime, having secured the return of Chainclaw. He tells Optimus Prime that the Decepticons double-crossed him and have kept the plans for themselves.

As Optimus Prime battles Scorponok for the plans, Double flees the scene; Double and Dealer are one and the same being, a mercenary named Doubledealer, who has just conned both factions to the tune of five thousand Energon units.

Notes:

This story features a group of Autobot Micromasters, the Race Car Patrol. Chronologically, therefore, it must be set after [54] 'King Con', in which they are seen to arrive on Earth for the first time.

(There's evidence to suggest that the publication order of the UK comic was in a state of flux at this time, as editor Euan Peters and writer Simon Furman got to grips with the new three-story format – it could well be the case that this story was originally intended to be published concurrently with [54] 'King Con', making the chronology much easier for readers to follow. Already, two stories, [52.1] 'The Fall and Rise of the Decepticon Empire' and [53.1] 'Survivors', had been cut into chunks in order to fit the newly-revamped comic, and even Marvel themselves seemed confused as to what was going on – their Marvel Checklist feature, a run-down of all Marvel UK titles available that week, claimed that UK#228 would contain the story [53.4] 'Hunting Party', which actually saw print in UK#229.)

There is talk of an 'Autobot resistance' on Cybertron, implying that things aren't going well for the Cybertronian Autobots since the clone Megatron's ascent to power in [52.1] 'The Fall and Rise of the Decepticon Empire'.

A Nebulous Concept

The *Transformers: Headmasters* comic mini-series showed a group of Transformers – the original Headmasters and Targetmasters – travel to the planet Nebulos, where they became binary-bonded to some of the native Nebulans. Later, when the Powermasters were introduced, the comic made a return trip to Nebulos, in [42] 'People Power', and a second group of Transformers gained Nebulan partners. Given that [42] 'People Power' established that the planet Nebulos was now deadly to Transformer life, it's uncertain how any Transformers not already bonded could suddenly gain Nebulan partners. Nevertheless, more and more Targetmasters, Headmasters and Powermasters were then introduced, with no explanation as to how they gained their Nebulan companions. Two possibilities present themselves: perhaps there is another planet full of Nebulans, either a sister planet or a colony, which has been visited by Transformers. The other explanation is that Nebulans have spaceflight technology and a group of them travelled to Cybertron, volunteering for the binary-bonding process.

Some of these new characters featured in the comic *without* any Nebulan partners. In this story, the Powermaster Doubledealer (whose action figure boasts two Powermaster engines) is depicted as a standard triple-changer, with no Nebulans in sight. In [53.2] 'Aspects of Evil', the Targetmasters Landfill and Quickmix appeared briefly, but if their Nebulan companions were featured at all, it certainly wasn't very clear.

Roll Call:

Autobots: Optimus Prime, Chainclaw, Roadhandler, Free Wheeler, Swindler and Tailspin.

Decepticons: Scorponok, Mindwipe, Weirdwolf and Doubledealer.

Nebulans: Zarak, Vorath and Monzo.

The three Nebulans appear only as the heads of Scorponok, Mindwipe and Weirdwolf respectively, rather than as individuals.

Data File: Andrew Wildman (artist)

After providing a number of covers for the title, Wildman soon graduated to interior strip work on *The Transformers*. With Simon Furman and a couple of others, he later moved to the US incarnation of the title, and from there to other American comics such as *X-Men Adventures*, *G.I. Joe: A Real American Hero* and *Spider-Man 2099*. He has returned to the franchise on many occasions, contributing to *Transformers: Generation 2*, *Transformers: The War Within* and *Transformers: Regeneration One*. He is now a concept and storyboard artist for television, with credits on shows such as *The Fades*, *Our Zoo* and *Doctor Who*.

Review:
By far the shortest individual Transformers story presented to this point, '[Double] Deal of the Century' nevertheless packs a lot into its meagre page count. It's a fun script, and Doubledealer's plan is certainly well-plotted and engaging, although perhaps more could have been done to disguise the 'twist' ending, which is obvious almost immediately. 3/5

[53.4] THE HUNTING PARTY
UK#229, 5 August 1989, 5 pages

Credits:
Simon Furman (script); Simon Coleby (art); Helen Stone (letters); Geoff Senior (cover).

This story was later reprinted in full colour in the *Transformers Annual 1992*; the new colours were provided by Euan Peters.

Plot:
A group of Decepticons attack Slaughter City, an Autobot-held region of Cybertron. Most of them begin striking down Autobots with ease; the exception is Needlenose, who is obviously not cut out to be a great warrior – he is hesitant, panics easily, and flees at the first sign of danger.

The lead Decepticon, Spinister, notices that Needlenose is ill-equipped to take on the Autobot hordes, and considers making an example of his craven colleague by killing him on the spot. However, he concludes that Needlenose has the makings of a good warrior, if only he could overcome his fear. To test this, he deliberately puts himself in harm's way, hoping that Needlenose will regain his wits and save him.

Needlenose duly 'rescues' Spinister, but he's still tentative and ill-at-ease. Suddenly, the Decepticons find themselves back in their headquarters – the entire battle was a holographic simulation to ascertain if the Decepticons were fit to be part of the new Mayhem Attack Squad. Despite Needlenose being patently unfit for such a group, Spinister lies and gets him onto the team.

Notes:
This story sees the formation of the new Mayhem Attack Squad, replacing the old unit, who were massacred in [48.2] 'Time Wars'. Their new mission will be to hunt down and kill the Decepticon traitors Carnivac and Catilla, who joined forces with a small band of Autobots in [53.1] 'Survivors'.

This story also marks the first appearance of the Decepticons Needlenose and Spinister. Despite their action figure counterparts being Targetmasters, it's quite clear that the comic versions are using standard weapons only (see the notes to [53.3] '[Double] Deal of the Century' for more on this).

This is the first present-day appearance of the Decepticon Pretenders Stranglehold, Bludgeon and Octopunch. They – or perhaps parallel versions of them – previously appeared in the 1990 sequence of [53.2] 'Aspects of Evil'. It's unclear when or how they gained their Pretender shells (the technology was invented by Scorponok in [40] 'Pretender to the Throne'); however, as with combiners, it would seem that Cybertron was quick to adopt Transformer advances that were first developed on Earth.

The Decepticons' ability to create realistic holographic environments was first demonstrated in [48] 'The Flames of Boltax'.

Roll Call:
'Autobots': Optimus Prime, Prowl, Ratchet, Slag, Kup, Fortress Maximus and Getaway.

No real Autobots appear in the story – all the above are merely projections in the Decepticon training simulation.

Decepticons: Snarler, Stranglehold, Bludgeon, Octopunch, **Needlenose** and **Spinister**.

Data File: Helen Stone (letterer)
Colourist and letterer Stone contributed to a number of Marvel UK titles, including *Death's Head II*, *The Knights of Pendragon* and *The Sleeze Brothers*. She was also an editor on *The Real Ghostbusters*.

Review:
A decent little character piece. The five page format means that it can't delve too deeply into the Decepticon psyche, but what this lacks in depth it makes up for in sheer economy of storytelling – there's no padding, because there's no *room* for padding. Sharp, concise and eminently readable. 4/5

Black and White and Read All Over
The move to a partially black-and-white format from UK#215 (see the notes to [52] 'Guess Who the Mecannibals Are Having for Dinner') went down like a lead balloon with the majority of readers, as did the increased reliance on reprints of old material (see the notes to [53.1] 'Survivors'). Here is a selection of readers' correspondence pertaining to these cost-saving measures, and the responses in the Transformation editorial page and the Dread Tidings letters page:

- UK#223: A reader writes in, complaining about the lack of full colour. Dreadwind: 'You obviously don't like the new black and white format. Why not colour the stories yourselves?'
- UK#224: Again, a complaint about the reduction in colour pages. Dreadwind: 'Another one that doesn't like the new black and white format, eh? Sorry to hear that – I thought it looked quite good.'
- UK#225: The Transformation editorial page weighs in: 'There's been an awful lot of moanin' and groanin' from you lot about the new black and white format … Well, it's time to come clean about it. Due to soaring production costs, we've had to drop the colour from some pages … This is, after all, better than no stories at all, wouldn't you agree?!'
- UK#226: Yet another reader complains about the black and white pages, and also bemoans the reprints of old stories. Dreadwind's response: 'I've already explained about the black and white strip – where were you?! As to repeating stories, it may surprise you to know that there may be a lot of people out there who haven't seen them yet … I don't know what you're complaining about – you're still getting new stories, even if they are in black and white. Surely that's better than no new stories at all, yes?'
- UK#230: Transformation: 'Judging from the mail that's been flooding in, a lot of

you out there don't like the recent repeats of classic *Transformers* tales.'

- UK#231: Dreadwind: 'I've said just about all I'm going to about the black and white dilemma, so there.'
- UK#255: Dreadwind: 'I'm getting a bit cheesed off with all these wingin' letters, always complainin' ... If you're gonna criticise, make it constructive, huh?'

There were no further complaints thereafter (so either readers got the message and stopped sending such letters, or the comic just refused to print them).

[53.5] THE BIG SHUTDOWN!
- UK#230, 12 August 1989 (Part One), 5 pages
- UK#231, 19 August 1989 (Part Two), 5 pages

This story was later reprinted in full colour in 1991, near the very end of the original UK run:

UK#330, 21 December 1991 (Part One), 5 pages
UK#331, 4 January 1992 (Part Two), 5 pages

Credits:
Simon Furman (script); Lee Sullivan (art); Helen Stones (letters, part 1); Stuart Bartlett (letters, part 2); Andrew Wildman (cover, UK#230); Lee Sullivan (cover, UK#231).

Euan Peters provided the colours for the later reprint.

Plot:
Nightbeat and Siren investigate the corpse of their fellow Autobot Playback, which has washed up on a beach in California. While Siren chases after a couple of Transformers spotted fleeing the scene, Nightbeat studies the corpse for clues.
When Siren catches up with his quarry, he finds they are actually Autobots – Hosehead and Horsepower, both of whom are being hunted by the Decepticon Thunderwing. Thunderwing is 'heir apparent to the Decepticon throne', and has been charged with hunting down three recently-released Autobot prisoners as a test of his mettle.

Horsepower is killed, but Hosehead and Siren return to the beach, where they are reunited with Nightbeat. Nightbeat's Headmaster companion, Muzzle, temporarily confuses Thunderwing by reanimating Playback's corpse. Muzzle gets to safety as the Autobots detonate Playback's fuel supply, injuring Thunderwing in the process.

Notes:
Part One is accompanied by a caption stating simply: 'With apologies to Raymond Chandler'. The opening few pages contain imagery and language paying homage to Chandler (1888-1959), an author and screenwriter famous for his hard-boiled detective fiction. The title of this story is a play on that of Chandler's debut novel *The Big Sleep* (1939); the opening lines ('Did it matter where you lay once you were dead?') misquote a famous passage from the end of that book. One of the ill-fated Autobots is named after another of his works, *Playback* (1958). Here the Autobot Headmaster Nightbeat plays detective, mirroring the role of Chandler's chief protagonist, Philip Marlowe. This adventure takes place in an unnamed Californian town with 'a dirty beach'; Chandler

lived and died in California, and many of his works are set there.

Thunderwing is a powerful Pretender Transformer, and next in line for the leadership of the Decepticons (or, at least, their Cybertronian branch – Scorponok is by now firmly entrenched as the commander of their Earth-based forces, since he took over from Ratbat in [50] 'Dark Star'). To prove his worthiness, the Decepticons have released on Earth three Autobot prisoners – Hosehead, Playback and Horsepower – and tasked Thunderwing to hunt them down. Such prisoners can be identified via a 'serial brand'.

Nightbeat's line on the cover of UK#230 ('Of all the beaches in all the world …') is a misquote of a line from *Casablanca* (Michael Curtiz, 1942). Siren's line 'Elementary, dear Nightbeat' is a play on the famous quote 'Elementary, my dear Watson' – often attributed to the fictional detective Sherlock Holmes, but actually first coined in *Psmith, Journalist*, a 1915 novel by P G Wodehouse.

Thunderwing's Story

Thunderwing makes his American debut in [60] 'Yesterday's Heroes', where he's depicted as the Decepticon Leader on Cybertron (and addressed as a 'Lord'). The story of Thunderwing's rise to power was depicted in the UK strips, albeit confusingly – his stories were published out of chronological sequence.

The nature of the Decepticon hierarchy also muddies the waters somewhat. Ratbat mentions a 'Decepticon Imperial Headquarters' in [47] 'Club Con', which is presumably the same body as the triumvirate seen in [52.1] 'The Fall and Rise of the Decepticon Empire' (although it's hard to imagine Ratbat – who doesn't suffer fools gladly – taking orders from the triumvirate, a trio of hedonistic slobs). There was also a 'Decepticon High Command' mentioned in 'Cybertron: The Middle Years', a text feature in UK#83. Given that Scorponok was also a Decepticon leader on Cybertron (until he left for Nebulos in [HDM1] 'Ring of Hate'), it seems likely that the Decepticon Nation is far from unified, and that there are many different Decepticon-affiliated political bodies scattered around the planet, each with a claim to authority – it's perhaps telling that the triumvirate held sway from their capital city Helex, whereas both Straxus and Ratbat ruled out of Polyhex.

It's entirely possible, then, that both Thunderwing and the triumvirate could have laid claim to the Decepticon leadership on Cybertron *at the same time* – the triumvirate in Helex, and Thunderwing (based in a Royal Palace elsewhere on the planet) having been appointed by a different 'High Council'.

Oddly, it appears as though Thunderwing has at least two separate stints as leader – Siren's reference to the *Ark* means that [53.5] 'The Big Shutdown' must be set at some point after the crews of the *Ark* and the *Steelhaven* merge under the leadership of Optimus Prime just prior to [47] 'Club Con' (i.e. after December 1988, assuming Siren and Nightbeat were part of the *Steelhaven* crew).

However, according to [54.1] 'A Small War', Thunderwing is Decepticon Leader (and is being addressed as 'Lord') 'fourteen months' prior to the events of [54] 'King Con'. (As 'King Con' is set roughly around March 1989, it means that Thunderwing was a leader at least as far back as January 1988.) In other words, 'A Small War', set in January 1988, *must* take place prior to 'The Big Shutdown', set at some point after December 1988. Bearing all that in mind, Thunderwing's story must go something like this:

- January 1988 ([54.1] 'A Small War'): Lord Thunderwing is a 'Decepticon Leader' in a story set 'fourteen months ago'. At some point afterwards (possibly due to the flux caused by Ratbat's death and/or the Clone Megatron's ascent to power), Thunderwing loses his rank, becoming merely the Decepticons' 'heir apparent'.
- February 1989 ([53.5] 'The Big Shutdown'): Thunderwing's leadership prowess is tested against a trio of Autobots; he is defeated off the Californian coast.
- May 1989 ([56.2] 'Rage'): Thunderwing emerges from the ocean, and is named Decepticon Leader shortly afterwards.
- May 1989 ([56.1] 'Out to Lunch'): Thunderwing is leader, in a story set shortly after Megatron's demise in [59] 'Skin Deep'.
- Late 1989 ([60] 'Yesterday's Heroes'): Thunderwing's first appearance in the American strips.

For more on the chronology of these (and other) stories, see the notes to [59] 'Skin Deep'.

Roll Call:
Autobots: **Nightbeat, Siren** and **Hosehead**.

Decepticons: **Thunderwing**.

Nebulans: **Muzzle, Quig** and **Lug**.

Quig appears only as Siren's head, rather than as an individual. All the characters featured in this story are making their debut appearances – the first time this has happened since [1] 'The Transformers'.

Review:
The main prerequisites for a story such as this is that all the new debutants are well established from the outset and are given good characterisation. Thankfully this story delivers in spades – Nightbeat is introspective and cynical, Siren is brash and reckless, Hosehead is the practical one and Thunderwing is just pure evil.

With all the introducing to do, the plot does suffer a bit – this is otherwise a fairly standard action run-around. However, the Raymond Chandler homages add an extra layer to proceedings. 4/5

[54] KING CON!
US#54, 'July 1989' (published March 1989), 22 pages.

British reprint: UK#232, 26 August 1989 (Part 1), 6 pages; UK#233, 2 September 1989 (Part 2), 5 pages; UK#234, 9 September 1989 (Part 3), 5 pages; UK#235, 16 September 1989 (Part 4), 6 pages.

In an unfortunate typographical error, the fourth and final part of the UK reprint was incorrectly billed as 'Part 3'.

Credits:
Bob Budiansky (script); José Delbo (pencil breakdowns); Danny Bulanadi (ink finishes);

Nel Yomtov (colours); Jim Massara (letters); Don Daley (editor); Tom DeFalco (editor-in-chief); José Delbo and Danny Bulanadi (cover). **UK:** Lee Sullivan (cover, UK#232); Jeff Anderson (cover, UK#233); Geoff Senior (covers, UK#234 and 235).

Plot:

To replenish the depleted Autobot ranks, Optimus Prime sends for the Micromasters – small Autobots not much bigger than a human – from Cybertron. However, the new arrivals are belligerent, argumentative and don't take kindly to orders.

Meanwhile, Scorponok has devised a new plan to create Energon cubes – a 'stormmaker' device is set up in the New Jersey swamps, and immediately begins to affect local weather conditions. By turning the Empire State Building into a giant lightning conduit, it will collect massive amounts of energy – but half of New York City will be wiped out in the process.

A local television journalist, Cecilia Santiago, travels to the swamps to investigate some recent 'creature' sightings, and finds the Decepticon Pretenders setting up the stormmaker. She is rescued by the Autobot Micromasters, and together they track the Decepticons back to the Empire State Building. There, Iguanus is setting up the equipment at the tip of the building, but is attacked by the Micromasters and falls to the street below. With the danger over, the Micromasters elect to stay with Cecilia rather than go back with Optimus Prime.

Notes:

This story's title and main action sequence, in which a monster climbs the Empire State Building while clutching a woman, are borrowed from *King Kong* (Merian C Cooper and Ernest B Schoedsack, 1933). This is the second Transformers comic story to homage that movie, after [45] 'Monstercon from Mars'. Indeed, 'Monstercon from Mars' is directly referenced here, as Skullgrin's exploits in that story are discussed by his Decepticon colleagues.

This story is set in and around the New York/New Jersey area: it opens in a New Jersey swampland, close to the Ramapo Mountains. The Empire State Building (completed 1931) features prominently and there are mentions of the Hudson River (which forms the border between New Jersey and Manhattan Island) and the Lincoln Tunnel (opened in 1937). The fare for the Lincoln Tunnel is three dollars, indicating that the action is set between 1987 and 1991. (Unlike its British counterpart, the American comic hardly ever clarifies when its adventures are set; the bridge toll here is the best dating clue we've had in a US story since [23] 'Decepticon Graffiti'.)

Scorponok's new base makes its debut here: it's an underground complex hidden beneath a garbage dump within a New Jersey swamp. (The site was probably selected by Skullgrin, who was sent to scout the Earth in [45] 'Monstercon from Mars'.) The Earthbound Decepticons were previously based in either Ratbat's or Scorponok's spacecraft, both of which were destroyed in [50] 'Dark Star'.

The Micromasters arrive on Earth via a 'dimensional transwarp' (essentially, a magic door). Optimus Prime worries that this new method of transportation is 'untested', but it works fine here. (It appears to be based on the teleportation method used by the Wreckers to visit Earth in stories such as [40.5] 'Wreking Havoc', but without the painful side effects. It seems to have supplanted the old space bridge, which made its final appearance in [46] 'Ca\$h and Car-nage'.) The small size of the Micromasters is due to them having 'downsized to conserve energy'. Although they are just slightly taller than humans, they still transform into normal-sized vehicles. Their mandate is to replace the Autobots who were killed in [50] 'Dark Star'. There's a reference to Cloudburst's and Landmine's failed mission to buy vital microchips, as seen in [53] 'Recipe for Disaster'.

Cecilia Santiago is host of the television news programme *New York Talks*; the hunters who appear on her show have a dog named Lady, a possible reference to the movie *Lady and the Tramp* (Clyde Geronimi, Wilfred Jackson and Hamilton Luske, 1955).

UK Notes:
Although this was the first American appearance of the Micromasters, they had previously featured in two British stories: [53.2] 'Aspects of Evil' and [53.3] '[Double] Deal of the Century'.

UK Changes:
Page 2, panel 1: credits replaced; image slightly cropped to fit the page.
Page 4, panel 6: the reference to issue #50 is changed to #208-210; 'see last issue – Don' becomes '217-220'.
Page 7, panel 1: 'The next day ...' caption is painted out.
Page 8, panel 2: editor Don Perlin's tag is removed from the caption.
Page 9, panel 3: the reference to issue #45 is changed to #190-191; Perlin's sig is again removed.
Page 11, pane 1: a colouring error (in which the background colour seeps onto a thought bubble, and a random white rectangle appears in the sky) is corrected.
Page 12, panel 3: 'recognizable' is changed to 'recognisable'.
Page 13, panel 3: oddly, the first three words of Powertrain's thought bubble ('a human ... and') have been removed.
Page 22, panel 7: 'The end' – caption deleted.

Roll Call:
Autobots: Optimus Prime, Roadhandler, Free Wheeler, Swindler, Tailspin, **Powertrain, Mudslinger, Highjump** and **Tote**.

Decepticons: Scorponok, Skullcruncher, Mindwipe, Weirdwolf, Bomb Burst, Skullgrin, Submarauder, Iguanus, Bugly and Finback.

Other: **Cecilia Santiago**.

Nebulans: Hi-Q.

Data File: Jim Massara (letterer)
Massara provided letters for a number of titles, including *The Real Ghostbusters*, *Marvel Fanfare* and *Nexus*. He was later an editor, with credits on *The Defenders* and *Rocket Raccoon: Tales from Half-World*.

Review:
We can forgive him as it's his penultimate story, but this is essentially Bob Budiansky's Greatest Hits. We have a group of new Autobots getting to grips with Earth culture and

foiling a wacky plan by the Decepticons to create Energon cubes. In other words, this is a virtual repeat of [14] 'Rock and Roll-Out'. We also have the human angle, as television host Cecilia Santiago gets caught up in the battle and ultimately proves vital to the Autobot cause – not unlike Bomber Bill in [10] 'The Next Best Thing to Being There'. We have references to New Jersey, Budiansky's home territory, and a King Kong homage as per [45] 'Monstercon from Mars', and some new Transformers introduce themselves using horribly clunky dialogue.

By rights, then, this should feel tired, perfunctory and by-the-numbers – and some critics have indeed argued that it is. But for all the repetition, this is what Budiansky does best – human drama, humour, adventure and atmosphere, topped off with an action-packed finale. This is the American Transformers comic in a nutshell, and it's great. 4/5

[54.1] A SMALL WAR!

- UK#232, 26 August 1989 (Part One), 5 pages
- UK#233, 2 September 1989 (Part Two), 5 pages

Credits:
Simon Furman (script); Jeff Anderson (art, part 1); Geoff Senior (art, part 2); Gary 'Glib' Gilbert (letters). For cover credits to issues 232 and 233, see the entry for [54] 'King Con' above.

Plot:
Learning that the Decepticons are developing a 'secret weapon', the new Autobot Battle Patrol – a team of Micromasters – infiltrate a Decepticon base in order to find out the exact nature of this weapon, and to destroy it – even at the cost of their own lives, if necessary.

It transpires that the rumours of a secret weapon were just a lure – Thunderwing has been trying to build Micromasters of his own, but needs to study the Autobot Micromasters in order to perfect his creations. The Battle Patrol defy orders and deactivate their 'suicide switches', preferring capture to death.

Emirate Xaaron sends the remainder of the Autobot Micromasters into the Decepticon base – not to rescue their allies but to destroy them, so that none of their secrets can fall into enemy hands. Once at the base, however, the Micromasters disobey orders and set out to rescue their captured comrades rather than kill them.

The rescue is a success, but thanks to the knowledge they have gleaned, the Decepticons now have Micromasters of their own. The Autobot Micromaster leader Roadhandler reports back to Xaaron, expecting a dressing-down; however, Xaaron absolves him of any blame, instead admitting that it was wrong for him to expect the Micromasters to lay down their lives.

Notes:
This is an origin story for the Micromasters, showing us how they were developed and why, and the special abilities they have. Originally devised by the Autobot resistance on Cybertron, these new Transformers are extremely fuel-efficient, and being so small – seven feet, or 2.1 metres, tall – they make for excellent spies and infiltrators.

It's stated twice that this story is set 'fourteen months ago' – relative to [54] 'King Con', which was printed simultaneously with this adventure in the UK. Thunderwing is Decepticon leader here (see the notes to [53.5] 'The Big Shutdown), and is building his own team of Micromasters. The Autobot Micromasters are initially deemed expendable by Xaaron, which goes some way toward explaining their later distrust of authority figures in [54] 'King Con'.

It is not clear how the Autobots and Decepticons can create these new Micromaster troops without access to the life-giving properties of the Matrix. Either these are pre-existing personalities that have been given new bodies, or both sides now have access to the Matrix Flame (see [20.2] 'Target: 2006').

Roll Call:
Autobots: Emirate Xaaron, Flak, Sunrunner, Roadhandler, Free Wheeler, Swindler, Tailspin, Powertrain, Tote, **Big Shot, Sidetrack, Red Hot, Fixit, Seawatch** and **Stakeout**.

It's heavily implied that all the Autobot Micromasters take part in the attack on the Decepticon base, but although Mudslinger and Highjump are seemingly present during these events, they're never clearly shown on the page.

Decepticons: Stormcloud, Whisper, Tailwind, Nightflight, Thunderwing, **Blackjack** and **Detour**.

Blackjack and Detour appear only as unconscious bodies. One of the Decepticon guards in this story bears a strong resemblance to Hun-Gurr; however, it's debatable whether or not this counts as a *bona fide* appearance by the character (especially considering that – 14 months ago – the Terrorcon would have been serving under Scorponok's command, rather than Thunderwing's).

Review:
In many ways, this is a retread of [31.1] 'Worlds Apart' – a group of new Autobots are lured into a Decepticon trap, because the Decepticons want to study them and perfect new troops of their own. It's a tried and trusted way of introducing a whole swathe of new characters in a single go.

However, unlike 'Worlds Apart', this story adds some extra ingredients to the mix – there is tension and urgency in the air, as Autobots armed with self-destruct devices sneak into a Decepticon compound, and a second team defies orders to go in after them. Combined with another star turn by the deliciously manipulative Thunderwing, what could have been a perfunctory introduction story is realised with much aplomb. 4/5

UK Advertisements, Part 3: Other *Transformers* Merchandise
Convertible action figures weren't the only things that Transformers fans could buy. A lot of Transformers-related merchandise was released, and some of it was advertised within the pages of the UK comic. In the following list, products marked with an asterisk were available by redeeming Robot Point tokens from Transformers toy packaging.

Arrival from Cybertron (a home video containing the first three cartoon episodes) – UK#56-58, 64, 66

Gold Distribution (videocassette retailer, includes Transformers titles) – UK#194
Lumobots (glow-in-the-dark 'plastic figures')* – UK#23-24
Tempo Video (includes *The Transformers*, *Action Force* and *Inhumanoids* VHS releases) – UK#138, 186, 193, 210, 215
Time Warrior watch* – UK#15, 25-26
Transform-a-Wall poster – UK#309
The Transformers/Action Force comic merger – UK#151-152
The Transformers Annual (1987) – UK#75-76, 78-79, 82, 84
The Transformers Annual (1989) – UK#181, 200
The Transformers Autumn Special (1989) – UK#241
The Transformers books, by Ladybird – UK#20-21, 36, 142
The Transformers comic (a 1-page promotional strip) – UK#170
The Transformers: Desertion of the Dinobots (videocassette release) – UK#290
Transformers Powermaster Torch, from Ever Ready – UK#196-197
Transformers 'S.T.A.R.S.' battle pack* – UK#89-91, 95, 98, 100, 102, 104, 106, 108, 110, 117
Transformers stunt kite – UK#23
The Transformers: The Complete Works (reprints of old issues) – UK#128, 133
Transformers: The Movie (poster magazine) – UK#92, 97
Transformers: The Movie (soundtrack album) – UK#92, 94
Transformers: The Movie (Tell-A-Tale book and cassette, by Ladybird) – UK#96
Transformers: The Movie (theatrical release) – UK#89, 94
Transformers: The Movie (videocassette release) – UK#130, 132, 136-137
The Transformers: The Rebirth (videocassette release) – UK#160
The Transformers: The Return of Optimus Prime (videocassette release) – UK#171

[54.2] PRIME'S RIB!
UK#234, 9 September 1989, 5 pages

Credits:
Simon Furman (script); Andrew Wildman (art); Helen Stone (letters). For cover credit, see the entry for [54] 'King Con' above.

Plot:
The year is 1995. Optimus Prime unveils the first female Transformer – Arcee. However, the stereotypically 'girly' design of the new warrior (slim, sexy and coloured pink), and indeed the Autobots' general attitude on her unveiling, are strongly criticised by women's rights activists.

The awkward situation is only exacerbated when a group of Decepticons launch an attack. Seeing that her colleagues are struggling to fend off the Decepticons, Arcee joins the fray and drives them off single-handedly.

Notes:
This story shows us the origin of the female Autobot Arcee. The Autobots in this era are on good terms with humans; a situation that will ultimately lead to the creation of an Autobot City on Earth. To cement this relationship, the Autobots have created a female Autobot to counter accusations of sexism.

This adventure is set in California in 1995 (in Timeline A – six years prior to [A3.4]

'*Ark* Duty', the next story chronologically). One of the demonstrators has a shopping bag featuring the logo of Tesco, a British supermarket chain whose real-world attempts to launch stores in the USA met with limited success.

The Autobots' attitudes toward sex and gender are consistent with those laid out in [53] 'Recipe for Disaster' – they are generally ignorant of such topics, which amuse and bewilder them in equal measure. (This is odd, especially considering that one of the Autobots present at the unveiling is Jazz, the one most in tune with Earth popular culture. Given that, in the Transformers universe, many other races are divided into genders – the Nebulans and the Femaxians being just two examples – it seems bizarre that the spacefaring Autobots are completely clueless when it comes to females.)

The title was inspired by that of *Adam's Rib* (George Cukor, 1949), a battle-of-the-sexes comedy movie. That title was in turn derived from the Biblical story of Genesis, in which the first woman, Eve, was created from Adam's side or rib. 'Prime rib' is also a cut of beef, making it a double play on words.

Roll Call:
Autobots: Optimus Prime, Jazz, Hot Rod and Arcee.

Decepticons: Shockwave, Fangry, Horri-Bull and Squeezeplay.

It's possible that the Nebulans Brisko, Kreb and Lokos appear in this story, as the heads of Fangry, Horri-Bull and Squeezeplay respectively; but it's impossible to be sure if those Decepticons are Headmasters in this alternative timeline.

Review:
If this is a 'message' story, then it's a very mixed message indeed. On the plus side, the Autobots' attitude to gender (or rather, their lack of attitude) is rather refreshing. Transformers are practically unique as action heroes, in that they're never driven or distracted by their libidos. If it's a trite moral, at least it's a good one – Autobots don't care what gender you're born with (or identify as), humans are all the same to them. Furthermore, this is a chance for the comic to correct a previous error of judgment – the stereotypical presentation of Arcee in [44.1] 'Space Pirates' – and portray the female Autobot as a brilliant warrior, dispatching the Decepticons with ease.

On the other side of the coin, however, this story comes across as decidedly smug and unfunny, not least when Jazz makes a reference to Arcee's 'upper chassis design'. The women's rights activists – whose point of argument seems quite valid – are portrayed as militant harpies who do nothing but wave placards and call the Autobots 'pigs'. Even worse is the exchange between Optimus Prime and Arcee, which includes lines such as 'Stay back, Arcee, these Decepticons look tough', and ends with Arcee exclaiming 'Honestly! Men!'

In short, this adventure tries to have its cake and eat it: on the one hand it seems to be espousing the idea that gender isn't and shouldn't be an issue, but at the same time it has Jazz, Prime and Arcee make 'humorous' sexist comments. It just doesn't work.

As a five-page action vignette, it succeeds on a basic level: it shows us Arcee's origin and gives us a decent fight scene. But in every other respect – the mixed messages, the sitcom dialogue, and the unfortunate tone – this is weak stuff. 1/5

The 'NEXT' Box, Part 4

More teasers from the 'NEXT' box that appeared in the UK comic – issues UK#199-264.

- UK#199: The ravages of time!
- UK#200: The Autobot/Autobot war!
- UK#201: Twins of evil!
- UK#202: Shockwaves!
- UK#203: When all have fallen…
- UK#204: The final battle!
- UK#205: Cold wars!
- UK#206: Iced!
- UK#207: Dark Star!
- UK#208: First blood!
- UK#209: The sting!
- UK#210: Beasts!
- UK#211: Slaughter on the slopes!
- UK#212: Grand central!
- UK#213: (US strip) The deal! (UK strip) The challenge!
- UK#214: (US strip) It's dinner time! (UK strip) Race with the devil!
- UK#215: (US strip) Double-cross! (UK strip) The devil's lair!
- UK#216: (US strip) The main course! (UK strip) Scream and scream again!
- UK#217: (US strip) A culinary delight! (UK strip) Power cut!
- UK#218: (US strip) Battle of the sexes! (UK strip) Survivors!
- UK#219: (US strip) A woman scorned! (UK strip) Nuclear nightmare!
- UK#220: (US strip) Wanted: Galvatron – dead or alive! (UK strip) Dream war!
- UK#221: (reprint story) The hunt begins! (new UK strip) To the rescue!
- UK#222: (reprint story) First blood! (new UK strip) Aspects of Evil!
- UK#223: (reprint story) The arrival! (new UK strip) Galvatron!
- UK#224: (reprint story) Headhunt! (new UK strip) Shockwave!
- UK#225: (reprint story) Killin' time! (new UK strip) …Megatron!
- UK#226: (reprint story) ..? (new UK strip) Unicron!
- UK#227: (reprint story) Drained! (new UK strip) Doubledealer!
- UK#228: (reprint story) Resurrection! (new UK strip) The hunting party!
- UK#229: (reprint story) Mind games! (new UK strip) The big shutdown!
- UK#230: (reprint story) Whose death is it anyway? (new UK strip) Thunder and lightning!
- UK#231: (reprint story) Chain reaction! (new UK strip) A small war!
- UK#232: (US strip) Stormbringer! (UK strip) Crisis of conscience!
- UK#233: (US strip) Off-road ruckus! (UK strip) Arcee's story!
- UK#234: (US strip) Elemental fury! (UK strip) Deathbringer!
- UK#235: (US strip) Wrestle-mania! (UK strip) The enemy within!
- UK#236: (US strip) The big match! (UK strip) Know your enemy!
- UK#237: (US strip) The fix! (UK strip) Survival run!
- UK#238: (US strip) No holds barred! (UK strip) A savage place!
- UK#239: (US strip) Ratchet's nightmare! (UK strip) Out to lunch!
- UK#240: (US strip) 'Plane crazy! (UK strip) Rage!
- UK#241: (US strip) A dream come true?! (UK strip) Under siege!
- UK#242: (US strip) He's back! (UK strip) Mind games!
- UK#243: (US strip) The plan! (UK strip) Two Megatrons!
- UK#244: (US strip) The patient! (UK strip) Underworld!

- UK#245: (US strip) Just pretending! (UK strip) Demons!
- UK#246: (US strip) Prime's last stand? (UK strip) The killing fiends!
- UK#247: (US strip) Ratchet's revenge! (UK strip) Fallen star!
- UK#248: (US strip) Skin deep! (UK strip) Longtooth's shame!
- UK#249: (US strip) When titans clash! (UK strip) The greatest gift!
- UK#250: (US strip) Deathgrip! (UK strip) The void!
- UK#251: (US strip) Yesterday's heroes! (UK strip) Edge of impact!
- UK#252: (US strip) Prime resigns! (UK strip) Genocide!
- UK#253: (US strip) Prime unleashed! (UK strip) White fire!
- UK#254: (US strip) Worlds apart! (UK strip) Heroes!
- UK#255: (reprint story) The sting! (UK strip) Ironhide!
- UK#256: (reprint story) Nok, nok! (UK strip) Sunstreaker!
- UK#257: (reprint story) The secret's out! (UK strip) Wheeljack!
- UK#258: (reprint story) Primal scream! (UK strip) Silverbolt!
- UK#259: (US strip) Mayhem! (UK strip) Sleep's end!
- UK#260: (US strip) A rude awakening! (UK strip) Starting over!
- UK#261: (US strip) The last hope! (UK strip) Two steps back!
- UK#262: (US strip) Fatale attraction! (UK strip) Breakaway!
- UK#263: (US strip) Gutt-ed! (UK strip) Devastation!
- UK#264: (US strip) To be continued! (UK strip) A fairy story?!

[54.3] DEATHBRINGER
- UK#235, 16 September 1989 (Part 1), 5 pages
- UK#236, 23 September 1989 (Part 2), 5 pages

Credits:
Simon Furman (script); Geoff Senior (art, part 1); Stewart 'Staz' Johnson (art, part 2); Gary 'Glib' Gilbert (letters); Lee Sullivan (cover, UK#236). For cover credit to issue 235, see the entry for [54] 'King Con' above.

Plot:
The Autobots are stunned to learn that Optimus Prime no longer carries the Matrix within him – it was in his old body, which was sent out into space. Shortly after this bombshell, the Autobots answer a distress call – an Earth city has been levelled by a mechanoid calling himself Deathbringer.

The Deathbringer was a previously benign robot, whose function was to offer a painless, dignified death to terminally-ill patients. It came into contact with the Matrix while out in space and was reborn as a killing machine, offering death to all, whether they request it or not.

Nightbeat figures out what's going on after consulting the Ark's record tapes, and realises that brute force alone won't be enough to defeat this seemingly unstoppable creature. The Deathbringer is slowly wasting away, having been overwhelmed by the Matrix's power; Optimus Prime convinces it to abide by its original program, and terminate itself.

Notes:
It's in this story that we discover the fate of the Matrix, following the destruction of Optimus Prime's original body in [24] 'Afterdeath'. Prime's remains were sent into

space aboard a small capsule, as seen in [26] 'Funeral for a Friend', and eventually came to rest on a moon. There it was encountered by a Deathbringer robot, who as a result was reformatted into the powerful killer we see here.

The events of this adventure are later alluded to in the American story [65] 'Dark Creation' (in which the moon is identified as VsQs) – the only time that the events of a UK story are specifically referenced in a later American strip. ('Deathbringer' and 'Dark Creation' were both written by Simon Furman.)

The coming of the Deathbringer is said to have been foretold in an ancient Cybertronian myth. (The Transformers – and the Matrix – seem to have a manifest destiny, i.e. that they will eventually join together to defeat Unicron. The way events pan out could well have been foreseen – if not actively manipulated - by the Transformers' godlike creator, Primus. So these myths of a Deathbringer could well have been seeded by Primus himself. That Siren chooses to read up on this myth only moments prior to meeting the Deathbringer in the flesh could appear a remarkable coincidence, but it's more likely that he's being subtly influenced by Primus, just as Unicron was able to influence some Transformers in [20.2] 'Target: 2006'.)

These events will be revisited in a latter-day sequel comic, *Transformers: Regeneration One* (specifically, issue zero of that title), which retrospectively sets these events in Denver, Colorado.

Ratchet is seen here tending to the deactivated Beachcomber, indicating that the mini-Autobot was one of the casualties of the mass deaths of either [50] 'Dark Star' or [48.2] 'Time Wars'.

Roll Call:
Autobots: Optimus Prime, Ratchet, Beachcomber (as a corpse), Landmine, Cloudburst, Waverider, Joyride, Getaway, Nightbeat, Siren and Hosehead.

Nebulans: Muzzle, Quig and Lug (only as the heads of their respective partners, rather than as individual characters).

Review:
The Matrix angle is interesting, as is the idea of a friendly robot who carries out euthanasia on request. Otherwise, this is just a mass of fight scenes and flashbacks, with very little substance. The one character who gets a bit of development is Optimus Prime – once again he's in self-doubt mode, but unsurprisingly he's able to get a grip on himself by the end of the story (see also [12.2] 'Crisis of Command, [23.3] 'Distant Thunder' and [48.1] 'Cold Comfort and Joy' for more examples of this trope). The ending, in which Prime talks a robot intelligence into killing itself, is very *Star Trek*. 2/5

[55] THE INTERPLANETARY WRESTLING CHAMPIONSHIP!
US#55, 'August 1989' (published April 1989), 22 pages.

British reprint: UK#236, 23 September 1989 (Part 1), 6 pages; UK#237, 30 September 1989 (Part 2), 5 pages; UK#238, 7 October 1989 (Part 3), 6 pages; UK#239, 14 October 1989 (Part 4), 5 pages.

Credits:
Bob Budiansky (script, also layouts, pages 1-10); Jim Fern (layouts, pages 11-22, plus

finished pencils throughout); Mike Gustovich (inks); Nel Yomtov (colours); Jim Massara (letters); Don Daley (editor); Tom DeFalco (editor-in-chief); José Delbo and Danny Bulanadi (cover). **UK:** Geoff Senior (covers, UK#237 and 239); Andrew Wildman (cover, UK#238). For cover credit to issue 236, see the entry for [54.3] 'Deathbringer' above.

Plot:

The Autobot Micromasters, rather than join up with Optimus Prime, decide instead to become crime-fighting vigilantes, cleaning up the streets of New York City. Roadhandler is invited onto Cecilia Santiago's television show, *New York Talk*. Amongst the other studio guests is Jake 'The Jackhammer' Jackson, a pro-wrestler. Jackhammer 'trash talks' Roadhandler live on air and challenges the Autobot to a wrestling match. After the cameras stop rolling, Jackson reveals that he doesn't really disrespect Roadhandler, but was just acting up on screen for publicity purposes.

Roadhandler beats Jackson after going through a routine of pre-choreographed moves, and is dubbed the Interplanetary Wrestling Champion. He goes on to engage in many such bouts, while continuing to fight crime on the side. He uses his new-found fame to become a moral campaigner and activist, even going so far as to teach self-defence classes to a group of fans.

The Decepticons decide to put an end to Roadhandler's crusade, and plot to discredit him publically. The Decepticon Micromaster Stormcloud challenges Roadhandler to a wrestling match. In front of a disbelieving audience, Stormcloud starts strongly and begins pummelling the Autobot. It transpires that the Decepticons have kidnapped a group of Roadhandler's fans and are threatening to kill them unless he throws the match.

Fortunately, the other Autobot Micromasters are wise to the plot, and they rescue the young fans just in time. Roadhandler, now free to give the bout his full effort, beats Stormcloud easily. Despite the victory, Roadhandler decides to give up the wrestling job, so as not to put any more innocent fans in jeopardy.

Notes:

Aside from a brief return in 2006 (for a twentieth anniversary adaptation of the animated movie), this was the final Transformers comic to be scripted by Bob Budiansky, who had been the main writer of the American stories and originator of many of the brand's core concepts. For his final Marvel issue, he also provided pencil layouts for the comic's first ten pages.

The story is heavily inspired by the then-burgeoning pro-wresting circuit; the third WWF (now WWE) WrestleMania event in 1987 broke the record for the highest ever attendance for a North American indoor sporting event, and superstar wrestler Hulk Hogan was appearing in movies such as *Rocky III* (Sylvester Stallone, 1982) and *No Holds Barred* (Thomas J Wright, 1989). Budiansky decided on the wrestling angle for his final story, as several other Marvel staffers were big fans, making it a hot topic of office discussion. The wrestler in this story, Jake 'The Jackhammer' Jackson, is probably based on the real-world WWE icon, Jake 'The Snake' Roberts.

This adventure continues and concludes the Micromaster story set up in [54] 'King Con', neatly tying up that loose end, allowing Budiansky's successor, Simon Furman, to start with a clean slate. That said, Budiansky does hint at events of the next American story – [56] 'Back from the Dead' – when he has the Micromaster Stormcloud let slip that he has a mysterious ulterior 'purpose'.

This story features the return of the chat show host and journalist Cecilia Santiago and her programme *New York Talks*, as previously seen in [54] 'King Con'. Amongst Santiago's guests are a woman dubbed 'The Bird Lady of Brooklyn' (presumably named after the 'Bird Lady' – a predynastic Egyptian sculpture on display in the Brooklyn Museum since its discovery in 1907). Roadhandler practices his wresting moves at Arnie's Gym (perhaps a reference to the musclebound actor Arnold Schwarzenegger.)

Mentioned in dialogue but not seen, it would appear that the Decepticons are still using the space bridge to transport troops between Cybertron and Earth. (The Autobots, as seen in [54] 'King Con', are utilising a more advanced method of teleportation.) Roadhandler claims to weigh 0.873 tons (equivalent to 792 kilograms – roughly half the weight of a real Pontiac Firebird, the model of car into which he transforms).

'Fighter blackmailed into throwing a match but wins anyway' is a popular trope in fiction, famously used in films such as *Kickboxer* (Mark DiSalle and David Worth, 1989) and in episodes of television series such as *Quantum Leap* ('Right Hand of God'), *Police Squad!* ('Ring of Fear') and *General Hospital*.

UK Notes:
Although this was the first appearance of the Decepticon Air Strike Patrol in the US comics, they had already featured in a UK story, [53.2] 'Aspects of Evil'.

UK Changes:
Page 1, panel 1: credits replaced.
Page 2, panel 2: editor Don Perlin's tag is excised from the 'see last issue' caption.

Roll Call:
Autobots: Optimus Prime (only as an image on a piece of paper), Roadhandler, Free Wheeler, Swindler, Tailspin, Powertrain, Mudslinger (flashback only) and Highjump.

Decepticons: Scorponok, Skullgrin, Submarauder, Iguanus (flashback only), Bugly, Stormcloud, Whisper, Tailwind and Nightflight.

Other: Cecilia Santiago.

Nebulans: Zarak.

Data File: Bob Budiansky (writer/editor/artist)
Although best known for his work writing and developing the Transformers franchise, Budiansky has a slew of other credits to his name. He wrote and provided art for *Ghost Rider* and created his own Marvel character, the eponymous *Sleepwalker*. He wrote for *The Avengers* and *Captain Britain*, provided art on *Thor* and *Captain America*, and edited a number of titles, including *Fantastic Four*, *Daredevil*, and many of the various *Spider-Man* titles, including the controversial 'Clone Saga' arc.

Review:
Bob Budiansky goes out on a bit of a whimper, in this rather uninspired tale that's more

WWE than *The Transformers*. He was known for occasionally delivering some rather offbeat instalments – such as [13] 'Shooting Star', [31] 'Buster Witwicky and the Car Wash of Doom' and [45] 'Monstercon from Mars' – but those were played as comedies, even if the humour didn't always hit the right notes. Here, for one last time, Budiansky presents us with a wacky story – but plays it absolutely straight. This results in an adventure that's tonally all over the place. We have the absurdity of a Transformer wrestling match, but instead of the scenario being played for laughs, it's all so *earnest*. It would seem that Budiansky was caught between two stools – trying to go out with a trademark breezy romp while simultaneously aiming for something with a bit of gravitas.

Rather than end the review on a low point (and a 1/5 score – even the best sometimes have off-days), here are some choice quotes from this story, a far more apt way of signalling the end of Budiansky's remarkable tenure:

'Thank you for your support.'
'Awesome. He even made a fan out of me.'
'Don't go looking for heroes to believe in … believe in *yourselves*.'

US Advertisements, Part 7: Miscellaneous (A-L)
A list of all advertisements that appeared in the American comic and don't really fit into any of the previously-listed categories (food, drink, books, films, television, games etc):

Acne-12 (skincare cream) – US#5
Adidas sportswear – US#23; MOV#1
ALF Fan Club – US#58
American Medallion Corp – US#42
Anti-sex abuse campaign – US#4, 6, 15-18
Captain America Broadway show (young actress tryouts) – US#14
Century Martial Art Supply – US#27; GIJ#4
Chicago Comicon (convention) – US#57, 68
Child World (toy store chain) – US#70
Clearasil Doubleclear (skincare pads) – US#53, 56
Colgate Junior (toothpaste) – US#58
Columbia Record & Tape Club (mail-order music service) – US#45-46
Drawing Comics Kit (art supplies) – US#33
DP Orbatron (gym equipment) – US#7, 10
F.I.S.T. (a play-by-telephone fantasy game) – US#51-54
G.I. Joe Trading Cards – US#80
Fleer MLB trading cards – US#77, 79
Fleer NBA trading cards – US#72-73
Fleer NFL trading cards – US#69-70
Great Eastern Conventions (convention organisers) – US#40-41, 43, 52, 54-57, 67-68, 76
Huffy BMX bicycles – US#6
Indiana Jones (play-by-telephone adventure game) – US#56
Johnson Smith Company (mail-order shopping) – US#33
Littleton Coin Company – US#24; MOV#1

[55.1] WAY OF THE WARRIOR

- UK#237, 30 September 1989 (Way of the Warrior), 5 pages
- UK#238, 7 October 1989 (Survival Run), 5 pages
- UK#239, 14 October 1989 (A Savage Place!), 5 pages

NB: As with [8.2] 'The Wrath of Grimlock' and [23.2] 'Under Fire', these three adventures essentially form a single three-part story, despite each having its own individual title. I have thus chosen to analyse them together, using the 'Way of the Warrior' moniker as an umbrella title for all three parts.

Credits:
Simon Furman (script); Simon Coleby (art, part 1); Lee Sullivan (art, part 2); Geoff Senior (art, part 3); Gary 'Glib' Gilbert (letters, parts 1-2); Helen Stone (letters, part 3). For cover credits, see the entry for [55] 'The Interplanetary Wrestling Championship' above.

This story was later re-printed in full colour in the *Transformers Annual 1992*; the new colours were provided by Steve White (parts 1-2) and Louise Cassell (part 3).

Plot:
Following a heated argument in Dallas, Carnivac leaves the Survivors group and heads out on his own. Separated from his former colleagues, he is confronted by the Decepticon Mayhem Attack Squad, who have been sent to execute him. The US Army begin attacking the Decepticons, and during the ensuing massacre, in which the soldiers are killed, Carnivac is able to make his escape, fleeing into the desert.

The Mayhems catch up to their quarry in Mexico, but before they can kill the deserter, the rest of the Survivors enter the fray. The Mayhems retreat, but not before killing Catilla. Carnivac swears revenge for the death of his comrade.

Notes:
This story is a sequel to two previous adventures: [53.1] 'Survivors', in which Carnivac and Catilla defected from the Decepticons to join with a band of disaffected Autobots, and [53.4] 'The Hunting Party', in which the Decepticon Mayhem Attack Squad were seen training for this mission. The Mayhems have access to a robotic dog – a non-sentient drone dubbed a 'Hellhound' – which has been programmed to wreak havoc in the city of Dallas and 'smoke out' the Survivors.

The Mayhems pursue Carnivac all the way from Dallas, in the north east of Texas, to Los Gravos, a (fictional) town in Mexico, which means that Carnivac is able to run at least 350 miles (563 kilometres) before the Decepticons catch up to him.

This is the final appearance of the Pretender Catilla; Carnivac's story will continue in [62.6] 'Wolf in the Fold'.

Roll Call:
Autobots: Inferno, Skids, Springer, Broadside and Catilla.

Decepticons: Carnivac, Snarler, Stranglehold, Bludgeon, Octopunch, Needlenose and Spinister.

Review:
Carnivac's journey here is an interesting one. At the start of this story he mocks the Survivors' do-gooding ('Saving humans might be your idea of fun, but it isn't mine!'), but over the course of the adventure he comes to change his mind ('Help others who can't fight!'). It's a fairly standard character arc, but makes for a nice subplot.

What elevates this story above the run-of-the-mill, however, is that Carnivac promptly does a U-turn when Catilla is killed. Any enlightenment he gained over the first 14 pages goes out of the window when his friend is murdered – from here on out, he's a vengeful killer.

It's a great hook, and what could have been a trite, pat ending is turned on its head in that final page. Add some excellent art and terrific battle sequences, and it all adds up to a great three-parter. Only the tired regional clichés (the Texan man wears a Stetson, while the Mexicans sport droopy moustaches and sombreros) disappoint. 4/5.

[56] BACK FROM THE DEAD
US#56, 'September 1989' (published May 1989), 16 pages.

British reprint: UK#240, 21 October 1989 (Part 1), 5 pages; UK#241, 28 October 1989 (Part 2), 5 pages; UK#242, 4 November 1989 (Part 3), 6 pages.

Credits:
Simon Furman (script); José Delbo (pencils); Dave Hunt (inks); Nel Yomtov (colours); Jim Massara (letters); Don Daley (editor); Tom DeFalco (editor-in-chief); Dan Reed (cover). **UK:** Andrew Wildman (cover, UK#240); Geoff Senior (cover, UK#241); Jeff Anderson (cover, UK#242).

Plot:
Autobot medic Ratchet is feeling the pressure – with Autobot forces depleted, the job of restoring his many fallen comrades to life weighs heavily upon him. After he wakes from another stress-induced nightmare, in which he dreams he is attacked by the corpses he's working to fix, Optimus Prime orders that he rest awhile.

Meanwhile, on Earth, the Decepticon Air Strike Patrol attacks an American airbase. Optimus Prime and a group of Autobots travel to Earth in a bid to stop them, leaving the *Ark* unguarded.

A group of Decepticon Micromasters, the Sports Car Patrol, pose as Autobots and transport onto the *Ark*. They manage to convince Ratchet to go with them to Cybertron, where some advanced medical equipment can be found. Ratchet realises too late that this is all a trap, and that the Decepticon mastermind behind the entire plot is none other than the supposedly 'dead' Megatron …

Notes:
This story focuses on Ratchet, and the impossible task he has in repairing the Autobots killed during the events of [50] 'Dark Star'. The stress is so great that he suffers from nightmares (Transformers were previously seen to dream in [20] 'Showdown'.)

This is the first (American) appearance of the Decepticon Sports Car Patrol, who arrive on the *Ark* via a 'trans-time dimensional portal' (an extremely recent invention: in [55] 'The Interplanetary Wrestling Championship', the Decepticons were still using the space bridge). This would appear to be similar to the 'dimensional transwarp' technology used by the Autobots in [54] 'King Con'.

The Air Strike Patrol attack MacDill Air Force Base (a real-life installation, located in Tampa, Florida), home of an advanced new jet, the (fictional) B-204 (a designation that implies this is a bomber plane). It's said to be the biggest jet of its kind. It doubles as a mid-air refuelling plane, boasting increased range and capacity.

The Autobots travel to Earth in an All-Terrain Turbo-Transport – a flat-bodied shuttlecraft, introduced in [39] 'The Desert Island of Space' and seen again in [50] 'Dark Star'.

Most notably, however, this story sees the long-awaited return of Megatron, who (barring flashbacks) hasn't appeared in the comic since [25] 'Gone But Not Forgotten'.

Ret-'Con

Megatron was killed off in the American story [25] 'Gone But Not Forgotten'. Rather than have him stay dead, as would be the case in the US-only strips, the UK team decided to bring him back in [29.1] 'Ancient Relics', and continued to feature him in many subsequent stories, all the way through to [52.1] 'The Fall and Rise of the Decepticon Empire'. Initially, this didn't affect continuity between the American and British strips – in both, Megatron was believed dead to the majority of Transformers, but in the UK stories Shockwave secretly recovered his body and revived him as a means to defeat Galvatron.

By 1989, American The Transformers writer Bob Budiansky was angling for a move off the comic and onto other projects. However, given the convoluted nature of some of the ongoing storylines, and the fact that there were by now roughly 350 characters to keep track of, the writers willing or able to replace Budiansky numbered exactly zero. A victim of his own success, Budiansky was unable to leave unless he could find a replacement.

Budiansky's solution was elegant in its simplicity – he contacted Simon Furman, writer of the British comics, and invited him to take his place at Marvel in America. Furman, eager to crack the US comic industry, was more than happy to make the switch – although he continued to pen the UK-exclusive strips on top of his new duties.

[56] 'Back from the Dead' was Furman's first US story, and, eager to make a splash in his big-time debut, he decided to reintroduce Megatron to the American comics after a two-and-a-half year absence. The problem was how to write the Decepticon leader back into the US storyline without contradicting his more recent appearances in the UK comic.

The solution he chose was messy, to say the least. Modern parlance would call it a 'retcon' – a piece of retroactive continuity – in which previously established facts are altered after the event. In short, Furman decided that the Megatron seen in the UK-only stories from [29.1] 'Ancient Relics' onwards was actually a clone, rather than the real Megatron. The Megatron returning in [56] 'Back from the Dead' is the 'proper' Megatron, finally awakened after his apparent demise in [25] 'Gone But Not Forgotten'.

While fine for Furman's new American audience, this had four unfortunate side effects for UK readers. First, this revelation served retrospectively to cheapen some of Megatron's later British appearances – many classic Megatron moments, in stories such as [39.1] 'Salvage' and [48.2] 'Time Wars', had now been demoted to the actions of a mere clone. Secondly, this development made an already complicated story even more confusing, especially to younger readers. As well as juggling multiple parallel realities, and stories printed out of chronological order, fans now had to consider that the

Megatron that had been running around for the last thirty months had been a clone all along. Thirdly, there were a couple of continuity problems caused by the retcon – one being the thorny issue of Galvatron having the clone-Megatron's memories, as already covered in the notes to [48.2] 'Time Wars'. Lastly, in the American story [56] 'Back from the Dead', both Optimus Prime and Ratchet are under the impression that the Decepticon Leader is 'dead'. Although it transpires that the Megatron in [48.2] 'Time Wars' was a clone, as far as the Autobots were aware, he was the genuine article. So why would they believe Megatron was dead when they'd only just encountered the clone relatively recently? (One possible solution to this problem: Autobots on Cybertron could have discovered the clone Megatron's corpse from [57.1] 'Two Megatrons' and relayed the news of 'Megatron's' death to Optimus Prime on Earth.)

UK Notes:
Although this was their American debut, the Decepticon Sports Car Patrol (or rather, two of them), had previously appeared in the UK-only story [54.1] 'A Small War' (albeit as unconscious bodies).

UK Changes:
Page 1, panel 1: the credits are replaced, the artwork is extended upwards and the story title is moved to the top of the page. The bottom left of the page, where the title was previously located, has been painted over. Finally, the reference to issue #50 is changed to #206-210.
Page 16, panel 1: the 'To be continued' caption is excised.

Roll Call:
Autobots: Optimus Prime, Jazz (as a corpse), Ratchet, Hound (as a corpse), Grimlock (as a corpse), Sludge (as a corpse), Blaster (as a corpse), Perceptor (as a corpse), Omega Supreme (as a corpse), Hot Rod, Goldbug (as a corpse), Pointblank, Landmine and Getaway.

Decepticons: Megatron, Stormcloud, Whisper, Tailwind, Nightflight, Blackjack, Detour, **Road Hugger** and **Hyperdrive**.

Review:
A decent set-up, if a little slow-moving and padded – the Air Strike Patrol argue amongst themselves for a full page, and Ratchet's encounter with the animated corpses happens twice (once as a dream, and then again in reality). The cliffhanger, though, is excellent. 3/5

[56.1] OUT TO LUNCH!
UK#240, 21 October 1989, 5 pages

Credits:
Simon Furman (script); Andrew Wildman (art); Annie Halfacree (letters). For cover credit, see the entry for [56] 'Back from the Dead' above.

Plot:
Darkwing and Dreadwind go to Maccadam's Old Oil House, a bar on Cybertron, to

drown their sorrows. Unbeknown to the two Decepticons, they have been followed by a pair of Mecannibals, who are hungry for metal.

Also in the bar is Quickswitch, an Autobot intelligence operative waiting to meet with an informant. At that moment the Mecannibals enter the bar and start causing havoc – the unfortunate bouncer is the first to be eaten.

Quickswitch decides to take action and, using his powers as a six-changer, defeats the Mecannibals by transforming into his many attack modes – including a puma, a gun and a drill-tank – eventually causing the floor to collapse, trapping the hungry aliens beneath tonnes of rubble.

Darkwing and Dreadwind, meanwhile, have imbibed so much oil that they are completely drunk, and oblivious to the carnage going on around them.

Notes:
This story is set inside Maccadam's Old Oil House, a drinking establishment on Cybertron. (It's depicted as a somewhat seedy back-alley bar here, whereas in its previous appearance – in [20.2] 'Target: 2006' – it was a bustling saloon with at least two floor levels. Either it has downsized considerably, or Maccadam's is the name of chain of pubs with multiple locations across the planet.)

Darkwing and Dreadwind discuss their recent travails, recounting how they narrowly survived fuel-poisoning (in [42] 'People Power'), and near-death at the hands of the Mecannibals (in [53] 'Recipe for Disaster'). They also mention that they've just lost a job with Megatron (which means that this story is set after the yet-to-be-published [59] 'Skin Deep', in which their boss is seemingly destroyed in an explosion). The Mecannibals' presence on Cybertron was established in [58] 'All the Familiar Faces', which although published later is actually set before this story.

(Continuity in the UK-only stories is a bit muddled by this point, with strips often being printed out of chronological order. See the notes to [53.3] '[Double] Deal of the Century' for more on this.)

It's established that Thunderwing is the current Decepticon leader on Cybertron (as previously discussed under the entry for [53.5] 'The Big Shutdown'). This is Quickswitch's first and only appearance in *The Transformers* comic.

What's With All These Drill Tanks?
It's not uncommon for a Transformer to have a 'drill tank' for an alternate mode – a vehicle with tank-like treads and, at the front, a spinning drill-shaped appendage, either for boring tunnels or breaking through barriers. Such vehicles are properly known as subterrenes, but the only practical real-world equivalents are the earth-boring machines used to create underground tunnels, which differ quite considerably from these fictional drill tanks, both in appearance and in principle.

Despite that, drill tanks are a popular type of vehicle in science fiction. Notable examples include the Mole from the *Thunderbirds* television series (1965-66), the mining vehicle from the movie *Total Recall* (Paul Verhoeven, 1990), and the Iron Mole in the Edgar Rice Burroughs novel *Pellucidar* (1915).

Drill tanks are especially prevalent in Japanese manga and anime, in franchises such as *Machine Robo*, *Astro Boy* and *Kaizoku Sentai Gokaiger*. It's no surprise, then, that the (Japanese designed) Transformers toy line featured a number of such vehicles. As well as Quickswitch we have Nosecone, Twin Twist, Powerdasher Drill and the Rescue Force drill. The Constructicons Bonecrusher and Scavenger could also be converted into drilling vehicles via the use of attachable accessories.

The phenomenon wasn't restricted to the original Transformers toy line: a number of figures from later iterations of the franchise would also boast a drill tank mode, including Drill Bit, from *Transformers: Armada*, and Galvatron, from *Beast Wars II: Super Lifeform Transformers*.

Roll Call:
Autobots: Quickswitch.

Decepticons: Darkwing and Dreadwind.

Other: Mecannibals.

Review:
An amusing farce. What's notable is that the writing and art are working in perfect harmony, Andrew Wildman's characterful and expressive inks bringing the best out of a firmly tongue-in-cheek Simon Furman script. 3/5

[56.2] RAGE!
- UK#241, 28 October 1989 ('Rage!'), 5 pages
- UK#242, 4 November 1989 ('Assault on the *Ark*!'), 5 pages

NB: This two-part story has no overall title – each segment was individually named. For the purpose of analysis, this book will refer to the two-parter as simply 'Rage!'.

Credits:
Simon Furman (script); Andrew Wildman (art); Stuart Bartlett (letters). For cover credits, see the entry for [56] 'Back from the Dead' above.

Plot:
Thunderwing rises from the sea following his recent defeat, and swears revenge on Nightbeat, Siren and Hosehead, the three Autobots who bested him. Thunderwing's fury is so great that he battles against a group of Decepticons led by Ruckus, sent to bring him back to Cybertron. Thunderwing might have been defeated once, but the High Council is still considering him as a contender for Decepticon Leader.

Deciding that his personal vengeance is more important than all other issues, Thunderwing defies the Council and convinces Ruckus's group to help him attack the *Ark* and kill the trio of Autobots who defeated him.

Thunderwing's blind determination and rage-fuelled zeal gets him aboard the *Ark*, but once there the sheer weight of Autobot numbers means that he cannot possibly hope to succeed. Thunderwing's calmer, more calculated side kicks in, and he decides to retreat rather than be destroyed.

Arriving back on Cybertron, Thunderwing is appointed Decepticon Leader.

Notes:
This story is a direct sequel to [53.5] 'The Big Shutdown' – Thunderwing emerges from the sea following his defeat in that adventure, and makes an immediate bee-line for the three Autobots responsible. See the notes under [53.5] 'The Big Shutdown' for more on

the series of events that lead to Thunderwing being installed as Decepticon commander.

The opening sequence of this story – a late-night beach party ends tragically after an attack by a creature from the sea – is reminiscent of the first scene in the film *Jaws* (Steven Spielberg, 1975). Indeed, the cover of UK#241, in which the horns of Thunderwing's helmet are seen ominously protruding from the ocean, mimics several scenes from the *Jaws* franchise where the shark's fin breaks the surface of the water just before an attack.

The emissaries from the Decepticon council include Ruckus, Windsweeper and Quake, all of whom were last seen in [52.1] 'The Fall and Rise of the Decepticon Empire', where they were witness to the clone Megatron's rise to power. This seems to imply that Thunderwing is directly replacing the Megatron clone as leader of the Decepticons on Cybertron. Presumably the clone was able to unite the various Decepticon factions during his brief spell in charge. Again, see the notes to [53.5] 'The Big Shutdown' for more thoughts on the Decepticon hierarchy on Cybertron during this time.

Review:
While it's good finally to see the events that led to Thunderwing assuming command of the Decepticons, there's a lot here that doesn't make any sense. The *Ark* is infiltrated and invaded all too easily, which only makes one wonder why the Decepticons never try it again. Worse, the powers-that-be appoint Thunderwing as Decepticon leader even though he's obviously inept. He's powerful, sure, but his mindless rage, coupled with his attitude toward his fellow Decepticons, make him totally unfit for command. This is a good, fast-paced action romp – just don't think about it too much! 3/5

[57] THE RESURRECTION GAMBIT!
US#57, 'October 1989' (published June 1989), 16 pages.

British reprint: UK#243, 11 November 1989 (Part 1), 5 pages; UK#244, 18 November 1989 (Part 2), 5 pages; UK#245, 25 November 1989 (Part 3), 6 pages.

Credits:
Simon Furman (script); José Delbo (pencils); Dave Hunt (inks); Nel Yomtov (colours); Jim Massara (letters); Don Daley (editor); Tom DeFalco (editor-in-chief); José Delbo and Danny Bulanadi (cover). **UK:** Andrew Wildman (covers, UK#243 and 245); Geoff Senior (cover, UK#244).

Plot:
Optimus Prime and the rest of the Autobots battle the Decepticon Air Strike Patrol over control of the B-204 jet. The Decepticons call for reinforcements, and Scorponok duly arrives. A battle takes place at the airbase, although Optimus Prime suspects something is amiss. He's right – the Air Strike Patrol are secretly working for Megatron and have arranged the battle as a diversion, giving Megatron time to carry out his plan.

Megatron explains to Ratchet how he survived the space bridge explosion, and how he spent most of the next two-and-a-half years as an amnesiac, wandering the slums of Cybertron until such time as his memory could repair itself. Now fully restored, he has devised a typically insane plot – he plans to have Ratchet reanimate his former lieutenant, Starscream …

Notes:
This adventure continues right where [56] 'Back from the Dead' left off, with Ratchet a prisoner of the newly-returned Megatron. Indeed, some scenes here are set contemporaneously with the events of [56] 'Back from the Dead' – we see Optimus Prime receive the message sent by Ratchet in that previous story.

This is Megatron's first full appearance since his apparent death in [25] 'Gone But Not Forgotten' (notwithstanding flashbacks, dreams and his cameo in [56] 'Back from the Dead'). Here we learn what happened to the Decepticon leader during the last two-and-a-half years: his 'death' was merely a cover to allow him to return to Cybertron undetected. However, the explosion of the space bridge severely damaged him – he awoke to find that he had lost all his memories. He wandered aimlessly until stumbling across the Decepticon Blackjack, who was being attacked by two Autobots – a visual trigger that caused all of Megatron's memories to come flooding back.

Megatron has readied four new Pretender shells. Three are unwanted prototypes; the fourth has been earmarked for Starscream, who was last seen (in the American comics) in [50] 'Dark Star', where he was destroyed.

Some of the Cybertronian scenes hark back to [17] 'The Smelting Pool' – Straxus is namechecked, and we revisit the slum area known as the Dead End, and its downtrodden inhabitants, the Empties. Ratchet's horrified reaction to seeing Megatron again is probably a reference to [8] 'Repeat Performance', the last time the pair met face to face.

This is the first (American) appearance of Darkwing and Dreadwind since [53] 'Recipe for Disaster' – they explain that they were able to shake off the pursuing Mecannibals.

UK Notes:
British readers got to see how Darkwing and Dreadwind were able to recover Starscream's corpse, in [52.2] 'Race with the Devil'.

The fact that Megatron regained his memories after a meeting with Blackjack means that that sequence must take place at some point after [54.1] 'A Small War', in which Blackjack and his fellow Micromasters were created by the then Decepticon leader, Thunderwing.

In an outburst that would have meant little to American readers at the time, Optimus Prime exclaims 'by Primus' – a reference to the Transformers' godlike creator, as seen in [36.2] 'The Legacy of Unicron'. This served to foreshadow Primus's debut appearance in the American comic, in [57] 'Yesterday's Heroes'.

UK Changes:
Page 1, panel 1: credits replaced, artwork extended upwards.
Page 2, panel 5: 'realized' is changed to 'realised'.
Page 3, panel 1: the reference to issue 25 is amended to 125. Editor Don Perlin's tag is removed from the caption.
Page 3, panel 3: 'favor' becomes 'favour'.
Page 3, panel 5: 'armor' is amended to read 'armour'.

Faking It?

In this story Megatron claims that, in the events of [25] 'Gone But Not Forgotten', he deliberately faked his own death.

At first glance, it would appear that Megatron is lying – around the time of [25] 'Gone But Not Forgotten', he was secure as leader of the Decepticon forces, and the Autobots were in disarray following the death of Optimus Prime in [24] 'Afterdeath'. There was no discernible reason for Megatron to play dead, so it's more likely that his disappearance was exactly how it seemed at the time – a crazed Transformer attempting to destroy himself. In other words, he's lying to Ratchet, embellishing his story to make himself look better. (He downplays his insanity as simply 'my, er, confused state of mind'.) Although Megatron tries to spin his apparent demise as part of some master plan, the far more likely scenario is that, due to his unstable frame of mind, he genuinely attempted to blow himself up.

But what if we take Megatron's word at face value? What if he *was* actually trying to fake his own death? What would he have sought to gain by doing so?

Megatron's leadership was coming under increasing scrutiny from the Decepticon hierarchy back on Cybertron. Soon after his 'death', Ratbat came to Earth and quickly assumed authority over the Decepticon forces there. It could be that Megatron was plotting to forestall any Cybertronian interference in his Earth operations, and went to Cybertron in an attempt to assassinate Ratbat and/or his superiors. Let's not forget that Megatron had only recently visited Cybertron, and had been returned to Earth against his will in [23.5] 'Resurrection'. He had good reasons, then, for trying to get back there.

Another possibility is that Megatron was being mentally controlled by Straxus. In [23.5] 'Resurrection', Straxus made an attempt to possess Megatron's body and, although the plan failed, it did result in Megatron showing signs of memory loss and confusion. It could be that Straxus had some lingering mental influence over Megatron, commanding him to return to Cybertron (so that Straxus could more easily substitute the real Megatron with his clone).

Roll Call:

Autobots: Optimus Prime, Jazz (as a corpse), Ratchet, Grimlock (as a corpse), Hot Rod, Blurr, Goldbug (as a corpse), Highbrow, Landmine, Cloudburst, Joyride (unconscious), Slapdash and Getaway.

Decepticons: Megatron, Starscream (as a corpse), Scorponok, Skullcruncher, Mindwipe, Weirdwolf, Bomb Burst, Skullgrin, Iguanus, Darkwing, Dreadwind, Stormcloud, Whisper, Tailwind, Nightflight, Blackjack, Detour, Road Hugger and Hyperdrive.

Nebulans: Gort, Recoil (unconscious) and Zarak.

Gort and Zarak appear only as the heads of Highbrow and Scorponok respectively. An oversized Recoil is seen amongst the *Ark*'s unconscious skeleton crew. This was an art error; it's almost certain that penciller José Delbo meant to draw Kup, but confused him with his Targetmaster partner.

Review:

In a way, this is the spiritual successor to [5] 'The New Order' and works for all the same reasons. It's big, epic and downright exciting – Megatron is back, and he plans to resurrect Starscream! Just as in 'The New Order', there are corpses galore, a flashback, a cryptic mention of a godlike creator and a ranting villain at the top of his game.

However, this story suffers from the same major drawback as that earlier one. Nothing much actually *happens*; the bulk of the story consists of Megatron just explaining the plot.

A delightfully fun read, 'The Resurrection Gambit' has big ideas and pushes a great many fan buttons. Fortunately, that's more than enough to take the attention away from the rather expository nature of the script. 4/5

[57.1] TWO MEGATRONS!

- UK#243, 11 November 1989 ('Mind Games'), 5 pages
- UK#244, 18 November 1989 ('Two Megatrons!'), 5 pages

NB: This two-part story has no overall title – each segment was individually named. For the purpose of analysis, this book will refer to the two-parter as simply 'Two Megatrons!'.

Credits:
Simon Furman (script); Stewart 'Staz' Johnson (art, part 1); Geoff Senior (art, part 2); Annie Halfacree (letters, part 1), Gary 'Glib' Gilbert (letters, part 2). For cover credits, see the entry for [57] 'The Resurrection Gambit' above.

Plot:
Cybertron: Megatron's will is weakening – the malign influence of Straxus is beginning to reassert itself. Megatron's trusty lieutenant Ravage secretly considers that he could have to kill the Decepticon leader if Straxus gains any more control over Megatron's mind.

Just then, the intruder alarm sounds – a mysterious infiltrator is approaching the Decepticon base. Ravage confronts the attacker, who turns out to be … another Megatron! The two Megatrons fight, each claiming to be the genuine article. The newcomer explains what happened – although Straxus failed to take over Megatron's mind completely, he had a back-up plan: he placed his consciousness within a clone of Megatron, and sent the clone to Earth to take the place of the real one, who had apparently died. However, the clone awoke before Straxus's consciousness had fully formed, and thus the copy of Megatron's original personality was able to come to the fore.

Realising that the newcomer speaks the truth, the clone Megatron shoots himself, allowing the real Megatron to take his place. Straxus is now dead for good.

Notes:
As previously discussed in the notes to [56] 'Back from the Dead', this story's sole purpose was to explain away a major continuity discrepancy between the US comic, in which Megatron had been missing for over two years, and its UK sister title, in which Megatron was still a prominent character. The solution was to claim retroactively that the Megatron seen in the UK comics over the past two hundred issues was, in fact, a clone.

Writer Simon Furman was possibly inspired to this solution by 'Blast from the Past' (1986), an episode of the US television soap opera *Dallas*, which revealed that an entire season of the show had been nothing more than a dream – one of the most infamous retcons in history. Indeed, the *Dallas* precedent was directly referenced in the editorial page of UK#244.

This story is a sequel to [52.1] 'The Fall and Rise of the Decepticon Empire'; the clone Megatron is still based in Helex, and indeed the throne/arena area seen in the earlier story also appears here. The real Megatron makes a reference to being found by Blackjack, a sequence we saw in [57] 'The Resurrection Gambit'.

Events of the stories [23.5] 'Resurrection', [25] 'Gone But Not Forgotten', [29.1] 'Ancient Relics' and [39.1] 'Salvage' are recalled (see below).

What was Straxus's Plan?

This is what we know: the Decepticon Lord Straxus was nearly killed during a fight with the Autobot Blaster ([18] 'The Bridge to Nowhere'). He survived, but only as a disembodied head (as revealed in [23.2] 'Under Fire'). When Megatron arrived on Cybertron, Straxus seized his opportunity – he decided that he would attempt to place his own consciousness within Megatron's body. Plan A involved a simple mind-swap – Straxus attempted to switch his brain with Megatron's. Straxus would then have been in control of Megatron' body, while Megatron's mind would have been stuck in Straxus's severed head. The mind-swap failed, and Megatron destroyed Straxus's head, seemingly killing the tyrant for good ([23.5] 'Resurrection').

However, this was not the end for Straxus, who had foreseen that his plan was a risky one. As a contingency, he had ordered the creation of a Megatron clone, into which a copy of his personality could be placed. When the real Megatron appeared to die (in [25] 'Gone But Not Forgotten'), the clone was activated. However, something went awry: when the clone awakened (in [29.1] 'Ancient Relics'), Straxus's personality was present, but only in a dormant state. The clone had a will of its own, and believed itself to be the real Megatron.

Straxus made one attempt to assert command of the clone body (in [39.1] 'Salvage'), but the clone was strong-willed and managed to fend off the mental attack. Now, having gathered enough strength to make another attempt for control, Straxus is finally destroyed when the clone commits suicide.

When one considers Straxus's plot in detail, it appears at first glance that there are a few holes in it. Here, then, is an attempt to explain away some of those supposed flaws:

Why try the mind-swap with Megatron at all, when simply implanting his mind into the clone would have been the better strategy from the off?

Well, the clone was created from the body of a hapless Decepticon trooper, whose original memories would eventually rise to the surface and confuse the clone. Perhaps Straxus knew that such an occurrence was inevitable, or at least that there was always a risk of the clone's mind being clouded by these flashbacks. The clone is host to three sets of memories (Megatron's, Straxus's and the trooper's), whereas in taking over Megatron's original body there would only be two consciousnesses fighting for dominance.

Why imprint the clone with Megatron's memories, when it would have been easier for Straxus to inhabit a body with no pre-existing mind?

Straxus knew that, in order to pose successfully as Megatron, it was not enough for him simply to look like the Decepticon leader. Megatron's unique personality wouldn't be easily imitable. Furthermore, the Decepticon Soundwave, one of Megatron's most trusted lieutenants, has mind-reading capabilities. Consequently Straxus knew that the only way to play Megatron convincingly would be to add an element of the Decepticon Leader's personality and memories into the mix.

Why impersonate Megatron? Why didn't Straxus just build a replacement body for himself that looked like his old one?

First, it would seem that are inherent dangers involved in moving a Transformer brain into a completely new body. The first time we see it happen, in [14] 'Rock and Roll-Out', Wheeljack worries about potential dangers, and of course Optimus Prime is present with the life-giving Creation Matrix to perhaps smooth the way.

Another time we see it happen, when Optimus Prime gets a new body in [42] 'People Power', the Autobots can't do it on their own, and ask for help from the highly-advanced Nebulans, whose resources and equipment are more advanced than the Transformers' own. ('The technology here is all Fortress Maximus said it would be, and more!'). It would be far less risky, then, to take control of an already-inhabited body (either Megatron's or the trooper's) than for Straxus to transfer his memory into a blank slate.

Another issue is that Straxus's reputation was on the wane. Defeated by Blaster and reduced to a mere head, he couldn't quite muster the authority or respect that he once did. Simply transferring his brain into a new body wouldn't have erased his humiliating defeat – possessing Megatron was perhaps the only way to regain his previous authority.

Roll Call:
Decepticons: Megatron, Ravage, Straxus (in flashback and also as a mental apparition), Clone Megatron, Blackjack (flashback only).

Review:
This story is as good as it could be, given that its sole purpose is to fudge the continuity so that the US and UK strips marry up. The art is excellent, and there are a couple of nice lines. Overall, though, this is ten pages of shameless backtracking and damage limitation rather than a story in its own right. 1/5

[57.2] DEMONS!
- UK#245, 25 November 1989 ('Underworld!'), 5 pages
- UK#246, 2 December 1989 ('Demons!'), 5 pages
- UK#247, 9 December 1989 ('Dawn of Darkness'), 5 pages

NB: This three-part story has no overall title – each segment was individually named. For the purpose of analysis, this book will refer to the adventure as simply 'Demons!'.

Credits:
Simon Furman (script); Jeff Anderson (art, parts 1 and 2); Geoff Senior (art, part 3); Helen Stone (letters, part 1), Annie Halfacree (letters, part 2); Gary 'Glib' Gilbert (letters,

part 3); Stewart 'Staz' Johnson (cover, UK#246); Jeff Anderson (cover, UK#247). For cover credit to issue 245, see the entry for [57] 'The Resurrection Gambit' above.

Plot:
Cybertron: a group of Autobot cadets choose to take their initiation – a final test of their prowess as warriors – in the Underworld, a system of dark, dank tunnels and sewers beneath the planet's surface.

The cadets are soon set upon by a group of sewer-dwelling mutant Transformers – sadistic killers who gleefully murder any trespassers. Two of the Autobot trainees, Subsea and Flattop, are brutally slain; a third, Tailgate, manages to escape after igniting one of the mutants' built-in gas tanks, causing a massive explosion. Unknown to Tailgate, the explosion frees a group of 'Demons' that dwell in the lower depths of the planet.

Later, the Autobot Micromaster Seawatch comes into contact with these Demons, and is so terrified by the experience that his mind shuts down. The Autobot resistance leader, Emirate Xaaron, sends the Classic Pretenders to investigate. After a brief skirmish with a group of Decepticons, the Autobots locate the monsters, but their attacks prove ineffective; the Demons seem actually to feed upon the energy blasts aimed at them.

Xaaron realises that the only way to kill these Demons is to over-feed them, and so hits them with a blast of pure Energon. Unable to cope with so much energy, the Demons explode.

Notes:
This story marks the first appearance of the titular Demons, creatures who lived on Cybertron 'long before the Transformers claimed [the planet] for their own.' According to legend, they represent the 'flip side' of the Transformers, and were entombed beneath the surface of Cybertron by Primus (the Transformers' god-like creator). They will reappear in [75] 'On the Edge of Extinction', and play a major role in the the original comics' 21st Century sequel, *Transformers: Regeneration One*.

This story seems very heavily influenced by the *Judge Dredd* strips that ran in rival comic *2000 AD* (then published by Fleetway, whose roster of titles would later include the short-lived *Transformers: Generation 2*). Similarities include:

- The 'cadet' Autobots' final 'initiation' mission recall the final assessments undertaken by Cadet Judges in the *Dredd* strips.
- The labyrinthine system of tunnels and sewers, inhabited by various criminal mutants, is not unlike the Undercity located beneath Judge Dredd's home, Mega-City One.
- The group of evil mutants, including one particular villain – Jackhammer – who is very fond of head-butting, recall Judge Dredd's nemeses the Angel Gang, whose most prominent member, Mean Machine, is similarly fond of head-butting.
- The Demons – demonic creatures who can't be killed by ordinary weapons – are reminiscent in both look and concept to *2000 AD*'s Dark Judges.

Here it's stated that Autobot cadets must undergo an initiation missions. Two of those seen here, Outback and Pipes, have previously been depicted amongst the Autobots' ranks (in [23.2] 'Under Fire' and [23.5] 'Resurrection' respectively), so this rite of passage must simply be Xaaron's way of testing the suitability of existing Autobots for entry into his resistance cell.

The Cybertron sewer system was established in [31.3] 'Headhunt'. It's never stated how or why any Transformers could be considered 'mutants', although later iterations of the franchise would introduce concepts such as 'budding' (a form of reproduction similar to that used by real-world creatures such as hydra or convolutriloba) and 'CNA' (Transformer genetic material), either of which could provide a retrospective explanation.

Given the appearance of the Autobot Classic Pretenders here, this adventure must be set after [59] 'Skin Deep', the story in which they make their full debut (chronologically speaking).

Roll Call:
Autobots: Jazz, Bumblebee, Grimlock, Emirate Xaaron, Outback, Pipes, Tailgate, Red Hot, Fixit and Seawatch.

Decepticons: Sparkstalker, Cindersaur, Ruckus and Windsweeper.

Cindersaur appears to die in this story, being reduced by the Demons to a pile of ash. Miraculously – according to dialogue in [79] 'The Last Autobot' – he manages to survive.

Other: **Demons**.

Named one-off Transformers who appear in this story include Rotgut, Slayride, Jackhammer, Warhead, Smeltdown, Subsea and Flattop.

Review:
This is a rather unusual entry in the Transformers canon. It's a notably darker and more sinister tale than we're used to; surprisingly so, given that this is a comic supposedly aimed at younger children.

As with the noir-ish [56.5] 'The Big Shutdown', this is a story that makes a virtue of the UK strip's new black-and-white format – the unnerving mood is undoubtedly helped by the judicious use of light and shadow, and indeed the art is excellent throughout.

The plotting is elegant in its simplicity – as any good horror should be – and the script even finds the time to add extra layers to Cybertron's origin story. 4/5

[58] ALL THE FAMILIAR FACES!
US#58, 'November 1989' (published July 1989), 16 pages.

British reprint: UK#246, 2 December 1989 (Part 1), 6 pages; UK#247, 9 December 1989 (Part 2), 5 pages; UK#248, 16 December 1989 (Part 3), 5 pages.

Credits:
Simon Furman (script); José Delbo (pencils); Dave Hunt (inks); Nel Yomtov (colours); Jim Massara (letters); Don Daley (editor); Tom DeFalco (editor-in-chief); José Delbo (cover). **UK:** Geoff Senior (cover, UK#248). For cover credits to issues 246 and 247, see

the entry for [57.2] 'Demons' above.

Plot:
Ratchet is blackmailed into rebuilding Starscream as a Pretender – Megatron threatens that otherwise he will destroy the *Ark* and all its occupants. Ratchet's work is completed, but Megatron reneges on the deal, and reveals that he will blow up the *Ark* anyway.

Back on Earth, Optimus Prime and Scorponok discover that they have been duped into fighting each other by the Air Strike Patrol, who have been working for Megatron this whole time. Prime sends the rest of his troops back to the *Ark*, while he and Scorponok debate how best to proceed. Their talks are interrupted by the arrival of the newly-resurrected Starscream, who immediately attacks.

Back on the *Ark*, a wounded Kup wakes to find that Blackjack has rigged the ship to explode. The two robots confront each other; Blackjack unwittingly drops the detonator device, which triggers a countdown to the *Ark*'s destruction.

On Cybertron, Megatron is just about to kill Ratchet when he realises that the Autobot medic has turned the tables on him: using Megatron's rejected prototype Pretender shells, Ratchet has been able to revive his fallen Autobot comrades Bumblebee, Jazz and Grimlock ...

Notes:
This story is the third and penultimate chapter in the American comic's 'Megatron Returns' story arc, which began in [56] 'Back from the Dead' and continued in [57] 'The Resurrection Gambit'.

There are copious references to [50] 'Dark Star' – the adventure in which Starscream, Bumblebee (as Goldbug), Jazz and Grimlock originally lost their lives. Scorponok recalls those events, and specifically the moment when Optimus Prime saved him from being destroyed by the Underbase.

There's a scene here in which Hot Rod defies orders to stay back, instead deciding to aid Optimus Prime in battle – this is a direct homage to {3-00} *The Transformers: The Movie*, in which the same thing happens.

Starscream and the other 'Classic Pretenders' are restored to life partly as a result of their new outer shells, which have special healing/restorative powers (going some way to explaining how Iguanus could recover so quickly from the injuries he sustained in [54] 'King Con').

There's a dialogue reference to the events of [53] 'Recipe for Disaster' – Darkwing and Dreadwind recall their escape from the Mecannibals, who, it transpires, have now arrived on Cybertron.

Megatron refers to 'Lysken crystals', apparently flawless gemstones known to Cybertronians. Hot Rod mentions the Red Cross, the humanitarian charity founded in 1885.

UK Notes:
The appearance of the Mecannibals on Cybertron was addressed in the UK-originated story [56.1] 'Out to Lunch'.

UK Changes:
Page 1, panel 1: credits replaced, artwork extended upwards.

Page 16, panel 4: the 'To be continued' caption is painted out.

At this time in the UK comic's history, its editorial team seemed less interested in making changes to the US stories it reprinted. This adventure is a prime example – mentions of the American issues #50 and #56 go unchanged (they should have been altered to issues #210 and #242 respectively), and the US spelling of 'honor' is retained.

Roll Call:
Autobots: Optimus Prime, Jazz, Ratchet, Bumblebee, Grimlock, Hot Rod, Kup, Blurr, Goldbug (corpse only), Chromedome, Landmine, Joyride, Slapdash and Getaway.

Decepticons: Megatron, Starscream, Scorponok, Skullcruncher, Mindwipe, Weirdwolf, Triggerhappy, Iguanus, Darkwing, Dreadwind, Blackjack, Detour, Road Hugger and Hyperdrive.

The Decepticon Whisper is briefly seen at the air base (page 8, panel 5), but this is probably an art error – the dialogue makes it clear that he and the rest of the Air Strike Patrol have already fled the scene.

Other: The Mecannibals.

Nebulans: Stylor, Zarak, Grax and Monzo.

Of the Nebulans, only Zarak is shown in his humanoid form – the remainder appear as the heads of their respective partners. As in [57] 'The Resurrection Gambit', an oversize Recoil appears in one of the scenes aboard the *Ark*, but again it's probably an error.
    Notably, all of the Targetmasters in this story (Hot Rod, Kup and Blurr) are using their standard weapons, rather than their Nebulan Targetmaster partners.

Review:
The third instalment of the four-part 'Megatron Returns' arc, this is a slight disappointment, simply marking time until the conclusion. The scenes in the air base, as Prime and Scorponok continue to argue with each other, are especially repetitive.
    Thankfully, we have a triple-whammy cliffhanger to end the story with, as events on Earth, Cybertron and the *Ark* all come to a head simultaneously, promising much for the concluding part. 2/5

[58.1] FALLEN STAR!
UK#248, 16 December 1989, 5 pages

Credits:
Simon Furman (script); Andrew Wildman (art); Helen Stone (letters). For cover credit, see the entry for [58] 'All the Familiar Faces' above.

Plot:
Following his recent resurrection as a Pretender, Starscream is suffering from a crisis of confidence. He believes that he is nothing more than a joke in the eyes of his fellow Decepticons – although in reality they still fear him immensely.

Starscream exits the Decepticons' New Jersey base and runs into a trio of Autobots. He misinterprets their fear, believing that they are mocking him. Angered, he beats the three Autobots to a pulp before declaring: 'I'm back!'

Notes:
This little adventure is narrated by the newly-resurrected Starscream, who recalls the events of [50] 'Dark Star', in which he was empowered by the Underbase, and his attack on Optimus Prime and Scorponok from [59] 'Skin Deep' (which at the time was yet to be published in the UK). At one point, Starscream even breaks the fourth wall, directly addressing the readers ('C'mon, I'll show you what I mean …').

This is the first appearance of Soundwave since his apparent destruction (at Starscream's hands) in [50] 'Dark Star' (indicating that at least some of the many casualties of that story were later repaired).

This is only the second appearance of the Autobot Chainclaw – as in his debut, in [53.3] '[Double] Deal of the Century', he gets absolutely battered here.

Roll Call:
Autobots: Optimus Prime (flashback only), Omega Supreme (flashback only), Hot Rod (flashback only), Fortress Maximus (flashback only), Cerebros (flashback only), Cloudburst, Getaway and Chainclaw.

Decepticons: Starscream, Soundwave, Scorponok (flashback only), Mindwipe and Weirdwolf.

Nebulans: Zarak (flashback only), Vorath and Monzo.

Cerebros, Vorath and Monzo are only seen as the heads of their larger companions.

Review:
Simon Furman uses one of his favourite tropes – character overcomes a crisis of confidence – to decent effect here, in a story that is both amusing and well-illustrated. A great use of the five-page format, but it loses points for unoriginality – it's especially reminiscent of [36.1] 'Stargazing'. 3/5

[59] SKIN DEEP
US#59, 'Mid November 1989' (published August 1989), 16 pages.

Up until now, the American comics had had cover dates four months in advance of their actual release dates. This forward-dating of comics was for marketing reasons – the later the date on a comic, the 'newer' it would appear to prospective buyers. In 1989 Marvel US decided gradually to reduce the interval between release dates and cover dates to just two months. So although the cover dates would seem to imply that there were two issues published in the month of November 1989, that wasn't actually the case: *The Transformers* continued to be published on a monthly basis; the 'Mid November' cover date was merely a way of reducing the four-month lag. Likewise, US#61 would bear the cover date 'Mid December'.

British reprint: UK#249, 23 December 1989 (Part 1), 5 pages; UK#250, 30 December 1989

(Part 2), 6 pages; UK#251, 6 January 1990 (Part 3), 5 pages.

Credits:
Simon Furman (script); José Delbo (pencils); Dave Hunt (inks); Nel Yomtov (colours); Jim Massara (letters); Don Daley (editor); Tom DeFalco (editor-in-chief); José Delbo and Danny Bulanadi (cover). **UK:** Mario Capaldi (cover, UK#249); Andrew Wildman (cover, UK#250); Gary Erskine (cover, UK#251).

Plot:
On Cybertron, the new Autobot Classic Pretenders battle Megatron and his Sports Car Patrol. Meanwhile, back on the *Ark*, the Autobots there frantically attempt to defuse the explosives set by Blackjack.

On Earth, Optimus Prime and Scorponok temporarily join forces against their common foe – the newly-resurrected Starscream. Thankfully, it transpires that Ratchet sabotaged Starscream's renewal: rather than him being rebuilt as a mindless drone as Megatron intended, his old personality comes to the fore, and the spineless Decepticon quickly surrenders.

Megatron discovers Ratchet's deception and is about to kill the Autobot medic, who reveals a final twist: he has used Megatron's space portal to transport the explosives out of the *Ark* and into Megatron's base. With the detonation imminent, Megatron attempts to flee through the portal, but is tackled by Ratchet just as the explosion occurs. Both robots are presumed killed by the blast.

Notes:
This is the fourth and final part of the 'Megatron Returns' arc, and as such, events of the previous three instalments are referenced heavily. Optimus Prime recalls the initial attack on the air base in [56] 'Back from the Dead', and his failed attempt to contact Ratchet in [57] 'The Resurrection Gambit'. Also, the Classic Pretenders were first seen in [58] 'All the Familiar Faces'.

There are also a couple of references to [50] 'Dark Star' – Grimlock mentions his previous 'death', and Scorponok has developed something of a phobia of Starscream following his rampage in that adventure.

Bumblebee claims that Ratchet is the 'best surgeon this side of Hydrus Four' – the planet Hydrus Four will play a big part in future stories, such as [72] 'All This and Civil War 2'. (Writer Simon Furman is a fan of foreshadowing future events, another example being the recent mention of Primus in [57] 'The Resurrection Gambit'.)

Blurr claims that he is four million years old, which makes him 'too young to die' (indicating that the natural lifespan of a Transformer is a great deal more than four million years; however, given that the Transformers are in the midst of a terrible war, their actual life-expectancy can't be nearly as impressive).

Although Ratchet and Megatron are seemingly killed here, their real fate, to be revealed in [69] 'Eye of the Storm', will be even more shocking. The title of this story is derived from the idiom 'Beauty is only skin deep', a turn of phrase usually attributed to Sir Thomas Overbury (1581-1631).

Order of Play
While the American stories ploughed ahead with a four-part epic (US#56-59), the UK adventures printed at the same time were far less beholden to continuity – they were

printed out of chronological order, making for a rather haphazard read. There are a couple of theories regarding this. The first is that the UK stories were put 'out of sync' with the American ones by the run of old reprints in the British comic (issues #221-232). The other is that they were switched around in order to promote new toy releases. Many of these UK strips, including [54.1] 'A Small War' and [58.1] 'Fallen Star', were deliberate attempts to showcase new figures, and their publication order could well have been dictated by Hasbro.

In addition, from [56] 'Back from the Dead' onwards, the American stories were a few pages shorter than usual, so the UK comic was now splitting them over three issues instead of the usual four. This was another barrier to the UK production team's attempts to sync the imported US material to their own strips.

Whatever the reasons for the situation, putting these adventures into chronological order is somewhat tricky, though not impossible. Here is one interpretation, covering UK and American strips published between [52] 'Guess Who the Mecannibals are Having for Dinner' and [59] 'Skin Deep':

January 1988: [54.1] 'A Small War'. Set 'fourteen months' before the events of [54] 'King Con'.

Early January 1989: [52] 'Guess Who the Mecannibals are Having for Dinner'/[53] 'Recipe for Disaster'. This American two-parter is set shortly after the mass deaths that occurred in [50] 'Dark Star' and [48.2] 'Time Wars', the latter of which was set around New Years' Day.

Early January 1989: [52.1] 'The Fall and Rise of the Decepticon Empire'. Takes place not long after [48.2] 'Time Wars'; we see the clone Megatron fleeing to Cybertron in the aftermath of that story.

Early January 1989: [53.1] 'Survivors'. This is another story that takes place shortly after the cataclysmic events of [48.2] 'Time Wars'.

February 1989: [53.4] 'The Hunting Party'. Takes place at some unspecified time after [53.1] 'Survivors', with Snarler directly referencing the events of that story.

February 1989: [57.1] 'Two Megatrons'. The clone Megatron is killed, leaving the Cybertronian Decepticons leaderless. This is set at some point after [52.1] 'The Fall and Rise of the Decepticon Empire' – it shows the clone Megatron in control of the Cybertronian Decepticons – but before [55] 'The Interplanetary Wrestling Championship'. After his victory here, the real Megatron sets in motion his master plan: his first task is to send the Air Strike Patrol to Earth.

February 1989: [53.5] 'The Big Shutdown'. After the death of the clone Megatron, the Cybertronian Decepticons immediately begin testing Thunderwing for his suitability to lead them.

March 1989: [54] 'King Con'. The first Micromasters arrive on Earth.

March 1989: [54.3] 'Deathbringer'. Hosehead is now part of the *Ark* crew, so this must be set after the events of [53.5] 'The Big Shutdown'.

March-April 1989: [55] 'The Interplanetary Wrestling Championship'. This story takes place over the course of a few weeks (at least), as we see Roadhandler make a career for himself as a famous wrestler. The real Megatron is active at this point (he sent the Air Strike Patrol to Earth), so this must be set after [57.1] 'Two Megatrons'.

April 1989: [55.1] 'Way of the Warrior'. Takes place at some point after [53.4] 'The Hunting Party'.

April-May 1989: [52.2] 'Race with the Devil'. We have definitive dates for this story, given within the strip itself. The Decepticon Powermasters retrieve Starscream's corpse.

Early May 1989: The 'Megatron Returns' American four-parter, [56] 'Back from the Dead' through to [59] 'Skin Deep'. This story is set shortly after [52.2] 'Race with the Devil – the Decepticon Powermasters deliver Starscream's corpse to Megatron.

May 1989: [56.2] 'Rage'. Thunderwing awakens and assumes Decepticon leadership. This story is set after [53.5] 'The Big Shutdown'.

May 1989: [56.1] 'Out to Lunch'. Set shortly after [59] 'Skin Deep' (as Megatron's recent demise is mentioned in dialogue). It also post-dates [56.2] 'Rage' (as Thunderwing is Decepticon leader by this point).

June 1989: [53.3] '[Double] Deal of the Century'. Setting unknown, though it seems to be quite a bit after [55] 'The Interplanetary Wrestling Championship' – the Micromasters' previously antagonistic attitude towards Optimus Prime has warmed considerably.

August 1989: [57.2] 'Demons'. Setting unknown, but must be at some point after [59] 'Skin Deep', as it features the Autobot Classic Pretenders.

October 1989: [58.1] 'Fallen Star'. Setting unknown, but must be set after the events of [59] 'Skin Deep', which are mentioned in dialogue.

That leaves just [53.2] 'Aspects of Evil' and [54.2] 'Prime's Rib', both of which are set in the future.

NB: Stories are placed in publication order unless there is evidence otherwise; for example this list places [54.3] 'Deathbringer' between [54] 'King Con' and [55] 'The Interplanetary Wrestling Championship', even though it could be set at any point after [53.5] 'The Big Shutdown'. [58.1] 'Fallen Star' is placed after [57.2] 'Demons' for the same reason.

UK Changes:
Page 1, panel 1: credits replaced; artwork extended upwards.

Roll Call:
Autobots: Optimus Prime, Jazz, Ratchet, Bumblebee, Grimlock, Hot Rod, Kup, Blurr,

Cloudburst and Getaway.

Decepticons: Megatron, Starscream, Scorponok, Skullcruncher, Mindwipe, Weirdwolf, Triggerhappy, Skullgrin, Darkwing, Dreadwind, Stormcloud (flashback only), Whisper (flashback only), Tailwind (flashback only), Nightflight (flashback only), Blackjack, Detour, Road Hugger and Hyperdrive.

Nebulans: Zarak, Grax, Vorath and Monzo.

Of the Nebulans, only Zarak appears in his humanoid mode; the rest feature only as the heads of their respective partners.

Data File: Mario Capaldi (artist)
Scottish-born Capaldi enjoyed a career in art that lasted over forty years. His work graced the covers of Enid Blyton's *Famous Five* series of books, and also Ladybird Books' *The Princess and the Frog*. His comic work included contributions to *Eagle*, *Care Bears*, *Roy of the Rovers*, *Battle*, *Bunty* and *Tiger*. He was responsible for the 'charging horses' illustration on the box of the board game Risk, and also provided art for a *Harry Potter* colouring book for BBC Worldwide.

Review:
Although the 'Megatron Returns' arc meandered somewhat in the middle, the finale is suitably excellent. One of the main criticisms of writer Simon Furman is that he can be prone to rushed or unsatisfying endings, but that's certainly not the case here, as the four-parter is wrapped up in dramatic (and clever) fashion – the action and explosions are all present and correct, but Ratchet's dramatic last-minute reveal (echoing the events of [8] 'Repeat Performance') makes for a superb twist ending. 5/5

[59.1] WHOSE LIFEFORCE IS IT ANYWAY?
UK#249, 23 December 1989, 5 pages

Credits:
Simon Furman (script); Stewart 'Staz' Johnson (art); Stuart Bartlett (letters). For cover credit, see the entry for [59] 'Skin Deep' above.

Plot:
Cybertron: the Autobot Pretender named Longtooth is a little idiosyncratic, to say the least. He is seemingly fearless – launching into battle without regard for his own personal safety – yet also prone to emotional outbursts, especially when the Autobot Matrix comes up in conversation.

Via flashback, we see the root of Longtooth's maladjustment. Years ago, he tended to a fallen Autobot in the aftermath of a battle – not for any altruistic reasons but rather because he was terrified of being left alone. Optimus Prime mistook his selfishness for selflessness, and granted him a wondrous gift indeed – a piece of the Matrix.

This small element of the Matrix essentially grants Longtooth an 'extra life' – if he ever dies in battle, it will resurrect him – hence his fearlessness in combat situations.

Wracked by guilt because he kept the fragment for himself rather than use it to heal injured colleagues, Longtooth eventually decides to send it back to Optimus Prime on

Earth.

Notes:
According to this story, the Matrix can be divided into fragments that can then be used to heal wounded or dying Transformers. The process of creating these fragments, however, causes Prime great pain. (See also [6] 'The Worse of Two Evils' for another example of Prime splitting up the Matrix in this fashion.)

In Longtooth's flashback, he is seen wearing his Pretender shell, despite those scenes being set over four million years in the past. As with Thunderwing's appearance in [54.1] 'A Small War', this would seem to be an indication that the Pretender process wasn't an invention of Scorponok's, as was previously implied in [40] 'Pretender to the Throne'. However, we have seen inaccurate flashbacks within the comic before (notably in [4.1] 'Man of Iron' and [47] 'Club Con'), so it's possible that Longtooth is misremembering.

This adventure is a prelude to the upcoming Matrix Quest storyline that will feature in the American comics (Emirate Xaaron discusses the forthcoming search for the Matrix), so it must be set between the American stories [61] 'The Primal Scream' and [62] 'Bird of Prey'.

This story's title is a riff on 'Whose Life is it Anyway?' a 1972 episode of the UK anthology series *ITV Sunday Night Theatre*, which was later adapted into a play (1978) and a feature film (John Badham, 1981).

Roll Call:
Autobots: Optimus Prime (flashback only), Emirate Xaaron, **Longtooth**, **Pincher** and **Doubleheader**.

Review:
The five-page black-and-white format doesn't really lend itself to involved or complicated plotting; but on the plus side it excels as a vehicle for character set-up and development. This time around it's Longtooth who gets the character study, and it's extremely refreshing to see one of the Autobots portrayed in an unflattering light. Longtooth is secretive and selfish; for years he stood by and watched others die when he had the means to save them. It's a novel hook, making for a surprisingly meaty story that belies its meagre page count. 4/5

[59.2] THE GREATEST GIFT OF ALL
UK#250, 30 December 1989, 5 pages

Later reprinted in what would be the final issue of the British comic, UK#332, 18 January 1992.

Credits:
Simon Furman (script); Stewart 'Staz' Johnson (art); Helen Stone (letters). For cover credit, see the entry for [59] 'Skin Deep' above.

Plot:
Optimus Prime is now in possession of the Matrix fragment, but he can't decide which of the many injured Autobots he should resurrect – Prowl, First Aid, Silverbolt,

Seaspray and one of the Dinobots are all considered for various reasons.

Meanwhile, the Autobot Rescue Patrol are chasing Whisper through a forest – the Decepticon Micromaster has orders from High Command to assassinate a number of key Autobots. When the rest of the Air Strike Patrol show up to aid Whisper, a battle breaks out between the two sets of Micromasters.

Prime realises that the forest battle is doing a lot of damage to the ecosystem; he orders the Rescue Patrol to retreat and uses the Matrix fragment to restore the damaged wildlife.

Notes:

As with the cartoon episode {2-25} 'The Golden Lagoon', this story has a very strong environmental message that's as relevant today as it was in the '80s. The dialogue makes explicit reference both to the destruction of the rainforests, and to 'the ozone layer [being] destroyed by aerosol sprays' – the latter picking up on the major news story broken in 1985 that CFCs (chlorofluorocarbons), chemicals used in refrigeration and aerosol sprays, were damaging the part of Earth's atmosphere that filters out harmful ultraviolet radiation.

Indeed, the 1980s saw a great increase in environmental awareness, prompted by events such as the Chernobyl nuclear disaster (1986), the Exxon Valdez oil spill (1989) and the Bhopal gas tragedy (1984). *Captain Planet and the Planeteers*, a cartoon series that strongly advocated environmentalism, would be launched in 1990.

This adventure is set on Christmas Day 1989; it would be the final special Christmas story to see print in the UK comic (the text-only 'Dreadwind's Xmas' notwithstanding), following a tradition established in [12.1] 'Christmas Breaker' and continued in [22.1] 'The Gift', [36.1] 'Stargazing' and [48.1] 'Cold Comfort and Joy'. (The forest we see here is remarkably verdant for a story set around Christmas. Either it's a temperate evergreen forest, or the action is taking place in the southern hemisphere.)

It's confirmed that both Seaspray and First Aid are long-term casualties (although neither were shown getting injured – indeed Seaspray was shown alive and well in [51] 'The Man in the Machine'). Prowl is also amongst the list of casualties, even though he was never shown to die on-panel; it's later confirmed in [62.7] 'Flashback' that he was one of Starscream's many victims in [50] 'Dark Star'.

This is a sequel to [59.1] 'Whose Lifeforce is it Anyway', and features the Matrix fragment that was introduced in that adventure. Since their commander Megatron was seemingly killed in [59] 'Skin Deep', the Air Strike Patrol have fallen in with the Decepticon High Command, and are now working as assassins. (It's therefore possible that they were the ones responsible for the deaths of Seaspray and First Aid.)

Roll Call:

Autobots: Optimus Prime, Silverbolt (as a corpse), Seaspray (as a corpse), Red Hot, Fixit, Seawatch and Stakeout.

Decepticons: Stormcloud, Whisper, Tailwind and Nightflight.

Review:

A worthy 'message' story, but it's about as subtle as a brick. Not particularly great, but at least its heart is in the right place. 2/5

[59.3] SHADOW OF EVIL

- UK#251, 6 January 1990 ('The Void!'), 5 pages
- UK#252, 13 January 1990 ('Edge of Impact'), 5 pages
- UK#253, 20 January 1990 ('Shadow of Evil'), 5 pages
- UK#254, 27 January 1990 ('White Fire'), 5 pages

NB: This four-part story has no overall title – each segment was individually named. For the purpose of analysis, this book will refer to the adventure as simply 'Shadow of Evil'. Part 1, 'The Void', shouldn't be confused with the identically-named American story [74] 'The Void'.

Credits:

Simon Furman (script); Stewart 'Staz' Johnson (art, parts 1-2); Cam Smith (art, parts 3-4); Gary 'Glib' Gilbert (letters, parts 1-2); Stuart Bartlett (letters, parts 3-4); Gary Erskine (cover, UK#252); Stephen Baskerville (cover, UK#253 and 254). For cover credit to issue 251, see the entry for [59] 'Skin Deep' above.

Annie Halfacree was incorrectly credited for the lettering on part 3; a correction and apology was printed in UK#259.

Plot:

The future: a group of Autobots led by Rodimus Prime flee Cybertron, which is now ruled by Galvatron. To speed up the journey to Earth, the Autobot ship enters the void-like realm known as hyperspace.

It transpires that someone aboard the ship is a saboteur – a guard is killed and the craft emerges from hyperspace too close to Earth: assuming it doesn't burn up in the planet's atmosphere, it will crash-land and kill everyone aboard.

In order to flush out the saboteur, Kup declares that Arcee should attempt to access the retro rockets by swimming through the ship's coolant tanks. In reality, Arcee reaches the retros by navigating the ship's narrow crawlspaces, allowing Kup to set a trap at the coolant tanks. Kup is shocked to discover that the saboteur is Rodimus Prime, who has once again been corrupted by the Unicron-tainted Matrix.

The ship makes it to Earth in one piece and, once disembarked, the Autobots battle their disturbed leader. Rodimus is too powerful, however, and begins obliterating his former friends.

Meanwhile, within Rodimus Prime's mind, a mental battle is taking place, as the souls of Rodimus and Unicron do battle for control of the Autobot leader's body. Rodimus is on the brink of victory …

… but Kup removes the Matrix from Rodimus's chest cavity, thereby separating him from Unicron's influence. His mind restored to normal, Rodimus muses that Unicron still exists within the Matrix, and that one day they will confront each other again.

Notes:

The captions in this story declare that these events are set on 'New Year's Day, 2009', contradicting [48.2] 'Time Wars', which also claimed to be set on that date. The Transformation page in UK#253 corrects the mistake, and confirms that 'Shadow of Evil' is actually set on New Year's Day 2010; any lingering confusion was settled in the letters page of UK#258: 'The date should read New Year's Day 2010, not 2009. New Year's Day 2009 was the time (no pun intended) that "Time Wars" began. And besides, the division between present and future has always been 20 years.'

Chronologically speaking, this story is set between the Galvatron (2009) and Unicron (2010) segments of [53.2] 'Aspects of Evil', and so takes place in the post-Time Wars future, in which Galvatron never fled to the past.

Hyperspace is depicted as a 'negative' of real space, with a white vacuum and dark stars. Rodimus Prime's mental battle against Unicron references similar scenes in [36.2] 'The Legacy of Unicron'. The Autobots arrive on Earth with a goodwill gift – a large supply of Energon.

While the last multi-part UK story – [57.2] 'Demons' – was a tribute to *Judge Dredd*, this one is heavily influenced by the *Star Trek* franchise, both in dialogue and in plot. There are references to 'warp space' and 'blasters set to stun' (misquoting the famous 'phasers set to stun' catchphrase). Kup brings readers up to speed with a *Trek*-style log recording ('First officer Kup reporting. Earth date: 1/1/2009'). The design of the Autobot ship mimics *Star Trek*'s *USS Enterprise*, especially the bridge, which features a forward-facing viewing screen and manned consoles dotted around the perimeter of the room. There is also a network of crawlspaces, similar to the 'Jefferies tubes' on *Star Trek* spacecraft.

Plot-wise, this adventure homages *Trek*'s 'The Enemy Within' (1966), in which the ship's captain battles against his own dark side, and 'The Alternative Factor' (1967), where two facets of the same alien being do battle in a bizarre negative space. Rodimus Prime's swim through a coolant tank to reach the retro boosters recalls a scene in *Star Trek IV: The Voyage Home* (Leonard Nimoy, 1986), in which Captain Kirk (William Shatner) swims through a flooded area in order to access a vital control.

The clinchers: the Autobot helmsman is none other than Red Alert (the *USS Enterprise* was often at 'red alert' status during the course of the show), and Arcee numbers the ship's crew at 'about four hundred and thirty or so': in *Star Trek*, the original *USS Enterprise* was home to exactly 430 crew.

Roll Call:
Autobots: Red Alert, Blaster, Perceptor, Kup, Rodimus Prime, Afterburner, Strafe, Getaway, Arcee, Quickmix, Flak, Sunrunner, Chainclaw, Siren, Hosehead, Big Shot, Sidetrack, Seawatch, Longtooth, Pincher and Doubleheader.

Decepticons: Galvatron III (flashback only).

Other: Unicron.

Data File: Gary Erskine (artist)
The Transformers was amongst Erskine's first ever work. He's since had a long and fruitful career in the comics industry, with credits on titles such as *2000 AD*, *Hellblazer*, *Fantastic Four: First Family*, *G.I. Joe: A Real American Hero*, *She-Hulk* and *Batman: Legends of the Dark Knight*.

Review:
This story starts out as an unassuming little murder mystery, but then, when the culprit is revealed exactly halfway through, the action ramps up as Rodimus is forced to

massacre his fellow Autobots while simultaneously engaging in a battle of wills on the astral plane.

It's a fitting finale to the future-set stories and, like other recent stories featuring the future Autobots ([A4.5] 'Peace' and [53.2] 'Aspects of Evil'), has a deliciously downbeat ending.

Bleak and nightmarish, but wonderfully so. 4/5

UK Straplines, Part 4

The penultimate assortment of straplines from the cover of *The Transformers* UK, covering issues #199 to #264.

- UK#199: Time Wars begins ... Unleash the apocalypse!
- UK#200: none
- UK#201: Autobot war!
- UK#202: Twins of evil!
- UK#203: 'It's okay, Carnivac – we beat him. It's over! Carnivac?'
- UK#204: Earth's last hope!
- UK#205: 'I beat them all!'
- UK#206: Starscream – traitor?
- UK#207: Decepticon vs Decepticon ... in a cold war!
- UK#208: Underbase belongs to ... 'Starscream!'
- UK#209: 'I can't get involved – I just can't!'
- UK#210: 'Now nothing can stop me!'
- UK#211: 'Meet the Pretender Beasts ...' 'And die!'
- UK#212: 'Don't lose your head!'
- UK#213: Pretenders – on the menu! Megatron – the homecoming! Visionaries – the origin!
- UK#214: The Mecannibals are ... 'Hungry!' Plus: Megatron vs Quake!
- UK#215: 'This is the life ...' 'Peace and quiet ...' 'Uh, fellas ...'
- UK#216: Staring death ... in the face!
- UK#217: 'You did this ... but you're dead!'
- UK#218: Dogfight ... Sky Lynx ... incoming!
- UK#219: ... Never in your wildest dreams!
- UK#220: Alas, poor Cloudburst!
- UK#221: He's mad ... he's bad!
- UK#222: Game over!
- UK#223: Air strike!
- UK#224: 'No!' 'If Galvatron dies, we all die!'
- UK#225: 'I calculate a 97.5% probability of your immediate termination, fleshlings!'
- UK#226: Traitor!
- UK#227: The true face of evil!
- UK#228: 'Two more satisfied customers!'
- UK#229: 'Spinister – what was that about Decepticons never retreating?' 'Just shut up, Needlenose, and run!'
- UK#230: Nightbeat P.I.? 'Of all the beaches in all the world, ya hadta get washed up on mine!'
- UK#231: Look out, Nightbeat – there's thunder in the air!
- UK#232: 'Micromasters, hah! Need a magnifying glass to find 'em!'
- UK#233: Be a robot in disguise ... with your free tattoo!

- UK#234: The gentle touch!
- UK#235: Deathbringer ... and all hell followed!
- UK#236: The dark side ... of the force!
- UK#237: Dogs of war!
- UK#238: No place to run!
- UK#239: Mayhem!
- UK#240: 'I don't feel so good, Dreadwind.' 'Me neither, Darkwing – must've been something we ate!'
- UK#241: Devil in the deep blue sea!
- UK#242: Raid on the *Ark*!
- UK#243: none
- UK#244: And the winner is – Megatron! But which one?
- UK#245: Dead end!
- UK#246: I spy, with my little eye ...!
- UK#247: 'Uh guys ... shouldn't we be fighting together?' 'We *are* fighting together!'
- UK#248: Four classic Transformers ... as you've never seen them before!
- UK#249: Longtooth's secret
- UK#250: Fabulous free cover poster!
- UK#251: Crash dive!
- UK#252: 'Murderer!'
- UK#253: 'Get out of my head!'
- UK#254: 'Battle for the Matrix!'
- UK#255: Perchance to dream!
- UK#256: 'Go ahead ... make my day!'
- UK#257: 'Who's a pretty boy then?!'
- UK#258: 'Hmm ... I wonder who ...?'
- UK#259: Battle of the giants!
- UK#260: Pawns of Galvatron!
- UK#261: 'There's one thing we gotta get, Wheeljack ...' 'Wassat, Prowl?' 'Outta this business!'
- UK#262: Beware the Shockwave(s)!
- UK#263: 'I quit!'
- UK#264: 'There's somethin' moving out here, an' it ain't us!'

[60] YESTERDAY'S HEROES!

US#60, 'December 1989' (published September 1989), 18 pages.

British reprint: UK#252, 13 January 1990 (Part 1), 6 pages; UK#253, 20 January 1990 (Part 2), 6 pages; UK#251, 27 January 1990 (Part 3), 6 pages.

Credits:

Simon Furman (script); José Delbo (pencils); Dave Hunt (inks); Nel Yomtov (colours); Jim Massara (letters); Don Daley (editor); Tom DeFalco (editor-in-chief); José Delbo and Danny Bulanadi (cover). **UK:** For cover credits see the entry for [59.3] 'Shadow of Evil' above.

Plot:

Aboard the *Ark*, Optimus Prime mulls over the deaths of the many Autobots who have fallen in battle during their war with the Decepticons. Shocked and appalled by the loss of life, he reasons that the only way to prevent further deaths is simply to cease fighting.

When Prime announces that he is leaving the Autobots, Hot Rod comes up with an idea to make him return to the fold. He decides to use a remote-controlled Guardian robot to fake an attack on the Autobots, so that Optimus Prime will rush in and save them. His plan works a little *too* well: the robot runs amok, attacking the Autobots for real until Prime duly returns to save his comrades. His determination restored, Prime vows that he will never stop until the Decepticon menace is finished forever.

Back on Cybertron, the newly-resurrected Classic Pretenders – Bumblebee, Jazz and Grimlock – have joined with the Autobot resistance, and have aided in attacks against numerous Decepticon fuel depots. With the trio of new Pretenders set to journey to Earth, a Decepticon strike results in a malfunction of their teleportation device. The Autobots instead materialise within the centre of Cybertron, where they come face to face with their dormant god, Primus …

Notes:

The first part of a new story arc, this instalment sees the US debut appearances of many characters, such as Thunderwing, Bludgeon, Landfill and the Autobot Rescue Patrol. Writer Simon Furman also uses the opportunity to add some previously UK-only concepts into the American comic, such as Primus, Emirate Xaaron, the Guardian robots and the Decepticon Mayhem Attack Squad.

While Scorponok leads the Earth-based Decepticons, it's confirmed here that Thunderwing leads their Cybertron contingent. It's stated that Powerglide and Perceptor are 'deceased': Powerglide's death presumably occurred off-panel at some point during the cataclysmic events of [50] 'Dark Star'.

There are many references back to [59] 'Skin Deep' – the death of Ratchet is mentioned on numerous occasions, and there is a flashback to the destruction of Megatron's base. The *Ark* again visits the Earth's moon, having previously done so in [41] 'Totaled'.

An 'Orn' is a Cybertronian time unit equivalent to a lunar day. (This is a bit strange, as Cybertron has two moons; perhaps they both have the exact same period of rotation, which again implies that these are not natural satellites.)

There is gravity at the centre of Cybertron. (Theoretically there should be zero gravity at the centre of a planet; presumably there's some artificial gravity generation going on here.) Upon being teleported underground, Jazz exclaims 'I don't think we're in Kansas anymore', a misquote of a line from *The Wizard of Oz* (Victor Fleming, 1939).

UK Notes:

The Guardian robot seen in this story is stated to be a 'Mark V'. This is the third type of Guardian depicted in the comics, after the 'Omega Class' first seen in [4.3] 'Raiders of the Last *Ark*' and the unnamed type seen in [23.2] 'Under Fire'.

Thunderwing's rise to power was documented in UK-only stories such as [53.5] 'The Big Shutdown' and [56.2] 'Rage'. Indeed, many Transformers making their US debuts in this story had previously featured in UK adventures: Emirate Xaaron in [A1.3] 'And There Shall Come … A Leader', Bludgeon and his Mayhem Attack Squad in [53.4] 'The Hunting Party', the Rescue Patrol in [59.2] 'The Greatest Gift of All', and Landfill and Quickmix in [53.2] 'Aspects of Evil'.

Optimus Prime has a lengthy discussion with the *Ark*'s computer, which was nicknamed 'Auntie' the last time it featured prominently in the comics, in [4.3] 'Raiders of the Last *Ark*.

Roll Call:
Autobots: Optimus Prime, Jazz, Prowl (viewscreen image only), Ratchet (viewscreen image only), Bumblebee, Grimlock, Powerglide (viewscreen image only), Perceptor (viewscreen image only), Emirate Xaaron, Hot Rod, Kup, Blurr, Fortress Maximus (flashback only), Cerebros (flashback only), Highbrow, Brainstorm, Cloudburst, Landfill, Quickmix, Fixit, Seawatch, Stakeout and **Scoop**.

Decepticons: Starscream (flashback only), Stranglehold, Bludgeon, Octopunch and Thunderwing.

Other: Primus.

Nebulans: Gort and Arcana.

Starscream and Fortress Maximus appear in a flashback alongside a mystery third Transformer (which appears to be an oddly-drawn Jazz – that's certainly his gun, waist and lower legs).

Gort, Arcana and Cerebros appear only as the heads of Highbrow, Brainstorm and Fortress Maximus respectively, rather than as individual characters.

Review:
Best described as an interlude story, this acts as a bridge between the two more substantial American stories either side of it. There's a lot of standing still: Optimus Prime talks to a computer, leaves the Autobots and then rejoins, while the Pretenders raid some Decepticon fuel facilities.
The cliffhanger is excellent, and there are a couple of good action sequences, but the low-key nature of this story does count against it. 2/5

US Advertisements, Part 7: Miscellaneous (M-Z)
The final list of advertisements from the American comic, the second half of the 'miscellaneous' category:

Marvel slumber bags – US#79
Marvel superhero pin badges – US#38-41
Marvel superhero poster offer – US#14, 49
Marvel T-shirt offer – US#79-80
Marvel Universe trading cards – US#73-74
Military Diamond Sales – US#2
Mr Bubble (bubble bath) – US#57-63
NBA Hoops (trading cards) – US#73, 75-76, 79
NFL 'SuperPro' fan club – US#3
Noxzema Clear-Ups (acne cleansing pads) – US#7
Olympic Sales Club (mail-order shopping) – US#1, 5, 10, 16, 20-21, 28, 32-33, 40, 44-45, 56, 58; HDM#2
Oxy (skincare products) – US#33-35; HDM#3
Pineapple (glow-in-the-dark posters/shoelaces etc.) – US#10-13

Pro Set NFL trading cards – US#70

Rip-Off's (sports shoes) – US#5, 9

Sales Leadership Club (mail-order shopping) – US#15, 20, 27, 32, 39-40, 44; GIJ#4; HDM#2

San Francisco Mint (*Star Trek* figurines) – US#59-61

Schwinn (bicycle manufacturer) – US#52, 54, 56

Score MLB trading cards – US#78

Score NFL trading cards – US#71, 80

Sears (US retailer) – US#55-57

SkyBox NBA trading cards – US#73, 79

Southern Cal. Comic Convention – US#68

Spider-Man Trivia Game (play-by-telephone quiz game) – US#78

Studio 4 Home DJ Machine – US#49-50

Super Mario Bros (shampoo and bubble-bath range) – US#73-74

'Time for Heroes, A' (7" single by Meatloaf and Brian May) – US#34; HDM#3

Win a job at Marvel Comics (winners included *Spider-Man* penciller Mark Bagley) – US#3

Yamaha DX100 synthesizer – US#19-20, 22, 24-25; MOV#2-3; GIJ#1-2

Young Astronaut Program – US#6, 8-10

[60.1] ...PERCHANCE TO DREAM

- UK#255, 3 February 1990 (1. Prowl), 5 pages
- UK#256, 10 February 1990 (2. Ironhide), 5 pages
- UK#257, 17 February 1990 (3. Sunstreaker), 5 pages
- UK#258, 24 February 1990 (4. Wheeljack), 5 pages
- UK#259, 3 March 1990 (5. Silverbolt), 5 pages
- UK#260, 10 March 1990 (6. Galvatron), 5 pages

Credits:

Simon Furman (script); Andrew Wildman (art, parts 1, 3 and 6); Stewart 'Staz' Johnson (art, parts 2 and 4); John Stokes (art, part 5); Gary 'Glib' Gilbert (letters, parts 1-2); Stuart Bartlett (letters, part 3-6); Stephen Baskerville (cover, UK#255 and 256); Art Wetherell (cover, UK#257); Jeff Anderson (cover, UK#258); Andrew Wildman (cover, UK#259); Geoff Senior (cover, UK#260).

Plot:

The Autobots are off on a mission, leaving the *Ark* deserted. A shadowy infiltrator sneaks aboard and begins tapping the minds of the many comatose Autobots lying dormant within the repair bay.

Prowl is the first Autobot to undergo the mind scan: he dreams of relentlessly pursuing the Decepticon Battlechargers across America, but is stopped by Optimus Prime. Prowl was so focused on hunting down his quarry that he neglected to think of the damage he was causing to the humans and their property.

The next dream we see is Ironhide's. He confronts a group of terrorists who have taken hostages within an abandoned warehouse. He is able to rescue the hostages, but no thanks to the human police, who just get in the way. Ironhide muses how dumb humans can be ...

Sunstreaker dreams of a reconnaissance mission to the Decepticon base. Jazz is attacked by Skywarp and Thundercracker but Sunstreaker – so vain that he avoids battles for fear that his bodywork could get damaged – decides to retreat. However, his actions are not purely driven by vanity or cowardice: Sunstreaker lures the attackers into a confrontation with some human fighter jets, who are able to drive the Decepticons away.

In Wheeljack's dream, we see him in the old Blackrock Aerospace facility, searching for the advanced Decepticon technology that allowed the creation of Jetfire. There he meets Ravage, who proposes a deal: the technology in exchange for Jetfire himself. Wheeljack seriously considers turning Jetfire over to the Decepticons, and only after some heavy soul-searching does he decide not to go through with it.

Silverbolt dreams of a time soon after his construction. The Autobot suffers from an irrational fear of heights, which he keeps from his fellow Aerialbots. However, during a battle with Menasor, the Aerialbots combine to form Superion – and this merging of minds results in his acrophobia becoming common knowledge. Silverbolt's rage at his most private secret being revealed causes Superion to lash out violently and launch a crazed attack on Menasor.

The shadowy infiltrator – Galvatron – watches these dreams with interest. His aim is to bring out the Autobots' character flaws and turn them into evil warrior-slaves. However, his mind probes instead have the effect of waking the Autobots from their comatose state; the newly-revived Autobots use Galvatron's own mind probe against him. In a reversal of roles, Galvatron is now permanently comatose, stuck in a terrible nightmare of his own.

Notes:

The storytelling technique here is similar to that in [53.2] 'Aspects of Evil': a number of individual character vignettes with a linking 'frame'. Each part focuses on a different Autobot. In 1990 Hasbro Europe were in the process of re-releasing a number of the older Transformers figures, as part of their 'Classics' sub-line; all Autobots featured here were amongst those included. (Two others, Jazz and Inferno, were omitted, due to them being already active in the current ongoing storylines.)

Although it's possible that the Autobots' dreams are simply products of their respective imaginations, the way the story is written heavily implies that these are actual flashbacks, rather than dreams *per se*.

Prowl's dream sees him pursue the Battlechargers, in a sequence that's clearly set at some point during the events of [23] 'Decepticon Graffiti'. Ironhide's flashback is harder to place, as it contains no reference to outside events. Given that Optimus Prime is alive, the Ironhide sequence could be set at almost any point between [12] 'Prime Time' and [24] 'Afterdeath'. The sign on the warehouse in this segment reads 'A Daley Import and Export Ltd', a reference to the popular British comedy-drama series *Minder*. Ironhide's line on the front cover of this issue (UK#256), 'Go ahead … make my day'), is a quote from the film *Sudden Impact* (Clint Eastwood, 1983). The exact same quotation was previously used by Wreck-Gar in [43] 'The Big Broadcast of 2006'.

The Sunstreaker segment is set at some point after the military surround Megatron's base in [3] 'Prisoner of War', but before Sunstreaker is shot by Shockwave in [5] 'The New Order' – probably during the events of [4] 'The Last Stand'. (Megatron orders his troops not to engage in hostilities with the humans; he had no such qualms in [3] 'Prisoner of War'.) Sunstreaker has to be told who Galvatron is, meaning that after his brief revival in [41] 'Totalled', he was somehow rendered inactive again prior to the major battle with Galvatron in [48.2] 'Time Wars'.

The Wheeljack chapter is set at some point after [12] 'Prime Time', and shows the Autobot investigating the Blackrock Aerospace plant that was abandoned by the Decepticons in that story. Jetfire is drawn without his Autobot insignia, so this is probably set between [12.4] 'Dinobot Hunt', where he loses his Decepticon insignia, and [14] 'Rock and Roll-Out', where he gains his Autobot badge. Ravage claims that Jetfire 'broke his programming, defected to the Autobots' (an inaccurate reading of events: Jetfire was a mindless Decepticon drone, later instilled with an Autobot personality). Ravage also states that Wheeljack could become the 'best engineer this side of Hydrus Four' – the planet Hydrus Four was previously mentioned in [59] 'Skin Deep', and will play an important part in upcoming stories.

The Silverbolt section is probably set between [21] 'Aerialbots over America' and [22] 'Heavy Traffic' – the Aerialbots are still new and this is the first time they've combined since they were given their 'proper' personalities. Menasor is seen attacking a Blackrock Fuel Depot (the Decepticons attacked a similar facility in [22.1] 'The Gift').

Galvatron knows Shakespeare (it was presumably programmed into him when the *Ark* reactivated Megatron in [1] 'The Transformers'); the title of this story is a quote from his play *The Tragedy of Hamlet, Prince of Denmark* (act III, scene i).

This Galvatron definitely isn't the same one who died in [48.2] 'Time Wars' ('A different Galvatron, I think'). Instead this is Galvatron III, the Decepticon leader from the post-Time Wars future (see [53.2] 'Aspects of Evil'). This will be Galvatron III's final appearance in the comics – being trapped inside a never-ending nightmare is a fitting fate for the villain who has caused so much trouble. (The letters page in UK#279 confirms that the Galvatron seen here is indeed the same one that appeared in [53.2] 'Aspects of Evil'.)

This story is the first part of the so-called 'Earthforce Saga', which consists of all the UK-printed stories from here until the end of the comic's run.

Roll Call:
Autobots: Optimus Prime (in a dream), Jazz (in a dream), Prowl, Ironhide, Sunstreaker, Wheeljack, Brawn (as a corpse), Jetfire (in a dream), Silverbolt, Air Raid (in a dream), Fireflight (in a dream), Skydive (in a dream), Slingshot (in a dream), Superion (in a dream) and Rodimus Prime (in a dream).

Decepticons: Megatron (in a dream), Skywarp (in a dream), Thundercracker (in a dream), Ravage (in a dream), Motormaster (in a dream), Drag Strip (in a dream), Dead End (in a dream), Wildrider (in a dream), Breakdown (in a dream), Menasor (in a dream), Galvatron III, Runabout (in a dream) and Runamuck (in a dream).

Motormaster, Drag Strip, Dead End, Wildrider and Breakdown appear only as part of their combined mode, Menasor.

Data File: Art Wetherell (artist)
Wetherell's other credits include *Action Force Monthly*, *The Incredible Hulk Presents*, *Death's Head* and *Star Wars*.

Review:
Basically, this is just [53.2] 'Aspects of Evil' but with Autobots, and done better. Not

only are all the individual parts very good (especially the Wheeljack and Sunstreaker segments, which are excellent), but it also has a very satisfactory ending.

Most of the time-travelling done in *The Transformers* is between the present day and the future, which means there's very little scope for celebrating and revisiting old events and characters. Part of the appeal here is that we're seeing classic characters such as Prowl, Skywarp and Jetfire, and old locations such as Fortress Sinister and the Blackrock Aerospace plant.

This would have been a fun nostalgia trip in any case; that it's actually a remarkably good story is just an added bonus. 5/5

[61] THE PRIMAL SCREAM
US#61, 'Mid December 1989' (published October 1989), 18 pages.

British reprint: UK#259, 3 March 1990 (Part 1), 6 pages; UK#260, 10 March 1990 (Part 2), 6 pages; UK#261, 17 March 1990 (Part 3), 6 pages.

Credits:
Simon Furman (script); Geoff Senior (art); Nel Yomtov (colours); Jim Massara (letters); Don Daley (editor); Tom DeFalco (editor-in-chief); Don Perlin and Vince Mielcarek (cover). **UK:** Stephen Baskerville (cover, UK#261). For cover credits to issues 259 and 260, see the entry for [60.1] 'Perchance to Dream' above.

The American comic had a little fun with the credits, amending the production team's names to sound like Transformers: Simon Furman Maximus, Geoffire Senior, Shrapnel Yomtov, Jim Lock Massara, Megadon Daley and Double Dealer DeFalco.

Plot:
At Cybertron's core, the misplaced Autobots are met by the Keeper, who explains that Primus is presently sleeping. He shares a mental link with the planet-devourer Unicron: if Primus is woken, it will alert Unicron to Cybertron's location. To prevent Unicron from attacking Cybertron, Primus must remain dormant.

Meanwhile, back on Earth, Scorponok is facing something of a mutiny – ever since he invited the unpopular Starscream to rejoin their ranks, his fellow Decepticons have begun to question his judgment.

At Cybertron's core, the Autobots are set upon by the Decepticon Mayhem Attack Squad, who were also inadvertently teleported to the planet's centre. During the ensuing battle, gunfire ricochets off Grimlock and hits Primus, waking him up. Primus lets out an almighty scream, the sound reverberating across the entire planet. Before anyone can react, Emirate Xaaron is able to fix the damaged teleport device, sending the Autobot Pretenders to Earth as originally intended.

Light years away, Unicron hears the scream and changes course for Cybertron ...

Notes:
A momentous story, this sees the Transformers' origins recounted in the American comic for the first time. It's the very first appearance of the contemporary, Timeline B iteration of Unicron, and the full debut of the present-day Primus, barring his cameo in the cliffhanger ending of [60] 'Yesterday's Heroes'.

Primus is psychically linked to Unicron – should Primus ever wake from his slumber, Unicron will be able to locate him. Primus is programmed to wake only when the Transformers have ceased their civil war and become a united people, strong enough to stand against Unicron; his early rousing here means that Unicron is now due to arrive ahead of schedule.

Primus is tended to by the Keeper, a belligerently devout Cybertronian who is able to project (holographic?) images from his hands. He is shot and killed by the Decepticons.

This story continues directly on from the previous American one, [60] 'Yesterday's Heroes'. Ratchet's recent death in [59] 'Skin Deep' is mentioned, as is Bumblebee's previous death in [50] 'Dark Star'. Starscream's treacherous attacks against his fellow Decepticons in [50] 'Dark Star' and [59] 'Skin Deep' are mentioned.

The Keeper confirms that the Matrix is the one thing that can kill Unicron, prompting the upcoming 'Matrix Quest' storyline beginning in [62] 'Bird of Prey'.

The title is derived from *The Primal Scream*, a 1970 pop-psychology book by Arthur Janov.

UK Notes:
For UK readers, the Transformers' origin story had already been recounted (see the notes to [36.2] 'The Legacy of Unicron). Unicron's advance toward Cybertron here is the final proof (if any were still needed) that the UK future-set stories take place in an alternative reality (Timeline A, in which Unicron doesn't attack Cybertron until the year 2006).

The Keeper seen here is only the second Cybertronian cleric seen in the comics; the first was the monk-like Transformer who tended to the Matrix Flame in [20.2] 'Target: 2006'.

UK Changes:
Page 1, panel 1: credits replaced.
Page 9, panel 4: the references to issues #50 and 59 are changed to #209, 210 and 248.

Roll Call:
Autobots: Jazz, Bumblebee, Grimlock, Emirate Xaaron, Red Hot, Fixit, Seawatch, Stakeout and Doubleheader.

Decepticons: Starscream, Soundwave, Scorponok, Mindwipe, Apeface, Snapdragon, Slugslinger, Misfire, Stranglehold, Bludgeon and Octopunch.

Other: Unicron and Primus.

Nebulans: Zarak, Vorath, Spasma and Krunk.

All Nebulans in this story appear only as the heads of their respective Transformer partners, rather than as individuals.
The 'first Transformer' seen in the Keeper's origin flashback would retroactively be named Prima in subsequent official Transformers media.

Review:
More than any other story, the merits of 'The Primal Scream' depend almost entirely on

whether one follows the American or the British comics. For the Americans, this was a truly momentous issue, with the Transformers' origin finally revealed, and the debut of Geoff Senior's artwork, in a style unlike anything seen previously in the US book.

For British readers, however, this wasn't as big a turning point – the Transformers' origin had been recounted twice before, in [36.2] 'The Legacy of Unicron' and 'The Transformers: The Facts', a booklet that came free with UK#200, and Geoff Senior's work was already familiar.

Despite consisting mainly of exposition and fight sequences, this is a satisfying read nevertheless. Even those already familiar with the Transformers' origin can't help but be awed at the mythic quality and scope of the storytelling on display, even though it's simply recycling old material. Also, it's quite ironic that an entire planet is threatened with destruction simply because a laser beam bounces off of Grimlock's backside.

More than anything, though, this is Geoff Senior's story. His art is spectacular here, papering over some of the cracks in the script and resulting in a comic that is simply a joy to look at. Big, bold and exciting, this is a great story, despite a few niggling flaws. 4/5

[61.1] STARTING OVER!
- UK#261, 17 March 1990 ('Starting Over!'), 5 pages
- UK#262, 24 March 1990 ('Two Steps Back!'), 5 pages
- UK#263, 31 March 1990 ('Break-Away!'), 5 pages
- UK#264, 7 April 1990 ('Desert Island Risks!'), 5 pages
- UK#265, 14 April 1990 ('Once Upon a Time ...'), 5 pages
- UK#266, 21 April 1990 ('Life in the Slow Lane'), 5 pages

While these strips form a single adventure of sorts (and will be analysed as such), the link is admittedly more tenuous than usual, each working equally well on a stand-alone basis. However, there are a couple of plot threads – the formation of Earthforce and Prowl's effort to prevent Megatron's gas attack – that bind the stories together; and, combined with the relatively-low page count, this makes it convenient to address them in a single block.

Credits:
Simon Furman (script); Stewart 'Staz' Johnson (art, parts 1 and 3); Andrew Wildman (art, parts 2 and 5); Pete Knifton (pencils, parts 4 and 6); Pete Venters (inks, parts 4 and 6); Stuart Bartlett (letters, parts 1-4); Peri Godbold (letters, part 5); Gary 'Glib' Gilbert (letters, part 6); Stephen Baskerville (cover, UK#262 and 263); Jeff Anderson (cover, UK#264); Gary 'Glib' Gilbert (cover design, UK#265); Andrew Wildman (cover, UK#266). For cover credit to UK#261, see the entry for [61] 'The Primal Scream' above.

Gary Gilbert gets an unusual 'cover design' credit for issue 265 – the image is merely a slightly modified blow-up of some of Andrew Wildman's interior art, although Gilbert's lettering features prominently.

Plot:
Having recently been reactivated, Prowl and Wheeljack are sent to check on reports of Decepticon activity in Arizona. While *en route* they reminisce about how much simpler things were in the old days: new-fangled types of Transformers such as Pretenders,

Powermasters and Micromasters have made life more complicated. Consequently they react with a certain amount of glee when they are attacked by a couple of 'old-school' Decepticons, Mixmaster and Long Haul – this is just how things used to be.

Eventually tracking the Decepticons to their outpost, they find that Megatron has hatched another lunatic scheme: he plans to launch a missile that will release gases into the atmosphere and cause the Earth to overheat – heat energy that can be converted into Energon cubes. Completely surrounded and seemingly defeated, Prowl and Wheeljack smile at each other before launching into a fierce attack on the Decepticons – it's just like old times.

Meanwhile, the Dinobots' methods are being questioned by Optimus Prime – their crude, unsubtle tactics, he claims, are a danger to humans. Prime also despairs that the Dinobots seem to take great delight in battling Decepticons – according to Prime, violence should be a last resort, not something to be relished.

Grimlock takes umbrage at Optimus Prime's words and threatens to leave the Autobots. The argument gets so heated that the two Autobots briefly fight. In the end, Prime relents, and gives Grimlock leadership of the Earth-based Autobot army, now dubbed Earthforce.

The first mission for Earthforce is to locate Prowl, last seen wrestling in mid-air with Megatron's deadly gas missile. The Autobots track some Transformer life-readings to the Bahamas, but it turns out to be a Decepticon encampment where they are in the midst of constructing a second Devastator robot. Ironhide is able to sabotage the half-built goliath before resuming the hunt for Prowl.

Regrouping at the new Earthforce base in Canada, Grimlock declares that his new team have to be prepared to fight fire with fire if they want to beat the Decepticons and not be slaves to the high-handed moralising that was Optimus Prime's philosophy.

Earthforce eventually track Megatron's planet-threatening gas missile to Louisiana – but so have the Decepticons. The Earth-based Decepticons have split into two factions, one led by Shockwave and one by Megatron. As the two rival bands of Decepticons fight over the gas, Earthforce find Prowl alive and well – having made the crashed missile safe, he is enjoying watching the Decepticons fight against each other for no reason.

Notes:
This story sees the Autobot 'Classic Heroes' – Wheeljack, Sunstreaker, Ironhide, Prowl and Silverbolt – alive and well, following their revival in [60.1] 'Perchance to Dream'. Also back in action are Skydive, Slag, Snarl, Sludge and Swoop, all of whom were previously established as being inactive. The circumstances surrounding the resurrection of these other Autobots are unclear here; the only explanation offered is: 'See upcoming US story for details!' (An explanation would actually be offered in a UK story, [62.11] 'Makin' Tracks'. See also the Earthforce essay below for more on this.) On a related note, we get the first hints that this latest run of UK strips, the so-called 'Earthforce Saga', isn't going to mesh well with the events of the American stories. Megatron is inexplicably alive, whereas in the contemporary American comics he is offline following the events of [59] 'Skin Deep', and he is 'not Decepticon leader anymore', hinting at a schism in the Decepticon ranks that will play out in the British stories but *not* in the American ones.

This Decepticon civil war is being contested by two factions, led by Megatron and Shockwave respectively. Oddly, Drag Strip and Dead End are shown working for

Megatron in part 1, but are members of Shockwave's army in part 6; similarly, Runabout and Runamuck are fighting alongside Shockwave in part 2, but in part 6 are part of Megatron's forces. (Either the Decepticons are such a divided force that the rank and file are constantly switching sides, or these four have been acting as double agents, infiltrating the opposite side. More likely, it's simply a production error.)

With the exception of Runamuck's cameo in [47] 'Club Con', this is the first contemporary appearance of the Decepticon Battlechargers since their debut in [23] 'Decepticon Graffiti'. This is also the first appearance of the Stunticons and Constructicons (in the present day) since [41] 'Totalled'. On the subject of the Constructicons, it would appear that they have lost their ability to combine, hence the Decepticons' attempt to build a new, separate Devastator robot – thereby providing an in-fiction explanation of the non-transforming Action Master Devastator figure released by Hasbro in 1990. (In the letters page of UK#279, a reader asks how the Constructicons lost their ability to combine. The answer: 'That's yet to be explained – bear with us!' No such explanation was ever forthcoming.)

The half-built Devastator is protected by an 'automated defence ring' that tests the knowledge and reasoning of those who attempt to cross it. Its tests are references to classic British game shows such as *Blockbusters* ('What "A" is a subterranean lifeform from the Hydrus Four system') and *Blankety Blank* ('For one hundred and fifty blanks …'). Ironhide responds with the line 'Devastator – come on down', a catchphrase from the internationally successful game show *The Price is Right*. Another of the tests is a variation of the classic Knights and Knaves logic puzzle, long a favourite of fantasy writers, having featured prominently in the 1975 *Doctor Who* serial 'Pyramids of Mars', and in the movie *Labyrinth* (Jim Henson, 1986). On the cover of UK#264, Ironhide says 'There's somethin' moving out here, an' it ain't us', a direct quote from the movie *Aliens* (James Cameron, 1986).

Prowl and Wheeljack lament the introduction of new types of Transformer and claim, 'Things sure have changed since we were deactivated.' Other than a smattering of cameos in stories such as [41] 'Totalled', [48.2] 'Time Wars' and [50] 'Dark Star', Wheeljack hasn't featured regularly in the comic since [36] 'Spacehikers', and Prowl not since [23.5] 'Resurrection'. (This is odd, considering that Wheeljack and Prowl should have been familiar with the Headmasters given their involvement in [41] 'Totalled'. It's likely that Wheeljack and Prowl have been offline for most of the recent past, and that their sporadic cameo appearances were the result of temporary repair jobs, rather than a return to full functionality. It's not hard to imagine that such an extended lay-off, coupled with exposure to Galvatron's mind-bug in [60.1] 'Perchance to Dream', could have affected their memories somewhat.)

The Earthforce base is located in 'Northern Canada, sixteen miles east of Churchill'. The town of Churchill is located in the province of Manitoba and is popularly nicknamed 'The Polar Bear Capital of the World'. (Apparently writer Simon Furman is a big fan of polar bears; locating the Autobot base near Churchill made for a good excuse to feature plenty of them in the comic.) Other locations in this story include a desert in Arizona, a state previously featured in stories such as [30] 'The Cure', [45] 'Monstercon from Mars' and [46] 'Ca$h and Car-nage', and Louisiana, just off 'Route 43 – Jacksonville to New Orleans'. (A geographical inaccuracy: in the real world, Route 43 runs north-south through Alabama and Tennessee; on a trip between Jacksonville and New Orleans, one would actually travel east-west along the I-10.)

The individual chapter titles contain a few pop-culture references. Part 1's is possibly derived from the 1980 number one hit single by John Lennon, '(Just Like) Starting Over'. Part 2's comes from the phrase 'One step forward, two steps back', which dates back to at least 1904, when it was used as the title of a work by Vladimir Lenin, and was memorably used in the chorus of a contemporary pop single, 'Opposites Attract' by Paula Abdul and the Wild Pair, still in the UK charts when this story went to press. 'Desert Island Risks' is a play on *Desert Island Discs*, the name of a long-running BBC radio programme (1942-present), and 'Life in the Slow Lane' is a spin on 'Life in the Fast Lane', a 1977 hit for rock group the Eagles.

This story seems especially constructed to rekindle memories of the old *The Transformers* cartoon series: two of the six parts are set entirely in a desert, as many of the earliest episodes were, and most of the featured Transformers are older, 'classic' characters introduced during the show's first two seasons. Furthermore, Megatron's insane plan is very reminiscent of some hatched by his animated counterpart.

Roll Call:
Autobots: Optimus Prime, Jazz, Prowl, Ironhide, Sunstreaker, Wheeljack, Bumblebee, Grimlock, Snarl, Slag, Sludge, Swoop, Silverbolt, Highbrow, Crosshairs, Cloudburst, Getaway and Tote.

Decepticons: Megatron, Starscream, Soundwave, Ravage, Shockwave, Mixmaster, Long Haul, Devastator, Motormaster, Drag Strip, Dead End, Blitzwing (flashback only), Runabout and Runamuck.

Nebulans: Gort (as a head only).

A Decepticon 'Seeker'-type robot is seen in part 2 (and in flashback in part 5). Given the lack of colour, this could be any of Starscream, Skywarp or Thundercracker, but Starscream is the most likely suspect, hence his inclusion in the list above.

Review:
Goofy fun, albeit with a couple of caveats. The comedy ranges from light humour to broad farce, much of which works well, despite a couple of ill-judged sequences. The main problem here is that the continuity is all messed up. What should have been a bit of light and frothy fun is instead a complicated mess. When one is busy wondering why Megatron is alive, whose side everybody is on, and why the Constructicons can no longer combine, it's a huge distraction.

All in all, a good tone-setter for the Earthforce stories to come, even if the execution is a little off. 3/5

The Earthforce Saga: A Continuity Conundrum
As we shall see, it's exceedingly hard to marry up the events of the Earthforce stories, i.e. all British-originated strips from [60.1] 'Perchance to Dream' to [64.1] 'Inside Story', with those of the 'main' strips that originated in the American comic – and this despite them being penned by the same man, Simon Furman.

There is a very good behind-the-scenes reason for the continuity discrepancies. When the three-strip format began in the British comic (in UK#213), it was relatively easy to synchronise the two – the debut of the Micromaster characters was timed so that the British story that introduced them ([54.1] 'A Small War') began in the same issue as their first US appearance ([54] 'King Con'). Similarly, the UK story that tied up the whole 'Clone Megatron' storyline ([57.1] 'Two Megatrons') was timed to correspond with the American one that saw the real Megatron return ([57] 'The Resurrection Gambit').

However, there were some problems with this tactic: while Simon Furman was busy writing both the American and the British strips, the editorial team of *The Transformers* UK had their hands full working out the logistics of publishing these stories. Matters weren't helped by production delays that meant many American stories were pre-empted by re-prints of previously-seen strips; and the old *G.I. Joe* crossover story was also printed as a stop-gap measure (see the notes under [53.1] 'Survivors' and [GIJ1] 'Blood on the Tracks' for more on this). Because of this, it became harder and harder to make the UK and US stories tie in with each other. (Take a look at the notes under [59] 'Skin Deep' to see how even the non-Earthforce adventures of this era are tricky to fit together.)

Furman's solution was to create Earthforce. He knew that the American comic's stories would be set largely away from Earth for the rest of its run, and would feature mainly the more modern Transformers such as Nightbeat, Fangry and Thunderwing. His best bet, then, would be to have the UK strips set on Earth, and showcase older, 'classic' Transformers, thereby avoiding treading on the toes of the American stories.

Unfortunately, such ideals quickly fell by the wayside: if the original plan was to avoid outright a continuity clash, it failed; the Earthforce stories represent the biggest ever continuity slip-up between the UK and US comics. This essay will look at all the discrepancies between the American strips and the Earthforce stories, and postulate a 'best fit' way of shoehorning the latter in.

In Transformers fandom, there are three main theories concerning the Earthforce stories:

1. They occur *concurrently* with the contemporary American strips – in other words, they show the events taking place on Earth while the 'Matrix Quest' saga (US#62-66) is going on in outer space.
2. They take place *after* the events of the final American story (post [80] 'End of the Road).
3. They don't tie up with the American strips at all, and therefore take place in a continuity all of their own, a parallel dimension if you will.

This essay will consider options 1 and 2 only. The Transformers continuity already has at least three different parallel universes going on (Timeline A, Timeline B, and the one-off alternate future seen in [67] 'Rhythms of Darkness' – see the notes under [27.1] 'Wanted: Galvatron – Dead or Alive for more on this), and adding another would just make a complex situation even more so. Another issue with the 'Earthforce happens in a parallel universe' idea is that it's the easy way out – treating the Earthforce stories as if they didn't really 'happen' is the simplest way to look at them; attempting to tie them into the events of the American strips requires a bit more imagination and is frankly more fun.

Option 1: The 'Concurrent' Theory

When the Earthforce Saga begins in [60.1] 'Perchance to Dream', the *Ark* is deserted, as the Autobots are on 'some mission or other' (a probable reference to the Matrix Quest of

US#62-66). According to 'Break-Away' – the third part of [61.1] 'Starting Over' – the time is 'now'. In that same segment, Optimus Prime mentions that Unicron is 'pressing ever closer to Cybertron', a major plot point in the Matrix Quest stories. In [62.1] 'Snow Fun', we get an exact date: 1 April 1990. (Compare with the later American story [78] 'A Savage Circle', set in 1991.) From these clues, then, it would seem as through these stories are set at some point during the Matrix Quest.

Sadly, things aren't that simple.

The main problem is the appearance of Megatron. In the American strips, he was trapped mid-teleport from [59] 'Skin Deep' until [69] 'Eye of the Storm', and when he reappeared, it transpired that he had merged with the Autobot Ratchet to become some kind of hybrid creature. He remained in that state until subdued in [70] 'The Price of Life', and thereafter remained in stasis until his revival in [77] 'Exodus', before he was seemingly killed in the *Ark*'s crash-landing at the end of [78] 'A Savage Circle'. So the question is: how can Megatron be active at the time of the Matrix Quest if he's either dead, hybridised or otherwise trapped in a transporter beam for the entirety of US#59-80?

A similar question can be asked of other characters who shouldn't really be active at this point. Prowl appears in the Earthforce stories, yet in the American strips he is confirmed dead in [60] 'Yesterday's Heroes' and isn't revived until [75] 'On the Edge of Extinction'. The Dinobots feature prominently in the Earthforce stories, but according to the US strips they are effectively dead from [50] 'Dark Star' all the way through to their revival in [72] 'All This and Civil War 2'.

Contemporary readers of the UK comics were quick to point out the discrepancies. In UK#287, the following correspondence featured on the letters page: 'Megatron … disappeared into the trans-dimensional portal. But Megatron is still featured in the UK strip! Please explain.' The response: 'This will be resolved very soon'. It wasn't.

Another attempt to placate confused readers appeared on the 'Transformation' editorial page of UK#290: 'Things have got a bit out of synch. But that, hopefully, should be resolved as we go on … All your questions will be answered (well a few of them anyway)!' Again, the promised explanations were not forthcoming.

Option 2: The 'Set in the Future' Theory

So, what if we disregard all the references to contemporary events? Can we set these stories after the action of the final US issue, in the near future? Unfortunately, that presents just as many problems, if not more.

First, the *Ark* crash-lands on Earth at the end of [78] 'A Savage Circle', and it's heavily implied that Megatron, Shockwave and Starscream are killed as a result – yet all three appear in the Earthforce stories, and the *Ark* itself is up and running in [60.1] 'Perchance to Dream, apparently none the worse for wear.

Furthermore, the Decepticon Runabout is eaten alive at the end of [75] 'On the Edge of Extinction'. While we can make the case that Starscream and company could have survived a crashing spaceship, it's a bit harder to rationalise how a Transformer could have survived being consumed by a Demon. Crosshairs, too, is killed in [66] 'All Fall Down', and both Highbrow and Cloudburst meet their maker in [75] 'On the Edge of Extinction' – and yet all three appear in 'Break-Away', the third episode of [61.1] 'Starting Over'.

Another issue is the physical appearance of Optimus Prime. Each time he shows up in the Earthforce stories, e.g. in [61.1] 'Starting Over', [62.10] 'The 4,000,000 Year Itch', he is in his Powermaster body. Yet by the end of the American comic, he had replaced that with a different-looking Action Master body, in [80] 'End of the Road'. Another Transformer who becomes a (non-transforming) Action Master is Grimlock, in [76] 'Still Life', yet in the Earthforce stories he has his classic body and the ability to transform (see, for example, 'Two Steps Back', the second chapter of [61.1] 'Starting Over').

The one positive aspect of the 'near future' theory is that, by the time the American strip ends, a lot of the older classic characters – Prowl, Wheeljack, the Dinobots – have been brought back to life, which would explain their appearances in Earthforce. But, as we have seen, the 'near future' theory is just as problematic as the 'concurrent' theory – if not more so.

So, what other clues do we have? What else does Earthforce tell us about the world in which it's set? Well, Megatron is not just alive, he's the leader of an offshoot Decepticon faction (he's 'not Decepticon leader anymore' according to [61.1] 'Starting Over').

Many classic Decepticons are also back from the dead, including the Stunticons, Predacons, Insecticons, Constructicons (who have somehow lost the ability to combine), Triple Changers, Thrust and Dirge. The Autobots have apparently found a way to restore 'warriors to life without the Creation Matrix', as stated in [61.1] 'Starting Over'. This is confirmed in [62.11] 'Makin' Tracks', where we discover that the Autobots have built the ACU, a device with which they can restore fallen Autobots. Other timing clues include the deaths of Spinister, Snarler and Needlenose in [62.6] 'Wolf in the Fold', and the presence in [62.7] 'Internal Affairs' of Shockwave's underwater base, which is the same as that seen in American stories such as [71] 'Surrender'.

Given all this information, is there a way to fit all these stories into the American continuity? Well, yes, but we have to make the following two assumptions: 1) that many of the Autobots revived by the ACU are later deactivated so that they can be revived *again* in the American strips; and 2) that the 'Megatron' who appears in the Earthforce stories is not the real Megatron (maybe he's another Straxus clone, a time traveller, or perhaps even a 'splinter' somehow created when Megatron jumped through the exploding teleporter in [59] 'Skin Deep'). Either way, this cannot be the real Megatron who appears in the US strips from [56] 'Back from the Dead' onwards.

With all that in mind, here is one possible chronology of events, which just about fits with what we know, without too many contradictions …

The Earthbound Decepticons are led by Scorponok. These forces consist mainly of newer Transformers (Headmasters, Targetmasters, Pretenders etc). Starscream leaves this group and teams up with Shockwave, who has formed a new army of older, 'classic' Decepticons. A third faction emerges, led by a faux-Megatron. While Scorponok's camp in New Jersey remain blissfully ignorant of these other factions, the Shockwave and Megatron groups are at war with each other.

[61] 'The Primal Scream'
Following the events of this story, the Matrix Quest begins. In its initial stages, most of the *Ark* crew are engaged in the search, leaving the ship near-deserted.

[60.1] 'Perchance to Dream'
Galvatron III travels back in time from the post-Time Wars Timeline A (see [53.2] 'Aspects of Evil', [59.3] 'Shadow of Evil' and the notes under [67] 'Rhythms of

Darkness') and his actions unwittingly awaken a number of previously-deactivated Autobots.

[A6.1] 'The Magnificent Six'
These newly-revived Autobots go on a mission to Cybertron.

[61.1] 'Starting Over'
Upon their return, the resurrected Autobots form the core of Earthforce, a new team set up by Optimus Prime to protect Earth.

Around this time, Wheeljack invents the ACU (Automated Construction Unit), a device that allows the Autobots to revive some of their fallen comrades, including the Dinobots and the Aerialbots.

[62.1] 'Snow Fun', [62.2] 'Flashback', [62.3] 'Mystery' and [62.4] 'The Bad Guy's Ball'
The Earthforce team have an initial series of adventures.

[62.5] 'The Living Nightlights'
In the only reference to Scorponok's faction within the Earthforce saga, we find that the treacherous Mindwipe has betrayed his leader and struck out on his own. After his defeat by Earthforce here, he returns to Scorponok (who, as we saw in [59] 'Skin Deep', is not above giving second chances to treacherous Decepticons). However, Mindwipe is still unhappy with Scorponok's leadership and will later defect *again* (in [69] 'Eye of the Storm').

[62.6] 'Wolf in the Fold'
The ranks of Earthforce are bolstered when they take in a second group of Autobots, the so-called Survivors. Although Snarler, Needlenose and Spinister are 'killed' here, the latter two are soon revived by Thunderwing and join him on the Matrix Quest.

[62] 'Bird of Prey'
Meanwhile, out in space, the Matrix Quest is by now in full swing.

[62.7] 'Internal Affairs', [62.8] 'The House that Wheeljack Built'
Further adventures for Earthforce.

[62.9] 'Divide and Conquer' (comic)
Megatron and Shockwave are usurped as leaders of their respective factions, and their two groups of 'classic' Decepticons are united under the joint leadership of Starscream and Soundwave.

[63] 'Kings of the Wild Frontier'
Out amongst the stars, the Matrix Quest rumbles on.

[62.10] 'The 4,000,000 Year Itch', [62.11] 'Makin' Tracks', [63.1] 'Shut Up', [63.2] 'Manoeuvres', [63.3] 'Assassins', [64.1] 'Inside Story'
The final Earthforce stories take place.

[64] 'Deadly Obsession'
The Matrix Quest continues.

[A5.2] 'Destiny of the Dinobots'
We have to ignore the '1992' date and set these events in 1991. Snarl's body is wracked with the debilitating disease Corrodia Gravis. Although his body dies, his mind is copied into a real dinosaur for safekeeping.

At this point, there is presumably a massive battle on Earth. The remainder of the Dinobots plus the rest of Earthforce and the Survivors are all killed in the conflict, as are the faux-Megatron and most of the 'classic' Decepticons. (Such bloodshed is not unprecedented: see [48.2] 'Time Wars', [50] 'Dark Star' and [75] 'On the Edge of Extinction' for more Transformer massacres.)

The only survivors would appear to be the Autobot Classic Pretenders (Grimlock, Jazz and Bumblebee), Starscream and Soundwave (who wheedle their way back into Scorponok's camp), Shockwave (who retreats to his underwater base), Ravage, Runabout and Runamuck (who all join Shockwave), plus Bludgeon, Stranglehold and Octopunch (who also eventually end up with Shockwave). Shockwave's situation is interesting. It would seem that he fakes his death before making his getaway – when he recruits Starscream in [68] 'The Human Factor', Starscream is surprised that he still functions.

Later, the *Ark* briefly returns to Earth to pick up Grimlock, Bumblebee and Jazz, plus the bodies of the fallen Autobots.

[65] 'Dark Creation'
Following their stint as members of Earthforce, Grimlock, Jazz and Bumblebee help their fellow Autobots on the Matrix Quest. The remainder of the American stories (US#66-80) then continue and conclude the story.

[62] BIRD OF PREY! (MATRIX QUEST Part One of Five)
US#62, 'January 1990' (published November 1989), 18 pages.

British reprint: UK#262, 24 March 1990 (Part 1), 6 pages; UK#263, 31 March 1990 (Part 2), 6 pages; UK#264, 7 April 1990 (Part 3), 6 pages.

Credits:
Simon Furman (script); Geoff Senior (art); Nel Yomtov (colours); Jim Massara (letters); Don Daley (editor); Tom DeFalco (editor-in-chief); Rod Ramos and Eliot R Brown (cover). **UK:** For UK cover credits, see the entry for [61.1] 'Starting Over' above.

Plot:
With Unicron awake and heading for Cybertron, the Autobots desperately search for the one thing that can stop him – the Creation Matrix. Having narrowed the search to a particular star system, Optimus Prime sends teams of Autobots to quest for their mystical talisman.

Nightbeat, Siren and Hosehead arrive on the planet Pz-Zazz, a corrupt and crime-ridden planet and home to rival mob bosses Gutt and B'hgdad. Both factions are searching for a bird of prey statue, which falls into the hands of the Autobots after a chance meeting with a dying alien.

The Autobots fall in with Miss Fatale, who claims that the statue belongs to her. In exchange for the bird of prey, she takes the Autobots to the top of a mountain said to have a 'font of life' at its peak. The Autobots assume it is somehow connected to the Matrix, and head to the summit.

The Autobots and mobsters converge at the top of the mountain, and a shootout ensues – Nightbeat realises that the bird of prey is actually a Matrix-like life-restoring talisman, and was the mountain's source of power. He replaces it on its podium and a massive transformation occurs – the decrepit old planet is restored to a paradise.

Before the Autobots can congratulate themselves on a job well done, they are shot by Thunderwing and his Mayhem Attack Squad …

Notes:

This is the first story in the 'Matrix Quest' arc, in which the Autobots search for the Creation Matrix, missing since it was sent into space with the remains of Optimus Prime's first body in [26] 'Funeral for a Friend'. This particular adventure focuses on one such search party, consisting of the Headmasters Nightbeat, Hosehead and Siren, making their first appearances in the American comic.

The planet Pz-Zazz, despite being populated by a number of different alien species, has a culture clearly based upon early 20th Century America, with its mobsters and mafiosos (similar in set-up to the *Star Trek* episode 'A Piece of the Action' (1968)).

However, the main influence is clearly the 1929 Dashiell Hammett novel *The Maltese Falcon* – or rather, its 1941 film adaptation by John Huston. This is reflected both in the main plot – a group of criminals seek a desirable bird statue – and in the characters: the rotund mob boss Gutt is based on the novel's Kasper Guttman (played in the film by the similarly rotund Sydney Greenstreet), and B'hgdad on Joel Cairo (Peter Lorre). Similarly, the alluring-but-manipulative Miss Fatale is clearly based on the femme fatale character Brigid O'Shaughnessy (Mary Astor) and the dying alien who hands Nightbeat the statue fulfils a role identical to that of Captain Jacobi (Walter Huston).

Other links to the film include a billboard image of Humphrey Bogart, who played the main character Sam Spade, and a dialogue reference to the aforementioned Peter Lorre. Gutt is seen crushing an Academy Award of Merit, popularly known as an Oscar statuette; a sly dig at the fact that *The Maltese Falcon* failed to win one, despite three nominations.

In the final scene, we get our first modern-day glimpse of a number of new Decepticons, including Windsweeper, Ruckus, Needlenose and Spinster (although Windsweeper and Ruckus had previously appeared – in flashback – in [48] 'The Flames of Boltax').

The American cover to this story includes a reference to Timely, the publishing house that was a precursor to Marvel Comics. (It existed between 1939 and 1950, thereby cementing the '40s feel of the issue.)

UK Notes:

For UK readers, there were no new Transformer characters debuting here. Nightbeat and the other Headmasters had debuted in [53.5] 'The Big Shutdown' (similarly full of references to classic detective fiction), and the Decepticons seen here had already been established in stories such as [53.4] 'The Hunting Party'.

UK Changes:
Page 1, panel 1: credits replaced.
Page 6, panel 5: 'last issue' becomes 'issue #259!'

Roll Call:
Autobots: Optimus Prime, Jazz (flashback only), Bumblebee (flashback only), Grimlock (flashback only), Emirate Xaaron, Hot Rod, Nightbeat, Siren and Hosehead.

Decepticons: Ruckus, Windsweeper, Needlenose, Spinister and Thunderwing.

Other: Unicron (flashback only) and Primus (flashback only).

Nebulans: Muzzle, Quig and Lug.

The three Nebulans appear only as the heads of their Autobot partners, rather than as individual entities.

Review:
[53.5] 'The Big Shutdown' succeeded because it worked on a couple of levels – at its core it was a good story in its own right, but the addition of the Raymond Chandler references gave it a welcome added layer. 'Bird of Prey' isn't as good, partly because *The Maltese Falcon* references are laid on so thick as to be overwhelming. If you get all the references there's some fun to be had, but for those who aren't familiar with the source material – which would have included most of the children reading this back in 1990 – there's not a lot else to chew on.

On the plus side, the art is again excellent, and Furman's dialogue and characterisation are absolutely sparkling, especially in the interplay between the three lead Autobots. 2/5

[62.1] SNOW FUN!
UK#267, 28 April 1990, 5 pages

Credits:
Simon Furman (script); Jeff Anderson (art); Stuart Bartlett (letters); John Marshall and Stephen Baskerville (cover).

The editorial page of UK#266 promised that the cover of issue 267 would feature inks by newcomer Michael Eve, yet within issue 267 itself only Marshall and Baskerville are credited. Either Eve worked on the cover uncredited or, more likely, there was a change of plans and Eve made no contribution.

Plot:
April Fools Day 1990. Having been challenged to a duel by Shockwave, Grimlock journeys out into the Canadian tundra to meet the Decepticon. Of course, it's all a prank, and Grimlock has been set up by his fellow Dinobots – arriving at the designated coordinates, he is met only by a snowman in the shape of Shockwave.

Grimlock is being tracked by the Predacons, who have been attempting in vain to locate the Earthforce base. Already enraged by the prank, Grimlock wastes no time venting his frustration on them.

Later, back at Earthforce HQ, the Dinobots await Grimlock's return and ponder what their leader's reaction might be. They don't realise that he is sneaking up behind them, ready to pelt them with the biggest snowball ever assembled ...

Notes:
Although set on April Fools Day, i.e. 1 April, this instalment went out in the issue published on 21 April (and cover-dated 28 April). Presumably it was originally scheduled for issue 265 but put back due to a late reshuffle.

Despite many previous issues having shown the Transformers comfortably operating in the vacuum of space (and on the sun-less rogue planet Cybertron), the cold Canadian climate causes the Dinobots some discomfort; the Earthforce base even has some kind of heating apparatus installed. (The Dinobots' new-found sensitivity to cold weather could be a side-effect of the process that revived them.) Grimlock travels 'three hundred miles' to his supposed rendezvous with Shockwave; which, considering the location of the Earthforce base established in [61.1] 'Starting Over', would place the meeting point near the Manitoba-Saskatchewan border.

This is the first appearance of the Predacons Rampage and Razorclaw since they were apparently destroyed by Starscream in [50] 'Dark Star'; their sudden reappearance is never explained.

Roll Call:
Autobots: Grimlock, Snarl, Slag, Sludge and Swoop.

Decepticons: Shockwave (only as a falsified image on a computer monitor), Razorclaw and Rampage.

Data File: John Marshall (artist)
Marshall's other credits include *Action Force*, *Doctor Who Magazine* and *The Incredible Hulk Presents* for Marvel UK.

Review:
Another humorous tale in the same vein as the [61.1] 'Starting Over' sextet, this can be best described as an amusing piece of fluff. While the plot is slight, there are some genuinely funny moments: Grimlock's battle with the Predacons is so vicious that a large 'CENSORED' caption covers the image; his reaction to the April Fools joke is absolutely priceless; and the scene where the Dinobots spy on Grimlock (peeking around the corner, *Scooby-Doo* style) is a hoot. A fun script, heightened by some hilarious visuals by Jeff Anderson, though its throwaway nature counts against it. 3/5

UK Advertisements, Part 4: Film, Television and Video Games
A list of all film, television and video game-related advertisements that appeared in the UK comic.

Action Force (video game) – UK#145
Action Force (videocassette releases) – UK#168
Action Force: The Movie (videocassette release) – UK#184
All Dogs Go to Heaven (movie) – UK#261

Amstrad GX4000 games console – UK#297-298, 300
Biggles (movie) – UK#59-63
Caravan of Courage (movie) – UK#7
Ewoks/Droids (videocassette release) – UK#161
Grandstand (handheld LCD electronic games) – UK#262, 275, 291
Karate Kid Part III, The (videocassette release) – UK#262
Leisure View Video (range of cartoons on VHS, including *RoboCop* and *Spider-Man*) – UK#320
Light Games (a video game cartridge system with built-in projector) – UK#241, 244
Short Circuit (movie) – UK#100
Short Circuit 2 (movie) – UK#204

[62.2] FLASHBACK!
NB: Within the strip itself, the title is parsed as 'FLASHKCAB!' (with the final four letters drawn back-to-front); the issue's editorial page opts for the simpler 'Flashback'.

UK#268 5 May 1990, 5 pages

Credits:
Simon Furman (script); John Marshall (pencils); Stephen Baskerville (inks); Gary 'Glib' Gilbert (letters); Stephen Baskerville (cover).

Plot:
Megatron escapes into the past via a 'Flashback Doorway', a form of time machine that allows one to possess the body of someone in the past. Prowl follows, and finds himself in New York, 1989 – where the Underbase-enhanced Starscream is in the process of massacring the Transformers.

Megatron's plan is to possess the body of Seacon leader Snaptrap and lead the Seacons to safety. If the Seacons survive, Megatron reasons, it will give him more troops to lead in the present day.

Prowl, having jumped into the body of his past self, confronts Megatron/Snaptrap, and the pair do battle. Prowl manages to knock the Decepticon unconscious, which automatically sends Megatron back to the present.

His job done, Prowl watches the destruction of the Seacons and makes sure that his own past self is destroyed, just as it originally happened. The explosion results in the destruction of the time machine.

Notes:
The time travel mechanism seen here, the Flashback Doorway, would appear to have been influenced by the television programme *Quantum Leap* (1989-1993), popular at the time this story was written. It's never stated how Megatron acquired the gateway, whether or not he built it himself, or where it's located. (Based on what we know of Megatron's technical abilities, it's likely he just found the device on an alien planet.)

Megatron and Prowl travel back in time to alter action previously seen in the comic, namely Starscream's attack in [50] 'Dark Star'. Although unconfirmed in the original issue, it's stated here that Prowl was one of Starscream's victims in that story.

As with Galvatron before him (in [20.2] 'Target: 2006'), Megatron believes that he can change the course of history. (Aside from the very special circumstances of the post-

Time Wars future seen in [53.2] 'Aspects of Evil' and [59.3] 'Shadow of Evil', Galvatron's tinkering in history never seems to affect the future that he originates from, indicating that Megatron's plan is doomed to failure anyway. See the notes to [21.1] 'Wanted: Galvatron – Dead or Alive'.)

Prowl's journey through history is illustrated by a series of melting clocks, a motif made famous by the 1931 Salvador Dali painting *The Persistence of Memory*.

Roll Call:
Autobots: Jazz and Prowl.

Decepticons: Megatron, Starscream, Snaptrap, Seawing, Skalor, Overbite, Nautilator and Tentakil.

Megatron's only appearances in this story are when he is in possession of Snaptrap – his own body is never seen.

Review:
After the jollity of recent UK-only strips, 'Flashback' sees a return to a more serious tone – and what a return! This is such a densely-written, tightly-scripted story, one wonders how it even fits into five pages. Coupled with art rich in texture and detail, this is a mini-masterpiece. 5/5

[62.3] MYSTERY!
UK#269 12 May 1990, 5 pages

Credits:
Simon Furman (script); Pete Knifton (pencils); Pete Venters (inks); Gary 'Glib' Gilbert (letters); Pete Knifton and Pete Venters (cover).

The cover of this issue was adapted from a panel of the interior artwork.

Plot:
It's Skydive's turn for guard duty but, upon arrival at his sentry post, he discovers that the previous guard, Wheeljack, is missing, amid signs of a struggle. Noticing animal prints leading away from the scene, he surmises that Wheeljack must have been attacked by a Predacon.

Skydive follows the tracks, and spies what appears to be the silhouette of the Predacon carrying Wheeljack's body. Skydive tackles the robot, only to discover that it is in fact Wheeljack himself, carrying a thermo-heating unit.

It transpires that Wheeljack was not attacked by a Predacon, merely startled by a polar bear.

Notes:
The story opens with the caption 'Twas a dark and stormy night', a piece of purple prose originated by novelist Edward Bulwer-Lytton in his 1830 book *Paul Clifford*. (To be fair to Bulwer-Lytton, he also coined the phrases 'the pen is mightier than the sword' and 'the great unwashed'; he was an inspiration to Bram Stoker, and invented the word 'vril', after which the meat extract product Bovril was named.)

While the Autobot Earthforce are using a spacecraft as their current base, a more permanent installation is currently under construction, although it currently consists of nothing but 'a mess of foundations and a few girders'. There are a couple of references back to [62.1] 'Snow Fun' – Grimlock has reported Predacon activity in the area, and thermo-heating units are regularly used to make the Autobots comfortable in the chilly tundra of the Canadian Shield.

As revealed in [61.1] 'Starting Over', the Aerialbots have recently been reactivated – Skydive and Air Raid make their first appearances since being zapped by Starscream in [50] 'Dark Star'.

Roll Call:
Autobots: Wheeljack, Air Raid and Skydive.

Review:
A weak shaggy-dog story, redeemed only by some excellent art by Petes Knifton and Venters. Silly in the extreme. 1/5

UK Straplines, Part 5
The final batch of straplines from the cover of *The Transformers* UK, covering issues #265 to #332.

- UK#265: The Autobot Code is rubbish!
- UK#266: Sudden fright chicken – Transformer style!
- UK#267: 'That ain't no polar bear!'
- UK#268: 'Perish at the hands of – Megatron?!'
- UK#269: Mystery! 'Wheeljack …?!'
- UK#270: Glasnost – Decepticon style! 'Cheers!'
- UK#271: Whatever you do … don't fall asleep!
- UK#272: Cry wolf!
- UK#273: Wolf in the fold!
- UK#274: Earthforce and Survivors unite!
- UK#275: none
- UK#276: Insecticon swat team!
- UK#277: Mayhem at Memphis!
- UK#278: 'Turn 'em off, turn 'em off!' 'Um …'
- UK#279: none
- UK#280: 'Help!'
- UK#281: 'No doubt, Optimus, we got us a saboteur!'
- UK#282: none
- UK#283: none
- UK#284: none
- UK#285: 'Say g'night, Soundwave!'
- UK#286: Friends at last?
- UK#287: 'Run – Superion's out of control!'
- UK#288: Stop the press!
- UK#289: Prisoner of the Stunticons!
- UK#290: The awakening!
- UK#291: none

- UK#292: 'Aarghh!' 'Ang about!
- UK#293: End of quest?
- UK#294: 'Landmine!' The late Pretender!
- UK#295: Unstoppable?
- UK#296: Dirty 'Trix!
- UK#297: 'Wing clipped!
- UK#298: I ♥ New York (with the heart replaced by a Decepticon logo)
- UK#299: Decepticon justice! 'Last request, Prime?'
- UK#300: none
- UK#301: New Glory! 'Primus Bless America' – Jazz
- UK#302: Past … present …future? Dreadwind's Xmas!
- UK#303: Star-scream!
- UK#304: 'Aargh!' 'Unnnn!'
- UK#305: none
- UK#306: 'By reason and calm judgement, the qualities specially appertaining to a leader.' – Tacitus
- UK#307: none
- UK#308: 'Chill-out, Mindwipe. Understand?!'
- UK#309: 21st Century schizoid!
- UK#310: none
- UK#311: Surrender!
- UK#312: none
- UK#313: Bomb the base!
- UK#314: Decepticon v Decepticon
- UK#315: Circuit broken!
- UK#316: The vanishing!
- UK#317: 'Hear me children. The chaos-bringer approaches …'
- UK#318: none
- UK#319: The jaws of death!
- UK#320: none
- UK#321: Death of a Decepticon
- UK#322: Showdown on Cybertron!
- UK#323: Aftermath …
- UK#324: 'I tell you there's something moving out here!' 'Uhh, well, it sure not me!' (as per US#76)
- UK#325: It's a knock-out!
- UK#326: Fall out! (as per US#77)
- UK#327: The one you've all been waiting for … past and future collide as … Galvatron battles Megatron!
- UK#328: Bad boys stick together!
- UK#329: The last Autobot? (as per US#79)
- UK#330: Iced!
- UK#331: Optimus Prime is back! – Just in time for … the Transformers' last stand!!
- UK#332: The final cut!

[62.4] THE BAD GUY'S BALL!
UK#270 19 May 1990, 5 pages

Credits:
Simon Furman (script); Pete Knifton (pencils); Michael Eve (inks); Gary 'Glib' Gilbert (letters); Stephen Baskerville (cover).

Plot:
The Enclave: a meeting of the disparate Decepticon factions, an attempt to set aside the in-fighting and call a truce. Shockwave's and Megatron's forces come together to discuss how they can pool their resources and concentrate on waging war against the Autobots instead of each other.

Spying on the meeting are four Autobots: Jazz, Sunstreaker, Bumblebee and Ironhide. Rather than sit back and watch the Decepticons become a unified force, they take matters into their own hands and sabotage the alliance. First, Jazz subdues Headstrong and, from a distance, uses the Decepticon's gun to take a pot-shot at Megatron. When the Decepticons fire back, they spot Headstrong's unconscious body and his recently-fired weapon. Believing that he has been betrayed, Megatron attacks Shockwave, an assault that leads to an all-out battle as the Decepticons fight each other. Their mission completed, the Autobots celebrate an important victory.

Notes:
The Decepticon gathering is known as an Enclave. In modern parlance, this is a term used to describe a territory that is completely surrounded by another (for example the nation of San Marino, which is completely surrounded by Italy). However, its root is the Old French word *enclaver*, meaning to lock in. Although not stated outright within the story itself, this would seem to imply that the attending Decepticons are not allowed to leave the venue until an accord has been reached.

The attending Decepticons are provided with drinks and snacks (hence the Autobots' nickname for the Enclave: 'the bad guy's ball'), including Energon snacks and the 'multi-carb special'. Such items appear to have an intoxicating effect on the Decepticons. (See [56.1] 'Out to Lunch' for another example of 'drunk' Transformers.)

This story marks the first appearance of the three original Insecticons – Shrapnel, Bombshell and Kickback – since [41] 'Totaled'.

Roll Call:
Autobots: Jazz, Ironhide, Sunstreaker and Bumblebee.

Decepticons: Megatron, Soundwave, Ravage, Shockwave, Scavenger, Mixmaster, Bonecrusher, Long Haul, Hook, Motormaster, Drag Strip, Dead End, Wildrider, Breakdown, Shrapnel, Bombshell, Kickback, Astrotrain, Blitzwing, Octane, Runabout, Razorclaw, Rampage, Tantrum, Headstrong and Divebomb.

Hook's appearance is hard to spot; only his weapon and the end of his arm appear in frame. Also in this story are one of the humanoid Decepticon cassettes (either Rumble or Frenzy) and a Decepticon jet (either Starscream, Skywarp or Thundercracker), but in black and white it's impossible to discern exactly which of them is being represented.

Review:
An amiable little story that manages to advance the ongoing 'civil war' plot while still delivering the fun and humour for which the Earthforce stories are known. Coupled

with some excellent art (the Decepticon-on-Decepticon battle is especially well-drawn), this is one of the better Earthforce episodes. 4/5

UK Advertisements, Part 5: Books and Comics
A list of all books and comics advertised within the pages of the British comic (excluding the 'classified' ad sections that would crop up from time to time).

Action Force (comic) – UK#99, 101, 103, 108, 111, 113, 121, 125, 132, 225-229
Action Force: The Official Collector Card Album – UK#194-195, 197-198, 205, 212
Adventures of the Galaxy Rangers, The (comic) – UK#174
ALF – UK#163, 188
American Football 89 (sticker album) – UK#234
Beauty and the Beast (graphic novel) – UK#244, 249
Captain Britain Monthly – UK#6-7, 18-19, 29-30
Captain Britain (trade paperback) – UK#190, 194, 197
Complete Spider-Man, The (comic) – UK#305, 307, 311, 322, 330
Death's Head (comic) – UK#191, 193-194, 197-200, 202-203, 206-207
Digitek (comic) – UK#331
Doctor Who Magazine – UK#14, 27, 187, 251-252, 259, 262, 291, 311, 317
Doctor Who Magazine 1991 Winter Special – UK#331
Doctor Who: Voyager (graphic novel) – UK#120, 213-215, 217
Doctor Who 25th Anniversary Special – UK#192
Dragon's Claws – UK#167 (under its working title, *Dragon's Teeth*), 171, 206
Get Along Gang (comic) – UK#14, 16
Ghostbusters II (graphic novel adaptation of the movie) – UK#254
Grandreams 1985 Annuals – UK#3-6
Harrison Ford Story, The – UK#7
Havoc (comic) – UK#320-323
How to Draw Comics the Marvel Way – UK#83
Incredible Hulk Presents, The – UK#241, 246, 248, 250
Indiana Jones comic – UK#1, 7
Knights of Pendragon, The – UK#268-270, 272-273, 276-278, 280, 285, 287, 290, 292, 293, 318, 325, 331
Marvel 1985 Summer Specials – UK#22-23
Marvel 1985 Winter Specials – UK#35-37, 40-41, 44
Marvel 1986 Spring Specials – UK#56-58, 60, 66
Marvel 1986 Summer Specials – UK#67-68, 70-73, 75
Marvel 1986 hardback books range – UK#62, 66
Marvel 1986 Winter Specials – UK#98
Marvel 1987 Summer Specials – UK#117
Marvel 1988 Annuals – UK#135-136, 144, 146, 148, 150
Marvel 1987 Winter Specials – UK#139, 141-142
Marvel 1988 Spring Specials – UK#163, 165, 167
Marvel 1988 Summer Specials – UK#169, 174
Marvel 1989 Annuals – UK#187
Marvel 1991 Annuals – UK#298, 300, 301, 303
Marvel 1991 Holiday Specials – UK#313, 315
Marvel 1992 Annuals – UK#327, 330, 332

Marvel Bumper Comic, The – UK#175-176, 179
Masters of the Universe (books, by Ladybird) – UK#19
Meltdown (comic) – UK#320, 323-324
Police Academy: The Comic Book – UK#304
Punisher, The – UK#232-233, 235-241, 247, 249, 251-253, 255-258, 260, 263
Real Ghostbusters, The – UK#153, 156-157, 178, 182-183, 252, 254-259, 267
Real Ghostbusters Puzzlebuster, The – UK#281-282, 285-286, 289
Savage Sword of Conan (comic) – UK#1
Secret Wars (comic) (Marvel UK version) – UK#15-16, 25-27, 34
Secret Wars II (comic) (Marvel UK version) – UK#45-46, 48-49
Sleeze Brothers, The – UK#224, 226-233, 235, 237, 238
Spider-Man Annual (1987) – UK#78
Spider-Man (comic) (Marvel UK version) – UK#4-5, 9, 11
Spider-Man and Zoids (comic) – UK#50-51, 53-54, 86
Star Trek: The Next Generation (comic) – UK#296, 304-305, 307, 310-311, 317
Star Trek: The Next Generation 1992 Annual – UK#330
Star Wars: Return of the Jedi (comic) – UK#9-10, 12-13, 21
Steeleye and the Lost Magic (book) – UK#121, 123
Strip – UK#277
Thundercats Annual (1987) – UK#79, 84
Thundercats (comic) – UK#104, 107, 133, 187
Visionaries Spring Special 1989 – UK#211
William Tell (graphic novel) – UK#211, 218, 220, 222-223
World Cup '86 (from Ladybird Books) – UK#61, 63
X-Men – UK#326
Zoids Annual (1987) – UK#76, 78

[62.5] THE LIVING NIGHTLIGHTS!
UK#271 26 May 1990, 5 pages

Credits:
Simon Furman (script); John Marshall (pencils); Stephen Baskerville (inks); Helen Stone (letters); Stewart 'Staz' Johnson (cover).

Plot:
A range of ugly, troll-shaped nightlights has gone on sale. Marketed as Sleepfast, these are thought-activated, allowing owners to turn them on or off with a simple mental command. Investigating this advanced technology, Wheeljack discerns that the lamps are of Cybertronian origin and – worse – are programmed to hypnotise any human who buys one.

Wheeljack and Snarl investigate the warehouse where the Sleepfast lights are being stored, but their investigations are being monitored by a shadowy observer, who activates a control on a computer console. Suddenly, the lamps come to life, with thousands of the impish creatures swarming to attack the two Autobots.

The mastermind behind the plot makes himself known – the Decepticon hypnotist Mindwipe, who has struck out on his own, having been booted out of the Decepticon ranks by Scorponok. Wheeljack and Snarl use their minds to activate all the lamps simultaneously – the resultant blast of hypnotic light damages Mindwipe and allows the Autobots to subdue him.

Notes:
The title is a play on the old English idiom 'the living daylights', which dates back to the 18ᵗʰ Century and refers to a person's eyes. It was famously used as the title of a then-recent James Bond film (John Glen, 1987).

This is the first (and only) reference to Scorponok and his group of Decepticons in the Earthforce stories – other instalments concentrate solely on the factions led by Shockwave and Megatron.

This issue's cover featured the slogan 'Whatever you do … don't fall asleep', a memorable line from the horror movie *A Nightmare on Elm Street* (Wes Craven, 1984).

The idea of nightlights shaped as characters with kid appeal was a popular one at the time, and the whole story reads as a spoof of the Playskool toy franchises *Glo Worm* and *Glo Friends*, which, like the Transformers, were stars of a cartoon series made by Sunbow Productions.

Roll Call:
Autobots: Wheeljack and Snarl.

Decepticons: Mindwipe.

Nebulans: Vorath (but only as Mindwipe's head).

Review:
A really bizarre story, this reads less like *The Transformers* and more akin to *The Twilight Zone*, with its mundane-looking objects that belie a surprising power, and the ironic way in which the villain meets his downfall.

The five-page format allows writer Simon Furman to play with storytelling techniques – while some of his experiments don't work ([62.3] 'Mystery' being a prime example), this one comes off, thanks mostly to the by-play between the two lead Autobots and the sheer audacity of the attempt. 4/5

[62.6] WOLF IN THE FOLD!
- UK#272, 2 June 1990 ('Cry Wolf!'), 5 pages
- UK#273, 9 June 1990 ('Wolf in the Fold!'), 5 pages
- UK#274, 16 June 1990 ('Where Wolf?'), 5 pages

NB: This three-part story has no overall title – each segment was individually named. For the purpose of analysis, this book will refer to the adventure as 'Wolf in the Fold!'.

Credits:
Simon Furman (script); Pete Knifton (pencils, part 1); Michael Eve (inks, part 1); Stewart 'Staz' Johnson (art, part 2); Jeff Anderson (pencils, part 3); Stephen Baskerville (inks, part 3); Gary 'Glib' Gilbert (letters, parts 1 and 2); Stuart Bartlett (letters, part 3); Stephen Baskerville (cover, UK#272); Stewart 'Staz' Johnson (cover, UK#273); Pete Venters (cover, UK#274).

This story was later reprinted in full colour in the *Transformers Annual 1992*; the new colours were provided by Louise Cassell (part 1), Caroline Steeden (part 2) and Euan Peters (part 3).

Plot:
The Decepticon Mayhem Attack Squad have set up camp on a fortified island. Having previously killed the Autobot Catilla, they understand that the Pretender Beast, Carnivac (Catilla's comrade), will soon attack the island in an attempt to seek revenge.

The Decepticons respond to a sighting of Carnivac on the island – but they are angered when they realise it's a false alarm. The cowardly and paranoid Needlenose is testing his fellow Decepticons to make sure they are prepared for a real attack. This fatally backfires on Needlenose – no-one believes him when Carnivac does attack for real, and he is slain.

Carnivac then makes an attempt on Bludgeon's life, but the rest of the Mayhem Squad come to his aid, and a well-placed shot by Spinister apparently destroys the vengeful Pretender Beast.

Meanwhile, the rest of the Autobot 'Survivors' team realise that Carnivac has gone missing, and so seek the help of Grimlock's Earthforce faction. A combined force of Survivor and Earthforce Autobots storm the island, and are shocked when Bludgeon reveals that Carnivac has been killed.

Carnivac is not dead, however: only his Pretender shell was destroyed in the blast, and he has been using the opportunity to pick off the Mayhem Squad one by one, starting with Snarler and Spinister.

On rejoining his fellow Autobots, Carnivac advises them not to kill Bludgeon – denying the Decepticon a warrior's death is punishment enough.

Notes:
This story merges two of the comic's ongoing plot threads, the 'Survivors' arc, which started in [53.1] 'Survivors, and the 'Earthforce' storyline, which began in [61.1] 'Starting Over'. The 'Survivors' storyline is particularly important here: we follow up on the death of Catilla in [55.1] 'Way of the Warrior' and also Needlenose's cowardly streak, first evidenced in [53.4] 'The Hunting Party'.

Here we get an insight into Bludgeon's strict code of honour – for him, a 'warrior's death' in battle is actually a great privilege; indeed, he is full of regret when he believes that Carnivac has been killed by a long-range shot rather than in hand-to-hand combat. Furthermore, he nearly kills his own colleague Needlenose when he feels he has been disrespected. When his life is spared by Carnivac at the end of the story, therefore, it is a great dishonour to him – death is preferable to failure.

The first part of this story is (as its title would suggest) heavily based on 'The Boy Who Cried Wolf', a fable attributed to Aesop, dating back to classical times. 'Cry Wolf' was also the title of a 1986 UK top 5 hit by the band A-ha.

The Autobots travel to the Decepticon island via some unnamed vehicles that look like a cross between motorcycles and hovercraft.

Roll Call:
Autobots: Jazz, Prowl, Ironhide, Grimlock, Slag, Inferno, Skids, Springer, Broadside and Catilla (flashback only).

Decepticons: Carnivac, Snarler, Stranglehold, Bludgeon, Octopunch, Needlenose and

Spinister.

Data File: Stephen Baskerville (artist)

Baskerville began at Marvel UK in 1987, and worked on titles such as *Doctor Who Magazine*, *Thundercats* and *The Real Ghostbusters*. As part of the British group who made the move to the American *The Transformers* comic, he got his foot in the door at Marvel US, and worked on *The Amazing Spider-Man* and *G.I. Joe: A Real American Hero*.

Review:

An action-packed revenge play that has the added bonus of tying together two disparate plot lines. This is another of those stories where everything comes together – the plotting is taut and clever (especially the way that Carnivac's Pretender shell is used as a red herring), the characterisation is rich and on-the-nose (Needlenose, Carnivac, Springer and Bludgeon all get particularly meaty roles), and there is some excellent art here too, not only in the obvious stuff (the splash page of part two is excellent), but also in the little details (like how Needlenose's wings slump when he's worried). 5/5

The Transformers UK: The Ident Box

Like the American comic, the British version featured an ident box showing the price, the date, the issue number and a piece of art. Here is a list of all the art to feature in the UK ident boxes:

- UK#1-26: no ident box.
- UK#27-28: the *Ark* attacks (in an animation still taken from a television ad).
- UK#29-37: over the course of a number of boxes, Optimus Prime is depicted transforming from truck to robot mode (again, in screengrabs from the television ads).
- UK#38-73: Optimus Prime (animation still from television ad).
- UK#74, 76-78, 88, 90, 92, 96: close-up of Optimus Prime's face (artwork taken from the first page of [16.1] 'Robot Buster').
- UK#75, 83-87, 89, 91, 94-95, 97: close-up of Megatron's face (artwork taken from the annual story [A2.3] 'State Games').
- UK#93: Optimus Prime in a Santa outfit (artwork taken from the cover of UK#41).
- UK#100, 103-105, 109-111, 113-115, 119: close-up of Optimus Prime's face (artwork taken from part two of [23.1] 'Prey').
- UK#101-102, 106-108, 112, 116-118, 120: close-up of Megatron's face (artwork taken from part five of [20.2] 'Target: 2006').
- UK#121, 124, 126-127, 135-137, 139, 143-144, 148-149, 151, 154, 156, 158, 164-168, 171, 174-175, 177, 179-181: close-up of Rodimus Prime's face (artwork taken from part one of [27.4] 'Fire on High').
- UK#123, 128-129, 134, 140, 142, 147, 155, 157, 159, 161, 169, 172-173, 176, 182: close-up of Galvatron's face (artwork taken from part two of [27.4] 'Fire on High').
- UK#133: a one off cover-box – Rodimus Prime screams in pain (an image taken from the interior art of that issue, i.e. part one of [31.3] 'Headhunt').
- UK#146: another one-off cover box – Rodimus Prime celebrates the New Year (this is an excerpt from the interior art of that issue – part one of [36.2] 'The Legacy of Unicron' – but with a clock and champagne glass painted in).
- UK#190-197, 199, 201-231, 235-241, 243-244, 246-249, 251-258, 261-263, 266-275, 278, 280-281: Optimus Prime (artwork taken from the cover of UK#177).

- UK#282-284: over the course of a few covers, Dreadwind reaches into the cover box, punches Optimus Prime in the head, then takes over the box himself.
- UK#285-293, 295, 297-299: Dreadwind and Hi-Test.
- UK#301-308, 311-332: Blaster.

Occasionally the usual ident box art would be replaced by a star, a circle or some other shape containing information about competitions or free gifts. This occurred on issues #65-70, #79-82, #98-99, #122, #125, #130-132, #138, #141, #145, #150, #152-153, #160, #162-163, #170, #178, #183-189, #198, #200, #232-234, #242, #245, #250,# 259-260, #264-265, #276-277, #279, #294, #296, #300 and #309-310.

Pricing information could also be found in the UK ident boxes, as follows:

- UK#1-10: 25p
- UK#11-26: 27p
- UK#27-93: 30p
- UK#94-96: 30p (US $1.25, CAN $1.75)
- UK#97-98: 32p (US $1.25, CAN $1.75)
- UK#99-125: 32p (US $1.00, CAN $1.50)
- UK#126-138: 32p (US $1.25, CAN $1.75)
- UK#139-155: 32p (US $1.30, CAN $1.70)
- UK#156-169: 32p (US $1.35, CAN $1.75)
- UK#170-199: 35p (US $1.45, CAN $1.85)
- UK#200-212: 35p
- UK#213-231: 38p
- UK#232-255: 40p
- UK#256-293: 45p
- UK#294-319: 50p
- UK#320-332: 55p

Other cover-related trivia. On issues #22, #24 and #25, the usual red Autobot Transformers logo was replaced by a purple Decepticon one, to reflect the fact that the Autobots had been temporarily defeated. The Decepticon sigil returned for UK#75, coinciding with Megatron's first appearance in the cover box. On issues #1-26, the Transformers logo was set against a black background. Issues #32 and #35 had the logo against a purple background, #42 against a blue one, and #66 against a white one. This was done to ensure that the logo retained visibility on similarly-coloured or busy backgrounds. On issue #116, to ensure that it stood out on an orange background, the logo was completely white.

The logo underwent a number of design changes over the years. It was originally displayed in painted, metallic-effect lettering until issue #113, when it was changed to a simplified (but bolder) blue/white/red colour scheme. From UK#200 it was completely revamped, in line with the design changes made to the packaging of the toys in 1989.

[62.7] INTERNAL AFFAIRS!
- UK#275, 23 June 1990 ('Secrets'), 5 pages
- UK#276, 30 June 1990 ('Bugged!'), 5 pages
- UK#277, 7 July 1990 ('Internal Affairs!'), 5 pages

NB: This three-part story has no overall title – each segment was individually named. For the purpose of analysis, this book will refer to the adventure as 'Internal Affairs!'.

Credits:

Simon Furman (script); Pete Knifton (pencils, part 1); Pete Venters (inks, part 1); Jeff Anderson (pencils, part 2); Michael Eve (inks, part 2); Simon Coleby (art, part 3); Gary 'Glib' Gilbert (letters, part 1); Stuart Bartlett (letters, parts 2 and 3); Stephen Baskerville (cover, UK#275); Pete Knifton (cover, UK#276); Stewart 'Staz' Johnson (cover, UK#277).

Simon Coleby was initially credited as providing just the pencils on part three (with Michael Eve listed as the inker). A correction and apology printed in UK#285 revealed that Coleby was responsible for both pencils *and* inks on that instalment.

Plot:

After Megatron sees one of his Energon shipments taken by Shockwave he realises that he has an informant within his ranks. Megatron tasks Soundwave with the job of determining the traitor's identity.

The twist is that Soundwave himself is the traitor, playing the rival Decepticon leaders against each other to further his own advancement. Soundwave tries to delay the investigation, but Megatron makes it clear in no uncertain terms that failure is not an option.

Soundwave decides to set up one of his colleagues as the traitor, and chooses the paranoid Wildrider. He asks him to transmit some 'secret battle plans', then informs Megatron that the 'traitor' is sending information to Shockwave. Megatron catches the nonplussed Wildrider in the act, and shoots him dead. Now cleared of suspicion, Soundwave is free to continue his scheming.

Meanwhile, Starscream – ostensibly second-in-command of Shockwave's Decepticon faction – is forced to work sentry duty, a monotonous task that involves watching security camera footage. When he spots the Insecticons – from Megatron's rival Decepticon group – infiltrating the base, he decides to have a little fun.

Starscream gleefully brandishes a Cybertronian 'rustbug hoop' (basically a high-tech fly-swatter) and uses it to attack the intruders. He then forces the Insecticons to feed false information back to Megatron, in an attempt to set up a Megatron/Shockwave confrontation. Starscream sees this as the perfect opportunity to get rid of the competition and claim the leadership for himself.

Megatron duly confronts Shockwave at Memphis airport, and the pair do battle. Starscream, meanwhile, anonymously reports the fight to the Autobot Earthforce, who are duty-bound to respond.

While the two Decepticon leaders continue to tussle, both with each other and with the Earthforce troops, Starscream and Soundwave come to an agreement of their own – *they* will be the new Decepticon leaders. Once this news reaches Megatron and Shockwave, the pair cease their fighting and make their escape, each vowing revenge against his respective usurper.

Notes:

Megatron has a new base of operations, a spider-like structure located in a Louisiana bayou. This isn't the first comic story to take place in the state of Louisiana: the final part of the [61.1] 'Starting Over' arc was also set there.

Shockwave also has a base of his own, an underwater headquarters that will later be seen in US-originated stories such as [71] 'Surrender'.

The Megatron/Shockwave fight occurs in Memphis International Airport, making this the first Transformers comic story to be set at least partly in Tennessee (like Louisiana, a state in the American South).

It's been already established that Transformers can get drunk (as recently evidenced in [62.4] 'The Bad Guy's Ball'), but here we discover that Transformers also do drugs. Mixmaster is a dealer of a substance called Syk, known as a 'forbidden circuit booster'. (The name hints at an association with Fort Scyk, a Decepticon base seen in the annual story [A6.1] 'The Magnificent Six' – perhaps the drug is produced there?)

The panel showing the Insecticons chewing through a wall (and the accompanying line: 'Tasty, eh, Bombshell') appears to be a deliberate homage to a similar scene in {3-00} *The Transformers: The Movie* (where the line was 'Delicious, eh, Shrapnel').

This story establishes Motormaster as part of Megatron's Decepticon faction, whereas in [61.1] 'Starting Over' he was fighting alongside Shockwave (so either he swapped sides or he's yet another double agent).

The title might well have been inspired by that of the movie *Internal Affairs* (Mike Figgis, 1990), which starred Richard Gere.

Roll Call:
Autobots: Jazz, Prowl and Grimlock.

Decepticons: Megatron, Soundwave, Shockwave, Scrapper, Mixmaster, Bonecrusher, Long Haul, Hook, Motormaster, Wildrider, Shrapnel, Bombshell, Kickback, Astrotrain, Blitzwing, Octane and Divebomb (only as an image on a security monitor).

One of the humanoid Decepticon cassettes (Frenzy or Rumble) is also visible on Starscream's security monitors, but without the benefit of colour it's impossible to discern which of the two it is.

Data File: Simon Coleby (artist)
After *The Transformers*, Coleby moved on to *2000 AD*, where his work was featured in *Judge Dredd* and *Sinister Dexter*. Later credits include *Punisher 2099*, *New X-Men*, *Fantastic Four* and *Batman*.

Review:
A mixed bag of interlinked vignettes that showcase the best and worst aspects of the five-page black-and-white format. To get the negatives out of the way first: the middle section, 'Bugged', is one of the most uninspired, ill-conceived strips the comic has ever produced. It basically boils down to nothing more than 'Starscream attacks the Insecticons with a fly-swatter'. Jokey issues can work well on occasion, but this attempt at farce falls well wide of the mark. Thankfully, then, the two parts that bookend this story are superb. The Decepticons are always at their best when scheming and hatching plots, so to see both Soundwave and Starscream finagling their way to the top here is a joy to behold. While the sly Starscream bargains and blackmails his way to the top, it's Soundwave who steals the show here, manipulating events (and even sacrificing a fellow Decepticon) as part of his power-play. These sequences are full of character, magnificently written, and the fight scenes in the final part add some action and

excitement to an otherwise cerebral tale.

A decent story overall, but it loses a lot of credit for the awful middle segment. 3/5

[62.8] THE HOUSE THAT WHEELJACK BUILT!
UK#278, 14 July 1990, 5 pages

Credits:
Simon Furman (script); Pete Knifton (pencils); Michael Eve (inks); Gary 'Glib' Gilbert (letters); Jeff Anderson (cover).

Plot:
At the grand opening of the new Earthforce base (designed by Wheeljack), Prowl voices his concerns that its defences might not be up to scratch. At the touch of a button, a number of hidden armaments become visible: laser turrets, heat-seeking drones, computer-controlled robotic 'acid bats' and electrified tendrils.

While the display is impressive, it transpires that this security grid can be deactivated only from *within* the base – meaning that the Autobots will have to overcome the various hazards themselves, just to turn them off.

Prowl makes a dash for the base, while Jazz, Bumblebee and the Aerialbots lay down covering fire. He is finally able to reach the control room and deactivate the defences. A relieved Prowl realises that, in retrospect, he was wrong to question Wheeljack's abilities.

Notes:
This story sees the full debut of the Earthforce Autobots' new headquarters. It was seen briefly in [62.7] 'Internal Affairs', and also in [62.3] 'Mystery', at which point it was still under construction.

Prowl does a quick headcount of the assembled Autobots before realising that there is no-one inside the base to switch off the defences – however, Springer's group of Survivors, who joined with Earthforce following the events of [62.6] 'Wolf in the Fold', are nowhere to be seen. The following story, [62.9] 'Divide and Conquer', will show that they have been placed 'on full alert', thereby providing an explanation for their absence from the opening ceremony.

The basic premise of the story – Autobots attacked by their own defences – is one we've seen a couple of times already in the comic: the scenes of Prowl getting past the various traps are highly reminiscent of Windcharger's and Ravage's journey in [4.3] 'Raiders of the Last *Ark*', and the Autobots were also attacked by their own weapons in [26] 'Funeral for a Friend'.

The story's title is from the English nursery rhyme 'This is the House That Jack Built'.

Roll Call:
Autobots: Jazz, Prowl, Ironhide, Sunstreaker, Wheeljack, Bumblebee, Grimlock, Snarl, Slag, Sludge, Swoop, Silverbolt, Air Raid, Fireflight, Skydive and Slingshot.

Review:
A recycled idea, with extra wit added: Grimlock's and Prowl's reactions to Wheeljack's

error are quite amusing. The art is great, but with such a slight plot there's very little to analyse here. It exists, it raises a smile, but ultimately it's too flimsy to have any real impact. 2/5

UK Advertisements, Part 6: Toys and Games
A list of all (non-Transformers-related) toys and games advertised within the UK comic.

Action Force toys ('Operation: Prisoner Release') – UK#104-105, 109
Action Force toys ('Striker Meets Stinger') – UK#115, 117, 121, 123, 125, 127, 129, 131, 135, 159, 170
Action Force toys ('Skystriker Strikes Back') – UK#137, 139, 141, 143, 145, 147, 149, 151, 154, 156, 158, 183
Action Force toys ('Rattler Battle') – UK#168
Action Force toys ('WHALE sinks Thunder Machine') – UK#178, 190, 196
Action Force toys (Special Corps figure offer) – UK#213, 217, 224, 231, 238, 240, 244, 247
Action Force toys (Weapon Transport/Night Landing vehicle offer) – UK#215, 221, 228, 236, 241, 246, 257
Back to the Future (board game) – UK#313
Battle Beasts (action figures) – UK#107, 110, 112, 114, 126-127
Dragon Lock (puzzle game) – UK#139
Dungeons and Dragons (role-playing game) – UK#30-32, 38-40, 83-85, 95-97
G.I. Joe: The Action Force toys (Destro's Despoiler/Desert Fox/D.E.M.O.N.) – UK#267
G.I. Joe: The Action Force toys (Tiger Force) – UK#269, 271, 273, 280, 286, 292
G.I. Joe: The Action Force toys (Rolling Thunder/X-19 Stealth Fighter) – UK#295, 298, 301, 317, 319
Lolobal (bouncing activity toy) – UK#80
M.A.N.T.A. Force (action figures and playsets) – UK#312-313
Marvel Super Heroes (role-playing game) – UK#88-90
Motivation, Health and Leisure Ltd (toy manufacturers) – UK#115, 119, 124
Mutant (a ball of green slime) – UK#177, 180
Real Ghostbusters, The (action figures; ad placed in association with Asda supermarkets) – UK#243
Record Breakers (customisable motorised car/racetrack system) – UK#263, 265, 268, 272, 275
Transforming robot watch – UK#2-5
Visionaries toys – UK#161-162, 165, 166, 171, 174, 176, 180-181, 186, 189, 192

[62.9] DIVIDE AND CONQUER! (comic)
UK#279, 21 July 1990, 5 pages

NB: Not to be confused with {1-06} 'Divide and Conquer' (cartoon episode).

Credits:
Simon Furman (script); Stewart 'Staz' Johnson (pencils); Michael Eve (inks); Gary 'Glib' Gilbert (letters); Bryan Hitch (cover).

Plot:
The Decepticons, now a united force under the joint leadership of Starscream and

Soundwave, launch a full-scale attack on the Earthforce base. However, it's all a diversion – while the Autobots are occupied, Starscream is free to steal an oil tanker in the Gulf of Mexico.

Or so he thinks – it's not just the Decepticons who can play the 'divide and conquer' card: the Autobots have also split their forces. Starscream is met by the Survivors, who manage to save the tanker and force Starscream into retreat.

Their ruse discovered, Starscream orders the rest of the Decepticons to end their attack on Earthforce HQ. Soundwave tells his fellow Decepticons that Starscream's failure means that he should take sole command of them – another instance of 'divide and conquer'.

Notes:
The principle of 'divide and conquer' forms the backbone of this story. The philosophy of *divide et impera* (as it was in the original Latin) breaks down into two basic ideas: in war, it's the act of creating divisions amongst the opposing force, thereby weakening them; in politics, it involves the act of dividing one's subjects into smaller factions, making them less likely to oppose a ruler than if they were united.

This is the first time in the 'Earthforce' saga that the Decepticons are seen as a united force, now under the joint leadership of Soundwave and Starscream following the deposal of Megatron and Shockwave in [62.7] 'Internal Affairs'. The schism was first revealed in [61.1] 'Starting Over'.

This adventure has many links with the previous one, [62.8] 'The House That Wheeljack Built'. We discover why the Survivors were not present in that story, and we find out that the Earthforce HQ's new security measures have temporarily been shut down following those events.

The Decepticons Thrust and Dirge make a welcome return. Although they have been seen in a couple of future-set stories, this is their first present-day appearance since [41] 'Totaled' and [39.1] 'Salvage' respectively.

This is the second time we have seen the Decepticons attack an oil tanker; their previous attempt, in [31] 'Buster Witwicky and the Car Wash of Doom', proved equally fruitless.

Roll Call:
Autobots: Jazz, Prowl, Wheeljack, Grimlock, Snarl, Slag, Swoop, Inferno, Skids, Springer and Broadside.

Decepticons: Starscream, Soundwave, Rumble, Ravage, Scrapper, Scavenger, Mixmaster, Long Haul, Hook, Drag Strip, Dead End, Breakdown, Bombshell, Kickback, Thrust, Dirge, Astrotrain, Blitzwing, Octane, Runabout, Runamuck, Rampage, Tantrum, Headstrong, Divebomb and Carnivac.

Data File: Stewart 'Staz' Johnson (artist)
Another *The Transformers* contributor who later went on to success with mainstream American titles, after a stint at *2000 AD*. His credits include *Robin*, *Catwoman* and *Dectective Comics* for DC, and *X-Men* and *Spider-Man* for Marvel.

Review:
Giant battles are common in *The Transformers* comic, but this isn't just action and

mayhem – some thought has obviously gone into the tactics of the various factions, making it a surprisingly fulfilling read. Starscream gets to be as funny and cowardly as ever, Soundwave is as sharp and manipulative as ever, and there's some great material for the Survivors, who get a chance to shine for the first time since their arc combined with the Earthforce one. 4/5

[62.10] THE 4,000,000 YEAR ITCH!
UK#280, 28 July 1990, 5 pages

Credits:
Simon Furman (script); Jeff Anderson (art); Stuart Bartlett (letters); Pete Venters (cover).

Plot:
A glitch in Slag's brain means that once every four million years he goes berserk, even turning on fellow Autobots if they happen to be close by. On such occasions, his fellow Dinobots make every attempt to keep Slag's episodes a secret, for fear he will be deactivated if anyone finds out.

In a feat of remarkably bad timing, Slag goes berserk at the same time Optimus Prime is taking a tour around the Earthforce base. Fortunately, however, the Dinobots are just about able to influence events enough so that the two don't come into contact with one another.

As the oblivious Optimus Prime departs, the Dinobots consider themselves grateful that this happens only once every four million years.

Notes:
The title of this story is derived from that of *The Seven Year Itch*, a 1952 play later adapted into a feature film starring Marilyn Monroe (Billy Wilder, 1955).

The plot, however, borrows from an altogether different source – the classic *Star Trek* episode 'Amok Time' (1967), in which it's revealed that members of the Vulcan species (including lead character Mr Spock) experience a violent 'blood fever' every seven years.

The plot reasoning behind Slag's malaise is interesting: apparently, all Transformers are essentially savage warriors (an 'age-old force … uncontrollable'), now held in check by 'emotional dampers' – a part of a Transformer brain that now regulates such impulses. Slag has no such dampers, so has to make a constant, conscious effort to keep his primal urges at bay – and every four million years, these primitive emotions take over.

It's revealed that, in Slag's last such relapse on Cybertron, he 'wiped out his entire unit', an event the rest of the Dinobots were guilty of covering up to protect their friend.

The story contains elements of classic French farce, in that Slag and Optimus Prime never actually meet here, despite several near misses.

Roll Call:
Autobots: Optimus Prime, Grimlock, Snarl, Slag, Sludge and Swoop.

Data File: Stuart Bartlett (letterer)
Bartlett lettered issues of *Doctor Who Magazine*, *Action Force Monthly*, *Knights of Pendragon* and *James Bond Jr*. He was also an editor, and in that capacity had credits on

The Real Ghostbusters, Death's Head II and *The Complete Spider-Man.*

Review:
After the action and excitement of [62.9] 'Divide and Conquer', we're back to the short comedy stories. This one is actually pretty funny – the sitcom-like way in which Optimus Prime is completely oblivious to the carnage going on around him is simply superb. It won't be everyone's cup of tea, but for those prepared to see a lighter take on the Autobots, this should hit the spot. 4/5

Free Gifts
The British comic would often include free gifts. There were two reasons for this – first, to make it look more appealing to potential buyers; secondly, more cynically, to appease regular readers when the price went up.
Here then is a list of all free items given out with *The Transformers* UK:

- UK#1: a set of transfers (based on toy box art).
- UK#2: another set of transfers.
- UK#3: an iron-on transfer (depicting Optimus Prime).
- UK#15: a 'badge' (actually a thick cardboard sticker depicting either Optimus Prime or Megatron) and a glossy poster.
- UK#16: another badge/sticker (Ravage).
- UK#17: yet another 'badge' (either Optimus Prime or Megatron).
- UK#18: a small model airliner (part of a Kellogg's Corn Flakes promotion).
- UK#27: giant poster (various Transformers and their planet against a starry backdrop).
- UK#28: giant poster (this time featuring the Dinobots).
- UK#29: giant poster (featuring box art of Megatron and Sideswipe).
- UK#30: giant poster (a promo image of Optimus Prime and Megatron).
- UK#45: giant poster (the Autobot mini-warriors).
- UK#52: a Transformers Panini sticker album.
- UK#53: some stickers (for the album given away with the previous issue).
- UK#54: a free Special Teams poster, the reverse of which features a comic strip.
- UK#63: another Special Teams poster, this time with profiles of each team member.
- UK#64-70: collectable Special Teams art cards, intended for use with the poster that came with the previous issue.
- UK#79-80: a two-part giant poster, featuring Ultra Magnus and Galvatron.
- UK#81: a *Secret Wars* Panini sticker album.
- UK#82: some stickers (for the album given away with the previous issue).
- UK#98: a badge/sticker of Ultra Magnus (similar to those given away in issues #15-17).
- UK#99: a badge/sticker of Galvatron.
- UK#130: a card 'data scan' with facts and statistics about the new Headmasters characters.
- UK#162: a sticker, depicting the Autobot Cloudburst.
- UK#186: an *Action Force* Panini sticker album.
- UK#187: some stickers (for the album given away with the previous issue).
- UK#188: a free can of the carbonated soft drink Tango (via a redeemable coupon).
- UK#200: a free booklet: *Transformers: The Facts.*
- UK#232: a magnifying glass.
- UK#233: a temporary tattoo.
- UK#234: more temporary tattoos.
- UK#259: a free sticker (bearing the slogan 'Caution – Transformers live here!').

- UK#260: a free poster, featuring the Classic Heroes.
- UK#274: a free Italia 90 World Cup Sticker Album (and stickers), via a redeemable coupon.
- UK#276: a free badge.
- UK#294: a free sew-on patch (bearing the Autobot insignia).
- UK#309: a free bookmark (with images of the Megatron/Ratchet hybrid monster).
- UK#310: a free poster, featuring a number of Autobots and Decepticons.
- UK#315: a *Beetlejuice*-themed joke book (actually, more of a small pamphlet than a book).
- UK#320-322: a giant poster of Unicron attacking Cybertron, split into three parts.

[62.11] MAKIN' TRACKS!
UK#281, 4 August 1990, 5 pages

Credits:
Simon Furman (script); Pete Knifton (pencils); Michael Eve (inks); Sophie Heath (letters); John Marshall and Pete Venters (cover).

Plot:
The Autobot Earthforce base is equipped with a state-of-the-art repair facility, the 'bodyshop', which is how they have been able to resurrect so many of their fallen warriors recently. However, Wheeljack has been having problems reviving the next Autobot on his list – Tracks. A series of computer glitches and equipment malfunctions have delayed Tracks' repair, and Optimus Prime suspects sabotage.

It transpires that the culprit is none other than the Earthforce leader, Grimlock. Grimlock hates Tracks, and begrudges the Autobot's position at the top of the repair list. As Tracks' body is placed in the ACU machine – the final stage of the repair effort – Grimlock also leaps into the machine in a last-ditch effort to stop the process.

While the machine rebuilds Tracks as planned, Grimlock isn't so lucky, as the device inflicts some significant damage on him. To make Grimlock's day even worse, Tracks is assigned to work closely with Grimlock as part of Earthforce.

Notes:
This story finally follows up on the promise in [61.1] 'Starting Over' that we would finally get an explanation for the fact that many 'dead' Autobots have been revived recently. We get our first look at the Autobot body shop and its revolutionary machine, the ACU (an acronym for Automated Construction Unit, according to the letters page in UK#292). This new technology involves placing a stricken Autobot into a repair chamber. (Its exact method is never elaborated upon, but the likely explanation is that it was reverse-engineered from the Pretender shells that Megatron created and that were able to restore Jazz, Bumblebee, Grimlock and Starscream in [58] 'All the Familiar Faces'. It might also be based upon the technology used by Galvatron in [60.1] 'Perchance to Dream', which reactivated a number of Autobots.)

Tracks' reintroduction here actually pre-dates the re-release of his toy by a full year. (Tracks would be part of the European Classic Hero range in 1991; an Action Master version of the character also saw release in 1991.)

Roll Call:
Autobots: Optimus Prime, Wheeljack, Grimlock and Tracks.

An unidentifiable corpse (damaged beyond recognition) can also be seen in the Autobot body shop.

Data File: Pete Knifton (artist)
After *The Transformers*, Knifton moved into the world of role-playing games, providing art for Games Workshop's range of games and publications, including *White Dwarf* magazine, and a couple of *Fighting Fantasy* gamebooks, 'Tower of Destruction' and 'Siege of Sardath'.

Data File: Sophie Heath (letterer)
Heath is best known for her colouring. Her work can be found in issues of *Biker Mice from Mars*, *James Bond Jr.* and *Knights of Pendragon*. She also coloured a number of the *Combat Colin* strips that appeared within *The Transformers* comic.

Review:
A curious story. It's played entirely for laughs, but essentially boils down to Grimlock actively attempting to keep a fellow Autobot 'dead'. It's not quite out of character for the morally-grey Grimlock (he has previous for turning on his comrades), but it still jars in comparison with the mellower, more comedic Grimlock we've seen in recent stories.

Also, this isn't really all that funny – it comes across like a bad *Tweety and Sylvester* cartoon, with Grimlock's ever-more desperate (and pitiful) attempts to kill Tracks resulting in his own downfall. One almost expects Porky Pig to show up at the final chase scene, declaring 'That's all, folks!' 1/5

[63] KINGS OF THE WILD FRONTIER. (MATRIX QUEST Part Two of Five)
US#63, 'February 1990' (published December 1989), 20 pages.

British reprint: UK#282, 11 August 1990 (Part 1), 5 pages; UK#283, 18 August 1990 (Part 2), 5 pages; UK#284, 25 August 1990 (Part 3), 5 pages; UK#285, 1 September 1990 (Part 4), 5 pages.

Credits:
Simon Furman (script); José Delbo (pencils); Dave Hunt (inks); Nel Yomtov (colours); Jim Massara (letters); Don Daley (editor); Tom DeFalco (editor-in-chief); Ian Akin (cover). **UK:** John Marshall and Pete Venters (cover, UK#282); Robin Smith (cover, UK#283); Kirk Etienne (cover, UK#284); Stewart 'Staz' Johnson (cover, UK#285).

Plot:
The Autobot Triggerbots arrive on the frontier planet Cheyne, hoping to find the Matrix. They witness a murderous lynch mob chasing after a young alien child, and decide to intervene, thereby saving the youngster.

The Triggerbots become friendly with the child's parents, settlers who claim to have angered the local populace by refusing to sell their farmland to unscrupulous town officials. The Triggerbots decide to rest up at the family's farm, where a change gradually overcomes them – they begin to forget about the Matrix Quest and become passive and docile, content to stay and work on the farm.

Having grilled the captive Headmasters – Nightbeat, Siren and Hosehead – about the Autobots' plans, Thunderwing decides to claim the Matrix for himself. He and a team of Decepticons arrive on Cheyne and confront the Triggerbot Dogfight – only to find that Dogfight's brain has been massively affected by his stay on the farm.

His altercation with the Decepticons causes Dogfight's memories to resurface – he recalls his original mission to search for the Matrix, and realises that the alien family have warped his mind.

Dogfight returns to the farm and confronts the alien family – they are actually Vrobians, 'psychic vampires' who feed on emotions. He rescues his fellow Triggerbots, and the Autobots continue their search for the Matrix.

Notes:
This story is a virtual compendium of Wild West and cowboy references. The main influence would appear to be the 1949 Jack Schaefer novel *Shane* and its later movie adaptation (George Stevens, 1953), which tells the story of a gunslinger out to protect a group of homesteaders against a ruthless baron trying to steal their land. In this retelling, the Triggerbots take the part of Shane while the Vrobians are the homesteaders.

The name of the planet here, Cheyne, could well be another reference to *Shane*, but the spelling hints at another Western influence: *Cheyenne*, a classic television series broadcast between 1955 and 1963, itself inspired by the Cheyenne tribe of Native Americans and the Wyoming city that bears their name.

The alien town is named Osaplam, which is Malpaso spelled backwards. Malpaso is the name of Clint Eastwood's production company, which was responsible for classic Westerns such as *Paint Your Wagon* (Joshua Logan, 1969), *Two Mules for Sister Sara* (Don Siegel, 1970) and *Unforgiven* (Clint Eastwood, 1992).

The name of the psychic vampire race, Vrobian, would seem to be a corruption/partial anagram of the title *Rio Bravo*, the classic John Wayne Western (Howard Hawks, 1959). The name of the lead Vrobian is Hud, presumably a reference to the Paul Newman movie *Hud* (Martin Ritt, 1963), also a Western.

This story was written during the brief fad for children's space-Westerns that began in the late '80s, with contemporary cartoon series such as *BraveStarr* and *The Adventures of the Galaxy Rangers* covering similar ground. Another influence would seem to include 'This Side of Paradise', an original *Star Trek* series episode in which the regular cast were reduced to vacant-minded farmers by way of an alien influence.

Plot-wise, this is a direct sequel to [62] 'Bird of Prey'. It features a flashback to that story, and we see that the Autobot Headmasters Siren, Hosehead and Nightbeat are still in Decepticon custody following their capture at the end of it.

We discover that the *Ark* contains an altar that allows Optimus Prime to form a mental link with the Matrix. We also get our first confirmation that the Matrix has been tainted, 'its pristine form defaced by the graffiti of evil'.

The title of this story comes from the popular nickname for Davy Crockett (1786-1836), the legendary American frontiersman; it was also the title of a 1980 UK chart-topping album by Adam and the Ants.

UK Notes:
Although the concept was new to American readers, British Transformers fans were

already aware that the Matrix could be tainted – indeed, this was an important plot point in the most recent future-set stories, such as [53.2] 'Aspects of Evil' and [59.3] 'Shadow of Evil'.

The altar in the *Ark* appears to be similar in function to the Matrix Flame altar seen in [20.2] 'Target: 2006'.

UK Changes:
Page 1, panel 1: credits replaced.
Page 9, panel 4: the reference to 'last issue' is changed to 'issue 264'
Pages 12-13: a printing error in the UK comic meant that, on these two pages, some of the colours (especially shades of blue) appeared washed-out.

Roll Call:
Autobots: Backstreet, Dogfight, Override, Nightbeat, Siren and Hosehead.

Decepticons: Ruckus, Windsweeper, Needlenose, Spinister and Thunderwing.

Other: Unicron (in a vision).

Nebulans: Muzzle, Quig and Lug (as the heads of Nightbeat, Siren and Hosehead respectively).

The Decepticon Crankcase appears on the cover of the issue, but not within the comic itself.

Review:
All the problems inherent in [62] 'Bird of Prey' resurface here, only to a greater extent. This isn't really a story, more a stitched-together series of references and pastiches. Take the homages out, and what we're left with is just as vacuous as the alien-influenced minds of the Triggerbots.

It's a clever, technical exercise in shoehorning Wild West trappings into a comic, but the basics - characterisation, pace, depth, urgency, emotion – seem to have been neglected. 1/5

US Straplines, Part 3
A list of all the slogans that graced the cover of the American comic between issues #61 and #80, plus all issues of the various spin-off comics. (NB: such straplines were absent on issue #62 of the regular comic, issues #1 and 3 of the *Transformers: The Movie* adaptation, issue #2 of *Transformers: Headmasters*, and all issues of *G.I. Joe and the Transformers*):

US#61: The primal scream!!
US#63: 'Ah've come fer mah Matrix!' You'll never forget the day they drifted in … Thunderwing and the Decepticons hit town!
US#64: To save Longtooth from himself … and a race from extinction … his fellow Autobots may just have to kill him!
US#65: Has Grimlock found the Matrix – or has *it* found *him*?!
US#66: By the Matrix … possessed!

US#67: The war is over – and the Decepticons have won!

US#68: The humans strike back!

US#69: Optimus Prime! Grimlock! Galvatron! Ravage! Shockwave! Starscream! The gathering storm!

US#70: 'Help us.' The ultimate Autobot/Decepticon team-up!

US#71: Surrender!

US#72: The war is over – and the war has begun!

US#73: Less than meets the eye – the vanishing!

US#74: Optimus Prime and Scorponok side-by-side ... against the hordes of Unicron!

US#75: Double-sized all-out action anniversary issue! The end?! ... or the beginning?

US#76: 'I tell you there's something moving out here!' 'Uhh, well, it sure not me!' The big freeze!

US#77: Fall out!

US#78: Past and future collide as ... Galvatron battles Megatron!

US#79: The last Autobot?

US#80: When all hope is gone ... one shall rise! The epic conclusion!

Transformers: The Movie #2: The Sharkticons strike!

Transformers Universe #1: 1st collector's item issue! Beginning a 4-issue guide to all the Autobots and Decepticons – their powers and weaknesses – and more!

Transformers Universe #2: 2nd sensational issue! Continuing a 4-issue guide to everything you ever wanted to know about the Autobots and Decepticons!

Transformers Universe #3: 3rd tantalising issue! Continuing a 4-issue guide to the biggest stars of TV, movies, and comics!

Transformers Universe #4: 4th final issue! Concluding a 4-part guide to all the Autobots and Decepticons! Bonus! All the new Transformers from the hit movie included in this issue!

Headmasters #1: Introducing an all-powerful, all-new generation of Transformers!

Headmasters #3: The love that kills

Headmasters #4: Enter: the Targetmasters! Fierce final issue!

[63.1] SHUT UP!
UK#282 11 August 1990, 5 pages

Credits:
Simon Furman (script); Stewart 'Staz' Johnson (art); Gary 'Glib' Gilbert (letters). For cover credits, see the entry for [63] 'Kings of the Wild Frontier' above.

Plot:
Inside the Earthforce base, Inferno keeps a watchful eye on three Decepticon prisoners – Bludgeon, Stranglehold and Octopunch. The Decepticons just sit in their cell, motionless, staring and silent, completely unnerving Inferno.

Suddenly, the unusually-mute Stranglehold starts tearing up the floor of the cell. The already-spooked Inferno opens the cell door in order to pacify the Decepticon, but is skewered by Bludgeon's sword – as a master of the ancient martial art of Metallikato, Bludgeon is able to control the weapon via telekinesis. The Decepticons then seize their opportunity and flee the base.

After being asked how the escape happened, the recovering Inferno replies, 'They did it by keeping quiet.'

Notes:
This story is a sequel to [62.6] 'Wolf in the Fold', in which Bludgeon, Stranglehold and Octopunch were captured by the Autobots.

We get a look at two previously-unseen areas of the Earthforce base here – the detention area (containing prison cells with 'doors' actually comprised of energy beams) and a secure storage room where confiscated Decepticon weaponry is kept.

Roll Call:
Autobots: Prowl, Grimlock and Inferno.

Decepticons: Stranglehold, Bludgeon and Octopunch.

Review:
A tense psychological thriller, this works both as a prison-escape adventure, and also as a gripping little character piece. Inferno gets some good development (his thoughts 'narrate' the story), and it also helps build up the growing threat of Bludgeon and his cronies, who easily outsmart the Autobots here. 4/5

[63.2] MANOEUVRES!
UK#283 18 August 1990, 5 pages

Credits:
Simon Furman (script); Pete Knifton (pencils); Pete Venters (inks); Sophie Heath (letters). For cover credits, see the entry for [63] 'Kings of the Wild Frontier' above.

Plot:
The Decepticon tanker Octane often gets bored with simply transporting fuel from A to B. As he ferries gasoline back to the Decepticon base, he often relieves the monotony by driving like a maniac, putting human vehicles at risk and lives in danger.

On one such trip, Octane begins 'toying' with a white Porsche, trying to make it crash. Not concentrating on his surroundings, he goes off-course and ends up in the middle of an army firing range. When it suddenly occurs to him that a single shot would ignite the fuel he carries within him, he contacts his fellow triple-changers – Astrotrain and Blitzwing – to rescue him.

Astrotrain and Blitzwing arrive on the scene and initially begin shooting at the army tanks and helicopters, until realising that Octane got himself into this mess. Angered by his recklessness, his Decepticon comrades flee the scene, leaving him to fend for himself.

In a final twist, it transpires that the white Porsche that led Octane into the firing range was, in fact, the Autobot Jazz.

Notes:
The logo on the gas station raided by Octane is only partially readable, but it ends in '-XXON', a reference to the real-world fuel company Exxon, or possibly its fictitious

Marvel counterpart Roxxon, previously mentioned in [12.3] 'The Icarus Theory'.

In his tanker truck mode, Octane has a capacity of ten thousand (presumably US) gallons, confirming a detail originally revealed on the character's toy packaging. This capacity corresponds to some real-world tankers, and is nothing out of the ordinary.

Jazz is able to hide his Autobot logo when in vehicle mode thanks to a sliding panel, an ability common to many Autobots, first established in [14] 'Rock and Roll-Out'.

Roll Call:
Autobots: Jazz.

Decepticons: Astrotrain, Blitzwing and Octane.

Data File: Pete Venters (artist)
Venters also worked on a few issues of *2000 AD*, including on a *Judge Dredd* strip. He's since gone on to be one of the most prolific artists on the *Magic: The Gathering* card game, with over 250 individual card illustrations to his name.

Review:
The last of the five-page, standalone British strips, 'Manoeuvres' is fairly typical of the genre: there is some decent focus on a single character – in this case, Octane – a bit of light-hearted comedy and a twist ending. The very epitome of 'run of the mill'. 3/5

The 'NEXT' Box, Part 5
A final round-up of captions from the 'NEXT' box that appeared in the UK comic – issues UK#265-332.

- UK#265: (US strip) Enter the Decepticons! (UK strip) Top gear!
- UK#266: (US strip) Launch day! (UK strip) Snow fun!
- UK#267: (US strip) Bumblebee – R.I.P. (UK strip) Flashback!
- UK#268: (US strip) Power struggle! (UK strip) Mystery!
- UK#269: (US strip) Blast off! (UK strip) Bad guy's ball!
- UK#270: (US strip) A bargaining chip! (UK strip) The living nightlights!
- UK#271: (US strip) Kindred spirits?! (UK strip) Cry wolf!
- UK#272: (US strip) The end of the world! (UK strip) Wolf in the fold!
- UK#273: (US strip) Devious dealings! (UK strip) XK9!
- UK#274: (US strip) Playing for high stakes! (UK strip) Secrets!
- UK#275: (US strip) Buzzy bee! (UK strip) Bugged!
- UK#276: (US strip) All fall down! (UK strip) Build up!
- UK#277: (US strip) One chance, one choice! (UK strip) Bodge job!
- UK#278: (US strip) Plan of action! (UK strip) The splits!
- UK#279: (US strip) Fish to fry! (UK strip) The itch!
- UK#280: (US strip) Loose ends! (UK strip) Makin' Tracks!
- UK#281: (US strip) Matrix Quest returns! (UK strip) Golden silence!
- UK#282: (US strip) Hung up! (UK strip) Muckin' about!
- UK#283: (US strip) Déjà vu? (UK strip) Assassins!
- UK#284: (US strip) Shifting shapes! (UK strip) External affairs!
- UK#285: (US strip) Deadly obsession! (UK strip) The lesser evil!
- UK#286: (US strip) Klud quest! (UK strip) Inside story!

- UK#287: (US strip) Lousy timing! (UK strip) Front line!
- UK#288: (US strip) Redemption! (UK strip) Road games!
- UK#289: (US strip) Dark creation! (UK strip) The war goes on ...
- UK#290: (UK reprint) A pile of junk! (US strip) Prey!
- UK#291: (UK reprint) Shock tactics! (US strip) Will to power!
- UK#292: (UK reprint) When the chips are down! (US strip) Homeward bound!
- UK#293: (UK reprint) Total war! (US strip) All fall down!
- UK#294: (UK reprint) In Death's Head's head! (US strip) Prime target!
- UK#295: (UK reprint) The hard fall! (US strip) Battleark!
- UK#296: (UK reprint) Towering Inferno! (US strip) The grappling!
- UK#297: (UK reprint) Mind games! (US strip) Rhythms of darkness!
- UK#298: (UK reprint) Origins of Transformers (2) (US strip) The human factor!
- UK#299: (UK reprint) Junk laid waste! (US strip) Powerbase!
- UK#300: (UK reprint) Two good reasons! (US strip) Stars 'n' stripes!
- UK#301: (UK reprint) In the national interest! (US strip) The human factor!
- UK#302: (UK reprint) Dinobot rescue! (US strip) Starscream!
- UK#303: (UK reprint) Gauntlet! (US strip) Circuit broken!
- UK#304: (UK reprint) Swoop to rescue! (US strip) Shockwave!
- UK#305: (UK reprint) Holocaust! (US strip) Eye of the storm!
- UK#306: (UK reprint) The Dinobots' last stand? (US strip) Galvatron v Unicron!
- UK#307: (UK reprint) The Enemy Within! (US strip) 'Con-fusion?!
- UK#308: (UK reprint) The best laid plans ... (US strip) The price of life!
- UK#309: (UK reprint) Enough is enough! (US strip) Kill or cure?
- UK#310: Surrender!
- UK#311: Chaos & uncreation!
- UK#312: ... All this and civil war 2!
- UK#313: (US strip) Clash of the titans! (UK reprint) Crime... and punishment!
- UK#314: (US strip) Out of time! (UK reprint) Battle plan!
- UK#315: (US strip) The vanishing! (UK reprint) Trial ... and error!
- UK#316: (US strip) none (UK reprint) Endings ... and beginnings
- UK#317: Mask of Unicron!
- UK#318: To be continued ...
- UK#319: The stand!
- UK#320: Suicide run!
- UK#321: Clash of the titans!
- UK#322: Still life!
- UK#323: -- Monsters!
- UK#324: Exodus!
- UK#325: A fond farewell?
- UK#326: A savage circle!
- UK#327: Planet fall!
- UK#328: The Last Autobot!
- UK#329: A hero rises!
- UK#330: (US strip) End of the road! (UK reprint) Thunder and lightning!
- UK#331: (US strip) The prime mover! (UK reprint) The greatest gift of all!
- UK#332: The end!

[63.3] ASSASSINS

UK#284 25 August 1990 ('Assassins'), 5 pages

UK#285 1 September 1990 ('External Forces!'), 5 pages
UK#286 8 September 1990 ('The Lesser Evil!'), 5 pages

NB: This three-part story has no overall title – each segment was individually named. For the purpose of analysis, this book will refer to the adventure as 'Assassins'.

Credits:
Simon Furman (script); Jeff Anderson (pencils, part 1; inks, part 3); Michael Eve (inks, part 1); Pete Knifton (pencils, part 2); Pete Venters (inks, part 2); John Marshall (pencils, part 2); Stuart Bartlett (letters, part 1); Julie Hughes (letters, part 2); Peri Godbold (letters, part 3); Andrew Wildman (cover, UK#286). For cover credits to UK#284 and 285, see the entry for [63] 'Kings of the Wild Frontier' above.

Plot:
After surviving a series of assassination attempts, Starscream eventually figures out that there is a bounty on his head. The prime suspect would appear to be his fellow Decepticon commander, Soundwave, who would stand to take sole control of the faction should he be killed.

Meanwhile, the Autobots determine that Snarl is suffering from the deadly rusting disease corrodia gravis. The only cure is a 'systems boost' from a compatible Transformer but, to make matters even more complicated, the only compatible donor is Starscream.

Starscream angrily confronts Soundwave, who is able to convince him that he wasn't the one who hired the assassins. The real culprits are the former Decepticon leaders Megatron and Shockwave, who have joined forces in a bid to oust the usurpers.

The Autobots arrive on the scene, only to find Starscream under fire from a combined force of Megatron, Shockwave, Bludgeon, Octopunch and Stranglehold. Realising that they must keep Starscream alive in order to save Snarl, the Autobots join the battle, aiding Starscream and eventually driving off the attackers.

Saved by the Autobots, Starscream agrees to help cure Snarl, on the proviso that the Autobots promise to protect him again should Megatron and Shockwave make another assassination attempt.

Notes:
This story is a sequel to [62.7] 'Internal Affairs', focusing on Megatron's and Shockwave's attempts to reclaim their position as Decepticon leaders. It is also a prequel to the previous year's [A5.2] 'Destiny of the Dinobots', in which Snarl was revealed to have the corrodia gravis disease. Given that Snarl is still afflicted by the illness two years later, we can infer that Starscream's 'system boost' fails to cure the Dinobot fully.

The name corrodia gravis is derived from Latin – 'corrodia' would appear to be a derivative of *corrodere* ('to gnaw completely' – the root of the English 'corrode'), and *gravis* ('heavy' or 'serious') – basically, then, it's a serious wasting disease, eating away at Snarl's body.

This is the first appearance of Bludgeon, Stranglehold and Octopunch since their escape from detention in [63.1] 'Shut Up'. The story is set mostly in Louisiana, in the environs of the Decepticon base previously introduced in [62.7] 'Internal Affairs'.

Roll Call:
Autobots: Prowl, Ironhide, Wheeljack, Grimlock, Snarl, Slag, Sludge and Swoop.

Decepticons: Megatron, Starscream, Soundwave, Shockwave, Stranglehold, Bludgeon and Octopunch.

Data File: Peri Godbold (letterer)
Originally hired as an art assistant to letterer/editor Richard Starkings, Godbold provided letters for *Apocalypse* and *Death's Head II*. She's best known these days as a designer/art editor for *Doctor Who Magazine* and *The Essential Doctor Who*, where her duties also involve restoration of vintage comic strips and photographs.

Review:
An exciting, imaginative action story with a neat premise – it's good to see the UK strips attempting something this big, considering that most of them in this era were little one-off comedy vignettes. In many ways, this adventure seems like the culmination of the Earthforce Saga, featuring a number of previously-established plot elements – the re-emergence of Bludgeon's group, the Decepticon leadership rivalries – and binding them together.

That said, this tale is a little too ambitious for its own good – even at 15 pages, there's a lot packed in here, meaning that some important story beats (Bludgeon's defeat, Soundwave's fate) get glossed over.

Despite some meaningful shortcomings, though, there's a lot to enjoy here. From the weird alien assassins to Prowl's 'brick' thought-bubble, this is a fun – if structurally-flawed – entry in the canon. 3/5

UK Advertisements, Part 7: Miscellaneous
A list of all companies and products advertised in the pages of *The Transformers* UK that don't readily fit into any of the previous categories.

3-in-One (BMX lubricant) – UK#77, 79-80
Abbey National Building Society – UK#7, 330
Dolphin Adventure Holidays – UK#64
Firework safety campaign – UK#3, 294-295
G-Force (a GI Joe fan club) – UK#303-308, 310
Ghostbusters fan club – UK#12, 15, 17-18
Grandstand (walkie-talkie/spy gear range) – UK#264, 278, 297
Halfords (bicycle retailer) – UK#240, 242, 244-245, 299
Harlequin wall clocks – UK#138
Indiana Jones Adventure Club – (coupons entitling readers to a discount on membership were printed in UK#269-271, with an order form printed in UK#272)
Initial Time Pieces – UK#11, 13
Just Comics (comic retailer) – UK#82
Nostalgia & Comics (comic retailer) – UK#76, 80
Pal dog food – UK#1
Panini Mega Stickers – UK#183
Perfect Mailing Company (comic back-issue specialist) – UK#8
Spider-Man wristwatches – UK#2-3, 8, 10

Thundercats toothbrushes – UK#205
UHU craft glue sticks – UK#26
Woolworths (UK retail chain) – UK#189

[64] DEADLY OBSESSION (MATRIX QUEST Part Three of Five)
- US#64, 'March 1990' (published January 1990), 20 pages.

British reprint: UK#286, 8 September 1990 (Part 1), 5 pages; UK#287, 15 September 1990 (Part 2), 5 pages; UK#288, 22 September 1990 (Part 3), 5 pages; UK#289, 29 September 1990 (Part 4), 5 pages.

NB: The issue's title page erroneously lists it as 'Matrix Quest Part Four of Five'.

Credits:
Simon Furman (script); José Delbo (pencils); Al Williamson (inks, pages 1-4); Dan Reed (inks, pages 5-20); Nel Yomtov (colours); Jim Massara (letters); Don Daley (editor); Tom DeFalco (editor-in-chief); Ian Akin (cover). **UK:** Stewart 'Staz' Johnson (cover, UK#287); Pete Knifton (covers, UK#288 and 289). For cover credit to UK#286, see the entry for [63.3] 'Assassins' above.

Plot:
The search for the Matrix brings three Autobots – the Pretenders Longtooth, Doubleheader and Pincher – to the mercury seas of the planet Pequod. They are investigating claims that a creature previously thought extinct – the whale-like Klud – is responsible for the numerous 'boating accidents' that have occurred recently. The Autobots figure that the creature might have been regenerated by the life-giving properties of the Matrix.

While searching for the Klud, Longtooth is seriously wounded by the leviathan. Delirious with pain and rage, he splits from the other Autobots and goes off on his own in an attempt to kill the creature.

Meanwhile, Thunderwing has an obsession of his own – he is hell-bent on securing the Matrix for himself. Indeed, he has a special affinity for the Transformers' sacred talisman and is able to connect his mind with that of the Klud. Thunderwing determines that the Klud came into contact with Matrix energy after eating an astronaut who had crash-landed on Pequod. That astronaut had himself encountered the Matrix on a nearby moon, so Thunderwing orders the Decepticons to leave Pequod and head there.

With the Decepticons in retreat, Doubleheader and Pincher convince the crazed Longtooth not to kill the Klud.

Notes:
As with the previous parts of the 'Matrix Quest' arc, this issue is heavily indebted to a couple of prior sources: the 1851 Herman Melville novel *Moby-Dick; or, The Whale* and (the film adaptation of) Peter Benchley's 1974 novel *Jaws* (Stephen Spielberg, 1975).

Moby-Dick provides the basis of the plot: a mariner who loses his leg to a whale attack is obsessed with hunting down and killing that same whale. In the original novel, the mariner in question was named Ahab; here Longtooth takes on that role, hunting the Klud after his own leg is mauled.

Other *Moby-Dick* references abound: the first line of the issue ('Call me Longtooth') is a play on the famous opening line of *Moby-Dick* ('Call me Ishmael'), and the planet Pequod is named after Captain Ahab's boat.

From *Jaws* we get the name of Longtooth's boat – the *Orca* – the name of the alien city – Gottlieb, after Carl Gottlieb, who co-wrote the film's screenplay – and the whole subplot about how the authorities were hushing up the reports of Klud attacks, calling them 'boating accidents', for fear it would harm the tourist trade.

A third inspiration would seem to have been the real-life story of the coelacanth, a type of fish previously believed extinct but rediscovered in 1938. The return of the Klud ('Thought they were extinct, you know, everyone did') appears to be based on those events.

In terms of continuity, we have the first US appearance of the Autobot Pretenders Longtooth, Pincher and Doubleheader. We also discover why Thunderwing is obsessed with the Matrix: 'Like a select few others, normally Autobots, I was created with an innate affinity with our sacred lifeforce! It calls to me, as it does to potential Autobot leaders.' Emirate Xaaron here provides a quick recap of the events so far, including a mention of Unicron's impending arrival (foreshadowed in [61] 'The Primal Scream'). There is a first mention of the planet Cameron and its moon, VsQs, which will play a pivotal role in the following US story, [65] 'Dark Creation'.

On Pequod, 'blug' would appear to be a word for 'hell', a 'guhk' is a length of time, and 'drax' is a currency.

UK Notes:
The UK-only story [59.1] 'Whose Lifeforce Is It Anyway' acts a prequel to this one, showing us the Autobot Pretenders being briefed on the quest for the Matrix. It also demonstrates that Longtooth's state of mind was already troubled, even before his run-in with the Klud.

UK Changes:
Page 1, panel 1: credits replaced; the 'Matrix Quest' logo has been painted out.
Page 5, panel 2: the reference to issue #61 is changed to issue #261.
Page 6, panel 2: 'harbor' is changed to 'harbour'.
Page 13, panel 1: 'savior' is altered to 'saviour'.

Roll Call:
Autobots: Emirate Xaaron, Longtooth, Pincher and Doubleheader.

Decepticons: Ruckus, Windsweeper, Needlenose, Spinister and Thunderwing.

Data File: Al Williamson (artist)
Now inducted into the Will Eisner Comic Book Hall of Fame, Williamson began his career in the '40s, working on *Tarzan* newspaper strips. His many, many credits include *Flash Gordon*, *Weird Science*, *Star Wars*, *Daredevil* and *The Amazing Spider-Man*. He has twice won the Eisner Award for Best Inker (1991 and 1997).

Review:
While the previous two instalments of the Matrix Quest storyline borrowed perhaps too heavily from other sources, 'Deadly Obsession' achieves a far better balance between

the various homages (in this case, *Jaws* and *Moby-Dick*) and being a good story in its own right. While there's still a sense that the characters are merely pawns in writer Simon Furman's game of 'spot the reference' (Longtooth, in particular, comes down with an ill-defined 'delirium' purely so as to cast him in the Ahab role), this feels far more substantial than the previous two outings.

For one thing, the story structure is unique and interesting (the plot is non-linear and unfolds mostly in a series of flashbacks), and there's some good work done with Thunderwing, too – he might be a deranged lunatic, but his mental link with the Matrix lends him some much-needed additional gravitas and threat.

Furthermore, this looks like no other Transformers comic. The combination of José Delbo's crisp, effective pencils with Dan Reed's more expressive inks lends the comic a unique style. The vibrant, almost neon colour palette, coupled with the ornate design of the captions (which are lettered and drawn to look like ancient scrolls) make this a visual treat.

An odd little story, but the appealingly experimental feel of both the script and the visuals makes it worth a read. 3/5

[64.1] INSIDE STORY!

- UK#287 15 September 1990 ('Inside Story!'), 5 pages
- UK#288 22 September 1990 ('Front Line!'), 5 pages
- UK#289 29 September 1990 ('End of the Road!'), 5 pages

NB: This three-part story has no overall title – each segment was individually named. For the purpose of analysis, this book will refer to it as 'Inside Story!'. The third episode, 'End of the Road', should not be confused with [80] 'End of the Road', the final issue of the comic in America.

Credits:

Simon Furman (script); Pete Knifton (pencils, parts 1-2); Pete Venters (inks, parts 1-2); Stewart 'Staz' Johnson (art, part 3); Stuart Bartlett (letters, parts 1-2); Gary 'Glib' Gilbert (letters, part 3). For cover credits, see the entry for [64] 'Deadly Obsession' above.

Plot:

The Decepticon Bombshell has injected one of his mind-altering cerebro-shells into the brain of the Autobot Superion, who runs amuck in Upper New York State. It's part of a plan by Starscream and Shockwave to discredit the Autobots, whom they fear might one day form an alliance with humanity. Grimlock and Prowl discover that journalist Irwin Spoon is covering Superion's rampage, and so co-opt him into venturing inside the haywire Autobot, to climb his way through Superion's inner workings and remove the cerebro-shell. In return, Prowl offers Spoon the story of a lifetime – a chance to look around the Earthforce base and an exclusive interview with Grimlock.

Despite some difficulty, Spoon is eventually able to remove the shell and restore Superion to normality. He is taken to the Earthforce base for the tour and interview, but the Decepticons get wind of this and send the Stunticons to kidnap Spoon – in their current campaign of disinformation, the last thing they need is a major piece of journalism portraying the Autobots as good and just.

As the Stunticons drive away with Spoon, the Autobots give chase. Despite their best efforts to evade their pursuers, the Stunticons are caught and defeated, and Spoon is rescued. Later, Spoon writes his article, and uses it to discredit the Autobots completely – he, too, is a victim of Bombshell's cerebro-shells.

Notes:
This was the last ever domestically-originated story to see print within the UK comic – from now on, all the adventures appearing within its pages would be either American material or reprints of old UK strips.

The Decepticons' 'Project Smear' plan is similar to their plot in [15] 'I, Robot Master' *et seq.*, in which they used popular media to convince the public that the Autobots were evil. Starscream and Soundwave are still the Decepticon leaders, having survived the events of [63.3] 'Assassins'. The Earthforce base features an equipment store (with contents including the jet-ski-like vehicles previously seen in [62.6] 'Wolf in the Fold') and a combat room where Autobots undergo training simulations (probably similar to that seen in [47] 'Club Con').

The Superion sequence is set in Upstate New York, where journalist Irwin Spoon is covering events. He likens Superion's rampage to that of the fictional monsters Godzilla (see [3] 'Prisoner of War') and King Kong (see [45] 'Monstercon from Mars' and [54] 'King Con'). His journey inside the giant Autobot is a mini-tribute to the classic sci-fi movie *Fantastic Voyage* (Richard Fleischer, 1966) (although *The Transformers* cartoon series had already explored a similar premise, in {2-18} 'Microbots'). He quotes the old journalistic aphorism 'Man bites dog – that's news', and his study contains a small replica of the Discobolus, the famous sculpture of a discus thrower by Myron of Eleutherae (c 460-450 BC). Spoon's surname was first revealed on the editorial page of UK#287 (the issue in which part one of this story saw print); it wasn't actually used within the strip itself until part three (UK#289).

Reformatted!
It was around this time that Euan Peters, the UK editor of *The Transformers*, stepped down. His period in charge had been nothing if not tumultuous – in order to contend with falling sales, he had split the comic into three strips and made the switch from full colour to partly black-and-white. His replacement was Harry Papadopoulos. According to the letters page of UK#302, the change of editors was somewhat problematic: '[Artist Stewart 'Staz' Johnson] helped us through a tricky editorial changeover.'

Once installed, Papadopoulos immediately set about making his mark. The UK-only strips were dropped and replaced with reprints; the money saved in this way meant that the comic could return to full colour (albeit partly funded by a 5p price increase from UK#294). The letter-answerer character changed from the tetchy Decepticon Dreadwind to the more upbeat Autobot Blaster from UK#300, and the style of the cover art changed – the covers became more detailed, textured and 'painterly', as opposed to the standard comic book art that had previously been the norm.

The long-running *G.I. Joe* back-up strip (a regular feature since early 1988) was finally dropped, and replaced with *Machine Man*. The comic also went back to being a fortnightly title, reverting to the classic two-strip format.

With all these changes taking place during the final year of the comic's life, readers were in for an interesting ride as the title fought a losing battle with cancellation.

Roll Call:
Autobots: Jazz, Prowl, Ironhide, Sunstreaker, Wheeljack, Bumblebee, Grimlock, Tracks,

Silverbolt, Air Raid, Fireflight, Skydive, Slingshot, Superion and Springer.

Decepticons: Starscream, Shockwave, Motormaster, Drag Strip, Dead End, Breakdown and Bombshell.

The five Aerialbots (Silverbolt, Air Raid, Fireflight, Skydive and Slingshot) appear only in their combined Superion mode, rather than as individual robots.

Data File: Harry Papadopoulos (editor)
An editor for Marvel UK titles such as *Care Bears*, *The Flintstones* and *Star Trek: The Next Generation*, Papadopoulos is far better known as a successful photographer in the music industry, having worked for *Sounds* magazine between 1979 and 1984. His photographs have graced art galleries and even been compiled into a book (*What Presence! The Rock Photography of Harry Papadopoulos*).

Review:
As the last ever UK-only story to see print in the original comic, this should be momentous. The final chapter is suitably entitled 'End of the Road', and the strip finishes with the caption 'The war goes on ...' Unfortunately, however, the content is not as substantial or powerful as the occasion would seem to demand. Not only is this fairly small-scale stuff, but the Decepticons' plan – to use a human writer to spread lies about the Autobots – has already been done once before. The middle issue is especially poor (nothing really happens until the cliffhanger ending), and the central character in all this, Irwin Spoon, isn't likeable or memorable enough to inspire any emotional investment.

There are some good ideas here – the scenes of Superion running amuck and Spoon's adventures inside the robot's body are good fun, if all-to-brief. The finale – a nicely-drawn car-chase set piece – is also quite diverting. All-in-all, though, this is a rather weak end to an era. 2/5.

[65] DARK CREATION (MATRIX QUEST Part Four of Five)
US#65, 'April 1990' (published February 1990), 20 pages.

British reprint: UK#290, 6 October 1990 (Part 1), 5 pages; UK#291, 13 October 1990 (Part 2), 5 pages; UK#292, 20 October 1990 (Part 3), 5 pages; UK#289, 27 October 1990 (Part 4), 5 pages.

Credits:
Simon Furman (script); Geoff Senior (art); Nel Yomtov (colours); Jim Massara (letters); Don Daley (editor); Tom DeFalco (editor-in-chief); Bill Sienkiewicz (cover). **UK:** Stewart 'Staz' Johnson (covers, UK#290-293).

Plot:
Bumblebee, Jazz and Grimlock investigate VsQs, a moon orbiting the planet Cameron, where astronauts have reported the presence of Optimus Prime's funeral bier. They discover that the astronauts have been killed by a monstrous alien that stalks the corridors and service ducts of their moonbase.

Prime's old body, and the Matrix, did indeed crash-land on the moon, and the creature that massacred the astronauts was a small alien life form that was enlarged and mutated after coming into contact with the Transformers' sacred life force.

Thunderwing arrives on the scene, also hoping to capture the Matrix, but his fellow Decepticons are perturbed by his increasingly erratic behaviour – at one point he is happy to sacrifice the life of Windsweeper rather than destroy the creature.

The Matrix is eventually found, and Thunderwing makes a desperate grab for it – but he is suddenly attacked by the creature, allowing the Autobots a chance to take it for themselves.

The Autobots' shuttle docks with the *Ark*, and Optimus Prime goes to greet them. When the shuttle door opens, however, Thunderwing emerges – with the Matrix!

Notes:
As per the previous instalments of the Matrix Quest saga, 'Dark Creation' is heavily based upon a piece of popular fiction; in this case, the film *Aliens* (James Cameron, 1986). The planet Cameron is a thinly-veiled nod to the film's director, and the moon VsQs is likely a reference to Vasquez, the memorable character played by Jennette Goldstein. The creature itself – a 'face-hugger' monster that later evolves into a large, black creature with a sharp-toothed maw – is extremely reminiscent of the titular Aliens, and the moonbase is similar in design to Hadley's Hope, the terraforming base seen in the film. Finally, Thunderwing's urge to keep the alien alive, even at the expense of his colleagues, mirrors the attitude of Carter Burke, the main human antagonist in *Aliens*.

Aside from a brief nod to [56.1] 'Out to Lunch' in [58] 'All the Familiar Faces', this is the first time that a UK Transformers story is directly referenced within the American strips. In this instance it's [54.3] 'Deathbringer', which is recapped and summarised for the benefit of American readers unfamiliar with the UK strips.

This story is a direct sequel to [64] 'Deadly Obsession'. Here, we find out how the astronaut from Cameron (later eaten by the Klud) became infused with Matrix energy (he was attacked by the evil Matrix creature). Thunderwing's attack on Ruckus (also from that issue) is referenced here too, as is the awakening of Primus (seen in [61] 'The Primal Scream').

There is also a lot of foreshadowing of future issues – Grimlock is determined to revive his fellow Dinobots ('We'll find a way – you'll see. One way or another the Dinobots will live again'), paving the way for their eventual resurrection in [72] 'All This and Civil War 2'. Also, a mysterious Transformer emerges from the sea; it's obviously Shockwave, but the comic will play his eventual full return in [68] 'The Human Factor' as a surprise 'reveal'.

UK Notes:
For American readers, this is Shockwave's first appearance since he fell to Earth at the end of [39] 'The Desert Island of Space', although the UK edit of that story made his 'demise' seem much less final, and indeed he continued to be a part of the UK stories, playing a major role in [48.2] 'Time Wars'.

Prime's Predecessor
According to [A1.3] 'And There Shall Come … A Leader', Optimus Prime was the very first military leader of the Autobots – prior to his promotion, the Autobots were commanded by civilian bureaucrats.

In a flashback sequence in [36.2] 'The Legacy of Unicron' we see Optimus Prime receive the Matrix from his predecessor – a battle-scarred, orange-coloured Autobot. In trying to identify this mysterious Autobot, a couple of options present themselves.

In the letters page of UK#56, it's High Councillor Traachon who is clearly and unambiguously named as the Matrix-bearer immediately prior to Optimus Prime. This actually makes a lot of sense; in [A1.3] 'And There Shall Come ... A Leader', Traachon's only other appearance, his head is shown in close-up but his full body is never clearly visible, so it's certainly possible for him to be the orange-bodied robot in the flashback. The design of his head is quite different, but this is nothing new in *The Transformers* (Bumblebee, Gears, Blaster, Skids and Megatron being just a few of the characters who have sported varying head designs during their time in the comic). Furthermore, in the text story [A2.3] 'State Games', Traachon is addressed as 'General Traachon'. As a civilian leader with military experience, his death on the battlefield – in the arms of his successor Optimus Prime – seems quite fitting. According to the Optimus Prime Datafile in the 1987 *The Transformers Annual* (see the entry under [A2.1] 'In the Beginning' for more on this), it was Traachon who surrendered 'complete control' to Prime.

All these events, however, occurred only in the UK comics and annuals. For contemporary American readers, the issue of Prime's predecessor was addressed somewhat differently. In the US-originated adventure [65] 'Dark Creation', the Matrix (now demonstrating sentience) makes the following proclamation: 'We are Primus. We are Prima. We are Prime Nova. We are Sentinel Prime. We are Optimus Prime.' In the context of that story, this reads like a complete list of all the Matrix-bearers in chronological order – in other words, an Autobot named Sentinel Prime was the leader immediately prior to Optimus. When illicit scans, and later official reprints, of the UK comics became readily available in America years later, it was logically and retrospectively assumed that the orange Autobot in [36.2] 'The Legacy of Unicron' was therefore meant to be Sentinel Prime.

The identity of Optimus Prime's predecessor, therefore, varies depending upon one's interpretation of the material. In the early UK comics it was General Traachon, otherwise it was Sentinel Prime. While the list of prior Matrix-bearers given in [65] 'Dark Creation' is strongly implied to be complete and exhaustive, the wording is ambiguous enough to ensure that the Traachon-as-Matrix-holder idea isn't *completely* contradicted.

We know that not every Matrix-bearer has what it takes to be a Prime. Galvatron, Ultra Magnus and General Ghyrik (see *The Transformers: The Movie* and [44.1] 'Space Pirates') have all held the Matrix but did not become one with it in the way that Hot Rod did when the Matrix transformed him into Rodimus Prime. It's therefore possible that many Autobots (including Traachon) held the Matrix between the tenures of Sentinel and Optimus, none of them worthy enough to be converted into a true Prime.

UK Changes:
Page 3, panel 3: credits excised.
Page 4, panel 4: the reference to issue #61 is changed to issue #261.
Page 8, panel 3: 'Last issue!' is amended to 'Issue 287!'
Page 10, panel 5: to prevent the cliffhanger falling mid-sentence, Thunderwing's interrupted 'But that –' is changed to 'But that is all!'

Roll Call:
Autobots: Optimus Prime, Jazz, Bumblebee, Grimlock, Hot Rod, Nightbeat, Siren and Hosehead.

Decepticons: Shockwave, Ruckus, Windsweeper, Needlenose, Spinister and Thunderwing.

Nebulans: Muzzle, Quig and Lug (as the heads of Nightbeat, Siren and Hosehead respectively).

Data File: Bill Sienkiewicz (artist)
The Kirby and Eisner Award-winning Sienkiewicz has provided art for a great many titles, including *Batman* (issue #400), *Superman* (issue #400), *Green Lantern*, *New Mutants* and *Moon Knight*. He has illustrated cards for the *Magic: The Gathering* card game, provided scenic art for concerts by ex-Pink Floyd bassist Roger Waters, painted covers for the magazine *Entertainment Weekly* and provided the box art for the video game *Resident Evil*.

Review:
'Dark Creation' doesn't just borrow some imagery, names and plot points from *Aliens*, it steals a lot more – genuine shocks, gut-wrenching action and an all-pervasive sense of fear and foreboding – bound together by some good character work and utterly spellbinding visuals.

While a lot of credit must go to Simon Furman – who gives us possibly the best script seen in an American Transformers comic since the Headmasters mini-series – this wouldn't have quite the same impact were it not for the sumptuous art by Geoff Senior. It's crisp, dynamic and expressive, with exquisite use of shadow and framing.

It's utterly unoriginal, granted, but that doesn't stop it from being a wonderfully beguiling synergy of script and art. 5/5

[66] ALL FALL DOWN (MATRIX QUEST Part Five of Five) (TF)
NB: Not to be confused with the fourth issue of the *G.I. Joe and the Transformers* comic series, [GIJ4] 'All Fall Down' (GIJ)

US#66, 'May 1990' (published March 1990), 20 pages.

British reprint: UK#294, 3 November 1990 (Part 1), 5 pages; UK#295, 10 November 1990 (Part 2), 5 pages; UK#296, 17 November 1990 (Part 3), 5 pages; UK#297, 24 November 1990 (Part 4), 5 pages.

Credits:
Simon Furman (script); Geoff Senior (art); Nel Yomtov (colours); Jim Massara (letters); Don Daley (editor); Tom DeFalco (editor-in-chief); Ian Akin (cover). **UK:** Stewart 'Staz' Johnson (covers, UK#294, 295 and 297); Stephen Baskerville (cover, UK#296).

Plot:
Now in possession of the Matrix, Thunderwing proves more than a match for the assorted Autobots within the *Ark*, injuring and killing many. However, he is not quite

himself – tainted by evil, the Matrix has developed a warped, twisted personality of its own, and is slowly taking control of his body.

Meanwhile, Unicron continues his journey toward Cybertron. *En route*, he destroys and devours the planet Ghennix, which lies in his path. Unicron spares three survivors from the planet and transforms them into a trio of robotic heralds, named Hook, Line and Sinker. He sends his new emissaries into a parallel future, with a mission to bring back a powerful being from another dimension who can act as his agent of havoc.

Back on the *Ark*, it transpires that the Autobot trio of Hosehead, Siren and Nightbeat were able to stow away on Thunderwing's stolen shuttle (having escaped from his 'mind-tap' machine). Nightbeat devises a dangerous plan – he sets the shuttle to self-destruct, then skewers Thunderwing by shooting him with the shuttle's grappling harpoon. When the *Ark*'s bay doors are opened, the shuttle is sucked out into space, with Thunderwing still attached. Once clear of the *Ark*, the shuttle explodes.

The Matrix Quest is over – the Autobots' sacred lifeforce has apparently been destroyed. A grim-faced Prime claims that, in defeating Thunderwing, the Autobots have won this particular battle – despite the loss of life and the seeming destruction of the one thing that could stop Unicron …

Notes:

As the final chapter of the Matrix Quest arc, this story ties up a number of loose ends, but also sows seeds for future issues. Hosehead, Siren and Nightbeat finally escape from Decepticon captivity here, having been abducted at the end of [62] 'Bird of Prey'. They are saved by a freak chain of events – the machinery they were hooked up to underwent a power surge (various cables and wires were shown sparking in [65] 'Dark Creation'), which itself was caused when Thunderwing attacked Ruckus in [64] 'Deadly Obsession'.

We also discover how Thunderwing was able to procure the Matrix – he killed the mutated alien on VsQs, then overpowered the Autobot Classic Pretenders, who were debilitated by the moon's high gravity, before stealing the Autobot shuttle.

Introduced here are Unicron's heralds, Hook, Line and Sinker. In order to pave the way for his arrival on Cybertron, Unicron sends them to find him an agent of chaos from 'one of my futures'. (As we shall see in the upcoming [67] 'Rhythms of Darkness' the agent in question turns out to be Galvatron II, a Decepticon leader from a parallel future.)

Also making an appearance is Shockwave (although still not identified as such). He is spying on Scorponok's New Jersey base (not seen since [61] 'The Primal Scream'), and plans to make a 'bid for power'. His recent disappearance is explained as follows: 'I have, up till now, laid low – let my name fade into Decepticon history.'

The tainted Matrix takes on the form of a demonic black energy creature, possibly based on the appearance of the alien from [65] 'Dark Creation'. Continuing the *Aliens* motif established in that story, Thunderwing is defeated when he is sucked through an airlock, mirroring the fate of the Alien Queen in the movie.

Hot Rod states that the battle with Thunderwing was fierce: 'Ten or more injured, three deactivated.' Only Landmine is definitively killed on-panel here. (Of all the Autobots featured in this story, the only other one who never appears again is Crosshairs, making him the likely second victim. If that is indeed the case, the third victim might therefore be Crosshairs' Targetmaster partner Pinpointer.)

This story's title is a lyric from the popular children's nursery rhyme 'Ring a Ring o'

Roses'.

UK Changes:
Page 1, panel 1: credits replaced.
Page 11, panel 2: the reference to issue #62 is changed to #264.

Roll Call:
Autobots: Optimus Prime, Jazz (flashback only), Bumblebee (flashback only), Grimlock (flashback only), Hot Rod, Kup, Blurr, Highbrow, Chromedome, Brainstorm, Crosshairs, Landmine, Waverider, Joyride, Getaway, Nightbeat, Siren and Hosehead.

Decepticons: Megatron, Starscream, Shockwave, Galvatron II (only as an image on a video screen), Ruckus, Windsweeper, Needlenose, Spinister and Thunderwing.

Other: Unicron, **Hook, Line** and **Sinker**.

Nebulans: Stylor, Muzzle, Quig and Lug (as the heads of Chromedome, Nightbeat, Siren and Hosehead respectively).

Review:
After all the build-up, the denouement of the Matrix Quest is basically an extremely satisfying fight scene, well scripted and drawn by the reliable pair of Furman and Senior. Amongst all the action and noise, there is still time for fine details – Thunderwing's increasing insanity/possession is well-played, and the tantalising glimpses of the Unicron and Shockwave storylines leave the reader eager for more.

The only minor gripe is that, after nearly half a year of questing, nobody has actually achieved anything – the Matrix remains just as lost at the end of the story as at the beginning. Although Thunderwing's defeat is satisfying, it doesn't quite merit the five-month build-up, and as such this feels naggingly anticlimactic. 4/5

[67] RHYTHMS OF DARKNESS!
US#67, 'June 1990' (published April 1990), 20 pages.

British reprint: UK#298, 1 December 1990 (Part 1), 5 pages; UK#299, 8 December 1990 (Part 2), 5 pages; UK#300, 15 December 1990 (Part 3), 5 pages; UK#301, 22 December 1990 (Part 4), 5 pages.

Credits:
Simon Furman (script); José Delbo (pencils); Danny Bulanadi (inks); Nel Yomtov (colours); Jim Massara (letters); Don Daley (editor); Tom DeFalco (editor-in-chief); Jim Lee (cover). **UK:** Stewart 'Staz' Johnson (cover, UK#298); John Marshall and Stewart 'Staz' Johnson (cover, UK#299); Stewart 'Staz' Johnson and John Burns (cover, UK#300); John Marshall, Stephen Baskerville and Robin Bouttell (cover, UK#301).

Plot:
New York, 2009, a 'possible future'. The Americas have been completely conquered by the Decepticons; only a handful of Autobots remain. Although victory seems impossible, the Autobots have allied themselves with a group of human resistance

fighters, led by this era's version of Spike Witwicky, for one final, possibly suicidal attack.

The rest of humanity, meanwhile, have come up with an alternative plan: the European Crisis Commission will nuke the Americas unless they see a sign that the Autobots are capable of fighting back. The Decepticon leader Galvatron is actually banking on a nuclear attack, and has constructed around his base a protective force field that will absorb the power of the explosions and convert it into Energon.

The Autobots strike against the Decepticon base, although many are killed in the attempt. After the Decepticons' force field is deactivated, Jazz distracts Galvatron while Spike scales the tower.

The diversion is a success; Galvatron realises too late what Spike was doing – he has placed a USA flag atop the Decepticon citadel. This sign of defiance is spotted by the European Crisis Commission, who stay the nuclear attack.

At that moment, Hook, Line and Sinker arrive from the past and kidnap Galvatron, whisking him back through time with them. With Galvatron out of the picture, the surviving Autobots and humans finally have a chance to defeat the remaining Decepticons.

Notes:

This story takes place in an alternative future version of the year 2009. In this reality, the events of *The Transformers: The Movie* played out slightly differently: although Galvatron, Cyclonus, Scourge and Rodimus Prime were created, here Unicron successfully destroyed Cybertron and Earth was claimed by the Decepticons, 'a present from Unicron before he departed'. Prowl is alive (in the 'proper' timeline he was killed in *The Movie*) and although Spike is present, there's no sign of his son Daniel.

Although America has been conquered, the rest of the world meets at the European Crisis Commission based in Geneva. Members of this commission would seem to include Russia and possibly also China.

This story sees the first appearances of Inferno and Chainclaw within the US comic; Crossblades and the Pretender Monsters had never been seen before in the UK comic either.

This story follows up on [66] 'All Fall Down' (TF), in which Unicron created Hook, Line and Sinker and sent them into the future to procure Galvatron's services.

UK Notes:

Although this was their first appearance in the US strips, Inferno had featured in numerous UK-only stories, dating back to [8.1] 'Decepticon Dam-Busters'. Likewise, Chainclaw had appeared in British adventures such as [53.3] '[Double] Deal of the Century'. The alternate version of 2009 seen here is different from any of the futures presented by the UK comic thus far – for one thing, Cybertron still exists in the others we've seen.

The cover of UK#301 is designed to resemble the famous World War Two photograph *Raising the Flag on Iwo Jima*, taken by Jim Rosenthal in 1945.

Three Galvatrons!

Confusingly, there have been three different versions of Galvatron seen in the comic up to this point. The aim of this section is to recap what we know of each version, and indeed why writer Simon Furman felt the need to have three versions of the same character running about.

Galvatron I:
The first Galvatron (from Timeline A) was created by Unicron in the future (*The Transformers: The Movie*) and subsequently travelled back in time, making two trips to the present day ([20.2] 'Target: 2006' and [23.4] 'Fallen Angel'). His excursions into the past caused damage to the fabric of space and time, causing a giant time-rift to appear. He was sucked into the rift and destroyed ([48.2] 'Time Wars').

Galvatron II:
After assuming writing duties on the American comic, Furman decided to introduce Galvatron into the storyline there, too. However, so as not to contradict his earlier strips for the UK comic, he created 'Galvatron II', a version from an alternative 2009. After leaving this parallel future (in [67] 'Rhythms of Darkness'), it's this second Galvatron that becomes a leading player in the remainder of the US issues.

The 'Galvatron II' name was given official sanction in 2006, when a toy was released in Japan specifically referencing the character.

Galvatron III:
A version unique to the tail end of the UK-only strips, Galvatron III was introduced in [53.2] 'Aspects of Evil' and also featured in [60.1] 'Perchance to Dream'. Presumably intended to become a main villain in the later UK strips, he was unceremoniously written out when Furman decided instead to concentrate on the 'Earthforce' saga.

This Galvatron is from a third version of the future, created when time 'corrected itself' in the aftermath of [48.2] 'Time Wars'. This post-Time Wars future was also glimpsed in [59.3] 'Shadow of Evil'.

The letters page in UK#279 stated that the Galvatron from [53.2] 'Aspects of Evil' was the same as that from [60.1] 'Perchance to Dream' – i.e. Galvatron III. This was confirmed in the letters page of UK#309, where a correspondent wrote: 'The Galvatron involved in the "Perchance to Dream" saga is, I take it, the Galvatron from "Aspects of Evil" [and [59.3] "Shadow of Evil"]?' Blaster affirms that 'the current Galvatron [II] is a separate entity.'

Confusingly, a more recent source (*Transformers: Dinobot Hunt*, a 2004 reprint compilation), instead claimed that the Galvatron in [60.1] 'Perchance to Dream' is actually the 'Galvatron II' from the American comics.

Given the choice between two official statements from the comic itself, printed in 1990 and 1991, around the time the stories were being written, and a statement 14 years after the fact in the editorial of a reprint compilation, this book prefers to accept the former as the most reliable source.

UK Changes:
Page 1, panel 1: new credits added.
Page 3, panel 1: original credits painted out.
Page 19, panel 7: 'as seen last issue' becomes 'issue 294'.

Roll Call:
Autobots: Jazz, Prowl, Inferno, Kup (flashback only), Blurr (flashback only), Rodimus Prime (in flashback, and as a corpse), Guzzle, Getaway, Chainclaw and **Crossblades**.

Decepticons: Laserbeak, **Galvatron II**, Cyclonus, Scourge, Astrotrain, Octane, Runabout, Runamuck, **Icepick, Bristleback, Scowl, Wildfly, Birdbrain** and **Slog**.

This is the first full appearance of Galvatron II, although his image featured on one of Unicron's monitor banks in [66] 'All Fall Down' (TF).

Other: Spike, Hook, Line and Sinker.

Data File: Jim Lee (artist)
Lee worked for both Marvel (*Fantastic Four, Iron Man, Alpha Flight*) and DC (*Batman, Superman*) before becoming one of the co-founders of Image Comics. He later returned to DC Comics in an executive role. He was the artist on *X-Men Volume 2* issue #1 (1991), the best-selling comic of all time (8.1 million copies).

Review:
An interesting 'what if?' scenario, notable for its unremittingly bleak outlook and funereal atmosphere. Writer Simon Furman milks the 'parallel future' idea for all it's worth, killing off numerous characters (including Rodimus Prime and Cyclonus), knowing full well that, as this is an alternate dimension, none of the events here will have any repercussions on the regular strips.

However, amongst the all-out carnage, there's a surprising amount of character work here, especially in the scenes where Spike and his fellow freedom-fighter Lisa argue with the Autobots about the merits of fighting and dying for the cause, even in a war that is essentially unwinnable.

If there's a downside, it's the decidedly cheesy ending, in which the American flag proves enough to prevent a nuclear launch. That mawkishness aside, however, this is another very strong story, and a great send-off for long-time artist José Delbo, whose final Transformers work is amongst his best. 4/5

[68] THE HUMAN FACTOR!
US#68, 'July 1990' (published May 1990), 21 pages.

British reprint: UK#302, 29 December 1990 (Part 1), 6 pages; UK#303, 5 January 1991 (Part 2), 5 pages; UK#304, 12 January 1991 (Part 3), 5 pages; UK#305, 19 January 1991 (Part 4), 5 pages.

Credits:
Simon Furman (script); Dwayne Turner (art); Nel Yomtov (colours); Rick Parker (letters); Don Daley (editor); Tom DeFalco (editor-in-chief); Dwayne Turner (cover). **UK:** Stewart 'Staz' Johnson and John Burns (cover, UK#302); Stewart 'Staz' Johnson and Robin Bouttell (cover, UK#303); John Marshall, Bambos Georgiou and Robin Bouttell (cover, UK#304); Richard Fisher (cover, UK#305).

Richard Fisher's painting of Shockwave used as the cover art for UK#305 had already been seen in the comic once before, back in UK#29, when it formed the basis of a pull-out poster/calendar for October 1985.

Stewart Johnson was erroneously credited as working on the cover art for UK#304 (rather than John Marshall); a correction and apology was printed in UK#308.

Plot:
Following the dissolution of RAAT – the US government's anti-robot team – G B Blackrock is in the process of forming a new group tasked with protecting Earth from the Decepticons.

His new recruits are mutants; gifted humans with special powers: Rapture, who has the power to entrance her enemies in a dream-like state, and Thunderpunch, who can energise his hands and feet so that his punches and kicks can harm even a Transformer.

They view video images of another potential recruit, Hector Dialonzo, who was recorded defeating the Decepticon Air Strike Patrol by tapping power from within the Earth. However, Dialonzo's whereabouts have been leaked somehow, and Blackrock suspects that there are other parties interested in the mutant.

Arriving at Dialonzo's location, these other parties make themselves known: Starscream, who wants to use the mutant as a Powermaster partner, and Circuit Breaker, still hell-bent on destroying all Transformers she encounters.

Following a brief battle between Dialonzo's various suitors, the mutant elects to team up with Blackrock's group. Blackrock is also able to convince Circuit Breaker to join them.

The defeated Starscream regains consciousness, only to be confronted by Shockwave, who makes his own proposition: 'Together the two of us can rule the Decepticons … and then two worlds!'

Notes:
A sidestep from the main ongoing storylines, this issue acts as an origin story for the superhuman team that will later become known as the Neo-Knights. It was hoped that the group would eventually spin off into their own comic series (much as Death's Head had done), but that never transpired.

The team are commanded by the entrepreneur G B Blackrock, last seen back in [31] 'Buster Witwicky and the Car Wash of Doom'. He's had some health problems recently ('Easy, G B! Remember the old ticker!').

Also on the team are Thunderpunch, aka Lee Gruber, a former freak-show act and general malcontent (described as a 'sexist redneck pig') and Rapture, real name Katrina Vesotzky, who was a homeless beggar before being recruited onto Blackrock's team. The third mutant is Hector Dialonzo (whose super-hero name will be confirmed as Dynamo in his next appearance), an immigrant from Mexico who is given temporary US citizenship in exchange for joining up. The final Neo-Knight is Circuit Breaker, who appears for the first time since [45] 'Monstercon from Mars'.

Blackrock Industries now has its corporate headquarters in Washington, DC. (Previous issues had the company located in Portland.) RAAT was disbanded once the 'Security Council' (of the United Nations?) became convinced that not all Transformers were evil (probably as a result of the events of [39] 'The Desert Island of Space').

Locations seen here include an oil refinery in Louisiana (possibly located near to the Decepticons' Louisiana base, seen in 'Earthforce' stories such as [63.3] 'Assassins'), the outskirts of Jacksonville, Florida, and Matacumbe Key, also in Florida. (In the real world, there is no Matacumbe Key, but there are two similarly-named islands in the Florida Keys – Upper Metecumbe Key and Lower Metecumbe Key. It's unknown whether this was a typographical error or a deliberate attempt to create a fictitious island.)

There are numerous references to previous stories: a flashback to Shockwave's oil rig attack that critically injured Circuit Breaker ([6] 'The Worse of Two Evils'); Circuit Breaker's previous battle with Starscream ([9] 'Dis-Integrated Circuits'); the attack at Macdill Air Force Base ([56] 'Back from the Dead'); and 'a trail of apparently random destruction across the Southern States' ([37] 'Toy Soldiers').

It's ambiguous, but the Decepticon Air Strike Patrol appear to be killed off here; this is their final appearance in the comic. Shockwave, who has been a 'mysterious' shadowy figure since his re-emergence in [65] 'Dark Creation', is finally revealed in full here.

'Dreadwind's Xmas!'

Issue #302 of the UK comic was the 1990 Christmas issue, and for the first time since 1984 there was no special festive strip – there was simply no room or budget for it, as by this point the comic had become a reprint-only title. Instead, the usual 'Transformation' editorial page was given over to a brief, tongue-in-cheek text story, in which Dreadwind is visited by the ghosts of Christmases past, present and future (a parody of Charles Dickens' 1843 novella *A Christmas Carol*). The story was untitled, but has become popularly known as 'Dreadwind's Xmas!' It does not fit into the standard comic continuity, and the premise is based on Dreadwind (formerly the UK's resident letter-answerer character) finally being persuaded to leave Marvel's offices in London.

UK Changes:

Page 1, panel 1: credits replaced.
Page 12, panel 5: the reference to issue 9 is changed to issue 33.

Roll Call:

Decepticons: Starscream, Shockwave, Scorponok (in a dream sequence), Stormcloud, Whisper, Tailwind and Nightflight. These last four, the Decepticon Air Strike Patrol, appear only in news footage seen on a television screen.

Other: G B Blackrock, Circuit Breaker, **Thunderpunch**, **Rapture** and **Dynamo**.

Nebulans: Zarak (as Scorponok's head, in a dream sequence).

Data File: Dwayne Turner (artist)

Turner's art can be found in many comics, including issues of *The Incredible Hulk*, *The Punisher* and *Spawn*. He now works as a storyboard artist in the film industry, with credits on *Tron: Legacy* (Joseph Kosinski, 2010), *Ender's Game* (Gavin Hood, 2013) and *The Jungle Book* (John Favreau, 2016).

Review:

The second atypical story in a row. In this one, the focus is firmly on set-up, as Blackrock and Circuit Breaker are reintroduced and the new super-hero gang is assembled. As with [3] 'Prisoner of War', the Transformers are reduced to bit parts in their own comic.

While this makes for a refreshingly different kind of Transformers adventure, by necessity there are compromises in the script, with reams of exposition, flashbacks and explanations to establish this new group of humans. It promises much for future stories, but doesn't make for an appealing read in itself.

The main talking-point, however, is Dwayne Turner's art, which has been almost universally panned, even by Simon Furman himself. It's scratchy, grubby and heavily-inked, like something out of a sketchbook. In conjunction with Nel Yomtov's muted colour palette, it gives the impression of being murky and unfinished.

While that's a valid viewpoint, there's also a case to be made that the art lends this story atmosphere, ambiance and character. What could have been a dull, talky comic has been transformed into a noir-ish grotesque – Starscream has often been menacing, but here he's actually *frightening*, thanks to Turner's off-model rendering of him. This is a Starscream that skulks rather than walks, looms rather than stands. It's foreboding, eerie and frankly unnerving.

All in all, this is a rather ordinary issue, enlivened by some extraordinary art – even if you think this looks terrible, at least it's a talking-point, in a comic that's otherwise devoid of any. 2/5

[69] EYE OF THE STORM
US#69, 'August 1990' (published June 1990), 20 pages.

British reprint: UK#306, 26 January 1991 (Part 1), 7 pages; UK#307, 2 February 1991 (Part 2), 6 pages; UK#308, 9 February 1991 (Part 3), 7 pages.

Credits:
Simon Furman (script); Andrew Wildman (pencils); Harry Candelario (inks, pages 1-6, 9-14 and 18-20); Bob Lewis (inks, pages 7-8 and 15-16); Nel Yomtov (colours); Rick Parker (letters); Don Daley (editor); Tom DeFalco (editor-in-chief); Andrew Wildman (cover). **UK:** Stewart 'Staz' Johnson and Robin Bouttell (cover, UK#306); Andrew Wildman and Robin Bouttell (cover, UK#307); Stephen Baskerville, Lesley Dalton and Robin Bouttell (cover, UK#308).

Plot:
In the aftermath of the Matrix Quest and the defeat of Thunderwing, the Autobots aboard the *Ark* are taking some much-needed rest and recuperation. Optimus Prime is not in the mood for relaxing, however. He is lost in thought and suffering from a bout of abdominal pains. Still obsessing over the death of his friend Ratchet, Prime has Nightbeat investigate the explosion that apparently killed the Autobot medic.

Grimlock is also in a bad mood – he has seen reports of a miraculous wonder cure, Nucelon, which can be found on the planet Hydrus Four. Forbidden by Optimus Prime to investigate the substance, due to it having some unforeseen side effects, Grimlock defies orders and leaves the *Ark* in a shuttle – taking the inert bodies of his fellow Dinobots with him.

Back on Earth, two Decepticons, Mindwipe and Triggerhappy, desert Scorponok's ranks, complaining of failures and empty promises. They are approached by Starscream, Shockwave and Ravage, who co-opt them into their new group, which plans to overthrow Scorponok.

In space, Galvatron arrives from a parallel future, summoned by the Unicron of this era. Although reluctant to obey Unicron's orders, Galvatron decides to play along with the world-devourer's plans … for now.

Back on the *Ark*, Nightbeat has determined there's a chance that Ratchet was pulled into a teleport beam just prior to the massive explosion that appeared to destroy him. He theorises that Ratchet might be simply trapped between realities, unable to rematerialise. He is able to home in on Ratchet's signal and beam the Autobot back onto the ship; but what materialises shocks everyone into silence.

It transpires that Ratchet wasn't the only Transformer stuck in mid-teleport when the explosion hit – Megatron was also trapped. The creature that has just appeared on the *Ark* is a grotesque hybrid of both Ratchet *and* Megatron ...

Notes:

This story sees the return of Megatron and Ratchet, albeit merged into a hybrid creature, after their apparent destruction in [59] 'Skin Deep'. Instead of perishing in the explosion of Megatron's base, they fell into the interdimensional portal but never reappeared, instead remaining trapped in what Nightbeat calls 'unspace'. Nightbeat's probe locks onto Ratchet's pattern and rematerialises both robots, in their new conjoined state.

After two stories that focused on events away from the *Ark*, we see the Autobots recuperating in the aftermath of the Matrix Quest, which concluded in [66] 'All Fall Down'. Chromedome, maimed in that story, is still undergoing repairs, while Grimlock, Bumblebee and Jazz have been rescued and retrieved after being abandoned on VsQs in [65] 'Dark Creation'.

The Autobots on the *Ark* relax by watching television and playing what appears to be a Cybertronian equivalent of chess. (Pieces include 'Quarg' and 'Vig'; 'Fullstasis' would seem to be analogous to checkmate.)

Optimus Prime is seen to be suffering from severe abdominal pains (a condition that, as we shall discover, is related to the upcoming metamorphosis of Prime's Powermaster partner, Hi-Q, in [80] 'End of the Road'). Optimus Prime remembers the words of the Keeper (in [61] 'The Primal Scream') who foretold that he would stand against Unicron only when the Transformers were 'united as one force'. To that end, Prime plans to surrender to the Decepticons.

Grimlock defies orders to travel to Hydrus Four, a planet first referenced in [59] 'Skin Deep'; it is located in the Styrakon system. ('Styrakon' is possibly a play on 'Styracosaurus', a genus of dinosaur – the perfect name for the place where the Dinobots are resurrected.) There he hopes to find Nucleon, a substance that both revives and strengthens mechanoids, but known side effects include madness. Grimlock has been itching to restore the Dinobots to life for some time, as previously evidenced in [65] 'Dark Creation'.

This is the first story set in the present day to feature Galvatron II, who was summoned from an alternate future in [67] 'Rhythms of Darkness'.

On Earth, the dissent amongst Scorponok's troops, as seen in [61] 'The Primal Scream', has intensified to the point where Triggerhappy and Mindwipe defect to the Starscream and Shockwave coalition formed in [68] 'The Human Factor'. Mindwipe and Triggerhappy are surprised to discover that Shockwave and Ravage were still alive following their apparent deaths in [39] 'The Desert Island of Space' and [20] 'Showdown' respectively.

UK Notes:

In the UK stories, both Shockwave and Ravage survived their 'deaths' in the American strips, resurfacing in stories such as [39.1] 'Salvage' and [48.2] 'Time Wars'. However, on no occasion during that time did Shockwave or Ravage cross paths with Scorponok's troops (although there were some near-misses during 'Time Wars'), so it's certainly feasible that Mindwipe and Triggerhappy were unaware that the pair had survived.

This isn't the first time the Autobots have been seen relaxing and playing a chess-like game while aboard the *Ark* – there was a similar scene in [56.2] 'Rage'.

The cover of UK#306 sees Optimus Prime posed in a manner akin to Le Penseur (The Thinker) a sculpture by Auguste Rodin (1840-1917). Appearing on the same cover is the quote 'By reason and calm judgement, the qualities specially appertaining to a leader' (original Latin: '*Ratione et consilio, propriis ducis artibus*'), from *Histories* (c100-110), a work by the Roman senator and historian Tacitus (c56-c117).

UK Changes:
Page 2, panel 1: credits replaced.
Page 3, panel 7: a reference to the events of issues #65-66 is changed to issues #290-297.
Page 7, panel 2: 'as seen in issue #59' becomes 'as seen in issue #251'
Page 17, panel 2: a reference to issue #20 is changed to issue #73 (although, oddly, a reference to US#39 on the same page goes uncorrected).

Roll Call:
Autobots: Optimus Prime, Jazz (flashback only), Ratchet (in flashback, and also as part of the Megatron/Ratchet hybrid), Bumblebee (flashback only), Grimlock, Snarl (as a corpse), Swoop (as a corpse), Hot Rod, Kup, Highbrow, Chromedome, Cloudburst, Waverider, Joyride, Getaway, Nightbeat, Siren, Hosehead and Fixit.

Decepticons: Megatron (in flashback, and also as part of the Megatron/Ratchet hybrid), Starscream, Ravage, Shockwave, Galvatron II, Scorponok, Mindwipe and Triggerhappy.

Other: Unicron, Hook, Line and Sinker.

Nebulans: Gort, Stylor, Zarak, Vorath, Muzzle, Quig and Lug (as the heads of Highbrow, Chromedome, Scorponok, Mindwipe, Nightbeat, Siren and Hosehead respectively).

Review:
As its name would imply, 'Eye of the Storm' is ostensibly a calm, character-led interlude between the mayhem of the Matrix Quest and the upcoming arrival of Unicron. Optimus Prime and Grimlock benefit the most from this. Optimus gets some excellent character development – he projects an outward image of strength and surety while constantly fretting about the future and agonising over difficult decisions. The only time he lets his guard down is when he's unable to contain his excitement at the prospect that Ratchet may still be alive.

Grimlock, too, gets a chance to shine. The bull-headed Autobot defies orders and heads off on a mission to save his fellow Dinobots – but there is some depth here also. Grimlock hates going against Prime like this, and he fully admits that he's compromising one of the principles he most admires – loyalty.

But while this appears to be a character piece on the surface, what's surprising is how tightly plotted it all is – writer Simon Furman expertly juggles a number of threads – Galvatron/Unicron, Starscream/Shockwave and Megatron/Ratchet – progressing the overall storyline while still managing to incorporate all the personal drama.

This is a story that in retrospect is massively pivotal – Optimus Prime decides to surrender to the Decepticons, Megatron returns and Galvatron arrives in the present day. But it almost lulls you into a false sense of calmness, until it slaps you full in the face with that cliffhanger ending. 'Eye of the Storm' – a title has never been more apt. 5/5

[70] THE PRICE OF LIFE!
US#70, 'September 1990' (published July 1990), 20 pages.

British reprint: UK#309, 2 March 1991 (Part 1), 10 pages; UK#310, 16 March 1991 (Part 2), 10 pages.

From UK#309, the comic reverted to a fortnightly schedule, as had been the case between issues 1 and 26.

Credits:
Simon Furman (script); Andrew Wildman (pencils); Stephen Baskerville (inks); Nel Yomtov (colours); Rick Parker (letters); Rob Tokar (editor); Tom DeFalco (editor-in-chief); Andrew Wildman (cover). **UK:** Frances Farmer (cover, UK#309); Stewart 'Staz' Johnson and Robin Bouttell (cover, UK#310).

Plot:
The Megatron/Ratchet hybrid creature goes on a rampage through the *Ark*, leaving a trail of destruction in its wake. Kup advocates destroying it, thus killing Megatron and putting Ratchet out of his misery, but Optimus Prime refuses, hoping that Ratchet can still be saved somehow.

Meanwhile, on Hydrus Four, Grimlock ventures across hostile terrain in order to find Nucleon, the substance that can revive dead mechanoids. His progress is halted by two robots who have already used the Nucleon and been driven mad as a result. Grimlock defeats both, and tests the Nucleon on himself – he's loath to use the substance on his fellow Dinobots if there is a risk of dangerous side effects. The Nucleon makes Grimlock feel more powerful than ever before, and he immediately sets about reviving the Dinobots.

Optimus Prime, meanwhile, manages to subdue the Megatron/Ratchet hybrid. The Autobot medic Fixit examines the creature and determines that it might be possible to separate the two Transformers and repair Ratchet. However, as the two are now linked on a mental level, Ratchet will live only as long as Megatron does. Prime orders that the operation go ahead, even if it means reviving Megatron …

Notes:
This is a direct sequel to [69] 'Eye of the Storm', and follows up on the shock cliffhanger ending to that issue. Here we see Grimlock become infused with Nucleon; and, although we don't know it yet, this action sets him on the path to becoming a non-transforming Action Master.

It's stated that there are 'thirty-or-so' active Autobots aboard the *Ark*, with another sixty lying deactivated in stasis pods (which means that the bulk of the Autobot forces are located elsewhere – either on Cybertron or on Earth). When speaking to Optimus Prime, Kup makes mention of 'all the knocks you've taken recently', a reference to his battle with Thunderwing in [66] 'All Fall Down'. There's another flashback to the explosion in [59] 'Skin Deep', which created this Megatron/Ratchet hybrid creature. As head of security, Kup has the authority to invoke the 'Crisis Act', and seize command of the Autobots if he considers that Prime's decision-making has become flawed.

Nucleon is a gold-coloured liquid that springs from 'The Well', located on Hydrus Four – specifically, within the Medi-Center on the island of Farooth. It's guarded by three powerful robots driven mad by the Nucleon. The substance 'affects no type of mechanoid in the same way'.

UK Notes:
The cover of UK#309, all screaming mouths and lolling tongues, seems designed to invoke the sleeve artwork for the 1969 King Crimson album *In the Court of the Crimson King*. The strapline to the same issue reads '21st Century schizoid!' a reference to the album's opening cut, '21st Century Schizoid Man'.

UK Changes:
Page 1, panel 1: credits replaced.
Page 3, panel 5: the reference to issue 59 is changed to 251.

Roll Call:
Autobots: Optimus Prime, Ratchet (in flashback, and as part of the Megatron/Ratchet hybrid), Grimlock, Snarl (corpse only), Slag (corpse only), Sludge (corpse only), Swoop (corpse only), Kup, Highbrow, Getaway, Nightbeat, Siren and Fixit.

Decepticons: Megatron (in flashback, and as part of the Megatron/Ratchet hybrid).

Nebulans: Gort, Muzzle and Quig (as the heads of Highbrow, Nightbeat and Siren respectively).

Data File: Rob Tokar (editor)
Tokar edited a number of Marvel titles, including *Alpha Flight*, *The Punisher* and *Web of Spider-Man*. He also provided edits on the relaunch title *Transformers: Generation 2*.

Review:
After the previous issue, which was heavy on talk but low on action, 'The Pri¢e of Life' redresses the balance somewhat, with the Megatron/Ratchet monster running amuck on the *Ark* and Grimlock battling some Nucleon-fuelled maniacs on Hydrus Four. There's still time for personal drama, though, as Optimus Prime and Kup clash over whether to save Ratchet or put him out of his misery.

The one drawback is that the plotting is a tad mechanical, as both Prime and Grimlock, in two completely separate story strands, are forced to weigh up the negative consequences of saving their dear friends. While the two plots work well enough, the fact that both characters are essentially facing identical dilemmas is just a little *too* neat. Otherwise, this is another top-quality instalment. 4/5

[71] SURRENDER!
US#71, 'October 1990' (published August 1990), 20 pages.

British reprint: UK#311, 30 March 1991 (Part 1), 10 pages; UK#312, 13 April 1991 (Part 2), 10 pages.

Credits:
Simon Furman (script); Andrew Wildman (pencils); Stephen Baskerville (inks); Nel Yomtov (colours); Rick Parker (letters); Rob Tokar (editor); Tom DeFalco (editor-in-chief); Andrew Wildman (cover). **UK:** Andrew Wildman and Robin Bouttell (cover, UK#311 – heavily altered version of US cover); Stephen Baskerville, Lesley Dalton and Robin Bouttell (cover, UK#312).

Plot:
Although his fellow Autobots are uncomfortable with the idea, Optimus Prime officially surrenders himself and his troops to Scorponok. Prime knows that only when the 'children of Primus' are united as one race can they hope to defeat Unicron. Initially though, Scorponok refuses to negotiate with Prime, and throws the Autobots into cells.

Meanwhile, on Cybertron, Galvatron II has arrived, and is causing total havoc. He destroys one of the Autobot bases, but Xaaron manages to escape into the tunnels beneath Cybertron.

Back on Earth, Optimus Prime and a group of Autobots escape from their cells and try to force Scorponok into talks. The Decepticon leader relents, and shakes hands with Prime. At that moment, Shockwave's rebel faction shows up and destroys Scorponok's base – with the Autobots still inside.

On Cybertron, Xaaron continues to make his way through the sewers. But his efforts are in vain – Galvatron has caught up with him …

Notes:
The story opens with a flashback to events on Cybertron, roughly four million years ago: heavily outnumbered, a small band of Autobots led by Optimus Prime manage to defend the city-state of Iacon against overwhelming odds. (Other than Prime himself, the other recognisable Autobots in this sequence were all part of the European Classic Heroes range of toys, thereby giving the figures some exposure despite the UK-only stories having now been cancelled.)

This is the first US sighting of Shockwave's underwater base off the coast of Blackpool. As well as Mindwipe, Triggerhappy, Starscream and Ravage, all previously seen in [69] 'Eye of the Storm', Shockwave has also recruited Runabout and Runamuck. There is another mention of Shockwave's apparent demise in [39] 'The Desert Island of Space'.

Bludgeon, Stranglehold and Octopunch are now a part of Scorponok's Decepticon faction, having been transported to Earth in [61] 'The Primal Scream'. There is a reference to the Matrix having been lost in [66] 'All Fall Down'. Optimus Prime's plan to surrender was previously revealed in [69] 'Eye of the Storm'.

UK Notes:
Shockwave's underwater base – seen here for the first time in the American strips – made its debut in [62.7] 'Internal Affairs'.

UK Changes:
Page 1: credits added.
Page 3, panel 1: the original credits box is turned into a 'Part 1' caption.
Page 6, panel 4: the reference to issue #66 is changed to issue #297.
Page 6, panel 5: 'issue #61' becomes 'issue's [sic] 259-261'.
Page 9, panel 3: the reference to issue #39 is altered to issue #159.
Page 10, panel 6: to make for a better mid-story cliffhanger, the caption is painted out.
Page 11, panel 1: similarly, the caption '– that was it!' is edited to read 'Cybertron ...'

Blackpool Illuminati

Shockwave's secret cabal of Decepticon renegades are based in an underwater complex off the coast of Blackpool, a popular resort town in Lancashire in the north west of England. However, there is some confusion as to the exact nature of Shockwave's base. A reader wrote in to the letters page of the American comic with a possible explanation, published in issue #74: 'Remember way back in issue #1, when Megatron and his army attacked the *Ark* after it had cleared a path for Cybertron through the asteroid field? We know they left Shockwave aboard their craft and that later he went down to Earth (where he met the Dinobots). It is logical that Shockwave would have hidden the Decepticon spacecraft, remote-landing it somewhere it would go unnoticed – as a contingency plan against possible disasters. Where better to hide it than on the ocean floor?' The response: 'Your explanation is pretty much spot on.' That would seem to be the final word on the matter – Shockwave's base is the Decepticon ship from [1] 'The Transformers'.

Except, it can't be, as that would contradict [20.2] 'Target: 2006', in which it's categorically stated that the Decepticon ship remained in orbit around the Earth until it was destroyed by Galvatron's solar-powered weapon. So what's going on here?

First, it should be noted that [20.2] 'Target: 2006' was a UK-only story. As far as American readers and editors knew, the Decepticon ship was still intact. Indeed, many Transformers fans even today consider the American strips to be the 'prime' storyline and treat the UK strips as some kind of offshoot continuity, even though Simon Furman went to great lengths to synchronise the two. So, for many people, this isn't even an issue: Shockwave's undersea base is the original Decepticon ship, end of story.

Equally, however, UK fans weren't privy to the letter in US#74, so from their point of view, Shockwave's Blackpool base was simply another new Decepticon HQ, with no obvious link to their spacecraft.

Is there any other evidence within the comics themselves? Not really. Every time we see the Decepticon ship ([1] 'The Transformers', [5] 'The New Order', [20.2] 'Target: 2006 etc) it looks different, and Shockwave's base doesn't really match any of the previously-seen configurations. One must also wonder, if this *is* the Decepticon spacecraft, why Shockwave has only just begun to use it as his headquarters – surely it would have been a better base of operations than, say, Blackrock's oil rig, Fortress Sinister or the 'makeshift' base we see in [16] 'Plight of the Bumblebee'?

As a proponent of the idea that the UK and US strips form a single continuity, this book is obviously biased toward the UK reading of events, and would propose that the events of [20.2] 'Target: 2006' supersede a reader's speculation that was never corroborated within the strips themselves. However, as with all these things, it should be down to individual readers to decide for themselves which version they prefer.

Roll Call:
Autobots: Optimus Prime, Jazz (flashback only), Prowl (flashback only), Ironhide (flashback only), Wheeljack (flashback only), Emirate Xaaron, Hot Rod, Kup, Blurr, Cloudburst, Getaway and Quickmix.

Decepticons: Starscream, Soundwave, Ravage, Shockwave, Galvatron II, Runabout, Runamuck, Scorponok, Mindwipe, Apeface, Triggerhappy, Misfire, Bomb Burst, Skullgrin, Fangry, Horri-Bull, Bludgeon, Octopunch and Thunderwing (flashback only).

Other: Unicron (in a dream/flash-forward), Hook, Line and Sinker.

Nebulans: Gort, Recoil, Zarak, Vorath, Spasma and Kreb. Of the Nebulans, only Zarak and Recoil appear in their humanoid modes; the remainder are only seen as the heads of their respective partners.

Review:
Another great story in what's fast becoming the best ever run of strips in the American comic. Each of the plot elements is engrossing in its own right: Shockwave planning a coup on Earth; Galvatron causing mayhem on Cybertron; and – the real meat of the story – Optimus Prime's surrender.

The focus is firmly on the two leaders, Prime and Scorponok, as they wrestle with discontent within their own ranks in the aftermath of the Autobot surrender. Is Optimus Prime betraying his principles by capitulating so meekly? Does joining forces with the Autobots go against everything Scorponok stands for? This is high drama indeed. 5/5

[72] ... ALL THIS AND CIVIL WAR 2
US#72, 'November 1990' (published September 1990), 20 pages.

British reprint: UK#313, 27 April 1991 (Part 1), 10 pages; UK#314, 11 May 1991 (Part 2), 10 pages.

Credits:
Simon Furman (script); Andrew Wildman (pencils); Stephen Baskerville (inks); Nel Yomtov (colours); Rick Parker (letters); Rob Tokar (editor); Tom DeFalco (editor-in-chief); Andrew Wildman (cover). **UK:** Stewart 'Staz' Johnson and Robin Bouttell (cover, UK#313); Andrew Wildman and Robin Bouttell (cover, UK#314 – adapted from US cover).

Plot:
Scorponok's base may have been destroyed, but many of the Autobots and Decepticons have survived in the underground tunnels. Scorponok himself is the first to emerge, and he immediately enters into a vicious hand-to-claw fight with his would-be usurper, Shockwave. The battle is fierce, and spreads from New Jersey across the Hudson River and into New York City.

Meanwhile, back on Cybertron, Galvatron confronts and interrogates the Autobot resistance leader Xaaron. With the Matrix lost, Xaaron confirms that the only way to fight Unicron is if the Autobots and Decepticons can somehow put aside their hostilities and unite as a single race.

On Earth, the remainder of the Autobots and Decepticons emerge from the rubble. While the bulk of the robots remain in New Jersey, Optimus Prime heads to New York City to stop the Scorponok/Shockwave fight and prevent any humans from being caught in the crossfire. As Prime confronts the two Decepticons, G B Blackrock's mutant task-force, the Neo-Knights, arrive on the scene …

Notes:

Set in and around the opposite banks of the Hudson River, this story features many local landmarks, including Liberty Island (see also [23] 'Decepticon Graffiti'), Ellis Island, the Verrazano-Narrows Bridge (opened in 1964) and Battery Park. The site of the Decepticons' (former) base in New Jersey is said to be 'four miles' from New York City.

Also appearing in this story is the US President, un-named in the text but drawn to resemble the then-current incumbent of that post, George H W Bush. His dialogue contains a couple of notable Bush catchphrases: 'read my lips' is from an infamous speech made during his Presidential campaign in August 1988, in which he promised 'no new taxes', only to renege on that vow when he got into power. 'It just wouldn't be prudent at this juncture' is not technically a George Bush quotation, but instead stems from a series of Bush impersonations by comedian Dana Carvey in episodes of *Saturday Night Live*.

A startled onlooker sees the explosion of the Decepticon base and questions if the blast is has been caused by 'the Iraqis', a topical reference to the Gulf War, which began the month before this issue went to press.

There are many references to previous issues: Starscream recalls being recruited by Shockwave in [68] 'The Human Factor', a story that also saw the introduction of Blackrock's team of Neo-Knights (named here for the first time). There is a flashback to the Autobot capitulation in [71] 'Surrender', and also a reference to the events of [59] 'Skin Deep' – Scorponok regrets sparing Starscream's life in that issue.

We also get another look at events on Hydrus Four: Grimlock has successfully resurrected his Dinobots, but the side-effects of the Nucleon (see [70] 'The Price of Life') are beginning to show – at one stage here, Grimlock's leg briefly seizes up.

The title of this story is a reference to the notorious box-office flop *All This and World War II* (Susan Winslow, 1976).

UK Notes:

The tagline for UK#313 reads 'Bomb the base!', a reference to the British dance/electronica act Bomb the Bass.

UK Changes:

Page 1, panel 1: credits replaced

Page 3, panel 1: the reference to issue #68 is changed to #305.

Pages 10-15: to make for a better cliffhanger, in the UK printing the pages were reordered: the two-page Cybertron scene that comprised the original pages 10 and 11 was deferred and placed instead after the original page 15.

Page 12, panel 1: to facilitate the reordering of pages, the caption '– when he knows no-one's out there to give it!' is changed to simply 'Hydrus Four …'

Roll Call:
Autobots: Optimus Prime, Grimlock, Snarl, Slag, Sludge, Swoop, Emirate Xaaron, Hot Rod, Kup, Highbrow and Nightbeat.

Decepticons: Starscream, Soundwave, Ravage, Shockwave, Galvatron II, Runabout, Runamuck, Scorponok, Mindwipe, Weirdwolf, Triggerhappy, Misfire, Skullgrin, Fangry, Horri-Bull, Bludgeon and Octopunch.

Other: Circuit Breaker, Thunderpunch, Rapture and Dynamo.

Nebulans: Gort, Zarak, Vorath, Monzo, Muzzle. Other than Zarak, all Nebulans appear in their head modes only.

Review:
After a heavy (but delicious) feast of dramatic, plot-laden issues, along comes '... All This and Civil War 2' to cleanse the palate. Lighter and breezier than many recent instalments, this sees the comic in full-on 'mindless action movie' mode.

On the negative side, this means that the strip doesn't feel as fresh or innovative as it has done in recent months – it quickly falls into standard 'comic fight' mode, as characters trade verbal barbs as well as blows: 'You can do nothing, traitors ... except die!' 'There is but one sentence – death!'

Fortunately, however, the sheer visceral thrill of this story outweighs its more clichéd elements. Andrew Wildman's dynamic and punchy pencils make it a joy to look at, and the overall feeling is that, even if it isn't a masterpiece, it's still a whole lot of fun. 4/5

[73] OUT OF TIME!
US#73, 'December 1990' (published October 1990), 20 pages.

British reprint: UK#315, 25 May 1991 (Part 1), 10 pages; UK#316, 8 June 1991 (Part 2), 10 pages.

Credits:
Simon Furman (script); Andrew Wildman (pencils); Stephen Baskerville (inks); Nel Yomtov (colours); Rick Parker (letters); Rob Tokar (editor); Tom DeFalco (editor-in-chief); Andrew Wildman (cover). **UK:** Andrew Wildman (covers, UK#315 & 316 – the latter of which is adapted from his US cover).

Plot:
At the centre of Cybertron, Galvatron and Xaaron enter the Primus chamber, hoping to revive the Transformers' creator. Unicron suspects Galvatron's treachery, so sends Hook, Line and Sinker to the planet's core in an attempt to find the errant Decepticon. Galvatron, as eager as anyone to destroy Unicron, easily dispatches the three heralds.

Back on Earth, the Neo-Knights attack the Transformers with abandon; both Scorponok and Optimus Prime feel the force of Circuit Breaker's electrical blasts. Circuit Breaker then vents her ire upon Shockwave, the Decepticon who nearly killed her over five years ago. Circuit Breaker uses up all her power on a massive energy discharge that sends the Decepticon reeling.

Back on Cybertron, Xaaron manages to awaken Primus – indeed, Primus takes possession of Xaaron's body in order to communicate with Galvatron. Galvatron asks Primus to unite the Transformer race for a final stand against Unicron – and at that moment, all the Transformers on Earth suddenly vanish into thin air. The helicopter carrying Blackrock and the Neo-Knights is unlucky enough to be in physical contact with Nightbeat just as the Autobot dematerialises, so that it also disappears.

Meanwhile, out in space, Thunderwing's body has come to rest on a planet. The Matrix rises from his corpse, hungry for revenge …

Notes:
This story sees the deaths of Hook, Line, Sinker and most notably Emirate Xaaron. (Although his body will survive until [75] 'On the Edge of Extinction', his personality is replaced by that of Primus here.) Other than his initial scream (in [61] 'The Primal Scream'), this is the first time that Primus is seen to talk.

On his long voyage to Cybertron, Unicron passes the planet Jhi, the dog-like inhabitants of which know of him. Their lineage can be traced 'back beyond the swarm', and in their native language, the word 'ke' means 'fate'.

There are references to Galvatron II's abduction by Hook, Line and Sinker in [67] 'Rhythms of Darkness', and to Shockwave's attack on the offshore oil rig in [6] 'The Worse of Two Evils', in which Josie Beller/Circuit Breaker was critically injured.

UK Changes:
Page 1, panel 1: credits replaced.
Page 2, panel 4: the reference to issue 67 is changed to 301.

Roll Call:
Autobots: Optimus Prime, Emirate Xaaron, Kup, Highbrow, Sureshot, Waverider, Landfill, Quickmix and Nightbeat.

Decepticons: Starscream, Soundwave, Shockwave, Galvatron II, Runamuck, Scorponok, Mindwipe, Weirdwolf, Triggerhappy and Thunderwing (as a corpse).

Other: G B Blackrock, Circuit Breaker, Primus, Hook, Line, Sinker, Thunderpunch, Rapture and Dynamo.

Nebulans: Gort, Zarak, Vorath, Monzo and Muzzle. All Nebulans appear only as the heads of their respective partners.

Review:
The weakest US issue for some considerable time, sabotaged by the infuriating Circuit Breaker, a character who has shown zero development or progression over the years. She's still doing exactly the same thing she's been doing since [9] 'Dis-Integrated Circuits' – zapping Autobots and Decepticons alike, hindering the Transformers … and the plot.

On the plus side, the scenes on Cybertron are great. Galvatron shows why he's the perfect villain – he is devious, intelligent and powerful, and his battle with Unicron's heralds is brilliantly done. Unfortunately, his scenes aren't enough to compensate for the deficiencies of the remainder of the story. 2/5.

Bullpen Bulletins

'Bullpen Bulletins' was a monthly editorial page syndicated throughout all of Marvel's core titles in America, full of Marvel-related news and gossip, a comics checklist, and sometimes a profile dedicated to a particular Marvel staffer. For a short run (US#58-66), this was temporarily replaced in *The Transformers* by 'Star Signals', a similar sort of thing but intended for the younger readers of Marvel's Star Comics imprint. Editions pertinent to *The Transformers* include:

US#17: It's revealed that *The Transformers'* main writer Bob Budiansky has recently moved to New Jersey (a state heavily featured in subsequent issues; it's the location of both RAAT's headquarters and Scorponok's base). Also, it's alleged that Bill Sienkewicz (cover art, US#1 & 65) uses a sun lamp to top up his tan, and that future editor-in-chief Tom DeFalco enjoys seal clubbing (a joke – hopefully). Meanwhile, entertainment at the Marvel Christmas Party was provided by a band called the K-Otics, whose members included regular *The Transformers* colourist Nel Yomtov on harmonica and occasional cover artist Mark Bright on bass. Other musicians on staff include Jim Owsley (former editor) and Don Daley (future editor), both drummers.

US#30/HDM#1: A look at the Marvel editorial staff. As well as writing *The Transformers*, Bob Budiansky is also the editor of *Psi-Force*, plus movie adaptations and special projects. There are also mentions of Ralph Macchio, Don Daley, Michael Higgins, Jim Salicrup, Tom DeFalco and Jim Shooter, all of whom have *The Transformers* credits to their name.

US#32/HDM#2: An announcement that Don Perlin has been promoted to the role of staff Art Director at Marvel; consequently, the upcoming [35] 'Child's Play' (comic) will prove to be his final issue as the regular penciller on *The Transformers*.

US#34/HDM#3: Confirmation that Marvel's Editor-in-Chief Jim Shooter has 'stepped down' (a euphemism; he was fired). His replacement is Tom DeFalco.

US#37: A Q&A with writer Bob Budiansky. The single work of which he's most proud is the cover of *Ghost Rider* #35, and one of his favourite performers is Bruce Springsteen (see [14] 'Rock and Roll-Out').

US#40: A Q&A with contributor Michael Higgins. He loves the Grateful Dead, Brooklyn, and van Gogh.

US#41: Another *The Transformers*-related Q&A, this time featuring Jim Salicrup. He takes early-morning aerobics, listens to Alice Cooper and would like Jerry Lewis to play him if there was ever a movie made about his life.

[74] THE VOID!

US#74, 'January 1991' (published November 1990), 20 pages.

British reprint: UK#317, 22 June 1991 (Part 1), 11 pages; UK#318, 6 July 1991 (Part 2), 10 pages.

The page count of the UK printing was increased by extending the first page (basically, an empty white void) into a double-page splash, encroaching onto the usual 'Transformation' editorial page. If the title 'The Void' seems familiar, that's because it was previously used for a UK-only story (part 1 of [59.3] 'Shadow of Evil').

Credits:
Simon Furman (script); Andrew Wildman (pencils); Stephen Baskerville (inks); Nel Yomtov (colours); Rick Parker (letters); Rob Tokar (editor); Tom DeFalco (editor-in-chief); Andrew Wildman (cover). **UK:** Andrew Wildman (cover, UK#317); Andrew Wildman and Robin Bouttell (cover, UK#318 – a re-coloured version of the American cover).

Due to the lack of a standard editorial page in UK#317, Andrew Wildman's cover credit for that comic was listed in the 'Next issue' preview, rather than on the 'Transformation' page as was the norm.

Plot:
With the Earthbound Transformers now transported to Cybertron, Primus urges the robots to put aside their differences and unite as one race to defeat the rapidly-approaching Unicron. Blackrock and the Neo-Knights have also been transported to the planet, and upon seeing an entire planet full of Transformers, the robophobic Circuit Breaker suffers a mental breakdown.

The Transformers' preparations are interrupted by a legion of brainwashed Cybertronians: Unicron cultists who set out to kill Optimus Prime. Primus is encouraged by the fact that the Autobots and Decepticons join forces to defeat the cult, although Optimus Prime is disappointed by the manipulative and callous personality of the Transformers' creator.

Meanwhile, the revived Dinobots return to Earth to find the *Ark* deserted; they pump Nucleon into the ship's medical stasis pods, hoping to revive all the fallen Autobots interred there – however they don't realise that Megatron's body also lies within one of the pods. Elsewhere, the Matrix restores Thunderwing to full health and plots a course to Cybertron, swearing revenge on all Transformers.

Back on the Transformers' home world, the Autobots and Decepticons look on in horror as Unicron – now in his planet-sized robot mode – appears in the skies and prepares to strike …

Notes:
The Transformers' origin story is retold here from Primus's point of view (having been previously related by the Keeper in [61] 'The Primal Scream'). We learn that, when Cybertron was young, Unicron affected the minds of a group of Transformers, making them his unwilling sleeper agents. As Unicron approaches the planet, his mental link with these agents is reactivated, and they form a 'Unicron cult', whose sole intention is to kill Primus's chosen leader – in this case, Optimus Prime.

The fact that G B Blackrock and the Neo-Knights are able to survive on Cybertron indicates that the planet's conditions (gravity, pressure, atmosphere) are close to those on Earth. (It's probable that Primus foresaw that the Neo-Knights would have a part to play in Unicron's destruction, and so created Cybertron's atmosphere to suit.)

When Grimlock finds that the *Ark* is empty, the editorial captions compare it to the *Mary Celeste*, the infamous merchant sailboat found mysteriously abandoned in 1872. The Dinobots douse with Nucleon a number of fallen Transformers, including Prowl, Wheeljack, Ratchet and Megatron. Grimlock is still feeling side-effects of the treatment, as he did in [72] 'All This and Civil War 2'. Here, his hand freezes for a few moments. The Dinobots can detect only a single Transformer life sign on Earth, although oddly it's split into two parts (apparently a reference to Spike Witwicky and his control helmet).

Optimus Prime is still suffering from intermittent stomach pains, as previously established in [69] 'Eye of the Storm'. This story sees the first appearances of Quake and Battletrap in the American strips (although Battletrap had previously featured in the *Headmasters* mini-series).

UK Notes:

The Transformers' origin story originally appeared in [36.2] 'The Legacy of Unicron'. Quake made his debut in the UK story [52.1] 'The Fall and Rise of the Decepticon Empire'.

UK Changes:

Page 1, panel 1: credits replaced. One of the speech bubbles has been painted out and moved across to the facing page, turning what was a single page in the original printing into a two-page spread.

Roll Call:

Autobots: Optimus Prime, Grimlock, Snarl, Slag, Sludge, Swoop, Emirate Xaaron (body only; as a receptacle for the Primus avatar), Hot Rod, Kup, Highbrow, Sureshot, Cloudburst, Waverider, Getaway, Backstreet, Landfill, Quickmix, Nightbeat, Siren, Hosehead and Fixit.

Decepticons: Starscream, Soundwave, Ravage, Shockwave, Galvatron II, Runabout, Runamuck, Scorponok, Skullcruncher, Mindwipe, Weirdwolf, Apeface, Triggerhappy, Battletrap, Bomb Burst, Darkwing, Dreadwind, Fangry, Horri-Bull, Squeezeplay, Crankcase, Quake, Stranglehold, Bludgeon, Octopunch and Thunderwing.

Other: G B Blackrock, Circuit Breaker, Unicron, Primus, Thunderpunch, Rapture and Dynamo.

Nebulans: Gort, Zarak, Grax, Vorath, Spasma, Kreb, Muzzle, Quig and Lug. (All Nebulans appear only as the heads of their respective partners.)

Review:

This is basically an issue of build-up, ratcheting up the tension and generally setting things in motion in preparation for the giant-sized issue #75 that follows. Surprisingly, then, this is a masterpiece in its own right – the perfect blend of action (the fight with the cultists) and character work (the excellent writing of Optimus Prime and Scorponok). Add in the battling gods, talk of manifest destinies and cosmic games of chess, and the end result is a truly marvellous piece of work. 5/5

Next Issue, Part 3

A list of all the 'next issue' teasers printed in issues #61-80 of the US comic, plus the associated spin-offs:

US#61: The only thing that can save them is the thing they haven't got – the Matrix quest begins!

US#62: The Matrix Quest continues as Backstreet, Override and Dogfight become Kings of the Wild Frontier!

US#63: Continuing the search for the Matrix, Doubleheader, Longtooth and Pincher voyage to an oceanic world and find themselves pitted against the last of the techno-organic whales, but what started as a quest soon becomes a Deadly Obsession! In thirty days!

US#64: Bumblebee! Jazz! Grimlock! Thunderwing's Decepticons! In an all-out war with the Dark Creation – in 30 days!

US#65: The Matrix Quest is finished – and so are the Autobots! The battle won't stop until All Fall Down!

US#66: Don't be too sure, Optimus, because the future holds … [image of Galvatron's head in silhouette].

US#67: Circuit Breaker! G B Blackrock! Starscream! There's a new side in the Autobot/Decepticon war: the Human Factor!

US#68: More shocks! More 'returns'! More out-and-out action! More thrills! And more stupid exclamations! 'The Eye of the Storm!' in 30 days.

US#69: Don't you dare miss next issue: The Price of Life!

US#70: The issue you thought you'd never see (heck, we didn't think we'd see it either, and we produced it): Surrender!

US#71: The wrath of Galvatron! The return of the Dinobots! The coming of Unicron! All this … and civil war 2!

US#72: Unicron's on the last leg of his journey to Cybertron, and that means that just about everyone is out of time!

US#73: All are one – but is one enough? The united Transformers prepare to attack on Unicron's arrival at Cybertron, only to find that Unicron has prepared an attack for their arrival as well! 'The Void' in 30 days!

US#74: The United Transformers fight for their very existence the awesome and unstoppable Unicron! [sic] Who will live? Who will … not live? Don't miss this double-sized slugfest of cosmic proportions as the Transformers find themselves On The Edge of Extinction!

US#75: A holiday? A chance to put your feet up? Nah! Even more: action, thrills, shocks and intrigue!

US#76: What is happening to Hi-Q? Sure, he finally has more hair, but is the price of his new 'do' his sanity? What is happening to the Ark? Will it actually be used as a tool for the invasion of a Neo-Knightless Earth? What is happening to Cybertron? The decreasingly-united Transformers find out what's making their home shake, rattle and roll, beginning their Exodus!

US#77: To be continued next issue! (But you knew that, didn't you?)

US#78: The Last Autobot!

US#79: All good things …

US#80: Next issue: whoops – force of habit. Sorry.

MOV#1: Continued next issue: Judgment Day!
MOV#2: The startling conclusion as the Autobots engage in final battle with the evil Decepticons … and the greatest menace of all – Unicron!
MOV#3: The end.

GIJ#1: An all-out air battle for control of Power Station Alpha and the beginning of an unholy alliance! Don't miss Power Struggle! On sale in thirty days!
GIJ#2: Ring of fire!
GIJ#3: All Fall Down!
GIJ#4: Finis

HDM#1: The Decepticons arrive … and the Headmasters are born!
HDM#2: The Decepticons strike back!
HDM#3: The climactic, cataclysmic conclusion of *Headmasters*!
HDM#4: Follow the saga of the Headmasters as it continues in *Transformers* #38

[75] ON THE EDGE OF EXTINCTION!
US#75, 'February 1991' (published December 1990), 36 pages.

British reprint: UK#319, 20 July 1991 (Part 1), 9 pages; UK#320, 3 August 1991 (Part 2), 9 pages; UK#321, 17 August 1991 (Part 3), 9 pages; UK#322, 31 August 1991 (Part 4), 9 pages.

Credits:
Simon Furman (script); Geoff Senior (art); Nel Yomtov (colours); Rick Parker (letters); Rob Tokar (editor); Tom DeFalco (editor-in-chief); Geoff Senior (cover).
UK: Geoff Senior and Robin Bouttell (cover, UK#319 – re-coloured version of US cover); Stewart 'Staz' Johnson (covers, UK#320-322).

Stewart Johnson's cover art for UK#322 was uncredited.

Plot:
Unicron begins attacking Cybertron, and the Transformers seem powerless to stop him. Primus, still inhabiting the body of Emirate Xaaron, confronts the chaos-bringer but is destroyed. Galvatron has a turn at shooting Unicron, but his blast proves ineffective. Inspired by Galvatron's defiance, Optimus Prime and Scorponok lead the Transformers into an all-out attack on Unicron – but even their combined efforts appear fruitless. Scorponok and many others are brutally slain while attempting to fight against the planet-sized behemoth. Grimlock arrives in the *Ark* with an army of previously-deactivated Autobots, now healed thanks to the restorative powers of Nucleon.

Suddenly, Thunderwing appears, wielding the tainted Matrix. The Matrix wants revenge on the Transformers and considers Unicron as an obstacle in its path. However, it is effective against Unicron only in its original, pure state – with the Transformers' sacred lifeforce corrupted and weakened, Unicron withstands the attack, and Thunderwing is destroyed.

However, Optimus Prime retrieves the Matrix, and by sheer strength of will is able to cleanse it of its evil taint. While Circuit Breaker distracts Unicron with an electrical blast, Prime flies into the mouth of the beast. The Matrix energy is now strong enough to defeat Unicron, and the chaos-bringer explodes, with Prime still inside.

Notes:

This bumper-sized issue was the culmination of the sixteen-month-long story arc that began in [60] 'Yesterday's Heroes'. Many Transformers are killed here, and – perhaps more importantly – so are their two gods, Primus and Unicron.

With the Transformers failing to destroy Unicron, it's Primus himself – or his essence within the Matrix – that finally succeeds. In facilitating all this, Optimus Prime finally realises the purpose of the Transformer race: 'I thought you created us to die, Primus – to perish in your place. But now I understand. You created us to carry on after you are gone! You must die, Primus – so that all might live!'

This story sees the return of many previously-deactivated Autobots, revived by Nucleon. Barring flashbacks and dream sequences, these characters hadn't been seen alive in the US comic since [41] 'Totaled' (in the case of Skids, Ironhide, Sunstreaker and Wheeljack) or [50] 'Dark Star' (in the case of Silverbolt and Blaster).

Transformers (and Nebulans) killed here include Brainstorm and Arcana (skewered on Unicron's fingernail and then eaten), Emirate Xaaron (killed by Unicron's eye lasers), Cloudburst (destroyed by Unicron's pink mist breath), Highbrow and Gort (crushed by Unicron's hands), Finback and Misfire (killed when a gun turret overloads), Hardhead, Duros and Bomb Burst (stepped on by Unicron), Waverider, Joyride and Hotwire (zapped by Unicron's eye lasers), Scorponok (destroyed by Unicron's heat breath), Thunderwing, Mindwipe and Vorath (caught in the blast when Unicron destroys the Matrix-creature) and finally Runabout (eaten by the Demons). Many more are presumably killed off-panel.

The pink mist that kills Cloudburst was previously seen in [MOV1] 'The Planet-Eater', part of the comic adaptation of *The Transformers: The Movie* (but not seen within the movie itself).

Optimus Prime is still suffering from the abdominal pains that have plagued him since [69] 'Eye of the Storm'; he leaves his Nebulan companion Hi-Q safe on Cybertron before he himself is destroyed with Unicron. This is Hi-Q's first appearance in the comic since [54] 'King Con'.

UK Notes:

With the exception of Blaster, all of the other Nucleon-cured Autobots in this story had featured prominently in the 'Earthforce saga' (i.e. the run of UK-only stories between [60.1] 'Perchance to Dream' and [64.1] 'Inside Story'). Presumably this was writer Simon Furman's attempt at bridging the gap between the UK and the US continuity – however, as we saw in the notes to [61.1] 'Starting Over', this only complicated matters even further.

UK Changes:

Page 1, panel 1: credits replaced.
Page 28, panel 1: to make for a better cliffhanger reprise, the caption '- with the Decepticon Thunderwing at its dark heart' is painted out.
Page 30, panel 3: the reference to issue #66 is changed to #296.

Roll Call:

Autobots: Optimus Prime, Jazz, Prowl, Ironhide, Sunstreaker, Wheeljack, Grimlock, Snarl, Slag, Sludge, Swoop, Skids, Silverbolt, Blaster, Hot Rod, Kup, Highbrow, Chromedome, Hardhead, Brainstorm, Sureshot, Cloudburst, Waverider, Joyride, Getaway, Nightbeat and Siren.

Decepticons: Starscream, Ravage, Shockwave, Galvatron II, Runabout, Scorponok, Skullcruncher, Mindwipe, Weirdwolf, Apeface, Misfire, Battletrap, Bomb Burst, Iguanus, Finback, Darkwing, Dreadwind, Fangry, Squeezeplay, Quake, Stranglehold, Bludgeon, Octopunch and Thunderwing.

Other: G B Blackrock, Circuit Breaker, Unicron, Primus, Demons, Thunderpunch, Rapture and Dynamo.

Nebulans: Duros, Arcana, Zarak, Grax, Vorath, Monzo, Spasma, Hi-Q, Lokos, Muzzle and Quig. Only Hi-Q is shown in his individual humanoid mode – the others only appear as the heads of their respective partners.

Review:

Originally intended to be the grand finale of *The Transformers* comic, until a further five issues were hastily commissioned, this would have seen the series go out with a triumphant bang, a synergy of script and art that still impresses today.

As with [20.2] 'Target: 2006' before it, it's almost a shame that this appeared in a toy tie-in comic, because it has a quality and substance worthy of more acclaimed titles. Like [50] 'Dark Star', this is an exercise in action and carnage, with many Transformers being killed off. Unlike 'Dark Star', however, it also has a lot of heart – underpinning all the action is an emotional centre that makes it a cut above.

The Decepticon leader Scorponok, so villainous when he made his debut in the *Headmasters* series, has slowly morphed into a noble, intelligent warrior, and his death here – in the mourning arms of Optimus Prime – shows how far the character has come.

The art by Geoff Senior is, once again, truly outstanding. Every frame has meaning, and it would be quite possible to follow the story without looking at the dialogue, such is the power of the imagery. It's a testament to Senior's skills that we see all the emotions running through Optimus Prime's head – sadness, shock, determination – even though most of his face is covered by his trademark faceplate. That the artist can convey so much emotion – using just body-language and the look in Prime's eyes – is perhaps more astonishing than his drawings of a planet-sized robot laying waste to Cybertron. 5/5

[76] STILL LIFE!

US#76, 'March 1991' (published January 1991), 20 pages.

British reprint: UK#323, 14 September 1991 (Part 1), 10 pages; UK#324, 28 September 1991 (Part 2), 10 pages.

Credits:

Simon Furman (script); Andrew Wildman (pencils); Stephen Baskerville (inks); Nel

Yomtov (colours); Rick Parker (letters); Rob Tokar (editor); Tom DeFalco (editor-in-chief); Andrew Wildman (cover). **UK:** Andrew Wildman (cover, UK#323); Andrew Wildman and Robin Bouttell (cover, UK#324 – adapted from US cover).

Plot:
In the aftermath of Unicron's attack on Cybertron, many Transformers lie dead or dying. They include Optimus Prime, whose remains temporarily cling to life, thanks to residual Matrix energy. Before passing away, he nominates Grimlock as his successor.

Meanwhile, Shockwave and Starscream are repairing the *Ark*. With all the Transformers now on Cybertron, they plan to conquer the Earth unopposed. Their scheming is overheard by Galvatron, who is watching nearby.

It transpires that Unicron's attack has disturbed a race of creatures who live beneath the surface of Cybertron. These 'Demons' are rising up and attacking the surviving Transformers. The Dinobots find Hi-Q amongst the ruins but are set upon by a horde of Demons. Grimlock, still suffering from the side-effects of Nucleon, is frozen in place, helpless to intervene as his Dinobots near defeat. However, Hi-Q realises that the statuesque Grimlock has gone into a 'chrysalis stage'. Using his Powermaster abilities, Hi-Q accelerates Grimlock's metamorphosis, changing him into an Action Master – more powerful than ever before, but unable to transform. Grimlock defeats the Demons with ease.

Hi-Q then makes a stunning announcement: 'I *am* Optimus Prime!'

Notes:
The cliffhanger ending to this story gives us the revelation that Hi-Q is now Optimus Prime. He calls it 'the change' and a 'metamorphosis', and it is somehow linked to the abdominal pains that Optimus Prime has been feeling since [69] 'Eye of the Storm'.

There are many references to the previous issue's battle, such as shots of dead Transformers littering the Cybertronian landscape, confirmation that the *Ark* has been damaged, and a flashback to Unicron's destruction. There is also a flashback to the events of [70] 'The Pri¢e of Life', showing Grimlock testing the Nucleon on himself.

Action Master Grimlock isn't the only such Transformer making his debut here – two other Action Masters, Rad and Krok, appear – although in story terms they haven't been exposed to Nucleon and so are not technically Action Masters, even though their action figure counterparts were sold as such.

There are two movie references in the dialogue. After using his flame breath on one of the demons, Slag exclaims 'frying tonight!', a quote from *Carry On Screaming!* (Gerald Thomas, 1966). (Writer Simon Furman must be a fan, as the same line was spoken by Wreck-Gar in [44.1] 'Space Pirates'.) Swoop's 'Let's make like shepherds' joke was popularised by the film *Lethal Weapon* (Richard Donner, 1987), the punchline being 'Get the flock out of here.'

Grimlock speculates that the reason why the Transformer race is split into two factions is purely down to 'genetics', a concept later expanded upon in *Transformers: Regeneration One*, a comic launched in 2012 that acted as a sequel to the original Marvel comics.

Amongst the dead Transformers are Apeface, Sureshot, Hosehead and

Runamuck, confirming that they were also killed (off-panel) during the battle with Unicron.

UK Notes:
The Demons had already been featured in the UK comic, in the story [57.2] 'Demons'.

UK Changes:
Page 1, panel 1: credits replaced.

American Comic Sales Data

So long as their titles were distributed by the US Postal Service, Marvel were legally-bound to print sales data for each of their titles, periodically and within the comics themselves (pursuant to title 39, part IV, chapter 36, subchapter 3685 of the US Code). This sales data was quite detailed, with breakdowns of over-counter sales, subscriptions and number of copies unsold. Such breakdowns appeared in issues #27, #39, #60, #66 and #76, and are reproduced below:

Date of filing [1]	6 October 1986	October 1987 [2]	1 October 1988	1 November 1989	1 October 1990
A: Sales (over counter)	287,440	200,425	138,075	89,730	65,450
B: Sales (mail subscriptions)	13,542	16,850	11,900	6,650	4,383
C: Total sales (A+B)	300,982	217,275	149,975	96,380	69,833
D: Samples /complimentary copies	525	132	132	150	100
E: Total distribution (C+D)	301,507	217,407	150,107	96,530	69,933
F: Copies returned unsold	201,747	224,945	200,525	115,365	76,626
G: Other copies undistributed	2,689	3,960	975	600	600
H: Total unsold/ undistributed (F+G)	204,436	228,905	201,500	115,965	77,226
I: Sum of copies printed (E+H)	505,983	446,312	351,607	212,495	147,159

[1] Basically, a 'year ending' date – figures are averages for the twelve month period immediately prior to the date of filing.

[2] Due to a typo, the date of filing wasn't listed with this set of figures; presumably the date would have been some time in October 1987 in line with the data surrounding it.

We can see that the comic was cancelled after losing roughly 77% of its circulation between 1986 and 1990. Roughly half of all copies printed were returned unsold to be pulped; mail subscribers made up between 4% and 8% of total sales.

By way of comparison, in 1990 the *G.I. Joe: A Real American Hero* comic was selling roughly 150,000 copies at around the time that *The Transformers* was cancelled. These days, due to a sea-change in the comics market, a comic selling roughly 70,000 copies would be considered a good seller, certainly in the top thirty, in line with titles such as *The Walking Dead* and *The Invincible Iron Man*. According to the major US distributor, Diamond Comics, the current Transformers titles from IDW Publishing usually sell around 10,000 copies per issue (excluding overseas and digital sales).

Roll Call:
Autobots: Optimus Prime, Jazz, Prowl, Wheeljack, Grimlock, Snarl, Slag, Sludge, Swoop, Blaster, Kup, Sureshot (as a corpse), Cloudburst (as a corpse), Nightbeat, Hosehead (as a corpse) and **Rad**.

Decepticons: Starscream, Shockwave, Galvatron II, Runamuck (as a corpse), Scorponok (as a corpse), Apeface (as a corpse), Bomb Burst (as a corpse), Darkwing, Quake, Bludgeon and **Krok**.

Other: Unicron (flashback only) and the Demons.

Nebulans: Zarak, Spasma, Hi-Q and Muzzle. Hi-Q appears in his humanoid mode and Muzzle only as the head of Nightbeat. Zarak and Spasma appear as heads only, and dead ones at that, as they form part of Scorponok's and Apeface's corpses.

Review:
Not as earth-shattering as recent issues, but then it doesn't try to be. It's a study of leadership, as Grimlock is lectured first by Prowl and then by Hi-Q on what it means to be the Autobot commander. Meanwhile, Bludgeon, Shockwave and Galvatron all start scheming, hinting at the conflicts that will form the basis of the four remaining issues.

A decent character piece, then, with the Demon sub-plot added to give the story a bit of action and excitement. 3/5

[77] EXODUS!

US#77, 'April 1991' (published February 1991), 20 pages.

British reprint: UK#325, 12 October 1991 (Part 1), 10 pages; UK#326, 26 October 1991 (Part 2), 10 pages.

Credits:
Simon Furman (script); Andrew Wildman (pencils); Stephen Baskerville (inks); Nel Yomtov (colours); Rick Parker (letters); Rob Tokar (editor); Tom DeFalco (editor-in-chief); Andrew Wildman (cover). **UK:** Andrew Wildman (cover, UK#325 and 326, the latter of which is adapted from his US cover).

Andrew Wildman's cover art for UK#326 went uncredited.

Plot:
The alliance between the Autobots and Decepticons is proving fragile – although an uneasy peace exists, tensions are running high. Matters are not helped by Blaster's revelation that the planet Cybertron is tearing itself apart – partly as a result of the damage caused by Unicron and partly due to the death of its binding force, Primus. The Autobots' plan is to evacuate Cybertron and seek a new world to colonise.

Bludgeon, having assumed the Decepticon leadership, hates the idea of the truce and itches for an excuse to end it. He's nearly given that opportunity when Grimlock and Fangry come to blows, but Prowl manages to calm the situation.

The Decepticon ships take off first, and the Autobots attempt to evacuate also – only to discover that Bludgeon has betrayed them and sabotaged the remaining spacecraft; the Autobots are stranded on the doomed planet.

Meanwhile, Starscream and Shockwave ready the *Ark* for take-off, as they plot to invade the Earth. They are unaware that Galvatron has stowed away with them. As Galvatron strolls through the ship's corridors, he is confronted by Megatron, restored to life once more …

Notes:
This story features the return of Megatron, his first appearance as a separate entity since the explosion at the end of [59] 'Skin Deep'. He later returned as part of the Megatron/Ratchet hybrid creature in [69] 'Eye of the Storm', and following the events of [70] 'The Price of Life', the Autobots were able to split the creature back into its two component parts. All fallen Transformers within the Autobot stasis pods were doused with the restorative chemical Nucleon in [74] 'The Void', hence Megatron's revival here.

Interestingly, Hi-Q insists that the Transformers' planet is not dying ('about Cybertron, they're wrong'), and that he needs help to 'wake the Last Autobot'. Given that he claims to be Optimus Prime, Hi-Q's desperate pleas are dismissed by the Neo-Knights as the ravings of a madman.

The Autobot and Decepticon ships are located in the 'Ibex Quadrant' of Cybertron, which boasts an impressive spaceport. (In real life, an ibex is a type of mountain goat.)

This story sees the debut of two new Transformers released as part of the Action Master range of figures: the Autobot Rollout and the Decepticon Treadshot. There are references to the death of Primus and Unicron's attack on Cybertron from [75] 'On the Edge of Extinction'.

UK Notes:
Ibex is the second Cybertronian quadrant to get a namecheck in the comic; Tyrest was also described as such in [40.4] 'Deadly Games'. The strapline to UK#325 reads 'It's a knock-out!', a reference to the long-running British game show *It's a Knockout*, first broadcast in 1966.

UK Changes:
Page 1, panel 1: credits replaced.

Roll Call:
Autobots: Jazz, Prowl, Sunstreaker, Wheeljack, Bumblebee, Grimlock, Snarl, Silverbolt, Blaster and **Rollout**.

Decepticons: Megatron, Starscream, Soundwave, Shockwave, Galvatron II, Darkwing, Dreadwind, Fangry, Squeezeplay, Crankcase, Quake, Bludgeon, Krok and **Treadshot**.

Other: G B Blackrock, Circuit Breaker, Thunderpunch, Rapture and Dynamo.

Nebulans: Hi-Q, Brisko and Lokos. Brisko and Lokos appear only as the heads of Fangry and Squeezeplay respectively.

Review:
Other than a minor skirmish between Grimlock and Fangry there is little action here – all the tension and excitement come from the unfolding character drama. The desperate Prowl struggles to hold the alliance together, but he's resentful that Grimlock was appointed Autobot leader in his stead. Meanwhile Bludgeon and Krok conspire to break the truce, while Grimlock formulates plans of his own. This is a dense, tightly-wound script that packs a lot into its twenty pages. 4/5

[78] A SAVAGE CIRCLE
US#78, 'May 1991' (published March 1991), 20 pages.

British reprint: UK#327, 9 November 1991 (Part 1), 10 pages; UK#328, 9 November 1991 (Part 2), 10 pages.

Credits:
Simon Furman (script); Andrew Wildman (pencils); Stephen Baskerville (inks); Nel Yomtov (colours); Rick Parker (letters); Rob Tokar (editor); Tom DeFalco (editor-in-chief); Andrew Wildman (cover). **UK:** Andrew Wildman (cover, UK#327 and 328, the former of which is adapted from his US cover).

Plot:
Aboard the Earth-bound *Ark*, Galvatron II and Megatron do battle – Galvatron figures that by killing Megatron, he will 'exorcise' his past and 'break the circle'. Elsewhere in the ship, Shockwave and Starscream detect the battle and head off to investigate.

Meanwhile, on the dying Cybertron, Hi-Q manages to convince the Neo-Knights to join him on a quest to awaken the so-called 'Last Autobot'. The remainder of the Autobots try to come to terms with the fact that they are stranded on the unstable planet, but Grimlock and the Dinobots ride to the rescue – Grimlock had a secret stash of stolen Decepticon battle-cruisers hidden away in Cybertron's 'rad zone'.

Bludgeon's Decepticons, meanwhile, have their sights set on the peaceful planet Klo, which they see as ripe for invasion, and a place from which to rebuild the Decepticon Empire.

Back on the *Ark*, Ratchet emerges from a stasis pod, having been revived by the Nucleon. Realising that the ship contains Shockwave, Starscream, Megatron and Galvatron, he decides to sabotage it, just as Optimus Prime did four million years earlier. There is a massive explosion, and the *Ark* free-falls towards Earth.

Notes:
Here we get an 'origin' story for Galvatron II, and more details of the parallel future we saw in [67] 'Rhythms of Darkness'. In the 'Rhythms' version of 2005, Megatron was

'destroyed by Optimus Prime' and 'cast into space by Starscream', where Unicron found him and reformatted him into Galvatron. (This is near-identical to the origin of Galvatron I in *The Transformers: The Movie*. We know from [67] 'Rhythms of Darkness' that Cyclonus II was also created by Unicron at some point, but he and Scourge are nowhere to be seen in this flashback – perhaps in the 'Rhythms' universe their creation was a completely separate event to that of Galvatron.)

We also get more details of the Megatron/Ratchet merger that occurred in [59] 'Skin Deep' – although their bodies have been separated, their minds remain linked (as Fixit predicted in [70] 'The Pri¢e of Life'). Ratchet is now able to see whatever Megatron sees, and also reacts in pain when Megatron is struck by Galvatron II and Shockwave.

We discover that the Dinobots stole three Decepticon Battle Cruisers over four million years ago, before they embarked on the original *Ark* mission. Grimlock explains, 'We did not care much for Prime's leadership, think he a bit soft in the head.' After they were stolen, the ships were hidden in Cybertron's rad zone for safekeeping.

The Decepticons' target is the planet Klo, located in 'Quadrant Alpha, Grid Ref B-B'. It is nicknamed 'the World of Enduring Peace', and its inhabitants, the Klovians, enjoy a good level of technology and abundant natural resources.

The events of this story are definitively dated to 1991 (the year of publication).

UK Notes:
Another difference between Galvatron II and Galvatron I: we learn here that, in the 'Rhythms' parallel timeline, Galvatron II was created in the year 2005; the Galvatron I from Timeline A was created in 2006 (according to [20.2] 'Target: 2006').

The Dinobots' disdain for Optimus Prime's leadership was originally explored in [12.3] 'The Icarus Theory', in which it was established that Swoop in particular has a longstanding resentment towards the Autobot leader, dating back to their time on Cybertron together.

Galvatron II holds back from destroying Megatron because 'a chance exists, however slight, that killing him may cancel me out!' this parallels Scourge's dilemma in [44.3] 'Dry Run', when he also considers killing Megatron.

This story recalls a similar Megatron/Galvatron fight in the UK annual story [A4.2] 'Altered Image'. Both end with the two Decepticons reconciling, and both feature extensive 'cracked mirror' imagery.

The cover strapline to UK#328 reads 'Bad boys stick together!', a lyric from 'Bad Boys', a 1983 hit single by the pop group Wham!.

UK Changes:
Page 1, panel 1: credits replaced.
Page 4, panel 5: the reference to issue #70 is changed to issue #311.
Page 10, panel 6: to make for a neater cliffhanger, Grimlock's line is truncated to omit the 'And surely –'.
Page 11, panel 1: similarly, the leading hyphens of Grimlock's next line are also painted out.

Roll Call:
Autobots: Optimus Prime (flashback only), Prowl, Ironhide, Ratchet, Wheeljack, Grimlock, Inferno, Blaster and Fixit (flashback only).

Decepticons: Megatron, Starscream, Shockwave, Galvatron II, Darkwing, Stranglehold and Bludgeon.

Other: G B Blackrock, Circuit Breaker, Unicron (flashback only), Thunderpunch, Rapture and Dynamo.

Nebulans: Hi-Q.

Review:
Very much a mixed bag. There are some fantastic lines here (the bickering between Shockwave and Starscream, Grimlock's verdict on the Decepticon 'truce', Ratchet's angry tirade at Starscream), but there are also some rather iffy moments. Grimlock 'just happens' to have three Decepticon ships up his sleeve (how convenient), and the story's centrepiece, the Megatron/Galvatron fight, doesn't really excite.

Some plotting issues are perfectly understandable, as writer Simon Furman struggles to wrap everything up by the end of issue #80 – but despite a few great moments, this is ultimately a bit of a misstep overall. 2/5

The Intro Text
Many comics titles have a standard piece of blurb or 'intro text' at the top of the first page, giving an overview for new readers. The American *The Transformers* comic was no exception; here's a run-down of all such introductory paragraphs used throughout the title's run:

US#2-59: 'Four million years ago they came from Cybertron, a world composed entirely of machinery … a world torn by an age-old war between the heroic Autobots and the evil Decepticons. These incredibly powerful living robots, capable of converting themselves into land and air vehicles, weapons and other mechanical forms, continue their conflict here on Earth. They are … *the Transformers.*'

US#33 only: 'This month we take you to – *England!* Yes, in response to your overwhelming demand, we're *finally* printing some of the British issues of your favorite mag, which have never seen print stateside until now. Incidentally, you'll notice *Optimus Prime* leading the Autobots this ish since the events depicted occurred a while back, so don't sweat it! And now, without further adieu [sic], from the land that gave us the Fab Four, Dickens and Princess Di, we bring you a tale of *the Transformers.*'

US#34 only: 'Tally-ho, faithful ones! Here it is, straight from Marvel U.K., Man of Iron! Get a hold of yer wig-hat! Dear old Aunt Petunia never read anything like: *Transformers.*'

US#60-75: 'They *were* the dream – mechanical beings able to transform their bodies into vehicles, machinery and weapons; a last line of defence against the chaos bringer, Unicron! They *are* at war, heroic Autobot pitted against evil Decepticon, both on their homeworld, the metal planet called Cybertron, and here on Earth. They *are* the galaxy's last hope, they *are* – *Transformers.*'

US#76-80: '*Transformers* – one race of sentient mechanoids, ever divided into two warring factions; heroic Autobot and evil Decepticon. Able to transform their bodies into likenesses of vehicles, machinery and weapons, these proud warriors have fulfilled their destiny, battling and defeating a malignant force from beyond time! But their victory is not without cost, and the aftershocks continue to ripple ...'

[79] THE LAST AUTOBOT?
US#79, 'June 1991' (published April 1991), 20 pages.

British reprint: UK#329, 7 December 1991 (Part 1), 10 pages; UK#330, 21 December 1991 (Part 2), 10 pages.

Credits:
Simon Furman (script); Andrew Wildman (pencils); Stephen Baskerville (inks); Nel Yomtov (colours); Rick Parker (letters); Rob Tokar (editor); Tom DeFalco (editor-in-chief); Andrew Wildman (cover). **UK:** Andrew Wildman (cover, UK#329 – adapted from his US cover); Stewart 'Staz' Johnson (cover, UK#330).

Plot:
The *Ark* crash-lands in northern Canada; all aboard appear to have perished in the ship's destruction – except for Galvatron, who emerges from the wreckage madder than ever. Spike Witwicky is drawn to the scene of the crash – called by his Headmaster partner Fortress Maximus, whose body is still on board the ship. Realising that he has a responsibility to defeat the lone Decepticon, Spike bonds with Fortress Maximus once more. He and Galvatron do battle, but the combined will of Spike and Fortress Maximus proves too much for the future Decepticon, who is thrown into an icy pool, seemingly to his death.

Meanwhile, on Klo, the Decepticons have set about conquering the planet and massacring the peaceful natives. Krok discovers that the Decepticon spaceships that fled Cybertron were equipped with an Autobot tracking device – with the Autobots on their way, the scene is set for a showdown on Klo.

Back on the unstable Cybertron, Hi-Q – still claiming to be Optimus Prime – leads the Neo-Knights on a quest to find the mythical Last Autobot. Using Dynamo's special power – he is able to tap into Cybertron's energies – the group finally finds the giant robot, who looms silently before them ...

Notes:
This story sees the first appearance of Spike, Cerebros and Fortress Maximus since [51] 'The Man in the Machine'. Spike's presence on Earth was previously detected by the Dinobots in [74] 'The Void'. After the demise of Galvatron here, Fortress Maximus appoints himself Defender of Earth ('I've had worse jobs!'), thus ending the Earthbound strand of stories that began way back in [1] 'The Transformers'.

On Cybertron, it's confirmed that the Neo-Knights, G B Blackrock and Hi-Q are the only life-forms remaining on the planet, following the departure of all the Transformers in [77] 'Exodus' and [78] 'A Savage Circle' ('Cybertron ... current population – six'). (So basically, the entire Transformer race can fit on six spaceships – presumably their number was drastically reduced by the attack by Unicron in [75] 'On the Edge of Extinction'. Given that the subterranean Demons from [76] 'Still Life' are obviously not included in this figure, we can assume they perished in the various earthquakes and tremors that wrack the planet.)

The Last Autobot is a large blue- and copper-coloured robot whose face resembles the Autobot insignia. Although not seen here, according to dialogue within the story, Sparkstalker is killed off-panel.

Roll Call:
Autobots: Prowl, Silverbolt, Fortress Maximus, Cerebros, Nightbeat and the **Last Autobot**.

Decepticons: Megatron (in flashback, also as a corpse), Galvatron II, Snapdragon, Battletrap, Darkwing, Dreadwind, Fangry, Horri-Bull, Squeezeplay, Crankcase, Quake, Stranglehold, Bludgeon, Octopunch and Krok. Darkwing and Dreadwind appear only in their 'Dreadwing' combined jet mode.

Other: G B Blackrock, Circuit Breaker, Spike, Thunderpunch, Rapture and Dynamo.

Nebulans: Hi-Q and Muzzle. Muzzle appears only as the head of Nightbeat.

Review:
As the penultimate story, this has to do an awful lot – tie up things on Earth, set up the final Autobot/Decepticon battle on Klo, and introduce the Last Autobot – to get things in place for the finale. Unfortunately, however, it spends most of its page-count focusing on Spike and Fortress Maximus. While the fight with Galvatron is good enough, the emotional throughline – Spike and Fortress Maximus must work together to succeed – is one we've seen before, both in the American comics ([61] 'The Man in the Machine') and in Britain ([31.1] 'Worlds Apart' and [A4.4] 'All in the Minds). With such little time left, it just seems a waste to spend so long on such tired material. 2/5.

[80] END OF THE ROAD!
US#80, 'June 1991' (published May 1991), 22 pages.

British reprint: UK#331, 4 January 1992 (Part One), 12 pages; UK#332, 18 January 1992 (Part Two), 10 pages.

Credits:
Simon Furman (script); Andrew Wildman (pencils); Stephen Baskerville (inks); Nel Yomtov (colours); Rick Parker (letters); Rob Tokar (editor); Tom DeFalco (editor-in-chief); Andrew Wildman (cover). **UK:** Andrew Wildman (cover, UK#331 and #332).

Andrew Wildman's covers were uncredited in both of these UK issues. That for UK#331 is adapted from an interior splash page, and that for UK#332 is a slightly altered version of the American one.

Plot:
The Autobots arrive on the planet Klo and are instantly set upon by the Decepticons, who lie in wait for them. Most of the Autobots are slaughtered, while a few survivors, including Grimlock and Prowl, hide and regroup.

Unfortunately, Grimlock's remaining Autobots are unable to stay undetected for long, and are confronted by a Decepticon patrol – it seems as though the Decepticons have finally won the Transformer War.

At that moment, the Neo-Knights arrive aboard a ship, and begin attacking the Decepticons. Also aboard is a resurrected Optimus Prime; the 'ship' is actually the Last Autobot, who reverts back to his robot mode. The Last Autobot explains that the Powermaster process fused Hi-Q and Optimus Prime in ways they could not have imagined – Prime's soul lived on within Hi-Q, so the Last Autobot converted the diminutive Nebulan into a new, powerful Optimus Prime.

The Last Autobot explains that he was built by Primus to watch over the Transformers after the death of their creator. Having slumbered for millions of years, he now heralds a new chapter in Transformers history.

As Prime and the Neo-Knights attack the Decepticons, the Last Autobot re-animates the fallen Autobots and they also join the battle. Finally defeated and dishonoured, Bludgeon leads the Decepticons into a self-imposed exile.

Optimus Prime reveals that Cybertron was not destroying itself, but rather regenerating, reborn as a new planet. After returning the Neo-Knights to Earth, the Autobots can finally go home and live in peace.

Notes:
The final Marvel 'Generation 1' Transformers comic.

The front cover bears the line '#80 in a four-issue limited series', a triumphant celebration of the fact that what had been initially conceived as a four-part toy tie-in had eventually lasted for seven years.

Many of the loose ends are tied up – the Decepticon invasion of Klo (conceived in [78] 'A Savage Circle') is halted, and the Decepticon leader Bludgeon, his actions tightly bound to a quasi-religious code of honour, takes the Decepticons into exile as a result. Cybertron, which has been ostensibly tearing itself apart since [77] 'Exodus', is revealed actually to have been renewing itself, meaning the Autobots are able to return to a completely restored version of their homeworld. (One wonders if the planet's aimless wandering through the galaxy has also been 'corrected', leaving the planet stable and stationary once again.) The Hi-Q/Optimus Prime plot (set up in [69] 'Eye of the Storm') leads to a total fusion of the two characters in a new body (based upon the Optimus Prime Action Master toy). Earth is safe (under the protection of Fortress Maximus and the Neo-Knights), Cybertron is now a safe haven for the Autobots, and the Decepticons are in exile. The war is over – finished.

UK Changes:
Page 1, panel 1: credits added to first page.

Roll Call:
Autobots: Optimus Prime, Prowl, Wheeljack, Grimlock, Snarl (in flashback, also as a corpse), Slag, Sludge, Swoop (flashback only), Silverbolt (as a corpse), Air Raid (as a corpse), Blaster, Hot Rod, Kup, Blurr (as a corpse), Slapdash (as a corpse), Getaway, Siren, and the Last Autobot. Although the dead bodies of many Autobots are seen here, it's heavily implied that all are subsequently resurrected by the Last Autobot.

Decepticons: Skullcruncher, Weirdwolf, Snapdragon, Battletrap, Darkwing, Dreadwind, Fangry, Horri-Bull, Squeezeplay, Crankcase, Quake, Stranglehold,

Bludgeon and Octopunch. Though it's not confirmed either way, the implication is that Fangry, Weirdwolf and Snapdragon are all killed here.

Other: G B Blackrock, Circuit Breaker, Thunderpunch, Rapture and Dynamo.

Nebulans: Grax, Krunk, Hi-Q (flashback only), Kreb and Quig. Other than Hi-Q, all other Nebulans appear only as heads.

Review:
Not quite as action-packed as [75] 'On the Edge of Extinction', this is still a suitably exciting send-off for the Robots in Disguise – especially when one considers than the cancellation forced the comic to condense drastically many of its planned plotlines. In the end it's Bludgeon and Grimlock who get the best lines here, proving that, even up to the end, this comic was just as concerned about its characters as it was about space battles and ancient gods.

Writer Simon Furman leaves a few strands hanging. Are Galvatron, Shockwave, Megatron and Starscream truly dead? Can we trust Bludgeon to honour his self-imposed exile? It opens the door for future writers to continue the adventures; an invitation that has since been graciously accepted by more than one author over the years.

Triumphant yet bitter-sweet, satisfying yet open-ended, this is as good an ending as anyone could have wished for, under the circumstances. 5/5

RIP Transformers
The cancellation of the Transformers comic (on both sides of the Atlantic) had been on the cards for a while, and indeed discussed within the pages of the comic itself:

The Transformers US:

- US#75: A reader writes in, having heard rumours that the comic is wrapping up. The candid response: 'Issue #75 is NOT the last issue of Transformers. If we have our way, it will reach and pass #200! BUT, and it's a big but, our position is beginning to look on the slightly shaky side. We've done pretty much all we can on our end, making the stories better and giving you a great regular art team, so the rest is up to you!'
- US#79: Another reader writes in, having heard rumours that the US comic will finish on issue #80. The reply: 'Your information was (as by now you'll know) correct. We like it no more than you, but sometimes the best will in the world cannot buck the system. Issue #75's letters page was written around the same time #72 was on sale, and at that time we genuinely thought we could save the book. The axe fell shortly afterwards, too late to pull the letter. Sorry, but like you say – *Transformers* will live on in the hearts and minds of the fans … and the creators!'
- Confirmation of the title's cancellation was also printed in US#79: 'We kick off this page with a heavy heart. We're sure you can guess the reason, though – like us – you've probably tried to convince yourself it wouldn't actually happen. Due to factors beyond our control and despite our most epic efforts to keep the book going, next issue is the last issue of *Transformers*.'
- US#80 featured letters by Simon Furman and Nel Yomtov. Furman: 'Though

Transformers had a dedicated and devoted readership, it was also a worryingly low readership. With the toy no longer a major force, with no *Transformers* TV show, with many of our original readers suddenly thinking themselves too old to be still picking up the book, our audience had dwindled (and was dwindling still) to a hard core of regular readers … The chances of *Transformers* ever being revived are incredibly small, so we'll not bother going into that … Did we do well? Yeah, I'd say so. Eighty issues of the regular series, three limited series, a series and book of *Transformers Universe*, 300-odd issues of *Transformers* UK, reprints around the world. All this from a dreaded "toy title", books which generally have a very limited life span. But then I guess all concerned with the book over its long history have always known it was more than that … *Transformers* took on a life of its own, and I am confident that it … will live on beyond its cancellation in the hearts and minds of those who read it and created it. For me, personally, it never ends!' Yomtov: 'We caught a lot of flak for publishing "another stupid comic about robots." Yet, as the robot craze subsided, sales on our book continued to be very healthy. We had made a point: a well-written and handsomely-illustrated comic could outlast the fad.'

The Transformers UK:

- UK#319: News of the US comic's cancellation reaches the UK. Blaster responds: 'Since Marvel US revealed that they would be canning *Transformers* in the States, we've received a great many letters from worried, nah frantic, readers deeply concerned that the Coolest Comic in the Cosmos faces imminent disaster. To put you all at ease, we have enough Yankee material to last at least until the end of 1991. "What happens after that?" you cry! Well, you know what they say: "Never stop fighting till the fight is done." Or something like that, anyway …'
- UK#321: More bad news from America, as the Transformers toy line is cancelled over there. Blaster: 'Although the toy range has been cancelled in the US, Hasbro will continue to produce *Transformers* in this country for at least another four years.'
- UK#324: Blaster writes: 'Whatever happens to *Transformers* in the future, there can be little doubt there will be no new stories, so apologies on that front. However, depending on our situation on reaching 332, things may not be as bleak as they seem. More on that in the future … many thanks to all those concerned readers who've written in and offered their support. Cheers, and remember what they say; "It's never over 'til Fortress Maximus sings!"'
- UK#328: Blaster again: 'Well, to set the record straight, it won't *all* come to an end when the comic goes into retirement, which is by no means certain anyway. Hasbro intend to produce toys for another couple of years, and videos will continue to be released. We are also planning another Winter Special to finish off [the re-print of] "Time Wars".'
- UK#330: There are plans to turn the UK comic into a monthly title from UK#333 onwards: '*Transformers* will get a bright, polished new look. What you'll be getting is a 36-page monthly containing 10 pages of newly-coloured *Transformers* classic adventures, 11 pages that feature the return of G.I. Joe, all the usual bits 'n' pieces, plus five originated … never seen before pages of *Transformers* that will continue the saga.' This plan was eventually nixed; issue #332 would be the comic's last.

- UK#332's editorial page broke the bad news: 'Alas poor readers! ... Issue 333 will not materialise! This is just as devastating for us as it is for you – our loyal readers ... Goodbye and farewell ...'

THE TRANSFORMERS: THE MOVIE (Comic Adaptation)

Throughout the years, Marvel Comics have published a number of movie adaptations in comic-book form. Given that they already had the rights to *The Transformers*, it was only natural that they would adapt the animated theatrical film into a comic.

In a happy coincidence, regular *The Transformers* writer Bob Budiansky was, at the time, Marvel's in-house editor of 'special projects' – a category that included movie adaptations. During his tenure at Marvel, Budiansky would edit comic or graphic novel adaptations of many popular films, including *Indiana Jones and the Last Crusade* (Steven Spielberg, 1989), *Labyrinth* (Jim Henson, 1986), *Who Framed Roger Rabbit?* (Robert Zemeckis, 1988) and *Willow* (Ron Howard, 1988).

Given the lead times required to turn a film into a comic, Marvel were given access to the script while the movie was still in production. This was a draft that was later (lightly) re-written, meaning that there are a few scenes and concepts within the comic adaptation that do not feature in the film itself. Consequently, Marvel's *The Transformers: The Movie* adaptation gives us an intriguing insight into the film's scripting process; a look at what might have been, if not for some late alterations to the shooting script.

[MOV1] THE PLANET-EATER!
US: 'December 1986' (published August 1986), 23 pages.
Published the same month as issue #23 of the main Transformers title, i.e. [23] 'Decepticon Graffiti'.

British reprint: all three issues of the movie adaptation were compiled into a single volume (not a comic *per se*, but a mini graphic novel with a card cover and spine) entitled *The Transformers: The Movie*. It was marketed as a 'Winter Special', and released in November 1986.

Credits:
Ralph Macchio (script), adapted from a screenplay by Ron Friedman (uncredited); Don Perlin (breakdowns); Ian Akin and Brian Garvey (finishes); Nel Yomtov (colours); Janice Chiang (letters); Bob Budiansky (editor); Jim Shooter (editor-in-chief); Don Perlin (cover). **UK:** Don Perlin (cover; adapted from the US cover).

Plot:
It is 2005. In this future, the Decepticons have reconquered Cybertron; the Autobots are based in a city on Earth, and also have secret bases on two of Cybertron's moons, where plans are afoot to retake the planet.

The Autobots make a shuttle run to Earth, to collect a shipment of Energon that will prove vital in their efforts to oust the Decepticons; however, the Decepticons become aware of the launch, and commandeer the shuttle, planning to use it as a 'Trojan horse', allowing them entry into the heart of Autobot City: Earth.

When the Decepticons reach Autobot City, a massive battle breaks out between the two factions. Optimus Prime and Megatron confront each other and engage in to hand-to-hand combat. The fight is so ferocious that both leaders are heavily damaged – Megatron's fall prompts the Decepticons to retreat, ending the battle. Optimus Prime dies of his wounds, but passes the Matrix of Leadership – a powerful glowing talisman safeguarded by Autobot leaders – to his chosen successor, an Autobot warrior named Ultra Magnus.

The Decepticons flee to Cybertron aboard the Decepticon space shuttle, Astrotrain. However, the combined mass of the Decepticon army is proving a drain on Astrotrain's fuel. Starscream recommends jettisoning into space all the injured and dying – a category that includes Megatron.

These abandoned Decepticons drift through space until they come near a planet, Unicron. Unicron is actually sentient, and sustains himself by destroying and eating other planets. Unicron completely rebuilds Megatron and his fallen troops into a new, powerful army, with the singular mission to destroy the Matrix – Unicron's only barrier to an attack on Cybertron ...

Notes:

In order to condense the plot of the movie into three comics, this adaptation omitted a number of scenes, notably involving the Decepticon attack on Autobot City. The scene in which Blaster and Soundwave's cassette minions do battle is excised, as is Starscream's pursuit of Arcee and Springer, Hot Rod's involvement in the Optimus/Megatron fight, Hot Rod's and Kup's encounter with the Insecticons, and the Autobots' struggle to move the rocket launcher into place. The end result is that the battle – which on screen was epic, chaotic and exciting – is reduced to a few pages and has far less of an impact.

Other scenes hint at earlier script revisions. In this version, the Lithonians – Unicron's victims in the film's opening 'teaser' – have the ability to transform, and Unicron destroys planets using a corrosive pink mist (seen again in the comics, in [75] 'On the Edge of Extinction') rather than physically consuming them as he does in the final film. The Autobots are caught unawares by the Decepticon attack on their shuttle because they are flying through an asteroid storm, and so mistake the initial blast for an asteroid impact.

In an example of the comic adding to our understanding of the film, we see that Megatron and the other injured Decepticons are pulled toward Unicron by a tractor beam – this is unexplained in the film itself; there, the Decepticons just seem to float toward him.

The Autobot City is at one stage referred to as Fortress Maximus, which is a little odd, as that's the name of an Autobot Headmaster character. Although Fortress Maximus does transform into a city mode, he looks completely different from the Autobot City seen here and in the movie itself.

UK Notes:

The UK story [20.2] 'Target: 2006' drew on an even *earlier* draft of the film's script than the one used for the comic adaptation. So while the final movie was set in 2005, 'Target: 2006' was written on the assumption that the film would be set a year later. The reference to the year '2005' here is changed to '2006' in the UK reprint, so that the movie adaptation marries up to the dates used in the UK comics.

UK Changes:
Page 1: a 'Chapter 1' caption is inserted at the top of the page.
Page 1, panel 3: 'Colored by' becomes 'Coloured by'.
Page 4, panel 1: '2005' is changed to '2006'.
Page 23, panel 4: the 'Continued next issue' caption is painted out.

Roll Call:
Autobots: Optimus Prime, Ironhide, Ratchet, Sunstreaker, Bumblebee, Cliffjumper, Brawn, Grimlock, Slag, Sludge, Perceptor, Ultra Magnus, Springer, Hot Rod, Kup, Blurr and Arcee.

Decepticons: Megatron, Starscream, Soundwave, Frenzy, Laserbeak, Scrapper, Scavenger, Mixmaster, Bonecrusher, Long Haul, Hook, Devastator, Shrapnel, Bombshell, Kickback, Galvatron, Cyclonus, Scourge and Astrotrain. Mixmaster, Scrapper and Scavenger appear only as components of the combined robot Devastator, rather than as individuals. Though he doesn't feature in the comic itself, the Decepticon Shockwave appears on the cover.

Other: Unicron, Spike, Daniel, Kranix and Arblus.

Data File: Ralph Macchio (writer)
A well-known figure in comics, Macchio wrote for titles such as *Fantastic Four*, *Captain America* and *Thor*. He later became an editor, helming (amongst others) *Daredevil*, *The Avengers* and the comic book adaptation of Stephen King's *The Dark Tower* novels.

Review:
It's so hard to judge this comic on its own merits, without the inevitable comparisons with the movie. Stripped of the stunning animation, the tremendous voice cast, the soundtrack and the cinematography, there's no denying that much is lost in translation.

On its own terms, though, this is a decent comic – the size and scope of the film are captured well, most of the key scenes are intact, as are most of the iconic lines ('All we need is a little Energon and a lot of luck'; 'I'll rip out your optics!'; 'Oh, how it pains me to do this!').

If there is a complaint, it's that the comic is a tad wordy: there's a lot of info-dump dialogue, and much of the story is conveyed by the captions rather than the visuals. Otherwise, this is a solid instalment. 3/5

[MOV2] JUDGMENT DAY!
US: 'January 1987' (published September 1986), 23 pages.
Published the same month as issue #24 of the main title, i.e. [24] 'Afterdeath'.

British reprint: for details, see [MOV1] 'The Planet-Eater' above.

Credits:
Ralph Macchio (script), adapted from a screenplay by Ron Friedman (uncredited); Don Perlin (breakdowns); Ian Akin and Brian Garvey (finishes); Nel Yomtov (colours); Janice Chiang (letters); Bob Budiansky (editor); Jim Shooter (editor-in-chief); Don Perlin (cover).

Plot:
The re-built Megatron – now called Galvatron – returns to Cybertron and assassinates Starscream. When he sees Unicron destroy one of Cybertron's two moons, he orders another attack on Earth.* When the Decepticons arrive on Earth, the Autobots flee in their ships and head out into space.

Ultra Magnus's ship is damaged by a Decepticon attack, forcing a landing on a nearby planet for repairs. Another fleeing Autobot shuttle, containing Hot Rod, Kup and the Dinobots, crash-lands on the planet Quintessa, home to the Quintessons, who get amusement from staging 'show-trials' on captured aliens, then killing their captives regardless whether they are found guilty or innocent. Hot Rod, Kup and Grimlock are tried in one such kangaroo court, but are rescued by the remainder of the Dinobots. Together with Wheelie, another young Autobot who has been living there, they escape the Quintesson planet.

Meanwhile, Unicron attacks Cybertron's second moon. Bumblebee and Spike flee in a spaceship, having set explosive charges on the doomed satellite. However, Unicron proves impervious to the blast, and consumes both the moon *and* the fleeing vessel …

Notes:
Again, there are a number of interesting differences between the comic adaptation and the movie itself. The biggest is that many scenes are shifted about to help the structure of the comic. In the film, the scenes of Hot Rod and company on Quintessa were intercut with those of Ultra Magnus's group on Junkion. Here, all the Junkion scenes are deferred until issue three. The destruction of the second moonbase, which in the film occurred soon after the first, is here moved to the end of the issue, which admittedly makes for a suitably exciting cliffhanger.

There are some other changes elsewhere: Hot Rod's ship crash-lands because is it attacked by a claw-like appendage that rises from the surface of the Quintesson planet; in the film, the crash was due solely to the damage caused by the Decepticons. Furthermore, Grimlock tags along with Hot Rod and Kup on the planet; in the film, he arrived later, with the other Dinobots.

One scene that didn't make it to the final movie is retained in this issue: during the space battle, Cyclonus chases Ultra Magnus's ship through an asteroid field. Conversely, one of the film's most memorable set-pieces, Hot Rod fighting the robot fish and octopus on Quintessa, is omitted entirely.

We also learn that the Quintessons are in league with Unicron, and are actively hunting creatures who have escaped the planet-eater – another element from earlier drafts that didn't make it to the shooting script.

UK Notes:
According to the UK comics, the asterisk inserted into the synopsis above marks the point at which Galvatron, Cyclonus and Scourge journey back in time and take part in the events of [20.2] 'Target: 2006'. This was confirmed in the letters page of UK#96.

UK Changes:
Page 1, panel 1: a 'Chapter 2' logo is added. 'Colored' is changed to 'coloured'.
Page 4, panel 1: righting a mistake in the original printing, the UK version has Cliffjumper and Jazz in their correct colours.
Page 4, panel 3: Jazz's and Cliffjumper's speech bubbles are swapped around.

Page 7, panels 5-6: Springer's line 'I remember it well' is expanded across two panels, and now reads: 'Yeah, the only way to buckle this Decepticon attack is to steer towards ... the nearest asteroid belt!'
Page 10, panel 2: 'maneuvers' is changed to 'manoeuvres'.
Page 15, panel 2: 'neighborly' becomes 'friendly'.
Page 16, panel 6: 'See the first issue' is altered to read 'See chapter one'. Editor Bob Budiansky's sign-off is excised from the caption.

Roll Call:
Autobots: Jazz, Bumblebee, Cliffjumper, Grimlock, Slag, Sludge, Swoop, Perceptor, Ultra Magnus, Springer, Hot Rod, Kup, Blurr, Arcee and Wheelie.

Decepticons: Starscream, Soundwave, Bonecrusher, Shrapnel, Galvatron, Cyclonus, Scourge, Astrotrain and Blitzwing.

Other: Unicron, Spike, Daniel and Kranix, plus various Quintessons.

Review:
Again, the wordy writing style and rather un-dynamic art take some of the punch out of proceedings, but otherwise this is an engaging read. The decision to reshuffle some of the movie's scenes around does help the comic's flow, and overall this is a decent adaptation.

That said, the middle third of the movie is probably its weakest segment, so despite a good effort in translating the script into a comic format, the limitations of the source material count against it. 2/5

[MOV3] THE FINAL BATTLE!
US: 'February 1987' (published October 1986), 24 pages.
Published the same month as issue #25 of the main title, i.e. [25] 'Gone but Not Forgotten'.

British reprint: for details, see [MOV1] 'The Planet-Eater' above.

Credits:
Ralph Macchio (script), adapted from a screenplay by Ron Friedman (uncredited); Don Perlin (breakdowns); Ian Akin and Brian Garvey (finishes); Nel Yomtov (colours); Janice Chiang (letters); Bob Budiansky (editor); Jim Shooter (editor-in-chief); Don Perlin (cover).

Plot:
Ultra Magnus's ship has landed on the planet Junkion, home to a strange robot species, the Junkions, who are led by the idiosyncratic Wreck-Gar and base their lives and speech-patterns around television broadcasts from Earth. Galvatron attacks the planet and has Ultra Magnus torn into pieces. Fortunately, the friendly Junkions are able to repair the Autobot.

Now in possession of the Matrix, Galvatron attempts to use it against Unicron, but is unable to activate it. In response, Unicron transforms into a planet-sized robot, swallows Galvatron whole, and begins attacking Cybertron. There he is confronted by the Autobot and Junkion ships; one of these is crewed by Hot Rod, Kup, Springer, Arcee and Daniel – the young son of Spike, who was on one of the destroyed moon bases. This ship crashes through one of Unicron's eyes, and its occupants find themselves within the belly of the beast.

Hot Rod becomes separated from his comrades and comes face to face with Galvatron. The two do battle, but Galvatron's superior strength is too much for Hot Rod, who is weakened and near defeat.

At that moment, however, Hot Rod makes a grab for the Matrix, and is able to activate it. Its energies transform him into Rodimus Prime, the new Autobot leader. He throws Galvatron through a wall and out into space. He then uses the power of the Matrix to destroy Unicron from within. The assorted Autobots trapped inside the giant robot manage to escape just in time as Unicron explodes.

The Autobots return to Cybertron, and begin the rebuilding process, reinvigorated by their courageous new leader.

Notes:
As per the draft script of the movie, the adaptation sees Ultra Magnus stretched and dismembered to death, in quite a disturbing scene – in the finished film he was merely shot at. Another change is that the Junkion planet transforms into a spacecraft, whereas in the film, the ship emerged from beneath the planet's surface.

The main changes are all omissions, presumably to enable the entire story to fit within three issues. Galvatron's first return to Unicron, in which he learns of Ultra Magnus's survival, is cut; instead Galvatron recounts this scene in dialogue. The sequences set inside Unicron's body are heavily truncated. The attack by the claw arms, the flooding of the tunnels, and Daniel's scene at the acid vat are all edited out. Consequently, to the general reader it is unclear whether or not the likes of Spike, Bumblebee, Jazz and Cliffjumper survive. (Eagle-eyed readers will spot them at the end, though their small size and erratic colouring makes identification difficult.)

UK Changes:
Page 1, panel 1: a 'Chapter 3' caption is added. '2005' is changed to '2006', 'defense' to 'defence' and 'coloring' to 'colouring'.
Page 3, panels 3-4: Bob Budiansky's tag is erased from both captions.
Page 5, panel 3: 'flavor' becomes 'flavour'.
Page 10, panel 2: 'See issue #2 for details – Bob' is changed to 'See chapter two for details.'

Roll Call:
Autobots: Jazz, Bumblebee, Grimlock, Sludge, Perceptor, Ultra Magnus, Springer, Hot Rod, Kup, Blurr, Wreck-Gar, Arcee and Wheelie.

Decepticons: Shockwave, Scavenger, Shrapnel, Galvatron, Cyclonus and Scourge.

Other: Unicron, Spike and Daniel.

Review:
A good finale to what's been a functional and workmanlike adaptation, the scenes starring robot-mode Unicron being the highlight. It's still unnecessarily wordy

(prime example: a caption tells us 'Galvatron strikes at his enemy by transforming into cannon mode', when we can easily tell what's going on by looking at the pictures), and the art is still a bit flat in places, but overall this does a decent job in getting the story across. 3/5

THE TRANSFORMERS UNIVERSE

Beginning in 1982, Marvel Comics published a periodical entitled *The Official Handbook of the Marvel Universe*. Serialised over fifteen issues, it was an alphabetical run-down of all major Marvel heroes, villains and weapons, with full-body portraits of most characters, plus details of their background, powers, weaknesses and vital statistics. It proved to be a popular series, and has been revised, collected and updated numerous times over the years.

With *The Transformers* at the peak of its popularity in 1986 (culminating in the release of *The Transformers: The Movie*), it was decided to commission a four-issue limited series called *The Transformers Universe*, which would do for this franchise what *The Official Handbook* had done for super-heroes.

Most of the art for the series had already been done: it was decided that the images used in the *The Transformers Universe* would be adapted from the character model sheets already in Marvel's possession. With these tweaked by Ian Akin and Brian Garvey and coloured by Nel Yomtov, the only thing remaining was the character profiles.

Except, writer Bob Budiansky had already written profiles for each Transformer, used for the back-of-package 'Tech Specs' information that came with every Transformers action figure and featured in the UK comic as part of that title's 'Interface' series of features. Budiansky combined these profiles with the newly spruced-up art; *The Transformers Universe* was born.

[UNI1] *The Transformers Universe* #1

US: 'December 1986' (published August 1986). 36 pages total (32 pages of profiles). Published the same month as issue #23 of the main title, i.e. [23] 'Decepticon Graffiti'.

Profiles: Air Raid, Astrotrain, Beachcomber, Blades, Blaster, Blast Off, Blitzwing, Blue Streak [sic], Bombshell, Bonecrusher, Brawl, Brawn, Breakdown, Broadside, Bruticus, Bumblebee, Buzzsaw, Cliffjumper, Cosmos, Dead End, Defensor, Devastator, Dirge, Divebomb, Drag Strip, Eject, Fireflight, First Aid, Frenzy, Gears, Grapple and Grimlock.

[UNI2] *The Transformers Universe* #2

US: 'January 1987' (published September 1986). 36 pages total (33 pages of profiles). Published the same month as issue #24 of the main title, i.e. [24] 'Afterdeath'.

Profiles: Groove, Headstrong, Hoist, Hook, Hot Spot, Hound, Huffer, Inferno, Ironhide, Jazz, Jetfire, Kickback, Laserbeak, Long Haul, Megatron, Menasor, Metroplex, Mirage, Mixmaster, Motormaster, Octane, Omega Supreme, Onslaught, Optimus Prime, Outback, Perceptor, Pipes, Powerglide, Predaking, Prowl, Ramhorn and Ramjet.

[UNI3] *The Transformers Universe* **#3**

US: 'February 1987' (published October 1986). 36 pages total (33 pages of profiles). Published the same month as issue #25 of the main title, i.e. [25] 'Gone But Not Forgotten'.

Profiles: Rampage, Ratbat, Ratchet, Ravage, Razorclaw, Red Alert, Rewind, Rumble, Runabout, Runamuck, Sandstorm, Scavenger, Scrapper, Seaspray, Shockwave, Shrapnel, Sideswipe, Silverbolt, Skids, Skydive, Sky Lynx, Skywarp, Slag, Slingshot, Sludge, Smokescreen, Snarl, Soundwave, Starscream, Streetwise, Sunstreaker, Superion and Swindle.

[UNI4] *The Transformers Universe* **#4**

US: 'March 1987' (published November 1986). 36 pages total (33 pages of profiles). Published the same month as issue #26 of the main title, i.e. [26] 'Funeral for a Friend'.

Profiles: Steeljaw, Swoop, Tailgate, Tantrum, Thrust, Thundercracker, Topspin, Tracks, Trailbreaker, Trypticon, Twin Twist, Vortex, Warpath, Wheeljack, Wildrider and Windcharger. And from *The Transformers: The Movie* ... Arblus, Arcee, Blurr, Cyclonus, Galvatron, Hot Rod, Rodimus Prime, Kranix, Kup, Quintessons, Scourge, Sharkticon, Springer, Ultra Magnus, Unicron, Wheelie and Wreck-Gar.

Credits for *The Transformers Universe* comics are as follows:

Editor-in-chief: Jim Shooter (#1-4); Editor and design director: Jim Salicrup (#1-4); Assistant editor: Adam Philips (#1-2), Dwight Jon Zimmerman (#3-4); Writer/consulting editor: Bob Budiansky (#1-4); Inkers/embellishers: Ian Akin and Brian Garvey (#1-4); Colourist: Nel Yomtov (#1-4); Cover artists: Herb Trimpe, Ian Akin and Brian Garvey (#1-4); Designer: Barbara Johnson (#1), Rich DuFour (#2-4); Art director: John Romita (#1-4); Assistant art director: Tom Morgan (#1-2); 'Romita's Raiders': Mark Alexander (#1-4), Jose Marzan (#1-4), Mark McKenna (#1-2), Bruce N Solotoff (#3-4); Art/production coordinator: Anita Duncan (#1-4); Production assistant: Doreen Frederick (#1-4); Typesetter: Brenda Mings (#1-4); Proof reader: Jack Abel (#1-4); Production: Paul Becton (#1-4), Pat Brosseau (#1-4), Harry Candelario (#1-4), Rob Carosella (#1-4), Hector Collazo (#1-4), Rich DuFour (#1), Dawn Geiger (#1-4), Barbara Johnston (#2-4), Veronica Lawlor (#1-4), Ken Lopez (#1-4), Michael Maier (#1-4), Bill Oakley (#1-4), Bill Vallely (#1-4), Michael Yee (#2-3); Traffic manager: Virginia Romita (#1-4).

From issue #2, a line was added to the credits: 'Artwork based on model sheets by Marvel Productions'. One 'Irving Forbush' was credited with the role of 'Spare Part' in #1, 'Less than meets the eye' in #2, as 'Major weakness' in #3, and 'Has seen movie 63 times' in #4. Irving Forbush is not a real person, and his appearance in the credits is merely part of a long-running Marvel in-joke.

Following the success of *The Transformers Universe*, plans were put in motion for a second run, featuring new characters that were introduced after 1986. However, due to the shrinking sales figures of the main comic, the proposal was put on hold, despite some work having been already completed. Some additional profiles eventually saw the light of the day within the main comic, as filler material:

US#47: Snapdragon, Highbrow and Apeface; US#48: Hardhead, Brainstorm, Chromedome, Crosshairs and Searchlight; US#49: Chase and Freeway; US#56: Battletrap, Blot, Cutthroat, Goldbug, Rollbar and Wideload; US#57: Cloudraker, Overkill and Slugfest; US#58: Afterburner, Lightspeed, Nosecone, Scattershot, Strafe and Computron; US#59: Nautilator, Overbite, Seawing, Skalor, Snaptrap, Tentakil and Piranacon; US#60: Misfire, Pointblank, Slugslinger and Sureshot; US#61: Triggerhappy, Landfill, Quickmix and Scoop; US#62: Hosehead, Nightbeat, Siren and Backstreet; US#63: Dogfight and Override; US#64: Crankcase and Needlenose; US#65: Spinister and Windsweeper; US#66: Quake and Ruckus; US#67: Getaway and Joyride; US#68: Slapdash; US#69: Fastlane and Mindwipe; US#70: Optimus Prime (Powermaster version); US#71: Punch and Counter Punch [sic]; US#72: Landmine and Skullgrin; US#74: Darkwing and Dreadwind; US#75: Fangry and Squeezeplay; US#76: Grotusque and Horri-Bull; US#77: Weirdwolf and Skullcruncher; US#78: Pounce and Repugnus; US#79: Fortress Maximus.

Furthermore, unused profiles for Swerve, Hubcap, Ransack, Chop Shop, Venom, Barrage, Roadbuster and Whirl were later discovered and posted on the personal website of Transformers writer and researcher Jim Sorenson.

The Transformers A to Z

The four issues of *The Transformers Universe* were compiled by Marvel into a trade paperback reprint in July 1987; this was also available in the United Kingdom. What the UK also got, however, were slightly edited and heavily redesigned versions of the *Universe* profiles, serialised alphabetically over the course of the comic (and a few annuals). These revised profiles (rebranded as 'Transformers A to Z') replaced a previous series of fact-files that briefly ran in *The Transformers* UK, called 'Interface' (see the notes under [8.1] 'Decepticon Dam-Busters').

Unlike the American *Universe* profiles, the British A to Z versions would often incorporate information from recent comic adventures, helping to tie them further into the ongoing narrative. A complete list of A to Z profiles printed in the UK is as follows:

- UK#89: Air Raid/Astrotrain
- UK#93: Beachcomber/Blades
- UK#101: Blaster/Blast Off
- UK#108: Blue Streak [sic]/Blitzwing
- UK#116: Bombshell/Bonecrusher
- UK#117: Brawl/Brawn
- UK#119: Breakdown/Bruticus
- UK#124: Buzzsaw/Cliffjumper
- UK#125: Cosmos/Dead End
- UK#133: Defensor/Devastator
- UK#138: Dirge/Divebomb
- UK#139: Dragstrip [sic]/Fireflight
- UK#143: First Aid/Frenzy
- UK#146: Gears/Grapple
- UK#148: Grimlock*/Groove

- UK#150: Rodimus Prime*
- UK#151: Headstrong/Hoist
- UK#155: Hook/Hotspot [sic]
- UK#156: Hound/Huffer
- UK#166: Inferno/Ironhide
- UK#174: Jazz/Jetfire
- UK#177: Optimus Prime*
- UK#190: Kickback/Laserbeak
- UK#195: Long Haul/Menasor
- UK#196: Megatron*
- UK#211: Metroplex
- UK#213: Mirage/Mixmaster
- UK#215: Motormaster/Octane
- UK#220: Omega Supreme
- UK#221: Onslaught/Outback
- UK#222: Perceptor/Pipes
- UK#223: Powerglide/Predaking
- UK#227: Prowl/Ramhorn
- UK#233: Rampage/Ratbat
- UK#239: Ratchet/Ravage
- UK#249: Razorclaw/Red Alert
- UK#250: Rewind/Rumble
- UK#251: Runabout/Runamuck
- UK#252: Sandstorm/Scavenger
- UK#253: Scrapper/Seaspray
- UK#265: Shockwave
- UK#267: Shrapnel/Sideswipe
- UK#269: Silverbolt/Skids
- UK#271: Skydive/Sky Lynx
- UK#273: Skywarp/Slag
- UK#276: Slingshot/Sludge
- UK#277: Smokescreen/Snarl
- UK#278: Soundwave/Starscream
- UK#279: Streetwise/Sunstreaker
- UK#280: Steeljaw/Superion
- UK#281: Swindle/Swoop
- UK#282: Tailgate/Tantrum
- UK#283: Thundercracker/Thrust (printed in black-and-white, as the feature's usual position in the colour section was taken by a competition page)
- UK#284: Topspin/Tracks
- UK#285: Trailbreaker/Trypticon
- UK#286: Twin Twist/Ultra Magnus
- UK#287: Unicron*
- UK#288: Vortex/Warpath
- UK#289: Wheelie/Wheeljack
- UK#290: Wildrider/Windcharger
- UK#309: Thundercracker/Thrust (re-printed in full-colour)
- UK#310: Optimus Prime (updated version)
- UK#311: Joyride/Getaway

- UK#313: Slapdash
- UK#314: Punch/Counter Punch [sic]
- UK#315: Landmine
- UK#317: Dreadwind
- UK#318: Darkwing
- UK#319: Fangry
- UK#320: Squeezeplay
- UK#321: Siren
- UK#322: Kup
- UK#323: Grotusque
- UK#324: Horri-Bull
- UK#325: Weirdwolf
- UK#326: Skullcruncher
- UK#327: Pounce
- UK#328: Repugnus
- UK#329: Fortress Maximus (a straight reprint of the US profile, not edited or reformatted into the standard UK 'A to Z' template)

1988 Annual: Brainstorm / Chromedome / Hardhead / Highbrow / Mindwipe / Skullcruncher / Weirdwolf
1989 Annual: Nautilator/Seawing/Skalor/Snap Trap [sic]/Tentakil/Jawbreaker
1990 Annual: Race Car Patrol/Off Road Patrol/Air Strike Patrol/Sports Car Patrol/ Rescue Patrol/Battle Patrol
1991 Annual: Inferno*/Ironhide*/Jazz*/Sunstreaker*/Prowl*/Wheeljack* (updated versions)

Profiles marked with an asterisk were altered to include recent story information. The entry for Bumblebee (who had, by that point, been reformatted as Goldbug) was not printed.

G.I. JOE AND THE TRANSFORMERS

The GI Joe and Transformers franchises share many links: they are both Hasbro toy lines that were adapted into Marvel comics and Sunbow animated television shows. In the 21st Century, both have been turned into series of live-action feature films. As such, it was only natural that they would star in a crossover event.

This crossover was designed to blend seamlessly with the mythology of both series, so there were many references to the recent events in both *The Transformers* and *G.I. Joe: A Real American Hero* – the latter being a Marvel publication that was launched in 1982 and ran for 155 issues before its cancellation in 1994. As *The Transformers* writer Bob Budiansky and *G.I. Joe* writer Larry Hama were busy working on their own titles, the task of writing *G.I. Joe and the Transformers* fell to Michael Higgins, who already had a prior *The Transformers* credit to his name, as co-letterer on [1] 'The Transformers'.

[GIJ1] BLOOD ON THE TRACKS
US: *G.I. Joe and the Transformers* #1 'January 1987' (published September 1986), 24 pages. Published the same month as issue #24 of the main *The Transformers* title, i.e. [24]

'Afterdeath', and #55 of *G.I. Joe: A Real American Hero*, 'Unmasking'.

British reprint: UK#265, 14 April 1990 (Part 1), 6 pages; UK#266, 21 April 1990 (Part 2), 6 pages; UK#267, 28 April 1990 (Part 3), 6 pages; UK#268, 5 May 1990 (Part 4), 6 pages.

Credits:
Michael Higgins (script); Herb Trimpe (pencils); Vince Colletta (inks); Nel Yomtov (colours); Joe Rosen (letters); Bob Harras and Don Daley (editors); Jim Shooter (editor-in-chief); Herb Trimpe (cover). **UK:** For UK cover credits, see the entries for [61.1] 'Starting Over', [62.1] 'Snow Fun' and [62.2] 'Flashback'.

Bob Harras and Don Daley were the then editors of the regular *G.I. Joe* and *The Transformers* comics respectively.

Plot:
A group of protestors demonstrate outside the gates of Power Station Alpha, a prototype mobile solar/nuclear power station that's about to be launched. The station is being guarded by the GI Joe team, who fend off an attack by the Dreadnoks, an evil biker gang affiliated to the terrorist organisation Cobra.

In the *Ark*, Optimus Prime realises that the station might well attract the attentions of the Decepticons, so he sends Bumblebee to scout the area surreptitiously. Prime is correct: Megatron does intend to seize the station for himself, and so sends Dirge and Bombshell to the site. Their plan: to use Bombshell's mind-controlling cerebro-shells to hack the station's computer.

By way of a diversion, Bombshell injects a cerebro-shell into the brain of a small boy, Tony Duranti, whom he then orders to walk onto the runway just as the station is about to take off. Unwilling to watch the boy die, Bumblebee blows his cover, assumes his robot mode, and saves the child. Believing him to be a threat to the station, the Joes launch everything they have at the Autobot, completely destroying him.

As Bombshell enters the station, Autobot reinforcements arrive in the form of Superion ...

Notes:
From the point of view of *The Transformers*, this story is set between [23] 'Decepticon Graffiti' (Optimus Prime references Decepticon activity in that issue) and [24] 'Afterdeath' (in which Optimus Prime is killed). This fits into the *G.I. Joe* chronology somewhere around the events of *G.I. Joe* #52 ('Snap Decisions'); there are explicit references to the 'debacle in Springfield' (*G.I. Joe* #50).

There are a number of other references to recent *The Transformers* issues, including [19] 'Command Performances' (Bumblebee recording Devastator's transformation sequence), [21] 'Aerialbots over America' (the Aerialbots' teething problems) and [22] 'Heavy Traffic' (Bombshell injecting Optimus Prime with a cerebro-shell).

The majority of this story takes place in and around Fort Lewis, a real-world army base near Tacoma, Washington. The protestors campaigning against the power station refer to many other 'science gone wrong' disasters over the years: Chernobyl (an accident at a Ukrainian nuclear power station in 1986), Three Mile Island (a partial nuclear meltdown at a power plant in Pennsylvania), Thalidomide (an over-the-counter morning sickness drug later found to cause birth defects) and DDT (or dichlorodiphenyltrichloroethane, a widely-used pesticide that also proved deadly to bird and fish populations and harmful to humans).

The Autobots' human friend G B Blackrock is mentioned in passing. The story shares its title with a classic 1975 album by Bob Dylan.

UK Notes:

The UK comic originally skipped over this crossover in its reprinting of the American strips, instead devising its own method of killing off Bumblebee and replacing him with Goldbug (see the notes under [27.3] 'Hunters'). However, circumstances forced it to turn to the story much later in its run, as a last-minute fill-in. The editorial page of UK#265 explained, rather apologetically: 'We've caught up with the Americans as regards the stories and, as a consequence of this, there's a somewhat long delay before we can print the US stories. So, in order for them to get ahead again, we'll be running the *Transformers/G.I. Joe* crossover story. Sorry 'bout that! Still, it gives you a chance to see a somewhat novel *Transformers* story, yeah? Incidentally, look out for the US version of the "birth" of Goldbug!'

On previous occasions where the UK comic had caught up with its American counterpart, the decision had been made to run repeats of stories from earlier in the British run (see the notes to [53.1] 'Survivors'), however this had proved unpopular with readers. With this *G.I. Joe* crossover, UK fans were at least getting material they had never seen before.

UK Changes:

Page 1, panel 1: credits replaced. 'Bloody buggers' is changed to 'morons'. The artwork is extended downwards to fill the page.

Page 3, panel 3: the reference to *G.I. Joe* #50 is changed to *The Transformers* issues #158-165.

Page 5, panel 1: the reference to *The Transformers* #23 is changed to #94 & 95.

Page 6, panel 7: to make for a cleaner cliffhanger, the ellipsis at the end of Hawk's line 'Don't worry, Barbara ...' is turned into an exclamation mark.

Page 7, panel 1: similarly, the leading dashes in Hawk's line '--I'll protect you!' are painted out.

Page 11, panel 6: Bombshell's line: 'That trip to the *Ark*' is changed to 'That trip to the dam', and the issue reference altered from #19 to #89; this corrects a mistake in the original printing – Bombshell's trip to the *Ark* occurred in US#22, not US#19.

Page 21, panel 2: 'center' becomes 'centre'.

Roll Call:

Autobots: Optimus Prime, Ratchet, Bumblebee, Silverbolt, Air Raid, Fireflight, Skydive, Slingshot and Superion.

Decepticons: Megatron, Bombshell and Dirge.

GI Joes: Hawk, Roadblock, Snake-Eyes, Beachhead, Scarlett, Junkyard and Mutt (plus the Armadillo, AWE Striker and VAMP Mark II vehicles).

Cobra, the Enemy: Ripper, Torch, Buzzer, Zartan, the Baroness, Cobra Commander, Dr Mindbender, Serpentor and Zarana.

Data File: Michael Higgins (letterer/writer)
The multi-talented Higgins was a comic artist, colourist and editor, as well as being a writer and letterer. He scripted issues of (amongst others) *Conan the Barbarian* and *Silver Surfer*. As an artist, he worked on *The Incredible Hulk* and *Star Wars*. He edited issues of titles such as *Captain America* and *Star Brand*. He was most prolific as a letterer, however, where his credits include (the English-language version of) *Akira*, *Thor*, *X-Men* and *Machine Man*.

Review:
It's all set-up, and boring set-up at that. While the Dreadnoks show a bit of character, everyone else has really stilted dialogue. This is a very bland story, with nothing in the way of flair or panache. The focus is very much on the human cast, which is very frustrating – the Transformers come across almost as guest stars in a GI Joe-focused story. It doesn't help that the Joes are able to blow Bumblebee to bits, even though previous *The Transformers* instalments have shown that Cybertronians are largely unfazed by regular human weaponry.

Interesting as a curio, but generally lacking in excitement, tension or character. 2/5

[GIJ2] POWER STRUGGLE
US: *G.I. Joe and the Transformers* #2 'February 1987' (published October 1986), 23 pages. Published the same month as issue #25 of the main *The Transformers* title, i.e. [25] 'Gone but Not Forgotten', and #56 of *G.I. Joe: A Real American Hero*, 'Jungle Moves'.

British reprint: UK#269, 12 May 1990 (Part 1), 5 pages; UK#270, 19 May 1990 (Part 2), 6 pages; UK#271, 26 May 1990 (Part 3), 6 pages; UK#272, 2 June 1990 (Part 4), 6 pages.

Credits:
Michael Higgins (script); Herb Trimpe (pencils); Vince Colletta (inks); Nel Yomtov (colours); Joe Rosen (letters); Don Daley (consulting editor); Bob Harras (editor); Jim Shooter (editor-in-chief); Herb Trimpe (cover). **UK:** For UK cover credits, see the entries for [62.3] 'Mystery', [62.4] 'The Bad Guy's Ball', [62.5] 'The Living Nightlights' and [62.6] 'Wolf in the Fold'.

Plot:
Superion attacks the GI Joes but is ordered to return to the *Ark* by Blaster, who has some bad news: Optimus Prime is dead! In the aftermath of the skirmish, the Joes collect Bumblebee's remains for study.

Under the control of one of Bombshell's cerebro-shells, Power Station Alpha takes off, much to the surprise of Hawk and his team. From his base on Cobra Island, Dr Mindbender uses a control helmet to take over the station's guidance systems for himself. He directs the station to Cobra Island.

The Decepticons follow the path of the power station and also show up on the island, whereupon Serpentor agrees to a truce between the Decepticons and Cobra. Dirge returns to the Decepticon base to discuss the proposal with Shockwave – Shockwave decides to play along with Cobra, until such time as he's ready to betray them and use the station to plunder energy from the Earth's core. Unbeknown to Shockwave, Dr Mindbender has placed a listening device on Dirge and so can hear every word of the Decepticons' plotting …

Notes:
As before, this story is set in and around the events of [24] 'Afterdeath' and [25] 'Gone but Not Forgotten'. Optimus Prime's destruction in the former is a current event, as is the Decepticons' move from their coal mine base in Wyoming to their island base in the latter. Megatron vanishes from this story after page 10, reflecting his own demise in the latter. (According to [25] 'Gone but Not Forgotten', the Decepticons don't decamp to the island base until *after* Megatron's 'death', and yet this story depicts him on the island. It's likely that Megatron and Shockwave are at the base only temporarily to oversee a 'set-up' phase prior to the final move.)

From the *G.I. Joe* point of view, this story takes place around the same time as issue #53, 'Pit-Fall', in which both Destro and Cobra Commander are believed killed. Destro vanishes from this issue after page 18, reflecting his status in the ongoing *G.I. Joe* comic. There's a specific reference to Cobra Commander's return in *G.I. Joe* #55, 'Unmasking'.

In contrast with other contemporary *The Transformers* strips, Ravage is seen here, alive and well – he was previously thought to have been deactivated after falling down a mineshaft in [20] 'Showdown' (see the notes under [A1.1] 'Plague of the Insecticons' for one possible explanation).

The GI Joe team have no prior knowledge of the Transformers and require G B Blackrock to fill them in on some of the details, contrary to the facts as established in *The Transformers* (such as in [15] 'I, Robot Master', where news of the Transformers was broadcast across America). Even stranger is the fact that Tony Duranti, the young boy whose mind was controlled by Bombshell in [GIJ1] 'Blood on the Tracks', is seen here playing with a Bumblebee toy.

UK Changes:
Page 1, panel 1: Credits replaced. The reference to the 'first issue' is changed to 'last issue'.
Page 5, panel 1: An additional clarification is added to the mention of Prime's death – readers are told to refer to 'issue 106'.
Page 7, panel 1: 'honor' is changed to 'honour'.
Page 15, panel 5: illustrating the difference between British and American sensibilities, 'bloody' is altered to read 'damn'.
Page 20, panel 2: the reference to *G.I. Joe* issue #55 is changed to issue #192.

Roll Call:
Autobots: Bumblebee (as a corpse), Silverbolt, Air Raid, Fireflight, Skydive, Slingshot, Superion and Blaster. The five Aerialbots – Silverbolt, Air Raid, Firelight, Skydive and Slingshot – appear only as part of their Superion combined mode.

Decepticons: Megatron, Ravage, Shockwave, Bombshell and Dirge.

Other: G B Blackrock.

GI Joes: Mutt, Scarlett, Junkyard, Snake-Eyes, Roadblock, Beachhead, Sgt Slaughter, Lady Jaye, Dial-Tone, Ace, Crankcase, Hawk, Mainframe, Wild Bill, Lift-Ticket and Slipstream (plus the Armadillo, Conquest X-30, Dragonfly XH-1, Mauler MBT, Skystriker XP-14F, Tomahawk and WHALE vehicles).

Cobra, the Enemy: the Baroness, Serpentor, Destro and Dr Mindbender (plus a number of Cobra Rattler vehicles).

Review:

This is a story where action and plot expediency take precedence over sense and motivation. While the various battles and alliances and back-stabbing seem superficially fine, delve beneath the surface and the story is built on shaky foundations. Why do the Decepticons entertain the notion of joining forces with Cobra, instead of just killing them and taking the power station for themselves? What does Superion hope to gain by shooting at the Joes? Why doesn't he take Bumblebee's remains with him when he flies off? Isn't it a massive coincidence that the cruise ship attacked by Cobra just happens to be owned by Transformer expert G B Blackrock?

This is a total mess, a series of events with little meaning. 1/5

[GIJ3] ASHES, ASHES ...

US: *G.I. Joe and the Transformers* #3 'March 1987' (published November 1986), 23 pages. Published the same month as issue #26 of the main *The Transformers* title, i.e. [26] 'Funeral for a Friend', and #57 of *G.I. Joe: A Real American Hero*, 'Strange Bedfellows'.

British reprint: UK#273, 9 June 1990 (Part 1), 5 pages; UK#274, 16 June 1990 (Part 2), 6 pages; UK#275, 23 June 1990 (Part 3), 6 pages; UK#276, 30 June 1990 (Part 4), 6 pages.

Credits:

Michael Higgins (script); Herb Trimpe (pencils); Vince Colletta (inks); Nel Yomtov (colours); Joe Rosen (letters); Don Daley (consulting editor); Bob Harras (editor); Jim Shooter (editor-in-chief); Al Milgrom (cover). **UK:** For UK cover credits, see the entries for [62.6] 'Wolf in the Fold' and [62.7] 'Internal Affairs'.

Plot:

Cobra decide to play along with the Decepticons; Dr Mindbender stays behind at Shockwave's island base while the remainder of Cobra, plus the Decepticon Dirge, make an attack on the *Ark*. Dr Mindbender watches as Bombshell undergoes some kind of systems glitch, caused when a doctor – on the other side of the continent – begins examining the cerebro-shell that he injected into Tony Duranti.

Meanwhile, at a top-brass meeting, it's discovered that Power Station Alpha is as dangerous as the protestors were claiming: riddled with weaknesses and lacking in fail-safes, the project went ahead only because Cobra themselves were bribing various officials. Hawk is shocked to discover that one of those corrupt officials was Senator Barbara Larkin, whom he had recently begun dating.

Back at Fort Lewis, the Joes are able to activate Bumblebee's brain, and he explains the situation to them. After learning all about the Transformers, the Joes decide to head for the *Ark* to get help from the other Autobots.

As the Decepticons launch Power Station Alpha, Cobra approach the *Ark* themselves, having been instructed by Shockwave to attack the Autobots. Instead, Cobra destroy Dirge and form an alliance with the Autobots – even Cobra have no wish to see the Decepticons use the station to destroy the Earth.

The GI Joe troops arrive on the scene and realise that they must join forces with both the Autobots *and* Cobra to defeat the Decepticons ...

Notes:
This story is set concurrently with [26] 'Funeral for a Friend' – in both stories we are shown segments of Optimus Prime's funeral.

We finally discover what Shockwave's plan is. He means to use the station to shoot 'intense waves' of energy at the Earth's geological fault lines, then to bore into the Earth and unleash subterranean magma, and finally to release radiation into the polar regions. This will turn the planet into a 'furious fireball', the energies of which can be transmitted back to Cybertron. (Although Power Station Alpha is dangerous by design, some modifications are required in order for it to be able to do everything Shockwave wants.)

As well as Fort Lewis, other locations seen in this story are the Pentagon (the headquarters of the US Department of Defence) and the Capitol Building (also seen in [14] 'Rock and Roll-Out'), both in Washington DC. We also get a glimpse of Richmond International Airport in nearby Virginia.

We learn here that Bombshell can be susceptible to involuntary partial transformations when his cerebro-shells are manipulated. (Presumably this is just a one-off glitch – it would be a major design flaw if all of his shells caused him to malfunction in such a manner.)

Dirge's destruction here marks his final sighting in the US storylines; conversely, the Autobot Red Alert makes his one and only American appearance here, during the Autobots' battle with Cobra.

The title of this story is taken from a line of the popular nursery rhyme 'Ring a Ring o' Roses' (aka 'Ring Around the Rosie'). The line 'Ashes, ashes' is often replaced with 'Atishoo, atishoo' in many (chiefly British) variants of the lyrics, meaning that many UK readers would not have got the reference.

UK Notes:
While Dirge would play no further part in the American strips, *The Transformers* UK considered the events of this *G.I. Joe* crossover apocryphal, and consequently he continued to appear sporadically in stories such as [39.1] 'Salvage' and [62.9] 'Divide and Conquer' (comic).

Red Alert made his UK comics debut in [4.2] 'The Enemy Within'.

UK Changes:
Page 1, panel 1: to help fill up the page, the line 'Scenario: the end of the world!' is enlarged to fit the page, and all but the word 'scenario' is recoloured pink for emphasis.
Page 1, panel 3: credits added.
Page 3, bottom panel: the original US credits are painted out.
Page 5, panel 3: 'honored' becomes 'honoured'.
Page 8, panel 1: the reference to issue #26 is changed to #109.
Page 23, panel 8: the 'Next issue' box is painted out and the panel is extended downwards, allowing us to see more of Slip-Stream's upper body.

Roll Call:
Autobots: Optimus Prime (as a corpse), Bluestreak, Ratchet, Bumblebee (as a voice, and also as a dismembered body), Cliffjumper, Red Alert, Jetfire, Blaster, Perceptor and Omega Supreme.

Decepticons: Laserbeak, Ravage, Shockwave and Dirge

Other: G B Blackrock.

GI Joes: Mainframe, Crankcase, Hawk and Slip-Stream (plus the Skystriker XP-14F, Dragonfly HX-1 and Conquest X-30 vehicles).

Cobra, the Enemy: Serpentor, the Baroness, Dr Mindbender, Zartan, Torch, Buzzer, Ripper and a Tele-Viper (plus a number of Cobra Rattler vehicles).

Data File: Herb Trimpe (artist)
Trimpe came to fame in the Silver Age of Comics, and was known specially for his work on classic issues of *The Incredible Hulk* (including the first appearance of Wolverine). During his long spell at Marvel, he provided art on a great many other comics, such as *The Avengers*, *Iron Man*, and *The Amazing Spider-Man*.

Review:
Again terrible, but at least we're now into so-bad-it's-unintentionally-amusing territory. We have Senator Larkin, a well-meaning but dim character who accepted 'incredible sums of money' to benefit her 'home state', in exchange for green-lighting a dangerously flawed power station that could potentially kill millions. For some bizarre reason, she's not arrested and pumped for information the moment her deal with Cobra is discovered. Instead, she has a tearful showdown with her boyfriend Hawk, with an exchange of dialogue that wouldn't look out of place in a bad daytime soap ('How could I have been so wrong about you? I trusted you … I loved you …')

In the meantime, the Decepticons keep Dr Mindbender around for no particular reason, except that the plot requires a human spy in their base. Furthermore, the Decepticons equip the power station with energy beams, an earth-boring mechanism, and the ability to transmit energy across the galaxy … which makes one wonder why they have gone to all this trouble, instead of just building their own such device from scratch.

Add all that to some over-the-top melodrama in the hospital scenes, plus the 'comedy' moment where Bumblebee realises that he no longer has a body, and you have a contender for one of the silliest Transformers comics ever published.

On the plus side, the cover is nice. 1/5

[GIJ4] … ALL FALL DOWN! (GIJ)
US: *G.I. Joe and the Transformers* #4 'April 1987' (published December 1986), 25 pages.
Published the same month as issue #27 of the main *The Transformers* title, i.e. [27] 'King of the Hill', and #58 of *G.I. Joe: A Real American Hero*, 'Desperate Moves'.

Not to be confused with the regular *The Transformers* comic story, [66] 'All Fall Down' (TF)

British reprint: UK#277, 7 July 1990 (Part 1), 5 pages; UK#278, 14 July 1990 (Part 2), 5 pages; UK#279, 21 July 1990 (Part 3), 5 pages; UK#280, 28 July 1990 (Part 4), 5 pages; UK#281, 4 August 1990 (Part 5), 5 pages.

Credits:
Michael Higgins (script); Herb Trimpe (pencils); Vince Colletta (inks); Nel Yomtov (colours); Joe Rosen (letters); Don Daley (consulting editor); Bob Harras (editor); Jim Shooter (editor-in-chief); Al Milgrom (cover). **UK:** For UK cover credits, see the entries for [62.7] 'Internal Affairs', [62.8] 'The House that Wheeljack Built', [62.9] 'Divide and Conquer' (comic), [62.10] 'The 4,000,000 Year Itch' and [62.11] 'Makin' Tracks'.

Plot:
Power Station Alpha begins drilling through Earth's geological fault lines, causing earthquakes. Shockwave sends Bombshell to dispose of Dr Mindbeder, but the Cobra scientist is saved by the Baroness, who arrives in the nick of time.

At Fort Lewis, Ratchet puts the finishing touches to Bumblebee's new body – the diminutive Autobot now wishes to be known by the name Goldbug. The Autobots, Joes and Cobra come up with a plan: while the bulk of their forces attack the Decepticons' island base, the trio of Goldbug, Scarlett and the Baroness head to the station and lay explosive charges around its surface.

Experimenting with the cerebro-shell that was removed from Tony Duranti's brain, Dr Mindbender realises that he can gain remote control of the station. After he commands the station to fly safely into space, the charges are detonated and it explodes safely above the atmosphere.

With the station destroyed, all four factions break off their fighting and regroup. Afterwards, Hawk watches on as Senator Larkin is led away by the authorities – however, she is assassinated by a Cobra agent before she can be interrogated.

Notes:
This story sees the American introduction of Goldbug, the rebuilt version of Bumblebee. Grimlock is nowhere in evidence, indicating that these events occur prior to [27] 'King of the Hill', in which he becomes Autobot leader. From the GI Joe point of view, there is a reference to Snake-Eyes' captivity and brain scan in 'Hush Job', an adventure that appeared in *G.I. Joe Yearbook* #3, cover-dated March 1987.

The Washington Monument is seen here; it's evidently been cleaned up since the Battlechargers defaced it in [23] 'Decepticon Graffiti'.

Amongst the Decepticons seen here are Starscream, Skywarp and Thundercracker, who at this point in the American continuity were in Autobot captivity within the *Ark*; this is a production error. One of the Decepticon jets seen in the air battle looks remarkably like Dirge, who was supposedly killed in [GIJ3] 'Ashes, Ashes'.

These events are definitively dated to December 1986 (the month of publication); this is specified on Senator Larkin's gravestone. As with the previous issue, the title comes from the nursery rhyme 'Ring a Ring o' Roses'.

UK Notes:
From the UK point of view, the appearance of Starscream and the other Decepticon jets is explainable: if we assume the entire *G.I. Joe* crossover series takes place in the parallel Timeline A, in which Galvatron never came back and changed history in [20.2] 'Target: 2006', then it's possible for all these jets to be active here. See also the notes to [27.1] 'Wanted: Galvatron – Dead or Alive', [27.3] 'Hunters' and [A2.3] 'The Return of the Transformers'.

UK Changes:
Page 1, panel 1: credits replaced; story title caption moved upwards slightly.
Page 5, panel 4: 'honor' is changed to 'honour'.
Page 7, panel 4: the reference to *G.I. Joe Yearbook* #3 is amended to *The Transformers* issues #199 and 201-203.
Page 18, panel 2: 'favor' is altered to read 'favour'.
Page 25, panel 6: the 'Finis' caption is changed to 'The end'

Roll Call:
Autobots: Ratchet, Jetfire, Silverbolt, Air Raid, Fireflight, Skydive, Slingshot, Superion, Blaster, Omega Supreme and Goldbug.

Decepticons: Starscream, Skywarp, Thundercracker, Ravage, Shockwave, Scrapper, Scavenger, Mixmaster, Bonecrusher, Long Haul, Hook, Devastator, Bombshell, Ramjet, Thrust and Dirge.

GI Joes: Wild Bill, Slip-Stream, Ace, Mainframe, Snake-Eyes, Scarlett, Beachhead, Roadblock and Hawk (plus the Conquest X-30, Skystriker XP-14F and Tomahawk vehicles).

Cobra, the Enemy: Buzzer, Torch, Ripper, Zartan, Serpentor, Dr Mindbender and the Baroness (plus a number of Cobra Rattler vehicles).

Review:
A decent, action-packed finale to what's otherwise been an awful mini-series, mostly due to the fact that it cuts out a lot of the talky scheming and gets down to the action. The dogfight over the Decepticon island is quite impressive-looking, and it's great to see Superion battle Devastator, an obvious match-up that was surprisingly absent from the main Transformers comics.

That said, there are still caveats: the Autobots oddly want to capture the power station rather than destroy it, all because Blaster has got it into his head that the Decepticon-augmented weapon of doom might now constitute a sentient being, which basically comes out of nowhere and makes little sense. The whole Hawk/Larkin subplot is still a bit naff, as are the Tony Duranti scenes (the boy stopped being relevant to the plot last issue).

As a whole, the *G.I. Joe and the Transformers* series can only be considered a disappointment, even though this final chapter marks a slight upturn in quality. 2/5

THE TRANSFORMERS: HEADMASTERS

Telling good stories was just a secondary aim of the *The Transformers* comic; its primary concern was to sell toys. As it progressed, it would regularly introduce new characters to tie in with the release of their toy counterparts. Issues #21 to 25 of the American comic, for example, saw the introductions of the Aerialbots, Stunticons, Battlechargers, Protectobots, Combaticons and Predacons – that's 32 new characters in the space of just five issues. Even then, Hasbro were releasing new figures faster than the comic could keep up.

1986 saw a compromise of sorts – *The Transformers: The Movie* was released theatrically, and it was deemed that the film and its Marvel comic adaptation would give more than adequate exposure to 'futuristic' figures such as Hot Rod and Galvatron; this allowed the American comic virtually to ignore those movie characters and concentrate on the remainder of the line.

When 1987 rolled around, the cartoon series was winding down, which meant that Hasbro could no longer afford Marvel any leeway when it came to featuring the new toys in the comic. The problem was that the 1987 range, when Headmaster and Targetmaster companions were factored in, was the biggest ever in terms of new Transformers characters – roughly 75 in total. *The Transformers* comic already had an extremely high turnover of characters, but this was something else.

The decision was made to launch a second Transformers comic, to help lighten the burden on the original title. Named *The Transformers: Headmasters*, this would do much of the legwork in introducing the new characters, leaving the main title to carry on as usual, relatively unencumbered.

[HDM1] RING OF HATE!
US: *The Transformers: Headmasters* #1 'July 1987' (published March 1987), 23 pages. Published the same month as issue #30 of the main title, i.e. [30] 'The Cure'

British reprint: UK#130, 12 September 1987 (Part 1), 6 pages; UK#131, 19 September 1987 (Part 2), 5 pages; UK#132, 26 September 1987 (Part 3), 6 pages; UK#133, 3 October 1987 (Part 4), 6 pages.

Credits:
Bob Budiansky (script); Frank Springer (pencils); Ian Akin, Brian Garvey (inks); Nel Yomtov (colours); Diana Albers (letters); Don Daley (editor); Jim Shooter (editor-in-chief); Bob Budiansky, Ian Akin and Brian Garvey (cover).

Plot:
After millions of years of war on Cybertron, a group of Autobots led by Fortress Maximus decide to leave the planet altogether and begin a new existence of peace on another planet. They construct a spaceship and head out into space.

These Autobots arrive on the planet Nebulos, a ringed world with natives that look very similar to humans. While the powerful Lord Zarak distrusts the Autobots, the moderate Galen, head of the World Watchers, advocates cooperation. When the Autobot envoy Blurr meets the council, the duplicitous Zarak uses a magnetic polariser on him, causing him to lash out involuntarily and destroy a nearby monument.

Zarak having convinced his fellow Nebulans that the Autobots are a threat, they launch an attack on the unsuspecting robots. Eager to maintain the peace, some of the Autobots surrender their weapons, and others their heads, in a desperate display of submission …

Notes:
Fortress Maximus reveals that the Autobot/Decepticon war began '50,000 vorns ago' (i.e. 4.15 million years ago, a vorn being equal to 83 Earth years). Given that Optimus Prime and Megatron left Cybertron four million years ago, it seems that the war was roughly a hundred and fifty thousand years old when the *Ark* left on its fateful mission.

(It must be remembered however that according to [1] 'The Transformers' the Decepticon faction was formed by Megatron 'eons' before war actually broke out, so there might have been a lengthy period of terrorist acts, battles and skirmishes prior to all-out war being declared.)

Fortress Maximus and his troops have a base in the Manganese Mountains, a 'remote' location on Cybertron that appears to be a natural formation. (Most depictions of Cybertron show the planet completely covered in cities, towers, ramps and other artificial constructs; the appearance of a naturally-occurring mountain range is our first indication that at least some of its original geography remains intact.)

Maximus and his group are seemingly unaware of Optimus Prime's fate ('they were never heard from again'). It's likely that their region of the planet is so remote that they are simply unaware of the various messages sent between Earth and Cybertron, beginning in [10] 'The Next Best Thing to Being There', or indeed of Optimus Prime's brief return to Cybertron, in [23.2] 'Under Fire'.

Although they look identical to humans, the Nebulans are an advanced species, with access to holographic playback devices, magnetic polarizer guns, laser pistols and flying 'hovercraft'. Even their ancestors thousands of years ago had advanced weaponry including tanks and missile launchers.

Koraja is the Nebulan capital, where the Council of Peers sit in session to debate global policy. Lord Zarak appears to have a lot of authority but can be overruled by Galen, leader of a party known as the World Watchers, established to 'maintain peace and environmental harmony'.

Ten thousand years ago Nebulos was devastated by a war that nearly destroyed it. Since then the government has maintained a strict policy of pacifism; all machines of war have been placed under lock and key in a secret stash in the Arvassian mountain range.

UK Changes:
Page 1, panel 1: the credits are replaced.
Page 17, panel 1: an oddly-positioned caption ('But the other Autobots feel differently …') is excised.
Page 23, panel 7: the final caption (trailing the next issue) is painted out, revealing more of Galen's upper body.

Roll Call:
Autobots: Optimus Prime (flashback), Hot Rod, Kup, Blurr, **Fortress Maximus, Highbrow, Chromedome, Hardhead, Brainstorm, Crosshairs, Pointblank, Sureshot, Scattershot, Lightspeed, Nosecone, Afterburner, Grotusque, Doublecross, Repugnus, Cog, Gasket** and **Grommet**.

Two Throttlebots appear to be present in the background of the opening splash page, but it's hard to ascertain exactly which they are supposed to be, or if indeed their appearance was intentional.

This is the first appearance of the present-day iterations of Hot Rod, Kup and Blurr; their future versions had previously been seen in stories such as [20.2] 'Target: 2006'.

Decepticons: **Scorponok, Skullcruncher, Apeface, Snapdragon, Slugslinger, Triggerhappy, Misfire, Blot, Flywheels, Battletrap** and **Fasttrack**.

Nebulans: **Galen**, **Gort**, **Duros**, **Zarak** and **Krunk**

The art and colouring make identifying some of the Transformers in this issue very difficult – Cerebros appears, for example, despite not having been created yet. The above list comprises only those characters whose appearances make sense from a narrative point of view.

Review:

As in [17] 'The Smelting Pool', writer Bob Budiansky shows a real flair for world-building. In just a few short pages we are told an awful lot about the planet Nebulos, its history and its culture. What could have been a boring, generic planet is a place we can actually buy into and care about.

Also notable is that, after the Decepticons are seen off within the first four pages, there are no real villains here; all of the conflict arises from characters being unable to understand or know the full picture. Even the belligerent Zarak, who wants the Autobots gone, acts only because he feels it's in the best interests of the planet.

Annoying art errors notwithstanding, this is an intelligent and absorbing piece of work. 4/5

[HDM2] BROKEN GLASS!

US: *The Transformers: Headmasters* #2 'September 1987' (published May 1987), 23 pages. Published the same month as issue 32 of the main title, i.e. [32] 'Used Autobots'

British reprint: UK#134, 10 October 1987 (Part 1), 5 pages; UK#135, 17 October 1987 (Part 2), 6 pages; UK#136, 24 October 1987 (Part 3), 6 pages; UK#137, 31 October 1987 (Part 4), 6 pages.

NB: On this and the remaining two issues, the cover gives the comic's title as simply *Headmasters*; however the indicia on the first page gives the full title as *The Transformers: Headmasters*, in line with issue 1.

Credits:

Bob Budiansky (script); Frank Springer (pencils); Ian Akin, Brian Garvey (inks); Nel Yomtov (colours); Pat Brosseau (letters); Don Daley (editor); Jim Shooter (editor-in-chief); Frank Springer, Ian Akin and Brian Garvey (cover).

For the British printing, Diana Albers (who worked on issue 1 in this series) was incorrectly credited as the letterer.

Plot:

Fortress Maximus and others having forfeited their heads, the remaining Autobots are allowed to live in peace on Nebulos. Lord Zarak, however, still isn't satisfied with the situation – he secretly incites a civil disturbance during an anti-Autobot rally in the Nebulan capital; and, worse, he invites the Decepticons to Nebulos in a bid to get rid of the Autobots.

Inevitably, the Decepticons arrive and start causing havoc, threatening not only the Autobots but the Nebulans also. The Autobots, disarmed and leaderless, are unable to help, so Galen and a group of like-minded Nebulans take matters into their own hands.

They undergo a radical and experimental surgery to become 'binary-bonded' to the headless Autobots. Effectively, this means that the Nebulans are able to transform into new heads for the five decapitated Autobots. This symbiotic relationship with the Autobots dramatically increases their battle-skills, and they drive the Decepticons back with ease.

Notes:

We learn a bit more about Nebulos this issue. The area where Highbrow first encountered Gort was called the Folassian Forest. Zarak has access to a hyper-galactic transceiver that can contact Cybertron. (As well as 'hyper-galactic', the terms 'interdimensional space' and 'endless void' are used, indicating that Cybertron is currently a great distance from Nebulos; contrast this with [HDM1] 'Ring of Hate', where the Transformers' homeworld was said to be relatively 'near' to Nebulos – evidence perhaps of Cybertron's great speed as it hurtles around the cosmos. See also the notes to [16.3] 'Second Generation'.) We see an example of untranslated Nebulan text; it appears to be some sort of complex logographic system.

The Headmaster process, as it's initially explained, would appear to be a simple matter of the Nebulans taking sole control of the Autobots' bodies. These Autobots – Fortress Maximus, Hardhead, Highbrow, Chromedome and Brainstorm – are 'no longer commanders of their own bodies' fates'; they merely 'maintain radio contact with their respective Nebulan successors'. However, as we shall see in later adventures, the Autobots' personalities will eventually reassert themselves on their new partners, the relationship becoming more symbiotic as time goes on. As a portent of this development, the Nebulans have started to refer to each other by their Transformer names ('I did indeed, Chromedome').

UK Notes:

Unfortunately, in both of his appearances in this story, Cyclonus is incorrectly drawn, resembling his future Nebulan companion Nightstick. As UK readers would have been bound to spot this error – the character had featured heavily in stories such as [20.2] 'Target: 2006' and [27.1] 'Wanted: Galvatron – Dead or Alive' – edits were made, and the mis-drawn Decepticon was referred to by the made-up name 'Krunix'.

UK Changes:

Page 1, panel 1: the credits are replaced.
Page 2, panel 2: 'see *Headmasters* #1' is changed to 'see issues 130-133'
Page 9, panel 3: 'gismo' is altered to read 'gizmo'
Page 10, panel 2: as discussed above, the reference to 'Cyclonus' is altered to 'Krunix'.
Page 12, panel 3: 'Save some for Cyclonus!' is altered to 'Save some for me too!'
Page 13, panel 1: the American 'defenses' is changed to the British 'defences'.
Page 14, panel 3: the reference to 'last issue' becomes 'issue 133'.
Page 15, panel 1: 'endeavor' is replaced by 'endeavour'.
Page 16, panel 2: 'armor' is amended to read 'armour'.
Page 17, panel 1: 'armored' becomes 'armoured'.
Page 19, panel 6: 'human' is corrected to 'Nebulan'.
Page 23, panel 8: 'savor' is changed to 'savour'; the next issue preview caption is also painted out.

Roll Call:
Autobots: Hot Rod, Kup, Blurr, Fortress Maximus, Highbrow, Chromedome, Hardhead, Brainstorm, Crosshairs and Pointblank.

Decepticons: Cyclonus (sort of, see the 'UK Changes' section above), Scorponok, Skullcruncher, **Mindwipe**, Apeface, Snapdragon, Slugslinger, Triggerhappy, Misfire, Blot, Flywheels, Battletrap, Fasttrack and **Sixshot**.

Nebulans: Galen, Gort, **Stylor**, Duros, **Arcana**, Zarak, **Grax**, **Vorath**, **Spasma** and Krunk.

Review:
Another fine instalment of the Headmasters saga; again, the political wrangling and scheming – a novelty for a Transformers comic – is just as interesting as the action and the fire fights. As this saga progresses, it becomes more and more obvious that the hero of the piece is not Autobot leader Fortress Maximus, but the noble and romantic Nebulan Galen.

That said, some of the twists and turns here are a little hard to swallow. Zarak is vehemently opposed to the Autobot encampment on Nebulos, so it's a bit odd that he chooses to invite yet more Transformers to the planet. Otherwise, this is an impressive second chapter in what's proving to be a refreshingly different take on the Transformers saga. 4/5

[HDM3] LOVE AND STEEL!
US: *The Transformers: Headmasters* #3 'November 1987' (published July 1987), 22 pages. Published the same month as issue #34 of the main title, i.e. the concluding part of the [4.1] 'Man of Iron' reprint.

British reprint: UK#138, 7 November 1987 (Part 1), 6 pages; UK#139, 14 November 1987 (Part 2), 5 pages; UK#140, 21 November 1987 (Part 3), 6 pages; UK#141, 28 November 1987 (Part 4), 5 pages.

Credits:
Bob Budiansky (script); Frank Springer (pencils); Ian Akin, Brian Garvey (inks); Nel Yomtov (colours); Pat Brosseau (letters); Don Daley (editor); Tom DeFalco (editor-in-chief); Frank Springer, Ian Akin and Brian Garvey (cover).

Again, Diana Albers was incorrectly credited as the letterer in the UK printing.

Plot:
A battle between the Technobots and the Terrorcons in the city of Splendora results in widespread damage. The Nebulan Council of Peers are growing increasingly distrustful of Autobots and Decepticons alike, despite Galen's involvement as an Autobot Headmaster.

Zarak, meanwhile, convinces the Decepticons that the only way they can defeat the Autobots is by undergoing the Headmaster process themselves. He lures the Autobot Headmasters into a trap, using as bait his own daughter, Galen's fiancée Llyra.

The Autobots duly arrive and battle the newly-created Decepticon Headmasters.

The Headmaster process having increased the Decepticons' battle prowess, this time the fight against the Autobot Headmasters is much more even. When Scorponok traps a group of council members sent to observe, Fortress Maximus and his Autobots break away from the battle in order to free the prisoners. This gives the Decepticons the opportunity to attack the Autobots in force.

With the Autobots defeated and their Nebulan companions unconscious, Zarak surveys the scene of his victory …

Notes:
This story sees the first appearance of Computron and Abominus, the combined forms of the Technobots and Throttlebots respectively. Previous adventures such as [16.2] 'Second Generation' and [19] 'Command Performances' have established that the combiner ability is novel and difficult to achieve, so it's unclear how the Autobots and Decepticons have been able to develop the technology independently on Cybertron. (It's possible that, at some point after [16.2] 'Second Generation', the Decepticons sent the schematics for these 'Special Teams' to Cybertron for further development, and that that communique was intercepted by the Autobots.)

More information is revealed about Nebulos; Splendora is a resort city but (as with the capital Koraja) its defenders have armed themselves with powerful weapons left over from the war, in order to counter the robot threat. Elsewhere, the Plains of Thok are said to be 'remote'.

Llyra inherits her father's seat on the Council of Peers when her father is taken by the Decepticons, indicating that at least some aspects of government are determined on the basis of bloodline, rather than through the democratic process.

Already, the Headmaster process is beginning to have an effect on the Nebulans and their Transformer counterparts, as the blending of minds is cemented. Notably, Scorponok momentarily hesitates when Zarak's daughter is threatened; this despite the Decepticon leader having previously shown no regard for Nebulan life.

UK Changes:
Page 1, panel 1: the credits are replaced. Also, completing a sentence left hanging in the original printing, the UK version adds an additional word to the end of one of the captions: '… when these seven living mechanical monsters – the Decepticons Apeface, Cutthroat, Snapdragon, Rippersnapper, Hun-Grr [sic], Sinnertwin and Blot – arrived!'
Page 10, panel 2: 'endeavoring' is changed to the British 'endeavouring'. Also, 'Headmasters #1 becomes 'issue #133'
Page 12, panel 1: 'armor' is changed to 'armour'
Page 21, panel 4: 'humans' is amended to 'Nebulans'

Roll Call:
Autobots: Fortress Maximus, Highbrow, Chromedome, Hardhead, Brainstorm, Scattershot, Lightspeed, Nosecone, Afterburner, **Strafe** and **Computron**.

Afterburner and Strafe are seen only as part of the giant combiner Computron, and do not appear in their individual guises.

Decepticons: Scorponok, Skullcruncher, Mindwipe, Weirdwolf, Apeface, Snapdragon, Slugslinger, **Hun-Gurr**, **Cutthroat**, Blot, **Sinnertwin**, **Rippersnapper** and **Abominus**.

It's unclear if Slugslinger's appearance is deliberate, or if it's another of the many art errors that blight the Headmasters mini-series – he's seen in a single panel, in a group of Decepticons retreating from the battle at Splendora.

Nebulans: Galen, Gort, Stylor, Duros, Arcana, Zarak, Grax, Vorath, **Monzo**, Spasma and Krunk.

Review:
Another decent chapter in the Headmasters saga, albeit spoiled by some rather odd characterisation. In previous issues Zarak has always put Nebulos first, even though his methods might have been underhand. Here, though, he persuades Scorponok to put him through the Headmaster process, despite having already criticised Galen for doing the same. Here is a character, unafraid to die for his beliefs, yet one who makes bizarre decisions (his plan to call the Decepticons to Nebulos in the first place being another) for the sake of plot expediency.

Another problem character is Llyra. A woman having to choose between the two men in her life, fighting on opposite sides of a war, is a great hook for a character. Sadly, however, she comes across as petty, easily led and wilfully ignorant. She castigates Galen for putting aside his peaceful ways, despite the fact that it was her father, Zarak, whose idea it was to wage war on the Autobots in the first place.

The problems are irksome precisely because the rest of this series has been so good. 'Love and Steel' has good action sequences and some emotional moments, but the intelligent plotting and politicking of the first two issues have made way here for melodrama and soap opera. 3/5

[HDM4] BROTHERS IN ARMOR!!
US: *The Transformers: Headmasters* #4 'January 1988' (published September 1987), 22 pages.
Published the same month as issue 36 of the main title, i.e. [36] 'Spacehikers'.

British reprint: UK#142, 5 December 1987 (Part 1), 6 pages; UK#143, 12 December 1987 (Part 2), 5 pages; UK#144, 19 December 1987 (Part 3), 5 pages; UK#145, 26 December 1987 (Part 4), 6 pages.

For the British printing, the title of this story was amended to 'Brothers in Armour!'

Credits:
Bob Budiansky (script); Frank Springer (pencils); Ian Akin, Brian Garvey (inks); Nel Yomtov (colours); Jack Morelli (letters); Don Daley (editor); Tom DeFalco (editor-in-chief); Frank Springer and Brian Garvey (cover).

Plot:
The Decepticons continue to wreak havoc across Nebulos; the Mercury Gardens of Melanossus, an agricultural research facility and even the capital city itself come under attack.

With their Headmaster compatriots under lock and key, some of the remaining Autobots decide to swing the tide of battle back in their favour. They become Targetmasters, with Nebulan allies bioengineered to transform into their handguns.

With these new weapons, the Autobots are able to drive the Decepticons away, but not before the Decepticons cause severe damage to the surrounding area. To counter this new technology, the Decepticons also decide to engineer some of their own warriors into Targetmasters.

Zarak, meanwhile, is a tortured soul. The Headmaster process has not gone well for him, and he is torn between his love for Nebulos and the new bloodlust that comes from being binary-bonded with the Decepticon leader Scorponok. In a brief moment of clarity, he frees the Autobot Headmasters. Galen decides that the only way to rid Nebulos of the Transformer menace is for the Autobots to flee the planet and hope that the Decepticons pursue. Following a distress signal to Earth, the Transformers depart Nebulos.

Notes:
Locations on Nebulos introduced here include the Nursery, a beautiful communal garden that doubles as a bio-research facility, and the Mercury Gardens of Melanossus, which boast stunning fountains of quicksilver. Both are destroyed here in Decepticon attacks. (Mercury is, of course, highly toxic; either the Nebulans have found a way to make it safe, or their physiology is so different from humans' that they are unaffected by it.)

The Nebulan code-named 'Peacemaker' reveals that the planet boasts an 'eons-old democracy'. (Compare this with the line in [HDM3] 'Love and Steel' in which Llyra talks about inheriting her father's seat on the council, albeit temporarily. It's possible that Nebulos has a two-tier government; one house for elected representatives and another for the nobility, similar to the British system. It's telling that many of these governmental characters are addressed as either 'Lord' or 'Peer' – titles that, in the British system, refer to the unelected gentry – whereas the likeable Galen is never titled as such – making it likely that he was one of the democratically elected council members.

NNN (the Nebulan News Network) is a popular news outlet (presumably named after the real-world news channel CNN). Nebulos practises capital punishment on (at least some of) its criminals.

The dark side of the Headmaster process is seen here, as Zarak is slowly driven mad by his blending with Scorponok. Publically he refuses to admit anything is wrong ('They have no influence on me! They can't!'), but finally he admits to Galen, 'Each time I combine with Scorponok, it gets worse – he's reprogramming my mind – making me do things!'

The signal from Earth that the Autobots detect was sent by Goldbug in [37] 'Toy Soldiers', a story that was still to be published when this issue went on sale.

The title is a play on the saying 'brothers in arms', popularised when used as the title of an international number one album by rock group Dire Straits in 1985.

UK Changes:
Page 1, panel 1: the credits are replaced, the title is amended, and an odd lettering anomaly (a random letter 'F' in the middle of Scorponok's speech bubble) is removed.
Page 4, panel 4: the reference to '*Headmasters* #'s 1-3' is changed to 'issues 130-141'.
Page 6, panel 2: '*Headmasters* 1' is altered to 'issue 133'.
Page 7, panel 3: the '*Headmasters* #2' citation note now reads 'issue #135'.
Page 10, panel 4: 'fibers' is changed to 'fibres'.

Page 11, panel 5: to make for a better cliffhanger ending when this story was split into four parts for the UK printing, the ellipsis at the end of the final sentence is changed to an exclamation mark.

Page 13, panel 6: compounding the confusion surrounding the correct spelling of the character's name, 'Hun-Grr' is changed to 'Hun-Garr'.

Roll Call:
Autobots: Hot Rod, Kup, Blurr, Fortress Maximus, Highbrow, Chromedome, Hardhead, Brainstorm, Crosshairs, Pointblank, Sureshot, Grotusque, Doublecross and Repugnus.

Decepticons: Cyclonus, Scourge, Scorponok, Skullcruncher, Mindwipe, Weirdwolf, Apeface, Snapdragon, Slugslinger, Triggerhappy, Misfire, Hun-Gurrr, Cutthroat, Blot, Sinnertwin, Rippersnapper and Sixshot (flashback only).

Nebulans: Galen, Gort, Stylor, Duros, Arcana, **Firebolt**, **Haywire**, **Recoil**, **Pinpointer**, **Peacemaker**, **Spoilsport**, Zarak, Grax, Vorath, Monzo, Spasma, Krunk, **Nightstick**, **Fracas**, **Caliburst**, **Blowpipe** and **Aimless**.

Hot Rod's Targetmaster partner, Firebolt, is incorrectly referred to as 'Sparks' in this story.

Review:
After the slight mis-step that was [HDM3] 'Love and Steel', this is a marked improvement. Zarak is better here: a man torn between his duty to his planet and the lust for power that comes from being a Decepticon.

The introduction of the Targetmasters is perfunctory at best (the Decepticon Targetmaster weapons aren't even named), but that's down simply to lack of space; this is a taut finale to what's been an excellent and intriguing series. 4/5

THE UK ANNUALS
In the UK, an annual is a traditional Christmas gift – a colourful, large format, hardback children's book, usually based on a particular topic (e.g. a recent film, a sports team, a television show, a popular celebrity etc.) From 1985, Marvel UK, in conjunction with book publishers Grandreams, produced a Transformers Annual. As well as containing facts, quizzes and activities, these presented new, exclusive fiction – often written so as to tie in with events in the comics.

Although each edition was simply titled *The Transformers Annual*, it is common practice in the UK to refer to annuals by the year *after* publication – so the first edition, published in 1985, is referred to as the 1986 Annual. This was traditionally done to extend the books' shelf-life, so that they would still be seen as 'current' even in the months after Christmas.

[A1.1] PLAGUE OF THE INSECTICONS!
20 pages; from the UK *The Transformers Annual 1986* (published August 1985)

NB: Even after much research, it's difficult to ascertain the precise release date for this year's annual. This conjectural date of August 1985 is based on the following evidence:

- The other Transformers annuals have known publication dates in July, August or September, so it's highly likely that this edition came out at a similar time of year.
- A reader's letter praising the annual was printed in UK#32 in October 1985, so it must have been available prior to that.
- Images from the annual's strips were used to illustrate the 'Robot War!' feature in UK#22 in July 1985, so production must have been at an advanced stage by then.

Credits:

Simon Furman (script); Mike Collins and Jeff Anderson (art); Gina Hart (colours); Richard Starkings (letters); Sheila Cranna (editor). The annual's cover was provided by John Higgins.

Plot:

Concerned that humans are unable to tell the Autobots from the Decepticons, Optimus Prime enters into peace talks with the President of the United States of America. The negotiations are interrupted when a trio of insectoid Decepticons – Insecticons – attack Washington DC in an attempt to discredit the Autobots.

It transpires that the Insecticons are being guided and controlled by the Decepticon Ravage. By an amazing stroke of luck, a brain-wiping cerebro-shell meant for the Autobot leader misses and instead hits Ravage. With the Insecticons rudderless, the Autobots emerge victorious.

The Autobots assume that their reputation is now in tatters, and elect to retreat rather than face the President again. Ironically, the President actually suspected that the Autobots were being set up, but their decision not to resume talks makes him doubt their good intentions.

Notes:

As with many of the stories in the 1986 Annual, the events of 'Plague of the Insecticons' are difficult to place within the timeline of the regular comics. As this was a standalone publication separate from the standard issues, the writers had free rein to come up with stories unhindered by the need to fit into the comics' continuity. A case in point: this story sees appearances by Warpath, Shrapnel, Bombshell and Kickback, who at the time were available as toys but still to be introduced in the comics.

If this story were to fit into the regular comic continuity, then it would have to be set in the short gap between Warpath joining the Earth-based Autobot ranks in [23.5] 'Resurrection' and Optimus Prime being killed in [24] 'Afterdeath'. (Although he is later resurrected in [42] 'People Power', it's unlikely that the Roller component survives his original demise.) However, that's impossible, as Ravage was inactive during that period – he was lost in [20] 'Showdown' and returned in [48.2] 'Time Wars. Therefore this story cannot really be slotted in at any point of the comic's chronology. It's best to assume that it takes place in Timeline A – the parallel dimension in which Galvatron never interfered with history – see [27.1] 'Wanted: Galvatron – Dead or Alive'.

The unnamed President is very obviously the then current incumbent, Ronald Reagan. His colleague, referred to only as 'Don', is possibly supposed to represent Reagan's chief of staff, Donald Regan, although it looks nothing like him.

While the ability was mentioned in his fact file piece in UK#6, this is the first time we actually see Optimus Prime dividing his consciousness between his three core components – the standard robot, the 'combat deck' trailer module, and Roller, a non-transforming scout car. Pain felt by any member of the trinity is also experienced by the other two.

The interior of the Decepticons' base is seen to have green walls, similar to its depiction in [4.2] 'The Enemy Within' – possibly inferring that they are still based in the mountaintop Fortress Sinister seen in that earlier story.

Businesses in Washington DC include Furman's Weight Watchers and Rimmer's Ooptician [sic], references to Marvel UK writer Simon Furman and editor Ian Rimmer.

Optimus Prime's vehicle mode is described by the President as a 'lorry', the British writing team obviously forgetting that, as an American, the President would be more likely to use the word 'truck'.

Pest Control

Why do the Insecticons need to be guided by Ravage here? Well, they are known for their ability to construct clones of themselves (especially in the cartoon series), so it's entirely possible that those seen in this story are mindless duplicates – perhaps similar to the Facsimile Constructs we see in adventures such as [20.2] 'Target: 2006'. Alternatively they could be less successful products of the mind-clone technique used by the Autobots in [14] 'Rock and Roll-Out'. The unusual colour schemes sported by the Insecticons in this story are extremely reminiscent of Salvo, Shothole and Zaptrap, limited-edition Japanese-exclusive toys released in 2004 with the specific intention of representing these unintelligent Insecti-clones.

In the real world, a toy ad for the Insecticons was placed in a couple of early issues of the UK comic (UK#17 and 19). This featured artwork of the figures, but in a reddish colour scheme clearly based on the early, pre-Transformers versions of the toys marketed in Japan as Dicalone Insecter Robo. Seemingly oblivious that the ad was unrepresentative of the actual toys, colourist Gina Hart probably used it as a reference for her work on this story.

Continuity Cat Flap

In [20] 'Showdown', the Decepticon cassette warrior Ravage falls down an old mineshaft, seemingly to his doom. He doesn't revive until [48.2] 'Time Wars' – and yet is still able to appear in stories such as [A1.1] 'Plague of the Insecticons', [A1.4] 'Hunted', [GIJ2] 'Power Struggle', [GIJ3] 'Ashes, Ashes' and [GIJ4] 'All Fall Down' (GIJ). It's therefore safe to assume that all of these stories are set in the parallel Timeline A (see above). In this, Ravage was revived and restored to full health earlier than in Timeline B.

Roll Call:

Autobots: Optimus Prime, Jazz (flashback only), Prowl, Hound (flashback only), Gears (flashback only) and **Warpath**.

During the flashback, a number of Autobots are seen in silhouette, but other than Jazz and Hound (both shown in the foreground) and also Gears (whose head shape is extremely distinctive), none of them is immediately recognisable.

Decepticons: Megatron, Soundwave (both flashback only), Ravage, **Shrapnel**, **Bombshell** and **Kickback**.

Data File: John Higgins (artist)
Writer, artist and colourist Higgins has done a lot of work for *2000 AD*, including *Judge Dredd*, *ABC Warriors* and *Chopper*. He successfully made the transition to American comics, where his credits include *Swamp Thing*, *Razorjack* and *The Hills Have Eyes: The Beginning*. However, he's best known for being the colourist on *Batman: The Killing Joke* and the comic classic *Watchmen*.

Review:
This is a surprisingly meaty story, full of incident and plot twists. The method of Ravage's defeat is ingenious, topped only by the marvellous epilogue in which it's revealed that the humans aren't quite as stupid as they look. 4/5

[A1.2] MISSING IN ACTION
7 pages; from the UK *The Transformers Annual 1986* (published August 1985)

NB: This is an illustrated prose story, rather than a comic strip *per se*.

Credits:
James Hill (writer); John Stokes (art); Sheila Cranna (editor).

Plot:
Badly injured after a skirmish with the Decepticon Rumble, the Autobot Tracks transforms into his car mode and becomes dormant. He is soon hijacked by two human criminals, Mark and J D, who use the unconscious Autobot as a getaway car in a series of armed robberies.

The Autobots eventually find Tracks at the scene of the latest bank robbery. Their appearance startles the two crooks, who accidentally set off a bomb they have brought with them. The bank goes up in flames, but the Autobot forces are able to rescue the trapped civilians – one of whom is a small boy, Danny.

Notes:
The opening scenes, in which Tracks is incapacitated and then stolen, are said to take place in 'Greater Portland', which has a population that 'never exceeds ten thousand'. In reality, the Greater Portland metropolitan area has a population of over two million, whereas Portland city itself was home to around 400,000 people during the '80s, when this story was set.

Mention is made of Woolworth's, the US department store chain that went out of business in 1997.

As previously evidenced by the incongruous use of the word 'lorry' in [A1.1] 'Plague of the Insecticons', this story is again very obviously written by a Briton; the word 'bonnet' is used to describe Tracks' front section, rather than the American 'hood'.

As discussed in the entry to [8.1] 'Decepticon Dam-Busters', Inferno was presumably part of the original group of Autobots who arrived on Earth in the *Ark*. However, his appearances in the comic are extremely rare, so either he's very injury-prone or he's always off on other missions. It's entirely possible that he was grievously wounded during Shockwave's attack in [4] 'The Last Stand' and this is his first adventure after a long lay-off.

Setting the Action
As with [A1.1] 'Plague of the Insecticons', ascertaining exactly how this fits into comic continuity is a bit tricky. If anywhere, the best place for it is between [18] 'The Bridge to Nowhere', in which Cosmos arrives on Earth, and [19] 'Command Performances', in which Rumble is rendered inoperable. However, rationalising Cosmos's appearance still requires some lateral thinking, as he doesn't actually join the ranks of the Earthbound Autobots until a bit later ([23.5] 'Resurrection'). So here's one possible theory:

Cosmos and the rest of the Cybertron Seven arrive on Earth ([18] 'The Bridge to Nowhere'). Thanks to his alternate mode (a UFO), he has the greatest range of any of the new arrivals, so he scouts ahead for other signs of Transformer activity. He comes into contact with Optimus Prime and the *Ark* crew, during which time he participates in the events of this story.

Armed with this knowledge, he returns to Blaster and the rest of the new Autobots, but before he can divulge any details, the seven are attacked and beheaded by RAAT ([22] 'Heavy Traffic'). This damage has an effect on Cosmos's memory, and he forgets that he ever met the rest of the Autobots.

(Although this just about works as an explanation, it is not one given the comics themselves.)

Given all the above, this story therefore takes place sometime in 1986. A New York kid, Danny, is ten years old here; his father died when he was four, in an accident involving a NASA test vehicle (which ties in quite neatly with real-world events: there were a handful of deaths in 1981 during launch preparations for the first US Space Shuttle, *Columbia*).

Alternatively, this story could just be set in the parallel Timeline A (see the essays under [27.1] 'Wanted: Galvatron – Dead or Alive' and [A2.3] 'The Return of the Transformers').

Roll Call:
Autobots: Optimus Prime, Jazz, Mirage, Brawn, **Inferno**, **Tracks**, **Grapple**, **Hoist** and **Cosmos**.

Decepticons: Rumble only, although Megatron is also name-checked.

Review:
An over-simplistic plot, definitely aimed toward the younger end of the readership. It's functional without being particularly engaging, although the accompanying illustrations are lovely. 2/5

[A1.3] TALES OF CYBERTRON: AND THERE SHALL COME... A LEADER!
10 pages; from the UK *The Transformers Annual 1986* (published August 1985)

Credits:
Simon Furman (script); John Stokes (art); Gina Hart (colours); Richard Starkings (letters); Sheila Cranna (editor).

Plot:
Cybertron: millions of years ago. Megatron and his Decepticons are on the verge of

complete victory over the Autobots, who are commanded by a council of elders and politicians. One of these governors, Emirate Xaaron, suggests that control of the Autobot forces should instead be entrusted to a military mind, and suggests a soldier, Optimus Prime, as the ideal candidate.

Re-galvanised under Prime's leadership, the Autobots enter into battle, and decimate the Decepticon forces by luring them onto a bridge booby-trapped with explosives. The bridge is demolished, and the Decepticon forces are defeated.

Unbeknown to the Autobots, Megatron has survived, and clambers out of the rubble swearing revenge ...

Notes:

This adventure is set some time before Optimus Prime and the Autobots leave for Earth as depicted in [1] 'The Transformers'. Given that the Cybertron seen here has bright skies and an atmosphere (weapon guidance systems have to compensate for 'wind vectors'), we can surmise that it is at this point still in orbit around Alpha Centauri.

Visually, this story owes much to the artwork seen in the very first issue; designs of buildings and background characters are carried over wholesale.

This story gives us a better glimpse of the Autobot city-state of Iacon, seen briefly in issue #1; in particular its Great Dome and the spires of the Celestial Temple within. It's the home of the Council of Autobot Elders (also referred to here as the High Council or simply the Council). It's obviously intended to be the same group of Autobot Elders we see convene in issue #1.

One of the Elders seen in that first comic – a white/blue Transformer – is here identified as Tomaandi. Others present include High Councillor Traachon and Emirate Xaaron, who will go on to become a prominent character in the later comics. (The three councillors named here have more alien-sounding names than most regular Transformers, all including two letter As in succession. It's tempting to believe these are actual Transformer names, rather than the usual nicknames sported by the general soldiers (such as Bluestreak or Windcharger). This ties in neatly with dialogue in [4.1] 'Man of Iron', where Jazz explained that his real name would be unpronounceable to humans.)

Incidentally, in English the word Emirate is not a rank, but rather the land or office held by an Emir, an Islamic prince or chieftain – presumably the term has a different meaning on Cybertron, or perhaps Emirate is not a title but is actually a part of Xaaron's name.

One-off Autobots named here include Pulsar, Tempest and Fusion, the latter of which transforms into a wheeled tank with a design clearly based on Optimus Prime's own Cybertronian vehicle mode as seen in issue #1. Bluestreak's Cybertron mode is a streamlined, futuristic-looking car.

'And there shall come ...' is a turn of phrase prevalent in some translations of the Bible, for example 'And there shall come forth a rod' (Isaiah 11:1), 'And there shall come forth a vessel' (Proverbs 25:4) and 'And there shall come a redeemer' (Isaiah 59:20), giving Optimus Prime's arrival an epic, mystical quality, almost as if it were predestined.

Roll Call:

In addition to the various one-off characters listed above, we also have ...

Autobots: Optimus Prime, Prowl, Bluestreak, Gears, Brawn, Windcharger and **Emirate Xaaron**.

Decepticons: Megatron and Soundwave.

Hound and Ratchet are mentioned in dialogue but not seen. It's possible that the winged black Decepticon who kills Fusion is Skywarp in a pre-Earth jet mode, but this is not confirmed in the story itself.

Review:
A nice glimpse of life in Cybertron's early years, and the bickering between the councillors in the opening pages is fun to read. However, the plot is very slight and not particularly memorable.

Pivotal for its introduction of Emirate Xaaron and for being the first story to delve into the ancient Cybertronian mythos, the story seems content just to present us with ancient Cybertron rather than bothering to tell a particularly interesting narrative within it. 3/5

[A1.4] HUNTED!
7 pages; from the UK *The Transformers Annual 1986* (published August 1985)

NB: This is another prose story.

Credits:
James Hill (writer); John Stokes (art); Sheila Cranna (editor).

Plot:
The Decepticons have set up a base in the South American jungle. Their plan: using human slave labour, they are mining for rare crystals that, when imprinted with intelligence, can be used to create new Decepticon troops.

Monitoring global news programmes, the Autobots pick up on a report about Dr John Butler, who managed to escape from the Decepticons' clutches; they head off to South America to investigate.

In the resulting battle, Starscream is shot down – he crashes directly into the Decepticon mine, completely destroying it. Megatron escapes yet again, but the Autobots manage to free the remainder of the human captives.

Notes:
The Decepticons' plan here is to use crystals as receptacles for Transformer intelligence; presumably a technology similar to the crystals seen in [14] 'Rock and Roll-Out', on which the Autobots store the minds of their troops.

The Decepticons here are based in a replica of Megatron's fortress on Cybertron: presumably the Castle Decepticon seen in [1] 'The Transformers'.

Aside from a few vague references to South America, there's no indication as to where exactly this adventure takes place – rainforests and boa constrictors are abundant throughout the continent. In the real world, South America is indeed famous for its gemstones and other minerals (Colombia being the world's largest exporter of emeralds).

Hunting for Explanations

Placing this story in the timeline is, again, an extremely difficult task and, like [A1.1] 'Plague of the Insecticons', it doesn't really fit into the standard comic continuity.

Problem #1: the presence of two Autobot 'Wreckers' (Twin Twist and Topspin) in this Earth-set story, even though at this point they should still be based on Cybertron. However, as seen in adventures such as [20.2] 'Target: 2006' and [40.5] 'Wrecking Havoc', the Cybertron-based Autobots *are* able to teleport to Earth when necessary. This would also explain the otherwise baffling appearances of Cybertron-based characters such as Broadside in (the original version of) [41] 'Totaled' and Twin Twist in [36] 'Spacehikers'. As such, this is the least problematic of the continuity issues posed by the adventure.

Problem #2: the presence of Starscream. Starscream is supposed to be dormant during this period, having been placed in suspended animation at the end of [19] 'Command Performances'. Except for a brief revival in [20.1] 'Target: 2006', he doesn't wake up again until the events of [36.1] 'Stargazing', a special festive story published for Christmas 1987, by which time Optimus Prime is dead.

Problem #3: the appearance of Ravage, who was inactive between [20] 'Showdown' and [48.2] 'Time Wars'.

As such, this story must surely take place in a parallel dimension, namely Timeline A (see the entries for [27.1] 'Wanted: Galvatron – Dead or Alive' and [A2.3] 'The Return of the Transformers').

Roll Call:

Autobots: Prowl, Bumblebee, **Twin Twist** and **Topspin**. Optimus Prime and Jazz are mentioned in dialogue.

Decepticons: Megatron, Starscream, Ravage, **Thrust** and **Dirge**.

Review:

Of the two prose stories in the 1986 Annual, this one is very slightly the better. The overall plot and writing style are still quite simplistic, but 'Hunted' just about edges it by giving Bumblebee and Prowl some decent characterisation. 2/5

[A2.1] IN THE BEGINNING... (THE STORY OF THE TRANSFORMERS... SO FAR.)

5 pages; from the UK *The Transformers Annual 1987* (published August 1986)

NB: As with the previous year's annual, the exact publication date has been lost in the mists of time. A recent volume of reprints suggests a date of September 1986, which is backed up by an editor's note in UK#65 ('on sale in September'). However, advertisements in UK#75 and #76 (published in August 1986) claimed that the Annual was already 'on sale now' – a claim also backed up by issue #76's editorial page.

This is an illustrated prose story.

Credits:

Simon Furman (writer); Sheila Cranna (editor). Stock artwork from previous issues was used to illustrate the story. John Stokes provided the annual's cover, while Steve Cook was credited as designer.

Plot:
Computer whizz Adam Reynolds accepts a bet to hack into some banking records; however he accidentally gains access to the Decepticon Mainframe Computer instead.

Adam uses the computer to find details of the Transformers' history and their adventures on Earth – unaware that the Decepticon computer's firewall system is preparing to send a deadly million-volt shock wirelessly into Adam's own terminal.

Luckily, Adam is distracted by his pet cat Ulysses, and is therefore at a safe enough distance from the resultant explosion of his computer.

Notes:
Adam's plan is to hack into 'Portland National Bank'. In the real world there are many Portland-area banks with the words 'National Bank' (or variations thereof) in their name, so it's impossible to narrow this down to a specific branch. It may or may not be the same institution as the First National Bank robbed by Joey Slick in [13] 'Shooting Star'.

Adam uses a Sinclair computer to perform his hacking. At the time this story was set, the latest model would have been the ZX Spectrum 128, or possibly the ZX Spectrum +2. Although Sinclair were a household name in the UK, they never really took off across the Atlantic, where their computers were branded Timex Sinclair as part of a joint venture with the well-known watch company. Given that Atari and Commodore had pretty much cornered the home computing market in mid-'80s America, the use of the Sinclair here seems like an out-of-place British-ism in a USA-set story.

Connection between the two computers is presumably via a modem, indicating that the Decepticon Mainframe is connected to a telephone line – presumably Adam is hacking into the Decepticons' old base at Fortress Sinister, which we know contains a computer of human construction. (Sparkplug used it when working on his fuel formula in [3] 'Prisoner of War'.)

If indeed the Decepticons had been using an Earth computer, not only would it explain why it's connected to the telephone system, but also why it has only a rudimentary security system and why the Decepticon logs are known as 'war tapes' – perhaps some of the Decepticon history files have been transferred onto half-inch reels. Such tapes might also be the source of the Tornado and Earthquake footage previously seen in [4.2] 'The Enemy Within'.

Some of the text here is quoted verbatim from [1] 'The Transformers', which raises the intriguing possibility that the opening scenes in that issue were actually being narrated by the Decepticon computer. 'Using his ability to transform into a combat vehicle, Prime possessed a firepower potential that only Megatron could match' is a sentence used word-for-word in both stories, for example.

This story can be set at any time between the events of [16.3] 'Second Generation' and [19] 'Command Performances' – Megatron and Shockwave are described as being in joint command of the Decepticons, and Robot-Master is a current news story according to the *Portland Chronicle* newspaper – the same publication that Circuit Breaker is seen reading in [12.1] 'Christmas Breaker'.

The backstory here is pretty straightforward, although there are a few new tidbits of information:

- Mount St Hilary, rather than being simply dormant, is here described as an 'extinct' volcano that suffered a 'freak' eruption.
- Buster used his Matrix-powers to aid Ratchet in the rebuilding of the Autobots. (Although in [8.2] 'The Wrath of Grimlock', Buster is nowhere to be seen when Ratchet fixes up his fellow Autobots.)
- The Creation Matrix deliberately triggered Buster's nightmares (in [16.3] 'Second Generation') to ensure the creation of the Special Teams – it's said here to have 'left behind a message'. This is the first hint that the Matrix could in fact be sentient.
- The UK 'last vestiges' theory of the Constructicons' creation is confirmed – see the notes section of [10] 'The Next Best Thing to Being There' for more on this.

Although the first UK Annual was pretty much its own entity, there's a real attempt here to make the 1987 one dovetail much better with the comics. As well as the improved storytelling continuity, there's a visual link to the comics – the main font used here is Optima (developed by Herman Zapf in the 1950s), the same one that, at the time, the UK *The Transformers* comic used throughout (most notably on the editorial and letters pages). Similarly, this story's title is rendered in the font Eras (created by Albert Boton and Albert Hollenstein and released in 1976), as used for the straplines on the front covers of most UK *The Transformers* comics.

The plot – young hacker accidentally connects to a war computer – is heavily reminiscent of that of the 1983 Matthew Broderick vehicle *WarGames* (John Badham, 1983). The title, 'In the Beginning', constitutes the first three words of the Bible.

Picture Sources:
- Megatron on the bridge: [A1.3] 'And There Shall Come ... A Leader'.
- Optimus Prime in Iacon: [A1.3] 'And There Shall Come ... A Leader'.
- Grimlock v Sludge: [12.4] 'Dinobot Hunt' (Conclusion).
- Frenzy in a frenzy: [16.1] 'Robot Buster' (Part One).
- Shockwave threatens Prime: [8.2] 'The Wrath of Grimlock' (Part One: 'The Wrath of Guardian').
- Guardian attacks: [8.2] 'The Wrath of Grimlock' (Part Two).
- 'Heads Up, Troops': [8.1] 'Decepticon Dam-Busters' (Conclusion).

Review:
A great way to give new readers the heads-up on the story so far, the framing device is an excellent hook for the story recaps. 3/5

The Annual Datafiles
Also from the 1987 Annual, these are page-long profiles of the two faction leaders, presented in a computer Datafile format (to tie in with the hacking of the Decepticon mainframe in [A2.1] 'In the Beginning'). These, too, contain some interesting new info:

Optimus Prime was inaugurated as Autobot leader on the Cybertronian date '1st cycle 820'. He originally planned to be a medic. His old job as commander of Elite Flying Corps (first mentioned in [12.3] 'The Icarus Theory') is alluded to. Before wresting the Autobot leadership from the High Council ([A1.3] 'And There Shall Come ... A Leader'), he was field commander of the Autobot army.

Megatron founded the Decepticons on the date '1st cycle 549' (so if the three-digit number in the dating system relates to the 'vorn' – a Cybertronian time period first described in [17] 'The Smelting Pool' – then there was a gap of 22,493 Earth years between the formation of the Decepticons and Prime's ascension to leadership). Megatron, together with Shockwave and Soundwave, formed the 'nucleus' of the Decepticon movement.

On the subject of recaps, this is the perfect opportunity to take a look at the other attempts to chronicle the Transformers' adventures …

Robot War! From Cybertron to Earth – The Story So Far!

Published in UK#22, at a time when continuity was at its most confusing (see the essay 'Early UK Stories: Continuity Nightmares', under the entry for [4] 'The Last Stand'), the first Robot War recap coincided with a mini-relaunch of the UK comic, with a new look and a change of editor.

According to this, the correct order of the early stories goes [2] 'Power Play', [4.1] 'Man of Iron', [3] 'Prisoner of War', [4.2] 'The Enemy Within', [4.3] 'Raiders of the Last Ark' and [4] 'The Last Stand' – although see the aforementioned essay for why that chronology is debatable.

There aren't many other nuggets here. Mount St Hilary was a 'dormant' volcano, rather than 'extinct' as described in [A2.1] 'In the Beginning'. We also learn that Soundwave had a previously unknown role in the events of [4.1] 'Man of Iron' – according to this, the Decepticon communications officer was the one who alerted Megatron to the signal emitted by the Cybertronian ship in that story.

Picture Sources:

- Decepticons attacking the dome of Iacon: [A1.3] 'And There Shall Come … A Leader'.
- Megatron stands supreme: [4] 'The Last Stand'.
- 'This car is different': [2] 'Power Play'.
- Spider-Man: image from 'Homecoming!' a story first seen in *The Amazing Spider-Man* #252 (May 1984), and later printed by Marvel UK in *Spider-Man* #631-632 (13-20 April 1985).
- Megatron taps a black hole: [4.3] 'Raiders of the Last Ark' (Part 4).
- The Celestial Spires: [A1.3] 'And There Shall Come … A Leader'.

Robot War II The Saga of the Transformers

First printed in UK#36. With more adventures to summarise, this edition of Robot War is slightly less detailed than its predecessor. Because of this, or perhaps partly because of the continuity headaches they caused, the UK 'flashback stories' ([4.1] to [4.3]) are described very minimally.

The Sherman Dam battle described by Ratchet in [8.1] 'Decepticon Dam-Busters' is placed just after [4.1] 'Man of Iron' and prior to [3] 'Prisoner of War'.

Picture Sources:

- Optimus Prime v Megatron: [8.1] 'Decepticon Dam-Busters' (Conclusion).
- Prime towers over his human friends: [2] 'Power Play'.
- Shockwave approaches Earth: [7] 'Warrior School'.
- The Decepticons attack Prime: [4] 'The Last Stand'.
- Ratchet in the forest: [7] 'Warrior School'.

- Shockwave v the Dinobots: [7] 'Warrior School'.

Robot War III
First published in UK#63, as part of yet another relaunch (the Special Teams issue with free poster).

There is some new information to be found here: it's stated that twelve Autobots in total were rendered inactive during the events of [12.4] 'Dinobot Hunt' (the five Dinobots, plus presumably Jazz, Bluestreak, Sideswipe, Cliffjumper, Huffer, Gears and Windcharger).

It's also revealed here that Soundwave deliberately agreed to withhold from Shockwave the news that Megatron had returned ([15] 'I, Robot-Master').

And finally, as with all these recaps, the Autobot computer is referred to throughout as 'Aunty' (as per her brief mention in [1] 'The Transformers'), rather than 'Auntie' (the spelling used in [4.3] 'Raiders of the Last *Ark*').

Picture Sources:
- Optimus Prime has a gleam in his eyes: [12.4] 'Dinobot Hunt' (Part 3).
- Ratchet and the Dinobots: [8.1] 'Decepticon Dam-Busters' (Conclusion).
- Megatron: [8.1] 'Decepticon Dam-Busters' (Part 1).
- Shockwave clenches his fist: [16.2] 'Devastation Derby' (Part 1).
- Circuit Breaker: [12.1] 'Christmas Brea*ker*'.
- The Autobots: [12.2] 'Crisis of Command' (Part 3).

[A2.2] TO A POWER UNKNOWN!
11 pages; from the UK *The Transformers Annual 1987* (published August 1986)

Credits:
Ian Mennell and Wilf Prigmore (script); Will Simpson (art); Josie Firmin (colours); Annie Halfacree (letters); Sheila Cranna (editor).

Plot:
Meet the Heroic Decepticons and the Evil Autobots! An experimental computer-scrambling weapon named PARD affects the Transformers, completely reversing their moral compasses. The genius behind the weapon is UK-based Professor Purnel, who hopes to use PARD as a means to reverse enemy missile attacks.

Tracking the weapon to its source, the Autobots and Decepticons converge on the UK, but are again confused when PARD is reactivated. Events come to a head when PARD's computer core is stolen by a rival scientist. Both the core and the scientist are destroyed by one of Jazz's heat-seeking missiles, originally meant for Starscream.

Notes:
There's no easy way to slot the events of this story into the comics' narrative, but the best place for it is immediately prior to the events of [19] 'Command Performances' – although we have to assume that Jazz and Sideswipe have been temporarily restored to full health here (and that the debilitating effect of the PARD is what causes them to go offline again shortly afterwards).

The evil scientist here is called Zeke Heilmann, a play on the German phrase *Sieg heil* (hail victory), a rallying cry associated with the Nazi regime.

The PARD (Purnel's Auto-Reverse Defence system) affects computers the world over – including the Transformers' brains, causing the inversion of their programming. (Presumably PARD doesn't affect *every* computer, instead specifically targeting enemy systems across the globe; its impact upon the alien minds of the Transformers appears to be an unforeseen side-effect.)

Three of the nations listed on PARD's readouts are the USSR, China and Libya. As this story was written in the middle of the Cold War (c 1947-91), it's no surprise to see two communist nations on the list of enemy states. The third, Colonel Gaddafi's Libya, had been engaged in hostilities against the US since the Gulf of Sidra Incident in 1981, and against the UK following the murder of WPC Yvonne Fletcher outside the Libyan Embassy in London in 1984. Other Libyan attacks on the West included the 1986 Berlin discotheque bombing and, after this story was published, the 1988 Lockerbie bombing.

Given that the story is set partly in Britain, there's a lot of its pop culture on display here. The opening scenes in America include a town named Pinewoodsville, a nod to the world-renowned Pinewood Studios in Buckinghamshire, where movies such as *The Ipcress File* (Sidney J Furie, 1965) and *Aliens* (James Cameron, 1986) were filmed, as well as the popular *James Bond* and *Carry On* series.

One scene features a cameo by the Red Arrows, the famous aerobatics display squadron of the Royal Air Force, founded in 1965. (Tellingly, their computer systems appear to be completely unaffected by PARD.) Given that this story seems to be set near the Red Arrows' training base, which in the mid-'80s was RAF Scampton in Lincolnshire, these events probably take place in that area, i.e. east-central England.

The effects of PARD cause Starscream to receive random television and radio transmissions. First we are treated to a scene from the world's longest-running soap opera, *Coronation Street* (1960-present), featuring the long-standing characters Bet Lynch (played by Julie Goodyear, a regular cast member between 1970 and 1995) and Ken Barlow (introduced in the very first episode and played by William Roache).

There is also a reference to *Doctor Who* (1963-present), which like *Coronation Street* is the world's longest running television show in its genre – in this case, science fiction. As well as the titular Doctor, we also hear mention of his mortal enemies, the alien Daleks. (This story's editor Sheila Cranna was also the then-current editor of Marvel UK's *Doctor Who Magazine*.)

Finally, we hear tell of popular disc jockey Gary Davies (although his surname is misspelled here as Davis, perhaps deliberately), who at the time hosted the popular lunchtime slot on the UK's number-one national radio station, BBC Radio 1, and was also a regular host of the music television show *Top of the Pops*. Davies's iconic 'Ooh Gary Davies' jingle is broadcast to an understandably confused Starscream.

Oddly, the Autobots are seen here to be able to fly. (If we're being *really* generous, we could posit that they are not flying, but instead riding face-down in an invisible shuttlecraft.)

The Heroic Decepticons' advice here is to 'Give Peace a Chance', an anti-Vietnam War mantra coined by John Lennon in his song of the same name. Officially credited to the Plastic Ono Band, it was a UK #2 hit single – and US #14 – upon its release in 1969.

Roll Call:
Autobots: Optimus Prime, Jazz, Prowl, Sideswipe and Mirage.

Decepticons: Megatron, Starscream, Skywarp, Thundercracker, Soundwave and

Shockwave.

Other: **Bet Lynch** and **Ken Barlow**.

Review:
A decidedly curious little story, and tonally very different from the strips featured in the regular comics. It's competently written and mildly amusing, if a little inconsequential. 2/5

[A2.3] THE RETURN OF THE TRANSFORMERS
8 pages; a text story from the UK *The Transformers Annual 1987* (published August 1986)

Credits:
James Hill (writer); John Stokes (art); Sheila Cranna (editor).

Plot:
The Decepticons attack a wave farm on the East Coast of the USA, and begin siphoning off its power into Energon cubes. Optimus Prime sees this as an ideal opportunity to test the prowess of the new Aerialbots, whom he sends to thwart the Decepticons' plans, with Jetfire acting as an observer.

Also present is Danny Phillips, a young boy whose life was previously saved by the Autobots. Since that incident, he's become obsessed with the Transformers. He's taken out of harm's way by the Aerialbot Fireflight, but comes to realise that the alien robots he once idolised are as petty and flawed as any human.

With the Decepticons defeated, Jetfire elects not to report the Aerialbots' many failings, feeling that their problems are better sorted out amongst themselves.

Notes:
The Decepticons' target in this adventure is a wave farm – a means to extract energy from the waves. In the real world, however, the first commercial wave farm, the Islay LIMPET on the coast of Scotland, wasn't built until 1991. Their means of converting the wave power into Energon cubes is via the use of a 'power siphon', according to the Autobot Air Raid. This technology is the same as that described in previous stories such as [8.1] 'Decepticon Dam-Busters', [14] 'Rock and Roll-Out' and [18] 'The Bridge to Nowhere'.

Danny and his mother are staying at a Charlton Hotel, the name of which is probably based upon the real-world Ritz-Carlton hotel chain. The resort's location is never specified, other than it being on the East Coast.

This story makes a point of correcting a continuity error in the comics, specifically Optimus Prime's change of heart – in [12.2] 'Crisis of Command' he was dead set against the use of the Matrix to create additional Autobot troops, and yet he's later seen giving life to the Aerialbots and Protectobots. It's established here that the return of Megatron in [15] 'I, Robot-Master' has turned the tide of war in the Decepticons' favour, prompting Prime to rethink his strategy.

It's stated here that the Aerialbot Silverbolt suffers from 'vertigo' (i.e. the medical condition caused by a dysfunction of the vestibular system). However, later stories will establish that his discomfort is instead a result of acrophobia (an irrational fear of heights).

Double Time

As we have already seen, a number of Transformers comic stories, especially those published in the early UK annuals, don't readily fit into the comics' established continuity. This book has tried its best to invent possible ways to shoehorn these stories into the regular narrative – see [A2.2] 'To a Power Unknown' for one such attempt – but here, with [A2.3] 'The Return of the Transformers', there's just no way to make it fit.

This is a sequel to Danny Phillips' previous appearance in [A1.2] 'Missing in Action', the events of which are said to have taken place 'last summer'. As explained in the notes to that story, its 'best fit' was between [18] 'The Bridge to Nowhere' and [19] 'Command Performances', i.e. around May/June 1986. Theoretically then, this story must be set in winter 1986. However, in this story the Autobots are testing out their new troops, the Aerialbots. The problem is that, in the comics, the Aerialbots are created in the middle of summer – see [21] 'Aerialbots over America' – so they can't possibly be new creations here, in a story that is categorically set in 'the depths of winter'. Even more jarring is the appearance of Skywarp, Starscream and Trailbreaker, who have all joined the long-term inactive list by the time the Aerialbots make their debut.

As previously discussed in the entry for [27.1] 'Wanted: Galvatron – Dead or Alive', there appear to be two different continuities running parallel to each other: Timeline A and Timeline B. [A2.3] 'The Return of the Transformers' must, then, be set in what I've called Timeline A – the original, unaltered timeline in which Galvatron never travelled back in time and tinkered with history. Here, the Aerialbots were created a few months later, winter rather than summer 1986. (Presumably in Timeline B they were rushed into action due to the events of [20.2] 'Target: 2006'.) Also it would appear that Skywarp has been revived (which might well have been possible had his body not been blown to pieces by Galvatron in 'Target: 2006'), and that Trailbreaker is still alive (which again stands to reason – if 'Target: 2006' never happened then he would never have been maimed during the battle at the steelworks). Also, Starscream is active (without the presence of the future-Autobots, he would never have been put into cold storage) – his continued presence in the unaltered Timeline A is confirmed in [A1.4] 'Hunted', another story that we can retrospectively set in that dimension.

Roll Call:

Autobots: Optimus Prime, Jetfire, **Silverbolt, Air Raid, Fireflight, Skydive, Slingshot** and **Superion**.

This is the first 'proper' sighting of the Aerialbots, notwithstanding their appearance in Buster's dream in [16.3] 'Second Generation'. Prowl and Trailbreaker are mentioned, but do not appear. Bumblebee and Ratchet feature in the montage of press cuttings; Inferno appears in an illustration recycled from [A1.2] 'Missing in Action'.

Decepticons: Starscream and Skywarp.

It's entirely possible that other Decepticons are involved in the attack on the power plant, but these are the only two named in the text. Megatron is name-checked; both he and Shockwave are shown in the press cuttings.

Review:

A story with a bit more emotional depth than we're used to: the Aerialbots' various neuroses are explored here, but the main focus is on the troubled adolescent, Danny. It's an interesting mix, and makes for a thought-provoking read. The only problem is the Decepticons' plan: a raid on a power station. While admittedly not the story's main focus, this element is extremely generic and keeps the story from achieving a perfect grade. 4/5

[A2.4] A TALE FROM CYBERTRON: STATE GAMES
8 pages; a text story from the UK *The Transformers Annual 1987* (published August 1986)

Credits:
James Hill (writer); John Stokes (art); Sheila Cranna (editor).

Plot:
Many millions of years ago, before the war. An energy crisis has resulted in Cybertron's devolution from a unified nation ruled by the Overlord into a planet of disparate city states. Tempers are temporarily calmed by a series of inter-state gladiatorial competitions, but tensions again reach boiling point when combatants from the state of Vos sabotage a power plant in a rival city, Tarn. Attempts to blame the destruction on yet another political power, Iacon, fail. War is declared, and Vos and Tarn destroy each other.

A disparate bunch of Transformers – Tarn's gladiatorial champion Megatron, Autobot warrior Optimus Prime, plus the ageing Overlord and his two bodyguards, Ravage and Nightstalker – attempt to flee the wreckage of Tarn and make the dangerous journey to Iacon. With Overlord on the verge of death, Optimus Prime splits from the group and forges ahead in a bid to secure aid.

Nightstalker sacrifices himself to save the Overlord from a group of attackers, but it is too late – the ancient Transformer expires anyway. Ravage allies himself with Megatron, who addresses the survivors of the now-ruined Vos and Tarn: 'We will have our revenge on the Iaconians!' Thus are born the Decepticons ...

Notes:
This story is set prior to the events of [A1.3] 'And There Shall Come ... a Leader' (another story billed as a 'Tale of Cybertron'), with the Decepticons on the verge of being founded and Optimus Prime not yet installed as Autobot leader.

According to the Megatron Datafile in this very same annual (see [A2.1] 'In the Beginning'), the foundation of the Decepticons seen here occurs on the Cybertronian date '1st cycle 549'. A 'quarter of a time cycle' is another time unit mentioned in this story.

In addition to the already-established Iacon, we learn of two other city states here: Tarn, ruled by Shockwave, and Vos, ruled by Starscream. Given his devious nature, it comes as no surprise to learn that Vosians under Starscream's rule resort to sneak tactics, specifically their plan to blow up a power plant and blame it on another party. Many of the Decepticons' strained relationships seen in the comics are shown in a new light, thanks to the revelations in this story. Starscream's and Megatron's antipathy toward one another likely stems from the fact that they are from rival cities, Vos and Tarn respectively.

At the beginning of this tale, Megatron is a citizen of Tarn, under Shockwave's rule; by the end of the story, it is Megatron who holds all the power – Shockwave's future resentment of Megatron is probably due to him having been usurped by, essentially, a former underling.

Mention is made of the fact that the Vosians are sporting a small rank insignia; it's hinted that this is the symbol that will, in the future, come to represent the entire Decepticon faction. (The Decepticon logo does, after all, vaguely resemble the letter 'V' for Vos.)

One of the Vosian saboteurs is Tornado, previously seen in archive tapes in [4.2] 'The Enemy Within'. As per those tapes, he later joined the ranks of the Decepticons, only to be declared a traitor and forced to undergo the Trial by Combat.

We are also reintroduced to the Autobot High Council, specifically Councillors Xaaron, Traachon (here described as a General) and Tomaandi, who were all previously in [A1.3] 'And There Shall Come ... a Leader'. We know from the text story 'Cybertron: The Middle Years' (covered in the notes of [20.2] 'Target: 2006') that the warlord Trannis will eventually brutally slay the council (except for Xaaron, who manages to escape).

Megatron gains his trademark fusion cannon here, salvaging it from the body of a dead warrior. This won't be the last reference to the inter-state gladiatorial competitions; Iacon's Imperial Amphitheatre will be seen in [20.2] 'Target: 2006'.

Let There Be Light!

Previously in the comics, we've seen a number of weapons described as using photons to various extents. In [9] 'Dis-Integrated Circuits', for example, G B Blackrock built an Anti-Robot Photonic Multi-Cannon to attack the Transformers. In this story, Optimus Prime wields a photon pistol, and the cities of Vos and Tarn are obliterated by photon missiles. Photons however, aren't dangerous at all – they are just particles of light, and are all around us in nature. So how can they be weaponised, to the extent that they can be used to destroy Transformers and indeed entire cities?

The obvious answer would be by way of a laser (Light Amplification by Stimulated Emission of Radiation), which of course has real-world applications as a cutting tool. But this only really works when the light is focused into a narrow beam, and the required power consumption makes it highly inefficient – why waste energy creating a laser beam, when even a simple substance such as gunpowder would give you a far better destructive yield using far less energy resource?

The television show *Star Trek* (1966-69) and its spin-offs postulated a futuristic device called a photon torpedo, indicating that the idea of using light quanta as a weapon is an appealing one in science-fiction. However, this doesn't help us much – according to the official literature, *Trek*'s photon torpedoes work by mixing matter with antimatter, rather than using photons as a weapon *per se*.

Perhaps the key is in a metal called hafnium. When 'excited' by high-energy photons, this element can be used to create what's known as a nuclear isomer, a gram of which contains approximately 1,330 megajoules of energy. In large enough quantities, this 'photon' weapon could indeed level an entire city (in theory, anyway).

More Than Meets the Ides

Cybertron is a ginormous metal planet populated by giant robots who can turn into cars and jets.

It's an outlandish premise, but as written, seems almost real to us. Scribes such as Bob Budiansky, Simon Furman, James Hill and latterly James Roberts have built this fictional world in such a way than one can *almost* believe it exists. So what's the secret here? How is such a bizarre premise moulded into something that can be accepted by readers? Just how can a sheen of verisimilitude be given to such an unbelievable concept?

The simple answer is, the writers take a leaf out of the history books. In other words, they steal from the past in order to make events on the Transformers' homeworld seem *familiar* and therefore relatable. Basically, Cybertron is an amalgam of the ancient Roman and Greek civilisations, which flourished from the 8th Century BCE until the 6th Century CE.

The first clue we had was the use of the term 'city states'. Ancient Greece was basically a huge conglomeration of allied but independent *poleis* such as Athens, Corinth, Sparta and Troy. Cybertron's Iacon, Vos and Tarn are just three more states of the same ilk.

The bickering and politicking of the Autobot High Council read not unlike the intrigues of the Roman Senate, and Megatron's popular uprising seen at the end of this story certainly mirrors Julius Caesar's rise to power on the back of support from the plebeian class, disenfranchised from the established senatorial nobility.

Nowhere is the Roman influence more obvious than in the names of the characters. Another term for the senatorial elite, and thus Megatron's/Caesar's direct rivals, is *optimates*, which sounds not unlike the name of a certain Autobot leader. Latin-sounding names abound in Transformers lore: Ultra Magnus, Fortress Maximus, Bruticus and many others all have names in the Latin style. Indeed the name Cybertron itself can be traced back, via English words such as cybernetic and electron, to the Greek *kubernao tron* – literally a 'steerable instrument', which ties in quite neatly with Megatron's plan to pilot the planet around the universe.

The parallels are plentiful. Some of the Greek constellations, for example Cepheus and Cassiopeia, were thought to be gods and goddesses who had been transformed into celestial bodies – compare this to the idea of Unicron and Primus (more names in the classical style), the Transformer gods who became planets. The melding of Megatron and Ratchet in [69] 'Eye of the Storm' evokes the mythical blending of Hermaphroditus and Salmacis. Shockwave is a one-eyed Cyclops. In this very story, Optimus Prime traverses a dangerous bridge (crosses the Rubicon), while the Overlord is betrayed by Ravage (Brutus). The myths of Icarus and the Argonauts have already been discussed, both having been referenced in previous stories ([12.3] 'The Icarus Theory' and [16.1] 'Robot Buster' respectively).

It can be argued that every piece of modern literature owes *something* to stories of the Romans and the Greeks; you could probably find coincidental parallels in any piece of fiction if you look hard enough. But in deliberately using terms such as 'city state', 'gladiator' and 'Omega Supreme', it's clear that in the Transformers comics, at least some of this was intentional.

And by drawing on this ancient store of recognisable history and mythology, Cybertron is not some generic alien world, but a recognisable and identifiable *place*, which makes reading about it so much more satisfying.

Roll Call :
Autobots: Optimus Prime and Sunstreaker.

Notwithstanding sightings of his corpse in [8] 'Repeat Performance' and [10] 'The Next

Best Thing to Being There', this is the first time Sunstreaker plays a major part in a story since way back in [5] 'The New Order', where he was effectively killed off.

Other Autobots seen here include Overlord, Nightstalker, Tomaandi and Traachon.

Not-yet Decepticons: Megatron and Ravage.

Shockwave and Starscream are mentioned but not seen. As noted above, Tornado also makes an appearance.

Review:
[17] 'The Smelting Pool' succeeded so well because of its ability to juggle good storytelling with some excellent world-building. Although 'State Games' does admirably well in setting up and realising pre-war Cybertron in some depth, it's more a series of disparate vignettes than a cohesive, well-rounded narrative.

We go from a gladiatorial bout, to a power station, to the Autobot High Council, to an adventure on an expressway. It's all excellent stuff, even if structurally it feels a little off. 4/5

[A2.5] 'VICTORY!'
11 pages; from the UK *The Transformers Annual 1987* (published August 1986)

Credits:
Simon Furman (script); Geoff Senior (art); Gina Hart (colours); Annie Halfacree (letters); Sheila Cranna (editor).

Plot:
Grimlock's dream. The Decepticons are victorious; Optimus Prime is dead. Grimlock brutally slays Megatron, and thinks he's turned the tide of the battle – only to be blasted dead by Starscream.

Swoop's dream. Swoop plucks Soundwave off the ground and soars into the air with his captive. However, he doesn't reckon on the Decepticon using a self-destruct device, obliterating both robots.

Sludge's dream. In the forest, and in the arms of his beloved Joy Meadows, Sludge is truly at peace; but Meadows is an android doppelganger controlled by the Decepticons, and she destroys the Dinobot with her laser-bolt eyes.

Snarl's dream. Guardian is back, and he's killed at least five Autobots! Luckily, Snarl is around, and he decapitates the errant sentry drone. However, he realises all too late that Guardian can operate without a head, and the decapitated sentinel duly bashes Snarl into a pulp.

Slag's dream. Once again, Shockwave and Slag do battle on a precipice overlooking a tar pit. The Dinobot launches himself over the edge, taking Shockwave with him. However, while the Decepticon lands safely on solid ground, Slag finds himself sinking into gooey oblivion.

Although physically fine, the Dinobots are comatose and unresponsive. Only when they achieve victory in their dreams can they ever wake again. In the dream world, the Dinobots commence battle once more, and the cycle begins again …

Notes:
Although notable for its sheer brutality, Grimlock's dream is the most disconnected from 'real' events in the comic. His nightmare is a world in which the Decepticons reign supreme, and where his bullish pride becomes his downfall. We discover that despite his dislike of Optimus Prime, he would still regret the Autobot leader's demise.

Swoop's dream death - midair destruction by means of an explosive – echoes his actual defeat by the exploding Guardian robot in [8.2] 'The Wrath of Grimlock'. His deliberate defiance of Prime's orders hints at a deeper distrust of the Autobot Leader that we eventually see confirmed in [A3.1] 'What's in a Name'.

Sludge's dream includes a nightmarish version of his crush, Joy Meadows, previously seen in [12.4] 'Dinobot Hunt' and [20.1] 'In the National Interest'. Here she's actually an android wearing a fleshy mask, in a disturbing image reminiscent of sources such as *The Terminator* (James Cameron, 1984), *Alien* (Ridley Scott, 1979) or, closer to home, the character Silverman from Marvel UK's *Spider-Man and Zoids*.

Snarl's nightmare is a rematch against Guardian, whom he'd previously met in [8.2] 'The Wrath of Grimlock'. Here Guardian operates without a head, which recalls the remote-controlled headless Optimus Prime corpse also seen in that story.

Slag, finally, has dreams based upon his previous fight against Shockwave seen in [8] 'Repeat Performance'.

These events are set at some point between [12.4] 'Dinobot Hunt', in which the Dinobots suffer brain-damage, and [16.3] 'Second Generation', when they finally wake from their dream state.

The idea of deadly dreams was popularised by the movie *A Nightmare on Elm Street* (Wes Craven, 1984).

Roll Call:
Autobots: Optimus Prime, Jazz (dream only), Prowl (dream only), Ratchet, Bumblebee (dream only), Grimlock, Snarl, Slag, Sludge and Swoop.

Decepticons: Megatron, Starscream, Thundercracker and Soundwave (all dream only)

Other: Joy Meadows (sort of; dream only)

Review:
A great collection of action set-pieces that, because this is all a dream, are allowed to be much more brutal than usual. With the shackles off, this story features many Transformer 'deaths'; it's a visceral thrill, to be sure.

Another plus point is that there are no easy answers here, no pat resolutions. As with many prior Furman stories, the ending is deliciously bittersweet. With the Dinobots doomed to a few more weeks of nightmares, there's a reason why the rather ironic title is written in inverted commas. 5/5

[A2.6] THE MISSION
8 pages; a story from the UK *The Transformers Annual 1987* (published August 1986).

Credits:
Jamie Delano (writer); John Stokes (art); Sheila Cranna (editor).

Plot:
Hoist is on a mission in Canada, spying on the Constructicons who have set up camp in the area. However, he accidentally steps into an old mineshaft and becomes stuck, wedged in the narrow opening.

Jazz picks up Hoist's distress signal, and rescues his comrade. However, the pair are discovered by the Constructicons, who attack – Jazz is shot in the head, which reduces the luckless Autobot to a primitive mental state.

Hoist drags the disoriented Jazz through the snowy forest, pursued by the mighty Devastator. They manage to evade their gargantuan pursuer by destroying a nearby dam. While Devastator is distracted by the raging torrent, the Autobots are swept away to safety.

Notes:
This tale was written as a deliberate homage to Jack London's seminal 1903 novel *The Call of the Wild*, which tells of a dog, Buck, who is shipped in a crate by sea from San Francisco to the port of Skagway in Alaska – the exact same route and method of transport taken by Jazz in this story. London's novel is set during the Klondike Gold Rush (1896-99), when a hundred thousand prospectors flocked to the river Klondike in Canada's Yukon Territory, which was rich in gold deposits. 'The Mission' is also set mostly in Yukon, and there is a direct reference to the gold rush when Jazz rescues Hoist from one of the abandoned mines.

Jazz's reversion to savagery after being zapped in the head by the Constructicons echoes Buck's own fate, as during the course of the novel, the canine reverts from a domesticated pup to a wild dog, living in the forest.

The Constructicons' defeat here echoes the fate of three characters from *The Call of the Wild*: the villains Hal, Charles and Mercedes, who are all drowned in a river while Buck makes his escape.

Finally, given the fact that *The Call of the Wild* is the tale of a sled dog, it's quite apt that the final scene of 'The Mission' has Hoist towing Jazz to safety, essentially taking the role of a husky.

Given that this story stars Jazz, Hoist and the Constructicons, it's a simple matter to fit it just prior to [20.2] 'Target: 2006', in which these characters also appear.

Jazz's mental problems are caused by damage to his 'sensory and logistic circuits' – presumably the author actually meant to say 'logic circuits'.

Roll Call:
Autobots: Jazz and Hoist.

Decepticons: Scrapper, Scavenger, Mixmaster, Bonecrusher, Long Haul, Hook and Devastator.

Data File: Jamie Delano (writer)
Delano started out at Marvel UK on titles such as *Captain Britain* and *Doctor Who Magazine*; he also wrote for *2000 AD*. He's best known, however, as the original writer on DC Comics' *Hellblazer*, a title that was later adapted into the film *Constantine* (Francis Lawrence, 2005).

Review:
This isn't just a homage to *The Call of the Wild*, but an excellent story in its own right. The Jack London-inspired prose is poetic and evocative, and the scenes told from the frazzled Jazz's point of view are a joy to read, especially the bit where he spots a wild caribou and wonders at its 'antennae'. The plot might be simple, but the use of language to create a unique sense of place and atmosphere is first-rate. 4/5

[A3.1] WHAT'S IN A NAME?
5 pages; from the UK *The Transformers Annual 1988* (published August 1987)

NB: The release month of this annual was revealed in the comic itself. (According to UK#126, dated 15 August 1987, the book was 'on sale now'.)

Credits:
Simon Furman (script); Will Simpson (pencils); Dave Elliott (inks); Jenny O'Connor (editor, uncredited). No letterer or colourist were credited and their identities remain a mystery, although it has been suggested that Steve White might have been the colourist. Robin Smith provided the annual's cover.

Plot:
Cybertron, millions of years ago. Swoop, disobeying orders, is on the hunt for a Decepticon named Divebomb. Swoop himself was once known as Divebomb, but this Decepticon stole his name after defeating him in battle.

Swoop is able to locate Divebomb, and the two do battle. Divebomb proves once again that he is the superior warrior, and is on the verge of victory when Optimus Prime intervenes and saves Swoop's life. Swoop, who hates Optimus Prime with a passion, is deeply embarrassed by the incident and keeps these events a secret for millions of years.

In the present day, Swoop discovers that Divebomb has arrived on Earth, and goes after the Decepticon once more …

Notes:
Swoop's strained relationship with Optimus Prime, and his previous identity as Divebomb, were established in [12.3] 'The Icarus Theory'.

This story would shortly spawn a related tale in the main comic, [31.4] 'Grudge Match', which acts both as a prequel and a sequel to this adventure. The present-day sequences of 'What's In a Name?' are set immediately after the third panel of the eighth page of 'Grudge Match'.

Swoop's and Divebomb's Cybertronian modes are seen here: Swoop used to transform into an alien-looking jet, whereas Divebomb's alternative mode was that of a wyvern-like creature.

Roll Call:
Autobots: Optimus Prime (flashback only), Grimlock, Sludge and Swoop.

Decepticons: Divebomb.

Review:
An exciting, incident-packed little strip that belies its low page-count. 4/5

[A3.2] HEADMASTERS SAGA
24 pages; from the UK *The Transformers Annual 1988* (published August 1987)

NB: This text story was split into three eight-page chapters spread throughout the annual. The individual parts were entitled 'Doomsday for Nebulos', 'Stylor's Story' and 'The Final Conflict' respectively.

Credits:
Ian Rimmer (writer, uncredited); Jenny O'Connor (editor, uncredited). The story is accompanied by a series of illustrations, but the artist went uncredited (although it appears to be the work of Phil Gascoine).

Plot:
Lord Zarak greets the Decepticons as they arrive on Nebulos, and remembers the circumstances that led to their arrival: the Autobots had recently landed on the planet and, fearful of these giant robots' presence, Zarak had requested the Decepticons' help in getting rid of them. Zarak is shocked to learn that the Decepticons are an even greater menace than the Autobots, and numbly watches on as Scorponok and his forces leave to wreak havoc across the planet.

The Nebulan Stylor might be known as a fashion-conscious party-goer, but it transpires that he's also a brave and clever individual. Shocked at the destruction that the Decepticons have wrought, he overhears a plan being hatched by the Nebulan leader, Kord, to bioengineer Nebulans to become the new heads for a group of decapitated Autobots. He immediately volunteers for this procedure, and is bonded to an Autobot, Chromedome. Armed with the new Headmaster technology, the Autobots defeat the Decepticons in battle.

Fortress Maximus is troubled: each time it seems as if the Autobots have got the upper hand, for instance by developing the Headmaster and Targetmaster processes, the Decepticons soon cancel out that advantage by following suit. The Autobots' latest advancement is a new device that can convert fuel into energy more efficiently than ever before. Fortress Maximus and Scorponok do battle – but it's all just a diversion, as the Decepticons sneak past the distracted Autobots and make off with the fuel converter. The Decepticons depart Nebulos and head for Earth, and the Autobots follow in hot pursuit.

Notes:
This is basically a truncated retelling of the *Headmasters* comic series ([HDM1] 'Ring of Hate' to [HDM4] 'Brothers in Armor') in the form of a text story. However, when it was being written, in the summer of 1987, the final two issues of that series had yet to be published, so the ending was unknown to the British writing team. Given that some of the names used here are also different from those seen in the *Headmasters* comics (Galen is called Kord here, and Gort is Grot), it's possible that author Ian Rimmer was working from a very early version of the *Headmasters* scripts.

Chapter one sees the meeting of Zarak and Scorponok that in strip form occurred in [HDM2] 'Broken Glass'. Their initial conversation is much longer here, and features a new sequence in which Scorponok picks Zarak off the ground and then drops him from ten feet in the air. Mention is made of 'Nebulos' moon', when the comic strip showed that Nebulos has at least two natural satellites. It's stated that Kord (Galen) is the Nebulan leader, and that his group, the World Watchers, are the ruling political party, whereas in the strip it's never stated that Galen is the overall leader of the planet; on the contrary, he's often seen deferring to other members of the Council.

The second part is told from Stylor's point of view, and again focuses on events from [HDM2] 'Broken Glass'. The Nebulan capital, Koraja, is never mentioned by name here, but referred to only as the City (always capitalised). Central City Park was a recreational area within Koraja, until it was destroyed by the Decepticons. Nebulans are 'six foot on average', making them slightly taller than humans. Stylor reports that Arcana studies 'ancient, mystical sciences', indicating that the enlightened, advanced Nebulans aren't as secular as they initially appear. The historical figure Quixotol was ridiculed when he suggested that Nebulos was round. This makes him the Nebulan equivalent of Galileo Galilei (1564-1642), who was branded a heretic for claiming that the Earth revolved around the Sun, rather than the other way around. Quixotol's name would seem to be derived from that of Don Quixote, the title character of Miguel de Cervantes' famous 1605 novel.

Scorponok's final plan – a duel to the death that turns out to be a mere diversion – is very similar to Megatron's scheme in the cartoon episode {1-16} 'Heavy Metal War'. In this story the Headmasters retain their original heads, which can be stored in a compartment in the robots' chests when not in use. This completely contradicts the *Headmasters* comic strip, in which the Autobots being separated from their heads is a non-negotiable aspect of the peace deal. In another radical departure, the Targetmaster weapons are not in fact Nebulans, but rather 'small, Nebulan-sized robots ... given minds which were duplicated from other Nebulans'.

Roll Call:
Autobots: Fortress Maximus, Highbrow, Chromedome, Hardhead and Brainstorm. Lightspeed and Nosecone are also referred to, having been injured in a previous battle.

Decepticons: Scorponok, Skullcruncher, Mindwipe, Weirdwolf, Apeface, Snapdragon, Slugslinger, Triggerhappy and Misfire.

Nebulans: Galen ('Kord'), Gort ('Grot'), Stylor, Duros, Arcana, Zarak, Grax, Vorath, Monzo, Spasma and Krunk.

As this story recounts a number of large battles, doubtless many more Transformers are involved than are listed above. However, the list is restricted to those characters mentioned by name in the text or depicted in the accompanying illustrations.

Review:
This story is very much an oddity. The fact that it contradicts much of the *Headmasters* mini-series means that it's very easy to dismiss out of hand for being non-canonical. That's a shame, because – inconsistencies aside – there's a lot to like here. The first part, focusing on Zarak, shows the Nebulan Lord in a new light – his outward arrogance and bluster belie an inner lack of self-confidence. Stylor, who gets only a couple of lines in the comic, is the narrator of the second chapter, and so we get our only real insight into

his character and motivations. This is strong character work, making what could have been a boring recap into a good story.

Chapter three, however, lets the side down somewhat – the new ending is a bit of a damp squib, and suffers in comparison with the *Headmasters* comic. Another issue is in the editing; the story is riddled with annoying typographical errors that should have been ironed out before going to print ('puzzeled' instead of 'puzzled' and so on). 3/5

[A3.3] VICIOUS CIRCLE!
11 pages; from the UK *The Transformers Annual 1988* (published August 1987)

Credits:
Simon Furman (script); Jeff Anderson (pencils); Dave Harwood (inks); Jenny O'Connor (editor, uncredited). As per [A3.1] 'What's in a Name', no letterer or colourist were credited, though again, Steve White was possibly the colourist.

Plot:
Ultra Magnus has survived his fall into the mouth of Mount Verona, the active volcano from which Galvatron hopes to absorb fantastic amounts of energy. He is helped to his feet by Goldbug, who recaps recent events – how Galvatron's power siphon threatens to destroy large swathes of the western United States, and how Galvatron's fellow time travellers (Rodimus Prime, Death's Head, Wreck-Gar *et al*) have been returned to the year 2007. Ultra Magnus is now the only thing that stands in Galvatron's way.

Magnus, however, is tired. Burnt-out and weary from so many battles with Galvatron, he knows that any further attack will be futile. Goldbug himself makes an attempt on Galvatron's life, but he is no match for the maniacal Decepticon.

Goldbug's valiant efforts shame Ultra Magnus into finally accepting his duty, and he battles Galvatron once more. During the ensuing battle, Galvatron's power siphon becomes damaged; instead of the volcanic energy being absorbed, it now manifests as a standard eruption. Goldbug manages to get clear, but Ultra Magnus and Galvatron are consumed by the blast.

Notes:
This story is a direct continuation of the cliffhanger ending of [27.4] 'Fire on High' in the main comic. As such, it ties up the long-running 'Volcano' arc that began with [27.1] 'Wanted: Galvatron – Dead or Alive'.

It's revealed that Ultra Magnus survived his apparent death in [27.4] 'Fire on High' by landing on a ledge rather than falling directly into the lava. (A similar escape was made by Shockwave in Slag's dream sequence in [A2.5] 'Victory'.)

Ultra Magnus has now lost count of the number of times he's fought Galvatron, referencing previous battles in [20.2] 'Target: 2006', [27.2] 'Burning Sky', [27.3] 'Hunters' and [27.4] 'Fire on High'.

The aftermath of the volcano's explosion will be explored in this story's sequel, [31.5] 'Ladies' Night'.

Roll Call:
Autobots: Ultra Magnus, Rodimus Prime (flashback only), Wreck-Gar (flashback only) and Goldbug.

Decepticons: Galvatron.

Other: Death's Head (flashback only).

Review:
The major problem with the 'Volcano' saga was that it dragged on for far too long in the comic itself – this final instalment does nothing to improve matters.

Yet again this all boils down to Galvatron doing battle with Ultra Magnus, punctuated by scenes of the lead Autobots standing around and wallowing in their angst. It's something that the comic might have gotten away with for a couple of issues, but this story arc was already a bloated 88 pages long, even before this concluding chapter.

Magnus and Galvatron get an epic send-off, and it's nice to see some of the loose ends finally tied up, but the execution is sorely lacking. 2/5

[A3.4] ARK DUTY
7 pages; from the UK *The Transformers Annual 1988* (published August 1987)

Credits:
Ian Rimmer (script, uncredited); Will Simpson (art, uncredited); Jenny O'Connor (editor, uncredited). Again, no colourist or letterer were credited, though Steve White and Annie Halfacree respectively appear the likely candidates.

Plot:
The year is 2003, and the Autobots are planning to build a new Autobot City on Earth. While most of them set out in convoy to collect materials, Kup's job is to transport the city's top-secret plans, leaving Hot Rod and Blurr to guard the *Ark*. The two reluctant sentries are told in no uncertain terms that they are not to leave their post under any circumstance, in case of Decepticon attack.

Ravage, who has been spying on the Autobot meeting, reports back to the Stunticons. With the secret city plans entrusted to the elderly Kup, it will seemingly be an easy task to steal them.

Having seen this via the *Ark*'s monitors, Hot Rod disobeys orders and leaves his post in order to save Kup from the Stunticon attack. Despite his best efforts, the Stunticons are able to make off with the plans.

Kup reveals that it was all a ruse – the plans were fake and the whole thing was a set-up to deliver false information to the Decepticons. After giving him a stern dressing-down for disobeying orders and leaving the *Ark*, Kup concedes that Hot Rod's attempts to stop the Stunticons added to the illusion that they were stealing the real plans.

Notes:
This is the first story to confirm positively that the UK 'future' stories are set in an alternate timeline caused by Galvatron's meddling with history (see the notes to [27.1] 'Wanted: Galvatron – Dead or Alive'). In this version of 2003, the *Ark* remains entombed beneath Mount St Hilary (compare this with the present-day stories, in which the *Ark* left Earth in [35] 'Child's Play' (comic)).

This alternative Earth would appear to have a singular, unified government (who are now allied to the Autobots and willing to supply them with raw materials). At least one office of this world government appears to be located within driving distance of the *Ark*'s location in Oregon.

This story acts as a prequel to *The Transformers: The Movie*, in which it's established that the Autobots have a massive city complex located on Earth. It was established in [20.2] 'Target: 2006' that the city's location was inspired by a mental suggestion from Unicron.

Although written first, this story is preceded chronologically by [54.2] 'Prime's Rib' (set in 1995). Autobot City's inauguration (in 2004) would later be seen in [53.2] 'Aspects of Evil'.

Roll Call:
Autobots: Ratchet, Jetfire, Hoist, Ultra Magnus, Hot Rod, Kup and Blurr.

Decepticons: Ravage, Motormaster, Drag Strip, Dead End, Wildrider and Breakdown.

A great many more Autobots appear as background characters in the initial briefing scene, but other than Ratchet, Hoist and Jetfire, they are drawn so indistinctly as to make positive identification extremely difficult.

Review:
Having an adventure set just prior to the movie is a neat concept, and makes for nice little story with some good action and a decent twist ending. It's nothing particularly stand-out, but given the low page-count that's only to be expected. 3/5

[A4.1] THE SAGA OF THE TRANSFORMERS – SO FAR!
7 pages; from the UK *The Transformers Annual 1989* (published September 1988)

NB: Again, the release date for the 1989 Annual can be gleaned from the comics themselves. A remark in the letters page of UK#169 indicated that the Annual 'should hit the shops around September time'; an advertisement for the annual appeared in UK#181, with the tag line 'It's arrived'.

This is an illustrated prose story.

Credits:
Simon Furman (writer); Robin Smith (art); Steve White (colours); Chris Francis (editor). In addition to the new art, stock images from previous issues were used to illustrate the story. Lee Sullivan provided the annual's cover, Gary 'Glib' Gilbert was the designer and Dan Reed/John Burns provided the inside cover art. 'Chris Francis' is a pseudonym for Simon Furman (it's his middle names); he used it to get around Marvel rules that forbade staff to write and edit the same title.

Plot:
Adam Reynolds, who once hacked into a Decepticon computer, is at it again. He's tracked down the old Autobot headquarters within Mount St Hilary, and although the *Ark* is no longer there, he accesses an Autobot computer left behind.

Scanning the Autobot files, he reads about the history of the Transformers – how their war started, how they came to Earth, and key events in the war over the last four years.

His interest piqued, Reynolds muses that he might like to become a Transformer himself, by undergoing the Headmaster process …

Notes:

As with the 1987 annual two years previously, it was decided to open the book with a recap of the events of the comics, for readers new to the franchise. Like [A2.1] 'In the Beginning', this took the form of computer hacker Adam Reynolds gaining access to a Transformer computer and accessing its files.

Although the *Ark* had departed Mount St Hilary in [35] 'Child's Play' (comic), the later story [38] 'Trial by Fire' established that the Autobots had left some computers and equipment behind. The Autobot computer contains details of the entire Transformers saga up to the events of [39.1] 'Salvage'.

There's an interesting insight into the events that sparked the Autobot/Decepticon war. As per [40.2] 'Legion of the Lost', the official Autobot history claims that Megatron rose to power within the Decepticons' ranks. (In [A2.4] 'State Games' we see the truth – Megatron was always their leader and indeed their founder member.) The war on Cybertron started when Megatron announced his plan to turn Cybertron into a spacefaring battle station, and 'thereby plunged headlong into war with those Transformers who would die before seeing their planet used in this fashion.'

(It's notable, then, that the war continues to this day, despite Megatron's 'cosmic juggernaut' plan having been long since abandoned. Obviously there are other major philosophical differences between the two factions, and Megatron's wild scheme was simply the last straw.)

The Transformers' initial revival on Earth is incorrectly dated to 1982. (It was 1984.)

Picture Sources:

Adam views events on the computer screen: original art

The Dinobots charge: [A2.5] 'Victory'

Megatron throws a rock: [23.1] 'Prey' (Part 1)

Shockwave beheads the Autobots: [16.3] 'Second Generation' (Part 1)

Lord Straxus: [23.5] 'Resurrection' (Part 1)

Galvatron aims his cannon: [20.2] 'Target: 2006' (Part 8)

Hot Rod, Kup and Blurr: [20.2] 'Target: 2006' (Part 6: Trios)

A battle-scarred Optimus Prime: [12.2] 'Crisis of Command' (Part 3)

Review:

More a summary of events rather than a story in its own right, but it gets the job done. 2/5

[A4.2] ALTERED IMAGE!

6 pages; from the UK *The Transformers Annual 1989* (published September 1988)

Credits:

Ian Rimmer (script); Simon Furman (plot); Lee Sullivan (art); Steve White (colours); Tom Frame (letters); Chris Francis (editor).

Plot:
Megatron, brainwashed by Shockwave into believing that Galvatron is his enemy, attacks Galvatron in the middle of a town. Galvatron's aim is to convince Megatron that they should be on the same side, but Shockwave's conditioning proves difficult to overcome.

The two titans clash. Megatron goes all-out in an attempt to kill his future self, while Galvatron holds back, all the while trying to convince Megatron of the truth.

After most of his pleas fall on deaf ears, it's an offhand remark by Galvatron about how he kills Starscream in the future that finally convinces Megatron to break off the attack. United by their common hatred of Starscream, the two Decepticon leaders form an alliance.

Notes:
A story that ties directly into the comics, this is set after [44.3] 'Dry Run', in which Shockwave sends Megatron out to kill Galvatron', and before [48.2] 'Time Wars', where Megatron and Galvatron are now allies.

Megatron's brainwashing occurred in [39.1] 'Salvage'; there's also a flashback to Megatron being rebuilt into Galvatron (from *The Transformers: The Movie*).

Though nobody knew it at the time, the Megatron seen in this story would retroactively be revealed to be a clone, rather than the genuine article. The clone was introduced in [29.1] 'Ancient Relics' and his true nature revealed in [57.1] 'Two Megatrons'.

Roll Call:
Decepticons: Galvatron and Clone Megatron.

Other: Unicron (flashback only).

Review:
This might just be a six-page fight sequence, but it's a good one. The fight itself is capably realised by artist Lee Sullivan, and both Galvatron and Megatron come across well here.

There's a recurring motif of mirrors and reflections, literally and figuratively – while Galvatron recognises himself in his own past incarnation, images of both Decepticons are reflected in the glass of a nearby skyscraper. It's a neat concept, and adds an extra layer to an otherwise simple tale. 4/5

[A4.3] PRIME BOMB!
14 pages; from the UK *The Transformers Annual 1989* (published September 1988)

NB: This illustrated text story was split into two chapters, spread across the annual. Part 1 was 6 pages long; Part 2 consisted of 8 pages.

Credits:
Ian Rimmer (writer); Robin Smith (art); Steve White (colours); Chris Francis (editor).

Plot:
Scorponok's Decepticons stage two daring raids, and on each occasion they manage to

outwit the Autobots. First the Decepticon Powermasters launch an assault on Ethan Zachary's company headquarters, where a copy of the disc housing Optimus Prime's personality is stored. The Decepticons manage to make off with not only the disc, but also the Autobot Getaway, who is captured while trying to defend the facility.

In the meantime, the Combaticons attack the Rutter Military Base and steal ABC – a computer built by humans using Transformer technology. The Decepticons' ultimate plan is to make a smart bomb, a homing missile controlled by ABC. Thanks to the stolen disc, the missile is programmed to home in relentlessly on Optimus Prime.

Getaway manages to escape his cell on the Decepticon ship and works out what the Decepticons are planning. He locates ABC and tries to reason with it, but his pleas seemingly fall on deaf ears. Getaway steals an escape pod and rejoins his fellow Autobots on Earth.

Optimus Prime heads to a deserted area to ensure that, if he is destroyed by the missile, there will be no other casualties. Attempts to shoot down or escape from the missile prove fruitless, and Optimus Prime is resigned to his fate – however, the missile isn't armed, and proves harmless.

Getaway muses that his talk with ABC must have persuaded the sentient computer to help them after all.

Notes:
This story is set at some point after [50] 'Dark Star', as Scorponok is in command of the Combaticons, rather than Ratbat, who is killed in that story. (It's heavily implied that both the Combaticons and Protectobots are also killed during the events of [50] 'Dark Star', but as their deaths are never shown, it's certainly possible that they could have survived.)

The floppy disc stolen by the Decepticons is a copy of the one created after Optimus Prime's destruction in [24] 'Afterdeath'. Optimus Prime apparently wanted the copy kept safe, as it was his only link to the many computer-generated characters he lived with while reduced to a mere program (as seen in [40] 'Pretender to the Throne'). The disc's creator, Ethan Zachary, gets a mention, as does his technology company, Alternate Reality Inc.

The (fictional) Rutter US Military Base seen here houses ABC, an advanced computer built using Transformer technology (either reverse-engineered from the many Autobots captured by RAAT in stories such as [22] 'Heavy Traffic', or salvaged from Mount Saint Hilary after it was abandoned by the Autobots in [35] 'Child's Play' (comic)).

Getaway uses an Earth credit card to escape from his cell, having seen similar escape sequences on television. He states that he doesn't 'leave home without one,' a catchphrase used in a series of commercials launched in 1975 for the financial services provider American Express.

In the comics, Darkwing and Dreadwind are depicted as mercenaries, happy to work for anyone so long as the pay is right. (They serve the Mecannibals in [52] 'Guess Who the Mecannibals are Having for Dinner' and Megatron in [52.2] 'Race with the Devil'.) Presumably their affiliation with Scorponok here is for business reasons rather than out of a blind loyalty to the Decepticon commander.

Roll Call:
Autobots: Optimus Prime, Hot Spot, Streetwise, Blades, Groove, First Aid, Defensor,

Joyride, Slapdash and Getaway.

Decepticons: Onslaught, Brawl, Blast Off, Swindle, Vortex, Scorponok, Darkwing and Dreadwind.

Nebulans: Hi-Q, Hotwire, Rev, Throttle and Hi-Test.

Another Nebulan, Lube, is mentioned but does not appear. Darkwing and Dreadwind combine to form the super jet Dreadwing.

Review:
A game of two halves. The first part, which focuses on the Decepticon raids, is pedestrian action fare, lacking in pace or urgency. The second half, however, is much better. Getaway's escape from the Decepticon ship is riveting stuff, and the action showdown, as Optimus Prime struggles to avoid the missile, is an excellently-written sequence. 3/5

[A4.4] ALL IN THE MINDS!
11 pages; from the UK *The Transformers Annual 1989* (published September 1988)

Credits:
Simon Furman (script); Dan Reed (art); Euan Peters (colours); Tom Frame (letters); Chris Francis (editor).

Plot:
Ambushed by the Decepticons, Highbrow finds himself in a one-on-one fight with the powerful Decepticon leader Scorponok. Highbrow converts to his helicopter mode in an attempt to escape, but while in the air he is confronted by the Decepticons' master hypnotist, Mindwipe. Under the Decepticons' control, Highbrow is convinced that the Decepticons are in fact his allies, and that he should attack the evil Autobots.

Although Highbrow has been brainwashed, his Nebulan Headmaster companion, Gort, is unaffected. As soon as Gort separates from the Autobot, he realises what has happened and again turns on the Decepticons. However, he has something of a dilemma – as a diminutive Nebulan, he has no chance of defeating the Decepticons … but recombining with the mesmerised Highbrow could see him once more under Mindwipe's control.

Gort reconnects with Highbrow and initially seems to be back under the Decepticons' power – however it is all a ruse and, when close to Scorponok, the Autobot rips the Decepticon leader's head right off his shoulders. It transpires that Gort's influence was strong enough to overcome Mindwipe's hold over Highbrow.

Notes:
This story is set immediately prior to (the present-day segments of) [48.2] 'Time Wars', with Highbrow's theft of Scorponok's head and Apeface's crash here both getting a mention in that comic adventure.

As the Fortress Maximus toy was never released in the UK, for the purposes of the British Transformers market Highbrow was given the role of the 'lead' Autobot Headmaster toy, and therefore Scorponok's opposite number. This resulted in the pair having a couple of face-offs in the British stories, both here and in [31.1] 'Worlds Apart'.

An editorial caption misquotes the nursery rhyme 'The Teddy Bears' Picnic', the lyrics of which were written by Jimmy Kennedy in 1932 (for a 1907 tune composed by John Walter Bratton).

Roll Call:
Autobots: Highbrow.

Decepticons: Scorponok, Mindwipe, Apeface and Snapdragon.

Nebulans: Gort, Zarak, Vorath and Krunk.

Krunk appears exclusively as the head of Snapdragon's dinosaur mode, rather than as a separate character in his own right.

Review:
A semi-remake of [31.1] 'Worlds Apart', with Highbrow again using his Headmaster powers to outmanoeuvre the stronger Scorponok. However, just as 'Worlds Apart' was a mundane adventure, this feels equally half-hearted, with the added problem that it's a bit of a rehash of old ideas. 1/5

[A4.5] PEACE
6 pages; from the UK *The Transformers Annual 1989* (published September 1988)

Credits:
Richard Alan (script); Robin Smith (art); Steve White (colours); Gary 'Glib' Gilbert (letters); Chris Francis (editor).

Richard Alan is a pseudonym of Richard Starkings (Alan is his middle name); he had already served *The Transformers* comic in the capacity of letterer and editor.

Plot:
Earth date: 2510. The Transformers' great war is over, as the last surviving Decepticon is killed in battle. His duty done, Rodimus Prime decides to step down as Autobot leader and chooses Springer to take his place.

Another Autobot, Triton, bemoans this decision, and assertively makes the case for Ultra Magnus to be the new leader, punching Whirl out of the way as he does so. This is the cue for a mass brawl between the various Autobots as they argue over who should be leader. During the skirmish, Roadbuster is killed.

As the battle becomes ever more intense and bloodthirsty, Rodimus Prime sinks to his knees in anguish – the Autobot/Decepticon war may be over, but a new one has just broken out to take its place.

The battling Autobots remain oblivious to the corpse of Triton, who has also been killed during the fracas. His Autobot badge has come loose to reveal a Decepticon logo. Triton was the last Decepticon, a spy in the Autobots' ranks, whose final action was to ensure that war would go on …

Notes:
When this story was written, the future shown here seemed like a logical progression from the future-set stories previously presented in the comic (or Timeline A, as discussed in the notes to [27.1] 'Wanted: Galvatron – Dead or Alive'). The Technobots are part of the future Autobot forces (as previously established in [44.1] 'Space Pirates'), and the Autobase seen here is the same one that had appeared in other future-set stories, such as [31.3] 'Headhunt'.

A later adventure, [48.2] 'Time Wars', complicates matters a little, establishing that characters such as Sandstorm and Twin Twist are killed in the present-day (and therefore shouldn't exist in the future). However, given that the future-set stories seem to be set in a different dimension from the present-day ones (again, see [27.1] 'Wanted: Galvatron – Dead or Alive' for an explanation), this is less of a problem than it first appears – the Autobots killed in [48.2] 'Time Wars' are alternative, parallel versions of their future incarnations seen here. Besides which, many Transformers have managed to cheat certain death before (Optimus Prime in [24] 'Afterdeath', Starscream in [50] 'Dark Star' and so on), so the future appearances of supposedly-dead present-day characters is not in itself a continuity problem.

The main sticking-point is the presence of Rodimus Prime, who in [53.2] 'Aspects of Evil' was shown as sickly and near death in the year 2356. However, according to the letters page of UK#236, Rodimus Prime was only temporarily ill and later made a full recovery.

Is This Just Fantasy?

As explained above, this story does (just about) fit into the same chronology as most other future-set adventures (dubbed Timeline A in this book). However, there have been several attempts to claim that this story is, in fact, apocryphal.

Editor Simon Furman said as much in the reprint compilation, *The Transformers Classics UK, Vol. 5*: 'I looked at it very much as a *What if …?* type story [a reference to a series of Marvel Comics that explored alternative fictional universes] … the Transformers annuals … opened up loopholes … These odd stories didn't have to fit quite so snugly into the prevailing continuity.'

The letters page of the Transformers comic, however, had a different idea: 'Peace' was canonical, but just took place in an alternate universe ('parallel dimensions an' all that stuff' – UK#221). However, given that *every* future story takes place in an alternate universe, it unclear if it's supposed to be set in the same timeline as the other future stories, or a different one entirely.

Roll Call:
Autobots: Ultra Magnus, Roadbuster, Whirl, Topspin, Twin Twist, Springer, Sandstorm, Broadside, Blurr, Rodimus Prime, Scattershot, Lightspeed, Nosecone, Afterburner and Strafe.

Plus, notably, the Decepticon double-agent Triton.

Review:
A sublime story about the futility of war, written with verve and suitably illustrated. Given this evidence, it's a shame that writer Richard Starkings wasn't invited back to

pen more Transformers stories, such is the power of his first effort. It might be only six pages long, but this little vignette is head and shoulders above any other story in the 1989 Annual. 5/5

[A5.1] THE QUEST!
7 pages; from the UK *Transformers Annual 1990* (published August 1989)

This is an illustrated prose story.

Credits:
Simon Furman (writer, uncredited); Art Wetherell and Stephen Baskerville (original art, uncredited); Chris Francis (editor). In addition to the new art, stock images from previous issues were used to illustrate the story. Lee Sullivan provided the annual's cover, Gary 'Glib' Gilbert was the designer and Art Wetherell/Stephen Baskerville/John Burns provided the inside cover art. 'Chris Francis' is a pseudonym of Simon Furman.

Plot:
In the far future, an alien boy named Dicet writes a report on the Autobot/Decepticon war for a school project. He decides to get a first-hand look at the Transformers by using an untested time machine on which his father had been working, and so visits a number of key events in Transformers history.

Although a 'cloaking screen' renders Dicet invisible, during one of his trips through time he 'interacts' with history when he stumbles and falls onto Ultra Magnus. After he returns home and completes his essay, his father is furious – the government have cancelled his time travel research as a result of Dicet's trip.

Dicet wonders if he might have inadvertently changed history. Is his father the same man as he always was, or has reality become altered ...?

Notes:
This is another 'recap' story in same vein as [A2.1] 'In the Beginning' and [A4.1] 'The Saga of the Transformers – So Far' in previous annuals. This time the framing story shows us an alien travelling to nine key points in Transformers history.

The first trip takes Dicet to the events of [1] 'The Transformers', where he witnesses the Decepticons' attack on the *Ark*. (These events are dated to '1st Cycle 931', in line with a dating format previously seen in the 'Datafiles' pages of the 1987 annual.) The next trip takes in the events of [4] 'The Last Stand', as we witness Sparkplug's heart attack and Shockwave's attack on the Autobots.

For the third trip, we revisit the events of [12] 'Prime Time' as Optimus Prime's body is reunited with his head. Next, Dicet visits Galvatron's arrival on Earth in [23.4] 'Fallen Angel'. Following that, we witness the destruction of Optimus Prime, from [24] 'Afterdeath'.

Trip number six takes Dicet to the battle atop Mount Verona in [A3.3] 'Vicious Circle'. After that, he witnesses the birth of Powermaster Optimus Prime in [42] 'People Power'. He then watches a scene never previously depicted in the comics – Grimlock ceding the Autobot leadership to Optimus Prime, at some point prior to [47] 'Club Con'. Finally, Dicet sees Galvatron's death in [48.2] 'Time Wars'.

Dicet hails from the planet Theturis, where 'gluxins' and 'anns' are measurements of time. His house (or 'culture pod') contains anti-grav pads and a holographic emitter (which projects an image of his teacher, allowing him to study from home). The plasma plains are a notable landmark, and the time machine is called a 'transtime pod'.

Picture Sources:
Optimus Prime, Megatron and Dicet: original art
Optimus Prime and Prowl: original art
Optimus Prime and Megatron: original art (loosely based on the cover art of US#2)
Prime passes the Matrix to Buster: [16.3] 'Second Generation' (Part 1)
Galvatron battles Centurion: [23.4] 'Fallen Angel' (Part 1)
Ultra Magnus: from the cover art of UK#171
Galvatron: from the cover art of UK#199

Roll Call:
Autobots: Optimus Prime, Jazz, Prowl, Ironhide, Ratchet, Sideswipe, Huffer, Grimlock, Snarl, Slag, Sludge, Swoop, Jetfire, Hot Spot, Streetwise, Blades, Groove, First Aid, Ultra Magnus, Rodimus Prime, Goldbug, Joyride, Slapdash and Getaway.

Decepticons: Megatron, Shockwave, Onslaught, Brawl, Blast Off, Swindle, Vortex, Galvatron, Cyclonus, Scourge, Darkwing and Dreadwind.

Other: Buster, Sparkplug, Centurion and Ethan Zachary.

Nebulans: Hi-Q.

Unicron, Kup, Blurr, Wreck-Gar, Death's Head, Fortress Maximus and Scorponok are all mentioned, but take no part in events. Ironhide is erroneously misspelt as 'Ironside' throughout. Many other Autobots and Decepticons are involved in the events herein; this list concerns itself only with those specifically named within the text.

Review:
A novel way of recapping events, but by now the chronology of the Transformers is so sprawling and dense that the story manages to give only a taster of this rich tapestry rather than a full account. 2/5

[A5.2] DESTINY OF THE DINOBOTS!
6 pages; from the UK *Transformers Annual 1990* (published August 1989)

Credits:
Steve White (plot, colours, and 'dinosaur consultant'); Steve Alan (plot and script); Andrew Wildman (art); Gary 'Glib' Gilbert (letters); Chris Francis (editor).

'Steve Alan' is a pseudonym of John Tomlinson.

Plot:
1992. The Dinobot Snarl is suffering from the deadly wasting disease Corrodia Gravis. However, his fellow Dinobots plan to store his mind on a control crystal, so that his brain might continue to exist when his body dies. One such control crystal can be found

on the shuttle that originally ferried the Dinobots to the Savage Land four million years ago.

The Dinobots arrive in the Savage Land – a tropical wilderness where dinosaurs still exist – but the crystal is nowhere to be seen. It soon transpires that it has been taken by a palaeontologist, Professor Embrey, who is using its powers to ward off a disease that has been killing off the region's dinosaurs.

Realising that taking back the crystal would doom the dinosaurs, the Dinobots instead use it to transfer Snarl's mind into the body of a real stegosaurus. There Snarl's consciousness will remain until a new body can be found for him.

Notes:
This story sees the Dinobots return to the Savage Land, a location not seen (outside of dreams and flashbacks) since [8] 'Repeat Performance'. The control crystal seen here is identical to the ones that appeared in [14] 'Rock and Roll-Out'. There they were used to store (copies of) the minds of Grapple, Tracks, Hoist, Smokescreen and Skids.

Although this story is supposed to be set in '1992', and therefore after the events of [80] 'On the Edge of Extinction', that cannot be the case, as Grimlock is able to transform into his tyrannosaurus mode here, and he lost that ability in [76] 'Still Life'. This is better set in 1991, prior to [65] 'Dark Creation'. (See the Earthforce essay under the entry for [61.1] 'Starting Over' for a rationale.)

For the continuity to work, we have to assume that Snarl's brain was merely 'copied' into the stegosaurus (just as the minds of Tracks and co were just copies in [14] 'Rock and Roll Out'), and that his original mind remains within his original body. His diseased body eventually ends up in stasis and is later revived with Nucleon.

Snarl's medical condition would be referenced in a later story (albeit one set before this), namely [63.3] 'Assassins'.

Roll Call:
Autobots: Grimlock, Snarl, Slag, Sludge and Swoop.

Review:
Everyone loves dinosaurs, don't they? Taking the Dinobots and putting them in a story with real dinosaurs is an idea so obvious, you wonder why the comic hadn't done it before. The plot is decent and carries the story well, and the Dinobots get some good character moments. 4/5

[A5.3] TRIGGER-HAPPY!
14 pages; from the UK *Transformers Annual 1990* (published August 1989)

NB: This illustrated text story was split into two chapters, spread across the annual. Part 1 was 6 pages long; Part 2 consisted of 8 pages.

Credits:
Ian Rimmer (writer, part 1); Dan Abnett (writer, part 2); Art Wetherell and Stephen Baskerville (art); Chris Francis (editor).

Plot:
A plan to ambush a group of Decepticons goes awry when the nervous Autobot

Backstreet panics and defies orders. Firing blindly, he damages a nearby town. When his colleague Override jokily suggests that he could face a court-martial and even termination, the anxious Backstreet drives off in terror. Matters aren't helped when he is confronted by a convoy of military vehicles – believing them to be Decepticons, he fires on the humans before fleeing.

Megatron tracks the terrified Backstreet to his hiding place in an abandoned fairground. Realising that the Autobot has deserted his comrades, he offers him the chance to join the Decepticons. Optimus Prime arrives on the scene and attacks Megatron, but the powerful Decepticon wins out and prepares to kill his opposite number.

Backstreet redeems himself by firing on Megatron and saving Prime. Once his earlier misunderstandings are cleared up, he is welcomed back into the Autobots' ranks.

Notes:
The setting of this story is somewhat problematic: Powermaster Optimus Prime and Megatron are both based on Earth, and there is a three-way power struggle for the Decepticon leadership, involving Megatron, Shockwave and Scorponok, a situation that never arises in the regular comic continuity. We can't set it in Timeline A (which, as explained in the notes to [27.1] 'Wanted: Galvatron – Dead or Alive', is a timeline in which Galvatron never arrived in the past), because Megatron here has the foreknowledge that he will one day become Galvatron. While not a perfect fit, this story is best set around the time of the Earthforce stories (see [61.1] 'Starting Over').

This story is set in and around the (fictional) settlement of Rivers' Town (presumably in the USA, though it's not stated categorically). There's an abandoned funfair nearby, the Riverway Fun Park, which boasts a 'Cyclorama' 3-D cinema. One of Backstreet's lines in this story ('A moment's indecision can be your last'), is taken directly from the 'Tech Spec' character profile found on the packaging of the Backstreet action figure.

Roll Call:
Autobots: Optimus Prime, Joyride, Getaway, Backstreet, Dogfight, Override, Landfill, Quickmix and Scoop.

Decepticons: Megatron, Crankcase, Ruckus, Windsweeper, Quake, Needlenose and Spinister.

Nebulans: Hi-Q and **Holepunch**.

This is the only comic-continuity story in which any of the Double Targetmasters' Nebulan companions is mentioned by name; indeed, it's never stated outright that the Double Targetmasters even *have* Nebulan companions in the comics (see the notes to [53.3] '[Double] Deal of the Century' for more on this). It's possible, then, that the 'Holepunch' mentioned here could be just a regular gun (it never transforms or displays any sentience here), rather than a Nebulan Targetmaster companion.

Scoop, incidentally, is misidentified as a Decepticon in the Dan Abnett-written second half of the story – in the Ian Rimmer-written first half, he's correctly written as an Autobot.

Scorponok, Shockwave, Galvatron, Warpath and the Combaticons are all mentioned in the text, but do not appear.

Data File: Dan Abnett (writer)
Abnett started out at Marvel UK on titles such as *Doctor Who Magazine*, *Knights of Pendragon* and *Death's Head II*, and then made the move to *2000 AD*, penning scripts for *Judge Dredd* and *Strontium Dog* and co-creating *Sinister Dexter*. For DC Comics he has credits on *Aquaman*, *Superman* and *The Legion*, and his Marvel US work includes *Iron Man*, *The New Mutants* and *Guardians of the Galaxy*; as co-creator of the latter, he received a credit on its film adaptation (James Gunn, 2014). As a novelist, Abnett has written a couple of books based on the television series *Torchwood*, but he's best known for his books based on the *Warhammer* franchise, which have sold a combined total of over a million copies.

Review:
The Autobot Triggerbots and Double Targetmasters had few opportunities to shine in the comics, so it's nice to see them feature so prominently here. It's especially gratifying to see the characters written to match their 'Tech Spec' toy bios (Backstreet is insecure and anxious, Override is horribly unsubtle, etc), which doesn't always happen.

While there's much about this story that's refreshing, however, the overall plot isn't that great, and Megatron's scheme to sow distrust between Autobots and humans is unengaging, low-key stuff. 2/5

[A5.4] DREADWING DOWN!
11 pages; from the UK *Transformers Annual 1990* (published August 1989)

Credits:
Simon Furman (script); Dan Reed (art); Euan Peters (colours); Gary 'Glib' Gilbert (letters); Chris Francis (editor).

Plot:
When Joyride chases a Decepticon down a winding mountain highway, a human vehicle is forced off the road, its driver left in critical condition. Optimus Prime's Powermaster partner Hi-Q can use Nebulan technology to heal the innocent driver, but when Dreadwing steals a vital power cell, the driver's life hangs in the balance.

Dreadwing is shot down over the ocean, so the Autobot Powermasters head to the sea bed to retrieve the power cell. There they are confronted by the Seacons, who are also after the cell. Matters are complicated by the fact that the Nebulan Powermaster partners have only enough air in their suits to last thirty minutes.

While the Autobots fend off the Seacons, the quartet of Nebulans are able to retrieve the power cell before their oxygen tanks run empty.

Notes:
Given that this story features the Powermasters, Aerialbots and Seacons, it is probably set just prior to [47] 'Club Con'. The location is somewhere off the Atlantic coast (presumably in North America, though it could really be anywhere).

It's revealed that the Nebulans have only enough air reserves in their suits to survive thirty minutes underwater. It's likely that – as a direct result of these events – the Nebulans' Powermaster suits were augmented to increase their oxygen capacity soon afterwards. Certainly, Optimus Prime later expresses no concerns about spending a lot of time in the vacuum of space in [50] 'Dark Star'.

Roll Call:
Autobots: Optimus Prime, Silverbolt, Air Raid, Fireflight, Skydive, Slingshot, Joyride, Slapdash and Getaway.

Decepticons: Snaptrap, Seawing, Skalor, Overbite, Nautilator, Tentakil, Darkwing, Dreadwind and Quake (flashback only). Darkwing and Dreadwind appear only in their combined 'Dreadwing' mode.

Nebulans: Hi-Q, Hotwire, Lube, Rev, Throttle and Hi-Test.

Review:
Slight and inconsequential, this is simply a vehicle for some underwater battle scenes and some rather heavy-handed 'value of life' moralising. It does a decent job, but it's ultimately forgettable. 2/5

[A5.5] THE CHAIN GANG!
6 pages; from the UK *Transformers Annual 1990* (published August 1989)

Credits:
Dan Abnett (script); Dan Reed (art); Euan Peters (colours); Gary 'Glib' Gilbert (letters); Chris Francis (editor).

Plot:
A group of Decepticon Pretenders attack an offshore oil rig. Using a device called a 'transmuter', they plan to turn the crude oil into a refined fuel source suitable for Transformers. A trio of Autobots arrive, having followed the Decepticons to the rig. A fight ensues, during which a passing aeroplane is hit by a stray blast. With the damaged plane on a potentially explosive collision course with the rig, the Autobot Cloudburst and Decepticon Bomb Burst join forces to redirect it.

When they land back on the rig, Bomb Burst discovers that, while he was otherwise occupied, the other Autobots have captured his comrades. Now outnumbered, Bomb Burst is also subdued.

Notes:
This story must be set at some point after the creation of the Pretenders in [40] 'Pretender to the Throne'. Within this story the Autobot Pretenders (Cloudburst, Splashdown and Landmine) act akin to an Autobot police force, tracking down the Decepticons, capturing them, and preparing them for a trial on Cybertron. (It was established in [36] 'Spacehikers' that – according to Autobot law – all sentient beings accused of crimes have the right to a trial.)

Contrary to the opening caption, there is no such body of water as the 'Gulf of New Mexico' (New Mexico is a landlocked state); presumably the writer meant the Gulf of Mexico. Similarly, the oil rig is referred to as an 'oil terminal' (a land-based depot where refined oil is stored), when it's actually drawn as an oil platform.

Roll Call:
Autobots: Landmine, Cloudburst and Splashdown.

Decepticons: Bomb Burst, Skullgrin and Iguanus.

Review:
Dan Reed's colourful and expressive art is a high-point in an otherwise unremarkable little strip. As with [A5.4] 'Dreadwing Down' in the same annual, this is mildly diverting but nothing more. 2/5

[A6.1] THE MAGNIFICENT SIX!
16 pages; from the UK *Transformers Annual 1991* (published July 1989)

NB: This illustrated text story was split into two chapters, spread across the annual. Each consisted of 8 pages.

Credits:
Simon Furman (writer); Stewart 'Staz' Johnson (art); Louise Cassell (colours); Euan Peters (editor). Geoff Senior provided the annual's cover, Jacqui Papp was the designer and Jeff Anderson provided the inside cover art (later reissued as a poster, included free with UK#310).

Plot:
Cybertron – millions of years ago. A group of Autobots, including Jazz, Inferno, Wheeljack, Sunstreaker and Prowl, are tasked with defending a settlement full of neutralists against a Decepticon raid. They are captured and tortured by the mad Decepticon Megadeath, who plans to cleanse Cybertron by detonating a series of nuclear blasts across the planet. The Autobots manage to escape the first such explosion, and Megadeath is assumed destroyed in the blast – along with the innocent neutralists. Wracked by guilt and the scars of torture, the Autobots vow never to talk about the incident again.

Cybertron – the present-day. These same five Autobots, along with Silverbolt, are tasked with returning to that nuclear wasteland to investigate the power source of the Underbase. Still emotionally scarred by the memories of their previous mission there, they are understandably nervous.

Their dread only increases when Megadeath appears and kidnaps the group. Seeing his comrades paralysed by fear, Silverbolt, who wasn't a part of the original mission all those years ago, manages to talk them into action. Galvanised by his words, the Autobots confront Megadeath. Rather than be captured, Megadeath commits suicide.

Notes:
The only original story in the 1991 Annual (the others were reprints of old comic material), this showcases the Autobot 'Classic Heroes' characters, which means that the 'present-day' sections are set after their reawakening in [60.1] 'Perchance to Dream'. Given that there is no mention of Earthforce, it would appear to be set in the gap between 'Perchance' and the following story, [61.1] 'Starting Over'.

Echoing events in the contemporary comics, the Matrix is missing and Unicron is approaching Cybertron. Optimus Prime hopes that the power source of the Underbase (see [48] 'The Flames of Boltax' and [50] 'Dark Star'), which is somehow linked to Primus, can be used as a weapon against Unicron.

Millions of years ago (before their first meeting with Optimus Prime), Wheeljack, Sunstreaker, Prowl, Jazz and Inferno were teamed up with an Autobot named Stampede in a group nicknamed the 'Magnificent Six'. They were tasked with defending Yuss, a neutralist town in the Stanix region of Cybertron that boasted a Justice Building and an 'Amprodrome' (museum). Located in the 'south west' of the planet, Stanix was one of its first regions to fall to the Decepticons, whose base there is called Fort Scyk. Decepticons based at Stanix included Steamhammer, Pounder, Claw, Ripsnorter, Switchblade and Backfire.

Also present was Megadeath, an insane Decepticon who planned to destroy huge swathes of Cybertron with nuclear weapons. When his plan was vetoed by the Decepticon High Command, he went rogue and nuked Stanix anyway. His lieutenant at the time was a young Thunderwing. Stampede was killed, and Megadeath and the neutralists were assumed dead in the explosion.

In reality, Megadeath survived to the present day, and created a base for himself in Yuss (now irradiated, the area is known colloquially as the 'Acid Wastes'), with the mutated, zombie-like neutralists acting as his minions.

On Cybertron, a 'joor' and a 'groon' are both units of time, and a 'hic' is a measurement of distance. Sunstreaker's pre-Earth alternative mode was that of a 'sleek, golden hovercar'. Optimus Prime mentions that the 'chances of an alliance with the Decepticons [are] wrecked beyond all hope of salvage' (a reference to an unseen adventure – in the comics, the Autobots and Decepticons eventually join forces in [71] 'Surrender').

The title is derived from that of the classic western, *The Magnificent Seven* (John Sturges, 1960).

Roll Call:
Autobots: Optimus Prime, Jazz, Prowl, Sunstreaker, Wheeljack and Silverbolt.

Decepticons: Thunderwing.

Megatron, Unicron, Primus, Starscream and the Aerialbots are also mentioned in the text, but do not appear.

Review:
An excellent story, proving that Simon Furman was just as proficient at writing prose as he was at writing comics. It's engaging, exciting and well-constructed, plus it adds extra depth to characters such as Prowl, Jazz and Silverbolt. 4/5

[A7.1] ANOTHER TIME & PLACE
18 pages; from the UK *Transformers Annual 1991* (published July1990)

NB: This illustrated text story was split into two chapters, spread across the annual. Part 1 was 8 pages long; Part 2 consisted of 10 pages.

Credits:

Simon Furman (writer); Stewart 'Staz' Johnson (pencils); Lesley Dalton (inks); Caroline Steenden (colours). Jeff Anderson provided the annual's cover, and the inside cover art was a collaboration between Stewart 'Staz' Johnson, Stephen Baskerville and Robin Bouttell. No editor was credited, but it was probably Harry Papadopoulos, then editor of the UK *The Transformers* comic.

Plot:

The Autobot/Decepticon war might be over, but tensions remain. Grimlock hates being unable to transform – a side-effect of the Nucleon treatment. Going against Prime's orders, he and the Dinobots return to Hydrus Four, where they hope a second dose of Nucleon (its formula now perfected) will restore their ability to convert between modes.

The Dinobots are followed by a ship full of Decepticons. While the former are distracted by a native beast, the latter beat them to the medical facility. Catching Grimlock's troops unawares, the Decepticons ambush the Dinobots and chain them up. Bludgeon explains that the Decepticons have retrieved Megatron's body and plan to revive him using the Nucleon.

Fortunately, the Dinobots had also been tracked to Hydrus Four by Optimus Prime, who leads a group of Autobots in an assault on the medical facility. The Dinobots are rescued and Bludgeon is disassembled by a robotic medical device. Although Megatron is resurrected, Grimlock uses the new-formula Nucleon to restore his ability to transform. Joining forces with Optimus Prime, Grimlock assumes his tyrannosaur mode and kills Megatron – this time for good.

Notes:

This was the 'official' final story of the Generation One comic continuity, trumpeted as such in the pages of the UK Transformers comic and also – uniquely for a British annual – in the letters page of the American comic. As such, there are a number of references to events within the later comics. Much of the story is set on the planet Hydrus Four, first seen in [70] 'The Pri¢e of Life'. There is a mention of the Decepticon betrayal in [77] 'Exodus', Ratchet's deliberate destruction of the *Ark* in [78] 'A Savage Circle', the Decepticon attack on Klo in [79] 'The Last Autobot', and their subsequent defeat in [80] 'End of the Road'.

Since that last comic story, the Autobots have rebuilt the planet Klo. On Cybertron, there is a building called the Nova Point observation bay. A 'holocaust trigger' is a device that can create disorientating lights and sounds, enough to render a Transformer unconscious.

Hydrus Four is a 'part-colonised' world in the Hunfi system. (In [69] 'Eye of the Storm', the planet was said to be located within the Styrakon system.) Hydrus Four is full of natural dangers, including fire winds, slime swamps and razor vines. Native fauna includes Energon limpets, spine hogs and terracowls.

This story is bookended by some short scenes set 'many thousands of years later'. Though the Autobot/Decepticon war has been over for millennia, Autobot probes have detected signs of Decepticon activity in 'the far reaches of the galaxy' – the story goes on …

Roll Call:

Autobots: Optimus Prime, Prowl, Ironhide, Sunstreaker, Grimlock, Snarl, Slag, Sludge,

Swoop, Silverbolt, Air Raid, Skydive, Blaster, Springer, Roadhandler, Nightbeat and Tote.

Decepticons: Megatron, Dreadwind, Fangry, Crankcase, Quake, Stranglehold, Bludgeon and Octopunch.

Unicron, Fortress Maximus and Ratchet are all mentioned, but do not appear. Hi-Q (the Nebulan who later amalgamated with Optimus Prime) is also mentioned.

Review:
An 'important' story (the final chapter of Marvel's Generation One storyline), but it's not a very good one. Megatron is resurrected but doesn't actually do anything, the Decepticons are defeated all too easily, and Grimlock's battle with the Hydrus Four monster goes on far too long. Prowl, Prime and Grimlock get some good lines and character beats, but otherwise this is painfully mundane, when the occasion perhaps warranted something a little more epic. [80] 'End of the Road' was a far better and more fitting finale to the series; this is merely an unnecessary postscript. 1/5

THE TRANSFORMERS IN 3-D

Marvel might have held the comic rights to the Transformers franchise, but rival publisher Blackthorne were able to negotiate the licence for a '3-D comic'. Using red/blue polarised glasses and stereogram art, the comics allowed readers to enjoy Transformers adventures in three dimensions.

A lot of Blackthorne's output consisted of 3-D comics in this vein; other titles in the range included *Star Wars*, *G.I. Joe* and *Battle Beasts*. After the company folded in 1990, these strips entered a rights limbo, and they have never been officially reprinted.

[3D1] THE TEST
Issue #1, 'Fall (September) 1987' (issue #25 overall in Blackthorne's 3-D series), 28 pages.

Credits: Tim Tobolski (script, uncredited); Tim Tobolski and Bob Versandi (art, uncredited); Bob and Nancy Fritsch (3-D effects, uncredited); John Stephenson (staff editor).

NB: According to the cover, the title of this series is simply *The Transformers 3-D*; however, the indicia on the inside front cover gives the full title as *The Transformers in 3-D*.

Plot:
Independently tracking an energy source to a barren asteroid, the Autobots and Decepticons discover a docile, reptilian animal whose waste matter contains Energon. Oblivious of each other's presence, the two factions set to work studying the creature – the Autobots treat their specimen kindly, whereas the Decepticons are less ethical.

After sending scouts to explore the rest of the asteroid, both factions become aware of each other, and a massive battle ensues. Notably, the giant Transformers Fortress

Maximus and Scorponok face off against each other.

It transpires that the alien Energon creatures are actually intelligent, and are agents of the Quintessons. As they survey the battlefield and compare notes, it's the aliens who are now doing the testing, and the battlefield is their laboratory.

Notes:
Completely independent from both Marvel and Sunbow, this story doesn't fit within either the regular comic continuity or the cartoon one. Hot Rod can seemingly change into his Rodimus Prime alter ego at will ('At the sign of any real trouble, "Rodimus" will pop up and save the day'). Although both Fortress Maximus and Scorponok are present, it would seem that neither has yet undergone the Headmaster process, although the Autobots are still researching it (Hot Rod: 'We started making some progress on the "Headmaster" technology').

Interestingly, Ratbat is posing as Galvatron's mindless, obedient pet, concealing his true nature as a devious, intelligent plotter. As in the cartoons, the Quintessons would appear to be major villains.

Roll Call:
Autobots: Ultra Magnus, Hot Rod, Blurr, Searchlight, Fortress Maximus, Lightspeed and Sky Lynx.

Decepticons: Galvatron, Cyclonus, Scourge, Ratbat, Scorponok, Flywheels, Sixshot, Wingspan and Pounce.

Review:
The 3-D gimmick, jocular tone and rather stylised art might be offputting to some, but this is actually a decent morality play – covering the topic of animal testing – and features a smart, *The Twilight Zone*-esque twist ending. Furthermore, there's an interesting narrative device – characters and situations mirroring each other on different sides of the asteroid before coming together in a big battle – that's very reminiscent of [4.2] 'The Enemy Within'. 3/5

[3D2] PRISM OF POWER
Issue #2, 'December 1987' (issue #29 overall in Blackthorne's 3-D series), 28 pages.

NB: No story title was given within the issue itself; 'Prism of Power' is an unofficial name coined for ease of reference. The definite article is missing from the cover, which calls the series simply *Transformers in 3-D*. Again, the indicia confirms the correct title as *The Transformers in 3-D*.

Credits: Andrea LaFrance (script); Dennis Francis (art); Bob and Nancy Fritsch (3-D effects, uncredited); John Stephenson (staff editor).

Plot:
The Decepticons have a new weapon – the suspension-ray beam – that has the ability to 'freeze' human victims. They test it on the occupants of space station Exton 9; in their suspended state, the humans can be transported to the Decepticons' energy research laboratory, where they will be used as slave labour.

Fortunately, a group of youngsters were away from the station's central laboratory when the Decepticons attacked. Unaffected, these five seek out the Prism of Power – a mystical object that has the power to nullify the effects of the ray.

Teaming up with the Autobots Cosmos and Ironhide, the kids travel to the planet Andellor, where the Prism is supposed to be located. The artefact is guarded by an alien called Grogg – it was created by advanced aliens who left it behind when they ascended to another dimension.

After passing Grogg's test of worthiness, the kids are allowed to borrow the Prism (with one of their number staying behind as collateral), and use it to reawaken the adults.

Notes:

The introductory caption presents this as a story of the 'bygone days of the Transformers', inferring that it is set in the past (meaning that the spacefaring 'humans' in this story are actually aliens). Compared with how they were presented in [3D1] 'The Test', the relationships between the Decepticons are very different here (probably as a result of different writers). Ratbat talks to Galvatron (in the last issue he posed as a dumb 'pet'), and Galvatron himself is considerably toned down from the ranting maniac of the previous issue.

Their main weapon is the 'suspension-ray beam', which the kids recognise on sight as a 'new scientific discovery' (probably stolen by the Decepticons). The children and the Transformers are aware of the legend of the Prism of Power, but don't consider it to be a real object. (Even if they did, the Prism is very well guarded, lying on the other side of an asteroid belt that's home to energy-sucking space vultures and located beyond a chamber full of snake-like monsters capable of beheading Transformers – such dangers would have either killed or dissuaded anyone curious enough to attempt to search for the Prism before, hence its now-legendary status.)

The Prism was created by a group of advanced aliens who lived on the planet Andellor. These futuristic librarians accumulated vast knowledge, of which the Prism is a repository. (The 'Prism' is technically not a prism at all; geometrically it's a prism*atoid* – specifically, a tetrahedron. The name is probably meant to be a metaphor: the device is capable of dispersing knowledge and power much as an optical prism disperses light.)

Borrowing the Prism requires one to prove one's wisdom by answering a riddle ('What … cannot be touched … has laid low the greatest of titans'), the correct answer being 'time'. A very similar riddle (with an identical answer) is spoken by the character Gollum in J R R Tolkein's 1937 novel *The Hobbit, or There and Back Again*.

Roll Call:

Autobots: Ironhide and Cosmos.

Decepticons: Galvatron, Cyclonus, Octane, Razorclaw, Ratbat and Scorponok.

Review:

[3D1] 'The Test' was great fun, and there was evidence of some thought going into that issue's script and characterisation. Here, sadly, there are no such positives, in a hokey space-opera full of annoying kids and terrible dialogue. The 3-D is great, though. 1/5

[3D3] THE WAR AGAINST THE DESTRUCTONS (Chapter 1 of 3)

Issue #3, 'March 1987' (issue #37 overall in Blackthorne's 3-D series), 28 pages.

Credits: John (?) Williams (script); Dante Fuget (pencils); Philip Haxo (inks); 'Noodles' (letters); Paul Tallerday and Barbara Marker (3-D effects); John Stephenson (staff editor).

Williams, Fuget and Haxo were credited by their surnames only; while Fuget and Haxo are distinctive enough names to make full identification easy, there were a few different Williamses who worked on Blackthorne comics, so the writer's identity is unconfirmed. It's been suggested that 'Noodles' is possibly a pseudonym of Pete Iro.

Plot:
On an alien world, a battle rages between the Andegeans and the Kalkars. During the skirmish, one of the Andegeans is tricked into releasing the Destructons: powerful techno-organic criminals who have been trapped behind a 'dimension barrier'. The Destructons kill everyone in sight. However, a tape containing a recorded warning message is shot out into space.

On the neighbouring world of Tau-Ursa, populated by harmless little robots, scientists have developed the Intergon Device, a contraption that has the ability to either increase or decrease the potency of Energon. The Decepticons attack the planet and steal the Intergon Device, then head to Cybertron for an assault on the Autobots. Galvatron uses the device on the Autobots' Energon plant, severely depleting their power reserves.

Despite their defeat, the Autobots travel to Tau-Ursa, hoping to rid the planet of the invading Decepticons. There, they discover the tape containing the warning message. Realising that the only beings that can defeat the Destructons are another alien race, the Logicons, the Autobots 'search across the galaxy' to find these Logicons and secure their aid.

The Autobots and Decepticons again do battle, but are stopped in their tracks by the arrival of the Destructons. The two factions reluctantly decide to join forces against their common foe …

Notes:
Despite its billing as 'Chapter 1 of 3', this was the final issue of *The Transformers in 3-D*, and as such the story remains incomplete. According to a caption on the last page, the next issue would have been 'Union of the Transformers'.

The Destructons are a group of four criminals whose sole aim is to kill every other life form in the universe. Their names are Bruton (a dim-witted brute, whose weapon of choice is the 'confusion club'), Medusa (who shoots 'Medusa beams' from her eyes), the samurai-like Psychokhan (who has a 'psychospear' weapon) and their leader, Lord Imperious Delerious (who can shoot 'delerious fire' from his mouth). (Medusa is a half-woman, half-snake creature, so in terms of Greek mythology she's actually closer in appearance to Echidna than to Medusa.)

The only beings who can stop the Destructons are the Logicons, from the Energon-rich planet Metascan Alpha, who look like giant bloated heads with tentacles. (Based on appearances, they might perhaps be related to the Quintessons.)

The Autobots are friends to the Tau-Ursans, whose people include Mini-Mayor

Monitorus. Until now they have shunned military aid from the Autobots for fear that it would incur the Decepticons' wrath. (Tau-Ursa has a name very similar to those of some real-world stars – Tau Ursae Majoris, a binary star, and Tau Ursae Minoris, a red giant. It's therefore feasible that the planet orbits one of these two stars.)

Other alien races seen here include the warring Andegeans and Kalkars. Named Andegeans include Doza and Charc Dulth, the latter of whom introduces himself as a 'fourth rank science counselor'.

In a scene set during a Cybertronian medical examination, Hot Rod states, 'It's good to have you back, Optimus', implying that the Autobot leader has just been repaired after a long period out of action.

Wreck-Gar makes a brief appearance here, and yet again his sentences are full of cultural references:

- 'Ambush at the OK Corral, sheriff!' is a reference to the infamous 1881 gunfight at the Old Kindersley Corral building in Tombstone, Arizona, depicted in many Westerns over the years, including *Gunfight at the O.K. Corral* (John Sturges, 1957).
- 'Tastes great, less filling!' is an advertising slogan for Miller Lite beer.
- 'Will the real Energon please stand up?' is a catchphrase from the American game show *To Tell The Truth* (launched 1956), in which celebrities have to guess which one of three 'challengers' is the named contestant.
- 'Hop Sing Chop! Chop!' is a reference to the character Hop Sing (played by Victor Sen Yung) in the television Western series *Bonanza* (1959-73).

Roll Call:
Autobots: Optimus Prime, Hoist, First Aid, Blaster, Ultra Magnus, Hot Rod, Kup, Blurr, Wreck-Gar, Sureshot, Grotusque, Doublecross, Repugnus, Sky Lynx, Rewind, Fastlane and Cloudraker.

Decepticons: Laserbeak (or possibly Buzzsaw – they look identical in monochrome), Blast Off, Galvatron, Cyclonus, Scourge, Scorponok, Apeface, Slugslinger, Triggerhappy, Misfire, Hun-Gurrr, Cutthroat, Blot, Sinnertwin, Rippersnapper, Abominus, Sixshot, Wingspan and Pounce.

Nebulans: Zarak, Spasma, Nightstick and Fracas. All Nebulans bar Zarak appear only in their head or gun modes.

This is the first appearance of Fastlane and Cloudraker in a Transformers comic.

The Missing Episodes
So, with this story ending on a cliffhanger, how would it have concluded? Well, much is set up within the story itself. Undoubtedly the Autobots would have located the Logicons and joined forces with them in an attempt to return the Destructons to their prison. Furthermore, the Autobot Kup would probably have been the one who makes first contact with the Logicons. He was last seen on the Logicons' planet and left for dead, having stayed behind to cover the escape of his comrades.

Not only are the Logicons the key to defeating the Destructons, but their planet contains vast amounts of Energon, which would have neatly solved the Autobots' energy crisis. Undoubtedly the Decepticons would have broken the truce at some point and turned on the Autobots, possibly in a bid to save their own skins.

Another dangling plot point here is the Galvatron/Scorponok relationship: Galvatron hates serving under Scorponok and believes that he should lead the Decepticons. This power struggle would probably have come to a head in the remaining two chapters.

Review:

It's so hard to judge a story when we can see only the first third of it. What we *can* say is that the art is very good, the dialogue is an improvement on that of the previous issues in the series, and the whole feel of the piece is much more adult and 'epic'.

The most interesting thing here is the depth given to the supporting players and new alien races. The Tau-Ursans, Destructons and Andegeans are all very well realised and unique creations. Rather than spout clunky exposition at each other, they reveal themselves through natural snippets of information and offhand mentions of concepts such as 'science counselors' and 'mini-mayors'.

It's a crying shame, then, that the concluding chapters were never published, because this offers a tantalising glimpse of what *The Transformers in 3-D* could have become, had it continued. 4/5

WOMAN'S DAY

The American-published lifestyle magazine *Woman's Day* is, as its name would suggest, aimed squarely at female readers, covering topics such as food, fashion, health and celebrities. A Christmas-themed issue in 1985 contained within its pages a short Transformers strip. Although no credits were provided, it's almost certainly a Marvel Comics production, and it's been claimed that the pencils were provided by Herb Trimpe, possibly inked by Al Gordon, and that colours were by Nel Yomtov. The latter is debatable: the colours definitely seem more nuanced than Yomtov's work for the regular comic, with highlights, lowlights and subtle gradients apparent; however, as a glossy magazine, *Woman's Day* was unfettered by Marvel's standard blocky, dotty printing techniques, so the extra subtleties could be due simply to Yomtov having extra scope to express himself.

As an officially-licensed comic adventure, it's included here for the sake of completeness …

[WD1] THE NIGHT THE TRANSFORMERS SAVED CHRISTMAS
Published in *Woman's Day*, 26 December 1985, 4 pages.

Plot:
Soundwave and Laserbeak are in the process of tapping energy from an electrical substation, causing a blackout in a nearby town. The Autobots arrive on the scene and chase the Decepticons away. During the pursuit, a human car is damaged in the crossfire. Calling off the chase to tend to the startled travellers – Bill and Cynthia Perry and their daughter Megan – Bumblebee learns that the town's Christmas tree lights were due to be switched on that evening.

As the Autobots struggle to effect repairs to the substation, Bumblebee – who has discovered the significance of Christmas following a conversation with the Perrys –

donates some of his own power to ensure the Christmas tree switch-on can go ahead as planned.

Notes:
This story features Tracks and Hoist, who debuted in [14] 'Rock and Roll-Out', and Prowl, who was incapacitated for reasons unknown around the time of [28] 'Mechaical Difficulties', meaning that it must be set at some point between those two adventures. The most likely placement would therefore seem to be around the time of the UK Christmas story [22.1] 'The Gift', i.e. December 1986. The 'energy siphon' used by the Decepticons to drain power from the substation appears to be the same kind of power-tapping technology used by the Decepticons in stories such as [14] 'Rock and Roll Out' and [18] 'The Bridge to Nowhere'.

Roll Call:
Autobots: Prowl, Bumblebee, Hoist and Tracks.

Decepticons: Soundwave and Laserbeak.

Review:
Many of the UK Christmas stories centred around the idea of Transformers learning about the 'Christmas spirit', and this – the only official American Christmas strip during the G1 era – follows the same basic (and obvious) idea.

For a simple four-page strip, however, this is surprisingly well-executed, and stacks up well against its longer British counterparts. Despite its inauspicious origins – printed in a lifestyle magazine as a means to keep the kids occupied over Christmas – it's worth checking out. 3/5

The Books

Although Marvel UK (in conjunction with Grandreams) had the rights to publish Transformers annuals in the UK, these weren't the only books published to tie in with the franchise. Other publishers were able to negotiate deals of their own, in various formats and markets, resulting in a number of Transformers-related books appearing. While it doesn't include every work of Transformers fiction released in the '80s (there were sticker albums and colouring books that had plots of sorts), what follows is a list (with brief synopses) of the most prominent examples released during the Generation 1 era.

Ladybird Books
Ladybird was a London-based imprint of the Penguin group, its titles specifically aimed at children and often found in primary schools across the UK (especially the 'Read it Yourself' range for novice readers). The books were pocket-sized hardbacks, measuring roughly 11.5 x 18.0 centimetres. In the '80s, Ladybird acquired the rights to a number of popular children's franchises including *The Transformers*, *Thomas the Tank Engine*, *Masters of the Universe* and *Action Force*. Often these titles would be packaged alongside cassette audiobooks, enabling children to follow the book while they listened to it being read out loud with music and sound effects. The Transformers titles formed part of this 'Tell-a-Tale' range.

Data File: Peter Marinker (narrator, Ladybird Tell-A-Tale audiobooks)
Although based in the UK, Marinker is a Canadian-born actor. His television credits include parts in *Z Cars*, *The Professionals*, *Casualty* and *Bugs*. His films include *Labyrinth* (Jim Henson, 1996), *Judge Dredd* (Danny Cannon, 1995), *Event Horizon* (Paul W S Anderson, 1997) and *Love Actually* (Richard Curtis, 2003).

Autobots' Lightning Strike (1985)
Written by John Grant. Art by Mike Collins and Mark Farmer.
ISBN 0721408958

The Autobots build a giant lightning conductor linked to an underground cavern. Their hope is that when lightning strikes the mast, they can harness its power and use it as a fuel source. The Decepticons infiltrate the cavern in the mistaken belief that the conductor is a radio mast. However, when lightning strikes the tower, the Decepticons within the cavern are badly damaged.

Megatron's Fight for Power (1985)
Written by John Grant. Art by Mike Collins and Mark Farmer.
ISBN 0721408966

The Decepticons attack a human solar power plant and use it to create Energon cubes. Starscream tries to overthrow Megatron but is unsuccessful. The Autobots monitor the Decepticons' transmissions and race to the scene; Spike infiltrates the station and focuses the solar power onto the Decepticons' stash of Energon cubes, destroying them.

Autobots Fight Back (1985)
Written by John Grant. Art by Mike Collins and Mark Farmer.
ISBN 0721409423

The Decepticons have set up camp in a disused railway tunnel where they can test a new propulsion system. The Autobots discover the Decepticon plot and decide to investigate. Under the pretence of being entrants in an organised car rally, they approach the tunnel and push a train of rusty hopper wagons down the track; the wagons collide with the Decepticons' machinery, foiling their plan.

Laserbeak's Fury (1985)
Written by John Grant. Art by Mike Collins and Mark Farmer.
ISBN 0721409431

On a recon mission, Laserbeak flies into an overhead power cable and shorts out, trapped in cassette mode. He is discovered by a local boy charged with arranging the music for a disco at the local village hall. When Laserbeak is inserted into the hall's hi-fi system he is recharged, and attacks the startled partygoers. The Autobots and Decepticons arrive at the scene. After Laserbeak is struck by the sails of a nearby windmill, the Decepticons assume that the windmill is a weapon and destroy it, before escaping into the night.

Galvatron's Air Attack (1986)

Written by John Grant. Art by Richard Dunn.
ISBN 0721409881

The Decepticons have launched three new spy satellites, capable of detecting Autobot activity. When the Autobots are discovered by Decepticon troops, they become suspicious of the satellites' existence and send Cosmos to investigate. Although the satellites have been rendered invisible via the use of a refraction shield, Cosmos is able to detect their radio signals. The Autobots send a false message to the satellites, ordering them to converge on the same point. Invisible to each other, the three satellites collide in space and are destroyed.

Decepticon Hideout (1986)
Written by John Grant. Art by Graham Potts.
ISBN 072140989X

The Decepticons attack Metroplex. Although they are driven away, Bumblebee is tasked with secretly following them home, in an attempt to locate their new base of operations, which is located within a construction/industrial complex. Biding their time until all humans have safely left the site, the Autobots make their move. With the help of some of the site's equipment (electromagnets, wrecking-balls and a large heater unit), they are able to defeat the Decepticons.

Transformers The Movie (1986)
Adapted by John Grant (from a script by Ron Friedman, uncredited). Designed by Howard Matthews. (There is no original art; all illustrations are screen-caps from the film.)
ISBN 072141009X

An adaptation of the theatrical film *The Transformers: The Movie*.

Decepticons at the Pole (1988)
Written by John Grant. Art by Barry Rowell.
ISBN 0721410685

The planet Nebulos draws its energy from cosmic radiation; the Decepticons decide to tap this by building a piece of 'pyramid energy technology' at the planet's North Pole. The Autobots get wise to the Decepticon plot and formulate a plan. The Autobot-affiliated Nebulans plant explosive charges around the base of the energy-intercepting tetrahedron, while the Autobots themselves melt the polar ice around where the Decepticons are standing. The Decepticons begin sinking into the layer of mud beneath the ice. The pyramid explodes, and Nebulos is saved.

Autobots Strike Oil (1988)
Written by John Grant. Art by Barry Rowell.
ISBN 0721410693

In need of oil, the Autobots build a pipeline to an underground oil well. Investigating what they are up to, the Decepticons damage the pipe, causing oil to spill out into the surrounding ravine. When the Autobots show up to repair the pipe, the Decepticons attack. After a brief chase, the Autobots lure the Decepticons full circle, back to where the section of broken pipe was – the Autobots manage to escape when the Decepticons skid on the spilled oil and crash into the wall of the ravine.

Autobot Hostage (1988)
Written by John Grant. Art by Glenn Steward.
ISBN 0721411185

When Highbrow is captured by the Decepticons, Scorponok suggests a prisoner exchange – Highbrow will be allowed to go free if Optimus Prime surrenders himself. Optimus Prime agrees, but secretly carries Hosehead and Fizzle in his trailer when he travels to the Decepticon base. The two passengers sneak away when Prime is captured, and free Highbrow. The trio then rescue Prime and make their escape.

Decepticons Underground (1988)
Written by John Grant. Art by Glenn Steward.
ISBN 0721411193

After a full search of the planet Nebulos, the Autobots determine that the Decepticons' only possible hiding-place is within the dreaded Nebulos Triangle, a region where many Nebulans have gone missing. Investigating, Quickswitch stumbles upon an underground lair that's being used as a base by the Decepticons. Escaping through a tunnel back to the surface, he shares his discovery with his Autobot colleagues Scoop and Quickmix, who seal the tunnel with a combination of rocks and fast-drying concrete, entombing the Decepticons within their own headquarters.

Ballantine Books
A major American publishing house founded in 1952, Ballantine had a catalogue including notable titles such as *Fahrenheit 451* and *The Lord of the Rings*, and a range of *Star Trek* tie-ins. Ballantine's Transformers range was part of a line called 'Find Your Fate … Junior': adventure gamebooks that allowed the readers to determine the outcome of the plot. Synopses for these books are necessarily vague, as the stories were shaped by the readers themselves.

Dinobots Strike Back (1985)
Written by Casey Todd. Art by William Schmidt.
ISBN 0345341503

The Dinobots go berserk after being affected by Bombshell's brain-altering cerebro-shells. Investigating, the Autobots find that the Decepticons have discovered an amazing new natural power source – black coral …

Battle Drive (1985)
Written by Barbara and Scott Siegel. Art by William Schmidt.
ISBN 0345341538

The Decepticons plot to lure the Autobots into a trap, by feeding them false information about their plans. Believing that the Decepticons are trying to destroy the planet's food supply, the Autobots race into battle ...

Attack of the Insecticons (1986)
Written by Lynn Beach. Art by William Schmidt.
ISBN 0345341511

Sparkplug has developed an experimental solar-powered battery, the Sun-Pak. However, Kickback is spying on the Autobots, and seeks the Sun-Pak for himself. Starscream also covets the device, and sees it as a means by which to usurp Megatron and claim the Decepticon leadership for himself ...

Earthquake (1986)
Written by Ann Matthews. Art by William Schmidt.
ISBN 0345330714

Beachcomber, Buster and Jessie accidentally stumble across a Decepticon plot to destroy Central City using their new Destruction Beam. Should the test prove successful, the Decepticons plan to target the world's capital cities ...

Desert Flight (1986)
Written by Jim Razzi. Art by William Schmidt.
ISBN 0345330722

The Autobots attempt to stop the Decepticons testing their gravity gun, but matters are complicated when Cosmos is captured and replaced by an identical duplicate ...

Decepticon Poison (1986)
Written by Judith Bauer Stamper. Art by William Schmidt.
ISBN 0345330730

With the bulk of their forces crippled by a poisoned fuel supply, a small group of unaffected Autobots, including Prowl, Bumblebee and Mirage, infiltrate the Decepticon base in search of an antidote ...

Autobot Alert! (1986)
Written by Judith Bauer Stamper. Art by William Schmidt.
ISBN 0345333888

The Autobots have to deal with a double peril – an ancient Cybertronian power formula that crash-landed on Earth centuries ago is coveted by the Decepticons. Meanwhile, the Decepticons have hacked into Earth's network of communications satellites ...

Project Brain Drain (1986)
Written by Barbara and Scott Siegel. Art by William Schmidt.
ISBN 0345333896

Experimenting with a new radio device, Sparkplug overhears a Decepticon plot to steal brain energy from thousands of revellers at a nearby rock concert – a concert that his son Spike is attending …

The Invisibility Factor (1986)
Written by Josepha Sherman. Art by William Schmidt.
ISBN 0345333918

Hot Rod and Kup encounter a pacifist human scientist who has developed an invisibility device. While the Autobots attempt to persuade her that the device could be used for good in their fight against the Decepticons, the Decepticons aren't so courteous …

Marvel Books
A division of Marvel Comics, Marvel's book-publishing arm was created in 1982 and focused on colouring books, sticker sets and trade paperback reprints of comics, as well as original prose stories.

Battle for Cybertron (1984)
Written by Scott Siegel. Art by Earl Norem.
ISBN 0871350165

After a battle, a spaceship carrying the Autobots and Decepticons crashes on Earth. On reawakening, the Decepticons drain energy from a nearby city and return to attack the Autobots. However, with the help of their new human friends Sparkplug and Spike, the Autobots are able to triumph.

The Great Car Rally (1984)
Written by Dwight Jon Zimmerman. Art by Earl Norem.
ISBN 0871350157

With free fuel and oil up for grabs as a prize, the Autobots enter a road race. Unfortunately, the Decepticons overhear their plans and attempt to sabotage their efforts. Thankfully, Megatron's efforts are thwarted and the Autobots are able to win.

Decepticon Hijack (1985)
Written by Regina Weyn. Art by John Speirs.
ISBN 0871350793

The Decepticons attempt to steal fuel from a broken-down oil tanker, but the Autobots are able to repair it. Still undeterred, the Decepticons chase after the tanker, but are again defeated. Although the tanker is destroyed, its human drivers are saved.

Insecticon Attack (1985)
Written by Dana Rosenfeld. Art by John Speirs.
ISBN 0871350785

Using his mind-altering cerebro-shells, the Insecticon Bombshell takes mental control of

Grapple and forces him to attack a fellow Autobot, Beachcomber. However, the Autobots attack the Decepticon base, and Grapple is cured. Not realising that Grapple is no longer under Decepticon control, the Autobot catches Megatron by surprise and defeats him.

Battle for Earth (1985)
Written by Max Z Baum. Art by Roberta Edelman.
ISBN 0871350629

The Global Building Corporation is responsible for impressive buildings all over the world. However, it is secretly being run by the Decepticons. The buildings are traps in which the Decepticons can hold millions of people hostage. Thankfully, the Autobots attack the Decepticon headquarters, and the hostages are saved.

The Autobots' Secret Weapon (1985)
Written by Nancy Krulik. Art by Charles Nicholas and Roberta Edelman.
ISBN 0871350610

When the Decepticons kidnap Sunstreaker and some of his comrades, they order the rest of the Autobots to surrender. Optimus Prime does so, and as a gesture of peace, the Autobots give the Decepticons a giant statue. However, the statue is hollow, and contains a number of Autobots. When the statue is wheeled inside the Decepticon base, the hidden Autobots emerge and rescue their friends.

Car Show Blow Up (1986)
Written by Dana Rosenfeld. Art by Earl Norem.
ISBN 0871351072

Galvatron plans to build an advanced Decepticon City. A nearby car show is demonstrating a new voice-activated robotic vehicle, so he decides to steal this and use it to build an army of subservient robot drones to build his city. Hot Rod realises what the Decepticons are planning and summons Autobot reinforcements. The Autobots emerge victorious, and the robot car is saved.

The Story of Wheelie, the Wild Boy of Quintesson (1986)
Written by Sonia Black Woods. Art by Earl Norem.
ISBN 0871351080

A spacecraft crashes on the planet Quintesson; the young Autobot Wheelie is the only survivor. For years, he spends his life living in the wilderness outside the city, evading capture by the evil Quintessons. Another Autobot ship is forced to land on the planet, its crew including Hot Rod and Kup. After Wheelie saves them from a Quintesson attack, they are able to repair the ship and escape.

Corgi Books
Counting Terry Pratchett and Anne McCaffrey amongst its roster of authors, Corgi (who alongside their publishing arm also used to make die-cast toy cars) had the rights to publish Transformers paperbacks in the United Kingdom. These consisted of six

adventure game books and a more traditional-type children's novel, *Battle Beneath the Ice.*

Dinobot War (1985)
Written by Dave Morris. Art by Bob Harvey.
ISBN 0552523143

A human is transported back in time by an alien device. Joining forces with the Dinobots, he uncovers a Decepticon plot to change history …

Peril from the Stars (1985)
Written by Dave Morris. Art by Bob Harvey.
ISBN 0552523151

The Decepticons attack an observatory, hoping to determine the location of a secret Cybertronian weapons pod …

Island of Fear (1986)
Written by Dave Morris. Art by John Higgins.
ISBN 055252316X

On an island in the South Pacific, the Autobot Beachcomber must foil a plot by the Decepticon Dirge to create energy from a nearby volcano …

Highway Clash (1986)
Written by Dave Morris. Art by John Higgins.
ISBN 0552523178

From a secret underground base in England, Megatron and Rumble plot to steal a number of valuable microchips, with which they hope to build a new army …

Swamp of the Scorpion (1987)
Written by Dave Morris. Art by Bob Harvey.
ISBN 0552525014

On Nebulos, the Decepticon Headmasters are planning to steal fuel from a local oil rig. All hopes depend on Highbrow, a lone Autobot against the Decepticon army …

Desert of Danger (1987)
Written by Dave Morris. Art by Bob Harvey.
ISBN 0552525022

The Decepticons attempt to smuggle additional troops to the planet Nebulos by hiding them in cargo ships arriving from Earth …

Battle Beneath the Ice (1987)
Written by Dave Morris. Art by Nik Spender.
ISBN 0552524026

In the year 2000, an aeroplane containing the Autobot Hot Rod and a group of human passengers is shot down over Antarctica. There, beneath the ice, the survivors discover an underground city populated by advanced humans. These Antarcticans plan to conquer Earth by programming themselves with more aggressive tendencies, thanks to footage of Autobot/Decepticon battles. The Autobots and Decepticons join forces against these creatures, and the battle footage is replaced by a recording of a cartoon show owned by one of the human crash survivors. Now programmed to act like zany animated characters, the Antarcticans no longer pose a threat.

PART THREE: THE CARTOON SERIES

Introduction

The Transformers animated television show was a co-production between two studios, Marvel Productions and Sunbow Entertainment.

Marvel Productions dates back to 1963, when it was formed as DePatie-Freleng Enterprises by two ex-employees of Warner Brothers' animation division. From the '60s to the early '80s, DFE (as it was also known) produced classic cartoons such as *Looney Tunes/Merrie Melodies* (1964-67) and *The Pink Panther Show* (1969-80) and many Dr Seuss television specials such as *The Cat in the Hat* (1971). It also produced animated segments for live-action shows, such as the title sequence of *I Dream of Jeannie* (1965). DFE was sold to Marvel in 1981 and, rebranded as Marvel Productions, began producing animated shows such as *Spider-Man and His Amazing Friends* (1981), *Dungeons and Dragons* (1983) and *Jim Henson's Muppet Babies* (1984).

Sunbow Entertainment, meanwhile, boasted close ties with Toei, a highly-regarded Japanese animation studio, and had impressed Marvel with its work on a series of animated *G.I. Joe* toy commercials. After successfully joining forces on the subsequent *G.I. Joe* television programme (1983), Marvel and Sunbow entered into a long-standing partnership that would result in the creation of further esteemed animation series, including *The Transformers*.

Written, directed, scored and voiced by a chiefly American cast and crew, much of the animation was handled by Sunbow's Japanese partners Toei.

{1-01} MORE THAN MEETS THE EYE, Part One
Also known as 'More Than Meets the Eye, Day One'

Production number: 4023 (1st episode produced of Season One)
Transmission date: 17 September 1984 (1st episode transmitted of Season One)

Written by George Arthur Bloom

Throughout Season One, no episode titles were shown on screen. Official sources for the titles include contemporary production documents (including a set of script scans that appeared as extras on a UK DVD release), listings magazines and the official VHS (and later DVD) range. Although these sources don't contradict each other in any significant way, there remains some slight variation in exact wording and punctuation. The episode titles employed by this book are those in most common usage (popularised by Jeff Lenburg's 1991 book *The Encyclopedia of Animated Cartoons*), with any alternatives also listed for the sake of completeness.

Plot:
The planet Cybertron: two factions of robots – the heroic Autobots and the evil Decepticons – are engaged in a long and bitter war. Collectively known as the Transformers, these metal armies have the uncanny ability to change shape into vehicles or other machinery, as a form of disguise.

With power reserves dwindling, the Autobots go off into space on a mission to seek out new supplies. Unfortunately, the Decepticons learn of their plan and chase their ship into a meteor shower. The Decepticons board the Autobot craft and, in the ensuing battle, it veers out of control and crashes into a volcano on the planet Earth.

Four million years later, the volcano erupts and awakens the Transformers once more, their civil war beginning anew on Earth. The Decepticons construct a base in the middle of the desert and plan to plunder energy from the Earth, then return to Cybertron in a newly-built starship. They attack an offshore oil rig, but while they are in the process of converting its oil into Energon cubes, the Autobots launch a strike against them. The Decepticons retreat with the Energon and destroy the oil rig, leaving the Autobots to pick up the pieces ...

Megatron's Rants:
- 'We shall return home with the power to build the ultimate weapon and conquer the universe!'
- 'I will plunder Earth, and steal its precious resources!'
- 'We must suck this planet Earth dry!'
- 'The Universe is mine!'

Witty Put-Downs:
- Cliffjumper, on Laserbeak's poor aim: 'You couldn't hit an Autobot with a moonbeam!'
- Megatron: 'You fool, Starscream!'

Roll Call (characters making their debut appearance are listed in **bold**):
Autobots: **Wheeljack, Bumblebee, Optimus Prime, Trailbreaker, Prowl, Jazz, Ratchet, Hound, Sideswipe, Ironhide, Mirage, Windcharger, Brawn, Sunstreaker, Cliffjumper** and **Huffer.**

Decepticons: **Skywarp, Starscream, Thundercracker, Soundwave, Laserbeak, Megatron, Shockwave, Reflector, Rumble** and **Ravage.**

Other: **the Narrator, Spike** and **Sparkplug.**

In addition to the Transformers listed above, there are some others who make a cameo appearance in this episode. Two one-off Decepticons appear in the early Cybertron scenes; similar in design to the Decepticon Planes such as Starscream, they are coloured yellow and purple respectively. Also, a truck crane that winches the injured Hound from a ravine is addressed by Cliffjumper as 'Hauler'. Although not seen to transform into a robot, this vehicle looks very much like the Earth mode of the Autobot Grapple, and could well rate as that character's first appearance in the show.

Spotlight: The First Episode

As was later to become the norm on Marvel/Sunbow co-productions, the first few episodes of the series were made as a multi-part pilot story broadcast over consecutive days. The same format had previously been used to great success on *G.I. Joe* and would later be repeated on series such as *Jem* (1985) and *The Visionaries* (1987).

Most of the core Transformers concepts had already been introduced in the Marvel comic books, but the cartoon show had a few new ideas of its own: the Autobots' young human friend is here known as Spike rather than Buster, and Transformers are powered by Energon, a glowing pink substance, rather than the modified gasoline seen in the comic's early issues. As well as their standard side-arms and missile launchers, the Transformers of the animated series have the ability to sprout weapons and useful tools from their hands – force-field emitters, grappling hooks, circular saws etc.

For the television series, the overall look of each Transformer was highly simplified, giving even the most unwieldy toy characters a more balanced, human-looking proportion on screen. These character designs were predominantly the work of artists Floro Dery and Shōhei Kohara, and were subsequently sent to Marvel Comics to ensure unity of design across the various media.

Making their debuts here are the famous 'ch-ch-ch-ch' transformation sound effect, copied by schoolchildren around the world and still used in modern iterations of the franchise, and the classic scene transition animation, in which a spinning faction logo accompanied by a brass jingle signifies a change of setting.

Data File: George Arthur Bloom (writer)
As well as the Transformers pilot, Bloom wrote for other Marvel/Sunbow cartoons, including an episode of *Jem and the Holograms*, and *My Little Pony: The Movie* (Michael Joens, 1986). Live action writing credits include episodes of television shows such as *The Incredible Hulk*, *Starsky and Hutch* and *The Billy Crystal Comedy Hour*. He was a 1973 Primetime Emmy Award co-nominee for his work on *The Julie Andrews Hour*, and co-won a 2007 Daytime Emmy for his work on the children's animated series *Cyberchase*.

Review:
'More than Meets the Eye, Part One' manages to reveal the origins of the Transformers, introduce viewers to around thirty characters, and set a plot in motion – all in the space of 22 fast-paced minutes. With its multitude of settings, crashes, space battles and action sequences, the episode is quick, relentless and visually appealing. 5/5

{1-02} MORE THAN MEETS THE EYE, Part Two
Also known as 'More Than Meets the Eye, Day Two'

Production number: 4024 (2nd episode produced of Season One)
Transmission date: 18 September 1984 (2nd episode transmitted of Season One)

Written by George Arthur Bloom

Plot:
The Autobots escape the burning oil rig, saving all of its human personnel in the process. Two of the crew – a mechanic nicknamed Sparkplug and his son, Spike – agree to join forces with the Autobots in their attempts to stop the Decepticons.

The Autobots intervene just as the Decepticons are creating Energon cubes at a hydroelectric power plant, but the evil robots continue to plunder the Earth's resources, attacking further oil wells and power stations in their bid to return to Cybertron.

The Decepticons now need just two more sources of energy before their work is complete. Their first target is a ruby mine in Burma, where the unique gems contain a powerful energy source. The Autobots again try to stop the Decepticons in their tracks, this time using a bomb. However, problems arise and the bomb goes off, blasting Autobot leader Optimus Prime from a cliff face in the process ...

Spotlight: Episode II – Attack of the Clones

The 'More than Meets the Eye' three-parter was originally produced as a pilot episode; at the time of production, further episodes were by no means guaranteed. After the pilot was finished, a few tweaks were made to the series' format going forward.

One of the main differences between the pilot trilogy and the rest of the series is that it features many more Transformer characters than existed as toys. From a marketing point of view, it's not hard to see why Hasbro would have wanted to ditch the generic troopers unavailable in the shops. Consequently, later episodes would focus on the core group of robots. Here, though, we are introduced to a multitude of Decepticon warriors, many of whom would never be seen again. To save on animation costs and time spent developing new character models, most of these 'generics' are based on existing designs, sometimes with new colour schemes.

In this particular episode there appears to be a massive army of Earth-based Decepticons, compared with the mere 12 in later first season episodes. For example, there are at least seven that look like the Decepticon Rumble. At one point during the attack on the dam, there are three in the same shot, while at the same time a fourth is causing the underwater quakes. Later, as the Decepticons line up in readiness to attack the mine, a further three are paraded, this time in alternative colour schemes (yellow, orange and green). In the same shot, it is possible to discern seven Reflector-style robots.

In the snow-bound sequence, at least nine Decepticons are seen, all of whom resemble the jet robots (Starscream, Thundercracker and Skywarp), but in various shades of blue, purple and green.

It is shown in the next episode that the Decepticons have the ability to construct identical (albeit fragile) facsimiles of themselves. From a story point of view, we can rationalise this early army as being largely made up of such replicas.

In later years, both Hasbro and Takara have seized upon such colour variations in the cartoon series and produced action figures based on these one-shot characters; fans can now own the newly-dubbed Acid Storm, Bitstream and Hotlink in their toy collection.

Megatron's Rants:

- 'Everything I touch is food for my hunger! My hunger for power!'
- 'I will build the ultimate weapon to defeat the Autobots! To control the planet! To conquer the universe!'
- And the old chestnut: 'Nothing can stop me now!'

Witty Put-Downs:

- Optimus Prime: 'You're old, Megatron! Yesterday's model! Ready for the scrap heap … Junk! That's what you are, junk!'
- Megatron takes it out on Starscream: 'Your knowledge is only overshadowed by your stupidity, Starscream!'
- 'You fool, Starscream!'
- And, after Starscream successfully proves that the Energon cubes work properly: 'You only proved your defective mentality!'

Roll Call:

Autobots: Huffer, Brawn, Optimus Prime, Trailbreaker, Wheeljack, Jazz, Ratchet,

Bumblebee, Ironhide, Sideswipe, **Gears**, Prowl, Sunstreaker, Cliffjumper, Mirage, Hound, Windcharger and **Bluestreak**.

Decepticons: Soundwave, Ravage, Megatron, Thundercracker, Starscream, Skywarp, Reflector and Rumble.

Other: the Narrator, Spike and Sparkplug.

Data File: Peter Cullen (voices, including Optimus Prime and Ironhide)
Forever associated with the character of Optimus Prime, Cullen also voiced him in the 21st Century live-action Transformers movies, and also in more recent offshoots of the franchise, such as *Transformers: Prime* and *Transformers: Robots in Disguise*. Away from *Transformers*, Cullen is the voice of Eeyore in *Winnie the Pooh*, KARR in *Knight Rider* and Mogwai in *Gremlins* (Joe Dante, 1984). He has a star on the Hollywood Walk of Fame.

Data File: Ken Sansom (voices, including Hound)
Sansom has numerous television credits to his name, on shows such as *Columbo*, *Charlie's Angels* and *Murder, She Wrote*. His film work includes parts in *The Long Goodbye* (Robert Altman, 1973), *The Sting* (George Roy Hill, 1973), *Herbie Rides Again* (Robert Stevenson, 1974) and *Airport 1975* (Jack Smight, 1974). However, he is best known as the voice of Rabbit in Disney's *Winnie the Pooh* franchise between 1988 and 2012.

Review:
After an excellent opening episode, part two falls flat. The fight atop the dam is a wonderful (and extremely memorable) set piece, but it's the only real high-point in an otherwise forgettable episode – it just about works as the middle segment of a longer story but doesn't have enough spark to stand up as a viewing experience in its own right. The idea that Burmese rubies are an enormous source of energy is frankly ludicrous, even for a children's television show. 2/5.

{1-03} MORE THAN MEETS THE EYE, Part Three
Also known as 'More Than Meets the Eye, Day Three'

Production number: 4025 (3rd episode produced of Season One)
Transmission date: 19 September 1984 (3rd episode transmitted of Season One)

Written by George Arthur Bloom

Plot:
Optimus Prime proves to be not too severely damaged from the mine blast. Nor, unfortunately, are the Decepticons, who escape with the Energon cubes they came for. With just one more energy source required in order to get back to Cybertron, they set their sights on a nearby military base, stocked with plenty of rocket fuel.

When the Autobots' plan to trick the Decepticons using a holographic projection fails, it looks as though the Decepticons have won. Their new ship blasts off, and even Optimus Prime, who gives chase using a rocket pack, is unable to stop them.

Fortunately, Mirage has used his powers of invisibility to good effect, and has stowed away on the Decepticon ship, sabotaging it before returning to Earth. The craft crash-lands into the sea, the Decepticons seemingly defeated for good.

Spotlight: The End …?

While everyone involved in the making of *The Transformers* hoped that the show would continue past its initial pilot trilogy, there was still a chance that it would not be renewed. Consequently the three-parter was written to be entirely self-contained, with an ending that would provide a sense of closure should this prove to be the Transformers' one and only adventure.

In 1984 it was still far from certain that the franchise would go on to be a major success. Many other '80s toy lines touted as being the 'next big thing' quickly disappeared into oblivion – Convertors, the Infaceables and Eagle Force being just three examples.

The ending of 'More Than Meets the Eye' was always intended to act as a possible end point for the young show. Also taken into consideration was the home video market, then in its infancy: a self-contained three-part story could easily be combined into a single movie-length edit, ideal for commercial release. By the story's conclusion, then, the Decepticons have been soundly defeated and the Autobots now have a fully-operational spacecraft in which to return to Cybertron.

This caused some headaches when the full series went into production. It was quickly decided that the majority of the first season would be set on Earth, so the notion that the Autobots were spaceflight-capable was quietly dropped. (An explanatory scene, in which it's stated that the Autobots have a new spaceship but refuse to launch it until the Earthbound Decepticons are defeated, was written but cut from the broadcast script for {1.04} 'Transport to Oblivion'.)

A similar scenario arose with {1-16} 'Heavy Metal War', the last episode of Season One. As it was again uncertain whether or not the series would continue, the finale ended with the Decepticons being swallowed by lava. When a second season was commissioned, this was likewise ignored, the Decepticons showing up alive and well in the very next episode.

(This of course mirrored the approach taken in Marvel's *The Transformers* comic series. If that had not continued beyond its originally-planned four-issue run, the ending of the fourth issue could easily have served as a grand finale with just a slight rewrite – and indeed one reprint compilation does have an alternative ending that omits the cliffhanger. Another 'climax' was included about a year into the run ([12] 'Prime Time'), which would presumably have been the final issue had sales figures not been up to scratch.)

By its second season, however, *The Transformers* had become established as a smash hit success – with an animated feature film ({3-00} *The Transformers: The Movie*) on the horizon and a third year assured, there was no need for any such 'final end' to be written into any of that year's scripts.

Megatron's Rants:

- 'We are indestructible! Power to the Decepticons! Forever!'
- And this amazing speech: 'I was onto your little scheme from the start! Did you really think you could fool me by allowing Ravage to escape? Did you? … While you and the other Autobots have been fighting a bunch of loose screws, the *real* Decepticons have been at the *real* rocket site! You've lost, Prime! The Decepticons have won!'

Witty Put-Downs:
- Megatron, on Starscream's prospects of becoming Decepticon leader: 'You couldn't lead androids to a picnic!'

Roll Call:
Autobots: Optimus Prime, Ironhide, Ratchet, Jazz, Prowl, Bluestreak, Mirage, Bumblebee, Hound, Gears, Huffer, Cliffjumper, Wheeljack, Sideswipe, Trailbreaker, Windcharger and Sunstreaker.

Decepticons: Soundwave, Skywarp, Thundercracker, Megatron, Starscream, Reflector, Ravage, Rumble and Laserbeak.

Other: the Narrator, Sparkplug, Spike.

Review:
This is a great end to the trilogy – the plotting might be unspectacular, but again the surfeit of action and drama make this an exciting episode. Megatron is at his cartoon-villain best here, and the climax is suitably epic. 4/5

Credits: Three-Part Pilot Episode
- Supervising Director: John Gibbs
- Sequence Directors: Dave Brain, Gerry Chiniquy, Jeff Hale, Norm McCabe, Tom Ray, Dan Thompson, James T Walker, John Walker, Warren Batchelder
- Voice Director: Wally Burr
- Voice Talents of: Michael Bell, Corey Burton, Peter Cullen, Dan Gilvezan, Casey Kasem, Chris Latta, Don Messick, Ken Sansom, Scatman Crothers, John Stephenson, Victor Caroli
- Voice Processing: Scott Brownlee, Soundtraxx
- Storyboard by: Floro Dery, Jim Fletcher, George Goode, Paul Grewell, Peter Chung, David Russell, Don Sheppard, Bob Smith, Vic Dalchele, Greg Davidson
- Model and Background Design by: Floro Dery, George Goode, Andy Kim
- Supervising Editor: Robert T. Gillis
- Music Editors: Joe Siracusa, Mark Shiney
- Sound Effects Editors: Richard Gannon, Bruce Elliott, Ron Fedele, Mike Tomack, Jim Blodgett, John Detra, Michael L DePatie
- Production Manager: Carole Weitzman
- Production Assistant: Yung Shin
- Creative Director: Jay Bacal
- Distributed by: Claster TV Productions, a division of Hasbro Industries
- © 1984 Hasbro Industries Inc. All rights reserved. Trademark of Hasbro Industries Inc. and is registered in the U.S. Patent and Trademark Office
- Produced in Association with: Toei Doga
- © 1984 Sunbow Productions Inc.
- Music by: Johnny Douglas
- Title Song by: Ford Kinder and Anne Bryant
- Executive in Charge of Production: Lee Gunther
- Written by: George Arthur Bloom

- Produced by: Nelson Shin
- Executive Producers: Joe Bacal, Margaret Loesch, Tom Griffin
- Sunbow Productions
- Marvel Productions Ltd, a Cadence Company

{1-04} TRANSPORT TO OBLIVION
Production number: 700-01 (4th episode produced of Season One)
Transmission date: 6 October 1984 (4th episode transmitted of Season One)

Written by Dick Robbins and Bryce Malek

Plot:
The Decepticons are still alive, and are using their crashed ship ({1-03} 'More Than Meets the Eye, Part Three') as an underwater base. Megatron is contacted there by Shockwave, who has built a space bridge on Cybertron, making transport back to the Transformers' home planet possible.

An unmanned test-run proves unsuccessful – a pilot is needed to steer the Decepticons' test vehicle as it crosses the bridge. The Decepticons capture Bumblebee and Spike – who have unwittingly stumbled across the Earth-bound terminus of the bridge – and force them to pilot the craft, together with a haul of Energon cubes, back to Cybertron.

Bumblebee manages to escape and, after almost falling foul of a Decepticon trap, returns to the terminus with his fellow Autobots as back-up. They contrive to rescue Spike and scatter the Energon cubes. Megatron tries to grab the cubes just as the bridge becomes active, and is himself transported to Cybertron.

With everyone assuming that Megatron has been killed, the Autobots rejoice as the Decepticons, now led by Starscream, make a hasty departure.

Megatron's Rants:
- 'We'll suck this Earth planet dry!'

Roll Call:
Autobots: Ironhide, Optimus Prime, Cliffjumper, Jazz, Ratchet, Prowl, Gears, Bumblebee, Brawn, Sideswipe, Trailbreaker and Sunstreaker.

Decepticons: Megatron, Shockwave, Soundwave, Laserbeak, Skywarp, Starscream, Ravage and Reflector.

Other: the Narrator, Spike and Sparkplug.

Data File: Bryce Malek (writer/story editor)
A specialist in children's television, Malek was a writer of animated shows such as *Defenders of the Earth*, *Scooby-Doo and Scrappy Doo* and *The Adventures of the Gummi Bears*. A successful script/story editor, he worked in this capacity on series such as *James Bond Jr* and the Emmy-nominated *Chip 'n' Dale Rescue Rangers*.

Data File: Dick Robbins (writer/story editor)
Robbins' television career began in the 1960s, when he worked as a writer for cartoons

such as *Rod Rocket* and *Spider-Man*. His CV reads like a 'greatest hits' of classic '70s and '80s animation, with credits including *The Flintstone Comedy Hour*, *The Scooby-Doo/Dynomutt Hour*, *The Smurfs* and *Godzilla*.

Review:
This is a decidedly average episode, focusing on the introduction of a new gimmick – the space bridge – at the expense of telling a particularly interesting story. That said, it is a really *good* gimmick (later adopted by the comics), both conceptually and visually. Eye candy then, rather than brain candy. 2/5

{1-05} ROLL FOR IT
Also known as 'Roll for It!'

Production number: 700-02 (5th episode produced of Season One)
Transmission date: 13 October 1984 (5th episode transmitted of Season One)

Written by Douglas Booth

Plot:
With Starscream now in charge, the Decepticons are in complete disarray - an attempted attack on a power plant is comfortably foiled by the Autobots. Megatron uses the space bridge to return to Earth and rally his troops for a bold plan: to create special Energon cubes using an anti-matter formula.

The revitalised Decepticons steal the formula despite the Autobots' best efforts. They then proceed to Autobot HQ in a bid to get rid of their enemies for good. However, with the help of a wheelchair-bound computer whizzkid, Chip Chase, the Autobots defeat the Decepticons, who are caught up in an anti-matter explosion.

Megatron's Rants:
* 'This time none of the Autobots will escape! Total victory shall be mine!'
* Ranting obviously comes with the job. Starscream's brief tenure as Decepticon leader means he gets in on the act as well: 'The Earth's energy shall be ours!'
* 'I am invincible! No-one can stand against me! No-one!'

Witty Put-Downs:
* Megatron again calls Starscream a 'fool', although not to his face.
* Mirage calls Starscream a 'garbage can'.

Roll Call:
Autobots: Optimus Prime, Bluestreak, Brawn, Cliffjumper, Prowl, Bumblebee, Gears, Hound, Ratchet, Sunstreaker, Wheeljack, Ironhide, Mirage, Jazz and Trailbreaker.

Decepticons: Starscream, Soundwave, Thundercracker, Megatron, Shockwave, Rumble, Laserbeak, Reflector, Skywarp and Ravage.

Other: Spike, **Chip**, Sparkplug.

Data File: Casey Kasem (voices, including Bluestreak and Cliffjumper)
Casey Kasem's unmistakeable voice originally came to prominence when the DJ hosted the hit radio show *American Top 40*. He is also much-loved for his role as the voice of Shaggy in the *Scooby-Doo* franchise. He has a star on the Hollywood Walk of Fame, and has been inducted into both the National Association of Broadcasters Hall of Fame and the National Radio Hall of Fame.

Review:
Reasonably entertaining, although the Decepticons' plan to create Energon cubes and use them to attack the Autobots is the same one they use in virtually every other first-season episode, and is already starting to wear a little thin. It's great that the Autobots' saviour is a wheelchair-bound geek, demonstrating to kids that you don't have to be superman to be a hero. Derivative, but fun. 3/5

{1-06} DIVIDE AND CONQUER (cartoon episode)
Also known as 'Divide & Conquer'

Production number: 700-03 (6th episode produced of Season One)
Transmission date: 20 October 1984 (6th episode transmitted of Season One)

NB: Not to be confused with [62.9] 'Divide and Conquer' (comic).

Written by Donald F Glut

Plot:
Trying to stop the Decepticons from attacking a munitions factory, Optimus Prime is severely damaged. His survival rests on a group of Autobots returning to Cybertron to find a device known as a Cosmotron, which has the ability to heal him.
    The Autobots locate the new site of the Decepticons' space bridge, and a group of them travel to Cybertron. Despite almost being killed when the Decepticons create a deluge of acid rain, they find the Cosmotron and return to Earth.
    The Decepticons, meanwhile, have taken advantage of the fact that Optimus Prime has been crippled, and launch an attack on Autobot HQ. Fortunately, however, the Autobot leader is repaired just in time, and the Decepticons are forced to retreat.

Spotlight: Transmision Dates
The Transformers was a syndicated show, sold to dozens of local US broadcasters, who would then transmit the episodes as they saw fit. Although most stations chose to show the episodes in the same order and on the same days, there were some exceptions. The transmission dates used in this book denote the US premiere of each episode – it should be kept in mind that the dates varied from station to station.

Megatron's Rants:
• 'We shall destroy the accursed Autobots, and none shall stand between us and the conquest of the Universe!'
• 'A new age of Decepticon supremacy is about to begin!'
• 'We are victorious! Is there anyone in the universe who'll challenge the might of Megatron?'

Witty Put-Downs:
- A great line from Skywarp: 'I think Laserbeak's chicken!'
- Reflector calls Spike an 'Earth germ'.

Roll Call:
Autobots: Ratchet, Bluestreak, Wheeljack, Trailbreaker, Bumblebee, Ironhide, Optimus Prime, Sunstreaker, Windcharger, Gears, Brawn, Sideswipe, Jazz, Huffer, Mirage, and Hound.

Decepticons: Starscream, Skywarp, Thundercracker, Soundwave, Reflector, Megatron, Laserbeak, Shockwave, Rumble and Ravage (plus three Cybertron-based Decepticons – green, yellow and purple jets – possibly the same as those previously seen in {1-01} 'More Than Meets the Eye, Part One').

Other: the Narrator, Chip, Sparkplug and Spike.

Data File: Dan Gilvezan (voices, including Bumblebee)
An actor who is just as comfortable on screen as he is behind the microphone, Gilvezan has appeared in a variety of live-action television shows, including *NYPD Blue*, *Moonlighting*, *The Twilight Zone* and *Parks and Recreation*. As a voice actor he has guested on animated series such as *Teenage Mutant Ninja Turtles*, *Centurions* and *Jem and the Holograms*. However, he is best known as the voice of Spider-Man in the 1981-83 series *Spider-Man & His Amazing Friends*.

Review:
At last, a plot that doesn't completely revolve around the search for Energon. Refreshingly, the Autobots are shown here to be less than indestructible, and the climactic fight at the end between Prime and Megatron is a great action sequence. Even the little-used Reflector and Trailbreaker get some decent screen time. Brilliant. 5/5

{1-07} FIRE IN THE SKY
Production number: 700-04 (7th episode produced of Season One)
Transmission date: 8 December 1984 (13th episode transmitted of Season One)

Written by Alfred A Pegal

Plot:
In order to create Energon cubes, the Decepticons are sucking heat energy from the Earth's core. As a result, the Earth's temperature has dropped alarmingly, even causing snow to fall in the middle of the desert. The Autobots get wise to this, and mount an attack on the Decepticons, who are camped out in the Arctic. However, they run into problems in the shape of a giant Decepticon, named Skyfire.

Skyfire was a scientist from Cybertron who, on a survey mission, crash-landed on Earth and became frozen in the ice. The Decepticons have repaired him and recruited him to their cause.

Upon discovering that the Decepticons are evil tyrants, Skyfire joins forces with the Autobots. In an aerial strike, he manages to foil the Decepticon plan, but crashes into the ice, apparently destroyed.

Megatron's Rants:
- 'Soon this entire planet will freeze into an icy tomb, and we will return to Cybertron with enough Energon cubes to dominate the Universe!'

Roll Call:
Autobots: Jazz, Bumblebee, Hound, Cliffjumper, Ratchet, Optimus Prime, Gears, Ironhide and **Skyfire**.

Decepticons: Skywarp, Reflector, Starscream, Megatron, Rumble, Soundwave, Thundercracker, Ravage and Laserbeak.

Other: Spike and Sparkplug,

Data File: Alfred A Pegal (writer)
Pegal (1913-1998) wrote for cartoon series such as *Defenders of the Earth*, *MASK*, and *G.I. Joe: A Real American Hero*.

Data File: Gregg Berger (voices, including Grimlock and Skyfire)
Prolific voice actor Gregg Berger is perhaps best known as the voice of Odie in the *Garfield* cartoons. His other television work includes shows such as *Men in Black: The Series*, *Star Wars: The Clone Wars* and the 1995-97 version of *Spider-Man*. His voice can also be heard in video game franchises such as *Call of Duty*, *Final Fantasy* and *Skylanders*. He provided voices for the film *Monsters University* (Dan Scanlon, 2013) and had a part in the live-action *Police Academy: Mission to Moscow* (Alan Metter, 1994).

Review:
This is another episode that follows the standard Season One formula: the Decepticons find a new means by which to create Energon cubes, and the Autobots turn up and stop them. Despite sticking rigidly to type, however, it is still highly enjoyable. The addition of the Skyfire character – and the fact that the icy setting makes a welcome break from the usual desert backdrops – gives it a sense of freshness despite the familiar plotting. 4/5

{1-08} S.O.S. DINOBOTS
Also known as 'S.O.S Dinobots!' and 'SOS – Dinobots'

Production number: 700-05 (8th episode produced of Season One)
Transmission date: 27 October 1984 (7th episode transmitted of Season One)

Written by Donald F Glut

Plot:
The Decepticons take over a dam, using it to create Energon cubes. They lay a trap for the Autobots, who after falling into the river are captured and placed in restrictive Energon chains.

Ratchet and Wheeljack, meanwhile, have discovered a horde of fossilised dinosaur bones in a cave adjoining the Autobot HQ. After a visit to a museum for more information on dinosaurs, they create three Dinobots – robots who, instead of transforming into vehicles, can change into massive robotic dinosaurs.

Despite the Dinobots being mentally unstable, they are used as a last resort in order to rescue Optimus Prime and the other captive Autobots. The Decepticons are defeated and, the new Dinobots having proved their worth, Optimus Prime welcomes them into the Autobots' ranks.

Witty Put-Downs:
- Starscream's taunting of Ironhide wouldn't sound out of place in a school playground: 'You're too slow, rusty pants!'
- Rumble on the Autobots' bad aim: 'Nice shooting … if you were aiming at the sky!'

Roll Call:
Autobots: Optimus Prime, Sideswipe, Ratchet, Ironhide, Wheeljack, Brawn, Hound, Huffer, Prowl, Mirage, Bluestreak, Trailbreaker, Sunstreaker, Jazz, Cliffjumper, Windcharger, Bumblebee, Gears, **Slag, Sludge** and **Grimlock**.

Decepticons: Soundwave, Reflector, Megatron, Thundercracker, Starscream, Skywarp, Ravage and Rumble.

Other: Spike and Sparkplug.

Review:
The 'Decepticons attempt to steal energy' plot is again re-hashed here, albeit spiced up by the introduction of (some of) the Dinobots. Although it's great finally to meet some Autobots whose loyalty and morality aren't perfect, the Dinobots come across as annoying oafs here, in stark contrast to their later characterisation as comic foils. 2/5

{1-09} FIRE ON THE MOUNTAIN
Production number: 700-06 (9th episode produced of Season One)
Transmission date: 22 December 1984 (15th episode transmitted of Season One)

Written by Douglas Booth

Plot:
The Decepticons learn of an ancient Incan legend that tells of 'the crystal of power'. They travel to Peru and use the crystal to supply energy to a devastatingly powerful weapon they have built atop an Incan pyramid. The crystal's main function was to prevent a fiery beam of heat energy from the Earth's core rising up and escaping. With the crystal gone, this energy beam now threatens the existence of a nearby villllage.

The Autobots learn of this, and after rescuing Skyfire from the Arctic ice (see {1-07} 'Fire in the Sky'), travel to the Andes to foil the Decepticons' plan. After an intense battle, the Autobots storm to the top of the pyramid and defeat Megatron, saving the village in the process.

Spotlight: The 1984 Christmas Toys
At first glance, the range of '80s Transformers toys can be split neatly by calendar year, with each twelve-month period having its own unique mix of characters. This idea of

'yearly waves' of figures was reinforced by annual changes to the packaging (most notably, the painted action scene on the rear of the boxes was changed every year) and by the series of pack-in toy catalogues included with most Transformers figures, which were refreshed each calendar year to reflect the then-current range. This book has followed convention by focusing on each years' worth of toys in turn, despite the fact that in reality the lines were sometimes blurred. Nowhere is this more evident than in the winter of 1984/85.

The first batch of Transformers toys had been released in the spring of 1984, promoted via a huge media campaign that included the tie-in comic and the animated television show. A second wave of figures was due for release in 1985, but in the run-up to Christmas 1984, toy manufacturers Hasbro needed new product on the shelves, so some of the figures that fans and collectors usually consider part of the 1985 range were actually brought forward and released in late 1984 (as evidenced by a number of contemporary store catalogues and newspaper advertisements).

Ultimately, it was Jetfire and Shockwave who were chosen to spearhead the new range of Transformers, both seeing release in late 1984. Both were large figures, and made for ideal Christmas presents.

Although Shockwave was already a regular face in the comics and cartoons, Jetfire was a complete unknown. To tie in with his winter toy release, the two animated episodes showcasing Jetfire were held back to near the end of Season One, eventually seeing broadcast in December 1984.

(As an aside, it's notable that Jetfire breaks the then-established mould of having the Autobots comprising only of land vehicles and the Decepticon faction of air vehicles and handheld devices. To get around this distinction from a storytelling point of view, both the cartoons and the comics initially depict Jetfire as being allied with the Decepticons before changing his allegiance.)

Another interesting oddity is the Autobot car, Skids. For the first two years of figures, the medium-sized Autobot car Transformers were sold to retailers in bulk cases of twelve. In 1984 there were eleven different toys of this type (Jazz, Prowl, Bluestreak, Ratchet, Ironhide, Mirage, Hound, Wheeljack, Sideswipe, Sunstreaker and Trailbreaker), so 'Assortment #5750' (as Hasbro called it) contained one of each figure, plus one random duplicate to make it up to an even dozen.

For the 1985 range, the roster was expanded with seven new Autobot car figures (Skids, Tracks, Red Alert, Bluestreak, Hoist, Inferno and Grapple), so there were now two different twelve-figure case assortments available to retailers, as follows:

Assortment #5765: Sunstreaker*, Bluestreak*, Jazz*, Ratchet*, Trailbreaker*, 2x Grapple, 2x Red Alert, 2x Hoist, Skids.

Assortment #5766: Sideswipe*, Hound*, Mirage*, Prowl*, Ironhide*, Wheeljack*, 2x Bluestreak, 2x Tracks, 2x Inferno

* Indicates a figure previously released as part of the original 1984 batch.

As indicated, all the new figures were packed two per case, with the sole exception of Skids who – like the older 1984 figures – was packed only one per case.

It was originally assumed that, because he was available only for a single year and packed only one per case, Skids was the rarest of all the Autobot cars. However, it was later discovered that the Skids toy actually made its debut in late 1984, replacing the random duplicate figure in the later batches of the original case #5750, which explains why he was shortpacked alongside the other older Autobots in 1985. Despite generally being considered a 1985 toy (thanks to the catalogues and other media appearances), Skids is known to exist in boxed examples of 1984 packaging.

Megatron's Rants:
- 'Now the power of the Earth's fiery core will serve the Decepticons!'
- 'The power of absolute destruction is mine!'

Witty Put-Downs:
- Megatron to Starscream on the new weapon frame: 'I hope it is stronger than your customary resolve in battle!'
- Brawn calls Soundwave a 'dipstick tapedeck' and Megatron an 'airborne garbage bucket', to which Megtron replies, 'You must have a blow-out in your logic circuits!'
- Both Starscream and Megatron scorn Thundercracker, calling him a 'putrid traitor' and a 'fool' respectively (hypocrites both!) Thundercracker later responds by calling them both 'real geeky'.

Roll Call:
Autobots: Brawn, Trailbreaker, Optimus Prime, Bumblebee, Ironhide, Wheeljack, Sideswipe, Windcharger, Skyfire, Bluestreak, Ratchet, Gears, Cliffjumper, Jazz and Sunstreaker.

Decepticons: Starscream, Thundercracker, Soundwave, Megatron, Skywarp, Reflector, Laserbeak, Rumble and Ravage.

Other: Spike.

Review:
An ancient Incan crystal serves as Energy Source of the Week, and unusually for this point in the show's history, there's not a desert nor an Energon cube in sight. The major problem with this episode is its depiction of the Peruvians, who are uncomfortably stereotyped as superstitious, poncho-wearing primitives. 1/5.

{1-10} WAR OF THE DINOBOTS
Also known as 'War on the Dinobots'

Production number: 700-07 (10th episode produced of Season One)
Transmission date: 24 November 1984 (11th episode transmitted of Season One)

Written by Donald F Glut

Plot:
A strange glowing meteor crashes into the Earth. The Autobots detect it, and order the Dinobots to stand guard in case of a Decepticon attack. Megatron tricks the Dinobots into turning against their fellow Autobots, and makes off with the meteor.

Meanwhile, the Autobots build two new Dinobots, Snarl and Swoop, and discover that the meteor is unstable: it could explode at any minute. Snarl and Swoop travel to the Decepticon camp, but are attacked by the three original Dinobots.

The meteor explodes, Optimus Prime risking his life to save Grimlock from the blast. Humbled by this selflessness, the Dinobots join forces and turn on the Decepticons, who are forced to retreat.

Witty Put-Downs:
* Megatron on the Dinobots: 'Those primitive pea-brain beasts!'

Roll Call:
Autobots: Ironhide, Sunstreaker, Hound, Optimus Prime, Wheeljack, Ratchet, Slag, Sludge, Grimlock, Prowl, Huffer, Gears, Brawn, **Snarl**, **Swoop**, Trailbreaker, Sideswipe and Bluestreak.

Decepticons: Thundercracker, Reflector, Megatron, Soundwave, Starscream, Rumble and Skywarp.

Other: Chip, Spike and Sparkplug.

Data File: Michael Horton (voices, including Chip Chase)
Horton is best known as Jessica Fletcher's nephew Grady in numerous episodes of *Murder, She Wrote*; he also played Lt Daniels in the movies *Star Trek: First Contact* (Jonathan Frakes, 1996) and *Star Trek: Insurrection* (Jonathan Frakes, 1998). Other live-action roles include parts in *Columbo*, *M*A*S*H*, *Baywatch* and *ER*. He also had a small part in the film *Dances With Wolves* (Kevin Costner, 1990); his appearance was excised from the theatrical release, but he can be seen in the extended cut put out on home video. His voice work includes parts in *Jem and the Holograms* and *G.I. Joe: A Real American Hero*.

Review:
This episode suffers from the same major flaw as its prequel, {1-08} 'S.O.S. Dinobots', in that the Autobots' troubles are caused by them having built the Dinobots with the brains of idiots – a design flaw that needn't have arisen. The Dinobots are impressive warriors, but their stupidity and ever-changing loyalties just make them frustratingly annoying – a far cry from the iconic comic-relief characters they later become. On the plus side, at least this week's powerful energy source, a meteor, is a little more interesting than an energy crystal or a dam, and the animation is of a notably better quality than usual. 2/5

{1-11} THE ULTIMATE DOOM, Part One
Also known as 'The Ultimate Doom, Part One: Brainwash'

Production number: 700-08 (11th episode produced of Season One)
Transmission date: 3 November 1984 (8th episode transmitted of Season One)

Teleplay by Larry Strauss; Story by Douglas Booth

Plot:
While many of the Autobots are away battling some of the Decepticons in India, Laserbeak takes the opportunity to infiltrate Autobot HQ and kidnap Sparkplug, who becomes a guinea-pig for the Decepticons' new hypno-chips. Invented by the Decepticon collaborator Dr Arkeville, these allow the Decepticons to control human minds.

The Autobots rescue Sparkplug who, under hypno-chip influence, sabotages Autobot HQ, allowing the Decepticons to attack. They are eventually thwarted when Spike manages to repair the damage his father caused to the computer.

The Decepticons meanwhile have set up a space bridge, which they use to transport the planet Cybertron itself into Earth orbit, an action that threatens to destroy Earth.

Megatron's Rants:
- 'You are the first of a new breed! A breed of slaves!'
- He later provides some necessary plot exposition: 'That devastation will create a tremendous flow of energy, energy which your hypno-chip slaves will collect into Energon cubes. The cubes will then easily be shipped to Cybertron for our use!'

Witty Put-Downs:
- Optimus Prime calls Megatron a 'fathead'.

Roll Call:
Autobots: Optimus Prime, Jazz, Sunstreaker, Wheeljack, Ratchet, Bumblebee, Sideswipe, Ironhide, Prowl, Hound, Brawn, Cliffjumper, Windcharger, Gears, Trailbreaker and Huffer.

Decepticons: Starscream, Thundercracker, Skywarp, Megatron, Soundwave, Rumble, Ravage, Laserbeak and Shockwave.

Other: The Narrator, **Dr. Arkeville**, Sparkplug and Spike.

Data File: Larry Strauss (writer)
Other than a couple of sitcom episodes, for the shows *227* and *The Facts of Life*, *The Transformers* is the only television credit on Strauss's CV. He is best known for his printed works, having written a number of articles, poems, novels and other books, including *The Magic Man*, a biography of basketball legend Magic Johnson.

Review:
Easily the worst episode to this point. The main plot – the transportation of Cybertron – doesn't get going until a minute before the end of the episode. The other 21 minutes are a plotless, padded mess, in which Sparkplug gets captured, is rescued, and then is captured again. 1/5

{1-12} THE ULTIMATE DOOM, Part Two
Also known as 'The Ultimate Doom, Part Two: Search'

Production number: 700-09 (12th episode produced of Season One)
Transmission date: 10 November 1984 (9th episode transmitted of Season One)

Teleplay by Earl Kress; Story by Douglas Booth

Plot:
Cybertron's appearance in orbit causes floods, quakes and other disasters to befall the Earth. The Decepticons are harnessing this destructive energy to create Energon cubes. The Autobots send the Dinobots to try to minimise the damage, but themselves almost fall foul of a volcanic eruption.

The brainwashed Sparkplug travels to Cybertron, together with a consignment of Energon cubes. The Autobots follow suit, and discover the plans for the hypno-chips. However, Sparkplug activates the alarm system, exposing the Autobots' presence.

Spotlight: The End Credits
For the makers of *The Transformers* cartoon in 1984, under time and budget pressures, any potential cost savings were regarded favourably. Once such measure was to create a single set of closing credits, listing all notable actors and production crew, that would be used unchanged throughout the first season.

In the end, external circumstances demanded that two different sets were made. The first was used only on the first three episodes and featured a number of errors – not least the omission of half the regular voice cast. As the author of the entire opening trilogy, writer George Arthur Bloom was given due acknowledgement in these end titles.

From {1-04} 'Transport to Oblivion' onwards, a second set of end credits was introduced. The full voice cast were now listed, and some behind-the-scenes reshuffles were also reflected. As these were 'catch-all' credits designed for use on multiple episodes, eight different writers were listed simultaneously. After all, how could individual writer credits (which changed from episode to episode) be reflected on a fixed set of titles intended for regular use?

Due to the nature of these credits, then, it was impossible to discern which episodes (with the exception of the first three) were written by which writers. The mystery remained until, prompted by fans, original script editor Bryce Malek, who had kept much of the original documentation, publically revealed the identities of the individual episodes' writers.

From Season Two onwards, all episodes of *The Transformers* featured a bespoke title caption and writer credit at the beginning, so thankfully all the confusion over writing credits and exact episode titles was restricted to the first year's run.

Megatron's Rants:
- 'Now there will be no power in the Universe to resist me! Decepticons will rule forever!'

Witty Put-Downs:
- Bluestreak calls Laserbeak a 'tinfoil turkey'.

Roll Call:
Autobots: Ironhide, Wheeljack, Jazz, Prowl, Optimus Prime, Bumblebee, Trailbreaker, Sunstreaker, Hound, Windcharger, Brawn, Bluestreak, Ratchet, Grimlock, Snarl, Slag, Sludge, Swoop, Skyfire and Huffer.

Decepticons: Megatron, Starscream, Soundwave, Skywarp, Ravage, Thundercracker, Rumble and Laserbeak.

Other: the Narrator, Spike, Sparkplug and Dr Arkeville.

Data File: Earl Kress (writer)
Writer, artist and story editor Earl Kress boasts credits on many much-loved children's series, including *Ewoks, Animaniacs, Tiny Toon Adventures* and *Pinky and the Brain* (for which he won a Daytime Emmy). He boasts a story credit on the Walt Disney animated classic *The Fox and the Hound* (Ted Berman, Richard Rich and Art Stevens, 1981), and also worked on *The Muppet Movie* (James Frawley, 1979).

Review:
Exciting and eventful, yet vacuous in the extreme, this middle part seems uninterested in driving the story forward; instead we get narrative *culs-de-sac* filling out most of the running-time. Examples of this include the 'audio disruptor wave', which deactivates all the hypno-chips, forcing the Decepticons to go back and capture a whole new batch of slaves, and the volcano sequence, in which the Autobots' base is briefly threatened with destruction. 2/5

{1-13} THE ULTIMATE DOOM, Part Three
Also known as 'The Ultimate Doom, Part Three: Revival'

Production number: 700-10 (13th episode produced of Season One)
Transmission date: 17 November 1984 (10th episode transmitted of Season One)

Teleplay by Leo D Paur; Story by Douglas Booth

Plot:
The Autobots escape from Cybertron with a device that can counteract the effects of the hypno-chips, and use it to free Sparkplug.

Back on Earth, Megatron's army of human slaves are collecting Energon cubes. Dr Arkeville, disenchanted with the Decepticons' plans, joins forces with the treacherous Starscream.

The Decepticons are in the process of loading the Energon onto their new ship when they are attacked by the Autobots, who realise that Cybertron's presence will soon cause the Earth's destruction.

The Autobots free the human slaves and destroy the Decepticon ship soon after it takes off. The energy of all the exploding Energon cubes pushes Cybertron out of Earth orbit, thereby saving the planet.

Witty Put-Downs:
* Soundwave, as described by Brawn: 'Tall, dark and gruesome.'

Roll Call:
Autobots: Bumblebee, Brawn, Skyfire, Wheeljack, Trailbreaker, Ratchet, Optimus Prime, Ironhide, Bluestreak, Jazz, Prowl, Cliffjumper and Mirage.

Decepticons: Shockwave, Soundwave, Rumble, Megatron, Reflector, Starscream, Skywarp and Thundercracker.

Other: the Narrator, Spike, Sparkplug and Dr Arkeville.

Data File: Leo D Paur (writer)
Writer/director Leo Paur has devoted his career to working with children – as well as his involvement in children's films such as *Rigoletto*, he is also a schoolteacher, American football coach and author of the book *How to Teach Your Children to Say 'No' to Drugs*.

Review:
Surprisingly good, and the best episode since {1-06} 'Divide and Conquer'. It has the same fast-paced, action-packed feel as the pilot episode, and all the plot threads are resolved nicely. Its only problem is that it didn't really warrant a two-episode build-up. 5/5

{1-14} COUNTDOWN TO EXTINCTION
Production number: 700-11 (14th episode produced of Season One)
Transmission date: 1 December 1984 (12th episode transmitted of Season One)

Written by Reed Robbins and Peter Salas

Plot:
Starscream, believing that Megatron perished in the explosion at the end of {1-13} 'The Ultimate Doom, Part Three', travels to Dr Arkeville's lab, which holds a powerful energy source known as an exponential generator. Starscream sets the device to explode. Although Earth will be destroyed in the process, Starscream plans to return to Cybertron and turn the resultant energy into Energon cubes.

The rest of the Decepticons travel to the lab to confront Starscream, but are followed by the Autobots, who have been helping to rebuild the Earth after recent events. The two factions join forces to prevent the Earth's destruction by launching the generator into space.

Megatron's Rants:
• Not Megatron, but Starscream: 'When Earth explodes, I will be on Cybertron collecting the resulting energy. It will give me limitless power, the power to dominate the universe!'

Witty Put-Downs:
• Winner of the prize of the most bizarre conversation ever: Skywarp calls Rumble a 'metallic mini-meatball'; in reply, Rumble accuses Skywarp of being a 'maxi-turkey'.

Roll Call:
Autobots: Wheeljack, Sludge, Grimlock, Optimus Prime, Ratchet, Ironhide, Gears, Brawn, Huffer, Hound, Cliffjumper, Jazz, Prowl, Bumblebee, Sideswipe and Mirage.

Decepticons: Rumble, Skywarp, Thundercracker, Soundwave, **Frenzy**, Megatron, Laserbeak, Starscream, Shockwave and Reflector.

Other: the Narrator and Dr Arkeville.

Data File: Chris Latta (voices, including Starscream, Sparkplug and Wheeljack)

An actor and stand-up comedian who was often credited under the name Christopher Collins, Latta excelled at voicing villains, including Cobra Commander in *G.I. Joe: A Real American Hero*, Darkstorm in *Visionaries* and the original Mr Burns in *The Simpsons*. He also appeared in live action television shows, including episodes of *Star Trek: The Next Generation*, *Seinfeld* and *NYPD Blue*. His film credits include *Road House* (Rowdy Herrington, 1989) and the Sylvester Stallone vehicle *Stop! Or My Mom Will Shoot* (Roger Spottiswoode, 1992).

Data File: Reed Robbins (writer):

Reed Robbins wrote for many animated television shows, including *Challenge of the GoBots*, *Defenders of the Earth* and *Captain Planet and the Planeteers*. He was also a composer, again for animation, with music credits on *Adventures of Sonic the Hedgehog* and *Hurricanes*.

Review:

This is pretty average fare, only the scenes involving Dr Arkeville being of any particular note. There are a number of plot points borrowed from previous episodes: Megatron's apparent death and eventual return ({1-05} 'Roll for It'); a timer counting down to an eventual explosion ({1-02} 'More Than Meets the Eye, Part 2'); and a human taken to Cybertron for a medical procedure ({1-12} 'The Ultimate Doom, Part Two'). 2/5

{1-15} A PLAGUE OF INSECTICONS

Production number: 700-12 (15th episode produced of Season One)
Transmission date: 29 December 1984 (16th episode transmitted of Season One)

Written by Douglas Booth

Plot:

When farmers are attacked by mysterious creatures on the island of Bali, their distress call is picked up by Autobots and Decepticons alike. The culprits are three Insecticons, Shrapnel, Bombshell and Kickback; Decepticons who crashed to Earth in an escape capsule, and who have been given the ability to transform into giant metallic insects.

The Insecticons and Decepticons join forces and attack the Autobots, but are eventually driven out when Autobot reinforcements arrive. They then begin an attack on a local oil refinery, but when met with stern Autobot resistance, the Insecticons betray Megatron's forces and fly off in retreat – with an angry mob of Decepticons in hot pursuit.

Spotlight: New Characters

Unlike the Jetfire/Skyfire situation, the introduction of the Insecticons in the cartoons did not coincide with the release of their action figures, which weren't made available until 1985. Other 1985 toys such as the Dinobots and Constructicons also appeared in

1984 episodes of the cartoon show. So why did the Insecticons appear in Transformers fiction this early, if their toy release was still months away?

In 1984, Hasbro's toy release schedule was in a state of flux. It would appear that both Shockwave and Reflector were due to be released alongside the original batch of Transformer figures in the spring of 1984, hence their early appearances in the comics and cartoon. Then, for whatever reason, the figures were delayed (Shockwave until later in 1984, Reflector until 1986).

(There's a scene in {1-16} 'Heavy Metal War' where images of the Decepticons are shown on a computer screen, and amongst the additional information provided is the official Hasbro reference number for each character's action figure. Notably, Reflector is given a 1984-style product code (5793).)

We can therefore surmise that, when a character makes his in-fiction debut long before the release of a corresponding action figure, it's a sign that the figure was originally due for release and then postponed. Given their relatively early appearances in the comics and cartoons, it is generally assumed that the Dinobots, Insecticons and Constructicons, first seen in shops in 1985, were originally pencilled in for a late 1984 release date.

(It's possible that Grapple, too, was originally earmarked for release as part of the original 1984 wave, before being deferred – a truck crane resembling Grapple's vehicle mode appeared in {1-01} 'More Than Meets the Eye, Part One'.)

Megatron's Rants:
- 'An oil refinery awaits our pleasure! Once we have taken its power, we will deal with our enemies once and for all!'

Witty Put-Downs:
- Kickback, after walloping Skyfire: 'Take that, you Autobot booby!'
- Brawn gets the better of Shrapnel: 'Gotcha, beetle-brain!'
- Shrapnel also gets a tongue-lashing from Wheeljack, who calls him an 'Insecti-twerp!'

Roll Call:
Autobots: Brawn, Windcharger, Bumblebee, Skyfire, Optimus Prime, Sunstreaker, Ironhide, Wheeljack, Trailbreaker and Sideswipe.

Decepticons: **Shrapnel, Bombshell, Kickback**, Laserbeak, Megatron, Soundwave, Thundercracker, Ravage, Rumble and Reflector.

Other: the Narrator, Spike and Sparkplug.

Data File: Johnny Douglas (music)
English composer and conductor Johnny Douglas was employed by record labels such as RCA and Decca, where he wrote, arranged and conducted literally hundreds of songs, working with renowned artists such as Mantovani, Shirley Bassey, Al Martino and Barbra Streisand. He composed many film soundtracks including that for *The Railway Children* (Lionel Jeffries, 1970), before moving on to scoring American animated shows such as *Spider-Man and his Amazing Friends* and *My Little Pony*.

Data File: Michael Bell (voices, including Prowl, Bombshell and Sideswipe)
A prolific voice actor, Bell is best known for his roles as Plastic Man in *The Plastic Man Comedy/Adventure Show*, Bruce Banner in the 1982-83 series *The Incredible Hulk* and Duke in *G.I. Joe: A Real American Hero*. In front of the camera, he has appeared in *Dallas*, *M*A*S*H*, and *Charlie's Angels*. He had a prominent role in the pilot episode of *Star Trek: The Next Generation*.

Review:
As with the Dinobots, the introduction of the Insecticons gives the series a much-needed shot in the arm. Fortunately, the script concentrates on these new characters and their abilities, drawing the focus away from the plot. The Decepticons' plan to attack an oil refinery and create Energon cubes is remarkable only for its unoriginality.
2/5

{1-16} HEAVY METAL WAR
Also known as 'Heavy Metal Wars' and 'The Heavy Metal War'

Production number: 700-13 (16th episode produced of Season One)
Transmission date: 15 December 1984 (14th episode transmitted of Season One)

Written by Donald F Glut

Plot:
The Decepticons have built six new Transformers. Collectively known as the Constructicons, they transform into their construction vehicle guises and steal a new energy system from a building site.
Megatron, meanwhile, has challenged Optimus Prime to a duel. The loser must face exile to deep space, along with all his forces. Megatron uses the stolen energy system to temporarily transfer all of his Decepticons' unique and individual powers into his own body. Armed with these new powers, he completely trounces Optimus Prime, who prepares the Autobots for exile.
The Constructicons infiltrate the Autobot base in an attempt to incapacitate the Autobot computer – the only thing that could potentially detect the fact that Megatron cheated. However, the Constructicons are caught in the act by the Dinobots.
The Constructicons then reveal their own special power – the ability to unite into one single giant Decepticon named Devastator. Devastator beats the Dinobots but is tricked into defeat by one of Hound's holograms.
Realising Megatron's deception, the Autobots send the Decepticons falling into a pit of lava, apparently defeated for good.

Megatron's Rants:
- 'Soon, Scrapper's invention will give me the power to defeat the Autobots once and for all!'
- Starscream's reply to this is one of the best lines in the series: 'Forgive me, but I believe your boast sounds vaguely familiar.'

Roll Call:
Autobots: Optimus Prime, Wheeljack, Bumblebee, Ratchet, Cliffjumper, Ironhide, Jazz,

Hound, Trailbreaker, Bluestreak, Prowl, Brawn, Sunstreaker, Sideswipe, Mirage, Huffer, Grimlock, Snarl, Slag, Sludge and Swoop.

Decepticons: **Scrapper, Scavenger, Bonecrusher, Hook, Long Haul, Mixmaster,** Megatron, Starscream, Thundercracker, Skywarp, Soundwave, Rumble, Reflector, Ravage, Laserbeak and **Devastator.**

Other: Spike, Sparkplug and Chip.

Data File: Arthur Burghardt (Devastator)
A familiar voice to fans of '80s cartoons, Burghardt played Destro in *G.I. Joe: A Real American Hero* and Turbo in *Challenge of the GoBots*. Other voice work includes parts in *Scooby-Doo and Scrappy-Doo, The Real Ghostbusters* and video games such as *Ultimate Spider-Man* and *World of Warcraft: Cataclysm*. Outside of the sound booth, he played Dr Jack Scott on the popular soap opera *Days of Our Lives*.

Review:
Season One of *The Transformers* ends on a high, with easily its best episode. A solid, coherent plot is coupled with an excellent introduction to the Constructicons. The revelation that they can combine into Devastator is left until right at the end, and when it does come, it ranks as one of the most memorable moments in the entire series. Central to the plot is the amazing duel between the two leaders, which makes all previous Prime v Megatron fights pale in comparison. 5/5

Credits: Season One
- Story Editors: Dick Robbins, Bryce Malek
- Written by: Douglas Booth, Donald F Glut, Alfred A Pegal, Larry Strauss, Earl Kress, Leo D Paur, Reed Robbins, Peter Salas
- Additional Dialogue by: Ron Friedman
- Voice Director: Wally Burr
- Voice Talents of: Michael Bell, Corey Burton, Peter Cullen, Dan Gilvezan, Casey Kasem, Chris Latta, Don Messick, Ken Sansom, Scatman Crothers, John Stephenson, Victor Caroli, Gregg Berger, Michael Horton, Mona Marshall, Hal Rayle, Clive Revill, Neil Ross, Frank Welker, Arthur Burghardt.
- Voice Processing: Scott Brownlee, Soundtraxx
- Director: John Walker
- Sequence Directors: John Gibbs, Norm McCabe, Jeff Hale, Brad Case
- Storyboard Supervision: Don Goodman
- Storyboard by: Floro Dery, George Goode, Peter Chung, Wendell Washer, David Russell, Bob Smith, Gregg Davidson, Lynsey Dawson, Doug Lefler, Gerald Moeller, Brian Ray, Roy Shishido, George Scribner
- Model and Background Design by: Floro Dery
- Assistant Design by: Gabriel Hoyos, Leondro Martinez
- Key Background: Dennis Venizelos
- Supervising Editor: Robert T Gillis
- Music Editors: Joe Siracusa, Mark Shiney
- Sound Effects Editors: Michael L DePatie, Richard Gannon, Richard Allen, Jim

Blodgett, Bruce Elliott, Mike Tomack, John Detra, Ron Fedele
- Director of Production: Carole Weitzman
- Production Assistant: Yung Shin
- Creative Director: Jay Bacal
- ©1985 Sunbow Productions Inc.
- Distributed by Claster TV Productions, a division of Hasbro Industries
- © 1984 Hasbro Industries Inc. All rights reserved. Trademark of Hasbro Industries Inc and is registered in the US Patent and Trademark Office
- Title Song by: Ford Kinder and Anne Bryant
- Music Composed and Conducted by: Johnny Douglas, Rob Walsh
- Executive in Charge of Production: Lee Gunther
- Produced by: Nelson Shin
- Executive Producers: Joe Bacal, Margaret Loesch, Tom Griffin
- Sunbow Productions
- Marvel Productions Ltd, a Cadence Company.

THE TELEVISION SERIES: SEASON TWO

By 1985, it was abundantly clear that the Transformers franchise was well on the way to becoming a massive hit. More and more action figures were being released to sate the demand from eager kids, the comic book was selling well, and a second season of the cartoon series was commissioned.

Although Season One was a success, it was felt that many of the episodes were a little samey: most weeks, Megatron would hit upon a new method of stealing Energon, only for Optimus Prime to foil him yet again. For the second year, then, the decision was taken to broaden the scope a little. The Decepticons were now intent on general villainy, rather than merely the pursuit of energy. In addition, the Transformers' exploits spread to other planets and locations, as ways were sought to make the stories more diverse, both narratively and visually.

Another innovation was the decision to make a number of episodes that would focus on a single, central Transformer. Season One concentrated on a core set of characters – Optimus Prime, Bumblebee, Megatron and Starscream – with the remaining robots getting comparatively little screen-time and coming across as fairly interchangeable. Now the balance was redressed, with instalments written specifically to showcase some of the lesser-known characters such as Mirage ({2-05} 'Traitor'), Red Alert ({2-17} 'Auto Berserk') and Beachcomber ({2-25} 'The Golden Lagoon').

Unlike Season One, which for the most part went out weekly, the second season was broadcast five times a week, Monday to Friday.

{2-01} AUTOBOT SPIKE
Production number: 700-16 (1st episode produced of Season Two)
Transmission date: 23 September 1985 (1st episode transmitted of Season Two)

NB: The premier broadcast of this episode actually occurred in Japan, where it went out on 14 September 1985.

Written by Donald F Glut

Plot:

Sparkplug builds a new robot, Autobot X, from spare parts. However, it goes mad, and the other Autobots are forced to disable it. Later, when the Decepticons attack a new rocket base, the Autobots rush to the scene. Although the Decepticons are quickly driven off, Spike is seriously injured during the battle.

As doctors battle to save his body, Spike's mind is temporarily transferred into the body of Autobot X. However, Spike becomes irrational and confused. Believing himself to be a monster, he goes on the run. He is quickly intercepted by Megatron, who talks Spike into attacking the Autobots.

It is only when his father Sparkplug is nearly killed that Spike comes to his senses and realises what he has done. He turns on the Decepticons, who quickly withdraw. With the operation on Spike's human body a success, his mind is transferred back to where it belongs.

Spotlight: Alternative Versions

As *The Transformers* cartoon grew in popularity, it was soon given a repeat run, and also sold around the world to foreign broadcasters. For this reason, a number of edits were made to the episodes' opening and closing sequences.

Each season of *The Transformers* had its own unique opening and closing animations, and different arrangements of the theme tune were also used – making it immediately obvious whether any given episode was part of Season One, Two, Three or Four.

For repeat and overseas broadcasts, networks wanted to give viewers the impression that they were watching 'current' episodes, so Season One and Season Two episodes were often broadcast with later versions of the signature tune and title sequence to make them seem newer and fresher.

Similarly, many episodes were shipped abroad with 'clean' closing sequences, lacking any captions. These were made so that non-English-speaking networks could add their own translations of the production credits.

By the time the episodes were eventually released on DVD, many variations of each episode existed, with 'wrong' title sequences and music, and sometimes blank closing sequences. Some of these alternative versions found their way onto official releases in many parts of the world – for the most part, this was because the original master tapes had become damaged or degraded, and putting out these higher-quality variants was cheaper than repairing and remastering the originals. As such, the commercially-available versions are not always those originally broadcast.

Megatron's Rants:

- Megatron decides to spell out this week's plot: 'Interesting! Perhaps I can turn the situation to my advantage, and use this Autobot Spike to destroy the other Autobots … What supreme irony! Turning their friend into their foe!'
- Starscream has heard it all already: 'You've made such boasts before, Megatron!'

Witty Put-downs:

- 'Mega-Crumb' is Spike's witty new name for the Decepticon leader.

Roll Call:
Autobots: Wheeljack, Optimus Prime, Bumblebee, Ironhide, Ratchet, Prowl, Trailbreaker, Windcharger, Brawn, Sideswipe, Sunstreaker, Bluestreak, Jazz, Huffer and Hound.

Decepticons: Megatron, Starscream, Thundercracker, Skywarp, Soundwave, Laserbeak, Rumble and Reflector.

Other: the Narrator, Sparkplug and Spike.

Data File: Lee Gunther (executive in charge of production)
Like his *The Transformers* colleague Nelson Shin, Gunther worked at DePatie-Freleng Enterprises after a stint at Warner Brothers in the '60s. As an editor, his credits include work on *Daffy Duck*, *Road Runner* and *Bugs Bunny* shorts. When DFE was sold to Marvel Productions in 1981, he became an executive vice president of the company. He later served as a vice president of the Fox Kids network.

Data File: Corey Burton (voices, including Spike, Shockwave and Brawn)
Burton has an extensive CV in the voice-over industry, and is famous for bringing life to characters such as *James Bond Jr.*, Dale in *Chip 'n' Dale Rescue Rangers* and Count Dooku in *Star Wars: The Clone Wars*. He has also provided voices for a range of films, including *Critters* (Stephen Herek, 1986), *Toy Story 2* (John Lasseter, 1999), *Planet Terror* (Robert Rodriguez, 2007) and *The A-Team* (Joe Carnahan, 2010).

Review:
Despite the advances made in the last couple of episodes of the first season, 'Autobot Spike' is back to *The Transformers* at its worst, with clunky dialogue and obvious plot 'twists'. Even the title is a dead giveaway as to what's about to happen. On the plus side, the new title sequence and music are a huge improvement, and the animation is a lot better throughout. 1/5

{2-02} CHANGING GEARS
Production number: 700-17 (2nd episode produced of Season Two)
Transmission date: 1 October 1985 (7th episode transmitted of Season Two)

NB: The premier broadcast of this episode actually occurred in Japan, where it went out on 21 September 1985.

Written by Larry Parr

Plot:
Megatron has created a new device, the Solar Needle, with which he plans to drain energy directly from the Sun. For it to function, however, the Decepticons need to steal a vital piece of circuitry from Gears, an Autobot. The removal of Gears' circuitry has an unforeseen side-effect: his personality is altered so that he becomes a slave to Megatron.

The Autobots attack the Solar Needle in an effort to rescue Gears, but the damage to the Sun proves cataclysmic, and the resulting earthquakes and solar flares are felt around the globe.

The Autobots win the battle when they manage to convince Gears to turn against the Decepticons. With only seconds remaining until the destruction of the Sun, Optimus Prime manages to deactivate the machinery. Gears is restored to normal, and the Solar Needle is destroyed.

Megatron's Rants:
- 'Behold my creation, the Solar Needle! And you, Autobot, you will help me pierce the fiery heart of the Sun, to harness its power!'
- 'The ultimate power of the Universe is mine! Mine! Mine! Nothing can stand against me!'

Witty Put-Downs:
Three classics from Gears, all aimed at Megatron:
- 'Ah, go dig your diodes and get defunct!'
- 'You are an evil son of a retro-rat!'
- 'You rotten hunk of scrap!'

Roll Call:
Autobots: Optimus Prime, Hound, Cliffjumper, Gears, Ratchet, Jazz, Wheeljack, Trailbreaker, Sunstreaker, Ironhide, Bumblebee, Mirage, Huffer, Bluestreak and Brawn.

Decepticons: Starscream, Skywarp, Thundercracker, Soundwave, Ravage, Laserbeak and Megatron.

Data File: Larry Parr (writer)
Larry Parr has written for a number of children's television shows, including *Defenders of the Earth*, *Fraggle Rock* and *X-Men*.

Data File: Don Messick (voices, including Ratchet, Scavenger and Gears)
Messick made his name at the famous Hanna-Barbera animation studio, where he voiced prominent characters such as Boo-Boo Bear and Ranger Smith in the *Yogi Bear* cartoons, Bamm-Bamm in *The Flintstones*, Dr Benton Quest in *Johnny Quest*, Muttley and Professor Pat Pending in *Wacky Races*, Papa Smurf in *The Smurfs*, and, most notably, both Scooby-Doo and Scrappy-Doo in the *Scooby-Doo* series.

Review:
A bog-standard episode, interesting for its heavy focus on Gears, until now a character who has never got any significant screen time. The Solar Needle storyline is par for the course, and the 'good guy goes crazy' sub-plot was used not only in the previous episode, but will also crop up in a number of others later in the season. 2/5

{2-03} CITY OF STEEL
Production number: 700-18 (3rd episode produced of Season Two)
Transmission date: 17 October 1985 (18th episode transmitted of Season Two)

Written by Douglas Booth

Plot:

With the help of the Constructicons, Megatron rebuilds New York in the style of a Decepticon city, renaming it New Cybertron. The Autobots arrive on the scene, but Optimus Prime is captured and disassembled. While his right arm and weapon become part of Megatron's defences, the Autobot leader's body is rebuilt into an 'Alligatorcon', which then goes on the rampage in the subway system. The Autobots eventually piece together their leader just in time for him to blast Devastator, who falls off of a skyscraper to his defeat. Foiled again, Megatron and his troops flee.

Megatron's Rants:

- 'Soon, all of New York City will be mine!'
- 'From now on Optimus Prime and this city belong to me!'
- 'I'll melt Optimus Prime down for paper clips!'

Witty Put-Downs:

- The Constructicons are 'hyper-driven chatter-oids', Laserbeak is a 'nosey no-good-nacon', and Megatron is a 'Mega-klutz.'
- The Decepticon leader is less than impressed: 'Mega-klutz! You dare to insult me!'

Roll Call:

Autobots: Bluestreak, Ratchet, Optimus Prime, Bumblebee, Ironhide, Trailbreaker, Sideswipe, Sunstreaker, Wheeljack, Mirage and Hound.

Decepticons: Laserbeak, Soundwave, Scrapper, Scavenger, Mixmaster, Hook, Bonecrusher, Long Haul, Reflector, Rumble, Frenzy, Starscream, Thundercracker, Skywarp, Devastator, **Buzzsaw**.

This was the first sighting of Buzzsaw, whose appearances in the cartoon were limited. Apparently this was at the behest of Hasbro, who didn't want undue screen-time given to a 'pack-in' toy (which could be purchased only as part of a set with Soundwave).

Other: Spike and Sparkplug.

Review:

After a dodgy start to the season, 'City of Steel' sees the show getting back on form. A larger-than-usual scale gives the Decepticons an extra air of menace, and there's a genuine sense that the Autobots are going to struggle to get out of this latest tight situation. The focus is well and truly on the Decepticons – and Megatron in general, who gets all the best lines. On the negative side, the premise is extremely silly, and the Decepticons give up far too easily after Devastator is defeated. 4/5

{2-04} ATTACK OF THE AUTOBOTS

Production number: 700-19 (4th episode produced of Season Two)
Transmission date: 4 October 1985 (10th episode transmitted of Season Two)

Written by David Wise

Plot:
While the Autobots are distracted during a Decepticon attack, Megatron and Soundwave infiltrate Autobot HQ and sabotage the Autobots' recharge pods. After the battle, the Autobots go to replenish their power, but the rewired pods alter their personalities. Now allied with Megatron, the afflicted Autobots proceed to an Air Force base and begin to destroy the aircraft stationed there.

Megatron's plan is to steal a rocket carrying a solar energy satellite. He intends to use the rocket to transport the Decepticons to Cybertron, and the satellite to end the energy crisis there.

Having been away from base while all this was going on, Jazz, Bumblebee, Spike and Sparkplug return to Autobot HQ, only to discover that the Autobots are now their enemies. Sparkplug invents a device with which to restore them to normal, and the satellite is saved.

Spotlight: Megatron's Master Plan?
In Season One and into Season Two, Megatron's basic goal is pretty simple: to create Energon cubes using Earth's resources, allowing him to restore Cybertron and ultimately to control the entire universe. In theory this plan is sound, but the way in which he implements it doesn't seem very sound at all.

Throughout these episodes, we see Megatron attacking dams, mines, oil platforms, laboratories, rocket sites and even ancient temples in his search for power. More outlandish plots involve the destruction of the Earth itself, as seen in {1-07} 'Fire in the Sky' and {1-13} 'The Ultimate Doom, Part Three'.

All these plans involve death and destruction to some extent. Only in {1-10} 'War of the Dinobots', in which the Decepticons create Energon cubes from a crashed meteor, do their plans not involve the theft of Earth resources.

On each and every occasion, these plans are foiled by the Autobots. So why do the Decepticons insist on accumulating energy by invasive or egregious means? Megatron's over-the-top antics invariably attract the Autobots' attentions, but he never seems to consider subtler methods.

Megatron's arm-mounted weapon is referred to as a 'fusion cannon', inferring that it works by nuclear fusion, an extremely powerful source of energy. Why not use this weapon to create Energon cubes? For that matter, why not attack high-yield nuclear power plants or weapons facilities, which would surely be much more efficient than storming a small hydroelectric dam every so often?

It would seem, then, that Energon can be made not simply from any energy source, but rather from substances found on Earth that no longer exist on Cybertron – water, fossil fuels, specific minerals – which would go some way to explaining the energy crisis the Transformers faced in {1-01} 'More Than Meets the Eye, Part One'.

Witty Put-Downs:
- Prowl calls Laserbeak a 'bird-brain'.
- Rumble is described as a 'turkey-tron' by Ratchet.

Roll Call:
Autobots: Ratchet, Optimus Prime, Bluestreak, Prowl, Gears, Trailbreaker, Hound, Skyfire, Sideswipe, Jazz and Bumblebee.

Decepticons: Thundercracker, Starscream, Skywarp, Soundwave, Rumble, Laserbeak, Megatron, Reflector and Frenzy.

Other: Spike and Sparkplug.

Data File: Scatman Crothers (Jazz)
Legendary singer, actor and musician Scatman Crothers once performed a concert for Al Capone. He was a great friend of Jack Nicholson, whom he appeared alongside in films such as *One Flew Over the Cuckoo's Nest* (Miloš Forman, 1975) and *The Shining* (Stanley Kubrick, 1980). He was the voice of Scat Cat in *The Aristocats* (Wolfgang Reitherman, 1970) and sang that film's main song, 'Ev'rybody Wants to be a Cat'. He also voiced Hanna-Barbera's *Hong Kong Phooey*. His live-action work includes parts in *Bewitched*, *Kojak* and *Magnum, P.I.*.

Data File: Morgan Lofting (voices)
Best known as the voice of the Baroness in *G.I. Joe: A Real American Hero*, Lofting has other credits in *Ben 10: Omniverse*, *Knots Landing* and *Total Recall* (Paul Verhoeven, 1990).

Review:
Terrible. Megatron's plan here is to steal energy and return to Cybertron, a plot strand pretty much exhausted in the first season. For the third time in four episodes (fourth if you count the Optimus alligator from {2-03} 'City of Steel'), Autobots are seen to be acting out of character. It wouldn't have been a good episode had it been original, but as a rehash, it's even worse. 1/5

{2-05} TRAITOR
Production number: 700-20 (5th episode produced of Season Two)
Transmission date: 27 September 1985 (5th episode transmitted of Season Two)

Written by George Hampton and Mike Moore

Plot:
The Decepticons have stolen some experimental electro-cells from a research lab. They hope to use the energy contained within the highly-volatile devices to create Energon cubes. To ensure that the Autobots don't defeat them, the Decepticons have once again teamed up with the Insecticons.

The Autobots have their own problems to worry about – it seems that one of their number, Mirage, has double-crossed them. First Mirage failed to report the location of the electro-cells, and then he was spotted by Cliffjumper delivering Energon cubes to the Decepticon base.

Of course, Mirage isn't really a traitor – it's all part of a plan to turn the Insecticons and Decepticons against each other. However, Mirage's ruse is discovered, and the Autobots are ambushed.

The Autobots manage to turn the tide and win the battle, during the course of which the electro-cells are eventually destroyed.

Megatron's Rants:
* 'Let us return to headquarters and begin the first chapter in the book of Decepticon

supremacy!'

Witty Put-Downs:
- Cliffjumper, after fooling Starscream: 'The oldest tricks only work on the biggest jerks!' He later calls Shrapnel 'beetle-breath.'

Roll Call:
Autobots: Cliffjumper, Optimus Prime, Bluestreak, Prowl, Ironhide, Mirage, Sunstreaker, Jazz and Ratchet.

Decepticons: Skywarp, Starscream, Megatron, Thundercracker, Soundwave, Laserbeak, Rumble, Shrapnel, Bombshell, Kickback, Frenzy and Reflector.

Data File: George Hampton and Mike Moore (writers)
The team of Hampton and Moore wrote for number of cartoon shows, including *The Get Along Gang*, *Thundercats* and *Police Academy: The Series*.

Review:
This episode continues the early-season theme of having Autobots act out of character – here, however, the twist is that it's all part of a ruse. Megatron's plan – find a power source; create Energon cubes – is nothing we've not already seen before, but the Mirage plot, coupled with the welcome return of the Insecticons, makes this an episode well worth a look. 3/5

{2-06} THE IMMOBILIZER
Production number: 700-21 (6th episode produced of Season Two)
Transmission date: 24 September 1985 (2nd episode transmitted of Season Two)

Written by Earl Kress

Plot:
Wheeljack invents a new device, an 'Immobilizer', which can render any object completely stationary. However, having planted a hidden camera on Bumblebee, the Decepticons find out about the device, and steal it.

Ironhide, who was supposed to be on watch when the Decepticons attacked, blames himself for the theft, and resigns from the Autobot ranks. He is persuaded to return to the fold by Carly, a young woman who had been kidnapped by the Decepticons.

The rest of the Autobots are having a tough time defeating the Decepticons, who are using the Immobilizer to gain the advantage. They are defeated only when Carly, an expert science student, reprograms the device. To prevent any further misuse, Ironhide destroys the device.

Megatron's Rants:
- 'As you can see, I've perfected your little toy! The effect is now permanent! Soon I shall immobilise the worthless population of this planet! The Earth will be mine! You and your friends will be the first to go!'

Witty Put-Downs:
- A policeman, after learning Bumblebee's name: 'Maybe it can buzz or make honey!'
- Trailbreaker calls Megatron 'Mega-turkey', and later 'Mega-jerk'.

Roll Call:
Autobots: Optimus Prime, Wheeljack, Jazz, Hound, Bumblebee, Huffer, Gears, Cliffjumper, Ironhide, Brawn, Bluestreak, Sunstreaker, Trailbreaker, Sideswipe, Ratchet, Prowl and Skyfire.

Decepticons: Ravage, Megatron, Starscream, Soundwave, Skywarp, Rumble, Thundercracker and Laserbeak.

Other: Spike, Sparkplug and **Carly**.

Review:
Yet another Autobot decides to break ranks, in a season where this is becoming a pattern. However, it's handled quite well here – no-one is forced to act out of character, or has their personality chip zapped; the split occurs naturally due to how events in the episode play out. It's also good to have the introduction of a recurring female character – something the show was crying out for – and the Immobilizer makes for an interesting weapon. Even better, this is an episode completely devoid of Energon cubes. 4/5

{2-07} THE AUTOBOT RUN
Production number: 700-22 (7th episode produced of Season Two)
Transmission date: 31 October 1985 (26th episode transmitted of Season Two)

Written by Donald F Glut

Plot:
The Decepticons have invented the Transfixatron, a weapon that can lock Transformers into their vehicle modes. When Megatron learns that the Autobots are planning to race for charity, he sees a perfect opportunity to defeat them.

With most of the Autobot forces trapped in vehicular form, only Bumblebee, Wheeljack, Ratchet, Brawn and Huffer remain unaffected. Together, they design a special grenade with which to counteract the effects of the Transfixatron.

When the grenade is unleashed, the Autobots are freed. However, Megatron orders Devastator to attack them. Some quick thinking allows Cliffjumper to take control of the Transfixatron and revert Devastator back into its component vehicle forms. The Decepticons retreat.

Spotlight: AKOM
Although most *The Transformers* episodes were animated by Sunbow's regular partners Toei, from Season Two onwards another name entered the fray. The AKOM (Animation Korea Movie) Production Company were founded by *The Transformers* producer Nelson Shin, and as the series progressed, he passed more and more of the animation responsibilities away from Toei and toward his own company.

AKOM's creation was thanks partly to Marvel Enterprises, who provided Shin with capital and loans; in exchange, they would reap the benefits of having a relatively inexpensive animation partner on board – AKOM's first project was *My Little Pony: The Movie* (Mike Joens, 1986), again based on a Hasbro toy franchise.

Today AKOM is still a major player in the world of animation, having handled numerous prestigious projects such as *Batman: The Animated Series* and *The Simpsons Movie* (David Silverman, 2007).

Witty Put-Downs:
- Soundwave calls Spike a 'human microbe'.

Roll Call:
Autobots: Bumblebee, Bluestreak, Gears, Ratchet, Trailbreaker, Mirage, Sunstreaker, Ironhide, Huffer, Optimus Prime, Brawn, Jazz, Prowl, Hound, Sideswipe, Cliffjumper, Wheeljack and Windcharger.

Decepticons: Laserbeak, Thundercracker, Soundwave, Megatron, Starscream, Scrapper, Scavenger, Mixmaster, Bonecrusher, Long Haul, Hook, Shockwave, Reflector, Skywarp, Ravage and Devastator.

Other: Spike and Chip.

Review:
An interesting concept on paper, but the execution is horrible. The episode can't seem to make up its mind which Autobots have been affected by the device and which haven't, and there are some serious flaws in the internal logic – at the beginning, the Transfixatron requires its victims to be already in their vehicle modes in order to work, yet later it converts the Constructicons into their vehicle modes automatically. Looks and feels like a first draft rather than a finished episode. 1/5

{2-08} ATLANTIS, ARISE!
Production number: 700-23 (8th episode produced of Season Two)
Transmission date: 3 October 1985 (9th episode transmitted of Season Two)

Written by Douglas Booth

Plot:
On a reconnaissance mission, Decepticons Laserbeak and Buzzsaw determine the location of Subatlantica, an Atlantis-like city populated by an aquatic race led by the evil King Nergill. The Subatlanticans form an uneasy partnership with the Decepticons, and their combined forces soon take over Washington DC. With Wheeljack as his captive, Nergill develops a weapon with which he can incapacitate the Autobots.

Spike and Bumblebee rescue Wheeljack and call for the help of the Dinobots, who breach the Subatlantican force-field, retake the capital, and revive the fallen Autobots. The battle then switches to Subatlantica itself, where Nergill is discovered to have betrayed the Decepticons.

Nergill sets Subatlantica to self-destruct, but the Autobot and Decepticon forces both manage to escape just in time.

Megatron's Rants:
- 'Yes! An underwater city of such size must generate enormous energy – energy that shall soon be ours!'

Witty Put-downs:
- Nergill calls Spike a 'land slug', and Megatron calls Grimlock a 'dino-goon'.

Roll Call:
Autobots: Hound, Grimlock, Sludge, Bumblebee, Snarl, Swoop, Slag, Wheeljack, Optimus Prime, Windcharger, Jazz, Sideswipe, Trailbreaker, Brawn, Ironhide, Prowl, Sunstreaker and Ratchet.

Decepticons: Laserbeak, Buzzsaw, Megatron, Soundwave, Starscream, Thundercracker, Skywarp, Rumble and Ravage.

Other: the Narrator and Spike.

Review:
Another large-scale episode, along the lines of {2-03} 'City of Steel'. The interplay between Megatron and Nergill, two villains both trying to betray each other, is excellent. It's also a good episode for the Dinobots, who finally seem to have found their feet after a poor introduction. 4/5

{2-09} DAY OF THE MACHINES
Production number: 700-24 (9th episode produced of Season Two)
Transmission date: 10 October 1985 (14th episode transmitted of Season Two)

Written by David Wise

Plot:
Megatron and company infiltrate a laboratory and reprogram Torq 3, an incredibly intelligent supercomputer. Giving it Megatron's personality, the Decepticons use the computer to take control of other machines with a special remote control chip. Soon hordes of tanks and other vehicles are all under Megatron's control. Furthermore, the Decepticons use Torq 3 to commandeer a flotilla of oil tankers and redirect them to their HQ, so that the oil can be converted into Energon cubes.

The Autobots answer a distress call from Torq 3's designers, and only narrowly manage to defeat all of Torq 3's security sentinels. Although Optimus Prime puts the computer out of commission, Megatron still has control of the oil tankers. The Autobots rush off to Decepticon HQ and destroy Megatron's remote control device. The Autobots manage to escape with the tankers as the Decepticon oil rig is destroyed.

Spotlight: Skyfire
As previously discussed, Hasbro's Transformers range was comprised primarily of figures repurposed from Takara's MicroChange and Diaclone lines. However, a few came from other sources. One such was Jetfire.

In Japan, the Jetfire toy was known as a Super Valkyrie, part of the Macross line of figures owned by toy company Bandai, a major rival of Takara. Macross was (and still is) a popular franchise in Japan – as well as a toy range there exist a number of movies, television shows and comics.

The plan was that *The Transformers* cartoon show would be sold to Japan to broadcast, but it was obvious from an early stage that Jetfire's inclusion would cause problems – Takara were reticent to endorse a show that featured characters based on its rivals' toys, and Bandai didn't want a likeness of their Super Valkyrie showing up outside of their own Macross series.

Ultimately, the decision was made to dramatically alter Jetfire's name and appearance in *The Transformers*, for fear of legal ramifications. Rather than transforming into a sleek jet like his toy version, the cartoon Jetfire, now renamed *Skyfire*, instead coverts into a blocky, chunky spacecraft.

To avoid any doubt whatsoever, Skyfire was soon written out of the show – other than the odd background cameo, {2-09} 'Day of the Machines' represented his final appearance.

Megatron's Rants:
- Not much from Megatron in this episode, but then he does download his personality into the Torq 3 computer, who certainly gets in on the act: 'I, Torq, will be master of everything!'

Witty Put-Downs:
- According to Hound, the Decepticon leader is named 'Mega-meatball'. Spike calls Laserbeak a 'beaky bird brain'.

Roll Call:
Autobots: Optimus Prime, Hound, Skyfire, Wheeljack, Prowl, Sideswipe, Ironhide, Grimlock, Snarl, Slag and Sludge.

Decepticons: Soundwave, Laserbeak, Megatron, Rumble, Frenzy, Hook, Ravage, Starscream and Thundercracker.

Other: the Narrator, Spike and Sparkplug.

Review:
The battle between the Autobots and the remote-controlled vehicles is the high spot in this atypical episode. The Torq 3 computer makes for an excellent villain, and it's a shame that he's killed off so early in the episode, because the climactic fight on the exploding oil rig is a bit of a let-down. 3/5

{2-10} ENTER THE NIGHTBIRD
Production number: 700-25 (10th episode produced of Season Two)
Transmission date: 30 September 1985 (6th episode transmitted of Season Two)

Written by Sylvia Wilson and Richard Milton

Plot:
Dr Fujiyama shows off his latest invention, a female Ninja robot named Nightbird, at a

gala press conference. Although the building is guarded by Autobots, the Decepticons inevitably gatecrash, making off with the new robot. They then reprogram her to follow Decepticon orders, and send her to raid the Autobot base.

The Autobots are safeguarding the World Energy Chip, an information storage device containing details of the entire world's energy stockpiles. Nightbird uses her Ninja skills against the Autobot defences, and easily steals the chip.

The Autobots follow her, and a battle ensues. Nightbird takes on the combined ranks of Autobots, and is only narrowly beaten. She is rescued by the Decepticons, who arrive to provide backup. Starscream, rightly concerned that Nightbird will replace him in the Decepticon ranks, shows up and incapacitates the Ninja. As the Decepticons chase off after him, the Autobots secure Nightbird and the World Energy Chip.

Megatron's Rants:
- 'I bring you greetings, Optimus Prime! Lethal greetings!'
- It appears that he has a bit of a crush on the new female Ninja robot: 'She's everything I've always wanted!'

Witty Put-downs:
- Prowl calls Rumble a 'dyno-metal delinquent'.
- Mirage calls Frenzy a 'punk'.
- Bombshell calls Starscream 'nitro-nose'.
- Megatron calls Cliffjumper an 'Auto-clot'.

Roll Call:
Autobots: Ratchet, Sunstreaker, Jazz, Cliffjumper, Huffer, Trailbreaker, Gears, Wheeljack, Optimus Prime, Ironhide, Sideswipe, Windcharger, Prowl, Hound, Mirage, Brawn and Bluestreak.

Decepticons: Rumble, Frenzy, Laserbeak, Megatron, Soundwave, Starscream, Thundercracker, Skywarp and Bombshell.

Other: Spike and Sparkplug.

Data File: Sylvia Wilson and Richard Milton (writers)
The Transformers was Sylvia Wilson's only television credit; her writing partner Richard Milton, however, wrote a couple of mid-'70s episodes for medical drama *Marcus Welby, M.D.*.

Review:
For the third episode in a row, the Decepticons play second fiddle to this week's guest villain. Their plan – reprogramming a machine to follow their orders – has been tried already this season, in episodes such as {2-04} 'Attack of the Autobots' and {2-09} 'Day of the Machines'. Fortunately, the focus this time is not the incompetent Decepticons or their tired plans, but the interesting and well-designed Nightbird robot. 3/5

{2-11} A PRIME PROBLEM
Production number: 700-26 (11th episode produced of Season Two)
Transmission date: 2 October 1985 (8th episode transmitted of Season Two)

Written by Dick Robbins and Bryce Malek

Plot:
The Decepticons locate a canyon filled with korlonium crystals, which destroy machinery on contact. Megatron hatches a plan to clone Optimus Prime, then have the imposter lead the Autobots into the canyon and to their doom.

Optimus Prime is cloned as planned, but when the real Prime returns, the Autobots don't know which one to trust. To circumvent this problem, Megatron has the fake Prime destroy an equally fake Starscream to convince the Autobots of his sincerity.

The Autobots are just about to journey into the deadly canyon when Windcharger appears and explains the deception – he had overheard Megatron's plans while spying on the Decepticon base. The final straw comes when the fake Prime fails to show any concern for Spike, a Decepticon captive. The Autobots quickly determine which Optimus Prime is which, and kill the clone. Spike is saved by Powerglide.

Megatron's Rants:
- 'I have written a brilliant scenario of Autobot destruction!'

Witty Put-downs:
- Starscream calls the Autobot leader 'Floptimus Prime'.
- Optimus Prime calls Laserbeak a 'tinfoil turkey'. This must be the common Autobot nickname for him, as Bluestreak also uses the term in {1-12} 'The Ultimate Doom, Part Two'.
- Spike calls Megatron 'Mega-rat'.

Roll Call:
Autobots: Optimus Prime, Ironhide, Trailbreaker, Jazz, Cliffjumper, Wheeljack, Sunstreaker, Bumblebee, Ratchet, Sideswipe, Gears, Prowl, Brawn, Mirage, Huffer, Bluestreak, Hound, **Warpath** and **Powerglide**.

Decepticons: Megatron, Soundwave, Starscream, Skywarp, Reflector, Rumble, Thundercracker and Laserbeak.

Soundwave's chest panel contains a special cassette, an auto-scout, which can transform into a mobile sensor probe.

Other: Spike.

Review:
A major step backward. The clone idea is not a particularly imaginative plot device, and were it not for the fleeting appearance of Powerglide, one could be forgiven for thinking this was a bad Season One episode. However, this is Season Two, and we should expect better than this by now. 1/5

{2-12} THE CORE
Production number: 700-27 (12th episode produced of Season Two)
Transmission date: 29 October 1985 (24th episode transmitted of Season Two)

Written by Dennis Marks

Plot:

The Decepticons are boring a hole to the centre of the Earth in order to tap energy from the core. Just in case anything goes awry, they have a space bridge nearby that can whisk them off to Cybertron at the first sign of trouble.

The Autobots arrive on the scene but are driven off by Devastator and forced to withdraw to Autobot HQ, where Chip has come up with a brilliant plan. He has designed six control discs that, when attached to the six Constructicons, will allow the Autobots to control Devastator.

Megatron learns of this plan and creates his own device to counteract Chip's control discs. However, with both factions trying to control Devastator's mind, the giant robot is driven insane. Devastator wrecks the Decepticon drill, which now threatens to destroy the Earth.

With the space bridge now inoperable, the Autobots and Decepticons team up in order to bring Devastator under control and prevent the drill from destroying the planet.

Spotlight: Megatron and Starscream

For many fans, one of the defining aspects of *The Transformers* animated series is the relationship between the two principal villains, Megatron and Starscream. While much of their success can be attributed to the excellent voice actors, Frank Welker and Chris Latta respectively, the scripts, too, had a part to play.

The two characters argue and fight like a married couple in a '70s sitcom, constantly insulting each other and making snide remarks yet never actually splitting up and going their separate ways. While their bickering makes for some of the show's best-loved and funniest scenes, it does beg the question: why does Megatron keep Starscream around?

Starscream follows Megatron's orders reluctantly; his aim is one day to usurp the Decepticon commander and claim the leadership for himself. The problem is that Starscream is obviously not cut out to be a leader (his brief stints in {1-05} 'Roll For It' and {1-14} 'Countdown to Extinction' both end in disaster), and his innate cowardice means that he's pretty unreliable in a battle. The episode {1-07} 'Fire in the Sky' established Starscream as a scientist, but that trait was soon forgotten when later episodes required him to act dumb, prompting Megatron to explain his latest evil scheme for the benefit of the viewers at home.

Because Starscream's so hapless, Megatron doesn't consider him a viable threat to his leadership. However, because *all* the Decepticons are pretty pathetic, Starscream, as the best of a bad bunch, still has a part to play in Megatron's army.

Megatron's Rants:

- 'We Decepticons will possess an energy source richer than any in the galaxy: the molten might of this planet itself!'

Witty Put-Downs:

- Megatron, on Starscream's chances of winning an Oscar: 'You're such a rotten actor you couldn't fool a Saturnian simpleton!'

Roll Call:
Autobots: Gears, Mirage, Jazz, Prowl, Sunstreaker, Optimus Prime, Wheeljack, Ironhide, Sideswipe, Bluestreak, Bumblebee, Huffer, Ratchet and Hound.

Decepticons: Scrapper, Scavenger, Mixmaster, Bonecrusher, Long Haul, Hook, Megatron, Starscream, Laserbeak, Devastator, Thundercracker, Skywarp and Ravage.

Other: Chip.

Review:
A simple story, told without much fuss. However, what would have been a distinctly average episode is saved by the wonderful Megatron/Starscream scenes. The show's two stand-out characters (by a long way) are at their bickering best here. 4/5

{2-13} THE INSECTICON SYNDROME
Production number: 700-28 (13th episode produced of Season Two)
Transmission date: 9 October 1985 (13th episode transmitted of Season Two)

Written by Douglas Booth

Plot:
Autobots and Decepticons alike converge on a forest where Insecticon activity has been reported. In exchange for giving the Insecticons a massive supply of energy, the Decepticons employ them to help break into the top security computer at Iron Mountain.

However, when the Insecticons consume huge amounts of energy at the Nova power plant, they grow to giant size and become virtually unstoppable. Pretending to go along with Megatron, they secretly use their cerebro-shells to enslave most of the Decepticon forces, who turn against their leader during the battle at Iron Mountain.

The Autobots, meanwhile, have discovered that the Nova power is unstable, and that the Insecticons will explode at any moment. Ratchet and Wheeljack come up with an antidote, and the Autobots team up with Megatron to return the Insecticons to normal.

With Bombshell's hold over them having worn off, the angry Decepticons withdraw to pursue the fleeing Insecticons.

Megatron's Rants:
• 'I will hold this world in the palm of my hand!'

Witty Put-Downs:
• Starscream calls Bombshell a 'rust-encrusted cockroach'.
• Megatron calls the Insecticons 'Insecti-clowns'.

Roll Call:
Autobots: **Beachcomber**, Hound, Bumblebee, **Inferno**, Ironhide, Ratchet, Jazz, Wheeljack and Optimus Prime.

Decepticons: Shrapnel, Bombshell, Kickback, Megatron, Soundwave, Starscream,

Skywarp, Thundercracker, Laserbeak and Buzzsaw.

Other: Spike.

Data File: Clive Revill (voices, including Kickback)
A star of stage and screen, New Zealander Revill was the original Emperor Palpatine in *The Empire Strikes Back* (Irvin Kershner, 1980), and is one of only a few actors to have appeared in both an original-trilogy *Star Wars* film and also in the *Star Trek* franchise (an episode of *The Next Generation*). He was the last ever murderer in the original 1970s series of *Columbo*, and his other television credits include parts in *Babylon 5*, *MacGuyver* and *Murder, She Wrote*. His film work includes roles in *One of Our Dinosaurs is Missing* (Robert Stevenson, 1975), *The Private Life of Sherlock Holmes* (Billy Wilder, 1970), *The Legend of Hell House* (John Hough, 1973) and *Let Him Have It* (Peter Medak, 1991). Other voice work includes parts in *DuckTales* and *Batman: The Animated Series*. He returned to the Transformers franchise in 2009, when he voiced Jetfire in the video game *Transformers: Revenge of the Fallen*.

Review:
The novelty of the Insecticons finally wears off in this rather lacklustre story. As a sub-group, they lack the charisma of the Dinobots or the wow factor of the Constructicons to be able to carry an episode on their own. With power plants, Decepticon treachery, unstable energy sources and supercomputers, this feels very much like a 'greatest hits' package rather than an episode in its own right. 2/5

{2-14} DINOBOT ISLAND, Part One
Production number: 700-29 (14th episode produced of Season Two)
Transmission date: 25 September 1985 (3rd episode transmitted of Season Two)

Written by Donald F Glut

Plot:
Searching for the source of some strange energy emissions, Powerglide and Bumblebee discover an island populated by flora and fauna from the dinosaur era. They believe it the perfect place for the Dinobots to practise their fighting skills. The Dinobots agree, and head out to the island, which Spike names Dinobot Island. There they discover that the Decepticons are creating Energon cubes from the island's natural resources.

Meanwhile, back in the city, a time-warp causes mammoths and cavemen to appear from out of nowhere. Bumblebee and Spike are caught up in the chaos and end up buried under a pile of rubble. On the island, the Dinobots launch an attack on the Decepticons. Megatron causes the indigenous dinosaur population to stampede, and the Dinobots fall to their apparent doom into a bubbling oil pit ...

Megatron's Rants:
- 'Do not stop until we have drained this island dry!'

Witty Put-Downs:
- Huffer on the Dinobots: 'Once a dino-klutz, always a dino-klutz!'
- Cliffjumper on the Dinobots: 'Clumsy oafs!'

- Megatron calls Swoop a 'dino-dolt'.

Roll Call:
Autobots: Bumblebee, Powerglide, Optimus Prime, Mirage, Huffer, **Tracks**, **Grapple**, Hound, Wheeljack, Sideswipe, Windcharger, Trailbreaker, Sunstreaker, Cliffjumper, Gears, Grimlock, **Blaster**, Slag, Sludge, Snarl, Swoop, **Red Alert**, **Smokescreen**, Inferno, Jazz, Brawn, Prowl, **Hoist** and Ratchet.

Decepticons: Ravage, Soundwave, Megatron, Laserbeak, Skywarp, **Thrust**, **Ramjet** and **Blitzwing**.

Other: Sparkplug and Spike.

Data File: Donald F Glut (writer)
Born in 1944, Donald Glut started out as an amateur director before moving into writing. He helped devise the backstory for *He-Man and the Masters of the Universe* and wrote the bestselling novelisation of the film *The Empire Strikes Back* (Irvin Kershner, 1980). He has many comic credits to his name, having scripted for titles such as *Captain America*, *Ghost Rider* and *Thor*. His television credits include *The Centurions*, *DuckTales* and the animated *X-Men*. A keen palaeontologist, he has written a number of books about dinosaurs.

Review:
Another excellent outing for the Dinobots, who by now have established themselves as some of the series' most popular characters, with their trademark blend of gruff action and child-like personalities. The plot is a little thin, but sets things up nicely; which, really, is what all good Part Ones should do. 3/5

{2-15} DINOBOT ISLAND, Part Two

Production number: 700-30 (15th episode produced of Season Two)
Transmission date: 26 September 1985 (4th episode transmitted of Season Two)

Written by Donald F Glut

Plot:
The Autobots rescue Bumblebee and Spike and send the mammoths and cavemen back through the time rift from whence they came. Then two more rifts open, spewing forth a pirate ship and a posse of cowboys. Thanks to the efforts of the Autobots, everyone is returned to their proper time periods and the time rifts are closed.

The rifts are being caused by the Decepticons' tampering with the natural energies of Dinobot Island, which turns out to be the focal point of the time disruptions. The Dinobots free themselves from the tar pit and rally the native dinosaurs in an attack on the Decepticons, who are forced to flee.

The Autobots release the stolen energy back into the Island, and everything is restored to normal.

Spotlight: Out of Order

As with Season One, this second year of episodes was broadcast in a very different order from that in which it was produced. Again, the primary reason for this was to maximise toy sales.

For the first ten episodes, the show used the same cast of characters that had been introduced during the first year. The 1985 mini-vehicles Powerglide and Warpath were the first new toys to make their Season Two debuts, in {2-11} 'A Prime Problem', closely followed by Beachcomber and Inferno, in {2-13} 'The Insecticon Syndrome'. This small trickle turned into a deluge in {2-14} 'Dinobot Island, Part One', with many more characters beginning to appear.

The problem for Hasbro was that they had dozens of new characters that they wanted to introduce quickly, but that didn't show up in the cartoon until over a quarter of the way through the season's production. To give the new characters some early exposure, the decision was taken to mix up the transmission order, so that episodes featuring new characters would be intermingled with those featuring only the Season One cast.

{2-01} 'Autobot Spike' was the first episode to be made, and was also the first broadcast. Then followed {2-06} 'The Immobilizer', to get Carly's introduction out of the way, and {2-14} 'Dinobot Island, Part One', the first episode to feature a good many of the new faces.

The episodes were deliberately written to facilitate being shown in a jumbled order: barring the occasional two-parter and a couple of other rare instances, each was a standalone adventure and could theoretically be viewed at any point during the season, making continuity and character development nearly impossible.

Roll Call:

Autobots: Sideswipe, Hound, Ratchet, Optimus Prime, Wheeljack, Sunstreaker, Ironhide, Huffer, **Perceptor**, Beachcomber, Cliffjumper, Tracks, **Seaspray**, Prowl, Red Alert, Inferno, Jazz, Warpath, Smokescreen, Trailbreaker, Grimlock, Snarl, Slag, Sludge and Swoop.

Decepticons: Megatron, Starscream, Soundwave, Ramjet, Thrust, Thundercracker, Skywarp, **Dirge** and Blitzwing.

Other: the Narrator, Sparkplug and Chip.

Review:

Instead of a plot, what we have here is a collection of entertaining set pieces – the mammoth fight, the pirate ship, the cowboys and the dinosaurs – and little else of worth. There's a conservation message buried in there somewhere, but this is an episode less than the sum of its parts. Although it has 'Dinobot' in its title, the Dinobots don't even appear until well over half way though. 3/5

{2-16} THE MASTER BUILDERS

Production number: 700-31 (16th episode produced of Season Two)

Transmission date: 8 October 1985 (12th episode transmitted of Season Two)

Written by David N Gottlieb and Herb Engelhardt

NB: Some versions of this episode have a title caption that reads 'The Master Builder' (singular). However, 'The Master Builders' is correct, as per the original broadcast and all surviving production documentation.

Plot:

The Autobots Grapple and Hoist have a plan to build a Solar Power Tower that will harness energy from the sun and provide all the Autobots' energy needs. However, Optimus Prime vetoes its construction, given that it would be dangerous should it ever fall into Decepticon hands.

Learning of this, the Constructicons convince Grapple and Hoist that they have defected from the Decepticon ranks, and offer to assist in building the Solar Power Tower. However, once construction is complete, the rest of the Decepticons arrive and imprison the two Autobots.

Realising that Grapple and Hoist have disappeared, the Autobots discover the Solar Power Tower and confront the Decepticons there. During the battle, they trick Devastator into destroying the tower, and rescue their friends.

Megatron's Rants:

- 'Magnificent! Now the gullible twosome will perish in their own tower!'

Witty Put-Downs:

- Ramjet calls Powerglide a 'flying scrap heap'.
- Smokescreen calls Devastator a 'scrap metal meatball'.

Roll Call:

Autobots: Powerglide, Grapple, Hoist, Wheeljack, Optimus Prime, Inferno, Smokescreen, Tracks, Brawn, Cliffjumper, Ironhide, Warpath and Inferno.

Decepticons: Thundercracker, Starscream, Scrapper, Scavenger, Mixmaster, Bonecrusher, Hook, Long Haul, Megatron, Dirge, Ramjet and Devastator.

Other: Spike.

Data File: David N Gottlieb (writer)

Aside from his animation credits on shows such as *MASK*, *The Jetsons* and *Star Street*, Gottlieb found the bulk of his work in documentary making, as a writer, producer and director.

Data File: Herb Engelhardt (writer)

As well as scripting for shows such as *The Jetsons*, *Punky Brewster* and *Thundercats*, Engelhardt was an assistant story editor on the animated show *Centurions*, for which he also wrote six episodes.

Data File: Peter Renaday (voices, including Grapple)

A prolific voice actor, Renaday is best known for playing Splinter in the original *Teenage Mutant Ninja Turtles* cartoon. He was also Mandrake in *Defenders of the Earth*. Other television voice work includes parts in *Animaniacs*, *Ben 10: Ultimate Alien* and *TaleSpin*. Live-action credits include parts in *The Love Bug* (Robert Stevenson, 1968) plus episodes of the television shows *Dallas* and *Angel*. Video game voice work includes the titles *Fallout: New Vegas*, *Dragon Age: Origins* and *Assassin's Creed*.

Review:
The first episode to really focus on some of the new 1985 Transformers is a major disappointment. Optimus Prime's stance is out of character – his basic point is that no-one should ever build any advanced technology whatsoever in case it falls into the wrong hands! – and the duo of Hoist and Grapple are so gullible that it becomes difficult to empathise with them. An episode so weak it has to be padded out with a subplot involving an Autobot basketball match. 1/5

{2-17} AUTO BERSERK
Production number: 700-32 (17th episode produced of Season Two)
Transmission date: 16 October 1985 (17th episode transmitted of Season Two)

Written by Antoni Zalewski

Plot:
The Autobots are testing a powerful new weapon, the Negavator, which shoots a beam that dematerialises objects on contact. During the test, the Decepticons attack, but are driven away, abandoning Starscream. Red Alert is damaged during the fracas, his logic circuits now unable to tell friend from foe.

Starscream and Red Alert team up and steal the Negavator for themselves, but set off the alarm, which draws the attention of both the Autobots and Decepticons. During the subsequent battle, Red Alert is shot again, restoring his sanity. Red Alert saves the day by setting the Negavator to self-destruct, forcing the Decepticons to retreat.

Megatron's Rants:
- 'You incompetent fools! I must have the Negavator!'
- 'You're too late, Prime! Next stop: oblivion!'
- He's just about to start another rant, when interrupted by Starscream: 'Save the oration!'

Witty Put-Downs:
- Megatron calls Rumble a 'clumsy oaf'.
- Megatron despairs when Ramjet collides with the Negavator: 'I've got morons on my team!' (A quote from *Butch Cassidy and the Sundance Kid* (George Roy Hill, 1969), where it's spoken by Strother Martin's character, Percy Garris.)

Roll Call:
Autobots: Optimus Prime, Smokescreen, Ironhide, Wheeljack, Grapple, Red Alert, Inferno and Hoist.

Decepticons: Soundwave, Rumble, Frenzy, Ravage, Buzzsaw, Megatron, Starscream, Thundercracker, Skywarp, Ramjet, Thrust and Dirge.

Review:
In the previous episode, Optimus Prime vetoed the construction of a relatively harmless

solar energy collector in case it fell into Decepticon hands; in this one he sanctions the creation of an advanced super-weapon – proof if any were needed that script editing isn't one of this show's strong points. As for the rest, well, it's all been done before: an Autobot goes rogue/mad/AWOL, only to redeem himself by the end of the episode, while the Decepticons try to get their hands on the technological gimmick of the week. Thankfully, an upturn in quality was just around the corner … 1/5

{2-18} MICROBOTS
Production number: 700-33 (18th episode produced of Season Two)
Transmission date: 7 October 1985 (11th episode transmitted of Season Two)

Written by David Wise

Plot:
A team of human archaeologists uncover a Decepticon ship buried beneath a hill. This was the ship in which Megatron's forces chased the Autobots to Earth, and as such it uses a powerful crystal, the Heart of Cybertron, as a power source.

Megatron removes the Heart of Cybertron and places it within himself. Now all-powerful, he defeats the Autobots with ease, forcing them to beat a hasty retreat.

Autobot scientist Perceptor leads a trio of Autobots into Megatron's inner workings, thanks to a shrink ray he uses for medical purposes. Just as Megatron is about to destroy Optimus Prime, Perceptor's team remove the Heart of Cybertron and destroy it. Without his new super powers, Megatron flees.

Spotlight: Production Problems
Within Transformers fandom, the original cartoon series has gained notoriety for its less-than-stellar production values and sometimes poor writing. To some extent these shortcomings are perfectly understandable – these were children's cartoon episodes, made to tight deadlines and even tighter budgets.

Notwithstanding the occasional negative review, this book's primary aim is to celebrate the earliest years of the Transformers franchise, rather than get bogged down by listing every single error or goof. However, such mistakes are so blatant and numerous that it would be remiss to pretend they don't exist.

According to one of the show's senior writers, Donald F Glut, episodes were often written very quickly, and given only a cursory check by the script editors before being sent into production. Furthermore, Hasbro would often have a say in the storyline process, stipulating which characters could or could not be used.

On the production side of things, no other cartoon show of the era featured as many different regular characters as *The Transformers*. By the end of Season Two, there were nearly a hundred Transformers to keep track of, each of whom had at least two modes (robot and vehicle). With 49 episodes produced during the course of the season, it's no wonder the animators were occasionally confused.

Given all these constraints and problems, then, it's a small miracle that the programme turned out as good as it did. At its very best, the show produced some outstanding episodes, on a par with any other cartoon series around at the time.

Megatron's Rants:
- 'After millions of years! It's mine!'

- 'Decepticons, a toast … to the imminent destruction of the accursed Autobots!'

Witty Put-downs:
- Megatron calls Perceptor's team 'filthy retro-rats'.

Roll Call:
Autobots: Perceptor, Ironhide, Brawn, Bumblebee, Optimus Prime, Ratchet, Cliffjumper, Bluestreak, Huffer, Smokescreen, Windcharger, Hoist, Gears, Wheeljack, Powerglide and Warpath. Grapple is mentioned but not seen.

Decepticons: Soundwave, Megatron, Bonecrusher, Thundercracker, Scavenger, Rumble, Starscream, Mixmaster, Ravage, Hook, Long Haul, Skywarp and Laserbeak.

Other: Sparkplug.

Data File: David Wise (writer)
The prolific David Wise is a famous name in animation, having been head writer and executive story editor on the original *Teenage Mutant Ninja Turtles* cartoon, for which he penned over seventy episodes. He was the most prolific of all *The Transformers* cartoon writers, contributing to fifteen scripts, and also wrote for *Batman: The Animated Series*, Disney's *Chip 'n' Dale Rescue Rangers* and *Star Trek: The Animated Series* ('How Sharper than a Serpent's Tooth'; the first *Star Trek* episode to win an Emmy). He also wrote for live-action series such as *Buck Rogers in the 25th Century* and *Wonder Woman*. A keen fan of *Doctor Who*, he often puts quotes from the series into his scripts, and even wrote a spin-off *Doctor Who* audio play, *Gallifrey: Forever*.

Review:
The Transformers does *Fantastic Voyage*! This is where Season Two really starts to get its act together, a tale in which Megatron finally comes across as a real threat, rather than a scenery-chewing buffoon. The episode has a relentless pace, loads of Autobots get blown to bits, and the scenes inside Megatron's body are excellently achieved. The only real drawback is the characterisation of Brawn, who comes across as a childish idiot; but this can be forgiven in an otherwise excellent episode. The hilarious drunken Decepticon scene has to be seen to be believed! 5/5

{2-19} MEGATRON'S MASTER PLAN, Part One
Production number: 700-34 (19th episode produced of Season Two)
Transmission date: 14 October 1985 (15th episode transmitted of Season Two)

Written by Donald F Glut

Plot:
Corporate fat cat and would-be Central City mayor Shawn Berger is duped by Megatron into believing that the Decepticons are the good guys and the Autobots are evil. As proof, a group of Decepticons attack an oil field disguised as Optimus Prime and company.

Armed with video evidence of the attack, Berger insists the Autobots be tried for the crime. This hard-line stance, Berger reasons, will boost his reputation and ensure his success in the next mayoral election.

Based on the video evidence, the Autobots are found guilty and banished from Earth in a spacecraft constructed by Berger's company. Once the Autobots are off-planet, Megatron sabotages their navigational computer and sets the controls for the heart of the sun ...

Megatron's Rants:
- 'Now nothing can save the Autobots ... they will become one with oblivion!'
- A villainous chess analogy: 'He thinks he will be king, but he will never be more than a pawn!'

Witty Put Downs:
- Megatron on Berger: 'The pompous, gullible fool!'

Roll Call:
Autobots: Optimus Prime, Ironhide, Warpath, Smokescreen, Bumblebee, Tracks, Wheeljack, Sunstreaker, Hound, Jazz, Hoist, Windcharger, Mirage, Huffer, Ratchet, Gears, Cliffjumper, Brawn, Red Alert, Grapple, Bluestreak, Beachcomber, Blaster, Prowl, Sideswipe, Trailbreaker and Inferno.

Decepticons: Starscream, Ramjet, Thrust, Dirge, Laserbeak, Megatron, Soundwave, Thundercracker, Skywarp and Ravage.

Other: Spike, Chip and Sparkplug.

Review:
An excellent episode, with a story that takes many twists on its way to that brilliant cliffhanger. True, there might be plot holes big enough for Unicron to fly through (the Autobots' guilt is based on a set of videotapes that no-one seems to have watched to the end), but the intriguingly epic premise and fast pace do a great job of mitigating any such concerns. 4/5

{2-20} MEGATRON'S MASTER PLAN, Part Two
Production number: 700-35 (20th episode produced of Season Two)
Transmission date: 15 October 1985 (16th episode transmitted of Season Two)

Written by Donald F Glut

Plot:
With the Autobots discredited and seemingly dead, the Decepticons are hailed by the mayor as heroes. However, in a live TV broadcast, Megatron reveals his plans to conquer the Earth.

Starting with Central City, the Decepticons send all the population to labour camps, where they toil to create Energon cubes. Berger sees the error of his ways and unsuccessfully attempts to help Spike escape; he is sent to one of the labour camps for his treachery.

The Autobots, meanwhile, have managed to escape their doomed ship, and return to Earth in order to liberate the Decepticon captives. In a furious battle, the Autobots emerge victorious and the Decepticons retreat.

The Autobots are given a full pardon and Berger is made to stand trial for his crimes.

Megatron's Rants:
- 'It's over! The Autobots are subatomic particles!'
- 'My plan is to conquer this mud-ball of a planet and suck it dry of energy!'
- 'I christen this city Megatronia One! Soon there will be many more!'

Witty Put-Downs:
- Megatron calls a reporter an 'Earth germ'.
- A reporter calls Berger a 'filthy swine'.

Roll Call:
Autobots: **Cosmos**, Cliffjumper, Huffer, Bumblebee, Hound, Brawn, Optimus Prime, Ironhide, Prowl, Jazz, Sideswipe, Ratchet, Smokescreen, Perceptor, Inferno, Beachcomber, Hoist, Powerglide, Red Alert, Seaspray, Gears, Tracks, Warpath and Bluestreak.

Decepticons: Megatron, Thundercracker, Soundwave, Starscream, Shrapnel, Bombshell, Long Haul, Hook, Bonecrusher, Mixmaster, Scrapper, Ravage, **Astrotrain**, Rumble and Scavenger.

Other: the Narrator, Sparkplug, Chip and Spike.

Data File: Victor Caroli (the Narrator)
The deep, authoritative voice of Victor Caroli is easily recognisable, having been heard in numerous advertisements, film trailers and documentaries. He narrated the animated series *Robotix*, and also the factual programme *Extreme Forensics*.

Review:
Another good episode, successfully tying up all the loose ends from Part One. But although successful in its own right, it doesn't quite reach the heights of that first episode, and as a result comes across as slightly anticlimactic. 3/5

{2-21} DESERTION OF THE DINOBOTS, Part One
Production number: 700-36 (21st episode produced of Season Two)
Transmission date: 21 October 1985 (19th episode transmitted of Season Two)

Written by Earl Kress

Plot:
The Autobots run into the Decepticons as they attempt to harvest Energon cubes from a power plant. During the battle, both factions begin to suffer from debilitating malfunctions and are forced to regroup.

It transpires that they are experiencing a deficiency of Cybertonium, an element common on Cybertron but not on Earth. The Dinobots, originated on Earth and therefore not Cybertonium-dependant, are sent to Cybertron via the space bridge to retrieve some. However, they rebel against their fellow Autobots, refusing to return home.

Spike and Carly go after the Dinobots, but just as they are about to materialise, Shockwave shoots the terminal on Cybertron, which explodes ...

Spotlight: Fists of Fun

The Transformers of the cartoon series boast the ability to convert their hands into various gadgets and gizmos. This was a convenient way for the show's writers to solve plot problems quickly and easily; a necessity due to each episode's limited 22-minute run-time. While this was an interesting addition to the Transformers' roster of powers, there have been criticisms that the show was perhaps over-reliant on such quick fixes. The most prominent example is a scene in {3-00} *The Transformers: The Movie* where Hot Rod is trapped by mechanical tendrils; he simply transforms his hand into a circular saw and frees himself.

This special power seems to have been influenced by the toys themselves, some of which (e.g. Trailbreaker and Inferno) had removable fists that could be replaced with weapons. Others (e.g. Megatron and Tracks) boasted weapons that fitted snugly over the hand, giving the impression that the hand (now hidden) had been replaced by a weapon.

The hand-transformations have proven to be quite popular in many quarters. A number of recent toy releases have seized on this ability – including a Soundwave figure with a sensor arm and a Sideswipe figure with piledriver hands. Furthermore, this trait has continued in Michael Bay's live-action Transformers movies, in which Bumblebee can change his hand into a cannon.

One of the most fondly-remembered scenes in the entire run of *The Transformers* came in {1-02} 'More Than Meets the Eye, Part Two', where Optimus Prime and Megatron engage in battle atop a dam, one with an axe for a hand and the other with a flail. What was initially a writer's 'cheat' has since become a much-loved part of the Transformers mythology.

Roll Call:
Autobots: Optimus Prime, Jazz, Hound, Mirage, Ironhide, Blaster, Bumblebee, Wheeljack, Grimlock, Snarl, Slag, Sludge, Swoop, Red Alert, Hoist, Inferno, Powerglide, Grapple, Ratchet, Perceptor and Prowl.

Decepticons: Soundwave, Ravage, Megatron, Starscream, Thundercracker, Thrust, Blitzwing, Rumble, Skywarp, Scrapper, Scavenger, Bonecrusher, Long Haul, Mixmaster, Devastator and Shockwave.

Other: Carly, Spike and Sparkplug.

Review:
Unlike in {2-19/2-20} 'Megatron's Master Plan', there's obviously not enough plot to go around here, so there's a lot of padding - Megatron's attack on the remote-controlled aircraft and the battle at the airport are inconsequential to the main Cybertonium plot. Once the story kicks in around half way through, this turns into a nice little set up for episode two. 2/5

{2-22} DESERTION OF THE DINOBOTS, Part Two

Production number: 700-37 (22nd episode produced of Season Two)
Transmission date: 22 October 1985 (20th episode transmitted of Season Two)

Written by Earl Kress

Plot:

Spike and Carly manage to survive their altercation with Shockwave and, with Sparkplug directing them from Earth, head off in search of Cybertonium. They meet Swoop, who reveals that his fellow Dinobots have been captured and taken to the Decepticons' Cybertonium mine.

Swoop, Spike and Carly are themselves captured and thrown into the mine, where the other Dinobots seem to be willingly working for the Decepticons. Carly realises that the Dinobots have been reprogrammed and manages to set their circuits straight. Tricking the guards, the humans and Dinobots make their escape with the Cybertonium.

With the Autobots now safe, they officially invite Spike and Carly into their ranks.

Witty Put-Downs:

- Megatron to Shockwave: 'I'll have you reprogrammed for maintenance!'
- Spike calls Grimlock a 'lumpy bag of bolts'.

Roll Call:

Autobots: Jazz, Brawn, Cliffjumper, Sunstreaker, Bumblebee, Sideswipe, Prowl, Ironhide, Swoop, Grimlock, Snarl, Slag, Sludge, Optimus Prime, Huffer, Windcharger, Gears, Hound, Wheeljack, Trailbreaker, Ratchet and Bluestreak.

Decepticons: Shockwave and Megatron.

Other: the Narrator, Spike, Carly and Sparkplug.

Plus numerous unnamed Cybertronian Transformers, including a speaking Decepticon listed only as 'Head Guard' in the script.

Data File: Hal Rayle (voices, including Snarl and Shrapnel)

Rayle's voice credits include work on *Teenage Mutant Ninja Turtles*, where he was briefly the voice of Raphael; *Galaxy High*, where he played the lead character, Doyle; and *Visionaries*, where he played Arzon. He was the voice of the Ghoulies in *Ghoulies II* (Albert Band, 1988) and that of the Predator in *Predator II* (Stephen Hopkins, 1990).

Review:

Plot plays second fiddle here as we are treated to a guided tour of Cybertron. A few nice action set-pieces keep up the entertainment in an episode that's basically just a vehicle for us to take a good look around the Transformers' home and history. It works very well on those terms, even if the Decepticons come across as particularly incompetent. 3/5

{2-23} BLASTER BLUES

Production number: 700-38 (23rd episode produced of Season Two)

Transmission date: 23 October 1985 (21st episode transmitted of Season Two)

Written by Larry Strauss

Plot:
Megatron steals a Voltronic Galaxer, a device designed for long-range communications with other galaxies. In his secret base on the moon, Megatron rewires the device so that it blocks all radio communications on Earth. Only when the governments of Earth give him all their energy reserves will Megatron deactivate the device.

Blaster and Cosmos stumble onto Megatron's plot, and are captured. However, they still manage to reprogram the device, allowing the rest of the Autobots to home in on their position. The Decepticons are defeated, and the Voltronic Galaxer is deactivated.

Witty Put-Downs:
- Cosmos is a 'useless piece of scrap!'
- Blaster is a 'son of an eight-track!'

Roll Call:
Autobots: Blaster, Cosmos, Optimus Prime, **Omega Supreme**, Jazz, Hoist, Ironhide, Ratchet, Cliffjumper, Trailbreaker, Hound, Sunstreaker, Sideswipe, Mirage, Bumblebee, Prowl, Wheeljack, Huffer, Tracks, Powerglide, Red Alert and Inferno.

Decepticons: Thundercracker, Megatron, Starscream, Astrotrain, Skywarp and Ramjet.

Other: Spike, Carly and Sparkplug.

Data File: Buster Jones (voices, including Blaster)
Although Jones had a couple of live-action roles in shows such as *The Six Million Dollar Man* and *Hill Street Blues*, he was best known as a voice actor. He played Black Vulcan in *Super Friends*, Winston Zeddemore in *The Real Ghostbusters*, Lothar in *Defenders of the Earth* and Doc in *G.I. Joe: A Real American Hero*.

Review:
An interesting worst-case-scenario – what would happen to the world if all radio communications were blocked? – is spoilt by poor execution. Vacuous and insubstantial, it's a forgettable, rather than bad, episode. 2/5

{2-24} A DECEPTICON RAIDER IN KING ARTHUR'S COURT
Production number: 700-39 (24th episode produced of Season Two)
Transmission date: 24 October 1985 (22nd episode transmitted of Season Two)

Written by Douglas Booth

(The original transmission of this episode featured a misspelling on the title caption and went out as 'A Deceptacon Raider in King Arthur's Court'. This was corrected for repeat broadcasts and on home video releases.)

Plot:

Desperately low on energy, Starscream and a small group of Decepticons track an energy source to a nearby cave. Followed by a group of Autobots, they are all transported to 6th Century England and become involved in a dispute between two local knights, Wigend and Aetheling. The Decepticons take over Wigend's castle and kidnap Aetheling's daughter, Nimue.

Thanks to the local wizard, Beorht, the depleted Autobots are revived long enough to defeat the Decepticons. After a short battle with a fire-breathing dragon, all are returned to the present day.

Spotlight: Alternative Transformers

Prior to their Hasbro release, the early Transformers had previously seen release in Japan as part of Takara's Diaclone and MicroChange lines. This isn't the whole story, however – these toys have seen additional official releases down the years, by companies other than Hasbro.

GiG

GiG is an Italian toy company that won the rights to release Diaclone figures in the early 1980s, prior to Hasbro getting involved. Figures released by GiG included versions of Tracks and the Dinobots in their original Diaclone colours.

When Hasbro launched the Transformers brand in 1984, their rights didn't extend to Italy, so GiG continued to release Takara figures under the name 'Trasformers' (sic). Eventually GiG reached a licencing agreement with Hasbro, finally allowing them to use the proper Transformers name and branding.

Joustra

In a scenario similar to GiG's, the French company Joustra had the Diaclone rights in central Europe. Rather than create an entirely new brand, they put the toys out under the Diaclone name. Figures included a set of yellow Constructicons, and others in their original Diaclone colours.

The Joustra Diaclone range was short-lived however, and soon superseded by official Transformers-branded figures bearing the logo of Hasbro's subsidiary Milton Bradley.

Takara

Before licensing their toys to Hasbro, Takara made their own attempts to sell their figures outside of Japan.

In the USA they launched a small number of toys under the name Diakron (due to an error in anglicising the word Diaclone). Takara also released some Diaclone figures in Finland, including a notoriously rare black version of Tracks. After Hasbro secured the rights to sell many of the Takara toys as Transformers, Takara began to withdraw from overseas markets.

'Shackwave'

The Hasbro Shockwave toy was not a Takara original; instead it was licensed from another Asian manufacturer, ToyCo. ToyCo also licensed the figure to US electrical chain RadioShack, who sold a grey-coloured version that they named 'Galactic Man'.

Plasticos IGA

Hasbro sold the licence to produce Transformers in Mexico to the company Plasticos IGA. However, as toy safety standards were more lax there than in other countries, the Mexican Transformers were notorious for containing lead-based paint, causing a stir in the UK national press when some of these figures were imported to Britain.

Convertors (US)

Convertors, a range of action figures released by the company Select, were a short-lived rival to the Transformers. The line was a mix of all-new toys bolstered by a number of pre-existing figures licensed from Japanese companies, including Bandai. This led to the situation where some figures were released both as Transformers and as Convertors, with both Hasbro and Select paying for the use of the exact same moulds. The Convertors figures Chopper, Wheels, Crawler and Morphus were basically the same toys, albeit with different colour schemes, as the Transformers figures Whirl, Roadbuster, Barrage and Ransack respectively.

Convertors (UK)

A seperate Convertors franchise, launched in the UK by the company Grandstand, best known for their range of handheld electronic games, also featured a range of robots co-opted from various Japanese toy lines. One such figure was Omegatron, which was also sold under the Transformers banner as Omega Supreme. It's been popularly theorised that Omegatron's existence is the reason why the Transformers Omega Supreme toy was never released in the UK.

Megatron's Rants:
- 'Starscream, you fool, you ruined my shot!' This familiar cry is recognised by Spike: 'It's the 20th Century, all right!'

Witty Put-Downs:
- Starscream: 'We have 1,451 years to go before we have to worry about the Autobots and that bungler Megatron!'
- Aetheling: 'I bid thee welcome!' Wigend: 'And I bid thee hold thy tongue!'
- Starscream, on the natives: 'You malingering peasants!'

Roll Call:
Autobots: Warpath and Hoist.

Decepticons: Starscream, Ramjet, Ravage, Rumble, Megatron, Skywarp, Thundercracker, Soundwave and Reflector.

Other: Spike.

Data File: Joy Grdnic (voices)
Primarily a comedian and radio DJ, Grdnic has released two Grammy-nominated comedy albums in conjunction with her long-time associate Ron Stevens. She also provided voices for animated series *The Dukes*, and scripted an episode of *The Munsters Today*.

Review:
A fun, colourful romp through Arthurian England, full of knights, castles, wizards, dragons, seagull poo, and maidens wearing conical hats. Many of the plot elements don't bear close scrutiny, and there are some very dodgy accents on display, but it's always nice to see a Starscream-heavy episode – he and Rumble steal every scene in what is, ultimately, a highly enjoyable half-hour. 5/5

{2-25} THE GOLDEN LAGOON
Production number: 700-40 (25th episode produced of Season Two)
Transmission date: 4 November 1985 (27th episode transmitted of Season Two)

Written by Dennis Marks

Plot:
Under attack from the Decepticons, Beachcomber discovers a picturesque meadow cut off from the rest of the world by mountains on all sides. In the centre of a field lies a golden pond of Electrum. Any Transformer who swims in this turns gold in colour and becomes invulnerable to weapons fire.

The Decepticons coat themselves with Electrum and trounce the Autobots. However, the effect soon wears off and the Decepticons are forced to retreat when confronted by an army of golden Electrum-infused Autobots. The Decepticons destroy the lagoon as they fly off.

Although the Autobots are victorious, a sombre Beachcomber sits in the smoking ashes of the meadow and reflects on the environmental damage caused by the recent battle.

Megatron's Rants:
* 'You see! Nothing can stop us now! The Autobots are finished!'

Witty Put-downs:
* Megatron: 'Show no mercy!' Starscream: 'Do we ever?'

Roll Call:
Autobots: Beachcomber, Seaspray, Powerglide, Perceptor, Warpath, Omega Supreme, Smokescreen, Mirage, Wheeljack, Bluestreak, Hound, Brawn, Sunstreaker, Optimus Prime, Ironhide, Ratchet, Jazz, Bumblebee, Sideswipe, Windcharger and Gears.

Decepticons: Blitzwing, Ramjet, Thrust, Skywarp, Thundercracker, Megatron, Starscream, Soundwave, Long Haul, Reflector and Dirge.

Plus either Rumble or Frenzy or perhaps both – it's impossible to be sure: every time we see one of the humanoid cassette Decepticons in this episode, they're coloured gold.

Data File: Dennis Marks (writer)
Marks' career in animation goes back to the '60s, when he wrote for shows such as *Batfink* and *The Beatles* television series. Later credits include *Josie and the Pussycats*, *Spider-Man & His Amazing Friends*, for which the multi-talented Marks also provided the voice of the villainous Green Goblin, and *Tom and Jerry: The Movie* (Phil Roman, 1992). In the early '80s he was Head of Development at Marvel Productions, where he was heavily involved in the *Dungeons & Dragons* cartoon, negotiating the rights and developing the premise. A keen comics fan, his mother was a personal friend of Harry Donnenfeld, one of the key players in the early days of the DC Comics company.

Review:
What could have been a preachy, overbearing episode is actually realised extremely well, with the environmental issues handled subtly using visuals only – they're not even mentioned in the dialogue. Add to that a number of excellent battle sequences and a lower-than-usual error-count, and what we have is a great little episode that manages to be thought provoking yet also viscerally exciting. 4/5

{2-26} THE GOD GAMBIT
Production number: 700-41 (26th episode produced of Season Two)
Transmission date: 28 October 1985 (23rd episode transmitted of Season Two)

Written by Buzz Dixon

Plot:
Cosmos, chased by Decepticons, is captured and deactivated on a moon populated by a primitive humanoid race, the Titans. These are led by a dictator named Jero, who keeps the masses in his thrall using an animated sky god statue. The Decepticon group, headed by Astrotrain, pose as sky gods and order the populace to mine an energy-rich crystal for them.

A heretic, Talaria, partly revives Cosmos and manages to send out a distress beacon. A group of Autobots arrive and defeat the Decepticons – but the retreating Astrotrain ignites the seam of crystals and starts a chain reaction.

The Autobots rescue the natives with seconds to spare, and they leave the Titans to rebuild, free from their false gods.

Witty Put-Downs:
- Astrotrain variously calls the natives 'worms' and 'maggots'. He also calls Cosmos a 'hunk of junk'.
- 'These fools worship Transformers!'

Roll Call:
Autobots: Cosmos, Optimus Prime, Perceptor, Jazz, Red Alert and Omega Supreme.

Decepticons: Astrotrain, Starscream and Thrust.

Review:
Starscream and Megatron are possibly the most entertaining double-act in cartoon history; their sniping banter can lift even the dullest of episodes. It's a shame, then, that

Megatron is entirely absent here and Starscream is nothing more than a background character. The episode itself is po-faced and desperately lacking in the wit that the Decepticons' repartee usually provides. There's nothing to particularly hate about this episode, but there's little to love, either. 2/5

{2-27} MAKE TRACKS

Production number: 700-42 (27th episode produced of Season Two)
Transmission date: 30 October 1985 (25th episode transmitted of Season Two)

Written by David Wise

Plot:

While riding around New York City at night, Tracks is attacked by would-be car thieves and ends up crashing into a lamp-post, severely damaging him to the extent that he can no longer transform into robot mode.

Tracks is found and fixed up by Raoul, a young mechanic who's being hired to find cars for a pair of mobsters, the Geddis Brothers. It transpires that the brothers are sending hundreds of vehicles to a new Decepticon base across the Jersey River.

Megatron's plan is to turn these cars into remote-controlled drone Transformers, who proceed to go on the rampage. Blaster is able to jam the Decepticons' frequency and render the drones lifeless.

Having now befriended the Autobots, Raoul is able to disable Megatron by spraying a can of aerosol paint into the Decepticon leader's inner workings.

Spotlight: Size Matters (Part One)

Transformers don't just change their shape – they also change their size. The massive robot Soundwave transforms into a small cassette player. Cosmos, one of the shorter Autobots, can transform into a giant spacecraft capable of holding numerous Autobot troops.

And it's not just a case of expanding or contracting; these Transformers seem to change their mass as well. Not only does Megatron shrink into a small handgun when he transforms, he becomes light enough to wielded by a human. So how does this ability work, exactly?

One of the more popular fan theories, which has since been ratified in official publications, is that the Transformers are able to 'mass-shift', temporarily shunting parts of their bodies into other dimensions. This same mass then returns to the Transformer whenever they 'grow'.

This raises the question: if the Transformers have the ability to access and draw matter from other dimensions, why is this 'wasted' on simply disguising themselves, when it could surely have more practical applications?

Well, the most likely explanation is that the Transformers are simply unable to harness this ability for other uses. In the comics, where the robots were the offspring of a mystical, god-like being, it stands to reason that their creator imbued them with this power but placed limitations upon it.

In the cartoons, however, the Transformers had rather different origins – there, they were built by the rather shady Quintessons. The Quintessons appear to be not that much more evolved than the Transformers themselves; from their appearances in the movie and television show, it seems unlikely they would have the necessary know-how to endow their creations with the ability to mass-shift. It's entirely possible that they once possessed great technologies and subsequently lost these due to some sort of cultural decline or dark age.

Witty Put-Downs:
- Blaster, on the subject of the Decepticon drones: 'They don't look that smart to me … Their aim's not too good, either'.
- Huffer: 'Talk about lousy shots.' (Huffer gets covered by falling debris.) 'Spoke too soon.'
- Optimus Prime: 'We're putting your company into bankruptcy, Megatron!'

Roll Call:
Autobots: Tracks, Blaster, Optimus Prime, Powerglide, Huffer, Hoist, Cosmos, Seaspray, Beachcomber, Sideswipe, Jazz, Bumblebee, Ratchet, Inferno, Ironhide and Windcharger.

Decepticons: Starscream, Megatron, Hook, Soundwave, Rumble, Scrapper, Ravage, Bonecrusher, Scavenger and Thundercracker.

Other: Sparkplug and **Raoul**.

Data File: Michael McConnohie (voices, including Tracks and Cosmos)
Writer and actor Michael McConnohie also provided voices for another iteration of the Transformers franchise, voicing Hot Shot and Ironhide in *Transformers: Robots in Disguise*. He voiced Ectar and Lexor in *Visionaries*, Cross-Country in *G.I. Joe: A Real American Hero* and Azulongmon in *Digimon*. He has also lent his voice to video games including *Mortal Kombat*, *World of Warcraft* and *Call of Duty III*.

Review:
This episode can be summed up by a single scene: the Autobot Seaspray, cruising down a grimy river in hovercraft mode, stops to aid a tow truck pulling an abandoned car from the murky depths. The scene has little relevance to the plot, but like much of this episode, demonstrates a grimness and dark realism we don't often get from this generally light-hearted show.

The script might demonstrate the less glamourous side of New York, replete with mobsters, traffic jams and carjackers, but it's the visuals that make the story. It's an episode set entirely at night, with glorious painted backdrops full of neon-signs, streetlights and shadows.

Plot-wise it's all a bit mundane (Megatron's plan is especially weak here), and there are a few token 'funny' lines, but there's a brooding atmosphere to the visuals that helps lift the episode above the script's limitations. 4/5

{2-28} CHILD'S PLAY (cartoon episode)
Production number: 700-43 (28th episode produced of Season Two)
Transmission date: 7 November 1985 (30th episode transmitted of Season Two)

Written by Beth Bornstein

NB: Not to be confused with [35] 'Child's Play' (comic).

Plot:
Following an accident with a space bridge, a group of Autobots and Decepticons are transported to a strange planet of giant humanoids, where Transformers are – relatively speaking – the size of toys.

After first evading the many dangers of a gigantic child's bedroom, including massive goldfish bowls, toy castles and pet cats, the Transformers are captured by the planet's scientists, who plan to dissect them for study.

Both factions manage to escape the clutches of the planet's authorities – the Decepticons return to Earth via a jury-rigged teleport beam, while the Autobots lift off aboard a converted toy rocket.

Witty Put-Downs:
- Starscream pursues the Autobot leader into a sewer: 'I see you are right where you belong, Optimus Prime!'

Roll Call:
Autobots: Optimus Prime, Brawn, Inferno, Perceptor, Ironhide, Bumblebee, Smokescreen, Trailbreaker, Wheeljack, Ratchet, Sideswipe, Gears and Huffer.

Decepticons: Megatron, Thrust, Starscream, Skywarp, Soundwave and Ravage.

Other: Spike and Chip.

Data File: Beth Bornstein (writer)
Bornstein's credits include scripts for animated television series such as *Jem and the Holograms*, *My Little Pony* and *Batman: The Animated Series*.

Data File: Mona Marshall (voices)
Marshall is best known to viewers as the voices of Sheila Broflovski and Linda Stotch in *South Park*, and Izzy Izumi in *Digimon*. Before then, she had voice parts in other animated series including *Rainbow Brite*, *My Little Pony* and *Jem and the Holograms*. She also voiced the character Penny in the pilot episode of *Inspector Gadget*. Her film credits include *Monsters University* (Dan Scanlon, 2013), *Despicable Me 2* (Pierre Coffin and Chris Renaud, 2013) and *Frozen* (Chris Buck and Jenifer Lee, 2013).

Review:
Kids across the world had their Transformers action figures play out battles across bedroom furniture and floors, so it's nice to see this acknowledged in the show itself. However, this is a very uneven episode. For every good scene (the initial exploration of the kid's bedroom) there is a poor one just around the corner (the seemingly advanced aliens who want to dissect the Transformers for no other reason than to add some further peril to the story). The animation, too, is especially poor in this instalment. Good fun overall, though. 3/5

{2-29} THE GAMBLER
Production number: 700-46 (31st episode produced of Season Two)

Transmission date: 11 November 1985 (31st episode transmitted of Season Two)

Written by Michael Charles Hill

NB: As stated in the introduction, this book lists the television episodes in a 'best viewing order', which has thus far corresponded to the order in which they were made. This is the first episode to buck that trend, being a direct continuation of {2-28} 'Child's Play' (cartoon episode). When originally transmitted, the two episodes were shown consecutively.

Plot:
En route to Earth aboard their toy rocket, Optimus Prime's small band of Autobots are kidnapped by a professional gambler, Bosch, who plans to trade his new captives for Energon. To facilitate this, all the Autobots bar Smokescreen have their personalities wiped, a process that depletes Bosch's Energon reserves. Without more power, he is unable to restore them to normal.

Smokescreen suggests an alternative plan: trade the lobotomised Autobots for Energon chips (a currency as well as an energy source), then cheat the tables in Monacus, a nearby casino planet. With the winnings, they can buy back the Autobots and use the remainder to power Bosch's ship and return the Autobots to normal.

Their plan goes awry, however, when they gamble all their chips and lose. Ownership of the captured Autobots passes to alien mob boss Gyconi, who made his fortune by betting on rigged gladiatorial tournaments; he plans to make the Autobots the next (losing) combatants.

Matters are complicated further by the arrival of a group of Decepticons, who themselves are being stalked by an Autobot bounty hunter named Devcon. With Devcon's help, Smokescreen and Bosch are able to rescue the Autobots from the arena.

The Decepticons are forced to retreat, Gyconi is humiliated, and the Autobots make off with the Energon chips.

Spotlight: Megatron, the Intergalactic Criminal Mastermind
In this story, the Decepticons appear to have a criminal relationship with the mobster Gyconi; they accuse him of skimming off their profits. Up until now, Megatron's plans have always focused on Earth and its unique natural resources; here we finally learn that his machinations have a wider scope than previously thought.

It would seem that at least some of the Energon that Megatron has plundered from the Earth is sent to other planets for investment purposes. Here Megatron appears to be funding Gyconi's tournaments in exchange for a cut of his revenue.

It's a neat way of accumulating Energon without risking the wrath of the Autobots, and seems to be a genuine effort on the part of the writing team to address many of the holes in Megatron's plans in previous episodes (see the Spotlight entry under {2-04} 'Attack of the Autobots' for more on this).

Witty Put-Downs:
- Gyconi sums up Ramjet and Thrust in a single word: 'Incompetents!'
- Gyconi again: 'You Autobots have caused more trouble than you're worth! I hope Megatron turns you into slag!'

Roll Call:
Autobots: Optimus Prime, Bumblebee, Inferno, Smokescreen and Perceptor.

The Autobot Devcon, invented especially for this episode, makes his one and only appearance here.

Decepticons: Astrotrain, Ramjet and Dirge.

Other: **Slizardo**, a non-speaking minion of Gyconi, who will turn up again in {3-24} 'Grimlock's New Brain'.

Data File: Michael Charles Hill (writer/associate producer)
Hill was also co-producer of the *G.I. Joe: A Real American Hero* animated series, and wrote for *Centurions, Challenge of the GoBots* and the *RoboCop* television show. He was an uncredited extra in the movie *Raging Bull* (Martin Scorsese, 1980).

Data File: Walker Edmiston (voices, including Inferno)
Edmiston is a familiar face and voice to generations of Americans. His numerous live-action credits include parts in *Maverick, The Monkees, Mission: Impossible* and *The Dukes of Hazzard*. He was the voice of the alien Balok in the first regular episode of *Star Trek* ('The Corbomite Maneuver'), the voice of the baby chimp in *Escape from the Planet of the Apes* (Don Taylor, 1971), and can also be heard in *The Andromeda Strain* (Robert Wise, 1971) and *Dick Tracy* (Warren Beatty, 1990). Other voice work included parts in *The Flintstones, Ben 10*, the radio show *Adventures in Odyssey*, and Disney's *The Great Mouse Detective* (Ron Clements et al, 1986).

Review:
This is a really good episode, with a complex yet accessible plot, some colourful alien locations, lots of action, and plenty of memorable one-off characters, such as Bosch, Gyconi and Devcon. 5/5

{2-30} QUEST FOR SURVIVAL
Production number: 700-44 (29th episode produced of Season Two)
Transmission date: 5 November 1985 (28th episode transmitted of Season Two)

Written by Reed Robbins and Peter Salas

Plot:
The Insecticons and their army of clones are on the rampage, devouring any and all plant life they come across, threatening the world's food supplies. After they feed, the resultant energy is siphoned off by the Decepticons, who turn it into Energon.

To combat this threat, the Autobots head out into space and obtain a can of robotic insecticide from the planet Floron 3. However, a fast-growing alien plant is also inadvertently brought back to Earth, and it soon begins spreading like wildfire across the landscape.

The Autobots and Decepticons do battle, and the insecticide is destroyed. However, it appears that the plant itself is hostile to robotic insect life, and indeed eats the majority of the Insecticon clones. The Autobots are able to round up the plant and send it back into space.

Megatron's Rants:
- The Decepticon leader lets others to do the dirty work: 'We'll let the Autobots get the insecticide for us!'
- 'Prime! You never learn, do you? Here's a demonstration of what's to become of all you pathetic Autobots!'

Witty Put-Downs:
- Megatron: 'If the Insecticons had brains they'd be dangerous!'
- Warpath and Optimus aren't fans of 1980s soft rock music: 'Prime! Blaster's music!' 'I know! It's frying my transistors, too!'
- Megatron pleads for rescue in his usual endearing way: 'Don't just stand there with your cockpits open, you fools!'
- Starscream, on the alien plant: 'Overgrown spinach patch!'

Roll Call:
Autobots: Huffer, Inferno, Smokescreen, Tracks, Warpath, **Skids**, Optimus Prime, Grapple, Hoist, Bumblebee, Cosmos, Beachcomber, Ratchet, Perceptor, Prowl, Ironhide and Blaster.

Decepticons: Shrapnel, Bombshell, Kickback, Dirge, Megatron, Starscream, Thundercracker, Rumble, Laserbeak, Soundwave, Skywarp, Thrust, Ramjet and Blitzwing.

Other: Spike.

Data File: Peter Salas (writer)
For the show *Challenge of the GoBots*, Salas contributed the script 'A New Suit for Leader-1', co-written with his *The Transformers* collaborator Reed Robbins.

Review:
The Transformers at its corniest, summed up by the scene in which Spike is dwarfed by a giant can of bug-spray. With the Autobots facing no fewer than three sets of antagonists – the Insecticons, the Decepticons and the killer plants – this is certainly an action-packed episode, but a little absurd in places. 3/5

{2-31} THE SECRET OF OMEGA SUPREME
Production number: 700-45 (30th episode produced of Season Two)
Transmission date: 6 November 1985 (29th episode transmitted of Season Two)

Written by David Wise

Plot:
There's trouble brewing out in space – the Constructicons are mining an energy-rich ore from an asteroid close to Earth. Omega Supreme is sent to deal with the situation, but his blind hatred of the Constructicons clouds his judgment – the 'asteroid' is actually the egg of a large alien creature and, while Omega Supreme's attention is focused on his

mortal nemeses, he ignores the alien as it heads toward Earth.

Optimus Prime discovers the root of Omega's problem – millions of years ago, he and the then-benign Constructicons were friends back on Cybertron. However, Megatron used his 'Robo-Smasher' device to convert the Constructicons into Decepticons, who then duped Omega into leaving Crystal City unguarded. The Constructicons reduced the city to rubble and Omega never forgave them. He himself was also a victim of the Robo-Smasher, but the process was interrupted half-way through, leaving him cold and detached – his only remaining emotion is his hatred of the Constructicons.

Omega Supreme eventually realises that if the alien creature is allowed to reach Earth, yet another city will have been destroyed on his watch. Vowing not to make the same mistake twice, he puts his feud with the Constructicons to one side and saves the planet.

Spotlight: What's the Origin of the Constructicons? (Redux)

As in the comics (see [10] 'The Next Best Thing to Being There'), the cartoon series' depiction of the Constructicons' origins is very confusing. In their debut appearance ({1-16} 'Heavy Metal War'), it's stated that they were built on Earth ('They were worth the time we spent building them in these caverns'). Here, though, they are shown to have been active on Cybertron, millions of years in the past. They were originally friendly (despite their Decepticon insignias), until Megatron converted them to the Decepticon cause using the Robo-Smasher. A further episode ({3.04}, 'Five Faces of Darkness, Part 4') features a flashback set on ancient Cybertron, showing that Megatron was actually built by the Constructicons. So how can we rationalise all this apparently conflicting information?

The simplest explanation is that, as with Skyfire, the Constructicons were originally Decepticons (during which time they built Megatron) but later saw the error of their ways and became 'good'. Later, Megatron used the Robo-Smasher to convert them back into Decepticons, this time permanently. And although their physical bodies were irreparably damaged when the Transformers arrived on Earth in 1984, Megatron built replacements for them on Earth.

Megatron's Rants:

- 'I'll blow that asteroid out of the sky, then sit back while the beast throws this planet into utter chaos!'

Roll Call:

Autobots: Sideswipe, Cosmos, Optimus Prime, Powerglide, Omega Supreme, Perceptor, Ironhide, Tracks, Beachcomber and Smokescreen.

Sideswipe's presence here – he's a non-speaking background character in a scene set in the Decepticon base – would seem to be an animation error, and as such probably doesn't rate as a *bona fide* appearance.

Decepticons: Bonecrusher, Scavenger, Scrapper, Long Haul, Mixmaster, Hook, Megatron, Soundwave, Astrotrain, Devastator and Starscream.

Data File: Wally Burr (voice director/additional voices)
The legendary Wally Burr directed the voice cast on shows such as *Inspector Gadget*, *Bucky O' Hare* and *Spider-Man*. A talented voice actor himself, he provided a number of voices for the English-language dub of *Akira* (Katsuhiro Otomo, 1988) and was credited as 'Newsreel Voice' in the movie *Pearl Harbor* (Michael Bay, 2001).

Data File: Jack Angel (voices, including Astrotrain, Omega Supreme and Smokescreen)
Voice actor Jack Angel lent his talents to numerous cartoon series, including *Scooby-Doo and Scrappy Doo*, *Darkwing Duck* and *Ben 10*. He can also be heard in a number of movies, including *Who Framed Roger Rabbit?* (Robert Zemeckis, 1988), *Beetlejuice* (Tim Burton, 1988) and notably *A.I. Artificial Intelligence* (Steven Spielberg, 2001), for which he voiced Teddy, the android teddy bear.

Review:
Origin stories, by their very nature, often appear more mythic and important than regular episodes, and this is no exception. The extended flashback sequence set in Cybertron's past is excellent, but sadly the framing sequence, in which Omega Supreme saves Earth from an alien monster and learns a life lesson in the process, is decidedly average. 3/5.

{2-32} KREMZEEK!
Production number: 700-47 (32nd episode produced of Season Two)
Transmission date: 27 December 1985 (46th episode transmitted of Season Two)

Written by David Wise

Plot:
While experimenting in his lab, Megatron creates a sentient energy creature, Kremzeek. Realising that the mischievous imp has the potential to cause mayhem, he dumps Kremzeek outside Autobot HQ.

The tricksy Kremzeek causes chaos in the base, before teleporting himself to Japan in a bid to wreak even more havoc. Optimus Prime and a group of Autobots give chase, but a mistake by Blaster serves only to worsen the problem and create a whole army of the pesky creatures.

The Autobots lure the multiple Kremzeeks to an electricity pylon and aim to merge them back into a single organism – unfortunately they succeed only in combining all the individual creatures into a single, giant Kremzeek, who proceeds to stomp through the streets of Tokyo.

Megatron, meanwhile, is busy testing his new 'energy magnet', with which he can remotely drain power from distant objects. He doesn't reckon on the arrival of Kremzeek, who proceeds to wreck the device and force the Decepticons into retreat.

The Autobots finally manage to disperse Kremzeek's energy, thereby defeating him. However, one of the smaller Kremzeek creatures remains uncaptured, and the Autobots once more head off in pursuit …

Megatron's Rants:
- 'Yes Kremzeek! You will be my ultimate weapon against the Autobots!'

- 'We will drain this planet dry!'
- 'Soon, all of this wretched planet's power will be mine, and nothing can stop me!

Witty Put-Downs:
- Both Bumblebee and Blaster call Kremzeek a 'little creep'.

Roll Call:
Autobots: Optimus Prime, Smokescreen, Hoist, Jazz, Ratchet, Huffer, Beachcomber, Sideswipe, Bluestreak, Bumblebee, Blaster, Inferno and Omega Supreme.

Decepticons: Starscream, Megatron, Soundwave and Thrust.

Other: Sparkplug

Review:
Lovable, mischievous antagonists were all the rage in mid-'80s cinema, thanks to characters such as Slimer from *Ghostbusters* (Ivan Reitman, 1984) and the titular *Gremlins* (Joe Dante, 1984). Kremzeek is another creature in the same mould – dangerous, but oddly cute.

The Transformers cartoon always boasted a strong sense of humour – here it's cranked up a notch, in a deliberately 'zany' episode that works really well. 4/5

{2-33} SEA CHANGE
Production number: 700-48 (33rd episode produced of Season Two)
Transmission date: 20 November 1985 (37th episode transmitted of Season Two)

Written by Douglas Booth

Plot:
The Decepticons have a squadron of droids based on the planet Tlalak; their mission is to suck the life-force out of the natives and convert it into Energon cubes. When the indigenous people begin a slaves' revolt, the droids send a distress call to Megatron on Earth.

The SOS is intercepted by the Autobots, who travel to the planet and investigate. The Autobots befriend the native Tlalakans, and discover that, despite looking much like humans, they have the ability to change their form by bathing in the Well of Transformation.

Seaspray, smitten by a female Tlalakan named Alana, dives into the pool and becomes an organic humanoid, similar in appearance to the natives.

The Decepticons are driven away when Seaspray – now returned to normal - destroys their stash of Energon cubes.

Megatron's Rants:
- On the Tlalakans' attack: 'The rebels have come to us to be destroyed! Let's oblige them immediately!'

Witty Put-Downs:
- Bumblebee to Seaspray, on his chances of wooing Alana: 'Dream on, bubble-brain!'

- Megatron, to the planet's Decepticon overlord: 'Keep your synthesizer shut!' He later calls Astrotrain a 'sponge'.

Roll Call:
Autobots: Seaspray, Bumblebee, Optimus Prime, Perceptor and Cosmos.

Decepticons: Dirge, Soundwave, Astrotrain, Megatron, Laserbeak and Rumble.

Data File: Alan Oppenheimer (voices, including Warpath, Beachcomber and Seaspray)
Alan Oppenheimer's acting career spans over six decades. On television he was Dr Rudy Wells in *The Six Million Dollar Man* and Ralph's father in *Happy Days*, and had guest roles in shows such as *Hogan's Heroes*, *Get Smart* and *Star Trek: Deep Space Nine*. On the silver screen, he appeared in films such as *Westworld* (Michael Crichton, 1973), *Freaky Friday* (Gary Nelson, 1976) and *Private Benjamin* (Howard Zeff, 1980). As a voice actor, he was the title character in *Mighty Mouse*, the Narrator in *The NeverEnding Story* (Wolfgang Petersen, 1984) and Skeletor, Man-at-Arms and Mer-Man in *He-Man and the Masters of the Universe*.

Review:
An odd episode that's all over the place tonally. On the one hand there are serious scenes of Decepticons whipping a disobedient slave girl, Seaspray risking his life for the woman he loves, and a strong underlying moral message (basically, don't judge by appearances). On the other side of the coin, there is a comedy Decepticon overseer who likes the sound of his own voice, a scene in which Bumblebee tries water-skiing with hilarious results, and best of all a moment where Rumble falls into the Well of Transformation and becomes a tree!

Overall, an episode that is big in concept and heart, but very rough around the edges. 2/5

{2-34} TRIPLE TAKEOVER
Production number: 700-49 (34th episode produced of Season Two)
Transmission date: 19 November 1985 (36th episode transmitted of Season Two)

Written by Larry Strauss

Plot:
Fed up with Megatron's leadership of the Decepticons, the two Triple-Changers Blitzwing and Astrotrain lure him into a trap, then assume joint command.

Astrotrain's stint in charge is initially successful – he converts a number of railway trains into remote-controlled drones, then uses them to tap the city's oil and gas pipelines and create Energon cubes.

Elsewhere, Blitzwing sets up a base in a football stadium, fortifying the entrance with an impenetrable maze so that no Autobot can get to him. He also begins shelling the city with long-range bombs.

After a promising start, it soon begins to unravel for the would-be usurpers. Astrotrain's drones malfunction, rupturing a water main and flooding the city. Blitzwing, meanwhile, comes under attack from Devastator.

Matters are further complicated when Megatron frees himself and makes a bee-line for the two traitors. He is able to reassert his authority, and normality is resumed.

Spotlight: Trail-blazing
Whenever Optimus Prime transforms into truck cab form, his trailer rolls into shot from off-camera and completes the vehicle mode. Likewise, when he returns to robot form, the trailer uncouples and wheels away, out of the picture.

This implies that, whenever Prime is in robot mode, his trailer is always lurking just out of shot, ready to enter the frame and reattach whenever called upon. The problem, however, is that Optimus Prime can summon his trailer even when he shouldn't be able to – it spontaneously appears in caves, inside buildings and even on alien planets.

Prime isn't the only Autobot who seems to lose and gain parts in unlikely places – Omega Supreme also demonstrates this ability. His robot arms can separate and form a space rocket – but when the rocket arrives at its destination, the rest of him appears out of nowhere and combines with the rocket to form the full robot mode.

It's possible that, as with those Transformers who change their mass when converting between modes (see the Spotlight entry under {2-27} 'Make Tracks' for more on this), Prime and Omega have the ability to teleport their unwanted parts into another dimension, for instantaneous retrieval as necessary.

Megatron's Rants:
- 'Megatron has no fear!'
- 'I am Decepticon leader, you are … recyclable.'

Witty Put-downs:
- Blitzwing discusses Starscream in less-than-glowing terms: 'He's been trying to dethrone Megatron for years! He's a failure!'
- Astrotrain also has a crack: 'No planet ever lost its orbit underestimating the stupidity of Starscream!'
- Megatron joins in the abuse: 'You have failed again Starscream!' And later: 'You are either lying, or stupid.' Starscream's reply: 'I'm stupid! I'm stupid!'
- Optimus Prime jumps on the bandwagon: 'You and Starscream are just a nuisance – a couple of metallic mosquitos!'
- Starscream gets his own back: 'Megatron is a wimp!'

Roll Call:
Autobots: Hoist, Tracks, Bluestreak, Skids, Prowl, Powerglide, Smokescreen, Optimus Prime, Ironhide and Trailbreaker.

Decepticons: Blitzwing, Astrotrain, Starscream, Megatron, Scrapper, Scavenger, Long Haul, Mixmaster, Bonecrusher, Hook, Thrust, Thundercracker, Ramjet, Dirge and Devastator.

Other: Spike.

Review:
The overthrow of Megatron is played entirely for laughs in a delightful episode full of Decepticons squabbling, fighting and double-crossing each other. The only real

negative is that the Autobots also feature – their perfunctory scenes do nothing other than interrupt the flow of the hilarious Decepticon action. 4/5

{2-35} PRIME TARGET
Production number: 700-50 (35th episode produced of Season Two)
Transmission date: 14 November 1985 (34th episode transmitted of Season Two)

Written by Flint Dille and Buzz Dixon

Plot:
Hunter and collector Lord Chumley steals an experimental aircraft from the Soviets, sparking tensions between East and West. His next target: the head of Optimus Prime.

To aid in his endeavour, Chumley successfully captures a number of Autobots and challenges Optimus Prime to rescue them. Prime approaches Chumley's castle, which is laden with various traps, monsters and weapons. Matters are further worsened when two Decepticons arrive on the scene.

Despite these hazards, Optimus Prime makes his way through the castle and rescues his fellow Autobots. Chumley and the experimental plane are delivered to the USSR.

Megatron's Rants:
- 'We shall finish off the Autobots once and for all!'

Witty Put-Downs:
- Starscream to Megatron, on the subject of Chumley's recent successes: 'He's done more in two days than you have in two years!'
- Chumley: 'Drat! Outsmarted by a lorry! I am disgraced!'
- Chumley to his manservant, Dinsmore: 'Decepticons! Trust them to spoil the hunt.' 'Yes sir, just like the Humane Society, in a way.'
- Optimus Prime, after Blitzwing falls foul of one of Chumley's traps: 'Amazing! A booby-trap that actually catches boobies!'

Roll Call:
Autobots: Tracks, Bumblebee, Blaster, Grapple, Beachcomber, Jazz, Optimus Prime, Inferno, Windcharger, Huffer, Hoist, Warpath, Ironhide, Cosmos, Mirage, Prowl, Bluestreak, Ratchet, Wheeljack, Trailbreaker, Sideswipe and Sunstreaker.

Decepticons: Blitzwing, Astrotrain, Megatron and Starscream.

Review:
The third out-and-out comedy in four episodes, this is, yet again, an absolute hoot. Lord Chumley is a brilliant creation, and gets the lion's share of the good lines. The Autobots are also great fun here, especially during the scene where they're caught watching a cheesy daytime soap opera. 5/5

{2-36} AUTO-BOP
Production number: 700-51 (36th episode produced of Season Two)
Transmission date: 13 November 1985 (33rd episode transmitted of Season Two)

Written by David Wise

Plot:
Things are very strange in New York City: Raoul (see {2-27} 'Make Tracks') is attacked by a street-gang whose members include a smartly-dressed businessman wielding a ray-gun; a subway driver sabotages his own train; and a housewife is amongst those working on a building site where a new and ominous-looking skyscraper is taking shape.

Investigating these events, Raoul, Tracks and Blaster determine that a popular nightclub, Dancitron, is the source of all the weirdness. It is controlled by the Decepticons, and they are using the music and light-show to hypnotise late-night revellers.

Blaster and Soundwave confront each other on the dance floor, the two cassette-player Transformers fighting each other with sonic blasts. Blaster is able to amplify his attacks using some of the nightclub's speakers, and the force of his blasts is so strong that Dancitron is utterly demolished.

Witty Put-Downs:
• Blaster, to Soundwave: 'You poor excuse for a sound system!'

Roll Call:
Autobots: Tracks and Blaster

Decepticons: Starscream, Soundwave and Megatron.

Other: Raoul.

Review:
An okay episode, its standing boosted by the long-awaited Blaster versus Soundwave showdown. Although some of the nightclub scenes are quite funny, it doesn't quite hang together, and a few plot points are left unresolved. 2/5

{2-37} THE SEARCH FOR ALPHA TRION
Production number: 700-52 (37th episode produced of Season Two)
Transmission date: 12 November 1985 (32nd episode transmitted of Season Two)

Written by Beth Bornstein

Plot:
A group of female Transformers storm the Decepticon base on Cybertron, and make off with a stack of Energon cubes. Shockwave calls on some reinforcements from Earth, and together the Decepticons are able to capture the female Autobot leader, Elita One. Using her as bait, the Decepticons lure Optimus Prime to Cybertron and into a trap. About to be executed, Prime is saved by Elita One, who has the power to freeze time. As the Decepticons stand motionless, Prime and Elita make their escape.

Using her special power leaves Elita One seriously drained and on the verge of death. Optimus Prime takes her to the wise old Autobot Alpha Trion, who is able to save her life.

The combined forces of the male and female Autobots are more than a match for the Decepticons, who are forced to retreat.

Spotlight: Female Transformers
This episode is notable for the first appearance of female Transformers in any medium. Despite the fact that (according to the Marvel comics, at least) Transformers are asexual alien robots, there are some valid reasons why gender exists amongst the Autobots ranks.

In the cartoon, the Autobots were built by the Quintessons as slave-bots – unsurprisingly then, they were created in male and female variants so as to 'fit in' with the alien species who bought them. In the comics, meanwhile, the Transformers were all male until Optimus Prime built the female Autobot Arcee in a misguided attempt to placate human feminist groups ([54.2] 'Prime's Rib').

In both media, the depiction of female Transformers is the same – they have thinner, curvier bodies than their male counterparts, and generally have lighter, pastel colour schemes (the two main female Autobots – Arcee and Elita One – are both pink).

At this point in the history of the franchise, female Transformers characters appeared only in the supporting media, and went completely unrepresented in the toy aisles. Although an Arcee toy was mooted in the mid-1980s, it wasn't until the release of Minerva in 1988 that an actual female Transformers toy was produced (albeit as a Japanese exclusive).

Megatron's Rants:
- 'You'll surrender immediately! If you ever want to see Elita One again … you have two Earth hours to make up your mind!'

Witty Put-Downs:
- Starscream: 'How quaint – the girls have come to rescue their boyfriends!'

Roll Call:
Autobots: **Elita One**, **Alpha Trion**, Optimus Prime, Cliffjumper, Powerglide, Inferno, Ironhide, Perceptor and Bumblebee.

Other, one-off Autobots include the female warriors Firestar, Chromia and Moonracer.

Decepticons: Shockwave, Astrotrain, Starscream, Rumble and Ramjet.

Data File: Paul Eiding (voices, including Perceptor)
Actor Paul Eiding boasts a lengthy CV, including live-action parts in shows such as *ER*, *The West Wing*, *CSI: Miami* and *Star Trek: The Next Generation*. As a voice artist, he plays Colonel Roy Campbell in the *Metal Gear Solid* video game series and is the narrator of the *Diablo* video game franchise. In television animation, he provides the voice of Max Tennyson, grandfather of the titular *Ben 10*.

Data File: Marlene Aragon (Elita One)
Marlene Aragon's other voice credits include the roles of Synergy in *Jem and the Holograms* and Cheetah in *Challenge of the Superfriends*. She also provided voices for *The Kwicky Koala Show* and *The Fonz and the Happy Days Gang*.

Review:
An exciting action/adventure episode, which makes full use of its Cybertronian setting. There's some neat foreshadowing here, setting up events of {2-42} 'War Dawn'; and the introduction of some rather different Autobots, such as the female Elita One and the wizened old Alpha Trion, adds a bit of variety to the mix. 3/5

{2-38} THE GIRL WHO LOVED POWERGLIDE
Production number: 700-53 (38th episode produced of Season Two)
Transmission date: 18 November 1985 (35th episode transmitted of Season Two)

Written by David Wise

Plot:
Astoria Carlton-Ritz, a spoilt young heiress, is the subject of a Decepticon kidnapping attempt. She is rescued by Powerglide, and is immediately smitten with the Autobot.

En route to Autobot HQ, the Decepticons attack again, and this time successfully abduct Astoria. Megatron believes she possesses a secret formula with which he can create Energon from the Earth's electromagnetic field.

Powerglide arrives at Megatron's flying platform base and, with Astoria's help, sends it plummeting into the Decepticons' undersea headquarters.

Megatron's Rants:
- 'Excellent! As soon as I find out what that girl knows, we can turn the Earth's electromagnetic field into raw Energon!'
- 'Attention Decepticons! This is Megatron! Your new orders are – uh – clean up this mess!'

Witty Put-Downs:
- Powerglide's new nickname for the enemy faction: 'Decepti-goons!'
- Megatron's withering dismissal of his minions: 'You are supposed to be the most powerful jets in the galaxy, and you were beaten by a pipsqueak Autobot plane?'
- Powerglide, to Astoria: 'You're a real pain in the afterburners, you know that?'
- Astoria, to the Decepticons: 'Let me go, you dirtbags! I hope your solenoids rot!' And later: 'Go blow a circuit, man!'

Roll Call:
Autobots: Powerglide, Optimus Prime, Ratchet, Wheeljack and Ironhide.

Decepticons: Ramjet, Thrust, Dirge, Megatron, Scrapper, Scavenger, Bonecrusher, Long Haul, Mixmaster, Hook, Soundwave and Rumble.

Other: Sparkplug, Spike.

Data File: Michael Chain (voices, including Powerglide and Hoist)
Although his contribution to *The Transformers* was all voice work, Michael Chain is best known as a writer. He supplied scripts for cartoons such as *Police Academy: The Series*, *Punky Brewster* and *She-Ra: Princess of Power*. He was head writer and story editor on the animated series *Rambo: The Force of Freedom*.

Review:
A silly idea on paper, but the finished product works extremely well, thanks to a tight script, some brilliant voice work and, as with all the best episodes, a wicked sense of humour. The mind-probe scene and Megatron's reaction to the sky-platform crashing into the Decepticon base are both priceless. 4/5

{2-39} HOIST GOES HOLLYWOOD
Production number: 700-54 (39th episode produced of Season Two)
Transmission date: 21 November 1985 (38th episode transmitted of Season Two)

Written by Earl Kress

Plot:
While on a drive with Spike and Carly, Hoist saves two movie stuntmen from falling to their deaths after an action scene goes horribly wrong. The director is so impressed by Hoist's exploits that he agrees to hire the Autobots as actors in the film.

Meanwhile, Dirge is transporting some stolen Autobot technology and crashes into the studio's swamp set. The Decepticons manage to retrieve him, but are caught on camera. Megatron orders a return to the film set in a bid to destroy the incriminating footage.

Spike and Carly find the tape, and are pursued by the Decepticons across the studio – through cave and jungle sets, and past animatronic dinosaurs. Megatron finally gives up the chase when Spike and Carly appear to be boiled in lava – in reality a special effect.

Megatron's Rants:
- 'This could be the ultimate weapon in defeating the Autobots!'

Witty Put-Downs:
- Megatron, to Starscream: 'Insolent pile of scrap iron!'
- 'Those are Decepticons!' says Spike, stating the obvious. Carly's sarcastic reply: 'Brilliant deduction, Sherlock!'

Roll Call:
Autobots: Hoist, Tracks, Warpath, Sunstreaker, Powerglide and Wheeljack.

Decepticons: Dirge, Starscream, Megatron, Astrotrain, Ramjet, Thrust, Soundwave and Rumble.

Other: Spike and Carly.

Data File: Margaret Loesch (executive producer)
Margaret Loesch worked her way up through the ranks at ABC, NBC and Hanna-Barbera before moving to Marvel Productions, for whom she oversaw the production of *The Transformers* and other toy tie-in cartoons. Since then, she has worked for Fox Kids and the Jim Henson Television Group. Consequently she boasts an impressive array of credits, on series such as *The New Scooby and Scrappy-Doo Show*, *The Smurfs*, *Muppet Babies* and *Fraggle Rock*. As CEO of the Hub Network, she again became

involved in the Transformers franchise, overseeing the production of *Transformers: Prime* (2010-14).

Data File: Arlene Banas (voices, including Carly)
Arlene Banas had roles in numerous live-action shows, including *Dynasty*, *Falcon Crest*, *Beauty and the Beast* and *Freddy's Nightmares*. Her voice work includes roles in *Street Fighter II: The Animated Movie* (Gisaburo Sugii, 1994) and *Codename: Robotech* (Robert V Barron, 1985).

Review:
An utterly ridiculous premise, milked for comedy gold. The Decepticons are as stupid and unthreatening as they ever get, but the laughs more than make up for the lack of peril. *The Transformers* goes sitcom. 4/5

{2-40} THE KEY TO VECTOR SIGMA, Part One
Production number: 700-55 (40th episode produced of Season Two)
Transmission date: 25 November 1985 (39th episode transmitted of Season Two)

Written by David Wise

Plot:
When an Autobot convoy evades an attack by the Decepticon planes by hiding in a tunnel, Megatron is determined to redress the balance and create some Decepticon car Transformers. Though their bodies are easily created, these new Stunticons lack personality or intelligence.

The Decepticons travel to Cybertron and seek out Vector Sigma, the computer that gave life to the Transformers. After stealing the computer's key from Alpha Trion, Megatron successfully imbues his new troops with minds of their own.

The Stunticons return to Earth and attack a military base that guards a new super-fuel. Seeing the driverless cars, the panicked soldiers naturally assume that the Autobots have turned against them ...

Spotlight: Combiners
The idea of combining robots was nothing new or innovative when introduced to the Transformers range in its second year. Some of the earliest examples came in episodes of Japanese animated series *Mighty Atom* (1963), which occasionally featured giant robots who could split into smaller individual components. So far as live-action productions were concerned, the first combiner robot was King Joe from the series *Ultra Seven* (1967). It wasn't until the early 1980s, though, that combiners became a mainstay of the Japanese robot scene. *Space Emperor God Sigma* (1980) was a series that featured a number of smaller humanoid robots that could combine into a larger one. Later examples included *Beast King GoLion* (1981) and *Armoured Fleet Dairugger XV* (1982), both of which were repackaged in the West as *Voltron: Defender of the Universe* (1984).

Megatron's Rants:
Megatron's proclamations are often used as info-dumps, explaining an episode's plot, and here we have some classic examples:

- 'Good work, Rumble! Now I will turn these cars into machines of total destruction!'
- 'To rule the roads, my Stunticons must have independently-functioning personalities of their own – and there is one place in the entire galaxy where they can receive them: Cybertron!'
- 'Yes! The mega-computer deep in the core of Cybertron which gave us all life!'
- 'The key to Vector Sigma! We're ready to give my Stunticons life!'

Witty Put-Downs:
- Megatron, on the Autobots: 'Motorised morons!'
- Optimus Prime goads Megatron: 'Frankly, I don't think you've got the guts!'

Roll Call:
Autobots: Optimus Prime, Prowl, Smokescreen, Warpath, Ratchet, Ironhide, Hoist, Omega Supreme, Blaster, Wheeljack, and Alpha Trion.

Decepticons: Megatron, Ramjet, Thrust, Dirge, Rumble, Soundwave, **Motormaster**, **Drag Strip**, **Dead End**, **Breakdown**, **Wildrider**, Shockwave, Ravage.

Data File: John Stephenson (voices, including Thundercracker, Alpha Trion and Kup)
Boasting an acting career dating back to the 1950s, John Stephenson appeared in numerous classic television shows, including *The Man from U.N.C.L.E.*, *The Lone Ranger*, *Perry Mason* and *I Love Lucy*. His many voice-only roles included Lazy Luke in *Wacky Races*, Fancy-Fancy in *Top Cat*, and Mr Slate in *The Flintstones*.

Data File: Terry McGovern (voices, including Wildrider)
Originally a radio DJ, Terry McGovern was a friend of director George Lucas, and had parts in a number of the latter's films, including *THX 1138* (1971), *American Graffiti* (1973) and, in an uncredited voice artist capacity, in *Star Wars* (1977), for which he coined the term 'Wookiee'. Other film work included roles in *The Enforcer* (James Fargo, 1976), *InnerSpace* (Joe Dante, 1987) and *Mrs. Doubtfire* (Chris Columbus, 1993). On the small screen, he had parts in shows such as *Happy Days*, *Mork & Mindy* and *The A-Team*. His other voice work includes the role of Launchpad McQuack in *DuckTales* and contributions to *Darkwing Duck* and many video games, including *The Walking Dead*, *The Sims: Superstar* and *Star Wars: Rogue Squadron*.

Review:
One of those rare occasions where Megatron's dastardly plan is actually quite clever, this is an action-packed adventure that bounds along at a good pace. As the introductory story for the Stunticons and Vector Sigma, it is an 'important' episode in the history of the show. Fortunately then, it's also a good one. 4/5.

{2-41} THE KEY TO VECTOR SIGMA, Part Two
Production number: 700-56 (41st episode produced of Season Two)
Transmission date: 26 November 1985 (40th episode transmitted of Season Two)

Written by David Wise

Plot:

In a bid to match the might of the Stunticons, the Autobots build their own new team – a squadron of jets known as the Aerialbots. Although Megatron still has Vector Sigma's key, Alpha Trion activates the computer by merging with it, thereby enabling Optimus Prime to give life to his new creations.

The Autobots return to Earth, but Omega Supreme sustains some damage and is on the verge of death. Furthermore, the new Aerialbots are aloof and argumentative, and want nothing to do with Earth or the Autobot cause. The Autobots travel to the military base and are able to reassure the base commander that they were not responsible for the fuel theft.

Meanwhile, Megatron has made an amazing discovery: Vector Sigma's key has the ability to turn organic matter into metal. He sets about converting America into a metal wasteland.

The Autobots show up, and are on the verge of defeat until the Aerialbots, who have had a change of heart, arrive on the scene. It transpires that the Stunticon and Aerialbot teams are combiners, and they do battle as giant gestalt robots, named Menasor and Superion respectively.

The battle of the behemoths is closely matched until the arrival of Omega Supreme, whose injuries have been repaired. The two massive Autobots are more than a match for Menasor, and Megatron orders a retreat. The key to Vector Sigma is destroyed.

Megatron's Rants:

- 'On this world, the key to Vector Sigma de-energises matter, turning it into metal! Why, I have the power to transform Earth into another Cybertron! We begin … now!'

Witty Put-Downs:

- Motormaster calls Slingshot a 'little runt.'
- Megatron calls Soundwave a 'clumsy fool.'

Roll Call:

Autobots: Optimus Prime, Alpha Trion, Blaster, Ironhide, Hoist, Ratchet, Wheeljack, **Silverbolt, Air Raid, Fireflight, Skydive, Slingshot**, Omega Supreme, Prowl, Jazz, Bluestreak, Smokescreen, Tracks and **Superion.**

Decepticons: Shockwave, Megatron, Soundwave, Rumble, Motormaster, Breakdown, Drag Strip, Dead End, Wildrider and **Menasor.**

Other: the Narrator and Sparkplug.

Data File: Jeff MacKay (voices, including Fireflight)

Jeff MacKay's television roles included parts in *Battlestar Galactica*, *Kung-Fu: The Legend Continues* and *Diagnosis Murder*. He also had a recurring role in *JAG* as Big Bud Roberts, but is best-known as Mac, Magnum's friend in *Magnum, P.I.*. His film career was modest, but included a role in the multi-Oscar-winning film *All the President's Men* (Alan J Pakula, 1976).

PART THREE: THE CARTOON SERIES

Review:
Finally, a two-parter where both instalments are equally good. On top of the great action set-pieces – Menasor versus Superion and Omega Supreme is an all-time classic Transformers fight – the episode also finds time to include a decent subplot, as Silverbolt overcomes his fear of heights and successfully convinces his fellow Aerialbots to join the rest of the Autobots in battle. 4/5

{2-42} WAR DAWN
Production number: 700-58 (43rd episode produced of Season Two)
Transmission date: 25 December 1985 (44th episode transmitted of Season Two)

Written by David Wise

NB: The 42nd episode produced in Season Two was {2-47} 'Aerial Assault'. However, as that instalment features the yet-to-be-created Combaticons, it has been shifted further down the list in order to achieve a 'best viewing order'.

Plot:
The Autobots travel to Cybertron in order to investigate some strange energy readings. The naïve young Aerialbots are also present; they still do not realise how evil the Decepticons truly are.

Megatron takes advantage of their trusting nature and lures them into a time-machine trap, sending them nine million years into Cybertron's past, to a time when the Autobot/Decepticon war was just beginning.

The Aerialbots meet the young Autobots Orion Pax and Ariel, who are heavily damaged by Megatron and his new Decepticon army. Fortunately, however, a young Alpha Trion is able to rebuild the two fallen Autobots into Optimus Prime and Elita One.

In the present, the Autobots are able to gain access to Megatron's time machine and retrieve the lost Aerialbots.

Spotlight: Repeat Performance
Season Two of *The Transformers* initially ran continuously from September 1985 to January 1986, five days a week. However, after {2-41} 'The Key to Vector Sigma, Part Two' in late November 1985, the remainder consisted of a handful of new episodes mixed in with a large number of repeats. Consequently the last few episodes have irregular broadcast dates; on some occasions a whole week would pass with no new ones. However, there was no break in transmission, the reruns filling in the gaps.

Megatron's Rants:
- 'So long as the Aerialbots live, my supremacy of the skies is threatened!'
- 'A time machine! I plan to use it to travel to the past, to steal energy from the era before the war, when Cybertron had plenty of power. But now, it will make a perfect trap for these miserable Aerialbots!'
- 'They'll be trapped forever in eternal nothingness, before the galaxy ever existed!'

Witty Put-Downs:
- Ironhide's not so keen on these new Aerialbots, calling them 'little twerps.'

Roll Call:
Autobots: Silverbolt, Air Raid, Fireflight, Skydive, Slingshot, Ironhide, Optimus Prime, Wheeljack, Ratchet, Omega Supreme, Elita One (in her previous guise as Ariel) and Alpha Trion.

Decepticons: Starscream, Skywarp, Thundercracker, Megatron, Soundwave and Shockwave.

Optimus Prime appears here both in his familiar body and as his previous incarnation, Orion Pax. Other notable characters seen in this episode include Dion, Megatron's drones and the Guardians (who look much like blue versions of Omega Supreme).

Data File: Rob Paulsen (voices, including Slingshot and Air Raid)
Legendary voice actor Rob Paulsen is best known for his role as Raphael in the original incarnation of *Teenage Mutant Ninja Turtles*, and also voiced Rude Dog in *Rude Dog and the Dweebs*, Jim Carrey's character Stanley Ipkiss in the animated version of *The Mask*, Pinky in *Animaniacs* and its spin-off *Pinky and the Brain* and Throttle in *Biker Mice from Mars*, to name just a few. His film work includes the role of Eric in *The Little Mermaid II: Return to the Sea* (Jim Kammerud and Brian Smith, 2000). His voice can also be heard in a number of advertisements, most notably the famous 'Got Milk?' ad campaign.

Data File: Samantha Newark (voices)
London-born actress and singer Samantha Newark will forever be associated with the title role in the '80s animated series *Jem and the Holograms*, and had a cameo role in its live-action film adaptation (Jon M Chu, 2015). She also voiced Peter Pan's mother in the film *Hook* (Steven Spielberg, 1991). As a musician, she has a couple of solo albums to her name, and co-wrote the song 'Deeper' for the chart-topping German group Fragma.

Review:
Another epic from the pen of David Wise, this episode gives us a glimpse of Golden-Age Cybertron, the beginnings of the war, and of course Optimus Prime's origins. The script deftly cuts between battles and action scenes nine million years apart, yet never feels complicated or cluttered. 5/5

{2-43} TRANS-EUROPE EXPRESS
Production number: 700-59 (44th episode produced of Season Two)
Transmission date: 23 December 1985 (43rd episode transmitted of Season Two)

Written by David Wise

Plot:
The Autobots are taking part in a charity race from Paris to Istanbul; their main rival for victory is expert race driver Augie Cahnay, whose own vehicle contains a new high-tech alloy.

Meanwhile, the Decepticons are digging for the legendary Pearl of Bahoudin, which is actually a Decepticon weather-control device that crashed in Turkey when their ship was wrecked four million years ago (as seen in {2-18} 'Microbots').

The Pearl is dangerously unstable outside of its protective casing, so Megatron steals Augie's car so that he can take advantage of its super-alloy to control the Pearl's power.

The Autobots race to Megatron's location – and, by doing so, win the race. The Pearl is activated, creating powerful electrical storms and tornadoes. Bumblebee, however, manages to destroy the Pearl and save the day.

Megatron's Rants:
- 'In a few moments, the Pearl of Bahoudin – and mastery of this entire planet – will be mine!'
- 'I shall be master of the very elements! Hahahahah! And, of the planet Earth itself!'
- 'We'll wait in our undersea headquarters, while the storm wipes humanity off the face of the Earth!'

Witty Put-Downs:
- Dead End calls the Autobots 'Auto-bozos'
- Bumblebee calls the Decepticon leader 'Mega-mouth'.
- Tracks isn't impressed by the Pearl of Bahoudin: 'Cooking up another sleazy scheme, eh, Megatron? What's that? Something the Easter Bunny brought you?'

Roll Call:
Autobots: Bluestreak, Bumblebee, Tracks, Wheeljack, Smokescreen, Sunstreaker and Sideswipe.

Decepticons: Soundwave, Megatron, Rumble, Scrapper, Scavenger, Breakdown, Wildrider, Motormaster, Drag Strip, Dead End and Menasor.

Data File: Ron Gans (Drag Drip)
Perhaps best known for providing the voice of Armus, the alien who killed regular character Tasha Yar in *Star Trek: The Next Generation*, Ron Gans appeared in shows such as *Perry Mason*, *Lost in Space* and *Quincy, M.E.*. Other voice credits include *Welcome to Pooh Corner*, *Pryde of the X-Men* and *Captain Planet and the Planeteers*. He also did many voice-overs for film trailers, including a radio spot for *Halloween* (John Carpenter, 1978).

Data File: Rege Cordic (voices, including Menasor)
Originally a disc jockey, Rege Cordic later moved into acting, appearing in episodes of *The Monkees*, *Gunsmoke* and *The Dukes of Hazzard*. He had an uncredited cameo role in the movie *Sleeper* (Woody Allen, 1973). As a voice actor, he can be heard in episodes of *The Scooby-Doo/Dynomutt Hour*, *Spider-Man* and *Challenge of the GoBots*.

Review:
Another good episode, made up of two seemingly disparate storylines – the race, and Megatron's hunt for the Pearl – that neatly tie up together at the end. As well as some taut, effective plotting, this episode also benefits from having a good variety of locations and action sequences. 4/5

{2-44} COSMIC RUST
Production number: 700-60 (45th episode produced of Season Two)
Transmission date: 26 December 1985 (45th episode transmitted of Season Two)

Written by Paul Davids

Plot:
The Decepticons explore a deserted planet, where they discover an ancient energy weapon, a 'lightning bug'. *En route* back to Earth, they are struck by an asteroid inhabited by 'cosmic rust' germs – a debilitating disease deadly to robot life.

Megatron is infected by the cosmic rust and so kidnaps Perceptor, who has recently perfected a compound called 'corrostop', an anti-corrosion agent and only cure for cosmic rust. Megatron heals himself, and infects Perceptor and through him the remainder of the Autobots.

The Autobots are initially unable to cure themselves – they have run out of an ingredient vital to production of corrostop. However, they recall that the Statue of Liberty has recently been coated with the compound, and after taking a sample, they use a matter duplicator to mass-produce the substance and cure themselves.

Megatron's Rants:
- 'How ironic! The Autobots will be destroyed by a device *they* created!'

Witty Put-Downs:
- Starscream, after Megatron becomes infected: 'Perhaps you are made of shoddy materials!'
- Megatron, after infecting the Autobots: 'Rust in peace, Prime!'

Roll Call:
Autobots: Perceptor, Silverbolt, Slingshot, Skydive, Air Raid, Fireflight, Optimus Prime, Mirage, Wheeljack, Ratchet, Red Alert, Ironhide, Bumblebee, Gears, Cosmos, Blaster, Inferno, Powerglide, Tracks, Hound, Beachcomber, Hoist, Trailbreaker, Sideswipe, Sunstreaker, Prowl, Jazz, Smokescreen and Superion.

Decepticons: Astrotrain, Rumble, Starscream, Megatron, Motormaster, Dead End, Breakdown, Drag Strip, Wildrider, Blitzwing, Dirge, Ramjet, Laserbeak and Menasor.

Other: Spike, Carly and Sparkplug.

Data File: Frank Welker (voices, including Megatron and Soundwave)
Frank Welker is one of the best voice actors in the business, with credits both iconic and numerous. He was the voice of Fred in *Scooby-Doo*, of Dr Claw in *Inspector Gadget* and of Ray in *The Real Ghostbusters*. He also voiced Soundwave, Galvatron and Shockwave in the 21st Century live-action Transformers movies, directed by Michael Bay. As well as voices, he excels at animal vocalisations, as demonstrated in films such as *Jumanji* (Joe Johnston, 1995), *Aladdin* (Ron Clements and John Musker, 1992) and *Gremlins* (Joe Dante, 1984). A study published in 2011 showed that Welker had acted in movies with a combined gross of over USD\$6 billion (a record), beating Samuel L Jackson (USD\$5.2 billion) and Tom Hanks (USD\$4.4 billion) into second and third place respectively.

Data File: Denise Mora (voices)
Mora's only other acting credit is for a role in the low-budget horror movie *Beasties* (Paul Contreras, 1989).

Review:
A fun little story, with an intriguing premise. Megatron's reaction to getting the cosmic rust plague is brilliantly funny, but on the whole the plot is just a tad too obvious. Perceptor creating an anti-corrosive agent just before the Autobots get infected by an alien rust plague is one of the most convenient coincidences in the history of the franchise. 3/5

{2-45} STARSCREAM'S BRIGADE
Production number: 700-61 (46th episode produced of Season Two)
Transmission date: 7 January 1986 (47th episode transmitted of Season Two)

Written by Michael Charles Hill

Plot:
Starscream makes an attempt to overthrow Megatron as Decepticon leader, but fails. Starscream is banished to the island of Guadalcanal, where he constructs his own troops, the Combaticons, using personality components stolen from a Decepticon prison on Cybertron.

Starscream and his new troops wage a campaign of evil, targeting Autobots and Decepticons alike. In a final battle, it is revealed that the Combaticons are a combiner team, and they force Megatron to declare Starscream the new leader. However, the Stunticons arrive on the scene and blast the Combaticons. Megatron reasserts his authority, and banishes Starscream again, this time to a small asteroid in deep space.

Spotlight: Size Matters (Part Two)
As toys, a lot of Transformers are horribly out of scale with each other. For example, the Air Raid and Starscream figures both transform into representations of an F-15 jet, yet Air Raid is a much smaller toy. Inferno's fire-engine mode is, in toy form, around the same size as the Octane figure, which is a Boeing 767 passenger jet. Robot modes can be a problem, too. In the comics and cartoon, Blaster is depicted as a regular-sized Autobot, yet his toy incarnation is one of the biggest in the range.

The Combaticons, introduced in this episode, take the issue to extremes – Blast Off and Swindle are identically-sized characters (both on-screen and in their toy incarnations), yet one is a space shuttle and the other a Jeep.

For one section of Transformers fandom, this issue can be a deal-breaker – sometimes even the best of toys can lose sales if they don't scale well or fit in with existing collections.

Megatron's Rants:
- 'The Autobots! Now they've really done it! They've gone too far this time! I shall crush them once and for all!'

Witty Put-Downs:
- Megatron: 'You're a fool, Starscream, if you think that anyone will ever follow your orders!'
- Starscream, to Skywarp and Thundercracker: 'You microchip morons!'
- Megatron thinks Optimus Prime has gone mad: 'Are Prime's microchips messed up?'

- Megatron, after Starscream's Combaticons fail to get the best of him: 'I see incompetence breeds even more incompetence!'
- Megatron again: 'Starscream is a child! Even with an army of thousands he couldn't lead them in a parade, let alone against us!'

Roll Call:
Autobots: Jazz, Cliffjumper, Gears, Bumblebee, Optimus Prime, Tracks, Powerglide, Brawn, Warpath, Ironhide, Prowl, Grapple and Ratchet.

Decepticons: Megatron, Starscream, Soundwave, Dirge, Ramjet, Thrust, Astrotrain, Laserbeak, Thundercracker, Skywarp, **Onslaught**, **Brawl**, **Blast Off**, **Swindle**, **Vortex**, Shockwave, Reflector, Rumble, Bonecrusher, Scavenger, Hook, Mixmaster, Long Haul, Scrapper, Drag Strip, Breakdown, Motormaster, Devastator, **Bruticus**, Wildrider, Dead End and Menasor.

Data File: Tony St James (voices, including Brawl and Blot)
Best known as a disc jockey, Tony St James also provided voice-overs for many commercials, including for Coors Extra Gold. His other credits include the animated show *Jem and the Holograms*.

Data File: S Marc Jordan (voices, including Onslaught)
Jordan had roles in a number of popular television series, such as *Hill Street Blues*, *The A-Team*, *Night Court* (where he played the recurring character Jack Griffin), *Seinfeld* and *Babylon 5*.

Review:
The Transformers cartoon is at its best when it focuses on its two best creations, Megatron and Starscream. This episode is no exception, and their sniping and bickering throughout are a delight to behold. The introduction of the new Combaticons is handled quite well, but Starscream's power-play is the main focus, and the episode is all the better for it. 4/5

{2-46} THE REVENGE OF BRUTICUS
Production number: 700-62 (47th episode produced of Season Two)
Transmission date: 8 January 1986 (48th episode transmitted of Season Two)

Written by Larry Strauss

Plot:
Starscream and the Combaticons escape their asteroid prison and travel to Cybertron. There, the Combaticons take over the planet and rig the space bridge to alter Earth's orbit, sending it toward the Sun. Starscream sends Megatron a message – accept him as leader or see the Earth destroyed.

Back on Earth, the Insecticons are running amok. Even worse, they have damaged the space bridge, preventing anyone from travelling to Cybertron and stopping the Combaticons. The Autobots and Decepticons join forces to repair the space bridge, then travel to Cybertron and defeat the Combaticons. Starscream's help in incapacitating the Combaticons is appreciated by Megatron, who invites him to rejoin the Decepticons' ranks.

Megatron's Rants:
- 'Once we finish reprogramming Bruticus to obey only me, we will be unstoppable! Hahaha!'

Witty Put-Downs:
- Starscream, to the Combaticons: 'You're all military morons! Anything is better than being stranded with you idiots!'
- Starscream calls Megatron 'Mega-bum.'

Roll Call:
Autobots: Tracks, Optimus Prime, Prowl, Sideswipe, **Hot Spot**, **Blades**, **First Aid**, **Groove**, **Streetwise**, Perceptor, Powerglide, Ratchet, Inferno, Red Alert and Sunstreaker.

Decepticons: Starscream, Onslaught, Swindle, Brawl, Vortex, Blast Off, Shockwave, Bruticus, Shrapnel, Bombshell, Kickback, Megatron, Thundercracker, Dirge, Ramjet and Skywarp.

Other: Spike.

Data File: Milt Jamin (voices, including Blast Off)
Also sometimes credited as Milton James, Jamin has had live-action parts in *Battlestar Galactica*, *Hill Street Blues*, *Babylon 5*, and *Law & Order: Criminal Intent*, amongst others. Much of his voice work has been in English-language dubs of overseas productions, including *Nikita*, *Macross Plus* and *Ghost in the Shell*. He often performs voices for video games, and can be heard in *Neverwinter Nights 2*, *Mafia II* and *Grand Theft Auto V*.

Review:
Another fine episode, full of delicious treachery and back-stabbing – Starscream betrays Megatron, the Combaticons betray Starscream, then Megatron teams up with the Autobots only to betray them too. 4/5

{2-47} AERIAL ASSAULT
Production number: 700-57 (42nd episode produced of Season Two)
Transmission date: 10 December 1985 (41st episode transmitted of Season Two)

Written by Douglas Booth

NB: As discussed in the entry for {2-42} 'War Dawn' above, this episode, although made and transmitted earlier in the season, features the Combaticons, who weren't created until the {2-45} 'Starscream's Brigade'/{2-46} 'The Revenge of Bruticus' two-parter. Chronologically, then, it is better placed here.

Plot:
The Aerialbots are in the Middle East, investigating the theft of a number of aeroplanes in the region. After an altercation with the Combaticons, Slingshot and Skydive decide

to go undercover and pretend to be Earth jets in a bid to ascertain who the crooks are.

A gang led by a man named Ali are the culprits – Ali is in league with Megatron, supplying him with the stolen planes in exchange for world domination. Megatron plans to turn the aircraft into unmanned drone warriors and take control of the Middle East's oil wells.

The Aerialbots arrive on the scene and, helped by a local kid, Hassan, are able to defeat the Combaticons and force Megatron into retreat. It later transpires that Hassan is the deposed Prince Jumal, who reclaims his crown, having previously been overthrown by Ali and the Decepticons.

Witty Put-Downs:
- Ali calls Hassan a 'Runny-nosed bazaar brat!'

Roll Call:
Autobots: Silverbolt, Air Raid, Fireflight, Slingshot, Sky Dive, Hoist, Jazz, Optimus Prime, Ratchet and Superion.

Decepticons: Swindle, Onslaught, Brawl, Vortex, Dirge, Blast Off, Megatron, Ramjet, Rumble, Frenzy and Bruticus.

Data File: Douglas Booth (writer)
Booth boasts a long career as a cartoon writer and producer. His many credits include *Spider-Man and His Amazing Friends*, *He-Man and the Masters of the Universe*, *Challenge of the GoBots* and *Teenage Mutant Ninja Turtles*.

Data File: Charlie Adler (voices, including Silverbolt)
A prolific voice actor, Adler has brought life to a great many animated characters, including Spike in *My Little Pony*, Eric Raymond in *Jem and the Holograms*, Deputy Fuzz and Tex Hex in *BraveStarr*, Buster Bunny in *Tiny Toon Adventures*, and both title characters in *Cow & Chicken*. For the silver screen, he provided voices in the films *The Little Mermaid* (Ron Clements and John Musker, 1989), *Cool World* (Ralph Bakshi, 1992) and *The Rugrats Movie* (Igor Kovalyov and Norton Virgien, 1998). Since the '90s he has also worked as a voice director, on shows such as *Bratz*, *Rugrats* and *The Wild Thornberrys*. He returned to the Transformers franchise in 2007, voicing Starscream in the live-action *Transformers* (Michael Bay, 2007) and its sequels.

Review:
Megatron is stealing vehicles to convert into drone warriors. The Autobots team up with a plucky young mechanic who helps save the day … yes, this is a blatant rehash of {2-27} 'Make Tracks', with none of that episode's sparkle. On the plus side, the Arabian setting makes for an interesting change, and the new Aerialbot and Combaticon teams get some welcome focus. 2/5

{2-48} MASQUERADE
Production number: 700-63 (48th episode produced of Season Two)
Transmission date: 16 December 1985 (42nd episode transmitted of Season Two)

Written by Donald F Glut

Plot:

Megatron is building a new energy weapon but needs three more components in order to complete it. He sends the Stunticons to steal the missing parts.

The Autobots, meanwhile, track the Stunticons' movements before moving in to attack them. The Stunticons are captured and placed in cells in Autobot HQ. Optimus Prime decides to disguise five Autobots as Stunticons and then infiltrate the Decepticons.

The Autobots enter the Decepticon camp unchallenged, but their ruse is eventually discovered when the real Stunticons escape and arrive on the scene. Megatron attempts to use his new energy weapon on the Autobots but it proves unstable, short-circuiting after only a few blasts. The Decepticons retreat.

Spotlight: Toei

For the majority of the first two seasons of *The Transformers*, the animation was produced by a company called Toei Animation (known as Toei Doga until 1998). This is a subsidiary of the Toei Company, a major film and television production and distribution corporation based in Japan. They are well known for their work on a number of Japanese anime series such as *Digimon* and long-running franchises such as *Sailor Moon* and *Dragonball*. Until the late '80s they also animated cartoon shows for Western companies, including the original *Teenage Mutant Ninja Turtles*, *The Real Ghostbusters*, *Inspector Gadget* and *The Jetsons*. Through their partnership with Sunbow, they worked on a number of cartoons based on Hasbro toy franchises, such as *Jem and the Holograms*, *Robotix*, *G.I. Joe: A Real American Hero* and of course *The Transformers*.

Megatron's Rants:

- 'It is complete! The most destructive weapon known to Decepticon science!'
- 'It will fire the most destructive ray of all, more powerful than any laser! It will create a chain reaction in whatever it touches, producing instantaneous destruction! Imagine my turning that ray on the Autobots' headquarters! Perhaps with it gone, someone will put up a memorial parking lot! Hahahahah!'

Witty Put-Downs:

- Motormaster goads Optimus Prime: 'Well, look who's here: the *old* king of the road! When I'm finished with you, you'll be king of the junkyard!'

Roll Call:

Autobots: Ironhide, Ratchet, Optimus Prime, Wheeljack, Bumblebee, Hoist, Inferno, Grapple, Blaster, Warpath, Tracks, Bluestreak, Hound, Sideswipe, Windcharger, Mirage, Trailbreaker, Prowl and Huffer.

Decepticons: Megatron, Motormaster, Breakdown, Dead End, Drag Strip, Wildrider, Starscream, Soundwave, Laserbeak, Hook, Scavenger, Mixmaster, Scrapper, Long Haul and Menasor.

Other: Spike.

Data File: Philip L Clarke (voices, including Dead End and Tantrum)

Philip L Clarke provided voices for many productions over the years. TV credits include *Scooby-Doo and Scrappy-Doo*, *Challenge of the GoBots* and *The Pirates of Dark Water*. His films include *The Little Mermaid* (Ron Clements and John Musker, 1989), *An American Tail: Fievel Goes West* (Phil Nibbelink and Simon Wells, 1991) and *Beauty and the Beast* (Gary Trousdale and Kirk Wise, 1991). His video game credits include *Tenchu 2: Birth of the Stealth Assassins*, and *Doom³*, in which he played the key villain, Dr Malcolm Betruger.

Review:
A solid enough episode. Megatron's villainous scheme is a little unoriginal, but the central premise of Autobots posing as Decepticons is quite appealing. 3/5

{2-49} B.O.T.
Production number: 700-64 (49th episode produced of Season Two)
Transmission date: 9 January 1986 (49th episode transmitted of Season Two)

Written by Earl Kress

Plot:
When the rest of the Combaticons are dismembered during a battle with Defensor, Swindle decides to sell his team-mates' body parts to a foreign dictator. Megatron, understandably annoyed, installs a bomb in Swindle's head, which will detonate if the Combaticon cannot rebuild his team-mates in time.

Brawl's personality component falls into the possession of a trio of students, who are building a home-made robot named B.O.T. for a science fair. After installing the component, B.O.T. goes on the rampage and attacks a number of Autobots. Eventually, Swindle is able to retrieve the personality component and rebuild the rest of the Combaticons.

Megatron is planning to use a new super-gun to blast the moon, then use the resulting tidal energy as a power source. The science fair kids overhear Megatron's scheming, and inform the Autobots.

The Autobots are in danger of losing the battle, but are saved when the kids use the remote-controlled B.O.T. to sabotage Megatron's giant gun.

Megatron's Rants:
- 'Once we have blasted the Earth's moon out of orbit, we will be able to control the tides with Soundwave's new device! Then we will flood the canyon, creating a nearly limitless power!'

Roll Call:
Autobots: **Defensor**, Hot Spot, Blades, First Aid, Groove, Streetwise, Gears, Optimus Prime, Bumblebee, Ironhide, Bluestreak, Prowl and Wheeljack.

Decepticons: Onslaught, Blast Off, Brawl, Swindle, Vortex, Bruticus, Astrotrain, Megatron, Skywarp, Starscream, Soundwave, Thundercracker, Ramjet.

Data File: Johnny Haymer (voices, including Swindle, Vortex and Highbrow)
Haymer has numerous acting credits to his name, but he's best remembered as the recurring character Sgt Zelmo Zale in twenty episodes of *M*A*S*H*. Other television

credits include *The Wild Wild West*, *Star Trek*, *Cagney & Lacey* and *Airwolf*. His film work includes parts in *Logan's Run* (Michael Anderson, 1976), *Annie Hall* (Woody Allen, 1977) and ... *And Justice For All* (Norman Jewison, 1979). Voice-only roles include parts in *Alvin & the Chipmunks*, *DuckTales*, and *G.I. Joe: A Real American Hero*.

Review:
The subplot, in which Swindle sells the body parts of his fellow Combaticons and then is forced to get them back, is quite fun. Unfortunately the main story – a trio of bratty kids foil Megatron's latest hare-brained scheme – is far less successful. 2/5

Credits: Season Two
NB: Two different sets of end credits were used during Season Two, with only minor differences in the copyright notices at the very end of the sequence.

- Supervising Producer: Nelson Shin
- Producers: George Singer, John Walker, Gwen Wetzler
- Production Coordinator: Paul Davids
- Director of Production: Jim Graziano
- Supervising Director: Terry Lennon
- Directors: Norm McCabe, Bob Shellhorn, Karen Peterson, Bob Kirk, Bob Treat, Tom Ray, Margaret Nichols, Bob Matz, Al Kouzel, Andy Kim
- Production Manager: Yung Shin
- Story Editors: Dick Robbins, Bryce Malek
- Additional Dialogue by: Ron Friedman
- Voice Director: Wally Burr
- Voice Talents of: Jack Angel, Arlene Banas, Michael Bell, Gregg Berger, Arthur Burghardt, Corey Burton, Michael Chain, Scatman Crothers, Peter Cullen, Bud Davis, Walker Edmiston, Paul Eiding, Ed Gilbert, Dan Gilvezan, Michael Horton, Buster Jones, Victor Caroli, Casey Kasem, Chris Latta, Morgan Lofting, Don Messick, Mike McConnohie, Allen Oppenheimer, Hal Rayle, Peter Reneday, Clive Revill, Neil Ross, Ken Sansom, John Stephenson, Frank Welker
- Voice Processing: Scott Brownlee, Wally Burr Recording
- Storyboard by: Peter Chung, Gregg Davidson, George Goode, Doug Lefler, Gerald Moeller, David Russell, David Shin, Roy Shishido, Vincenzo Tripetti, Wendall Washer
- Model and Background Design by: Floro Dery, Gabriel Hoyos, Dell Barras, Fred Carrillo, Romeo Tanghal, Pat Agnasin, Romeo Francisco
- Color Models: Phyllis Craig
- Key Backgrounds: Dennis Venizelos, Bob Schaffer, Phil Philipson
- Supervising Editor: Robert T Gillis
- Music Editors: Joe Siracusa, Mark Shiney, Peter Collier
- Sound Effects Editors: Richard Gannon, Jim Blodgett, Michael L DePatie, Nicholas James, Efraim Reuveni, Bruce Elliott, Michael Tomack, John Detra, Ron Fedele, Allison Cobb
- Sunbow Productions:
- Associate Producers: Flint Dille, Roger Slifer
- Production Manager: Carol Weitzman

- Production Assistant: Terri Gruskin
- Creative Director: Jay Bacal
- ©1985 Sunbow Productions Inc
- Distributed by: Claster TV Productions, a division of Hasbro Industries (early Season Two)/Sunbow Productions International (late Season Two)
- © 1984 Hasbro Industries Inc. All rights reserved. Trademark of Hasbro Industries Inc and is registered in the US Patent and Trademark Office (early Season Two)/Hasbro, Inc © 1985 Hasbro Industries Inc. All rights reserved. Trademark of Hasbro Industries Inc and is registered in the US Patent and Trademark Office (late Season Two)
- Title Song by: Ford Kinder and Ann Bryant
- Music Composed and Conducted by: Johnny Douglas, Rob Walsh
- Executive in Charge of Production: Lee Gunther
- Executive Producers: Joe Bacal, Margaret Loesch, Tom Griffin
- Sunbow Productions
- Marvel Productions Ltd, a Cadence Company

{3-00} *THE TRANSFORMERS: THE MOVIE*
Theatrical release date: 8 August 1986 (USA); 5 December 1986 (UK).

Directed by Nelson Shin
Written by Ron Friedman
Story Consultant: Flint Dille

Tagline: 'Beyond good. Beyond evil. Beyond your wildest imagination.'

Plot:
It is the year 2005. Since the events of Season Two, the Decepticons have reconquered the planet Cybertron; the Autobots are based in a city on Earth, and also have secret bases on two of Cybertron's moons, where plans are afoot to retake the planet.

The Autobots make a shuttle run to Earth, to collect a shipment of Energon that will prove vital in their efforts to oust the Decepticons; however, the Decepticons become aware of the launch and commandeer the shuttle, planning to use it as a 'Trojan horse' allowing them entry into the heart of Autobot City: Earth.

Fortunately, the young Autobot Hot Rod notices that the approaching shuttle is damaged, thus alerting everyone that the Decepticons are aboard. A massive and (metaphorically) bloody battle breaks out between the two factions, during which a number of Transformers on both sides are killed or maimed.

Optimus Prime and Megatron confront each other and agree to hand-to-hand combat, in which 'one shall stand, one shall fall.' In the event, the fight is so ferocious that both leaders are heavily damaged. Megatron's fall prompts the Decepticons to retreat, ending the battle.

The Decepticons flee to Cybertron aboard the Decepticon space shuttle, Astrotrain. However, the combined mass of the Decepticon army is proving a drain on his fuel. Starscream recommends jettisoning into space the injured and dying – a category that includes Megatron.

These abandoned Decepticons drift through space until they come near a planet,

Unicron. Unicron is actually sentient, and sustains himself by destroying and eating other planets. Unicron's one weakness is the Matrix of Leadership, a glowing talisman that is safeguarded by Autobot leaders. Unicron completely rebuilds Megatron and his fallen troops into a new, powerful army, whose singular mission is to destroy the Matrix – Unicron's only barrier to an attack on Cybertron.

The rebuilt Megatron, now called Galvatron, returns to Cybertron and assassinates Starscream, then leads the Decepticons for another attack on the Autobots' city on Earth – this time with the aim of destroying the Matrix.

On Earth, Optimus Prime dies of his wounds, but passes the Matrix to his chosen successor, an Autobot warrior named Ultra Magnus. When the Decepticons attack Earth, the Autobots flee in their ships and head out into space.

Ultra Magnus's ship lands on the planet Junkion, home to a strange robot species, the Junkions, led by the idiosyncratic Wreck-Gar, who base their lives and speech patterns around television broadcasts from Earth. Galvatron attacks the planet and has Ultra Magnus killed. Now in possession of the Matrix, he plans to use it against Unicron and usurp his new master.

Another fleeing Autobot shuttle, containing Hot Rod, Kup and the Dinobots, crash-lands on the planet Quintessa, home to the Quintessons, who get amusement from staging 'show trials' of captured aliens, then killing their captives regardless whether they are found guilty or innocent.

Hot Rod and Kup are tried in one such kangaroo court, but are rescued by the Dinobots and Wheelie, another young Autobot who has been living on the planet. Together, they escape Quintessa and rendezvous with their fellow Autobots on Junkion. There, the native Junkions are able to rebuild Ultra Magnus, and a combined force of Autobots and Junkions head to Cybertron, where Unicron has already 'eaten' the two moons that were home to Autobot bases.

Galvatron attempts to use the Matrix against Unicron, but he is unable to activate it. In response, Unicron transforms into a giant planet-sized robot, swallows Galvatron whole, and begins attacking Cybertron. There he is confronted by the Autobot and Junkion ships; one of these craft is crewed by Hot Rod, Kup, Springer, Arcee and Daniel – the young son of Spike, who was on one of the destroyed moonbases. This ship crashes through one of Unicron's eyes, and its occupants find themselves within the belly of the beast.

Daniel becomes separated from the rest of the group, and finds himself in a room where living beings – occupants of the planets and moons devoured by Unicron – are being dropped one by one into an acid-like substance. Daniel is able to destroy the mechanism seconds before his father is due to be killed.

Hot Rod has also become separated from his comrades, and comes face to face with Galvatron. The two do battle, but Galvatron's superior strength is too much for Hot Rod, who is weakened and near defeat. At that moment, however, Hot Rod makes a grab for the Matrix, and is able to activate it. Its energies transform him into Rodimus Prime, the new Autobot leader. He throws Galvatron through a wall and out into space. He then uses the power of the Matrix to destroy Unicron from within. The assorted Autobots trapped inside the giant robot manage to escape just in time as Unicron explodes.

The Autobots return to Cybertron and begin the rebuilding process, reinvigorated by their courageous new leader.

Production:

After the more-or-less instant success of the Transformers brand in 1984, it was decided fairly early on that an animated movie would be produced to cash in. *The Transformers: The Movie* went into production concurrently with Season Two of the animated cartoon, which is why some characters introduced late in that season – including Omega Supreme, the Aerialbots and the Stunticons – do not feature.

Translating a pre-existing cartoon and/or toy franchise into a feature film was a popular move in the mid-'80s, probably prompted by the runaway success of *The Care Bears Movie* (Arna Selznik, 1985), which made a profit of over thirty million US dollars at the box office – and that's before home video sales and rentals are taken into account, or indeed the spike in sales of Care Bears merchandise that followed. Other such theatrical releases pre-dating *The Transformers: The Movie* included *Rainbow Brite and the Star Stealer* (Bernard Dyriés and Kimio Yabuki, 1985), *He-Man and She-Ra: The Secret of the Sword* (Ed Friedman et al., 1985) and *GoBots: Battle of the Rock Lords* (Ray Patterson, 1986).

The animation was carried out by Sunbow's Japanese partners Toei, under the aegis of Nelson Shin. The budget of five million dollars was roughly equivalent to the cost of eighteen regular half-hour episodes of the cartoon. The voice recordings were completed in autumn 1985, and featured many famous names, including Leonard Nimoy, Judd Nelson, Eric Idle and, in his final role, Orson Welles.

Developing the script for the film proved problematic, not least because (according to Shin) Hasbro were dictating which characters should be killed off. From a toy point of view, Hasbro were using the movie as a means whereby new characters could be introduced and advertised, at the expense of older ones whose toys were being discontinued.

Writer Ron Friedman had a number of passes at writing a script – preliminary drafts were set just five (rather than nineteen) years in the future, and included many concepts that were eventually dropped, such as 'Ani-bots' (combining Autobots with animal modes) and 'life sparks' (Transformer souls). Another writer, Flint Dille, also had a lot of input, essentially taking over from Friedman and indeed performing the final rewrite. Friedman's contract stipulated that he should be given sole writer credit, so Dille was listed as a 'story consultant' only (although he is billed *before* Friedman in the opening titles of the film).

Many of the new characters featured in the movie were designed, devised and created especially for it; a complete departure from the normal procedure whereby the toys would be designed first, then named and given personalities by Bob Budiansky, the writer of the Marvel Comics series. Here, the toys were based on designs and personalities developed for the movie, so Budiansky had very little involvement – which is one of the reasons why many of these movie characters seldom appeared in the American comics.

Theme/Influences:

The film is clearly influenced by the *Star Wars* franchise, on a number of levels. For example, Arcee's head features circular bun-like designs over her ears, which seem to be a deliberate reference to the distinctive hairstyle sported by Carrie Fisher in her role as *Star Wars'* Princess Leia; Megatron wields an energy-dagger not unlike *Star Wars'* famous lightsabers; and the film's European cut opens with a similar crawler caption providing background information to the story.

Characters seem deliberately set up as analogies to *Star Wars* ones. Hot Rod is very much in the Luke Skywalker mould, starting out as an impetuous young hot-head and ending up as a wise and respected leader; Optimus Prime, his mentor who dies part-way through the action, clearly takes the Obi-Wan Kenobi role; while Springer is a conceptual match for Han Solo. Unicron – a planet that destroys other planets – is clearly based on *Star Wars'* Death Star. Indeed, the sci-fi spoof film *Spaceballs* (Mel Brooks, 1987) makes comment on this similarity, having its parody version of the Death Star (named Spaceball One), transform into a giant robot.

But both *Star Wars* and *The Transformers: The Movie* are informed by an even older common source – archetypes. In myths, legends and fiction, there are a number of common tropes that always seem to reoccur. The psychologist Carl Jung postulates that these archetypes are an innate part of the human psyche (the collective subconscious), and include familiar roles and ideas such as the Wise Old Man, the Hero, the Trickster, the Devil and the Apocalypse. Similar ideas were posited by scholar Joseph Campbell, whose seminal 1949 book *The Hero with a Thousand Faces* inspired George Lucas when he wrote *Star Wars*.

Campbell postulates that myths from all over the world share a fundamental structure, the 'monomyth'. In it, a hero from an 'ordinary' background goes on a great journey or quest, separated from his home, undergoes some sort of initiation, obtains a great gift (or 'boon'), and learns about himself in the process. In *The Transformers: The Movie*, Hot Rod is Campbell's 'ordinary hero' (his very first scene shows him on a fishing trip with Daniel), and the Matrix is both his boon, and also what Campbell calls the 'stolen elixir'. Hot Rod's adventure sees him go on an archetypal 'wonder journey' (through space and all sorts of bizarre alien landscapes), he is victim of an 'abduction' (by the Quintessons) and goes into the 'whale's belly' (inside Unicron).

Many other myths and stories follow the same basic structure, from those of Moses, Jesus, Buddha and King Arthur, through to more modern works such as *The Lord of The Rings*, *The Lion King* and the *Harry Potter* books.

There are other religious parallels here as well: Unicron, with his horns, beard and wings, is very Satanic-looking; and the fate of the Autobots – driven from their home land, persecuted and scattered across the universe – evokes the plight of the Jewish diaspora.

But while the Transformers movie follows a familiar structure, it does fold a number of other ingredients into the mix. Although dictated by Hasbro's edict to get rid of many of the older characters, one of its most notable aspects is its high body-count. For the first time the cartoon's history, well-known Transformers are seen to die – much-loved characters such as Optimus Prime, Wheeljack and Ironhide are mercilessly dispensed with. There was some consternation about this at the time – there are contemporary reports of children being reduced to tears by the film – and this prompted the addition at the end of some edits of a specially-recorded voice-over ('The greatest Autobot of them all, Optimus Prime, will return!') in an attempt to lessen the impact. As a result of this backlash, the planned death of the leading character Duke in *G.I. Joe: The Movie* – which was in production when *Transformers: The Movie* was released – was hastily revised.

In retrospect, however, the many deaths in *The Transformers: The Movie* do lend the film some extra gravitas. Although the reasoning behind it was pretty cynical (killing off characters whose toys were no longer on sale), it works in the film's favour. The general sense of foreboding and jeopardy is heightened when it becomes clear that, at any given time, characters could actually *die*.

The Music:

While animation usually ages very well, it's the incidental music of *The Transformers: The Movie* that immediately dates it to the mid-'80s. It's very much of-its-time, all synthesizers and driving drum beats. It's also quite loud; hardly a moment goes by without a keyboard riff or Fairlight flourish, leading some critics to comment that the production seems more akin to an extended music video than a film – and one can see their point. While the music might be intrusive, overbearing and irritating to some, fans of '80s AOR (adult-orientated rock) will applaud the catchy melodies and soaring crescendos that add to the film's 'retro' flavour. Whatever one's opinion, the music is inarguably one of the production's most memorable aspects.

The score was composed by Vince DiCola, the regular keyboardist for singer Frank Stallone, brother of the famous actor and director Sylvester Stallone. Through this connection, DiCola had been asked to contribute to the soundtrack of the film *Staying Alive* (Sylvester Stallone, 1983), and had so impressed with his work – which had included the memorable song 'Far From Over', a US top ten hit – that he had then been hired to provide the score for *Rocky IV* (Sylvester Stallone, 1985). He was a rising star in the film score business, hence it was somewhat of a coup when he agreed to provide the incidental music for *The Transformers: The Movie*.

DiCola's score has proved popular with Transformers fans, and after two convention-only releases, it finally saw a wider release in 2013, when it became volume 263 of Sony's Intrada soundtrack range. DiCola has also released a number of other Transformers-related albums, including *The Protoform Sessions*, consisting of edits, outtakes and alternative versions of music from the film, and *Artistic Transformations*, in which elements from the soundtrack are reinterpreted as a solo piano pieces.

In addition to the incidental music, seven rock songs feature in the film. These have been compiled and rereleased on numerous occasions, usually in conjunction with a selection of DiCola's pieces, most recently in 2007. The most famous of them are 'Dare' and 'The Touch', both performed by singer/songwriter Stan Bush, who has over a dozen albums to his name, and who also contributed songs to the soundtracks of *Kickboxer* (Mark DiSalle and David Worth, 1989) and *Bloodsport* (Newt Arnold, 1988).

Also featured in the film is 'Dare to be Stupid' by multi-platinum and Grammy Award-winning singer 'Weird Al' Yankovic, best-known for his parody songs (such as 'Eat It', a spoof of Michael Jackson's 'Beat It'). This was facilitated by the fact that Yankovic shared the same record label – Scotti Bros – as the film's soundtrack LP. Yankovic would go on to voice the character Wreck-Gar in the cartoon series *Transformers: Animated*.

Another band to contribute songs was Kick Axe, a well-supported Canadian heavy metal group – although, due to legal complications, they were credited as 'Spectre General'. They performed 'Hunger', later covered by King Kobra, and 'Nothing's Gonna Stand in My Way', itself a cover of a track by John Farnham.

The short-lived glam-metal group Lion, whose guitarist Doug Aldrich is a rock legend, having also been a member of the bands Dio and Whitesnake, contributed a rock version of the theme song to *The Transformers* cartoon; and N.R.G.'s 'Instruments of Destruction' was memorably played over a scene of Autobots being massacred.

The Cast:
This being a big-budget movie, a number of well-known actors filled out the cast, in tandem with the regular voice actors from the cartoon show.

Eric Idle (Wreck-Gar)
Idle gained international recognition as part of the Monty Python comedy group, with whom he appeared in films such as *Monty Python's Life of Brian* (Terry Jones, 1979). He also devised the sketch show *Rutland Weekend Television*, whose best-known characters were the Rutles – a Beatles parody group who also made appearances on the American comedy show *Saturday Night Live* and in a spin-off TV movie, *All You Need is Cash* (Eric Idle, Gary Weis, 1978). Other film work includes *Nuns on the Run* (Jonathan Lynn, 1990), *The Adventures of Baron Munchausen* (Terry Gilliam, 1988) and *Casper* (Brad Silberling, 1995). His voice work includes parts in *South Park: Bigger, Longer & Uncut* (Trey Parker, 1999), *102 Dalmatians* (Kevin Lima, 2000) and *Shrek the Third* (Chris Miller and Raman Hui, 2007).

Judd Nelson (Hot Rod/Rodimus Prime)
A huge star at the time *The Transformers: The Movie* was released, Judd Nelson was part of a collective of young actors dubbed 'the Brat Pack', coming to prominence in films such as *The Breakfast Club* (John Hughes, 1985) and *St Elmo's Fire* (Joel Schumacher, 1985). Since then, Nelson has built up quite a CV: television roles include parts in *Moonlighting*, *CSI: Crime Scene Investigation*, *Family Guy* and *Two and a Half Men*; his other film work includes *New Jack City* (Mario Van Peebles, 1991), *Airheads* (Michael Lehmann, 1994) and *Jay and Silent Bob Strike Back* (Kevin Smith, 2001). He later reprised his role as Rodimus Prime in the series *Transformers: Animated*.

Leonard Nimoy (Galvatron)
Nimoy was a familiar face for American television audiences in the '50s and '60s, guesting in shows such as *Wagon Train*, *The Outer Limits* and *The Man from U.N.C.L.E.* before winning the role that would make him a worldwide star – the half-Vulcan Mr Spock in *Star Trek* and its later feature-film spin-offs. After *Star Trek* was cancelled, he quickly found himself another regular part, playing the Great Paris in *Mission: Impossible*. He also found some success as a director, helming blockbuster movies such as *Star Trek IV: The Voyage Home* (1986) and *Three Men and a Baby* (1987). His other acting credits included parts in *Fringe*, *The Simpsons* and *Columbo*. He was also a noted writer, photographer and singer. His wife Susan Bay was the cousin of Michael Bay, and it was through that connection that he came to voice Sentinel Prime in *Transformers: Dark of the Moon* (Michael Bay, 2011). He died in 2015.

Robert Stack (Ultra Magnus)
As a young man, Robert Stack was a prodigious sportsman and set two world records in skeet (clay pigeon) shooting. After training to become an actor, he went on to a highly successful movie career, in films such as *The Mortal Storm* (Frank Borzage, 1940), where he appeared alongside James Stewart; *A Date with Judy* (Richard Thorpe, 1948), whose cast also included Elizabeth Taylor; the John Wayne vehicle *The High and the Mighty* (William A Wellman, 1954); and *Written on the Wind* (Douglas Sirk, 1956), for which he was nominated for a Best Supporting Actor Oscar. In later years he appeared in a number of comedies, including *Airplane!* (Jim Abrahams, David Zucker and Jerry

Zucker, 1980), *Caddyshack II* (Allan Arkush, 1988) and *BASEketball* (David Zucker, 1998). He is best remembered, however, for his appearances on the small screen: as the presenter of *Unsolved Mysteries*, and an unforgettable, Emmy-winning turn as Eliot Ness in *The Untouchables*.

Lionel Stander (Kup)
Stander's up-and-down acting career began in the 1920s, when he rubbed shoulders with the likes of Bing Crosby, Danny Kaye, Noël Coward and Bob Hope. His films included *The Scoundrel* (Ben Hecht and Charles McArthur, 1935), *Mr. Deeds Goes to Town* (Frank Capra, 1936) and *A Star is Born* (William A Wellman, 1937). A keen political activist and union man, he was a founding member of the Screen Actors Guild. In 1938 he was accused of being a Communist, and his roles began to dry up. He was called to testify before the House Un-American Activities Committee (HUAC) and subsequently blacklisted, despite a lack of evidence against him. His name besmirched, he moved to Europe, during which time he appeared in the spaghetti Western *Once Upon a Time in the West* (Sergio Leone, 1968). Stander eventually moved back to the USA, and took on the role with which he became synonymous, the butler Max in the television series *Hart to Hart*, for which he won a Golden Globe.

Orson Welles (Unicron)
Welles is a true legend of stage, screen and radio, and it's difficult to sum up his career in just a single paragraph. On the stage, he was founder of the Mercury Theatre company, and his productions included *Caesar* (1937); an adaptation of Shakespeare's *Macbeth* (1936) with an all-African-American cast and voodoo substituting for witchcraft; and *Chimes at Midnight* (1966). On the radio, he is best known for his adaptation of H G Wells' *The War of the Worlds*, which apparently panicked some listeners who mistook it for fact. He has been acclaimed by the British Film Institute and the American Film Institute as one of the best movie directors of all time, and his *Citizen Kane* (1941) is regarded as one of the best ever films. His other works include *The Magnificent Ambersons* (1942), *Touch of Evil* (1958) and, as an actor, *The Third Man* (Carol Reed, 1949) and *A Man for All Seasons* (Fred Zinnemann, 1966).

Release, Reception and Legacy:
Despite being based on an extremely popular franchise and boasting an excellent voice cast, *The Transformers: The Movie* was a box-office failure – it cost a reported five million dollars to make, but managed to recoup only around two point six million (domestic). It was also universally panned by critics. The general consensus was that it was loud, messy, uninspiring, and confusing for all but Transformers aficionados. The failure of both this and another Sunbow movie, *My Little Pony: The Movie*, resulted in a rethink for the studio – *G.I. Joe: The Movie* became a straight-to-video release, and a proposed film based on the *Jem and the Holograms* cartoon was scrapped altogether. After its poor performance in the USA, its UK release was postponed several times before finally, almost grudgingly, it was accorded a short theatrical run.

Although its reception was disappointing for many of the parties involved, *The Transformers: The Movie* has had a lasting legacy within the franchise, and to this day is one of the cornerstones of the entire Transformers phenomenon. Its influence was felt immediately: Season Three of *The Transformers* cartoon show would be set in its aftermath and would delve deeper into the stories of the Quintessons, Junkions and

Unicron himself. It was also a huge influence on the storyline of the UK comics; and although the American comics largely ignored it, a time-travelling Galvatron would eventually appear near the tail-end of their run.

Unicron was such an excellent villain that he has appeared in later iterations of the franchise, too, including *Transformers: Armada* and *Transformers: Prime*. The Matrix of Leadership, seen here for the first time, became such an integral part of the Transformers mythos that it was even a major plot point in *Transformers: Revenge of the Fallen* (Michael Bay, 2009).

Megatron's/Galvatron's Rants:

- 'When we slip by their early warning systems in their own shuttle, and destroy Autobot City, the Autobots will be vanquished forever!'
- 'Their defences are broken! Let the slaughter begin!'
- 'No! I'll crush you with my bare hands!'
- 'I'll rip out your optics!'
- 'I would've waited an eternity for this! It's over, Prime!'
- 'I have already crushed Optimus Prime with my bare hands … the point is, he's dead! And the Matrix died with him!'
- 'I will rip open Ultra Magnus, and every other Autobot, until the Matrix has been destroyed!'
- 'Cybertron and all its moons belong to me!'
- 'I, Galvatron, shall crush you, just as Megatron crushed Prime!'
- 'Ultra Magnus is dead, and the Matrix destroyed!'
- 'Unicron, my master – with this, I shall make you my slave!'
- 'Unicron, answer me! See this – the Matrix! I now possess that which you most fear! You will do my bidding, or taste my wrath!'
- 'First Prime, then Ultra Magnus and now you. It's a pity you Autobots die so easily or I might have a sense of satisfaction now!'

Witty Put-Downs:

- Ironhide calls the Decepticons both 'Decepti-chops' and 'Decepti-creeps'.
- Megatron: 'You're an idiot, Starscream!'
- Kup, after Hot Rod slams through a barrier: 'Turbo-revvin' young punk! I'll straighten ya out yet!'
- Blitzwing calls Hot Rod an 'Auto-brat'.
- Starscream, to the retreating Springer and Arcee: 'Pathetic fools! There's no escape!'
- Rumble smashes his way into the Autobot communication tower: 'First we crack the shell, then we crack the nuts inside!'
- Soundwave makes his case to be the Decepticon leader: 'Soundwave superior; Constructicons inferior'. The Constructicons beg to differ. Bonecrusher: 'Who are you calling inferior?' Hook: 'Nobody would follow an uncharismatic bore like you!'
- Unicron, to Megatron: 'The point is, you are a fool!'
- Hot Rod calls Grimlock 'A big bozo'. Twice.
- Scavenger calls Daniel a 'human germ'.
- Kup, on the Sharkticons: 'Cam-diggin' grill-crackin' things!'

Roll Call:
Autobots: Slag, Swoop, Sludge, Grimlock, Optimus Prime, Ironhide, Gears, Jazz, Cliffjumper, Bumblebee, Prowl, Brawn, Ratchet, **Hot Rod, Kup**, Huffer, Hound, Bluestreak, Sunstreaker, Perceptor, **Ultra Magnus**, **Springer**, **Arcee**, **Blurr**, Blaster, **Rewind, Eject, Ramhorn, Steeljaw**, Wheeljack, Windcharger, Grapple, Snarl, **Wreck-Gar, Wheelie** and **Rodimus Prime**.

Decepticons: Laserbeak, Thundercracker, Starscream, Shockwave, Soundwave, Megatron, Scavenger, Long Haul, Scrapper, Hook, Mixmaster, Bonecrusher, Dirge, Ramjet, Skywarp, Shrapnel, Blitzwing, Kickback, Reflector, Thrust, Rumble, Frenzy, Ravage, **Ratbat**, Devastator, Bombshell, Astrotrain, **Galvatron, Scourge** and **Cyclonus**.

Other: **Unicron, Kranix, Arblus**, the Narrator, Spike and **Daniel**.

Also seen are a number of unnamed Junkions, Sweeps, Lithionians, Sharkticons and Quintessons. The Autobot Inferno is listed in the end credits but makes no on-screen appearance.

Data File: Ron Friedman (writer)
The Emmy-nominated Ron Friedman has written over 700 hours of television going back to the mid '60s, on shows such as *My Favourite Martian*, *Bewitched*, *Happy Days*, *Charlie's Angels* and *The Dukes of Hazzard*. As well as scripting *The Transformers: The Movie*, he was the credited writer on *G.I. Joe: A Real American Hero: The Movie* (Don Jurwich, 1987).

Data File: Norm Alden (Kranix)
The Transformers: The Movie is Norm Alden's only contribution to the franchise. His biggest (and best) part was the title role in the award-winning *Andy* (Richard C Sarafian, 1965), in which he played a mentally handicapped man. His long career took in series such as *Leave It to Beaver*, *Batman*, *The A-Team* and *Dynasty*. His film work included parts in *Ed Wood* (Tim Burton, 1994), *They Live* (John Carpenter, 1988), *Everything You Always Wanted to Know About Sex but Were Afraid to Ask* (Woody Allen, 1972) and the Oscar-winning *Tora! Tora! Tora!* (Richard Fleischer, Toshio Masuda and Kinji Fukasaku, 1970). Modern audiences will probably know him best as café owner Lou in *Back to the Future* (Robert Zemeckis, 1985).

Review:
A film beloved by fans yet detested by critics. A fair assessment lies somewhere in between. Let's get the negatives out of the way first: the soundtrack is a great listen on CD, but when laid over the film it's loud, intrusive and overbearing. The plot meanders all over the place, the pace is uneven, and there are many scenes that contribute nothing to the story. The annoying kid character, Daniel, gets far too much screen time. More so than any episode of the regular cartoon, this is, to all intents and purposes, merely a toy commercial, with character deaths and introductions dictated by Hasbro.

So, what is there to enjoy here, other than simple nostalgia? Well, for one thing, it's very well made. The animation is generally good, the backgrounds amazingly so. Great use is made of light, shadow, colour and framing. Indeed, there is so much detail here that multiple rewatches are required to take it all in. From the little animated control panels to the robot fish of Quintessa, the Hollywood budget is certainly apparent on screen.

Yet again, the voice cast impresses greatly. There is a lot of clunky dialogue in the script (in amongst some really great lines, it must be said), but the quality of the acting makes it all palatable. Special mention must go to Corey Burton as Spike (the terror and panic in his voice when he is about to be dropped in a vat of acid are truly spine-chilling), but the rest of the cast are uniformly excellent also.

This is a well-produced, expertly-made animation with enough quotable lines, awesome imagery and iconic moments to ensure its cult status. It's almost painfully retro, and watching it inevitably brings forth warm feelings of nostalgia for those who were there to appreciate it the first time round. A guilty pleasure – just don't think about it too much. 4/5

Credits: *The Transformers: The Movie* **(selected)**

- A Sunbow and Marvel Production
- Starring: Eric Idle, Judd Nelson, Leonard Nimoy, Robert Stack, Lionel Stander and Orson Welles as 'Unicron'.
- Casting by Reuben Cannon & Associates, Carol Dudley
- Music Score by Vince DiCola
- Story Consultant: Flint Dille
- Written by Ron Friedman
- Executive Producers: Margaret Loesch and Lee Gunther
- Supervising Producer: Jay Bacal
- Produced by Joe Bacal and Tom Griffin
- Co-Produced and Directed by Nelson Shin
- Other Cast: Norm Alden, Jack Angel, Michael Bell, Gregg Berger, Susan Blu, Arthur Burghardt, Corey Burton, Roger C. Carmel, Victor Caroli, Rege Cordic, Peter Cullen, Scatman Crothers, Bud Davis, Walker Edmiston, Paul Eiding, Ed Gilbert, Dan Gilvezan, Buster Jones, Stan Jones, Casey Kasem, Chris Latta, David Mendenhall, Don Messick, John Moschitta, Hal Rayle, Clive Revill, Neil Ross, Frank Welker
- Voice Recording and Processing by Wally Burr Recording
- Voice Director: Wally Burr
- Sound Processing: Scott Brownlee
- Score Arranged and Produced by Vince DiCola and Ed Frugé
- Music Editor: Ed Frugé
- Executive in Charge of Production: Jim Graziano
- Senior Manager in Charge of Production: Carole Weitzman
- Production Managers: Gerald L Moeller, Koh Meguro, Satoru Nakamura, Tayuka Igarashi
- Executive Production Coordinator: Gene Pelc
- Production Staff: Mark Bakshi, Paul Davids, Yung Shin
- Original Concept Design: Floro Dery
- Character and Background Design: Fred Carillo, Rico Rival, Delfin Barras, Romeo Tanghal, Lew Ott, Romeo Francisco, Pat Agnasin, Ernie Guanlao, Eufronio R Cruz, Mike Sekowsky

- Supervising Animation Director: Kozo Morishita
- Animation Directors: John Patrick Freeman, Norm McCabe, Gerald L. Moeller, Bob Matz, Margaret Nichols
- Associate Story Consultants: Doug Booth, Roger Slifer
- Supervising Film Editor: Steven C Brown
- Film Editor: David Hankins
- Supervising Sound Effects Editor: Brian Courcier
- Dialogue Editor: Jerry Jacobson
- Main Title Design: Bill Millar, Deena Burkett
- Animated by Toei Animation Co, Ltd
- Associate Producers: Mashaharu Etoh, Tomoh Fukumoto
- Final Checker (Chief Animator): Koichi Tsunoda
- Special Effects: Masayuki Kawachi , Shoji Sato
- Background Art Direction: Robert Schaefer, Takao Sawada, Dario Campanile
- Chief Cameraman: Masatoshi Fukui
- © MCMLXXXVI Sunbow Productions, Inc
- © MCMLXXXVI Hasbro, Inc. All rights reserved.

THE TELEVISION SERIES: SEASON THREE

Season Three was a massive departure from what had gone before; instead of sticking to the tried-and-tested formula that had made Season Two so popular, Marvel and Sunbow made the decision to fast-forward twenty years and set the show in the future, in the immediate aftermath of *The Transformers: The Movie*.

Although there had been some off-world adventures in Season Two, Season Three was pure space opera, with episodes set all over the galaxy. Episodes set on Earth became far rarer.

To reflect the change in style and content, the title sequence was again updated, and radically so. Previously an orchestral piece, the theme tune was re-presented as a synth-pop number much more reflective of the futuristic setting. This also marked the point at which Nelson Shin's AKOM was animating the majority of the episodes, with Toei falling by the wayside.

The episodes were broadcast on weekdays between September 1986 and February 1987, interspersed with repeats using the Season Two opening sequence with Season Three music.

{3-01} FIVE FACES OF DARKNESS, Part One

Production number: 700-86 (1st episode produced of Season Three)
Transmission date: 15 September 1986 (1st episode transmitted of Season Three)

Written by Flint Dille

Plot:
The year is 2005. The Decepticons are licking their wounds following their defeat in {3-00} *The Transformers: The Movie*, and have relocated to the planet Chaar, where they are

suffering from an acute energy crisis – so much so that some of their number are barely able to transform. Meanwhile the triumphant Autobots are in a celebratory mood, participating in the Galactic Olympics.

Elsewhere, Blurr and Wheelie are sent on a mission to deliver a new transformation cog to Metroplex on Earth. Back at the games, an alien Skuxxoid sabotages the Olympic flame, sending smoke billowing out around the arena. With visibility poor, a spaceship lands in the vicinity and a group of shadowy attackers emerge. They are driven away, but when the smoke clears, it becomes apparent that Spike, Kup and Ultra Magnus have been kidnapped.

Meanwhile, a group of Decepticons arrive at Unicron's head, which is still in orbit around Cybertron. They use the sensors there to calculate the location of their missing leader, Galvatron.

Rodimus Prime concludes that the Decepticons are to blame for the attack on the Olympics, and so heads to Chaar to investigate, with Grimlock in tow. When he sees that the Decepticons are leaderless and down to their last reserves of power, Prime realises that the Decepticons can't have been the culprits.

While musing on this fact, Prime and Grimlock are spotted by the Decepticons, who close in for the kill …

Witty Put-Downs:
- Ultra Magnus, when he thinks that his leader is acting oddly: 'Rodimus is losing a few chips!'

Roll Call:
Autobots: Rodimus Prime, Kup, Arcee, Jazz, Bumblebee, Cliffjumper, Springer, Ultra Magnus, Blurr, Sludge, Perceptor, Slag, Wreck-Gar, Warpath, Wheelie, **Outback**, Blaster and Grimlock.

Decepticons: Astrotrain, Scrapper, Scavenger, Hook, Bonecrusher, Mixmaster, Long Haul, Devastator, Menasor, Motormaster, Dead End, Drag Strip, Breakdown, Wildrider, Bombshell, Kickback, Cyclonus, Scourge, Galvatron, Dirge, Ramjet, Onslaught, Blast Off, Soundwave, Rumble, **Octane**, **Tantrum** and Swindle.

Other: the Narrator, Spike, Daniel, Carly, **Abdul Fakkadi** and the Quintessons.

Spotlight: Carbombya
This story sees the debut of recurring character Abdul Fakkadi, ruler of the nation of Carbombya. He's a none-too-subtle parody of Colonel Gaddafi, who governed Libya at the time. As mentioned in the notes to [A2.2] 'To a Power Unknown', there were during the '80s a number of terrorist attacks attributed to Libya. So here we have a 'comedy' character based on a then-current dictator famous for his appalling human rights record and his support of terrorism. Sadly, the insensitivity on display here was okayed by numerous script editors, producers and executives, and was deemed fit for broadcast.

The one person who realised that the 'joke' was in poor taste was voice actor Casey Kasem (Bluestreak, Cliffjumper etc), who himself was of Arabic descent (his family was Lebanese). Kasem was a long-time campaigner for a fair and balanced portrayal of Arabs in American media, going on record to criticise popular films such as *Back to the Future* (Robert Zemeckis, 1985) and *The Black Stallion* (Carroll Ballard, 1979). He had no concerns about {2-47} 'Aerial Assault', on the other hand, because it featured both good *and* evil Arabian characters. Abdul Fakkadi (seen here and also in {3-11} 'Thief in the Night') proved a step too far, and prompted Kasem to quit the cast of *The Transformers*.

Thankfully, a letter of protest that Kasem sent to *The Transformers* Executive Producer Margaret Loesch was met with a warm response: 'I share your concerns. Your letter has been distributed to our writing staff and our voice directors in the hopes that they can be more sensitive to this issue and therefore more responsive to the problem.'

After {3-11} 'Thief in the Night', Abdul Fakkadi and Carbombya never appeared again.

Review:
Above all else, this looks really unprofessional. The quality of the animation is distinctly sub-par, and this is made doubly obvious by the reuse of some greatly superior footage taken from the movie, which sticks out like a sore thumb.

On the plus side, this is a decently-paced episode, with a lot going on – there's so much packed into these 22 minutes that the time seems to whizz by.

A fresh and breezy episode to set up this epic five-parter, marred by some horrible animation and editing. 3/5

{3-02} FIVE FACES OF DARKNESS, Part Two
Production number: 700-87 (2nd episode produced of Season Three)
Transmission date: 16 September 1986 (2nd episode transmitted of Season Three)

Written by Flint Dille

Plot:
The Decepticons attack Rodimus Prime and Grimlock. Despite their lack of power, by sheer force of numbers they are able to seriously damage Rodimus. Thankfully, Springer and Arcee arrive on the scene and rescue the pair.

The unconscious Rodimus Prime experiences a Matrix-induced vision in which the Quintessons feature prominently. Realising that they were behind the recent attack on the Olympics, Rodimus orders that they head to Quintessa.

Meanwhile, Cyclonus and Scourge find Galvatron and pull him free of a lava flow. Galvatron is quite mad, but as dangerously powerful as ever. He resumes his place as leader of the Decepticons.

On Quintessa, Ultra Magnus, Kup and Spike are about to be executed by Sharkticons when Springer's group shows up in the nick of time and saves them. The Quintessons flee their planet, having rigged it to explode – they reason that it's a price worth paying if it results in the destruction of Rodimus Prime and the Matrix.

Fortunately the Aerialbots are on hand to mount a rescue, and the Autobots prepare to leave Quintessa. However, at that moment, the planet explodes …

Galvatron's Rants:
• 'My empire of ash! My bastion of brimstone! My kingdom of desolation!'
• 'Decepticons! Your leader has returned! Long live the empire! Long live – ha ha ha ha ha ha – Galvatron! Ha ha ha ha ha!'

Witty Put-Downs:

- Quintesson: 'You are the Autobot called Kup; you are Cybertron's chief of security.' Kup: 'No, my name's Teaspoon, and I'm Cybertron's chief dishwasher.'
- Spike calls the Quintessons 'funky aliens'.

Roll Call:
Autobots: Bumblebee*, Ultra Magnus, Jazz*, Kup, Sludge*, Perceptor*, Slag*, Springer, Arcee, Wreck-Gar*, Cliffjumper*, Rodimus Prime, Blurr*, Wheelie*, Outback*, Grimlock, Optimus Prime (only as part of a dream sequence), Broadside, Skydive, Air Raid, Silverbolt, Silverbolt and Fireflight.

Decepticons: Astrotrain*, Bonecrusher*, Hook*, Scrapper*, Long Haul*, Scavenger*, Menasor*, Dead End, Breakdown, Wildrider, Motormaster, Drag Strip, Cyclonus, Scourge, Mixmaster*, Galvatron, Soundwave, Tantrum*, Swindle, Vortex, Blast Off, Rumble, Octane, Onslaught and Kickback.

Others: The Narrator, Daniel*, Spike, Carly*, Quintessons, and Unicron's head.

Characters marked with an asterisk (*) appear only as part of the recap of the previous episode.

Data File: Flint Dille (writer/story editor/associate producer/story consultant):
Dille began his career writing and producing animated television series such as *Bigfoot and the Muscle Machines*, *G.I. Joe: A Real American Hero* and *Inhumanoids*, and the theatrically-released *An American Tail: Fievel Goes West* (Phil Nibbelink and Simon Wells, 1991). His more recent work has concentrated on scripts for video games, including *Ghostbusters* (which reunited the original cast of the '80s feature films), *Diablo III* and *Wheelman* (whose voice cast included Vin Diesel).

Review:
Again, this is a fun, action-packed episode. The events on Quintessa are deliberately evocative of similar scenes in {3-00} *The Transformers: The Movie* – possibly overly so, as yet again a group of Autobots are captured by Quintessons, dropped into the Sharkticon pool and rescued at the last second.

The star of the show is Galvatron. Following his defeat in the movie and a lengthy sojourn at the bottom of a lava pool, he is now a raving lunatic, and his single scene here – he rants like a madman, turns on his own troops, then blasts an entire planet to dust – is both riveting and hilarious in equal measure. 3/5

{3-03} FIVE FACES OF DARKNESS, Part Three
Production number: 700-88 (3rd episode produced of Season Three)
Transmission date: 17 September 1986 (3rd episode transmitted of Season Three)

Written by Flint Dille

Plot:
The Autobots manage to escape the exploding planet just in time, but they are adrift in space. They float toward the planet Goo, the terrain of which is covered in a sticky ooze that traps them on the surface. To make matters worse, a giant drone vehicle is

sweeping the immediate area, sucking up the gunge and everything in it. Springer is caught in the machine's path, and is ground down into his constituent parts. However, Rodimus is able to disable the drone before it can cause further damage.

Meanwhile, Blurr and Wheelie are still heading back to Earth with the transformation cog. Their ship is destroyed by Galvatron in the vicinity of Jupiter, but the two Autobots are able to evacuate and crash-land on the moon Io. A group of menacing-looking alien creatures approach their position ...

The Quintessons travel to the Decepticon base on Chaar and offer them a deal, promising a supply of Energon cubes in exchange for attacking the Autobots stranded on Goo. Galvatron returns to Chaar to find the planet nearly deserted. Upon hearing that his troops are now following Quintesson orders, he vows to reclaim his leadership.

The Decepticons and Quintessons reach Goo, and begin shooting at the Autobots ...

Galvatron's Rants:
- 'Strike a blow for the honour of all Decepticons!'
- 'Bring me their heads as souvenirs!'
- 'Please meet your end with dignity; I despise whiners.'
- 'It's music! The symphony of destruction and the anthem of agony!'

Roll Call:
Autobots: Rodimus Prime, Grimlock, Springer, Arcee, Ultra Magnus, Kup, Optimus Prime (as a dream image)*, Silverbolt, Air Raid, Fireflight, Slingshot*, Skydive*, Broadside, Blurr, Wheelie, Blaster, Eject, and Bumblebee.

Aside from the recap, Fireflight's only other appearance in this episode is as a background character in the Decepticon camp. This is surely an animation error, so probably shouldn't count as a genuine appearance.

Decepticons: Cyclonus, Rumble, Soundwave, Breakdown, Swindle, Blast Off, Motormaster, Octane, Drag Strip, Vortex, Onslaught, Scourge, Galvatron, Blitzwing, Wildrider, Dead End, Hook, Scavenger, Mixmaster, Long Haul, Dirge, Astrotrain, Brawl, Bruticus, Shockwave and Shrapnel.

Bruticus, the combined form of the five Combaticons, actually appears in the same shot as the other Combaticons; so, as with Fireflight, his appearance must be a production mistake. Also appearing in this episode is a Seeker-type robot (i.e. the same body-type as Starscream), but bedecked in an unusual all-grey livery.

Other: the Narrator, Quintessons, Spike and **Marissa Faireborn**.

Characters marked with an asterisk (*) appear only as part of the recap of the previous episode.

Data File: Neil Ross (voices, including Springer, Slag and Bonecrusher)
London-born Neil Ross is best-known for his work as a narrator or announcer. He was heard in *Back to The Future Part II* (Robert Zemeckis, 1989), *Being John Malkovich* (Spike Jonze, 1999) and *Dick Tracy* (Warren Beatty, 1990). He also does a lot of voice work for video games, including the *Mass Effect* and *Metal Gear Solid* series. In animation, he has

had roles in series such *Galaxy High, Pinky and the Brain* and *Voltron*. He was the voice of the lead character Leoric in *Visionaries*, and Morocco Mole in *Secret Squirrel*.

Review:

The epitome of middle-episode filler, this third instalment of 'Five Faces of Darkness' does little to advance the plot – there are some nice space battles and some good lines, but there's a pervading sense that, story-wise, this is merely running on the spot.

The visuals are also quite frustrating – there are some lovely individual shots (the explosion in Jupiter's atmosphere, Galvatron and company travelling through the warp gate), but a number of obvious animation errors spoil things somewhat. 2/5

{3-04} FIVE FACES OF DARKNESS, Part Four

Production number: 700-89 (4th episode produced of Season Three)
Transmission date: 18 September 1986 (4th episode transmitted of Season Three)

Written by Flint Dille

Plot:

Galvatron arrives on Goo and questions why his troops are now following Quintesson orders. As the Decepticons argue over who exactly is in charge, this gives the Autobots an opportunity to escape: they contact Wreck-Gar for help, and he comes to the rescue in a spaceship.

On Io, Blurr and Wheelie are attacked by the native alien creatures, but are rescued by Marissa Faireborn, who has been monitoring their situation. Unfortunately, the creatures destroy Faireborn's ship, leaving the trio stranded.

Seeking answers to his questions, Rodimus Prime goes on a spiritual journey within the Matrix itself, and comes to understand the nature of the Transformer race, and why the Quintessons are so interested in them (see below).

Meanwhile, the duplicitous Quintessons form an alliance with the Decepticons and propose a two-pronged assault on Cybertron and Earth. The giant Decepticon Trypticon is unleashed upon the Earth, while on Cybertron the Decepticons render the Autobots helpless by sabotaging a power station, then move in for the kill …

Spotlight: Prepare to Meet Your Maker

This is the episode in which we discover the origin of the Transformers (at least, according to the cartoon; the comics had an entirely different take).

Cybertron was a factory planet, ruled by the Quintessons. The Transformers started out as mindless robots, sold across the galaxy. There were two main product lines: 'military hardware' and 'consumer goods'. Fed up with doing all the menial labour themselves, the Quintessons gave their robots artificial intelligence and – using them like slaves – tasked them with running the factory, while they themselves had the easy life as cruel overseers.

Not content with literally whipping the robots into shape, the Quintessons also used them for amusement, specifically in gladiatorial combat, where they would be forced to kill each other. Appalled at their slavery, the robots rose up against their masters, driving them from the planet.

There was peace for a time – however, the planet was still split into the two product lines, with different programming. While those robots built as 'consumer goods' (the

Autobots) wanted peace, the 'military hardware' ones (Decepticons) began a long war that decimated the planet. By way of tactical advantage, the Autobots developed the ability to transform into other modes. This advantage was soon nullified, however, when the Decepticons also re-engineered themselves with this ability. Thus, the Transformers were born!

Galvatron's Rants:
- 'Decepticons, learn the price of your disloyalty!
- 'You have forsaken the Decepticons' one true leader, and for your treachery, you will pay!'
- 'With your intellect and the strength of my Decepticons, we shall blast the Autobots and the humans off the map of the galaxy!'

Witty Put-Downs:
- Marissa Faireborn is unimpressed with Blurr: 'He ran right back into the danger! My digital watch is smarter than that!'
- Springer to Rodimus Prime: 'Wake up, you moron!'

Roll Call:
Autobots: Blurr, Wheelie, Rodimus Prime, Kup, Ultra Magnus, Grimlock, Arcee, Springer, Silverbolt, Broadside (recap only), Air Raid, Slag, Wreck-Gar, Blaster, Alpha Trion (flashback only), Optimus Prime (only as part of a vision), Perceptor, Cosmos, Fireflight, Skydive and Slingshot.

Decepticons: Galvatron, Soundwave, Astrotrain (recap only), Dirge (recap only), Shockwave, Blast Off, Ramjet, Blitzwing, Swindle, Dead End, Octane, Motormaster, Cyclonus, Scourge, Onslaught, Scrapper, Scavenger, Bonecrusher, Long Haul, Mixmaster, Hook, Megatron (flashback only), Vortex and **Trypticon**. Some of the Decepticons are drawn or coloured incorrectly, making positive identification difficult. Shockwave and Blitzwing, for example, are almost unrecognisable, and therefore it's debatable whether this counts as a valid appearance or not.

Other: the Narrator, the Quintessons, Marissa Faireborn and Spike.

Data File: John Moschitta, Jr (Blurr, Punch and Counterpunch)
Moschitta first came to fame in 1981 on an episode of *That's Incredible!*, where he demonstrated an amazing ability – he can speak up to 586 words per minute, and was credited in the *Guinness Book of World Records* as the World's Fastest Talker. This lead to a number of offers, including notable turns as the fast-talking voice of advertisements for FedEx and *Micro Machines*. His television roles included parts in *The A-Team*, *Sesame Street* and *Ally McBeal*. He also had a part in the film *Dick Tracy* (Warren Beatty, 1990). His voice-acting work includes parts in *Garfield and Friends*, *Adventure Time* and *Family Guy*. He reprised the part of Blurr in 2008, for the cartoon show *Transformers: Animated*.

Review:
After a rather laboured three-episode set-up, we finally get to the meat of the story, as the Decepticons attack Earth and Cybertron and – more importantly – we get the Transformers' origin story. It's really decent stuff, with the idea of the two 'product

types' neatly explaining why there are two factions, and on the whole it seems fitting that the Transformers had a noble origin, rising up against their enslavers to gain their freedom.

The animation is still quite poor, but when the episode otherwise hits its mark – as this one does – such annoyances become only minor quibbles. 4/5

{3-05} FIVE FACES OF DARKNESS, Part Five
Production number: 700-90 (5th episode produced of Season Three)
Transmission date: 19 September 1986 (5th episode transmitted of Season Three)

Written by Flint Dille

Plot:
The battles rage simultaneously on Earth and Cybertron. While the Autobots on Cybertron seem to be holding their own against the Decepticons, the same cannot be said for the those based on Earth, who are no match for the giant Trypticon. Of all the Autobots, only Metroplex is large or powerful enough to stop Trypticon, but without his transformation cog, he is stuck in city mode.

The Autobots send Sky Lynx to rescue Blurr, Wheelie and Faireborn, who are stranded on Io with the cog. However, the Quintessons intercept the transmission and send the Predacons to intercept. Thankfully, Sky Lynx is able to defeat the Predacons and shuttle his friends back to Earth. With his transformation cog in place, Metroplex transforms into robot mode and sends Trypticon plummeting to the bottom of the ocean.

Galvatron sends Blitzwing back to the Quintesson ship to give the aliens an update on how the battle is progressing. Blitzwing overhears the Quintessons plotting the destruction of the entire Transformer race: in a sub-level of Cybertron there exists a switch that will deactivate all Transformer life across the galaxy. When Galvatron refuses to listen, Blitzwing instead presents this news to Rodimus Prime. Blitzwing and Rodimus join forces to stop the Sharkticons pulling the lever, but Galvatron, unaware of its function, activates the switch, freezing all Transformers in their tracks. The Quintessons land on the now-pacified Cybertron and prepare to colonise it.

Unaffected by the switch, Spike is able to deactivate it, reawakening all of the Cybertronians. Faced by the combined might of the Autobots and Decepticons, the Quintessons flee. Irate that Blitzwing joined forces with the Autobots, Galvatron kicks him out of the Decepticon army.

Galvatron's Rants:
- 'Prepare, Autobots, to die in darkness!'
- 'Deceivers! Betrayers! Five-faced slime of the nebula! I will rip your tentacles!'
- 'You will suffer for this, Blitzwing! You will suffer unimaginably!'

Witty Put-Downs:
- Wheelie calls Tantrum a 'sucker'.

Roll Call:
Autobots: Blurr, Wheelie, Wreck-Gar (recap only), Rodimus Prime, Springer, Arcee, Kup, Ultra Magnus, Powerglide, Warpath, **Pipes**, **Swerve**, **Tailgate**, Bumblebee,

Beachcomber, Outback, **Metroplex**, **Scamper**, Rewind, Eject, **Sky Lynx**, Perceptor, First Aid, Slingshot, Air Raid, Jazz, Sunstreaker, Sludge and Grimlock.

Decepticons: Blitzwing, Octane (recap only), Ramjet, Blast Off, Dead End, Swindle, Galvatron, Scrapper, Scavenger, Mixmaster, Long Haul, Scrapper, Hook, Cyclonus, Scourge, Trypticon, Dirge, **Razorclaw**, Tantrum, **Headstrong**, **Divebomb**, **Rampage**, **Predaking**, Thrust, Laserbeak, Shrapnel, Bombshell, Kickback, Vortex, Brawl and Soundwave.

Other: the Narrator, Marissa Faireborn, Quintessons, Spike and Daniel.

Additionally, mis-coloured versions of Ratchet and Sandstorm appear. Both must rate as animation glitches rather than *bona fide* appearances, as Ratchet died in {3-00} *The Transformers: The Movie* and Sandstorm had yet to arrive on Cybertron.

Data File: Ed Gilbert (voices, including Blitzwing and Thrust)
Best known for playing Fenton Hardy in *The Hardy Boys/Nancy Drew Mysteries*, Ed Gilbert has a multitude of acting credits to his name, in series such as *The Wild Wild West*, *Mission: Impossible*, *Dallas* and *The A-Team*. As a voice actor, he played Hawk in *G.I. Joe: A Real American Hero*, Thirty-Thirty in *BraveStarr*, and Looten Plunder in *Captain Planet and the Planeteers*.

Data File: Joe Leahy (voices, including Razorclaw)
Joe Leahy is a voice-over artist with over ten thousand commercials to his name. His other credits are extremely varied, ranging from a part in the Kevin Bacon movie *Quicksilver* (Tom Donnelly, 1986) to *Batman: The Animated Series*, via Disneyland's Haunted Mansion attraction and twenty-plus years' worth of trailers for *The Simpsons*.

Data File: Ted Schwartz (voices, including Tailgate)
Ted Schwartz is best known for voicing the title role in the 1981/82 *Spider-Man* cartoon. He also voiced Thrasher in *G.I. Joe: A Real American Hero*, and can be heard in *Scooby-Doo and Scrappy-Doo*. His live-action work includes parts in long-running soap opera *The Doctors*, sitcom *Barney Miller* and the film *American Hot Wax* (Floyd Mutrux, 1978).

Review:
A patchy five-parter goes out with a bang, in an ending that is high on action, thrills and incident. The animation mistakes are still rife, but when the episode is this good, a few glitches here and there hardly seem to matter.

'The Five Faces of Darkness' would have made an excellent three-parter, but dragged over five. Some of the earlier episodes are quite hard-going, but thankfully the last two are good enough to redeem it. 4/5

{3-06} THE KILLING JAR
Production number: 700-91 (6th episode produced of Season Three)
Transmission date: 29 September 1986 (6th episode transmitted of Season Three)

Written by Michael Charles Hill and Joey Kurihara Piedra

Plot:
Hoping to study the Transformers and their allies, a Quintesson scientist kidnaps Ultra Magnus, Cyclonus, Wreck-Gar and Marissa Fairebon and sets about studying them. When the Quintesson ship is overcome by an electron storm, the captives are able to escape and confront the Quintesson scientist.

However, another menace threatens the ship – a black hole. With only a single one-man escape pod functional, the passengers argue over who gets to use it. In the event, the escape pod is jettisoned with no-one aboard, leaving everybody at the mercy of the black hole.

The ship is pulled into the black hole, but survives – on the other side of the black hole is a negative universe. All aboard the Quintesson ship join forces to make repairs, and eventually the ship is taken through a 'white hole' and back into the regular universe.

Everyone goes their separate ways, and – despite gaining grudging respect for each other during the crisis – Ultra Magnus and Cyclonus promise that, when next they meet, it will be as enemies.

Roll Call:
Autobots: Ultra Magnus, Wreck-Gar and Sky Lynx. Holographic images of Rodimus Prime and Broadside are also seen.

Decepticons: Cyclonus and Astrotrain, plus a holographic version of Galvatron.

Others: Quintessons and Marissa Fairebon. A holographic image of Marissa's father is also seen.

Data File: Aron Kincaid (voices, including Sky Lynx)
A successful artist as well as an actor, Kincaid played Laurence Olivier's standard-bearer in *Spartacus* (Stanley Kubrick, 1960) before going on to a successful acting and modelling career, notably in beach movies such as *The Girls on the Beach* (William N Witney, 1965), *Beach Ball* (Lennie Weinrib, 1965) and *Ski Party* (Alan Rafkin, 1965). Other work included appearances in the television shows *Get Smart*, *The Beverly Hillbillies* and *Lassie*. As a voice actor, he had parts in *DuckTales* and *Jonny Quest* and played villain Killer Croc in *Batman: The Animated Series*.

Data File: Bill Ratner (voices)
A prolific voice artist, Bill Ratner portrayed Flint in *G.I. Joe: A Real American Hero* (and reprised the part in episodes of *Family Guy* and *Community*), and is known to video game fans as the voice of Ambassador Donnel Udina in the *Mass Effect* franchise. He is the narrator on the *Ben 10* cartoon show and a radio announcer in the *Grand Theft Auto* video game series. He also narrates film trailers, and can be heard on the promo spots for movies such as *Kung Fu Panda* (John Stevenson and Mark Osborne, 2008), *Ant-Man* (Peyton Reed, 2015) and *Tenacious D in The Pick of Destiny* (Liam Lynch, 2006).

Review:
The first stand-alone episode of Season Three is a pretty mundane affair, and consists simply of a bunch of characters stuck in a damaged ship together. While this had the potential to give us some meaty character-based drama, we don't really learn anything

new about any of the characters here, except that Cyclonus seems pretty honourable for a Decepticon.

This is small-scale, low-key stuff. 2/5

{3-07} CHAOS
Production number: 700-92 (7th episode produced of Season Three)
Transmission date: 30 September 1986 (7th episode transmitted of Season Three)

Written by Paul Davids

Plot:
After a chance meeting with a Skuxxoid mercenary, the Decepticons discover a powerful new type of ammunition: death crystals. When shot out of a suitable launcher, these cause massive damage to anything they hit.

Investigating the crash of an Earth space station, Kup and a group of Autobots discover death crystals at the scene. Kup is only too familiar with these – many years ago, he was captured by aliens on the planet Dread and forced to work in a mine, digging for the crystals. Dread was also home to Chaos, a giant creature whose skin is made of death crystals. Kup recounts how he only barely escaped the planet with his life.

The Autobots arrive on Dread to find that the Decepticons have built a giant cannon, loaded with death crystals and aimed straight at Cybertron. The Autobots free the slaves who have been mining crystals for the Decepticons, while Kup confronts Chaos.

Kup uses the Decepticon death crystal cannon and aims it at Chaos, destroying the creature.

Witty Put-Downs:
• Sky Lynx calls the Predacons 'scrawny beasts'.

Roll Call:
Autobots: Kup, Wheelie, Blurr, Grimlock, Wreck-Gar and Sky Lynx.

Decepticons: Blast Off, **Runamuck**, Galvatron, Astrotrain, Razorclaw, Rampage, Tantrum, Headstrong, Divebomb and Predaking.

Other: An alien Skuxxoid is seen (possibly the same one previously featured in {3.01} 'Five Face of Darkness, Part One', though it's hard to tell).

Data File: Paul Davids (writer/production coordinator)
Davids wrote for '80s animated series such as *Defenders of the Earth*, *Bionic Six* and *C.O.P.S.* before moving into producing and directing films and documentaries about fringe subjects, including *The Life After Death Project* (2013), *Jesus in India* (2008) and *Roswell* (1994). He is married to Hollace Davids, a Senior Vice-President of Special Projects at Universal Pictures, with whom he has written a number of officially-licensed young adult *Star Wars* novels.

Laurie Faso (voices, including Skydive and Rampage)

Laurie Faso has provided his vocal talents to shows such as *Jem and the Holograms*, *Richie Rich* and *The New Yogi Bear Show*. As a live-action actor, he featured in episodes of *Family Law* and *Home Improvement*. He was the host of game show *I'm Telling!* and voiced Raphael in the movie *Teenage Mutant Ninja Turtles II: The Secret of the Ooze* (Michael Pressman, 1991).

Review:

Much better. The animation is of excellent quality, and the script is full of action scenes and excitement. The Chaos monster is an impressive creation and – most important of all – there's some good character work for Kup.

Polished, solid and a lot of fun. 4/5

Spotlight: Transformers that Never Were

Most transforming figures from Takara's Diaclone and MicroChange lines eventually saw rerelease as part of the Transformers range. However, there were exceptions. Here is a non-exhaustive list of the most notable examples:

No. 3 Countach Patrol Car Type

Part of the Diaclone 'Car Robots' line, this was very similar to the Sunstreaker figure, but decorated like a police car and incorporated a lightbar on the roof. Although the 'standard' version became Sunstreaker in Transformers, the lightbar version was never released as part of the Transformers line.

No. 6 Honda City R

As with the Countach figure above, the Honda City R was only a minor retool of a very similar figure, in this case the Honda City Turbo toy that eventually became Skids. The City R version was available in either red or silver, and had a different headsculpt and chest. This version eventually did see release as a Transformer in 2002, as a Japanese store exclusive named Crosscut.

Powered Buggy

A red, car-like vehicle that transformed into a robot, in Japan it came packed with Powered Convoy – the figure that would eventually become Ultra Magnus in the west.

Train Robo

Six robot action figures from Diaclone, each of which could convert into a train. All six could combine to form a larger robot. Although these were never released in the west, they were repackaged as Transformers in Japan in 1987.

- No. 1 Tôkaidô Bullet Train. Colours: white and blue. Transformer name: Shouki.
- No. 2 EF65 Blue Train. Colours: blue and yellow. Transformer name: Getsuei.
- No. 3 Tôhoku Jôetsu Bullet Train. Colours: white and blue. Transformer name: Yukikaze.
- No. 4 Tôkai-Type Express Train. Colours: red and green. Transformer name: Suiken.
- No. 5 L-Special-Express-485 System Special Express Train. Colours: yellow and red. Transformer name: Seizan.

- No 6. DE10 Diesel Locomotive. Colours: red and grey. Transformer name: Kaen.

These six were sold separately, and as part of a gift set. They were also re-released in alternative colours, as follows:

- No. 7 Tôkaidô Bullet Train. Colour: chromed silver.
- No. 8 ED67 Blue Train Pulling Train. Colour: red.
- No. 9 Doctor Yellow Bullet Train Comprehensive Test Train. Colours: yellow and blue.
- No. 10 Kuha 111-Type Express Train. Colours: white and blue.
- No. 11 L Special Express 583-Type Sleeping Car. Colours: yellow and blue.
- No. 12 DE10 Diesel Locomotive, Crystal Type. Colours: red and grey.

No. 2 Helicopter Type
A blue Diaclone triple-changer that could switch between robot, jet and helicopter modes.

MC-06 Watch Robo
A small MicroChange robot that transformed into a real working digital watch, available in black, blue, gold or silver. Although it never became a Transformer, the model was licensed to other companies around the world, including Kronoform in the USA.

MC-07 1910 Browning
As with the toy that would eventually become Megatron, Browning was part of a MicroChange sub-line called 'Gun Robo'. As the name would suggest, it transformed from a robot into a gun. As with the Diaclone Train Robos, this eventually saw release in 1988 as a Japanese-exclusive Transformer, called Browning.

MC-11 S&W Magnum 44
Another Gun Robo, this one was actually larger than Megatron and transformed into a revolver.

Key Robo
MicroChange figures that transformed into working padlocks. MC-17 Dial Man became a combination lock, while MC-18 Magneman was operated by a magnetic 'key' that doubled as a gun in robot mode.

MC-19 Scope Man
A robot that transformed into a set of binoculars.

MC-22 Beam Robo
A robot that transformed into a working flashlight. Although this figure was seen in toy catalogues, apparently it never actually saw release, even in Japan.

Bonaparte Tulcas
Not actually a Takara figure, this was a Takatoku design and part of the same Dorvack toy line that gave us Mugen Calibur (Roadbuster) and Ovelon Gazette (Whirl). It

transforms from a (rather stocky) robot into a tank.

Beet-Papil
Another Takatoku design, this one from the Beetras line that also spawned the Deluxe Insecticons. This toy never made it past the design phase, but would have been a ladybird that transformed into a female robot.

{3-08} DARK AWAKENING
Production number: 700-93 (8th episode produced of Season Three)
Transmission date: 1 October 1986 (8th episode transmitted of Season Three)

Written by Antoni Zalewski

Plot:
Chased through space by the Decepticons, an Autobot ship seeks refuge on the creepiest space station imaginable – a floating mausoleum containing bodies of fallen Autobots. One such is Optimus Prime who, to the surprise of everybody, is walking around the space-tomb alive and well!

Rodimus Prime is quick to hail the inexplicable return of their dead leader, and in returning the Matrix to Optimus Prime, reverts back to his old Hot Rod guise. Just then, however, Optimus Prime goes berserk and turns on his fellow Autobots, before fleeing the tomb in an escape craft. With the mausoleum locked on a course for a nearby sun, Hot Rod and the other Autobots trapped aboard appear doomed.

Optimus Prime returns to Cybertron and informs the Autobots there that Hot Rod and the others were murdered by Quintessons. Optimus proposes to lead the entire Autobot fleet in a revenge attack. In reality, Hot Rod and company have survived, having escaped the mausoleum shortly before its destruction.

It transpires that Optimus Prime's resurrection is actually a Quintesson ploy. The Quintessons have reanimated and reprogrammed Prime's corpse, and the Autobot fleet is being led into a deadly trap.

Hot Rod catches up with the Autobot armada and confronts Optimus Prime. After a brief battle, Optimus's old personality begins to reassert itself. He orders the rest of the Autobots to flee the scene while he alone activates the Quintesson trap and is destroyed once again.

Galvatron's Rants:
- The Decepticon leader relishes the irony of battling Rodimus Prime within a tomb: 'How convenient, Rodimus! We can lay your wreckage beside that of your mentor!'

Witty Put Downs:
- The Autobots really don't like the Decepticons. Ultra Magnus: 'There are too many of them!' Kup: '*One* Decepticon is one too many!'
- Springer, on the Quintessons: 'Five-faced tentacled slime!'

Roll Call:
Autobots: Ultra Magnus, Rodimus Prime/Hot Rod, Arcee, Kup, Optimus Prime, Perceptor, Grimlock, Springer, Skydive, Snarl, Sludge, Blurr, Blaster, Jazz and Wheelie.

Amongst the armada of Autobot ships, the likes of Air Raid, Slingshot, Broadside, Skyfire and Powerglide can all be seen, but given that many of these characters are duplicated in the same shot (and end up being destroyed) it would seem that these jets are actually supposed to represent Autobot spacecraft rather than specific characters.

Decepticons: Galvatron, Scourge, Cyclonus, Dirge and Thrust.

Other: Spike, Daniel and the Quintessons

Ironhide, Ratchet, Prowl and Huffer are all mentioned in dialogue (their bodies are said to be interred within the mausoleum), but are not seen on screen.

Data File: David Mendenhall (Daniel)
Former child actor David Mendenhall came to national prominence with a recurring role in the hit sitcom *Taxi* before having an award-winning stint as Mike Webber in the daytime soap *General Hospital*. Other live-action work includes parts in *Roseanne* and the '80s incarnation of *The Twilight Zone*. His voice work includes parts in *Rainbow Brite*, *G.I. Joe: A Real American Hero* and *The Centurions*. He played the son of star Sylvester Stallone's character in the movie *Over the Top* (Menahem Golan, 1987).

Data File: Antoni Zalewski (writer)
Wrote for many cartoon series, including *He-Man and the Masters of the Universe*, *Challenge of the GoBots*, *Defenders of the Earth*, and *G.I. Joe: A Real American Hero*.

Review:
The Transformers cartoon, while always full of drama and peril, is by nature quite a light-hearted, fun programme to watch. 'Dark Awakening', then, comes as something as a shock to the system – this is as grim and downbeat as it ever gets. Set in a dingy tomb and featuring an evil zombie Optimus Prime as the main villain, this is dark stuff. Even the hand-to-hand battle between Hot Rod and Optimus is quite nasty – Prime crushes Hot Rod until his chest bursts open and starts spewing gunge, and Hot Rod responds by ripping Optimus's arm off.

This is a taut, tense adventure with a line in black humour and a sense of dread that pervades throughout. It's a bold move, but it works brilliantly. 5/5

{3-09} FOREVER IS A LONG TIME COMING
Production number: 700-94 (9th episode produced of Season Three)
Transmission date: 8 October 1986 (11th episode transmitted of Season Three)

Written by Gerry Conway and Carla Conway

Plot:
On an asteroid, the Quintessons are working on a time window – a portal that will allow them to travel through time. Their target is Cybertron, eleven million years ago: they seek to change history and quash the slave rebellion that ousted them from the planet.

The Autobots detect an unusual energy signature emanating from the asteroid, and go to investigate. During the ensuing battle, a group of them are accidentally transported through the time window and into Cybertron's past. Matters are further complicated when a Cybertronian from the past, A3, arrives in the present. A3 was part of the rebel force involved in ridding Cybertron of the Quintessons.

While Blaster, Blurr and the other Autobots help the rebels in the distant past, strange things are occurring in the present: time loops, time going in reverse, people de-aging and Transformers appearing in two places at once. The Quintessons explain that the time window needs to be shut down – and fast – or the time damage will threaten the entire universe.

A3 returns through the window into the past, and helps the present-day Autobots return home. Once everyone has returned to their correct times, Rodimus Prime deactivates the time window. The Autobots realise that A3 was in fact Alpha Trion, the ancient Autobot who created Optimus Prime!

Witty Put-Downs:
- Slingshot is unimpressed with A3: 'Where'd this dinkoid come from? A toy store?'

The Secret Files of Teletraan II:
Presumably introduced as a means to reduce costs, 'The Secret Files of Teletraan II' were short segments incorporated into a number of Season Three episodes. Consisting of clips from prior episodes and narrated by Victor Caroli, they provided background information on key characters and concepts from the show. Teletraan II is the name of the Autobots' computer.

This episode was the first to incorporate a 'Secret Files' segment, and it focused on the Predacons, the Decepticon combiner team. All the footage was recycled from {3-07} 'Chaos'.

Roll Call:
Autobots: Wreck-Gar, Perceptor, Blurr, Blaster, Rewind, Ramhorn, Rodimus Prime, Superion, Silverbolt, Slingshot, Fireflight, Air Raid, Skydive, Alpha Trion, Pipes, Bumblebee, Swerve, Springer, Jazz, Wheelie, and Kup.

Others: the Quintessons, and Marissa Faireborn. The Decepticons do not appear, though a dummy of Cyclonus is seen as part of Faireborn's training simulation.

Data File: Tom Griffin and Joe Bacal (executive producers)
The pair founded the Griffin-Bacal advertising agency (at one point the sixty-seventh largest such company in the world) in 1978, and soon boasted Hasbro as one of their clients. It was Griffin-Bacal who came up with the terms 'Transformers', 'Autobot' and 'Decepticon', and developed all the logos for the franchise. Sunbow Productions was a subsidiary of Griffin-Bacal, and consequently the two men were credited in executive roles for a great many animated series, including *G.I. Joe: A Real American Hero*, *Visionaries*, *My Little Pony* and *The Tick*.

Data File: John Hostetter (Ramhorn)
John Hostetter has appeared in many television series, including *Moonlighting*, *L.A. Law*, *NYPD Blue* and *ER*, though he's best known for playing the part of John the stage manager in *Murphy Brown*. His film credits include parts in *Beverly Hills Cop II* (Tony Scott, 1987), *The People Under the Stairs* (Wes Craven, 1991) and *Star Trek: Insurrection*

(Jonathan Frakes, 1998). As a voice actor, he's had parts in *Spawn*, and *G.I. Joe: A Real American Hero*, in which he played Bazooka.

Review:
A high-concept time travel story with some big ideas and even bigger stakes, this episode gives us a look at what Cybertron was like under Quintesson rule, and we get to meet some of the rebels who helped to create an independent Cybertron. Coupled with this is the 'time gone nuts' subplot, which results in a couple of amusing scenes.

These last three episodes have given us a character piece, a zombie horror story and now an intriguing slice of classic science fiction – the eclectic and unpredictable third season is now in full swing. 4/5

{3-10} FIGHT OR FLEE
Production number: 700-106 (21st episode produced of Season Three)
Transmission date: 15 October 1986 (15th episode transmitted of Season Three)

Written by Tony Cinciripini and Larry Leahy

NB: This episode is an 'origin story' for the Autobot Sandstorm, and as such must be set prior to his appearance in {3-12} 'Starscream's Ghost', which is itself a sequel to {3-11} 'Thief in the Night'. So despite this being the twenty-first episode of Season Three to go into production, to maintain the 'best viewing order' we have to slot it in prior to those other two.

Metrodome, the company that produces and distributes the series on DVD in the United Kingdom (and that was once part of the same conglomerate that owned Sunbow Productions) concurred with this ordering, and put 'Fight or Flee' tenth in the running order on its Season Three DVD sets.

Plot:
Fleeing from a space battle with the Aerialbots, Scourge and Cyclonus risk flying through a glowing energy vortex. They emerge on the other side to find themselves on Paradron, a perfect recreation of pre-war Cybertron, populated entirely by meek, naïve (and unarmed) Transformers. What's more, the planet boasts an abundant supply of Energon.

The two Decepticons relay their discovery to Galvatron, who sends reinforcements to invade the planet. They seize the Energon for themselves and enslave the native Paradronians, forcing them to build an arsenal of weapons. One of the Paradronians, Sandstorm, manages to escape in a spacecraft and make his way to Cybertron.

Sandstorm meets with Rodimus Prime and explains the history of Paradron. Years before, a group of Autobots fled the war on Cybertron to settle on a planet free of conflict. Given that the planet was hidden on the other side of a vortex, they assumed that they would be safe from invaders.

The Autobots and Sandstorm go on a mission to retake the planet, arming the Paradronians and advising them to rise up against their invaders. Unfortunately, the Autobots are unable to wrest control of Paradron from the Decepticons, so – with Sandstorm's approval – they plant a bomb in its vast underground Energon core, and remotely destroy the planet. The evacuated Paradronians are invited to live on Cybertron.

Witty Put-Downs:
- Scourge: 'Have I got the wrong idea, or are these guys a bunch of wimps?' Cyclonus: 'Yes, they appear to be wimps.'
- Scourge describes the planet Paradron in his report to Galvatron: 'It's controlled by a bunch of sissy Autobots!'
- Cyclonus waxes philosophical after a Paradronian is sent crashing through a wall: 'Hey! I'm stuck up here!' 'Everybody's gotta be *somewhere*.'

The Secret Files of Teletraan II:
A brief history of the Quintessons, with clips taken from parts two to four of 'Five Faces of Darkness' ({2-02} to {2-04}).

Spotlight: 'He's Still Using My Name'
Trademark law can be a tricky and contentious subject, and nowhere is this more apparent than in the names of the Transformers themselves. In order to strengthen their claim on some of the of their better-known characters, Hasbro have taken to adding prefixes to the names on the toy packaging, hence we get figures named 'Autobot Jazz' and 'Battle Ravage'. But there are some names apparently off-limits to Hasbro, even taking prefixes into account.

Hot Rod is the most prominent example – until very recently, modern iterations of this classic character (and re-releases of the original toy) were not allowed to be sold under the Hot Rod moniker. Various different alternative names have been used over the years, including 'Rodimus' and 'Rodimus Major'. Other such victims include Fireflight (now 'Firefly' or 'Firestrike'), Slingshot ('Quickslinger') and Shrapnel ('Skrapnel').

It's not just legal reasons that have forced changes to Transformers' names – matters of culture and taste have also played a part. Recent iterations of the Dinobot Slag have been renamed 'Slug' by Hasbro, as the word 'slag' has a rather torrid alternative definition in the United Kingdom, Australia and other English-speaking countries outside of the USA. (A similar scenario occurred in 2010, when Hasbro solicited a Transformers figure by the name of 'Spastic' – a word that, in the United Kingdom, is deemed extremely offensive. After stories of the proposed toy made the British national press, it was renamed 'Over-Run'.)

Data File: Tony Cinciripini (writer)
Cinciripini has written a number of movie scripts, including *Confessions of a Hitman* (1994; directed by his *The Transformers* co-writer Larry Leahy and starring James Remar), and *Hell's Kitchen* (1998; which he also directed, and which starred Angelina Jolie).

Data File: Larry Leahy (writer)
Since his contribution to *The Transformers*, Leahy has gone on to have a decent career in Hollywood: as well as producing, writing and directing a few modestly successful films, he has been script coordinator on a number of blockbusters, including *Deep Impact* (Mimi Leder, 1998), *The Kid* (John Turteltaub, 2000) and *Road to Perdition* (Sam Mendes, 2002).

Roll Call:
Autobots: Air Raid, Silverbolt, Skydive, Fireflight, Slingshot, Superion, **Sandstorm**, Blurr, Springer, Rodimus Prime, Kup, Ultra Magnus, Sky Lynx, First Aid, Hot Spot, Wheelie, Groove and Sunstreaker. Ironhide, Ratchet and Wheeljack are also briefly glimpsed in a crowd scene, but as those characters were killed off in {3-00} *The Transformers: The Movie*, their appearance here can be best put down to an animation error.

Decepticons: Scourge, Cyclonus, Soundwave, Bonecrusher, Galvatron, Long Haul, Brawl, Razorclaw, Divebomb, Bruticus, Astrotrain, Blitzwing, Headstrong, Swindle, Blast Off, Onslaught, Vortex, Scrapper and Mixmaster.

Review:
While its plot is never going to win any points for originality, 'Fight or Flee' scores highly for presentation. It zips along at a fast pace, the script is full of quotable lines, and – most importantly – there's a sparkle here, a sense of fun that underpins the entire episode.

While it's a bit odd in places (Rodimus Prime's decision to nuke the planet is a little extreme, and it's remarkable that everyone appears to escape the exploding planet unscathed), one can overlook such quibbles when the end result is so entertaining. 4/5

{3-11} THIEF IN THE NIGHT
Production number: 700-96 (11th episode produced of Season Three)
Transmission date: 6 October 1986 (10th episode transmitted of Season Three)

Written by Paul Davids

NB: Although made and aired after {3-12} 'Starscream's Ghost', chronologically it is set beforehand, hence its placement here.

Plot:
Following his defeat at the hands of Metroplex in {3-05} 'Five Faces of Darkness, Part Five', Trypticon has been recuperating on Dinobot Island. However, the Decepticon Octane has other ideas. Defying Galvatron's orders, he persuades Trypticon to decamp to the African nation of Carbombya, where the oil wells are full of such high-grade fuel that Octane is able to create a 'super-Energon' power source.

When Carbombya's ruler, Abdul Fakkadi, asks the two Decepticons to leave his country, Trypticon bribes him off by stealing Fort Knox and bringing it all the way to Africa. Before long, the Taj Mahal and the Eiffel Tower are also relocated to Carbombya.

When Trypticon attempts to steal the Kremlin, Metroplex is on hand to stop him. Trypticon flees into the foggy night, leaving Metroplex holding the building. When the giant Autobot is spotted with the Kremlin in his hands, world leaders instantly accuse the Autobots of stealing the other monuments.

Meanwhile, Galvatron and the other Decepticons confront Octane, and demand to know why he 'stole' Trypticon. Their fury is temporarily assuaged when they discover Octane's super-Energon, and the power it brings them. Tracing the missing buildings to Carbombya, the Autobots enter the scene. After Metroplex manages to subdue Trypticon, the rest of the Decepticons flee.

Galvatron's Rants:
- 'You're a traitor, Octane! You had no permission to take Trypticon away from Dinobot Island! I need Trypticon for my plans of conquering the Earth! Now, because of you, he may never recover!'

Witty Put-Downs:
- Galvatron dismisses Fakkadi: 'You ridiculous little flesh creature!'

The Secret Files of Teletraan II:
A potted history of the Decepticon faction, with clips from numerous episodes, including {1-04} 'Transport to Oblivion', {2-01} 'Autobot Spike' and {2-44} 'Cosmic Rust'.

Roll Call:
Autobots: Metroplex, Rodimus Prime, Perceptor, Grimlock, Silverbolt, Air Raid, Skydive, Slingshot, Fireflight, Broadside, Seaspray, Sandstorm, **Six-Gun**, **Slammer**, Scamper, Slag, Snarl, Sludge, Swoop, Sky Lynx, Wheelie, Blurr and Ultra Magnus. Although this is Slammer's debut appearance as an individual character, in his alternate mode he transforms into a tower/city parts for Metroplex's base mode, and so technically he has made prior appearances as part of Metroplex.

Decepticons: Trypticon, Octane, Galvatron, Blast Off, Cyclonus, Thrust, Ramjet, Bombshell, Dirge and Scourge.

Other: Abdul Fakkadi.

Data File: Brad Garrett (Trypticon)
Brad Garrett is a popular actor and stand-up comedian who gained international recognition and three Emmy awards for his role as Raymond's brother Robert Barone in the successful sitcom *Everybody Loves Raymond*. Other live-action credits include parts in *Roseanne*, *Seinfeld*, *The Fresh Prince of Bel-Air* and *Monk*; his films include *Finding Nemo* (Andrew Stanton and Lee Unkrich, 2003), *Tangled* (Nathan Greno and Byron Howard, 2010), *Night at the Museum* (Shawn Levy, 2006), *Music and Lyrics* (Marc Lawrence, 2007) and *The Pacifier* (Adam Shankman, 2005). He has also entered professional poker tournaments, and appears on the back cover of the Electric Light Orchestra's 1979 album *Discovery*.

Data File: Beau Weaver (Octane)
A prolific actor, Weaver has also provided voice-overs for a great many advertisements, trailers and documentaries. He voiced Feryl in *Visionaries*, Mr Fantastic in *Fantastic Four* and the title role in the 1988 *Superman* animated series. Other voice work includes parts in *Mighty Mouse*, *The Incredible Hulk* and *Teenage Mutant Ninja Turtles*.

Data File: Maurice LaMarche (Six-Gun)
Emmy-winning voice actor LaMarche has hundreds of credits to his name, including Chief Quimby in *Inspector Gadget*, Egon in *The Real Ghostbusters*, Duke Nukum in *Captain Planet and the Planeteers*, the Brain in *Animaniacs* and its spin-off, *Pinky and the Brain*, and numerous roles in *Futurama*, including Kif Kroker and Morbo. Other voice work includes television series such as *The Simpsons*, *Heroes*, *Tiny Toon Adventures*, *Robot*

Chicken and *Adventure Time*. In films, he voiced Pepe Le Pew in *Space Jam* (Joe Pytka, 1996), Alec Baldwin in *Team America: World Police* (Trey Parker, 2004), Orson Welles in *Ed Wood* (Tim Burton, 1994) and the King of Arendelle (Anna and Elsa's father) in *Frozen* (Chris Buck and Jennifer Lee, 2013). He also voiced numerous characters in the series *Transformers: Rescue Bots*.

Review:
The cast may be full of 'new' characters, but deep down, this is a bit of a throwback to seasons past: an Earth setting, in-fighting amongst the Decepticons, the Autobot computer warning of trouble, and an almost sitcom line in humour.

The end result is an episode that looks and feels a bit tired and predictable, with jokes that fall flat and an overriding feeling of 'seen it all before'. 2/5

{3-12} STARSCREAM'S GHOST
Production number: 700-95 (10th episode produced of Season Three)
Transmission date: 2 October 1986 (9th episode transmitted of Season Three)

Written by Megeen McLaughlin

Plot:
Still angry about Octane's 'theft' of Trypticon (in {3-11} 'Thief in the Night'), Galvatron hires an alien Skuxxoid to assassinate the errant Decepticon. The paranoid Octane, however, is able to survive the Skuxxoid attack, and seeks protection from the Autobot Sandstorm. After being attacked again on Earth, Octane is given refuge on Cybertron.

Even on the Autobot-occupied Cybertron, Octane is not safe. When Cyclonus and Scourge sneak onto the planet, he hides in a crypt, only to stumble upon ... the ghost of Starscream!

Starscream possesses the body of Cyclonus and takes Octane back to Galvatron's base on Chaar. The pair collude: Starscream/Cyclonus pretends to 'torture' Octane for information. In reality, Octane is unharmed, and feeds false information that sends Galvatron into an Autobot trap.

Galvatron isn't defeated, however, and angrily returns to Chaar to seek revenge on Starscream. A swift cannon blast to the chest is enough to exorcise Starscream's spirit from Cyclonus's body. Galvatron reflects on a job well done, unaware that Starscream has merely jumped into the body of another Decepticon ...

Galvatron's Rants:
- '*Starscream*? I shall enjoy destroying you even more this time than the last!'
- On Octane's fate: 'We shall interrogate him! Even if it's not informative, it'll be fun!'

Witty Put-Downs:
- The Skuxxoid calls Octane an 'overgrown tin can'.
- Cyclonus, after Octane hides from him: 'How dare you disgrace your ancestors by cowering like a pocket computer?'
- Starscream to Octane, during the fake capture: 'Look scared, moron, or I will have to destroy you!'
- One of the Sweeps notices that Cyclonus's voice has changed: 'He sounds like

Starscream!' Scourge replies, 'No need to be insulting!'

The Secret Files of Teletraan II:
A beginner's guide to the Autobots. The clips are taken from numerous episodes, including {2-44} 'Cosmic Rust', {3-04} 'Five Faces of Darkness, Part Four' and {3-00} *The Transformers: The Movie*.

Roll Call:
Autobots: Sandstorm, Kup, Ultra Magnus, Rodimus Prime, Silverbolt, Slingshot, Skydive, Air Raid, Fireflight and Perceptor.

Decepticons: Octane, Galvatron, Brawl, Blast Off, Onslaught, Scourge, Cyclonus and Starscream (as a ghost). A statue of Thundercracker is seen in the Cybertronian crypt.

Data File: Megeen McLaughlin (writer)
Meg McLaughlin (as she is sometimes credited) began in animation as a production assistant, working on shows such as *Mister T* and *Alvin and the Chipmunks*. As a writer, she has contributed scripts to series such as *Spider-Man*, *The Incredible Hulk* and *The Smurfs*. McLaughlin returned to the Transformers franchise in the year 2000, penning 'Home Soil', an episode of *Transformers: Beast Machines*.

Data File: Jerry Houser (voices, including Sandstorm)
Houser is best known for playing Oscy Seltzer, one of the lead roles in the Oscar-winning *Summer of '42* (Robert Mulligan, 1971), and a supporting part opposite Paul Newman in *Slap Shot* (George Roy Hill, 1977). He also played Wally Logan in the '80s *Brady Bunch* spin-offs, including *The Brady Girls Get Married*, *The Brady Brides* and *The Bradys*. Other live-action work includes parts in *M*A*S*H*, *CHiPs* and *T.J. Hooker*. His voice-only credits include *G.I. Joe: A Real American Hero*, *Goof Troop* and *The Smurfs*.

Review:
The first eleven minutes focus on Octane and his various lucky escapes from the Decepticons and the Skuxxoid assassin. The humour is broad and almost slapstick in nature, and the various bizarre settings, including an alien equivalent of a truck stop diner, give it a unique colour and ambience.

Then Starscream arrives on the scene, and the 'proper' plot clicks into gear. Even then, the great lines continue to flow, especially when Octane overacts during his show-torture.

But while this is a gloriously funny episode, what really makes it is the return of Starscream, probably the best character of the show's first two seasons. Bringing him back as a ghost is an inspired idea, and his scene with Galvatron is electric. Marvellous. 5/5

{3-13} SURPRISE PARTY
Production number: 700-97 (12th episode produced of Season Three)
Transmission date: 9 October 1986 (12th episode transmitted of Season Three)

Written by Steve Mitchell and Barbara Petty

Plot:
The Autobots are hosting a galactic peace conference on Cybertron. The Combaticons attempt to sabotage the conference but are driven off. During the battle, Ultra Magnus risks his own life to protect Wheelie. Eager to repay Ultra Magnus for his selfless act, Wheelie and Daniel decide to throw him a surprise birthday party – but first they must determine when the Autobot's birthday actually *is*. Cybertron's own history records are tantalisingly incomplete, so Wheelie and Daniel go off in search of an Autobot archive, missing in space.

The two friends trace the archive to a small asteroid, but are kidnapped by Scourge and Cyclonus, who have followed them. Cyclonus sets the asteroid on a collision course for Cybertron and threatens to kill Wheelie and Daniel if the Autobots try to stop it.

Ultra Magnus and Sky Lynx arrive on the asteroid and battle the Decepticons. In the confusion, Wheelie sets the asteroid to self-destruct. Everyone flees before the asteroid harmlessly explodes in space. As they are still unsure of when Ultra Magnus's birthday is, Wheelie and Daniel decide to have the party there and then.

Galvatron's Rants:
- He's not happy about the peace conference: 'So, the Autobots seek to make peace throughout our galaxy? There shall be no peace!'

The Secret Files of Teletraan II:
Another sighting of the Predacon segment, previously seen in {3-09} 'Forever is a Long Time Coming'.

<u>Spotlight: Breaking the Mould</u>
Many of the classic Transformers toys have since been reissued, allowing collectors to own fresh new copies of the original figures. Unfortunately, not every figure has had this treatment – some, such as Jetfire, Whirl and Ransack, were licensed to Hasbro only for a limited time; Hasbro simply don't own the moulds any more, or have the rights to use them.

Other figures have seen their moulds go missing or become damaged: there have been no recent reissues of Wheeljack, Sunstreaker, Mirage or the Dinobots, as the moulds simply don't exist any more, at least in a usable state.

Some of the classic figures that *have* been reissued a number of times are now starting to show a little wear and tear. Recent releases of the Combaticons and Seacons have had a number of quality control issues that have been put down to mould degradation.

However, a problem of this kind need not be terminal – in recent years a couple of figures have surfaced that prove Hasbro and Takara are not averse to repairing damaged moulds. The Constructicons were re-released in 2011 – the first appearance of these toys since 1993 – with a number of slight changes from the originals, indicating that the moulds had been either extensively restored or recreated from scratch. In 2004, the Japanese character Stepper, basically a black version of Jazz, saw a re-release, but with a pristine headsculpt – correcting a fault that had previously afflicted Jazz reissues for years.

But while the fandom eagerly awaits news of further reissues – especially given the rising prices of vintage figures on the secondary market – another option presents itself: fakes and knock-offs.

To sate fans' demands for reissues of 'missing' figures such as Grimlock or Wheeljack, unscrupulous companies have taken to reverse-engineering the original toys and putting out their own versions, many of which are of questionable quality. Often these knock-offs ('KOs') are sold in replicas of the original packaging, making it difficult for the uninitiated to determine whether they are buying a mint original vintage toy or a fake. Nevertheless, some would argue that it's better to have black-market versions of these figures than none at all.

Roll Call:
Autobots: Warpath, First Aid, Rodimus Prime, Wheelie, Groove, Ultra Magnus, Perceptor, Blaster and Sky Lynx.

Decepticons: Galvatron, Scourge, Cyclonus, Swindle, Blast Off, Brawl, Onslaught and Vortex. Bruticus also makes an appearance, but as it's alongside the Combaticons, it must be an animation error (as he is their combined form).

Other: Daniel and Spike

Data File: Steve Mitchell (writer)
Mitchell's eclectic writing career spans animation (*G.I. Joe: A Real American Hero*, *Jem and the Holograms*), live action television (*Viper*, *Pacific Blue*) and movies, including cult comedy/horror film *Chopping Mall* (Jim Wynorski, 1986) and the action crime drama *Against the Law* (Jim Wynorski, 1997), which starred a pre-fame Jaime Pressly.

Data File: Barbara Petty (writer)
Petty wrote for a number of Sunbow cartoons, including *G.I. Joe: A Real American Hero*, *Jem and the Holograms*, and *My Little Pony*, for which she contributed the five-part 'Bright Lights' story.

Review:
As a showcase for the show's two juvenile, 'kid-friendly' characters, Wheelie and Daniel, it's easy to see why this episode grates on many adult fans. While the clear intention is to be whimsical and charming, it instead comes across as twee and inessential to adult eyes.

Even for Wheelie and Daniel fans, this still doesn't quite work: the plot is full of amazing coincidences that strain credulity: Cyclonus just happens to be monitoring Autobot garbage scows at the exact moment that Wheelie and Daniel steal one; the asteroid they crash on just happens to be the one containing the Autobot archive. While such plot shortcuts are forgivable if the episode is otherwise good, they become far more noticeable when viewers are less engaged. 1/5

{3-14} MADMAN'S PARADISE
Production number: 700-98 (13th episode produced of Season Three)
Transmission date: 13 October 1986 (13th episode transmitted of Season Three)

Written by Craig Rand

Plot:
While the Autobots hold a reception for a visiting alien dignitary, a bored Daniel slinks off, followed by Grimlock. Wandering the corridors of Cybertron, the pair find a secret tunnel leading to an underground chamber. They accidentally activate some machinery, and are transported to a bizarre alien planet.

There they are met by the Red Wizard, who explains that his castle is under siege from a group of evil usurpers. Grimlock agrees to help the Red Wizard fend off the attackers. Unbeknown to Grimlock and Daniel, they are being conned – the Red Wizard is an evil overlord, and the revolutionaries attacking the castle are actually on the side of good.

A group of Autobots search for the missing Grimlock and Daniel, and find the hidden transporter chamber. It's a relic from when the Quintessons used to rule Cybertron – they used it to exile criminals to remote worlds. The Red Wizard is a Quintesson criminal by the name of Mara Al-Utha, who has kept the benign Golden Wizard a captive for many years.

A group of Autobots transport to the planet and free the Golden Wizard, who uses his magic to defeat Mara Al-Utha. Daniel and the rest of the Autobots return to Cybertron.

Witty Put-Downs:
- Daniel thinks the alien world very strange indeed: 'Even California's not *this* weird!'

The Secret Files of Teletraan II:
A second outing for the Decepticon segment, previously seen in {3-11} 'Thief in the Night'.

Roll Call:
Autobots: Rodimus Prime, Ultra Magnus, Blaster, Ramhorn, Steeljaw, Elect, Rewind and Perceptor.

Data File: Craig Rand (writer)
Craig Rand also wrote for *Potato Head Kids* and provided the screenplay for the action movie *Land of Doom* (Peter Maris, 1986).

Data File: Townsend Coleman (voices, including Rewind)
A voice actor of some repute, Coleman is best known as the original Michaelangelo in *Teenage Mutant Ninja Turtles*, plus the title roles in *The Tick*, *Where's Waldo* and the animated *Teen Wolf* series. Other voice work includes parts in *Inspector Gadget*, *Fraggle Rock*, *Animaniacs* and *Timon and Pumbaa*. He later returned to the Transformers franchise, playing Sentinel Prime and Tracks in the revival show *Transformers: Animated*.

Review:
Dropping the Transformers into a setting full of magic and wizards has been done before, and better, in {2-24} 'A Decepticon Raider in King Arthur's Court'. While this desperately wants to be an all-out romp, it's not quite witty or funny enough to pull it off. It is amiable enough, and full of action, but in the final analysis it is less than the sum of its parts. 2/5

{3-15} NIGHTMARE PLANET

Production number: 700-99 (14th episode produced of Season Three)
Transmission date: 31 October 1986 (19th episode transmitted of Season Three)

Written by Beth Bornstein

Plot:

Rodimus Prime comforts Daniel after the boy begins suffering from a recurring nightmare in which he is threatened by a giant Galvatron. Soon afterwards, the Autobots trace an electromagnetic disturbance to a remote location on Cybertron. They are attacked by the Predacons ... and an array of monsters.

This area seems to be home to many bizarre creatures, including killer clowns, dragons, witches, snake monsters and evil hall-of-mirrors reflections. When the Transformers are attacked by a giant Galvatron, Rodimus deduces that somehow Daniel's nightmares have been made manifest.

It transpires that the Quintessons have kidnapped Daniel and hooked him up to a device that can turn the boy's nightmares into reality. However, Daniel is able to fight against the machine's effects, and provides the Autobots with the means by which to overcome their attackers: a magic lance to slay the dragon, weed-killer to thwart some robot-eating plants, and a giant Rodimus to attack the giant Galvatron.

The Autobots find Daniel, but it's the young human who thwarts the Quintessons – Daniel's dreams overload the machine, which explodes, apparently killing his kidnappers.

Nightmare Galvatron's Rants:

- Daniel's dream version of Galvatron is just as mad as his real-world counterpart: 'Human, your time has come! Prepare to meet your maker! You can't get away, Danny! I've got you! Hahahahaha!'
- After Rodimus questions how Galvatron can grow to giant size: 'Fool! Galvatron can be any size he wants!'

Witty Put-Downs:

- The nightmare Galvatron calls Headstrong a 'puny robot'.

The Secret Files of Teletraan II:

The main action comprises only seventeen-and-a-half minutes of this episode's twenty-two minute running time, so two of the 'Secret Files' segments were used to fill up the remainder: the Quintesson segment previously seen in {3-10} 'Fight or Flee', and the Decepticon segment previously seen in {3-11} 'Thief in the Night' and {3-14} 'Madman's Paradise'.

Roll Call:

Autobots: Rodimus Prime, Springer and Ultra Magnus.

Decepticons: Galvatron (or rather, a fake nightmare version of Galvatron), Razorclaw, Rampage, Headstrong, Tantrum, Divebomb and Predaking.

Other: Daniel, Spike, Carly and the Quintessons.

Data File: Nelson Shin (producer/supervising producer)
Nelson Shin is the owner and founder of AKOM, the animation studio that produced many episodes of *The Transformers*. He was previously at DePatie-Freleng Enterprises (DFE), where he worked on the *Pink Panther* series of shorts; DFE was then acquired by Marvel Productions. He provided animated lightsaber effects for the film *Star Wars* (George Lucas 1977), and, via his role at AKOM, is credited as the overseas animation producer/director on over a hundred episodes of *The Simpsons*.

Data File: Linda Gary (numerous one-off and background voices)
Acclaimed voice actor Linda Gary is best known for her work on the *Masters of the Universe* franchise and its spin-offs, where she provided voices for most of the female characters, including Teela, the Sorceress and Evil-Lyn. Her other voice credits include the animated shows *BraveStarr*, *The Real Ghostbusters*, *Batman: The Animated Series* and the 1994 *Spider-Man*.

Review:
A difficult episode to rate; it's simultaneously terrible and riotously funny. You have to be prepared to switch your brain off to be able to enjoy watching the Transformers fight against Frankenstein's Monster and the Wicked Witch of the West – certainly, the tech rationale for their appearance fails to convince – but if you're in the right frame of mind and willing to overlook the sheer stupidity of it all, this is a delightful little episode that revels in its own risibility. 3/5

{3-16} GHOST IN THE MACHINE
Production number: 700-100 (15th episode produced of Season Three)
Transmission date: 21 October 1986 (17th episode transmitted of Season Three)

Written by Michael Charles Hill and Joey Kurihara Piedra

Plot:
Starscream's ghost is up to no good again (see {3-12} 'Starscream's Ghost') – this time he possesses Scourge and travels to Unicron's dormant head, still in orbit around Cybertron. Starscream awakens Unicron and agrees to carry out three 'labours' in exchange for a new body. Scourge, who shot at Galvatron while possessed and is now believed to be a traitor, agrees to help Starscream carry out these tasks.

The first task is to steal Metroplex's eyes. Scourge and Starscream infiltrate the Autobot city-bot and steal his eyes, but one is broken during the ensuing battle. To replace the broken eye, they travel to the Decepticon planet Chaar and steal an optic from Trypticon.

Once the eyes are installed in Unicron's head, the decapitated world-devourer makes his second request – he wants Trypticon. Starscream and Scourge return to Chaar and capture the giant Decepticon. It seems that Unicron is after Trypticon's transformation cog, and Scourge installs it within his head.

For Unicron's third and final request, he asks that his head be connected to Cybertron, so that he can have a body again. Scourge baulks at this and flees, leaving Starscream to make the attachment.

Meanwhile, the Autobots deduce what Starscream and Unicron are up to, and so set an explosive charge at the base of Unicron's head. Unicron makes good his half of the bargain and provides Starscream with a body. The bomb goes off, however, flinging Unicron back into orbit around Cybertron, whist Starscream is also catapulted into space.

Galvatron's Rants:
- When Scourge goes berserk: 'There's no reasoning with him! Destroy him, he's lost his mind!'
- 'So Scourge is helping Starscream voluntarily and you four were unable to stop them? Well, all I can say is… *raaaagh!*'
- 'Silence, you cowards – and prepare to be scrapped!'

Witty Put-Downs:
- Cyclonus isn't impressed with his troops: 'Scourge is but one mad warrior. Get up and face him, you cowards!'
- Starscream to Scourge: 'Y'know, for the strong, silent type, you sure talk too much!'

Roll Call:
Autobots: Metroplex, Scamper, Slammer (only as part of Metroplex), Sky Lynx, Kup, Warpath, Bumblebee, Powerglide, Blaster, Silverbolt, Skydive, Groove, Hot Spot, Rodimus Prime, Ultra Magnus, Wheelie, Blurr, Springer and Arcee.

Decepticons: Scourge, Razorclaw, Headstrong, Starscream, Cyclonus, Galvatron, Trypticon, **Runabout**, Runamuck, Thrust, Dirge, Astrotrain and Divebomb.

Other: Spike and Unicron.

Data File: Joey Kurihara Piedra (writer)
Joey Kuihara Piedra is an American writer whose only television credits are two *The Transformers* episodes, both co-written with Michael Charles Hill.

Data File: Stan Jones (voices, including Scourge and Zarak)
An actor whose career dates back to the '50s, Stan Jones appeared in series including *Alfred Hitchcock Presents*, *Voyage to the Bottom of the Sea*, *The Twilight Zone* and *Beverly Hills, 90210*. As a voice actor, he can be heard in episodes of *Spider-Man & His Amazing Friends*, *TaleSpin* and *Alvin & the Chipmunks*. He was the narrator of the film *Little Shop of Horrors* (Frank Oz, 1986).

Data File: Roger Behr (Runabout and Runamuck)
Actor and comedian Behr also lent his voice to *Yogi's Space Race* and *The All-New Popeye Hour*. His films include the Meryl Streep-starring *Defending Your Life* (Albert Brooks, 1991) and the Saturn Award-nominated *Explorers* (Joe Dante, 1985).

Review:
A strong, plot-heavy episode that – like all the best ones – is littered with quotable dialogue and a strong line in wit. Yet again it is Starscream who steals the show, proving that the decision to kill him off in the movie was a mistake.

With Galvatron at his insane best, Unicron attempting to resurrect himself and

Scourge getting his best material yet, all the ingredients are in place for a classic episode. 5/5

Spotlight: Why were the Transformers such a success?

The temporary demise of the Transformers franchise in the early 1990s, and the reasons behind it, will be covered in Appendix 2, so here's a chance to look at the flipside of the coin: why did it become so huge in the first place?

The Transformers were America's biggest-selling toys of 1984, and Optimus Prime himself was the UK's biggest-selling toy of 1985 (according to figures released by the Toys 'Я' Us chain of toyshops). Transformers toys, comics and merchandise were everywhere in the mid-'80s. So why did the idea catch on?

Sometimes, of course, things don't need any particular reason to catch on: fads come and go all the time, and certain toy brands just get lucky. Often such fads start as the result of peer pressure, or the desire to own what the 'cool kids' are talking about, and then snowball into a national or international craze – what's known as the Bandwagon Effect. The '80s were a hotbed of such crazes, from the Cabbage Patch Kids riots in 1983 through to the Teenage Mutant Ninja Turtles in 1988.

But while it's seemingly arbitrary which toys become hits and which are misses (see also Pogs, Furby and the *Thunderbirds* Tracy Island playset), it does seem to help if they are of a good quality and are supported by a strong advertising campaign, tie-in media and other merchandise.

Hasbro really couldn't have done more to sell Transformers across the globe. Advertisements for the figures were all over children's television; the tie-in comics and cartoon episodes were on a par with or superior to those produced by rival brands; and the toys themselves were surprisingly durable, especially considering their complexity and the number of moving parts.

But while the toys were ingenious – because of the two modes, kids were essentially getting two toys in one – it was the quality of the tie-in media that elevated Transformers above (say) GoBots or Manta Force. Marvel's *The Transformers* comic was arguably one of the best toy tie-in comics ever produced, and reprints of those classic adventures are still sold today.

While *The Transformers* cartoon show wasn't so much of a market leader, certainly in terms of animation and storylines, it nevertheless captured the imaginations of children across the globe, thanks largely to the exacting voice director Wally Burr and his company of stellar voice actors, who could breathe magic into even the weakest of scripts.

The Transformers were a hit due to a combination of luck and hard work. While their success was never guaranteed – and the difference between success and failure can be extremely fine when it comes to toy lines – Hasbro and their partners did all they could to secure it. The toy-buying public did the rest.

Ultimately, this meant that the franchise was on solid enough ground that it became more than just a passing fad, and despite a few peaks and troughs in popularity, the 'Robots in Disguise' remain firm favourites even today, over thirty years later.

{3-17} WEBWORLD

Production number: 700-101 (16th episode produced of Season Three)
Transmission date: 20 October 1986 (16th episode transmitted of Season Three)

Written by Len Wein and Diane Duane

Plot:
The Autobots are mining for isidrite on an asteroid when they are attacked by the Decepticons. Thankfully, the increasingly erratic behaviour of the Decepticon leader Galvatron means that an Autobot victory is relatively routine stuff.

Back on Chaar, the Decepticons implore Cyclonus to do something about Galvatron's madness. A brief encounter with a Quintesson then inspires Cyclonus to send Galvatron to the planet Torkulon – basically, a mental health clinic in space.

The native Torkuli restrain Galvatron in a web-like material that emanates from the planet's surface. They try a number of different therapeutic techniques, but these only serve to enrage Galvatron even further. The Torkuli eventually conclude that Galvatron is a lost cause, and that the only way to cure him is via a special lobotomy, which involves linking his brain into the planet itself – Torkulon is actually a living creature, rather than a standard planet.

Galvatron's madness is so intense than linking with Torkulon corrupts the planet, which is suddenly beset by earthquakes. Galvatron travels to the planet's underground control core and destroys it, effectively killing the planet.

Galvatron's Rants:
- 'Crush the Autobots to scrap! Crush the Earth and its puny humanity! Crush anyone! Anything that dares to oppose us!'
- 'Strategy is for cowards!'
- 'You're finished, Magnus! I shall use your head as a doorstop!'
- 'I'm not beaten! Galvatron cannot be beaten! I will destroy you all!'
- A Torkulon therapist tries word-association on Galvatron:
    - Therapist: 'Don't fight it, just say whatever comes to mind'.
    - Galvatron: 'Kill! Smash! Destroy!'
    - Therapist: 'Uh, yes, go on …'
    - Galvatron: 'Rend! Mangle! Distort! … I'll destroy everything here! Everything! And then I'll destroy the Autobots!'
    - Therapist: 'Tell me about the Autobots.'
    - Galvatron: 'I hate the Autobots! I hate Cyclonus! And I'm not very fond of *you*, either! Crush you! Destroy you!'

Witty Put-Downs:
- Cyclonus, on the Quintesson: 'I trust you no further than I can throw Trypticon!'

The Secret Files of Teletraan II:
Another outing for the Autobot history clip, last seen in {3-12} 'Starscream's Ghost'.

Roll Call:
Autobots: Perceptor, Springer, Ultra Magnus, Sludge and Sky Lynx.

Decepticons: Galvatron, Soundwave, Ratbat, Swindle, Motormaster and Laserbeak.

Other: a lone Quintesson.

Data File: Len Wein (writer)

Legendary comic writer and editor Len Wein worked for both Marvel and DC Comics, where he co-created *X-Men* characters including Wolverine, Nightcrawler, Storm and Colossus, and also *Swamp Thing* (later adapted into a 1982 movie, directed by Wes Craven). He was the editor of the seminal *Watchmen* comic book series. In animation, he wrote for shows such as *Spider-Man*, *Ben 10* and *Iron Man*. In the Transformers universe, he also wrote for the shows *Beast Wars: Transformers* ('Tangled Web') and *Transformers: Beast Machines* ('Savage Noble'). To honour his contribution to the *X-Men* universe, he was given a cameo role in the movie *X-Men: Days of Future Past* (Bryan Singer, 2014).

Data File: Diane Duane (writer)

Duane has written for animated shows such as *DuckTales*, *Scooby-Doo and Scrappy-Doo* and *Batman: The Animated Series*. However, she is best known as a popular author, having created the *Young Wizards* series and penned tie-in novels for franchises such as *X-Men*, *The Outer Limits* and *Star Trek*. She was the co-writer, with fellow *The Transformers* alumnus Michael Reaves, of the *Star Trek: The Next Generation* episode 'Where No One Has Gone Before'.

Review:

While this episode doesn't really have much to say about mental illness (instead using the crazy aliens for cheap laughs), or go into any depth as to the root cause of Galvatron's malaise, it nevertheless works quite well, if only on a superficial level of zany humour.

Plot-wise this is pretty slight – the Autobots barely feature and most of the scenes centre on Galvatron's treatment on Torkulon. However, despite the atypical set-up this is a decent episode, due mostly to Frank Welker, who steals the show with his deliciously unhinged portrayal of Galvatron. The Decepticon leader's irate ranting is a delight to behold, as are his minions' increasing frustrations at their embarrassing boss. 3/5

{3-18} CARNAGE IN C-MINOR

Production number: 700-102 (17th episode produced of Season Three)
Transmission date: 14 October 1986 (14th episode transmitted of Season Three)

Written by Buzz Dixon

Plot:

The Decepticons have fitted a giant engine to an asteroid – their plan is to steer it on a collision course with Metroplex. The Autobots attack, and the engines are blown up, sending the asteroid toward an inhabited alien planet, Eurythma. To everyone's surprise, a wave of harmonic energy rises from the planet and destroys the asteroid. Intrigued by this powerful sonic weapon, the Autobots and Decepticons visit the planet.

The native Eurythmans have a culture based entirely on music – even down to the architecture of their cities. It transpires that their sonic weapon is in fact a vocal harmony, sung by three of the planet's natives. While the Decepticons capture one of the three singers, the Autobots befriend the second.

Over the course of various skirmishes on the planet, Soundwave is able to record the individual elements of the three-part harmony on his cassette tapes. He plays back the finished sound, causing havoc on the planet. Galvatron and Soundwave then head to Earth and play the sonic weapon for Metroplex, causing great damage to the Autobot city.

The Autobots, meanwhile, have gained the trust of the three Eurythman singers, and they all head to Earth. The Eurythmans sing an 'anti-sound' that nullifies the sonic weapon, and Blaster is able to wipe Soundwave's tapes. The Decepticons retreat.

Galvatron's Rants:
- 'No! Not when we're so close to victory!'
- 'They thwarted me! Make them suffer!'
- 'Why should you submit to that old fool's will? We are the future! As our ally, *you* can have the power!'

The Secret Files of Teletraan II:
Another outing for the Quintesson segment, which debuted in {3-10} 'Fight or Flee'.

Roll Call:
Autobots: Ultra Magnus, Perceptor, Grimlock, Superion, Blaster, Broadside, Hot Spot, Silverbolt, Skydive, Air Raid, Slingshot, Fireflight, Defensor, Streetwise, Groove, Blades, First Aid, Scamper and Metroplex. The Autobots Brawn and Huffer appear in a single shot, however this is probably an animation error, as they were both killed in {3-00} *The Transformers: The Movie*.

Decepticons: Galvatron, Soundwave, Hook, Bonecrusher, Devastator, Cyclonus, Mixmaster, Long Haul, Scrapper and Scavenger.

Data File: Buzz Dixon (writer)
Best known as the long-serving story editor for the *G.I. Joe: A Real American Hero* cartoon, Dixon also scripted episodes of *Alvin & the Chipmunks*, *Visionaries*, *Teenage Mutant Ninja Turtles* and *Tiny Toon Adventures*. In the medium of comic books, he wrote for titles such as *The Sensational She-Hulk* and *Disney's Aladdin*.

Data File: Bill Martin (Broadside)
The multitalented William E Martin made his name as a songwriter, penning or co-penning the songs 'All of Your Toys' and 'The Door into Summer' for the Monkees, 'Rainmaker' for Harry Nilsson and 'Evergreen (Earth Anthem)' recorded by The Turtles. He later appeared alongside the Monkees in the 1997 documentary film *Hey, Hey It's the Monkees* (Michael Nesmith, 1997) and co-wrote the screenplay for the film *Harry and the Hendersons* (William Dear, 1987). His voice work includes turns on *Challenge of the GoBots* and *Teenage Mutant Ninja Turtles*, for the latter of which he played the villainous Shredder between 1994 and 1996.

Review:
This is the episode that's harmed more than any other by animation errors; characters change size, colour, appearance and location from shot-to-shot; robots appear in places they shouldn't; characters switch sides and faction symbols ... It's all a bit of a mess.

Which is a crying shame, because the plot, ideas and dialogue here are actually rather good. Having an alien culture based totally on music is a brilliant science-fiction concept, bettered only by the notion of the vocal harmony that can be used as a weapon. The aliens 'sing' all of their lines, making this – essentially – *The Transformers: the Musical*.

If this episode had been animated with care, it would have been up there with the very best. As it is, the concepts and voice work are forced to carry it due to the failings of the visuals, and that's a huge shame. 3/5

{3-19} THE BIG BROADCAST OF 2006 (cartoon episode)
Production number: 700-105 (20th episode produced of Season Three)
Transmission date: 12 November 1986 (22nd episode transmitted of Season Three)

Written by Michael Reaves

NB: Although made and transmitted later in the season, this is set before {3-20} 'The Quintesson Journal', and as such is best placed here in the viewing order.

Plot:
The year 2006: the Quintessons are seeking a mysterious canister located on the planet Junkion. However, their efforts to retrieve the canister are thwarted by Wreck-Gar and his fellow Junkions.

The Quintessons decide on a more subtle tactic: realising that the Junkions are addicted to television broadcasts from Earth, they doctor the transmissions to incorporate hypnotic, subliminal messages. However, when their ship is attacked by the Aerialbots, the hypnotic command becomes scrambled.

Now broadcasting galaxy-wide, the transmissions encourage viewers to seek out and attack alien life – a situation that whips up an interplanetary war. Fortunately, the Autobot Blaster is able to broadcast a jamming frequency that counteracts the effect of the Quintesson signal. The Quintessons retreat, their canister lost in the vacuum of space.

Galvatron's Rants:
- 'A scrapyard! What an appropriate place to meet your end, Rodimus Prime!'

Witty Put-Downs:
- Galvatron calls the Junkions 'rattletrap robots'.

The Secret Files of Teletraan II:
A segment on the Autobots, last seen in {3-17} 'Webworld'.

Spotlight: Junk Culture
As in the comics, Wreck-Gar and his fellow Junkions 'talk TV' – their speech and mannerisms are taken wholesale from 20th Century pop culture. Here is a list of such cultural references in the cartoon show:

{3-00} *The Transformers: The Movie*
- 'Don't look behind door number two, Monty.' From the game show *Let's Make a Deal* (1963-present). 'Monty' is a reference to host Monty Hall.

- 'You check in, but you don't check out.' A misquote of an advertising slogan for Roach Motel insect traps ('Roaches check in but they don't check out'). ·
- 'Film at 11.00.' In old news broadcasts, newsreaders would promise viewers that filmed footage of breaking news stories would be shown during the evening bulletin.
- 'Please close cover before striking.' A warning message usually found on books of matches.
- 'Aw, rootie.' From the lyrics of 'Tutti Frutti', a classic rock and roll number by Little Richard.
- 'Kemosabe.' A term of endearment used by *The Lone Ranger* to refer to his trusty sidekick, Tonto. Also heard in {3-04} 'Five Faces of Darkness, Part Four'.
- 'Happy motoring.' An advertising slogan used by the fuel company Esso.
- 'Kill the Grand Poobah.' Pooh-Bah was a self-important, officious character from Gilbert and Sullivan's comic opera *The Mikado* (1885). 'Grand Poobah' has since become a mocking title referring to people of a similar bent.

{3-04} 'Five Faces of Darkness, Part Four'
- 'Hello, you out there in television land!' Another misquote, this time from 'Mr and Mrs TV Show', a 1955 episode of the sitcom *I Love Lucy* (the exact quote is 'Hello out there in TV land!'), later also used as a catchphrase in the *Rocky and Bullwinkle Show* (1959-64).
- 'Glad you used the dial'. Based on 'Aren't you glad you use Dial', an advertising slogan for Dial, a popular brand of soap.
- 'Come on down.' A catchphrase from the game show *The Price is Right* (1972-present). Also heard in {3-12} 'Starscream's Ghost'.
- 'Let's all be there'. (Actually spoken by Rodimus Prime, trying to communicate with Wreck-Gar on the same level.) An advertising slogan for the NBC television network.
- 'Wreck-Gar will put you in good hands.' 'You're in good hands' is a famous advertising slogan for Allstate Insurance.
- 'I've got a secret.' *I've Got a Secret* was a celebrity panel game show launched in 1952.
- 'You'll have Springer back faster than snap-crackle-pop.' 'Snap, crackle and pop' is the advertising slogan for Kellogg's Rice Krispies breakfast cereal.
- 'I believe in me.' Advertising slogan for Crystal Light, a brand of fruit-flavoured drink mixes. Also heard in {3-19} 'The Big Broadcast of 2006'.

{3-06} 'The Killing Jar'
- 'Smile. No candid camera insta-clicks me!' *Candid Camera* was a hidden-camera reality show launched in 1948. The show's catchphrase was 'Smile, you're on *Candid Camera*.'
- 'Home, sweet home'. A phrase first heard in the song 'Home! Sweet Home!' from John Howard Payne's 1823 opera *Clari, or the Maid of Milan*.
- 'Book me, Danno. I have the right to remain silent.' 'Book him, Danno' was a catchphrase of the cop show *Hawaii Five-O* (1968-1980).
- 'What a revoltin' development!' Catchphrase of Chester A Riley, lead character in the radio, film and television sitcom *The Life of Riley* (launched 1944).

- 'We've gotta get out of this place!' From 'We Gotta Get out of This Place', a 1965 hit single by the Animals.
- 'And away go troubles down the drain' advertising slogan for Roto-Rooter, an American plumbing company.
- 'Marissa's stayin' up all night long.' A misquote of some lyrics from 'All Night Long', a 1980 solo single for the Eagles' guitarist Joe Walsh.
- 'Wreck-Gar phoned home!' A misquote of a famous line ('ET phone home') from the movie *E.T. The Extra-Terrestrial* (Steven Spielberg, 1982).
- 'Go back, Jack, and do it again.' Lyrics from 'Do it Again', a 1972 single by Steely Dan.

{3-07} 'Chaos'
- 'Nine out of ten Autobots and the Surgeon General agree that death crystals can be hazardous to your health'. A spoof of the health warnings commonly found on tobacco products.

{3-09} 'Forever is a Long Time Coming'
- 'Golly, Mr Wizard.' A reference to the educational children's programmes *Watch Mr. Wizard* (1951-72) and its successor series *Mr. Wizard's World* (1983-90).
- 'And that's the way it is.' Catchphrase of popular CBS news anchor Walter Cronkite.
- 'We've come a long way, baby'. From the advertising slogan of Virginia Slims cigarettes ('You've come a long way, baby').

{3-12} 'Starscream's Ghost'
- 'Head 'em up and move 'em out!' A misquote of some lyrics to the theme tune of the television Western *Rawhide* (1959-1966).
- 'A day without scrap metal is like a breakfast without sunshine.' A mangled version of the slogan for Florida Orange Juice: 'Breakfast without orange juice is like a day without sunshine.'
- 'Can't please all of the people all of the time'. A rewording of the popular idiom 'Can't fool all of the people all of the time', often incorrectly attributed to Abraham Lincoln but in fact derived from a French-language text by Jacques Abbadie.
- 'The best to you each morning.' An advertising slogan for Kellogg's breakfast cereals.

{3-19} 'The Big Broadcast of 2006' (NB: the following is a list of references exclusive to the television script. For the remainder, see the entry for the comic adaptation, [43] 'The Big Broadcast of 2006'.)
- 'Your hit parade!' *Your Hit Parade* was a radio and television programme (1935-1959).
- 'Say goodnight, Gracie.' Catchphrase from the television sitcom *The George Burns and Gracie Allen Show* (1950-58).
- 'Oh, Cisco', 'Oh Pancho'. From the television Western series *The Cisco Kid* (1950-56).
- 'Find somebody else's friendly skies.' A reference to 'Fly the friendly skies of United', an advertising slogan for United Airlines.
- 'And that's the name of *that* tune.' Catchphrase of the title character in the cop

show *Baretta* (1975-78), which is itself derived from the game show *Name That Tune* (launched 1952).

- 'Warning, Will Robinson! Danger! Danger!' Another television catchphrase, this time from *Lost in Space* (1965-68).

- 'I pity the fool!' Catchphrase of actor Mr T, who spoke the line in the television series *The A-Team* (1983-87) and also in the film *Rocky III* (Sylvester Stallone, 1982). Also the title of a 1961 single by Bobby Bland, later covered by David Bowie's group the Manish Boys.

- 'Let's consume mass quantities.' From Dan Aykroyd's 'Coneheads' sketches on *Saturday Night Live* (which began in 1977), later adapted into the film *Coneheads* (Steve Barron, 1993).

- 'Look! Up in the sky! It's a bird! It's a plane! It's –' 'Great Caesar's ghost!' Quotes from *The Adventures of Superman*, the television series that ran between 1952 and 1958.

- 'Missed me by that much!' Catchphrase from the spy sitcom *Get Smart* (1965-70).

- 'Lassie!' Lassie is a fictional dog created by author Eric Knight for his 1940 novel *Lassie Come Home*, later adapted into a film (Fred M Wilcox, 1943) and the television series *Lassie* (1954-73).

- 'And I'm beautiful!' 'Baby, you're the greatest.' Lines regularly heard in television sitcom *The Honeymooners* (1955-56). For more on *The Honeymooners*, see the entry for [5] 'The New Order'.

- 'There is nothing wrong with your television set. We are controlling transmission. We control the horizontal. We control the vertical.' Narration from the opening titles to sci-fi show *The Outer Limits* (1963-65).

- 'We've got the touch!' Advertising slogan for the CBS television network. Possibly also a reference to 'The Touch', a song by Stan Bush that appeared on the soundtrack to {3-00} *The Transformers: The Movie*.

{3-22} 'The Dweller in the Depths'

- 'Yo Joe!' rallying cry used by the GI Joe team in the animated series *G.I. Joe: A Real American Hero* (1983-86).

- 'Here I come to save the day!' Lyrics from the theme tune to the cartoon series *Mighty Mouse* (created 1942).

- 'Can this be the end of little Wreck-Gar?' The Junkion leader paraphrases the final words of the titular gangster in the film *Little Caesar* (Mervyn LeRoy, 1931).

- 'Feed me!' Catchphrase of Audrey II, the evil alien plant from *The Little Shoppe of Horrors* (Frank Oz, 1986).

- 'Y'all don't come back now, y'hear'. A misquote of lyrics from 'The Ballad of Jed Clampett', the theme music to the sitcom *The Beverly Hillbillies* (1962-71).

{3-29} 'The Return of Optimus Prime, Part One'

- 'Ayayayayay! Lucy, Lucy, what have you done now?' As spoken by the character Ricky Ricardo in the sitcom *I Love Lucy* (1951-57).

- 'I'm a doctor, not a forklift!' 'His engines, they cannae take the strain!' 'He's dead, Jim'. All quotes or parodies of quotes from the television sci-fi show *Star Trek* (1966-69).

- 'Well excuuuse us!' A riff on 'Well excuuuse me', a catchphrase of American

comedian Steve Martin.
- 'I'm a pepper! Wouldn't you like to be a pepper, too?' Two advertising slogans for the carbonated drink Dr Pepper.

Roll Call:
Autobots: Powerglide (appears on Wreck-Gar's television screen), Wreck-Gar, Sky Lynx, Rodimus Prime, Ultra Magnus, Silverbolt, Skydive, Air Raid, Slingshot, Fireflight, Superion, First Aid, Omega Supreme, Blaster and Kup.

Decepticons: Astrotrain, Cyclonus, Galvatron, Scourge, Blast Off and Soundwave.

Other: Quintessons.

Data File: Michael Reaves (writer)
As well as his solitary original-series *The Transformers* episode, Reaves also wrote three of *Transformers: Beast Machines*. He was a prolific scriptwriter, with credits on a vast array of television shows, ranging from live-action (*The Twilight Zone*, *Buck Rogers in the 25th Century*, *The Incredible Hulk*, *Star Trek: The Next Generation*) to animation (*He-Man and the Masters of the Universe*, *Droids*, *Dungeons & Dragons*, *Teenage Mutant Ninja Turtles*). His work on *Batman: the Animated Series* won him an Emmy, and he has also written a number of *Star Wars* tie-in novels.

Data File: Tony Pope (voices, including Wreck-Gar in Season Three)
A prolific voice actor, Pope was the voice of Disney's Goofy for a number of years, most notably in *Who Framed Roger Rabbit?* (Robert Zemeckis, 1988). While he has voiced numerous Western animations, including *Pole Position*, *James Bond Jr.* and *Teenage Mutant Ninja Turtles*, much of his work has been English-language dubs of Japanese anime, including *Hello Kitty*, *Mobile Suit Gundam* and the film *Akira* (Katsuhiro Otomo, 1988).

Review:
A superficially fun episode – the Junkions and the Quintessons are hilarious here – but it doesn't really hold up under any sort of scrutiny. The Quintessons want to find a canister that's landed on the surface of Junkion, and to retrieve it they hypnotise the Junkions into becoming xenophobic and belligerent – which seems completely counterproductive to their aims. Why not instead hypnotise the Junkions into accepting the Quintessons as friends, allowing them free access to the canister?
A poorly thought-out plot, masked by a witty script. 2/5

{3-20} THE QUINTESSON JOURNAL
Production number: 700-103 (18th episode produced of Season Three)
Transmission date: 11 November 1986 (21st episode transmitted of Season Three)

Written by Richard Merwin

Plot:
The Quintesson canister (see {3-19} 'The Big Broadcast of 2006') lands on an alien world. Detecting its signal, both the Autobots and Decepticons send teams to investigate. After

a series of battles, during which the Autobots and Quintessons both briefly seize the canister, it is eventually taken by the Decepticons.

Meanwhile, Rodimus Prime is chairing a peace conference between two warring planets: Xetaxxis and Lanarq. The talks are not going well, and both sides secretly plan to destroy each other using an 'ultimate weapon'.

Galvatron opens the canister and discovers that it is a journal, with details of all the Quintessons' shady business deals. One such scheme involves them deliberately perpetuating the Xetaxxis/Lanarq war so that they can sell weapons to both sides.

The Autobots make a grab for the journal and head back to the peace conference, where the footage is shown to the warring aliens. Realising that their entire war has been engineered by the Quintessons, they agree to a cease fire. The Quintesson ship arrives, carrying the 'ultimate weapons' they had promised to deliver to the two sides, but the Aubotots blast at it – the weapons ignite, and the Quintessons perish in the ensuing explosion.

Galvatron's Rants:
- 'No mercy! And no mistakes!'
- '*I* decide who dies, and when!'

Witty Put-Downs:
- Sky Lynx isn't too impressed with Predaking's aim: 'You need more target practice!'

The Secret Files of Teletraan II:
Profiles on Metroplex and Trypticon, including clips taken from episodes such as {3-05} 'The Five Faces of Darkness, Part Five' and {3-11} 'Thief in the Night'.

Roll Call:
Autobots: Rodimus Prime, Ultra Magnus, Blurr, Blaster, Perceptor, Sky Lynx, Outback, Ramhorn and Steeljaw.

Decepticons: Predaking, Cyclonus, Tantrum, Headstrong, Razorclaw, Rampage, Divebomb, Scourge and Galvatron.

Other: Spike and the Quintessons.

Data File: Richard Merwin (writer)
Richard Merwin contributed scripts to cartoon shows such as *The Smurfs*, *Teenage Mutant Ninja Turtles* and *The New Adventures of He-Man*. He was also a writer and story editor on the animated show *Police Academy: The Series*.

Data File: Ron Feinburg (voices, including Headstrong)
The distinctive (6' 8" tall) Feinburg has many live-action television credits to his name, including on *Mission: Impossible*, *Hawaii Five-O* and *Hill Street Blues*. As a voice actor he played the villain Titanus in three episodes of *Teenage Mutant Ninja Turtles*, Vladimir Grizzlikof in *Darkwing Duck* and Ming the Merciless in *Defenders of the Earth*.

Review:
An exciting episode, full of battles, captures and escapes. There's depth here too – it's an examination of the futility of war, advocating that talks and negotiations are the best way to build peace. And after their inept showing in the previous episode, the Quintessons are much more of a threat here: their portrayal as shadowy intergalactic troublemakers gives them some much-needed credibility. 4/5

{3-21} THE ULTIMATE WEAPON

Production number: 700-104 (19th episode produced of Season Three)
Transmission date: 10 November 1986 (20th episode transmitted of Season Three)

Written by Arthur Byron Cover

Plot:
Galvatron attacks the Autobots in a small town, and boasts of having at his disposal an ultimate weapon that he can use at any time. However, the battle is merely a diversion, allowing the Decepticon Swindle to sneak into Metroplex and steal the transformation cog, leaving the Autobot city unable to assume robot mode. First Aid witnesses the theft, but his pacifist nature means he is unable to fight Swindle and prevent it.

First Aid feels guilty and useless, so decides to leave the Autobot ranks. Rodimus Prime also begins to question his own judgment and leadership skills. Spike and Daniel infiltrate Trypticon and steal his transformation cog, and install it in Metroplex. However, Metroplex's body rejects the new cog, causing incomplete and involuntary transformations.

In response, the Decepticons install Metroplex's cog in Trypticon. That operation is more successful, albeit that Trypticon loses the use of an arm. The giant robots do battle, and the unstable Metroplex looks like being the loser.

In the end, the Autobots are able to convince First Aid to rejoin their ranks, and he is able to adapt the cog in Metroplex to work correctly. Fully recovered, Metroplex throws Trypticon into a swamp.

Galvatron taunts Rodimus with more goading about his ultimate weapon, but the Autobot leader, now recovered from his crisis of confidence, sees through this bluff and forces the Decepticons into retreat.

Galvatron's Rants:
- 'Too late, Autobots! I, Galvatron, will destroy you all!'
- 'If my current plan fails, there's always my ultimate weapon! Nothing can stand in its wake!'

Witty Put-Downs:
- A great one from Rodimus Prime: 'Why don't you get used to losing, Galvatron? It's all you ever do!'
- Galvatron is not impressed by his troops: 'Weaklings! Wimps!'

Roll Call:
Autobots: Ultra Magnus, Blades, Hot Spot, First Aid, Groove, Rodimus Prime, Steeljaw, Ramhorn, Metroplex, Scamper, Slammer, Silverbolt, Air Raid, Slingshot, Skydive and Fireflight.

Decepticons: Galvatron, Cyclonus, Brawl, Octane, Predaking, Vortex, Swindle, Trypticon and Blitzwing.

Other: Spike and Daniel.

Data File: Bud Davis (voices, including Dirge, Metroplex and Predaking)
Davis has had a few acting credits, in shows such as *Remington Steele, Knots Landing* and *The Colbys*. However, he is best known as a stuntman, and latterly a stunt coordinator, on films such as *Tango & Cash* (Andrei Konchalovsky, 1989), *Forrest Gump* (Robert Zemeckis, 1994) and *Inglorious Basterds* (Quentin Tarantino, 2009).

Data File: Arthur Byron Cover (writer)
Arthur Byron Cover is best known as novelist. His first book, *Autumn Angels*, was nominated for the Nebula Prize. His writing career includes a *Buffy the Vampire Slayer* novel ('Night of the Living Rerun') and the official novelisation of the movie *Flash Gordon* (Mike Hodges, 1980), and he has also co-written with Harlan Ellison some issues of Marvel's *Daredevil* comic. In the field of animation, he wrote scripts for shows such as *The Real Ghostbusters* and *Defenders of the Earth*.

Review:
A mature script, in which two Autobots, First Aid and Rodimus Prime, overcome personal problems and end up saving the day. Considering it's only a children's cartoon, it's nice to see some conflict and drama arise from the characters and their relationships with each other, rather than simply have plot-driven stories all the time. But that's not to say the episode is totally serious either: there are some genuinely funny moments too, such as the scene in which Swindle tries to sell the transformation cog to Galvatron.

What's great is that the backdrop to all these character moments – the plot about transformation cogs and Galvatron's 'ultimate weapon' bluff – also work really well, leaving us with one of the most well-rounded and satisfying episodes of the entire run. 5/5

{3-22} THE DWELLER IN THE DEPTHS
Production number: 700-107 (22nd episode produced of Season Three)
Transmission date: 30 October 1986 (18th episode transmitted of Season Three)

Written by Paul Dini

Plot:
Prior to the creation of the Transformers, the Quintessons built a legion of hideous techno-organic creatures, which they then sealed beneath Cybertron's surface. They now plan to conquer the planet by unleashing these hellish monsters to kill all the inhabitants.

The Quintessons trick Galvatron into travelling to Cybertron and releasing the creatures. The lead monster, known as the Dweller, is able to suck the life force from any Transformers it touches, turning them into zombies.

The Dweller runs riot on Cybertron, amassing a zombie army that attacks the Autobots. Perceptor, however, discovers a way to re-convert zombified Transformers back to normal.

The Dweller feeds on energy, and to that end heads toward the Autobots' new power core. However, Rodimus launches the power core into space, and the creature along with it. The Quintessons approach Cybertron in their ship, hoping to find that the Transformers have been wiped out, but their ship is met by the Dweller, who proceeds to feast on them instead.

Galvatron's Rants:
- 'You cringing, cowardly, weak-willed fools! Why am I still stuck on this worthless cosmic trash bin? Why have I not retaken Cybertron? And – most importantly – why have I been saddled with such a useless pile of rusting junk for followers?!'

The Secret Files of Teletraan II:
A fourth outing for the Decepticon clip, introduced in {3-11} 'Thief in the Night'.

Roll Call:
Autobots: Springer, Rodimus Prime, Ultra Magnus, Perceptor, Arcee, Kup, Wreck-Gar, Streetwise and Groove.

Decepticons: Galvatron, Scourge and Cyclonus.

Other: the Quintessons.

Data File: Paul Dini (writer)
A legendary writer for animation, Dini has dozens of script credits to his name, for shows such as *He-Man and the Masters of the Universe*, *Star Wars: The Clone Wars* and *Tiny Toon Adventures*. He is especially well-known for his work on cartoon series based on DC comics characters, including *Krypto the Superdog*, *Justice League* and various *Batman* shows, including the Emmy-winning *Batman: The Animated Series*, *The New Batman Adventures* and *Batman Beyond*, and is the creator of the iconic villainess Harley Quinn. More recently, he has moved into writing scripts for video games, including *Lego Batman: The Videogame* and *Batman: Arkham Knight*. He was a writer/story editor on the popular live-action fantasy series *Lost*, and had a cameo role in the cult classic film *Jay and Silent Bob Strike Back* (Kevin Smith, 2001).

Data File: Roger C Carmel (voices, including Cyclonus and Motormaster)
Carmel's acting credits date back to the 1960s, when he appeared in episodes of famous series such as *The Munsters*, *The Man from U.N.C.L.E.*, *Hawaii Five-O* and *Batman*. In his later career he did a lot of voice work on cartoons including *Jonny Quest*, *DuckTales* and *Adventures of the Gummi Bears*. He will be forever associated with the character Harry Mudd, whom he played in three *Star Trek* episodes, 'Mudd's Women', 'I, Mudd' and the animated adventure 'Mudd's Passion'.

Review:
This is basically the Transformers equivalent of a monster movie – a Quintesson has his face smashed to pieces, a number of much-loved Autobots are turned into zombies, and hideous creatures go on the rampage, attacking our heroes. It's well-animated, unpretentious, visceral, highly-charged and action-packed. 4/5

Spotlight: Joe in the Show

While *The Transformers* comics made a big song and dance about their crossovers with the *G.I Joe* franchise ([29.1] 'Ancient Relics', [GIJ1] 'Blood on the Tracks' *et al*), *The Transformers* cartoon paid homage to the 'Real American Heroes' using much subtler means.

On three separate occasions, a character from *G.I Joe: A Real American Hero* made an appearance in *The Transformers* cartoon, and each time those characters went unnamed. The first such instance was in {2-35} 'Prime Target', in which we see a moustachioed, Hispanic news anchor. Although the character was not named within the episode itself, writer Buzz Dixon later confirmed that he was none other than Hector Ramirez, who debuted in the *G.I. Joe: A Real American Hero* episode 'Twenty Questions'. Ramirez would also appear in other Sunbow-produced cartoon shows, such as *Inhumanoids* and *Jem and the Holograms*.

But Ramirez was only ever a minor character; the next *G.I. Joe* cameo would prove to be a big-hitter. Marissa Faireborn is a recurring human character in *The Transformers*, making her debut in {3-03} 'Five Faces of Darkness, Part Three'. In {3-06} 'The Killing Jar' we see an image of her father. Although her father goes unnamed in the episode itself, the 'Faireborn' surname and the identity of the voice actor (Bill Ratner) point to the fact that Marissa is the daughter of Dashiell R Faireborn – aka Flint from *G.I. Joe*.

The third and final guest appearance by a *G.I. Joe* character would also be a popular one. The lead villain in {3-23} 'Only Human' is identified only as 'Old Snake' and wears a trenchcoat that disguises most of his body. However, the rasping voice and the silver faceplate are unmistakable: this is none other than Cobra Commander, leader of *G.I. Joe*'s villainous Cobra organisation. (At one point in the episode, 'Old Snake' even attempts to let out his famous 'Cobraaaa' battle-cry – but is cut off when he starts having a coughing fit.)

There are a number of other *G.I Joe* references in *The Transformers* cartoon. The Oktober Guard, a Russian military unit from the *G.I. Joe* universe, are seen in {2-35} 'Prime Target'. Artificial creatures known as Synthoids, from the *G.I. Joe* cartoon two-parter 'The Synthoid Conspiracy', show up in {3-23} 'Only Human'. GI Joe vehicles such as the MOBAT and the Armadillo can be seen during the army base scene in {2-41} 'The Key to Vector Sigma, Part Two'. In {3-22} 'The Dweller in the Depths', Wreck-Gar even lets out the famous 'Yo Joe!' rallying cry. Finally, in {3-19} 'The Big Broadcast of 2006', a parody of *G.I. Joe* entitled *Space Age Jack* can be seen on one of Wreck-Gar's television screens.

As the *G.I. Joe* and *The Transformers* cartoons were made by the same production company, many of the writers, staff and voice cast worked on both shows. Even the stock incidental music was shared between them. Once such piece was a rock song, 'Cold Slither', from the *G.I. Joe* episode of the same name, which Cobra used to feed subliminal messages to an unsuspecting public. That same music later saw use in *The Transformers*: Jazz played it in {2-07} 'The Autobot Run', Blaster played it in both {2-23} 'Blaster Blues' and {2-30} 'Quest for Survival', and it was heard at the Dancitron nightclub in {3-26} 'Auto-Bop'.

{3-23} ONLY HUMAN

Production number: 700-108 (23rd episode produced of Season Three)
Transmission date: 13 November 1986 (23rd episode transmitted of Season Three)

Written by Susan K Williams

Plot:
When the Autobots foil a plot by crime lord and terrorist Victor Drath, who has attacked New York as a cover to steal some explosive Newtronium, Drath becomes determined to destroy them.

Drath contacts the mysterious 'Old Snake', who has the technology to transfer brains into Synthoids – replica human bodies. Drath lures four Autobots – Springer, Arcee, Rodimus Prime and Ultra Magnus – into a trap. Once disabled, Drath and Old Snake transfer the Autobots' minds into human bodies.

These four Autobots – now creatures of flesh and blood – manage to survive Drath's assassination attempt and go on the run. Arcee goes to Autobot City – but as she is stuck in the body of a human, no-one believes her when she claims to be an Autobot. Ultra Magnus and Rodimus Prime are captured while investigating Drath, but Springer is able to infiltrate the ranks of Drath's minions.

Drath plans to load the Autobots' old bodies with explosives, then have them enter Autobot City. Once inside, the explosives will detonate and destroy the city. However Springer is able to commandeer his old body and fires on Autobot City – prompting the rest of the Autobots to activate their defences, and thus prevent the bomb-filled bodies of their colleagues from entering.

With Drath's plan foiled, the Autobots use his machinery to restore Rodimus Prime, Arcee, Springer and Ultra Magnus to their proper bodies.

Witty Put-Downs:
- One of Drath's minions, after failing to kill the human Autobots: 'Your trash got up and took a hike, before I could squash 'em!'

Roll Call:
Autobots: Springer, Arcee, Ultra Magnus, Rodimus Prime, Kup, Blaster, Perceptor and Grimlock.

Data File: Susan K Williams (writer)
The Transformers is one of just two credits Williams has to her name, the other being the *G.I. Joe: A Real American Hero* episode 'The Spy who Rooked Me'.

Data File: Susan Blu (voices, including Arcee and Marissa Faireborn)
Susan Blu began as a voice actress before moving into voice directing and casting. Her live-action roles included parts in *Kojak*, *St Elsewhere* and *Knight Rider*. As a voice actress, she played Aimee in *Galaxy High*, Galadria in *Visionaries* and Judge McBride in *BraveStarr*, and also contributed to *Scooby-Doo and Scrappy-Doo*, *The Simpsons* and the feature film *Cars* (John Lasseter and Joe Ranft, 2006). Behind the scenes, she performed voice casting for *Star Wars: The Clone Wars* and *Ben 10: Omniverse*, amongst others. As a voice director, she worked on *Teenage Mutant Ninja Turtles*, *Extreme Ghostbusters* and *Handy Manny*. She has continued to be involved in the Transformers franchise, contributing voices and/or her directorial talents to *Beast Wars: Transformers*, *Transformers: Beast Machines*, *Transformers: Animated* and *Transformers: Prime*.

Review:

A concept so good you wonder why no-one had done it before, 'Only Human' shows us how the Autobots would fare if they became human. Arcee is mistaken for a lunatic and locked away, Rodimus Prime is seduced by a duplicitous female villain, and Ultra Magnus … just gets captured. In the end it's Springer who has to save the day, posing as one of the villain's henchmen in order to foil their plans from within.

While it's an unusual and action-packed episode, however, it does seem like a missed opportunity to shed new light on the Autobots. The four converts don't stop to reflect on what has happened to them, or appear to gain any new understanding of humans; they just act and talk like they normally would, without missing a beat. There's nary a mention of their new-found fragility and mortality, and Rodimus Prime casually drinks a bad-tasting drink as if eating and drinking was something he did every day. Considering that they have become fundamentally changed, their response to their situation is just so casual and restrained.

This really needed to be a two-parter, as the ideas presented here warranted more examination than a single episode had time to give them. While it's a novelty watching human Transformers foil a terrorist group, it would have been preferable to have some time set aside to focus on the emotional and metaphysical implications of their situaton. 3/5

{3-24} GRIMLOCK'S NEW BRAIN

Production number: 700-110 (24th episode produced of Season Three)
Transmission date: 14 November 1986 (24th episode transmitted of Season Three)

Written by Paul Davids

Plot:

The Autobots unveil a new power generator, but two of Galvatron's alien agents infiltrate Cybertron and sabotage the device using anti-electrons; this causes it to break down, sending out beams of energy that cause the Autobots to malfunction.

The Autobots head underground to the generator's core, and Grimlock deactivates it by biting through the controls. In severing the connection, Grimlock is zapped by a beam of energy that gives him super-intelligence.

Now incredibly smart, Grimlock deduces that the Decepticons's next strike will be at Unicron's head, in an attempt to procure more anti-electrons. The Autobots travel to the head but are stopped in their tracks by the Terrorcons, Galvatron's new combiner team.

Grimlock slips away and creates a combiner team of his own, the Technobots, and transfuses his super-intelligence into them, thereby returning him to his old, dim-witted self. The Technobots are able to take down the Terrorcons with ease, and the Decepticons retreat.

Galvatron's Rants:

- 'You insolent organics! You failed in your mission!'
- 'I want those Autobots turned into so many pieces that we couldn't even sell them as junk to the Junkions!'

Witty Put-Downs:
- Grimlock: 'Grimlock smartest Dinobot of them all!' 'Unfortunately,' laments Perceptor, 'that's probably true.'
- Grimlock turns the tables on Perceptor after being given super-intelligence: 'Your mental abilities are so limited.'

The Secret Files of Teletraan II:
A profile of Ultra Magnus. Footage includes clips from {3-13} 'Surprise Party', {3-14} 'Madman's Paradise' and {3-18} 'Carnage in C-Minor'.

Roll Call:
Autobots: Ultra Magnus, Perceptor, Rodimus Prime, Grimlock, Sludge, Wheelie, Springer, Kup, Blurr, Snarl, Broadside, Slag, Cosmos, Sky Lynx, Blaster, **Nosecone, Lightspeed, Strafe, Scattershot, Afterburner, Computron** and Skydive.

Decepticons: Scourge, Galvatron, Cyclonus, **Rippersnapper, Blot, Sinnertwin, Cutthroat, Hun-Gurr** and **Abominus**.

Other: the Skuxxoid, Slizardo and Unicron.

Data File: Jered Barclay (voices, including Cerebros and Sinnertwin)
Jered Barclay's career dates back to the '50s, where he was cast predominantly in television Westerns, such as *Cheyenne, Rawhide, Gunslinger* and *Bonanza*. He later moved into voice work, and can be heard in shows such as *The Jetsons, Pole Position* and *Foofur*.

Data File: Bert Kramer (Computron)
Kramer's other television credits include *Mission: Impossible, M*A*S*H, Kojak* and *The Six Million Dollar Man*. On the silver screen, he can be seen in *Lady Sings the Blues* (Sidney J Furie, 1972) and *Volcano* (Mick Jackson, 1997).

Review:
A fun, breezy episode, in which Grimlock turns the tables on every Transformer to have called him 'stupid' over the years. He saves the day – twice – and ends up giving life to five new Autobots … not bad for a day's work!

That said, it's an episode that's all froth and no meat: light, with little in the way of depth, meaning or sense of threat, making it just a little *too* laid back for its own good. 3/5

{3-25} MONEY IS EVERYTHING
Production number: 700-111 (25th episode produced of Season Three)
Transmission date: 17 November 1986 (25th episode transmitted of Season Three)

Written by Carla and Gerry Conway

Plot:
Marissa Faireborn and the Technobots come to the rescue when intergalactic trader and rogue Dirk Manus is attacked by Hun-Gurr in space. Manus tries to woo Faireborn, but it's all a deception: he is in league with the Quintessons, and plans to sell them a

'recreator': a device that can heal injuries and diseases – but can also dematerialise people.

The trade is made, but the Quintessons double-cross Manus by giving him fake cash and planting a bomb on his ship. Manus crash-lands, only to be met by Faireborn and the Technobots – who aren't very happy to see him. The Technobots are injured in a battle with the Sharkticons and are thus unable to resist when Manus steals Faireborn's handgun and forces them at gunpoint to travel to the Quintesson base.

There, Manus turns the tables on the Quintessons by using the recreator to heal the Technobots' injuries. The Quintessons retreat and Manus flies off, having seemingly stolen all the Quintessons' cash.

However, Faireborn has a double-cross of her own up her sleeve – she knows that all the Quintesson money is in fact comprised of worthless 'mimic dust', and that Manus's shady schemes have gone unrewarded.

Witty Put-Downs:
- Dirk Manus and the Quintessons regard each other with disgust: 'Slimy, worm-fingered creep!' 'Unlikable, dry-skinned biped!'

The Secret Files of Teletraan II:
A look at the various cassette Transformers, illustrated via clips from {2-19} 'Megatron's Master Plan, Part One', {3-09} 'Forever is a Long Time Coming', {3-14} 'Madman's Paradise' and {3-17} 'Webworld'.

Roll Call:
Autobots: Scattershot, Strafe, Afterburner, Nosecone, Lightspeed and Computron.

Decepticons: Hun-Gurrr, Abominus, Rippersnapper, Cutthroat, Sinnertwin and Blot.

Other: Marissa Faireborn and the Quintessons.

Data File: Gerry Conway and Carla Conway (writers)
The (later divorced) husband-and-wife writing team had numerous credits to their name, both in television and in comics. Gerry is the most notable of the two, having co-created the title character of *The Punisher* for Marvel Comics (for whom he served briefly as Editor-in-Chief), plus Killer Croc, a notable *Batman* villain, for DC Comics. He wrote an infamous issue of *The Amazing Spider-Man* – #121, 'The Night Gwen Stacy Died' – and scripted the Marvel/DC crossover, *Superman vs. The Amazing Spider-Man*. Later moving into television, he wrote for *Perry Mason*, *Baywatch Nights* and *Law and Order* and was co-executive producer on *Law and Order: Criminal Intent*.

Carla Conway wrote for animated shows such as *My Little Pony 'n' Friends*, *Jem and the Holograms* and *Centurions*, and scripted for comics such as *Superman* and *Ms. Marvel*.

Data File: Steve Bulin (voices, including Strafe and Sureshot)
Steve Bulin is best known for voicing English-language dubs of Japanese anime. His credits in the genre include *Ghost in the Shell*, *Mobile Suit Gundam* and the title role in *Crying Freeman*. His work for Western productions includes *DuckTales*, *Dawson's Creek*, and movies such as *Shrek* (Andrew Adamson and Vicky Jensen, 2001) and *Turner & Hooch* (Roger Spottiswoode, 1989).

Review:

It seems that the writers must have been given a brief to develop the new Technobot and Terrorcon characters, as no other Transformers feature here. However, instead of light being shed on these new characters, we get a tale that focuses on a galactic con-man and his shady double-dealing. It is an episode in which the Transformers are virtual bystanders in their own show.

Up until the final twist, where she gets her own back, Faireborn is disappointingly stupid here, getting conned by Manus twice, getting tied-up, and easily losing her gun to him. The Technobots and Quintessons are equally gullible, trusting Manus time and again even though he's a proven liar.

Poor, and frustratingly so. 1/5

Spotlight: *The Transformers* on Home Video

The complete animated adventures of the Generation One Transformers had their first commercial release on DVD, in both the USA and Europe, in 2004. Numerous reissues and rereleases have ensured that they have been continually available to buy since then.

In the USA, the rights to the episodes are currently licensed to a company called Shout! Factory, who have released the series on DVD as both individual season sets and a complete box set. Prior to Shout! Factory gaining the licence in 2009, individual season sets were released by Kid Rhino. In the United Kingdom, DVD releases have long been handled by Metrodome, who themselves took over the licence from Sony/Maverick.

But while all the episodes are available to us today, only a selection were released to fans back in the '80s. In North America, the VHS video cassette rights were held by Family Home Entertainment (FHE). They put out every episode of Season One but, probably due to dwindling sales, the initial steady stream of releases soon turned into a trickle; only two episodes of Season Two were released ({2-31} 'The Secret of Omega Supreme' and {2-42} 'War Dawn'), and Season Three fared little better, with only the multi-part stories 'Five Faces of Darkness' ({3-01 to 05}) and 'The Return of Optimus Prime' ({3-29 to 30}) seeing the light of day. {3-00} *The Transformers: The Movie* was also released on VHS by FHE.

Possibly the heavy schedule of reruns in America meant that fan demand to own individual episodes on videotape was not as great there as in other parts of the world. In the United Kingdom, only Season One episodes were ever broadcast on free-to-air television, and even then in a seemingly haphazard and irregular way (see Appendix 1 for more on this). Consequently, the VHS releases, which tended to concentrate on later episodes, were more of a draw.

Only four Season One episodes – the three-part pilot episode, plus {1-16} 'Heavy Metal War' – made it to home video in the UK; Season Two and Three episodes made up the remainder of the releases. Most of these were two-parters – 'Megatron's Master Plan', 'Desertion of the Dinobots' etc – but a number of other random episodes also featured, including {2-38} 'The Girl Who Loved Powerglide', {3-26} 'Call of the Primitives' and {3-08} 'Dark Awakening'. A few different companies released these videos as the licence changed hands through the decade, including Video Gems, Entertainment UK and Tempo Video. It would seem that only a limited number of episodes were covered by the licence, as the various companies all seemed to release the same batches of episodes again and again in different permutations ('The Girl Who Loved Powerglide', for example, saw at least four separate releases).

{3-26} CALL OF THE PRIMITIVES

Production number: 700-112 (26th episode produced of Season Three)
Transmission date: 18 November 1986 (26th episode transmitted of Season Three)

Written by Donald F Glut

Plot:

A strange and destructive force is unleashed upon the galaxy: Tornedron, an energy creature who can suck the energy (and indeed life) from stars, planets, comets … and Transformers. After completely draining Cybertron of all life, Tornedron heads to Earth's moon, where the Autobots and Decepticons are engaged in battle. During the conflict, a strange ethereal voice contacts the 'primitives' (i.e. those Transformers with animal or creature modes) and entices them to leave the battlefield. While Galvatron and Rodimus Prime ponder why a number of their troops have deserted them, Tornedron arrives and consumes their life energy, before doing the same to the planet Earth.

The primitive Transformers are drawn to a barren planetoid where they come into contact with the bodiless intelligence that drew them there. The voice explains that Tornedron is just the latest planet-devouring creation of an evil genius called Primacron. Primacron's other creations include a number of the primitive Transformers – and also Unicron!

Tornedron arrives and begins sucking the life from the primitives one by one – the only survivor is Grimlock, who was presumed dead after Trypticon's giant corpse fell on him. Grimlock tracks down Primacron's lab and confronts the creature.

Unfortunately for them both, Tornedron is no longer responding to Primacron's remote commands, and is now threatening to attack the lab. Although a genius, Primacron is so smart that he often over-thinks things – it is the uncluttered, primitive mind of Grimlock that simply presses the 'reverse switch', destroying Tornedron and restoring the life to all of his victims. Grimlock then proceeds to destroy Primacron's lab, thereby ensuring that the alien will never again give life to a planet-eating monstrosity.

Galvatron's Rants:

- 'Hahahaha! The Autobots are being destroyed, and I don't even have to soil my hands!'
- 'Get back here, deserter! Let us seize them, and make them pay for their disloyalty!'

Witty Put-Downs:

- Rodimus is glad his enemies are cowards: 'If the Decepticons had any guts, we'd be taking a serious pounding!'
- Springer, on the Dinobots: 'I'd say they were losing their minds … *if* they had any to lose!'
- Headstrong, after Grimlock admits he doesn't know where they're headed: 'That's not surprising, Grimlock don't know nothing!' Snarl: 'Stupid Decepticon rhino make fun of our leader!'
- Grimlock is unimpressed with Primacron: 'Grimlock laugh at little wimp who make big trouble!'

The Secret Files of Teletraan II:
A second showing for the cassette fact-file, previously seen in {3-25} 'Money is Everything'.

Roll Call:
Autobots: Rodimus Prime, Springer, Ultra Magnus, Blaster, Slag, Snarl, Grimlock, Sludge, Kup, Bumblebee, Jazz, Wheelie, Slingshot, Blades, Swoop, Sky Lynx, Steeljaw and Ramhorn. Windcharger is also (briefly) seen, but given that he dies in {3-00} *The Transformers: The Movie*, his appearance must be an animation error.

Decepticons: Tantrum, Rampage, Blot, Soundwave, Galvatron, Cyclonus, Headstrong, Cutthroat, Hun-Gurrr, Razorclaw, Divebomb, Sinnertwin, Rippersnapper, Scourge, Abominus, Predaking, Trypticon, Ravage, Ratbat, **Slugfest** and **Overkill**.

Other: Unicron (as a dismembered head, and also in flashback).

Data File: Jim Cummings (voices, including Afterburner and Rippersnapper)
Jim Cummings has one of the longest CVs in the voice-acting business. He's the current voice of Winnie the Pooh and Tigger, played Monterey Jack in *Chip 'n' Dale Rescue Rangers*, Witterquick in *Visionaries*, the title role in *Darkwing Duck*, Dr Robotnik in *Sonic the Hedgehog*, Warner Brothers' Taz/Tasmanian Devil and Sly Sludge in *Captain Planet and the Planeteers*. He's also voiced characters in *The Simpsons*, *Family Guy* and *Adventure Time*. His movies include *Shrek* (Andrew Adamson and Vicky Jensen, 2001), *Aladdin* (Ron Clements and John Musker, 1992) and *Wreck-It Ralph* (Rich Moore, 2012). He later returned to the Transformers franchise to play Colonel Quint Quarry in *Transformers: Rescue Bots* and Clampdown in *Transformers: Robots in Disguise*.

Data File: Marshall Efron (Hun-Grrr)
Actor and humourist Marshall Efron's voice work includes the roles of Sloppy Smurf in *The Smurfs* and Ratso in *The Kwicky Koala Show*, as well as parts in *The 13 Ghosts of Scooby-Doo* and *Pink Panther and Sons*. His film work includes parts in *THX 1138* (George Lucas, 1971), *Robots* (Chris Wedge, 2005) and *Ice Age: the Meltdown* (Carlos Saldanha, 2006).

Review:
The obvious thing to say about this episode is that it looks completely unlike any other *The Transformers* episode: there is more fine detail, the character models are highly stylised, and there is good use of light and shadow – making this the best-looking instalment bar *The Movie*.

The script is also 'bigger' than we are used to, as it delves into the origins of Unicron and sees both Cybertron and Earth on the brink of death. Certainly the ideas and concepts are worthy enough of the impressive visuals.

Plot-wise, there are some issues: it's hard to believe that Primacron is so stupid that he forgets the existence of the reverse switch, and two new Decepticons – Slugfest and Overkill – vanish almost as soon as they are introduced. Such niggles aside, the script is excellent, with a number of great moments and quotable lines.

While some viewers might quibble that Unicron's origin, as presented here, is a little underwhelming – it turns out he was simply built by a diminutive alien – it could equally be argued that it's a clever reversal of expectations. Considering that the comic-book version of Unicron is a Lord of Chaos from the dawn of time, his cartoon origin is almost subversive in its simplicity.

A striking episode, in terms of both script and visuals. 5/5

{3-27} THE FACE OF THE NIJIKA

Production number: 700-113 (27th episode produced of Season Three)
Transmission date: 20 November 1986 (28th episode transmitted of Season Three)

Written by Mary Skrenes and Steve Skeates

Plot:

Travelling to the source of some strange sensor readings in deep space, the Autobots stumble upon a skirmish between the Quintessons and Galvatron. The Quintessons have set up a 'quadrant lock' – a device that seals off a section of space from the outside universe – and Galvatron is determined to find out what's inside.

Realising that they could use the lock to trap the Autobots and Decepticons on the other side, the Quintessons open it. The Autobots and Cyclonus make it through, as does the Quintesson ship. The quadrant lock closes behind, and the Quintessons are alarmed to discover that their 'key' to reopen it has been damaged. Fortunately, they learn that the Autobot Perceptor has a built-in device, a 'universal emulator', that could be used as a substitute key.

Perceptor crash-lands on the planet Zamojin and is discovered by the locals, a primitive people whose culture is reminiscent of feudal Japan. One of the natives, Katsu Don, removes Perceptor's Autobot insignia, and the internal circuitry behind it, and fuses it to the head of an android, Nijika, whose own face has been damaged. It transpires that Perceptor's brain was housed in the transplanted circuitry, giving him control of Nijika. To complicate matters, the universal emulator was also part of this circuitry.

Perceptor learns that, long ago, Zamojin was a thriving culture on the verge of a great evolutionary leap – the natives have great telephathic abilities, but their powers are linked to the stars. Fearful that the Zamojin could become a threat to them, the Quintessons quadrant-locked the planet to halt their development.

The Quintessons retrieve the emulator from Nijika and use it to open the lock so that they can escape. However, Perceptor has sabotaged the device, and the quadrant lock is opened permanently. The stars return to the sky above Zamojin, allowing its people to harness their telepathic powers once again.

Galvatron's Rants:

- 'I found it, it's mine! Don't let them steal it! Stop them!'

The Secret Files of Teletraan II:

For the third episode in a row, we get a profile of the cassette Transformers.

Roll Call:

Autobots: Sky Lynx, Ultra Magnus, Rodimus Prime, Perceptor and Blurr.

Decepticons: Galvatron and Cyclonus.

Other: the Quintessons.

Data File: Mary Skrenes (writer)

Primarily a writer for comics, Skrenes created *Omega the Unknown* for Marvel, and has also written for titles such as *Detective Comics* and *Howard the Duck*. As well as *The Transformers*, she wrote for other Sunbow-produced cartoon shows such as *G.I. Joe: A Real American Hero* and *Jem and the Holograms*.

Data File: Steve Skeates (writer):

A prolific comic writer, the Bill Finger Award-winning Steve Skeates has written extensively for both Marvel and DC, including on titles such as *Aquaman*, *The Flash* and *The Sub-Mariner*, to name just a few.

Review:

There have been episodes in the past where the villains have conquered an alien world for their own ends (for example, {2-26} 'The God Gambit' and {2-33} 'Sea Change'), but this one is different: while the surface trappings are quite familiar, there are a lot of interesting sci-fi ideas that serve to elevate it above others of its type.

Here we are presented with a telepathic alien race who revere a faceless android, a region of space that is 'quadrant-locked' away from the rest of the universe, and another dark chapter in the Quintessons' back story. The plot is not one that cannot be easily summarised in a single line or even a couple of paragraphs: of all *The Transformers* episodes, this is probably the most complex and tightly-packed. 4/5

{3-28} THE BURDEN HARDEST TO BEAR

Production number: 700-114 (28th episode produced of Season Three)
Transmission date: 19 November 1986 (27th episode transmitted of Season Three)

Written by Michael Charles Hill

Plot:

As the Autobots struggle to repel a constant stream of Decepticon attacks in Japan, Rodimus Prime is feeling the pressure – even the Prime Minister is unhappy, because the constant Transformer battles have caused untold damage to the country.

Rodimus is therefore relieved when – after an attack by Wildrider and Breakdown – the Matrix is stolen from him. Reverting to his Hot Rod form, he no longer has to bear the burden of responsibility, leaving his fellow Autobots in a bit of a crisis.

Galvatron discovers that he's unable to access the Matrix's power, and so gives it to Scourge to dispose of. Scourge instead takes the Matrix for himself, which makes him exponentially more powerful. He shoots Galvatron, assumes leadership of the Decepticons and leads them on another assault on Japan.

Hot Rod, meanwhile, has been getting some much-needed lessons in life and wisdom from a local kendo instructor, and when he sees a Matrix-enhanced Scourge run riot, he knows what he must do.

Besting Scourge in battle and reclaiming the Matrix, Hot Rod becomes Rodimus Prime once more, and drives the Decepticons away.

Galvatron's Rants:

- 'For years, the Matrix has eluded us, but now it is finally ours! At last, all shall be one … under Galvatron's rule!'
- 'With the Matrix destroyed, now – *now* – is the time to unleash our fury upon them!'
- 'I will not rest until the Matrix and Scourge have been destroyed!'

Witty Put-Downs:

- Marissa is unimpressed by Rodimus Prime's juvenile posturing: 'Okay, Mr Macho-bot!'
- Kup isn't too impressed by Scourge's new appearance: 'What kind of Decepticon are you, ugly?'

The Secret Files of Teletraan II:
The fifth and final sighting of the Decepticon segment.

Roll Call:
Autobots: Broadside, Superion, Silverbolt, Air Raid, Skydive, Slingshot, Fireflight, Defensor, Sky Lynx, Rodimus Prime/Hot Rod, Kup, Ultra Magnus and Springer. The Protectobots (Hot Spot, Streetwise, Groove, Blades and First Aid) appear in this episode, but only as part of their combined mode (Defensor), rather than as individuals.

Decepticons: Devastator, Predaking, Mixmaster, Hook, Long Haul, Astrotrain, Bruticus, Cyclonus, Scourge, Onslaught, Vortex, Blast Off, Swindle, Brawl, Wildrider, Dead End, Galvatron, Scrapper, Scavenger, Bonecrusher, Drag Strip and Breakdown. As with the Protectobots above, the Predacons (Razorclaw, Rampage, Divebomb, Tantrum and Headstrong) appear only in their combined Predaking guise.

Other: Marissa Faireborn.

Data File: Dick Gautier (voices, including Rodimus Prime and Apeface)
Dick Gautier began his acting career on the stage, and was Tony-nominated for his role in the Broadway production of *Bye-Bye Birdie*. On screen, he had guest parts in shows such as *Bewitched*, *Knight Rider* and *Nip/Tuck*, although he is probably best known for his recurring role as Hymie the Robot in *Get Smart*. In the '70s and '80s he became a mainstay of the celebrity game show circuit, with appearances on programmes such as *Win, Lose or Draw* and *Family Feud*. As a voice actor, he was the villainous Serpentor in *G.I. Joe: A Real American Hero* and also had parts in *Cow and Chicken*, *Batman: the Animated Series* and *DuckTales*.

Review:
A pretty simple character piece, as Rodimus Prime suffers from the responsibilities of leadership. But what's memorable here is the setting (the Japanese locations are very-well rendered) and the grotesquely mutated Scourge, who goes on the rampage after being corrupted by the Matrix.

There are some great lines here (especially from Galvatron), but the final result is an episode where the strong visuals are masking a rather by-the-numbers plot. 2/5

Spotlight: How Does the Cartoon Differ from the Comics?

As already noted, the main difference between the comic and the cartoon adventures of the Transformers is in the storytelling format: the comic tended to recount long, sprawling arcs that sometimes spanned years at a time, whereas the cartoon concentrated on telling mostly self-contained, stand-alone adventures, with only a few multi-part ones here and there.

While it would've been nice if the comics and cartoons had been compatible with each other, sadly it wasn't the case: the two different media tell two completely different versions of the Transformers story.

The biggest divergence is in the origin of the Transformers themselves. The comics depicted them as the children of the ancient god Primus, built to defeat one day the evil chaos-bringer Unicron. The cartoon origin, on the other hand, was more low-key: there, the Cybertronians were built by the Quintessons as slaves and commodities, but then rose up and overcame their masters. In the cartoon, Unicron was not a demonic being from the end of time, but merely a powerful robot built by the evil scientist Primacron.

In the comics, Transformers could be given life only by the Matrix. In the cartoons, however, the process was apparently much easier – the Dinobots, Technobots and Combaticons are all brought to life without the Matrix.

Another major difference is in the portrayal of the human characters. In the comics, Sparkplug was a mechanic and his son Spike a college student; in the cartoons, father and son were colleagues on an oil platform. As we shall see, another fundamental difference is in the depiction of Nebulans: in the comics, the alien race are physically no different from humans, but in the cartoons, they are green-skinned and clearly alien.

Another change is in the setting. In the television series, the *Ark* crashed in the middle of a desert, and many episodes (especially in Season One) were set in dry, arid landscapes. Compare this with the comic stories, in which the *Ark* was located on the outskirts of a major American city, Portland.

While both continuities gave the Transformers access to a space bridge leading from Cybertron to Earth, these looked and operated quite differently. The one in the comics was a literal bridge, with one end on Earth and the other on Cybertron. In the cartoons, the bridge was more of a transporter beam, which could zap the Transformers across the galaxy at a touch of a button.

There are other, more subtle differences. Reflector was a prominent character in the early episodes of the cartoon show but barely featured in the comics. Conversely, in the comics Shockwave was a major player, but in the cartoons he was a glorified caretaker, remaining on Cybertron while everybody else battled on Earth.

Another change is that, in the comics, humans are extremely distrustful of the Transformers; indeed some (RAAT, Circuit Breaker, the Neo-Knights) have made it their goal to rid the Earth of this 'menace'. In the cartoons, however, the Autobots and humans live in relative harmony.

Oddly, one of the smallest and most insignificant differences between the comics and cartoons is the one that has caused the most arguments amongst fans. In the cartoon series, Rumble is blue and Frenzy is red; however in the comics, and the toy line, these liveries are reversed, leading to endless arguments as to what the 'correct' colours ought to be.

{3-29} THE RETURN OF OPTIMUS PRIME, Part 1

Production number: 700-115 (29th episode produced of Season Three)

PART THREE: THE CARTOON SERIES

Transmission date: 24 February 1987 (29th episode transmitted of Season Three)

Written by Marv Wolfman and Cherie Wilkerson

Plot:
A pair of human astronauts, in space testing a new heat-resistant alloy, stumble upon the ship carrying the corpse of Optimus Prime. Despite the reservations of her co-pilot Gregory Swofford, who hates the Transformers after his face was scarred during a fight between Optimus Prime and Megatron, Jessica Morgan is able to retrieve Prime's body just in time. But while the alloy protects them from the effects of a supernova, some strange alien spores are disturbed by the explosion and attach themselves to their ship.

Once the spacecraft lands, the Decepticons attack the lab and steal the new alloy. Jessica's father, Dr Mark Morgan, also hates the Transformers, and so develops a plan to get back at them. It transpires that the spores carry a 'hate plague' transmitted by touch. Those afflicted become irrational, enraged and violent. Using Optimus Prime's body as a lure, Dr Morgan and Swofford plan to infect the Autobots.

The Autobots walk right into the trap. Although Optimus Prime's body is recovered, many of the Autobots become infected by the hate plague and turn on one another. The plague is eventually passed to the human population, and chaos spreads across the Earth.

Meanwhile, Sky Lynx, one of the few Autobots to remain uninfected, enlists the help of a Quintesson to restore Optimus Prime's body to life. The operation is a success: a newly-revived Prime vows to save the day ...

Galvatron's Rants:
- 'So ... Optimus Prime may yet live ... but not for much longer!'

Witty Put-Downs:
- Gregory calls Optimus Prime a 'lousy robot'.
- The plague-ridden Ultra Magnus searches for Rodimus Prime: 'There you are, you puny wimp!'

The Secret Files of Teletraan II:
The Autobot segment, first seen in {3-12} 'Starscream's Ghost'.

Roll Call:
Autobots: Optimus Prime, Afterburner, Lightspeed, Nosecone, Strafe, Scattershot, Computron, First Aid, Blades, Hot Spot, Ultra Magnus, Rodimus Prime, Groove, Streetwise, Defensor, Silverbolt, Air Raid, Skydive, Fireflight, Slingshot, Superion, **Searchlight**, **Chase**, **Wideload**, **Freeway**, Wheelie, Blurr, Bumblebee, Steeljaw, Kup, Wreck-Gar, Sky Lynx and Metroplex (voice only).

Decepticons: Megatron (flashback only), Blot, Cutthroat, Rippersnapper, Sinnertwin, Hun-Gurrr, Abominus, Ratbat, Soundwave, Galvatron, Cyclonus, Scourge, Bruticus, Breakdown, Dead End, Drag Strip, Motormaster, Wildrider, Brawl, Headstrong, Razorclaw and Vortex. Onslaught and Blast Off also appear, but only as parts of the Bruticus combiner, not as individuals. Swindle also appears, both as part of Bruticus, and as an animation error – oddly, as part of an Autobot team guarding the hospital.

Other: the Quintessons.

Data File: Danny Mann (voices, including Lightspeed)

Danny Mann's voice credits are numerous. On television they include the cartoons *Heathcliff and the Catillac Cats, Galaxy High* and *The Real Ghostbusters*. On the big screen they include *Babe* (Chris Noonan, 1995), *Pocahontas* (Mike Gabriel and Eric Goldberg, 1995), *Open Season* (Jill Culton and Roger Allers, 2006) and *Planes* (Klay Hall, 2013).

Data File: David Workman (Nosecone and Sinnertwin)

Workman's other credits include voice work on *Where's Waldo* (as Waldo's dog, Woof), *Johnny Bravo* and the animated movie *Rainbow Brite and the Star Stealer* (Bernard Deyriès and Kimio Yabuki, 1985). Live action credits include Martin Lawrence's sitcom *Martin* and the film *Banzai Runner* (John G Thomas, 1987).

Data File: Jim Gosa (Abominus)

Jim Gosa had a long career on radio, stage and screen. Television credits include roles in *The Man from U.N.C.L.E., Lost in Space, Starsky and Hutch* and *MacGuyver*. He also had a part in the movie *High Plains Drifter* (Clint Eastwood, 1973).

Review:

It's the first part of a two-parter, so a lot of this is just set-up for the conclusion, as it tries gradually to ramp up tension toward the cliffhanger. While its aims might be limited, it does the job relatively successfully: the action and excitement never let up. While the central concept – a hate-inducing plague that spreads across the Earth – is a little hokey, the execution is top notch. A promising beginning. 4/5

{3-30} THE RETURN OF OPTIMUS PRIME, Part 2

Production number: 700-116 (30th episode produced of Season Three)
Transmission date: 25 February 1987 (30th episode transmitted of Season Three)

Story by Cherie Wilkerson and Marv Wolfman
Teleplay by Michael Charles Hill

Plot:

The newly-revived Optimus Prime realises that the only way to combat the spores is to seek guidance from the Matrix, which contains the combined knowledge of past Autobot leaders. However, the only way to get the Matrix from the infected Rodimus Prime is through direct contact, and that means contracting the plague.

Jessica Morgan, who has decided to help the Autobots, realises that if Optimus Prime were to coat himself with the impervious alloy that the Decepticons stole from her lab, he would be immune to the spores' effects.

The captive Quintesson agrees to help fix up the remaining uninfected Autobots – during the operation, Bumblebee is given a new, upgraded body and a new name: Goldbug. Optimus leads these Autobots to the Decepticon base on Chaar, when they convince Galvatron that the only way to fight the plague is by retrieving the alloy. Despite Galvatron's attempts to betray him, Optimus Prime is able to do this.

Optimus coats himself with the alloy and goes after Rodimus. The two Primes do battle, but in the end Optimus is victorious and manages to secure the Matrix.

Connecting his brain to the Matrix, Optimus seeks the guidance of his forebears, and discovers that pure wisdom – such as that accumulated within the Matrix itself – could be the cure to the plague.

Optimus Prime unleashes the full power of the Matrix, its energies spreading across the galaxy, curing all the infected. Galvatron, impressed with Optimus Prime's performance in this crisis, agrees to a temporary cessation of hostilities as a show of respect for the Autobot leader.

The Autobots seem worried when they discover that the Matrix is now completely empty, its energies drained. Optimus responds: 'It's up to all of us to fill it again, with the wisdom we accumulate from this moment on. Autobots: transform and roll out!'

Galvatron's Rants:
- 'The Autobots are trying to save me! What madness is this?'
- 'I don't need you any more, Optimus! So much for your resurrection!'
- 'The world is ours! Optimus Prime shall die again!'

Witty Put-Downs:
- An infected Cyclonus, on Galvatron: 'What have we here? Looks like something the cat dragged in!'
- Jessica, to Galvatron: 'You jerk!'
- Galvatron, to the infected Cyclonus: 'Die, you worthless piece of slag!'

The Secret Files of Teletraan II:
A profile of Ultra Magnus, last seen in {3-24} 'Grimlock's New Brain'.

Roll Call:
Autobots: Optimus Prime, Sky Lynx, Slingshot (flashback only), Chase, Silverbolt (flashback only), Blaster, Goldbug, Steeljaw, Blurr, Kup, Rodimus Prime/Hot Rod, Searchlight, Freeway and Alpha Trion.

Decepticons: Dead End (flashback only), Wildrider (flashback only), Breakdown (flashback only), Motormaster (flashback only), Cyclonus, Scourge, Galvatron, Predaking, Razorclaw, Rampage, Tantrum, Headstrong and Divebomb.

Other: the Quintessons.

Data File: Cherie Wilkerson (writer/executive script consultant)
Wilkerson scripted episodes for a number of animated shows, including *DuckTales*, *Batman: The Animated Series* and *Jem and the Holograms*. She has also written a number of short stories and comics.

Data File: Marv Wolfman (writer/story editor)
A legendary comic writer, Marv Wolfman created the characters Blade for Marvel Comics and Tim Drake (aka Robin III) for DC. He wrote or edited many much-loved comic books, including *The Amazing Spider-Man*, *The Avengers*, *Batman*, *Captain America*, *Fantastic Four*, *Superman* and the landmark series *Crisis on Infinite Earths*. In the field of children's television, he penned episodes of series such as *Fraggle Rock*, *Batman: The Animated Series* and *ReBoot*. He also wrote for the shows *Beast Wars: Transformers* and

Transformers: Beast Machines.

Review:
A straight-up action-adventure episode that makes for a decent – if flawed – finale to Season Three. The animation is of excellent quality, the excitement never lets up, and there's an overall sense of fun about proceedings.

Unfortunately, there's a major drawback here: Optimus Prime uses the Matrix to magically cure the entire galaxy, in one of the most terrible cop-out endings imaginable, which really mars the entire endeavour.

An otherwise decent episode spoiled by a terrible ending. The final coda is just sublime, however. 3/5

As with Season One, Season Three's ending has a note of finality to it. Optimus Prime is back and has finally earnt the respect of Galvatron. The Matrix is gone. Even the sequence of Optimus contacting the Matrix acts as a fitting bookend to the series, mirroring the journey Rodimus Prime made in {3-04} 'Five Faces of Darkness, Part Four'. The soundtrack even reprises 'The Touch' – the song by Stan Bush from {3-00} *The Transformers: The Movie.*

Complaints about the pat resolution aside, narratively this episode would have made a good ending to the series as a whole – and it would seem that, for a time, this was indeed the intention. Fortunately, however, the series was given a stay of execution, albeit a very brief one …

Credits: Season Three
- Supervising Director: Rae Lee, Andy Kim
- Sequence Directors: Warren Batchelder, Bob Bemiller, Rudy Cataldi, Gerry Chiniquy, Charlie Downs, Lillian Evans, John Freeman, Caroline Heyward, Bob Kirk, Bill Knoll, Bob Matz, Norm McCabe, Joe Morrison, Margaret Nichols, Spencer Peel, Karen Peterson, Stan Phillips, Tom Ray, Bob Treat, Neal Warner
- Assistants to the Supervisors: Myrna Bushman, Lisa Wilson
- Background Supervisor: Dennis Venizelos
- Voice talents of: Charlie Adler, Jack Angel, Arlene Banas, Roger Behr, Michael Bell, Gregg Berger, Susan Blu, Corey Burton, Roger C. Carmel, Victor Caroli, Michael Chain, Phillip Clarke, Rege Cordic, Peter Cullen, Bud Davis, Paul Eiding, Laurie Faso, Ron Feinberg, Ron Gans, Linda Gary, Brad Garrett, Dick Gautier, Ed Gilbert, Dan Gilvezan, Joy Grdnic, John Haymer, John Hostetter, Jerry Houser, Milt Jamin, Buster Jones, Stan Jones, S Marc Jordan, Casey Kasem, Aron Kincaid (misspelled as 'Kindaid' on the caption), Chris Latta, Joe Leahy, Jeff MacKay, Terry McGovern, David Mendenhall, Denise Mora, John Moschitta, Allen Oppenheimer, Rob Paulsen, Tony Pope, Bill Ratner, Hal Rayle, Clive Revill, Neil Ross, Ted Schwartz, Tony St James, John Stevenson, Frank Welker, Beau Weaver
- Voices Directed By: Wally Burr
- Voice Recording Engineer: Joel Iwataki
- Recording Coordinator: Eileen Burr
- Storyboard Artists: Dell Barras, Bill Barry, Danny Bulanadi, Soo Young Chung, Joo In Kim, David Shin, Leo Sullivan, Young Sang Yoon
- Model and Background Design: Pat Agnasin, Fred Carrillo, Eufronio R Cruz, Romeo Francisco, Ernie Guanlao, Gabriel Hoyos, Rico Rival

- Key Background design: Dennis Venizelos, Bob Schaeffer, Andrew Phillipson, Jeff Richards, Fred Warter
- Colour Models: Phyliss Craig
- Supervising Editor: Steven C Brown
- Assistants to the Supervising Editor: Larry Whelan, Rick Gehr
- Effects Editors: Jim Blodgett, Matt Cope, Mike DePatie, John Detra, Karen Doulac, Ron Fedele, Allison Cobb, Lenny Geschke, Brad Gunther, David Hankins, Nick James, Richard Raderman, Jospeh Sorokin, Warren Taylor, Peter Tomaszewicz
- Music Editors: Marc Shiney, Peter Collier, Robert Randles, Bob Mayer, Richard Allen
- Dubbing Supervisors: Jacquie Freeman, John Hart
- Telecine Supervisors: Sarah Swiskow, Andrew Golov
- Post-Production Supervisors: Eric Early, Steven Heth
- Production Managers: Carole Weitzman, Yung Shin
- Production Coordinators: Paul Davids, Elise Goyette, Hildy Mesnik
- Production Assistants: Mitsuko Hayes, Lizabeth Elliott
- Director of Production: Jim Graziano
- Supervising Producer: Nelson Shin
- Producers: Gerald Modeller, George Singer
- Original Music Score Composed and Conducted by: Robert J. Walsh, Johnny Douglas
- Main Title Theme: Music and Lyrics by Ford Kinder and Anne Bryant
- Post-Production Services: L Ed Walsh, Terry Jennings, Saturday Morning Incorporated
- Co-Producer: Roger Slifer
- Story Editors: Flint Dille, Steve Gerber, Marv Wolfman
- Creative Director: Jay Bacal
- ©1986 Sunbow Productions, Inc
- ©1986 Wildstar Music, Inc
- © 1986 Starwild Music, Inc
- Distributed by Claster Television Productions, a division of Hasbro, Inc.
- Hasbro, Inc
- © 1986 Hasbro, Inc. All rights reserved. Trademark of Hasbro, Inc and is registered in the US Patent and Trademark Office.
- Executive in Charge of Production: Lee Gunther
- Executive Producers: Joe Bacal, Margaret Loesch, Tom Griffin
- Sunbow Productions/Marvel Productions Ltd

THE TELEVISION SERIES: SEASON FOUR

By 1987, the popularity of *The Transformers* had begun to wane from its peak of around two years earlier. New episodes of the cartoon show were becoming less and less economically viable to produce, as their viewing figures – and therefore the television stations' willingness to pay for them – declined.

However, Hasbro had a new slew of figures to promote: Headmasters, Targetmasters, Clones, Horrorcons, a Six-Changer and a Double Spy. It would seem that they urged Sunbow to make one final season, specifically to introduce these new characters and finally close the series – it's entirely possible that they themselves pumped additional money into the production, just to make it worth Sunbow's while.

Even so, budget cuts were soon implemented. What was originally written as a five-part storyline eventually got truncated to three. Even the title sequence and music, which were traditionally altered every season, were retained from Season Three, albeit with some elements replaced with 'new' animation – itself recycled from old footage originally created for the toy advertisements.

{4-01} THE REBIRTH, Part 1
Production number: 6701-1 (1st episode produced of Season Four)
Transmission date: 9 November 1987 (1st episode transmitted of Season Four)

Written by David Wise

Plot:
Optimus Prime has been having premonitions that something 'big' is about to happen. His fears are confirmed when Autobot City is attacked by a legion of Decepticons. A pitched battle ensues, during which two Decepticons – Wingspan and Pounce – slink into the city and steal an artefact from a safe. This achieved, the Decepticons call off their attack. The Autobots realise too late that the entire attack was a diversion, and that the key to the Plasma Energy Chamber is now in Galvatron's hands.

On Cybertron, the Autobots are engaged in a little experiment. The scientist Brainstorm postulates that they would function better with human pilots. His theory is proved when Hot Rod, aided by Daniel, beats Blurr to the finish line in a race-cum-assault course.

Their peace is shattered when the Decepticons show up and use the key to activate the Plasma Energy Chamber. Scourge is overcome by the released energies, allowing Spike and Cerebros to retrieve the key and escape with a group of Autobots in a shuttle. However, the ship is hit by a Plasma Energy spike and zapped across the cosmos, crash-landing on the planet Nebulos.

There, the Autobots are attacked by the native Nebulans, who have a distrust of all machinery. They explain that their people live in thrall to the Hive, a collective of evil Nebulans who live underground, using thought-control to activate machinery that keeps the rest of the population in check.

The Decepticons track the Autobots to the planet in the hope of recovering the key, but are driven off – but not before they capture six of the Autobots. The remaining Autobots realise that the only way to fight back is to team up with a group of Nebulan resistance fighters and put Brainstorm's theory to the test. The Autobots and Nebulans are about to become … Headmasters!

Galvatron's Rants:
- 'The key is gone! You miserable pile of junk! I ought to have you stamped down into tinfoil for losing it!'

Witty Put-Downs:
- Searchlight describes the Decepticons: 'Big, ugly guys made out of metal.'
- Hardhead has no time for Brainstorm's theories: 'The problem is you, and your

stupid ideas.'
- Slugslinger: 'You're history now, Auto-bozos!'
- Triggerhappy: 'Welcome to the scrapyard, Auto-bums!'

Roll Call:
Autobots: Lightspeed, Strafe, Goldbug, Scattershot, Ultra Magnus, Optimus Prime, Afterburner, Nosecone, Freeway, Wideload, Searchlight, Chase, **Rollbar**, **Punch**, Blurr, Hot Rod, Arcee, **Sureshot**, **Hardhead**, **Chromedome**, **Pointblank**, **Brainstorm**, **Highbrow**, **Crosshairs**, **Cerebros**, Kup, Silverbolt, Skydive, Air Raid, Slingshot, Fireflight, First Aid, Hotspot, **Fastlane** and **Cloudraker**.

Decepticons: Cutthroat, **Misfire**, **Skullcruncher**, Hun-Gurrr, **Apeface**, Cyclonus, Scourge, Galvatron, **Mindwipe**, **Weirdwolf**, **Snapdragon**, **Triggerhappy**, **Wingspan**, **Pounce**, **Counterpunch**, Rippersnapper, Sinnertwin, Blot, Hook, Long Haul, Mixmaster, Bonecrusher, **Sixshot** and **Slugslinger**.

Nebulans: **Duros, Pinpointer, Haywire, Firebolt, Recoil, Gort, Arcana, Stylor, Peacemaker** and **Spoilsport**. A number of the evil Nebulans are also seen, but from the back only, so it's not clear which ones they are.

Other: Daniel, Spike and the Narrator.

Review:
Perhaps due to the story's development as a five-parter that was eventually condensed into a three-parter, this is a dense, eventful and plot-driven episode. Considering the sheer number of new characters that writer David Wise had to introduce, he did well to fit in a lot of nice little character moments that demonstrate the new robots' personalities with the minimum of fuss: Hardhead is gruff, Brainstorm is a thinker, Cerebros is a pacifist, Gort is practical and so on.

There's some real meat here, too: the planet Nebulos is well-established; the villainous Hive are set up as a major threat without them even saying a word; and there's time for a little foreshadowing as well, with Optimus Prime's grave premonitions, and Brainstorm's theories about humans and Transformers cooperating with each other.

This is an episode that covers a lot of ground in 22 minutes. Given its rather cynical mandate – to squeeze in as many new characters as possible – it's astonishing how well it actually works. 4/5

Spotlight: Transformers in Japan
In the beginning, the Japanese Transformers line was much the same as its Hasbro equivalent. Buyers there got pretty much the same toys as the rest of the world, and the American cartoon show was dubbed and broadcast under the name *Fight! Super Robot Lifeform Transformers* (Seasons One and Two), and *Fight! Super Robot Lifeform Transformers 2010* (Season Three).

But then, in 1987, things changed. As the toy line and the cartoon both began to wane in popularity in the rest of the world, Takara, who oversaw the franchise in Japan, went in a completely different direction. Instead of the three-part Season Four, there were 119 Japanese-exclusive episodes, split into themed seasons as follows:

Transformers: The Headmasters (1987-88), *Transformers: Super-God Masterforce* (1988-89), *Fight! Super Robot Lifeform Transformers: Victory* (1989) and the one-off special *Transformers: Zone* (1990). These animated series complemented a whole host of Japanese-exclusive figures, such as Dai Atlas (a robot/tank/jet/battle station quad-changer), Deszaras (a dragon Transformer, and leader of the evil Breastforce) and the wonderfully-named Rodney, who transforms into a Headmaster head.

While this book focuses solely on the American and European aspects of the Transformers franchise, that shouldn't be construed as an attempt to legitimise them over and above the Japanese ones. The Japanese-only series and toy lines are considered part of the original Generation One Transformers line, just as valid as those we got in the rest of the world. Indeed, they continue to be a huge influence on the current Transformers, with new versions of Japanese-only characters such as Soundblaster, Star Saber and Metalhawk seeing release in the past few years.

{4-02} THE REBIRTH, Part 2
Production number: 6701-2 (2nd episode produced of Season Four)
Transmission date: 10 November 1987 (2nd episode transmitted of Season Four)

Written by David Wise

Plot:
The Autobots Arcee, Brainstorm, Chromedome, Hardhead and Highbrow are converted into Headmasters: their heads can transform into their Nebulan partners (or human partner in the case of Arcee, who is bonded with Daniel). First the Headmasters make short work of some automated Hive robots, then they attack the Decepticons, rescue their friends and take back the key to the Plasma Energy Chamber.

The Hive watch these events on their monitor screens, and decide to enter the fray. They force the Decepticons into becoming Headmasters and Targetmasters – with Hive members becoming the Decepticons' new heads and weapons. The Hive leader Zarak remains behind to run a special project: he plans to use the Hive city itself as the basis for a new, giant Decepticon.

The newly-energised Decepticons launch an attack on the Autobots and – thanks to the advantage of the new Targetmaster process – are able to get the key back for themselves.

On Cybertron, Optimus Prime uses the Vector Sigma computer to find out what's going on. Speaking with Alpha Trion, whose life essence exists within the computer, he discovers that the war has spread to Nebulos, and also that it was Vector Sigma itself who arranged for Galvatron to learn of the key's existence. It transpires that the super-computer is playing the long game, setting this entire chain of events in motion in the hope that it will lead to a new 'Golden Age' on Cybertron.

Optimus Prime travels to Nebulos where, in order to match the Decepticons, some of the Autobots have undergone the Targetmaster process too. They launch an attack on the Decepticons, and once more gain control of the key.

However, a giant city-sized Decepticon enters the fray: the Autobots look on helplessly as Scorponok makes his entrance …

Witty Put-Downs:
• Scourge calls the Autobots 'Auto-fools.'

- Kup: 'Go stick your head in a black hole, Scourge!'
- Brainstorm isn't very happy when the Decepticons undergo the Headmaster process: 'Those creeps, swiping my idea! I'll sue!'
- Brainstorm: 'Go hang upside-down from a tree, Mindwipe!'

Roll Call:
Autobots: Brainstorm, Arcee, Highbrow, Chromedome, Hardhead, Silverbolt, Skydive, Fireflight, Slingshot, Optimus Prime, Ultra Magnus, Punch, Fastlane, Cloudraker, Crosshairs, Sureshot, Blurr, Kup, Hot Rod, Pointblank, Alpha Trion (in a vision) and Cerebros. Hotspot and Fortress Maximus appear in the teaser for the following episode.

Decepticons: Abominus, Skullcruncher, Apeface, Weirdwolf, Mindwipe, Triggerhappy, Misfire, Scourge, Cyclonus, Slugslinger, **Scorponok** and Snapdragon. Abominus comprises the five Terrorcons (Hun-Gurrr, Sinnertwin, Blot, Cutthroat and Rippersnapper), but they don't appear here as individuals. Wingspan and Pounce appear in the recap from the previous episode; Galvatron appears only in the preview for Part Three.

Nebulans: Stylor, Gort, Arcana, Duros, Peacemaker, Firebolt, **Zarak**, **Nightstick**, **Monzo**, **Aimless**, **Caliburst**, **Blowpipe**, **Vorath**, **Fracas**, **Spasma**, **Krunk**, **Grax**, Haywire, Recoil, Pinpointer and Spoilsport.

Other: the Narrator, Spike and Daniel.

Review:
Coming after the frantic set-up and before the grand finale, this suffers from 'middle episode syndrome'. While there are some nifty battles and impressive dialogue, the plot slows down for a spot of housekeeping: we get the creation of the Headmasters and the Targetmasters, a big chunk of exposition from Alpha Trion, and very little else.

There's some clever misdirection here – in amongst all the firefights and action, it's easy to get swept up in it all, and not notice that this episode basically boils down to 'Autobots take the key, Decepticons take it back, Autobots steal it back again'. The plot is jogging on the spot, but it's entertaining enough. 3/5

{4-03} THE REBIRTH, Part 3
Production number: 6701-3 (3rd episode produced of Season Four)
Transmission date: 11 November 1987 (3rd episode transmitted of Season Four)

Written by David Wise

Plot:
With the mighty Scorponok on their side, the Decepticons gain control of the key to the Plasma Energy Chamber and head back to Cybertron. The Autobots set off after them – with the exception of Spike and Cerebros, who stay behind on Nebulos. Spike plans to rebuild an old Hive city into a giant Autobot powerful enough to take on Scorponok.

On Cybertron, Galvatron has built a giant rocket engine powerful enough to transport the planet into Earth's solar system. Galvatron uses the key to activate the Plasma Energy Chamber, but sets a timer on it: in ten minutes, the Chamber will open and its energies will overload every robot on the planet. It will also overload the sun, and cause it to go nova.

As the Decepticons attempt to flee the doomed Cybertron, Spike and Cerebros arrive, with Fortress Maximus in tow – a giant, city-sized Autobot. The Decepticons' retreat is delayed, and the Plasma Energy Chamber opens.

As Transformers all around them begin to overload, the humans and Nebulans remain unaffected. Spike shuts down the Chamber but it is too late: the sun has already absorbed too much plasma energy and is beginning to go critical.

The Decepticons, meanwhile, have escaped Cybertron, but they are hit by a bolt of plasma energy on take-off, catapulting them to the other side of the galaxy and far away from Cybertron.

Spike and the Nebulans reverse the flow of Galvatron's planet-engines, so that instead of emitting energy, they suck the excess from the sun. This energy is then filtered through the Vector Sigma computer and flooded back into Cybertron – this revives all the fallen Autobots, and restores the planet to a new Golden Age.

Galvatron's Rants:
- 'At last, Cybertron is mine!'
- 'Are you out of your minds! You call yourselves Decepticons? Allowing these filthy organic beings to co-habitate your bodies! ... You morons! ... I'm going to blow those creepy creatures clear out of you!'
- 'The Plasma Energy Chamber! A ten-minute delay should give us enough time to get clear. Then, this entire solar system will be destroyed!'
- 'There is much to do! We will attack the planets! We will suck them dry! We will rebuild the planet a hundred times more powerful than Cybertron! *And I will rule the galaxy! ... It is my destiny!*'

Witty Put-Downs:
- Combination insult/exposition from Chromedome: 'You little creeps! We're stuck being vehicles without our heads!'
- Spike: 'Kiss your afterburners goodbye, Decepticon slime!'
- Galvatron calls Scorponok an 'oversized shopping centre'.

Roll Call:
Autobots: Crosshairs, Sureshot, Hardhead, Optimus Prime, Arcee, Blurr, Brainstorm, Highbrow, Chromedome, Pointblank, Hot Rod, Kup, Alphas Trion (as a ghostly vision), Chase, Strafe, Afterburner, Freeway, Searchlight, Silverbolt, Fireflight, Ultra Magnus, Hotspot, Groove, First Aid, Streetwise, Blades, Cerebros, Rollbar, Wideload, **Fortress Maximus**, Goldbug, Nosecone and Lightspeed. Bumblebee is also seen in a crowd shot, but as he no longer exists (he was rebuilt into Goldbug), it must be an animation error. Additionally, Slingshot and Skydive are shown in the opening recap.

Decepticons: Scorponok, Triggerhappy, Cyclonus, Scourge, Skullcruncher, Mindwipe, Misfire, Slugslinger, Rippersnapper, Sinnertwin, Blot, Hun-Gurrr, Cutthroat, Blast Off, Galvatron, Onslaught, Swindle, Brawl, Weirdwolf, Apeface, Vortex and Snapdragon. Sixshot also appears, but only in a reprise of Part 1.

Nebulans: Grax, Spoilsport, Zarak, Arcana, Stylor, Gort, Nightstick, Fracas, Aimless,

Caliburst, Blowpipe, Vorath, Monzo, Spasma, Pinpointer, Peacemaker, Haywire, Recoil, Firebolt and Duros.

Other: the Narrator, Daniel and Spike.

Data File: Stephen Keener (voices, including Hardhead and Mindwipe)
Although *The Transformers* is his only credited acting work, Keener did a lot of voice-overs for television commercials and documentaries, and also taught acting and directing in colleges across the USA.

Review:
A worthy end to the series: Cyberton enters a Golden Age and the Decepticons are zapped across space. The dangling plot threads are tied up, the Scorponok v Fortress Maximus battle is pretty epic – and with the entire solar system at risk, the stakes couldn't be higher.

While the science might be a bit dodgy (the whole planet-engine thing, and the 'suck power from the sun' resolution), it works on an aesthetic level, at least.

All in all, this is a fine resolution to *The Transformers* cartoon series. 4/5

Credits: Season Four
- Director: Jaeho Hong
- Assistant Directors: Mooyoung Song, Kyungme Kim
- Animators: Youngduk Kim, Byungnam Choi, Kyungkwan Kim, Eynam Park, Baekyup Sung, Myunghi Park, Sungok Cho, Ghigeun Kang, Chiman Park, Hanyong Chung, Byungchong Oh, Sangil Shimi, Nosoo Kwak, Namyul Baik, Youngchan Shin
- Voice Talents of: Charlie Adler, Jack Angel, Jared Barclay, Michael Bell, Sue Blu, Steve Bulin, Corey Burton, Victor Caroli, Peter Cullen, Dick Gautier, Dan Gilvezan, Johnny Haymer, Milt Jamin, Stan Jones, Stephen Keener, Chris Latta, Danny Mann, David Mendenhall, Rob Paulsen, Neil Ross, John Stephenson, Frank Welker
- Voices Directed by: Wally Burr
- Voice Recording Engineers: Joel Iwataki, Sylvester Rivers, Scott Brownlee
- Recording Coordinator: Ellen Burr
- Editor: Al Breitenbach
- Assistant Editor: David Weathers
- Post-Production Services: Paul Vitello & Associates
- Telecine Supervisor: Sarah Swiskow
- Post-Production Supervisor: Eric Early
- Production Managers: Gerald Moeller, Elise Goyette
- Production Assistant: Laurie Pessell
- Director of Production: Jim Graziano
- Senior Production Manager: Carole Weitzman
- Original Music Score Composed and Conducted by: Robert J. Walsh, Johnny Douglas
- Main Title Theme by: Kinder and Bryant
- © Copyright 1987 Sunbow Productions, Inc
- © Copyright 1987 Wildstar Music, Inc

SEASON FIVE/GENERATION 2

{4-03} 'The Rebirth, Part 3' might have been the final *bona fide* original episode of *The Transformers*, but the series did actually go to a fifth season. With a new title sequence, made up of footage from toy advertisements and clips from {3-00} *The Transformers: The Movie*, 'Season Five', broadcast in 1988, consisted entirely of repeats of old episodes. However, there was more to it than that, as the decision was taken to film and incorporate new live-action 'umbrella' footage, consisting of Optimus Prime – realised by a combination of stop-motion puppetry and a large animatronic prop – recounting his old adventures to a young boy, Tommy Kennedy, played by actor Jason Jansen.

The season consisted of twenty episodes total: {1-01 to 1-03} 'More than Meets the Eye, Parts One to Three', {3-00} *The Transformers: The Movie* (split across five episodes), {3-01 to 3-05} 'Five Faces of Darkness, Parts One to Five', {3-13} 'Surprise Party', {3-08} 'Dark Awakening', {3-29 to 3-30} 'The Return of Optimus Prime, Parts 1 and 2' and {4-01 to 4-03} 'The Rebirth, Parts 1 to 3'.

More repackaging of old episodes was to follow. When the *Transformers: Generation 2* brand was launched in 1993, fifty-two of the classic cartoon episodes were selected for rebroadcast over two seasons. Other than a new CGI title sequence, and newly-animated scene transitions, these were as originally broadcast.

APPENDICES

Appendix 1:
The Transformers In The Uk

The history of the Transformers franchise in its core markets of the USA and Japan has been well-researched. For example, television airdates for the cartoon show in those territories are widely known, having been investigated by fans and then disseminated across the internet. Despite the UK being a mini-hotbed of Transformers fandom (it sustained its own long-running Transformers comic, after all), information is extremely thin on the ground when it comes to this country.

As this book is a UK publication, it's therefore an ideal opportunity to look into two aspects of *The Transformers* that have never been properly researched before: UK transmission dates for the cartoon episodes, and sales data for the UK Marvel comic.

Transmission Dates

There's a good reason why the UK transmission dates have not been properly researched before: it's a daunting proposition. Just one listings magazine – *The TV Times* – covered the channel on which the show was broadcast. Moreover, *The Transformers* was seldom aired as a discrete entity in its own right – instead, it almost always went out as part of a larger umbrella or 'magazine' programme.

What we *do* know is that the British television rights to *The Transformers* were first held by TV-am, which, by a strange quirk of the UK broadcasting system, was a station that transmitted only in the early mornings, until 9.25 am.

TV-am's flagship show was *Good Morning Britain*. Aimed squarely at adults, it was a mix of news, chat and current affairs, with only a token gesture (usually an old *Popeye* cartoon) toward younger audiences.

However, ratings and advertising revenues began to flag, and for a time it looked as if TV-am might have to cease transmission. Enter Roland Rat, a puppet character that delighted the station's younger viewers so much that viewing figures shot from 0.1 million to 1.8 million.

From April 1983, Roland Rat was the star of his own show on TV-am, broadcast on weekdays during the school holidays when children would be at home watching. The Roland Rat segment went through various iterations such as *Rat on the Road* and *Roland Goes East*, each a variation on the same basic theme.

In the summer of 1985, we finally get the first mention of *The Transformers* in British television listings. Each (roughly) 25-minute episode was divided into five-minute chunks and serialised over the course of a week. This cut-up version of *The Transformers* was broadcast as part of *The OWRRAS Summer Spectacular* (the acronym stood for Official Worldwide Roland Rat Appreciation Society), which also contained a mix of film reviews, pop videos and competitions. The full broadcast dates are as follows:

Monday 5 August 1985 – Friday 9 August 1985
Monday 12 August 1985 – Friday 16 August 1985
Monday 19 August 1985 – Friday 23 August 1985
Monday 26 August 1985 – Friday 30 August 1985
Each episode went out between 9.04 am and 9.25 am

Sadly there is no indication as to which episodes of *The Transformers* were chosen for broadcast. One would assume that it was the opening four episodes, serialised one per week, but there's no way to know for certain. What we *can* say for sure, though, is that the first time UK viewers saw *The Transformers* cartoon was on Monday 5 August 1985.

Roland Rat left TV-am in autumn 1985, defecting to the rival BBC, so the next school holiday, the October half-term, saw the debut of a new programme, *WACaday*. This was a spin-off of another TV-am children's programme, *The Wide Awake Club*.

The Wide Awake Club was broadcast every Saturday. Its first episode went out on 13 October 1984, featuring live music by XTC and an episode of the *Marvel Super-Heroes* cartoon. Because of its longer running-time – 7.30am to 9.25 am – it was able to incorporate a number of complete episodes of shows such as *Challenge of the Go-Bots*, *Flipper* and the 1960s live-action *Batman*, rather than simply chunks of programmes. Again, it was a mixture of competitions, games, pop performances and special guests. One notable episode, on 19 October 1985, featured an in-studio appearance by Marvel's American Editor-in-Chief, Jim Shooter.

While the *Wide Awake Club* went out on Saturdays, the shorter, sharper spin-off *WACaday* was shown on weekdays during the school holidays, in the old Roland Rat slot. Again, it was this weekday show that serialised episodes of *The Transformers*, still cut into chunks. Thanks to the *TV Times* listings magazine we can identify some episodes of *WACaday* that contained these five-minute instalments:

Monday 21 October 1985 – Friday 25 October 1985
Monday 28 October 1985 – Friday 1 November 1985
Monday 23 December 1985 – Friday 27 December 1985
Monday 30 December 1985 – Friday 3 January 1986

Again, each episode went out between 9.04 am and 9.25 am. Notably, the *TV Times* listing magazine has a publicity still from *The Transformers* alongside its schedule for 3 January 1986.

For the next school holiday, the spring half-term, *WACaday* was temporarily replaced by a new show, *Pop Shots*, a chart music programme hosted by Julie Brown, but *The Transformers* still featured, again split into segments. Transmission dates are as follows:

Monday 10 February 1986 – Friday 14 February 1986
Monday 17 February 1986 – Friday 21 February 1986

It's here that the *TV Times* listings become a bit hazy – from this point on, not every single broadcast of *The Transformers* would be noted by the magazine. This is where Associated Press comes in.

Associated Press is a Pulitzer Prize-winning global news service, based in New York. Its extensive archive includes over ten thousand hours' worth of footage from the old TV-am station, and its website contains (at time of writing) a searchable index of the footage held. Though tantalisingly incomplete, this does at least give us some more dates on which *The Transformers* was broadcast:

As part of *WACaday* (episodes edited into chunks and stripped across a week):

Monday 7 April 1986 – Friday 11 April 1986
(The AP website lists *The Transformers* only on 7 April and 9 April, but it's reasonable to conclude that it ran all week.)

As part of *The Wide Awake Club* (whole episodes):

Saturday 19 July 1986 (as per Associated Press)
Saturday 26 July 1986 (listed in the *TV Times*)
Saturday 2 August 1986 (as per Associated Press)
Saturday 13 September 1986 (confirmed by both the *TV Times* and Associated Press)

It's tempting to surmise that *The Transformers* was a regular constituent of *The Wide Awake Club*'s Saturday line-up throughout the summer and autumn of 1986, but with only these four listings to go on, all we can do is speculate. However, it would seem reasonable to assume that *The Transformers* was also broadcast on 9 August, 16 August, 23 August, 30 August and 6 September, making for a nine-week continuous run at the very least.

The next definitive *The Transformers* listing comes during Christmas Week of 1986 (courtesy of the *TV Times*, though the 2 January edition is also confirmed by AP), where it was again split into chunks and serialised across the week, as follows:

Monday 22 December 1986 – Friday 26 December 1986
Monday 29 December 1986 – Friday 2 January 1987

The 1986 Christmas Day segment was, uniquely, listed as a separate entity and not part of *WACaday*, because the schedules for that day were rejigged to accommodate special festive programmes.

This would appear to be the final broadcast of *The Transformers* on UK network television for some time, as new shows such as *Jem and The Holograms*, *Galaxy High* and *The Bionic Six* soon replaced it in TV-am's children's schedules.

The Transformers would next resurface in the summer holidays of 1987 (according to Associated Press), with episodes once more cut up and serialised over the course of a week:

Monday 27 July 1987 – Friday 31 July 1987
Monday 3 August 1987 – Friday 7 August 1987
Monday 10 August 1987 – Friday 14 August 1987
Monday 17 August 1987 – Friday 21 August 1987
Monday 24 August 1987 – Friday 28 August 1987
Monday 31 August 1987 – Friday 4 September 1987

A final batch of dates (again from AP) is the most interesting, as it's the only one for which we have some actual episode titles:

Tuesday 24 November 1987: {1-05} 'Roll for It'
Wednesday 25 November 1987: {1-08} 'S.O.S. Dinobots'
Thursday 26 November 1987: {1-10} 'War of the Dinobots'
Friday 27 November 1987: {1-14} 'Countdown to Extinction'

Monday 30 November 1987: {1-16} 'Heavy Metal War'
Tuesday 1 December 1987: no title given

Presumably this was a full two-week run, which would mean that there were also episodes broadcast on 23 November and 2 – 4 December, not listed by Associated Press. This batch was broadcast in full as an emergency measure, to cover for a technicians' strike that disrupted TV-am's regular schedules for a period from 23 November 1987.

Although we don't know exactly which episodes went out on which specific dates, it would seem to be the case that only Season One episodes were shown. Thankfully, as noted above, the British VHS videocassette labels Video Gems and Tempo Video concentrated on releasing episodes from Seasons Two and Three (with a smattering from Season One), so viewers had the opportunity to see at least *some* of the later ones.

After TV-am stopped showing *The Transformers*, the rights were bought by the Sky Channel, a subscription-only service that required viewers to install a special satellite dish. Although much more mainstream now, in the late-'80s and early-'90s Sky subscriptions were rare. The complete run of *The Transformers* was shown on this channel (later renamed Sky One), beginning in early 1988, as part of *The D.J. Kat Show* on weekdays and *Fun Factory* on Saturday mornings. As Sky was a new, expensive channel, however, many UK fans were unable to watch these broadcasts.

Comic Sales:
In the UK, publishers of comics, magazines and periodicals will often hire an independent company, the Audit Bureau of Circulations, to calculate sales data. As well as being interesting figures in their own right, these data have the practical application of allowing a publisher to set rates for would-be advertisers – the higher the circulation, the more a publisher can charge for advertising space. For most of the run of the UK *The Transformers* comic, Marvel paid the ABC to provide sales information. Published here for the very first time are those sales figures – alongside, for purposes of comparison, those of its main rival, the boys' adventure comic *2000AD*, published by Fleetway.

Time Period	2000AD	The Transformers
Jul-Dec 1984	99,663	No data
Jan-Jun 1985	99,611	No data
Jul-Dec 1985	101,748	70,228
Jan-Jun 1986	No data	101,947
Jul-Dec 1986	No data	103,916
Jan-Jun 1987	No data	99,920
Jul-Dec 1987	111,540	78,145
Jan-Jun 1988	112,688	73,789
Jul-Dec 1988	112,699	64,821
Jan-Jun 1989	106,019	51,608
Jul-Dec 1989	104,216	41,055
Jan-Jun 1990	97,055	31,809
Jul-Dec 1990	96,805	23,864
Jan-Jun 1991	90,957	19,839
Jul-Dec 1991	85,871	No data
Jan-Jun 1992	81,989	No data

Source: Audit Bureau of Circulations

The figures listed are the average sales per issue during the indicated time period. Some issues might have seen higher sales spikes (perhaps due to a television advertisement or a free gift), but over any six-month period the *average* sales never exceeded 103,916. One must also bear in mind that these are independent figures, sourced from an outside auditor; Marvel and Fleetway might have also had their own methods of calculating sales, giving different figures from those above.

Many sources, supported by some anecdotal evidence from Marvel and Fleetway employees, claim that the readership for both comics sometimes exceeded 200,000. This is no doubt true: even if the actual sales figures were lower, individual copies would often be read by a number of people, as kids lent or gave them to siblings or school friends. It was believed that, on average, each copy sold would be read by 2.5 people. Fleetway and Marvel would therefore take ABC's circulation figures and apply this 2.5 multiplier to give a total readership that did exceed 200,000 on occasion.

From the above, we can see that both titles saw sales dwindle over the course of the late '80s and into the early '90s, an indication that comic sales in general were falling at the time.

As we can see, sales of *The Transformers* comic suffered overall a spectacular slump, with average per-issue numbers falling over 80% between 1986 and 1991.

For the eighteen month period between July 1986 and December 1987, additional sales information is available. Average sales of *The Transformers* outside of its key markets of the UK and Eire were 2,532 copies per issue in the second half of 1986; 2,867 copies per issue in the first half of 1987, and 1,113 copies per issue in the second half of 1987. These overseas sales figures are included in the numbers in the table above.

Additionally, we can compare sales of *The Transformers* during this period to other British publications, as follows:

Title	Jul-Dec 1986	Jan-Jun 1987	Jul-Dec 1987
Radio Times (TV listings)	3,235,977	3,044,679	3,209,697
Smash Hits (music)	515,427	512,317	533,930
Cosmopolitan (lifestyle)	369,878	375,894	386,919
Look-In (comic)	195,949	208,838	204,003
Shoot (football)	158,617	157,922	163,388
My Little Pony (comic)	125,144	101,196	83,112
The Transformers	**103,916**	**99,920**	**78,145**
Care Bears (comic)	91,633	79,716	62,315
Masters of the Universe (comic)	90,299	65,254	50,073
Disney Magazine (comic)	50,465	55,301	50,114

Average per-issue sales figures. Source: *ABC Circulation Review*, Serial 112, December 1987

Appendix 2:
Why Did *The Transformers* Die?

The Transformers brand is still going strong today, and indeed Transformers and related figures have graced toy aisles around the world pretty much continuously since *Beast Wars: Transformers* was launched to good success in 1996. But for a time in the early '90s the brand was all but dead, at least in its core market of America. While the original Generation 1 (G1) line did soldier on in Japan and Europe, in America the toys, the cartoon and the comic were all cancelled. Even in countries where G1 *did* survive, its popularity was a mere fraction of what it had been in the mid-'80s.

So what changed? How did such a behemoth of a brand collapse so massively? It seems strange to us now – some younger fans will never have known the toyshops to be completely bereft of Transformers. So why did it all go wrong in the '90s? It certainly wasn't for lack of innovation. Hasbro launched all sorts of gimmicks as they tried time and again to reinvigorate the brand. Headmasters, Pretenders, Micromasters, Action-Masters … all intriguing attempts at something new, and yet none was enough to see the brand to safety. Why?

One of the obvious differences between more modern Transformers lines and the old G1 range is the astounding contrast in the number of 'classic' names that saw multiple releases. Nowadays, no sub-line is complete without an Optimus Prime, a Grimlock, a Bumblebee or a Starscream. With that in mind, it's amazing to think that, before the last-ditch releases of Classic Pretenders and Action Masters at the end of the run, only one character name was ever reused between 1984 and 1988 – and that was Optimus Prime himself. Nowadays we get at least two or three toys named Megatron per year. In G1, we got just one in the first six years.

While some of the later G1 characters have their fans, it remains the case that less popular figures such as Longtooth and Crankcase were filling up the toy stores while many kids were pining for their favourites to return. Powermaster Optimus Prime (1988) was immensely popular when it came out, not just because it was a good toy, but because it was *Optimus Prime.* This prompted Hasbro to release other core characters as part of their Classic Pretender and Action Master ranges, but by then the writing was already on the wall.

Another factor in the demise of G1 was the diminishing amount of tie-in media support as time went on. As toys, Transformers are obviously great fun to play with. But kids like to use them to re-enact favourite scenes from the cartoons or the comics, or to create new adventures based on the characters therein. While the back-of-the-box character profiles were good for what they were, robots like Optimus Prime and Bumblebee have distinct voices and personalities, informed by the cartoon and the comics, and to a lesser extent the books. Even today, those toys that featured prominently in the associated media, such as Bludgeon and Thunderwing, sell for far more money on the secondary market than other, similar Transformers released at the same time.

This wouldn't have been such a huge problem if the television show or the comic had continued, and given focus to some of the more obscure characters such as Vroom or Skyfall, but falling ratings and circulations meant that they were cancelled, leaving many of the toys woefully under-represented in the media. It was a vicious circle – the toys decreased in popularity, which meant that the opportunities for tie-in media were less viable, which in turn decreased the desirability of the toys.

Another reason for the decline in popularity was the inability of the franchise to 'recycle' its fan-base. Long-term success is particularly hard to maintain in a brand aimed squarely at children. Kids quickly grow up and become 'too old' for toys, or gain other interests. The key is to continuously attract new young fans, to replace those who will naturally lose interest. This the Transformers franchise singularly failed to do.

One need only look at the G1 comic book to see a prime example. Early issues were great for the kids, with even Spider-Man of all people popping up to help save the day. Here were some simple, well-told tales of adventuring robots that any child could pick up and enjoy. However, the comic grew up with its audience. By the end of its run, it was presenting a more adult narrative, with complex stories of time paradoxes and revenge, and using phrases such as 'charnel house' and 'somnolent' in the dialogue. Great for the original fans, who were now approaching their teens and able to appreciate more sophisticated plots, but not so great for attracting new seven-year-olds.

Compare this with how the Transformers brand operates today, with all ages of fans catered for. The adults have the comics published by IDW, the Masterpiece line of collector-orientated toys and sub-lines like Generations, where classic characters from the '80s are reinterpreted for a modern audience. Younger fans can enjoy television shows such as *Transformers: Rescue Bots* and *Transformers: Robots in Disguise* and play with a slew of simpler toys designed for smaller fingers.

There is also an argument – slightly controversial amongst fans – that the quality of the G1 figures themselves decreased as the line went on. While the tail-end of the G1 era has its staunch defenders – and indeed Habsro's willingness to refresh the brand with new characters and gimmicks is to be generally applauded – it's arguable that the company perhaps lost sight of what fans loved in the first place.

The original idea of Transformers was that they were 'Robots in Disguise'. Back then, anything could potentially be a Transformer. A toy gun, a toy car, a toy jet, a toy robot dinosaur (there were lots of toy robot dinosaurs in the '80s), even a toy microscope. For many kids, much of the appeal was the realistic alt-mode, which the uninitiated could easily mistake for a 'regular' non-transforming toy. That these disguises also had a practical use in the comics and the TV show was just an added bonus.

However, when the movie came along in 1986, a trend began whereby Transformers would be released that converted into futuristic, alien or Cybertronian vehicles. While some of these – Hot Rod and Hardhead, for example – were still excellent, the lack of recognisable real-world alternative modes became an excuse for less-well-executed engineering. For example, Roadblock's alternative mode is some kind of a car/tank 'thing', with obvious robot arms sticking out of the back, sold as an example of a 'futuristic' vehicle. Furthermore, some later Transformers toys had ill-defined 'creature' modes. Gone were the well-crafted animals of the past such as the Dinobots or the Predacons, replaced by toys such as Cindersaur, Icepick and Blot, whose beast modes were just random, made-up 'monsters'.

Unusual or alien alternative modes aren't a bad idea *per se*: the 'Unicron Trilogy' of Transformers toy lines (2002-2005) featured plenty of figures with more abstract alternative modes, and some of them were brilliant toys. Unfortunately, in the '80s, a lot of these modes looked more like badly folded-up robots and less like feasible vehicles.

It got worse. Some of these vehicle modes were so bad, one needed accessories to make them look like anything at all. Stick two wheels onto a jumble of robot limbs and – hey, presto! – you have yourself a 'futuristic motorbike', namely Iguanus. Then there was Doubleheader. In this case, in order to turn him into a jet, you had to attach the *entire back half of a jet, including the wings* onto the folded-up Autobot. Given these ill-thought-out alternative modes and transformation cheats, it's no wonder that some of these toys proved less popular than their forerunners.

Another possible reason for the end of G1 is the increase in competition. In the '80s, Transformers seemed to coexist happily with other popular boys' franchises such as GI Joe, Masters of the Universe and MASK. It didn't really have any sort of competition that could blow it out of the water.

In the late '80s and early '90s, things changed. Rivals such as Power Rangers and Teenage Mutant Ninja Turtles took off in a major way. Transformers was no longer the giant it had once been – it had been supplanted by the new kids on the block. Additionally, the market for home video games exploded around this time. Computers and games consoles might have been available prior to the launch of the Transformers brand, but by the end of the '80s their quality and affordability were such that kids were more interested in their Sega Genesis or Nintendo Entertainment Systems than they were in Transformers. To illustrate the point: of the first forty issues of the American *The Transformers* comic, only nine carried advertisements for video games, consoles or accessories; of the remaining forty, thirty-six did so.

In conclusion, then, Transformers wasn't laid low by any one particular thing – a whole slew of factors helped bring about the end of G1. Thankfully, Hasbro were able to learn from these mistakes, and have since ironed out many of the issues that plagued the initial toy line. There's absolutely no reason to think that Transformers as a franchise won't be able to continue into the foreseeable future and beyond.

Appendix 3:
The Comics – What Happened Next?

The American *The Transformers* comic might have ceased publication in 1991, but that wasn't quite the end of the road for the original G1 characters. Since 1991, there have been a number of attempts to continue the story from where [80] 'End of the Road' left off.

Transformers: Generation 2 (1993-1994)

The Transformers franchise got the first of its many relaunches in 1993, as Transformers: Generation 2. An American Marvel comic, written by Simon Furman, was launched to tie in with the new figure range. However, Furman decided to use this book to continue the story arcs of the previous G1 comic. *Transformers: Generation 2* lasted only twelve issues, but the complex storylines and unique art style combined to form an excellent series that still holds up well today. A UK *Generation 2* comic was published by Fleetway and featured a mix of new material and American reprints; however it lasted for just five issues, plus an annual.

The Transformers: Classics (2006-2016)

An interesting strand of Transformers fiction, the *Classics* stories are works developed for the *Official Transformers Collectors' Club Magazine*, and also the annual BotCon convention, all fully-authorised by Hasbro. The stories generally follow the mantra 'by fans, for fans', and are not widely distributed to the general public. They are based largely on Hasbro's The Transformers: Classics range of figures – classic characters reimagined for a modern audience.

The Transformers: Regeneration One (2012-2014)

IDW Publishing are the current rights-holders to the Transformers comic range, and their many Transformers-related titles include this series, set twenty years after [80] 'End of the Road' and boasting the talents of G1 alumni Simon Furman, Andrew Wildman and Stephen Baskerville. Unlike the *Generation 2* comic, which ended on a cliffhanger, this leads up to a definitive ending, and ties up many of the original comic's loose ends.

None of these titles is compatible with each other; each purports to continue from [80] 'End of the Road' and each makes a point of ignoring the events of the UK comics (understandably, given their limited distribution in the core American market).

Appendix 4: Comic Reprints

The best way to appreciate the classic original Transformers comics is in their original format. Unfortunately, collecting a complete run of all the American and British comics (and annuals) is quite an expensive process these days. While many of the 'middle' issues can be bought for not much more than the original cover price (their high print runs mean that they aren't particularly rare), the very earliest and very latest issues can be quite scarce, and can fetch quite high sums online, especially if all the free gifts, posters etc are still attached.

Thankfully, however, most of the comics have been reprinted, and those that haven't are (at the time of writing) planned for release over the next couple of years. Here then, is a list of US and UK publications in which reprinted Transformers comics can be found:

MARVEL US
The American branch of Marvel Comics reprinted a number of the strips even while the original *The Transformers* comic was still ongoing.

The Transformers: Collected Comics
Available in both hardback and paperback editions, this was a short-lived series of reprint collections.

- #1: The Story Begins … (November 1985). Reprints [1] 'The Transformers', [2] 'Power Play' and [3] 'Prisoner of War'.
- #2: The Battle Continues … (November 1985). Reprints [4] 'The Last Stand', [5] 'The New Order' and [6] 'The Worse of Two Evils'.

The Transformers Comics Magazine
A bi-monthly series of magazines, in a smaller, digest-sized format. Each issue contained two complete stories, plus a selection of character profiles taken from the *Transformers Universe* comic series.

- #1 (January 1987). Reprints [1] 'The Transformers' and [2] 'Power Play'.
- #2 (March 1987). Reprints [3] 'Prisoner of War' and [4] 'The Last Stand'.
- #3 (May 1987). Reprints [5] 'The New Order' and [6] 'The Worse of Two Evils'.
- #4 (July 1987). Reprints [7] 'Warrior School' and [8] 'Repeat Performance'.
- #5 (September 1987). Reprints [9] 'Dis-Integrated Circuits' and [10] 'The Next Best Thing to Being There'.
- #6 (November 1987). Reprints [11] 'Brainstorm' and [12] 'Prime Time'.
- #7 (January 1988). Reprints [13] 'Shooting Star' and [14] 'Rock and Roll-Out'.
- #8 (March 1988). Reprints [15] 'I, Robot-Master' and [16] 'Plight of the Bumblebee'.
- #9 (May 1988). Reprints [17] 'The Smelting Pool' and [18] 'The Bridge to Nowhere'
- #10 (July 1988). Reprints [19] 'Command Performances' and [20] 'Showdown'

Miscellaneous
Marvel US produced two other reprint compilations, focusing on two of the spin-off comic series:

- *Transformers Universe* (July 1987). Reprints the character profiles seen in the *Transformers Universe* comic series [UNI1] to [UNI4], with some edits/omissions.
- *G.I. Joe and the Transformers* (February 1993). Reprints the crossover series: [GIJ1] 'Blood on the Tracks' to [GIJ4] 'All Fall Down' (GIJ).

MARVEL UK
Specials/*Collected Comics*
In line with many other British comic publishers, Marvel UK released a number of 'Specials' (larger-format comics timed to coincide with the school holidays) that reprinted collections of old material. The comic adaptation of *The Transformers: The Movie* ([MOV1] to [MOV3]) took the slot of the 1986 Winter Special, but that material was new to the UK, and so not classed as a reprint for the purposes of this list.
- *Collected Comics* #1 (June 1985). Reprints [1] 'The Transformers' and [2] 'Power Play'. Unlike the majority of the UK specials, this publication had a card cover and spine. Although the terminology was never used on the special itself, this has been retrospectively dubbed *Collected Comics #1*, in line with the specials that were published subsequently.
- *Collected Comics* #2 (October 1985). Reprints [3] 'Prisoner of War' and [4] 'The Last Stand'.
- *Collected Comics* #3 (March 1986). Reprints [4.1] 'Man of Iron' (in full colour for the first time).
- *Collected Comics* #4 (June 1986). Reprints [4.2] 'The Enemy Within' (in full colour for the first time).
- *Collected Comics* #5 (April 1987). Reprints [8.1] 'Decepticon Dam-Busters'.
- *Collected Comics* #6 (May 1987). Reprints [8.2] 'The Wrath of Grimlock'.
- *Collected Comics* #7 (October 1987). Reprints [12.4] 'Dinobot Hunt'.
- *Collected Comics* #8 (April 1988). Reprints [12.2] 'Crisis of Command'.
- *Collected Comics* #9 (May 1988). Reprints [16.1] 'Robot Buster' and [31.2] 'Kup's Story'
- *Collected Comics* #10 (July 1988). Reprints [16.3] 'Second Generation'.
- *Collected Comics* #11 (November 1988). A Christmas themed collection, reprinting [12.1] 'Christmas Break*er*', [22.1] 'The Gift' and [36.1] 'Stargazing'.
- *Collected Comics* #12 (June 1989). Reprints [23.1] 'Prey' and 'The Harder They Fall' (the first part of the [23.2] 'Under Fire' two-parter)
- *Collected Comics* #13 (July 1989). Reprints 'Under Fire' (i.e. the second part of the [23.2] 'Under Fire' two-parter) and [23.3] 'Distant Thunder'.
- *Collected Comics* #14 (September 1989). Reprints [36.3] 'Enemy Action' and an abridged version of [A2.5] 'Victory'.
- *Collected Comics* #15 (February 1990). Reprints the prologue, part 1 and part 2 of [20.2] 'Target: 2006'. Further issues of *Collected Comics* were supposed to continue the reprints of this story, but the masters got lost in the post.
- *Collected Comics* #16 (May 1990). Reprints [40.5] 'Wrecking Havoc' and [44.3] 'Dry Run'.
- *Collected Comics* #17 (September 1990). Reprints [44.1] 'Space Pirates' (parts 1-3). Again, this story was left half-finished, and the next special moved on to another story.
- *Collected Comics* #18 (December 1990). Reprints [48.2] 'Time Wars' (parts 1-3).

- *Collected Comics* #19 (February 1991). Reprints [48.1] 'Cold Comfort and Joy' and [48.2] 'Time Wars' (parts 4-5). Yet again, the reprints of 'Time Wars' stopped partway through without explanation. This was the last UK Special to be labelled as a *Collected Comics* issue.
- *Transformers* Summer Special (July 1992). Reprints [31.4] 'Grudge Match' and an abridged version of [A2.5] 'Victory'. The first UK special to see print after the comic itself had ceased publication.
- *Transformers* Autumn Special (September 1992). Reprints [40.1] 'City of Fear' and part one of [40.2] 'Legion of the Lost'.
- *Transformers* Easter Special (April 1993). Reprints part two of [40.2] 'Legion of the Lost', plus [40.3] 'Meltdown'.
- *Transformers* Holiday Special (July 1993). Reprints [40.4] 'Deadly Games' and [52.1] 'The Fall and Rise of the Decepticon Empire'.
- *Transformers* Winter Special (December 1993). Reprints [8.1] 'Decepticon Dam-Busters' and [53.5] 'The Big Shutdown' (colour version).
- *Transformers* Holiday Special (April 1994). Reprints [8.2] 'The Wrath of Grimlock' and [A1.2] 'And There Shall Come ... A Leader'.
- *Transformers* Summer Special (July 1994). Reprints [39.1] 'Salvage' and [44.3] 'Dry Run'.
- *Transformers* Winter Special (December 1994). Reprints [55.1] 'Way of the Warrior' and [62.6] 'Wolf in the Fold' (colour versions).

Miscellaneous

As well as the specials, there were some other Marvel UK titles that contained reprint material:
- *The Complete Works, Part 1* (April 1986). Hardback, large format book similar in size to the UK annuals. Reprints [1] 'The Transformers' and [2] 'Power Play'.
- *The Complete Works, Part 2* (April 1987). Reprints [3] 'Prisoner of War' and [4] 'The Last Stand'. The ending of 'The Last Stand' was modified to ensure that the story didn't finish on a cliffhanger.
- *The Transformers: Plague of the Insecticons* (1986). Reprints [A1.1] 'Plague of the Insecticons' and [A1.3] 'And There Shall Come ... A Leader'.
- *Transformers Universe Vol. One* (December 1988). Reprints the character profiles seen in the *Transformers Universe* comic series [UNI1] to [UNI4], with some edits/omissions. Despite the title implying that further volumes would be forthcoming, this was the only one published.

Titan

In 2001, UK publisher Titan Books acquired the rights to reprint Marvel's old Transformers comics, and so released a series of trade paperbacks that collected almost the entire run of UK and US Marvel strips. For many years, these were regarded as the best collections of Generation 1 Transformers strips on the market. They were published out of chronological order; for ease of reference the list below rearranges the books into reading order.

American Strips

All of the following were available in both softcover and hardback options. All of the

American issues were reprinted in this series, with the exception of [4.1] 'Man of Iron' (the British story that was published in US#33-34 as a fill-in), [43] 'The Big Broadcast of 2006' (an adaptation of a cartoon episode that didn't really fit, continuity-wise), The *G.I. Joe and the Transformers* spin-off series, the *Transformers: The Movie* comic adaptation and the *Transformers Universe* character profiles.

- *Transformers: Beginnings* (March 2003). Reprints all US stories from [1] 'The Transformers' to [6] 'The Worse of Two Evils'.
- *Transformers: New Order* (June 2003). Reprints all US stories from [7] 'Warrior School' to [12] 'Prime Time'.
- *Transformers: Cybertron Redux* (September 2003). Reprints all US stories from [13] 'Shooting Star' to [18] 'The Bridge to Nowhere'.
- *Transformers: Showdown* (December 2003). Reprints all US stories from [19] 'Command Performances' to [24] 'Afterdeath'.
- *Transformers: Breakdown* (March 2004). Reprints all US stories from [25] 'Gone but Not Forgotten' to [30] 'The Cure'.
- *Transformers: Treason* (June 2004). Reprints all US stories from [31] 'Buster Witwicky and the Car Wash of Doom' to [37] 'Toy Soldiers' (excluding [4.1] 'Man of Iron, the UK-originated story printed in US#33-34).
- *Transformers: Trial by Fire* (September 2004). Reprints *The Transformers: Headmasters* mini-series ([HDM1] 'Ring of Hate' to [HDM4] 'Brothers in Armor'), plus [38] 'Trial by Fire' and [39] 'The Desert Island of Space'.
- *Transformers: Maximum Force* (November 2004). Reprints all US stories from [40] 'Pretender to the Throne' to [45] 'Monstercon from Mars (with the exception of [43] 'The Big Broadcast of 2006', due to it being an adaptation of a cartoon episode).
- *Transformers: Dark Star* (January 2005). Reprints all US stories from [46] 'Ca$h and Car-nage' to [50] 'Dark Star'.
- *Transformers: Last Stand* (March 2005). Reprints all US stories from [51] 'The Man in the Machine' to [55] 'The Interplanetary Wrestling Championship'.
- *Transformers: Primal Scream* (April 2002). Reprints all US stories from [56] 'Back from the Dead' to [62] 'Bird of Prey'.
- *Transformers: Matrix Quest* (July 2002). Reprints all US stories from [63] 'Kings of the Wild Frontier' to [68] 'The Human Factor'.
- *Transformers: All Fall Down* (November 2001). Reprints all US stories from [69] 'Eye of the Storm' to [74] 'The Void'.
- *Transformers: End of the Road* (February 2002). Reprints all US stories from [75] 'On the Edge of Extinction' to [80] 'End of the Road'.
- *Best of Transformers: Eye of the Storm* (April 2008). A last hurrah for the Titan reprint books, this was a 'best of' compilation of strips that had been already reprinted in other titles. Contains [62] 'Bird of Prey' to [66] 'All Fall Down', plus [69] 'Eye of the Storm' to [75] 'On the Edge of Extinction'.

British Colour Strips

Again, these were available as either hardbacks or paperbacks. Stories omitted from this reprint series were [4.1] 'Man of Iron', [4.2] 'The Enemy Within', [4.3] 'Raiders of the Last Ark', [8.1] 'Decepticon Dam-Busters', [8.2] 'The Wrath of Grimlock, [12.1] 'Christmas Breaker', [12.2] 'Crisis of Command' and the *Action Force* crossover story [29.1] 'Ancient Relics'. Many of the UK Annual stories were left unprinted also.

- *Transformers: Dinobot Hunt* (March 2004). A collection of UK stories: [12.3] 'The Icarus Theory', [12.4] 'Dinobot Hunt', [20.1] 'In the National Interest' and [A2.5] 'Victory'.
- *Transformers: Second Generation* (August 2004). A collection of UK stories: [16.1] 'Robot Buster', [16.2] 'Devastation Derby', [16.3] 'Second Generation', [22.1] 'The Gift, [36.1] 'Stargazing', [48.1] 'Cold Comfort and Joy' and [A5.4] 'Dreadwing Down'.
- *Transformers: Target: 2006* (October 2002). Reprints [20.2] 'Target: 2006'.
- *Transformers: Prey* (May 2004). A collection of UK stories: [23.1] 'Prey', [23.2] 'Under Fire', [23.3] 'Distant Thunder', [23.5] 'Resurrection', [A3.1] 'What's in a Name', [31.4] 'Grudge Match' and [A5.5] 'The Chain Gang'.
- *Transformers: Fallen Angel* (February 2003). A collection of UK stories: [23.4] 'Fallen Angel', [27.1] 'Wanted: Galvatron – Dead or Alive', [27.2] 'Burning Sky', [27.3] 'Hunters', [27.4] 'Fire on High' and [A3.3] 'Vicious Circle'.
- *Transformers: Legacy of Unicron* (March 2003). A collection of UK stories: [31.3] 'Headhunt', [31.5] 'Ladies' Night', [36.2] 'The Legacy of Unicron' and [36.3] 'Enemy Action'.
- *Transformers: City of Fear* (November 2003). A collection of UK stories: [31.2] 'Kup's Story', [40.1] 'City of Fear', [40.2] 'Legion of the Lost', [40.3] 'Meltdown', [40.4] 'Deadly Games', [44.2] 'Firebug' and [52.1] 'The Fall and Rise of the Decepticon Empire'.
- *Transformers: Space Pirates* (July 2003). A collection of UK stories: [39.1] 'Salvage', [40.5] 'Wrecking Havoc', the UK-exclusive prologue and epilogue to [43] 'The Big Broadcast of 2006', [44.1] 'Space Pirates' and [A3.4] '*Ark* Duty'.
- *Transformers: Time Wars* (August 2003). A collection of UK stories: [31.1] 'Worlds Apart', [44.3] 'Dry Run', [48.2] 'Time Wars', [A4.2] 'Altered Image' and [A4.4] 'All in the Minds'.

British Black-and-White Strips
The tail-end of the UK *The Transformers* comic featured a number of black-and-white strips. Rather than these being given the full-size, glossy trade paperback treatment, they were instead shrunk down to near digest size and released as cheaper paperbacks.
- *Transformers: Aspects of Evil* (June 2005). Small-format paperback, reprinting the UK black-and-white stories [53.2] 'Aspects of Evil', [54.3] 'Deathbringer', [56.1] 'Out to Lunch', [57.2] 'Demons' and [59.3] 'Shadow of Evil'.
- *Transformers: Way of the Warrior* (July 2005). Small-format paperback, reprinting the UK black-and-white stories [53.1] 'Survivors', [53.4] 'The Hunting Party', [55.1] 'Way of the Warrior', [59.1] 'Whose Lifeforce is it Anyway?', [59.2] 'The Greatest Gift of All', [62.6] 'Wolf in the Fold', [63.1] 'Shut Up' and [63.2] 'Manoeuvres'.
- *Transformers: Fallen Star* (November 2005). Small-format paperback, reprinting the UK black-and-white stories [52.2] 'Race with the Devil', [57.1] 'Two Megatrons', [58.1] 'Fallen Star', [62.2] 'Flashback', [62.4] 'The Bad Guy's Ball', [62.7] 'Internal Affairs' and [63.3] 'Assassins'.
- *Transformers: Earthforce* (December 2005). Small-format paperback, reprinting the UK black-and-white stories [53.3] '[Double] Deal of the Century', [54.2] 'Prime's Rib', [61.1] 'Starting Over', [62.1] 'Snow Fun', [62.3] 'Mystery', [62.5] 'The Living Nightlights', [62.8] 'The House that Wheeljack Built', [62.9] 'Divide and Conquer'

(comic), [62.10] 'The 4,000,000 Year Itch' and [62.11] 'Makin' Tracks'.

- *Transformers: Perchance to Dream* (February 2006). Small-format paperback, reprinting the UK black-and-white stories [53.5] 'The Big Shutdown', [54.1] 'A Small War', [56.2] 'Rage', [60.1] 'Perchance to Dream' and [64.1] 'Inside Story'.

IDW Publishing
US-based comic-book publisher IDW are the current rights-holders for Transformers comics – both their own original series, and also reprints of the old Marvel ones.

The Transformers: Generations
IDW's first attempt at reprinting the classic Marvel strips was not as a collected trade paperback, but instead as an ongoing comic series of their own. Each issue of *The Transformers: Generations* reprinted a single American issue; a compilation of the first six issues was also released.

- #1 (March 2006). Reprints [7] 'Warrior School'.
- #2 (April 2006). Reprints [13] 'Shooting Star'.
- #3 (May 2006). Reprints [14] 'Rock and Roll-Out'.
- #4 (June 2006). Reprints [16] 'Plight of the Bumblebee'.
- #5 (July 2006). Reprints [17] 'The Smelting Pool'.
- #6 (August 2006). Reprints [18] 'The Bridge to Nowhere'.
- #7 (September 2006). Reprints [24] 'Afterdeath'.
- #8 (October 2006). Reprints [25] 'Gone But Not Forgotten'.
- #9 (November 2006). Reprints [27] 'King of the Hill'.
- #10 (December 2006). Reprints [29] 'Crater Critters'.
- #11 (February 2007). Reprints [30] 'The Cure'.
- #12 (March 2007). Reprints [31] 'Buster Witwicky and the Car Wash of Doom'.
- *The Transformers: Generations* (January 2007). Trade paperback collection; reprints [7] 'Warrior School, [13] 'Shooting Star', [14] 'Rock and Roll-Out', [16] 'Plight of the Bumblebee', [17] 'The Smelting Pool' and [18] 'The Bridge to Nowhere'.

The Transformers: Target: 2006
Following on from their *Generations* comic, IDW's next reprint title was a serialisation of [20.2] 'Target: 2006'. Again, this comic was collected as a trade paperback at the end of the run.

- #1 (April 2007). Reprints the prologue and part 1 of [20.2] 'Target: 2006'.
- #2 (May 2007). Reprints parts 2 and 3 of [20.2] 'Target: 2006'.
- #3 (June 2007). Reprints parts 4 and 5 of [20.2] 'Target: 2006'.
- #4 (July 2007). Reprints parts 6, 7 and 8 of [20.2] 'Target: 2006'.
- #5 (August 2007). Reprints parts 9 and the epilogue of [20.2] 'Target: 2006'.
- *The Transformers: Target: 2006* (January 2008). Trade paperback compilation reprinting the entirety of [20.2] 'Target: 2006'.

The Best Of
IDW then hit upon the idea of themed trade paperback compilations, containing a choice selection of Transformers strips from across the entire history of the franchise, from the classic Marvel strips to more recent efforts.

- *The Transformers: Greatest Battles of Optimus Prime and Megatron* (June 2007). A themed collection of issues spanning several years. Its contents include [4] 'The Last Stand' and [24] 'Afterdeath'.

- *The Transformers: The Best of Simon Furman* (July 2007). A collection of stories by author Simon Furman, including parts 3 and 8 of [20.2] 'Target: 2006', [40.5] 'Wrecking Havoc', [62] 'Bird of Prey', [70] 'The Price of Life', [71] 'Surrender' and [75] 'On the Edge of Extinction'.
- *The Transformers: Best of Optimus Prime* (June 2010). A themed collection of issues spanning several years. Its contents include [48] 'The Flames of Boltax' and [A1.3] 'And There Shall Come … A Leader'.
- *The Transformers: Best of Megatron* (September 2010). A themed collection of issues spanning several years. Its contents include [24] 'Afterdeath', [78] 'A Savage Circle' and part four of [53.2] 'Aspects of Evil'.
- *The Transformers: Best of Grimlock* (November 2010). A themed collection of issues spanning several years. Its contents include [8.2] 'The Wrath of Grimlock', [A2.5] 'Victory', [27] 'King of the Hill', [62.10] 'The 4,000,000 Year Itch' and [76] 'Still Life'.
- *The Transformers: Best of Starscream* (December 2010). A themed collection of issues spanning several years. Its contents include [4.2] 'The Enemy Within', [36.1] 'Stargazing', [50] 'Dark Star', [58.1] 'Fallen Star' and 'The Lesser Evil' (i.e. part three of [63.3] 'Assassins').

The Transformers Magazine

Similar to the 'Best Of' themed books listed above, this was a short-lived run of comics, each issue reprinting three strips from various eras of Transformers history.

- #1 (June 2007). Features strips from numerous eras, including [42] 'People Power'.
- #2 (August 2007). Features strips from numerous eras, including [44] 'The Cosmic Carnival'.
- #3 (October 2007). Features strips from numerous eras, including [56] 'Back from the Dead'.
- #4 (December 2007). Features strips from numerous eras, including [57] 'The Resurrection Gambit'.

The Transformers: Best of UK

Another run of reprints in a monthly comic format, this time reprinting UK material.

- *Dinobots* #1 (September 2007). Reprints [12.3] 'The Icarus Theory'.
- *Dinobots* #2 (October 2007). Reprints parts one and two of [12.4] 'Dinobot Hunt'.
- *Dinobots* #3 (November 2007). Reprints parts three and four of [12.4] 'Dinobot Hunt'.
- *Dinobots* #4 (December 2007). Reprints [A2.5] 'Victory' and part one of [20.1] 'In the National Interest'.
- *Dinobots* #5 (January 2008). Reprints parts two and three of [20.1] 'In the National Interest'.
- *Dinobots* #6 (January 2008). Reprints part four of [20.1] 'In the National Interest', plus the American story [8] 'Repeat Performance'.
- *The Transformers: Best of UK – Dinobots* (May 2008). Trade paperback collection of the *Dinobots* comics; reprints [12.3] 'The Icarus Theory', [12.4] 'Dinobot Hunt', [A2.5] 'Victory', and [20.1] 'In the National Interest'.
- *Space Pirates* #1 (March 2008). Reprints parts 1 and 2 of [44.1] 'Space Pirates'.

- *Space Pirates* #2 (April 2008). Reprints parts 3 and 4 of [44.1] 'Space Pirates'.
- *Space Pirates* #3 (May 2008). Reprints parts 5 and 6 of [44.1] 'Space Pirates'.
- *Space Pirates* #4 (June 2008). Reprints [31.1] 'Worlds Apart'.
- *Space Pirates* #5 (July 2008). Reprints [40.5] 'Wrecking Havoc'.
- *The Transformers: Best of UK – Space Pirates* (October 2008). Trade paperback compilation of the *Space Pirates* comics, reprinting [31.1] 'Worlds Apart', [40.5] 'Wrecking Havoc' and [44.1] 'Space Pirates'.
- *Time Wars* #1 (August 2008). Reprints [44.3] 'Dry Run', [A4.2] 'Altered Image' and [A4.4] 'All in the Minds'.
- *Time Wars* #2 (September 2008). Reprints [44.2] 'Firebug', and part 1 of [48.2] 'Time Wars'.
- *Time Wars* #3 (October 2008). Reprints parts 2-3 of [48.2] 'Time Wars'.
- *Time Wars* #4 (November 2008). Reprints parts 4-5 of [48.2] 'Time Wars'.
- *Time Wars* #5 (December 2008). Reprints parts 6-7 of [48.2] 'Time Wars'.
- *The Transformers: Best of UK – Time Wars* (March 2009). Trade paperback compilation of the *Time Wars* comics, reprinting [44.2] 'Firebug', [44.3] 'Dry Run', [48.2] 'Time Wars', [A4.2] 'Altered Image' and [A4.4] 'All in the Minds'.
- *Transformers: Best of UK Omnibus* (August 2009). A compilation of the *Dinobots, Space Pirates* and *Time Wars* series: [12.3] 'The Icarus Theory', [12.4] 'Dinobot Hunt', [20.1] 'In the National Interest', [31.1] 'Worlds Apart', [40.5] 'Wrecking Havoc', [44.1] 'Space Pirates, [44.2] 'Firebug', [44.3] 'Dry Run', [48.2] 'Time Wars', [A2.5] 'Victory', [A4.2] 'Altered Image' and [A4.4] 'All in the Minds'.
- *City of Fear* #1 (February 2009). Reprints [40.1] 'City of Fear'.
- *City of Fear* #2 (March 2009). Reprints [40.2] 'Legion of the Lost'.
- *City of Fear* #3 (April 2009). Reprints [40.3] 'Meltdown'.
- *City of Fear* #4 (May 2009). Reprints [36.3] 'Enemy Action'.
- *City of Fear* #5 (June 2009). Reprints [40.4] 'Deadly Games'.
- *The Transformers: Best of UK – City of Fear* (November 2009). Trade paperback compilation of the *City of Fear* reprint series, comprising [36.3] 'Enemy Action', [40.1] 'City of Fear', [40.2] 'Legion of the Lost', [40.3] 'Meltdown' and [40.4] 'Deadly Games'.
- *Prey* #1 (August 2009). Contains [23.1] 'Prey'.
- *Prey* #2 (September 2009). Contains [23.2] 'Under Fire'.
- *Prey* #3 (October 2009). Contains [23.3] 'Distant Thunder' and [A3.1] 'What's in a Name'.
- *Prey* #4 (November 2009). Contains [23.5] 'Resurrection'.
- *Prey* #5 (December 2009). Contains [31.4] 'Grudge Match'.
- *The Transformers: Best of UK – Prey* (March 2010). Trade paperback compilation, reprinting the *Prey* series: [23.1] 'Prey', [23.2] 'Under Fire', [23.3] 'Distant Thunder', [23.5] 'Resurrection', [31.4] 'Grudge Match' and [A3.1] 'What's in a Name'.

Classic Transformers

After testing the market for reprints with their themed comic series and compilations, IDW finally decided to do a sequential run of the original American Transformers comics, in a six-volume book series. Unfortunately, rights issues involving two Marvel-owned characters – Spider-Man and Circuit Breaker – meant that a number of the comics were edited or omitted altogether (text summaries were provided to bridge the gaps).

- *Classic Transformers Volume 1* (February 2008). Reprints all US stories from [1] 'The Transformers' to [16] 'Plight of the Bumblebee', with the exception of [3] 'Prisoner of War' (which starred Spider-Man) and [9] 'Dis-Integrated Circuits' (which featured Circuit Breaker).
- *Classic Transformers Volume 2* (July 2008). Reprints all US stories from [17] 'The Smelting Pool' to [32] 'Used Autobots', with the exception of [22] 'Heavy Traffic' and [23] 'Decepticon Graffiti', both of which featured Circuit Breaker.
- *Classic Transformers Volume 3* (February 2009). Reprints all US stories from [35] 'Child's Play' to [46] 'Ca$h and Car-nage', with the exception of [45] 'Monstercon from Mars', a Circuit Breaker story. Also included is [4.1] 'Man of Iron', the UK story that saw print in US#33-34.
- *Classic Transformers Volume 4* (July 2009). Reprints all US stories from [47] 'Club Con' to [61] 'The Primal Scream'.
- *Classic Transformers Volume 5* (December 2009). Reprints all US stories from [62] 'Bird of Prey' to [74] 'The Void'.
- *Classic Transformers Volume 6* (August 2010). Reprints all US stories from [75] 'On the Edge of Extinction' to [80] 'End of the Road', plus *The Transformers: Headmasters* mini-series ([HDM1] 'Ring of Hate' to [HDM4] 'Brothers in Armor'), and *The Transformers: The Movie* comic adaptation ([MOV1] 'The Planet-Eater' to [MOV3] 'The Final Battle').

The Transformers Classics

Less than a year after the *Classic Transformers* book series finished, IDW were able to negotiate a deal with Marvel which allowed then to reprint those stories featuring Spider-Man and Circuit Breaker. This prompted yet another series of reprints, finally collecting every Marvel US Generation 1 Transformers comic for the very first time. This series of books is presently the definitive collection of the American material.

- *The Transformers Classics, Volume 1* (August 2011). Reprints all US comics from [1] 'The Transformers' to [13] 'Shooting Star'. ISBN 1600109357.
- *The Transformers Classics, Volume 2* (January 2012). Reprints all US comics from [14] 'Rock and Roll-Out' to [25] 'Gone but Not Forgotten'. ISBN 161377091X.
- *The Transformers Classics, Volume 3* (April 2012). Reprints all US comics from [26] 'Funeral for a Friend' to [38] 'Trial by Fire'. Also included is [4.1] 'Man of Iron', the UK story that saw print in US#33-34. ISBN 1613771630.
- *The Transformers Classics, Volume 4* (October 2012). Reprints all US comics from [39] 'The Desert Island of Space' to [50] 'Dark Star'. ISBN 1613774974.
- *The Transformers Classics, Volume 5* (August 2013). Reprints all US comics from [51] 'The Man in the Machine' to [62] 'Deadly Obsession'. ISBN 1613776330.
- *The Transformers Classics, Volume 6* (October 2013). Reprints all US comics from [63] 'Dark Creation' to [76] 'Still Life'. ISBN 1613777647.
- *The Transformers Classics, Volume 7* (July 2014). Reprints all US comics from [77] 'Exodus' to [80] 'End of the Road', plus *The Transformers: Headmasters* mini-series ([HDM1] 'Ring of Hate' to [HDM4] 'Brothers in Armor'), and the *Transformers: The Movie* comic adaptation ([MOV1] 'The Planet-Eater' to [MOV3] 'The Final Battle'). ISBN 1613779879.
- *The Transformers Classics, Volume 8* (March 2015). Reprints the *Transformers Universe*

comic series ([UNI1] to [UNI4]), the character profiles that appeared semi-regularly throughout the later issues of the US Transformers comic (#47-49, 56-72, 74-79), plus the *G.I. Joe and the Transformers* comic series ([GIJ1] to [GIJ4]). ISBN 1631401335.

The Transformers Classics UK

As with the American volumes above, this series aims to reprint the complete run of Marvel UK Transformers stories, including those that appeared only in the annuals. As an added bonus, these books contain historical and background information pertaining to the UK comic and interviews with some of those who worked on the series. At time of writing, only the first five volumes have seen print (although cover art and contents for the sixth volume have been announced).

- *The Transformers Classics UK, Volume 1* (October 2011). Reprints [4.1] 'Man of Iron', [4.2] 'The Enemy Within', [4.3] 'Raiders of the Last Ark', [8.1] 'Decepticon Dam-Busters', [8.2] 'The Wrath of Grimlock, [12.1] 'Christmas Breaker', [12.2] 'Crisis of Command, [A1.1] 'Plague of the Insecticons, [A1.2] 'Missing in Action', [A1.2] 'And There Shall Come … A Leader', and [A1.4] 'Hunted'. ISBN 1600109438.
- *The Transformers Classics UK, Volume 2* (March 2012). Reprints [12.3] 'The Icarus Theory', [12.4] 'Dinobot Hunt', [16.1] 'Robot Buster', [16.2] 'Devastation Derby', [16.3] 'Second Generation', [20.1] 'In the National Interest', [A2.1] 'In the Beginning', [A2.2] 'To a Power Unknown', [A2.3] 'The Return of the Transformers', [A2.4] 'State Games', [A2.5] 'Victory' and [A2.6] 'The Mission'. ISBN 161377141X.
- *The Transformers Classics UK, Volume 3* (July 2012). Reprints [20.2] 'Target: 2006', [22.1] 'The Gift', [23.1] 'Prey, [23.2] 'Under Fire', [23.3] 'Distant Thunder', [23.4] 'Fallen Angel' and [23.5] 'Resurrection'. ISBN 1613772319.
- *The Transformers Classics UK, Volume 4* (June 2013). Reprints [27.1] 'Wanted: Galvatron – Dead or Alive', [27.2] 'Burning Sky', [27.3] 'Hunters', [27.4] 'Fire on High', [29.1] 'Ancient Relics', [31.1] 'Worlds Apart', [31.2] 'Kup's Story', [31.3] 'Headhunt', [31.4] 'Grudge Match', [31.5] 'Ladies' Night', [36.1] 'Stargazing', [A3.2] 'Headmasters Saga', [A3.3] 'Vicious Circle' and [A3.4] 'Ark Duty'. ISBN 1613775172.
- *The Transformers Classics UK, Volume 5* (August 2014). Reprints [36.2] 'The Legacy of Unicron', [36.3] 'Enemy Action', [39.1] 'Salvage', [40.1] 'City of Fear', [40.2] 'Legion of the Lost', [40.3] 'Meltdown', [40.4] 'Deadly Games', [40.5] 'Wrecking Havoc', [A4.1] 'The Saga of the Transformers – So Far', [A4.3] 'Prime Bomb' and [A4.5] 'Peace'. ISBN 1613777140.
- *The Transformers Classics UK, Volume 6* (release date to be confirmed). Reprints [43] 'The Big Broadcast of 2006' (the UK printing of that American story featured British-exclusive pages), [44.1] 'Space Pirates', [44.2] 'Firebug', [44.3] 'Dry Run', [48.1] 'Cold Comfort and Joy', [48.2] 'Time Wars', [52.1] 'The Fall and Rise of the Decepticon Empire', [A4.2] 'Altered Image' and [A4.4] 'All in the Minds'. ISBN 1631404946.

Miscellaneous

- *The Transformers: Regeneration One – 100-Page Spectacular 2012* (July 2012). As a lead-in to their sequel series *The Transformers: Regeneration One*, this comic reprinted the final five issues of the original US comic, [76] 'Still Life' to [80] 'End of the Road' (although, for legal reasons, Circuit Breaker's appearances were altered or edited out).

- *G.I. Joe/Transformers Volume 1* (August 2012). Part of a series of paperbacks reprinting the various Transformers/GI Joe crossovers, it included [GIJ1] 'Blood on the Tracks' through to [GIJ4] 'All Fall Down' (GIJ).

Hachette Livre

Hachette are one of the 'big five' English-language publishers in the world. Headquartered in France, their roster of authors includes David Baldacci, Jeffrey Deaver and Stephenie Meyer. As well as regular books, Hachette also produce a vast array of part-works – longer collections split over a number of regular volumes, ordered via a subscription service. Titles include *Marvel Ultimate Graphic Novel Collection*, *Doctor Who: The Complete History* and *The Art of Quilting*.

In 2016, Hachette's UK part-works division announced a new title, *Transformers: The Definitive G1 Collection*, which aimed to collect all the Marvel US and UK comics (as well as later comics originally published by Dreamwave and IDW) in a series of attractive hardbacks. Notably, the volumes would include new behind-the-scenes information, and present the UK black-and-white strips in full colour.

To gauge the size of the potential market, a limited trial run of the first four issues went on sale in the Greater Manchester area from September 2016; the series was launched nationally in December 2016.

Appendix 5: Issue Contents

The Transformers **(Marvel US)**

Four-Issue Limited Series (bi-monthly):

#1: September 1984. Cover (1p); [1] 'The Transformers' (25p); advertisements (10p). 36 pages total.

#2: November 1984. Cover (1p); [2] 'Power Play' (23p); Bullpen Bulletins (1p); advertisements (11p). 36 pages total.

#3: January 1985. Cover (1p); [3] 'Prisoner of War' (23p); Bullpen Bulletins (1p); advertisements (11p). 36 pages total.

#4: March 1985. Cover (1p); [4] 'The Last Stand' (22p); Bullpen Bulletins (1p); Transmissions (1p); advertisements (11p). 36 pages total.

Regular Series (monthly):

#5: June 1985. Cover (1p); [5] 'The New Order' (22p); Bullpen Bulletins (1p); Transmissions (1p); advertisements (11p). 36 pages total.

#6: July 1985. Cover (1p); [6] 'The Worse of Two Evils' (22p); Bullpen Bulletins (1p); advertisements (12p). 36 pages total.

#7: August 1985. Cover (1p); [7] 'Warrior School' (23p); Bullpen Bulletins (1p); Transmissions (1p); advertisements (10p). 36 pages total.

#8: September 1985. Cover (1p); [8] 'Repeat Performance' (22p); Bullpen Bulletins (1p); advertisements (12p). 36 pages total.

#9: October 1985. Cover (1p); [9] 'Dis-Integrated Circuits' (22p); Bullpen Bulletins (1p); advertisements (12p). 36 pages total.

#10: November 1985. Cover (1p); [10] 'The Next Best Thing to Being There' (22p); Bullpen Bulletins (1p); advertisements (12p). 36 pages total.

#11: December 1985. Cover (1p); [11] 'Brainstorm' (22p); Bullpen Bulletins (1p); advertisements (12p). 36 pages total.

#12: January 1986. Cover (1p); [12] 'Prime Time' (22p); Bullpen Bulletins (1p); advertisements (12p). 36 pages total.

#13: February 1986. Cover (1p); [13] 'Shooting Star' (23p); Bullpen Bulletins (1p); advertisements (11p). 36 pages total.

#14: March 1986. Cover (1p); [14] 'Rock and Roll-Out' (22p); Bullpen Bulletins (1p); Transmissions (1p); advertisements (11p). 32 pages total.

#15: April 1986. Cover (1p); [15] 'I, Robot Master' (22p); Bullpen Bulletins (1p); advertisements (12p). 36 pages total.

#16: May 1986. Cover (1p); [16] 'Plight of the Bumblebee' (22p); Bullpen Bulletins (1p); advertisements (12p). 36 pages total.

#17: June 1986. Cover (1p); [17] 'The Smelting Pool' (22p); Bullpen Bulletins (1p); Transmissions (1p); advertisements (11p). 36 pages total.

#18: July 1986. Cover (1p); [18] 'The Bridge to Nowhere' (22p); Bullpen Bulletins (1p); Transmissions (1p); advertisements (11p). 36 pages total.

#19: August 1986. Cover (1p); [19] 'Command Performances' (22p); Bullpen Bulletins (1p); Transmissions (1p); advertisements (11p). 36 pages total.

#20: September 1986. Cover (1p); [20] 'Showdown' (22p); Bullpen Bulletins (1p); Transmissions (1p); advertisements (11p). 36 pages total.

#21: October 1986. Cover (1p); [21] 'Aerialbots over America' (23p); Bullpen Bulletins (1p); advertisements (11p). 36 pages total.

#22: November 1986. Cover (1p); [22] 'Heavy Traffic' (23p); Bullpen Bulletins (1p); advertisements (12p). 36 pages total.

#23: December 1986. Cover (1p); [23] 'Decepticon Graffiti' (22p); Bullpen Bulletins (1p); Transmissions (1p); advertisements (11p). 36 pages total.

#24: January 1987. Cover (1p); [24] 'Afterdeath' (23p); Bullpen Bulletins (1p); Advertisements (11p). 36 pages total.

#25: February 1987. Cover (1p); [25] 'Gone but Not Forgotten' (22p); Bullpen Bulletins (1p); Transmissions (1p); advertisements (11p). 36 pages total.

#26: March 1987. Cover (1p); [26] 'Funeral for a Friend' (22p); Transmissions (1p); advertisements (12p). 36 pages total.

#27: April 1987. Cover (1p); [27] 'King of the Hill' (22p); Transmissions (1p); advertisements (12p). 36 pages total.

#28: May 1987. Cover (1p); [28] 'Mechanical Difficulties' (22p); advertisements (13p). 36 pages total.

#29: June 1987. Cover (1p); [29] 'Crater Critters' (22p); Bullpen Bulletins (1p); Transmissions (1p); advertisements (11p). 36 pages total.

#30: July 1987. Cover (1p); [30] 'The Cure' (22p); Bullpen Bulletins (1p); advertisements (12p). 36 pages total.

#31: August 1987. Cover (1p); [31] 'Buster Witwicky and the Car Wash of Doom' (23p); Transmissions (1p); advertisements (11p). 36 pages total.

#32: September 1987. Cover (1p); [32] 'Used Autobots' (22p); Bullpen Bulletins (1p); Transmissions (1p); advertisements (11p). 36 pages total.

#33: October 1987. Cover (1p); [4.1] 'Man of Iron' (1/2; reprints of UK material) (22p); Bullpen Bulletins (1p); Transmissions (1p); advertisements (11p). 36 pages total.

#34: November 1987. Cover (1p); [4.1] 'Man of Iron' (2/2; reprints of UK material) (22p); Bullpen Bulletins (1p); Transmissions (1p); advertisements (11p). 36 pages total.

#35: December 1987. Cover (1p); [35] 'Child's Play' (comic) (23p); Bullpen Bulletins (1p); advertisements (11p). 36 pages total.

#36: January 1988. Cover (1p); [36] 'Spacehikers' (22p); Bullpen Bulletins (1p); Transmissions (1p); advertisements (11p). 36 pages total.

#37: February 1988. Cover (1p); [37] 'Toy Soldiers' (22p); Bullpen Bulletins (1p); Transmissions (1p); advertisements (11p). 36 pages total.

#38: March 1988. Cover (1p); [38] 'Trial by Fire' (22p); Bullpen Bulletins (1p); Transmissions (1p); advertisements (11p). 36 pages total.

#39: April 1988. Cover (1p); [39] 'The Desert Island of Space' (22p); Bullpen Bulletins (1p); Transmissions (1p); advertisements (11p). 36 pages total.

#40: May 1988. Cover (1p); [40] 'Pretender to the Throne' (22p); Bullpen Bulletins (1p); Transmissions (1p); advertisements (11p). 36 pages total.

#41: June 1988. Cover (1p); [41] 'Totaled' (22p); Bullpen Bulletins (1p); Transmissions (1p); advertisements (11p). 36 pages total.

#42: Jul 1988. Cover (1p); [42] 'People Power' (22p); Bullpen Bulletins (1p); Transmissions (1p); advertisements (11p). 36 pages total.

#43: Aug 1988. Cover (1p); [43] 'The Big Broadcast of 2006' (22p); Bullpen Bulletins (1p); Transmissions (1p); advertisements (11p). 36 pages total.

#44: September 1988. Cover (1p); [44] 'The Cosmic Carnival' (22p); Bullpen Bulletins (1p); Transmissions (1p); advertisements (11p). 36 pages total.

#45: October 1988. Cover (1p); [45] 'Monstercon from Mars' (22p); Bullpen Bulletins (1p); Transmissions (1p); advertisements (11p). 36 pages total.

#46: November 1988. Cover (1p); [46] 'Ca$h and Car-nage' (22p); Bullpen Bulletins (1p); Transmissions (1p); advertisements (11p). 36 pages total.

#47: December 1988. Cover (1p); [47] 'Club Con' (20p); Bullpen Bulletins (1p); *Transformers Universe* profiles (Snapdragon/Highbrow/Apeface) (3p); advertisements (11p). 36 pages total.

#48: January 1989. Cover (1p); [48] 'The Flames of Boltax' (18p); Bullpen Bulletins (½p); *Transformers Universe* profiles (Hardhead/Brainstorm/Chromedome/Crosshairs/Searchlight) (5p); advertisements (11½p). 36 pages total.

#49: February 1989. Cover (1p); [49] 'Cold War' (18p); Bullpen Bulletins (½p); *Transformers Universe* profiles (Chase/Freeway) (2p); advertisements (14½ p). 36 pages total.

#50: March 1989. Cover (1p); [50] 'Dark Star' (38p); Bullpen Bulletins (1p); advertisements (12p). 52 pages total.

#51: April 1989. Cover (1p); [51] 'The Man in the Machine' (22p); Bullpen Bulletins (1p); advertisements (12p). 36 pages total.

#52: May 1989. Cover (1p); [52] 'Guess Who the Mecannibals are Having for Dinner?' (21p); Bullpen Bulletins (1p); advertisements (13p). 36 pages total.

#53: June 1989. Cover (1p); [53] 'Recipe for Disaster' (22p); Bullpen Bulletins (1p); Transmissions (1p); advertisements (11p). 36 pages total.

#54: July 1989. Cover (1p); [54] 'King Con' (22p); Bullpen Bulletins (1p); advertisements (12p). 36 pages total.

#55: August 1989. Cover (1p); [55] 'The Interplanetary Wrestling Championship' (22p); Bullpen Bulletins (1p); advertisements (12p). 36 pages total.

#56: September 1989. Cover (1p); [56] 'Back from the Dead' (16p); Bullpen Bulletins (1p); *Transformers Universe* profiles (Battletrap/Blot/Cutthroat/Goldbug/Rollbar/Wideload) (6p); advertisements (12p). 36 pages total.

#57: October 1989. Cover (1p); [57] 'The Resurrection Gambit' (16p); Bullpen Bulletins (1p); Transmissions (1p); *Transformers Universe* profiles (Cloudraker/Overkill/Slugfest) (6p); advertisements (11p). 36 pages total.

#58: November 1989. Cover (1p); [58] 'All the Familiar Faces' (16p); Star Signals (1p); *Transformers Universe* profiles (Afterburner/Lightspeed/Nosecone/Scattershot/Strafe/Computron) (6p); advertisements (12p). 36 pages total.

#59: Mid November 1989. Cover (1p); [59] 'Skin Deep' (16p); Star Signals (1p); *Transformers Universe* profiles (Nautilator/Overbite/Seawing/Skalor/Snaptrap/Tentakil/Piranacon) (7p); advertisements (11p). 36 pages total.

#60: December 1989. Cover (1p); [60] 'Yesterday's Heroes' (18p); Star Signals (1p); Transmissions (1p); *Transformers Universe* profiles (Misfire/Pointblank/Slugslinger/Sureshot) (4p); advertisements (11p). 36 pages total.

#61: Mid December 1989. Cover (1p); [61] 'The Primal Scream' (18p); Star Signals (1p); Transmissions (1p); *Transformers Universe* profiles (Triggerhappy/Landfill/Quickmix/Scoop) (4p); advertisements (11p). 36 pages total.

#62: January 1990. Cover (1p); [62] 'Bird of Prey' (18p); Star Signals (1p); Transmissions (1p); *Transformers Universe* profiles (Hosehead/Nightbeat/Siren/Backstreet) (4p); advertisements (11p). 36 pages total.

#63: February 1990. Cover (1p); [63] 'Kings of the Wild Frontier' (20p); Star Signals (1p); Transmissions (1p); *Transformers Universe* profiles (Dogfight/Override) (2p); advertisements (11p). 36 pages total.

#64: March 1990. Cover (1p); [64] 'Deadly Obsession' (20p); Star Signals (1p); Transmissions (1p); *Transformers Universe* profiles (Crankcase/Needlenose) (2p); advertisements (11p). 36 pages total.

#65: April 1990. Cover (1p); [65] 'Dark Creation' (20p); Star Signals (1p); Transmissions (1p); *Transformers Universe* profiles (Spinister/Windsweeper) (2p); advertisements (11p). 36 pages total.

#66: May 1990. Cover (1p); [66] 'All Fall Down' (TF) (20p); Star Signals (1p); Transmissions (1p); *Transformers Universe* profiles (Quake/Ruckus) (2p); advertisements (11p). 36 pages total.

#67: June 1990. Cover (1p); [67] 'Rhythms of Darkness' (20p); Bullpen Bulletins (1p); Transmissions (1p); *Transformers Universe* profiles (Getaway/Joyride) (2p); advertisements (11p). 36 pages total.

#68: July 1990. Cover (1p); [68] 'The Human Factor' (21p); Bullpen Bulletins (1p); Transmissions (1p); *Transformers Universe* profile (Slapdash) (1p); advertisements (11p). 36 pages total.

#69: August 1990. Cover (1p); [69] 'Eye of the Storm' (20p); Bullpen Bulletins (1p); Transmissions (1p); *Transformers Universe* profiles (Fastlane/Mindwipe) (2p); advertisements (11p). 36 pages total.

#70: September 1990. Cover (1p); [70] 'The Price of Life' (20p); Bullpen Bulletins (1p); Transmissions (1p); *Transformers Universe* profile (Powermaster Optimus Prime) (2p); advertisements (11p). 36 pages total.

#71: October 1990. Cover (1p); [71] 'Surrender' (20p); Transmissions (1p); *Transformers Universe* profiles (Punch/Counterpunch); advertisements (12p). 36 pages total.

#72: November 1990. Cover (1p); [72] 'All This and Civil War 2' (20p); Bullpen Bulletins (1p); Transmissions (1p); *Transformers Universe* profiles (Landmine/Skullgrin) (2p); advertisements (11p). 36 pages total.

#73: December 1990. Cover (1p); [73] 'Out of Time' (20p); Transmissions (1p); double-page spread of Optimus Prime v Megatron artwork (2p); advertisements (12p). 36 pages total.

#74: January 1991. Cover (1p); [74] 'The Void' (20p); Bullpen Bulletins (1p); Transmissions (1p); *Transformers Universe* profiles (Darkwing/Dreadwind) (2p); advertisements (11p). 36 pages total.

#75: February 1991. Cover (1p); [75] 'On the Edge of Extinction' (36p); Transmissions (2p); *Transformers Universe* profiles (Fangry/Squeezeplay) (2p); advertisements (11p). 52 pages total.

#76: March 1991. Cover (1p); [76] 'Still Life' (20p); Transmissions (1p); *Transformers Universe* profiles (Grotusque/Horri-Bull) (2p); advertisements (12p). 36 pages total.

#77: April 1991. Cover (1p); [77] 'Exodus' (20p); Bullpen Bulletins (1p); Transmissions (1p); *Transformers Universe* profiles (Weirdwolf/Skullcruncher) (2p); advertisements (11p). 36 pages total.

#78: May 1991. Cover (1p); [78] 'A Savage Circle' (20p); Bullpen Bulletins (1p); Transmissions (1p); *Transformers Universe* profiles (Pounce/Repugnus) (2p); advertisements (11p). 36 pages total.

#79: June 1991. Cover (1p); [79] 'The Last Autobot?' (20p); Bullpen Bulletins (1p); Transmissions (1p); *Transformers Universe* profile (Fortress Maximus) (2p); advertisements (11p). 36 pages total.

#80: July 1991. Cover (1p); [80] 'End of the Road' (22p); Bullpen Bulletins (1p); Transmissions (1p); advertisements (11p). 36 pages total.

Some of the later issues (between US#70 and US#80) featured an additional four-page glossy pull-out featuring extra advertisements. Variations of the comics exist with and without these pull-outs.

Transformers: The Movie (Marvel US)

Three-Issue Limited Series (monthly):

#1: December 1986. Cover (1p); [MOV1] 'The Planet-Eater' (23p); Bullpen Bulletins (1p); advertisements (11p). 36 pages total.

#2: January 1987. Cover (1p); [MOV2] 'Judgment Day' (23p); Bullpen Bulletins (1p); advertisements (11p). 36 pages total.

#3: February 1987. Cover (1p); [MOV3] 'The Final Battle' (24p); Bullpen Bulletins (1p); advertisements (10p). 36 pages total.

The Transformers Universe (Marvel US)

Four-Issue Limited Series (monthly):

#1: December 1986. Cover (wraparound) (2p); contents page (1p); *Transformers Universe* profiles (Air Raid to Grimlock) (32p); endpaper (1p). 36 pages total.

#2: January 1987. Cover (wraparound) (2p); contents page (1p); *Transformers Universe* profiles (Groove to Ramjet) (33p). 36 pages total.

#3: February 1987. Cover (wraparound) (2p); contents page (1p); *Transformers Universe* profiles (Rampage to Swindle) (33p). 36 pages total.

#4: March 1987. Cover (wraparound) (2p); contents page (1p); *Transformers Universe* profiles (Steeljaw to Windcharger, plus Movie characters) (33p). 36 pages total.

G.I. Joe and the Transformers (Marvel US)

Four-Issue Limited Series (monthly):

#1: January 1987. Cover (1p); [GIJ1] 'Blood on the Tracks' (24p); Bullpen Bulletins (1p); advertisements (10p). 36 pages total.

#2: February 1987. Cover (1p); [GIJ2] 'Power Struggle' (23p); Bullpen Bulletins (1p); advertisements (11p). 36 pages total.

#3: March 1987. Cover (1p); [GIJ3] 'Ashes, Ashes' (23p); advertisements (12p). 36 pages total.

#4: April 1987. Cover (1p); [GIJ4] 'All Fall Down' (GIJ) (25p); advertisements (10p). 36 pages total.

The Transformers: Headmasters (Marvel US)

Four-Issue Limited Series (bi-monthly):

#1: July 1987. Cover (1p); [HDM1] 'Ring of Hate' (23p); Bullpen Bulletins (1p); advertisements (11p). 36 pages total.

#2: September 1987. Cover (1p); [HDM2] 'Broken Glass' (23p); Bullpen Bulletins (1p); advertisements (11p). 36 pages total.

#3: November 1987. Cover (1p); [HDM3] 'Love and Steel' (22p); Bullpen Bulletins (1p); advertisements (12p). 36 pages total.

#4: January 1988. Cover (1p); [HDM4] 'Brothers in Armor' (22p); Bullpen Bulletins (1p); advertisements (12p). 36 pages total.

The Transformers (Marvel UK)

Fortnightly publication, partially black-and-white:

#1: 20 Sep – 3 Oct 1984. Cover (1p); Openers (2p); [1] 'The Transformers' (1/2) (11p); *Machine Man* (9p); Robot Round-Up (2p); competition page (1p); pull-out posters (2p); next issue preview/subscription offer (1p); advertisements (3p). 32 pages total, full colour.

#2: 4 Oct – 17 Oct 1984. Cover (1p); Openers (2p); [1] 'The Transformers' (2/2) (12p); *Machine Man* (6p); Robot Round-Up (2p); competition page (1p); feature article: '*Doctor Who* Meets the Robots' (1p); pull-out posters (4p); next issue preview/subscription offer (1p); advertisements (2p). 32 pages total (of which 16 are black-and-white only). NB: the actual Transformers strip was missing two pages, which instead appeared (with amendments) as part of the pull-out poster section in the centre of the comic.

#3: 18 Oct – 31 Oct 1984. Cover (1p); Openers (2p); [2] 'Power Play' (1/2) (14p); *Machine Man* (5p); Robot Round-Up (2p); competition page (1p); pull-out posters (2p); next issue preview/subscription offer (1p); advertisements (4p). 32 pages total (16 b/w).

#4: 1 Nov – 14 Nov 1984. Cover (1p); Openers (2p); [2] 'Power Play' (2/2) (9p); *Machine Man* (10p); Robot Round-Up (2p); competition page (1p); pull-out posters (2p); next issue preview/subscription offer (1p); advertisements (4p). 32 pages total (16 b/w).

#5: 17 Nov – 30 Nov 1984. Cover (1p); Openers (2p); [3] 'Prisoner of War' (1/2) (12p); *Machine Man* (7p); Robot Round-Up (2p); competition page (1p); feature article: 'His Name's Sieve-Head…' (1p); pull-out poster (1p); next issue preview/*Matt and the Cat* (1p); advertisements (4p). 32 pages total (16 b/w).

#6: 1 Dec – 14 Dec 1984. Cover (1p); Openers (2p); [3] 'Prisoner of War' (2/2) (11p); *Machine Man* (9p); Robot Round-Up (2p); competition page (1p); pull-out poster (1p); next issue preview/*Matt and the Cat* (1p); advertisements (4p). 32 pages total (16 b/w).

#7: 15 Dec – 28 Dec 1984. Cover (1p); Openers (2p); [4] 'The Last Stand' (1/1) (12p); *Machine Man* (8p); Robot Round-Up (2p); reader-submitted artwork (2p); next issue preview/*Matt and the Cat* (1p); advertisements (4p). 32 pages total (16 b/w).

#8: 29 Dec 1984 – 11 Jan 1985. Cover (1p); Openers (2p); [4] 'The Last Stand' (2/2) (10p); *Machine Man* (10p); Robot Round-Up (2p); January calendar (2p); next issue preview/*Matt and the Cat* (1p); advertisements (4p). 32 pages total (16 b/w).

#9: 12 Jan – 25 Jan 1985. Cover (1p); Openers (2p); [4.1] 'Man of Iron' (1/4) (11p); *Machine Man* (8p); Robot Round-Up (2p); toy check-list (1p); reader-submitted artwork (2p); next issue preview/*Matt and the Cat* (1p); advertisements (4p). 32 pages total (16 b/w).

#10: 26 Jan – 8 Feb 1985. Cover (1p); Openers (2p); [4.1] 'Man of Iron' (2/4) (11p); *Machine Man* (8p); Robot Round-Up (2p); February calendar (2p); feature article: 'Robby the Robot' (2p); next issue preview/*Matt and the Cat* (1p); advertisements (3p). 32 pages total (16 b/w).

#11: 9 Feb – 22 Feb 1985. Cover (1p); Openers (2p); [4.1] 'Man of Iron' (3/4) (11p); *Machine Man* (9p); Robot Round-Up (1p); competition page (1p); reader-submitted artwork (2p); next issue preview/*Matt and the Cat* (1p); advertisements (4p). 32 pages total (16 b/w).

#12: 23 Feb – 8 Mar 1985. Cover (1p); Openers (2p); [4.1] 'Man of Iron' (4/4) (11p); *Machine Man* (6p); Robot Round-Up (2p); *The Chromobots* (2p); competition page (1p); March calendar (2p); next issue preview/*Matt and the Cat* (1p); advertisements (4p). 32 pages total (16 b/w).

#13: 9 Mar – 22 Mar 1985. Cover (1p); Openers (2p); [4.2] 'The Enemy Within' (1/5) (11p); *Machine Man* (6p); Robot Round-Up (2p); *The Chromobots* (2p); reader-submitted artwork (2p); competition page (1p); next issue preview/*Matt and the Cat* (1p); advertisements (4p). 32 pages total (16 b/w).

#14: 23 Mar – 5 Apr 1985. Cover (1p); Openers (2p); [4.2] 'The Enemy Within' (2/5) (11p); *Machine Man* (5p); Robot Round-Up (2p); *The Chromobots* (2p); reader-submitted artwork (1p); competition page (1p); April calendar (2p); next issue preview/*Matt and the Cat* (1p); advertisements (4p). 32 pages total (16 b/w).

#15: 6 Apr – 19 Apr 1985. Cover (1p); Openers (2p); [4.2] 'The Enemy Within' (3/5) (11p); *Machine Man* (5p); *The Chromobots* (2p); *From the Fact Files* (6p); competition page (1p); next issue preview/*Matt and the Cat* (1p); advertisements (3p). 32 pages total. (16 b/w).

#16: 20 Apr-3 May 1985. Cover (1p); Openers (2p); [4.2] 'The Enemy Within' (4/5) (6p); *Machine Man* (7p); Robot Round-Up (2p); *The Chromobots* (2p); *Planet Terry* (5p); competition page (1p); May calendar (2p); next issue preview/*Matt and the Cat* (1p); advertisements (3p). 32 pages total (16 b/w).

#17: 4 May – 17 May 1985. Cover (1p); Openers (2p); [4.2] 'The Enemy Within' (5/5) (5p); *Machine Man* (5p); *The Chromobots* (2p); *From the Fact Files* (5p); *Planet Terry* (5p); competition page (1p); pull-out poster (1p); next issue preview/*Matt and the Cat* (1p); advertisements (4p). 32 pages total (16 b/w).

#18: 18 May – 31 May 1985. Cover (1p); Openers (2p); [4.3] 'Raiders of the Last *Ark*' (1/4) (6p); *Machine Man* (8p); Robot Round-Up (2p); *The Chromobots* (2p); *Planet Terry* (5p); June Calendar (2p); next issue preview/*Matt and the Cat* (1p); advertisements (3p). 32 pages total (16 b/w).

#19: 1 Jun – 14 Jun 1985. Cover (1p); Openers (2p); [4.3] 'Raiders of the Last *Ark*' (2/4) (5p); *Machine Man* (7p); *The Chromobots* (2p); *From the Fact Files* (4p); *Planet Terry* (7p); next issue preview/*Matt and the Cat* (1p); advertisements (3p). 32 pages total (16 b/w).

#20: 15 Jun – 28 Jun 1985. Cover (1p); Openers (2p); [4.3] 'Raiders of the Last *Ark*' (3/4) (6p); *Machine Man* (7p); Robot Round-Up (2p); *The Chromobots* (2p); *Planet Terry* (6p); competition page (1p); toy checklist (1p); next issue preview/*Matt and the Cat* (1p); advertisements (3p). 32 pages total (16 b/w).

#21: 29 Jun – 12 Jul 1985. Cover (1p); Openers (2p); [4.3] 'Raiders of the Last *Ark*' (4/4) (5p); *The Chromobots* (2p); *From the Fact Files* (4p); *Planet Terry* (9p); competition page (1p); July calendar (2p); toy checklist (1p); story recap (reprint of the final page of [4] The Last Stand) (1p); next issue preview/*Matt and the Cat* (1p); advertisements (3p). 32 pages total (16 b/w).

#22: 13 Jul – 26 Jul 1985. Cover (1p); Transformation (1p); [5] 'The New Order' (1/2) (9p); *Machine Man* (7p); *The Chromobots* (2p); *Planet Terry* (4p); Soundwaves (1p); feature: 'Robot War!' (2p); competition page (1p); next issue preview/*Matt and the Cat* (1p); advertisements (3p). 32 pages total (16 b/w).

#23: 27 Jul – 9 Aug 1985. Cover (1p); Transformation (1p); [5] 'The New Order' (2/2) (13p); *Machine Man* (5p); *The Chromobots* (2p); *Planet Terry* (3p); competition page (1p); August calendar (2p); next issue preview/*Matt and the Cat* (1p); advertisements (3p). 32 pages total (16 b/w).

#24: 10 Aug – 23 Aug 1985. Cover (1p); Transformation (1p); [6] 'The Worse of Two Evils' (1/2) (11p); *Machine Man* (5p); *The Chromobots* (3p); *Planet Terry* (5p); Soundwaves (2p); competition page (1p); next issue preview/*Matt and the Cat* (1p); advertisements (2p). 32 pages total (16 b/w).

UK#25: 24 Aug – 6 Sep 1985. Cover (1p); Transformation (1p); [6] 'The Worse of Two Evils' (2/2) (11p); *Machine Man* (5p); *The Chromobots* (2p); *Planet Terry* (3p); Soundwaves (1p); Interface (Warpath/Ramjet) (1p); competition page (1p); September calendar (2p); feature: 'The New Machine Man' (1p); next issue preview/*Matt and the Cat* (1p); advertisements (2p). 32 pages total (16 b/w).

UK#26: 7 Sep – 14 Sep 1985. Cover (1p); Transformation (1p); [7] 'Warrior School' (23p); *The Chromobots* (2p); full-page next-issue preview (advertising the new full-colour weekly incarnation of the comic) (1p); *Matt and the Cat* (½p); advertisements (3½p). 32 pages total (16 b/w).

Weekly publication, full colour:

UK#27: 21 Sep 1985. Cover (1p); Transformation (1p); [8] 'Repeat Performance' (1/2) (11p); *Machine Man* (8p); *Matt and the Cat* (½p); advertisements (2½p). 24 pages total.

UK#28: 28 Sep 1985. Cover (1p); Transformation (1p); [8] 'Repeat Performance' (2/2) (10½p); *Machine Man* (6p); Soundwaves (1p); Interface (Snarl) (½p); competition page (1p); next issue preview/*Matt and the Cat* (1p); advertisements (2p). 24 pages total.

UK#29: 5 Oct 1985. Cover (1p); Transformation (1p); [8.1] 'Decepticon Dam-Busters' (1/2) (11p); *Machine Man* (5p); Soundwaves (1p); October calendar (2p); comic order form/*Matt and the Cat* (1p); next issue preview (½p); advertisements (1½p). 24 pages total.

UK#30: 12 Oct 1985. Cover (1p); Transformation (1p); [8.1] 'Decepticon Dam-Busters' (2/2) (11p); *Machine Man* (6p); Soundwaves (1p); next issue preview (½p); advertisements (3½p). 24 pages total.

UK#31: 19 Oct 1985. Cover (1p); Transformation (1p); [8.2] 'The Wrath of Grimlock' (1/2) (11p); *Machine Man* (6p); competition page (1p); next issue preview/Interface (Bombshell) (1p); *Matt and the Cat* (1p); advertisements (2p). 24 pages total.

UK#32: 26 October 1985. Cover (1p); Transformation (1p); [8.2] 'The Wrath of Grimlock' (2/2) (11p); *Machine Man* (6p); Soundwaves (1p); next issue preview/Interface (Inferno) (1p); list of competition winners/*Matt and the Cat* (1p); advertisements (2p). 24 pages total.

UK#33: 2 November 1985. Cover (1p); Transformation (1p); [9] 'Dis-Integrated Circuits' (1/2) (11p); *Machine Man* (5p); Soundwaves (1p); November calendar (2p); competition page (1p); *Matt and the Cat*/next issue preview (1p); advertisements (1p). 24 pages total.

UK#34: 9 November 1985. Cover (1p); Transformation (1p); [9] 'Dis-Integrated Circuits' (2/2) (11p); *Machine Man* (5p); Soundwaves (1p); competition page (1p); *Matt and the Cat*/next issue preview (1p); advertisements (3p). 24 pages total.

UK#35: 16 November 1985. Cover (1p); Transformation (1p); [10] 'The Next Best Thing to Being There' (1/2) (11p); *Machine Man* (6p); Soundwaves (1p); competition page (1p); *Matt and the Cat*/next issue preview (1p); advertisements (2p). 24 pages total.

UK#36: 23 November 1985. Cover (1p); Transformation (1p); [10] 'The Next Best Thing to Being There' (2/2) (11p); *Machine Man* (5p); Soundwaves (1p); feature: 'Robot War II' (2p); advertisements (3p). 24 pages total.

UK#37: 30 November 1985. Cover (1p); Transformation (1p); [11] 'Brainstorm' (1/2) (11p); *Machine Man* (6p); Soundwaves (1p); competition page (1p); *Matt and the Cat*/next issue preview (1p); advertisements (2p). 24 pages total.

UK#38: 7 December 1985. Cover (1p); Transformation (1p); [11] 'Brainstorm' (2/2) (11p); *Machine Man* (6p); Soundwaves (1p); December calendar (2p); advertisements (2p). 24 pages total.

UK#39: 14 December 1985. Cover (1p); Transformation (1p); [12] 'Prime Time' (1/2) (11p); *Machine Man* (5p); Soundwaves (1p); *Matt and the Cat* (1p); Interface (Scavenger)/next issue preview (1p); advertisements (3p). 24 pages total.

UK#40: 21 December 1985. Cover (1p); Transformation (1p); [12] 'Prime Time' (2/2) (11p); *Machine Man* (6p); Soundwaves (1p); *Matt and the Cat*/next issue preview (1p); advertisements (3p). 24 pages total.

UK#41: 28 December 1985. Cover (1p); Transformation (1p); [12.1] 'Christmas Breaker' (11p); *Machine Man* (6p); Rat-Chat (1p); competition page (1p); *Matt and the Cat*/next issue preview (1p); advertisements (2p). 24 pages total.

UK#42: 4 January 1986. Cover (1p); Transformation (1p); [12.2] 'Crisis of Command' (1/3) (11p); *Machine Man* (6p); Soundwaves (1p); Interface (Blitzwing/Tracks) (1p); *Matt and the Cat* (1p); order coupon/next issue preview (1p); advertisements (1p). 24 pages total.

UK#43: 11 January 1986. Cover (1p); Transformation (1p); [12.2] 'Crisis of Command' (2/3) (11p); *Iron Man* (7p); Soundwaves (1p); *Matt and the Cat*/next issue preview (1p); advertisements (2p). 24 pages total.

UK#44: 18 January 1986. Cover (1p); Transformation (1p); [12.2] 'Crisis of Command' (3/3) (11p); *Iron Man* (6p); Soundwaves (1p); feature/advertorial: 'The Do-it-Yourself Transformer!' (1p); *Matt and the Cat*/next issue preview (1p); advertisements (2p). 24 pages total.

UK#45: 25 January 1986. Cover (1p); Transformation (1p); [12.3] 'The Icarus Theory' (1/2) (11p); *Iron Man* (6p); Soundwaves (1p); Interface (Cosmos/Beachcomber) (1p); *Matt and the Cat*/next issue preview (1p); advertisements (2p). 24 pages total.

UK#46: 1 February 1986. Cover (1p); Transformation (1p); [12.3] 'The Icarus Theory' (2/2) (11p); *Iron Man* (6p); Soundwaves (1p); *Matt and the Cat* (1p); order coupon/next issue preview (1p); advertisements (2p). 24 pages total.

UK#47: 8 February 1986. Cover (1p); Transformation (1p); [12.4] 'Dinobot Hunt' (1/4) (11p); *Iron Man* (7p); Soundwaves (1p); *Matt and the Cat*/next issue preview (1p); advertisements (2p). 24 pages total.

UK#48: 15 February 1986. Cover (1p); Transformation (1p); [12.4] 'Dinobot Hunt' (2/4) (11p); *Iron Man* (6p); Soundwaves (1p); Feature: 'The Decepticon Who's Who' (1p); *Matt and the Cat*/next issue preview (1p); advertisements (2p). 24 pages total.

UK#49: 22 February 1986. Cover (1p); Transformation (1p); [12.4] 'Dinobot Hunt' (3/4) (11p); *Iron Man* (6p); Soundwaves (1p); *Matt and the Cat*/competition results (1p); order coupon/next issue preview (1p); advertisements (2p). 24 pages total.

UK#50: 1 March 1986. Cover (1p); Transformation (1p); [12.4] 'Dinobot Hunt' (4/4) (11p); *Iron Man* (7p); Soundwaves (1p); *Matt and the Cat*/next issue preview (1p); advertisements (2p). 24 pages total.

UK#51: 8 March 1986. Cover (1p); Transformation (1p); [13] 'Shooting Star' (1/2) (12p); *Robotix* (6p); Soundwaves (1p); *Matt and the Cat*/next issue preview (1p); advertisements (2p). 24 pages total.

UK#52: 15 March 1986. Cover (1p); Transformation (1p); [13] 'Shooting Star' (2/2) (11p); *Robotix* (7p); Interface (Smokescreen/Mixmaster) (1p); *Matt and the Cat*/next issue preview (1p); advertisements (2p). 24 pages total.

UK#53: 22 March 1986. Cover (1p); Transformation (1p); [14] 'Rock and Roll-Out' (1/2) (11p); *Robotix* (6p); Soundwaves (1p); Feature: 'The Autobot Who's Who' (1/2) (1p); *Matt and the Cat*/next issue preview (1p); advertisements (2p). 24 pages total.

UK#54: 29 March 1986. Cover (1p); Transformation (1p); [14] 'Rock and Roll-Out' (2/2) (11p); *Robotix* (6p); Soundwaves (1p); Feature: 'The Autobot Who's Who' (2/2) (1p); *Matt and the Cat*/next issue preview (1p); advertisements (2p). 24 pages total.

UK#55: 5 April 1986. Cover (1p); Transformation (1p); [15] 'I, Robot-Master' (1/2) (11p); *Rocket Raccoon* (7p); Soundwaves (1p); Interface (Kickback/Slag) (1p); *Matt and the Cat*/next issue preview (1p); advertisements (1p). 24 pages total.

UK#56: 12 April 1986. Cover (1p); Transformation (1p); [15] 'I, Robot-Master' (2/2) (11p); *Rocket Raccoon* (6p); Soundwaves (1p); *Matt and the Cat*/next issue preview (1p); advertisements (3p). 24 pages total.

UK#57: 19 April 1986. Cover (1p); Transformation (1p); [16] 'Plight of the Bumblebee' (1/2) (11p); *Rocket Raccoon* (7p); Soundwaves (1p); order coupon/next issue preview (1p); advertisements (2p). 24 pages total.

UK#58: 26 April 1986. Cover (1p); Transformation (1p); [16] 'Plight of the Bumblebee' (2/2) (11p); *Rocket Raccoon* (7p); Soundwaves (1p); *Matt and the Cat*/next issue preview (1p); advertisements (2p). 24 pages total.

UK#59: 3 May 1986. Cover (1p); Transformation (1p); [16.1] 'Robot Buster' (1/2) (11p); *Rocket Raccoon* (6p); Soundwaves (1p); Feature: 'The Human Who's Who' (1p); order coupon ($\frac{1}{2}$p); *Matt and the Cat*/next issue preview (1p); advertisements (1½p). 24 pages total.

UK#60: 10 May 1986. Cover (1p); Transformation (1p); [16.1] 'Robot Buster' (2/2) (11p); *Rocket Raccoon* (5p); Soundwaves (1p); competition page (1p); next issue preview (½p); advertisements (3½p). 24 pages total.

UK#61: 17 May 1986. Cover (1p); Transformation (1p); [16.2] 'Devastation Derby' (1/2) (11p); *Rocket Raccoon* (6p); Soundwaves (1p); Interface (Devastator) (½p); *Matt and the Cat*/competition page (1p); next issue preview (½p); advertisements (2p). 24 pages total.

UK#62: 24 May 1986. Cover (1p); Transformation (1p); [16.2] 'Devastation Derby' (2/2) (11p); *Rocket Raccoon* (6p); Soundwaves (1p); next issue preview (1p); competition (½p); advertisements (2½p). 24 pages total.

UK#63: 31 May 1986. Cover (1p); Transformation (1p); [16.3] 'Second Generation' (1/3) (11p); *Rocket Raccoon* (5p); Soundwaves (1p); Feature: 'Robot War III' (3p); advertisements (2p). 24 pages total.

UK#64: 7 June 1986. Cover (1p); Transformation (1p); [16.3] 'Second Generation' (2/3)

(11p); *Rocket Raccoon* (6p); Soundwaves (1p); feature/advertorial 'Transform Your Summer!' (2p); *Matt and the Cat*/next issue preview (1p); advertisement (1p). 24 pages total.

UK#65: 14 June 1986. Cover (1p); Transformation (1p); [16.3] 'Second Generation' (3/3) (11p); *Rocket Raccoon* (6p); Soundwaves (1p); Interface (Soundwave/Blaster) (1p); *Matt and the Cat*/next issue preview (1p); advertisements (2p). 24 pages total.

UK#66: 21 June 1986. Cover (1p); Transformation (1p); [17] 'The Smelting Pool' (1/2) (11p); *Rocket Raccoon* (6p); Soundwaves (1p); *Matt and the Cat* (1p); advertisements (3p). 24 pages total.

UK#67: 28 June 1986. Cover (1p); Transformation (1p); [17] 'The Smelting Pool' (2/2) (11p); *Rocket Raccoon* (6p); Soundwaves (1p); puzzle page/Interface (Perceptor) (1p); *Matt and the Cat*/next issue preview (1p); advertisements (2p). 24 pages total.

UK#68: 5 July 1986. Cover (1p); Transformation (1p); [18] 'The Bridge to Nowhere' (1/2) (11p); *Rocket Raccoon* (6p); Soundwaves (1p); order coupon/Interface (Long Haul) (1p); *Matt and the Cat*/next issue preview (1p); advertisements (2p). 24 pages total.

UK#69: 12 July 1986. Cover (1p); Transformation (1p); [18] 'The Bridge to Nowhere' (2/2) (11p); *Rocket Raccoon* (5p); Soundwaves (1p); order coupon/Interface (Swoop) (1p); *Matt and the Cat*/next issue preview (1p); advertisements (3p). 24 pages total.

UK#70: 19 July 1986. Cover (1p); Transformation (1p); [19] 'Command Performances' (1/2) (11p); *Hercules* (6p); Soundwaves (1p); Interface (Omega Supreme) (1p); *Matt and the Cat*/next issue preview (1p); advertisements (2p). 24 pages total.

UK#71: 26 July 1986. Cover (1p); Transformation (1p); [19] 'Command Performances' (1/2) (11p); *Hercules* (6p); Soundwaves (1p); order coupon/Interface (Thrust) (1p); *Matt and the Cat*/next issue preview (1p); advertisements (2p). 24 pages total.

UK#72: 2 August 1986. Cover (1p); Transformation (1p); [20] 'Showdown' (1/2) (11p); *Hercules* (6p); Soundwaves (1p); *Matt and the Cat*/next issue preview (1p); advertisements (3p). 24 pages total.

UK#73: 9 August 1986. Cover (1p); Transformation (1p); [20] 'Showdown' (2/2) (11p); *Hercules* (5p); Soundwaves (1p); Interface (Ravage)/*Matt and the Cat* (1p); next issue preview (1p); advertisements (3p). 24 pages total.

UK#74: 16 August 1986. Cover (1p); Transformation (1p); [20.1] 'In the National Interest' (1/4) (11p); *Hercules* (6p); Feature: Hercules Fact File (1p); *Robo-Capers* (1p); next issue preview (1p); advertisements (2p). 24 pages total.

UK#75: 23 August 1986. Cover (1p); Transformation (1p); [20.1] 'In the National Interest' (2/4) (11p); *Hercules* (6p); Grim Grams (1p); *Robo-Capers* (½p); order coupon/next issue preview (1p); advertisements (2½p). 24 pages total.

UK#76: 30 August 1986. Cover (1p); Transformation (1p); [20.1] 'In the National Interest' (3/4) (11p); *Hercules* (5p); Grim Grams (1p); Features: 'And Now… the Dinobots'/*Transformers Annual* preview (2p); *Robo-Capers*/next issue preview (1p); advertisements (2p). 24 pages total.

UK#77: 6 September 1986. Cover (1p); Transformation (1p); [20.1] 'In the National Interest' (4/4) (11p); *Hercules* (6p); Grim Grams (1p); competition page (1p); *Robo-Capers* (½p); advertisements (2½p). 24 pages total.

UK#78: 13 September 1986. Cover (1p); Transformation (1p); [20.2] 'Target: 2006' (1/11) (11p); *Hercules* (6p); Grim Grams (1p); order coupon (½p); *Robo-Capers*/next issue preview (1p); advertisements (2½p). 24 pages total.

UK#79: 20 September 1986. Cover (1p); Transformation (1p); [20.2] 'Target: 2006' (2/11) (11p); *Hercules* (5p); Grim Grams (1p); *Robo-Capers* (½p); order coupon/next issue preview (1p); advertisements (3½p). 24 pages total.

UK#80: 27 September 1986. Cover (1p); Transformation (1p); [20.2] 'Target: 2006' (3/11) (11p); *Hercules* (6p); Grim Grams (1p); next issue preview (½p); advertisements (3½p). 24 pages total.

UK#81: 4 October 1986. Cover (1p); Transformation (1p); [20.2] 'Target: 2006' (4/11) (11p); *Hercules* (5p); Grim Grams (1p); Feature: 'Introducing the New Leaders: Ultra Magnus' (1p); *Robo-Capers* (½p); order coupon/next issue preview (1p); advertisements (2½p). 24 pages total.

UK#82: 11 October 1986. Cover (1p); Transformation (1p); [20.2] 'Target: 2006' (5/11) (11p); *Hercules* (6p); Grim Grams (1p); *Robo-Capers* (½p); order coupon/next issue preview (1p); advertisements (2½p). 24 pages total.

UK#83: 18 October 1986. Cover (1p); Transformation (1p); [20.2] 'Target: 2006' (6/11) (11p); *Hercules* (5p); Grim Grams (1p); Feature: 'Cybertron: The Middle Years!' (1p); *Robo-Capers* (½p); order coupon/next issue preview (1p); advertisements (2½p). 24 pages total.

UK#84: 25 October 1986. Cover (1p); Transformation (1p); [20.2] 'Target: 2006' (7/11) (11p); *Hercules* (6p); Grim Grams (1p); *Robo-Capers*/next issue preview (1p); advertisements (3p). 24 pages total.

UK#85: 1 November 1986. Cover (1p); Transformation (1p); [20.2] 'Target: 2006' (8/11) (11p); Hercules (5p); Grim Grams (1p); Hercules pull-out poster (1p); *Robo-Capers*/next issue preview (1p); advertisements (3p). 24 pages total.

UK#86: 8 November 1986. Cover (1p); Transformation (1p); [20.2] 'Target: 2006' (9/11) (11 p); *Spitfire and the Troubleshooters* (6p); Grim Grams (1p); *Robo-Capers* (½p); order coupon/next issue preview (1p); advertisements (2½p). 24 pages total.

UK#87: 15 November 1986. Cover (1p); Transformation (1p); [20.2] 'Target: 2006'

(10/11) (11 p); *Spitfire and the Troubleshooters* (6p); Grim Grams (1p); Feature: 'Introducing the New Leaders: Galvatron' (1p); *Robo-Capers*/next issue preview (1p); advertisements (2p). 24 pages total.

UK#88: 22 November 1986. Cover (1p); Transformation (1p); [20.2] 'Target: 2006' (11/11) (12p); *Spitfire and the Troubleshooters* (4p); Grim Grams (1p); *Robo-Capers*/next issue preview (1p); advertisements (4p). 24 pages total.

UK#89: 29 November 1986. Cover (1p); Transformation (1p); [21] 'Aerialbots over America' (1/2) (11p); *Spitfire and the Troubleshooters* (5p); Grim Grams (1p); Transformers A to Z (Air Raid/Astrotrain) (1p); *Robo-Capers*/next issue preview (1p); advertisements (3p). 24 pages total.

UK#90: 6 December 1986. Cover (1p); Transformation (1p); [21] 'Aerialbots over America' (2/2) (12p); *Spitfire and the Troubleshooters* (5p); Grim Grams (1p); competition page (1p); *Robo-Capers*/next issue preview (1p); advertisements (2p). 24 pages total.

UK#91: 13 December 1986. Cover (1p); Transformation (1p); [22] 'Heavy Traffic' (1/2) (12p); *Spitfire and the Troubleshooters* (5p); Feature: 'Film 2006' (1p); competition page (1p); *Robo-Capers*/next issue preview (1p); advertisements (2p). 24 pages total.

UK#92: 20 December 1986. Cover (1p); Transformation (1p); [22] 'Heavy Traffic' (2/2) (11p); *Spitfire and the Troubleshooters* (5p); Grim Grams (1p); competition/*Robo-Capers* (1p); next issue preview ($\frac{1}{2}$p); advertisements (3$\frac{1}{2}$p). 24 pages total.

UK#93: 27 December 1986. Cover (1p); Transformation (1p); [22.1] 'The Gift' (1/1) (11p); Spitfire and the Troubleshooters (6p); Grim Grams (1p); Transformers A to Z (Beachcomber/Blades) (1p); competition page (1p); *Robo-Capers*/next issue preview (1p); advertisements (1p). 24 pages total.

UK#94: 3 January 1987. Cover (1p); Transformation (1p); [22] 'Decepticon Graffiti' (1/2) (11p); *Spitfire and the Troubleshooters* (7p); Grim Grams (1p); *Robo-Capers*/next issue preview (1p); advertisements (2p). 24 pages total.

UK#95: 10 January 1987. Cover (1p); Transformation (1p); [22] 'Decepticon Graffiti' (2/2) (11p); *Spitfire and the Troubleshooters* (5p); Grim Grams (1p); *Robo-Capers*/next issue preview (1p); advertisements (4p). 24 pages total.

UK#96: 17 January 1987. Cover (1p); Transformation (1p); [22.1] 'Prey' (1/2) (11p); *Spitfire and the Troubleshooters* (5p); Grim Grams (1p); *Robo-Capers*/next issue preview (1p); advertisements (4p). 24 pages total.

UK#97: 24 January 1987. Cover (1p); Transformation (1p); [22.1] 'Prey' (1/2) (11p); *Spitfire and the Troubleshooters* (6p); Grim Grams (1p); *Robo-Capers* ($\frac{1}{2}$p); next issue preview/order coupon (1p); advertisements (2$\frac{1}{2}$p). 24 pages total.

UK#98: 31 January 1987. Cover (1p); Transformation (1p); [23.2] 'Under Fire' (1/2) (11p); *Spitfire and the Troubleshooters* (5p); Grim Grams (1p); competition page (1p); *Robo-*

Capers/next issue preview (1p); advertisements (3p). 24 pages total.

UK#99: 7 February 1987. Cover (1p); Transformation (1p); [23.2] 'Under Fire' (2/2) (11p); *Action Force* (5p); Grim Grams (1p); *Robo-Capers*/order coupon (1p); next issue preview (1p); advertisements (3p). 24 pages total.

UK#100: 14 February 1987. Wraparound cover (2p); Transformation (1p); [23.3] 'Distant Thunder' (1/1) (19p); *Action Force* (6p); competition page (1p); order coupon (½p); *Robo Capers*/next issue preview (1p); advertisements (1½p). 32 pages total (special bumper issue).

UK#101: 21 February 1987. Cover (1p); Transformation (1p); [23.4] 'Fallen Angel' (1/2) (11p); *Action Force* (6p); Grim Grams (1p); Transformers A to Z (Blaster/Blast Off) (1p); *Robo-Capers*/next issue preview (1p); advertisements (2p). 24 pages total.

UK#102: 28 February 1987. Cover (1p); Transformation (1p); [23.4] 'Fallen Angel' (2/2) (11p); *Action Force* (6p); Grim Grams (1p); *Robo-Capers*/next issue preview (1p); advertisements (3p). 24 pages total.

UK#103: 7 March 1987. Cover (1p); Transformation (1p); [23.5] 'Resurrection' (1/2) (11p); *The Inhumanoids* (5p); competition page (1p); *Robo-Capers*/next issue preview (1p); advertisements (4p). 24 pages total.

UK#104: 14 March 1987. Cover (1p); Transformation (1p); [23.5] 'Resurrection' (2/2) (11p); *The Inhumanoids* (5p); competition page (1p); *Robo-Capers*/next issue preview (1p); advertisements (4p). 24 pages total.

UK#105: 21 March 1987. Cover (1p); Transformation (1p); [24] 'Afterdeath' (1/2) (11p); *The Inhumanoids* (6p); *Robo-Capers*/next issue preview (1p); advertisements (4p). 24 pages total.

UK#106: 28 March 1987. Cover (1p); Transformation (1p); [24] 'Afterdeath' (2/2) (12p); *The Inhumanoids* (5p); Grim Grams (1p); *Robo-Capers*/next issue preview (1p); advertisements (3p). 24 pages total.

UK#107: 4 April 1987. Cover (1p); Transformation (1p); [25] 'Gone but Not Forgotten' (1/2) (11p); *The Inhumanoids* (5p), Grim Grams (1p); *Robo-Capers*/next issue preview (1p); advertisements (4p). 24 pages total.

UK#108: 11 April 1987. Cover (1p); Transformation (1p); [25] 'Gone but Not Forgotten' (2/2) (11p); *The Inhumanoids* (5p); Grim Grams (1p); Transformers A to Z (Bluestreak/Blitzwing) (1p); *Robo-Capers*/next issue preview (1p); advertisements (3p). 24 pages total.

UK#109: 18 April 1987. Cover (1p); Transformation (1p); [26] 'Funeral for a Friend' (1/2) (11p); *The Inhumanoids* (6p); Grim Grams (1p); *Robo-Capers*/next issue preview (1p); advertisements (3p). 24 pages total.

UK#110: 25 April 1987. Cover (1p); Transformation (1p); [26] 'Funeral for a Friend' (2/2) (11p); *The Inhumanoids* (6p); Grim Grams (1p); *Robo-Capers*/next issue preview (1p); advertisements (3p). 24 pages total.

UK#111: 2 May 1987. Cover (1p); Transformation (1p); [27] 'King of the Hill' (1/2) (11p); *The Inhumanoids* (5p); Grim Grams (1p); order coupon/competition results (1p); *Robo-Capers*/next issue preview (1p); advertisements (3p). 24 pages total.

UK#112: 9 May 1987. Cover (1p); Transformation (1p); [27] 'King of the Hill' (2/2) (11p); *The Inhumanoids* (6p); Grim Grams (1p); *Robo-Capers*/next issue preview (1p); advertisements (3p). 24 pages total.

UK#113: 16 May 1987. Cover (1p); Transformation (1p); [27.1] 'Wanted: Galvatron – Dead or Alive' (1/2) (11p); *The Inhumanoids* (6p); Grim Grams (1p); *Robo-Capers*/next issue preview (1p); advertisements (3p). 24 pages total.

UK#114: 23 May 1987. Cover (1p); Transformation (1p); [27.1] 'Wanted: Galvatron – Dead or Alive' (2/2) (11p); *The Inhumanoids* (6p); Grim Grams (1p); competition page (1p); *Robo-Capers*/next issue preview (1p); advertisements (2p). 24 pages total.

UK#115: 30 May 1987. Cover (1p); Transformation (1p); [27.2] 'Burning Sky' (1/2) (11p); *The Inhumanoids* (6p); Grim Grams (1p); *Robo-Capers*/next issue preview (1p); advertisements (3p). 24 pages total.

UK#116: 6 June 1987. Cover (1p); Transformation (1p); [27.2] 'Burning Sky' (2/2) (11p); *The Inhumanoids* (6p); Grim Grams (1p); Transformers A to Z (Bombshell/Bonecrusher) (1p); *Robo-Capers*/next issue preview (1p); advertisements (2p). 24 pages total.

UK#117: 13 June 1987. Cover (1p); Transformation (1p); [27.3] 'Hunters' (1/2) (11p); *The Inhumanoids* (5p); Grim Grams (1p); Transformers A to Z (Brawl/Brawn) (1p); *Robo-Capers*/next issue preview (1p); advertisements (3p). 24 pages total.

UK#118: 20 June 1987. Cover (1p); Transformation (1p); [27.3] 'Hunters' (2/2) (11p); *The Inhumanoids* (6p); Grim Grams (1p); *Robo-Capers*/next issue preview (1p); advertisements (3p). 24 pages total.

UK#119: 27 June 1987. Cover (1p); Transformation (1p); [27.4] 'Fire on High' (1/2) (11p); *The Iron Man of 2020* (6p); Grim Grams (1p); Transformers A to Z (Breakdown/Bruticus) (1p); *Robo-Capers*/next issue preview (1p); advertisements (2p). 24 pages total.

UK#120: 4 July 1987. Cover (1p); Transformation (1p); [27.4] 'Fire on High' (2/2) (11p); *The Iron Man of 2020* (5p); Grim Grams (1p); *Robo-Capers* (½p); Next issue preview/annual preview (1p); advertisements (3½p). 24 pages total.

UK#121: 11 July 1987. Cover (1p); Transformation (1p); [28] 'Mechanical Difficulties' (1/2) (11p); *The Iron Man of 2020* (6p); Grim Grams (1p); *Robo-Capers*/next issue preview (1p); advertisements (3p). 24 pages total.

UK#122: 18 July 1987. Cover (1p); Transformation (1p); [28] 'Mechanical Difficulties' (2/2) (11p); *The Iron Man of 2020* (5p); *Action Force* (6p); Grim Grams (1p); *Robo-Capers*/next issue preview (1p); advertisements (2p). 28 pages total. (Bumper issue with bonus Action Force strip.)

UK#123: 25 July 1987. Cover (1p); Transformation (1p); [29] 'Crater Critters' (1/2) (11p); *The Iron Man of 2020* (6p); Grim Grams (1p); *Robo-Capers*/next issue preview (1p); advertisements (3p). 24 pages total.

UK#124: 1 August 1987. Cover (1p); Transformation (1p); [29] 'Crater Critters' (2/2) (11p); *The Iron Man of 2020* (6p); Grim Grams (1p); Transformers A to Z (Buzzsaw/Cliffjumper) (1p); *Robo-Capers*/next issue preview (1p); advertisements (2p). 24 pages total.

UK#125: 8 August 1987. Cover (1p); Transformation (1p); [29.1] 'Ancient Relics' (1/5) (11p); *The Iron Man of 2020* (5p); Grim Grams (1p); competition page (1p); *Robo-Capers*/next issue preview (1p); advertisements (3p). 24 pages total.

UK#126: 15 August 1987. Cover (1p); Transformation (1p); [30] 'The Cure' (1/2) (11p); *Iron Man* (5p); Grim Grams (1p); *Transformers Annual* preview (1p); *Robo-Capers*/next issue preview (1p); advertisements (3p). 24 pages total.

UK#127: 22 August 1987. Cover (1p); Transformation (1p); [30] 'The Cure' (2/2) (11p); *Iron Man* (6p); Grim Grams (1p); *Robo-Capers*/next issue preview (1p); advertisements (3p). 24 pages total.

UK#128: 29 August 1987. Cover (1p); Transformation (1p); [31] 'Buster Witwicky and the Car Wash of Doom' (1/2) (11p); *Iron Man* (5p); Grim Grams (1p); Transformers A to Z (Cosmos/Dead End) (1p); *Robo-Capers*/next issue preview (1p); advertisements (3p). 24 pages total.

UK#129: 5 September 1987. Cover (1p); Transformation (1p); [31] 'Buster Witwicky and the Car Wash of Doom' (2/2) (12p); *Iron Man* (6p); Grim Grams (1p); next issue preview (1p); advertisements (3p). 24 pages total.

UK#130: 12 September 1987. Cover (1p); Transformation (1p); [31.1] 'Worlds Apart' (1/2) (11p); [HDM1] 'Ring of Hate' (1/4) (6p); Grim Grams (1p); competition page (1p); *Robo-Capers*/next issue preview (1p); advertisements (2p). 24 pages total.

UK#131: 19 September 1987. Cover (1p); Transformation (1p); [31.1] 'Worlds Apart' (2/2) (11p); [HDM1] 'Ring of Hate' (2/4) (5p); Grim Grams (1p); competition page (1p); *Robo-Capers*/next issue preview (1p); advertisements (3p). 24 pages total.

UK#132: 26 September 1987. Cover (1p); Transformation (1p); [31.2] 'Kup's Story' (1/1) (11p); [HDM1] 'Ring of Hate' (3/4) (6p); *Spider-Man: Children in Danger!* (4p); Grim Grams (1p); *Robo-Capers*/next issue preview (1p); advertisements (3p). 28 pages total.

UK#133: 3 October 1987. Cover (1p); Transformation (1p); [31.3] 'Headhunt' (1/2) (11p);

[HDM1] 'Ring of Hate' (4/4) (6p); Grim Grams (1p); competition pages (2p); Transformers A to Z (Defensor/Devastator) (1p); *Robo-Capers*/next issue preview (1p); advertisements (4p). 28 pages total.

UK#134: 10 October 1987. Cover (1p); Transformation (1p); [31.3] 'Headhunt' (2/2) (11p); [HDM2] 'Broken Glass' (1/4) (5p); Grim Grams (1p); competition page (1p); *Robo-Capers*/next issue preview (1p); advertisements (3p). 24 pages total.

UK#135: 17 October 1987. Cover (1p); Transformation (1p); [31.4] 'Grudge Match' (1/2) (11p); [HDM2] 'Broken Glass' (2/4) (6p); Grim Grams (1p); *Robo-Capers*/next issue preview (1p); advertisements (3p). 24 pages total.

UK#136: 24 October 1987. Cover (1p); Transformation (1p); [31.4] 'Grudge Match' (2/2) (11p); [HDM2] 'Broken Glass' (3/4) (6p); Grim Grams (1p); *Robo-Capers*/next issue preview (1p); advertisements (3p). 24 pages total.

UK#137: 31 October 1987. Cover (1p); Transformation (1p); [31.5] 'Ladies' Night' (1/2) (11p); [HDM2] 'Broken Glass' (4/4) (6p); Grim Grams (1p); *Robo-Capers*/next issue preview (1p); advertisements (3p). 24 pages total.

UK#138: 7 November 1987. Cover (1p); Transformation (1p); [31.5] 'Ladies' Night' (2/2) (11p); [HDM3] 'Love and Steel' (1/4) (6p); Grim Grams (1p); competition page (1p); Transformers A to Z (Dirge/Divebomb) (1p); *Robo-Capers*/next issue preview (1p); advertisements (5p). 28 pages total.

UK#139: 14 November 1987. Cover (1p); Transformation (1p); [32] 'Used Autobots' (1/2) (11p); [HDM3] 'Love and Steel' (2/4) (5p); Grim Grams (1p); Transformers A to Z (Drag Strip/Fireflight) (1p); *Robo-Capers*/next issue preview (1p); advertisements (3p). 24 pages total.

UK#140: 21 November 1987. Cover (1p); Transformation (1p); [32] 'Used Autobots' (2/2) (11p); [HDM3] 'Love and Steel' (3/4) (6p); Grim Grams (1p); *Robo-Capers*/next issue preview (1p); advertisements (3p). 24 pages total.

UK#141: 28 November 1987. Cover (1p); Transformation (1p); [35] 'Child's Play' (comic) (1/2) (12p); [HDM3] 'Love and Steel' (4/4) (5p); Grim Grams (1p); competition page (1p); *Robo-Capers*/next issue preview (1p); advertisements (2p). 24 pages total.

UK#142: 5 December 1987. Cover (1p); Transformation (1p); [35] 'Child's Play' (comic) (2/2) (11p); [HDM4] 'Brothers in Armor' (1/4) (6p); Grim Grams (1p); *Robo-Capers*/next issue preview (1p); advertisements (3p). 24 pages total.

UK#143: 12 December 1987. Cover (1p); Transformation (1p); [36] 'Spacehikers' (1/2) (11p); [HDM4] 'Brothers in Armor' (2/4) (5p); Grim Grams (1p); Transformers A to Z (First Aid/Frenzy) (1p); *Robo-Capers*/next issue preview (1p); advertisements (3p). 24 pages total.

UK#144: 19 December 1987. Cover (1p); Transformation (1p); [36] 'Spacehikers' (2/2)

(11p); [HDM4] 'Brothers in Armor' (3/4) (5p); Grim Grams (1p); competition result/*Robo-Capers* (1p); next issue preview/order coupon (1p); advertisements (3p). 24 pages total.

UK#145: 26 December 1987. Cover (1p); Transformation (1p); [36.1] 'Stargazing' (1/1) (11p); [HDM4] 'Brothers in Armor' (4/4) (6p); Grim Grams (1p); competition page (1p); *Robo-Capers*/next issue preview (1p); advertisements (2p). 24 pages total.

UK#146: 2 January 1988. Cover (1p); Transformation (1p); [36.2] 'The Legacy of Unicron' (1/6) (11p); *Iron Man* (6p); Grim Grams (1p); Transformers A to Z (Gears/Grapple) (1p); *Robo-Capers*/next issue preview (1p); advertisements (2p). 24 pages total.

UK#147: 9 January 1988. Cover (1p); Transformation (1p); [36.2] 'The Legacy of Unicron' (2/6) (11p); *Iron Man* (6p); Grim Grams (1p); competition results (1p); *Robo-Capers*/next issue preview (1p); advertisements (2p). 24 pages total.

UK#148: 16 January 1988. Cover (1p); Transformation (1p); [36.3] 'The Legacy of Unicron' (3/6) (11p); *Iron Man* (6p); Grim Grams (1p); Transformers A to Z (Grimlock/Groove) (1p); *Robo-Capers*/next issue preview (1p); advertisements (2p). 24 pages total.

UK#149: 23 January 1988. Cover (1p); Transformation (1p); [36.3] 'The Legacy of Unicron' (4/6) (11p); *Iron Man* (6p); Grim Grams (1p); *Robo-Capers*/next issue preview (1p); advertisements (3p). 24 pages total.

UK#150: 30 January 1988. Wraparound cover (2p); Transformation (1p); [36.3] 'The Legacy of Unicron' (5/6) (11p); *Iron Man* (5p); Grim Grams (1p); Transformers A to Z (Rodimus Prime) (1p); *Robo-Capers*/next issue preview (1p); advertisements (2p). 24 pages total.

UK#151: 6 February 1988. Cover (1p); Transformation (1p); [36.3] 'The Legacy of Unicron' (6/6) (11p); *Iron Man* (5p); Grim Grams (1p); Transformers A to Z (Headstrong/Hoist) (1p); *Robo-Capers*/next issue preview (1p); advertisements (3p). 24 pages total.

UK#152: 13 February 1988. Cover (1p); Transformation (1p); [36.4] 'Enemy Action' (1/2) (11p); *Iron Man* (5p); Grim Grams (1p); competition page (1p); *Robo-Capers*/order coupon (1p); next issue preview (1p); advertisements (2p). 24 pages total.

UK#153: 20 February 1988. Cover (1p); Transformation (1p); [36.4] 'Enemy Action' (2/2) (11p); Feature – '*Action Force*: An Introduction' (2p); *Action Force* (5p); Grim Grams (1p); *Combat Colin*/next issue preview (1p); advertisements (2p). 24 pages total.

UK#154: 27 February 1988. Cover (1p); Transformation (1p); [37] 'Toy Soldiers' (1/2) (11p); *Action Force* (6p); Grim Grams (1p); *Combat Colin*/next issue preview (1p); advertisements (3p). 24 pages total.

UK#155: 5 March 1988. Cover (1p); Transformation (1p); [37] 'Toy Soldiers' (2/2) (11p); *Action Force* (5p); Grim Grams (1p); Transformers A to Z (Hook/Hot Spot) (1p); *Combat Colin*/next issue preview (1p); advertisements (3p). 24 pages total.

UK#156: 12 March 1988. Cover (1p); Transformation (1p); [38] 'Trial by Fire' (1/2) (11p); *Action Force* (6p); Grim Grams (1p); *Combat Colin*/next issue preview (1p); advertisements (3p). 24 pages total.

UK#157: 19 March 1988. Cover (1p); Transformation (1p); [38] 'Trial by Fire' (1/2) (11p); *Action Force* (5p); Grim Grams (1p); *Combat Colin*/next issue preview (1p); advertisements (4p). 24 pages total.

UK#158: 26 March 1988. Cover (1p); Transformation (1p); [39] 'The Desert Island of Space' (1/2) (11p); *Action Force* (6p); Grim Grams (1p); Transformers A to Z (Hound/Huffer) (1p); *Visionaries* advertisement/feature (4p); *Combat Colin*/next issue preview (1p); advertisements (2p). 28 pages total.

UK#159: 2 April 1988. Cover (1p); Transformation (1p); [39] 'The Desert Island of Space' (2/2) (11p); *Action Force* (6p); Grim Grams (1p); *Combat Colin*/next issue preview (1p); advertisements (3p). 24 pages total.

UK#160: 9 April 1988. Cover (1p); Transformation (1p); [39.1] 'Salvage' (1/2) (11p); *Action Force* (5p); Grim Grams (1p); competition page (1p); *Combat Colin*/next issue preview (1p); advertisements (3p). 24 pages total.

UK#161: 16 April 1988. Cover (1p); Transformation (1p); [39.1] 'Salvage' (2/2) (11p); *Action Force* (7p); Grim Grams (1p); *Combat Colin*/next issue preview (1p); advertisements (2p). 24 pages total.

UK#162: 23 April 1988. Cover (1p); Transformation (1p); [40] 'Pretender to the Throne' (1/2) (12p); *Action Force* (5p); Grim Grams (1p); *Combat Colin*/next issue preview (1p); advertisements (3p). 24 pages total.

UK#163: 30 April 1988. Cover (1p); Transformation (1p); [40] 'Pretender to the Throne' (2/2) (10p); *Action Force* (6p); Grim Grams (1p); competition page (1p); *Combat Colin*/next issue preview (1p); advertisements (3p). 24 pages total.

UK#164: 7 May 1988. Cover (1p); Transformation (1p); [40.1] 'City of Fear' (1/2) (11p); *Action Force* (5p); Grim Grams (1p); competition results (1p); *Combat Colin*/next issue preview (1p); advertisements (3p). 24 pages total.

UK#165: 14 May 1988. Cover (1p); Transformation (1p); [40.1] 'City of Fear' (2/2) (11p); *Action Force* (6p); Grim Grams (1p); *Combat Colin*/next issue preview (1p); advertisements (3p). 24 pages total.

UK#166: 21 May 1988. Cover (1p); Transformation (1p); [40.2] 'Legion of the Lost' (1/2) (11p); Action Force (5p); Grim Grams (1p); Transformers A to Z (Inferno/Ironhide) (1p); *Combat Colin*/next issue preview (1p); advertisements (3p). 24 pages total.

UK#167: 28 May 1988. Cover (1p); Transformation (1p); [40.2] 'Legion of the Lost' (2/2) (11p); *Action Force* (5p); *Death's Head* (1p); Grim Grams (1p); order coupon (½p); *Combat Colin*/next issue preview (1p); advertisements (2½p). 24 pages total.

UK#168: 4 June 1988. Cover (1p); Transformation (1p); [40.3] 'Meltdown' (1/2) (11p); *Action Force* (6p); Grim Grams (1p); *Combat Colin*/next issue preview (1p); advertisements (3p). 24 pages total.

UK#169: 11 June 1988. Cover (1p); Transformation (1p); [40.3] 'Meltdown' (2/2) (11p); *Action Force* (6p); Grim Grams (1p); *Combat Colin*/next issue preview (1p); advertisements (3p). 24 pages total.

UK#170: 18 June 1988. Cover (1p); Transformation (1p); [40.4] 'Deadly Games' (1/2) (11p); *Transformers* - 'A Bonus Story' (1p); *Action Force* (5p); Grim Grams (1p); competition page (1p); *Combat Colin*/next issue preview (1p); advertisements (2p). 24 pages total.

UK#171: 25 June 1988. Cover (1p); Transformation (1p); [40.4] 'Deadly Games' (2/2) (11p); *Action Force* (5p); Grim Grams (1p); *Combat Colin*/next issue preview (1p); advertisements (4p). 24 pages total.

UK#172: 2 July 1988. Cover (1p); Transformation (1p); [40.5] 'Wrecking Havoc' (1/2) (11p); *Action Force* (6p); Grim Grams (1p); *Combat Colin*/next issue preview (1p); advertisements (3p). 24 pages total.

UK#173: 9 July 1988. Cover (1p); Transformation (1p); [40.5] 'Wrecking Havoc' (2/2) (11p); *Action Force* (6p); Grim Grams (1p); *Combat Colin*/next issue preview (1p); advertisements (3p). 24 pages total.

UK#174: 16 July 1988. Cover (1p); Transformation (1p); [41] 'Totaled' (1/2) (11p); *Action Force* (5p); Grim Grams (1p); Transformers A to Z (Jazz/Jetfire) (1p); *Combat Colin*/next issue preview (1p); advertisements (3p). 24 pages total.

UK#175: 23 July 1988. Cover (1p); Transformation (1p); [41] 'Totaled' (2/2) (11p) *Action Force* (6p); Grim Grams (1p); *Combat Colin*/next issue preview (1p); advertisements (3p). 24 pages total.

UK#176: 30 July 1988. Cover (1p); Transformation (1p); [42] 'People Power' (1/2) (11p); *Action Force* (6p); Grim Grams (1p); *Combat Colin*/next issue preview (1p); advertisements (3p). 24 pages total.

UK#177: 6 August 1988. Cover (1p); Transformation (1p); [42] 'People Power' (2/2) (11p); *Action Force* (5p); Grim Grams (1p); Transformers A to Z (Optimus Prime) (1p); *Combat Colin*/next issue preview (1p); advertisements (3p). 24 pages total.

UK#178: 13 August 1988. Cover (1p); Transformation (1p); [44] 'The Cosmic Carnival' (1/2) (11p); *Action Force* (5p); Grim Grams (1p); competition page (1p); *Combat Colin*/next issue preview (1p); advertisements (3p). 24 pages total.

UK#179: 20 August 1988. Cover (1p); Transformation (1p); [44] 'The Cosmic Carnival' (2/2) (11p); *Action Force* (7p); Grim Grams (1p); *Combat Colin*/next issue preview (1p); advertisements (2p). 24 pages total.

UK#180: 27 August 1988. Cover (1p); Transformation (1p); [43] 'The Big Broadcast of 2006' (1/2) (12p); *Action Force* (5p); *Combat Colin*/next issue preview (1p); advertisements (3p). 24 pages total.

UK#181: 3 September 1988. Cover (1p); Transformation (1p); [43] 'The Big Broadcast of 2006' (2/2) (12p); *Action Force* (5p); *Combat Colin*/next issue preview (1p); advertisements (3p). 24 pages total.

UK#182: 10 September 1988. Cover (1p); Transformation (1p); [44.1] 'Space Pirates' (1/6) (11p); *Combat Colin* (6p); Grim Grams (1p); competition (1½p); order coupon (½p); next issue preview (½p); advertisements (1½p). 24 pages total.

UK#183: 17 September 1988. Cover (1p); Transformation (1p); [44.1] 'Space Pirates' (2/6) (11p); *Visionaries* (including 'story so far' recap) (6p); *Robo-Capers* (1p); next issue preview (1p); advertisements (3p). 24 pages total.

UK#184: 24 September 1988. Cover (1p); Transformation (1p); [44.1] 'Space Pirates' (3/6) (11p); *Visionaries* (6p); Dread Tidings (1p); competition page (1p); *Combat Colin*/next issue preview (1p); advertisements (2p). 24 pages total.

UK#185: 1 October 1988. Cover (1p); Transformation (1p); [44.1] 'Space Pirates' (4/6) (11p); *Visionaries* (6p); Dread Tidings (1p); competition page (1p); *Combat Colin*/next issue preview (1p); advertisements (2p). 24 pages total.

UK#186: 8 October 1988. Cover (1p); Transformation (1p); [44.1] 'Space Pirates' (5/6) (11p); *Visionaries* (6p); Dread Tidings (1p); *Combat Colin*/next issue preview (1p); advertisements (3p). 24 pages total.

UK#187: 15 October 1988. Cover (1p); Transformation (1p); [44.1] 'Space Pirates' (6/6) (11p); *Visionaries* (5p); Dread Tidings (1p); *Combat Colin*/next issue preview (1p); advertisements (4p). 24 pages total.

UK#188: 22 October 1988. Cover (1p); Transformation (1p); [44.2] 'Firebug' (1/1) (11p); *Visionaries* (6p); Dread Tidings (1p); Marvel Checklist/free drink offer (1p) *Combat Colin*/next issue preview (1p); advertisements (2p). 24 pages total.

UK#189: 29 October 1988. Cover (1p); Transformation (1p); [44.3] 'Dry Run (1/1) (11p); Visionaries (5p); Dread Tidings (1p); competition page (1p); Marvel Checklist/order coupon (1p); *Combat Colin*/next issue preview (1p); advertisements (2p). 24 pages total.

UK#190: 5 November 1988. Cover (1p); Transformation (1p); [45] 'Monstercon from Mars' (1/2) (11p); *Visionaries* (6p); Dread Tidings (1p); Transformers A to Z (Kickback/Laserbeak) (1p); *Combat Colin*/next issue preview (1p); advertisements (2p). 24 pages total.

UK#191: 12 November 1988. Cover (1p); Transformation (1p); [45] 'Monstercon from Mars' (2/2) (11p); *Action Force* (5p); Dread Tidings (1p); Marvel Checklist (½p); *Combat Colin*/next issue preview (1p); advertisements (3½p). 24 pages total.

UK#192: 19 November 1988. Cover (1p); Transformation (1p); [46] 'Ca$h and Car-nage' (1/2) (11p); *Action Force* (6p); Dread Tidings (1p); Marvel Checklist/order coupon (1p); *Combat Colin*/next issue preview (1p); advertisements (2p). 24 pages total.

UK#193: 26 November 1988. Cover (1p); Transformation (1p); [46] 'Ca$h and Car-nage' (2/2) (11p); *Action Force* (5p); Dread Tidings (1p); *Combat Colin*/next issue preview (1p); advertisements (4p). 24 pages total.

UK#194: 3 December 1988. Cover (1p); Transformation (1p); [47] 'Club Con' (1/2) (10p); *Action Force* (6p); Dread Tidings (1p); next issue preview (½p); advertisements (4½p). 24 pages total.

UK#195: 10 December 1988. Cover (1p); Transformation (1p); [47] 'Club Con' (2/2) (10p); *Action Force* (5p); Dread Tidings (1p); Transformers A to Z (Long Haul/Menasor) (1p); *Combat Colin*/next issue preview (1p); advertisements (4p). 24 pages total.

UK#196: 17 December 1988. Cover (1p); Transformation (1p); [48] 'The Flames of Boltax' (1/2) (9p); *Action Force* (6p); Dread Tidings (1p); Transformers A to Z (Megatron) (1p); Marvel Checklist/order coupon (1p); *Combat Colin*/next issue preview (1p); advertisements (3p). 24 pages total.

UK#197: 24 December 1988. Cover (1p); Transformation (1p); [48] 'The Flames of Boltax' (2/2) (10p); *Action Force* (6p); Dread Tidings (1p); *Combat Colin*/next issue preview (1p); advertisements (4p). 24 pages total.

UK#198: 31 December 1988. Cover (1p); Transformation (1p); [48.1] 'Cold Comfort and Joy' (1/1) (11p); *Action Force* (5p); Dread Tidings (1p); competition page (1p); Marvel Checklist/order coupon (1p); *Combat Colin*/next issue preview (1p); advertisements (2p). 24 pages total.

UK#199: 7 January 1989. Cover (1p); Transformation (1p); [48.2] 'Time Wars' (1/7) (11p); *Action Force* (5p); Dread Tidings (1p); Marvel Checklist/*Combat Colin* (1p); next issue preview (1p); advertisements (3p). 24 pages total.

UK#200: 14 January 1989. Wraparound cover (2p); Transformation (1p); [48.2] 'Time Wars' (2/7) (11p); Feature: A Pictorial History of the Transformers! (2p); January calendar (2p); *Combat Colin/Robo-Capers* crossover (1p); competition page (1p); next issue preview/Marvel checklist (1p); advertisements (3p). 24 pages total.

UK#201: 21 January 1989. Cover (1p); Transformation (1p); [48.2] 'Time Wars' (3/7) (11p); *Action Force* (6p); Dread Tidings (1p); Marvel Checklist/order coupon (1p); *Combat Colin*/next issue preview (1p); advertisements (2p). 24 pages total.

UK#202: 28 January 1989. Cover (1p); Transformation (1p); [48.2] 'Time Wars' (4/7)

(11p); *Action Force* (6p); Dread Tidings (1p); Marvel Checklist/order coupon (1p); *Combat Colin*/next issue preview (1p); advertisements (2p). 24 pages total.

UK#203: 4 February 1989. Cover (1p); Transformation (1p); [48.2] 'Time Wars' (5/7) (11p); *Action Force* (6p); Dread Tidings (1p); Marvel Checklist/order coupon (1p); *Combat Colin*/next issue preview (1p); advertisements (2p). 24 pages total.

UK#204: 11 February 1989. Cover (1p); Transformation (1p); [48.2] 'Time Wars' (6/7) (11p); *Action Force* (4p); February calendar (2p); Marvel Checklist (½p); Combat Colin/order coupon (1p); next issue preview (1p); advertisements (2½p). 24 pages total.

UK#205: 18 February 1989. Cover (1p); Transformation (1p); [48.2] 'Time Wars' (7/7) (11p); *Action Force* (5p); Dread Tidings (1p); Marvel Checklist/order coupon (1p); *Combat Colin*/next issue preview (1p); advertisements (3p). 24 pages total.

UK#206: 25 February 1989. Cover (1p); Transformation (1p); [49] 'Cold War' (1/2) (10p); *Action Force* (7p); Dread Tidings (1p); *Combat Colin*/next issue preview (1p); advertisements (3p). 24 pages total.

UK#207: 4 March 1989. Cover (1p); Transformation (1p); [49] 'Cold War' (2/2) (10p); *Action Force* (6p); Dread Tidings (1p); Marvel Checklist/order coupon (1p); *Combat Colin*/next issue preview (1p); advertisements (3p). 24 pages total.

UK#208: 11 March 1989. Cover (1p); Transformation (1p); [50] 'Dark Star' (1/3) (12p); *Action Force* (4p); Dread Tidings (1p); March calendar (2p); *Combat Colin*/next issue preview (1p); advertisements (2p). 24 pages total.

UK#209: 18 March 1989. Cover (1p); Transformation (1p); [50] 'Dark Star' (2/3) (12p); *Action Force* (6p); Marvel Checklist/order coupon (1p); *Combat Colin*/next issue preview (1p); advertisements (2p). 24 pages total.

UK#210: 25 March 1989. Cover (1p); Transformation (1p); [50] 'Dark Star' (3/3) (12p); *Action Force* (5p); Dread Tidings (1p); Marvel Checklist/order coupon (1p); *Combat Colin*/next issue preview (1p); advertisements (2p). 24 pages total.

UK#211: 1 April 1989. Cover (1p); Transformation (1p); [51] 'The Man in the Machine' (1/2) (11p); *Action Force* (4p); Dread Tidings (1p); Marvel Checklist/order coupon (1p); Transformers A to Z (Metroplex) (1p); *Combat Colin*/next issue preview (1p); advertisements (3p). 24 pages total.

UK#212: 8 April 1989. Cover (1p); Transformation (1p); [51] 'The Man in the Machine' (2/2) (11p); *Action Force* (4p); Dread Tidings (1p); April calendar (2p); Marvel Checklist/order coupon (1p); *Combat Colin*/next issue preview (1p); advertisements (2p). 24 pages total.

UK#213: 15 April 1989. Cover (1p); Transformation (1p); [52] 'Guess Who the Mecannibals are Having for Dinner?' (1/4) (5p); [52.1] 'The Fall and Rise of the Decepticon Empire' (1/2) (6p); *Visionaries* (5p); Dread Tidings (1p); Marvel Checklist/

order coupon (1p); Transformers A to Z (Mirage/Mixmaster) (1p); *Combat Colin*/next issue preview (1p); advertisements (2p). 24 pages total.

UK#214: 22 April 1989. Cover (1p); Transformation (1p); [52] 'Guess Who the Mecannibals are Having for Dinner?' (2/4) (6p); [52.1] 'The Fall and Rise of the Decepticon Empire' (2/2) (5p); Visionaries (5p); Dread Tidings (1p); Marvel Checklist/order coupon (1p); *Combat Colin*/next issue preview (1p); advertisements (3p). 24 pages total.

Partly black-and-white:

UK#215: 29 April 1989. Cover (1p); Transformation (1p); [52] 'Guess Who the Mecannibals are Having for Dinner? (3/4) (5p); [52.2] 'Race with the Devil' (1/4) (6p); *Visionaries* (5p); Dread Tidings (1p); Marvel Checklist/order coupon (1p); Transformers A to Z (Motormaster/Octane) (1p); *Combat Colin*/next issue preview (1p); advertisements (2p). 24 pages total (6 b/w).

UK#216: 6 May 1989. Cover (1p); Transformation (1p); [52] 'Guess Who the Mecannibals are Having for Dinner?' (4/4) (5p); [52.2] 'Race with the Devil' (2/4) (5p); *Visionaries* (5p); Dread Tidings (1p); June calendar (2p); Marvel Checklist/order coupon (1p); *Combat Colin*/next issue preview (1p); advertisements (2p). 24 pages total (5 b/w).

UK#217: 13 May 1989. Cover (1p); Transformation (1p); [53] 'Recipe for Disaster' (1/4) (5p); [52.2] 'Race with the Devil' (3/4) (6p); *Visionaries* (5p); Dread Tidings (1p); Marvel Checklist/order coupon (1p); *Combat Colin*/next issue preview (1p); advertisements (3p). 24 pages total (6 b/w).

UK#218: 20 May 1989. Cover (1p); Transformation (1p); [53] 'Recipe for Disaster' (2/4) (6p); [52.2] 'Race with the Devil' (4/4) (5p); *Visionaries* (6p); Dread Tidings (1p); Marvel Checklist/order coupon (1p); *Combat Colin*/next issue preview (1p); advertisements (2p). 24 pages total (5 b/w).

UK#219: 27 May 1989. Cover (1p); Transformation (1p); [53] 'Recipe for Disaster' (3/4) (6p); [53.1] 'Survivors' (1/4) (6p); *Visionaries* (7p); *Combat Colin*/next issue preview (1p); advertisements (2p). 24 pages total (6 b/w).

UK#220: 3 June 1989. Cover (1p); Transformation (1p); [53] 'Recipe for Disaster' (4/4) (5p); [53.1] 'Survivors' (2/4) (5p); *Action Force* (4p); Dread Tidings (1p); Transformers A to Z (Omega Supreme) (1p); May calendar (2p); Marvel Checklist/order coupon (1p); *Combat Colin*/next issue preview (1p); advertisements (2p). 24 pages total (5 b/w).

UK#221: 10 June 1989. Cover (1p); Transformation (1p); Reprint: [27.1] 'Wanted: Galvatron – Dead or Alive' (1/4) (6p); [53.1] 'Survivors (3/4) (5p); *Action Force* (5p); Dread Tidings (1p); Transformers A to Z (Onslaught/Outback) (1p); Marvel Checklist/order coupon (1p); *Combat Colin*/next issue preview (1p); advertisements (2p). 24 pages total (5 b/w).

UK#222: 17 June 1989. Cover (1p); Transformation (1p); Reprint: [27.1] 'Wanted:

Galvatron – Dead or Alive' (2/4) (5p); [53.1] 'Survivors' (4/4) (6p); *Action Force* (5p); Dread Tidings (1p); Transformers A to Z (Perceptor/Pipes) (1p); Marvel Checklist/ order coupon (1p); *Combat Colin*/next issue preview (1p); advertisements (2p). 24 pages total (6 b/w).

UK#223: 24 June 1989. Cover (1p); Transformation (1p); Reprint: [27.1] 'Wanted: Galvatron – Dead or Alive' (3/4) (6p); [53.2] 'Aspects of Evil' (1/5) (5p); *Action Force* (4p); Dread Tidings (1p); Transformers A to Z (Powerglide/Predaking) (1p); Marvel Checklist/order coupon (1p); *Combat Colin*/next issue preview (1p); advertisements (3p). 24 pages total (5 b/w).

UK#224: 1 July 1989. Cover (1p); Transformation (1p); Reprint: [27.1] 'Wanted: Galvatron – Dead or Alive' (4/4) (5p); [53.2] 'Aspects of Evil' (2/5) (5p); *Action Force* (4p); Dread Tidings (1p); July Calendar (2p); competition results (1p); *Combat Colin* (1p); next issue preview/Marvel Checklist (1p); advertisements (2p). 24 pages total (7 b/w).

UK#225: 8 July 1989. Cover (1p); Transformation (1p); Reprint: [31.3] 'Headhunt' (1/4) (6p); [53.2] 'Aspects of Evil' (3/5) (5p); *Action Force* (4p); Dread Tidings (1p); competition page (1p); Marvel Checklist (½p); *Combat Colin* (1p); next issue preview/order coupon (1p); advertisements (2½p). 24 pages total (6 b/w).

UK#226: 15 July 1989. Cover (1p); Transformation (1p); Reprint: [31.3] 'Headhunt' (2/4) (5p); [53.2] 'Aspects of Evil' (4/5) (5p); *Action Force* (5p); Dread Tidings (1p); Marvel Checklist (½p); *Combat Colin* (1p); next issue preview/order coupon (1p); advertisements (3½p). 24 pages total (8 b/w).

UK#227: 22 July 1989. Cover (1p); Transformation (1p); Reprint: [31.3] 'Headhunt' (3/4) (5p); [53.2] 'Aspects of Evil' (5/5) (5p); *Action Force* (4p); Dread Tidings (1p); Transformers A to Z (Prowl/Ramhorn) (1p); Marvel Checklist (½p); *Combat Colin* (1p); next issue preview/order coupon (1p); advertisements (3½p). 24 pages total (8 b/w).

UK#228: 29 July 1989. Cover (1p); Transformation (1p); Reprint: [31.3] 'Headhunt' (4/4) (6p); [53.3] '[Double] Deal of the Century' (1/1) (5p); *Action Force* (4p); Dread Tidings (1p); Marvel Checklist (½p); *Combat Colin* (1p); next issue preview/order coupon (1p); advertisements (3½p). 24 pages total (8 b/w).

UK#229: 5 August 1989. Cover (1p); Transformation (1p); Reprint: [23.5] 'Resurrection' (1/4) (5p); [53.4] 'The Hunting Party' (1/1) (5p); *Action Force* (5p); August calendar (2p); Marvel Checklist (½p); *Combat Colin* (1p); next issue preview/order coupon (1p); advertisements (2½p). 24 pages total (8 b/w).

UK#230: 12 August 1989. Cover (1p); Transformation (1p); Reprint: [23.5] 'Resurrection' (2/4) (6p); [53.5] 'The Big Shutdown' (1/2) (5p); *Action Force* (5p); Dread Tidings (1p); *Combat Colin* (1p); next issue preview/order coupon (1p); advertisements (3p). 24 pages total (8 b/w).

UK#231: 19 August 1989. Cover (1p); Transformation (1p); Reprint: [23.5] 'Resurrection' (3/4) (6p); [53.5] 'The Big Shutdown' (2/2) (5p); *Action Force* (4p); Dread Tidings (1p);

Marvel Checklist (½p); *Combat Colin* (1½p); next issue preview/order coupon (1p); advertisements (3p). 24 pages total (8 b/w).

UK#232: 26 August 1989. Cover (1p); Transformation (1p); [54] 'King Con' (1/4) (6p); [54.1] 'A Small War' (1/2) (5p); Reprint: [23.5] 'Resurrection (4/4) (5p); competition page (1p); Marvel Checklist (½p); *Combat Colin* (1p); next issue preview/order coupon (1p); advertisements (2½p). 24 pages total (8 b/w).

UK#233: 2 September 1989. Cover (1p); Transformation (1p); [54] 'King Con' (2/4) (5p); [54.1] 'A Small War' (2/2) (5p); *Action Force* (5p); Dread Tidings (1p); *Combat Colin* (1p); Transformers A to Z (Rampage/Ratbat) (1p); next issue preview/competition (1p); advertisements (3p). 24 pages total (8 b/w).

UK#234: 9 September 1989. Cover (1p); Transformation (1p); [54] 'King Con' (3/4) (5p); [54.2] 'Prime's Rib' (1/1) (5p); *Action Force* (4p); *Combat Colin* (1p); Marvel Checklist/order coupon (1p); September calendar (2p); next issue preview/competition (1p); advertisements (3p). 24 pages total (8 b/w).

UK#235: 16 September 1989. Cover (1p); Transformation (1p); [54] 'King Con' (4/4) (6p); [54.5] 'Deathbringer' (1/2) (5p); *Action Force* (4p); Dread Tidings (1p); *Combat Colin* (1p); competition page (1p); next issue preview/order coupon (1p); advertisements (3p). 24 pages total (8 b/w).

UK#236: 23 September 1989. Cover (1p); Transformation (1p); [55] 'The Interplanetary Wrestling Championship' (1/4) (6p); [54.5] 'Deathbringer' (2/2) (5p); *Action Force* (5p); Dread Tidings (1p); *Combat Colin* (1p); Marvel Checklist (½p); next issue preview/order coupon (1p); advertisements (2½p). 24 pages total (7 b/w).

UK#237: 30 September 1989. Cover (1p); Transformation (1p); [55] 'The Interplanetary Wrestling Championship' (2/4) (5p); [55.1] 'Way of the Warrior' (1/3) (5p); *Action Force* (4p); October calendar (2p); *Combat Colin* (1p); Marvel Checklist (½p); next issue preview/order coupon (1p); advertisements (3½p). 24 pages total (8 b/w).

UK#238: 7 October 1989. Cover (1p); Transformation (1p); [55] 'The Interplanetary Wrestling Championship' (3/4) (6p); [55.1] 'Way of the Warrior' (2/3) (5p); *Action Force* (4p); Dread Tidings (1p); *Combat Colin* (1p); Marvel Checklist (½p); next issue preview/order coupon (1p); advertisements (3½p). 24 pages total (8 b/w).

UK#239: 14 October 1989. Cover (1p); Transformation (1p); [55] 'The Interplanetary Wrestling Championship' (4/4) (5p); [55.1] 'Way of the Warrior' (3/3) (5p); *Action Force* (5p); Dread Tidings (1p); *Combat Colin* (1p); Transformers A to Z (Ratchet/Ravage) (1p); Marvel Checklist (½p); next issue preview/order coupon (1p); advertisements (2½p). 24 pages total (7 b/w).

UK#240: 21 October 1989. Cover (1p); Transformation (1p); [56] 'Back from the Dead' (1/3) (5p); [56.1] 'Out to Lunch' (1/1) (5p); *Action Force* (4p); Dread Tidings (1p); *Combat Colin* (1p); Marvel Checklist (½p); next issue preview/order coupon (1p); advertisements (4½p). 24 pages total (7 b/w).

UK#241: 21 October 1989. Cover (1p); Transformation (1p); [56] 'Back from the Dead' (2/3) (5p); [56.2] 'Rage' (1/2) (5p); *Action Force* (4p); Dread Tidings (1p); *Combat Colin* (1p); Marvel Checklist (½p); next issue preview/order coupon (1p); advertisements (4½p). 24 pages total (8 b/w).

UK#242: 4 November 1989. Cover (1p); Transformation (1p); [56] 'Back from the Dead' (3/3) (6p); [56.2] 'Rage' (2/2) (5p); *Action Force* (4p); Dread Tidings (1p); *Combat Colin* (1p); competition page (1p); next issue preview/order coupon (1p); advertisements (3p). 24 pages total (6 b/w).

UK#243: 11 November 1989. Cover (1p); Transformation (1p); [57] 'The Resurrection Gambit' (1/3) (5p); [57.1] 'Two Megatrons' (1/2) (5p); *Action Force* (4p); *Combat Colin* (1p); November calendar (2p); next issue preview/Marvel Checklist (1p); advertisements (4p). 24 pages total (7 b/w).

UK#244: 18 November 1989. Cover (1p); Transformation (1p); [57] 'The Resurrection Gambit' (2/3) (5p); [57.1] 'Two Megatrons' (2/2) (5p); *Action Force* (5p); Dread Tidings (1p); *Combat Colin* (1p); Marvel Checklist (½p); next issue preview/order coupon (1p); advertisements (3½p). 24 pages total (6 b/w).

UK#245: 25 November 1989. Cover (1p); Transformation (1p); [57] 'The Resurrection Gambit' (3/3) (6p); [57.2] 'Demons' (1/3) (5p); *Action Force* (9p); Dread Tidings (1p); *Combat Colin* (1p); next issue preview/order coupon (1p); advertisements (3p). 28 pages total (6 b/w).

UK#246: 2 December 1989. Cover (1p); Transformation (1p); [58] 'All the Familiar Faces' (1/3) (6p); [57.2] 'Demons' (2/3) (5p); *Action Force* (5p); *Combat Colin* (1p); Marvel Checklist/order coupon (1p); next issue preview (½p); advertisements (3½p). 24 pages total (7 b/w).

UK#247: 9 December 1989. Cover (1p); Transformation (1p); [58] 'All the Familiar Faces' (2/3) (5p); [57.2] 'Demons' (3/3) (5p); *Action Force* (5p); *Combat Colin* (1p); December calendar (2p); Marvel Checklist (½p); next issue preview/order coupon (1p); advertisements (2½p). 24 pages total (8 b/w).

UK#248: 16 December 1989. Cover (1p); Transformation (1p); [58] 'All the Familiar Faces' (3/3) (5p); [58.1] 'Fallen Star' (1/1) (5p); *G.I. Joe: The Action Force* (5p); *Combat Colin* (1p); Dread Tidings (1p); Marvel Checklist/order coupon (1p); next issue preview (½p); advertisements (3½p). 24 pages total (7 b/w).

UK#249: 23 December 1989. Cover (1p); Transformation (1p); [59] 'Skin Deep' (1/3) (5p); [59.1] 'Whose Lifeforce is it Anyway' (1/1) (5p); *G.I. Joe: The Action Force* (4p); *Combat Colin* (1p); Dread Tidings (1p); Transformers A to Z (Razorclaw/Rampage) (1p); Marvel Checklist/order coupon (1p); next issue preview (1p); advertisements (3p). 24 pages total (8 b/w).

UK#250: 30 December 1989. Wraparound cover (2p); Transformation (1p); [59] 'Skin Deep' (2/3) (6p); [59.2] 'The Greatest Gift of All' (1/1) (5p); *Combat Colin* (1p); Dread

Tidings (1p); Transformers A to Z (Rewind/Rumble) (1p); competition (2p); next issue preview/Marvel Checklist (1p); advertisements (4p). 24 pages total (5 b/w).

UK#251: 6 January 1990. Cover (1p); Transformation (1p); [59] 'Skin Deep' (3/3) (5p); [59.3] 'Shadow of Evil' (1/4) (5p); *G.I. Joe: The Action Force* (5p); *Combat Colin* (1p); Dread Tidings (1p); Transformers A to Z (Runabout/Runamuck) (1p); order coupon (½p); next issue preview (½p); advertisements (3p). 24 pages total (8 b/w).

UK#252: 13 January 1990. Cover (1p); Transformation (1p); [60] 'Yesterday's Heroes' (1/3) (6p); [59.3] 'Shadow of Evil' (2/4) (5p); *G.I. Joe: The Action Force* (4p); *Combat Colin* (1p); Dread Tidings (1p); Transformers A to Z (Sandstorm/Scavenger) (1p); next issue preview (½p); advertisements (3½p). 24 pages total (8 b/w).

UK#253: 20 January 1990. Cover (1p); Transformation (1p); [60] 'Yesterday's Heroes' (2/3) (6p); [59.3] 'Shadow of Evil' (3/4) (5p); *G.I. Joe: The Action Force* (4p); *Combat Colin* (1p); Dread Tidings (1p); Transformers A to Z (Scrapper/Seaspray) (1p); next issue preview/order coupon (1p); advertisements (3p). 24 pages total (6 b/w).

UK#254: 27 January 1990. Cover (1p); Transformation (1p); [60] 'Yesterday's Heroes' (3/3) (6p); [59.3] 'Shadow of Evil' (4/4) (5p); *G.I. Joe: The Action Force* (5p); *Combat Colin* (1p); Dread Tidings (1p); next issue preview/order coupon (1p); advertisements (3p). 24 pages total (7 b/w).

UK#255: 3 February 1990. Cover (1p); Transformation (1p); Reprint: [31.1] 'Worlds Apart' (1/4) (5p); [60.1] 'Perchance to Dream' (1/6) (5p); *G.I. Joe: The Action Force* (6p); *Combat Colin* (1p); Dread Tidings (1p); next issue preview/order coupon (1p); advertisements (3p). 24 pages total (8 b/w).

UK#256: 10 February 1990. Cover (1p); Transformation (1p); Reprint: [31.1] 'Worlds Apart' (2/4) (6p); [60.1] 'Perchance to Dream' (2/6) (5p); *G.I. Joe: The Action Force* (5p); *Combat Colin* (1p); Dread Tidings (1p); next issue preview/order coupon (1p); advertisements (3p). 24 pages total (8 b/w).

UK#257: 17 February 1990. Cover (1p); Transformation (1p); Reprint: [31.1] 'Worlds Apart' (3/4) (5p); [60.1] 'Perchance to Dream' (3/6) (5p); *G.I. Joe: The Action Force* (6p); *Combat Colin* (1p); Dread Tidings (1p); next issue preview/order coupon (1p); advertisements (3p). 24 pages total (8 b/w).

UK#258: 24 February 1990. Cover (1p); Transformation (1p); Reprint: [31.1] 'Worlds Apart' (4/4) (6p); [60.1] 'Perchance to Dream' (4/6) (5p); *G.I. Joe: The Action Force* (5p); *Combat Colin* (1p); Dread Tidings (1p); next issue preview/order coupon (1p); advertisements (3p). 24 pages total (8 b/w).

UK#259: 3 March 1990. Cover (1p); Transformation (1p); [61] 'The Primal Scream' (1/3) (6p); [60.1] 'Perchance to Dream' (5/6) (5p); *G.I. Joe: The Action Force* (5p); *Combat Colin* (1p); Dread Tidings (1p); next issue preview/order coupon (1p); advertisements (3p). 24 pages total (8 b/w).

UK#260: 10 March 1990. Cover (1p); Transformation (1p); [61] 'The Primal Scream' (2/3) (6p); [60.1] 'Perchance to Dream' (6/6) (5p); *G.I. Joe: The Action Force* (6p); *Combat Colin* (1p); Dread Tidings (1p); competition page (1p) next issue preview/order coupon (1p); advertisements (1p). 24 pages total (8 b/w).

UK#261: 17 March 1990. Cover (1p); Transformation (1p); [61] 'The Primal Scream' (3/3) (6p); [61.1] 'Starting Over' (1/6) (5p); *G.I. Joe: The Action Force* (6p); *Combat Colin* (1p); Dread Tidings (1p); competition page (1p) next issue preview/order coupon (1p); advertisements (1p). 24 pages total (7 b/w).

UK#262: 24 March 1990. Cover (1p); Transformation (1p); [62] 'Bird of Prey' (1/3) (6p); [61.1] 'Starting Over' (2/6) (5p); *G.I. Joe: The Action Force* (5p); *Combat Colin* (1p); Dread Tidings (1p); next issue preview/order coupon (1p); advertisements (3p). 24 pages total (7 b/w).

UK#263: 31 March 1990. Cover (1p); Transformation (1p); [62] 'Bird of Prey' (2/3) (6p); [61.1] 'Starting Over' (3/6) (5p); *G.I. Joe: The Action Force* (6p); *Combat Colin* (1p); Dread Tidings (1p); next issue preview/order coupon (1p); advertisements (2p). 24 pages total (8 b/w).

UK#264: 7 April 1990. Cover (1p); Transformation (1p); [62] 'Bird of Prey' (3/3) (6p); [61.1] 'Starting Over' (4/6) (5p); *G.I. Joe: The Action Force* (6p); *Combat Colin* (1p); Dread Tidings (1p); competition page (1p); next issue preview/order coupon (1p); advertisements (1p). 24 pages total (7 b/w).

UK#265: 14 April 1990. Cover (1p); Transformation (1p); [GIJ1] 'Blood on the Tracks' (1/4) (6p); [61.1] 'Starting Over' (5/6) (5p); *G.I. Joe: The Action Force* (5p); *Combat Colin* (1p); Dread Tidings (1p); Transformers A to Z (Shockwave) (1p); competition page (1p); next issue preview/order coupon (1p); advertisements (1p). 24 pages total (7 b/w).

UK#266: 21 April 1990. Cover (1p); Transformation (1p); [GIJ1] 'Blood on the Tracks' (2/4) (6p); [61.1] 'Starting Over' (6/6) (5p); *G.I. Joe: The Action Force* (6p); *Combat Colin* (1p); Dread Tidings (1p); next issue preview/order coupon (1p); advertisements (2p). 24 pages total (8 b/w).

UK#267: 28 April 1990. Cover (1p); Transformation (1p); [GIJ1] 'Blood on the Tracks' (3/4) (6p); [62.1] 'Snow Fun' (1/1) (5p); *G.I. Joe: The Action Force* (5p); *Combat Kate* (1p); Dread Tidings (1p); Transformers A to Z (Shrapnel/Sideswipe) (1p) next issue preview/order coupon (1p); advertisements (2p). 24 pages total (8 b/w).

UK#268: 5 May 1990. Cover (1p); Transformation (1p); [GIJ1] 'Blood on the Tracks' (4/4) (6p); [62.2] 'Flashback' (1/1) (5p); *G.I. Joe: The Action Force* (6p); *Combat Colin* (1p); Dread Tidings (1p); next issue preview/order coupon (1p); advertisements (2p). 24 pages total (8 b/w).

UK#269: 12 May 1990. Cover (1p); Transformation (1p); [GIJ2] 'Power Struggle' (1/4) (5p); [62.3] 'Mystery' (1/1) (5p); *G.I. Joe: The Action Force* (5p); *Combat Colin* (1p); Dread Tidings (1p); Transformers A to Z (Silverbolt/Skids) (1p); next issue preview (½p);

advertisements (3½p). 24 pages total (8 b/w).

UK#270: 19 May 1990. Cover (1p); Transformation (1p); [GIJ2] 'Power Struggle' (2/4) (6p); [62.4] 'The Bad Guy's Ball' (1/1) (5p); *G.I. Joe: The Action Force* (6p); *Combat Colin* (1p); Dread Tidings (1p); next issue preview/order coupon (1p); advertisements (2p). 24 pages total (8 b/w).

UK#271: 26 May 1990. Cover (1p); Transformation (1p); [GIJ2] 'Power Struggle' (3/4) (6p); [62.5] 'The Living Nightlights' (1/1) (5p); *G.I. Joe: The Action Force* (5p); *Combat Colin* (1p); Dread Tidings (1p); Transformers A to Z (Skydive/Sky Lynx) (1p); next issue preview/order coupon (1p); advertisements (2p). 24 pages total (8 b/w).

UK#272: 2 June 1990. Cover (1p); Transformation (1p); [GIJ2] 'Power Struggle' (4/4) (6p); [62.6] 'Wolf in the Fold' (1/3) (5p); *G.I. Joe: The Action Force* (5p); *Combat Colin* (1p); Dread Tidings (1p); next issue preview/order coupon (1p); advertisements (3p). 24 pages total (8 b/w).

UK#273: 9 June 1990. Cover (1p); Transformation (1p); [GIJ3] 'Ashes, Ashes' (1/4) (5p); [62.6] 'Wolf in the Fold' (2/3) (5p); *G.I. Joe: The Action Force* (6p); *Combat Colin* (1p); Dread Tidings (1p); Transformers A to Z (Skywarp/Slag) (1p); next issue preview/order coupon (1p); advertisements (2p). 24 pages total (8 b/w).

UK#274: 16 June 1990. Cover (1p); Transformation (1p); [GIJ3] 'Ashes, Ashes' (2/4) (6p); [62.6] 'Wolf in the Fold' (3/3) (5p); *G.I. Joe: The Action Force* (6p); *Combat Colin* (1p); Dread Tidings (1p); next issue preview/order coupon (1p); advertisements (2p). 24 pages total (8 b/w).

UK#275: 23 June 1990. Cover (1p); Transformation (1p); [GIJ3] 'Ashes, Ashes' (3/4) (6p); [62.7] 'Internal Affairs' (1/3) (5p); *G.I. Joe: The Action Force* (6p); *Combat Colin* (1p); Dread Tidings (1p); next issue preview (½p); advertisements (2½p). 24 pages total (8 b/w).

UK#276: 30 June 1990. Cover (1p); Transformation (1p); [GIJ3] 'Ashes, Ashes' (4/4) (6p); [62.7] 'Internal Affairs' (2/3) (5p); *G.I. Joe: The Action Force* (5p); *Combat Colin* (1p); Dread Tidings (1p); Transformers A to Z (Slingshot/Sludge) (1p); next issue preview/order coupon (1p); advertisements (2p). 24 pages total (8 b/w).

UK#277: 7 July 1990. Cover (1p); Transformation (1p); [GIJ4] 'All Fall Down' (GIJ) (1/5) (5p); [62.7] 'Internal Affairs' (3/3) (5p); *G.I. Joe: The Action Force* (5p); *Combat Colin* (1p); Dread Tidings (1p); Transformers A to Z (Smokescreen/Snarl) (1p); next issue preview/competition coupon (1p); advertisements (3p). 24 pages total (8 b/w).

UK#278: 14 July 1990. Cover (1p); Transformation (1p); [GIJ4] 'All Fall Down' (GIJ) (2/5) (5p); [62.8] 'The House That Wheeljack Built' (1/1) (5p); *G.I. Joe: The Action Force* (6p); *Combat Colin* (1p); Dread Tidings (1p); Transformers A to Z (Soundwave/ Starscream) (1p); next issue preview/competition coupon (1p); advertisements (2p). 24 pages total (8 b/w).

UK#279: 21 July 1990. Cover (1p); Transformation (1p); [GIJ4] 'All Fall Down' (GIJ)

(3/5) (5p); [62.9] 'Divide and Conquer' (1/1) (5p); *G.I. Joe: The Action Force* (5p); *Combat Colin* (1p); Dread Tidings (1p); Transformers A to Z (Streetwise/Sunstreaker) (1p); competition page (1p); next issue preview/order coupon (1p); advertisements (2p). 24 pages total (8 b/w).

UK#280: 28 July 1990. Cover (1p); Transformation (1p); [GIJ4] 'All Fall Down' (GIJ) (4/5) (5p); [62.10] 'The 4,000,000 Year Itch' (1/1) (5p); *G.I. Joe: The Action Force* (5p); *Combat Colin* (1p); Dread Tidings (1p); Transformers A to Z (Steeljaw/Superion) (1p); next issue preview (½p); order coupon (½p); advertisements (3p). 24 pages total (8 b/w).

UK#281: 4 August 1990. Cover (1p); Transformation (1p); [GIJ4] 'All Fall Down' (GIJ) (5/5) (5p); [62.11] 'Makin' Tracks' (1/1) (5p); *G.I. Joe: The Action Force* (6p); *Combat Colin* (1p); Dread Tidings (1p); Transformers A to Z (Swindle/Swoop) (1p); next issue preview/order coupon (1p); advertisements (2p). 24 pages total (8 b/w).

UK#282: 11 August 1990. Cover (1p); Transformation (1p); [63] 'Kings of the Wild Frontier' (1/4) (5p); [63.1] 'Shut Up' (1/1) (5p); *G.I. Joe: The Action Force* (6p); *Combat Colin* (1p); Dread Tidings (1p); Transformers A to Z (Tailgate/Tantrum) (1p); next issue preview/order coupon (1p); advertisements (2p). 24 pages total (8 b/w).

UK#283: 18 August 1990. Cover (1p); Transformation (1p); [63] 'Kings of the Wild Frontier' (2/4) (5p); [63.2] 'Manoeuvres' (1/1) (5p); *G.I. Joe: The Action Force* (5p); *Combat Colin* (1p); Dread Tidings (1p); competition page (1p); Transformers A to Z (Thundercracker/Thrust) (1p); next issue preview (½p); order coupon (½p); advertisements (2p). 24 pages total (8 b/w).

UK#284: 25 August 1990. Cover (1p); Transformation (1p); [63] 'Kings of the Wild Frontier' (3/4) (5p); [63.3] 'Assassins' (1/3) (5p); *G.I. Joe: The Action Force* (6p); *Combat Colin* (1p); Dread Tidings (1p); Transformers A to Z (Topspin/Tracks) (1p); next issue preview/order coupon (1p); advertisements (2p). 24 pages total (8 b/w).

UK#285: 1 September 1990. Cover (1p); Transformation (1p); [63] 'Kings of the Wild Frontier' (4/4) (5p); [63.3] 'Assassins' (2/3) (5p); *G.I. Joe: The Action Force* (5p); *Combat Colin* (1p); Dread Tidings (1p); Transformers A to Z (Trailbreaker/Trypticon) (1p); next issue preview/order coupon (1p); advertisements (3p). 24 pages total (8 b/w).

UK#286: 8 September 1990. Cover (1p); Transformation (1p); [64] 'Deadly Obsession' (1/4) (5p); [63.3] 'Assassins' (3/3) (5p); *G.I. Joe: The Action Force* (6p); *Combat Colin* (1p); Dread Tidings (1p); Transformers A to Z (Twin Twist/Ultra Magnus) (1p); next issue preview/order coupon (1p); advertisements (2p). 24 pages total (8 b/w).

UK#287: 15 September 1990. Cover (1p); Transformation (1p); [64] 'Deadly Obsession' (2/4) (5p); [64.1] 'Inside Story' (1/3) (5p); *G.I. Joe: The Action Force* (6p); *Combat Colin* (1p); Dread Tidings (1p); Transformers A to Z (Unicron) (1p); competition page (1p); next issue preview/order coupon (1p); advertisements (1p). 24 pages total (8 b/w).

UK#288: 22 September 1990. Cover (1p); Transformation (1p); [64] 'Deadly Obsession'

(3/4) (5p); [64.1] 'Inside Story' (2/3) (5p); *G.I. Joe: The Action Force* (5p); *Combat Colin* (1p); Dread Tidings (1p); Transformers A to Z (Vortex/Warpath) (1p); competition page (1p); next issue preview/order coupon (1p); advertisements (2p). 24 pages total (8 b/w).

UK#289: 29 September 1990. Cover (1p); Transformation (1p); [64] 'Deadly Obsession' (4/4) (5p); [64.1] 'Inside Story' (3/3) (5p); *G.I. Joe: The Action Force* (5p); *Combat Colin* (1p); Dread Tidings (1p); Transformers A to Z (Wheelie/Wheeljack) (1p); competition page (1p); next issue preview/order coupon (1p); advertisements (2p). 24 pages total (8 b/w).

Comic returns to full-colour:

UK#290: 6 October 1990. Cover (1p); Transformation (1p); Reprint: [36.2] 'The Legacy of Unicron' (1/12) (5p); [65] 'Dark Creation' (1/4) (5p); *G.I. Joe: The Action Force* (5p); *Combat Colin* (1p); Dread Tidings (1p); Transformers A to Z (Wildrider/Windcharger) (1p); next issue preview/order coupon (1p); advertisements (3p). 24 pages total.

UK#291: 13 October 1990. Cover (1p); Transformation (1p); Reprint: [36.2] 'The Legacy of Unicron' (2/12) (6p); [65] 'Dark Creation' (2/4) (5p); *G.I. Joe: The Action Force* (5p); *Combat Colin* (1p); Dread Tidings (1p); (1p); next issue preview (½p); order coupon (½p); advertisements (3p). 24 pages total.

UK#292: 20 October 1990. Cover (1p); Transformation (1p); Reprint: [36.2] 'The Legacy of Unicron' (3/12) (5p); [65] 'Dark Creation' (3/4) (5p); *G.I. Joe: The Action Force* (6p); *Combat Colin* (1p); Dread Tidings (1p); next issue preview/order coupon (1p); advertisements (3p). 24 pages total.

UK#293: 27 October 1990. Cover (1p); Transformation (1p); Reprint: [36.2] 'The Legacy of Unicron' (4/12) (6p); [65] 'Dark Creation' (4/4) (5p); *G.I. Joe: The Action Force* (6p); *Combat Colin* (1p); Dread Tidings (1p); next issue preview/order coupon (1p); advertisements (2p). 24 pages total.

UK#294: 3 November 1990. Cover (1p); Transformation (1p); Reprint: [36.2] 'The Legacy of Unicron' (5/12) (6p); [66] 'All Fall Down' (TF) (1/4) (5p); *G.I. Joe: The Action Force* (5p); *Combat Colin* (1p); Dread Tidings (1p); next issue preview/order coupon (1p); advertisements (3p). 24 pages total.

UK#295: 10 November 1990. Cover (1p); Transformation (1p); Reprint: [36.2] 'The Legacy of Unicron' (6/12) (5p); [66] 'All Fall Down' (TF) (2/4) (5p); *G.I. Joe: The Action Force* (6p); *Combat Colin* (1p); Dread Tidings (1p); next issue preview (½p); order coupon (½p); advertisements (3p). 24 pages total.

UK#296: 17 November 1990. Cover (1p); Transformation (1p); Reprint: [36.2] 'The Legacy of Unicron' (7/12) (6p); [66] 'All Fall Down' (TF) (3/4) (5p); *G.I. Joe: The Action Force* (5p); *Combat Colin* (1p); Dread Tidings (1p); competition pages (1½p); next issue preview (½p); advertisements (2p). 24 pages total.

UK#297: 24 November 1990. Cover (1p); Transformation (1p); Reprint: [36.2] 'The

Legacy of Unicron' (8/12) (5p); [66] 'All Fall Down' (TF) (4/4) (5p); *G.I. Joe: The Action Force* (6p); *Combat Colin* (1p); Dread Tidings (1p); next issue preview/order coupon (1p); advertisements (3p). 24 pages total.

UK#298: 1 December 1990. Cover (1p); Transformation (1p); Reprint: [36.2] 'The Legacy of Unicron' (9/12) (5p); [67] 'Rhythms of Darkness' (1/4) (5p); *G.I. Joe: The Action Force* (6p); *Combat Colin* (1p); Dread Tidings (1p); next issue preview/order coupon (1p); advertisements (3p). 24 pages total.

UK#299: 8 December 1990. Cover (1p); Transformation (1p); Reprint: [36.2] 'The Legacy of Unicron' (10/12) (6p); [67] 'Rhythms of Darkness' (2/4) (5p); *G.I. Joe: The Action Force* (5p); *Combat Colin* (1p); Dread Tidings (1p); next issue preview (1p); advertisements (3p). 24 pages total.

UK#300: 15 December 1990. Cover [wraparound] (2p); Transformation (1p); Reprint: [36.2] 'The Legacy of Unicron' (11/12) (6p); [67] 'Rhythms of Darkness' (3/4) (5p); *G.I. Joe: The Action Force* (5p); *Combat Colin* (1p); Darn 'n' Blast (1p); next issue preview/order coupon (1p); advertisements (2p). 24 pages total.

UK#301: 22 December 1990. Cover (1p); Transformation (1p); Reprint: [36.2] 'The Legacy of Unicron' (12/12) (5p); [67] 'Rhythms of Darkness' (4/4) (5p); *G.I. Joe: The Action Force* (6p); *Combat Colin* (1p); Darn 'n' Blast (1p); next issue preview/order coupon (1p); advertisements (3p). 24 pages total.

UK#302: 29 December 1990. Cover (1p); Transformation (1p); Reprint: [20.1] 'In the National Interest' (1/6) (6p); [68] 'The Human Factor' (1/4) (6p); *G.I. Joe: The Action Force* (5p); *Combat Colin* (1p); Darn 'n' Blast (1p); next issue preview/order coupon (1p); advertisements (2p). 24 pages total.

UK#303: 3 January 1991. Cover (1p); Transformation (1p); Reprint: [20.1] 'In the National Interest' (2/6) (5p); [68] 'The Human Factor' (2/4) (5p); *G.I. Joe: The Action Force* (6p); *Combat Colin* (1p); Darn 'n' Blast (1p); next issue preview/order coupon (1p); advertisements (3p). 24 pages total.

UK#304: 12 January 1991. Cover (1p); Transformation (1p); Reprint: [20.1] 'In the National Interest' (3/6) (6p); [68] 'The Human Factor' (3/4) (5p); *G.I. Joe: The Action Force* (6p); *Combat Colin* (1p); Darn 'n' Blast (1p); advertisements (3p). 24 pages total.

UK#305: 19 January 1991. Cover (1p); Transformation (1p); Reprint: [20.1] 'In the National Interest' (4/6) (5p); [68] 'The Human Factor' (4/4) (5p); *G.I. Joe: The Action Force* (6p); *Combat Colin* (1p); Darn 'n' Blast (1p); next issue preview/order coupon (1p); advertisements (3p). 24 pages total.

UK#306: 26 January 1991. Cover (1p); Transformation (1p); Reprint: [20.1] 'In the National Interest' (5/6) (11p); [69] 'Eye of the Storm' (1/3) (7p); *Combat Colin* (1p); Darn 'n' Blast (1p); advertisements (2p). 24 pages total.

UK#307: 2 February 1991. Cover (1p); Transformation (1p); Reprint: [20.1] 'In the

National Interest' (6/6) (11p); [69] 'Eye of the Storm' (2/3) (6p); *Combat Colin* (1p); Darn 'n' Blast (1p); advertisements (3p). 24 pages total.

UK#308: 9 February 1991. Cover (1p); Transformation (1p); Reprint: [4.2] 'The Enemy Within' (1/7) (11p); [69] 'Eye of the Storm' (3/3) (7p); *Combat Colin* (1p); Darn 'n' Blast (1p); Feature: *Machine Man* Update (1p); advertisements (1p). 24 pages total.

Fortnightly publication:

UK#309: 2 March 1991. Cover (1p); Transformation (1p); Reprint: [4.2] 'The Enemy Within' (2/7) (5p); [70] 'The Pri¢e of Life' (1/2) (10p); *Machine Man* (7p); *Combat Colin* (1p); Darn 'n' Blast (1p); Transformers A to Z (Thundercracker/Thrust) (1p); advertisements (1p). 28 pages total.

UK#310: 16 March 1991. Cover (1p); Transformation (1p); [70] 'The Pri¢e of Life' (2/2) (10p); *Machine Man* (7p); *Combat Colin* (1p); Darn 'n' Blast (1p); Transformers A to Z (Optimus Prime) (1p); advertisements (2p). 24 pages total.

UK#311: 30 March 1991. Cover (1p); Transformation (1p); [71] 'Surrender' (1/2) (10p); *Machine Man* (5p); *Combat Colin* (1p); Darn 'n' Blast (1p); Transformers A to Z (Joyride/Getaway) (1p); competition page (1p); advertisements (3p). 24 pages total.

UK#312: 13 April 1991. Cover (1p); Transformation (1p); [71] 'Surrender' (2/2) (10p); *Machine Man* (6p); *Combat Colin* (1p); Darn 'n' Blast (1p); next issue preview/readers' poll (1p); advertisements (3p). 24 pages total.

UK#313: 27 April 1991. Cover (1p); Transformation (1p); [72] 'All This and Civil War 2' (1/2) (10p); Reprint: [4.2] 'The Enemy Within' (3/7) (6p); *Combat Colin* (1p); Darn 'n' Blast (1p); Transformers A to Z (Slapdash) (1p); next issue preview (½p); advertisements (2½p). 24 pages total.

UK#314: 11 May 1991. Cover (1p); Transformation (1p); [72] 'All This and Civil War 2' (2/2) (10p); Reprint: [4.2] 'The Enemy Within' (4/7) (5p); *Combat Colin* (1p); Darn 'n' Blast (1p); Transformers A to Z (Punch/Counterpunch) (1p); next issue preview (½p); advertisements (3½p). 24 pages total.

UK#315: 25 May 1991. Cover (1p); Transformation (1p); [73] 'Out of Time' (1/2) (10p); Reprint: [4.2] 'The Enemy Within' (5/7) (6p); *Combat Colin* (1p); Darn 'n' Blast (1p); Transformers A to Z (Landmine) (1p); next issue preview/order coupon (1p); advertisements (2p). 24 pages total.

UK#316: 8 June 1991. Cover (1p); Transformation (1p); [73] 'Out of Time' (2/2) (10p); Reprint: [4.2] 'The Enemy Within' (6/7) (6p); *Combat Colin* (1p); Darn 'n' Blast (1p); competition page (1p); next issue preview/order coupon (1p); advertisements (2p). 24 pages total.

UK#317: 22 June 1991. Cover (1p); [74] 'The Void' (1/2) (11p); Reprint: [4.2] 'The Enemy Within' (7/7) (5p); *Combat Colin* (1p); Darn 'n' Blast (1p); Transformers A to Z

(Dreadwind) (1p); next issue preview (½p); order coupon (½p); advertisements (3p). 24 pages total.

UK#318: 6 July 1991. Cover (1p); Transformation (1p); [74] 'The Void' (2/2) (10p); *Machine Man* (6p); *Combat Colin* (1p); Darn 'n' Blast (1p); Transformers A to Z (Darkwing) (1p); next issue preview/order coupon (1p); advertisements (2p). 24 pages total.

UK#319: 20 July 1991. Cover (1p); Transformation (1p); [75] 'On the Edge of Extinction' (1/4) (9p); *Machine Man* (6p); *Combat Colin* (1p); Darn 'n' Blast (1p); Transformers A to Z (Fangry) (1p); competition page (1p); next issue preview/order coupon (1p); advertisements (2p). 24 pages total.

UK#320: 3 August 1991. Cover (1p); Transformation (1p); [75] 'On the Edge of Extinction' (2/4) (9p); *Machine Man* (5p); *Combat Colin* (1p); Darn 'n' Blast (1p); Transformers A to Z (Squeezeplay) (1p); next issue preview/order coupon (1p); advertisements (4p). 24 pages total.

UK#321: 17 August 1991. Cover (1p); Transformation (1p); [75] 'On the Edge of Extinction' (3/4) (9p); *Machine Man* (5p); *Combat Colin* (1p); Darn 'n' Blast (1p); Transformers A to Z (Siren) (1p); competition pages (2p); next issue preview/order coupon (1p); advertisements (2p). 24 pages total.

UK#322: 31 August 1991. Cover (1p); Transformation (1p); [75] 'On the Edge of Extinction' (4/4) (9p); *Machine Man* (6p); *Combat Colin* (1p); Darn 'n' Blast (1p); Transformers A to Z (Kup) (1p); next issue preview/order coupon (1p); advertisements (3p). 24 pages total.

UK#323: 14 September 1991. Cover (1p); Transformation (1p); [76] 'Still Life' (1/2) (10p); *Machine Man* (5p); *Combat Colin* (1p); Darn 'n' Blast (1p); Transformers A to Z (Grotusque) (1p); next issue preview/order coupon (1p); advertisements (3p). 24 pages total.

UK#324: 28 September 1991. Cover (1p); Transformation (1p); [76] 'Still Life' (2/2) (10p); *Machine Man* (6p); *Combat Colin* (1p); Darn 'n' Blast (1p); Transformers A to Z (Horri-Bull) (1p); next issue preview/competition results (1p); advertisements (2p). 24 pages total.

UK#325: 12 October 1991. Cover (1p); Transformation (1p); [77] 'Exodus' (1/2) (10p); *Machine Man* (6p); *Combat Colin* (1p); Darn 'n' Blast (1p); Transformers A to Z (Weirdwolf) (1p); next issue preview/competition page (1p); advertisements (2p). 24 pages total.

UK#326: 26 October 1991. Cover (1p); Transformation (1p); [77] 'Exodus' (2/2) (10p); *Machine Man* (5p); *Combat Colin* (1p); Darn 'n' Blast (1p); Transformers A to Z (Skullcruncher) (1p); next issue preview/order coupon (1p); advertisements (3p). 24 pages total.

UK#327: 9 November 1991. Cover (1p); Transformation (1p); [78] 'A Savage Circle' (1/2) (10p); *Machine Man* (6p); *Combat Colin* (1p); Darn 'n' Blast (1p); Transformers A to Z (Pounce) (1p); competition page (1p); next issue preview/order coupon (1p); advertisements (1p). 24 pages total.

UK#328: 23 November 1991. Cover (1p); Transformation (1p); [78] 'A Savage Circle' (2/2) (10p); *Machine Man* (6p); *Combat Colin* (1p); Darn 'n' Blast (1p); Transformers A to Z (Repugnus) (1p); competition page (1p); next issue preview/order coupon (1p); advertisements (1p). 24 pages total.

UK#329: 7 December 1991. Cover (1p); Transformation (1p); [79] 'The Last Autobot' (1/2) (10p); *Machine Man* (6p); *Combat Colin* (1p); Darn 'n' Blast (1p); *Transformers Universe* profile (Fortress Maximus) (2p); next issue preview/Annual order coupon (1p); advertisements (1p). 24 pages total.

UK#330: 21 December 1991. Cover (1p); Transformation (1p); [79] 'The Last Autobot' (2/2) (10p); Reprint: [53.5] 'The Big Shutdown' (1/2) (5p) *Combat Colin* (1p); Darn 'n' Blast (1p); next issue preview/Annual order coupon (1p); advertisements (4p). 24 pages total.

UK#331: 4 January 1992. Cover (1p); Transformation (1p); [80] 'End of the Road' (1/2) (10p); Reprint: [53.5] 'The Big Shutdown' (2/2) (5p) *Combat Colin* (2p); next issue preview/Annual order coupon (1p); advertisements (4p). 24 pages total.

UK#332: 18 January 1992. Cover (1p); Transformation (1p); [80] 'End of the Road' (2/2) (12p); Reprint: [59.2] 'The Greatest Gift of All' (1/1) (5p) *Combat Colin* (2p); Darn 'n' Blast (1p); Annual order coupon (1p); advertisements (1p). 24 pages total (5 b/w).

THE TRANSFORMERS ANNUAL (MARVEL UK/GRANDREAMS)

The Transformers Annual (1986):
Cover price £3.25
P1: Front cover
P2: Endpaper (b/w image of Optimus Prime)
P3: Title page
P4-5: Decepticon roll-call (using stock box-art pictures)
P6-7: Autobot roll-call (reprint of the poster from UK#2)
P8-13, 15-18, 51-60: [A1.1] Plague of the Insecticons (20p)
P14: Puzzle – match the Transformers' names to the pictures of their heads
P19: Puzzle – which is the correct picture of the Autobot Cliffjumper?
P20-24, 30-31: [A1.2] Missing in Action (7p)
P25: Puzzle – solve the anagrams
P26: Puzzle – match the Decepticons to their alt modes
P27-29, 32-38: [A1.3] And There Shall Come… A Leader (10p)
P39: Puzzle – match the Autobots to their alt modes
P40-41: *Hexagonal Attack on Castle Decepticon* – board game
P42-46, 48-49: [A1.4] Hunted (7p)
P47: Puzzle – wordsearch

P50: Puzzle – solve the anagrams
P61: Puzzle – maze
P62: solutions to puzzles
P63: Endpaper (b/w image of Megatron)
P64: Back cover

The Transformers Annual (1987):
Cover price £3.50
P1: Front cover
P2-3: Endpaper splash (the Dinobots, reuse of art from UK#28's free poster)
P4: Title page
P5-9: [A2.1] In the Beginning (5p)
P10-20 [A2.2] To a Power Unknown (11p)
P21: Datafile: Optimus Prime
P22-29: [A2.3] The Return of the Transformers (8p)
P30-32: 'Threeplay' trivia quiz
P33: Datafile: Megatron
P34-41: [A2.4] State Games (8p)
P42-52: [A2.5] Victory (11p)
P53-60 [A2.6] The Mission (8p)
P61: Decepticon Who's Who (previously printed in UK#48)
P62-63: Endpaper splash: Autobot Who's Who (previously printed in UK#53-54)
P64: Back cover

The Transformers Annual (1988):
Cover price £3.75
P1: Front cover
P2-3: Endpaper splash: Ultra Magnus and Galvatron
P4: Title page
P5-9: [A3.1] What's in a Name? (5p)
P10-17: [A3.2] Headmasters Saga (chapter one) (8p)
P18-20: Transformers trivia quiz
P21-31: [A3.3] Vicious Circle (11p)
P32-39: [A3.2] Headmasters Saga (chapter two) (8p)
P40: Transformers A to Z: Brainstorm
P41: Transformers A to Z: Chromedome
P42: Transformers A to Z: Hardhead
P43: Transformers A to Z: Highbrow
P44-50: [A3.4] _Ark_ Duty (7p)
P51-58: [A3.2] Headmasters Saga (chapter three) (8p)
P59: Transformers A to Z: Mindwipe
P60: Transformers A to Z: Skullcruncher
P61: Transformers A to Z: Weirdwolf
P62-63: Endpaper splash: Ultra Magnus and Galvatron
P64: Back cover

The Transformers Annual (1989):
Cover price £3.95

P1: Front cover
P2-3: Endpaper splash: Hot Rod and Highbrow surrounded
P4: Title page
P5: Contents
P6-12: [A4.1] The Saga of the Transformers – So Far (7p)
P13-18: [A4.2] Altered Image (6p)
P19: Mini-poster (reprint of UK#107 cover art)
P20: Transformers A to Z: Nautilator
P21: Transformers A to Z: Seawing
P22-27, 44-51: [A4.3] Prime Bomb (14p)
P28-29: 'Puzzle Pathway' (trivia quiz)
P30-40: [A4.4] All in the Minds (11p)
P41: Mini-poster (reprint of UK#157 cover art)
P42: Transformers A to Z: Skalor
P43: Transformers A to Z: Snap Trap
P52: Quiz answers
P53-58: [A4.5] Peace (6p)
P59: Mini-poster (reprint of UK#113 cover art)
P60: Transformers A to Z: Tentakil
P61: Transformers A to Z: Jawbreaker (aka Overbite)
P62-63: Endpaper splash: Hot Rod and Highbrow surrounded
P64: Back cover

The Transformers Annual (1990):
Cover price £3.99
P1: Front cover
P2-3: Endpaper splash: Megatron
P4: Title page
P5: Contents
P6-12: [A5.1] The Quest (7p)
P13: Mini-poster (reprint of UK _Collected Comics_ #6 cover art)
P14-19: [A5.2] Destiny of the Dinobots (6p)
P20-21 'Duel of Wits' trivia quiz
P22-27, 43-50: [A5.3] Trigger-Happy (14p)
P28: Transformers A to Z: Autobot Race Car Patrol
P29: Transformers A to Z: Autobot Off Road Patrol
P30-40: [A5.4] Dreadwing Down (11p)
P41: Quiz answers
P42: Mini-poster (reprint of UK#160 cover art)
P51: Mini-poster (reprint of interior art from UK#185)
P52: Transformers A to Z: Decepticon Air Strike Patrol
P53: Transformers A to Z: Decepticon Sports Car Patrol
P54-59 [A5.5] The Chain Gang (6p)
P60: Transformers A to Z: Autobot Rescue Patrol
P61: Transformers A to Z: Autobot Battle Patrol
P62-63: Endpaper splash: Megatron
P64: Back cover

The Transformers Annual (1991):
Cover price £4.25
P1: Front cover
P2-3: Endpaper splash: Autobots v Decepticons
P4: Title page
P5: Contents
P6-16, 28-38 [23.4] Fallen Angel (22p; reprint)
P17: Transformers A to Z: Inferno (update)
P18-25, 40-47 [A6.1] The Magnificent Six (16p)
P26-27: Feature – 'Mechanoids and Their Spacecraft'
P39: Transformers A to Z: Ironhide (update)
P48: Transformers A to Z: Jazz (update)
P49: Transformers A to Z: Sunstreaker and Prowl (updates)
P50-60: [44.2] Firebug (11p; reprint)
P61: Transformers A to Z: Wheeljack (update)
P62-63: Endpaper splash: Autobots v Decepticons
P64: Back cover

The Transformers Annual 1992:
Cover price £4.50
P1: Front cover
P2-3: Endpaper splash: Optimus Prime
P4: Title and contents
P5-9: [53.4] The Hunting Party (5p; newly-coloured reprint)
P10-17, 36-45: [A7.1] Another Time & Place (18p)
P18-22, 24-28, 30-34: [55.1] Way of the Warrior (15p; newly-coloured reprint)
P23, 29, 35, 56: _Combat Colin_ (humour strip first printed in UK#290-293)
P46-55, 57-61: [62.6] Wolf in the Fold (15p; newly-coloured reprint)
P62-63: Endpaper splash: Optimus Prime
P64: Back cover

About the Author

Ryan Frost fell in love with the Transformers at the age of four and now owns so many of the toys and comics that he is starting to run out of room to put them.

When not obsessing over plastic action figures, he enjoys pub quizzes, rock concerts, mini-golf, real ale and the FIFA video game series (although not all at the same time).

He lives in Rayne, Essex and is *definitely* not too old to play with toy robots.